Red Hat® Linux® 9 Professional Secrets®

Red Hat® Linux® 9
Professional Secrets®

Naba Barkakati

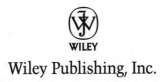

Wiley Publishing, Inc.

Library of Congress Control Number: 2003105672

ISBN: 0-7645-4133-1

Manufactured in the United States of America

10 9 8 7 6 5 4 3 2 1

1O/SS/QX/QT/IN

Credits

Executive Editor
Chris Webb

Acquisitions Editor
Debra Williams Cauley

Development Editor
Kenyon Brown

Technical Editor
Matt Hayden

Copy Editor
Foxxe Editorial Services

Editorial Manager
Kathryn A. Malm

Project Coordinators
Maridee Ennis
Nancee Reeves

Graphics and Production Specialists
Beth Brooks
Jennifer Click
Sean Decker
Heather Pope

Quality Control Technicians
John Tyler Connoley
Susan Moritz
Kathy Simpson

Permissions Editor
Laura Moss

Media Development Specialist
Greg Stafford

Media Development Coordinator
Sarah Cummings

Proofreader
Sossity R. Smith

Indexer
Tom Dinse

About the Author

Naba Barkakati is an electrical engineer and a successful computer-book author who has experience in a wide variety of systems, ranging from MS-DOS and Windows to UNIX and the X Window System. He bought his first personal computer—an IBM PC-AT—in 1984 after graduating with a Ph.D. in electrical engineering from the University of Maryland.. While pursuing a full-time career in engineering, Naba dreamed of writing software for the emerging PC software market. As luck would have it, instead of building a software empire like Microsoft, he ended up writing successful computer books. Currently, Naba is a senior level technologist at the Center for Technology and Engineering in the U.S. General Accounting Office.

Over the past 14 years, Naba has written over 25 computer books on a number of topics ranging from Windows programming with C++ to Linux. He has authored several best-selling titles such as *The Waite Group's Turbo C++ Bible*, *Object-Oriented Programming in C++*, *X Window System Programming*, *Visual C++ Developer's Guide*, and *Borland C++ 4 Developer's Guide*. His books have been translated into many languages, including Spanish, French, Polish, Greek, Italian, Chinese, Japanese, and Korean. Naba's most recent book is *Red Hat Linux All-in-One Desk Reference For Dummies*, also published by Wiley Publishing, Inc.

Naba lives in North Potomac, Maryland, with his wife Leha, and their children, Ivy, Emily, and Ashley.

This book is dedicated to my wife, Leha, and daughters, Ivy, Emily, and Ashley.

Introduction

If you are just beginning to use Linux, what you need is a practical guide that not only gets you going with the installation and set up of Linux, but also shows you how to use Linux for specific functions, such as a Web server or a software development platform.

Red Hat continues to improve its version of Linux. The recently released Red Hat Linux 9 includes many new system components, including the Linux 2.4.20 kernel, XFree86 4.3.0, GCC 3.2.2 compiler, and the glibc 2.3.2 system libraries. The X Window System is XFree86 version 4.3.0 with support for many more new and powerful graphics cards than the previous versions. Red Hat has improved the desktop experience by providing many more graphical tools to configure and manage the system. For productivity applications, Red Hat includes the Mozilla Web browser, Ximian Evolution personal information manager, and the OpenOffice.org office suite. Red Hat has also unified the look and feel of GNOME and KDE desktops, so the user feels at home regardless of the selected desktop. There are many under-the-hood improvements as well. For example, Red Hat Linux now uses the Common UNIX Printing System (CUPS) as the default printing system, and it includes the Native POSIX Thread Library, which offers performance improvements with Pentium Pro processors or better.

Red Hat Linux 9 Professional Secrets follows the successful model of the *Professional Secrets* series and highlights crucial, little-known facts as "secrets." The focus is on providing insights into the inner workings of Red Hat Linux—which configuration files control what, which commands to type in what sequence to perform a key task. In addition to these insights, the book also provides all the usual information on many of the applications—such as email, the Web, and news, plus graphics and text utilities—that are included on the book's companion CD-ROMs.

The book's companion CD-ROMs come with the Publisher's Edition of Red Hat Linux 9. The CD-ROMs are packed with all the software needed to turn your PC into a powerful Linux desktop and server. The book provides detailed technical information on installing and customizing Linux for use with various types of computers and peripherals.

The unique aspects of *Red Hat Linux 9 Professional Secrets* are the details of how things work behind the scenes. The book includes tips, techniques, shortcuts, and little-known facts about using Red Hat Linux in various real-world tasks that range from simply learning UNIX commands to setting up a secure, Java-capable Web server for your business.

By reading this book you can:

- Learn how to install and set up Red Hat Linux from the CD-ROMs included with the book
- Learn how to use various peripherals (video cards, hard disks, and network cards) in Red Hat Linux
- Learn about dial-up networking (with SLIP and PPP) under Red Hat Linux
- Get tips, techniques, and shortcuts for specific uses of Red Hat Linux, such as:
    - Setting up and using Internet services such as Web, Mail, News, FTP (File Transfer Protocol), NFS (Network File System), NIS (Network Information Service), and DNS (Domain Name System)
    - Setting up a Windows server using Samba
    - Learning UNIX on Red Hat Linux
    - Learning Perl, shell, and Tcl/Tk programming on Red Hat Linux
    - Learning Java programming on Red Hat Linux

◆ Understand the basics of system and network security

◆ Learn to perform system and network administration tasks

◆ Receive many Red Hat Linux tools and utilities

◆ Learn about Linux resources that can serve as continuing sources of information in the ever-changing world of Linux

Organization of the Book

Red Hat Linux 9 Professional Secrets contains 26 chapters, organized into five parts and eight appendixes covering topics such as installation and setup, routine use, networking and server setup, system administration, and programming.

Part I: Setting Up Red Hat Linux

Part I includes six chapters that introduce you to Linux, guide you through Red Hat Linux installation, and show you how to configure various types of hardware in Linux. The first chapter provides an overview of Linux in general. The second chapter takes you through the steps needed to install Red Hat Linux from this book's companion CD-ROMs. The next four chapters explain how to configure the X Window System, printers using the Common Unix Printing System (CUPS), and sound and network components.

Part II: Exploring Red Hat Linux

This part acquaints you with Red Hat Linux. The six chapters in this section describe the popular GNU utilities, the GUI desktops—GNOME and KDE, and the applications included with Red Hat Linux on the companion CD-ROMs. You will also learn how to edit text files, prepare DocBook documentation, and perform basic systems administration functions.

Part III: Internetworking with Red Hat Linux

The seven chapters in Part III focus on connecting the Red Hat Linux system to the Internet and setting up various Internet services on the system. After describing dial-up networking, the chapters in this part walk you through the setup and configuration of a number of servers including Web, FTP, SMTP (Simple Mail Transfer Protocol for mail), news, DNS, NIS, NFS, and Samba.

Part IV: Managing Red Hat Linux

The three chapters in Part IV cover systems administration and security. The first chapter in this part—Chapter 20—starts by discussing a number of advanced system administration topics. The next two chapters show you how to install and upgrade software using the Red Hat Package Manager (RPM), how to build software from source files, how to rebuild and install a new kernel, and how to secure the system and the network.

Part V: Programming Red Hat Linux

The four chapters in Part V turn to the subject of programming in Linux. The first chapter—Chapter 23—covers the basics as well as a number of software development tools and the GNU Public License that affects software developed in Linux. Then, that chapter briefly touches on C and C++ programming. The next two chapters cover scripting using the shell, Perl, and Tcl/Tk. Finally, the last chapter in this section introduces you to writing applet, servlets, and standalone applications using Java.

Part VI: Appendixes

This section includes eight appendixes:

♦ Appendix A, "Linux Commands," presents alphabetically arranged reference entries for the many commonly used Linux commands.

♦ Appendix B, "Disk Drives," describes IDE and SCSI disk controllers and lists driver modules needed for specific SCSI controllers.

♦ Appendix C, "CD-ROM Drives," lists specific types of Linux-supported CD-ROM drives, categorized by interface type.

♦ Appendix D, "Ethernet Cards," describes the physical setup of an Ethernet LAN and lists the Ethernet cards that Linux supports.

♦ Appendix E, "Modems and Terminals," explains how to connect, set up, and use modems and terminals in Linux.

♦ Appendix F, "PC Cards," briefly describes PC Cards that use the PCMCIA interface and the PCMCIA support package for Linux.

♦ Appendix G, "Linux Resources," lists resources on the Internet where you can obtain the latest information about Linux.

♦ Appendix H, "About the CD-ROMs," summarizes the contents of the book's companion CD-ROMs.

If you are a new user, you should start reading Part I, which guides you through installing Red Hat Linux from the CD-ROMs that accompany the books (see Appendix H also). If you have specific hardware questions, you should go directly to the relevant appendix (see Appendixes B through F). If you have already installed Red Hat Linux, you might want to begin with Part II, where you'll learn how to make the most of Red Hat Linux in everyday use (see Appendix G also). For questions related to Internet services, consult the appropriate chapter in Part III. Part IV gets you going with various systems administration tasks and explains how to maintain system and network security. To learn about programming in specific languages, consult the relevant chapters in Part V. When you need information on a specific Linux command, turn to Appendix A and look for that command in the alphabetically arranged reference entries.

Conventions Used in This Book

Red Hat Linux 9 Professional Secrets uses a simple notational style. All listings, filenames, function names, variable names, and keywords are typeset in a `monospace font` for ease of reading. The first occurrences of new terms and concepts are in *italic*. Text you are directed to type is in **boldface**. The output of commands follow the typed command and the output is shown in a `monospace font`.

Each chapter starts with a short list that highlights the "secrets" you will find in that chapter. The summary at the end of the chapter tells you a bit more about what the chapter covered.

Following the time-honored tradition of the *Professional Secrets* series, I use icons to help you quickly pinpoint useful information. The icons include the following:

note

The Note icon marks a general interesting fact—something that I thought you'd like to know.

insider insight

The Insider Insight icon marks things that you should know to make your job easier and to work smarter.

caution

The Caution icon highlights potential pitfalls. With this icon, I'm telling you: "Watch out! This could hurt your system!"

cross ref

The Cross-Reference icon points out other chapters in the book for a deeper discussion of a specific topic.

Secret

The Secret icon marks facts that explain the inner working of some aspect of Linux and related software. These are details that may not be that well-documented, but are important to know. It's not that no one knows this fact—it's just hard to find; and knowing this fact usually clears up many other questions that you may have. This icon also marks technical information that will be of interest to an advanced user.

About the Companion CD-ROMs

Red Hat Linux 9 Professional Secrets addresses the needs of new users who want to put Red Hat Linux to some productive use on their home or office PC. To ensure that readers have everything they need to start using Red Hat Linux, this book includes a copy of Red Hat Linux 9 (with Linux kernel 2.4.20) on the companion CD-ROMs. Red Hat Linux is easy to install and is well supported by Red Hat (http://www.redhat.com).

See Appendix H for a summary description of the contents of the companion CD-ROMs. As you browse the contents of the CD-ROMs, you'll notice that there is a huge amount of software included in Red Hat Linux. The long list of software shouldn't overwhelm you. You only have to learn to use what you need. Besides, this book will show you how to install Red Hat Linux and use most of this software.

If you have enough space (at least 4GB) available on your PC's hard disk (or, better yet, a spare second hard disk) and your PC can boot from the CD-ROM drive, Red Hat Linux installation can be as simple as plopping the first CD-ROM into the CD-ROM drive, booting the PC, and filling up information in a series of dialog boxes. You don't have to take my word for it—you can see for yourself.

It's time to get started on your Linux adventure. Take out the companion CD-ROM, turn to Chapter 1, and let the fun begin. Before you know it, you'll be a Linux expert!

I hope you enjoy this book as much as I enjoyed writing it!

Reach Out

The publisher and I would like your feedback. After you have had a chance to use this book, if you want to share any thought, please feel free to contact me directly at:

    naba@ieee.org

Acknowledgments

I am grateful to Chris Webb and Debra Williams Cauley for getting me started on writing *Red Hat Linux 9 Professional Secrets*. Ken Brown and Angela Smith guided me through the manuscript review process and kept everything moving. I really appreciated the thorough copyediting by the wonderful folks at Foxxe Editorial Services.

I would like to thank Matt Hayden for reviewing the manuscript for technical accuracy and providing many useful suggestions for improving the book's content.

Thanks to everyone at Wiley Publishing, Inc., for transforming my raw manuscript into this well-edited and beautifully packaged book.

Of course, there would be no reason for this book if it were not for Linux. For this, we have Linus Torvalds and the legions of Linux developers around the world to thank. Thanks to Red Hat for providing beta copies of Red Hat Linux and the publisher's edition CD-ROMs that are bundled with this book.

Finally, and as always, my greatest thanks go to my wife, Leha, and our daughters, Ivy, Emily, and Ashley—it is their love and support that keeps me going. Thanks for being there!

Contents at a Glance

Contents

Part V: Programming Red Hat Linux 709

Chapter 23: Software Development in Linux 711

Chapter 24: Shell and Perl Scripting 749

Part I

Setting Up Red Hat Linux

An Overview of Red Hat Linux

Chapter
1

◆ ◆

Secrets in This Chapter

◆ ◆

The world of operating systems changed forever when Linus Torvalds of the University of Helsinki in Finland decided to build a UNIX-like operating system for the PC. What started as a simple task-switching example, with two processes that printed AAAA . . . and BBBB . . . on a dumb terminal, has grown into a full-fledged, multitasking, multiuser operating system that rivals commercially available UNIX systems for Intel 80x86 systems. Many programmers around the world have contributed code and collaborated to bring Linux to its current state. With the release of version 1.0 in March 1994, Linux became an operating system of choice for UNIX enthusiasts, as well as for people looking for a low-cost UNIX platform for a specific purpose, such as developing software or running an Internet host.

This chapter provides a broad-brushstroke picture of Red Hat Linux, one of several well-known Linux distributions (other well-known Linux distributions are Mandrake, Debian, Slackware, and S.u.S.E.). The chapter describes how you can get the most out of the built-in capabilities of Red Hat Linux, such as networking, developing software, and running applications.

After you overcome your initial fear of the unknown and install Linux, you will see how you can use it to turn your PC into a UNIX workstation. The best part is that you can get Linux for free—just download it from one of several Internet sites (for example, you'll find links to many Linux distributions from the Linux Online website at `http://www .linux.org/dist/`). The best way for beginners and experts alike to get started, though, is to buy a book (such as this one) that comes with a Linux distribution on CD-ROM. This book is your guide to the inner workings of Red Hat Linux. The next chapter shows how to install Red Hat Linux, and subsequent chapters describe specific tasks (such as connecting to the Internet or developing software) that you may want to perform with your Red Hat Linux PC. In addition to many utilities with graphical user interfaces (GUIs), this book provides you the details such as what commands to use and what configuration files to edit.

What Is Red Hat Linux?

Linux is a freely available UNIX-like operating system that runs on a wide variety of systems. Linus Torvalds and other programmers originally developed Linux for the Intel 80x86 processor. Nowadays, Linux is also available for systems based on other processors, such as Intel's new 64-bit Itanium IA64 architecture processor, the Motorola 68000 family, the Alpha AXP processor, the Sun SPARC and UltraSPAC processors, Hewlett-Packard's HP PA-RISC processor, the PowerPC and PowerPC64 processors, ARM family of processors, and the MIPS R4x00 and R5x00 processors. More recently, IBM has announced Linux for its S/390 and zSeries mainframes. This book covers Red Hat Linux for the Intel 80x86 and Pentium processors (these are known as the IA32 architecture processors, or i386, because they support the instruction set of the 80386 processor).

Red Hat Linux is a specific Linux distribution. A Linux distribution is essentially a package consisting of the Linux operating system and a collection of applications, together with an easy-to-use installation program. All Linux distributions include the core Linux operating system (the kernel); the XFree86 X Window System for x86 systems; one or more graphical desktops, such as GNOME and KDE; and a large selection of applications. Everything comes in ready-to-run binary format, but the source code and documentation are also included. By now, each Linux distribution includes so much software that it comes on multiple CD-ROMs. For example, this book comes with two CD-ROMs containing the Publisher's Edition of Red Hat Linux. The source code CD-ROM is not included but is available upon request (see coupon on the final page of this book).

Like many other Linux distributions, Red Hat Linux is a commercial distribution. You can buy Red Hat Linux in computer stores and bookstores. The GNU (which stands for "GNU's Not UNIX") General Public License that applies to Linux allows for such commercial, for-profit distribution, but requires that the software be distributed in source-code form, and stipulates that anyone can copy and distribute the software in source-code form to anyone else.

---

insider insight   In an effort to unite several different Linux distributions and promote widespread adoption, a number of Linux companies (Conectiva, The SCO Group, SuSE, and Turbolinux) have formed the UnitedLinux group, and in November 2002, the group released version 1.0 of its UnitedLinux product. UnitedLinux is expected to compete with the Red Hat Linux distribution.

Both the Linux kernel and Red Hat Linux have gone through a number of versions. The version numbers are unrelated, but each has particular significance.

Linux Kernel Version Numbers

After Linux version 1.0 was released on March 14, 1994, the loosely organized Linux development community adopted a version-number scheme. Versions 1.x.y and 2.x.y, where x is an even number, are stable versions. The number y is the *patch level*, which is incremented as problems are fixed. Notice that these version numbers are of the form *Major.Minor.Patch*, where *Major* and *Minor* are integers denoting the major and minor version numbers, and *Patch* is another integer representing the patch level.

Versions 2.x.y with an odd x number are beta releases for developers only; they may be unstable, so you should not adopt these versions for day-to-day use. Developers add new features to these odd-numbered versions of Linux.

When this book was written, the latest stable version of the Linux kernel was 2.4.20 (note that information about the latest version of the Linux kernel is available at http://www.kernel.org/). This book's companion CD-ROMs contain the latest version of the Linux kernel as of Spring 2003.

---

cross ref   If you hear about a later version of Linux or about helpful patches (minor corrections) to the current version, you can obtain the patches and rebuild the kernel by following the instructions in Chapter 21. That chapter also describes how you can download the new kernel from Red Hat.

Red Hat Linux Version Numbers

Red Hat assigns the Red Hat Linux version numbers, such as 7.3 or 8.1. They are of the form x.y, where x is the major version and y the minor version. Unlike with the Linux kernel version numbers, there is no special meaning associated with odd and even minor versions. Nowadays if the minor version number is zero, it's simply dropped — as in Red Hat Linux 9. Each version of Red Hat Linux includes specific versions of the Linux kernel and other major components, such as the XFree86, GNOME, KDE, and various applications such as the OpenOffice.org suite.

Red Hat releases new versions of Red Hat Linux on a regular basis. For example, Red Hat Linux 5.2 came out in November 1998, 6.0 in April 1999, 7.0 in September 2000, 8.0 in September 2002, and Red Hat Linux 9 on March 31, 2003. Typically, each new major version of Red Hat Linux provides significant new features. Red Hat Linux 6.x brought in the GNOME and KDE graphical desktops; Red Hat Linux 7.0 offered features such as support for the Universal Serial Bus (USB) keyboard and mice, XFree86 4.0, and strengthened network security with Kerberos. Red Hat Linux 8.0 provided a uniform look-and-feel for both GNOME and KDE desktops, included the OpenOffice.org office suite, and added many graphical configuration tools. Red Hat Linux 9 includes the Common UNIX Printing System (CUPS), Apache 2.0 Web server, and the Native POSIX Thread Library. In all major versions, Red Hat also updates the core components from the kernel to the GNU C Compiler and associated libraries. Often these behind-the-scenes changes to the core operating system provide significant benefits such as support for newer interfaces and a more secure system.

Linux as a UNIX Platform

Like other UNIX systems, Linux is a multiuser, multitasking operating system, which means that it enables multiple users to log in and to run more than one program at the same time.

Secret

UNIX was developed in the early 1970s at AT&T Bell Laboratories. Its development came on the heels of another operating system called MULTICS; developers are said to have come up with the name UNIX by changing the MULT in MULTICS to UN (meaning one). Bell Laboratories continued to develop UNIX and released several versions: System III, followed by System V Release 1, or SVR1, and SVR2, SVR3, and SVR4.

As it maintained and enhanced UNIX, Bell Laboratories distributed source code to educational institutions. The University of California at Berkeley2 (UC Berkeley) was one of the schools that received a copy of UNIX and added many new features to the operating system. Eventually, UC Berkeley released its version of UNIX, called Berkeley Software Distribution (BSD) UNIX. The most widely used versions of BSD UNIX are 4.3 and 4.4 (known as 4.4BSD).

By the time 4.4BSD UNIX came out, UC Berkeley realized that there was very little original Bell Laboratories UNIX code in the source code. Soon, several groups wrote new code to replace the small amount of leftover Bell Laboratories code and adapted BSD UNIX to the Intel 386 processor. This resulted in the FreeBSD and NetBSD versions of freely available BSD UNIX for Intel PCs.

Note that UNIX System V, Release 4—SVR4—combines all features of System V and BSD UNIX.

POSIX Compliance

Linux is designed to comply with IEEE Std 1003.1 1996 Edition (POSIX). This standard defines the functions that applications written in the C programming language use to access the services of the operating system—for tasks ranging from opening a file to allocating memory. On March 8, 1996, the Computer Systems Laboratory of the National Institute of Standards and Technology (NIST), a U.S. government agency, confirmed that

Linux version 1.2.13, as packaged by Open Linux Ltd., conforms to the POSIX standard. To see a list of POSIX-validated products, point your Web browser to http://www.nist .gov/itl/div897/ctg/posix/finalreg4.htm. Note that the NIST POSIX testing program ended on December 31, 1997. Of course, POSIX compliance, while commendable, is not synonymous with a high-quality operating system.

Along with POSIX conformance, Linux includes many features of other UNIX standards, such as the System V Interface Document (SVID) and the Berkeley Software Distribution (BSD) version of UNIX. Linux takes an eclectic approach, picking the most-needed features of several standard flavors of UNIX.

Secret

POSIX stands for Portable Operating System Interface (abbreviated as POSIX to make it sound like UNIX). The Institute of Electrical and Electronics Engineers (IEEE) began developing the POSIX standards to promote the portability of applications across UNIX environments. POSIX is not limited to UNIX, however. Many other operating systems, such as Hewlett-Packard OpenVMS and Microsoft Windows NT/2000/XP, implement POSIX—in particular, the IEEE Std. 1003.1 1996 Edition, or POSIX.1, which provides a source-level C-language Application Program Interface (API) to the services of the operating system, such as reading and writing files. POSIX.1 has been accepted by the International Organization for Standardization (ISO) and is known as the ISO/IEC 9945-1:1996 standard.

Incidentally, the term POSIX is used interchangeably with the IEEE 1003 and 2003 family of standards. There are several other IEEE standards besides the 1003 and 2003 family—such as 1224 and 1228—that also provide APIs for developing portable applications. For the latest information on all IEEE standards, visit the IEEE Standards Home Page at http://standards.ieee.org/. To read summary information about the POSIX standards, visit the IEEE Web page at http://standards .ieee.org/reading/ieee/std_public/description/posix/.

In addition to POSIX (IEEE 1003.1) compliance, Linux supports the IEEE 1003.2 standard, which focuses on the operating system's command interpreter (commonly referred to as the shell) and a standard set of utility programs. If you know UNIX or you've had some exposure to it, you know that UNIX takes a tools-oriented view of the operating system. It provides a tool for almost anything you might want to do, and the shell enables you to combine several tools to perform tasks more complicated than those the basic tools handle. The IEEE 1003.2 standard maintains this tools-oriented view, providing the following features:

- A shell with a specified set of built-in commands and a programming syntax that can be used to write shell programs, or scripts
- A standard set of utility programs—such as sed, tr, and awk—that shell scripts and applications can call. Even the vi editor and the mail electronic-mail program are part of the standard set. You will learn more about these utilities in Chapters 8, 10, and 11.
- A set of C functions, such as system and getenv, that applications can use to access features of the shell
- A set of utilities, such as Perl and Tcl, for developing shell applications

The default Linux shell is called Bash, which stands for Bourne-Again Shell—a reference to the Bourne shell, which has been the standard UNIX shell since the early days of UNIX. Bash incorporates many of the features IEEE 1003.2 requires and then some. It essentially inherits the features and functionality of the Bourne shell. In case of any discrepancy between the Bourne shell and IEEE 1003.2, Bash follows IEEE 1003.2. For stricter IEEE 1003.2 compliance, Bash even includes a POSIX mode.

All in all, Linux serves as a good platform for learning UNIX because it offers a standard set of UNIX commands (the IEEE 1003.2 standard, as well as the best features of both System V and BSD UNIX).

Linux's support for POSIX and other common UNIX system calls (the functions that applications call) makes it an excellent system for software development. Another ingredient of modern workstation software, the X Window System, is also available in Linux in the form of XFree86.

Linux Standard Base (LSB)

Linux has become important enough that there is now a standard for Linux called the Linux Standard Base, or LSB for short. LSB is a set of binary standards that should help reduce variations among the Linux distributions and promote portability of applications. The idea behind LSB is to provide application binary interface (ABI) so that software applications can run on any Linux (or other UNIX) systems that conform to the LSB standard. The LSB specification references the POSIX standards as well as many other standards such as the C programming language standard and the X Window System version 11 release 6 (X11R6). LSB version 1.2 (commonly referred to as LSB 1.2) was released on June 28, 2002. LSB 1.3 went through a public review in early November 2002.

Secret

The LSB specification is organized into two parts—a common specification that remains the same across all types of processors and a set of hardware-specific specifications, one for each type of processor architecture. For example, LSB 1.2 has architecture-specific specifications for Intel 32-bit (IA32) and Power PC 32-bit (PPC32) processors. LSB 1.3 adds a specification for the Intel 64-bit (IA64) architecture, in addition to the ones for IA32 and PPC32.

There is an LSB certification program, and by now a number of Linux systems, such as Red Hat Linux 8.0, Mandrake Linux ProSuite 9.0, SuSE Linux 8.1, and UnitedLinux 1.0 LSB, are certified to be LSB 1.2–compliant IA32 runtime environments.

To learn more about LSB, visit `http://www.linuxbase.org/`. **The latest list of LSB-certified systems is available at** `http://www.opengroup.org/lsb/cert/cert_prodlist.tpl`.

Linux Desktop

Let's face it—typing cryptic UNIX commands on a terminal is boring. Those of us who know the commands by heart may not realize it, but the installed base of UNIX is not going to increase significantly if we don't make the system easy to use. This is where the X Window System, or X, comes to the rescue.

X provides a standard mechanism for displaying device-independent bitmapped graphics. In other words, an X application can display its graphic output on many different machines that use different methods to display text, graphics, and images on the monitor. X is also a windowing system, meaning it enables applications to organize their output in separate windows. X uses a client/server architecture and works over the network, so you can run X applications on various systems on the network while the output appears in windows that are managed by an X server running on your system.

Although X provides the mechanism for windowed output, it does not offer any specific look or feel for applications. The look and feel comes from GUIs, such as GNOME and KDE, which are based on the X Window System.

<table>
<tr>
<td>

cross
ref

</td>
<td>

The Red Hat Linux distribution on this book's CD-ROMs comes with the X Window System in the form of XFree86 4.3—an implementation of X11R6 (X Window System version 11, release 6, which is the latest release of X) for 80x86 systems. A key feature of XFree86 is its support for a wide variety of video cards available for today's PCs. As you will learn in Chapter 3, XFree86 supports hundreds of PC video cards, ranging from the run-of-the-mill Super Video Graphics Array (SVGA) to accelerated graphics cards such as the ones based on the 3Dfx, ATI, Intel, Matrox, NVIDIA, and S3 video chipsets. However, XFree86 may not work well on some generic video cards containing variants of popular chipsets such as S3.

</td>
</tr>
</table>

As for the GUI, Linux includes two powerful graphical desktop environments: KDE (K Desktop Environment) and GNOME (GNU Network Object Model Environment). When you install Red Hat Linux, you can choose which desktop you want or can install both and switch between the two. GNOME and KDE provide desktops similar to the ones in Microsoft Windows and the Apple Mac OS. GNOME also comes with the Nautilus graphical shell that makes it easy to find files, run applications, and configure your Linux system. With GNOME or KDE, you can begin using your Linux workstation without having to learn UNIX commands. However, if you should ever need to use UNIX commands, all you have to do is open a terminal window and type the commands at the shell prompt.

Red Hat Linux also comes with many graphical applications that run under X. The most noteworthy programs relate to image display and editing. The first is GIMP—the GNU Image Manipulation Program—a program with capabilities on a par with Adobe Photoshop; the second program is ImageMagick.

Another important aspect of the X Window System is that you can run applications across the network because X uses a client/server architecture. The X server runs at the workstation and controls the display, keyboard, and mouse. Client applications send requests to the X server to receive user input and display output. For example, you might run an X application on a server somewhere on the network but view that application's output and interact with it from your Linux desktop that's running a X-based GUI. In other words, with X, your Linux PC becomes a gateway to all the other systems on the network.

Motif is the dominant GUI in the UNIX marketplace, but it's not packaged with Linux because the Open Software Foundation does not distribute Motif for free. Motif has a look and feel similar to Microsoft Windows and includes the Motif Window Manager (MWM) and the Motif toolkit for programmers. You can download OpenMotif for Linux from http://www.motifzone.net/. In addition to Open Motif from The Open Group, another option for Motif for Linux is LessTif, a free version of Motif distributed under the GNU

General Public License (visit the LessTif home page at http://www.lesstif.org for the latest information on LessTif). Red Hat Linux comes with LessTif and is automatically installed if you select the X Software Development package group during Red Hat Linux installation.

If you need Motif for a project, using a Linux PC with a copy of OpenMotif or LessTif installed is an economical way to set up a software-development platform. If you have a consulting business, or if you want to develop X and Motif software at home, Linux is definitely the way to go.

Along with GNOME and KDE, you get two more options for developing GUI applications in Linux. GNOME comes with a toolkit called Gtk+ (GIMP toolkit), and KDE comes with the Qt toolkit. If you do not want to learn Motif, you may want to use Gtk+ or Qt for your GUI applications.

cross
ref

Chapter 3 shows you how to set up **XFree86** on your system, and Chapter 8 presents the GNOME and KDE desktops.

Secret

Office productivity software—such as word-processing, spreadsheet, and database applications—is an area in which Linux used to be lacking. This situation has changed, though. Red Hat Linux comes with the OpenOffice.org office-productivity applications. In addition, there are several prominent commercially available office-productivity applications for Linux that are not included on the companion CD-ROMs. Applixware Office—now called Anyware Desktop for Linux—is a good example of productivity software for Linux (http://www.vistasource.com/products/). Another well-known productivity-software package is StarOffice from Sun Microsystems (http://www.sun.com/staroffice/). CrossOver Office, from CodeWeavers, is a commercially available software package that enables you to install your Microsoft Office applications (only Office 97 or Office 2000, not Office XP) in Linux. Furthermore, many existing software packages (designed for UNIX workstations with the X Window System) can be readily ported to Linux, thanks to Linux's support for portable standards such as POSIX and the X Window System.

Linux Networking

Networking refers to all aspects of data exchange within one computer or between two or more computers, ranging from the physical connection to the protocol for the actual data exchange. A network protocol is the method the sender and receiver agree upon for exchanging data across a network.

Different network protocols are used at different levels of the network. At the physical level—at which the data bits travel through a medium, such as a cable—Ethernet and Asynchronous Transfer Mode (ATM) are two commonly-used protocols. Application programs don't really work at the physical level, however. Instead, they rely on protocols that operate on blocks of data. These protocols include Novell's Internet Packet Exchange (IPX) and the well-known Transmission Control Protocol/Internet Protocol (TCP/IP).

cross ref
The different levels of network protocols can be represented by a networking model such as the seven-layer Open Systems Interconnection (OSI) reference model, developed by ISO. Chapter 6 includes a discussion of this model.

Standard network protocols such as TCP/IP have been key to the growth of interconnected computers, resulting in local area networks (LANs), as well as wide area networks (WANs). Protocols have enabled these smaller networks to communicate with each other, and we now have interconnected networks that form an internetwork: the Internet.

TCP/IP

The ability to network has been one of the strengths of UNIX since its early days. In particular, the well-known TCP/IP protocol suite has been an integral part of UNIX ever since TCP/IP appeared in BSD UNIX around 1982. By now, TCP/IP is the wide area and local area networking protocol of choice in the global Internet. TCP/IP does not depend on the physical communication media. This media independence enables TCP/IP to work in a wide variety of networks.

Linux supports the TCP/IP protocol suite and includes all common network applications such as Telnet, FTP, and sendmail. At the physical-network level, Linux includes drivers for many Ethernet cards. Token ring is also an integral part of the Linux kernel source; all you have to do is load the token ring driver to enable support for token ring.

cross ref
You might say that Linux's support for TCP/IP—the dominant protocol suite of the Internet—comes naturally. The rapid development of Linux itself would not have been possible without the collaboration of so many developers from Europe, America, and other parts of the world. That collaboration, in turn, has been possible only because of the Internet. Chapters 13 through 19 show you how to set up TCP/IP networking and to use various servers to offer services such as Web, email, and domain name service.

Linux also includes the Berkeley Sockets programming interface (so named because the Sockets interface was introduced in Berkeley UNIX around 1982), a popular interface for network programming in TCP/IP networks. For those of you with C programming experience, the Sockets interface consists of several C header files and several C functions that you call to set up connections and to send and receive data. Chapter 6 describes sockets.

You can use the Berkeley Sockets programming interface to develop Internet tools such as Web browsers. Because most TCP/IP programs (including those available for free at various Internet sites) use the Sockets programming interface, it is easy to get these programs up and running on Linux because it includes the Sockets interface.

PPP and SLIP

Not everyone has an Ethernet connection to the Internet (although a growing number of us are beginning to have high-speed always-on connections to the Internet, thanks to cable modems or DSL). Most of us still connect to the Internet and communicate by using the TCP/IP protocol over a phone line and a modem. To do this, what you need is access to a server—a system that has an Internet connection and that accepts a dial-in connection from your system.

Commercial outfits known as Internet service providers (ISPs) offer this type of service for a fee. If you don't want to pay for such a connection, find out whether a computer at your place of business provides this access. That option may not be unreasonable, especially if you are doing UNIX software development (for your company) on your Linux PC at home.

When you access the Internet through a server, the server runs the Point-to-Point Protocol (PPP), which works over any serial link, including dial-up conenctions.

---

cross ref   Linux supports PPP for dial-up Internet connections. You can also turn your Linux system into a PPP server so that other computers can dial in to your computer and establish a TCP/IP connection over the phone. Chapter 13 explains how to set up a PPP dial-up Internet connection on your Red Hat Linux system.

Cable/DSL and Wireless Networks

If you have high-speed Internet access through cable modem or DSL (Digital Subscriber Line), you can easily hook up a Ethernet-equipped Linux PC to the Internet. For the most part, the configuration of the Linux PC is the same as that for TCP/IP networking. However, for ISPs that use PPP over Ethernet (PPPoE), you may have to do some additional configuring. Linux includes support for PPPoE.

Linux also supports wireless Ethernet cards that you can use to connect laptop PCs to an existing wired Ethernet local area network (LAN). These wireless Ethernet cards conform to the IEEE 802.11b standard, also known as Wi-Fi. If your LAN connects to the Internet through a cable/DSL router and hub, you can extend the LAN by connecting a wireless access point to the hub. Then, any Wi-Fi-equipped laptop or desktop PC can connect to the Internet through the cable or DSL connection.

---

cross ref   Chapter 13 describes how to configure Linux for a wireless Ethernet network.

File Sharing with NFS

In the Microsoft Windows or Novell NetWare world, you may be familiar with the concept of a file server—a system that maintains important files and allows all other systems on the network to access those files. Storing files on a central server provides for better security and enables convenient backups. Essentially, all PCs on the network share one or more central disks. In Windows and Novell, users see the file server's disk as just another drive, with its own drive letter (such as U). Typically in PC networks, you implement file sharing with Novell NetWare or Microsoft LAN Manager protocols.

File sharing exists in UNIX as well. The Network File System (NFS) provides a standard way for a system to access another system's files over the network. To the user, the remote system's files appear to be in a directory on the local system.

cross ref NFS is available in Linux; you can share your Linux system's directories with other systems that support NFS. The other systems that access your Linux system's files via NFS do not necessarily have to run UNIX; NFS is available for DOS, Windows, OS/2, and NetWare as well. Therefore, you can use a Linux PC as the file server for a small workgroup of PCs that run DOS and/or Windows. Chapter 19 further explores the use of a Linux PC as a file server. Chapter 19 also explains how to use the Samba package to set up your Linux PC as a server in a Windows network.

Linux System Administration

System administration refers to tasks that someone must perform to keep a computer system up and running properly. Now that almost all computers are networked, it's necessary to perform another set of tasks to keep the network up and running. All these tasks are collectively called network administration. A site with many computers probably has a full-time system administrator who takes care of all system-administration and network-administration tasks. Really large sites may have separate system-administration and network-administration personnel. If you are running Linux on a home PC or on a few systems in a small company, you are probably both the system administrator and the network administrator.

cross ref Linux supplies all the basic commands and utilities you need for system and network administration. Chapters 12 and 20 briefly cover some of these commands. Chapter 6 describes some network-administration tools.

GNOME's Nautilus graphical shell comes with many GUI tools that enable you to perform most system-administration and network-administration tasks without having to edit configuration files manually or type cryptic commands. However, you should always learn the key commands and be proficient with a plaintext editor such as vi, for those times when you must use a text-only login and the GUI tools are not available. Additionally, you need to understand the layout of the key configuration files. I cover this type of information throughout this book, even when describing GNOME and KDE, because they too depend on configuration files for correct operation.

System-Administration Tasks

As a system administrator, your tasks typically are the following:

◆ **Installing, configuring, and upgrading the operating system and various utilities.** You learn how to install Red Hat Linux and other software packages in Chapter 2. Chapter 3 tells you how to install and configure the X Window System, and Chapter 21 shows you how to upgrade the operating system—the Linux kernel.

◆ **Adding and removing users.** As shown in Chapter 18, you can use Nautilus's Red Hat User Manager graphical tool or the useradd command to add a new user after you install Linux. If a user forgets a password, you can change the password from the Red Hat User Manager or can use the passwd command to change it.

◆ **Installing new software.** For the typical Linux software, which you get in source-code form, this task involves using tools such as gunzip (to uncompress the software), tar (to unpack the archive), and make (to build the executable programs). For software, Red Hat distributes in Red Hat Package Manager (RPM) files, use the rpm command to install the software. Chapter 21 describes RPM.

◆ **Making backups.** You can use the tar program to archive one or more directories and to copy the archive to a floppy disk (if the archive is small enough) or to a tape (if you have a tape drive). Chapter 20 covers backing up and restoring files and directories.

◆ **Managing file systems.** When you want to read an MS-DOS floppy disk, for example, mount that disk's MS-DOS file system on one of the directories of the Linux file system. Use the mount command to do this. You can also use mount an NT file system (NTFS) after installing a kernel module that supports NTFS. You also want to monitor the file system to ensure that users or some errant process have not filled them up.

◆ **Monitoring the system's performance.** You have to use a few utilities, such as top (to see where the processor is spending most of its time) and free (to see the amount of free and used memory in the system).

◆ **Monitoring the system's integrity.** You want to make sure that no one has tampered with key system files. You can use tools such as Tripwire to perform this task. Chapter 22 covers how to maintain system security.

◆ **Starting and shutting down the system.** Although starting the system typically involves nothing more than powering up the PC, you do have to take some care when you want to shut down your Linux system. Use the shutdown command to stop all programs before turning off your PC's power switch. If your system is set up for a graphical login screen, you can perform the shutdown operation by selecting a menu item from the login screen.

Network-Administration Tasks

Typical network-administration tasks are the following:

◆ **Maintaining the network configuration files.** In Linux (as well as in other UNIX systems), several text files hold the configuration information for the TCP/IP network. You may have to edit these files to make networking work. You may have to edit one or more of the following files: /etc/hosts, /etc/networks, /etc/host.conf, /etc/resolv.conf, /etc/HOSTNAME, /etc/hosts.allow, /etc/hosts.deny, and the scripts in the /etc/sysconfig/network-scripts directory. You can either edit these files manually or use the graphical Network Configuration tool to configure them.

◆ **Setting up PPP.** You may use tools such as wvdial to set up and use PPP connections. You can also use the Red Hat Dialup Configuration Tool to set up PPP connections. Chapter 13 shows you how to work with PPP commands and configuration files.

◆ **Monitoring network status.** You have to use tools such as netstat (to view information about active network connections), /sbin/ifconfig (to check the status of various network interfaces), and ping (to make sure that a connection is working).

◆ **Securing Internet services.** If your system is connected to the Internet (or if it is on an internal network), you have to secure the system against anyone who might use one of many Internet services to gain access to your system. Each service—such as email, Web, or FTP—requires running a server program that responds to client requests arriving over the TCP/IP network. Some of these server programs have weaknesses that may enable an outsider to log in to your system—maybe with root privileges. Turn off services you do not need, and edit configuration files to restrict access to those services you are running. Chapter 22 covers network security and how to use commands such as chkconfig to turn Internet services on or off.

Windows and Linux

As you probably know, MS-DOS used to be and Microsoft Windows (in its various versions from Windows 95/98 to Windows XP) continues to be the most popular operating system for 80386, 80486, and Pentium PCs. Because Linux started on 80386/80486 PCs, a connection between DOS/Windows and Linux has always existed. Typically, you start the Linux installation with some steps in DOS.

Linux has maintained its connection to DOS/Windows in several ways:

 ◆ Linux supports the older MS-DOS file system called FAT (file allocation table), as well as the newer Windows VFAT (long filenames) and FAT32 file systems. From Linux, you can access MS-DOS and Windows files on a hard disk or a floppy disk.

 ◆ Linux supports read-only access to NTFS file system that is used in Windows NT/2000/XP. You can build (or download) and load a driver module to incorporate the NTFS support.

 ◆ Linux features a set of tools (called mtools) that manipulates DOS/Windows files from within Linux.

An ongoing project called WINE is developing a free implementation of Windows for the X Window System under UNIX (see http://www.winehq.com/). WINE enables you to run Windows 3.1/95/NT programs. WINE works on some versions of UNIX for the Intel x86 systems, including Linux and FreeBSD.

---

cross ref
Chapter 12 describes how you can access DOS from Linux and explains the use of the mtools utilities.

Software Development in Linux

Of all its potential uses, Linux is particularly well suited to software development. Software-development tools, such as the compiler and libraries, are included because you need them when you rebuild the Linux kernel. If you are a UNIX software developer, you already know UNIX, so you will feel right at home in Linux.

As far as the development environment goes, you have the same basic tools (such as an editor, a compiler, and a debugger) that you might use on other UNIX workstations, such as those from IBM, Sun Microsystems, and Hewlett-Packard (HP). Therefore, if you work by day on one of the mainstream UNIX workstations, you can use a Linux PC at home to duplicate that development environment at a fraction of the cost. Then, you can either complete work projects at home or devote your time to software you write for fun and share on the Internet.

Just to give you a sense of Linux's software-development support, the following is a list of various features that make Linux a productive software-development environment:

♦ GNU's C compiler, gcc, which can compile ANSI-standard C programs

♦ GNU's C++ compiler (g++), which supports ANSI-standard C++ features

♦ The GNU compiler for the Java programming language, gcj

♦ The GNU debugger, gdb, which enables you to step through your program to find problems and to determine where and how a program has failed. (The failed program's memory image is saved in a file named core; gdb can examine this file.)

♦ The GNU profiling utility, gprof, which enables you to determine the degree to which a piece of software uses your computer's processor time

♦ The GNU make utility, which enables you to compile and link large programs

♦ Concurrent Versions System (CVS) and Revision Control System (RCS), which maintain version information and control access to the source files so that two programmers don't modify the same source file inadvertently

♦ The GNU Emacs editor, which prepares source files and even launches a compile-link process to build the program

♦ The Perl scripting language, which you can use to write scripts that tie together many smaller programs with UNIX commands to accomplish a specific task

♦ The Tool Command Language and its X toolkit (Tcl/Tk), which enable you to prototype X applications rapidly

♦ The Python language, an interpreted language comparable to Perl and Tcl (the Red Hat Linux installation program, called anaconda, is written in Python)

♦ Dynamically linked shared libraries, which allow the actual program files to be much smaller because all the library code that several programs may use is shared, with only one copy being loaded in the system's memory

♦ POSIX header files and libraries, which enable you to write portable programs

cross ref   Chapter 23 covers software development in Linux. Read Chapters 24 and 25 to learn about Perl and Tcl/Tk programming. Chapter 26 covers Java programming in Red Hat Linux.

Linux as an Internet On-Ramp

Most likely, you have experienced much of what the Internet has to offer: electronic mail, newsgroups, and the Web. So you may be happy to learn that a Red Hat Linux system includes everything you need to access the Internet. In fact, your PC can become a first-class citizen of the Internet, with its own Web server on which you can publish any information you want.

Although Linux includes TCP/IP and supporting network software with which you can set up your PC as an Internet host, there is one catch: First, you have to obtain a physical connection to the Internet. Your Linux PC has to be connected to another node (which can be another computer or a networking device, such as a router) on the Internet. This requirement is the stumbling block for many people—an Internet connection costs money, the price proportional to the data-transfer rate.

Many commercial ISPs provide various forms of physical connections to the Internet. In the United States, if you are willing to spend between $15 and $30 a month, you can get an account on a PPP server. Then you can run PPP software on your Linux system, dial in via a modem, and connect to the Internet at data-transfer rates ranging from 28,800 bits per second (bps) to 56,000 bps, depending on your modem.

Although a dial-up connection is adequate for accessing the Internet, receiving email, and reading news, it may not be adequate if you want your system to provide information to other people through the Web or FTP (File Transfer Protocol). Besides your ISP may not allow you to use the dial-up connection to run a Web server. To set up a useful Web server, you need a connection that is available 24 hours a day, because other systems may try to access your system any time of day. For a few hundred dollars a month, you can get a dedicated connection and make your system a permanent presence on the Internet. Other options that offer higher-capacity Internet connections than dial-up modems are cable modems and Digital Subscriber Lines (DSL). You may also opt to run the server at the ISP's facility—something many people do because it's very convenient.

Another requirement for a business—or for anyone who has a few networked PCs—is connecting a local area network (LAN) to the Internet. You can run Linux on one of the PCs and use it as the Internet gateway to accomplish this task. Typically, you have an Ethernet LAN running TCP/IP connected to all of the PCs on the network, including the Linux machine. The Linux PC sets up a PPP connection to the Internet (via a dial-up or dedicated connection). You then set up the Linux PC to act as a gateway between the Ethernet LAN and the Internet so that the PCs on your LAN can access other systems on the Internet.

**cross
ref** In Chapter 13, you learn to configure your Linux system to access the Internet.

Summary

After you get Linux going on your PC, you can turn your attention to the work you plan to do with it. Whether you want to develop software or set up your PC as an Internet host, you can use Linux wisely if you know its overall capabilities. Accordingly, this chapter provided an overview of various aspects of Linux, ranging from software development to networking and system administration. In the next chapter, I will show you how to install Red Hat Linux from this book's companion CD-ROMs and get started on using Linux.

By reading this chapter, you learned the following:

♦ Linux is a freely available UNIX-like operating system that runs on a wide variety of systems. Red Hat Linux is a specific Linux distribution—a package incorporating the Linux operating system and a huge collection of applications, together with an easy-to-use installation program.

♦ Linux developers use a version-number scheme to help you understand what the various versions of Linux kernel—the core operating system—mean. Kernel versions 2.x.y, where x is an even number, are stable versions. The number represented by y is the patch level, which is incremented as problems are fixed. Versions 2.x.y, where x is an odd number, are beta releases for developers only, because these releases may be unstable.

◆ POSIX stands for Portable Operating System Interface (abbreviated as POSIX to make it sound like UNIX). The Institute of Electrical and Electronics Engineers (IEEE) began developing the POSIX standards to promote the portability of applications across UNIX environments.

◆ Red Hat Linux conforms to a binary standard called Linux Standard Base (LSB), which promotes compatibility among Linux systems so that applications built for one system can run on all LSB-compliant systems with the same processor architecture.

◆ This book's Red Hat Linux distribution comes with XFree86 (X Window System Version 11 Release 6 or X11R6), GNOME, and KDE software. After you install XFree86 and GNOME or KDE, you have a graphical user interface (GUI) for Linux. In addition, X enables you to run applications across the network—which means that you can run applications on another system on the network and can have the output appear on your Linux PC's display.

◆ Linux effectively supports TCP/IP networking. TCP/IP is the networking protocol of choice on the Internet. Therefore, a Linux PC is ideal as an Internet host, providing services such as FTP and World Wide Web access. You can also use the Linux PC as your Internet ramp by connecting to an Internet service provider through a dial-up, cable, or DSL connection and running a Web browser to surf the Net. You can configure Linux to support wireless Ethernet network cards.

◆ The Red Hat Linux distribution on the companion CD-ROM also includes Nautilus with many graphical tools that enable you to perform most system-administration and network-administration tasks from a GUI.

◆ Red Hat Linux provides all the software development tools you need to write UNIX and X applications. You'll find the GNU C and C++ compiler for compiling source files, `make` for automating the compiling, the `gdb` debugger for finding bugs, and Concurrent Versions System (CVS) and Revision Control System (RCS) for managing various revisions of a file. Thus, a Linux PC is the software developer's ideal workstation.

Red Hat Linux Installation

Chapter

2

♦ ♦

Secrets in This Chapter

♦ ♦

Red Hat Linux installation can be either straightforward or complicated, depending on the specific type of hardware in your PC. If your PC is relatively new and the installer detects all the peripherals such as the video card and network interface card correctly, then you can sail through the installation. On the other hand, if your PC has components that Red Hat Linux does not support, you'd have to perform additional steps to install Red Hat Linux. Typically, you are more likely to find Linux drivers for common name-brand hardware, but these drivers may not work properly for generic hardware. In all cases, if you decide to keep your existing Microsoft Windows installation and install Red Hat Linux as a second operating system, you have to go through the trouble of creating the disk partitions for Red Hat Linux.

You need some specific information about your PC's hardware, such as the type of disk controller, video card, and network card to figure out whether you can install Red Hat Linux easily or not. The Linux operating system controls the hardware through drivers (software through which the operating system accesses the hardware), so you need to make sure that the current release of Linux includes drivers for your hardware. If your hardware is popular enough, there's a good chance that someone has developed a driver for it. The version of Red Hat Linux on the companion CD-ROMs supports a wide variety of hardware, so all of your PC's peripherals are probably supported.

In this chapter, you learn how to install Red Hat Linux from the companion CD-ROMs. The chapter starts with an overview of the entire installation process, then it guides you through the installation process, highlighting the critical parts and providing technical information necessary to complete these installation steps.

cross
ref

If you have installed Red Hat Linux already, Chapter 7 shows you how to get started with Red Hat Linux.

Understanding the Red Hat Linux Installation Process

Before starting a big job, I always find it helpful to visualize the entire sequence of tasks I must perform. The process is similar to studying a map before you drive to a place you have never been. Red Hat Linux installation can be a big job, especially if you run into snags. This section shows you the road map for the installation process. After reading this section, you should be mentally prepared to install Red Hat Linux.

Here are the general steps for installing Red Hat Linux:

1. Gather information about your PC's hardware before you install Red Hat Linux. The Linux operating system accesses and uses various PC peripherals through software components called *drivers*. You have to make sure that the version of Red Hat Linux you are about to install has the necessary drivers for your system's hardware configuration. Conversely, if you do not have a system yet, look at the list of hardware that Linux supports, and make sure you buy a PC with components that Red Hat Linux supports.

2. Because most PCs come with Microsoft Windows preinstalled on the hard disk, you have to perform a step known as *partitioning* to allocate parts of your hard

disk for Linux's use. If you have a spare hard disk, you should keep Windows on the first hard disk and install Linux on the second hard disk. With a spare second disk, you don't need to worry about partitioning under DOS or Windows. If you have only one hard disk, however, you have to partition that disk into several parts. Use a part for Windows, and leave the rest for Linux. For Windows 95/98/Me, you can use the nondestructive repartitioning program FIPS to repartition your hard disk without destroying the existing contents. FIPS creates a new partition by shrinking the existing DOS partition. For Windows NT/2000/XP systems with disk partitions that use the NT file system (NTFS), use a commercial hard-drive partitioning tool such as PartitionMagic from PowerQuest. You can, of course, install Linux as the sole operating system on a PC; in that case, you can ignore this step and simply let the Red Hat Linux installation program automatically create the necessary partitions.

3. Under DOS or Windows, create a Red Hat Linux installer boot disk. This boot disk is used to boot your PC and to start an initial version of the Linux operating system. If your PC is configured to boot from the CD-ROM drive, you can skip this step—instead, you can boot Linux directly from the CD-ROM. Even if your PC normally does not boot from the CD-ROM drive, you can usually press one or more keys as the PC boots and enter the BIOS setup screen from which you can select the CD-ROM drive as the boot device. You may want to consult your PC's manual to see how you can boot from the CD-ROM.

4. Boot your PC from the first CD-ROM or with the Red Hat Linux installer boot disk. This procedure automatically loads the Linux kernel and runs anaconda, the Red Hat Linux installation program. From this point on, you respond to a number of dialog boxes as the Red Hat installation program takes you through the steps. You have the option of using a text mode or a graphical user interface (GUI). You have to use the text mode if, for some reason, the installation program fails to start the X Window System. In addition, you have to type the `linux noprobe` command if the Linux kernel does not detect some of the older hardware, such as the SCSI controller and network adapter installed in your system. When you type the `linux noprobe` command, you have to either provide a driver disk or load the drivers for your SCSI controller and network adapter by selecting them from a list of drivers.

5. Respond to the dialog box that asks you to choose a language to be used during installation. From subsequent dialog boxes, select the keyboard type, and the mouse type. If you have already placed the CD-ROM in the CD-ROM drive, the installation program uses the CD-ROM as the source of all Red Hat Linux files. Otherwise, the installation program starts in text mode and displays a dialog box from which you have to select the storage medium in which the Red Hat Linux files are located.

6. Choose whether you want to install a new system or to upgrade an existing installation. For a new installation, you also have to decide whether you want to set up a Personal Desktop, Workstation, Server, or a Custom system. Select a Custom installation for maximum flexibility.

7. Prepare the hard disk partitions on which you plan to install Linux. If you have created space for Linux by reducing the size of an existing Windows partition, now you have to create the partitions for Linux. Typically, you need at least two partitions: one for the Linux files and the other for use as the swap partition, which is a form of virtual memory. You can have the installation program automatically perform this disk-partitioning step for you, or you can manually create the partition using Disk Druid, a graphical partitioning utility. If you manually create the hard disk partitions, indicate which partition is the swap, and specify the partition on which you want to install Linux (this is called the root partition).

8. Specify options for installing a boot loader—the GNU GRand Unified Bootloader (GRUB) or the Linux Loader (LILO)—on your hard disk, so you can boot Linux when you power up your PC after shutting it down. For the GRUB boot loader, you can also enable a password that has to be typed every time the system boots. If you are squeamish about installing a boot loader, you can skip installing the boot loader. If you do so, you have to boot Linux using a boot disk that you create a few steps later during the installation process.

9. If the initial Linux kernel detects a network card (assuming that you have one installed on your system), the installation program lets you configure the network (the local area network, not the dial-up network). If the Linux kernel does not detect your network card, you can type the `linux noprobe` command and select your network card from a list. To configure the network, you can either identify a DHCP server (a DHCP server provides IP addresses to systems in a network) or specify a number of parameters, including an IP address, a host name, the IP address of name servers, and a domain name for your Linux system.

10. Configure the firewall security level for your system by selecting one of three predefined levels of security—high, medium, or none.

11. Select one or more languages to be used on your Linux system.

12. Specify the local time zone. For the United States, you can also enable the use of daylight saving time.

13. Select a root password. The root user is the super user—a user who can do anything—in Linux. You can also add one or more other users. Then, select the password-authentication method.

14. Select various software package groups to install. Each package represents a part of Red Hat Linux, from the base operating system to packages such as the GNOME and KDE graphical desktops, the Emacs editor, programming tools, and the X Window System (a graphical windowing system that GNOME and KDE require). Select the package groups you need, and let the Red Hat installation program do its job.

15. The installation program formats the disk partitions and installs the selected package groups.

16. Create a boot disk you can use to boot your Red Hat Linux system if the Linux kernel on the hard disk is damaged or if the boot loader—LILO or GRUB—does not work or if you have chosen not to install any boot loader.

17. Configure the X Window System. In response to dialog boxes that the installation program presents, provide information about your video card and monitor. In most cases, the installation program automatically detects the video card and the monitor. The installation program also lets you enable graphical login, so that when you boot your Linux system, it displays a graphical login window and (after you enter your user name and password) starts the GNOME or KDE graphical desktop after successful login.

18. If you find that Linux does not work properly with one or more of your system components (such as the network card or sound card), you may have to reconfigure the Linux operating system to add support for those system components.

The following sections guide you through the basic installation steps and the initial booting of Linux.

insider insight   Your PC must have a CD-ROM drive—one that Linux supports—to install Linux from this book's companion CD-ROM. Most new PCs have CD-ROM drives that connect to the hard disk controller (called IDE for Integrated Drive Electronics). Any IDE CD-ROM works in Red Hat Linux. If your PC does not have a CD-ROM drive but is on a network, you can use another PC's CD-ROM drive and can install Linux over the network by using NFS or FTP. To install Linux over the network, you must use the Red Hat installer boot disk along with a driver disk—one that contains the `drvnet.img` file from the `\images` directory of the Red Hat Linux CD-ROM.

Preparing Your PC for Linux Installation

Before you install Linux, you should prepare your PC for the installation. You can be in either of two situations:

- You already have a PC that runs some version of Microsoft Windows.
- You are about to buy a new PC, and you plan to run Red Hat Linux on that PC at least some of the time.

If you are about to purchase a PC, you are lucky because you can get a PC configured with peripherals that Red Hat Linux supports. To pick a Red Hat Linux-compatible PC, simply consult the current list of hardware that Red Hat Linux supports, and select a PC certified by Red Hat. If you don't see the PC model you are considering listed as Red Hat–certified, you can still make sure that key hardware components in the PC will work with Red Hat Linux. You may have to ask the PC vendor explicitly for detailed information about hardware, such as the video card, CD-ROM drive, and networking card, to ensure that you can use the peripherals under Red Hat Linux. Selecting a PC with Red Hat Linux–supported hardware minimizes the potential for problems when you install Red Hat Linux.

If you want to install Red Hat Linux on an existing PC, verify that the latest Red Hat Linux distribution supports all of the hardware on your PC. In other words, you have to take an inventory of your PC's hardware components and determine whether Red Hat Linux currently supports all of them.

Checking the Red Hat Hardware Compatibility List

Like many other operating systems, Linux supports various types of hardware through device drivers. For each type of peripheral device, such as a networking card or a CD-ROM drive, Linux needs a driver. In fact, each kind of peripheral needs a separate driver. Because Linux is available free (or relatively inexpensively) and because many programmers scattered throughout the world cooperate to develop Linux, you cannot demand support for a specific kind of hardware. You can only hope that someone who can write a Linux driver has the same hardware you do. In all likelihood, that person will write a driver, which eventually will find its way into a version of Linux, then you can use that hardware under Linux. It may take a while for Linux to support new interfaces.

Secret

Red Hat categorizes all hardware into four categories depending on their compatibility with Red Hat Linux:

- **Certified** hardware has been tested and certified by Red Hat. This type of hardware is fully supported. The installation program automatically detects such hardware and installs the appropriate drivers.
- **Compatible** hardware has been reviewed by Red Hat and is supported. Such hardware is generally known to work, but Red Hat has not certified the hardware. The installation program should be able to detect and use compatible hardware.
- **Community Knowledge** hardware is not tested and not supported by Red Hat. To support Community Knowledge hardware, you may have to perform some explicit steps, such as manually loading the driver module or editing the /etc/ modules.conf file.
- **Not supported** hardware may be compatible with Linux but is not officially supported by Red Hat Linux.

For the most recent and detailed list of hardware Red Hat Linux supports, as well as the level on which a specific hardware belongs, check Red Hat's Hardware Compatibility List at http://hardware.redhat.com/hcl/.

cross
ref

Appendixes B through F provide more information about whether or not Linux supports your system's unique hardware configuration. In these Appendixes, you can also find information about how to get the most from your PC's hardware under Linux.

Making a Hardware Checklist

After you have seen a list of various hardware peripherals Red Hat Linux supports, you should have a rough idea of whether or not you have the right PC hardware to use it. If you are buying a new PC to run Red Hat Linux, the hardware-compatibility list at http://hardware.redhat.com/hcl/ should help you decide the hardware configuration of your new PC.

To summarize, go through the following checklist to see whether or not you are ready to install Red Hat Linux:

- ◆ Does your PC have an 80386 or better processor, with the ISA, EISA (Extended Industry Standard Architecture), VLB (VESA Local-Bus), MCA (Micro Channel Architecture), or PCI (Peripheral Component Interconnect) bus; at least 64MB of RAM; a high-density floppy disk drive; and a large hard drive (at least 4GB)? Remember that to comfortably run both Windows and Red Hat Linux on your PC, you need at least 10GB of disk space.
- ◆ Does your PC have a CD-ROM drive that Red Hat Linux supports? (This is not a problem for new PCs with IDE CD-ROM drives. You need a CD-ROM drive to install Red Hat Linux from this book's companion CD-ROMs.)
- ◆ Can you get a second hard drive? (If so, you can install Red Hat Linux on that hard drive. Installing Red Hat Linux on a second drive prevents you from having to repartition your first hard drive, which usually has Windows loaded on it.)

♦ If you have a SCSI (Small Computer System Interface) controller with any SCSI devices that you want to use under Red Hat Linux, does Linux support the SCSI controller?

♦ Does XFree86 support your video card? (If not, you won't be able to set up and run the X Window System.)

As the comments after the questions indicate, you do not necessarily have to answer yes to each question. You must answer yes to the first two items, however, because without that basic hardware configuration, Red Hat Linux cannot run on your system.

insider insight

If you plan to install Red Hat Linux on an empty second hard disk or if you want to install Linux over an existing DOS/Windows partition, you do not have to go through the process of partitioning (dividing) your hard disk under MS-DOS. You can skip the next few sections and proceed to "Creating the Red Hat Installer Boot Disk." Then you can boot Linux from the CD-ROM or the installer boot disk and proceed to install Red Hat Linux.

Repartitioning Your Hard Drive

If your PC has a single hard disk drive, chances are good that you have some version of Microsoft Windows installed on that drive. If your hard drive is at least 10GB, I recommend that you keep Windows installed on your system, even if you want to work mostly in Linux. After all, you may have Windows applications that you paid for and would like to use now and then. You can access the Windows files from Linux. You get the best of both worlds if you keep Windows around when you install Linux.

Secret

Typically, your PC hard disk is set up as a single large partition, designated by the drive letter C (Windows XP installations often have a hidden first partition and the second partition designated as drive C). Unless you can scrounge up a second hard disk for your PC, or you already have a second disk, your first task is to shrink the existing partition on your one and only hard disk and create free space on the disk for Red Hat Linux.

You can use one of the following tools to resize the existing partition on your hard disk:

• **PartitionMagic:** This is a commercial product that can resize hard disk partitions and create new partitions on any version of Microsoft Windows and Linux. In particular, PartitionMagic can resize partitions that contain NTFS file systems used in Windows NT/2000/XP.

• **FIPS:** This is a free program that comes with Red Hat Linux and runs in MS-DOS mode and can split an existing partition into two. FIPS works only with Windows 95/98/Me systems that use the FAT or FAT32 file system. FIPS does not work with the NTFS file system that's often used in Windows NT/2000/XP systems. For those systems, your best bet is PartitionMagic.

continues

continued

With both of these tools, the idea is to shrink the existing Windows partition and to create unused disk space for the Linux partition. Later on, during Red Hat Linux installation, you have to create new partitions for Red Hat Linux in the unused space. You can either let the Red Hat installer automatically partition the unused disk space or create the partitions yourself by using the Disk Druid tool.

The bottom line is that once you have successfully shrunk the existing Microsoft Windows partition and created a block of unused disk space for Red Hat Linux, you are past the biggest hurdle in installing Red Hat Linux while retaining Windows intact.

Repartitioning with PartitionMagic

PartitionMagic, from PowerQuest, can resize and split disk partitions in all Microsoft operating systems from Windows 95/98/Me to Windows NT/2000/XP. It's a commercial product, so you have to buy it to use it. At the time I'm writing this, the list price of PartitionMagic 8.0 is $69.95. You can read about it and buy it at `http://www.powerquest.com/partitionmagic`.

caution   Resizing the disk partition always involves the risk of losing all data on the hard disk. Therefore, before you resize hard disk partitions using a disk partitioning tool such as PartitionMagic, you should back up your hard disk. After making your backup, please make sure that you can restore files from the backup.

When you run PartitionMagic, it shows the current partitions in a window. If you are running Windows XP, you probably have two partitions—one small hidden partition that contains Windows XP installation files and a huge second NTFS partition that serves as the C drive. You have to reduce the size of the existing C drive, which creates unused space following that partition. Then, during Red Hat Linux installation, the installation program can create new Linux partitions in the unused space.

To reduce the size of the partition, follow these steps:

1. In the partition map in PartitionMagic's main window, right-click the partition and select Resize/Move from the menu (see Figure 2-1). The Resize Partition dialog box appears.
2. In the Resize/Move Partition dialog box, click and drag the right edge of the partition to a smaller size. For a large hard disk (anything over 10GB), reduce the Windows partition to 5GB and leave the rest for Red Hat Linux. If possible, try to leave 5GB or more for Red Hat Linux.

Figure 2-1: Right-Clicking on the Partition to Resize in PartitionMagic 8.0.

3. Click OK and then Apply to apply the changes. After PartitionMagic has made the changes, click OK.
4. Reboot the PC.

You do not have to do anything with the disk space left over after shrinking the partition that used to be the C drive. Later, in the "Partitioning and Using the Hard Disk" section, you learn to use the free disk space to install Red Hat Linux.

Repartitioning with FIPS

Red Hat Linux comes with a utility program called FIPS (The First Nondestructive Interactive Partition Splitting Program), which can split an existing primary DOS partition into two partitions. FIPS cordons off the unused part of a hard disk, making a new partition out of it without destroying any existing data.

---

insider insight Before using FIPS, make sure that the hard disk has only a FAT or FAT32 partition and that there is enough free space to install Linux. You need 3GB to 4GB of free space for a useful Red Hat Linux installation.

The FIPS.EXE program and related files are located in the `\DOSUTIL` subdirectory of the first CD-ROM. To use FIPS, follow these steps:

1. For FIPS to work, all used areas of the disk must be contiguous or at least as tightly packed as possible. You can prepare the disk for FIPS by running a defragmenter. In Windows 95/98/Me, click the right mouse button on the disk symbol in the Explorer window, select Properties from the pop-up menu, click the Tools tab, and click the Defragment Now button. Another way to start the defragmenter is to select Start⇨Programs⇨Accessories⇨System Tools⇨ Disk Defragmenter.

2. Create a bootable disk by using the command `FORMAT A: /S`. In Windows 95/98/Me, create a startup disk by using the Add/Remove Programs option in the Control Panel and then following the instructions on the Startup Disk tab.

3. Copy the following files from the CD-ROM to the formatted disk (the following example assumes that D: is the CD-ROM drive):

   ```
   COPY D:\DOSUTILS\FIPS.EXE A:
   COPY D:\DOSUTILS\RESTORRB.EXE A:
   COPY D:\DOSUTILS\FIPSDOCS\ERRORS.TXT A:
   ```

   FIPS.EXE is the program that splits partitions. ERRORS.TXT is a list of FIPS error messages. You consult this list for an explanation of any error messages displayed by FIPS. RESTORRB.EXE is a program that allows you to restore certain important parts of your hard disk from a backup of those areas FIPS has created.

4. Leave the bootable disk in the A drive, and restart the PC. The PC boots from the A drive.

5. Type **FIPS**. The FIPS program runs and shows you information about your hard disk. FIPS gives you an opportunity to save a backup copy of important disk areas before proceeding. After that, FIPS displays the first free cylinder on which the new partition can start (as well as the size of the partition, in megabytes).

6. Use the left and right arrow keys to adjust the starting cylinder of the new partition (the one that results from splitting the existing partition) to change the partition size. Press the right arrow to increase the starting cylinder number (this leaves more room in the existing partition and reduces the size of the new partition you are creating).

7. When you are satisfied with the size of the new partition, press Enter. FIPS displays the modified partition table and prompts you to enter C to continue or R to re-edit the partition table.

8. Press C to continue. FIPS displays some information about the disk and asks whether you want to write the new partition information to the disk.

9. Press Y. FIPS writes the new partition table to the hard disk and exits.

Remove the disk from the A drive, and reboot the PC. When the system comes up, everything in your hard disk should be intact, but the C drive will be smaller. You have created a new partition from the unused parts of the old C drive.

You needn't do anything with the newly created partition under DOS. Later, in the "Partitioning and Using the Hard Disk" section, you will learn to use the new partition under Linux.

Creating the Red Hat Installer Boot Disk

After you repartition the hard disk and make room for Linux, you can begin the next step of installing Red Hat Linux from this book's CD-ROM: creating the Red Hat installer boot disk. (For this step, you should turn on your PC without any disk in the A drive and run Windows as usual.)

note
This book comes with the Publisher's Edition version of Red Hat Linux 9 that was provided by Red Hat. Unfortunately, these CDs do not include the DOSUTILS directory. If you have full Red Hat Linux distribution, you can use the following directions to create the boot disk. Otherwise, please download rawrite.exe from one of the FTP sites listed at

http://www.redhat.com/download/mirror.html

Click on one of the *Distribution* links and then look in the directory corresponding to the Red Hat Linux version number. For example, rawrite.exe for Red Hat Linux 9 should be in the 9/en/os/i386/dosutils directory. Use a Web browser to download the rawrite.exe file. Then, follow the steps outlined next, but run the version of rawrite.exe that you have downloaded from the FTP site.

insider insight
You do not need the Red Hat installer boot disk if you can boot your PC from the CD-ROM. You may have press a key (such as the F2 key) to go into the SETUP mode as the PC powers up and change the boot device to the CD-ROM. If you can boot directly from the first companion CD-ROM, skip this section and proceed to the section entitled "Booting the Red Hat Installer."

Like the MS-DOS or Windows boot disk, the Red Hat installer boot disk is used to start your PC, start Linux, and run the Red Hat installation program. Once you have installed Red Hat Linux, you no longer need the Red Hat installer boot disk.

The Red Hat installer boot disk contains an initial version of Linux that you use to start Linux, run the installer, prepare the hard disk, and load the rest of the files from the CD-ROMs to the hard disk. Creating the Red Hat installer boot disk involves using a utility program called RAWRITE.EXE to copy a special file called the Red Hat Linux boot image to a disk.

To create the Red Hat boot disk under Windows, follow these steps:

1. In Windows 95/98/Me, open an MS-DOS Prompt window by selecting Start⇨Run and then typing the word Command in the text field.
2. In Windows NT/2000/XP, select Start⇨Run. Click the Browse button and go to the WINNT folder; then open the SYSTEM32 folder, and select the CMD.EXE file in that folder. Click OK to run that program.

3. Put the first companion CD-ROM in the CD-ROM drive. Then, type the following commands in the window you opened in Step 1 or 2 (my comments are in parentheses, and your input is in boldface):

```
d:     (use the drive letter for the CD-ROM drive)
cd \dosutils
rawrite
Enter disk image source filename: \images\bootdisk.img
Enter target diskette drive: a
Please insert a formatted diskette into drive A: and press -ENTER- :
```

4. As instructed, you should put a formatted disk into your PC's A drive and press Enter. RAWRITE copies the boot-image file to the disk.

After you see the DOS prompt again, you can take the Red Hat boot disk out of the A drive and (if you haven't done so already) label it so you know what it is.

> **cross ref**
>
> If you are installing Red Hat Linux on a laptop, please see the "Installing Linux on a Laptop" section for more information.

Booting the Red Hat Linux Installer

The Red Hat Linux installer runs under Linux; therefore, you need to boot Linux on your PC before you can go through the installation steps. This initial version of Linux can come from the installer boot floppy or the frist CD-ROM. The initial Linux operating system, in turn, runs the Red Hat installation program, which prepares the disk partitions and copies all necessary files from the CD-ROM to the disk.

You can boot your PC with an initial version of the Linux operating system in one of the following ways:

✦ Boot your PC from the first CD-ROM (this works only if your PC is bootable from the CD-ROM; most PCs can boot from the CD-ROM drive, as I explain a little later).

✦ Load the initial Linux kernel by executing the AUTOBOOT.BAT command file (from the DOSUTILS directory of the CD-ROM) while your PC is running MS-DOS.

✦ Boot your PC from the Red Hat installer boot floppy you created earlier.

The following sections describe these approaches to booting Linux and initiating the Red Hat installation.

Booting from the Red Hat Linux CD-ROM

Most new PCs can boot directly from the CD-ROM. To do so, you have to go into SETUP as the PC powers up. The exact steps for entering SETUP and setting the boot device depend on the PC, but they typically involve pressing a key such as F2. As the PC powers up, a brief message should tell you what key to press to enter SETUP. Once you are in SETUP, you can designate the CD-ROM drive as the boot device.

After your PC is set up to boot directly from the CD-ROM drive, place the first Red Hat Linux CD-ROM into the CD-ROM drive, and reboot the PC. The PC should power up and start the Linux kernel from the CD-ROM. After Linux starts from the CD-ROM, the Red Hat installation program begins to run. The section "Installing from the Red Hat Linux CD-ROM" describes this process in detail.

Starting the Red Hat Linux Installer from DOS

You can start Linux directly from the CD-ROM while your PC is running MS-DOS. An MS-DOS program called LOADLIN.EXE can load a Linux kernel into memory and begin running Linux. The Linux kernel itself is in another file. You do not need to understand all of the details about how LOADLIN starts Linux. In fact, the Red Hat CD-ROM provides a DOS batch file, AUTOBOOT.BAT, in the \DOSUTILS directory that runs LOADLIN with appropriate arguments.

Secret

You can use AUTOBOOT to start Linux directly from the CD-ROM only if your PC is running MS-DOS alone (not an MS-DOS window under Windows 95/98 or a command window under Windows NT/2000/XP). In addition, you must be able to use the CD-ROM from MS-DOS. If your PC runs Windows, select Shutdown from the Start menu, and click the button labeled Restart the Computer in MS-DOS Mode. From the DOS prompt, try to see the directory of the CD-ROM with the command DIR D: where D is the drive letter of the CD-ROM drive. If this works, you can start Linux directly from the CD-ROM. Otherwise, you have to use a boot floppy.

To start Linux, place the Red Hat CD-ROM in the CD-ROM drive, and use the following commands from the DOS prompt:

```
D:           (use the drive letter for the CD-ROM drive)
cd \dosutils
autoboot
```

After Linux starts, the Red Hat installation program begins to run. The section "Installing Linux from the Red Hat CD-ROM" describes this process in detail.

The AUTOBOOT.BAT file runs the LOADLIN program with two arguments: the name of a Linux kernel file and a file that contains an initial file system (known as initial RAM disk, or initrd, because this file system is loaded into memory). If the autoboot command gives you an error message, type the following command to run loadlin and to start Linux from the CD-ROM:

```
loadlin autoboot\vmlinuz initrd=autoboot\initrd.img ramdisk_size=
9216 %1 %2 %3 %4 %5 %5 %7 %8 %9
```

Booting from the Red Hat Installer Boot Floppy

To start Linux for installation, put the Red Hat boot floppy in your PC's A drive and restart your PC. Your PC goes through its normal startup sequence, such as checking memory and running the ROM BIOS code. Then, the PC loads Linux from the floppy and begins running the Red Hat installation program.

Watching the Boot Process during Installation

A few moments after you start the boot process, an initial screen appears—the screen displays a welcome message and ends with a boot: prompt. The welcome message tells you that help is available by pressing one of the function keys, F1 through F5.

If you want to read the help screens, press the function key corresponding to the help you want. If you don't press any keys, after a minute the boot process proceeds with the loading of the Linux kernel into the PC's memory. To start booting Linux immediately, press Enter. After the Linux kernel loads, it automatically starts the Red Hat Linux installation program, which, in turn, starts the X Window System and provides a GUI for the installation.

Installing from the Red Hat Linux CD-ROM

After you start the initial version of Linux following the procedures described in the section "Booting the Red Hat Installer," Linux runs the Red Hat Linux installation program—called anaconda—from the CD-ROM. The rest of the installation occurs under the control of the installation program. The default Red Hat installation program uses a GUI. You can go through the installation steps by pointing and clicking with the mouse.

If, for some reason, the installer fails to detect your IDE CD-ROM drive and prompts you for the type of CD-ROM drive, restart the installation by pressing Ctrl-Alt-Del. When you see the boot prompt, type **linux hdx=cdrom** where x is a single letter— a, b, c, or d—identifying the IDE interface to which the CD-ROM drive is connected. The letter a refers to the master or primary connector of the first IDE controller, b is the slave on the first IDE controller. The letters c and d refer to the master and slave of the second IDE controller. Thus, if your CD-ROM drive is connected as the master on the second IDE controller, you would type the following at the boot prompt:

```
linux hdc=cdrom
```

Monitoring the Installation Process

As the installation progresses, you respond primarily to various dialog boxes, entering information the installation program needs. The installation program displays useful information about a number of virtual consoles—these are screens of text in memory that you can view on the physical screen by pressing the key sequences shown in Table 2-1.

insider insight

You work mostly in the main console—virtual console 7 in GUI installation and 1 in text mode. To switch to another virtual console, press the appropriate keystroke shown in Table 2-1. For example, to view the install log on virtual console 3, press Ctrl-Alt-F3. After you are done viewing the log, press Ctrl-Alt-F7 to return to the GUI console so you can continue with the installation.

Typically, you can get by without ever having to switch to the other screens, but if something goes wrong, you can switch to the install log screen by pressing Ctrl-Alt-F3, where you can get more information about the problem.

Table 2-1: Virtual Consoles Available During Red Hat Linux Installation

Virtual Console	Keystroke	Description
1	Ctrl-Alt-F1	This is the main console on which the installation program displays the text-based user interface through which you install Linux.
2	Ctrl-Alt-F2	This console displays a shell prompt from which you can use Linux commands to monitor the progress of installation. The shell prompt appears only after you insert the CD-ROM and press Enter in response to a dialog box that the installation program displays.
3	Ctrl-Alt-F3	This is the install log. Messages from the installation program appear here.
4	Ctrl-Alt-F4	The Linux kernel displays its messages on this console. After Linux initially boots, you may want to switch to this console to see the kernel messages because they include information about hardware that Linux detects in your PC.

(continued)

Table 2-1: *(continued)*

Virtual Console	Keystroke	Description
5	Ctrl-Alt-F5	This console shows the output of any other programs run during the installation process.
7	Ctrl-Alt-F7	This is where the anaconda installer displays the X Window System-based graphical user interface.

Understanding the Red Hat Installation Phases

Installing Red Hat Linux is a fairly lengthy process that contains the following major phases:

1. **Getting Ready to Install**—Choose the language to be used during the installation process. Indicate the type of keyboard. If you haven't already placed the first Red Hat CD-ROM into the CD-ROM drive, you also have to specify the media from which Red Hat Linux is to be loaded (for example, the CD-ROM). After the graphical installation screen appears, configure the mouse. Then specify whether you are installing or upgrading and, if you are installing, the type of installation: workstation, server, or custom. I show a custom system installation in this chapter.

2. **Partitioning and Using the Hard Disk**—This step is to prepare the hard disk space you plan to use for Red Hat Linux. Select the automatic partition option to let the installation program perform this step, or partition the disk manually using Disk Druid. At minimum, you need two partitions—one to be used as swap area and the other for the Linux root file system (represented by /). The partitions are also formatted before use. Appendix B discusses typical partitioning strategies in an operational Linux system.

3. **Configuring Linux**—In this phase, specify where the GRUB boot loader or Linux Loader (LILO) should be loaded. For GRUB, you can also specify a password that has to be entered to load Linux at system startup. You set up the TCP/IP network, the firewall, the language support, and the time zone, and you specify a password for the root—the super user. The final configuration step is to set up the authentication mechanism.

4. **Selecting the Package Groups to Install**—Select which package groups—such as X Window System, GNOME desktop, KDE Desktop, Editors, and Web server—you want to install. Up to this point, you can abort the installation without writing anything to the hard disk. After you select the package groups, the installation program prepares the hard disk and installs the selected packages on the hard disk. At the end of the installation, create a boot disk.

5. **Completing the Installation**—Configure the X Window System. This is the X configuration used when you reboot the system after the installation finishes. You have to identify your video card, monitor, select your GUI (GNOME or KDE), and indicate whether you want a graphical or text login screen.

If you have all configuration information handy (such as video card, monitor, network card details, IP addresses, and host names for the TCP/IP network configuration) and all goes well, installing Red Hat Linux from the companion CD-ROM on a fast Pentium PC should take approximately an hour (assuming that you select nearly all packages). For example, on 1 GHz Pentium PC with 128MB RAM and a 6GB-disk partition devoted to Linux, the entire installation took about an hour.

Secret

The Red Hat installer uses kudzu (a utility program) to probe—attempt to determine the presence of—specific hardware, and tailors the installation steps accordingly. For example, if the installation program detects a network card, the program automatically displays the screens on which you can configure the TCP/IP network. Therefore, you may see some variation in the sequence of steps, depending on your specific hardware configuration.

Kudzu is a configuration program as well as library of object code that can probe and determine what hardware is installed on your system. The anaconda installation program uses kudzu to detect hardware during installation.

To learn more about kudzu, visit Red Hat's kudzu website at `http://rhlinux.redhat.com/kudzu/`.

The following sections describe each of the Red Hat Linux installation phases in detail.

Getting Ready to Install

In this phase, you perform the following steps before moving on to disk setup and the actual installation of Linux:

1. A text screen appears with a welcome message and a prompt. Press Enter to begin installing in GUI mode or type **linux text** to install in text mode. If you have a SCSI controller or network card that the Linux kernel may not automatically detect, you should type **linux noprobe** to manually install the hardware (in this case, you have to select the hardware from a list or provide a driver disk; see Appendix B for more information on setting up SCSI controllers). Typically, you press Enter to continue the installation in GUI mode.

2. The installation program starts the X Window System and displays a list of languages to be used during the installation. The list includes languages such as English, French, German, Icelandic, Italian, Norwegian, Romanian, Russian, Slovak, Spanish, and Ukrainian. Use your mouse to select the language you want to use for the installation screens, then click the Next button to continue.

   In the graphical mode installation, each screen has online help available on the left side of the screen. You can read the help message to learn more about what you are supposed to select in a specific screen.

3. The installation program displays a list of keyboard layouts. Select a keyboard layout suitable for your language's character set (for example, U.S. English in the United States).

   Note that you can always reconfigure your keyboard after finishing the installation. Simply log in as `root` at a text console (you can get one by pressing, for example, Ctrl-Alt-F2) and type **setup**. This runs a text-mode setup utility that enables you to configure, among other things, the keyboard, the mouse, and the printer.

4. The installation program displays a screen from which you configure the mouse in your system. The various mouse types are listed in a tree structure organized alphabetically by manufacturer. You need to know your mouse type and whether or not it is connected to the PC's serial port or the PS/2 port (this uses a small round connector). If your mouse type appears in the list, select it. Otherwise, select a generic mouse type. Most new PCs have a PS/2 mouse. Finally, for a two-button mouse, you should select the Emulate 3 Buttons option. Because many X applications assume that you are using a three-button mouse, go ahead and select this option. On a typical two-button mouse, you can simulate a middle-button click by pressing both buttons simultaneously. On a Microsoft Intellimouse, the wheel acts as the middle button.

If you select a mouse with a serial interface, you have to specify the serial port where the mouse is connected. For COM1, specify /dev/ttyS0 as the device; for COM2, the device name is /dev/ttyS1.

5. The installation program searches for any existing Red Hat Linux installation on your PC and then prompts you for the installation type—whether you want to install a new system or upgrade any older Red Hat installation. If you are performing a fresh installation, you have to select the installation type: Personal Desktop, Workstation, Server, or Custom. The Personal Desktop, Workstation, and Server installations simplify the installation process by partitioning the disk in a predefined manner. The Personal Desktop installation creates a Red Hat Linux system for home, laptop, or desktop use. A graphical environment is installed along with productivity applications.

A Workstation installation installs graphical environment as well as software development tools. This type of installation also deletes all currently existing Linux-related partitions and creates a set of new partitions for Linux. A Server installation deletes all existing disk partitions, including any existing Windows partitions, and creates a whole slew of Linux partitions. By default, the Server installation does not install the graphical environment, but you can always add the packages for the GUI desktops. For maximum flexibility, select the Custom installation, but note that the other installation types can be easier because many choices are already made for you.

caution
Do not select the Server installation if you want to retain any existing Windows partitions.

The next major phase of installation involves partitioning the hard disk for use in Linux.

Partitioning and Using the Hard Disk

Like Windows, Linux requires you to partition and prepare a hard disk before you can install Red Hat Linux. You usually do not perform this step; when you buy your PC from a vendor, the vendor takes care of preparing the hard disk and installing Windows and all other applications on the hard disk. Because you are installing Red Hat Linux from scratch, however, you have to perform this crucial step yourself. As you see in the following sections, this task is just a matter of following instructions.

When the Red Hat Linux installation program reaches the disk-partitioning phase, it displays a screen from which you can select a partitioning strategy. The screen gives you three options for partitioning and using the hard disk:

♦ **Automatically partition:** This option causes the Red Hat installation program to create new partitions for installing Linux, based on your installation type, such as workstation or server. After the automatic partitioning, you get a chance to customize the partitions. This is the option most users choose.

♦ **Manually partition with Disk Druid:** With this option, you can use the Disk Druid program that lets you partition the disk any way you want and, at the same time, specify which parts of the Linux file system are to be loaded on which partition.

From the disk-partitioning strategy screen, select the Automatically partition option to have the installer automatically partition the disk for you. The Red Hat Linux installation program, then displays another screen (see Figure 2-2) that asks you how you want the automatic partitioning to be done.

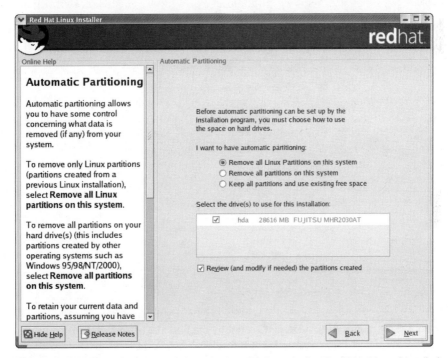

Figure 2-2: Selecting Automatic Partitioning Options during Red Hat Linux Installation.

As Figure 2-2 shows, you can select from three automatic partitioning options:

♦ **Remove all Linux partitions on this system**—This option causes the Red Hat installation program to remove all existing Linux partitions and to create new partitions for installing Red Hat Linux. You can use this option if you already have Linux installed on your PC and want to wipe it out and install the latest version of Red Hat Linux.

♦ **Remove all partitions on this system**—This option is similar to the first option, except that the installation program removes all partitions, including those used by other operating systems such as Microsoft Windows.

♦ **Keep all partitions and use existing free space**—If you have created space for Linux by using PartitionMagic or the FIPS utility, select this option to create the Linux partitions using the free space on the hard disk. If you are installing Red Hat Linux on a new PC after resizing the partition, this is the option to choose.

Select the appropriate option, and click Next. For example, if you select the first option, the Red Hat Linux installation program displays a dialog to confirm your choice and to point out that all data in the existing Linux partitions will be lost. Click Yes to continue. In the next screen (see Figure 2-3) the installer shows the partitions it has prepared. The exact appearance of this screen depends on your hard disk's capacity and its current partitions.

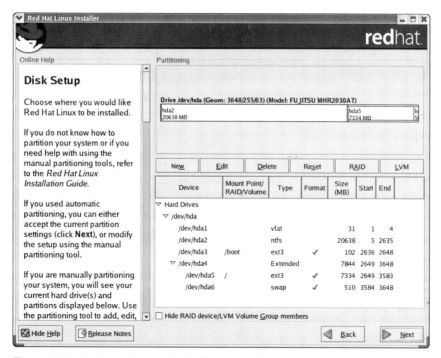

Figure 2-3: Partitions Automatically Created by the Red Hat Linux Installer.

The screen displays the disk drives and the current partition information for the drives. If you want to accept the partitions as is, click Next to proceed.

---

caution   If your PC does not have enough memory (typically less than 128MB), the installer asks if it can write the partition table and activate the swap partition. Once you do this, your hard disk partitions will be changed. Click Yes only if you are committed to the new partitions and definitely want to install Red Hat Linux.

You can also perform specific disk-setup tasks through the six buttons that run across the middle of the screen. Specifically, the buttons perform the following actions:

- ◆ *New* lets you create a new partition, assuming there is enough free disk space available to create a partition. When you click this button, another dialog box appears, in which you can fill in information necessary to create a partition.
- ◆ *Edit* lets you alter the attributes of the partition currently highlighted in the partitions list. You make changes to the current attribute in another dialog box that appears when you click the Edit button.
- ◆ *Delete* is used to delete the partition currently highlighted in the partitions list.
- ◆ *Reset* causes the installation program to ignore any changes you may have made.
- ◆ *RAID* is used to set up a RAID (Redundant Array of Independent Disks) device— a technique that combines multiple disks to improve reliability and data transfer rates. There are several types of RAID configurations. You have to select at least two partitions to make a RAID device.
- ◆ *LVM* creates a logical volume for Logical Volume Management (LVM).

For this discussion, I assume that the installer-created partitions are acceptable and that you click Next to continue with the installation.

Configuring Red Hat Linux

When the installation program finishes loading all of the selected packages, it moves on to some configuration steps. The typical configuration steps are as follows:

- ◆ Install boot loader
- ◆ Configure the network
- ◆ Configure the firewall
- ◆ Select languages to support
- ◆ Set the time zone
- ◆ Set the root password
- ◆ Configure password authentication

The following sections describe each of these configuration steps.

Installing a Boot Loader

You can install one of two boot loaders—GRUB or LILO. GRUB stands for Grand Unified Bootloader, and LILO stands for Linux Loader—each of these boot loader programs can reside on your hard disk, and each can start Linux when you power up your PC. If you have Microsoft Windows on your hard disk, you can configure the boot loader to load Windows as well. You perform this step from the boot loader installation screen (see Figure 2-4).

The boot loader installation screen (see Figure 2-4) shows you information about the boot loader to be installed and the partitions from which that the boot loader boots the PC. You also get a chance to change the boot loader or add other partitions that contain non-Linux operating systems.

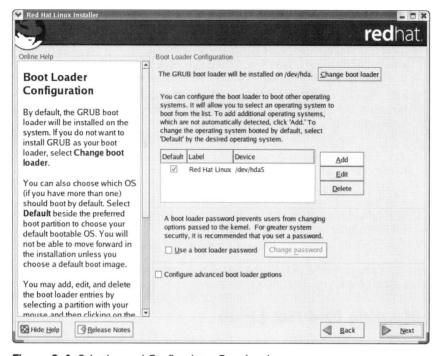

Figure 2-4: Selecting and Configuring a Boot Loader.

GRUB is the default boot loader, and it's installed by default in the master boot record (MBR) of the hard disk. If you want to change the boot loader from GRUB to LILO or not install it at all, click the "Change boot loader" button near the top of the window. From the dialog box that appears, either select the older LILO boot loader or skip the boot loader installation entirely. If you choose not to install any boot loader, you should definitely create a boot disk later on. Otherwise, you won't be able to start Red Hat Linux when you reboot the PC. You get a chance to create the boot disk at the very end of the installation.

In the middle of the boot loader installation screen a table lists the disk partitions from which the boot loader can boot the PC. That table lists the Linux partition and any other partitions that may contain another operating system (such as Windows XP or 2000). Each entry in that table is an operating system that the boot loader can load and start. The default operating system is the one with a check mark in the Default column.

Secret

You must assign a label to the Windows XP partition that appears in the list of partitions—click that line and enter the label. If there is no label, GRUB will not display that partition as a choice in its boot screen, and you won't be able to boot Windows XP after you finish installing Red Hat Linux.

If GRUB fails to detect and list an existing Windows XP partition in the list, you should click the Add button and fill in the information about the Windows XP partition, as shown in Figure 2-5. Typically, the Windows XP partition should be the /dev/hda2 device (the first partition—/dev/hda1—is usually a hidden partition that holds files used to install Windows XP).

Figure 2-5: Adding a Windows XP Partition to the List of Partitions to Boot.

If you forget to enter a label for the Windows XP partition or add the XP partition to the list, that does not mean that all is lost. The XP partition is still there on the hard disk. It's just that GRUB does not show it as an option to boot from. To fix the problem, you have to manually edit the GRUB configuration file, `/etc/grub.conf`. See Appendix B for information on configuring bootloaders such as GRUB and LILO. After you fix the `/etc/grub.conf` file, you should get the option to boot XP from the initial GRUB screen the next time you reboot the PC.

If you decide to install the GRUB bootloader, consider adding a password for GRUB. Click the "Use a boot loader password" check box and make sure that a check mark appears there. The installer displays a dialog box where you can specify a password for GRUB. With a GRUB password, your system is more secure because no one can boot your system without a password given that GRUB will not load the operating system without the password.

If you select the "Configure advanced boot loader options" check box and click Next, the installer displays the Advanced Boot Loader Configuration screen, as shown in Figure 2-6.

The screen of Figure 2-6 gives you the option to install the boot loader in one of two locations:

- Master Boot Record (MBR), which is located in the first sector of your PC's hard disk (the C drive)
- First sector of the Linux boot partition

You can also add any necessary boot options in the text field labeled "General kernel parameters." These are options passed to the kernel as the system boots.

You should install the boot loader in the Master Boot Record unless you are using another operating system loader, such as BootMagic or Windows NT/2000/XP Boot Manager. After making your selections for the boot loader, click Next to continue.

Configuring the Network

Assuming that the Linux kernel has detected a network card, the Red Hat installation program displays the Network Configuration screen, which enables you to configure the local area network (LAN) parameters for your Linux system.

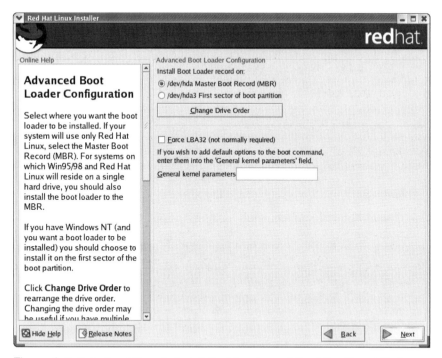

Figure 2-6: Selecting Where to Install Boot Loader and Providing Kernel Options.

This step is not for configuring the dial-up networking. You need to perform this step if your Linux system is connected to a TCP/IP LAN through an Ethernet card.

> **cross ref**
>
> If the Red Hat installation program does not detect your network card, you should restart the installation and type **linux noprobe** at the boot prompt. Then, you will be to select your network card manually. See the "Troubleshooting the Installation" section for more information.

The Network Configuration screen displays a list of the network devices (for example, Ethernet cards) installed in your PC. For each network device, you can indicate how the IP (Internet Protocol) address is set. Click the Edit button next to the list, and a dialog box appears from which you can specify the options.

You have two choices for specifying the IP address for the network card:

♦ **Configure using DHCP:** Enable this option if your PC gets its IP address and other network information from a Dynamic Host Configuration Protocol (DHCP) server. This is often the case if your PC is connected to a DSL or cable modem router.

♦ **Activate on boot:** Enable this option to turn on the network when your system boots.

You should select DHCP only if a DHCP server is running on your local area network. If you choose DHCP, your network configuration is set automatically, and you can skip the rest of this section.

If you do not select the "Configure using DHCP" option, you have to provide an IP address and a network mask that indicates which part of the IP address represents the network and which part the host address. After entering the requested parameters in the text input fields, click OK to close the dialog box.

> **cross ref**
>
> If you have a private LAN (one that is not directly connected to the Internet), you may use an IP address from a range that has been designated for private use. Common IP addresses for private LANs are in the range 192.168.0.1 through 192.168.0.254. You will learn more about TCP/IP networking and IP addresses in Chapter 6.

In the rest of the Network Configuration screen, you have to specify how to set the host name. You have two options to set the host name:

- ◆ **Automatically via DHCP:** Enable this option to assign a host name automatically using DHCP (the name is of the form dhcppc1, dhcppc2, and so on).
- ◆ **Manually:** Use this option to manually specify a host name—type the name in the text field next to the radio button.

After you enter the requested parameters, click the Next button to proceed to the firewall configuration step.

Configuring the Firewall

In this step, you configure the built-in packet filter that comes with Red Hat Linux and that enables you to control how various types of IP packets are handled. You can select a predefined level of security from the Firewall Configuration screen (see Figure 2-7), and customize these security levels to suit your needs.

The installer offers the following predefined security levels:

- ◆ *High security* means that your system does not accept any connections other than those that you explicitly enable. By default, a system with high security accepts only Domain Name Service (DNS) requests and DHCP requests.
- ◆ *Medium security* means that the system does not accept any connection requests for ports numbered 1023 and lower, or connections to the NFS server at port 2049, remote connections to the X Window System, and the X Font Server port.
- ◆ *No firewall security* means your system accepts connections at all ports and does not perform any security checking. Use this option only if your system runs in a trusted network, if it is already inside a firewall, or if you plan to set up a more elaborate firewall configuration later on.

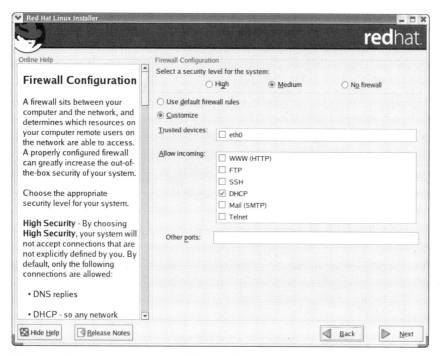

Figure 2-7: Setting up the Packet Filtering Firewall Built into Your System.

insider insight

Think about how you plan to use the Red Hat Linux system before selecting a predefined security level. For example, if you plan to use the system as a boot server on an internal network, you have to set the security level to No firewall security. Otherwise, the other PCs on the network cannot download the kernel using TFTP. If one of your system's network interface such as eth0 is only connected to your trusted internal network, you can indicate eth0 as a trusted device. If you do not configure the firewall correctly here, you can do so late ron by following instructions outlined in Chapter 22.

After you select a predefined security level, you can click the Customize button and select other services that you might want to enable. When you're done configuring the firewall, click the Next button to proceed to the next step.

Selecting Languages to Support

In this step, you select one or more languages that your Red Hat Linux system will support once the installation is complete. This step is similar to the language selection step you perform at the beginning of the installation when you select the language to be used during the installation. Now, you have to select the languages the system will support when you reboot the PC after completing the Red Hat Linux installation. From the Language Support Selection screen, select one or more languages to support. You must also select a default language. Then click the Next button to continue.

Setting the Time Zone

After completing the network configuration, you have to select the time zone—the difference between the local time and the current time in Greenwich, England, which is the standard reference time (also known as Greenwich Mean Time, or GMT, and UTC, or Universal Coordinated Time). The installation program shows you a screen with two tabs—Location and UTC Offset—from which you can select the time zone, either in terms of a geographic location or as an offset from the UTC. Initially, the screen shows the Location tab. This tab lets you pick a time zone by simply clicking your geographic location. As you move the mouse over the map, the currently selected location's name appears in a text field. If you want, you can also select your location from a long list of countries and regions. If you live on the East Coast of the United States, for example, select USA/Eastern. Of course, the easiest way is to simply click the eastern United States on the map.

If the World view of the map is too large for you to select your location, click the View button on top of the map. A drop-down list of views appears with the following options: World, North America, South America, Pacific Rim, Europe, Africa, and Asia. You can then click the view appropriate for your location.

The other way to set a time zone is to specify the time difference between your local time and UTC. Click the UTC Offset tab to select the time zone this way. For example, if you are in the eastern part of the United States, select UTC-05:00 as the time zone. This tab also allows you to enable Daylight Saving Time, which applies to the United States only.

After you select your time zone, click the Next button to proceed to the next configuration step.

Setting the Root Password

After completing the time zone selection, the installation program displays a screen from which you can set the root password. Earlier versions of the Red Hat installer enabled you to add one or more user accounts at the step, but now you get a chance to add user accounts when the system boots for the first time. You can also use the `useradd` command or the User Manager tool to add more user accounts later on.

The root user is the super user in Linux. Because the super user can do anything in the system, you should assign a password that you can remember but that others cannot guess easily. Make the password at least eight characters long, include a mix of letters and numbers, and, for good measure, throw in some special characters, such as + or *.

Type the password on the first line, and reenter the password on the next line. Each character in the password appears as an asterisk (*) on the screen. You have to type the password twice, and both entries must match before the installation program accepts it. This ensures that you do not make any typing mistakes.

After you type the root password twice, click the Next button to continue with the installation.

Configuring Password Authentication

The installation program displays a screen from which you can enable or disable several password-authentication options.

The first two check boxes that are checked by default have the following purposes:

◆ **Enable MD5 passwords:** Select this option to enable users to use long passwords of up to 256 characters instead of the standard password that can be, at most, eight characters. Note that MD5 refers to Message Digest 5, an algorithm developed by RSA, Inc., to compute the digest of the entire data of a message. Essentially, MD5 reduces a message to a digest consisting of four 32-bit numbers.

◆ **Enable shadow passwords:** This option causes the password to be stored in the /etc/shadow file instead of the older /etc/passwd file (the /etc/passwd file is still used to store account information). The /etc/shadow file can only be read by the super user (root). This provides an added level of security against someone getting access to the encrypted passwords (crackers may use tools to break these password, so it's critical to protect the password even though they are already encrypted).

The remaining authentication options on this screen are for different types of network-wide authentication protocols. The options appear in four tabs:

◆ **NIS:** Click this tab and select the Enable NIS check box to authenticate users on multiple systems in the same Network Information Service (NIS) domain with a common password and group file. Select the NIS domain option to specify the domain to which your system belongs. Otherwise, select the NIS server option to use a specific NIS server for authentication. To enable NIS, your Linux system must be connected to a network with an NIS server. Chapter 18 has more information on NIS.

◆ **LDAP:** Click this tab and select the Enable LDAP check box to use the Lightweight Directory Access Protocol (LDAP) as a unified authentication mechanism for logging into your Linux system, as well into other systems on the network. If you enable LDAP, you have to specify the LDAP Server and LDAP Base DN. For the LDAP Server, specify the full domain name of a server running LDAP. In the LDAP Base DN text field, enter the distinguished name (DN) to look up the authentication information. To learn more about using LDAP in Linux, consult the LDAP Linux HOWTO on the Web (http://www.ibiblio .org/pub/Linux/docs/HOWTO/LDAP-HOWTO).

◆ **Kerberos 5:** Click this tab and select the Enable Kerberos check box to use Kerberos for secure, network-based authentication. If you enable Kerberos, you have to specify the Realm, KDC, and Admin Server. The Realm is the network that uses Kerberos. KDC is the Key Distribution Center, also known as the Ticket Granting Server, or TGS. Admin Server runs kadmind, through which the Kerberos realm is managed. To learn more about Kerberos, visit the Kerberos home page at the Massachusetts Institute of Technology's (MIT) Website (http://web.mit.edu/kerberos/www/).

◆ **SMB:** Click this tab and select the Enable SMB authentication to use an SMB server running on a Windows system to authenticate users. If you enable SMB authentication, you have to specify the name of an SMB server and the workgroup to which the SMB server belongs. Chapter 19 shows you how to set up a Samba server on your Red Hat Linux system.

By default, only the Enable Shadow Passwords and Enable MD5 Passwords options are selected. Unless your network is set up to use NIS, LDAP, Kerberos, or SMB for authentication, you should use these default settings for authentication; click the Next button to proceed to the next configuration step.

Selecting the Package Groups to Install

After you complete the key configuration steps, the installation program displays a message about reading package information and, after a short while, shows a screen (see Figure 2-8) from which you can select the Red Hat Linux package groups you want to install.

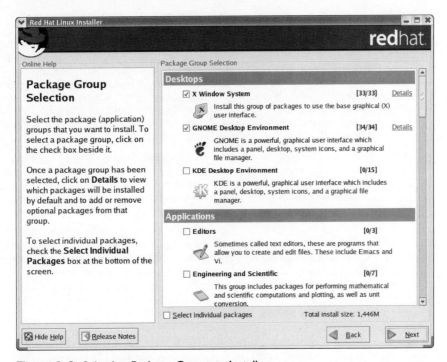

Figure 2-8: Selecting Package Groups to Install.

After you select the package groups, you can take a coffee break, and the Red Hat installation program can format the disk partitions and copy all selected files to those partitions.

---

cross ref

Red Hat uses special files called *packages* to bundle a number of files that make up specific software. For example, all configuration files, documentation, and binary files for the Perl programming language come in a Red Hat package. You use a special program called Red Hat Package Manager (RPM) to install, uninstall, and get information about packages. Chapter 21 shows you how to use RPM. For now, just remember that a package group is made up of several Red Hat packages.

As Figure 2-8 shows, the package groups are organized into broad categories such as Desktops, Applications, Servers, and so on. Within each category, each package group is shown with a label, an icon, a brief description, and a check box. To select a package group, you should click on the check box so that a check mark appears in the box. As you select package groups, the installer shows the total disk space needed for the installation.

Some of the package groups are already selected, as indicated by the check marks in the check boxes. You can think of the selected package groups as the minimal set of packages recommended by Red Hat for installation for the type of installation (personal desktop, workstation, server, or custom) you have chosen. You can, however, choose to install any or all of the components. Use the mouse to move up and down in the scrolling list and click the mouse on a check box to select or deselect that package group.

Secret

In an actual production installation of Red Hat Linux, you should install exactly those package groups that you need. However, when you are trying to learn everything about Red Hat Linux, you need many different packages. If you have enough disk space (at least 6GB) for the Linux partition, go ahead and select the package group labeled Everything—this installs all the package groups. Being able to install everything makes it easy for you to try out everything. Note that Everything is much more than the package groups that you see listed during installation—everything includes nearly all the packages on the companion CD-ROMs.

I must repeat that you should install Everything only when you are trying to play with all the packages on a system that is specifically meant for experimenting with Red Hat Linux. Do not install Everything on a system that will be used for anything critical. Installing everything is likely to open up too many security holes in your system.

Table 2-2 shows the package groups organized by the categories as they appear on the Package Group Selection screen. In addition to these user-selectable package groups, the Red Hat installation program automatically installs a number of packages needed to run Linux and the applications you select. In other words, even if you do not select any of the package groups, the installation program installs a number of packages needed simply to run the core Linux operating system and a minimal set of utilities.

insider
insight

Because each package group is a collection of many different Red Hat packages, the installation program also gives you the option to select individual packages. If you select the button labeled "Select Individual Packages" that appears below the list and click the Next button, the installation program takes you to another screen from which you can select individual packages.

If you are installing Linux for the first time, you do not need to go down to this level of detail to install specific packages. Simply pick the package groups you think you need from Table 2-2. If you forget something, you can always install additional packages later with the RPM utility program or the graphical Red Hat Package Management utility, described in Chapter 21. After you have selected the package groups you want, click the Next button to continue with the rest of the installation.

Table 2-2: List of Package Groups in Red Hat Linux

Package Group	Description
Desktops	
X Window System	Packages that make up XFree86, the X Window System for Intel x86 systems; includes all fonts, libraries, and GUI tools for configuring X, adding users, configuring printers, and so on
GNOME Desktop Environment	Packages for the GNOME (GNU Network Object Model Environment) graphical desktop, including the Nautilus graphical shell
KDE Desktop Environment	Packages for the KDE—K Desktop Environment—another graphical desktop for Linux
Applications	
Editors	Text editors such as Emacs and vi
Engineering and Scientific	Packages such as blas, octave, and gnuplot for performing math and science computations and plotting
Graphical Internet	Graphical email, Web, chat, and instant messaging clients included in packages such as evolution, mozilla, xchat, and gaim
Text-based Internet	Text-based email, Web, FTP, and news reader clients included in packages such as pine, lynx, xchat, ncftp, and slrn
Office/Productivity	Office suites, PDF viewers, and more in packages such as openoffice, abiword, xpdf, koffice, and kghostview
Sound and Video	Multimedia applications for tasks such as playing audio CDs and burning CDs in packages such as cdda2wav, cdp, cdrecord, dvdrecord, grip, xcdroast, and xmms
Authoring and Publishing	Tools to create documentation in TeX (pronounced "tech") and DocBook document-formatting system, provided in packages such as docbook-utils, tetex-latex, and xmlto
Graphics	Packages such as xsane, gimp, ImageMagick, and gtkam to scan and manipulate images and work with digital camera
Games and Entertainment	A number of computer games provided in packages such as Maelstrom, gnome-games, and kdegames
Servers	
Server Configuration Tools	Red Hat's custom server configuration tools in packages such as redhat-config-bind, redhat-config-httpd, redhat-config-nfs, redhat-config-network, redhat-config-printer, redhat-config-printer-gui, redhat-config-samba, redhat-config-securitylevel, and redhat-config-services
Web Server	Packages such as httpd, php, mod_perl, mod_ssl, and php-pgsql needed to run the Apache Web server
Mail Server	Packages such as sendmail, imap, and sendmail-cf used to set up a mail server

(continued)

Table 2-2: *(continued)*

Package Group	Description
Servers	
Windows File Server	Samba and other supporting packages needed to use the Linux PC as a LAN Manager server
DNS Name Server	The bind and caching-nameserver packages needed to provide Domain Name Service (DNS) on the Red Hat Linux system
FTP Server	The vsftpd and anonftp packages needed to run an FTP server
SQL Database Server	Packages such as postgresql-server and mysql-server that enable you to implement an SQL server (a database) on the Red Hat Linux system
News Server	The inn package for setting up an Internet News server
Network Servers	Packages such as cipe, dhcp, and telnet-server that enable you to run other services such as CIPE (Cryptographic IP Encapsulation), DHCP (Dynamic Host Configuration Protocol), and Telnet
Development	
Development Tools	Software development tools in packages such as gcc, gcc-c++, gcc-java, gdb, perl-CPAN, python-devel, cvs, rcs, and so on
Kernel Development	The kernel-source package and other libraries needed to rebuild the kernel
X Software Development	Packages such as XFree86-devel, lesstif-devel, and openmotif-devel needed to develop GUI applications for the X Window System
GNOME Software Development	Packages such as gtk+-devel, gtk2-devel, libgnome-devel, and bonobo-devel needed to develop GTK+ and GNOME graphical applications
KDE Software Development	Packages such as PyQt-devel, kdebase-devel, kdelibs-devel, qt-designer, and qt-devel needed to develop QT and KDE graphical applications
System	
Administration Tools	Graphical system administration tools in packages such as redhat-config-date, redhat-config-keyboard, redhat-config-kickstart, redhat-config-language, redhat-config-mouse, redhat-config-rootpassword, redhat-config-soundcard, redhat-config-users, redhat-config-packages, redhat-config-proc, and redhat-logviewer
System Tools	System administration and networking tools in packages such as ethereal, gnome-lokkit, nmap, samba-client, and vnc
Printing Support	Packages such as cups, cups-drivers, LPRng, and ghostscript needed to print from the system

Package Group	Description
Miscellaneous	
Minimal	Select this to install a minimal system.
Everything	Select this item to install all of the package groups plus many more additional packages.

Completing the Installation

After you complete the key configuration steps and select the package groups to install, the installer displays a screen informing you that installation is about to begin and that a log of the installation will be in the /root/install.log file. That file essentially lists all the Red Hat packages installed in your system. You can review the install log later and move the file to another directory for future reference. The content of the install log depends on the exact packages you choose to install.

The message also tells you that a kickstart file containing the installation options used in this installation is stored in the /root/anaconda-ks.cfg file. If you are going to repeat the same installation configuration on many more PCs, you can use this file along with a kickstart installation. See the "Using Kickstart Installation" section for a discussion of kickstart installation.

caution   This is your last chance to abort the installation without doing anything to the hard disk. To abort, simply press Ctrl-Alt-Delete to restart the PC. To proceed with installation click Next.

After you click Next at this step, the Red Hat installer formats the disk partitions and installs the packages one by one. As it installs packages, the installation program displays a status screen showing the progress of the installation, including information such as total number of packages to install, number installed so far, estimated amount of disk space needed, and estimated time remaining to install.

Secret

After the Red Hat Linux installation begins, the hard disk formatting and package installation can take quite a bit of time—so you can take a break and check back in 20 minutes or so (don't take too long a break though or you may come back to find the installer waiting for you to insert CD #2). When you come back, you should be able to get a sense of the time remaining from the status screen, which is updated continually.

After all the packages are installed, the Red Hat installer displays a screen that asks you to insert a blank floppy into your PC's A drive. This floppy is the boot disk that you can use to start Red Hat Linux if something happens to the hard disk or if you have not installed the boot loader. You should definitely create this boot disk if you did not install the boot loader. Otherwise, you will have no way to boot Red Hat Linux.

Insert a blank floppy into your PC's A drive, and click the Next button (note that all data on the floppy is destroyed). The installer copies the Linux kernel and some other files to the floppy so that you can boot Linux from that floppy.

After preparing the boot disk, the installation program configures the X Window System. In this step, the installation program prepares the configuration file to be used by the X server when your system reboots.

The installation program tries to detect the video card and displays the result in a screen, as shown in Figure 2-9.

Figure 2-9: Selecting the Video Card for X Configuration.

The detected card appears as the selected item in a long list of video cards. If you know the exact name of the video card, or the name of the video chipset used in the video card, select that item from the list. Also select the amount video memory from the drop-down list at the bottom of the screen. Click Next to continue.

Next, the installer tries to detect the monitor, displaying a screen (see Figure 2-10) with the results, whether successful or not.

If the installation program displays a wrong monitor or a generic one as the choice, you should enter a range of values for the two parameters that appear along the bottom of the screen:

- ◆ **Horizontal Sync:** This is the number of times per second that the monitor can display a horizontal raster line in kilohertz (kHz). A typical range might be 30–64 kHz.
- ◆ **Vertical Sync:** This is how many times a second the monitor can display the entire screen in Hertz (Hz). Also known as vertical refresh rate, the typical range is 50–90 Hz.

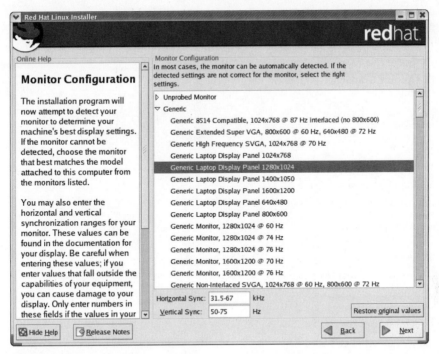

Figure 2-10: Configuring the Monitor.

Typically, the monitor's documentation includes all this information. If you have bought your PC recently, you may still have the documentation. If you have lost your monitor's documentation, one way to find the information might be from your Microsoft Windows setup. If your system comes with a Windows driver for the display, that driver may display information about the monitor. Another possibility is to visit your computer vendor's web-site and look for the technical specification of the monitor. I was able to locate useful information about my system's monitor from the vendor's website.

---

caution

Do not specify a horizontal synchronization range beyond the capabilities of your monitor. A wrong value can damage the monitor.

Next, the installation program displays a screen from which you can customize the system's GUI, as shown in Figure 2-11.

Select the color depth and screen resolution from drop-down lists. Then, click one of two check boxes—Text or Graphical—for a text or graphical login screen when the system restarts.

After you finish selecting X configuration options, click the Next button. At this point, you are basically done. Remove the floppy from the A drive (if you used a boot floppy), and click Exit to reboot your PC.

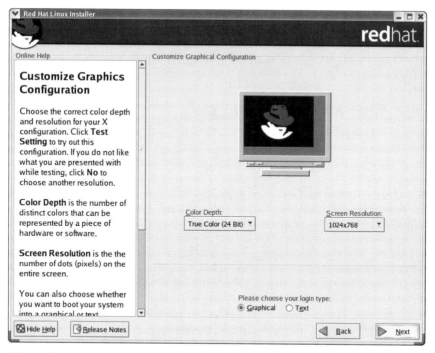

Figure 2-11: Customizing X and the Login Type.

insider
insight When Red Hat Linux boots for the first time, a server named `firstboot` runs and gives you an opportunity to perform some initial setup tasks such as setting the date and time and installing any other CDs that you might have.

Troubleshooting the Installation

One common installation problem is that the Red Hat installer may not detect some key hardware such as the SCSI controller and network interface card on your system. The installer takes you through a sequence of installation steps that depends on what hardware the installer detects. For example, if the installer cannot detect the network card, it skips the network configuration step.

Another common installation problem crops up when you restart the PC and, instead of a graphical login screen, you get a text terminal or worse, the system seems to be hung. This means that there is something wrong with the X Window System (or X) configuration.

There is an alternate way to install Red Hat Linux so that you can force it to configure the network card and the SCSI controller (if you have one). You can also troubleshoot any problems with X by reconfiguring X.

cross ref If you have problems with X Window System, printer, sound, or network, consult Chapters 3 through 6 for more information. In particular, Chapter 3 shows you how to configure X, and Chapter 4 shows you how to set up printers.

Using Text Mode Installation

The Red Hat installation program attempts to use a minimal X server to display the GUI mode installation screens. If the program fails to detect a video card, X does not start. If—for this reason or any other reason—it fails to start X, you can always fall back on the text mode installation program.

To use text mode installation, type **linux text** at the boot: prompt after you start the PC from the Red Hat Linux boot floppy. From then on, the basic sequence is similar to that of the graphical installation described previously in this chapter. However, many small details are different. You should be able to respond to the prompts and perform the installation.

In text mode, when the installation program fails to detect the video card, it displays a list of video cards from which you can select one. By selecting the video card, X may work when you install in text mode. If it does not, you can configure X using the information in Chapter 3.

Using the linux noprobe Command

If the Red Hat installation program does not detect your SCSI controller or network card, you can specify these devices manually by typing the linux noprobe command at the boot prompt.

Look for any indication of SCSI or network devices in the messages the Linux kernel displays as it boots. To view these boot messages during installation, press Ctrl-Alt-F4. This switches to a text-mode virtual console on which the messages appear. (A virtual console is a screen of text or graphical information stored in memory that you can view on the physical screen by pressing the appropriate key sequence.)

Another sign of undetected hardware is when the installation program skips a step. For example, if the Linux kernel does not detect the network card, the installation program skips the network configuration step.

To manually install devices, type **linux noprobe** at the boot: prompt in the initial text screen. The installation program then displays a dialog box that gives you the opportunity to add devices. Press Tab to highlight the Add Device button, then press Enter. The installation program then displays a dialog box that prompts you to select a driver from a list. You can then select the driver and press Enter. Repeat the process for as many drivers as you want to load.

After you finish adding any SCSI controllers and network cards, the installation program switches to graphics mode and guides you through the rest of the installation, as described previously in this chapter.

Troubleshooting X at the First Reboot

Sometimes you may run into a curious installation problem. During installation, the X configuration step works fine. But when you reboot the PC for the first time after installation, the graphical login screen does not appear. Instead, the boot process seems to hang just as it starts something called `firstboot`. If this happens to you, here's how you can troubleshoot the problem.

Secret

When the firstboot process runs during the first system startup, it can either be uneventful or an aggravation. If all goes well, firstboot runs the Red Hat Setup agent that enables you to perform one-time setups such as date and time configuration as well as install any other CDs. Unfortunately firstboot may get stuck if the X Window System is not working on your system. You have to get around the firstboot process to configure X again and continue with the normal course of events that Red Hat planned for you. Here's how you can stop firstboot and configure X to tide you over this problem:

1. Press Ctrl-Alt-F1 to get back to the text-mode boot screen. You see the text display with the boot messages that stop at a line displaying information about firstboot.

2. Press Ctrl-Alt-Del to reboot the PC. The PC starts to boot, and you get to a screen where the GRUB boot loader prompts you to press Enter to boot the Red Hat Linux (if you have GRUB password, you have to enter that password before you get to this point).

3. Press *a* to add an option for use by the Linux kernel. The GRUB boot loader then displays a command line for the Linux kernel and prompts you to add what you want.

4. Type a space followed by the word `single` and then press Enter. The Linux kernel boots in a single-user mode and displays a prompt that looks like the following:

   `sh-2.05b#`

   Now you can configure X.

X uses a configuration file, called XF86Config, to figure out the type of display card, monitor, and the kind of screen resolution you want. The Red Hat installer prepares the configuration file, but sometimes the configuration is not correct.

To quickly create a working XF86Config file, follow these steps:

1. Type the following command:

   `/usr/X11R6/bin/XFree86 -configure`

   The screen goes blank and then XFree86 exists after displaying some messages. The last line of the message says the following:

   `To test the server, run 'XFree86 -xf86config //XF86Config.new'`

2. Try the new configuration file by typing the command:

   `/usr/X11R6/bin/XFree86 -xf86config //XF86Config.new`

   If you see a blank screen with a X-shaped cursor, the configuration file is probably working fine.

3. Press Ctrl-Alt-Backspace to kill the X server.
4. Copy the new XF86Config file to the /etc/X11 directory with the following command:

```
cp //XF86Xonfig.new /etc/X11/XF86Config
```

That should provide a working X configuration file. Now, you can reboot the PC by pressing Ctrl-Alt-Del or typing reboot.

---

cross ref

The XF86Config file created by using the -configure option of the X server is not displayed at the best resolution possible. To fine-tune the configuration file, you should turn to Chapter 3, where you can learn more about configuring the X Window System and editing the /etc/X11/XF86Config file further.

Resolving Other Installation Problems

I am sure I have not covered all the installation problems that at least someone out there may encounter. There are so many different combinations of components in Intel x86 PCs that there is bound to be some combination of hardware that the installation program cannot handle. This section lists a few known problems. For others, I would advise you to go to Google Groups (groups.google.com) and type in some of the symptoms of the trouble. Assuming that others are running into similar problems, you should get some indication of how to troubleshoot out of your particular predicament.

Not Being Able to Boot from Boot Disk

Sometimes the PC does not seem to boot with the Red Hat installation boot disk. If this happens to you, try creating another boot disk using a fresh floppy disk and see if that takes care of the problem. Otherwise, you may need updated boot images. New boot images, if any, should be available at Red Hat's support website (http://www.redhat .com/apps/support/errata/). After you download the image file, save it on your Windows system, give it a short name such as new.img. Then, create a new boot disk by following the steps explained in the "Creating the Red Hat Boot Disk" section. Remember to specify the new boot image file in response to the question that asks for the image source filename.

Understanding the Fatal Signal 11 Error

Some people get a fatal signal 11 error during installation. This usually happens past the initial boot screen as the anaconda installer is starting its GUI or text interface. The most likely cause of a signal 11 error during installation is a hardware error related to memory or the cache associated with the CPU (microprocessor).

Secret

Signal 11, also known as SIGSEGV (short for Segment Violation Signal), can occur in other Linux applications. A segment violation occurs when a process tries to access a memory location that it is not supposed to access. The operating system catches the problem before it happens and stops the offending process by sending it a signal 11. When it happens during installation, it means that anaconda had error accessing memory, and the most likely reason is some hardware problem.

A commonly suggested cure for the signal 11 problem is to turn off CPU cache in the BIOS. To do this, you have to enter setup as the PC boots (by pressing a function key such as F2) and then turn off CPU cache from the BIOS setup menus.

If the problem is due to hardware error in memory (in other words, the result of bad memory chips), you could try swapping the memory modules around in their slots. You may also consider replacing an existing memory module with another memory module, if you have it handy.

You can read more about the signal 11 problem at the following website:

```
http://www.bitwizard.nl/sig11/
```

Using Boot Commands during Installation

When you boot the PC for installation, either from a boot disk or directly from the first CD-ROM, you get a text screen with the `boot:` prompt. Typically, you press Enter at that prompt or do nothing and the installation begins shortly. You can, however, type quite a variety of commands at the boot prompt. The commands can provide options to the Linux kernel that takes care of the installation and controls various aspects of the installation such as whether the kernel should probe for hardware or whether to use GUI screens for the installation. Some of these commands can be helpful in bypassing problems that you may encounter during installation.

To use these boot commands, you type the word `linux` followed by the boot command. For example, to perform text-mode installation and tell the kernel that your PC has 256MB of memory, you'd type the following at the boot prompt:

```
linux text mem=256M
```

Consult Table 2-3 for a brief summary of the boot commands.

insider insight A few of the boot commands do not require you to type `linux` first. You can simply type `text` to enter text-mode installation and `expert` to run the installation in expert mode.

Table 2-3: Linux Boot Commands for Red Hat Linux Installation

Command	Description
askmethod	Prompts you for other installation methods such as install over the network using NFS, FTP, or HTTP
apic	Works around a bug commonly encountered in the Intel 440GX chipset BIOS and should only be executed with the installation program kernel
apm=allow_ints	Changes how the laptop can be suspended
apm=off	Disables APM (Advanced Power Management) in case a BIOS has a buggy APM
apm=power_off	Causes Red Hat Linux to power off the system (useful for symmetric multiprocessing—SMP—systems that do not shut down by default)
apm=realmode_ power_off	Causes APM to work the way it does in Windows 95 instead of how it works in Windows NT (useful if BIOS crashes when trying to shut down the machine)
dd	Prompts for a driver disk during the installation of Red Hat Linux
display=IP_ address:0	Causes installer GUI to appear on the remote system identified by the IP address (make sure that you run the command xhost +hostname on the remote system where hostname is the host where you are running the installer)
driverdisk	Performs the same function as the dd command
expert	Enables you to partition removable media and prompts for a driver disk
ide=nodma	Disables DMA (direct memory access) on all IDE devices and can be useful when you are having IDE-related problems
isa	Prompts you for the configuration of older ISA devices—the older IBM-compatible PC architecture) devices
ks	Configures the Ethernet card using DHCP and then runs a kickstart installation by using a kickstart file from an NFS server identified by the bootServer parameters provided by the DHCP server
ks=kickstartfile	Runs a kickstart installation by using the kickstart file specified by kickstartfile (see the "Using kickstart Installation" section for the format of the kickstartfile specification)
lowres	Forces the installer GUI to run at a lower resolution (640x480)
mediacheck	Prompts you if you want to check the integrity of the CD image (also called ISO image). This is done by computing the MD5 checksum and comparing that with the official Red Hat provided value. It can take a few minutes to check a CD-ROM.
mem=xxxM	Overrides the amount of memory the kernel detects in the PC (some older machines could detect only 16MB of memory, and on some new machines the video card may use a portion of the main memory). Replace xxx with the number representing the megabytes of memory in your PC.

(continued)

Table 2-3: *(continued)*

Command	Description
nmi_watchdog=1	Enables the built-in kernel deadlock detector that makes use of Non Maskable Interrupt (NMI)
noapic	Prevents the kernel from using the Advanced Programmable Interrupt Controller (APIC) chip (use this on motherboards known to have a bad APIC)
nofirewire	Does not load support for FireWire
noht	Disables hyperthreading (a feature available in some SMP systems)
nomce	Disables self-diagnosis checks performed on the CPU by using Machine Check Exception (MCE). On some machines these checks are performed too often and need to be disabled.
nomount	Does not automatically mount any installed Linux partitions in rescue mode
nopass	Does not pass the keyboard and mouse information to stage 2 of the installation program
nopcmcia	Ignores any PCMCIA controllers in system
noprobe	Disables automatic hardware detection and instead prompts the user for information about SCSI and network hardware installed on the PC. You can pass parameters to modules by using this approach.
noshell	Disables shell access on virtual console 2 (the one you get by pressing Ctrl-Alt-F2) during installation
nousb	Disables the loading of USB support during the installation (may be useful if the installation program hangs early in the process)
nousbstorage	Disables the loading of the usbstorage module in the installation program's loader. It may help with device ordering on SCSI systems.
reboot=b	Changes the way the kernel tries to reboot the PC so that it can reboot even if the kernel hands during system shutdown
rescue	Starts the kernel in rescue mode where you get a shell prompt and can try to fix problems
resolution=HHHxVVV	Causes the installer GUI to run in the specified video mode (replace HHH and VVV with standard resolution numbers, such as 640x480, 800x600, 1024x768, and so on)
serial	Turns on serial console support during installation
skipddc	Skips the Display Data Channel (DDC) probe of monitors (useful if the probing causes problems)
text	Runs the installation program in text mode
updates	Prompts for a floppy disk containing updates (bug fixes)

Learning Other Installation Methods

anaconda, the Red Hat installer, supports a number of installation methods. The CD-ROM method is one that you see described in this chapter. The other methods involve installing from different types of servers or even a hard disk partition that holds exact copy of the Red Hat Linux CD-ROMs. These images of a CD-ROM are known as ISO images.

Here are all the installation methods that anaconda supports:

♦ **CD-ROM:** This method installs Red Hat Linux from CD-ROMs. You can either boot from the CD-ROM or by using a boot disk with the bootdisk.img boot image. For laptop installations, use the boot disk together with a PCMCIA driver disk containing the pcmciadd.img image. This chapter describes the CD-ROM installation method in detail.

♦ **Hard Drive:** If you have copied the Red Hat Linux ISO images to a local hard drive with either FAT or Linux (ext2 or ext3) file systems, you can use this method to install Red Hat Linux. You have to boot from a boot disk and then identify the hard drive partition and the directory that contains the ISO images.

♦ **NFS:** This method installs from ISO images made available on a Network File System (NFS) server on the network. You have to boot the PC with a boor disk and then specify the NFS server and the directory as the source of the ISO images.

♦ **FTP:** This method installs Red Hat Linux from ISO images located on an FTP server. You have to boot from a boor disk and then specify the FTP server and the directory that contains the ISO images.

♦ **HTTP:** In this method, the Red Hat Linux ISO images are on a Web server and anaconda gets them by using HTTP (the Web server protocol). You have to boot the PC using a boot disk and then identify the Web server the directory where the ISO images are located.

Using kickstart Installation

If you need to install Red Hat Linux on many PCs, you need a way to automate the process so that you do not have to respond to the GUI installer prompts for each PC. kickstart is the answer to this need. It's an automated installation method that enables you to install Red Hat Linux with very little interaction from you.

The idea behind kickstart is to create a text file with all the installation options and then "kick start" the installation by booting and then providing the kickstart file as input.

Starting a kickstart Installation

Setting aside for the moment how to prepare a kickstart file, I want to briefly explain how you can start a kickstart installation. The common use of kickstart installation is to place the Red Hat Linux ISO images on a server on the network and then perform kickstart installations at all the PCs. Let's assume that you have the ISO images on a Web server and you want to install over the network using the HTTP installation method, but do this under the control of a kickstart file. Here's what you would do:

1. Prepare a boot disk with the `bootdisk.img` file (located in the images directory of the first Red Hat Linux CD-ROM).

2. Prepare a network driver disk with the `drvnet.img` file.

3. Place the ISO images and the kickstart file on the Web server and make note of the directory where the kickstart file is located.

4. Boot the PC using the boot disk. At the boot prompt, type the following command:

   ```
   linux ks=http://<server>/<pathname of kickstart file>
   ```

   where `<server>` stands for the name of the Web server and `<pathname of kickstart file>` is the complete pathname of the kickstart file. Thus, if the server is mycompany.com and the kickstart file's pathname is `/redhat8/ks.cfg`, then you type the following at the boot prompt:

   ```
   linux ks=http://mycompany.com/redhat8/ks.cfg
   ```

After that the installation should proceed under the control of the kickstart file.

If the kickstart file is on an NFS server, all you have to do is specify the kickstart file appropriately. The kickstart syntax for NFS is

```
linux ks=nfs:<server>:/<path>
```

Thus, if the NFS server is `someserver.com` and the location of the kickstart file is `/somedir/ks.cfg`, then you type the following command at the boot prompt:

```
linux ks=nfs:someserver.com:/somedir/ks.cfg
```

You can also place a kickstart file named ks.cfg on a floppy (type **mcopy ks.cfg a:** to copy the file to a floppy), and then install it with the following command at the boot prompt:

```
linux ks=floppy
```

You can also use a very simple form of the kickstart installation command that looks like this:

```
linux ks
```

In this case, the installation program configures the Ethernet card using DHCP and then uses the `bootServer` item from the DHCP response as the NFS server from which to get the kickstart file. The name and location of the kickstart file depends on the bootfile specified by DHCP. If the DHCP server does not specify a bootfile, the installler tries to read the file `/kickstart/A.B.C.D-kickstart`, where `A.B.C.D` is the numeric IP address of the PC on which you are installing Red Hat Linux.

Preparing the kickstart File

One way to get a kickstart file is to perform the installation on one PC. The Red Hat installer saves the installation options in the `/root/anaconda-ks.cfg` kickstart file. You can then use this kickstart file to repeat the installation on other PCs. You can also use this kickstart file as a starting point and edit it to create a custom kickstart file suitable for your situation.

Here's a typical anaconda-generated kickstart file:

```
# Kickstart file automatically generated by anaconda.
install
lang en_US.UTF-8
langsupport --default en_US.UTF-8 en_US.UTF-8
keyboard us
mouse generic3ps/2 --device psaux
xconfig --card "nVidia GeForce 2 Go" --videoram 16384 --hsync 31.5-48.5 --
vsync
40-70 --resolution 1024x768 --depth 24 --startxonboot  --defaultdesktop
gnome
network --device eth0 --bootproto dhcp
rootpw --iscrypted $1$7oGAOtge$Q7PCOe2sIRSwRouqxlyMS.
firewall --disabled
authconfig --enableshadow --enablemd5
timezone America/New_York
bootloader --location=mbr
... other kickstart options deleted ...

%packages
@ Administration Tools
@ GNOME Desktop Environment
@ Office/Productivity
@ Printing Support
.... other package groups...
@ X Window System
gnome-audio
tk
... other individual packages...
xmms
firstboot

%post
```

As you can see, the file starts with a long list of kickstart options that essentially mirrors the installation steps that you normally go through when you install Red Hat Linux interactively. After the kickstart options comes a `%packages` section that lists the package groups and individual packages to install. Finally, you see a `%post` section that contains any commands to execute after the installation is complete. For example, you could add commands in the `%post` section to add one or more user accounts.

As this example illustrates, a kickstart file has the following sections, in the exact order shown:

- ◆ **Command section**—This section lists all the kickstart options that control various aspects of the installation
- ◆ **%packages section**—This section lists the package groups (with names that have an @ prefix) and individual package names.
- ◆ **%pre and %post sections**—These two sections are optional, and they can appear in any order.

The command section of the kickstart file contains, at minimum, all the required options shown in Table 2-4. That table shows all the kickstart options and briefly describes each option.

The package group names listed in the `%package` section are defined in the `RedHat/base/comps.xml` file on the first Red Hat Linux CD-ROM. The `comps.xml` file uses XML to define the package database. Each package group contains one or more packages. The `comps.xml` file also defines the dependencies for each package—the other packages that a package needs in order to work properly.

The `%pre` section includes commands to be executed immediately after the kickstart file has been processed but before any installation steps are performed. In the `%pre` section, you can place a shell script to perform any preparatory tasks that have to be performed before installation can begin.

The `%post` section contains the commands to be executed after installation complete. In this section, you can place commands to turn services on or off and add user accounts.

---

insider insight

If you have a working Red Hat Linux system with a GUI desktop, you can use a GUI tool, called Kickstart Configurator, to create the kickstart file. To use the tool, select Main Menu⇨System Tools⇨Kickstart. You can also start the tool by typing the `redhat-config-kickstart` command in a terminal window.

Table 2-4: kickstart Options

Option	Optional (O) or Required (R)	Description
`autostep`	O	Similar to interactive, except that it goes to the next screen for you. It is used mostly for debugging.
`auth or authconfig`	R	Specifies the authentication options. Use one or more of following arguments after this option:
		—`enablemd5` (use MD5 encryption for passwords)
		—`enablenis` (turns on NIS support)
		—`nisdomain=<nisdomain>` (specifies NIS domain name)
		—`nisserver=<nisserver>` (specifies the NIS server name)
		—`useshadow` or —`enableshadow` (turns on shadow passwords)
		—`enableldap` (turns on LDAP support in /etc/nsswitch.conf and requires the nss_ldap package)
		—`enableldapauth` (enables LDAP as an authentication method)
		—`ldapserver=<LDAPserver>` (specifies the LDAP server name)
		—`ldapbasedn=<LDAP-DN>` (specifies LDAP distinguished name)

Option	Optional (O) or Required (R)	Description
		—enableldaptls (uses transport layer security during LDAP lookups)
		—enablekrb5 (turns on Kerberos 5 for authenticating users)
		—krb5realm=<KRBrealm> (specifies the Kerberos realm)
		—krb5kdc=<KDCserver> (specifies the Key Distribution Center)
		—krb5adminserver=<Kadminserver> (specifies the server running kadmind)
		—enablehesiod (enables Hesiod support for looking up user information)
		—hesiodlhs (specifies the Hesiod left-hand side)
		—hesiodrhs (specifies the Hesiod right-hand side)
		—enablesmbauth (enables authentication of users by an SMB server)
		—smbservers=<SMBservers> (specifies the servers to use for SMB authentication)
		—smbworkgroup=<WkGrpName> (specifies the workgroup name)
		—enablecache (enables the nscd service that caches user information)
bootloader	R	Specifies where the boot loader is installed and, optionally, which boot loader to install. Use one or more of following arguments after this option:
		—append=<kernel-params> (specifies kernel parameters)
		—location=[mbr|partition|none] (tells where to write the boot loader,: one of mbr, part, or none)
		—password=<GRUB-passwd> (specifies the GRUB password)
		—md5pass=<encrypted-GRUB-pass> (encrypted GRUB password)
		—useLilo (forces installation of LILO instead of GRUB)
		—lba32 (when using LILO, force use of LBA32 mode of hard disk access)
		—upgrade (upgrades existing boot loader configuration)

(continued)

Table 2-4: (continued)

Option	Optional (O) or Required (R)	Description
clearpart	O	Removes partitions from the system before creating new partitions. Use one or more of following arguments after this option:
		—linux (erases all existing Linux partitions)
		—all (erases all existing partitions)
		—drives=<drivenames> (specifies which drives to clear partitions from)
		—initlabel (initializes the disk label to the default for PC's architecture)
device <type> <moduleName> —opts=<options>	O	Instructs installer to load extra device driver modules. Use the following arguments:
		<type> (either scsi or eth—for a SCSI or Ethernet card)
		<moduleName> (the name of the driver module)
		—opts=<options> (options for the module, these depend on the driver)
deviceprobe	O	Probes the PCI bus for devices and loads modules for all the devices found (assuming that a module is available for the device)
driverdisk	O	Instructs the installer to look for driver disks in the specified disk partition. Use the following arguments:
		<partition> (disk partition containing the driver disk contents)
		—type=<fstype> (optional argument that specifies file system type: vfat, ext2, or ext3)
firewall	O	Configures the firewall based on the arguments:
		<securitylevel> (one of —high, —medium, or —disabled)
		—trust=<device> (trusted network device such as eth0)
		<incoming> (one of —dhcp, —ssh, —telnet, —smtp, —http, —ftp)
		—port=<portnum:protocol> (ports allowed through firewall)
install	O	Indicates that you want to do a fresh install. Specify the install method with one of the following arguments:
		cdrom (installs from the first CD-ROM drive)

Option	Optional (O) or Required (R)	Description
		`harddrive —partition=<part> — dir=<dirname>` (installs from a directory on hard disk partition)
		`nfs —server=<servername> —dir=<dir>` (installs from a directory on the NFS server)
		`url —url http://<server>/<dir>` (installs from a Web server)
		`url —url ftp://<username>:<password>@ <server>/<dir>` (installs from a FTP server)
interactive	O	Allows you to view and modify options as kickstart install progresses
keyboard	R	Sets the keyboard type. Here is the list of available keyboards on i386, Itanium, and Alpha machines: `be-latin1, be-latin2, bg, br-abnt2, cf, cz-lat2, cz-us-qwertz, de, de-latin1, de-latin1-nodeadkeys, dk, dk-latin1, dvorak, es, et, fi, i-latin1, fr, fr-latin0, fr-latin1, fr-pc, fr_CH, fr_CH-latin1, gr, hu, hu101, is-latin1, it, it-ibm, it2, jp106, no, no-latin1, pl, pt-latin1, ro, ru, ru-cp1251, ru-ms, ru1, ru2, ru_win, se-latin1, sg, sg-latin1, sk-qwerty, slovene, speakup, speakup-lt, trq, ua, uk, us`
lang	R	Sets the language to use during installation. Valid language codes are `cs_CZ, da_DK, en_US, fr_FR, de_DE, is_IS, it_IT, ja_JP.eucJP, ko_KR.eucKR, no_NO, pt_PT, ru_RU.koi8r, sl_SI, es_ES, sv_SE, uk_UA, zh_CN.GB18030, zh_TW.Big5`
langsupport	R	Sets the languages to install on the system. Use the same language codes as the ones for the `lang` option. If you install more than one language, indicate the default with the following argument: `—default=<lang>` (sets default language)
logvol	O	Creates a logical volume for Logical Volume Management (LVM). Provide the following arguments: `<mountpoint>` (name of directory where volume is mounted) `—vgname=<groupname>` (name of volume group) `—size=<size>` (size in megabytes) `—name=<volname>` (name of logical volume)

(continued)

Table 2-4: *(continued)*

Option	Optional (O) or Required (R)	Description
mouse	R	Specifies the mouse type and configures it. Use the following arguments:
		—device=<devname> (name of mouse device such as psaux or ttyS0)
		—emulthree (enable emulation of a three-button mouse)
		<mousetype> (specifies mouse type such as genericps/2 or generic3ps/2)
network	O	Configures the local area network information. For installations over network, the installation uses the first Ethernet card (eth0) and configures is dynamically using DHCP. Use the following arguments to configure network:
		—bootproto=<protocol> (one of dhcp, bootp, or static)
		—device=<netdevice> (Ethernet device name such as eth0 or eth1)
		—ip=<IPaddress> (the IP address for static addressing)
		—netmask=<Netmask> (for static addressing)
		—gateway=<gateway_IP> (default gateway IP address)
		—nameserver=<nameserver_IP> (primacy nameserver's IP address)
		—nodns (do not configure any DNS server)
		—hostname=<hostname> (hostname of the system)
part or partition	R	Creates a partition on the hard drive. Use the following arguments to specify details:
		<mntpoint> (the directory where the partition is mounted or the keyword swap for swap partition)
		—recommended (use with swap to size the partition automatically)
		raid.<id> (to use partition in a software RAID device)
		pv.<id> (to use partition in a logical volume)
		—size=<megabytes> (size in megabytes)
		—grow (causes partition to grow up to available space)
		—maxsize=<maxMB> (maximum size in megabytes)
		—noformat (do not format partition)

Option	Optional (O) or Required (R)	Description
		—onpart=<partname> (puts partition on already existing device)
		—usepart=<partname> (puts partition on already existing device)
		—ondisk=<diskname> (creates partition on the specified disk)
		—ondrive=<diskname> (creates partition on the specified disk)
		—asprimary (creates a primary partition)
		—bytes-per-inode=<numbytes> (number of bytes per inode on the filesystem)
		—fstype=<filesystem> (name of file system—one of ext2, ext3, swap, or vfat)
		—start=<startCylinder> (starting cylinder of partition)
		—end=<endCylinder> (ending cylinder of partition)
		—badblocks (checks partition for bad blocks)
raid	O	Creates a software RAID device. Use the following arguments:
		<mntpoint> (the directory where the RAID device is mounted)
		—level=<RAID_level> (the RAID level to use—0, 1, or 5)
		—device=<devname> (name of RAID device such as md0 or md1)
		—spares=<number> (number of spare drives allocated for the RAID array)
		—fstype=<filesystemType> (filesystem type—one of ext2, ext3, swap, or vfat)
		—noformat (does not format the RAID array)
reboot	O	Reboots after the installation is complete
rootpw	R	Sets the system's root password. Use the following arguments:
		—iscrypted (password is already encrypted)
		<password> (the encrypted root password)
skipx	O	Skips configuration of X Window System.
text	O	Performs the installation in text mode (instead of the default graphical mode).

(continued)

Table 2-4: *(continued)*

Option	*Optional (O) or Required (R)*	*Description*
timezone	R	Sets the system time zone. Use the following arguments:
		—utc (indicates that hardware clock is set to UTC— Greenwich Mean Time)
		<timezone> (the time zone name such as America/New_York or EST5EDT)
upgrade	O	Upgrades an existing system rather than installing a fresh system
xconfig	O	Configures the X Window System. Use the following arguments:
		—noprobe (does not probe the monitor)
		—card=<videcardName> (name of video card from list in /usr/share/hwdata/Cards)
		—videoram=<kilobytes> (amount of video RAM in kilobytes)
		—monitor=<monitorName> (name of monitor from list in /usr/share/hwdata/MonitorsDB)
		—hsync=<HSyncRange> (range of horizontal synchronization frequencies in kHz such as —hsync 31.5-69.0)
		—vsync=<VSyncRange> (range of vertical synchronization frequencies in Hz such as —vsync 55-120)
		—defaultdesktop=<DesktopName> (GNOME or KDE)
		—startxonboot (provides a graphical login screen)
		—resolution=<HHHxVVV> (default resolution in terms horizontal and vertical pixels such as 640x480 or 1024x768)
		—depth=<defaultDepthBits> (default color depth—one of 8, 16, 24, or 32)
volgroup	O	Creates a Logical Volume Management (LVM) group. Use following arguments:
		<name> (name of logical volume group)
		<partition> (partition to use)
zerombr	O	Initializes any invalid partition tables found on disks. Use the following argument:
		yes (destroy disks with invalid partition tables)

Option	Optional (O) or Required (R)	Description
`%include`	O	Includes the content of another file into this kickstart file. Use the following arguments: `<pathname>` (the file to include)

Installing Red Hat Linux on a Laptop

Laptops (also called notebook computers) are more integrated than desktops are; a laptop's video card, monitor, and hard disk are all built into a compact package. In other words, you cannot easily mix and match components with laptops as you do with desktop systems, so you have to make sure that Linux supports all components of your laptop system.

Laptops typically have a PCMCIA adapter where you can plug in many peripherals such as a wireless Ethernet network card or a modem. When installing Red Hat Linux on a laptop with a CD-ROM drive, you can either boot from the CD-ROM or prepare an additional driver disk for PCMCIA support. To prepare the PCMCIA driver disk, follow the same steps used for the Red Hat boot disk, but specify \images\pcmcia.img as the image filename. As with desktop PCs, you do not have to worry about the boot disk if you can boot the laptop directly from the CD-ROM drive.

If your laptop does not have a CD-ROM drive, then you have to use one of the other installation methods. See the "Learning Other Installation Methods" section of this chapter for brief descriptions of these other methods. Typically, you'd need a network interface and would then install using one of the network installation methods from another system on your local area network.

Most laptops with Intel 80386 or better processors should be able to run plain Linux without any problems. If you want to install XFree86, however, you may have some trouble if XFree86 does not support the video card (on a laptop, video circuitry is built into the motherboard) and the pointing device. With the Linux kernel versions 2.4 and later, you can use the VESA driver to get X working on most laptops even if XFree86 doesn't natively support the laptop's graphics chipset. Also, nowadays, most laptop pointing devices can at least emulate a standard PS/2 Mouse, so all pointing devices should work with XFree86.

Secret

This section barely touches upon the subject of how to run Linux on laptops. Installing Linux on a specific laptop model is a unique experience, and there are simply too many different models to describe here. As users install and run Linux on a variety of laptops, the user community's cumulative experience of Linux on laptops continues to grow. Much of this information is summarized and made available on the Web. For detailed information on how to install and run Linux on laptops, point your Web browser to the Linux on Laptops Home Page: http://www.linux-laptop.net/.

This page includes links to many more Web pages, each documenting the details of how to install and run Linux on a specific laptop model. In particular, you will find out if you have to do anything special to get Linux and X running on your laptop.

PCMCIA

Laptops typically include the PCMCIA (commonly referred to as PC Card) interface through which you can connect many different peripheral devices to the laptop. As this chapter explained earlier, the version of Red Hat Linux on the companion CD-ROMs supports PCMCIA. The current PCMCIA drivers support most common PCMCIA controllers, including Intel, Cirrus, Vadem, VLSI, Ricoh, and Databook chipsets. See Appendix F for a discussion of specific PC Cards that Linux supports.

Advanced Power Management

Another laptop-specific feature is power management, which refers to the capability of a laptop to suspend its activities so as to conserve battery power. Laptops that have Advanced Power Management (APM) capability can suspend and resume power-consuming components (such as the display and hard drive), as well as provide information on battery life.

The version of Red Hat Linux on the companion CD-ROMs supports APM. You can learn more about how to support APM under Linux by visiting the website at

http://www.worldvisions.ca/~apenwarr/apmd/

Sound on Laptops

Many high-end laptops come with built-in sound. Using the sound capabilities under Linux is a straightforward process, provided that you can figure out what type of sound card your laptop has. Chapter 5 covers sound cards in detail.

Red Hat's kudzu program—used to probe and detect hardware—should detect your laptop's sound card and set it up correctly. If your sound card is not detected, you can still get it to work by locaing the appropriate driver module with the modprobe command. To determine the driver, you would need information about the sound card. If sound support is not automatically set up, you should check your laptop's documentation for clues about the make and model of the sound card before you set up sound support.

The bottom line is that you can set up Linux to support sound on a laptop the same way you can for a desktop PC.

X on Laptops

Users have reported success in running Linux together with XFree86 on many 386, 486, and Pentium laptops. Nowadays, laptops support high-resolution LCD screens with capabilities on a par with those of desktop PCs. You can configure X to work as long as the laptop's video chipsets are supported by XFree86.

Most laptops use one of the following types of video chipsets:

- ATI Radeon Mobility M1-M7, Rage 128 Mobility
- Intel i810, i830M
- NVidia GeForce2 Go, GeForce4 Go
- Chips & Technology 655xx series chipset
- NeoMagic NM20xx and NM21xx chipsets

XFree86 4.3.0 supports these chipsets. You can learn more about the details of X configuration in Chapter 3.

Summary

Linux is a UNIX-like operating system for Intel 80x86, Pentium, and compatible systems. The CD-ROMs that accompany this book include the latest version of the popular Red Hat Linux distribution. This chapter guides you through the process of installing Red Hat Linux on your PC. The next chapter turns to another configuration task—how to configure and run the X Window System on your Red Hat Linux PC. You need X because with it you can have a GUI for Red Hat Linux.

By reading this chapter, you learned the following:

- Information you should gather about your PC before installing Red Hat Linux
- The overall process of installing Red Hat Linux (including the X Window System, GNOME, and KDE) from the companion CD-ROMs
- Steps you may need to perform under MS-DOS or Microsoft Windows before installing Linux
- How to boot Linux initially, partition the hard disk, and load the various software packages from the companion CD-ROMs by using the Red Hat Linux installer
- How to troubleshoot some common installation problems
- How to perform a kickstart installation
- How to install Red Hat Linux on laptops

X Window
System Setup

Chapter

3

♦ ♦

Secrets in This Chapter

♦ ♦

I f you have used Apple Mac OS or Microsoft Windows, you are familiar with the convenience of a graphical user interface (GUI, pronounced gooey). In Linux, the GUI is not an integral part of the operating system. Instead, Linux distributions, such as Red Hat Linux, typically provide GNOME and KDE as the GUI. GNOME and KDE are, in turn, built on a windowing system called the X Window System, or X. Red Hat Linux includes a version of X called XFree86, which is designed to work with your PC's video card and monitor. The video card and monitor you use do not matter much if you work only with text. But to install XFree86, you need detailed information about your video card and monitor.

The companion CD-ROMs contain the XFree86 software, which you might have installed on your hard disk during the installation process shown in Chapter 2. At that time, the Red Hat installation program would have detected your video card and monitor, and configured XFree86. This chapter describes the attributes of video cards and monitors and explains the X Window System. It also shows you how to use the redhat-config-xfree86 GUI utility to configure X in case the Red Hat installer fails to configure XFree86 properly on your PC.

Understanding Video Cards and Monitors

The video card or graphics adapter contains the electronics that control the monitor. On most systems, the video card takes the form of a circuit board that plugs into a slot on your PC's motherboard. On many new systems, however, the motherboard itself contains the necessary graphics chipsets.

Raster-Scan Display

All video cards operate on the same principle: They store an image in video memory (also called video RAM or VRAM for short) and generate the appropriate signals to display the image on the monitor's screen.

The monitor is the physical device that contains the display screen where the graphic and text output appears. The display screen is typically a phosphor-coated glass tube on which an electron beam traces the output image. On laptop computers, the display screen is a *liquid crystal display* (LCD). More expensive laptops use active-matrix LCD-display screens.

The image that appears on the monitor is made up of many horizontal lines, known as raster lines. An electron beam in the monitor generates the *raster lines* by sweeping back and forth on a phosphor-coated screen, as illustrated in Figure 3-1.

The phosphor on the screen glows in proportion to the intensity of the electron beam. The glowing dot on the screen represents a picture element, or pixel. Thus, a line of the image is generated by controlling the intensity of the beam as it scans across the screen. The phosphor fades in a while, but if the lines are redrawn repeatedly, our persistence of vision creates an illusion of a steady image. Most PC monitors redraw an entire screenful of raster lines 50 to 90 times per second.

Figure 3-1: A Typical Raster-Scan Display.

As Figure 3-1 shows, the electron beam scans an area larger than the actual view area of the display screen, but the electron beam is active only when the beam is in the viewable area. Also, after reaching the end of a line, the beam has to return to the start of the next raster line. This part of the beam's motion is known as the *horizontal retrace*. Similarly, when the beam reaches the bottom of the screen, it has to return to the first line to start another cycle of drawing. This period is known as the *vertical retrace*. The beam's intensity is reduced (the beam is blanked) during horizontal and vertical retrace so that those lines do not appear on the screen.

The video card generates the signals necessary to sweep the electron beam across the display and refresh the display at a rapid rate. There are two types of refreshing: *interlaced* and *noninterlaced*. In an interlaced refresh, each screen is drawn in two steps. First, the electron beam sweeps across the screen, drawing all the odd-numbered raster lines. Then the electron beam goes back to the beginning of the screen and draws all the even-numbered raster lines. Broadcast television uses interlaced refreshing. A noninterlaced refresh involves drawing all raster lines in a single step. Most video cards refresh the screen 60 times or more per second and use a noninterlaced refresh.

Color Display

Color display screens represent any color with a combination of the three primary colors: red (R), green (G), and blue (B). Most color displays use three electron beams, one for each primary color.

The screen in a color display has a repeated triangular pattern of red, green, and blue phosphor dots. Each phosphor dot glows in its color when the electron beam impinges on it. A perforated metal screen, known as a shadow mask, ensures that each electron beam strikes the phosphor of the intended color. The video card varies the intensity of the red, green, and blue electron beams, thereby displaying many colors.

Color Palette and Resolution

Typically, a video card allows a palette of 256 colors, and each pixel's color is stored in an 8-bit value. The actual color (in terms of R, G, B components) that corresponds to a pixel's 8-bit value is determined by consulting a color lookup table or colormap.

Today's high-performance video cards allow three bytes of storage per pixel, so that each pixel's value can directly specify the RGB components that determine that pixel's color. These so-called 24-bit video cards provide true color display but require more video memory to store the entire image.

The resolution of a display screen is expressed in terms of the number of visible dots (pixels) across a raster line and the total raster lines. A common resolution is 640 dots across by 480 lines vertically, which is commonly expressed as 640×480. Other common screen resolutions are 800×600, 1,024×768, and 1,280×1,024.

Video RAM

The video card stores the contents of the pixels in random-access memory (RAM), known as video RAM. The number of colors and the display resolution supported by a video card depends on the amount of video RAM. To store the information content of a 256-color 1,024×768 display screen, for example, the video card needs 1,024×768, or 786,432 bytes of video RAM (because an 8-bit pixel value represents 256 colors and 1 byte = 8 bits). On the other hand, to display 24-bit color at 1,024×768 resolution, the video card needs three times as much video RAM: 3×786,432 = 2,359,296 bytes, or about 2.3MB of video RAM (because 24 bit = 3 bytes).

Typical video cards have 4, 8, 16, 32, or 64MB of video RAM. A video card with 1MB of video RAM can comfortably handle a 256-color, 1,024×768-resolution display.

Dot clock

You run across the term dot clock when you configure a video card to work with XFree86 (the X Window System). This term refers to the rate at which the video card can traverse the raster lines that make up a complete display screen. The value of the dot clock is expressed in terms of the number of dots drawn per second.

To get a rough idea of the dot clock, consider a 640×480 display, which has 640×480 = 307,200 dots (visible ones, anyway). To produce the appearance of a steady display, these dots should be repainted at least 72 times per second. Thus, the video card has to paint 640×480×72 = 22,118,400 dots a second. This rate amounts to approximately 22 million dots a second, which is expressed as a dot clock of 22 MHz (1 MHz = a million times per second).

In reality, an even higher dot clock is required for a 640×480 display refreshed at 72 Hz (which means 72 times per second) because the electron beam cannot turn around on a dime. As illustrated in Figure 3-1, the electron beam has to traverse a scan line beyond the visible number of dots before it can snap back to the beginning of the next line. The required dot clock for a 640×480 display at a 72-Hz refresh rate, for example, is 25.2 MHz.

As you must realize by now, a higher-resolution display requires an even higher dot clock. A 1,024×768 display at a 72-Hz refresh rate implies 1,024×768×72 = 56,623,104 dots per second, at minimum. Thus, you can tell that the dot clock necessary for a 1,024×768 display will be somewhat higher than 56.6 MHz.

Older video cards support a fixed set of dot clocks, but many advanced video cards include a programmable dot clock. When a video card has a programmable dot clock, the X server can set the video card to operate at any dot clock that lies in a range of acceptable values. For a video card with a programmable dot clock, however, you may need to specify the name of the chip that controls the dot clock (known as the clock chip).

Importance of Video Card and Monitor

Linux works with any video card/monitor combination in text mode. If a video card and monitor work under MS-DOS or Windows, the combination also works under Linux in text mode. The story is different when you install XFree86, the X Window System for Linux. Because XFree86 controls the video card directly (MS-DOS typically uses standard predefined modes of the video card and Windows has its own video drivers), getting XFree86 running with a specific video card takes more work.

The monitor also is important for XFree86. Electrical signals from the video card control the monitor, so the monitor must be compatible with the video card. The output on the monitor is the result of a rapidly moving electron beam that the video card's signals control. A monitor's compatibility with a video card has to do with how fast the video card attempts to move the electron beam on the display screen.

The resolutions a video card/monitor combination supports depend on the amount of video memory on the card and on how fast the monitor's electron beam can move. XFree86 gets the necessary information about the monitor and the video card from a special text file named `XF86Config` in the `/etc/X11` directory.

Understanding the X Window System

The name *X Window System* (*X* for short) is loosely applied to several components that facilitate window-based graphics output (or a graphical interface) on a variety of bitmapped displays. A bitmapped display has two distinct components: a *video monitor* on which the graphics output appears and a *video card* (or *graphics card*)—either a plug-in card or some circuitry built into the system's motherboard—that causes the output to appear on the monitor.

At the heart of X is the *X server*—a process (computer program) running on a computer that has a bitmapped display, a keyboard, and a mouse. Applications—*X clients*—that need to display output do so by communicating with the X server via one of several possible interprocess communication mechanisms. The communications between the X clients and the X server follow a well-defined protocol: the *X protocol*. In addition to the X server, the clients, and the X protocol, the term X encompasses a library of routines known as *Xlib*, which constitutes the C-language interface to the facilities of the X server.

Secret

The development of the X Window System started in 1984 at the Massachusetts Institute of Technology (MIT), under the auspices of the MIT Laboratory for Computer Science and MIT/Project Athena. X had industry support from the beginning because Digital Equipment Corporation (DEC) and IBM were involved in Project Athena. By early 1986, DEC had introduced the first commercial implementation of X running on the VAXstation-II/GPX under the Ultrix operating system: X version 10, release 3 (X10R3). Soon X attracted the attention of other prominent workstation vendors such as Hewlett-Packard, Apollo Computer (which has since merged with Hewlett-Packard), Sun Microsystems, and Tektronix.

Feedback from users of X10 urged project members to start a major redesign of the X protocol. While the design of what would become X version 11 (X11) proceeded, X10R4 was released in December 1986. X10R4 was the last release of X version 10.

continues

continued

In January 1987, during the first X technical conference, 11 major computer vendors announced a joint effort to support and standardize on X11. The first release of X11—X11R1—became available in September 1987. To ensure the continued evolution of X under the control of an open organization, the MIT X Consortium was formed in January 1988. Under the leadership of Robert W. Scheifler, one of the principal architects of X, the consortium was a major cause of the success of X. Since then, control of the X Window System has been passed on to the X Consortium, Inc., a not-for-profit corporation.

In March 1988, release 2 of X11—X11R2—became available. X11 release 3—X11R3—appeared in late October 1988. In January 1990, the MIT X Consortium released X11R4; X11R5 followed in August 1991. X11R6—the latest release of X—was released in April 1994. Throughout these releases, the X11 protocol has remained unchanged. All enhancements have been made through the X11 protocol's ability to support extensions.

X Server and Clients

When you run X on your system, the X server runs on your computer and controls the monitor, keyboard, and mouse. The server responds to commands that X clients send that open windows and draw in those windows. The X clients may run locally or on remote systems. This arrangement is known as the *client/server model*. As the name implies, the server provides a service that the client requests. Usually, clients communicate with the server through a network, with client and server exchanging data using a protocol that both understand.

You may already have seen the client/server model in action. A *file server*, for example, stores files and allows clients to access and manipulate those files. Another common application, the *database server*, provides a centralized database from which clients retrieve data by sending queries. Similarly, the X display server offers graphics-display services to clients that send X protocol requests to the server.

One major difference exists between the X server and other servers, such as file and database servers. File servers and database servers are usually processes executing on remote machines, but the X server is a process executing on the computer where the monitor is located. The X clients may run locally or on remote systems.

---

insider insight
In the PC LAN's client/server model, applications are typically stored on a central server. Users access these server-based applications from client PCs. When you run an application from a PC, the application executes in your PC's processor. In the X client/server model, the situation is reversed. The X server runs on your PC and manages the display, keyboard, and mouse. The X clients—graphical applications that display output using X—are the ones that run in the server's processor. In other words, the X server runs in a location you typically associate with the client (as in the client PC in a PC LAN). Keep this distinction in mind when working with the X client/server model.

Graphical User Interfaces and X

An application's user interface determines its appearance (*look*) and behavior (*feel*). When the user interface uses graphic objects, such as windows and menus, we call it a *graphical user interface* (GUI). You can also call a GUI a point-and-click user interface because users generally interact with a GUI by moving the mouse pointer onscreen and clicking the mouse button. To confirm the closing of a file, for example, the user may click the mouse button while the mouse pointer is inside a button labeled OK. By now everyone is so used to GUIs that you'd describe that action of clicking the OK button as "click OK."

GUIs were originally developed at the Xerox Palo Alto Research Center (PARC). Subsequently, Apple Computer made such interfaces popular in its Lisa and Macintosh systems. Today, GUIs are available for most systems. Microsoft Windows is available for most IBM-compatible PCs; Motif, GNOME, and KDE (built on X) are avaialble for Linux and UNIX systems.

Most GUIs, including Motif, GNOME, and KDE, have three components:

- ◆ A window system
- ◆ A window manager
- ◆ A toolkit

The graphical window system organizes graphics output on the display screen and performs basic text- and graphics-drawing functions. The X Window System is the window system used by all X-based GUIs, such as GNOME and KDE.

The window manager enables the user to move and resize windows. The window manager is also partly responsible for the appearance of the windows because it usually adds a decorative frame to them. The window manager also manages input focus, the mechanism by which the user can select one of several windows onscreen and make that one the current active window (the window with which the user intends to interact). This process is called giving the input focus to a window. For GUIs based on the X Window system, a window manager is an X client, just like any other X application. For example, GNOME comes with the metacity window manager.

The third component, the toolkit, is a library of routines with a well-defined programming interface. This toolkit is primarily of interest to programmers because it enables them to write applications that use the facilities of the window system and that have a consistent look and feel. For example, GNOME comes with a toolkit named Gtk+ (GIMP toolkit), and KDE comes with the Qt toolkit.

X on Red Hat Linux

The X Window System for Red Hat Linux comes from the XFree86 project—a cooperative project of programmers who bring X to the PC. (You can access the XFree86 home page at `http://www.xfree86.org/`.) As a result, the Linux version of X is called XFree86.

insider insight The X server configures the display (number of colors, resolution in terms of number of pixels horizontally and vertically), mouse, and keyboard based on information stored in a configuration file. Red Hat Linux comes with XFree86 version 4.2.0 that uses a single X server that loads different driver modules to support different video cards. A configuration file—/etc/X11/XF86Config—configures the X server to work on a specific video card and display output in a specific resolution.

To configure X, you must prepare the X configuration file. The configuration file contains information about your video card, monitor, keyboard, and mouse. Red Hat Linux comes with a GUI utility program called redhat-config-xfree86 that enables you to create the XF86Config configuration file.

Setting up X on Red Hat Linux

You want to get X set up and going quickly; without it, Red Hat Linux has no GUI. If you are used to other graphical environments (perhaps on another UNIX workstation or on a PC running Microsoft Windows), you probably want a similar graphical environment on Red Hat Linux.

If you plan to develop software on your Red Hat Linux system, chances are good that your software has a graphical component that must be implemented and tested under X. You have to set up and run X to perform this implementation and testing.

No matter what your purpose, if you want to set up XFree86, you have to prepare a special configuration file named XF86Config (which must be present in the /etc/X11 directory) that contains information about your hardware. You can use the redhat-config-xfree86 utility to create the XF86Config file. The next few sections guide you through the process of configuring XFree86 and starting X on your Red Hat Linux PC.

cross ref You do not have to configure XFree86 if you have already successfully installed X during the Red Hat Linux installation, as explained in Chapter 2.

Knowing Your Video Hardware before Configuring XFree86

To configure XFree86, you must know the hardware that X must access and use. From this chapter's brief introduction to X, you know that the X server controls the following hardware:

- ◆ The video card
- ◆ The monitor
- ◆ The keyboard
- ◆ The mouse

The X server needs information about these components to work properly.

The Monitor

XFree86 controls the monitor through the video card. This means that an XFree86 server can cause a video card to send a wide range of signals to the monitor (to control how fast a raster line is drawn, for example, or how often the entire screen is redrawn). If a video card causes the monitor to perform some task beyond its capabilities (drawing each raster line much faster than it was designed to do, for example), the monitor may actually be damaged. To ensure that the signals from the video card are within the acceptable range for a monitor, XFree86 needs information about some key characteristics of the monitor.

At minimum, you have to provide the following information about the monitor:

- ◆ The range of acceptable horizontal synchronization frequencies. A typical range might be 30–64 kHz.
- ◆ The range of allowable vertical synchronization rates (also known as *vertical refresh rates*), such as 50–90 Hz
- ◆ If available, the bandwidth in megahertz, such as 75 MHz

Typically, the monitor's documentation includes all this information. If you bought your PC recently, you may still have the documentation. If you have lost your monitor's documentation, one way to find the information might be to check your Microsoft Windows setup. If your system came with a Windows driver for the display, that driver may display information about the monitor. Another possibility is to visit your computer vendor's website and look for the technical specification of the monitor. I found useful information about my system's monitor on the vendor's website. You can also try searching on a search engine such as Google (http://www.google.com/).

The Video Card

XFree86 already provides X servers designed to work with a particular video chipset (the integrated circuit chips that generate the signals needed to control the monitor). To select the correct X server, you have to indicate the video chipset your video card uses.

Even within a family of video cards based on a specific chipset, many configurable parameters may vary from one card to another. Therefore, you also must specify the vendor name and the model of your video card.

At a minimum, you have to provide the following information about the video card:

- ◆ Video chipset, such as S3, NVidia RIVA TNT, or ATI Mach64
- ◆ Vendor name and model, such as Diamond Stealth 64 VRAM, Diamond Viper V550, Number Nine GXE64, or ATI Graphics Xpression
- ◆ Amount of video RAM (random access memory), such as 16MB or 32MB.

Most PC vendors indicate only the make and model of the video card in advertisements; ads rarely mention the video chipset. You should ask explicitly about the video chipset and for as much information as the vendor can provide about the video card's model.

insider insight

If you are going to use an old PC to run Linux, you can try to find the video chipset information by opening your computer's case and looking at the video card. The vendor name and model number may be inscribed on the card. For the video chipset, you have to look at the markings on the different chips on the video card and try to guess. For example, if you find a chip with the following markings (only part of the markings are shown here):

```
S3 Trio 64 (GACC 2)

86C764 - P
```

You might then guess that this card uses the S3 chipset. In fact, markings on the chip show the 86C764 number as well (either in the full form or as the number 764). Now, if you can locate the vendor name and model of this card, you may be all set to configure the X server to run properly on your PC.

To find out if your video card or chipset is supported by XFree86 4.2.0, visit `http://www.xfree86.org/4.2.0/Status.html`. This Web page provides links to information on XFree86 support for specific video cards or chipsets from the following vendors (I briefly summarize the information here):

- **3Dfx**—Voodoo Graphics and Voodoo2 supported by glide driver. Voodoo Banshee, Voodoo3, Voodoo4, and Voodoo5 chipsets supported by `tdfx` driver.
- **3Dlabs**—Permedia series (including 1, 2, 2a, 2v, 3, and 4) and GLINT series (including 300SX, 500TX, MX, R3 and R4) with the Gamma, Gamma2, or Delta coprocessor are supported by the `glint` driver.
- **Alliance**—AT24, AT25, and AT3D are supported by the `apm` driver. AP6422 is partially supported.
- **ARK Logic**—ARK1000PV, ARK2000PV, and ARK2000MT are supported by the `ark` driver.
- **ATI**—All hardware except for Mach8 and some old Mach32 chips are supported by the `ati` driver. Accelerated support provided for Mach64, Rage, Rage 128, and Radeon chipsets only.
- **Avance Logic**—These chipsets are not supported.
- **Chips and Technologies**—All chipsets (65520, 65525, 65530, 65535, 65540, 65545, 65546, 65548, 65550, 65554, 65555, 68554, 69000, 64200, and 64300) are supported by the `chips` driver.
- **Cirrus Logic**—The Alpine (5430, 5434, 5436, 5446, 5480, 7548) and Laguna (5462, 5464, 5465) chipsets are supported by the `cirrus` driver. Other Cirrus Logic chipsets are not supported.
- **Compaq/Digital**—DEC 21030 TGA 8 plane and 24 plane chipsets are supported by the `tga` driver.
- **Cyrix**—The Cyrix MediaGX chipset is supported by the `cyrix` driver.
- **Epson**—These chipsets are not supported.
- **Genoa**—These chipsets are not supported.
- **IBM**—VGA chipsets (and compatibles) are supported by the `vga` driver. IBM 8514/A and XGA-2 are not supported.
- **IIT**—These chipsets are not supported.

- **Integrated Micro Solutions (IMS)**—IMS Twin Turbo 128 and Twin Turbo 3D are supported by the `imstt` driver.
- **Intel**—The i740 is supported by the i740 driver. Intel i810 (including i810-dc100 and i810e), i815, and i830 are supported by the `i810` driver.
- **Matrox**—MGA2064W (Millennium I), MGA1064SG (Mystique), MGA2164W (Millennium II, both PCI and AGP), G100, G200, G400, G450, and G550 are supported by the `mga` driver
- **Micronix, Inc. (MX)**—These chipsets are not supported.
- **NCR**—These chipsets are not supported.
- **NeoMagic**—NeoMagic NM2070, NM2090, NM2093, NM2097, NM2160, NM2200, NM2230, NM2360, and NM2380 chipsets are supported by the `neomagic` driver.
- **NVIDIA**—Riva 128, 128ZX, TNT, TNT2 (Ultra, Vanta, M64), GeForce (DDR, 256), Quadro, GeForce2 (GTS, Ultra, MX, Go), GeForce3, and Quadro2 are supported by the `nv` driver.
- **Number Nine**—Imagine 128, Ticket 2 Ride, Revolution 3D, and Revolution IV are supported by the `i128` driver.
- **Oak Technologies, Inc.**—These chipsets are not supported.
- **Paradise/Western Digital**—These chipsets are not supported.
- **RealTek**—These chipsets are not supported.
- **Rendition/Micron**—Verite 1000, 2100, and 2200 are supported by the rendition driver.
- **S3**—The 964 (revisions 0 and 1), 968, Trio32, Trio64, Trio64, Trio64V+, Trio64UV+, Aurora64V+, Trio64V2, and PLATO/PX chipsets are supported by the s3 driver when they are used with the IBM RGB 524, Texas Instruments 3025, or an internal TrioDAC RAMDAC chip. The ViRGE, ViRGE/VX, ViRGE/DX, ViRGE/GX, ViRGE/GX2, ViRGE/MX, ViRGE/MX+, Trio3D, and Trio3D/2X are supported by the `s3virge` driver. Savage3D, Savage3D/MV, Savage4, Savage2000, and SuperSavage are supported by the `savage` driver. Other S3 chipsets are not yet supported.
- **Silicon Graphics, Inc. (SGI)**—SGI Indy's Newport cards (also known as XL) are supported by the `newport` driver.
- **Silicon Integrated Systems (SiS)**—SiS 530, 620, 6326 are supported by the `sis` driver. SiS 630, 300, and 540 are also supported, but there are some problems with the support for these chipsets.
- **Silicon Motion, Inc**—Lynx, LynxE, Lynx3D, LynxEM, LynxEM+, and Lynx3DM chipsets are supported by the `siliconmotion` driver.
- **Sun Microsystems**—Sun BW2 framebuffers are supported by the `sunbw2` driver. Sun CG3 framebuffers are supported by the `suncg3` driver. Sun CG6 framebuffers are supported by the `suncg6` driver. Sun CG14 framebuffers are supported by the `suncg14` driver. Sun FFB framebuffers are supported by the `sunffb` driver. Sun LEO framebuffers are supported by the `sunleo` driver. Sun TCX framebuffers are supported by the `suntcx` driver.
- **Trident Microsystems**—TVGA8900B, TVGA8900C, TVGA8900CL, TVGA9000, TVGA9000i, TVGA9100B, TVGA9200CXr, TVGA8900D, TGUI9440AGi, TGUI9660, TGUI9680, ProVidia 9682, ProVidia 9685, 3DImage975, 3DImage985, Blade3D, Cyber9320, Cyber9382, Cyber9385, Cyber9388, Cyber9397,

Cyber9397/DVD, Cyber9520, Cyber9525/DVD CyberBlade/Ai1, CyberBlade/i7, CyberBlade/i1, CyberBlade/DSTN/Ai1, CyberBlade/DSTN/i7, CyberBlade/DSTN/i1, CyberBlade/e4, CyberBladeXP, and BladeXP are supported by the `trident` driver. The old TVGA ISA/VLB card has not been fully tested.

◆ **Tseng Labs**—ET4000AX, ET4000/W32, ET4000/W32i, ET4000/W32p, ET6000, and ET6100 are supported by the `tseng` driver.

◆ **Video 7**—This chipset is not supported.

◆ **Weitek**—These chipsets are not supported.

The Mouse

The mouse is an integral part of a GUI because users indicate choices and perform tasks by pointing and clicking. The X server moves an onscreen pointer as you move the mouse. The X server monitors all mouse clicks and sends these mouse-click events to the appropriate X client application—the one whose window contains the mouse pointer.

Although you may have set up the mouse during Linux installation, you still have to provide information about the mouse to the X server. The XFree86 X server needs a mouse to start; if the X server cannot access and control the mouse, it won't start.

To specify the mouse, you need to know the following things:

◆ The mouse type, such as Microsoft, Logitech, BusMouse, or PS/2-style mouse

◆ The type of connection between your mouse and the system (serial or bus)

◆ The mouse's device name. You can leave this as the generic name `/dev/mouse` because the Red Hat installation program sets up a link between `/dev/mouse` and the actual mouse device; the actual device name depends on the type of mouse and where it is connected—the exact serial port for a serial mouse, for example.

You should not have any problem with the mouse as long as the mouse type and device names are correct.

Configuring XFree86 Using redhat-config-xfree86

Up until version 8.0, Red Hat Linux came with xf86config—a text-mode utility to configure X. Now Red Hat provides a GUI utility called redhat-config-xfree86, written in the Python programming language.

Secret

The redhat-config-xfree86 utility provides a convenient way to configure X through a GUI that itself uses X. The utility probes the monitor and video card. Then it starts X and displays a window from which you can further configure the settings such as resolution and color.

To probe the monitor, redhat-config-xfree86 uses the Display Data Channel (DDC)—a command interface developed by the Video Electronics Standards Association (VESA) to support plug-and-play setup of monitors. The DDC interface enables bidirectional communication between the computer and the monitor. Older monitors are not fully DDC compliant, and they may not return information needed by display configuration programs such as redhat-config-xfree86. If it does not get the needed information, redhat-config-xfree86 makes some assumptions about the monitor and shows it as a unknown monitor.

If there is an existing X configuration file—/etc/X11/XF86Config—redhat-config-xfree86 reads and uses the existing configuration information to start X. If there is no XF86Config file, redhat-config-xfree86 creates a new file based on information it gathers and your input.

The only problem occurs when the initial probing by redhat-config-xfree86 does not result in good information and you get a blank screen. When this happens, try pressing Ctrl-Alt-Keypad- and then waiting for a few moments. This causes the X server (which redhat-config-xfree86 has started) to switch to a lower screen resolution (for example, 800x600 instead of 1024x768). Sometimes that's all it takes to get X going. You'll know when X is working because you should see the main window of redhat-config-xfree86, as shown in Figure 3-2.

Figure 3-2: Main Window from redhat-config-xfree86.

The window has two tabs—Display and Advanced. Initially redhat-config-xfree86 shows the Display tab. On that tab, the utility shows a summary line about the monitor and the video card. For example, in Figure 3-2, the monitor appears as unknown monitor because DDC probing of the monitor did not return the information needed by redhat-config-xfree86. When that happens, you can configure the monitor from the Advanced tab.

Two drop-down lists enable you to change the resolution and colors. The initial settings show what redhat-config-xfree86 has been able to determine through its own probing. You can change these to different values after changing the monitor type from the Advanced tab.

Clicking the Advanced tab causes redhat-config-xfree86 to display that tab, as shown in Figure 3-3. The Advanced tab enables you to configure the monitor and the vide card. Initially, redhat-config-xfree86 shows the current settings for the monitor and the video card.

Figure 3-3: You Can Configure the Monitor and the Video Card from the Advanced Tab.

In this example, the monitor is shown as unknown and the video card type is a generic S3 ViRGE chipset. To configure the monitor, click the Configure button in the Monitor section of the tab. This causes a new window to appear, as shown in Figure 3-4.

Figure 3-4: Configuring the Monitor in redhat-config-xfree86.

If you know your monitor's make and model, select it from the list. Otherwise, you can specify the ranges of values for the horizontal and the vertical synchronization rates (or frequencies) of your monitor. These two critical parameters of your monitor have the following meanings:

 ♦ **Horizontal synchronization frequency**—the number of times per second that the monitor can display a horizontal raster line, in kilohertz (kHz).
 ♦ **Vertical synchronization rate or vertical refresh rate**—how many times a second the monitor can display the entire screen.

You can enter the numbers in the text-entry fields on the right-hand side of the window.

Click OK after entering the information about the monitor. The window closes, and you get back to the Advanced tab in the redhat-config-xfree86 utility's main window.

Check the video card information—the video card type, the amount of video memory, and the driver. Typically, redhat-config-xfree86 does a good job of detecting the video card. If you need to change the video card information, click the Configure button next to the video card information (refer to Figure 3-3). This causes redhat-config-xfree86 to display a new window, as shown in Figure 3-5.

Figure 3-5: Configuring the Video Card in redhat-config-xfree86.

Initially redhat-config-xfree86 shows the detected video card type and the driver it has selected for that card (that driver is an XFree86 driver, used by the XFree86 server to control the video card). If you want to change the video card type, scroll through the list on the left and pick your video card from the list. The driver for the selected card should appear in the Driver field.

Sometimes you may know that a certain XFree86 driver would work for your video card (perhaps you have read that on a newsgroup or found from an Internet search). To select a specific driver, click the arrow button for the drop-down list of drivers, as shown in Figure 3-6.

Figure 3-6: Selecting a Specific XFree86 Driver for Your Video Card.

After configuring the video card, click OK to return to the main window of redhat-config-xfree86. Then, click OK to complete the X configuration. The redhat-config-xfree86 writes the configuration to the /etc/X11/XF86Config file and displays a dialog box informing you what has been done, as shown in Figure 3-7.

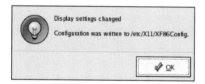

Figure 3-7: Completing X Configuration with redhat-config-xfree86.

Click OK to close the dialog box. That completes the X configuration. You can now restart your PC and get the graphical login screen (assuming that the default run level is 5).

Examining the XF86Config File

The XF86Config file describes your video card, monitor, and mouse to the X server. By default, the X server first looks for the configuration file in the /etc/X11 directory (/etc/X11/XF86Config), which is where you should save the configuration file.

If you study the /etc/X11/XF86Config file (I refer to this file generically as XF86Config), you see that the configuration file consists of several sections. Each section has the following format:

```
# This a comment
Section "SectionName"
    EntryName  EntryValue
    ...
```

```
    ...
    Subsection "SubsectionName"
        EntryName EntryValue
        ...
        ...
    EndSubsection
EndSection
```

Sections consist of a sequence of entries; each entry has a name and a value. A section may contain one or more subsections. A hash mark (#) at the beginning of a line marks a comment line.

In XFree86 4.x, the XF86Config file contains one or more of the following sections:

- **ServerFlags**—This section lists various X server options, such as DontZap (which means "do not allow the Ctrl-Alt-Backspace keystroke to terminate the X server") and DontZoom (which means "do not accept special keystrokes to change screen resolution").

- **Files**—This section lists the pathnames (full directory names) of font files and the file that contains the color database, called the *RGB file*. RGB stands for red, green, and blue—the three primary components of color. The font pathname typically specifies the port number where the X font server provides font information.

- **Module**—This section specifies which X server extension modules and font modules should be loaded. The modules are object code and libraries that add specific functionality to the X server.

- **InputDevice**—This section lists information about the keyboard and the mouse or pointer. (In the X Window System's terminology, the mouse is known as the *pointer*.)

- **Device**—This section describes the characteristics of a video card (or *graphics device*). The configuration file may have more than one Device section. The Driver entry in the Device section specifies the XFree86 4.2.0 driver for the video card.

- **Monitor**—This section includes the specifications of a monitor (such as horizontal and vertical synchronization rates) and a list of video modes that the monitor supports. In XFree86 4.2.0, a set of VESA modes is defined internally in the server, so for most monitors it isn't necessary to specify any modes explicitly in the Monitor section.

- **Screen**—This section describes a combination of a video card and monitor to be used by the X server. This section includes a Display subsection that the depth (number of colors) and the modes (supported screen resolutions) in terms of the numbers of horizontal and vertical pixels (for example, 1,024×768).

- **ServerLayout**—This section combines one or more Screen sections and one or more InputDevice sections to specify the complete layout of the display screens and input devices.

- **DRI**—This optional section provides information for the Direct Rendering Infrastructure that enables the X server to use the hardware acceleration capabilities of modern video cards. (To learn more about DRI, read the *DRI User Guide* online at http://www.xfree86.org/current/DRI.html.)

You should not have to learn all the details of these sections, and you need not change the configuration file manually. If you need to edit the configuration file, start with an XF86Config file generated by the redhat-config-xfree86 utility.

Secret

Three sections in XF86Config deal with the video card and monitor:

- The Screen section combines a video card and monitor with the video modes to be used by the X server for that screen. Each Screen section typically contains several Display subsections—one for each depth and display mode. The configuration can have multiple Screen sections, one for each display screen, if the system has multiple displays.
- The Device section describes the characteristics of a video card (also known as a graphics device) as well as the driver that XFree86 needs to use that video card. The configuration file can have several Device sections, one for each video card, if the system has multiple video cards.
- The Monitor section lists the technical specifications of a monitor, specifically the horizontal and vertical synchronization rates.

As you learned earlier in this chapter, you can create the XF86Config file by running the redhat-config-xfree86 utility program. If redhat-config-xfree86 correctly detects your video card and monitor, the generated XF86Config file may work as is. Typically, you run into problems only when you attempt to use the full capabilities of advanced video cards.

Understanding the Screen Section

The X server determines the settings of the video card and the monitor from the Screen section meant for that server. The Screen section specifies the names of a Device (video card) and a Monitor that make up this screen. Following is a Screen section from a typical XFree86 4.2.0 configuration file:

```
Section "Screen"
    Identifier    "Screen0"
    Device        "S3 ViRGE/DX (generic)"
    Monitor       "Monitor0"
    DefaultDepth   16

    Subsection "Display"
        Depth       8
        Modes       "1024x768" "800x600" "640x480"
        ViewPort  0 0
        Virtual   1024 768
    EndSubsection

    Subsection "Display"
        Depth       16
        Modes       "1024x768" "800x600" "640x480"
    EndSubsection
    ... other Display subsections ...
EndSection
```

Comment lines start with the hash mark (#). The section's definition is enclosed in the Section . . . EndSection block.

The Identifier line gives a name to this screen. This name is used to refer to the screen in the ServerLayout section. Following the Device and Monitor names are several Display subsections. Each Display subsection applies to a specific Depth (the number of bits of storage per pixel, which also determines the number of colors that can be displayed at a time).

Secret

The X server automatically uses the first Display subsection in the Screen definition, but you can start the server with command-line options that specify a different Depth. If you have set up your Red Hat Linux system for a graphical login screen, you can start the X server with a Depth of 24 by having the following line in the [servers] section of the /etc/X11/gdm/gdm.conf file:

```
0=/usr/bin/X11/X -bpp 24
```

The -bpp option for the X server program stands for bits per pixel, which is the same as Depth. Selecting a value for the Depth works, provided that the video card and the monitor are capable of supporting that Depth. You can also specify a default depth through the DefaultDepth entry in the Screen section.

The Modes line in the Display subsection lists the names of video modes that the monitor and video card can support. The names of these modes appear in the Monitor section of the XF86Config file.

For some video cards, if the card has more memory than is needed to hold the information for all visible pixels in a specific mode, the X server can use the leftover memory to give the appearance of a much larger array of pixels than the 640×480 or 1,024×768 that a video mode may specify. In other words, you get a large virtual screen from which you can select a smaller area to view. The Virtual line indicates the size of this virtual screen, whereas ViewPort specifies which part of the virtual screen is mapped to the physical display.

Understanding the Device Section

The Device section of the XF86Config file provides information about the video card. For a video card based on the S3 ViRGE/DX chipset, XF86Config has a Device section that looks like this:

```
Section "Device"
    Identifier    "S3 ViRGE/DX (generic)"
    Driver        "s3virge"
    VendorName    "S3 ViRGE/DX (generic)"
    BoardName     "S3 ViRGE/DX (generic)"
EndSection
```

Each line in the section provides some information about the video card. In this case, the Identifier indicates the name assigned to this video card; this identifier is used in the Screen section to refer to this specific video card. If the information is available, the VendorName and BoardName further identify the video card.

For older video cards that do not have a programmable dot clock, an important line in the Device section is the Clocks line. The values in this line indicate the dot clocks that the video card supports. A typical Clocks line looks like this:

```
Clocks     25.2 28.3
```

Nowadays, most video cards do not require the Clocks line because the cards have programmable dot clocks. In addition to the Clocks line, you can specify one or more flags meant for the X server for the type of video card that you are specifying in the Device section.

Secret

If your PC has more than one video card, you also need in the Device section of the XF86Config file a BusID line identifying the location of this particular video card on the bus. For PCI bus video cards, type the lspci command to find this information. For example, here's the output from lspci on a PC:

```
00:00.0 Host bridge: Intel Corp. 82845 845 (Brookdale) Chipset Host
Bridge (rev 05)
00:01.0 PCI bridge: Intel Corp. 82845 845 (Brookdale) Chipset AGP
Bridge (rev 05)
00:1d.0 USB Controller: Intel Corp. 82801CA/CAM USB (Hub #1) (rev 02)
00:1d.1 USB Controller: Intel Corp. 82801CA/CAM USB (Hub #2) (rev 02)
00:1e.0 PCI bridge: Intel Corp. 82801BAM/CAM PCI Bridge (rev 42)
00:1f.0 ISA bridge: Intel Corp. 82801CAM ISA Bridge (LPC) (rev 02)
00:1f.1 IDE interface: Intel Corp. 82801CAM IDE U100 (rev 02)
00:1f.3 SMBus: Intel Corp. 82801CA/CAM SMBus (rev 02)
00:1f.5 Multimedia audio controller: Intel Corp. 82801CA/CAM AC'97
Audio (rev 02)
00:1f.6 Modem: Intel Corp. 82801CA/CAM AC'97 Modem (rev 02)
01:00.0 VGA compatible controller: nVidia Corporation NV11 [GeForce2
Go] (rev b2)
02:01.0 Ethernet controller: 3Com Corporation 3c905C-TX/TX-M
[Tornado] (rev 78)
02:04.0 CardBus bridge: O2 Micro, Inc. OZ6912 Cardbus Controller
```

The first part of the output shows the bus ID of PCi devices. In this case, the ID 01:00.0 refers to the video card. Therefore, the BusID line should look like this:

```
BusID      "PCI:01:00:0"
```

Understanding the Monitor Section

The Monitor section lists the technical specifications of the monitor: the horizontal synchronization (or *horizontal sync*) frequency and vertical refresh rate. You can get these two values from your monitor's manual.

Secret

The horizontal-sync signal occurs at the end of each raster line; this signal moves the electron beam from the end of one line to the beginning of the next raster line. The horizontal-sync frequency is essentially the number of times per second that the monitor can trace a raster line on the display screen. If the monitor can display 480 lines (at 640×480 resolution, for example) and repaint the screen 72 times per second (a vertical refresh rate of 72 Hz), the horizontal-sync frequency is at least 480×72 = 34,560 times per second = 34,560 Hz = 34.56 kHz. The actual value is higher because the monitor always has to trace more lines than are displayed.

You have to be careful when specifying the values of horizontal sync and vertical refresh rates because the X server uses these values to select the signals sent from the video card. A monitor may be physically damaged if the video card sends signals that are beyond the monitor's specifications.

Most new monitors are multisync and support a range of horizontal-synchronization frequencies (as opposed to a fixed set of values). If you have the monitor's manual, you can specify the range of frequencies for the horizontal sync that the monitor supports.

The Monitor section may also include ModeLine lines that define video modes suitable for use with the monitor. Typically, a set of VESA standard video modes is defined internally in the X server, so there is no need to define any video modes explicitly in the Monitor section, for most monitors.

Following is a typical Monitor section (comments show the format of video-mode specification):

```
Section "Monitor"
    Identifier    "Monitor0"
    VendorName    "Monitor Vendor"
    ModelName     "Monitor Model"
    HorizSync     30.0-69.0
    VertRefresh   55.0-120.0
# Modes can be specified in two formats. A compact one-line format, or
# a multiline format.

# The following two are equivalent

#ModeLine "1024x768i" 45 1024 1048 1208 1264 768 776 784 817 Interlace

#   Mode "1024x768i"
#     DotClock  45
#     HTimings  1024 1048 1208 1264
#     VTimings  768 776 784 817
#     Flags     "Interlace"
#   EndMode

EndSection
```

The Monitor section's Identifier field gives a name to this monitor; this name is used in the Screen section to refer to this monitor. You should fill in the HorizSync and VertRefresh lines with information from the monitor's manual.

Computing a ModeLine

Although you can live with the VESA standard video modes defined in the XFree86 4.2.0 server, you may sometimes have to add a `ModeLine` manually to get a video mode to work for a specific video card/monitor combination.

Secret

You specify a `ModeLine` on a single line with the following syntax:

```
ModeLine "name"  CLK  HRES HSS HSE HTOT  VRES VSS VSE VTOT flags
```

You must fill in all arguments, except the last argument, which is an optional keyword that indicates the type of the mode. The flags field, for example, can be `Interlace` for an interlaced mode (alternateraster lines are drawn through the image each time) or `DoubleScan` (each scan line is doubled). Other flags indicate the polarity of the sync signal. The values can be `+HSync`, `-HSync`, `+VSync`, or `-VSync`, depending on the polarities you are specifying.

The arguments on the `ModeLine` have the following meanings:

- **"name"**: The name of this mode, in double quotes. Usually, the resolution of the mode is used as its name. Thus, you'll see mode names such as "640x480" and "1024x768". These mode names are used in the `Display` subsection of the Screen section.

- **CLK**: The dot clock to be used for this mode. For a video card with a fixed set of dot clocks, the dot clock should be one of the values on the `Clocks` line in the Device section of the `XF86Config` file.

- **HRES HSS HSE HTOT**: The horizontal timing parameters. `HRES` is the horizontal resolution in terms of the number of pixels visible on a raster line. As Figure 3-1 shows, the actual number of pixels on a raster line exceeds the number of visible pixels. `HTOT` is the total pixels on the line. `HSS` is where the horizontal-sync signal begins, and `HSE` is the pixel number where the horizontal-sync signal ends. The horizontal-sync signal moves the electron beam from one line to the next. For a 640 ×480 video mode, these four parameters might be `640 680 720 864`. That sequence of numbers expresses that 864 pixels are on the raster lines but that only 640 are visible. The horizontal-sync signal begins at pixel 680 and ends at pixel 864.

- **VRES VSS VSE VTOT**: The vertical timing parameters. `VRES` is the vertical resolution in terms of the number of visible raster lines on the display screen. As Figure 3-1 shows, the actual number of raster lines exceeds the number of visible raster lines. `VTOT` is the total raster lines. `VSS` is the line number where the vertical-sync signal begins, and `VSE` is the line number where the vertical-sync signal ends. The vertical-sync signal moves the electron beam from the bottom of the screen to the beginning of the first line. For a 640×480 video mode, these four parameters might be **480 488 491 521**.

From a monitor's manual, you can get two key parameters: the vertical refresh rate (in Hz) and the horizontal synchronization frequency (in kHz). The monitor's manual provides these two values as ranges of valid values. The vertical refresh rate is typically between

50 Hz and 90 Hz; the horizontal sync frequency can be anywhere from 30 kHz to 135 kHz. Following are two equations that define the relationship between the dot clock and some of the horizontal and vertical timing parameters on the `ModeLine`:

```
CLK = RR * HTOT * VTOT
CLK = HSF * HTOT
```

In these equations, `RR` is a screen refresh rate within the range of the vertical refresh rate of the monitor, and `HSF` is a horizontal-scan frequency the monitor supports. Remember to convert everything to a common unit (for example, make sure that all values are in Hz) when you apply these formulas.

To define a mode, you can start with a desired refresh rate (`RR`) such as 72 Hz. For a given dot clock, you then can compute the product `HTOT * VTOT` from the first equation. Next, plug in a value for `HSF` within the range of supported horizontal-scan frequencies for the monitor. Because the dot clock is already known, you can compute `HTOT` from the second equation. After you know `HTOT`, you can determine `VTOT` because you have already computed the product of `HTOT * VTOT`.

At this point, you know `HTOT` and `VTOT`. You have to select the arguments `HSS`, `HSE`, `VSS`, and `VSE`, which you need for the `ModeLine`. Unfortunately, figuring out these four parameters requires some trial and error. You can pick the `HRES` and `VRES` values first (`HRES` and `VRES` determine the resolution of the mode). Then, you have to select `HSS` and `HSE` to lie between `HRES` and `HTOT` and ensure that `HSE > HSS`. Similarly, `VSS`, and `VSE` should be between `VRES` and `VTOT`; make sure that `VSE > VSS`.

If the display area looks small or not centered, you have to alter the values `HSS`, `HSE`, `VSS`, and `VSE` to tweak the display. One way to correct any minor display problems is to run the xvidtune utility that comes with XFree86. If your X display is working but the display does not look as good as you think it should (for example, if it does not fill the whole screen or is skewed to one side), type **xvidtune** in a terminal window. The program prints a few lines of information about the monitor on the terminal window. The xvidtune window and a dialog box appear. The dialog box (see Figure 3-8) displays a message that warns you about the possibility of damaging your monitor and video card if you use the xvidtune program improperly.

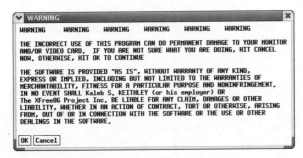

Figure 3-8: Warning Message from xvidtune.

If you decide to proceed, click OK to dismiss the dialog box. You have to interact with xvidtune through its main window, as shown in Figure 3-9.

Image of xvidtune window showing the following fields:

HDisplay: 1024 VDisplay: 768
HSyncStart: 1040 VSyncStart: 769
HSyncEnd: 1136 VSyncEnd: 772
HTotal: 1288 VTotal: 800

Left Right Wider Narrower Up Down Shorter Taller

Flags (hex): 0005 Pixel Clock (MHz): 78.80

Quit Apply Auto Test Restore Horizontal Sync (kHz): 61.18

Fetch Show Next Prev Vertical Sync (Hz): 76.47

Figure 3-9: Adjust ModeLine Parameters from the Main Window of xvidtune.

Click the Auto button. Then, click the appropriate buttons (Up, Down, Left, Right, Shorter, Taller, Wider, and Narrower) to adjust the display. After each click, the display changes. After you have adjusted the display to your liking, click Show. This prints a ModeLine of the following form on the terminal window:

```
"1024x768"     78.80   1024 1040 1136 1288    768  769  772  800 +hsync +vsync
```

The idea is that you can use this ModeLine in the Monitor section of the /etc/X11/ XF86Config file, save the file, and restart the X display (press Ctrl-Alt-Backspace to kill the X server).

If you want to adjust the other video modes, you can click the Next and Prev buttons to switch modes. The effect of these buttons is equivalent to pressing Ctrl-Alt-Keypad+ and Ctrl-Alt-Keypad– (Keypad– means the minus key in the numeric keypad), respectively.

When you are through using xvidtune, click the Quit button to exit the program.

Running X

After you have a complete XF86Config file, your X server should be ready to run. Typically, you have already selected a graphical login option during installation, so that X starts automatically when you reboot your system.

Secret

If you are not already running X, you can start the X server from the text console by running the startx script, which is a file that contains Linux commands. This script is in the /usr/X11R6/bin directory, but that directory should already be in your PATH environment variable. Therefore, to run that script, type **startx** at the shell prompt.

The startx script looks for another script file, named .xinitrc, in your home directory. If startx does not find any .xinitrc file in your home directory, it runs the xinit command with the default script /etc/X11/xinit/xinitrc. Notice that unlike the .xinitrc file in your home directory, the default script file does not have a period as the first character of its name.

The result of running startx depends on the commands in `.xinitrc` in your home directory, if you have one. Otherwise, the result depends on the commands in the `/etc/X11/xinit/xinitrc` file. The net effect of running `/etc/X11/xinit/xinitrc` is to execute the /etc/X11/xinit/Xclients script. That script, in turn, starts a GNOME or KDE session with a window manager and several other applications.

There are some special keystrokes you can use to control the X server. The following sections describe these methods of controlling X.

Aborting X Using Ctrl-Alt-Backspace

If you have created a new XF86Config file to try out some new video modes, you can press Ctrl-Alt-Backspace to kill the X server. (In Linux, the term kill refers to exiting a program abnormally. Linux even has a `kill` command that stops errant programs.)

If you have selected the graphical login option, the X server immediately restarts but this time with the configuration options in the new XF86Config file. If your system is not set up for a graphical login screen, you go back to the text display.

insider insight

If you have enabled the graphical login screen and X does not work properly because of erroneous configuration options in the XF86Config file, press Ctrl-Alt-F1 to get a text-mode login screen. Log in as root, and run `redhat-config-xf86config` to configure X, carefully selecting the options for monitor, video card, and video mode (resolution and depth). After preparing the new XF86Config file, press Ctrl-Alt-F7 to get back to the graphical login screen, and press Ctrl-Alt-Backspace to kill the X server and to force it to restart with the new configuration options.

Trying Different Video Modes

In your XF86Config file, if you look at the Screen section that applies to your X server, you notice several Display subsections. Each Display subsection lists the video modes supported for a specific depth—the number of bits in each pixel's value. An X server typically supports a depth of 8, which means that each pixel has an 8-bit value and that the server can display up to 28 = 256 distinct colors. The Display subsection lists the video modes in terms of the display resolution, which in turn is expressed in terms of the number of pixels horizontally and vertically. For example, here is a partial listing of a Screen section of the X configuration file:

```
Section "Screen"
    Identifier    "Screen0"
    Device        "S3 ViRGE/DX (generic)"
    Monitor       "Monitor0"
    DefaultDepth  16

    Subsection "Display"
        Depth     8
        Modes     "640x480" "800x600" "1024x768"
```

```
        ViewPort   0 0
        Virtual    1024 768
    EndSubsection
    ... other Display subsections ...
EndSection
```

Secret

When the X server starts, it configures the video card at the first listed resolution (in this case, 640×480, or 640 pixels horizontally by 480 pixels vertically) that corresponds to the first mode shown in the Modes entry, as follows:

```
Modes       "640x480" "800x600" "1024x768"
```

You can try the other video modes without having to exit the X server. Press Ctrl-Alt-Keypad+ (Keypad+ means the plus key in the numeric keypad). The X server switches to the next mode—in this case 800×600. Press Ctrl-Alt-Keypad+ again, and the X server switches to 1,024×768 mode. When you press Ctrl-Alt-Keypad+, the X server cycles forward to the next mode listed in the Modes entry.

Press Ctrl-Alt-Keypad+ several times to make sure that the X server works in all video modes.

To cycle backward to the preceding mode, press Ctrl-Alt-Keypad–. Therefore, if the X server is displaying in 800×600 mode and you press Ctrl-Alt-Keypad–, the server switches to 640×480 mode.

You can make the X server start in any of the supported modes. If you want the X server to start at the highest-resolution mode, simply change the Modes entry in the Screen section that corresponds to your X server (the Driver entry in the Screen section indicates the X server type) to the following:

```
Modes       "1024x768" "800x600" "640x480"
```

This change makes X start in 1,024×768 mode, which gives you much more screen area than 640×480 mode.

The screen resolutions in the Modes entry determine several things:

♦ The first resolution is the default (the resolution in which the X server starts).

♦ When you alter screen resolutions, the X server scrolls through them in the order shown in the Modes entry. When you press Ctrl-Alt-Keypad+, the X server changes resolutions in the left-to-right order; the order is reversed when you press Ctrl-Alt-Keypad–.

Some applications, such as some office suites and graphics software, require you to run the X server in 16 bits per pixel mode (also referred to as a 16-bit color depth). To make the X server start with a 16-bit color depth, perform the following steps:

1. Open the /etc/X11/XF86Config file by using your favorite text editor.

2. Locate the Screen section corresponding to the X section that corresponds to your X server. For example, if you use the SVGA server, look for the Screen section that has svga as the Driver entry.

3. Just before the first Display subsection, insert the following line:

   DefaultColorDepth 16

   This forces the X server to use a 16-bit color depth. The server uses the information from the Display subsection that specifies Depth as 16.

4. Save the XF86Config file.

5. If X is running (and assuming you have enabled the graphical login screen), press Ctrl-Alt-Backspace to stop the X server and force it to restart. It should now use a 16-bit color depth.

Adjusting the Display Settings

After you get X running, you can adjust the display settings—the resolution, color depth, monitor type, and video card—by using the Display Settings utility from the GNOME or KDE desktops. Select Main Menu⇨Display and the Display Settings window appears, as shown in Figure 3-10. In fact, this is the same redhat-config-xfree86 utility that you use to configure X initially. That's why Figure 3-10 looks similar to Figure 3-2 (except that Figure 3-2 lacks the window frame).

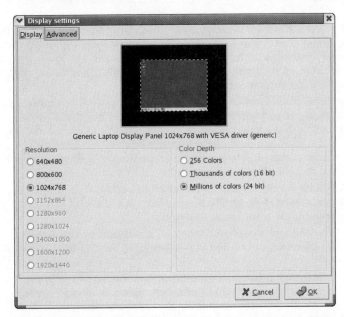

Figure 3-10: Adjusting Display Settings from GNOME or KDE.

The window has two tabs—Display and Advanced. From the Display tab you can adjust the resolution and the number of colors (also known as color depth or the bits per pixel).

To adjust the monitor type or video card, click the Advanced tab. On that tab, click the Configure button for whichever component—monitor or video card—you want to modify. When you click Configure, another window appears from which you can configure that component.

Summary

Video cards and monitors don't matter much if you use Linux in text mode only. If you want to use the XFree86 X Window System, however, you have to pay attention to the video card and monitor. You need X to run graphical desktops such as GNOME and KDE. The X Window System (X) is a popular window system that serves as the basis of GUIs and graphical output on most UNIX workstations. XFree86 is a free implementation of X for Intel 80x86 and compatible PCs. XFree86 works with a variety of video cards, but you have to configure it to use the appropriate parameters for your video card and monitor. This chapter showed you how to configure and run X on your Red Hat Linux system.

By reading this chapter, you learned the following:

- In a PC, the video card stores the array of pixels that constitutes the image you see onscreen. The video card converts the pixel values to analog signals that drive the red (R), green (G), and blue (B) electron guns in a monitor. These RGB electron beams, in turn, paint the color image on the phosphor-coated display screen. The combination of the video card and monitor is important to the X Window System because the X server controls the video card directly and because the monitor must be capable of handling the signals the video card generates.

- X Window System is a network-transparent windowing system based on the client/server model. The X server, running on a workstation with a bit-mapped graphics display, manages regions of the screen known as windows, where the output from X client applications appears. The X clients often run on remote systems, but their output appears on the local X display.

- The term graphical user interface (GUI—pronounced *gooey*) describes a user interface that makes use of windows, menus, and other graphical objects, so that users can interact with the application by pointing with the mouse and clicking mouse buttons. From an application developer's point of view, a GUI is a combination of a window manager, a style guide, and a library of routines or a toolkit that can be used to build the user interface.

- X provides the basic functions that can be used to build a GUI. Many GUIs are built upon X. Motif, GNOME, and KDE are examples of such GUIs. GNOME and KDE are popular GUIs for Linux systems.

- XFree86 is the X Window System for Linux PCs; it comes on this book's companion CD-ROMs. When you install Red Hat Linux from the CD-ROMs, you also install XFree86.

- When the X server runs, it consults a configuration file named XF86Config (in the /etc/X11 directory) to select an appropriate video mode and to configure the video card and monitor for proper operation. Computing the valid video-mode parameters is complicated. As long as you know the technical specification of your monitor (such as horizontal-synchronization frequency and refresh rate), you do not need to compute the video-mode information.

- You configure XFree86 as you install Red Hat Linux. However, you can reconfigure XFree86 by running the redhat-config-xfree86 program. This program prompts you for some technical information about your PC's video card, monitor, and mouse.

♦ You should specify the correct information about your monitor because incorrect information may damage it.

♦ You can kill the X server by pressing Ctrl-Alt-Backspace. If you have a graphical login screen, this key combination restarts the X server.

♦ You can switch among different modes (screen resolutions such as 1,024×768 and 800×600) by pressing special key combinations: Ctrl-Alt-Keypad+ and Ctrl-Alt-Keypad–.

Printer Setup

Chapter

4

♦ ♦

Secrets in This Chapter

♦ ♦

When you set up Red Hat Linux on a PC, the printer probably is the last thing on your mind. First, you want to get Red Hat Linux running on the PC., then you may decide to make the modem work to dial up your your Internet service provider. When you begin to depend more on Red Hat Linux, however, you'll want to print documents that you prepare or get from the Internet, and that's when you want to know how to make the printer work with Red Hat Linux.

As you might guess, physically connecting a printer to the PC's parallel port is straightforward; that part doesn't depend on the operating system. The software setup for printing is the part that takes some effort. Accordingly, this chapter provides information on setting up the printing environment in Red Hat Linux.

Configuring CUPS Print Queues

Setting up a printer in Red Hat Linux involves setting up a queue for the print spooler or scheduler—the process that accepts and sends files for printing and does whatever is needed to get them printed. The queue is essentially a holding place for files that are to be sent to a printer. Before being sent to the printer, however, the files are usually processed to convert them to a form that the printer can understand. For example, to print on a PostScript printer, the files have to be converted to PostScript, which is a page description language (from Adobe Systems Incorporated) that many printers understand.

If you have printed under Microsoft Windows, you may already be familiar with spooling. Spooling refers to the ability to print in the background. When you print from a word processor in Windows, for example, the output first goes to a file on the disk. Then, while you continue working with the word processor, a background process sends that output to the printer.

The Red Hat Linux printing environment, which consists of several programs described later in this chapter, also supports spooling. The spool directory refers to the directory that contains output files intended for the printer.

Print job refers to what you print with a single print command. The printing environment queues print jobs by storing them in the spool directory. A background process periodically sends the print jobs from the spool directory to the printer.

Secret

Red Hat Linux uses the Common UNIX Printing System (CUPS) for its printing environment. CUPS is a printing system based on the Internet Printing Protocol (IPP)—an application-level protocol for distributed printing using Internet technologies. IPP assumes a client/server model with the client being an application and the server a "Printer"—an abstraction of an output device or a printing service provider. IPP supports a distributed printing environment with the clients and Printer servers communicating over the Internet. You could use an IPP client to print on a printer anywhere on the Internet. The client and Printer exchange data using the HTTP 1.1 protocol. The client application uses IPP to inquire about capabilities of a printer, submit print jobs, and inquire about and cancel print jobs. Because IPP uses HTTP—the same protocol that Web servers use, CUPS configuration directives are similar to those used by the Apache Web server (Chapter 14 describes the Apache Web server configuration files).

CUPS has been developed by Easy Software Products and is distributed under the GNU General Public License (GPL), version 2. The CUPS application programming interface (API) library is distributed under the GNU Library General Public License (LGPL), version 2. For a discussion of GPL and LGPL, see Chapter 23.

You can configure CUPS print queues through the graphical Red Hat printer configuration tool or by typing the `lpadmin` command in a terminal window (a print queue or printer queue is a mechanism for scheduling printing on a specific printer). You can also manage CUPS print queues through the Web browser. To access the CUPS administration functions, point the Mozilla Web browser to `http://localhost:631/`.

Your Red Hat Linux system should have CUPS already installed. That installation also includes documentation on CUPS. To read the CUPS documentation, start the Mozilla Web browser and open the file `/usr/share/doc/cups*/documentation.html`. You can also read CUPS documentation from the Internet at `http://www.cups.org/documentation.php`.

For the latest information about CUPS and to read the CUPS Frequently Asked Questions (FAQ), visit the CUPS website at `http://www.cups.org/`.

At the user level, you can use either System V UNIX commands or Berkeley Software Distribution (BSD) UNIX commands to submit and manage print jobs. Although CUPS supports both BSD and System V-style print commands, it favors the System V print commands such as `lp` to print a file and `lpstat` to check the status of the print queues. As you become more knowledgeable about UNIX (or if you are a UNIX old-timer), you may find this bit of information useful because it tells you the printing commands you can use in Red Hat Linux. If you don't know anything about System V or BSD UNIX, don't worry; you will learn about the printing commands in the following sections.

Using the Red Hat Printer Configuration Tool

In Red Hat Linux, you can configure a printer by using the printer configuration GUI tool. To configure printers with this tool, you must be running GNOME or KDE. From the graphical login screen, log in as root, and select Main Menu⇨System Settings⇨Printing from the GNOME or KDE desktop. You can also start the tool by typing the command `redhat-config-printer` in a terminal window.

The main window of the printer configuration tool appears (see Figure 4-1).

Figure 4-1: The Main Window of the Printer Configuration Tool.

You can create and manage print queues by using the printer configuration tool. Each *print queue* refers to a holding place for files that are to be sent to a specific printer (note that the terms *print queue* and *printer queue* are typically used interchangeably). Thus, a print queue is associated with at least one printer. To add a printer to your Red Hat Linux system is equivalent to creating a printer queue and associating that queue with the printer.

To add a new printer queue, click the New button on the toolbar. The printer configuration tool displays the *Add a new print queue* Wizard that takes you through the process of adding a new printer queue. The initial step shows a message that assures you that nothing will be changed until you click the Apply button at the end of all the steps. Click the Forward button to continue. The next screen prompts you for the print queue's name and a short description, as shown in Figure 4-2.

Figure 4-2: Set the Print Queue Name and Description.

Enter a name for the queue and description. You should use some systematic approach when naming the print queue. For example, if I have a HP Laserjet 4 printer on the second floor in Room 210, I might name the queue *Room-210-HPLJ4* because this makes it easy to find the printer. Sometimes systems administrators choose cute names such as kermit, piggy, elmo, cookiemonster, and so on, but once you have too many printers, such cute schemes do not work well. It's best to provide a clue about the printer's location as well as the make and model in the print queue's name. After entering the queue name and description, click Forward.

The Queue Type window appears. You have to select a queue type from the drop-down selection box (see Figure 4-3). As the drop-down list shows, you have to select the queue type from the following list:

- ♦ **Locally-connected printer**—Refers to a printer connected directly to the serial, parallel, or USB port of the PC
- ♦ **Networked IPP (CUPS) queue**—Refers to a CUPS print queue at another server on the network (IPP refers to the Internet Printing Protocol that is used to communicate with the remote CUPS server)

- ◆ **Networked UNIX (LPD) printer**—Refers to a print queue managed by the LPD server on another UNIX system on the local network (LPD refers to Line Printer Daemon—another print spooler for UNIX systems)
- ◆ **Networked Windows (SMB) printer**—Refers to a printer connected to another PC on the local network and that uses the Server Message Block (SMB) protocol, the underlying protocol in Windows file and print sharing
- ◆ **Networked Novell (NCP) printer**—Refers to a printer connected to a Novell Netware server on the local network
- ◆ **Networked JetDirect queue**—Refers to a network-connected printer that prints data received at a specific TCP/IP port (typically, port number 9100). HP JetDirect cards use this method of printing.

Figure 4-3: Select the Print Queue Type.

Select the print queue type that applies to your configuration. When you select any of the networked print queues, you have to identify the server and remote queue name using the syntax appropriate for that type of queue. For example, if you want to set up a print queue directed at a Windows (SMB) printer, you have to identify the printer by using the following syntax:

```
//WindowsMachine/PrinterName
```

On the other hand, for remote CUPS or LPD queues, you specify the server's hostname and the queue's name (as defined on that remote server).

If you select a locally-connected printer, you should see the parallel port device (/dev/lp0) listed. If you want to connect the printer to another port (such as serial port or USB), you can click the *Custom device* button. Then enter the device name (such as /dev/ttyS0 for the first serial port or /dev/usb/lp0 for the first USB printer) in the dialog box that appears. After specifying the device, click Forward and the wizard takes you to the next step, where you select a print driver from a list. Click the drop-down list (above the scrolling list) and a list of printer manufacturers appear. Select the printer manufacturer, and the scrolling list displays the names of different printer models from that manufacturer, as shown in Figure 4-4 (for Epson).

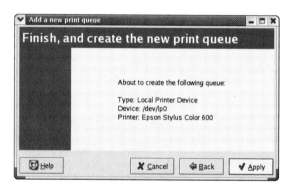

Figure 4-4: Select a Printer Manufacturer and Model.

You can then select your printer model from the list. If you have a PostScript printer, you can simply go to the Generic list (Generic is one of the choices in the manufacturer list) and select PostScript printer. After selecting the print driver, click Forward to continue. This brings you to the final screen, as shown in Figure 4-5.

Figure 4-5: Finish Creating the New Print Queue.

This step displays a message that tells you what print queue you are about to create. Click Apply to complete the task.

A dialog box prompts you if you want to print a test page. Click Yes. This applies all the changes and restarts cupsd—the print scheduler daemon that takes care of printing (a daemon is essentially a background process that runs as long as the system is up). The printer should print a test page. A message box appears asking you to check the test page. Click OK to dismiss the message box.

Now, the new print queue should appear in the printer configuration window, and you should be able to submit print jobs to this queue. To quit the printer configuration tool select Action⇨Quit or close the printer configuration window by clicking the X button in the upper-right corner of the window's frame.

insider insight If you did not print a test page when you initially set up the print queue, you can always do so from the Test menu in the Red Hat printer configuration tool. Click the print queue in the Printer configuration window, and then select Test⇨CUPS Test page from the menu to print a test page on the printer.

The next section describes some of the commands you can use to print and check the status of print jobs.

Administering Printers with CUPS Web Interface

Although you can use the Red Hat printer configuration tool to configure CUPS printers, there is another way to administer CUPS. You can also administer CUPS printers through its Web interface. In fact, the Web interface is the method used to configure CUPS printers on non-Red Hat systems because the Red Hat configuration tool is meant for Red Hat Linux systems only.

The CUPS scheduler—cupsd—listens on port 631 on your system. Port 631 is assigned to the IPP service. For example, here's what you should get when you search for ipp in the /etc/services file:

```
grep ipp /etc/services
ipp              631/tcp          # Internet Printing Protocol
ipp              631/ucp          # Internet Printing Protocol
```

When you use a Web browser to connect to port 631 on your system, cupsd displays its Web interface, as shown in Figure 4-6.

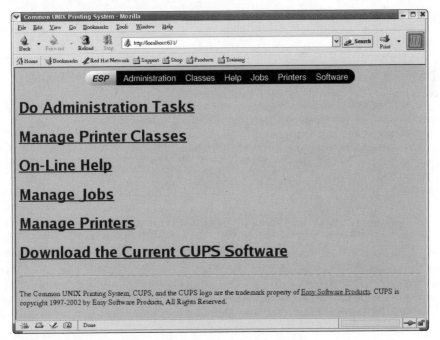

Figure 4-6: Accessing the CUPS Web Interface at Port 631.

You can perform a variety of administration tasks through the links and the buttons on the CUPS Web interface. If you click the *Do Administration Tasks* link, CUPS displays a new Web page from which you can manage printer classes (explained later in this section), jobs, and printers.

Secret

To add a printer through the CUPS Web interface, follow these steps:

1. Start the CUPS Web interface by pointing the Mozilla Web browser at `http://localhost:631/`. The Web interface appears, as shown in Figure 4-6.

2. Click the Manage Printers link. CUPS displays information about each of the current printers as well as buttons for performing many different tasks (Figure 4-7). A set of buttons enable you to perform tasks such as print a test page and stop a printer. Additionally, a single Add Printer button enables you to add a printer.

Figure 4-7: Managing Printers through the CUPS Web Interface.

3. Click the Add Printer button. CUPS prompts for information about the new printer.

4. Enter the printer's name, location, and description, then click Continue. CUPS asks you to select the device from a drop-down list. The list is more extensive than what the Red Hat printer configuration tool shows.

5. Select printer device, and click Continue. CUPS prompts for the make of the printer. The list is much shorter than what you get from the Red Hat printer configuration tool.

6. Select the printer make and click Continue. CUPS prompts for the printer model. That list depends on the make you selected.

7. Select the model, and click Continue. CUPS adds the printer by adding the new printer's information to the `/etc/cups/printers.conf` file and creating a PPD file for the printer in the `/etc/cups/ppd` directory.

insider insight

A key concept in CUPS is the idea of a class of printers. You can define a class consisting of a number of printers and then send print jobs to the class (instead of individual printers). CUPS then sends the print job to the first available printer in the class. This is a good way to share the printing load among a number of printers. You can print on a class just as you print on an individual printer. For example, if your system has the class pr5 defined, then you can print the `sample.ps` file on this class with the following lp command:

```
lp -d pr5 sample.ps
```

To define a class of printers from the CUPS Web interface point the Web browser to `http://localhost:631/` and then follow these steps:

1. Click Classes on the tool bar in the Web interface. CUPS displays the current classes, if any, and an Add Class button.

2. Click the Add Class button. A dialog box prompts for a user name and password. Enter the root as user name and the root password. CUPS then prompts for information about the class.

3. Enter the following identifying information about the new class:
   - **Name**—The class name, up to 127 printable characters (no embedded spaces)
   - **Location**—Information about where this class of printes is located
   - **Description**—A brief description of this class of printers

   Click Continue. CUPS asks you to select which of the currently defined printers should be members of this class.

4. Click the printers you want to add to the class, then click Continue. CUPS creates the new class.

When you create a new class, the class definition is added to the `/etc/cups/classes.conf` file. For example, here's the definiton of a class named pr5:

```
<Class pr5>
Info Printers on 5th Floor
Location 5th Floor
State Idle
Accepting Yes
JobSheets none none
```

```
Printer 5N28-hplj4
Printer 5X15-hplj5000
Printer 5Z15-hplj4200
QuotaPeriod 0
PageLimit 0
KLimit 0
</Class>
```

In this case, the `pr5` class contains three printers idenfied by the `Printer` lines inside the class definition.

Learning the Printing Commands

After you have set up the print queue for a printer on your Red Hat Linux system, you can type commands in a terminal window to print and check the status of the print queue. The following sections provide an overview of the basic printing commands. You can use either System V or BSd UNIX print commands. Table 4-1 summarizes the two sets of print commands. In addition to these commands, you can use `lpadmin` to manage the printer queues and `lpoptions` to set default options for a print queue.

Table 4-1: System V and BSD Print Commands

Task	System V Command	BSD Command
Submit a print job	`lp`	`lpr`
Cancel a print job	`cancel`	`lprm`
Check status of a print job	`lpstat`	`lpq`

Printing a File

You can use the `lp` or `lpr` command to print a file. For example, to print the file `rfc1789.txt`, you can type the following `lp` command in a terminal window:

```
lp rfc1789.txt
```

This `lp` command then queues the `rfc1789.txt` file for printing on the default printer. The default printer is identified by the `<DefaultPrinter` *queuename*`>` entry in the CUPS configuration file `/etc/cups/cupsd.conf` (where `queuename` is the name of the print queue).

---

insider insight   When you use the `lp` command to print a file, `lp` sends that file along with information about the print job to the `cupsd` print scheduler that stores this information in a control file and a data file in the `/var/spool/cups` directory. The `cupsd` scheduler then processes the files according to the file extension (such as `.txt` or `.ps`) and sends them to the printer using its backend interfaces. Thanks to various configuration files, the cupsd scheduler knows what to do to make sure that the file—be it a text file or an image file—gets printed properly.

You can embellish the simple lp command with some options. If you have many different print queues defined, you can specify the destination of the print job with the -d option. For example, to send a print job to the Hewlett-Packard LaserJet 5000 printer named Rm5N28hplj5000 you would type the following command (later, in the "Understanding the CUPS Configuration Files" section, you'll see that the print queue name appears in the /etc/cups/printers.conf file),

```
lp -d Rm5N28hplj5000  rfc1789.txt
```

If you mistakenly print a large file and want to stop the print job before you waste too much paper, you can use the lpstat or lpq command to look at the current print jobs and then cancel the large print job. Here is a typical output from the lpstat command after I typed the lp command to print a file on the queue named Office-ES600:

```
lpstat
Office-ES600-2          root          15360   Wed 15 Jan 2003 04:25:48 PM EST
```

The first field of the output shows the name of the queue with a job number appended to it (that number identifies the print job). You need that job number to cancel the print job.

When I typed lpq for the same print job, here is the output I get:

```
lpq
Office-ES600 is ready and printing
Rank    Owner   Job    File(s)                    Total Size
active  root    2      testprint.ps               15360 bytes
```

The lpq command also shows the job number. It also shows the name of the file that I am printing (testprint.ps).

To remove a job from the print queue, use the cancel or lprm command. For example, to remove print job 2, type the following command:

```
cancel 2
```

You can get the same result with the following lprm command:

```
lprm 2
```

insider insight

If you are in a hurry and want to cancel all print jobs you have submitted so far, use cancel or lprm with -a as the argument, as follows:

```
cancel -a
```

Specifying Print Options

You can use the -o option with the lp and lpr commands to specify print job options such as paper size, whether to print in landscape orientation, and whether to print a banner page at the start and the end of a print job. For example, suppose that you want to print a file on a A4-size paper instead of U.S. letter-size paper that happens to be the default. You can specify this in the print command, as follows:

```
lp -o media=A4 letter.pdf
```

That part—-o media=A4—specifies the value of the standard option named media that can set the size, type, and source of the output media (paper or transparency). If you also want a standard banner page at the start of the print job, you can add the job-sheets option and specify the type of banner you want:

```
lp -o media=A4 -o job-sheets=standard letter.pdf
```

There is an extensive set of standard options, but some of them would work only if your printer supports that option. You can specify these options the -o option of the lp command.

Use the lpoptions command to see what options a printer supports. Suppose that you have a print queue named hpdj8 for a HP Deskjet printer. You can query the options it accepts with the following command:

```
lpoptions -p hpdj8 -l
ColorModel/Output Mode: CMYK2 *CMYK Gray
Resolution/Output Resolution: *300dpi 600x300dpi 600dpi
Duplex/Double-Sided Printing: *None DuplexNoTumble DuplexTumble
PageSize/Media Size: *Letter Legal Executive Tabloid A3 A4 A5 B5 EnvISOB5
Env10
EnvC5 EnvDL EnvMonarch
InputSlot/Media Source: *Tray Manual Envelope Auto
MediaType/Media Type: *Plain Bond Special Transparency Glossy
PageRegion/PageRegion: Letter Legal Executive Tabloid A3 A4 A5 B5 EnvISOB5
Env10
 EnvC5 EnvDL EnvMonarch
Option1/Duplexer: True *False
```

The first field on each line is the name of the option. The text between the forward slash (/) and the colon (:) is the description of that option. The rest of the lines show the possible values you can specify for that option. The default value is marked with an asterisk (*).

Controlling the Print Queue

To see the names of printers connected to your system, use the lpc status command. On my system, the lpc status command shows the following:

```
lpc status
Office-ES600:
        printer is on device 'parallel' speed -1
        queuing is enabled
        printing is enabled
        no entries
        daemon present
```

Notice that queuing and printing are both enabled for this printer. The last line tells you that the cupsd daemon is running and available to handle print jobs.

You can use the accept and reject commands to enable or disable queuing for a print queue. For example, to stop queuing further print jobs for the Office-ES600 printer, I would type:

```
reject Office-ES600
```

This command disables queuing jobs for this printer. If anyone tries to send a print job using the lp command, the user receives an error message like this:

```
lp: unable to print file: server-error-not-accepting-jobs
```

If you want to allow queuing of print jobs, but want to start or stop the printing, use the enable and disable commands. When you disable printing, users can submit print jobs, but nothing gets printed until you enable printing again. For example, here is the command I use to disable printing on the Office-ES600 printer:

```
disable Office-ES600
```

insider insight

If you are trying to print, but nothing seems to be coming out of the printer, check the printer status with the lpc status command and make sure that the daemon is present and that both queuing and printing are enabled. To allow the queuing of print jobs, use the accept command and to start printing, use the enable command.

Understanding the CUPS Printing System

In Red Hat Linux, with the CUPS printing system, the user's view of printing is based on the basic printing commands: lp, lpr, lpq, lprm, and lpc status. A bit more information will help you understand how printing works behind the scenes. As with so many things in Linux, support for the CUPS printing system is all a matter of having the right files in the right places. This becomes apparent after you have configured Linux for networking and have set up dial-in modems, for example. In each case, you have to make sure that several configuration files appear in the correct places. The printing environment has the same requirement: configuration files that specify how printing occurs.

Although nowadays you can use graphical configuration tools to set up services such as printing and dial-up networking, it is useful to know the names of the text-configuration files because you can then fix problems even if you do not have access to a graphical login.

If you have experience with MS-DOS from a long time ago, you might have printed files by simply copying them to the printer port (LPT1, for example). You might think that a similar approach is good enough for Linux. As you see in the next section, such a brute-force approach to copying a file to the physical printer port is not appropriate for a multi-user system such as Linux. You need a way to queue print jobs and to have a separate printing process take care of the printing.

Copying to the Printer: Brute-Force Printing

If you have a printer connected to the /dev/lp0 parallel port, you can print a text file simply by sending the file to the printer with the following command:

```
cat webstat.txt > /dev/lp0
```

This command indeed produces a printout of the file `webstat.txt`, provided that the following conditions are true:

◆ You are logged in as `root` (Linux allows only `root` and certain processes direct access to physical devices, such as printers).

◆ The printer is connected to the /dev/lp0 port, powered up, and online.

The problem with copying a file directly to the printer device is that the command completes only when the copying (which, in this case, is equivalent to printing) is completed. For a large file, this process can take a while. In fact, if the printer is not turned on, the command appears to hang (if this happens, just press Ctrl-C to abort the command).

Printing the CUPS Way

On a multitasking and multiuser system such as Linux, a better way to print is to spool the data and schedule the printing: send the output to a file, and have a separate process send the output to the printer. That way, you can continue with your work while the printing takes place in the background. In addition, if your system has more than one user, everyone can print on the same printer, without worrying about whether or not the printer is available; the background printing process can take care of all the details.

That's how the CUPS printing environment works. Users use a client program—lp or lpr—to send the files to be printed to a server called cupsd—the printer daemon—over a TCP/IP connection. The cupsd server then queues the files, filters the file (to get them ready for the printer), and sends them to the printer.

Although you typically have only one printer connected to your PC, one advantage of the CUPS printing system is the capability to print on a printer connected to another system on a network. Printing to a remote printer is handled in the same fashion as printing to a local printer; the local cupsd daemon simply sends the files to the remote system's server.

As explained earlier, the user-level programs for spooling a file are lp and lpr. When lp or lpr runs, it sends the data to the cupsd server that manages the specified print queue. Other user-level commands for working with print queues are `lpstat`, `lpq`, `cancel`, `lprm`, and `lpc`. The program that completes the CUPS printing environment is the CUPS scheduler: `cupsd`.

In addition to the commands `lpd`, `lpr`, `lpq`, `lprm`, `cancel`, and `lpc`, the configuration files in `/etc/cups` directory play a crucial role in the CUPS printing environment. The "Understanding the CUPS Configuration Files" section describes the key configruation files.

Secret

A good way to understand CUPS is to take a look at the *CUPS architecture*—the parts that make up CUPS and how they fit together. CUPS is designed around the cupsd print scheduling process that accepts print jobs submitted through printing commands, spools print files, uses filters to convert filesto a form acceptable to the printer, and sends the data to printers using backends. Figure 4-8 shows the basic architecture of CUPS.

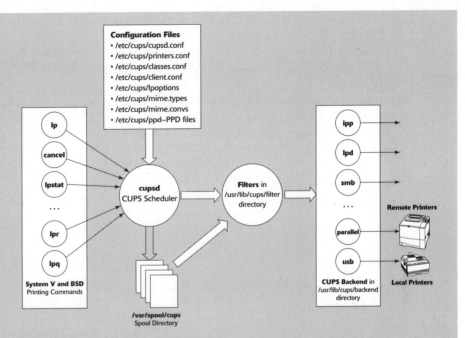

Figure 4-8: The CUPS Architecture.

As Figure 4-8 shows, the makor components of CUPS are as follows:

1. **CUPS Scheduler**—cupsd is the scheduling process that acts as an HTTP 1.1 server and handles printing requests sent by clients using the Internet Printing Protocol (IPP). cupsd also acts as a Web server and provides a Web interface for administering CUPS print queues.

2. **Configuration Files**—The configuration files in /etc/cups directory control how CUPS works. The "Understanding the CUPS Configuration Files" section further describes these files.

3. **Printing Commands**—System V and BSD printing commands enable you to submit print jobs and check printer status from the command line.

4. **Filters**—The filter programs located in the /usr/lib/cups/filter directory convert various input file formats (such as text, PostScript, and Image) into output understood by the printer on which the file is being printed. CUPS uses Ghostscript to convert PostScript page description language into output suitable for a specific printer.

5. **Backend**—The backend programs located in the /usr/lib/cups/backend directory send the output of the filters to the destination printer. Each backend takes care of sending output to a specific type of connection such as locally connected parallel printer or a remote Windows printer that communicates with the SMB protocol.

Understanding the CUPS Configuration Files

You can learn a lot about the CUPS configuration files by examining the entries in various configuration files that the Red Hat printer configuration tool creates when you set up a new print queue. The CUPS configuration files are in /etc/cups directory.

Consider the example of adding a new print queue named Office-ES600 for an Epson Stylus Color 600 printer that is connected to the parallel port of the PC. Here are the files that contain information about this print queue and the printer model:

◆ **/etc/printcap**—This file used to be the printer capabilities database and was very important to the LPD print spooler that used to be popular before CUPS came along (not that I miss LPD; CUPS is much better). CUPS generates single entry in the /etc/printcap file for each printer. For example, here is the /etc/printcap file that CUPS generates for a print queue named Office-ES600 (the details of the printer are in the /etc/cups/printers.conf file):

```
# This file was automatically generated by cupsd(8) from the
# /etc/cups/printers.conf file.  All changes to this file
# will be lost.
Office-ES600:
```

◆ **/etc/cups/printers.conf**—This is the printer configuration file with entries for each print queue. The information includes the device where the printer is connected and other parameters of the queue. Here is the entry for the Epson Stylus Color 600 printer:

```
<DefaultPrinter Office-ES600>
Info Created by redhat-config-printer 0.6.x
DeviceURI parallel:/dev/lp0
Location Epson Stylus 600
State Idle
Accepting Yes
JobSheets none none
QuotaPeriod 0
PageLimit 0
KLimit 0
</Printer>
```

◆ **/etc/cups/cupsd.conf**—This is the configuration file for cupsd, the CUPS print scheduler. The syntax of the configuration file is similar to that of Apache httpd, the Web server (see Chapter 14 for a description of Apache httpd configuration). The similarities with the Apache httpd configuration files are to be expected because cupsd is also an HTTP server. Here are the entries in /etc/cups/cupsd .conf for the print queue names Office-ES600:

```
<Location /printers/Office-ES600>
Order Deny,Allow
Deny From All
Allow From 127.0.0.1
AuthType None
</Location>
<Location />
Order Deny,Allow
Deny From All
Allow From 127.0.0.1
```

```
</Location>
Browsing Off
Listen 127.0.0.1:631
```

There are many more directives in the /etc/cups/cupsd.conf file that apply all print queues managed by the cupsd server.

♦ **/etc/cups/lpoptions**—This file stores the default option settings that apply to all print jobs when you create a print queue as root. Note that users can specify other options when they print with the lp commands. Here is the /etc/cups/lpoptions file with the default options for the Office-ES600 printer:

```
Dest Office-ES600 page-bottom=36 cpi=12 lpi=7 scaling=100 page-right=36
page-left=36 wrap=true page-top=36
```

♦ **/etc/cups/ppd**—This is a directory that contains the PostScript Printer Description (PPD) file for the Epson Stylus Color 600 printer in a file named Office-ES600 .ppd (the name I had assigned to that print queue). Each PPD file is a text file containing information about the printer capability (similar to the old /etc/ printcap file in intent, but PPD files have much more detailed information). Here are the first few lines from the PPD file /etc/cups/ppd/Office-ES600.ppd:

```
*PPD-Adobe: "4.3"
*%
*% For information on using this, and to obtain the required backend
*% script, consult http://www.linuxprinting.org/ppd-doc.html.
*%
*% PPD-O-MATIC generated this PPD file. It is for use with all programs
*% and environments which use PPD files for dealing with printer
capability
*% information. The printer must be configured with a Foomatic backend
*% filter script. This file and the backend filter script work together
to
*% support PPD-controlled printer driver option access with arbitrary
free
*% software printer drivers and printing spoolers.
*%
*% You may save this file as 'Epson-Stylus_Color_600-gimp-print.ppd'
*%
*%
*FormatVersion: "4.3"
*FileVersion:   "1.1"
*LanguageVersion: English
*LanguageEncoding: ISOLatin1
*PCFileName:    "GIMP-PRI.PPD"
*Manufacturer:  "EPSON"
*Product:       "Stylus COLOR 600"
*cupsVersion:   1.0
*cupsManualCopies: True
*cupsModelNumber:  2
*cupsFilter:    "application/vnd.cups-postscript 0 cupsomatic"
*ModelName:     "Epson Stylus Color 600, Foomatic + gimp-print"
*NickName:      "Epson Stylus Color 600, Foomatic + gimp-print"
```

```
*ShortNickName: "Epson Stylus Color 600"
*PSVersion:     "(3010.000) 550"
*PSVersion:     "(3010.000) 651"
*PSVersion:     "(3010.000) 652"
*PSVersion:     "(3010.000) 653"
*PSVersion:     "(3010.000) 704"
*PSVersion:     "(3010.000) 705"
*LanguageLevel: "3"
*ColorDevice:   True
*DefaultColorSpace: RGB
*FileSystem:    False
*Throughput:    "1"
*LandscapeOrientation: Plus90
*VariablePaperSize: False
*TTRasterizer:  Type42

*HWMargins: 0 0 0 0
*VariablePaperSize: True
*MaxMediaWidth: 100000
.... many lines deleted ...
```

That should give you an idea of the kind of information stored in PPD files. You don't have to understand or prepare the PPD files manually. CUPS generates the PPD file automatically from descriptions in the Foomatic printer drivers that come with Red Hat Linux (described later in this chapter).

As this example shows, for each print queue it manages, CUPS needs a considerable amount of information stored in multiple configuration files. So far, I have shown you only the configuration files affected by the definition of a new print queue. It's helpful to know the full extent of the configuration files, understand their purpose, and have a rough idea of what each of these files contain.

Secret

CUPS replies on a large number of configuration files to provide a comprehensive printing solution for Red Hat Linux. Although you do not have to manually edit these configuration files, be aware of what these files are and where they are stored. The key configuration files are located in the /etc/cups directory and its subdirectories. Here is a brief summary of the configuration files:

- **/etc/cups/cupsd.conf**—The CUPS HTTP server configuration file, used by cupsd, the CUPS scheduler and HPP server process. The directives in this file are similar to those used by the Apache httpd (Web server). This means that if you know how to read Apache httpd configuration file, you can also read and understand cupsd.conf. In particular, cupsd.conf defines access control for a printer in the same way that Apache httpd defines access control for a directory.

- **/etc/cups/printers.conf**—Defines all available print queues. Information about each printer is in a `<Printer PrinterName>` ... `</Printer>` block. A `<DefaultPrinter>` tag identifies the default printer.

- **/etc/cups/classes.conf**—Contains definitions of all printer classes. A *printer class* is a collection of printers. Print jobs sent to a class are forwarded to the first available printer in the class.

- **/etc/cups/mime.types**—Lists the supported MIME, types such as text/plain and application/postscript, and the rules for automatically detecting the format of a file. (MIME stands for *Multipurpose Internet Mail Extensions,* which began life as a way to send attachments in a single message file.) The cupsd server uses these rules to determine the type of a file.
- **/etc/cups/mime.convs**—Contains the MIME conversion rules to convert a file into a format acceptable to a printer. The conversion is achieved by using filters. Each filter has a relative cost associated with it, and the filtering algorithm selects the set of filters that will convert the file to the needed format with the lowest total cost.
- **/etc/cups/ppd**—Is a directory with the PostScript Printer Description (PPD) files for the printers being managed by CUPS. These PPD files describe the capabilities of all printers, not just PostScript printers. There is one PPD file for each printer. A PPD file for a non-PostScript printer identifies a filter with the `cupsFilter` attribute. CUPS uses that filter to convert a file into a firm suitable for sending to the printer. For example, the `cupsFilter` attribute for an Epson Stylus Color 600 printer identifies `cupsomatic` as the filter, like this:

  `*cupsFilter:    "application/vnd.cups-postscript 0 cupsomatic"`

  The `cupsomatic` filter is located in the `/usr/lib/cups/filter` directory.
- **/etc/cups/client.conf**—Specifies the default options for clients (in particular, the default server name and whether encryption is to be used or not). Note that a client is any machine that sends print jobs to another machine for final printing. This means that when your system prints to a local printer, it's a client to the cupsd scheduler running on your system.

Summary

Printing under Red Hat Linux is simple, provided that the CUPS printing environment is set up properly. You do have to learn a small set of commands to submit a print job and to check the status of pending print jobs. This chapter explained the CUPS printing system from the user's point of view and how to set everything up as a system administrator.

By reading this chapter, you learned the following things:

- ◆ Red Hat Linux comes with the CUPS printing system, which is an open-source implementation of a printing system based on the Internet Printing Protocol (IPP) and integrated with other tools such as Foomatic filter scripts and Ghostscript printer drivers.
- ◆ As a user, you print with the lp or lpr command, check the status of the print queue with lpq or lpstat, cancel print jobs with lprm or cancel, and check the printer's status with lpc status.
- ◆ Behind the scenes, the lp command sends the print file and a control file to the cupsd server (the print scheduler daemon), which places the files in a holding directory called the spool directory. Then cupsd processes the spooled print files through filters and sends them to the printer by using backend interface programs.
- ◆ You can use the Red Hat printer configuration tool or the CUPS Web interface (http://localhost:631/) to set up printers.
- ◆ CUPS relies on a number of configuration files, located in the /etc/cups directory, for its operation. This chapter explains these configuration files.

Sound Setup

Chapter
5

♦ ♦

Secrets in This Chapter

♦ ♦

Without a sound card, the PC's built-in speaker can only play a single note; you can't even vary the loudness of the note. Luckily, most PCs nowadays come with a sound card—either a separate card or some sound circuitry built into the motherboards—that greatly improves the sound-output capability of the PC. The sound card is an adapter that plugs into a slot on your PC's motherboard and includes the electronic circuitry needed to play and record sound. You can plug speakers and a microphone into the back of a sound card.

When a microphone is hooked up to the sound card, the card can convert the analog (continuously varying) sound waves into 8-bit or 16-bit numbers, sampling the wave at rates ranging from 4 kHz (4,000 times a second) to 44 kHz (44,000 times a second) and more. Higher sampling rates and a higher number of bits (16) provide better quality, but you need more disk space to store high-quality sound. In addition, the sound card can convert digital sound samples to analog signals you can play on a speaker.

Most sound cards, including the popular Sound Blaster, also support MIDI (Musical Instrument Digital Interface) commands, in addition to recording and playing back waveform sound. MIDI is commonly used to record and play back musical sounds that a synthesizer can create. (Most sound cards have built-in synthesizers.)

This chapter describes specific types of Linux-supported sound cards and how you can set up a sound card after you have successfully installed Red Hat Linux.

Sound Cards Supported by Red Hat Linux

Table 5-1 lists the sound cards that Red Hat Linux supports and shows the name of the driver module that supports a specific set of sound cards. For the most recent (and more detailed) list of sound cards Red Hat Linux supports, consult the Red Hat hardware-compatibility list at `http://hardware.redhat.com/hcl/`.

Table 5-1: Supported Sound Cards

Sound Card	*Linux Driver Module*
Acer Notebook sound, Avance Logic (ALS-007, ALS-100, ALS-110), Creative Labs SoundBlaster cards, ESS1868 AudioDrive, Logitech SoundMan Games, MediaVision Jazz16 (ProSonic, SoundMan Wave)	`sb`
AdLib	`adlib_card`
Allied Telesyn AT1700	`at1700`
Analog Devices AD1816	`ad1816`
Analog Devices AD1848, Compaq DeskPro XL sound, Ensoniq SoundScape VIVO	`ad1848`
Aztech Sound Galaxy Waverider Pro 32-3D	`sgalaxy`
C-Media CMI8x38	`cmpci`
Creative Labs SoundBlaster Live!	`emu10k1`
Ensoniq AudioPCI (ES1371)	`es1371`
Crystal Audio SoundFusion (CS46xx)	`cs46xx`

Sound Card	Linux Driver Module
Ensoniq AudioPCI (ES1370)	es1370
Ensoniq AudioPCI (ES1371)	es1371
Ensoniq SoundScape	sscape
ESS Maestro 1, Maestro 2, and Maestro 2E	maestro
ESS Solo 1	esssolo1
Gravis UltraSound, UltraSound MAX, UltraSound PnP,	gus
Intel i810/i810E Integrated AC97 Audio	i810_audio
MediaTrix AudioTrix Pro	trix
microSOUND PCM12, OPTi MAD16 Pro (82C929, 82C930), OPTi Mozart/MAD16 (82C928)	mad16
NeoMagic MagicMedia 256AV	nm256
Pro Audio Spectrum Studio 16 and SoundMan 16	pas2
Personal Sound System (PSS) Orchid SW32 and Cardinal DSP16	pss
S3 SonicVibes	sonicvibes
Trident 4D-Wave NX/DX	trident
Turtle Beach MultiSound Classic, MultiSound Monterey, and MultiSound Tahiti	msnd_classic
Turtle Beach MultiSound Fiji, MultiSound Pinnacle	msnd_pinnacle
VIA 82Cxxx chipset, Windows Sound System	via82cxxx
Yamaha OPL3-SA1	opl3sa
Yamaha OPL3-SA2, OPL3-SA3, OPL3-SAx	opl3sa2
Yamaha YMF PCI Audio	ymfsb

insider insight

Many sound cards include a built-in interface through which you can attach a CD-ROM drive. Linux needs a separate device driver to access a CD-ROM drive connected to a sound card; the sound driver does not have anything to do with the CD-ROM drive, even though the drive is attached to the sound card. By the same token, the sound driver has nothing to do with the joystick port that many sound cards include.

Configuring the Sound Card

Linux needs a driver to control the sound card. The initial Linux kernel (after you install Linux from the companion CD-ROMs) does not load the sound driver. The sound drivers are provided as loadable modules you can load after booting Linux. You will find the sound drivers in the /lib/modules/2.4.*/kernel/drivers/sound directory, where

VERSION is the kernel version number. If you look at the names of the module files, you see that each filename ends with the extension `.o.gz` (the `.o` extension identifies an object file—a file containing binary instructions that implements the driver and `.gz` means that the files are compressed).

Secret

Whenever you boot Red Hat Linux, the kernel runs kudzu, a tool that detects new hardware. Whenever kudzu runs, it detects the current hardware and checks it against a list stored in a text file, `/etc/sysconfig/hwconf`. It then determines if any hardware has been added or removed. Kudzu gives the user an opportunity to configure new hardware or remove the support for hardware no longer installed on the system. Configuring new hardware includes adding appropriate lines to the `/etc/modules.conf` file so that the proper driver modules will be loaded when needed. Typically, a sound card should be detected by kudzu and configured during the boot sequence, but sometimes kudzu seems to load the incorrect driver for a card.

As Linux boots and kudzu detects hardware, it displays messages about the detected hardware. The boot messages scroll by too fast to read, but you can look at them with the dmesg command. Type **dmesg | more** and then look for one or more lines that mention your sound card's name or model number. You can also look at the `/etc/sysconfig/hwconf` file where kudzu stores information about hardware it detects.

If you have older ISA bus plug-and-play (PnP) sound cards, look for any occurrence of lines containing the word isapnp in the boot messages—these lines show the result of kudzu detecting the PnP devices. On one of my PCs, for example, I have a Yamaha OPL3-SA3 PnP sound card. In this case, when I type dmesg | more, I see the following messages:

```
kernel: isapnp: Scanning for PnP cards...
kernel: isapnp: Card 'OPL3-SA3 Snd System'
kernel: isapnp: 1 Plug & Play card detected total
```

For this sound card, the `/etc/modules.conf` file should have the following lines:

```
alias sound-slot-0 opl3sa2
```

Unfortunately, instead of opl3sa2, kudzu specifies the ad1848 driver that is not appropriate (as you can tell by consulting Table 5-1).

Red Hat provides a sound card configuration tool (redhat-config-soundcard), but that tool does not work with ISA PnP cards. It can detect only PCI sound cards. Select Main Menu⇨System Settings⇨Soundcard Detection. If the tool detects your sound card, it displays the information in a small window, as shown in Figure 5-1.

You can play a test sound with the sound card configuration tool, but the tool does not provide for any way to configure the sound card (for example, to load a different driver module). The bottom line is that newer PCI sound cards should work without much trouble in Linux, but for older ISA PnP sound cards you have to do some work to get sound going.

Figure 5-1: Sound Card Detected by redhat-config-soundcard Tool.

If you know your sound card type, one way to configure it is to manually load the driver and to set up information in the /etc/modules.conf file so that the correct driver is loaded.

The next few sections describe how to maually configure sound on Red Hat Linux.

Checking Information about a Sound Card

Typically, you can find out information about your PC's sound card from what kudzu finds as it probes the hardware. Kudzu stores the information about all detected hardware in the following file:

```
/etc/sysconfig/hwconf
```

You can open that file in a text editor and look for a line that looks like this:

```
class: AUDIO
```

The information about the sound card is in the lines that follow, up to the next line that has a lone hyphen. For example, here is the information for an ISA bus Yamaha OPL3SA2 sound card:

```
class: AUDIO
bus: ISAPNP
detached: 0
driver: ad1848
desc: "OPL3-SA3 Snd System:Unknown"
deviceId: YMH0021
pdeviceId: YMH0030
native: 1
active: 0
cardnum: 0
logdev: 0
dma: 0,0
```

The desc line tells you the name of the sound card. As you can see from the driver line, kudzu specifies ad1848 as the driver for this sound card. Unfortunately, the correct driver is opl3sa2. To correct the problem, you have to do some work yourself.

Manually Configuring the Sound Card

When you know the sound card type and the driver that you must load, it's a simple procedure to load the driver manually. All you have to do is log in as root and use the modprobe command with the following syntax:

```
modprobe drivername
```

where drivername is the name of the driver module to load. Thus, you can load the opl3sa2 driver by typing:

```
modprobe opl3sa2
```

That's all you need to do. After loading the driver, you can verify that it's loaded by typing the lsmod command. For example, here are a few lines of output from the lsmod command on a PC after loading the opl3sa2 driver:

```
Module            Size   Used by    Not tainted
opl3sa2           10256  0  (unused)
mpu401            24068  0  [opl3sa2]
ad1848            28556  0  [opl3sa2]
sound             74164  0  [opl3sa2 mpu401 ad1848]
soundcore         6404   6  [sound]
... rest of the lines deleted...
```

I want to point to the fact that loading the opl3sa2 driver with the modprobe command causes the loading of the other modules—mpu401, ad1848, sound, and soundcore—that opl3sa2 needs. As you can see, opl3sa2 needs ad1848, but ad1848 is not enough for the Yamaha OL3SA2 sound card.

After you load the driver manually with the modprobe command, the sound card should work. You can test it by playing an audio CD-ROM, as explained in the "Testing the Sound Card" section.

Secret

To test a sound driver, you can load it manually with the modprobe command, but for automatic loading you should also edit the /etc/modules.conf file and add the following line:

```
alias sound-slot-0 drivername
```

where drivername is the sound driver you want to load. That way, when the kernel needs to load the sound driver (perhaps because you have started playing an audio CD-ROM with the CD Player application), the correct driver will be loaded.

Typically, the sound driver can probe any PnP sound card to determine its hardware parameters such as the I/O port addresses, the interrupt request numbers (IRQs), and the direct memory access (DMAs) channel. If you do not have a PnP sound card, you have to specify the I/O address, the IRQ, and the DMA channel number of the sound card. You can specify these parameters by adding options lines in the

/etc/modules.conf file. For example, the following lines in /etc/modules.conf specify the parameters for a Creative Labs SoundBlaster sound card:

```
alias sound-slot-0 sb
options sb io=0x220 irq=5 dma=1
```

For a PnP or PCI sound card, all you have to do is have an alias line for sound-slot-0 with the correct driver name. For example, here is the line for a laptop with the Intel i810 Integrated AC97 Audio:

```
alias sound-slot-0 i810_audio
```

Learning Sound Device Names

Like any other devices in Linux, the sound devices have files in the /dev directory with specific names. Table 5-2 lists the standard device filenames that provide sound capability in Linux (you may not have all these devices on your system).

Table 5-2: Standard Sound Device Filenames in Linux

Device Filename	Description
/dev/audio	An audio device capable of playing Sun workstation–compatible audio files (typically with a .au extension). The device does not support all capabilities of the Sun workstation audio device but can play Sun audio files.
/dev/audio1	A Sun workstation–compatible audio device for the second sound card (if any)
/dev/dsp	A digital signal-processing device that also can play Sun audio files
/dev/midi00 - 03	MIDI ports
/dev/mixer	A sound-mixer device
/dev/mixer1	A second sound-mixer device
/dev/sequencer	A MIDI sequencer device

Testing the Sound Card

To test the sound driver, you should try playing a sound file. A good way to do this is to insert an audio CD-ROM into your CD-ROM drive, and play a sound track. See the section "Playing Audio CD-ROMSs" for more information about various CD Player applications.

If you don't have an audio CD-ROM handy, you can use the X Multimedia System (XMMS) to open and play a sound file. XMMS can play many types of sound files, including MP3 and Windows WAV. You will find many WAV sound files—which usually have names that end with the .wav extension—in the /usr/share/sounds directory of your Red Hat Linux system.

Secret

To play a sound file, start XMMS from the GNOME desktop by selecting Main Menu⇨Sound & Video⇨Audioo Player. The X Multimedia System has a simple user interface. To open a sound file, select Window Menu⇨Play File, or press L and select a `.wav` file from the Open dialog box. Select a file from the `/usr/share/sounds` directory, and then click the play button. XMMS starts playing the sound file.

If you get an error message from XMMS, select Window Menu⇨Options⇨Preferences, and select the OSS Driver as the Output Plugin. If you want to adjust the volume or other attributes of the sound, start the volume control by selecting Main Menu⇨ Sound & Video⇨Volume Control from the GNOME desktop.

If you have a microphone connected to your sound card, you can try recording a 10-second sound file with the following command:

```
dd bs=8k count=10 </dev/audio >test.au
```

The `dd` command simply copies a specified amount of data from one file to another. In this case, the input file is the audio device (which records from the microphone), and the output file is the sound file. You may have to run the volume control program to set the recording-gain level for the microphone. After recording the sound file, you can play it back by sending the data back to `/dev/audio` with the following command:

```
cat test.au > /dev/audio
```

Playing Audio CD-ROMs

You need a special application to play audio CD-ROMs in the CD-ROM drive. Both GNOME and KDE come with CD Players.

Before using any CD Player program, make sure you unmount any CD-ROM currently in the drive (use the `umount/dev/cdrom` command), remove the CD-ROM, and place an audio CD-ROM in the drive. To play the audio CD-ROM, you must also have a sound card and the appropriate sound drivers installed, as described in earlier sections of this chapter.

If you are using the GNOME desktop, you can play audio CD-ROMs by using the CD Player application. You can launch the GNOME CD Player by selecting Main Menu⇨ Sound & Video⇨CD Player. Figure 5-2 shows this CD player playing a track from an audio CD. As you can see, the CD Player displays the title of the CD and the name of the current track. The CD Player gets the song titles from CDDB—a CD database on the Internet. This means you need an active Internet connection for the CD Player to download song information from the CD database. Once the CD Player downloads information about a particular CD, it caches that information in a local database for future use.

Figure 5-2: The GNOME CD Player Playing a Track from an Audio CD.

The CD Player's user interface is intuitive, and you can learn it easily. One nice feature is that you have the ability to select a track by title, as shown in Figure 5-3.

Figure 5-3: Selecting a Specific Audio Track to Play with the CD Player.

insider
insight

To learn more about CDDB, read the Frequently Asked Questions at `http://www.cddb.com/faq.html`.

Secret

If you want to log in as a normal user and play audio CD-ROMs on the CD-ROM drive, you should first log in as `root` and set the permissions settings on the CD-ROM device so that anyone can read it. (You have to set the permissions for the actual CD-ROM device, not the generic `/dev/cdrom` device.) To do this, follow these steps:

1. Log in as `root`. If you are already logged in, type **su -**, and enter the super user's password to assume the identity of **root.**

2. Type **ls –l /dev/cdrom** and find the actual device for which `/dev/cdrom` is a symbolic link. For example, in my case, `/dev/hdc` is the physical device, as the output of the `ls -l /dev/cdrom` command indicates:

   ```
   lrwxrwxrwx  1 root  root  8 Jan 23 19:16 /dev/cdrom -> /dev/hdc
   ```

3. Make the CD-ROM device readable by all users by using the `chmod` command as follows:

   ```
   chmod o+r /dev/hdc
   ```

   Anyone who has access to your Red Hat Linux PC can now play audio CD-ROMs and access the CD-ROM drive. Note, however, that anyone with access to the PC, including anyone who can remotely log in, can now read data CD-ROMs as well.

If you use KDE as your desktop, you can find a similar audio CD Player in KDE. Start the KDE CD Player by selecting Main Menu⇨Sound & Video⇨KsCD.

Troubleshooting Sound Cards

If, after you configure the sound driver, the sound card does not produce sound when you play a sound file or an audio CD-ROM, try the following steps to diagnose and fix the problem:

1. Check to see whether or not the sound driver is included in the kernel. One way to check is to look at the contents of the `/proc/devices` file. The following is an example:

```
cat /proc/devices | more
Character devices:
  1 mem
  2 pty
  3 ttyp
  4 ttyS
  5 cua
  6 lp
  7 vcs
 10 misc
 13 input
 14 sound
 29 fb
 36 netlink
128 ptm
... lines deleted ...
```

The listing should show the character device `14 sound`. If you don't see this device, the kernel may not be configured properly or the sound driver module may not be loaded properly.

2. Verify that the sound driver detected the sound card when it was loaded. Type **tail 100 /var/log/messages** to look at the recent log messages; then check for a line reporting that the sound card was found. If the sound driver does not report the sound card, it's possible that the sound card is not properly installed and configured.

   First, make sure that the sound card works under DOS or Windows. Determine the I/O address, IRQ, and DMA channel, and reconfigure the kernel to include support for your sound card with the same parameters as under DOS.

3. If nothing works, you may want to read the latest Sound-HOWTO file. To read this file, point your Web browser to `http://www.ibiblio.org/pub/Linux/docs/HOWTO/Sound-HOWTO`. You can also find documentation for specific sound drivers in the `/usr/src/linux-2.4/Documentation/sound` directory. Note that this directory exists only if you have installed the Linux source code (see Chapter 21 for more information).

insider insight If you still cannot get the sound card to work under Linux, you may want to post a news item to one of the comp.os.linux newsgroups. Chapter 16 discusses how to connect to the Internet and access the newsgroups. You might also consider purchasing the low-cost ($20) commercial version of the Open Sound System (OSS) driver from 4Front Technologies (http://www.opensound.com/). The commercial OSS driver supports more sounds cards (in particular, sound cards with proprietary programming information) than the OSS driver included with the Linux kernel.

Summary

Unlike many UNIX workstations, a typical PC nowadays comes with a sound card. This chapter describes the sound cards that Red Hat Linux supports and shows you how to detect and correct some common sound-card installation problems.

By reading this chapter, you learned the following:

- Sound cards often include interfaces for CD-ROM drives and joysticks. The sound driver supports only the sound card's sound capabilities; you need separate drivers for the CD-ROM drive and the joystick.
- To use a sound card, you have to load the sound driver module. The kudzu program can detect and load the correct driver module for PCI and plug-and-play (PnP) sound cards.
- If kudzu does not load the correct driver, you can use the modprobe command to load the correct driver. You should also edit the /etc/modules.conf file so that the correct sound driver is automatically loaded whenever the kernel needs it.
- Both GNOME and KDE desktops come with CD Player applications that enable you to play sound tracks from audio CDs. You can use these CD Players to test your sound card.

Network Setup

◆ ◆

Secrets in This Chapter

◆ ◆

U NIX and networking go hand in hand; TCP/IP (Transmission Control Protocol/ Internet Protocol) networking is practically synonymous with UNIX. As a UNIX clone, Linux includes extensive built-in networking capabilities. In particular, Linux supports TCP/IP networking over several physical interfaces, such as Ethernet cards, serial ports, and parallel ports.

Typically, you use an Ethernet network for your local area network (LAN)—at your office or even your home (if you happen to have several systems at home). TCP/IP networking over the serial port enables you to connect to other networks by dialing out over a modem. Linux supports both Serial Line Internet Protocol (SLIP) and Point-to-Point Protocol (PPP).

This chapter focuses on Linux's support for Ethernet and TCP/IP. The chapter starts with a discussion of networking in general and TCP/IP in particular, then it covers the physical setup of an Ethernet LAN, including information about specific brands of Ethernet cards. Finally, the chapter describes how to set up a TCP/IP network on a Linux system.

---

cross
ref

Although much of this applies to TCP/IP over the serial line, this chapter does not dwell on the specific details of dial-up networking; that topic is the focus of Chapter 13. That chapter also describes how to connect to the Internet using cable modem and DSL as well as how to configure a wireless Ethernet LAN in Red Hat Linux.

Laptops often use PCMCIA cards (also called PC cards) for networking. Appendix F describes the PC cards that Linux supports.

Networking Basics

Like any other technical subject, networking is full of terminology and jargon that a newcomer might find daunting. This section introduces some basic concepts of networking, starting with a layered model of networking and proceeding to details of Ethernet and TCP/IP network protocols.

The OSI Seven-Layer Model

A widely used conceptual model of networking is the seven-layer Open Systems Interconnection (OSI) reference model, developed by the International Organizaton for Standardization (ISO). The OSI reference model describes the flow of data between the physical connection to the network and the end-user application. Each layer is responsible for providing particular functionality, as shown in Figure 6-1.

As Figure 6-1 shows, the OSI layers are numbered from bottom to top. Basic functions, such as physically sending data bits through the network cable, are at the bottom; functions that deal with higher-level abstractions of the data are at the top. The purpose of each layer is to provide services to the next-higher layer in a manner such that the higher layer does not have to know how the services are actually implemented. In fact, each layer is designed so that it does not have to know how the other layers work.

7	Application
6	Presentation
5	Session
4	Transport
3	Network
2	Data Link
1	Physical

Figure 6-1: The OSI Seven-Layer Reference Model of Networking.

The purposes of the seven layers in the OSI reference model are as follows:

♦ **Physical layer (Layer 1)**—Transmits raw bits of data across the physical medium (the networking cable or electromagnetic waves, in the case of wireless networks). This layer carries the data generated by all the higher layers. The physical layer deals with three physical components:

   • Network topology (such as bus or star), which specifies how various nodes of a network are physically connected

   • Transmission medium (such as RG-58 coaxial cable, shielded or unshielded twisted pair, fiber-optic cable, and microwave) that carries the actual signals representing data

   • Transmission technique (such as Carrier Sense Multiple Access with Collision Detection [CSMA/CD], used by Ethernet; and token-based techniques, used by token-ring and Fiber Distributed Data Interface [FDDI]), which defines the hardware protocols for data transfer

♦ **Data link layer (Layer 2)**—Deals with logical packets (or frames) of data. This layer packages raw bits from the physical layer into frames, the exact format of which depends on the type of network, such as Ethernet or token ring. The frames the data-link layer uses contain the physical addresses of the sender and the receiver of data.

♦ **Network layer (Layer 3)**—Contains information about the logical network addresses and how to translate logical addresses to physical ones. At the sending end, the network layer converts larger logical packets to smaller physical data frames. At the receiving end, the network layer reassembles the data frames into their original logical packet structure.

♦ **Transport layer (Layer 4)**—Responsible for the reliable delivery of messages that originate at the application layer. At the sending end, this layer divides long messages into several packets. At the receiving end, the transport layer reassembles the original messages and sends an acknowledgment of receipt. The transport layer also ensures that data is received in the correct order in a timely manner. In case of errors, the transport layer requests retransmission of data.

◆ **Session layer (Layer 5)**—Enables applications on different computers to initiate, use, and terminate a connection (the connection is called a session). The session layer translates the names of systems to appropriate addresses (for example, IP addresses in TCP/IP networks).

◆ **Presentation layer (Layer 6)**—Manages the format used to exchange data between networked computers. Data encryption and decryption, for example, are in this layer. Most network protocols do not have a presentation layer.

◆ **Application layer (Layer 7)**—The gateway through which application processes access network services. This layer represents services (such as file transfers, database access, and electronic mail) that directly support applications.

The OSI model is not specific to any hardware or software; it simply provides an architectural framework and gives us a common terminology for discussing various networking capabilities.

A Simplified Four-Layer TCP/IP Network Model

The OSI seven-layer model is not a specification; it provides guidelines for organizing all network services. Most implementations adopt a layered model for networking services, and these layered models can be mapped to the OSI reference model. The TCP/IP networking model, for example, can be adequately represented by a simplified model.

Network-aware applications usually deal with the top three layers (session, presentation, and application) of the OSI seven-layer reference model. Thus, these three layers can be combined into a single layer called the application layer.

The bottom two layers of the OSI model—physical and data link—also can be combined into a single physical layer. These combinations result in a simplified four-layer model, as shown in Figure 6-2.

4	Application	Mail, File transfer, Telnet
3	Transport	TCP (Transmission Control Protocol) UDP (User Datagram Protocol)
2	Network	IP (Internet Protocol)
1	Physical	Ethernet

Figure 6-2: A Simplified Four-Layer TCP/IP Networking Model.

At each of these layers, information is exchanged through one of many network protocols.

Network Protocols

A *network protocol* refers to a detailed process the sender and receiver agree upon for exchanging data at a specific layer of the networking model. Thus, you find the following protocols in the simplified four-layer network model of Figure 6-2:

◆ Physical-layer protocols, such as Ethernet, token ring, and FDDI

◆ Network-layer protocols, such as the Internet Protocol (IP), which is part of the TCP/IP protocol suite

♦ Transport-layer protocols, such as the Transmission Control Protocol (TCP) and User Datagram Protocol (UDP), which are part of the TCP/IP protocol suite

♦ Application-layer protocols, such as File Transfer Protocol (FTP), Simple Mail Transfer Protocol (SMTP), Domain Name Service (DNS), Telnet, HyperText Transfer Protocol (HTTP), and Simple Network Management Protocol (SNMP), which are also part of the TCP/IP protocol suite

The term protocol suite refers to a collection of two or more protocols from these layers that form the basis of a network. The following are some of the well-known protocol suites:

♦ IPX/SPX (Internet Packet Exchange/Sequenced Packet Exchange) protocol suite, used by Novell NetWare

♦ NetBIOS and NetBEUI (Network BIOS Extended User Interface), used by Microsoft's operating systems

♦ TCP/IP protocol suite

Of these protocol suites, you are probably most interested in the TCP/IP protocol suite, because that's what Linux and other UNIX systems support well.

---

cross
ref

In addition to the TCP/IP protocol, Linux supports the IPX protocol but not the SPX protocol necessary for NetWare. Linux's support for NetBIOS comes in the form of a software package named Samba, included on the companion CD-ROMs and described in Chapter 19.

Learning More about TCP/IP

This chapter gives you an overview of TCP/IP and Ethernet networking, then moves on to Linux-specific instructions for setting up TCP/IP networking. A single chapter simply isn't enough to provide all available information about TCP/IP. For more information on TCP/IP, consult one of the following books:

♦ Douglas E. Comer and Ralph E. Droms, *Computer Networks and Internets, with Internet Applications*, 3rd Edition, Prentice Hall, 2001

♦ Douglas E. Comer, *Internetworking with TCP/IP, Volume 1: Principles, Protocols, and Architecture*, Fourth Edition, Prentice Hall, 2000

♦ W. Richard Stevens, *UNIX Network Programming*, Second Edition, Prentice Hall, 1998

TCP/IP and the Internet

TCP/IP has become the protocol of choice on the Internet—the "network of networks" that evolved from ARPAnet, a packet-switching network that itself evolved from research the U.S. government's Advanced Research Projects Agency (ARPA) initiated in the 1970s. Subsequently, ARPA acquired a Defense prefix and became DARPA. Under the auspices of DARPA, the TCP/IP protocols emerged as a popular collection of protocols for internet-working—a term used to describe communication among networks.

TCP/IP has flourished for several reasons. A significant reason is that the protocol is open, which means the technical descriptions of the protocol appear in public documents, so anyone can implement TCP/IP on specific hardware and software.

Another, more important, reason for TCP/IP's success is the availability of sample implementation. Instead of describing network architecture and protocols on paper, each component of the TCP/IP protocol suite began life as a specification with a sample implementation.

Taking Stock of RFCs

The details of each TCP/IP protocol (including TCP and IP, as well as specific service protocols such as SMTP and FTP) are described in documents known as Requests for Comments (RFCs). These documents are freely distributed on the Internet. You can get RFCs from `http://www.cis.ohio-state.edu/hypertext/information/rfc.html` (click the Index link for a complete index of the RFC or search by keyword). Another good URL for RFCs is `http://www.faqs.org/rfcs/`.

In fact, the notation used to name Internet resources in a uniform manner is itself documented in an RFC. The notation, known as the Uniform Resource Locator (URL), is described in RFC 1738, "Uniform Resource Locators (URL)," written by, among others, T. Berners-Lee, the originator of the World Wide Web (WWW).

You can think of RFCs as the working papers of the Internet research-and-development community. All Internet standards are published as RFCs. However, many RFCs do not specify any standards; they are informational documents only.

The following are some RFCs you may find interesting:

- ◆ RFC 768, "User Datagram Protocol (UDP)"
- ◆ RFC 791, "Internet Protocol (IP)"
- ◆ RFC 792, "Internet Control Message Protocol (ICMP)"
- ◆ RFC 793, "Transmission Control Protocol (TCP)"
- ◆ RFC 854, "TELNET Protocol Specification"
- ◆ RFC 950, "Internet Standard Subnetting Procedure"
- ◆ RFC 959, "File Transfer Protocol (FTP)"
- ◆ RFC 1034, "Domain Names: Concepts and Facilities"
- ◆ RFC 1058, "Routing Information Protocol (RIP)"
- ◆ RFC 1112, "Host Extensions for IP Multicasting"
- ◆ RFC 1155, "Structure and Identification of Management Information for TCP/IP-based Internets"
- ◆ RFC 1157, "Simple Network Management Protocol (SNMP)"
- ◆ RFC 1519, "Classless Inter-Domain Routing (CIDR) Assignment and Aggregation Strategy"
- ◆ RFC 1661, "The Point-to-Point Protocol (PPP)"
- ◆ RFC 1738, "Uniform Resource Locators (URL)"
- ◆ RFC 1796, "Not All RFCs Are Standards"
- ◆ RFC 1855, "Netiquette Guidelines"
- ◆ RFC 1886, "DNS Extensions to Support IP Version 6"
- ◆ RFC 1918, "Address Allocation for Private Internets"
- ◆ RFC 1939, "Post Office Protocol, Version 3 (POP3)"

- RFC 1945, "HyperText Transfer Protocol—HTTP/1.0"
- RFC 2026, "The Internet Standards Process—Revision 3"
- RFC 2028, "The Organizations Involved in the IETF Standards Process"
- RFC 2045 through 2049, "Multipurpose Internet Mail Extensions (MIME)" (Parts One through Five)
- RFC 2060, "Internet Message Access Protocol—Version 4rev1 (IMAP4)"
- RFC 2131, "Dynamic Host Configuration Protocol (DHCP)"
- RFC 2146, "U.S. Government Internet Domain Names"
- RFC 2151, "A Primer on Internet and TCP/IP Tools and Utilities"
- RFC 2305, "A Simple Mode of Facsimile Using Internet Mail"
- RFC 2328, "Open Shortest Path First Routing (OSPF) Version 2"
- RFC 2368, "The mailto URL scheme"
- RFC 2373, "IP Version 6 Addressing Architecture"
- RFC 2396, "Uniform Resource Identifiers (URI): Generic Syntax"
- RFC 2460, "Internet Protocol, Version 6 (IPv6) Specification"
- RFC 2535, "Domain Name System Security Extensions"
- RFC 2616, "HyperText Transfer Protocol—HTTP/1.1"
- RFC 2660, "The Secure HyperText Transfer Protocol"
- RFC 2821, "Simple Mail Transfer Protocol (SMTP)"
- RFC 2822, "Internet Message Format"
- RFC 2853, "Generic Security Service API Version 2: Java Bindings"
- RFC 2854, "The 'text/html' Media Type"
- RFC 2865, "Remote Authentication Dial In User Service (RADIUS)"
- RFC 2870, "Root Name Server Operational Requirements"
- RFC 2871, "A Framework for Telephony Routing over IP"
- RFC 2900, "Internet Official Protocol Standards"
- RFC 2910, "Internet Printing Protocol/1.1: Encoding and Transport"
- RFC 2911, "Internet Printing Protocol/1.1: Model and Semantics"
- RFC 3013, "Recommended Internet Service Provider Security Services and Procedures"
- RFC 3022, "Traditional IP Network Address Translator (Traditional NAT)"
- RFC 3076, "Canonical XML Version 1.0"
- RFC 3130, "Notes from the State-Of-The-Technology: DNSSEC"
- RFC 3174, "US Secure Hash Algorithm 1 (SHA1)"
- RFC 3196, "Internet Printing Protocol/1.1: Implementer's Guide"
- RFC 3275, "(Extensible Markup Language) XML-Signature Syntax and Processing"
- RFC 3330, "Special-Use IPv4 Addresses"
- RFC 3344, "IP Mobility Support for IPv4"

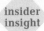

insider insight

The RFCs continue to evolve as new technology and techniques emerge. If you work in networking, you should keep an eye on the RFCs to monitor emerging networking protocols. You can check up on the RFCs at http://www.faqs.org/rfcs/.

Understanding IP Addresses

When you have many computers on a network, you need a way to identify each one uniquely. In TCP/IP networking, the address of a computer is known as the IP address. Because TCP/IP deals with internetworking, the address is based on the concepts of a network address and a host address. You might think of the idea of a network address and a host address as having to provide two addresses to identify a computer uniquely:

◆ **Network address**—Indicates the network on which the computer is located

◆ **Host address**—Indicates a specific computer on that network

Secret

The IP address is a 4-byte (32-bit) value with some of the bits devoted to the network address and the rest used for host address. The convention is to write each byte as a decimal value and to put a dot (.) after each number. Thus, you see network addresses such as 132.250.112.52. This way of writing IP addresses is known as *dotted-decimal* or *dotted-quad* notation. Each of the four decimal numbers in the dotted-decimal notation is often referred to as an octet. Note that each decimal number in the dotted-decimal notation must be between 0 and 255 because that's the range of values a byte can hold.

The bits in an IP address are organized in the following manner:

```
<Network Address, Host Address>
```

In other words, a specified number of bits of the 32-bit IP address are used as a network address, and the rest of the bits are interpreted as a host address. The network address identifies the LAN to which your PC is connected and the host address identifies your PC one of many hosts within the LAN. Other PCs in the LAN share the same network address, but have different bits in the host address portion fo their IP addresses.

When IP addresses were initially allocated to organizations, a class system was devised to accommodate networks of various sizes (the network size is the number of computers in that network). Although the network classes are largely ignored nowadays, it is important to understand what the network classes are and how they work because they linger on in the backbone of the Internet. In place of predefined classes, IP networks use classless addressing schemes with network marks to separate out the network address from the host address.

There are five classes of IP addresses, named class A through class E, as shown in Figure 6-3.

Of the five address classes, only classes A, B, and C are used for addressing networks and hosts; classes D and E addresses are reserved for special use.

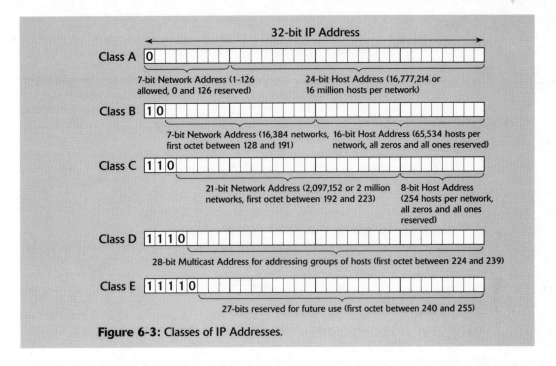

Figure 6-3: Classes of IP Addresses.

Class A addresses support 126 networks, each with up to 16 million hosts. Although the network address is 7-bit, two values (0 and 127) have special meaning; therefore, you can have only 1 through 126 as Class A network addresses. There can be approximately 2 billion class A hosts.

Class B addresses are for networks with up to 65,534 hosts. There can be at most 16,384 class B networks. All class B networks, taken together, can have approximately 1 billion hosts.

Class C addresses are meant for small organizations. Each class C address allows up to 254 hosts, and there can be approximately 2 million class C networks. Therefore, there can be at most approximately 500 million class C hosts. If you are in a small company, you probably have a class C address. Nowadays, it is customary to aggregate multiple class C addresses into a single block and use them for efficient routing.

All together, class A, B, and C networks can support at most approximately 3.5 billion hosts.

You can tell the class of an IP address by the first number in the dotted-decimal notation, as follows:

- ◆ Class A addresses: 1.xxx.xxx.xxx through 126.xxx.xxx.xxx
- ◆ Class B addresses: 128.xxx.xxx.xxx through 191.xxx.xxx.xxx
- ◆ Class C addresses: 192.xxx.xxx.xxx through 223.xxx.xxx.xxx

Even within the five address classes, the following IP addresses have special meaning:

◆ An address with all zeros in its network portion indicates the local network—the network where the data packet with this IP address originated. Thus, the address 0.0.0.200 means host number 200 on this class C network.

◆ The class A address 127.xxx.xxx.xxx is used for loopback—communications within the same host. Conventionally, 127.0.0.1 is used as the loopback address. Processes that need to communicate through TCP with other processes on the same host use the loopback address to avoid having to send packets out on the network.

◆ Turning on all the bits in any part of the address indicates a broadcast message. The address 128.18.255.255, for example, means all hosts on the class B network 128.18. The address 255.255.255.255 is known as a limited broadcast; all work-stations on the current network segment will receive the packet.

Getting IP Addresses for Your Network

If you are setting up an independent network of your own that will be connected to the Internet, you need unique IP addresses for your network. You would typically get a range of IP addresses for your network from the ISP who connects your network to the Internet. You can get the domain name from one of the Internet domain name registration services. For example, for the .com domain, you can obtain domain names from VeriSign located on the Web at http://www.networksolutions.com/. To learn more about domain name and IP address services, point your Web browser to the InterNIC website at http://www.internic.net/.

ISPs typically get their IP address allocation in large blocks from regional Internet registries such as ARIN (American Registry for Internet Numbers, http://www.arin.net/) in the United States, RIPE (Réseaux IP Européens, http://www.ripe.net/) in Europe, and APNIC (Asia Pacific Network Information Centre, http://www.apnic.net/) for the Asia-Pacific region. For more information about IP address allocation services, visit the Internet Assigned Numbers Authority (IANA) website at http://www.iana.org/ipaddress/ip-addresses.htm.

Secret

If you don't plan to connect your network to the Internet, you really don't need a unique IP address. RFC 1918 (the "Address Allocation for Private Internets" section) provides guidance about what IP addresses you can use within private networks (the term private Internet refers to any network not connected to the Internet). Three blocks of IP addresses are reserved for private Internets:

• 10.0.0.0 to 10.255.255.255

• 172.16.0.0 to 172.31.255.255

• 192.168.0.0 to 192.168.255.255

You can use addresses from these blocks for your private network without having to coordinate with an organization. For example, I (and many others) use the 192.168.0.0 Class C address for a home network. Additionally, the cable/DSI routers use one of these private Class C addresses for the local network interface.

If you have only one public Internet address from your ISP, you can still use a Network Address Translation (NAT) router to connect your network with private IP addresses to the public Internet.

Figuring Out Network Masks

The network mask is an IP address that has 1s in the bits that correspond to the network address, and 0s in all other bit positions. The class of your network address determines the network mask.

If you have a class C address, for example, the network mask is 255.255.255.0. Thus, class B networks have a network mask of 255.255.0.0, and class A networks have 255.0.0.0 as the network mask. Of course, you do not have to use the historical class A, B, or C network masks. Nowadays, you can use any other network mask that's appropriate for your network address.

Extracting Network Addresses

The network address is the bitwise AND of the network mask with any IP address in your network. If the IP address of a system on your network is 206.197.168.200, and the network mask is 255.255.255.0, the network address is 206.197.168.0. The network address is written with zero bits in the part of the address that's supposed to be for the host address.

Using Subnets

If your site has a class B address, you get one network number, and that network can have up to 65,534 hosts. Even if you work for a megacorporation that has thousands of hosts, you may want to divide your network into smaller subnetworks (or *subnets*). If your organization has offices in several locations, for example, you may want each office to be on a separate network. You can do this by taking some bits from the host-address portion of the IP address and assigning those bits to the network address. This procedure is known as defining a subnet mask.

---

caution   Do not confuse an IP subnet, which is a logical division of a network, with Ethernet segments, which refer to physical divisions of an Ethernet network.

Essentially, when you define a subnet mask, you add more bits to the default network mask for that address class. If you have a class B network, for example, the default network mask would be 255.255.0.0. Then, if you decide to divide your network into 128 subnetworks, each of which has 512 hosts, you would designate 7 bits from the host address space as the subnet address. Thus, the subnet mask becomes 255.255.254.0.

Using Supernets or CIDR

There are so few class A and B network addresses that they are becoming scarce. Class C addresses are more plentiful, but the proliferation of class C addresses has introduced a unique problem. Each class C address needs an entry in the network routing tables—the tables that contain information about how to locate any network on the Internet. Too many class C addresses means too many entries in the routing tables, which causes the router's performance to deteriorate. One way to get around this problem is ignore the predefined address classes and let the network address be any number of bits. All you need is for the network mask to figure out which part of the 32-bit IP address is the network address. Based on this idea the Classless Inter-Domain Routing (CIDR)—documented in RFC 1519—was developed to enable routing of contiguous blocks of class C addresses with a single entry in the routing table. CIDR is used in the Internet as the primary mechanism to improve scalability of the Internet routing system.

Secret

The basis of CIDR is the idea of supernets—arbitrarily-sized networks created by combining contiguous class C addresses that satisfy some criteria. For example, to create a supernet from two class C networks, the two network addresses must satisfy the following properties:

- The network addresses must be consecutive (for example, 198.41.18.0 and 198.41.19.0 are consecutive class C addresses).
- The third number of the first network address must be divisible by 2 (for example, the third number of 198.41.18.0 is 18, and 18 is divisible by 2).

Thus, you could combine 198.41.18.0 and 198.41.19.0 into a single block, but you cannot combine 198.41.15.0 with 198.41.16.0 because 15 is not divisible by 2. When you create a supernet of two class C networks, the network can have up to 512 host addresses, and the network mask becomes 255.255.254.0, which leaves 9 bits for the host address.

You can also supernet any number of class C networks in powers of two. The only requirement is that the third number (in the dotted-decimal notation) of the first address must be divisible by the number of networks you are combining. Thus, if you are supernetting eight networks, the third number of the first address must be divisible by 8. Thus, you could supernet the following eight consecutive class C networks:

```
198.41.16.0
198.41.17.0
198.41.18.0
198.41.19.0
198.41.20.0
198.41.21.0
198.41.22.0
198.41.23.0
```

The network mask of this supernet would be 255.255.248.0, which provides for 21 bits of network address and leaves 11 bits for 8×256 = 2,048 host addresses.

Such a network address is written with the notation /21 to indicate that there are 21 bits in the network address.

Learning about IPv6

When the 4-byte IP address was created, the number of addresses seemed to be adequate. By now, however, class A and B addresses are running out, and class C addresses are being depleted at a fast rate. The Internet Engineering Task Force (IETF) recognized the potential for running out of IP addresses in 1991, and work began then on the next-generation IP addressing scheme, named IPng, which will eventually replace the old 4-byte addressing scheme (called IPv4, for IP Version 4).

Several alternative addressing schemes for IPng were proposed and debated. The final contender, with a 128-bit (16-byte) address, was dubbed IPv6 (for IP Version 6). On September 18, 1995, the IETF declared the core set of IPv6 addressing protocols to be an IETF Proposed Standard. By now, there are many RFCs dealing with various aspects of IPv6, from IPv6 over PPP for the transmission of IPv6 packets over Ethernet.

IPv6 is designed to be an evolutionary step from IPv4. The proposed standard provides direct interoperability between hosts using the older IPv4 addresses and any new IPv6 hosts. The idea is that users can upgrade their systems to use IPv6 when they want and that network operators are free to upgrade their network hardware to use IPv6 without affecting current users of IPv4. Sample implementations of IPv6 are being developed for many operating systems, including Linux. For more information about IPv6 in Linux, consult the Linux IPv6 FAQ/HOWTO at `http://www.linuxhq.com/IPv6/`.

The IPv6 128-bit addressing scheme allows for 170,141,183,460,469,232,000,000,000,000,000,000,000 unique hosts! That should last us for a while!

Routing TCP/IP Packets

Routing refers to the task of forwarding information from one network to another. Consider the two class C networks 206.197.168.0 and 164.109.10.0. You need a routing device to send packets from one of these networks to the other.

Because a routing device facilitates data exchange between two networks, it has two physical network connections, one on each network. Each network interface has its own IP address, and the routing device essentially passes packets back and forth between the two network interfaces. Figure 6-4 illustrates how a routing device has a physical presence in two networks and how each network interface has its own IP address.

Figure 6-4: A Routing Device Allows Packet Exchange between Two Networks.

The generic term "routing device" can refer to a general-purpose computer with two network interfaces or a dedicated device designed specifically for routing. Such dedicated routing devices are known as *routers*.

insider insight

The generic term "gateway" also refers to any routing device regardless of whether the device is another PC or a router. For good performance (a high packet-transfer rate), you want a dedicated router, whose sole purpose is to route packets of data in a network.

Later, when you learn how to set up a TCP/IP network in Linux, you'll have to specify the IP address of your network's gateway. If your Linux system gets its IP address from a DHCP (Dynamic Host Configuration Protocol) server, then that DHCP server can also provide the gateway address.

A single routing device, of course, does not connect all the networks in the world; packets get around in the Internet from one gateway to another. Any network connected to another network has a designated gateway. You can even have specific gateways for specific networks. As you'll learn, a routing table keeps track of the gateway associated with an external network and the type of physical interface (such as Ethernet or Point-to-Point Protocol over serial lines) for that network. A default gateway gets packets that are addressed to any unknown network.

Secret

In your local area network, all packets addressed to another network go to your network's default gateway, except for those addresses that are explicitly directed elsewhere by static routes. If that gateway is physically connected to the destination network, the story ends there because the gateway can physically send the packets to the destination host. If that gateway does not know the destination network, however, it sends the packets to the next default gateway (the gateway for the other network on which your gateway also "lives"). In this way, packets travel from one gateway to the next until they reach the destination network (or you get an error message saying that the destination network is unreachable).

To send packets around in the network efficiently, routers exchange information (in the form of routing tables), so that each router can have a "map" of the network in its vicinity. Routers exchange information by using a routing protocol from a family of protocols, known as the Interior Gateway Protocol (IGP). A commonly used Interior Gateway Protocol is the Routing Information Protocol (RIP). Another, more recent, Interior Gateway Protocol is the Open Shortest Path First (OSPF) protocol.

In TCP/IP routing, any time a packet passes through a router, it has made what is considered a hop. In RIP, the maximum size of the Internet is 15 hops. A network is considered to be unreachable from your network if a packet does not reach the destination network within 15 hops. In other words, any network more than 15 routers away is considered to be unreachable. The newer OSPF routing protocol uses a different metric for measuring the quality of different network paths; therefore, it can have hops greater than 15.

Within a single network, you don't need a router as long as you do not use a subnet mask to break the single IP network into several subnets. In that case, however, you have to set up routers to send packets from one subnet to another.

Understanding the Domain Name System (DNS)

You can access any host computer in a TCP/IP network with an IP address. Remembering the IP addresses of even a few hosts of interest, however, is tedious. This fact was recognized from the beginning of TCP/IP, and the association between a hostname and IP address was created. The concept is similar to that of a phone book, in which you can look up a telephone number by searching for a person's name.

In the early days of the Internet, the association between names and IP addresses was maintained in a text file named HOSTS.TXT at the Network Information Center (NIC), which was located in the Stanford Research Institute (SRI). This file contained the names and corresponding IP addresses of networks, hosts, and routers on the Internet. All hosts on the Internet used to transfer that file by FTP. (Can you imagine all hosts getting a file from a single source in today's Internet?) As the number of Internet hosts increased, the single file idea became unmanageable. The hosts file was becoming difficult to maintain, and it was hard for all the hosts to update their hosts file in a timely manner. To alleviate the problem, RFC 881 introduced the concept of and plans for domain names in November 1983. Eventually, in 1987 this led to the Domain Name System (DNS) as we know it today (documented in RFCs 1032, 1033, 1034, and 1035).

DNS provides a hierarchical naming system much like your postal address, which you can read as "your name" at "your street address" in "your city" in "your state" in "your country." If I know your full postal address, I can locate you by starting with your city in your country. Then, I'd locate the street address to find your home, ring the doorbell, and ask for you by name.

Secret

DNS essentially provides an addressing scheme for an Internet host that is much like the postal address. The entire Internet is subdivided into several domains, such as gov, edu, com, mil, and net. Each domain is further subdivided into subdomains. Finally, within a subdomain, each host is given a symbolic name. To write a host's fully qualified domain name (FQDN), string together the hostname, subdomain names, and domain name with dots (.) as separators. Following is the full domain name of a host named ADDLAB in the subdomain NWS within another subdomain NOAA in the GOV domain: ADDLAB.NWS.NOAA.GOV. Note that domain names are not case sensitive. By the way, a single dot (.) represents the topmost level (root) of the domain-name hierarchy.

Figure 6-5 illustrates part of the Internet Domain Name System, showing the location of the host ADDLAB.NWS.NOAA.GOV.

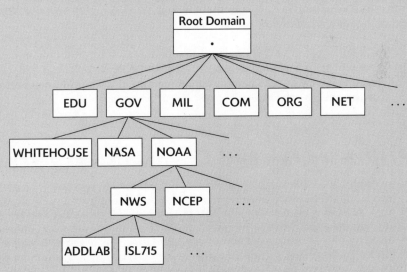

Figure 6-5: Part of the Internet Domain-Name Hierarchy.

For a commercial system in the COM domain, the name of a host might be as simple as REDHAT.COM. Of course, within REDHAT.COM you could have many subdomains such as FTP.REDHAT.COM, MAIL.REDHAT.COM, and so forth.

The convention for the email address of a user on a system is to append an at sign (@) to the user name (the name under which the user logs in) and then append the system's fully qualified domain name. Thus, refer to the user named webmaster at the host gao.gov as webmaster@GAO.GOV (unlike hostnames, user names are case sensitive).

TCP/IP network applications resolve a hostname to an IP address by consulting a name server, which is another host that's accessible from your network. If you decide to use the Domain Name System (DNS) on your network, you have to set up a name server in your network or indicate a name server (by an IP address).

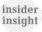

cross ref Later sections of this chapter discuss the configuration files /etc/host.conf and /etc/resolv.conf, through which you specify how hostnames are converted to IP addresses. In particular, you specify the IP addresses of a name server in the /etc/resolv.conf file.

If you do not use DNS, you still can have host name-to-IP address mapping through a text file named /etc/hosts. The entries in a typical /etc/hosts file might look like the following example:

```
# Lines like these are comments
# You must have the localhost line in /etc/hosts file
127.0.0.1        localhost.localdomain localhost
192.168.0.100    lnbp933  lnbp933.local.net
192.168.0.60     lnbp600
192.168.0.200    lnbp200  lnbp200.local.net
192.168.0.40     lnbp400  lnbp400.local.net
192.168.0.25     mac      lnbmac  lnbmac.local.net
```

As the example shows, the file lists a hostname for each IP address. The IP address and hostnames are different for your system, of course.

insider insight One problem with relying on the /etc/hosts file for name lookup is that you have to replicate this file on each system on your network. This procedure can become a nuisance even in a network that has only five or six systems.

TCP/IP Services and Client/Server Architecture

By design, a typical Internet service is implemented in two parts—a server that provides information and one or more clients that request information. Such client/server architecture has been gaining popularity as an approach for implementing distributed information systems. The client/server architecture typically consists of a collection of computers connected by a communication network. The functions of the information system are performed by processes (computer programs) that run on these computers and communicate through the network.

In recent years, the client/server architecture has become commonplace as the mechanism that brings the centralized corporate databases to desktop PCs on a network. In a client/server environment, one or more servers manage the centralized database and clients gain access to the data through the server.

Like a database server, an Internet service such as FTP or the Web also provides a service using the client/server model. A user who wants to access information uses a client (for example, a Web browser) to connect to a server and download information (for example, Web pages from a Web server). In this case, the Web server acts as a database manager—the data are the HTML files (Web pages).

insider insight   Client/server architecture requires clients to communicate with the servers. That's where TCP/IP comes in—TCP/IP provides a standard way for clients and servers to exchange packets of data. The next few sections explain how TCP/IP-based services communicate. From this discussion, you learn about the port numbers associated with many well-known Internet services.

Understanding TCP/IP and Sockets

Client/server applications such as Web servers and browsers use TCP/IP to communicate. These Internet applications perform TCP/IP communications using the Berkeley Sockets interface (so named because the socket interface was introduced in Berkeley UNIX around 1982). The sockets interface consists of a library of routines that an application developer can use to create applications that can communicate with other applications on the Internet. There is even a Windows Sockets API (application programming interface—a fancy name for a library of programming functions that can be called by C programs) modeled after the Berkeley Sockets interface. The Winsock interface, as it's known, provides a standard API that Windows programmers can use to write network applications.

Even if you do not write network applications using sockets, you have to use many network applications. Knowledge of sockets can help you understand how network-based applications work, which, in turn, helps you find and correct any problems with these applications.

Socket Definition

Network applications use sockets to communicate over a TCP/IP network. A socket is an abstraction that represents an endpoint of a connection. Because a socket is bidirectional, data can be sent as well as received through it. A socket has three attributes:

- The network address (the IP address) of the system
- The port number identifying the process (a process is a computer program running on a computer) that exchanges data through the socket
- The type of socket (such as stream or datagram) identifying the protocol for data exchange

Essentially, the IP address identifies a network node, the port number identifies a process on the node, and the socket type determines the manner in which data is exchanged—through a connection-oriented or connectionless protocol.

Connection-Oriented Protocols

The socket type indicates the protocol being used to communicate through the socket. A connection-oriented protocol works like a normal phone conversation. When you want to talk to your friend, you have to dial your friend's phone number and establish a connection before you can have a conversation. In the same way, connection-oriented data exchange requires both the sending and receiving processes to establish a connection before data exchange can begin.

In the TCP/IP protocol suite, TCP—Transmission Control Protocol—supports a connection-oriented data transfer between two processes running on two computers on the Internet. TCP provides a reliable two-way data exchange between processes.

As the name TCP/IP suggests (and as the "Network Protocols" section indicates), TCP relies on IP—Internet Protocol—for delivery of packets. IP does not guarantee delivery of packets, nor does it deliver packets in any particular sequence. IP does, however, efficiently deliver packets from one network to another. TCP is responsible for arranging the packets in the proper sequence, detecting whether or not errors have occurred, and requesting retransmission of packets in the case of an error.

TCP is useful for applications that plan to exchange large amounts of data at a time. In addition, applications that need reliable data exchange use TCP. For example, FTP uses TCP to transfer files.

In the sockets model, a socket that uses TCP is referred to as a *stream* socket because TCP provides an illusion of a continuous stream of data.

Connectionless Protocols

A connectionless data-exchange protocol does not require the sender and receiver to explicitly establish a connection. It's like shouting to your friend in a crowded room—you can't be sure if your friend hears you, and if you can't tell whether or not he or she heard you, after a certain amount of time, you shout again to see if he or she hears you.

In the TCP/IP protocol suite, the User Datagram Protocol (UDP) provides connectionless service for sending and receiving packets known as datagrams. Unlike TCP, UDP does not guarantee that datagrams ever reach their intended destination. Nor does UDP ensure that datagrams are delivered in the order they have been sent.

UDP is used by applications that exchange small amounts of data at a time or by applications that do not need the reliability and sequencing of data delivery. For example, SNMP (Simple Network Management Protocol) uses UDP to transfer data. UDP is generally used by applications where each message is largely self-contained so that even if some of the messages don't get through, it's not critical.

In the sockets model, a socket that uses UDP is referred to as a *datagram* socket.

Sockets and the Client/Server Model

It takes two sockets to complete a communication path. When two processes communicate, they use the client/server model to establish the connection. The server application listens on a specific port on the system—the server is completely identified by the IP address of the system where it runs and the port number where it listens for connections. The client initiates connection from any available port and tries to connect to the server (identified by the IP address and port number). Once the connection is established, the client and the server can exchange data according to their own protocol.

The sequence of events in sockets-based data exchanges depends on whether the transfer is connection oriented (TCP) or connectionless (UDP).

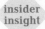

insider
insight

For a connection-oriented data transfer using TCP sockets, the server "listens" on a specific port, waiting for clients to request connection. Data transfer begins only after a connection is established. The server is a program that responds when a connection is attempted at a certain port.

For connectionless data transfers using UDP sockets, the server waits for a datagram to arrive at a specified port. The client does not wait to establish a connection; it simply sends a datagram to the server.

Performing Client/Server Communications with TCP/IP

Client/server applications use the following basic steps to exchange data in a TCP/IP network:

1. Create a socket. If the socket already exists, you can skip this step.
2. Bind an IP address and port to the socket.
3. Listen for connections if the application is a server using a stream socket.
4. Establish connection if the application is a client using a stream socket.
5. Exchange data.
6. Close the socket when done.

Connectionless sockets (that implement data transfer using UDP) do not require Steps 3 and 4.

Regardless of whether it's a server or a client, each application first creates a socket. Then it associates (binds) the socket with the local computer's IP address and a port number. The IP address identifies the machine (where the application is running), and the port number identifies the application using the socket.

Secret

Servers typically listen to a well-known port number so that clients can connect to that port to access the server. For a client application, the process of binding a socket to the IP address and port is the same as that for a server, but the client can use zero as the port number—the sockets library automatically uses an unused port number for the client.

For a connection-oriented stream socket, the communicating client and server applications have to establish a connection. The exact steps for establishing a connection depend on whether the application is a server or a client.

In the client/server model, the server has to be up and running before the client can run. After creating a socket and binding the socket to a port, the server application sets up a queue of connections, which determines how many clients can connect to the server. Typically, a server listens to anywhere from one to five connections. However, the size of the listen queue is one of the parameters you can adjust (especially for a Web server) to ensure that the server responds to as many clients as possible.

After setting up the listen queue, the server waits for a connection from a client.

continues

continued

Establishing the connection from the client side is somewhat simpler. After creating a socket and binding the socket to a network address, the client establishes connection with the server. To make the connection, the client needs to know the network name or IP address of the server, as well as the port on which the server accepts connections. As the next section shows, all Internet services have well-known standard port numbers.

After a client establishes connection to a server using a connection-oriented stream socket, the client and server can exchange data by calling appropriate sockets API functions. Like a conversation between two persons, the server and client alternately send and receive data—the meaning of the data depends on the message protocol the server and clients use. Usually, a server is designed for a specific task; inherent in that design is a message protocol that the server and clients use to exchange necessary data. For example, the Web server and the Web browser (client) communicate using HTTP.

Exploring Internet Services and Port Numbers

The TCP/IP protocol suite has become the lingua franca of the Internet because many standard services are available on all systems that support TCP/IP. These services make the Internet tick by enabling the transfer of mail, news, and Web pages. These services go by well-known names such as the following:

◆ **DHCP (Dynamic Host Configuration Protocol)** is for dynamically configuring TCP/IP network parameters on a computer. DHCP is primarily used to assign dynamic IP addresses and other networking information such as name server, default gateway, domain names that are needed to configure TCP/IP networks. The DHCP server listens on port 67.

◆ **FTP (File Transfer Protocol)** enables the transfer of files between computers on the Internet. FTP uses two ports—data is transferred on port 20, while control information is exchanged on port 21.

◆ **HTTP (HyperText Transfer Protocol)** is a recent protocol for sending HTML documents from one system to another. HTTP is the underlying protocol of the Web. By default, the Web server and client communicate on port 80.

◆ **SMTP (Simple Mail Transfer Protocol)** is for exchanging email messages between systems. SMTP uses port 25 for information exchange.

◆ **NNTP (Network News Transfer Protocol)** is for distribution of news articles in a store-and-forward fashion across the Internet. NNTP uses port 119.

◆ **Telnet** enables a user on one system to log in to another system on the Internet (the user must provide a valid user ID and password to log in to the remote system). Telnet uses port 23 by default. However, the Telnet client can connect to any specified port.

◆ **SNMP (Simple Network Management Protocol)** is for managing all types of network devices on the Internet. Like FTP, SNMP uses two ports: 161 and 162.

◆ **TFTP (Trivial File Transfer Protocol)** is for transferring files from one system to another (typically used by X terminals and diskless workstations to download boot files from another host on the network). TFTP data transfer takes place on port 69.

◆ **NFS (Network File System)** is for sharing files among computers. NFS uses Sun's Remote Procedure Call (RPC) facility, which exchanges information through port 111.

A well-known port is associated with each of these services. The TCP protocol uses this port to locate a service on any system. (A server process—a computer program running on a system—implements each service.)

Note that many applications use specific port ranges that are outside the typical list of well-known ports.

As with the /etc/hosts file, which stores the association between host names and IP addresses, the association between a service name and a port number (as well as a protocol) is stored in another text file, named /etc/services. Following is a small subset of lines from the /etc/services file in a Red Hat Linux system:

```
# /etc/services:
# $Id: services,v 1.32 2003/01/09 17:56:30 dwalsh Exp $
#
# Network services, Internet style
#
# Note that it is presently the policy of IANA to assign a single
# well-known port number for both TCP and UDP; hence, most
# entries here have two entries even if the protocol doesn't
# support UDP operations.
# Updated from RFC 1700, ``Assigned Numbers'' (October 1994).
# Not all ports are included, only the more common ones.
#
# The latest IANA port assignments can be gotten from
#       http://www.iana.org/assignments/port-numbers
# The Well Known Ports are those from 0 through 1023.
# The Registered Ports are those from 1024 through 49151
# The Dynamic and/or Private Ports are those from 49152
# through 65535.
#
# Each line describes one service, and is of the form:
#
# service-name  port/protocol  [aliases ...]   [# comment]
tcpmux          1/tcp      # TCP port service multiplexer
tcpmux          1/udp      # TCP port service multiplexer
ftp-data        20/tcp
ftp-data        20/udp
# 21 is registered to ftp, but also used by fsp
ftp             21/tcp
ftp             21/udp        fsp fspd
ssh             22/tcp                    # SSH Remote Login Protocol
ssh             22/udp                    # SSH Remote Login Protocol
telnet          23/tcp
telnet          23/udp
# 24 - private mail system
smtp            25/tcp        mail
smtp            25/udp        mail
... many lines deleted ...
```

You'll find browsing through the entries in the /etc/services file to be instructive because they show the breadth of networking services available under TCP/IP.

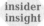

Note that port number 80 is designated for WWW service. In other words, if you set up a Web server on your system, that server listens to port 80. By the way, IANA—the Internet Assigned Numbers Authority (http://www.iana.org/)—is responsible for coordinating the assignment of port numbers below 1,024.

Running the xinetd Superserver

The client/server model requires that the server be up and running before a client makes a request for service. A simplistic idea would be to run all the servers and have them listen to their respective ports all the time. However, this idea is not practical because each server process would use up system resources in the form of memory and processor time. Besides, you don't really need all the services up and ready at all times. A smart solution to this problem is to run a single server, xinetd, which listens to all the ports, then starts the appropriate server when a client request comes in.

The xinetd server is a replacement for an older server named inetd but with improved accesses control and logging. The name xinetd stands for *extended* inetd. You can learn more about xinetd by visiting http://www.xinetd.org/.

Learning How xinetd Works

The xinetd server is designed to monitor the ports for the services it is configured to start. When a client requests connection to one of the monitored ports, xinetd starts the corresponding server. The client then directly communicates with that server while xinetd goes on to listening to the ports again. For example, when a client tries to connect to the Telnet port, xinetd starts the Telnet server and lets it communicate directly with the client (and the Telnet server exits when the client disconnects). xinetd also logs the connection requests in a log file based on settings in its configuration file.

Secret

The xinetd server is known as the Internet superserver because it starts various servers on demand. Typically, a Red Hat Linux system starts xinetd when the system boots. The xinetd server reads a configuration file named /etc/xinetd.conf at startup. This file tells xinetd which ports to listen to and what server to start for each port. The file can contain instructions that include other configuration files. In Red Hat Linux, the /etc/xinetd.conf file looks like the following:

```
#
# Simple configuration file for xinetd
#
# Some defaults, and include /etc/xinetd.d/

defaults
```

```
{
        instances               = 60
        log_type                = SYSLOG authpriv
        log_on_success          = HOST PID
        log_on_failure          = HOST
        cps                     = 25 30
}
```

```
includedir /etc/xinetd.d
```

Comment lines begin with the pound sign (#). The `defaults` block, enclosed in curly braces ({ . . . }) specifies default values for some attributes. These default values apply to all other services that `xinetd` is set up to start. The `instances` attribute is set to 60, which means there can be, at most, 60 servers simultaneously active for any service. The other attributes have the following meanings:

- The `log_type` attribute specifies how xinetd should log error or status information. In this case the `log_type` is `SYSLOG authpriv`, which means that xinetd will use the **SYSLOG** facility's `authpriv` log. The `/etc/syslog.conf` file defines the `authpriv` log as the file `/var/log/secure`. This means that the `/var/log/secure` file contains the logs for services started by xinetd.

- The `log_on_success` attribute tells xinetd what information to log when a server is started and when the server exits. In this case, the attribute is set to `HOST` and `PID`. The result is that if the startup of a service such as Telnet is successful, then xinetd logs the name of the remote host that has requested the service and the process ID of the Telnet server (that it starts). This setting for the `log_on_success` attribute results in entries in the `/var/log/secure` file of the following form:

  ```
  Feb  1 13:52:57 dhcppc7 xinetd[2241]: START: telnet pid=2627
  from=192.168.0.4
  ```

- The `log_on_failure` attribute tells xinetd what information to log when it cannot start a server. In this case, the attribute is set to `HOST`, which means that if xinetd cannot start a service such as Telnet, it logs the name of the remote host that requested the service.

- The `cps = 25 30` line tells xinetd to allow no more than 25 connections per second to a given service. If this limit is reached, the service is turned off for 30 seconds. Placing a limit such as this protects your system against denial of service attacks that attempts to overwhelm the system by requesting too many connections.

The last line in the `/etc/xinetd.conf` file uses the `includedir` directive to include all files inside the `/etc/xinetd.d` directory, excluding files whose names begin with a period (.). The idea is that the `/etc/xinetd.d` directory would contain all service configuration files—one file for each type of service the xinetd server is expected to manage. You should study the files in `/etc/xinetd.d` directory to see what services xinetd can start and how each service is configured. You can enable or disable a service by editing that service's configuration file in `/etc/xinetd.d` (you can also perform this task through the `chkconfig` command, as described in Chapter 22).

Here is the listing of files in the `/etc/xinetd.d` directory on a typical Red Hat Linux system:

```
ls /etc/xinetd.d
chargen        daytime-udp   imap    kotalk   rexec   servers   telnet
chargen-udp    echo          imaps   ktalk    rlogin  services  time
cups-lpd       echo-udp      ipop2   ntalk    rsh     sgi_fam   time-udp
daytime        finger        ipop3   pop3s    rsync   talk
```

Each file specifies the attributes for one service. As this listing shows, there are more than two dozen services that xinetd can start. Whether all the services are enabled or not, depends on the settings in each configuration file.

Understanding the xinetd Configuration Files

For example, the following listing shows the contents of the `/etc/xinetd.d/telnet` file, which specifies the `xinetd` configuration for the `telnet` service:

```
# description: The Telnet server serves Telnet sessions; it uses
#       unencrypted username/password pairs for authentication.
service telnet
{
        flags           = REUSE
        socket_type     = stream
        wait            = no
        user            = root
        server          = /usr/sbin/in.telnetd
        log_on_failure  += USERID
        disable         = yes
}
```

The filename (in this case, `telnet`) can be anything; what matters is the service name that appears next to the `service` keyword in the file. In this case, the line `service telnet` tells xinetd the name of the service. xinetd uses this name to look up the port number from the `/etc/services` file. If you use the `grep` command to look for `telnet` in the `/etc/services` file, here's what you'll find:

```
grep telnet /etc/services
telnet        23/tcp
telnet        23/udp
rtelnet       107/tcp                          # Remote Telnet
rtelnet       107/udp
telnets       992/tcp
telnets       992/udp
```

As the first two lines that begin with `telnet` show, the port number of the Telnet service is 23. This tells xinetd to listen to port 23 for Telnet service requests.

The attributes in the `/etc/xinetd.d/telnet` file, enclosed in curly braces, have the following meanings:

     ✦ The `flags` attribute provides specific instructions about how to run the servers that xinetd starts. The `REUSE` flag means that the service is left running even if xinetd is restarted. Note that the `REUSE` flag is now implicitly assumed to be set for all services.

     ✦ The `socket_type` attribute is set to `stream`, which tells xinetd that the Telnet service uses a connection-oriented TCP socket to communicate with the client.

For services that use the connectionless UDP sockets, this attribute would be set to `dgram`.

♦ The `wait` attribute is set to `no`, which tells xinetd to start a new server for each request. If this attribute is set to `yes`, xinetd waits until the server exits before starting the server again.

♦ The `user` attribute provides the user ID that xinetd uses to run the server. In this case, the server runs the Telnet server as `root`.

♦ The `server` attribute specifies the program to run for this service. In this case, xinetd runs the `/usr/sbin/in.telnetd` program to respond to requests for Telnet service.

♦ The `log_on_failure` attribute tells xinetd what information to log when it cannot start a server. In this case, the attribute appends the `USERID` flag to the default setting of `HOST` (set through the `defaults` block in the `/etc/xinetd.conf` file). The result is that if the Telnet service fails, xinetd logs the name of the remote host that requested the service as well as the user ID of the remote user.

♦ The `disable` attribute turns off the service if it's set to `yes`. By default the `disable` attribute is set to `yes` and Telnet is turned off.

Secret

The xinetd server uses the facilities of the `libwrap` library (called the *TCP wrapper*), which provides an access-control facility for Internet services. The TCP wrapper can start other services such as FTP and Telnet, but before starting the service, the wrapper consults the `/etc/hosts.allow` file to see if the host requesting service is allowed that service. If there is nothing in `/etc/hosts.allow` about that host, the TCP wrapper checks the `/etc/hosts.deny` file to see if the service should be denied. If both files are empty, the TCP wrapper allows the host access to the requested service. You can place the line `ALL:ALL` in the `/etc/hosts.deny` file to deny all hosts access to any Internet services, and then enable specfic hosts to access the services by listing them in the `/etc/hosts.allow` file (see the "/etc/hosts.allow" and "/etc/hosts.deny" sections to learn more about these access control files).

In addition to the access control provided by the TCP wrapper files—`/etc/hosts.allow` and `/etc/hosts.deny`—you can also control access to each service by using the following attributes in xinetd configuration files:

• *only_from* attribute specifies a list of IP addresses that are the only ones allowed to connect to the server. To deny all connections, use the following line:

```
only_from =
```

On the other hand, to allow access to all hosts in the 192.168.1.0 class C network, add the following line:

```
only_from = 192.168.1.0/24
```

• *no_access* attribute specifies the IP addresses of remote hosts that are not allowed to connect to xinetd services. For example, to deny access to the host with IP address 192.168.1.64, write:

```
no_access = 192.168.1.64
```

continues

continued

Browse through the files in the /etc/xinetd.d directory on your Red Hat Linux system to find out the kinds of services that xinetd is set up to start. By default nearly all of these services are turned off by setting the disable attribute to yes. You should leave them disabled, unless you need a service such as Telnet for your internal network.

If you need to connect to your Red Hat Linux system by using telnet and you get an error message, check the appropriate Telnet file in the /etc/xinetd.d directory and make sure the disable attribute it set to no or the disable line is commented out by placing a # at the beginning of the line. You can also turn the service on or off by using the chkconfig command. For example, to turn Telnet service on, type:

```
chkconfig telnet on
```

After you make any change to the xinetd configuration files or turn a service on or off, you must restart the xinetd server by typing the following command:

```
service xinetd restart
```

Starting Standalone Servers

Although starting servers through xinetd is a smart approach, xinetd is not efficient if a service has to be started very often. The Web server typically has to be started often because every time a user clicks on a link on a Web page, a request arrives at the Web server. For such high-demand services, it's best to start the server in a standalone manner. Such standalone servers are designed to run as daemons—processes that run continuously. That means the server listens on the assigned port; whenever a request arrives, the server handles it by making a copy of itself. In this way, the server keeps running forever. A more efficient strategy, used for Web servers, is to run multiple copies of the server and let each copy handle some of the incoming requests.

Secret

To help you manage standalone servers, Red Hat Linux includes scripts (called *initscripts*) in the /etc/init.d directory as well as symbolic links to enable execution of these scripts at various run levels (run levels are discussed in Chapter 20). You can log in as root and manage the standalone servers through the initscripts in the following ways:

- Use the service command to start, stop, or restart a server. The service command has the following syntax:

```
service <servicename> <action>
```

Here, <servicename> is the name of the service such as httpd for the Web server, sendmail for the mail server, and so on. The last field, <action>, must be one of start, stop, or restart with the obvious meaning—start runs the server, stop terminates it, and restart stops the server first and then runs it again. Typically, you must restart a server after you have made changes to the server's configuration file.

- Use the chkconfig command to set up a service to start automatically when the system boots into a run level. For example, to set up httpd to run in run levels 3 and 5, you would type:

```
chkconfig --level 35 httpd on
```

If a service is already set to start automatically at boot time, you can disable it with the following `chkconfig` command:

```
chkconfig --level 35 <servicename> off
```

where `<servicename>` is the name of the service that you want to turn off.

Note that services can typically be configured to run under xinetd or on a standalone basis. For example, prior to version 9, Red Hat Linux used to start the FTP service under control of xinetd. Starting with version 9, however, the Very Secure FTP server (`vsftpd`) is set up as a standalone server. Nowadays, if you need to start the FTP service, type **service vsftpd start**. To start the FTP service automatically at boot time, type **chkconfig vsftpd on.**

TCP/IP Setup in Linux

Like almost everything else in Linux, TCP/IP setup is a matter of preparing numerous configuration files (text files you can edit with any text editor). Most of these configuration files are in the `/etc` directory. The Red Hat installation program helps by hiding the details of the TCP/IP configuration files. Nevertheless, it's better if you know the names of the files and their purposes so that you can edit the files manually, if necessary.

> **cross ref**
>
> The next few sections show you how to set up TCP/IP for an Ethernet LAN. Chapter 13 covers dial-up networking under Linux, including topics such as PPP. Appendix D discusses physical set up of Ethernet networks and types of Ehternet cards supported by Linux.

Before you look at TCP/IP setup, make sure your system's Ethernet card is properly installed and detected by the Linux kernel. Also, you need to know the device names for the network devices.

Learning Network-Device Names

For most devices, Linux uses files in the `/dev` directory. The networking devices, however, have names defined internally in the kernel; no files for these devices exist in the `/dev` directory. Following are the common network-device names in Linux:

- **lo**—The loopback device. This device is used for efficient handling of network packets sent from your system to itself (when, for example, an X client communicates with the X server on the same system).
- **eth0**—The first Ethernet card or 802.11b wireless network card. If you have more Ethernet cards, they get device names `eth1`, `eth2`, and so on.
- **ppp0**—The first serial port configured for a point-to-point link to another computer, using Point-to-Point Protocol (PPP). If you have more serial ports configured for PPP networking, they are assigned device names `ppp1`, `ppp2`, and so on.
- **sl0**—The first serial port configured for Serial Line Internet Protocol (SLIP) networking. SLIP is used for establishing a point-to-point link to a TCP/IP network. If you use a second serial port for SLIP, it gets the device name `sl1`. SLIP is not used much anymore; it has been superseded by PPP.

You always have a loopback device (lo), whether or not you have a network. The loopback device passes data from one process to another without having to go out to a network. In fact, the whole point of the loopback device is to allow network applications to work, as long as the communicating processes are on the same system.

PPP is popular in dial-up networks, in which you use a modem to dial in to an Internet host (typically, a system at your work or your ISP) and establish a connection to the Internet. Chapter 13 covers this subject in detail.

If you want to see the names of installed network devices on your system, try the following command:

```
cat /proc/net/dev
```

This command shows the network-device names, as well as statistics on the number of packets sent and received for a specific device.

Using Red Hat's Network Configuration Tool

After you ensure that the Linux kernel is properly configured for TCP/IP, you have to make sure that the appropriate configuration files exist. Red Hat Linux includes a network configuration tool that enables you to configure various network interfaces on your system for TCP/IP networking. You can run the network configuration tool to add a new network interface or to alter information such as name servers and hostnames (you can also directly edit the configuration files listed in the "Using TCP/IP Configuration Files" section).

Log in as root and from the GNOME desktop, select Main Menu⇨Programs⇨System⇨ Network Configuration to run the Network Configuration tool. The Network Configuration tool displays a tabbed dialog box, as shown in Figure 6-6.

Figure 6-6: Configuring a TCP/IP Network with the Red Hat Network Configuration Tool.

You can configure various aspects of your network through the four tabs that appear along the top of the dialog box. Specifically, the tabs enable you to do the following:

- ◆ **Devices**—Lets you add a new network interface, specify the IP address of the interface, and activate the interface. This information is stored in various files in the /etc/sysconfig directory.
- ◆ **Hardware**— Lets you add a new hardware device such as an Ethernet card, modem, or an ISDN device. You can then provide information such as interrupt request (IRQ) and I/O port numbers, and DMA channels for the device.
- ◆ **DNS**—Lets you enter the hostname for your system and the IP addresses of name servers. The name server addresses are stored in the /etc/resolv.conf file. The host name is stored in the HOSTNAME variable in the /etc/sysconfig/ network file.
- ◆ **Hosts**—Shows you the current contents of the /etc/hosts file and lets you add, remove, or edit entries.

To configure the network interfaces, you need to assign IP addresses to each interface. If you are running a private network, you may use IP addresses in the range 192.168.0.0 to 192.168.255.255. (There are other ranges of addresses reserved for private networks, but this range should suffice for most needs.) For example, I use the 192.168.0.0 address for a small private network.

Testing the Network

After you run the Network Configuration tool, you may want to check whether or not the network is up and running. If you have not rebooted your system yet, you have to run /sbin/ifconfig to configure the Ethernet interface for your IP address. On a system whose IP address is 192.168.0.4, you would type the following command (you have to be logged in as root to do this):

```
/sbin/ifconfig eth0 192.168.0 netmask 255.255.255.0 broadcast 192.168.0.255
```

Now, you should use the ping utility program to verify whether or not another system on your network is accessible. You need the IP address of another system on the network to use ping. On my PC, I might try the following:

```
ping 192.168.0.1
PING 192.168.0.1 (192.168.0.1) from 192.168.0.2 : 56(84) bytes of data.
64 bytes from 192.168.0.1: icmp_seq=1 ttl=254 time=1.45 ms
64 bytes from 192.168.0.1: icmp_seq=2 ttl=254 time=1.35 ms
64 bytes from 192.168.0.1: icmp_seq=3 ttl=254 time=1.34 ms
64 bytes from 192.168.0.1: icmp_seq=4 ttl=254 time=1.35 ms
          (press Ctrl-C here)

--- 192.168.0.1 ping statistics ---
4 packets transmitted, 4 received, 0% loss, time 3006ms
rtt min/avg/max/mdev = 1.347/1.378/1.457/0.058 ms
```

If the ping command shows that other systems on your network are reachable, you can proceed to use other network programs, such as FTP and Telnet.

Using TCP/IP Configuration Files

Running the Red Hat network configuration tool may be enough to get TCP/IP configured on your system. You may want to be familiar with the configuration files, however, so that you can edit the files if necessary. For example, you can specify the name servers through the network configuration tool, but you may want to add an alternate name servers directly to the configuration file. To do so, you need to know about the /etc/resolv.conf file, which stores the IP addresses of name servers.

The following sections describe the basic TCP/IP configuration files.

/etc/hosts

The /etc/hosts text file contains a list of IP addresses and hostnames for your local network. In the absence of a name server, any network program on your system consults this file to determine the IP address that corresponds to a hostname.

Following is the /etc/hosts file from my system, showing the IP addresses and names of other hosts on my LAN:

```
# Lines like these are comments.
# You must have the localhost line in the /etc/hosts file.
127.0.0.1        localhost.localdomain localhost
192.168.0.100    lnbp933  lnbp933.local.net
192.168.0.60     lnbp600
192.168.0.200    lnbp200  lnbp200.local.net
192.168.0.40     lnbp400  lnbp400.local.net
192.168.0.25     mac      lnbmac  lnbmac.local.net
```

As the example shows, each line in the file starts with an IP address, followed by the hostname for that IP address. You can have more than one hostname for a given IP address.

/etc/networks

/etc/networks is another text file that contains the names and IP addresses of networks. These network names are commonly used in the routing command (/sbin/route) to specify a network by name instead of by its IP address.

Don't be alarmed if your Linux PC does not have the /etc/networks file. Your TCP/IP network works fine without this file. In fact, the Red Hat Linux installation program does not create a /etc/networks file.

/etc/host.conf

Linux uses a resolver library to obtain the IP address that corresponds to a hostname. The /etc/host.conf file specifies how names are resolved. A typical /etc/host.conf file might contain the following lines:

```
order hosts, bind
multi on
```

The entries in the /etc/host.conf file tell the resolver library what services to use (and in which order) to resolve names.

The order option indicates the order of services. The sample entry specifies that the resolver library should first consult the /etc/hosts file, then check the name server to resolve a name. In other words, this host.conf file says: "use static resolution prior to dynamic resolution."

The multi option determines whether or not a host in the /etc/hosts file can have multiple IP addresses. Hosts that have more than one IP address are called multihomed because the presence of multiple IP addresses implies that the host has several network interfaces (the host "lives" in several networks simultaneously).

/etc/resolv.conf

The /etc/resolv.conf file is another text file used by the resolver—a library that determines the IP address for a hostname. Following is a sample /etc/resolv.conf file:

```
domain local.net
nameserver 164.109.1.3
nameserver 164.109.10.23
```

The first line specifies your system's domain name. The nameserver line provides the IP addresses of name servers for your domain. If you have multiple name servers, you should list them on separate lines. They are queried in the order in which they appear in the file.

If you do not have a name server for your network, you can safely ignore this file. TCP/IP should still work, even though you may not be able to refer to hosts by name. You do, however, have to make sure that you have a /etc/host.conf file that is set up to use the /etc/hosts file.

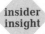

If your system gets its IP address from a DHCP server, the DHCP client also receives the IP addresses of name servers as well as the domain name from the DHCP service. In this case, the DHCP client automatically creates a /etc/resolv.conf file with the name server information it obtains from the DHCP server.

/etc/hosts.allow

This file specifies which hosts are allowed to use the Internet services such as Telnet running on your system. As explained in the section "Understanding the xinetd Configuration Files," the TCP wrapper consults the /etc/hosts.allow file before starting Internet services. It starts the service only if the entries in the hosts.allow file imply that the requesting host is allowed to use the services.

The entries in /etc/hosts.allow are in the form of a *server:IP address* format, where *server* refers to the name of the program providing a specific Internet service, and *IP address* identifies the host allowed to use that service. For example, if you want all hosts in your local network (which has the class C address 192.168.0.0) to access the Telnet service (which is provided by the in.telnetd program), add the following line in the /etc/hosts.allow file:

```
in.telnetd:192.168.0.
```

If you want to let all local hosts have access to all Internet services, you can use the ALL keyword and rewrite the line as follows:

```
ALL:192.168.0.
```

Finally, to open all Internet services to all hosts, you can replace the IP address with ALL, as follows:

```
ALL:ALL
```

You can also use host names in place of IP addresses.

insider insight **To learn the detailed syntax of the entries in the** /etc/hosts.allow **file, type** man hosts.allow **at the Linux shell prompt.**

/etc/hosts.deny

This file is just the opposite of /etc/hosts.allow—whereas hosts.allow specifies which hosts may access Internet services (such as TELNET and FTP) on your system, the hosts.deny file identifies the hosts that must be denied services. As explained in the section "Understanding the xinetd Configuration Files," the TCP wrapper consults the /etc/hosts.deny file if it does not find any rules in the /etc/hosts.allow file that apply to the requesting host. The TCP wrapper denies service if it finds in the hosts.deny file a rule that applies to the host.

The entries in /etc/hosts.deny file follow the same format as those in the /etc/hosts.allow file—they are in the form of a *server:IP address format*, where *server* refers to the name of the program providing a specific Internet service and *IP address* identifies the host allowed to use that service.

If you have already set up entries in the /etc/hosts.allow file to allow access to specific hosts, you can place the following line in /etc/hosts.deny to deny all other hosts access to any service on your system:

```
ALL:ALL
```

insider insight **To learn the detailed syntax of the entries in the** /etc/hosts.deny **file, type** man hosts.deny **at the Linux shell prompt.**

/etc/nsswitch.conf

This file, known as the name service switch (NSS) file, specifies how services, such as the name resolver library, NIS, NIS+, and local configuration files such as /etc/hosts and /etc/shadow, interact. Newer versions of Linux that use GNU C Library version 2 (glibc 2) or later rely on the /etc/nsswitch.conf file to determine what takes precedence: a local configuration file or a service such as DNS or NIS (see Chapter 18 to learn more about DNS and NIS).

As an example, the following hosts entry in the /etc/nsswitch.conf file specifies that the resolver library should first try the /etc/hosts file, then try NIS+, and finally try DNS:

```
hosts:      files nisplus dns
```

◆ **insider insight** You can learn more about the `/etc/nsswitch.conf` file by typing `info libc` "`Name Service Switch`" in a terminal window.

Configuring Networks at Boot Time

You want to start your network automatically every time you boot the system. For this to happen, you have to put the appropriate commands in one or more startup scripts. The init process runs immediately after Linux boots. The process consults the `/etc/inittab` file and executes various commands (typically, shell scripts), depending on the current run level. For example, in run level 3—the multiuser level—`/etc/inittab` specifies that init should run the script file `/etc/rc.d/rc` with the argument 3.

Secret

In run levels 3 and 5, the startup script ends up executing the `/etc/rc.d/init.d/network` script to activate all networking interfaces. If you consult the `/etc/rc.d/init.d/network file`, you will notice that network initialization is done by using another set of files in the `/etc/sysconfig` directory. The network activation script checks the variables defined in the `/etc/sysconfig/network` file to decide whether or not to activate the network. In `/etc/sysconfig/network`, you should see a line with the `NETWORKING` variable as follows:

```
NETWORKING=yes
```

The network is activated only if the `NETWORKING` variable is set to `yes`.

The `/etc/rc.d/init.d/network` script, in turn, executes a number of scripts in the `/etc/sysconfig/network-scripts` directory to activate specific network interfaces. For example, to activate the Ethernet interface eth0, the `/etc/sysconfig/network-scripts/ifup` script is executed with `/etc/sysconfig/network-scripts/ifcfg-eth0` as the configuration file. Here is what a typical `/etc/sysconfig/network-scripts/ifcfg-eth0` file contains:

```
DEVICE=eth0
IPADDR=192.168.0.200
NETMASK=255.255.255.0
BROADCAST=192.168.0.255
ONBOOT=yes
BOOTPROTO=none
```

As you can see, this file contains the network device name, as well as the IP address of the interface and several other TCP/IP parameters. The `ONBOOT` variable indicates whether this network interface should be activated when Linux boots. If your PC has an Ethernet card, you want to activate the interface at boot time; therefore, `ONBOOT` is set to `yes`.

The files in the `/etc/sysconfig` directory are created by the Red Hat Linux installation program as you install Linux and also by the Red Hat network configuration tool when you configure the network later on.

continues

continued

The `/etc/sysconfig/network-scripts/ifup` script essentially runs the following commands:

- `/sbin/ifconfig`, to configure the specified network interface; in this case, the Ethernet card (eth0)
- `/sbin/route`, to set up the routing table for the activated network interface

If you have PCMCIA network cards, those network interfaces are configured and activated by the `/etc/init.d/pcmcia` script, which, in turn, calls the `/etc/pcmcia/network` script. The `/etc/pcmcia/network` script then runs the `/etc/sysconfig/network-scripts/ifup` script to bring the interface up and `/etc/sysconfig/network-scripts/ifdown` script to bring the interface down.

TCP/IP Network Diagnostics

After you configure Ethernet and TCP/IP (during Red Hat Linux installation or by running netcfg later on), you should be able to use various networking applications without any problem. The TCP/IP protocol suite includes several tools that help you monitor and diagnose problems.

Looking at Network Interface Status

Use the `/sbin/ifconfig` command to view the currently configured network interfaces. The `ifconfig` command is used to configure a network interface (that is, to associate an IP address with a network device). If you run `ifconfig` without any command-line arguments, the command displays information about the current network interfaces. The following is a typical invocation of `ifconfig` and the resulting output:

```
/sbin/ifconfig
eth0      Link encap:Ethernet  HWaddr 02:60:8C:8E:C6:A9
          inet addr:192.168.0.4  Bcast:192.168.0.255  Mask:255.255.255.0
          UP BROADCAST NOTRAILERS RUNNING  MTU:1500  Metric:1
          RX packets:2738 errors:0 dropped:0 overruns:0 frame:0
          TX packets:1397 errors:0 dropped:0 overruns:0 carrier:0
          collisions:6
          RX bytes:638288 (623.3 Kb)  TX bytes:575658 (562.1 Kb)

lo        Link encap:Local Loopback
          inet addr:127.0.0.1  Mask:255.0.0.0
          UP LOOPBACK RUNNING  MTU:16436  Metric:1
          RX packets:48 errors:0 dropped:0 overruns:0 frame:0
          TX packets:48 errors:0 dropped:0 overruns:0 carrier:0
          collisions:0
          RX bytes:3148 (3.0 Kb)  TX bytes:3148 (3.0 Kb)
```

This output shows that two interfaces—the loopback interface (`lo`) and an Ethernet card (`eth0`)—are currently active on this system. For each interface, you can see the IP address, as well as statistics on packets delivered and sent. If the Red Hat Linux system had a dial-up PPP link up and running, you'd also see an item for the `ppp0` interface in the output.

Viewing the IP Routing Table

The other network configuration command, /sbin/route, also provides status information when it is run without any command-line argument. If you are having trouble checking a connection to another host (that you specify with an IP address), check the IP routing table to see whether a default gateway is specified. Then check the gateway's routing table to ensure that paths to an outside network appear in that routing table.

A typical output from the /sbin/route command looks like the following:

```
/sbin/route
Kernel IP routing table
Destination    Gateway       Genmask          Flags Metric Ref   Use Iface
192.168.0.0    *             255.255.255.0    U     0      0       0 eth0
127.0.0.0      *             255.0.0.0        U     0      0       0 lo
default        192.168.0.1   0.0.0.0          UG    0      0       0 eth0
```

As this routing table shows, the local network uses the eth0 Ethernet interface, and the default gateway is also that Ethernet interface. The default gateway is a routing device that handles packets addressed to any network, other than the one in which the Linux system resides. In this example, packets addressed to any network address other than ones that begin with 192.168.0 are sent to the gateway—192.168.0.1. The gateway forwards those packets to other networks (assuming, of course, that the gateway is connected to another network).

Checking Connectivity to a Host

To check for a network path to a specific host, use the ping command. Ping is a widely used TCP/IP tool that uses a series of Internet Control Message Protocol (ICMP, often pronounced as *eye-comp*) messages. (ICMP provides for an Echo message to which every host responds.) Using the ICMP messages and replies, Ping can determine whether or not the other system is alive and can compute the round-trip delay in communicating with that system.

The following example shows how I run Ping to see whether or not one of the systems on my network is alive:

```
ping 192.168.0.1
PING 192.168.0.1 (192.168.0.1) from 192.168.0.4 : 56(84) bytes of data.
64 bytes from 192.168.0.1: icmp_seq=0 ttl=254 time=2.116 msec
64 bytes from 192.168.0.1: icmp_seq=1 ttl=254 time=1.770 msec
64 bytes from 192.168.0.1: icmp_seq=2 ttl=254 time=1.759 msec
64 bytes from 192.168.0.1: icmp_seq=3 ttl=254 time=1.778 msec

--- 192.168.0.1 ping statistics ---
4 packets transmitted, 4 packets received, 0% packet loss
round-trip min/avg/max/mdev = 1.759/1.855/2.116/0.159 ms
```

In Red Hat Linux, Ping continues to run until you press Ctrl+C to stop it, then it displays summary statistics showing the typical time it takes to send a packet between the two systems. On some systems, Ping simply reports that a remote host is alive. However, you can still get the timing information with appropriate command-line arguments.

You can also use the traceroute command to check connectivity to a host and more. The traceroute command prints the route that packets take from your system to another system on the Internet. For example, here is an example of using `traceroute` to print the route from a system to `www.noaa.gov`:

```
traceroute www.noaa.gov
traceroute to www.noaa.gov (192.64.69.81), 30 hops max, 38 byte packets
 1  192.168.0.1 (192.168.0.1)  1.509 ms  1.431 ms  4.980 ms
 2  10.75.216.1 (10.75.216.1)  11.286 ms  11.882 ms  9.594 ms
 3  172.30.103.65 (172.30.103.65)  11.734 ms  10.752 ms  9.883 ms
 4  172.30.103.131 (172.30.103.131)  10.438 ms  10.372 ms  14.481 ms
 5  172.30.100.186 (172.30.100.186)  11.101 ms  11.662 ms  12.423 ms
 6  68.48.0.174 (68.48.0.174)  10.901 ms  9.610 ms  9.946 ms
 7  12.126.168.5 (12.126.168.5)  11.715 ms  11.852 ms  11.880 ms
 8  * * *
 9  ggr1-p3100.wswdc.ip.att.net (12.122.11.238)  12.151 ms  12.659 ms  11.249 ms
10  dca-brdr-02.inet.qwest.net (205.171.1.137)  16.740 ms  28.900 ms  15.532 ms
11  dca-core-02.inet.qwest.net (205.171.9.57)  17.833 ms  14.777 ms  16.378 ms
12  dca-edge-03.inet.qwest.net (205.171.9.62)  17.521 ms  17.292 ms  17.737 ms
13  65.125.14.202 (65.125.14.202)  16.435 ms  15.841 ms  15.776 ms
14  140.90.76.106 (140.90.76.106)  15.904 ms  16.826 ms  17.882 ms
15  140.90.111.36 (140.90.111.36)  18.668 ms  17.289 ms  16.816 ms
16  rainbow.hpcc.noaa.gov (192.64.69.81)  17.532 ms  19.369 ms  19.142 ms
```

Checking Network Status

To check the status of the network, use the `netstat` command. This command displays the status of network connections of various types (such as TCP and UDP connections). You can view the status of the interfaces quickly with the `-i` option, as follows:

```
netstat -i
Kernel Interface table
Iface   MTU Met RX-OK RX-ERR RX-DRP RX-OVR   TX-OK TX-ERR TX-DRP TX-OVR Flg
eth0   1500   0  2963      0      0      0    1531      0      0      0 BNRU
lo    16436   0    48      0      0      0      48      0      0      0 LRU
```

In this case, the output shows the current status of the loopback and Ethernet interfaces. Table 6-1 describes the meanings of the columns.

Table 6-1: Columns in the Kernel Interface Table

Column	Meaning
Iface	Name of the interface
MTU	Maximum Transfer Unit—the maximum number of bytes that a packet can contain
RX-OK, TX-OK	Number of error-free packets received (RX) or transmitted (TX)
RX-ERR, TX-ERR	Number of packets with errors
RX-DRP, TX-DRP	Number of dropped packets

Column	Meaning
RX-OVR, TX-OVR	Number of packets lost due to overflow
Flg	A = receive multicast; B = broadcast allowed; D = debugging turned on; L = loopback interface (notice the flag on lo); M = all packets received; N = trailers avoided; O = no ARP on this interface; P = point-to-point interface; R = interface is running; U = interface is up.

Another useful `netstat` option is `-t`, which shows all active TCP connections. Following is a typical result of `netstat -t` on one of my Linux PCs:

```
netstat -t
Active Internet connections (w/o servers)
Proto Recv-Q Send-Q Local Address        Foreign Address        State
tcp       0      0 dhcppc3:ftp          192.168.0.2:1454       ESTABLISHED
tcp       0      0 dhcppc3:ftp-data     192.168.0.2:1455       TIME_WAIT
tcp       0    138 dhcppc3:telnet       192.168.0.2:1250       ESTABLISHED
tcp       0      0 dhcppc3:1054         ftp25c.newaol.com:ftp  ESTABLISHED
tcp       0      1 dhcppc3:1055         ftp25c.newaol.com:59095 LAST_ACK
```

In this case, the output columns show the protocol (`Proto`), the number of bytes in the receive and transmit queues (`Recv-Q`, `Send-Q`), the local TCP port in *hostname:service* format (`Local Address`), the remote port (`Foreign Address`), and the state of the connection.

insider insight

If you want `netstat` to display all addresses in numeric format, use the `-n` option of `netstat`, like this:

```
netstat -tn
```

Many of us prefer the numeric address format because the output looks cleaner and `netstat` does not have to figure out the name corresponding to each address.

Using the ip Command

The Linux kernel comes with a powerful IP routing engine together with an `ip` command that looks similar to the command with the same name that Cisco IOS supports (Cisco IOS is the operating system that runs on Cisco routers). You can use the `ip` command to manage or get information about network objects. The general syntax of the `ip` command is as follows:

```
ip [options] OBJECT [command [arg1 arg2 ...]]
```

where `options` are flags that modify the behavior of the command, `OBJECT` is the network object you want to manage or view, and `command` is the action you want to perform. The command may take zero or more arguments, as indicated by `arg1`, `arg2`, `...` in the syntax.

The objects you can manage or view with the ip command are the following:

- **link**—Refers to network devices such as eth0 and ppp0
- **address**—Refers to the IP or IPv6 address of a network device
- **neighbor**—Refers to an entry in the Address Resolution Protocol (ARP) that associates an IP address to a physical Ethernet address
- **route**—Refers to entries in the routing table
- **rule**—Refers to rules in the routing policy database
- **maddress**—Refers to multicast address
- **mroute**—Refers to entries in the multicast routing cache
- **tunnel**—Refers to a tunnel over IP

To view information about the network interfaces, use the following ip command:

```
ip address show
1: lo: <LOOPBACK,UP> mtu 16436 qdisc noqueue
    link/loopback 00:00:00:00:00:00 brd 00:00:00:00:00:00
    inet 127.0.0.1/8 brd 127.255.255.255 scope host lo
2: eth0: <BROADCAST,MULTICAST,UP> mtu 1500 qdisc pfifo_fast qlen 100
    link/ether 00:08:74:e5:eb:56 brd ff:ff:ff:ff:ff:ff
    inet 192.168.0.7/24 brd 192.168.0.255 scope global eth0
```

This tells you that the eth0 interface is associated with the inet address 192.168.0.7/24. The /24 stands for the number of bits that are in the network address. There are 32 bits, of which 24 are network address, so there are 8 bits left for the hosts in this network.

To see routes, type **ip route show**. Here is a typical example of the output of that command:

```
192.168.0.0/24 dev eth0   proto kernel   scope link   src 192.168.0.7
169.254.0.0/16 dev eth0   scope link
127.0.0.0/8 dev lo   scope link
default via 192.168.0.1 dev eth0
```

You can try out ip to view the other network objects, but the greatest power of ip is in configuring the network objects to turn your Linux system into a sophisticated router.

---

insider insight

The ip **command's capabilities are too extensive to cover in this chapter. To learn more about the** ip **command and what you can do with it, visit** http://www.ibiblio.org/ pub/Linux/docs/HOWTO/Adv-Routing-HOWTO, **and consult the documentation in** /usr/share/doc/iproute* **directory of your Red Hat Linux system.**

Summary

Linux has extensive built-in support for TCP/IP and Ethernet networks. This chapter explained the basics of TCP/IP networking and showed you how to set up TCP/IP networking on your Linux PC.

By reading this chapter, you learned the following things:

♦ The OSI seven-layer model provides a framework for making various networks work together. The OSI layered model also sets the stage for various networking protocols.

♦ The Transmission Control Protocol and Internet Protocol (TCP/IP) originated from research the U.S. Government's Advanced Research Projects Agency (ARPA) initiated in the 1970s. The modern Internet evolved from the networking technology developed during that time.

♦ All Internet protocols are documented in Requests for Comments (RFC) documents. The RFCs are available from the Internet resource `http://www.cis`
`.ohio-state.edu/hypertext/information/rfc.html.` or `http://www.faqs`
`.org/rfcs/.` All Internet standards are in RFCs, but many RFCs simply provide information to the Internet community.

♦ Internetworking is at the heart of the TCP/IP protocol; that is the purpose of the Internet Protocol. The TCP/IP protocol identifies a host by using a 32-bit IP address that has two parts: a network address and a host address.

♦ Typically, an IP address is expressed in dotted-decimal notation, in which each byte's value is written in decimal format and separated from the adjacent byte by a dot (.). A typical IP address is 132.250.112.52.

♦ IP addresses are grouped in classes. Class A addresses use a 1-byte network address and 3 bytes for the host address, class B addresses use a 2-byte network and host address, and class C addresses use a 3-byte network address and a single byte for the host address. The values of the first byte indicate the type of address: 1–126 are class A, 128–191 are class B, and 192–223 are class C.

♦ The IP address space is filling rapidly. To alleviate this problem, the Internet Engineering Task Force has adopted a new 16-byte (128-bit) addressing scheme known as IPv6 (or IP Version 6). Hosts that use the new IPv6 addresses will work with hosts that use the older IPv4 (32-bit) addresses.

♦ The use of private IP addresses (as specified by RFC 1918) and Classless Inter-Domain Routing (CIDR) are interim, but proven, approaches to manage the diminishing IPv4 address pool.

♦ Setting up TCP/IP on Linux requires setting up various configuration files. The Red Hat network-configuration tool provides a convenient way to set up these files. You need some information—such as an IP address, the address of a gateway, and the address of a name server—to set up TCP/IP networking on your system. If you do not plan to connect your local network to the Internet, you can use a range of IP addresses (such as 192.168.0.0 to 192.168.255.255) without having to coordinate with any organization.

♦ Linux comes with many TCP/IP utilities, such as FTP (File Transfer Protocol) and Telnet (for logging in to another system on the network).

♦ To diagnose TCP/IP networking problems, you can use the `ifconfig`, `ping`, `route`, and `netstat` commands. You can also use the `ip` command to view as well as manage network objects such as interfaces, addresses, and routing table entries.

Part II

Exploring Red Hat Linux

Red Hat Linux Basics

Chapter
7

♦ ♦

Secrets in This Chapter

♦ ♦

Now that you have installed Red Hat Linux from this book's companion CD-ROMs, you are ready to explore and learn the basics of Red Hat Linux. This chapter shows you how to log in, log out, and shut down your Linux system. Then, you power up again and learn about Linux commands.

Although Red Hat Linux comes with the GNOME and KDE graphical user interfaces (GUIs), you can't do everything from the graphical environment. It's not impossible to design a graphical interface that enables you to perform most chores, but sometimes you may have to perform system-administration tasks when the graphical environment is not available. You may be logged in through a terminal session, or you may have problems with X. In such cases, you have to use Linux commands to accomplish specific tasks.

This chapter also shows you how to work with files and directories in Red Hat Linux. To use files and directories, you need to understand the concept of a hierarchical file system. The chapter provides a quick introduction to the Linux file system. Then, you learn to explore the file system with the Nautilus graphical shell. Finally, you learn several Linux commands that you can use to work with files and directories.

Starting Red Hat Linux for the First Time

After the installation is complete, the Red Hat Linux installation program automatically reboots the system. The PC goes through its normal power-up sequence and loads the boot loader—GRUB or LILO, depending on which one you selected when you installed Red Hat Linux. A graphical screen appears with the names of the partitions the boot loader can boot. You can press the up and down arrow keys to select the partition from which the system should boot. When you installed the boot loader, if you specified the Linux partition as the default one, you can simply wait; after a few seconds, Red Hat Linux starts.

Controlling Linux with Boot Parameters

Before you select a partition to boot, you can get a text-mode prompt from the bootloader and enter other commands. If you use LILO as the boot loader, press Ctrl-X and you get the following prompt:

```
LILO boot:
```

You can view the names of the available bootable partitions by pressing the Tab key. For example, a typical result of pressing Tab might be the following:

```
linux windows
```

Then, you can type the name of the partition from which LILO should boot.

Secret

Sometimes you need the text-mode LILO boot prompt so that you can specify boot-time arguments that LILO passes to the Linux kernel. For example, if you want to mount your root file system read-only so that you can run the file system consistency checking program (called fsck), you can specify this by typing the following line in response to the LILO boot prompt:

```
linux ro
```

Note that after you boot your Linux system with the root file system mounted read-only, no processes can write to the file system until you remount the file system again with the `mount -w -n -o remount /` command.

If you use GRUB as the bootloader, press a when the GRUB screen appears. This causes GRUB to prompt you for commands to add to its default boot command (which, I assume, is set to boot Red Hat Linux). Then, you can type anything else you want to add to that command. For example, to boot the system into single user mode, press the Spacebar and type:

```
single
```

You can pass many more parameters to the Linux kernel. To learn the kernel boot parameters, type **man bootparam** in a terminal window (after you boot Linux).

After Linux starts, you should see a long list of opening messages, including the names of the devices that Linux detects. One of the messages says `Calibrating delay loop...` `xxx.xx BogoMIPS`, where `xxx.xx` is some number. BogoMIPS is one of those words that confound new Linux users.

insider insight

As you may know, MIPS is an acronym for millions of instructions per second—a measure of how fast your computer runs programs. As such, MIPS is not a very good measure of performance because comparing the MIPS of different types of computers is difficult. *BogoMIPS* is bogus MIPS, which refers to an indication of the computer's speed. Linux uses the BogoMIPS number to calibrate a delay loop, in which the computer processes some instructions repeatedly until a specified amount of time has passed.

The BogoMIPS numbers can range anywhere from 1 to 3,000 or more, depending on the type of processor (386, 486, or Pentium). An older 33MHz 80386DX system has a BogoMIPS of about 6, whereas a 66MHz 80486DX2/66 system shows a BogoMIPS of about 33. The BogoMIPS for newer Pentium systems is much higher. For example, on an old 200MHz Pentium MMX system, Linux reports a BogoMIPS of 398.13. However, on a laptop with a 1.5GHz Celeron processor, the BogoMIPS is 2,971.18. It's higher yet on more recent 3GHz or better Pentium 4 systems.

Configuring for the First Time with Firstboot

If you are booting Red Hat Linux for the first time after installation, a server named first-boot runs and displays a welcome screen about setting up Red Hat Linux. The firstboot server (Red Hat calls it the Red Hat Setup Agent) takes you through date and time setup, gives you a chance to register with Red Hat Network, and install any additional CDs.

caution
If the screen goes dark and there is no activity, the first-time configuration utility may be having trouble starting the X Window System. Unfortunately, you cannot proceed any further without fixing this problem. Sometimes the graphical environment fails even though the graphical interface seems to work fine during installation. There are ways to fix this problem. Go to Chapter 2 for more information on how to troubleshoot this problem.

The Red Hat Setup Agent takes you through the following steps (you can skip these steps if you want)

1. Set the date and time from a GUI screen. If your system is connected to the Internet, click the check box labeled Enable Network Time Protocol and then select a server from the drop-down list labeled Server. This way, the system is going to get its time directly from one of the superaccurate time servers on the Internet using the Network Time Protocol (NTP). After setting the date and time, click Forward.

2. The Red Hat Setup Agent then prompts you if you want to register with Red Hat Network. To register, click Forward and respond to the requested information. After that step is done, click Forward again.

3. The Red Hat Setup Agent displays a window from which you can install additional CDs. If you have additional CDs to install, click the appropriate icon. Otherwise, click Forward.

Secret

When you're done with the Red Hat Setup Agent you're really done for good because it is set to run only once when you boot for the first time. If, for some reason, you want to go through these steps again, you can run the firstboot server again. Log in as `root`, and type the following command in a terminal window (to open a terminal window select Main Menu⇨System Tools⇨Terminal):

```
rm /etc/sysconfig/firstboot
chkconfig --level 5 firstboot on
```

That's it! Next time you reboot the PC, firstboot should run again. If you want to run firstboot interactively from GNOME or KDE, you can do so by logging in as `root` and typing the following commands in a terminal window:

```
rm /etc/sysconfig/firstboot
firstboot
```

Logging in at Graphical Login Screen

On first-time boot, you get the graphical login screen after you're through with the Red Hat Setup Agent. At other times, you would first see the boot messages, and at the end of all the messages, if all goes well, you get a graphical login screen, such as the one shown in Figure 7-1.

Figure 7-1: Graphical Login Screen in Red Hat Linux.

Secret

You won't get a graphical login screen if your system is set for text-mode login or if there is something wrong with your X Window System setup. If you get a text-mode login screen, log in as usual and then you can configure X or switch to a graphical login. First check the runlevel with the following command:

```
runlevel
```

If you see a response with the number 3, then your system is set for text-mode login. You can enter graphical login with the following command

```
telinit 5
```

On the other hand, if the output of runlevel contains the number 5, then there may be something wrong with the X setup. You should consult Chapter 3 for more information on how to set up X.

continues

continued

If you get the graphical login screen, a login window in the middle of the screen displays a welcome message with your system's hostname—the name you assign to your system when you configure the network. If the network is not configured, localhost.localdomain is the hostname. If you use DHCP to configure the network, the DHCP server provides a hostname for your system. The login window also has a text input field that prompts you for your user name.

You can log in using any of the accounts you define during the installation, including root. For example, to log in as root, type **root** in the first text field, and press Enter (move the mouse over the login dialog box before you begin typing). Then, type the root password (the one you set during installation) to log in as the super user.

Because the default GUI is GNOME, the GNOME desktop appears, as shown in Figure 7-2. As you can see, the desktop is similar to the Windows desktop. Now, you can perform a few initial chores and learn how to shut down your Red Hat Linux system.

Figure 7-2: Initial GNOME Desktop.

Take a moment to look at the initial GNOME desktop as it appears in Figure 7-2. The GNOME desktop is very much like the Windows desktop. The GNOME Panel—similar to the Windows taskbar—appears along the bottom edge of the screen. You can access various menus and launch applications from the GNOME Panel. The Panel also contains such applets as the Clock, which displays the time in a small area at the right edge of the Panel.

cross ref You learn more about the GNOME desktop in Chapter 9. For now, all you need to know is that the red hat icon at the left edge of the GNOME Panel is the Main Menu button. This button is like the Start button in Microsoft Windows. You can access many programs from the Main Menu button (the red hat icon). You can also start some programs by clicking the icons on the Panel. For example, to start the Mozilla Web browser, click the earth-and-mouse icon on the Panel.

The following sections show you how to log out of and shut down your Red Hat Linux system.

Logging Out

Now that you have seen how to log in, you should learn how to log out. To log out, select Main Menu (the red hat icon)⇨Log Out. The screen is grayed out, and a dialog box asks you if you really want to log out. Click the OK button to log out.

cross ref After a few moments, the graphical login screen (refer to Figure 7-1) appears again so that another user can log in and use the system. The graphical login window is displayed by a display manager such as xdm (X Display Manager), gdm (GNOME Display Manager), or kdm (KDE Display Manager). You learn more about the display managers and configuration of the graphical logins in Chapter 9.

Shutting Down Linux

When you are ready to shut down Red Hat Linux, you should do so in an orderly manner. Even if you are the sole user of a Linux system, several other programs are usually running in the background. In addition, operating systems such as Linux try to optimize the way in which they write data to the disk. Because disk access is relatively slow (compared with the time needed to access memory locations), data usually is held in memory and written to the disk in large chunks. Therefore, if you simply turn the power off, you run the risk that some files will not be updated properly.

Any user (you do not have to be logged in as root) can shut down the system from the GNOME desktop. The Logout dialog box provides the options for rebooting or halting the system. To shut down the system, simply select Shutdown, and click OK. The system then shuts down in an orderly manner.

caution Note that it does not require root access to shutdown or reboot the system in this manner. This is why you need to make sure that physical access to the console is protected adequately.

As the system shuts down, you see messages about processes being shut down. You may be surprised how many processes there are, even though no one is explicitly running any programs on the system. If your system does not automatically power off on shut down, you can manually turn the power off.

Secret

If you are already logged in as root, you can use the shutdown command to halt or reboot the system. If you are already logged in using another user name, you can become the super user by typing the following command (your input is shown in boldface; my comments are in italic):

```
su -
Password:    (type the root password and press Enter)
```

When you become root by typing su - (instead of su alone), you also get root's environment, including settings such as the PATH environment variable. This enables you to run many system utilities without having to explicitly specify their path.

After you become a super user, type the following command to halt the system:

```
shutdown -h now
```

After a few moments, you see many more messages about processes being stopped. On older systems, you see a message about the system's being halted. You can then turn the power off. On newer systems, the shutdown process also turns the power off.

If you want to reboot the system instead of halting it, use the shutdown command with the -r option, as follows:

```
/sbin/shutdown -r now
```

On the other hand, you can also simply type **reboot** to restart the system.

Looking up Online Documentation

You should familiarize yourself with an important source of information in Red Hat Linux. Every so often, you see instructions that ask you to enter a Linux command. After a while, you are bound to get to the point at which you vaguely recall a command's name, but you cannot remember the exact syntax of what you are supposed to type. This is a situation in which the Linux online manual pages can come to your rescue.

insider insight

To try out the commands described in this section, you have to open a terminal window in GNOME. Select Main Menu⇨System Tools⇨Terminal (refer to Figure 7-2). This opens a terminal window in which you can type Linux commands.

You can view the manual page—commonly referred to as the *man page*—for a command by using the man command. (You do have to remember that command to access online help.) For example, to view the man page for the modprobe command, type the following command in a terminal window:

```
man modprobe
```

The man command then displays the help information page by page. Press the Spacebar to move to the next page. Press b to move backward by a page. To look for a specific word in the man page, press the forward slash, type the word, and press Enter. For example, to search for the word "debug," type **/debug**, and press Enter. When you finish reading the man page, press q to return to the Linux command prompt.

Having touted the usefulness of the online help pages, I must point out that the term Linux command refers to any executable file, ranging from a script file that contains other Linux commands to standard Linux executable programs. Although man pages exist for most standard programs, many programs do not have any online help. Nevertheless, whenever you are having difficulty recalling some command, it is worthwhile to use the man command to see whether any online help for that command exists.

If you do not want to read the full man page, you can use whatis to read a one-line summary of a command. For example, here's how you use whatis to see a brief description of the modprobe command:

```
whatis modprobe
modprobe                (8)  - high level handling of loadable module
```

The number (8) indicates the man page section where the modprobe command is listed. You should try the whatis command to view one-line descriptions of a few other commands.

You can use the shell's wildcard feature and the whatis command to explore the files in various system directories such as /bin, /sbin, /usr/sbin, /usr/bin, and so on. Simply change the directory to one of interest and type **whatis *** to view one-line descriptions of the programs in that directory. (whatis displays information for those programs for which such information is available.) For example, here is how you can explore the /sbin directory:

```
cd /sbin; whatis * | more
addpart: nothing appropriate
adsl-connect        (8)  - Shell script to manage a PPPoE link
adsl-setup          (8)  - Shell script to configure Roaring Penguin PPPoE clie
nt
adsl-start          (8)  - Shell script to bring up a PPPoE link
adsl-status         (8)  - Shell script to report on status of PPPoE link
adsl-stop           (8)  - Shell script to shut down a PPPoE link
agetty              (8)  - alternative Linux getty
arp                 (7)  - Linux ARP kernel module
arp                 (8)  - manipulate the system ARP cache
arping              (8)  - send ARP REQUEST to a neighbour host
arytst: nothing appropriate
avmcapictrl         (8)  - Add, reset or remove active AVM cards and load firmw
are
badblocks           (8)  - search a device for bad blocks
blockdev            (8)  - call block device ioctls from the command line
capiinit: nothing appropriate
cardctl             (8)  - PCMCIA card control utility
cardmgr             (8)  - PCMCIA device manager
chkconfig           (8)  - updates and queries runlevel information for system
services
clock               (3)  - Determine processor time
... rest of the output not shown ...
```

As you can see, the output is an alphabetic list of all programs in the current directory, along with the one-line descriptions where available. The whatis command displays a message saying nothing appropriate if there is no information available for a program.

The man and whatis commands are useful when you know the name of a command. If you do not know the exact name of a command, you can use the apropos command to search for a command by a keyword (or even a part of a word). For example, if you remember that the command contains the word probe, type the following apropos command to search:

```
apropos probe
modprobe              (8)  - high level handling of loadable modules
partprobe             (8)  - inform the OS of partition table changes
scanpci              (1x)  - scan/probe PCI buses
```

In this case, the search result shows three candidate commands, each with a brief description. You can then select the command that does what you want to do.

insider insight   If apropos **displays a long list of commands that scroll by too fast for you to read, you can type** apropos keyword | more **to view the output one screen at a time.**

Another form of online documentation you can refer to are the HOWTO files, which you can access by visiting the Linux Documentation Project (LDP) website http://www. redhat.com/mirrors/LDP/. (Click the earth icon on the GNOME Panel to launch the Mozilla Web browser.) On that Web page, you find (among other things) links to Frequently Asked Questions (FAQs) and HOWTOs. You can click the HOWTOs link and download (or read) HOWTO documents in several formats, including text and HTML. For example, if you click to view plain-text HOWTOs, the Web browser shows a list of HOWTO files.

Each HOWTO file contains information about some area of Linux, such as the hardware it supports or how to create a boot disk. As you scroll through the list, you find over 230 HOWTO files. Table 7-1 lists and briefly describes some of these HOWTO files. To view any of these files, click the name; the Web browser should display the full text file.

insider insight   Near the beginning of the list of HOWTO files, you find a folder named mini. **Click that link to view a list of mini-HOWTOs, which cover many more narrowly focused topics.**

Table 7-1: Some Linux HOWTO Files

HOWTO Filename	*Contents*
ADSL-Bandwidth-Management-HOWTO	How to configure a Linux router to more effectively manage outbound traffic on an ADSL modem or cable modem
ATA-RAID-HOWTO	How to install Linux on an Intel Pentium–compatible PC with an ATA RAID Controller and at least two hard disks
AX25-HOWTO	How to install and configure Linux to support the AX.25 packet radio protocol used by Amateur Radio Operators worldwide

HOWTO Filename	*Contents*
Accessibility-HOWTO	How to make Linux accessible to persons with disabilities
Adv-Routing-HOWTO	How to do perform advanced routing with the IP routing capabilities built into Linux 2.2 and 2.4 kernels
Apache-Compile-HOWTO	How to compile the Apache Web server with the modules such as mod_perl, mod_jserv, and mod_php
Apache-Overview-HOWTO	An overview of the Apache Web server and other associated commercial and open source software
Apache-WebDAV-LDAP-HOWTO	How to set up an Apache-based WebDAV (Web enabled Distributed Authoring and Versioning) server that can authenticate against a LDAP server
Assembly-HOWTO	How to program in assembly language in Linux
Authentication-Gateway-HOWTO	How to set up an authentication gateway for wireless networks in Linux
Bash-Prompt-HOWTO	How to use the Bash shell (command processor)
Belgian-HOWTO	How to configure Linux for Belgian users
BootPrompt-HOWTO	A list of arguments that can be passed to Linux at boot time (at the LILO boot: prompt)
Bootdisk-HOWTO	How to create boot, root, and other utility disks for Linux
C-C++Beautifier-HOWTO	How to beautifully format C and C++ programs so that they are more readable
Cable-Modem-HOWTO	How to connect a Linux system to a cable modem or cable Internet service provider
CD-Distributions-EN-HOWTO	A list of English-language Linux distributions, with particular focus on commercial CD-ROM distributions
CD-Writing-HOWTO	How to record a CD-ROM using a CD Recorder installed in a Linux system
CDROM-HOWTO	How to install, configure, and use CD-ROM drives with Linux
CVS-RCS-HOWTO	How to set up CVS and RCS source code control systems
Cable-Modem-Providers-HOWTO	How to connect a Linux system with various cable modem–based Internet service providers

(continued)

Table 7-1: *(continued)*

HOWTO Filename	*Contents*
Chroot-BIND HOWTO	How to install and configure a BIND 8 name server in a secure manner
Clone-HOWTO	How to boot Linux using GRUB and save partition images to and restore from a TFTP server
Cluster-HOWTO	How to build and configure high-performance Linux computing clusters
Config-HOWTO	How to configure the most common applications in Linux
DB2-HOWTO	How to install DB2 Universal Database Version 7.1 for Linux
DNS-HOWTO	How to set up Domain Name Service (DNS) on a Linux system
DOS-Win-to-Linux-HOWTO	How to apply your DOS and Windows knowledge to the Linux environment
DOS-to-Linux-HOWTO	How to apply your knowledge of MS-DOS in Linux
DSL-HOWTO	How to set up and use high-speed DSL (Digital Subscriber Line) connections to the Internet
DVD-HOWTO	How to play DVD movies in Linux
Diskless-HOWTO	How to set up a diskless Linux system
DocBook-Demystification-HOWTO	Explanation of the DocBook markup system, used to write technical documentation for open-source projects hosted on Linux
DocBook-OpenJade-SGML-XML-HOWTO	How to set up OpenJade to process SGML/XML DocBook documents
Emacs-Beginner-HOWTO	How to use the Emacs editor in Linux
Enterprise-Java-for-Linux-HOWTO	How to set up an Enterprise Java environment on Linux
Ethernet-HOWTO	How to configure and use Ethernet network adapters with Linux
Filesystems-HOWTO	How to access various file systems
Finnish-HOWTO	How to set up Linux for the Finnish language. (Except for the initial paragraph, the HOWTO itself is in Finnish.)
Firewall-HOWTO	How to set up an Internet firewall on a Linux system
Font-HOWTO	A comprehensive source of information about using different types of fonts in Linux

HOWTO Filename	Contents
Framebuffer-HOWTO	How to use framebuffer devices (an abstraction of graphics hardware) in Linux
Francophones-HOWTO	How to set up Linux for the French language. (This HOWTO is in French.)
From-PowerUp-To-Bash-Prompt-HOWTO	How Linux boots itself
Ftape-HOWTO	How to set up and use floppy tape drives (QIC-40, QIC-80, QIC-3010, and QIC-3020-compatible tape drives that connect to your PC through the floppy disk controller) in Linux
Game-Server-HOWTO	How to install, configure, and maintain servers for some popular multiplayer games such as Quake II and Quake III Arena
GCC-HOWTO	How to set up and use the GNU C compiler and development libraries in Linux
German-HOWTO	How to use Linux with the German character set. (This HOWTO is in German.)
Glibc2-HOWTO	How to install and use the GNU C Library version 2 (libc 6) on Linux systems
Hardware-HOWTO	A list of hardware known to work with Linux; and how to locate any necessary drivers
Hebrew-HOWTO	How to support the Hebrew character set in X Window System and text-mode screens
Hellenic-HOWTO	How to use Linux with the Greek character set. (This HOWTO is in Greek.)
HighQuality-Apps-HOWTO	How to create Linux applications that are highly integrated with the operating system and provides security and ease of use
HOWTO-HOWTO	How to write a HOWTO document
HOWTO-INDEX	Index of all HOWTOs
Infrared-HOWTO	How to use IrDA-compliant infrared devices in Linux (IrDA is a standard for infrared wireless communication at speeds ranging from 2400bps to 4Mbps)
IngresII-HOWTO	How to install the Ingres II Relational Database Management System on Linux
Installation-HOWTO	How to obtain and install Linux
Intranet-Server-HOWTO	How to use a Linux system in an Intranet that ties together Unix, Novell Netware, Windows NT, and Windows 95 systems

(continued)

Table 7-1: *(continued)*

HOWTO Filename	*Contents*
IP-Masquerade-HOWTO	How to enable the IP Masquerading feature on a Linux system
IPCHAINS-HOWTO	How to obtain, install, and configure the enhanced IP firewall chains software for Linux, including some ideas about how you might use the ipchains tool (ipchains replaces the older ipfwadm tool)
IPX-HOWTO	How to obtain, install, and configure various software that use the Linux support for IPX protocol (IPX is used by Novell NetWare)
ISP-Hookup-HOWTO	How to connect a Linux system to an Internet service provider (ISP) via a dial-up modem connection
ISP-Setup-RedHat-HOWTO	How to set up a Red Hat Linux system for dial-in, virtual Web hosting, email, POP3, and FTP
Italian-HOWTO	How to set up Linux for the Italian language. (This HOWTO is in Italian.)
Java-CGI-HOWTO	How to develop and use Java programs in Linux
Java-Decompiler-HOWTO	How to decompile the Java class files
Jaz-Drive-HOWTO	How to use 1GB and 2GB Iomega Jaz drives in Linux
KDE-GUI-Login-Configuration-HOWTO	How to customize the KDE GUI login screen
Kernel-HOWTO	How to upgrade and rebuild the Linux kernel
KernelAnalysis-HOWTO	Description of the Linux kernel and how it works
Keyboard-and-Console-HOWTO	How to use various Linux utilities to configure the keyboard and the console (the text-mode screen)
Kickstart-HOWTO	How to use the Red Hat Linux Kickstart system to install an identical version of Linux on a large number of systems
Kiosk-HOWTO	How to set up a Web-based kiosk using Linux, X, Netscape Navigator, and a trackball
Kodak-Digitalcam-HOWTO	How to get a Kodak digital camera to work in Linux
Laptop-HOWTO	How to install and use Linux on laptop computers
LDAP-HOWTO	How to install, configure, run, and maintain a Lightweight Directory Access Protocol (LDAP) server on a Linux system

HOWTO Filename	Contents
LDP-Reviewer-HOWTO	How to review Linux Documentation Project (LDP) documentation
LILO-crash-rescue-HOWTO	How to recover from Linux system failures when you use the LILO boot loader
Linmodem-HOWTO	How to use Winmodems in Linux
Linux+IPv6-HOWTO	How to install, configure, and use IPv6 applications in Linux
Linux+Win9x+Grub-HOWTO	How to use the GRUB boot loader to support dual-booting of Windows and Linux
Linux+XFS-HOWTO	How to build a Linux system that uses the SGI XFS journaling file system
Linux-Complete-Backup-and-Recovery-HOWTO	How to back up a Linux system so as to be able to recover from a complete disk crash and how to make that recovery
LinuxDoc+Emacs+Ispell-HOWTO	How to use Emacs and ispell to write documents such as HOWTOs for the Linux Documentation Project
Linux-Init-HOWTO	Description of the Linux 2.4 kernel initialization sequence on IA-32 processors
LVM-HOWTO	How to build, install, and configure Logical Volume Manager (LVM) for Linux
MIDI-HOWTO	Description of hardware, software, and procedures needed to play and sequence using MIDI devices in Linux
MILO-HOWTO	How to set up and use the Miniloader (MILO) for Linux on Alpha AXP-based systems. (Just as LILO loads and starts Linux on Intel-based PCs, MILO loads Linux on Alpha systems.)
Mail-Administrator-HOWTO	How to perform system-administration tasks related to electronic mail (email) systems in Linux
Mail-User-HOWTO	Information for users of the email system
Majordomo-MajorCool-HOWTO	How to install Majordomo Mailing List Software and the MajorCool utility to manage Majordomo lists on Linux
Masquerading-Simple-HOWTO	How to set up IP masquerading using iptables
Medicine-HOWTO	Description of Linux software for medical sciences
MIPS-HOWTO	How to obtain and use the version of Linux for the MIPS processors from Silicon Graphics. (The MIPS processors are used in many systems, ranging from Silicon Graphics workstations to Nintendo 64 game consoles.)

(continued)

Table 7-1: *(continued)*

HOWTO *Filename*	*Contents*
Modem-HOWTO	How to select, connect, configure, and use modems in Linux
Modem-Dialup-NT-HOWTO	How to set up the modem to support dial-up networking with a remote server such as Windows NT Remote Access Server (RAS) or Linux
Module-HOWTO	How to create and use loadable kernel modules (LKMs) in Linux
Mosix-HOWTO	How to use openMosix, a software package that turns a network of Linux systems into a computer cluster
MP3-HOWTO	How to encode and play MP3 sound files in Linux
Multi-Disk-HOWTO	How to best use multiple disks and partitions in Linux
Multicast-HOWTO	Information about multicasting over TCP/IP networking
Mutt-GnuPG-PGP-HOWTO	How to configure Mutt-i, PGP, and various versions of GnuPG in order to set up a mail reader with encryption and digital-signing capabilities
Net-HOWTO	Description of all Linux Networking implementations
NetMeeting-HOWTO	How to configure Linux for interoperability with Microsoft NetMeeting
Network-boot-HOWTO	How to set up a Linux server to support booting diskless Linux clients using an IP network
Network-Install-HOWTO	How to install Linux over a local area network (LAN)
Networking-Overview-HOWTO	An overview of networking capabilities of Linux
NFS-HOWTO	How to set up an NFS (Network File System) server and client in Linux
NIS-HOWTO	How to configure NIS (Network Information Service) in Linux
Online-Troubleshooting-HOWTO	How to use resources available on the Internet to troubleshoot Linux-related problems
Optical-Disk-HOWTO	How to install and configure optical disk drives in Linux (includes detailed coverage of the Panasonic LF1000 PD Phase change optical drive with the SCSI-II interface)

HOWTO Filename	**Contents**
Oracle-7-HOWTO	How to install and configure the Oracle Database Server on a Linux system
Oracle-8-HOWTO	How to install and get started with Oracle 8i Enterprise Edition for Linux
Oracle8-on-RH7X-HOWTO	How to install Oracle 8i, version 8.1.7 Enterprise Edition for Linux on a Red Hat 7.x system
PalmOS-HOWTO	How to use a PalmOS device (such as Palm III) with Linux
Parallel-Processing-HOWTO	How to use parallel processing approaches such as SMP (Symmetric Multiprocessing) Linux systems, clusters of networked Linux systems, and parallel execution using multimedia instructions (e.g., MMX), and attached (parallel) processors hosted by a Linux system
PCI-HOWTO	Information on Linux's support for the PCI (Peripheral Component Interconnect) bus architecture
PCMCIA-HOWTO	How to install and use PCMCIA (Personal Computer Memory Card International Association) Card Services in Linux
PHP-HOWTO	How to develop Web applications using PHP, a server-side HTML scripting language
Plug-and-Play-HOWTO	How to support Plug-and-Play (PnP) devices in Linux
Polish-HOWTO	How to set up Linux for the Polish language. (This HOWTO is in Polish.)
Portuguese-HOWTO	How to set up Linux for the Portuguese language. (This HOWTO is in Portuguese.)
PostgreSQL-HOWTO	How to set up and use the PostgreSQL database engine in Linux
PPP-HOWTO	How to set up and use Point-to-Point Protocol (PPP) networking in Linux
Printing-HOWTO	How to set up printing in Linux
Printing-Usage-HOWTO	How to use the print spooling system in Linux
Program-Library-HOWTO	How to create and use program libraries in Linux (aimed at programmers)
Quake-HOWTO	How to install, run, and troubleshoot Quake, QuakeWorld and Quake II in Linux (these are 3D action games developed by id Software)
Querying-libiptc-HOWTO	How to use the libiptc library included in the iptables package

(continued)

Table 7-1: *(continued)*

HOWTO Filename	*Contents*
RedHat-CD-HOWTO	How to make your own CDs from the Red Hat Linux distribution that are equivalent to the ones commercially available from Red Hat
Remote-Serial-Console-HOWTO	How to set up Linux to support a terminal or modem attached to the serial port
Root-RAID-HOWTO	How to create a root-mounted RAID (Redundant Array of Inexpensive Disks) file system in Linux
RPM-HOWTO	How to use the Red Hat Package Manager (RPM) in Linux
RTLinux-HOWTO	How to set up and run RTLinux (real-time Linux)
SCSI-2.4-HOWTO	Description of the SCSI subsystem in the Linux 2.4 kernel
SCSI-Generic-HOWTO	Description of the SCSI Generic driver (sg) found in the Linux 2.4 kernel
SCSI-Programming-HOWTO	Information on programming the SCSI device driver in Linux (useful for programmers who want to add support for a new SCSI device in Linux)
Secure-Programs-HOWTO	How to write secure programs for Linux and UNIX systems
Security-HOWTO	An overview of security issues in a Linux system
Security-Quickstart-HOWTO	An overview of the basic steps required to secure a Linux system from intrusion
Security-Quickstart-Redhat-HOWTO	An overview of the basic steps required to secure a Red Hat Linux system from intrusion
Sentry-Firewall-CD-HOWTO	How to set up a firewall using the Sentry Firewall CD (http://www.SentryFirewall.com/)
Serbian-HOWTO	How to configure Linux for Serbian users. (This HOWTO is in Serbian.)
Serial-HOWTO	How to set up serial communication devices in Linux
Serial-Programming-HOWTO	How to program the serial port in Linux
Shadow-Password-HOWTO	How to obtain, install, and configure the password Shadow Suite in Linux (password shadowing provides for more secure passwords than the ones stored in the /etc/passwd file)

HOWTO Filename	Contents
Slovenian-HOWTO	How to configure Linux for Slovenian users. (This HOWTO is in Slovenian.)
SMB-HOWTO	How to use the Server Message Block (SMB) protocol, also called the NetBIOS or LAN Manager protocol, with Linux
SMP-HOWTO	Information on configuring Symmetric Multiprocessing (SMP) on Linux systems with multiple processors
Snort-Statistics-HOWTO	How to configure Snort version 1.8.3, a Network Intrusion Detection System (NIDS), to gather statistics about network packets
Software-Building-HOWTO	How to build and install UNIX software distributions in Linux
Software-RAID-HOWTO	How to use Software RAID (software-supported virtual redundant disks) in Linux
Software-Release-Practice-HOWTO	Describes the good software release practices of Linux Open Source projects
Sound-HOWTO	How to enable support for sound hardware in Linux
Sound-Playing-HOWTO	Lists many sound file formats and the applications that can be used to play sound in Linux
Spanish-HOWTO	How to configure Linux for Spanish-speaking users. (This HOWTO is in Spanish.)
Speech-Recognition-HOWTO	Description and use of automatic speech recognition software in Linux
SRM-HOWTO	How to boot an Alpha-based Linux system using the SRM (System Reference Manual) firmware, which is the firmware normally used to boot DEC Unix on Alpha
SSL-Certificates-HOWTO	How to manage a certificate authority (CA) and issue or sign certificates to be used for secure Web or secure email using Secure Sockets Layer (SSL)
SSL-RedHat-HOWTO	How to build a secure Apache Web server in Red Hat Linux
TclTk-HOWTO	How to install, configure, and use the Tcl/Tk programming environment in Linux
TeTeX-HOWTO	How to install and use the teTeX TeX (pronounced tech as in technology) and LaTeX document formatting software in Linux

(continued)

Table 7-1: *(continued)*

HOWTO Filename	*Contents*
Text-Terminal-HOWTO	How to install and use text terminals (typically connected to multiport serial cards or a terminal server) with a Linux host
Thai-HOWTO	How to set up Linux for the Thai language
TimePrecision-HOWTO	How to maintain accurate date and time in Linux
Tips-HOWTO	Hints and tips to make Linux more useful and fun
UMSDOS-HOWTO	How to install and use the UMSDOS file system that lets you install Linux in an MS-DOS directory
Unicode-HOWTO	How to set up a Linux system so that it uses UTF-8 as text encoding
Unix-Internet-Fundamentals-HOWTO	Nontechnical description of how PCs, UNIX-like operating systems, and the Internet work
UPS-HOWTO	How to use an uninterruptible power supply (UPS) with Linux
USB-Digital-Camera-HOWTO	How to use in Linux a digital camera with Universal Serial Bus (USB) mass storage capabilities
Usenet-News-HOWTO	How to set up and access Usenet news in Linux
User-Authentication-HOWTO	How to secure user authentication in Linux
User-Group-HOWTO	How to establish and run a Linux User Group
UUCP-HOWTO	How to set up and use the Unix-to-Unix Copy (UUCP) software in Linux
VAR-HOWTO	Lists Linux Value Added Resellers (VARs)
Vim-HOWTO	How to set up and use the vim (Vi Improved) editor with color highlighting
Virtual-Services-HOWTO	How to support virtual services on a Linux system so that a single machine can recognize multiple IP addresses without multiple network cards
VME-HOWTO	How to run Linux on VMEbus systems
VMS-to-Linux-HOWTO	How to transition from VMS to Linux. (VMS is an operating system that runs on VAX systems from Digital Equipment Corporation.)
VoIP-HOWTO	Description of voice over IP (VoIP) system and software
VPN-HOWTO	How to configure a Linux system to support a virtual private network (VPN)

HOWTO Filename	*Contents*
VPN-Masquerade-HOWTO	How to configure a Linux firewall to masquerade IPsec and Point-to-Point Tunneling Protocol (PPTP) traffic to support a virtual private network (VPN)
WWW-HOWTO	How to set up a World Wide Web (WWW) service in Linux
WWW-mSQL-HOWTO	How to use the mSQL database server with a Web server in Linux
Winmodems-and-Linux-HOWTO	How to get a Winmodem (which normally needs a Windows driver to work) working in Linux
Wireless-HOWTO	How to setup wireless networking in Linux
XDMCP-HOWTO	How to set up remote X terminals using X Display Manager (xdm, gdm, or kdm) and XDMCP (X Display Manager Control Protocol)
XFree86-HOWTO	How to install and configure the XFree86 (X Window System Version 11 Release 6—X11R6) in Linux
XFree86-Video-Timings-HOWTO	How to create a modeline in the X configuration file for a specific video card. (See Chapter 10 for a description of modeline and the format of the X configuration file.)
XWindow-User-HOWTO	How to configure the X Window environment for a Linux user
Xinerama-HOWTO	How to configure XFree86 Version 4.0 with multiple monitors and the Xinerama extension

Understanding the Linux File System

Like any other operating system, Linux organizes information in files and directories. The files, in turn, are contained in directories (a directory is a special file that can contain other files and directories). A directory can contain other directories, giving rise to a hierarchical structure. This hierarchical organization of files is called the file system.

The Linux file system provides a unified model of all storage in the system. The file system has a single root directory, indicated by a forward slash (/). Then there is a hierarchy of files and directories. Parts of the file system can reside in different physical media, such as hard disk, floppy disk, and CD-ROM. Figure 7-3 illustrates the concept of the Linux file system and how it spans multiple physical devices.

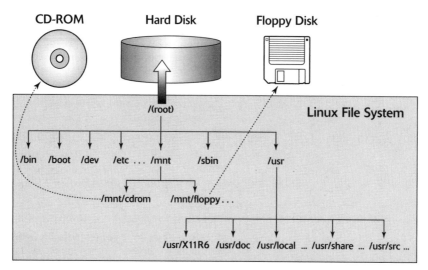

Figure 7-3: The Linux File System Provides a Unified View of Storage That May Span Multiple Drives.

If you are familiar with MS-DOS or Windows, notice that there is no concept of a drive letter in UNIX. You can have long filenames (up to 256 characters), and filenames are case sensitive. Often, UNIX filenames have multiple extensions, such as `sample.tar.Z`. Some UNIX filenames include the following: `index.html`, `Makefile`, `kernel-enterprise-2.4.18-3.i686.rpm`, `.bash_profile`, and `httpd_src.tar.gz`.

To locate a file, you need more than just the file's name; you also need information about the directory hierarchy. The term *pathname* refers to the complete specification necessary to locate a file—the complete hierarchy of directories leading to the file—and the filename. Figure 7-4 shows a typical Linux pathname for a file.

Figure 7-4: A Typical Linux Pathname.

As you can see from Figure 7-4, a Linux pathname consists of the following parts:

1. The root directory, indicated by a forward slash (/) character.
2. The directory hierarchy, with each directory name separated from the previous one by a forward slash (/) character. A / appears after the last directory name.
3. The filename, with a name and one or more optional extensions.

Many directories have specific purposes. If you know the purpose of specific directories, finding your way around Linux directories is easier. Another benefit of knowing the typical use of directories is that you can guess where to look for specific types of files when you face a new situation. Table 7-2 briefly describes the directories in a Linux system:

Table 7-2: Linux System Directories

Directory	Description
/	Root directory that forms the base of the file system. All files and directories are contained logically in the root directory, regardless of their physical locations.
/bin	Contains the executable programs that are part of the Linux operating system. Many Linux commands, such as cat, cp, ls, more, and tar, are located in /bin.
/boot	Contains the Linux kernel and other files the LILO and GRUB boot managers need (the kernel and other files can be anywhere, but it is customary to place them in the /boot directory).
/dev	Contains all device files. Linux treats each device as a special file; all such files are located in the device directory /dev.
/etc	Contains most system configuration files and the initialization scripts (in the /etc/rc.d subdirectory)
/home	Conventional location of the home directories of all users. User naba's home directory, for example, is /home/naba.
/lib	Contains library files, including the loadable driver modules, needed to boot the system
/lost+found	Directory for lost files. Every disk partition has a lost+found directory.
/mnt	A directory, typically used to mount devices temporarily, such as floppy disks and disk partitions. Also contains the /mnt/floppy directory for mounting floppy disks and the /mnt/cdrom directory for mounting the CD-ROM drive. (Of course, you can mount the CD-ROM drive on another directory as well.)
/proc	A special directory that contains information about various aspects of the Linux system
/root	The home directory for the root user
/sbin	Contains executable files representing commands typically used for system-administration tasks. Commands such as mount, halt, umount, and shutdown reside in the /sbin directory.
/tmp	Temporary directory that any user can use as a scratch directory, meaning that the contents of this directory are considered unimportant and usually are deleted every time the system boots
/usr	Contains the subdirectories for many important programs, such as the X Window System, and the online manual
/var	Contains various system files (such as logs), as well as directories for holding other information, such as files for the Web server and anonymous FTP server

The /usr and /var directories also contains a host of useful subdirectories. Table 7-3 lists a few of the important subdirectories in /usr. Table 7-4 shows a similar breakdown for the /var directory.

Table 7-3: Important /usr Subdirectories

Subdirectory	Description
/usr/X11R6	Contains the XFree86 (X Window System) software
/usr/bin	Contains executable files for many more Linux commands, including utility programs commonly available in Linux, but is not part of the core Linux operating system
/usr/games	Contains some Linux games such as Chromium, and Maelstrom
/usr/include	Contains the header files (files with names ending in .h) for the C and C++ programming languages; also includes the X11 header files in the /usr/include/X11 directory and the kernel header files in the /usr/include/linux directory
/usr/lib	Contains the libraries for C and C++ programming languages; also contains many other libraries, such as database libraries, graphical toolkit libraries, and so on
/usr/local	Contains local files. The /usr/local/bin directory, for example, is supposed to be the location for any executable program developed on your system.
/usr/sbin	Contains many administrative commands, such as commands for electronic mail and networking
/usr/share	Contains shared data, such as default configuration files and images for many applications. For example, /usr/share/gnome contains various shared files for the GNOME desktop; and /usr/share/doc has the documentation files for many Linux applications (such as the Bash shell, mtools, and the GIMP image processing program).
/usr/share/man	Contains the online manual (which you can read by using the man command)
/usr/src	Contains the source code for the Linux kernel (the core operating system)

Table 7-4: Important /var Subdirectories

Subdirectory	Description
/var/cache	Storage area for cached data for a applications
/var/lib	Contains information relating to the current state of applications
/var/lock	Contains lock files to ensure that a resource is used by one application only

Subdirectory	Description
/var/log	Contains log files organized into subdirectories. The syslogd server stores its log files in /var/log and the exact content of the files depend on the syslogd configuration file: /etc/syslog.conf. For example, /var/log/messages is the main system log file, /var/log/secure contains log messages from secure services such as sshd and xinetd, and /var/log/maillog contains the log of mail messages.
/var/mail	Contains user mailbox files
/var/opt	Contains variable data for packages stored in /opt directory
/var/run	Contains data describing the system since it was booted
/var/spool	Contains data that's waiting for some kind of processing
/var/tmp	Contains temporary files preserved between system reboots
/var/yp	Contains Network Information Service (NIS) database files

Using the Nautilus Shell

Now that you know the basics of the Linux file system, you can explore it. You can access the files and directories in two ways:

♦ By using a graphical file manager such as the Nautilus shell in GNOME
♦ By typing appropriate Linux commands in a terminal window or a text console

The Nautilus graphical shell is intuitive to use—it is similar to Windows' Active Desktop—and you can perform many tasks such as navigating the file system and performing system-management tasks with Nautilus. You may want to spend a few minutes now exploring the file system by using the Nautilus (the KDE file manager works in a similar manner, so it isn't covered here).

To start Nautilus, double-click the home icon in the upper-left corner of the GNOME desktop (refer to Figure 7-2). Nautilus runs and displays the contents of your home directory, as shown in Figure 7-5.

The Nautilus window is vertically divided into two windows—the left side can show different views of the file system and other objects you can browse with Nautilus; the right side shows the files and directories in the currently selected directory. As you can see from the Location text box along the top of the window, Figure 7-5 shows the content of the /home/naba directory. The title bar shows the name of the currently selected directory.

If you have used Windows Explorer, you can use Nautilus in a similar manner. Folders represent directories and you can open them by double-clicking. To move to other directories, click the up button on the toolbar as many times as necessary, and then navigate to whichever directory you want to see.

Figure 7-5: My Home Directory, as It Appears in Nautilus.

In addition to moving around the file system and viewing contents of directories, you can use Nautilus to perform tasks such as moving a file from one directory to another and deleting a file. I won't outline each step, but you can take a few moments to try the following tasks:

◆ To move a file to a different directory, drag and drop the file's icon on the directory where you want the file.

◆ To copy a file to a new location, select the file's icon and select Edit⇨Copy File. You can also right-click the file's icon and select Copy File from the pop-up menu. Then move to the directory where you want to copy the file, and select Edit⇨Paste Files.

◆ To delete a file or directory, right-click the icon, and select Move to Trash from the pop-up menu. To really delete the file, right click the Trashcan icon on the desktop, and select Empty Trash from the pop-up menu.

◆ To rename a file or a directory, right click the icon, and select Rename from the pop-up menu. Then, you can type the new name or edit the name.

◆ To create a new directory, right-click in an empty area of the right-hand window, and select New Folder from the pop-up menu. After the new folder icon appears, you can rename it by right-clicking and selecting Rename from the pop-up menu.

Navigating the File System with Linux Commands

Although graphical shells such as Nautilus are easy to use, you can use them only if you have a graphical login. Sometimes, you may not have a graphical environment to run a graphical file manager. For example, you might be logged in through a text terminal, or X might not be working on your system. In those situations, you have to rely on Linux commands to work with files and directories. Of course, you can always use Linux commands, even in the graphical environment—all you have to do is open a terminal window and type the Linux commands. Click the terminal icon in the GNOME Panel (refer to Figure 7-2) to start a terminal emulation program that displays a terminal window.

Using Directory Navigation Commands

In Red Hat Linux, when you log in as root, your home directory is /root. For other users, the home directory is usually in the /home directory. My home directory (when I log in as naba) is /home/naba. This information is stored in the /etc/passwd file. By default, only you (and root, of course) have permission to save files in your home directory, and only you can create subdirectories in your home directory to further organize your files.

Linux supports the concept of a current directory, which is the directory on which all file and directory commands operate. After you log in, for example, your current directory is the home directory. To see the current directory, type the pwd command.

To change the current directory, use the cd command. To change the current directory to /usr/share/doc, type the following:

```
cd /usr/share/doc
```

Then, to change the directory to the bash-2.05b subdirectory in /usr/share/doc, type this command:

```
cd bash-2.05b
```

Now, if you use the pwd command, that command shows /usr/share/doc/bash-2.05b as the current directory. Therefore, you can refer to a directory's name in two ways:

♦ An absolute pathname (such as /usr/share/doc), which specifies the exact directory in the directory tree

♦ A relative directory name (such as bash-2.05b, which represents the bash-2.05b subdirectory of the current directory)

If you type **cd bash-2.05b** in /usr/share/doc, the current directory changes to /usr/share/doc/bash-2.05b; the same command in /home/naba tries to change the current directory to /home/naba/bash-2.05b.

Secret

Use the cd command without any arguments to change the current directory to your home directory. Actually, the lone cd command changes the current directory to the directory listed in the HOME environment variable; that environment variable contains your home directory by default.

Notice that the tilde character (~) also refers to the directory the HOME environment variable specifies. Thus, the command cd ~ changes the current directory to whatever directory the HOME environment variable specifies.

You can use a shortcut to refer to any user's home directory. Prefix a user's login name with a tilde (~) to refer to that user's home directory. Therefore, ~naba refers to the home directory of the user naba, and ~root refers to the home directory of the root user. If your system has a user with the login name emily, you can type **cd ~emily** to change to Emily's home directory.

The directory names . and .. have special meanings. A single period (.) indicates the current directory, whereas two periods (..) indicate the parent directory. If the current directory is /usr/share/doc, for example, you can change the current directory to /usr by typing the cd .. command (if you are a DOS/Windows user, note that there is a space between cd and the two periods). Essentially, this command takes you up one level in the file-system hierarchy.

Showing the Current Directory in the Shell Prompt

Note that you can display the current directory in the shell prompt. The Bash shell uses the value of the environment variable PS1 as the primary prompt. Another variable, PS2, functions as the secondary prompt when a command requires further input from the user. You can view these variables with the echo command (for example, type **echo $PS1** to view the setting of PS1).

Secret

By default, the PS1 environment variable is defined in Red Hat Linux as follows:

```
echo $PS1
[\u@\h \W]\$
```

With this setting for PS1, the prompt looks like this:

```
[username@hostname dirname]$
```

In this example, username is the login name of the user; hostname is the system's name (Excluding the domain name), and dirname is the last part of the current working directory. Thus, if the current directory is /usr/src/linux, the dirname is linux. Thus, when a usernamed joe on a system with hostname mycompany.com changes the directory to /usr/share/doc, the shell prompt appears as follows:

```
[joe@mycompany doc]$
```

For the root user, the $ sign changes to a number sign (#) and the prompt looks like this:

```
[root@mycompany doc]#
```

Table 7-5 shows the character sequences you can use in the PS1 environment variable to customize your prompt.

Table 7-5: Character Sequences in the PS1 Environment

Code	What Appears in Prompt
\t	Current time in HH:MM:SS format
\d	Date in "Weekday Month Date" format, such as "Sun Oct 26"
\n	Newline
\s	Name of the shell, such as bash
\w	Full name of the current working directory, such as /usr/src/linux
\W	Basename of the current working directory, such as linux for /usr/src/linux
\u	User name of the current user
\h	Hostname
\#	Command number of this command
\!	History number of this command
\$	# if the effective user ID is 0 (indicating the user is root); otherwise, a $
\nnn	Character corresponding to the octal number nnn
\\	A backslash
\[	Begins a sequence of nonprinting characters, which could be used to embed a terminal control sequence into the prompt
\]	Ends a sequence of nonprinting characters

Given this information, you can show the full directory name (enclosed in square brackets) in the prompt by using the following command:

```
export PS1="[\w]"
```

If the current directory is /usr/src/linux-2.4, the prompt appears as follows:

```
[/usr/src/linux-2.4]
```

Interpreting Directory Listings and Permissions

As you move around the Linux directories, you may want to check the contents of a directory. You can get a directory listing by using the ls command. By default, the ls command—without any options—displays the contents of the current directory in a compact, multicolumn format. For example, type the following commands to see the contents of the /etc/X11 directory. (Type the commands shown in boldface; I have omitted the command prompts from the listing):

```
cd /etc/X11
ls
applnk          prefdm      sysconfig    XftConfig.README-OBSOLETE  xserver
desktop-menus   proxymngr   twm          xinit                      xsm
```

```
fs              rstart          X           xkb
gdm             serverconfig    xdm         Xmodmap
lbxproxy        starthere       XF86Config  Xresources
```

From this listing, you cannot tell whether an entry is a file or a directory. To tell the directories and files apart, use the -F option with ls, as follows:

```
ls -F
applnk/          prefdm*         sysconfig/   XftConfig.README-OBSOLETE  xserver/
desktop-menus/   proxymngr/      twm/         xinit/                     xsm/
fs/              rstart/         X@           xkb@
gdm/             serverconfig/   xdm/         Xmodmap
lbxproxy/        starthere/      XF86Config   Xresources
```

Now, the directory names have a slash (/) appended to them. Plain filenames appear as is. The at sign (@) appended to the first filename indicates that that file is a link to another file (in other words, this filename simply refers to another file). An asterisk (*) is appended to executable files (see, for example, the prefdm file in the listing).

You can see even more detailed information about the files and directories with the -l option:

```
ls -l
```

For the /etc/X11 directory, a typical output from ls -l looks like the following:

```
total 80
drwxr-xr-x   5 root     root     4096 Jan 18 21:15 applnk
drwxr-xr-x   2 root     root     4096 Jan 18 20:47 desktop-menus
drwxr-xr-x   2 root     root     4096 Jan 18 21:36 fs
drwxr-xr-x   6 root     root     4096 Jan 18 21:33 gdm
drwxr-xr-x   2 root     root     4096 Jan 18 21:31 lbxproxy
-rwxr-xr-x   1 root     root     1419 Jan 15 22:38 prefdm
drwxr-xr-x   2 root     root     4096 Jan 18 21:31 proxymngr
drwxr-xr-x   4 root     root     4096 Jan 18 21:31 rstart
drwxr-xr-x   2 root     root     4096 Dec  2 12:03 serverconfig
drwxr-xr-x   2 root     root     4096 Dec  2 12:03 starthere
drwxr-xr-x   2 root     root     4096 Dec  2 12:03 sysconfig
drwxr-xr-x   2 root     root     4096 Jan 18 21:33 twm
lrwxrwxrwx   1 root     root       27 Jan 18 21:39
                                        X ->../../usr/X11R6/bin/XFree86
drwxr-xr-x   3 root     root     4096 Jan 18 21:32 xdm
-rw-r--r--   1 root     root     3184 Jan 18 21:39 XF86Config
... lines deleted ...
```

Secret

The detailed directory listing displayed by the ls -l command shows considerable information about each directory entry, which can be a file or another directory. A typical line in the detailed directory listing has the following appearance:

```
drwxr-xr-x   6 root       root     4096 Oct 26 21:18 gdm
```

Looking at a line from the right column to the left, you see that the rightmost column shows the name of the directory entry. The date and time before the name show when the last modifications to that file were made. Before the date and time is the size of the file, in bytes.

The file's group and owner appear to the left of the column that shows the file size. The next number to the left indicates the number of links to the file. (A link is like a shortcut in Windows.) Finally, the leftmost column shows the file's permission settings, which determine who can read, write, or execute the file.

The first letter of the leftmost column has a special meaning, as the following list shows:

- **-** means an ordinary file
- **b** means a block special file
- **c** means a character special file
- **d** means a directory
- **l** means a symbolic link to another file
- **p** means a first-in first-out (FIFO) special file (also known as a *pipe* file)
- **s** means a local socket

After that first letter, the leftmost column shows a sequence of nine characters, which appears as `rwxrwxrwx` when each letter is present. Each letter indicates a specific permission; a hyphen (-) in place of a letter indicates no permission for a specific operation on the file. Think of these nine letters as three groups of three letters (`rwx`), interpreted as follows:

- The leftmost group of `rwx` controls the read, write, and execute permission of the file's owner. In other words, if you see `rwx` in this position, the file's owner can read (`r`), write (`w`), and execute (`x`) the file. A hyphen in the place of a letter indicates no permission. Thus, the string `rw-` means that the owner has read and write permission but not execute permission. Typically, executable programs (including shell programs) have execute permission. However, for directories, execute permission is equivalent to use permission—a user must have execute permission on a directory to open and read the contents of the directory.
- The middle three `rwx` letters control the read, write, and execute permission of any user belonging to that file's group.
- The rightmost group of `rwx` letters controls the read, write, and execute permission of all other users (collectively referred to as the world).

Thus, a file with the permission setting `rwx——` is accessible only to the file's owner, whereas the permission setting `rwxr–r–` makes the file readable by the group and the world.

An interesting feature of the `ls` command is that it does not list any file whose name begins with a period. To see these files, you must use the `ls` command with the `-a` option, as follows:

```
ls -a
```

Try this command in your home directory, and compare the result with what you see when you don't use the `-a` option:

1. Type **cd** to change to your home directory.
2. Type **ls -F** to see the files and directories in your home directory.
3. Type **ls -aF** to see everything, including the hidden files.

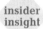

---

insider insight   Most Linux commands take single-character options, each with a minus sign (think of this sign as a hyphen) as a prefix. When you want to use several options, type a hyphen and concatenate the option letters one after another. Therefore, `ls -al` is equivalent to `ls -a -l`. However, if an option requires a value, then you have to first list the option and then its value.

Learning the Bash Shell

If you have used MS-DOS, you may be familiar with COMMAND.COM, the DOS command interpreter. That program displays the infamous C:\> prompt. Linux provides a command interpreter that resembles COMMAND.COM in DOS. In UNIX, the command interpreter traditionally is referred to as a shell. The original UNIX shell was called the Bourne shell, and its executable program was named sh. The default Linux shell is Bash, and its program name is bash (found in the /bin directory). Bash is compatible with the original sh, but includes many desirable features of other well-known shells, such as the C shell and the Korn shell. For example, Bash enables you to recall commands you have entered previously, and it even completes partial commands (this is called *command completion*).

The purpose of a shell such as Bash is to display a prompt and execute the command you type at the keyboard. Some commands, such as cd (change directory) and pwd (print working directory), are built into Bash. Other commands, such as cp (copy) and ls (list directory), are separate programs (a file representing these commands resides in one of the directories on your system). As a user, however, you really do not have to know or care whether a command is built in or is in the form of a separate executable program. Note that shell built-in commands are executed before executable files with the same name.

In addition to the standard Linux commands, Bash can execute any program stored in an executable file. Bash can even execute a shell script (a text file that contains one or more commands). As you learn in Chapter 24, you can use the shell's built-in commands to write programs (also known as shell scripts). Type **help** at the shell prompt to see a list of the built-in commands.

The shell enables you to run any Linux command, but you need to know the commands before you can run them. Because Linux is a UNIX clone, all Linux commands essentially are UNIX commands. Some of the most important commands, summarized earlier in the chapter, are for moving around the Linux file system. A large number of the Linux commands are GNU utilities—Chapter 8 provides an overview of GNU utilities.

---

cross ref   Consult Appendix A for a Linux command reference to learn about many more Linux commands, including most GNU utilities. Chapter 8 describes the GNU utilities and Chapter 24 shows you how to write shell programs (also called *shell scripts*).

The next few sections give you a feel for the various features of a shell, ranging from the general command syntax to defining aliases for long commands.

The discussions in this chapter assume that you use Bash as your shell because Bash is the shell you get when you install Linux from the CD-ROMs that accompany this book.

Learning Shell Command Syntax

Because a shell interprets what you type, it is important to know how the shell processes the text you enter. All shell commands have the following general format:

```
command option1 option2 ... optionN
```

A single line of command commonly is referred to as a command line. On a command line, you enter a command followed by one or more options (or arguments), known as command-line options (or command-line arguments). Sometimes the command-line options are also called switches.

Here are the basic command-line rules:

◆ Use a space or a tab to separate the command from the options.
◆ Separate individual options with a space or a tab.
◆ If you use an option that contains embedded spaces, you have to put that option inside quotation marks.

To search for my name in the password file, for example, I enter the `grep` command as follows:

```
grep "Naba Barkakati" /etc/passwd
```

When `grep` prints the line with my name, it looks like this:

```
naba:x:500:500:Naba Barkakati:/home/naba:/bin/bash
```

I use shadow passwords on my system (Chapter 22 describes shadow passwords). That's why the password field (the characters between the first and second colon) is a single letter x. Nevertheless, this line contains some useful information; the most interesting information (for the purposes of this discussion) is the field that follows the last colon (:). That field shows the name of the shell I am running.

The number and the format of the command-line options, of course, depend on the actual command. When you learn more about the commands, you see that the command-line options that control the behavior of a command are of the form $-X$, in which X is a single character.

Because various GNU tools and utilities implement most Linux commands, you should know that GNU command-line options begin with two dashes followed by a descriptive word. Thus, the GNU options are of the form $-xxxx$, where xxxx is a word denoting the option. For example, the GNU `ls -all` command shows all directory entries, including those that begin with a period (.). This is the same as the `ls -a` command in all UNIX systems.

If a command is too long to fit on a single line, you can press the backslash (\) key, followed by Enter. Then continue entering the command on the next line. In addition, you can concatenate several shorter commands on a single line by using the semicolon (;) as a separator between the commands. For example, when rebuilding the Linux kernel (as explained in Chapter 21), you can complete three sequential tasks by typing the following commands on a single line:

```
make dep; make clean; make zImage
```

Combining Commands

Linux follows the UNIX philosophy of giving the user a toolbox of many simple commands. You can, however, combine these simple commands to create a more sophisticated command. Suppose that you want to determine whether a device file named sbpcd resides in your system's /dev directory because you need that device file for a Sound Blaster Pro CD-ROM drive. You can use the command ls /dev to get a directory listing of the /dev directory and to see whether anything that contains sbpcd appears in the listing. Unfortunately, the /dev directory has a great many entries, and it may be difficult to locate any item that has sbpcd in its name. You can, however, combine the ls command with grep to come up with a command that does exactly what you want:

```
ls /dev | grep sbpcd
```

The shell sends the output of the ls command (the directory listing) to the grep command, which searches for the string sbpcd. That vertical bar (|) is known as a pipe because it acts as a conduit between the two programs; the output of the first command becomes the input of the second one.

For example, to see roughly how many processes running on your system, type:

```
ps ax | wc -l
```

This sends the output of the ps ax command (which lists all the processes) to the wc command that counts the number of lines and that count is one more than the total number of processes.

Here is another example of combining commands with pipes. Suppose you are having a meeting with a rather larger number of attendees and you have several sign-up sheets for attendees to put down their names. The attendees sign up on one or more of the sign-up sheets. Then, your assistant types each sheet into separate text files (named list1, list2, list3, and so on), one name per line. You can then combine the lists, sort the names, get rid of duplicates, and view the list with the following command:

```
cat list* | sort -u | more
```

The cat command simply turns all the names from the files into a stream of text. The sort -u command sorts the lines alphabetically and also removes any duplicates. Then more shows you the list a page at a time.

---

insider insight   Most Linux commands are designed in a way that enables the output of one command to be fed into the input of another. To do this, simply concatenate the commands, placing pipes between them.

Using I/O Redirection

Linux commands designed to work together have a common feature—they always read from the *standard input* (usually, the keyboard) and write to the *standard output* (usually, the screen). Error messages are sent to the *standard error* (usually, the screen). These three devices often are referred to as *stdout*, *stdin*, and *stderr*.

If you want a command to read from a file, you can redirect the standard input to come from that file. Similarly, to save the output of a command in a file, redirect the standard output to a file. These features of the shell are called input and output redirection, or I/O redirection.

Using the following command, for example, you can search through all files in the /usr/include directory for the occurrence of the string typedef and save that list in a file called typedef.out:

```
grep typedef /usr/include/* > typedef.out
```

This command also illustrates another feature of Bash. When you use an asterisk (*), Bash replaces the asterisk with a list of all the filenames in the specified directory. Thus, /usr/include/* means all the files in the /usr/include directory.

Table 7-6 shows the syntax of common I/O redirection commands.

Table 7-6: Common Standard I/O Redirections

Task	Command Syntax
Send stdout to a file	command > file
Send stderr to file	command 2> file
Send stdout and stderr to file	command > file 2>&1
Read stdin from a file	command < file
Read stdin from file.in and send stdout to file.out	command < file.in > file.out
Append stdout to the end of a file	command >> file
Append stderr to the end of a file	command 2>> file
Append stdout and stderr to the end of a file	command >> file 2>&1
Read stdin from the keyboard until the character c	command <<c
Pipe stdout to command2	command | command2
Pipe stdout and stderr to command2	command 2>&1 | command2

Using the I/O redirection commands is fairly straightforward. For example, suppose that you want to create a new file where you want to keep storing all text until you type **ZZ**. Here is how you can accomplish that task:

```
cat <<ZZ > input.txt
```

After you type this command, you can keep typing lines and type **ZZ** on a line when done. Everything you type should be saved in the file `input.txt`.

To save the list of files in the current directory in a file named `filelist`, type:

```
ls > filelist
```

To append the listing of the `/etc/X11` ditrecory to the same `filelist` file, type:

```
ls /etc/X11 >> filelist
```

To alphabetically sort that list of files, you can feed it to the `sort` command, like this:

```
sort < filelist
```

You should see the sorted list of files scroll by on the screen. To save that sorted list in another file named `sortedlist`, type:

```
sort < filelist > sortedlist
```

Now, the sorted list of files are saved in the `sortedlist` files.

Understanding Environment Variables

The shell and other Linux commands need information to work properly. If you type a command that isn't one of that shell's built-in commands, the shell has to locate an executable file (whose name matches the command you type). The shell needs to know which directories to search for those files. Similarly, a text editor, such as vi, needs to know the type of terminal (even if the terminal happens to be a terminal window in GNOME or KDE).

One way to provide this kind of information to a program is through command-line options. However, if you use that approach, you may have to enter many options every time you start a program. UNIX provides an elegant solution through environment variables.

When you log in as a user, you get a set of environment variables that control many aspects of what you see and do on your Red Hat Linux system. If you want to see your current environment, go ahead and type the following command in a terminal window:

```
env
```

By the way, the `printenv` command also displays the environment, but `env` is shorter.

The `env` command should print a long list of lines. That whole collection of lines is the current environment and each line defines an environment variable. For example, here is a typical line displayed by the `env` command:

```
HOSTNAME=localhost.localdomain
```

This line defines the environment variable HOSTNAME, and it's defined as `localhost.localdomain`.

Secret

An environment variable is nothing more than a name associated with a string. On my system, for example, when I log in with the user name `naba`, the environment variable named `PATH` is defined as follows:

```
PATH=/usr/local/bin:/bin:/usr/bin:/usr/X11R6/bin:/home/naba/bin
```

The string to the right of the equal sign is the value of the `PATH` environment variable. By convention, the `PATH` environment variable is a sequence of directory names, each name separated from the preceding one by a colon (`:`).

When the shell has to search for a file, it simply searches the directories listed in the `PATH` environment variable. The shell searches the directories in `PATH` in the order of their appearance. Therefore, if two programs have the same name, the shell executes the one it finds first.

In a fashion similar to the shell's use of the `PATH` environment variable, an editor such as vi uses the value of the `TERM` environment variable to figure out how to display the file you are editing with vi. To see the current setting of `TERM`, type the following command at the shell prompt:

```
echo $TERM
```

If you type this command in a terminal window, the output is as follows:

```
xterm
```

To define an environment variable in Bash, use the following syntax:

```
export NAME=Value
```

Here, `NAME` denotes the name of the environment variable, and `Value` is the string representing its value. Therefore, you set `TERM` to the value `vt100` by using the following command:

```
export TERM=vt100
```

You can set `TERM` to any of the terminal types defined in the `/etc/termcap` file, assuming, of course, that the terminal window or physical terminal matches the capabilities of that terminal type.

After you define an environment variable, you can change its value by simply specifying the new value with the syntax `NAME=new-value`. For example, to change the definition of `TERM` to `ansi`, type **TERM=ansi** at the shell prompt.

With an environment variable such as `PATH`, you typically want to append a new directory name to the existing definition, rather than define the `PATH` from scratch. The following example shows how to accomplish this task:

```
export PATH=$PATH:/sbin
```

This command appends the string `:/sbin` to the current definition of the `PATH` environment variable. The net effect is to add `/sbin` to the list of directories in `PATH`.

After you type that command, you can access programs in the `/sbin` directory such as `ifconfig`, a program that displays information about the network interfaces.

Note that you also can write this export command as follows:

```
export PATH=${PATH}:/sbin
```

PATH and TERM are only two of a handful of common environment variables. Table 7-7 lists some of the useful environment variables in Bash.

Table 7-7: Useful Bash Environment Variables

Environment Variable	Contents
BASH	The full path name of the Bash executable program (usually, /bin/bash)
BASH_VERSION	The version number of the Bash program
DISPLAY	The name of the display on which the X Window System displays output (typically set to :0.0)
HOME	Your home directory
HOSTNAME	The hostname of your system
LOGNAME	Your login name
MAIL	The location of your mail directory
PATH	The list of directories in which the shell looks for programs
PS1	The shell prompt. (The default is bash$ for all users except root; for root, the default prompt is bash#.)
SHELL	Your shell (SHELL=/bin/bash for Bash)
TERM	The type of terminal

Viewing Process Information

Every time the shell acts on a command that you type, it starts a process. The shell itself is a process, so are any scripts or programs that the shell executes. Examples of such programs are the metacity window manager and Nautilus graphical shell in GNOME. You can use the ps command to see a list of processes. When you type **ps ax**, for example, Bash shows you the current set of processes. Following is a typical report displayed when you enter the ps ax command in a terminal window (I also include the —cols 256 option to ensure that you can see each command in its entirety):

```
ps ax --cols 256
  PID TTY      STAT   TIME COMMAND
    1 ?        S      0:03 init
    2 ?        SW     0:00 [keventd]
    3 ?        SW     0:00 [kapmd]
    4 ?        SWN    0:00 [ksoftirqd_CPU0]
    7 ?        SW     0:00 [bdflush]
    5 ?        SW     0:01 [kswapd]
    6 ?        SW     0:00 [kscand]
```

```
   8 ?          SW       0:00 [kupdated]
   9 ?          SW       0:00 [mdrecoveryd]
  13 ?          SW       0:00 [kjournald]
  71 ?          SW       0:00 [khubd]
1178 ?          SW       0:00 [kjournald]
... lines deleted ...
2601 ?          S        0:00 in.telnetd: dhcppc3
2602 ?          S        0:00 login -- naba
2603 pts/1      S        0:00 -bash
2715 pts/1      R        0:00 ps ax --cols 256
```

In the default output format, the COMMAND column shows the commands that create the processes. This list shows the bash shell and the ps command as the processes. Other processes include all the programs the shell starts when I log in at the graphical login screen and start a GNOME session. In particular, the list includes the metacity (window manager) and the nautilus (graphical shell) processes.

Secret

The ps ax form of the command is the BSD UNIX format of the ps command. You also can write the command as ps -ax—with a hyphen prefix for the options as in most other Linux commands. The Linux ps command accepts options both with and without a hyphen prefix. In a typical output of the ps ax command you should expect to see anywhere from 60 to 70 processes in the list. Quite a few processes are running in your Red Hat Linux system even when you are the only user on the system. Hare are the first two lines of output from ps ax:

```
PID TTY       STAT   TIME COMMAND
  1 ?          S      0:04 init
```

In the output of the ps command, the first column has the heading PID and it shows a number for each process. PID stands for process ID (identification), which is a sequential number the Linux kernel assigns. If you look through the output of the ps ax command, you should see that the init command is the first process; it has a PID or process number of 1. That's why init is referred to as the mother of all processes.

The process ID or process number is useful when you have to stop an errant process forcibly. Look at the output of the ps ax command, and note the PID of the offending process. Then use the kill command with that process number. To stop process number 12318, for example, type **kill -9 12318**.

UNIX systems, including Linux, use signals to notify a process that a specific event has occurred. The kill command enables you to send a signal to a process (identified by a process number). The -9 part of the kill command indicates the signal to be sent; 9 happens to be the number of the SIGKILL signal that causes a process to exit.

Running Commands in the Background or in Virtual Consoles

When using MS-DOS, you have no choice but to wait for each command to complete before you enter the next command. (You can type ahead a bit, but the MS-DOS system can hold only a few characters in its internal buffer.) Linux, however, can handle multiple tasks simultaneously. The only problem you may have is that the terminal or console is tied up until a command completes.

If you work in a terminal window and a command takes too long to complete, you can open another terminal window and continue to enter other commands. If you work in text mode, however, and a command seems to take too long, you need some other way to access your system.

Several methods enable you to continue working while your Linux system handles a lengthy task:

♦ You can start a lengthy command in the background, which means that the shell starts the process corresponding to a command and immediately returns to accept more commands. The shell does not wait for the command to complete; the command runs as a distinct process in the background. To start a process in the background, simply place an ampersand (&) at the end of a command line. When I want to run the convpcx shell script to convert an image file named imagel to PCX format, for example, I run the script in the background by using the following command:

```
convpcx imagel &
```

♦ If you want a command to continue running in the background after you log out, use nohup to start the command using the following syntax:

```
nohup command
```

This causes the *command* to run in the background and all output is redirected to a file named nohup.out.

♦ If a command (that you have not run in the background) seems to be taking a long time, press Ctrl-Z to stop it; then type **bg** to put that process in the background.

♦ Use the virtual-console feature of Linux. Even though your Linux system has only one physical terminal or console (the combination of monitor and keyboard is called the terminal or console), it gives you the appearance of having multiple consoles. The initial text screen is the first virtual console. Press Alt-F2 to get to the second virtual console, Alt-F3 for the third virtual console, and so on. From the GUI desktop, you have to press Ctrl-Alt-F1 to get to the first virtual console, Ctrl-Alt-F2 for the second one, and so on.

Typing Less with Filename Completion

Many commands take a filename as an argument. When you want to browse through a file named /etc/X11/XF86Config, for example, type the following:

```
more /etc/X11/XF86Config
```

That entry causes the more command to display the file /etc/X11/XF86Config one screen at a time. For commands that take a filename as an argument, Bash includes a feature that enables you to type short filenames. All you have to type is the bare minimum— just the first few characters—to identify the file uniquely in its directory.

To see an example, type more /etc/X11/XF, but don't press Enter; press Tab instead. Bash automatically completes the filename, so that the command becomes more /etc/X11/XF86Config. Now, press Enter to run the command.

insider insight

Whenever you type a filename, press Tab after the first few characters. Bash probably can complete the filename, so that you don't have to type the entire name. If you don't enter enough characters to identify the file uniquely, Bash beeps. Just type a few more characters and press Tab again.

Using Wildcards in Filenames

Another way to avoid typing too many filenames is to use wildcards, special characters, such as the asterisk (*) and question mark (?), that match zero or more characters in a string. If you are familiar with MS-DOS, you may use commands such as COPY *.* A: to copy all files from the current directory to the A drive. Bash accepts similar wildcards in filenames. In fact, Bash provides many more wildcard options than MS-DOS does.

Bash supports three types of wildcards:

- ◆ The asterisk (*) character matches zero or more characters in a filename. Therefore, * denotes all files in a directory.
- ◆ The question mark (?) matches any single character.
- ◆ A set of characters in brackets matches any single character from that set. The string [xX]*, for example, matches any filename that starts with x or X.

Wildcards are handy when you want to perform a task on a group of files. To copy all the files from a directory named /mnt/cdrom to the current directory, for example, type the following:

```
cp /mnt/cdrom/* .
```

Bash replaces the wildcard character * with the names of all the files in the /mnt/cdrom directory. The period at the end of the command represents the current directory.

You can use the asterisk with other parts of a filename to select a more specific group of files. Suppose that you want to use the grep command to search for the string typedef struct in all files of the /usr/include directory that meet the following criteria:

- ◆ The filename starts with s.
- ◆ The filename ends with .h.

The wildcard specification s*.h denotes all filenames that meet these criteria. Thus, you can perform the search by using the following command:

```
grep "typedef struct" /usr/include/s*.h
```

The string contains a space that you want the grep command to find, so you have to enclose that string in quotation marks. This method ensures that Bash does not try to interpret each word in the string as a separate command-line argument.

Although the asterisk (*) matches any number of characters, the question mark (?) matches a single character. Suppose that you have four files—image1.pcx, image2.pcx, image3.pcx, and image4.pcx—in the current directory. To copy these files to the /mnt/floppy directory, use the following command:

```
cp image?.pcx /mnt/floppy
```

Bash replaces the single question mark with any single character and copies the four files to /mnt/floppy.

The third wildcard format—[...]—matches a single character from a specific set. You may want to combine this format with other wildcards to narrow the matching filenames to a smaller set. To see a list of all filenames in the /etc/X11/xdm directory that start with x or X, type the following command:

```
ls /etc/X11/xdm/[xX]*
```

Viewing the Command History

To make it easy for you to repeat long commands, Bash stores up to 500 old commands. Essentially, Bash maintains a command history (a list of old commands). To see the command history, type history. Bash displays a numbered list of the old commands, including those you have entered during previous logins. That list may resemble the following:

```
1  cd
2  ls -a
3  more /etc/X11/XF86Config
4  history
```

If the command list is very long, you may choose to see only the last few commands. To see the last 10 commands only, type the following:

```
history 10
```

To repeat a command from the list the history command has generated, simply type an exclamation point (!), followed by that command's number. To repeat command 3, type **!3**.

You also can repeat an old command without knowing its command number. Suppose that you typed **more /usr/lib/X11/xdm/xdm-config** a while ago, and now you want to look at that file again. To repeat the previous more command, type the following:

```
!more
```

Often, you may want to repeat the last command you typed, perhaps with a slight change. For example, you may have displayed the contents of the directory by using the ls -l command. To repeat that command, type two exclamation points as follows:

```
!!
```

Sometimes, you may want to repeat the previous command but add extra arguments to it. Suppose that ls -l shows too many files. Simply repeat that command, but pipe the output through the more command as follows:

```
!! | more
```

Bash replaces the two exclamation points with the previous command and appends |
more to that command.

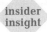

An easy way to recall previous commands is to press the up arrow key, which causes
Bash to go backward in the list of commands. To move forward in the command history, press the down arrow key.

Editing Recalled Commands

After you recall a command, you do not have to use the command as is; you can edit the
command. Bash supports a wide variety of command-line editing commands. These commands resemble those the emacs and vi editors use.

Suppose that you want to look at the file /etc/X11/XF86Config, but you type the following:

```
more /etc/X11/XF86config
```

After you press Enter and see an error message stating that no such file exists, you realize
that the c in config should have been uppercase. Instead of retyping the entire line, you
can type the following editing command to fix the problem:

```
^con^Con
```

Bash interprets this command to mean that it should replace the string con with Con in the
previous command.

Secret

By default, Bash enables you to edit the command line by using a small subset of
commands that the emacs editor supports.

Because I am already familiar with emacs, I use emacs commands to edit commands.
To bring back a previous command line, for example, I press Ctrl-P. Then I use the following keystrokes to edit the command line:

- Ctrl-B to go backward a character
- Ctrl-F to go forward a character
- Ctrl-D to delete the character on which the text cursor rests

I can also recall previous command lines by pressing the up arrow and then edit the
command line. To move about the command line, I can use the left and right arrow
keys.

To insert text, I type the text. Although emacs has a huge selection of editing commands, you can edit Bash command lines adequately with the preceding small set.

By default, the Bash shell supports emacs-style editing of command lines. To edit the
command line by using the vi editor's commands, type **set -o vi** at the shell prompt.
In vi mode, you have to press Esc to enter editing commands and press i to switch
back to interacting with the shell. From vi mode, you can return to emacs editing by
typing **set -o emacs** at the shell prompt.

Using Aliases

While configuring the Linux kernel and creating a new Linux boot floppy, I found myself changing the directory to /usr/src/linux-2.4/arch/i386/boot quite a few times. After typing that directory name twice, I immediately set up a shortcut using Bash's alias feature:

```
alias goboot='cd /usr/src/linux-2.4/arch/i386/boot'
```

I intentionally did not use any underscore characters or uppercase letters in goboot because I wanted the alias to be quick and easy to type (and it had to mean something to me only). Now that I've defined the alias, I can go to that directory by typing the following at the Bash prompt:

```
goboot
```

As you can see, an alias simply is an alternate (and usually shorter) name for a lengthy command. Bash replaces the alias with its definition and performs the equivalent command.

Secret

Many users use the alias feature to give more familiar names to common commands. If you are familiar with DOS/Windows commands and you use the dir command to get a directory listing, you can simply define dir as an alias for ls (the Linux command that displays the directory listing), as follows:

```
alias dir=ls
```

Now, you can type **dir** whenever you want to see a directory listing.

Another good use of an alias is to redefine a dangerous command, such as rm, to make it safer. By default, the rm command deletes one or more specified files. If you type **rm *** by mistake, rm deletes all files in your current directory. I learned this the hard way one day when I wanted to delete all files that ended with .xwd. (These files contained old screen images I no longer needed.) I intended to type **rm *.xwd**, but somehow I ended up typing **rm * .xwd**. I got the following message:

```
rm: .xwd: No such file or directory
```

At first I was puzzled by the message, so I typed **ls** to see the directory's contents again. When the listing showed nothing, I realized that I had an extra space between the * and .xwd. Of course, all the files in that directory were gone forever.

The rm command provides the -i option, which asks for confirmation before deleting a file. To make that option a default, add the following alias definition to the .bash_profile file in your home directory:

```
alias rm='rm -i'
```

That's it! From now on, when you use rm to delete a file, the command first asks for confirmation, as follows:

```
rm .bash_profile
rm: remove `.bash_profile'? n
```

Press y to delete the file; otherwise, press n.

If you type the same long command often, you should define an alias for that command. To make sure that the alias is available whenever you log in, place the definition in the .bash_profile file in your home directory.

Summary

Once you have installed Red Hat Linux on your PC, you can begin learning how to use and operate a Red Hat Linux system. Some of the basic steps are to log in, log out, and shut down the system. You also need to learn how to navigate the file system. At heart, Linux is still UNIX, and you have to learn to use a shell—a command interpreter—to perform many common tasks. Even when you use a graphical interface, you sometimes have to open a terminal window and type commands at the shell prompt. This chapter has gotten you started with Red Hat Linux operations and Bash—the Bourne Again shell—and some Linux commands for navigating the file system. You also have learned to use the Nautilus shell to explore the file system.

By reading this chapter, you learned the following:

- With graphical login enabled, you can log in, log out, and shut down a Red Hat Linux system from the graphical screen. You can also use `/sbin/shutdown` to shut down the system from the shell prompt.

- Online documentation is available to help with many aspects of the Linux operating system. You can also read online HOWTO documents that describe how to perform specific tasks or use specific software in Linux.

- The Linux directory structure is organized logically as a single tree, regardless of the physical location of subdirectories. Linux includes many commands for navigating directories and manipulating files.

- GNOME includes the Nautilus graphical shell, which you can use to work with files and directories.

- Even when you stay in the graphical environment of the X Window System and GNOME (or KDE), you may have to type Linux commands in a terminal window to perform many routine tasks. This especially is true when you log in using Telnet or when you have problems with X.

- A shell is a program that runs commands for you. Bash is the default shell in Linux. Bash is compatible with the Bourne shell that comes with all other UNIX systems.

GNU Utilities

Chapter

8

◆ ◆

Secrets in This Chapter

◆ ◆

ed Hat Linux includes the Linux kernel and a large collection of utilities and applications that make it a complete operating system. Most of these utilities and applications are from the GNU Project. In a way, Linux has become a full-fledged UNIX-like operating system primarily because of the GNU software. The GNU Project provided everything from the software development tools—assembler, compiler, and make—to GNOME, the graphical user interface (GUI) desktop. This chapter gives you an overview of the GNU software and introduces you to some of the GNU utilities.

cross
ref

Chapter 10 describes several applications, such as The GIMP, Ghostscript, and Ghostview. Chapter 11 describes the GNU Emacs editor, one of the most well-known software packages from the GNU Project. Other GNU software, such as the Bash shell, C/C++ compiler, the make utility, and other software packages, are described in several chapters throughout this book.

An Overview of GNU Software

As a Red Hat Linux user, you may not realize the extent to which Red Hat Linux (and, for that matter, all Linux distributions) relies on GNU software. Nearly all tasks you perform in a Red Hat Linux system involve one or more GNU software packages. For example, the GNOME GUI and the Bash shell are both GNU software. If you rebuild the kernel or develop software, you do so with the GNU C and C++ compiler and the make utility; both are parts of the GNU software packages that accompany all Linux distributions. If you edit text files with the ed or Emacs editor, you are again using a GNU software package. The list goes on and on. It's a safe bet that when you are using any Linux system, you are running some GNU software all the time.

Secret

If you are wondering what GNU is, here's the scoop. GNU is a recursive acronym that stands for *GNU's Not Unix*. The GNU Project was launched in 1984 by Richard Stallman to develop a complete UNIX-like operating system. The GNU Project developed nearly everything needed for a complete operating system except for the operating system kernel. All GNU software was distributed under the GNU General Public License (GPL). GPL essentially requires that the software be distributed in source-code form and stipulates that any user can copy, modify, and distribute the software to anyone else in source-code form. Users may, however, have to pay for their copy of GNU software.

The Free Software Foundation (FSF) is a tax-exempt charity that raises funds for work on the GNU Project. To learn more about the GNU Project, visit their home page at http://www.gnu.org/. There you can find information about how to contact the Free Software Foundation and how you can help the GNU Project.

One way to appreciate the extent of GNU software in Linux is to take stock of various GNU software packages. Table 8-1 briefly describes some of the well-known GNU software packages that come with Red Hat Linux. You can browse the table to get a feel for the types of tasks you can perform with GNU software.

Table 8-1: Well-Known GNU Software Packages

Software Package	Description
Autoconf	Generates shell scripts that automatically configure source-code packages
Automake	Generates `Makefile.in` files for use with Autoconf
Bash	The default shell—command interpreter—in Red Hat Linux. (Bash is compatible with the UNIX sh shell and offers many extensions found in csh and ksh shells.)
bc	An interactive calculator with arbitrary precision numbers
Binutils	A package that includes several utilities for working with binary files: `ar`, `as`, `gasp`, `gprof`, `ld`, `nm`, `objcopy`, `objdump`, `ranlib`, `readelf`, `size`, `strings`, and `strip`
gnuchess	A chess-playing program that regularly beats many good players
GNU C Library	For use with all Linux programs
cpio	Copies file archives to and from disk or to another part of the file system
diff	Compares files, showing line-by-line changes in several different formats
ed	A line-oriented text editor
Emacs	An extensible, customizable full-screen text editor and computing environment
Fileutils	A package that implements the following Linux commands: `chgrp`, `chmod`, `chown`, `cp`, `dd`, `df`, `dir`, `dircolors`, `du`, `install`, `ln`, `ls`, `mkdir`, `mkfifo`, `mknod`, `mv`, `rm`, `rmdir`, `sync`, `touch`, and `vdir`
Findutils	A package that includes the `find`, `locate`, and `xargs` utilities
Finger	A utility program designed to enable users of UNIX systems (including Red Hat Linux) on the Internet to get information about one another
Gawk	The GNU Project's implementation of the AWK programming language that conforms to the definition of the language in the POSIX 1003.2 Command Language and Utilities Standard
GCC	Compilers for C, C++, Objective C, and other languages
gdb	Source-level debugger for C, C++ and Fortran
gdbm	A replacement for the traditional dbm and ndbm database libraries
gettext	A set of utilities that enables software maintainers to internationalize a software package's user messages
Ghostscript	An interpreter for the Postscript and Portable Document Format (PDF) languages

(continued)

Table 8-1: *(continued)*

Software Package	Description
Ghostview	An X Window System application that provides a graphical front end to Ghostscript, and enables users to view Postscript or PDF files in a window
The GIMP	The GNU Image Manipulation Program is an Adobe Photoshop-like image-processing program
GNOME	Provides a GUI for a wide variety of tasks that a Linux user might perform
Gnumeric	A graphical spreadsheet (similar to Microsoft Excel) that works in GNOME and can work with Excel 95 format files
grep package	Includes the `grep`, `egrep`, and `fgrep` commands that are used to find lines that match a specified text pattern
Groff	A document formatting system similar to `troff`
GTK+	A GUI toolkit for the X Window System (used to develop GNOME applications)
gzip	A GNU utility for compressing and decompressing files
indent	Formats C source code by indenting it in one of several different styles
less	A page-by-page display program similar to `more`, but with additional capabilities
libpng	A library for image files in the Portable Network Graphics (PNG) format
m4	An implementation of the traditional UNIX macro processor that is commonly used to create the `sendmail` configuration file
make	A utility that determines which files of a large software package need to be recompiled, and issues the commands to recompile them
mtools	A set of programs that enables users to read, write, and manipulate files on a DOS file system (typically a floppy disk, but also Windows partitions of hard drives)
ncurses	A package for displaying and updating text on text-only terminals
patch	A GNU version of Larry Wall's program to take the output of `diff` and apply those differences to an original file to generate the modified version
RCS	The Revision Control System is used for version control and management of source files in software projects
sed	A stream-oriented version of the `ed` text editor
sharutils	A package that includes shar (used to make shell archives out of many files), unshar (to unpack these shell archives), as well as uuencode and uudecode utilities (some open source software installers need uudecode)

Software Package	Description
shellutils	A package that includes the following utilities, which are part of the Bash shell: basename, chroot, date, dirname, echo, env, expr, factor, false, groups, hostname, id, logname, nice, nohup, pathchk, printenv, printf, pwd, seq, sleep, stty, su, tee, test, true, tty, uname, uptime, users, who, whoami, and yes
tar	A tape archiving program that includes multivolume support; the capability to archive sparse files, handle compression and decompression, and create remote archives; and other special features for incremental and full backups
texinfo	A set of utilities that generates printed manuals, plain ASCII text, and online hypertext documentation (called Info), and that enables users to view and read online Info documents
textutils	A set of utilities such as cut, join, nl, split, tail, wc, and so on, for manipulating text
time	A utility that reports the user, system, and actual time a process uses

The remainder of this chapter introduces you to several categories of GNU utilities.

Shell Utilities

The shell utilities implement a number of shell commands you can use interactively or in shell scripts. Each utility program performs a specific task. The idea is that you can combine these commands in shell scripts to perform more complicated tasks.

Table 8-2 briefly describes each shell utility. You can try out some of these utilities by typing the program name at the shell prompt. Each program takes command-line options. You should first type **man *progname***, where *progname* is the name of the utility, to learn more about the command-line options. Then try the utility with appropriate options.

---

cross ref   You encounter some of these shell utilities again in Chapter 24 in the section covering shell programming.

Table 8-2: GNU Shell Utilities

Program	Description
[	Evaluates an expression and returns zero if the result is true (same as test)
basename	Removes the path prefix from a given pathname
chroot	Changes the root directory
date	Prints or sets the system date and time

(continued)

Table 8-2: *(continued)*

Program	Description
dirname	Removes the last level or filename from a given pathname
echo	Prints a line of text
env	Prints environment variables or runs a command with modified environment variables
expr	Evaluates expressions
factor	Prints prime factors of a number
false	Returns an unsuccessful exit status
groups	Prints the names of the groups to which a user belongs
hostid	Prints the numeric identifier for the host
id	Prints the real and effective user and group IDs
logname	Prints the current login name
nice	Runs a program with specified scheduling priority
nohup	Allows a command to continue running after the user logs out
pathchk	Checks whether filenames are valid and portable
pinky	Prints information about users. (This is similar to the finger program; in fact, the name pinky refers to a lightweight finger.)
printenv	Prints environment variables
printf	Formats and prints data
pwd	Prints the working (current) directory
seq	Prints numeric sequences
sleep	Suspends execution for a specified time
stty	Prints or changes terminal settings
su	Enables the user to adopt the ID of another user, or the super user (root)
tee	Sends output to multiple files
test	Evaluates an expression and returns zero if the result is true
true	Returns a successful exit status
tty	Prints the terminal name
uname	Prints system information
users	Prints current user names
who	Prints a list of all users currently logged in
whoami	Prints the user name for the current effective user ID
yes	Prints a string repeatedly until the process is killed

File Utilities and the find Command

The file utilities include programs you can use to work with files and directories in your Red Hat Linux system. Table 8-3 briefly describes each of these programs. You can copy and delete files, create new directories, and change file permissions and ownerships. You can also list directories and see the amount of disk space the files use.

Because you need to use the file utilities often, the next few sections show you how to use some of them. Also provided is a brief introduction to the find command, which enables you to locate all files that meet specified criteria.

Table 8-3: GNU File Utilities

Program	Description
chgrp	Changes group ownership of files
chmod	Changes the permissions of files
chown	Changes the ownership of files
cp	Copies files
dd	Converts a file according to a specified format and then copies the file
df	Shows storage space (hard disk, CD-ROM, floppy, and so on) usage for the file systems
dir	Prints a brief directory listing
dircolors	Prints the command to set the LS_COLORS environment variable, used by the color version of the GNU ls program
du	Shows disk space used by files and directories
install	Copies files and sets permissions
ln	Creates links between files
ls	Lists the contents of a directory
mkdir	Creates directories, if they do not already exist
mkfifo	Creates named pipes, used for data transfer between programs (FIFO stands for first-in first-out, which is how the named pipes transfer data)
mknod	Creates special block or character device files (usually located in the /dev directory)
mv	Renames files
rm	Deletes files
rmdir	Deletes empty directories
shred	Deletes a file securely by first overwriting it to make it harder to recover the data
sync	Flushes file system buffers to disk, thereby synchronizing memory and disk
touch	Changes the timestamps of files
vdir	Prints detailed directory listings (similar to ls -l)

Working with Files

Often, you may copy files from one directory to another. Use the `cp` command to perform this task. To copy the file `/usr/X11R6/lib/X11/xinit/Xclients` to the `Xclients.sample` file in the current directory (such as your home directory), type the following:

```
cp /usr/X11R6/lib/X11/xinit/Xclients Xclients.sample
```

If you want to copy a file to the current directory and retain the same name, use a period (.) as the second argument of the `cp` command. Thus, the following command copies the `XF86Config` file from the `/etc/X11` directory to the current directory (denoted by a single period):

```
cp /etc/X11/XF86Config .
```

The `cp` command makes a new copy of a file and leaves the original intact.

Secret

If you want to copy the entire contents of a directory—including all subdirectories and their contents—to another directory, use the command `cp -ar sourcedir destdir` (this copies everything under `sourcedir` directory to `destdir`). For example, to copy all files from the `/etc/X11` directory to the current directory, type the following command:

```
cp -ar /etc/X11 .
```

Another GNU utility command, `mv`, moves a file to a new location. The original copy is gone, and a new copy appears at the specified destination. You can use `mv` to rename a file. If you want to change the name of the `today.list` to `old.list`, use the `mv` command, as follows:

```
mv today.list old.list
```

On the other hand, if you want to move the `today.list` file to a subdirectory named `saved`, use this command:

```
mv today.list saved
```

An interesting feature of `mv` is the fact that you can use it to move entire directories, with all their subdirectories and files, to a new location. If you have a directory named `data` that contains many files and subdirectories, you can move that entire directory structure to `old_data` by using the following command:

```
mv data old_data
```

Another common file operation is deleting a file. Use the `rm` command to delete a file named `old.list`, for example, by typing the following command:

```
rm old.list
```

Be careful with the `rm` command—in particular, when you log in as `root`. Inadvertently deleting important files with `rm` is very common. One way to avoid problems is to add the command `alias rm='rm -i'` to the `.bash_profile` file in your home directory. With that in place, whenever you use the `rm` command to delete a file, the command first asks for confirmation.

Manipulating Directories

To organize files in your home directory, you have to create new directories. Use the `mkdir` command to create a directory. For example, to create a directory named `images` in the current directory, type the following:

```
mkdir images
```

After you create the directory, you can type the `cd images` command to change to that directory.

You can create an entire directory tree by using the `-p` option of the `mkdir` command. For example, suppose that your system has a `/usr/src` directory and you want to create the directory tree `/usr/src/book/java/examples/applets`. You can create this directory hierarchy by typing the following command:

```
mkdir -p /usr/src/book/java/examples/applets
```

When you no longer need a directory, use the `rmdir` command to delete it. You can delete a directory only when the directory is empty.

To remove an empty directory tree, you can use the –p option, like this:

```
rmdir -p /usr/src/book/java/examples/applets
```

This command removes the empty parent directories of `applets`. The command stops when it encounters a directory that's not empty.

Copying Disks with dd

The `dd` command is useful for copying binary data to a floppy disk (or to other devices, such as tape). For example, if you want to make a Red Hat boot disk on a Linux system, you can use the `dd` command to prepare the boot disk before you install Red Hat Linux from this book's companion CD-ROMs. Perform the following steps to prepare the boot disk:

1. Log in as `root` and mount the first CD from this book's companion CD-ROMs on `/mnt/cdrom` (type **mount /mnt/cdrom**). Change to the directory with the boot images as follows:

   ```
   cd /mnt/cdrom/images
   ```

2. Place a formatted floppy disk in the floppy drive, then type the following command to copy the `bootdisk.img` file to the floppy disk:

   ```
   dd if=bootdisk.img of=/dev/fd0 bs=1440k
   ```

If you want to copy another boot image to the floppy, replace `bootdisk.img` with that file's name.

Viewing Disk Usage Information

Two programs in the GNU file utilities—df and du—enable you to check disk-space usage. These commands are simple to use. The df command shows you a summary of disk-space usage for all mounted devices, as shown in the following example:

```
df
Filesystem           1K-blocks       Used  Available  Use%  Mounted on
/dev/hda5             7392428      3412688    3604224   49%  /
/dev/hda3              101107         8865      87021   10%  /boot
none                  127328            0     127328    0%  /dev/shm
/dev/cdrom             75322        75322          0  100%  /mnt/cdrom
```

The output is a table that shows the device, the total kilobytes of storage, how much is in use, how much is available, the percentage being used, and the mount point. For example, on my system, the /dev/hda5 device (a disk partition) is mounted on the Linux file system's root directory; it has about 7.4GB of space, of which 3.4GB (or 49 percent) is being used, and 3.6GB is available. Similarly, you can see from the last line that the CD-ROM has about 75MB of storage in use.

The other command, du, is useful for finding out how much space a directory is using. For example, type the following command to view the contents of all the subdirectories in the /var/log directory (this directory contains various error logs):

```
du /var/log
4         /var/log/vbox
12528     /var/log/cups
4         /var/log/samba
4         /var/log/news/OLD
8         /var/log/news
60        /var/log/httpd
4         /var/log/squid
36        /var/log/gdm
14764     /var/log
```

Each directory name is preceded by a number—that number denotes the number of kilobytes of disk space that directory uses. Thus, the /var/log directory, as a whole, uses 14764KB, or about 14.7MB, of disk space, whereas the /var/log/httpd subdirectory uses 60KB.

You can use the -h option with the du command to view the disk-space usage in human-readable format. For example, here's what you get when you type **du -h /var/log** to view the disk space used by the /var/log directory and its contents:

```
du -h /var/log
4.0K      /var/log/vbox
13M       /var/log/cups
4.0K      /var/log/samba
4.0K      /var/log/news/OLD
8.0K      /var/log/news
60K       /var/log/httpd
4.0K      /var/log/squid
36K       /var/log/gdm
15M       /var/log
```

If you simply want the total disk space a directory uses (including all the files and subdirectories contained in that directory), use the -s option together with the -h option, as follows:

```
du -sh /var/log
15M    /var/log
```

Notice that the -s option causes du to print just the summary information for the /var/log directory.

Learning the find Command

The find command is very useful for locating files (and directories) that meet specified search criteria. The Linux version of the find command also comes from GNU, and it has more extensive options than the standard UNIX version. I show the syntax for the standard UNIX find command, however, because it syntax works in GNU find, and you can use the same format on other UNIX systems.

I must admit that when I began using UNIX many years ago (Berkeley UNIX in the early 1980s), I was confounded by the find command. I stayed with one basic syntax of find for a long time before graduating to more complex forms. The basic syntax I learned first was for finding a file anywhere in the file system.

Suppose that you want to find any file or directory with a name that starts with gnome. You can use find to perform this search, as follows:

```
find / -name "gnome*" -print
```

This command tells find to start looking at the root directory (/), to look for filenames that match gnome*, and to display the full pathname of any matching file.

You can use variations of this simple form of find to locate a file in any directory (as well as any subdirectories contained in the directory). If you forget where in your home directory you have stored all files named report* (names that start with the text string report), you can search for the files by using the following command:

```
find ~ -name "report*" -print
```

When you become comfortable with this syntax of find, you can use other options of find. For example, to find only specific types of files (such as directories), use the -type option. The following command displays all top-level directory names in your Linux system:

```
find / -type d -maxdepth 1 -print
```

To find all files that exceed 20,000KB (20MB) in size, you can use the following find command:

```
find / -size +20000k -print
```

Secret

You can also execute some command [i1]on a file after you find it. For example, suppose that you want to search for the files that exceed 20,000KB in size and then print a detailed directory listing of that file. You can use the `-exec` operator of `find` to execute the `ls -l` command on each file that matches the search criteria, like this:

```
find / -size +20000k -exec ls -l {} \;
```

The `-exec` operator enables you to run any command on the files that meet whatever search criteria you use with `find`. You can type the command to execute following the `-exec` operator, then list any arguments, and end the list with a semicolon (`;`). However, the shell treats semicolon as command-separator, so you must place a backslash (`\`) in front of the semicolon to stop the shell from interpreting it. That's why every `-exec` operator ends with the characters `\;`. The curly brace pair `{}` is also has special meaning. The `find` command replaces the characters `{}` with the name of the file it has found—the file that satisfies whatever search criteria you have provided.

Another good use of `find`'s `-exec` operator is to find the files with permission settings that may be too dangerous and then change the permission by using the `chmod` command. For example, suppose you want to locate any file with a group-write permission (that means the group owner is allowed to alter the file) and take away that permission. Here is a `find` command that uses the `-exec` operator to accomplish this task:

```
find / -perm -20 -exec chmod g-w {} \;
```

You probably do not have to use the complex forms of `find` very often in a typical Linux system, but you can look up the rest of the find options by using the following command:

```
man find
```

Text Utilities

The GNU text utility package includes a large number of utilities to manipulate the contents of text files. These utilities are patterned after the UNIX commands of the same name. The GNU versions of the programs usually have additional options and are optimized for speed. In general, the GNU utilities do not have any of the arbitrary limitations of their UNIX counterparts.

Table 8-4 briefly describes each text utility. The best way to learn these utilities is to try each one out. Before trying out a program, type **info _progname_** or **man _progname_** (where _progname_ is the name of the program) to view the online help information.

cross ref

A few selected text utilities are described in the following sections. You can find reference pages for many of these utilities in Appendix A.

Table 8-4: GNU Text Utilities

Program	Description
cat	Concatenates files and writes them to standard output
cksum	Prints the cyclic redundancy check (CRC) checksums and byte counts of files (used to verify that files have not been corrupted in transmission, by comparing the cksum output for the received files with the cksum output for the original files)
comm	Compares two sorted files line by line. (The sort command sorts files.)
csplit	Splits a file into sections determined by text patterns in the file and places each section in a separate file named xx00, xx01, and so on
cut	Removes sections from each line of files and writes them to standard output
expand	Converts tabs in each file to spaces and writes the result to standard output
fmt	Fills and joins lines, making each line roughly the same length, and writes the formatted lines to standard output
fold	Breaks lines in a file so that each line is no wider than a specified width, and writes the lines to standard output
head	Prints the first part of files
join	Joins corresponding lines of two files using a common field and writes each line to standard output
md5sum	Computes and checks the MD5 message digest (a 128-bit checksum using the MD5 algorithm)
nl	Numbers each line in a file and writes the lines to standard output
od	Writes the contents of files to standard output in octal and other formats. (This is used to view the contents of binary files.)
paste	Merges corresponding lines of one or more files into vertical columns separated by tabs, and writes each line to standard output
pr	Formats text files for printing
ptx	Produces a permuted index of file contents
sort	Sorts lines of text files
split	Splits a file into pieces
sum	Computes and prints a 16-bit checksum for each file and counts the number of 1,024-byte blocks in the file
tac	Writes each file to standard output, last line first
tail	Prints the last part of files
tr	Translates or deletes characters in files
tsort	Performs a topological sort (used to organize a library for efficient handling by the ar and ld commands)
unexpand	Converts spaces into tabs
uniq	Removes duplicate lines from a sorted file
wc	Prints the number of bytes, words, and lines in files

Counting Words and Lines in a Text File

For example, suppose that you want to use the `wc` command to display the character, word, and line count of a text file. Try the following:

```
wc /etc/inittab
     54      236     1698 /etc/inittab
```

This causes `wc` to display the number of lines (54), words (236), and characters (1698) in the /etc/inittab file. If you simply want to see the number of lines in a file, use the `-l` option:

```
wc -l /etc/inittab
     54 /etc/inittab
```

As you can see, in this case, `wc` simply displays the line count.

If you don't specify a filename, the `wc` command expects input from the standard input. You can use the pipe feature of the shell to feed the output of another command to `wc`. This can be handy sometimes. Suppose that you want a rough count of the processes running on your system. You can get a list of all processes with the `ps ax` command, but instead of manually counting the lines, just pipe the output of `ps` to `wc`, and you can get a rough count, as follows:

```
ps ax | wc -l
     65
```

That means that the `ps` command has produced 65 lines of output. Because the first line simply shows the headings for the tabular columns, you can estimate that about 64 processes are running on your system. (Of course, this count probably includes the processes used to run the `ps` and `wc` commands as well, but who's counting?)

Sorting Text Files

You can sort the lines in a text file by using the `sort` command. To see how the `sort` command works, first type **more /etc/passwd** to see the current contents of the /etc/passwd file. Now, type **sort /etc/passwd** to see the lines sorted alphabetically. If you want to sort a file and save the sorted version in another file, you have to use the Bash shell's output redirection feature, as follows:

```
sort /etc/passwd > ~/sorted.text
```

This command sorts the lines in the /etc/passwd file and saves the output in a file named sorted.text in your home directory.

Substituting or Deleting Characters from a File

Another interesting command is `tr`—it substitutes one group of characters for another (or deletes a selected character) throughout a file. The `tr` command is useful when you want to convert a text file from one operating system to another because different operating systems use different special characters to mark the end of a line of text.

Secret

Suppose that you occasionally have to use MS-DOS text files on your Linux system. Although you might expect to use a text file on any system without any problems, there is one catch: DOS uses a carriage return followed by a line feed to mark the end of each line, whereas Linux (and other UNIX systems) use only a line feed. Therefore, if you use the vi editor with the -b option to open a DOS text file (for example, type **vi -b filename** to open the file), you see ^M at the end of each line. That ^M stands for Ctrl-M, which is the carriage-return character.

On your Linux system, you can easily rid the DOS text file of the extra carriage returns by using the tr command with the -d option. Essentially, to convert the DOS text file filename.dos to a Linux text file named filename.linux, type the following:

```
tr -d '\015' < filename.dos > filename.linux
```

In this command, '\015' denotes the ASCII code in octal notation for the carriage-return character.

You can use the tr command to translate or delete characters from the input. When you use tr with the -d option, it deletes all occurrences of a specific character from the input data. Following the -d option, you must specify the character to be deleted. Like many UNIX utilities, tr reads the standard input and writes its output to standard output. As the sample command shows, you must employ input and output redirection to use tr to delete all occurrences of a character in a file and save the output in another file.

Splitting a File into Several Smaller Files

The split command is handy when you want to copy a file to a floppy disk but the file is too large to fit on a single floppy. You can then use the split command to break up the file into smaller files, each of which can fit on a floppy.

By default, split puts 1,000 lines into each file. The files are named by groups of letters such as aa, ab, ac, and so on. You can specify a prefix for the filenames. For example, to split a large file called hugefile.tar into smaller files that fit onto several high-density 3.5-inch floppy disks, use split as follows:

```
split -b 1440k hugefile.tar part.
```

This command splits the hugefile.tar file into 1,440K chunks so that each can fit onto a floppy disk. The command creates files named part.aa, part.ab, part.ac, and so on.

To combine the split files back into a single file, use the cat command as follows:

```
cat part.?? > hugefile.tar
```

Binary Utilities

Just as the text utilities are meant for working with text files, the GNU binary utilities are meant for performing various tasks on binary files. Some of these utilities, such as ar, as, and ld, are used when building and managing object files that are generated when source files are compiled. A number of other binary utilities enable you to examine the contents of binary files. For example, the strings command prints all strings of printable characters in a file. Here is what the `strings` command displays for a simple C program that prints `Hello, World!` (the name of the binary executable is `a.out`):

```
strings a.out
/lib/ld-linux.so.2
libc.so.6
printf
_IO_stdin_used
__libc_start_main
__gmon_start__
GLIBC_2.0
PTRh
QVh(
Hello, World!
```

Notice that the output includes the `Hello World!` string, as well names of libraries (`/lib/ld-linux.so.2` and `libc.so.6`) and C functions (`printf`).

You can use the `size` command to look at the number of bytes that various sections (such as the code size, data area, and stack space) of a program would need. Here is the output of size for the `a.out` file that contains the Hello, World! program:

```
size a.out
   text    data     bss     dec   hex filename
    790     256       4    1050   41a a.out
```

In this case, the program requires 790 bytes for the code (called text, but it's the binary executable code of a program), 256 bytes for the data, and 4 bytes for stack. Thus, the program requires a total of 1,050 bytes of memory. Note that the actual size of the `a.out` file is about 10KB, which is much larger than 1,050 bytes because other information, such as symbols, is included in the file. Programmers would find the output of the `size` command useful because it tells them about the memory required to load and run a program.

Table 8-5 briefly describes the programs in the GNU binary utilities package. You can try some of these programs on any binary file in the system. For example, here's the result of running size on `/bin/bash`—the executable for the Bash shell:

```
size /bin/bash
   text    data     bss     dec    hex filename
 602431   22200   17044  641675  9ca8b /bin/bash
```

Table 8-5: GNU Binary Utilities

Program	Description
addr2line	This uses debugging information in an executable file to translate program addresses into filenames and line numbers
ar	This creates and modifies archives and extracts from archives. (An archive is a library holding the object code of commonly needed subroutines.)
as	This is the portable GNU assembler
gasp	This is a filter program to translate encoded C++ symbols
gprof	This is the GNU profiler, used to determine which parts of a program are taking most of the execution time

Program	Description
ld	This the GNU linker, used to combine a number of object and archive files and create executable files
nm	This lists symbols from object files
objcopy	This copies the contents of an object file to another (can also translate the format, if required)
objdump	This displays information from object files
ranlib	This generates an index to the contents of an archive
readelf	This displays information about one or more Executable and Linking Format (ELF) object files
size	This lists the section sizes of an object or archive file
strings	This lists printable strings from files
strip	This discards symbols from object files

Other Utilities

This section introduces you to a few more utilities from the GNU software packages shown in Table 8-1. The list is not exhaustive; I include only a few selected utilities. Following are the utilities summarized in the following sections:

- GNU bc: Arbitrary precision calculator
- gzip: Utility for compressing and expanding files
- patch: Utility for applying changes to a text file

GNU bc

GNU bc enables you to enter arbitrary precision numbers and to perform various calculations with these numbers. GNU bc implements the arbitrary precision-calculation capability the POSIX P1003.2/D11 draft standard specifies.

GNU bc is installed as part of the base operating system during the Red Hat Linux installation on the companion CD-ROMs.

If you have GNU bc installed, you should be able to run it with the following command:

```
bc
bc 1.06
Copyright 1991-1994, 1997, 1998, 2000 Free Software Foundation, Inc.
This is free software with ABSOLUTELY NO WARRANTY.
For details type `warranty'.
```

After displaying the banner, bc waits for your input (there is no prompt), then you can enter numbers and expressions by using syntax similar to that of the C programming language.

Numbers are the basic elements in bc. A number is treated as an arbitrary precision number with an integral and fractional part. You can enter numbers and evaluate expressions just as you write expressions in C, as the following example shows:

```
1.000000000000000033 + 0.1
1.100000000000000033
```

As soon as you enter an expression, bc evaluates the it and displays the result.

You can also define variables and use them in expressions, as follows:

```
cost=119.95
tax_rate=0.05
total=(1+tax_rate)*cost
total
125.94
```

If you check this result with your calculator, you'll notice that bc truncates the result of multiplication (it does the same with division). If you want, you can retain more significant digits by setting the scale variable, as follows:

```
scale=10
total=(1+tax_rate)*cost
total
125.9475
```

In this case, the result has more significant digits.

The bc utility supports an entire programming language with a C-style syntax. You can write loops and conditional statements and even define new functions with the define keyword. The following example shows how you might define a factorial function:

```
define factorial (n) {
  if(n <= 1) return (1);
  return (factorial(n-1)*n);
}
```

As you can see, the factorial function is recursive; it calls itself. Entering the lines as shown in the example is important. In particular, bc needs the open curly brace ({) on the first line because that brace tells bc to continue reading input until it comes to a closing brace (}).

After you define the factorial function, you can use it just as you might call a C function. Following are some examples:

```
factorial(3)
6
factorial(4)
24
factorial(10)
3628800
factorial(40)
815915283247897734345611269596115894272000000000
factorial(50)
30414093201713378043612608166064768844377641568960512000000000000
factorial(100)
9332621544394415268169923885626670049071596826438162146859296389521751\
9999322991560894146397615651828625369792082722375825118521091686400000\
00000000000000000000
```

As the example shows, you can use bc to represent as large a number as you want; no limit exists. When necessary, bc displays the result on multiple lines, with each continuation line ending in a backslash (\) followed by a new line.

To quit bc, type the following command:

```
quit
```

To learn more about bc, consult its man pages by using the `man bc` command. After you learn about new features of bc, try them interactively.

gzip

The gzip program is the GNU zip compression utility used to compress all Linux software distributions. When you run gzip with a filename as an argument, it reduces the file's size by using the Lempel-Ziv (LZ77) compression algorithm and stores the result in a file with the same name, but with an additional `.gz` extension. Thus, if you compress a file with the gzip `files.tar` command, the result is a compressed file with the name `files.tar.gz`.

The same gzip program can decompress any file gzip has compressed. To decompress the file `files.tar.gz`, for example, you can simply type the following:

```
gzip -d files.tar
```

Notice that you do not have to type the `.gz` extension explicitly; gzip automatically appends a `.gz` extension when it is looking for the compressed file. After decompressing, the utility creates a new file with the name `files.tar`.

Instead of `gzip -d`, you can use the `gunzip` command to decompress a file:

```
gunzip files.tar
```

This command also looks for a file named `files.tar.gz` and decompresses the file, if found.

By default, gzip stores the original filename and timestamp in the compressed file. You can decompress a file with the `-N` option to restore the original filename and timestamp.

Following is the basic syntax of the `gzip` command:

```
gzip [-cdfhlLnNrtvV19] [-S .xxx] [file ...]
```

The options have the following meanings:

- `-c` writes output to standard output.
- `-d` decompresses the file.
- `-f` forces compression or decompression, even if the file has multiple links or the corresponding file already exists.
- `-h` displays a help screen and quits.
- `-l` lists files sizes before and after compression.
- `-L` displays the gzip license and quits.
- `-n` stops gzip from storing the original filename in the compressed file.
- `-N` restores the original filename during decompression.
- `-q` suppresses all warnings.

- ♦ -r causes gzip to traverse the directory structure recursively and operate on all files.
- ♦ -S .xxx causes gzip to use the suffix .xxx instead of .gz.
- ♦ -t tests the integrity of a compressed file.
- ♦ -v displays the name and percentage of compression for each file.
- ♦ -V displays the version number and the compiler options used to build that version of gzip.
- ♦ -1 uses the fastest compression method (even though compression may not be as much).
- ♦ -9 uses the slowest compression method (provides the most compression).
- ♦ file ... specifies one or more filenames (the files to be compressed or decompressed).

The gzip utility is installed automatically when you install Red Hat Linux from the companion CD-ROMs.

patch

The GNU patch utility is designed to apply patches, or corrections, to files. The basic idea behind patch is that when you want to distribute changes in a file, you run the standard UNIX diff command and generate a diff file that indicates how the file should be changed, then you distribute that diff file to everyone who has the original file. The recipient runs the patch utility with the diff file as input and patch makes the changes in the original files.

---

cross ref
The patch utility is installed automatically when you install Linux from the companion CD-ROMs. Chapter 21 discusses how to use patch to apply changes to the Linux kernel sources when you upgrade the kernel from one version to the next.

You can learn more about patch through a simple example. Assume that you have a file named original.txt that contains the following text:

```
Version: 1.0

Revision history:
  10/26/2002: Original file (NB)
```

This text file is used as an example to illustrate how to use diff and patch to update a file.

Suppose that you already distributed the original.txt file to several users. (Pretend that the file is the source file of a computer program.) After a while, you make some changes in this file. The new file, named revised.txt, looks like the following:

```
Version: 1.1

Revision history:
  10/26/2002: Original file (NB)
  4/19/2003: Added a new line (LB)
```

Now, you want to provide these changes to your users so they can use the new file. Your first task is to create a `diff` file that captures the changes you have made.

To create the `diff` file, run `diff` with the `-u` option, and specify the two filenames as arguments—the original file, followed by the revised one. Thus, the following command creates the `diff` file for the current example:

```
diff -u original.txt revised.txt > patch-1.1
```

This command creates the file `patch-1.1`, which is what you distribute to your users who are currently using the file `original.txt`. This `diff` file is also referred to as the *patch file*.

When a user receives the patch file, all he or she needs to do is put the `patch` file in the same directory where the file `original.txt` resides and type the following command:

```
patch < patch-1.1
patching file 'original.txt'
```

The `patch` command applies the changes directly to the file `original.txt`. After `patch` finishes, you'll find that the content of the `original.txt` file matches that of `revised.txt`. This example should give you a good idea of how to use the `patch` utility to update text files.

Stream Editor – sed

The sed program is a text editor similar to ed (described in Chapter 11); unlike ed, sed is not interactive. Instead, sed is meant for editing a stream of input coming from standard input and for writing the edited text to standard output. The name sed stands for *stream editor* because it operates on a stream of text.

---

cross ref **To read more about standard input and standard output, consult Chapter 7.**

The sed editor is typically used to edit one or more files automatically through a shell script or to simplify repetitive edits on multiple files. The following sections provide an overview of sed.

Running sed

The sed editor expects to read from the standard input and write to the standard output. You can provide a filename on the command line, but sed still writes the output to standard output. This means that sed does not change the file it edits. You can redirect the output to another file or to the original file, thereby changing that file.

By default, sed applies each editing command globally to all lines in the file. You can, however, use line addresses or patterns to restrict the lines to which the editing commands apply.

To use sed on the fly from the shell prompt, you can run it as follows:

```
somecommand | sed 'editcommand' | anothercommand
```

In this case, feed the output of somecommand to sed (sed applies editcommand to each line); sed's output goes to anothercommand. For example, to see all the current processes that have gnome in their name, you can type the following command, which uses sed to edit the stream:

```
ps ax | sed -n /gnome/p | cut -c 28-80
/usr/bin/gnome-session
gnome-settings-daemon --oaf-activate-iid=OAFIID:GNOME
gnome-panel --sm-config-prefix /gnome-panel-9pyRb5/ -
gnome-terminal --sm-config-prefix /gnome-terminal-sHh
gnome-pty-helper
sed -n /gnome/p
```

In this case, each line in the output of the ps command is edited by sed, and a part of each line is extracted by using the cut command. Here, sed [i2]is invoked as follows:

```
sed -n '/gnome/p'
```

The -n option stops sed from printing each line to standard output. The '/gnome/p' part of the command line is an editing command—it means print each line containing the string gnome.

If you want to apply multiple sed commands, use the -e option to specify each editing command. For example, the following sed command takes the output of ps and deletes all lines that do not contain gnome (this is the edit command -e '/gnome/!d') and then deletes any line that contains the string sed (this is done by -e '/sed/d'):

```
ps ax | sed -e '/gnome/!d' -e '/sed/d' | cut -c 28-80
/usr/bin/gnome-session
gnome-settings-daemon --oaf-activate-iid=OAFIID:GNOME
gnome-panel --sm-config-prefix /gnome-panel-9pyRb5/ -
gnome-terminal --sm-config-prefix /gnome-terminal-sHh
gnome-pty-helper
```

Of course, you typically do not type long sed commands at the shell prompt. Instead, sed is used in shell scripts. You can also place sed commands in a file and edit a text file by running sed with the -f option, as follows:

```
sed -f sedscriptfile myfile
```

This command edits myfile by using the sed commands in sedscriptfile, and writes the lines to standard output. If you want to save the output in another file, redirect the output as follows:

```
sed -f sedscriptfile myfile > editedfile
```

Learning the Basics of sed Commands

All sed commands have the following general form:

```
[address][,address][!]command[arguments]
```

The parts shown in square brackets are optional. The command is an editing command (similar to those for the ed editor) that specifies the action sed takes on a line. The address specifies the lines to which the commands apply. The exclamation mark (!) applies the command to all lines that do not match the address. The arguments are needed by some editing commands, such as the w or r command, that read a file for which you have to provide the filename as an argument.

cross ref

As you can see, the basic syntax of sed commands is simple; but the address usually includes regular expressions, which cause the sed commands to appear very cryptic. Chapter 24 describes regular expressions.

Secret

Understanding the address is the key to learning sed. A sed command can have zero, one, or two addresses. The addresses identify lines to which sed commands are to be applied. An address is a regular expression or a line number, or a symbol such as $ that refers to a line number. Use the following guidelines to understand how addresses control what gets edited:

- If there are no addresses, sed applies the command to each line. For example, if a script has the command s/UNIX/Linux/, sed changes every occurrence of UNIX to Linux.
- If there is only one address, sed applies the command to any lines matching the address. For example, 1d deletes the first line of the stream.
- If you specify two comma-separated addresses, sed applies the command to the first matching line and to all subsequent lines up to, and including, the line matching the second address. Thus, the following command deletes everything from line 26 to the last line in the file:

```
26,$d
```

- If you add an exclamation mark (!) after an address, the command applies to all lines that do not match the address. For example, the command /gnome/!d deletes all lines that do not contain the string gnome.

You can use curly braces to apply more than one editing command to an address. The syntax is as follows:

```
[/pattern/][,/pattern]{
command1
command2
...other commands...
}
```

Note that the opening curly brace ({) must end a line, and the closing curly brace (}) must be on a line by itself. You should ensure that there are no blank spaces after the curly braces.

Sometimes you need to delete a line but to hold it in temporary storage and insert it elsewhere in the output stream. There are sed commands, such as h and g, for such operations. To use these commands, you need to understand the concept of pattern space and hold space. The *pattern space* is the buffer holding the current input line. The *hold space* is a separate set-aside buffer used for temporary storage. You can copy the contents of the hold space to the pattern space, and vice versa. For example, suppose that you want to extract all lines containing the string Item: and move them to a location later in the file (assume that the place is a line that has the string List of items:). You can do this with the following sed script:

```
/Item:/{
H
d
}
/List of items:/G
```

The first four lines of the script apply the commands H and d to the lines that contain Item:. The H command appends the line to the hold space; the d command deletes it. Then the G command on the last line of the script inserts the contents of the hold space after the string List of Items:.

Because of limited space, this section does not show you all the sed commands in detail. However, Table 8-6 provides a summary of commonly used sed commands, grouped by function.

Table 8-6: Commonly Used sed Commands

Command	Meaning
Editing	
=	Prints the line number of a line. For example, /ORDER/= prints the line number of the lines containing the ORDER string (the line number is printed before each matching line).

a\	Appends text after a line. For example, the following script appends a few lines to the file at the end of the output:
	
	`$a\`
	`This line goes at the end of the file.\`
	`Then this one.`

c\	Replaces text. For example, the following script replaces the first 50 lines of text with a single line that says <50 lines deleted>:
	
	`1,50c\`
	`<50 lines deleted>`

i\	Inserts text before a line. For example, the following script inserts text before a line containing SKU 53055:
	
	`/SKU 53055/i\`
	`*** THE FOLLOWING ITEM IS OUT OF STOCK ***`

d	Deletes lines. The command 1,20d deletes the first 20 lines.
l	Prints the line showing nonprinting characters as ASCII codes. For example, 5l prints the fifth line.

Command	Meaning
Editing	
n	Skips the current line. For example, suppose a file contains section headers on a line right after a SECTION line. The following script extracts all section headers from the file (run this script with sed -n -f scriptfile, where scriptfile contains the following script):

```
/^SECTION/{
n
p
}
```

Command	Meaning
p	Prints a line. For example, the /gnome/p command prints the lines containing the string gnome. Because sed prints each line anyway, this causes duplicate lines to be printed. You can use the p command with sed -n to print only selected lines (-n stops sed from printing lines by default).
q	Quits sed. For example, /Detailed Report/q quits the editor after printing the first line that contains this string.
s	Substitutes one pattern with another. For example, s/UNIX/Linux/ replaces all occurrences of UNIX with Linux.
y	Translates characters (similar to what the tr command does). For example, /^Appendix [1-9]/y/123456789/ABCDEFGHI/ replaces Appendix 1, 2, and so on, to Appendix A, B, and so on.
Working Multiple Lines	
D	Deletes the first part of pattern space (up to a newline) created by the N command. For example, the following script deletes multiple blank lines:

```
/^$/
{
N
/^\n$/D
}
```

Command	Meaning
N	Appends the next input line to the pattern space (a newline character separates the two lines). See the example for D.
Copying and Pasting	
h	Copies the pattern space to the hold space, wiping out what was in the hold space. For example, the following script finds an order number (assumed to be four digits) in a file and prints a note followed by the order number:

```
/Order/{
h
s/Order \#[0-9]\{4\}$/We have shipped your order:/
p
x
}
```

Command	Meaning
H	Appends the pattern space to the hold space. See example earlier in the "Learning the Basics of sed Commands" section.

(continued)

Table 8-6: *(continued)*

Command	Meaning
Copying and Pasting	
g	Pastes the contents of the hold space into the pattern space, overwriting the previous contents
G	Pastes the contents of the hold space after the current line. See example earlier in the "Learning the Basics of sed Commands" section.
x	Exchanges contents of pattern space with the contents of hold space. See example for h.
File Input and Output	
r	Reads a file into the input stream. For example, /^Dear/r letter inserts the contents of the letter file into the input stream after the line that begins with Dear.
w	Writes input lines to a file. For example, /^Order/w orders writes all lines that begin with Order to the file named orders.

Summary

Software from the GNU Project has helped make Linux a complete operating system. Many components of Linux—from the Bash shell to the GNOME GUI—come from the GNU Project. This chapter provided an overview of the GNU software packages and described some of the utility programs in those packages. Other GNU software packages are covered in other parts of this book.

By reading this chapter, you learned the following things:

♦ The GNU Project, supported by the Free Software Foundation, provided many software packages that make Linux a complete operating system. More information about the GNU Project is available online at http://www.gnu.org/.

♦ The GNU software packages include such well-known software as the Bash shell, the GNOME GUI, the GIMP image-processing program, the gzip compression/decompression utility, the tar archiving program, the Emacs editor, and a large number of other utilities that Linux users and programmers use.

GUI Desktops

Chapter
9

By now, you have installed Red Hat Linux and X, and you have had your first taste of Red Hat Linux. During Red Hat Linux installation, the installation program configures X and gives you an option to use a graphical login screen. If you have opted for the graphical login screen, X starts automatically, and you get a graphical screen with a login dialog box.

This chapter explains how Linux automatically starts in graphics mode. If you have not enabled the graphical login screen, you can easily do so by reading this chapter. You also learn about GNOME and KDE—two graphical environments in Red Hat Linux.

cross
ref
Turn to Chapter 2 if you have not installed Red Hat Linux and X. Turn to Chapter 3 if you have installed Red Hat Linux but have not configured X. Then, return to this chapter to learn how Linux automatically starts X and displays a graphical login screen.

Setting up a Graphical Login

Setting up your Linux workstation to display a graphical login screen is easy—all you have to do is make the appropriate selection during the installation. Even if you have not initially elected to have a graphical login screen, you can easily set it up once you know the details. The following sections explain how your Red Hat Linux system displays the graphical login screen.

Understanding How init Starts the Display Manager

A process named init starts the initial set of processes on your Red Hat Linux system. What init starts depends on the current run level, the contents of the /etc/inittab file, and the shell scripts located in the /etc/rc.d directory and its subdirectories. For now, you don't need to understand the details; you must know, however, that the graphical login screen starts at run level 5.

cross
ref
Chapter 20 describes in detail the init process, the /etc/inittab file, and the Red Hat Linux boot process.

The last line of the /etc/inittab file is responsible for starting the graphical login process with the following entry (the number 5 denotes run level 5):

```
x:5:respawn:/etc/X11/prefdm -nodaemon
```

This command runs /etc/X11/prefdm, a shell script that contains the following lines:

```
#!/bin/sh
PATH=/sbin:/usr/sbin:/bin:/usr/bin:/usr/X11R6/bin

# Shut down any graphical boot that might exist.
if [ -x /usr/bin/rhgb-client ]; then
    /usr/bin/rhgb-client -quit
fi
```

```
# We need to source this so that the login screens are translated.
[ -f /etc/profile.d/lang.sh ] && . /etc/profile.d/lang.sh

# Run preferred X display manager
# Try autologin first, if wanted...
if [ -f /etc/sysconfig/autologin -a -x /usr/sbin/autologin ]; then
    if /usr/sbin/autologin; then
          exit 0
    fi
    # If autologin fails (bad permissions, etc.), we get here -
    # time to start a real display manager.
fi


preferred=
if [ -f /etc/sysconfig/desktop ]; then
    . /etc/sysconfig/desktop
    if [ "$DISPLAYMANAGER" = GNOME ]; then
          preferred=gdm
    elif [ "$DISPLAYMANAGER" = KDE ]; then
          preferred=kdm
    elif [ "$DISPLAYMANAGER" = XDM ]; then
          preferred=xdm
    fi
fi


if [ -z "$preferred" ]; then
    if which gdm >/dev/null 2>&1; then
          preferred=gdm
    elif which kdm >/dev/null 2>&1; then
          preferred=kdm
    elif which xdm >/dev/null 2>&1; then
          preferred=xdm
    fi
fi

if [ -n "$preferred" ] && which $preferred >/dev/null 2>&1; then
    exec `which $preferred` $* >/dev/null 2>&1
fi

if which gdm >/dev/null 2>&1; then
    exec `which gdm` $* >/dev/null 2>&1
elif which kdm >/dev/null 2>&1; then
    exec `which kdm` $* >/dev/null 2>&1
elif which xdm >/dev/null 2>&1; then
    exec `which xdm` $* >/dev/null 2>&1
fi

# Catch all exit error
exit 1
```

This script starts a specific display manager—gdm, kdm, or xdm—depending on the setting of the `DISPLAYMANAGER` variable in the `/etc/sysconfig/desktop` file. The *display manager* is a program responsible for displaying the graphical login window, authenticating users who log in, running initialization scripts at the start of a session, and cleaning up after the session. The display manager process manages the display, making it available to the users and cleaning up after the user finishes a session. Note that of the three display managers—gdm, kdm, or xdm—xdm is the most generic.

Secret

If the `DISPLAYMANAGER` variable is not defined, the `/etc/X11/prefdm` script checks for gdm, kdm, and xdm—in that order—and runs whichever display manager it finds first. The end result is that you get gdm if you installed GNOME and kdm if you installed KDE as your sole desktop. If you install both GNOME and KDE, you get gdm by default because the `prefdm` script looks for gdm first. If you do have both GNOME and KDE installed on your system and you want the kdm as the display manager, define the `DISPLAYMANAGER` variable in `/etc/sysconfig/desktop` like this:

```
DISPLAYMANAGER="KDE"
```

Then, the next time you reboot the system, the kdm display manager will run.

To summarize, regardless of your choice of GUI, at run level 5 init starts a display manager. The display manager, in turn, displays the graphical login dialog box, which enables you to log in to the system.

If you have not enabled the graphical login screen during Red Hat installation, you can do so by editing the `/etc/inittab` file. Locate the line containing `initdefault`, and make sure that it reads as follows:

```
id:5:initdefault:
```

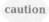

caution

Before you edit the `/etc/inittab` file, you should know that any errors in this file may prevent Linux from starting up to a point at which you can log in. If you cannot log in, you cannot use your system.

After editing the default run level in `/etc/inittab`, you can either reboot the system or type the following command to switch to run level 5:

```
telinit 5
```

Learning the GNOME Display Manager (gdm)

The gdm program is a display manager similar to xdm, the X display manager. Like xdm, gdm starts an X server for each local display, displays a login dialog box, and enables the user to log in to the system. Figure 9-1 shows a typical graphical login screen displayed by gdm.

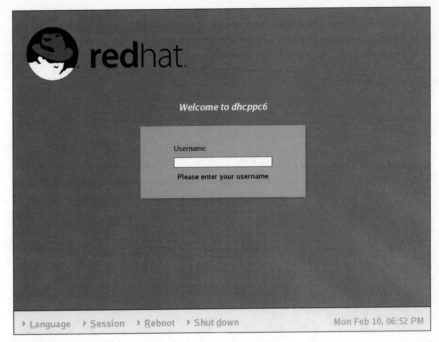

Figure 9-1: Graphical Login Screen Managed by gdm.

When gdm runs, it reads various configuration parameters from the configuration file /etc/X11/gdm/gdm.conf, which has a structure similar to a Windows INI file. For example, here is a typical gdm.conf file:

```
[daemon]
AlwaysRestartServer=false
AutomaticLogin=
AutomaticLoginEnable=false
Chooser=/usr/bin/gdmchooser
Configurator=/usr/sbin/gdmsetup --disable-sound --disable-crash-dialog
DefaultPath=/usr/local/bin:/usr/bin:/bin:/usr/X11R6/bin
DisplayInitDir=/etc/X11/gdm/Init
FailsafeXServer=
FirstVT=7
FlexibleXServers=5
GnomeDefaultSession=/usr/share/gnome/default.session
Greeter=/usr/bin/gdmgreeter
Group=gdm
HaltCommand=/usr/bin/poweroff;/sbin/poweroff;/sbin/shutdown -h now;/usr/sbin/shutdown
-h now
KillInitClients=true
LocalNoPasswordUsers=
LogDir=/var/log/gdm
PidFile=/var/run/gdm.pid
PostSessionScriptDir=/etc/X11/gdm/PostSession/
```

```
PreSessionScriptDir=/etc/X11/gdm/PreSession/
RebootCommand=/sbin/shutdown -r now;/usr/sbin/shutdown -r now
RemoteGreeter=/usr/bin/gdmlogin
RootPath=/usr/local/sbin:/usr/local/bin:/sbin:/bin:/usr/sbin:/usr/bin:/usr/X11R6/bin
ServAuthDir=/var/gdm
SessionDir=/etc/X11/gdm/Sessions/
StandardXServer=/usr/X11R6/bin/X
SuspendCommand=
TimedLogin=
TimedLoginDelay=30
TimedLoginEnable=false
User=gdm
UserAuthDir=
UserAuthFBDir=/tmp
UserAuthFile=.Xauthority
VTAllocation=true
XKeepsCrashing=/etc/X11/gdm/XKeepsCrashing
Xnest=/usr/X11R6/bin/Xnest -name Xnest

[security]
AllowRemoteAutoLogin=false
AllowRemoteRoot=true
AllowRoot=true
RelaxPermissions=0
RetryDelay=1
SessionMaxFile=524388
UserMaxFile=65536

[xdmcp]
DisplaysPerHost=1
Enable=false
HonorIndirect=true
MaxPending=4
MaxPendingIndirect=4
MaxSessions=16
MaxWait=15
MaxWaitIndirect=15
Port=177
Willing=/etc/X11/gdm/Xwilling

[gui]
GtkRC=/usr/share/themes/Bluecurve/gtk-2.0/gtkrc
MaxIconHeight=128
MaxIconWidth=128

[greeter]
BackgroundColor=#27408b
BackgroundImage=
BackgroundProgram=
BackgroundRemoteOnlyColor=true
BackgroundScaleToFit=true
```

```
BackgroundType=0
Browser=false
ConfigAvailable=false
DefaultFace=/usr/share/pixmaps/nobody.png
Exclude=
bin,daemon,adm,lp,sync,shutdown,halt,mail,news,uucp,operator,nobody,gdm,postgres,pvm,r
pm
GlobalFaceDir=/usr/share/faces/
GraphicalTheme=Bluecurve
GraphicalThemeDir=/usr/share/gdm/themes/
Icon=/usr/share/pixmaps/gdm.png
LocaleFile=/etc/X11/gdm/locale.alias
LockPosition=true
Logo=
MinimalUID=500
PositionX=0
PositionY=0
Quiver=true
RunBackgroundProgramAlways=false
SetPosition=false
ShowGnomeChooserSession=false
ShowGnomeFailsafeSession=false
ShowXtermFailsafeSession=false
SystemMenu=true
TitleBar=false
Use24Clock=false
UseCirclesInEntry=false
Welcome=Welcome to %n
XineramaScreen=0

[chooser]
Broadcast=true
DefaultHostImg=/usr/share/pixmaps/nohost.png
HostImageDir=/usr/share/hosts/
Hosts=
ScanTime=3

[debug]
Enable=false

[servers]
0=Standard

[server-Standard]
command=/usr/X11R6/bin/X
flexible=true
name=Standard server
```

The [servers] section of the file specifies the displays on which gdm displays the login dialog box. Each line of this section starts with a display number and shows the command needed to start the X server.

You see the term `greeter` used often in the display manager configuration file. *Greeter* refers to the login screen—the user interface through which the display manager prompts the user to log in to the system.

The different sections in the configuration file control different aspects of the graphical login screen as well as the tasks the user can perform from that screen. Table 9-1 describes the gdm configuration options, organized by sections.

---

insider insight

Edit the `Welcome=` line to change the welcome message on the graphical login screen. The default message says welcome to the hostname, which can be somewhat cryptic. You can edit that line and change the message to something more meaningful with the syntax `Welcome=Welcome to XYZ Corp.`

Table 9-1: The gdm Configuration Options

Configuration Option	Description
[daemon] section	
`AlwaysRestartServer=true or false`	If set to true, gdm always kills the existing X server and starts a new one.
`AutomaticLoginEnable=true or false`	If set to true, automatically log in the user specified in the `AutomaticLogin` option without asking for any password.
`AutomaticLogin=username`	If a user name is specified and `AutomaticLogin Enable` is true, that user is logged without asking for a password.
`Chooser=chooserprogram`	Full path and name of the `gdmchooser` executable file (typically, this should be `/usr/bin/gdmchooser`)
`Configurator=chooserprogram`	Full path and name of the `gdmconfig` executable file (typically, this should be `/usr/bin/gdmconfig`)
`DefaultPath=pathname`	Path (names of directories separated by colons) to be used for the user's session
`DisplayInitDir=pathname`	Directory containing the initialization scripts (the default is `/etc/X11/gdm/Init`)
`FailsafeXServer = safex-script`	Full path name of script that gdm should run to provide a failsafe GUI login screen
`FirstVT =number`	The virtual terminal (VT) number where X should be run (default is 7)
`FlexibleXServers =count`	Maximum number of X servers to run
`GnomeDefaultSession= sessionfile`	Full path name of file that gdm should read if there are no user GNOME session files (the default is `/usr/share/gnome/default.session`)
`Greeter=greeterprogram`	Full path and name of the greeter executable file, followed by arguments (typically, this should be `/usr/bin/gdmlogin`)

Configuration Option	Description
Group=groupname	Group name under which gdmlogin and gdmchooser are run (the default is gdm)
HaltCommand=haltprogram	Full path and arguments to the commands to be executed when the user selects Halt from the System menu (typically, this should be /sbin/shutdown -h now)
KillInitClients=true or false	When set to true, gdm kills the X clients started by the Init scripts after the user logs in (the default is true).
LocalNoPasswordUsers = userlist	Comma-separated list of users that are allowed to log in without password
LogDir=pathname	Directory containing the log files for the displays (the default is /var/log/gdm)
PidFile=pidfile	Name of the file where the process ID (pid) of the gdm process is stored (the default is /var/run/gdm.pid)
PostSessionScriptDir= pathname	Directory that contains the PostSession scripts—scripts run after the user logs out (the default is /etc/X11/gdm/ PostSession/)
PreSessionScriptDir=pathname	Directory that contains the PreSession scripts—scripts run right after the user logs in (the default is /etc/X11/ gdm/PreSession/)
RebootCommand=rebootprogram	Full path and arguments to the command to be executed when the user selects Reboot from the System menu (typically, this should be /sbin/shutdown -r now)
RemoteGreeter =pathname	Full path name of the greeter executable file for remote displays
RootPath=pathname	Path (names of directories separated by colons) to be used for the root user's session
ServAuthDir=pathname	Directory (the default is /var/gdm) containing the X authentication files for the displays (this directory should be owned by user gdm, group gdm, with permission 750)
SessionDir=pathname	Directory containing scripts for all session types available on the system (the default is /etc/X11/gdm/Sessions)
StandardXServer =pathname	Path name of standard X server (the default is /usr/X11R6/bin/X)
TimedLogin=username	If a user name is specified and TimedLoginEnable is true, then that user is logged without asking for any password after the login screen is inactive for the number of seconds specified in the TimedLoginDelay option
TimedLoginDelay=N	The number of seconds delay before the user specified in TimedLogin is automatically logged in
TimedLoginEnable=true or false	If set to true, automatically logs in the user specified in the TimedLogin option without asking for any password

(continued)

Table 9-1: *(continued)*

Configuration Option	Description
User=username	User name under which gdmchooser and gdmlogin are run (the default is gdm)
UserAuthDir=pathname	Directory where the user's .Xauthority file should be saved (if this field is empty, the user's home directory is used, which is the default)
UserAuthFBDir=pathname	Directory where a fallback cookie (which simply refers to the small amount of authentication information) is created if gdm fails to update the user's .Xauthority file (the default is /tmp)
UserAuthFile=filename	Name of the file for storing the user's authentication cookies (the default is .Xauthority)
VTAllocation =true or false	If true, automatically allocate virtual terminal (VT) for use by X server (default is true)
XKeepsCrashing=sessionfile	Full path name of a script that gdm should run if X keeps crashing (the default script is /etc/X11/gdm/XKeepsCrashing)
Xnest = pathname	Full path name of the nested X server (Xnest) that runs as an X client, but also manages graphics on behalf of the X server (default is /usr/X11R6/bin/Xnest -name Xnest)
[security] section	
AllowRemoteAutoLogin =true or false	When set to true, allows remote timed login (the default is false)
AllowRemoteRoot=true or false	When set to true, the root user can log in remotely (the default is true)
AllowRoot=true or false	When set to true, the root user can log in at the console (the default is true)
RelaxPermissions=0, 1, or 2	0 = gdm only accepts files and directories owned by the user; 1 = gdm allows group writeable files and directories; 2 = gdm allows world writeable files and directories (the default is 1)
RetryDelay=N	Number of seconds to wait before gdm displays the login window again after a failed login (the default is 3 seconds)
UserMaxFile=N	Maximum size (in bytes) of files that gdm will read or write (the default is 64KB, or 65,536 bytes)
[xdmcp] section	
DisplaysPerHost =number	Number of displays per host (the default is 1)
Enable=true or false	When set to true, gdm listens on port 177 and supports the X Display Manager Control Protocol (XDMCP) that enables users to log in to other hosts on the network (the default is false)

Configuration Option	Description
HonorIndirect=true or false	When set to true, gdm allows remote execution of the gdmchooser client on X terminals (the default is true)
MaxPending=N	Maximum number of pending connections (the default is 4) that gdm should allow (this helps avoid any denial of service attacks)
MaxPendingIndirect=N	Maximum number of gdmchooser clients that gdm will run simultaneously on remote displays (the default is 4)
MaxSessions=N	Maximum number of remote display connections that gdm will accept (the default is 16)
MaxWait=N	Maximum number of seconds that gdm waits for a response from a display before assuming that the display is not active anymore (the default is 15 seconds)
MaxWaitIndirect=N	Maximum number of seconds that gdm waits for a remote display to complete protocol negotiations after the display requests a chooser (the default is 15 seconds)
Port=177	The UDP port number where gdm listens for XDMCP requests (the default is 177)
Willing =pathname	Full path name of script to run to generate replies to XDMCP BroadcastQuery requests (the default is /etc/X11/gdm/Xwilling)

[gui] section

Configuration Option	Description
GtkRC=pathname	Path name of file that contains the theme to be used by the gdmlogin and gdmchooser programs (the default is the BlueCurve theme, defined in the file /usr/share/themes/Bluecurve/gtk-2.0/gtkrc)
MaxIconWidth=N	Maximum width (the default is 128 pixels) of icons that the face browser will display (gdmlogin can display a face browser containing icons for all the users on a system; these icons can be installed globally by the system administrator or in the users' home directories)
MaxIconHeight=N	Maximum height (the default is 128 pixels) of icons that the face browser will display

[greeter] section

Configuration Option	Description
BackgroundColor =#colornum	Background color
BackgroundImage =pathname	Pathname of image to use as background (when BackgroundType=1)
BackgroundProgram =pathname	Pathname of program to run to draw the background
BackgroundRemoteOnlyColor = true or false	When set to true, displays a solid color background for remote displays (the default is true)
BackgroundScaleToFit = true or false	When set to true, scales image to fit screen (the default is true)

(continued)

Table 9-1: *(continued)*

Configuration Option	*Description*
`BackgroundType =0, 1, or 2`	Type of background for the greeter, 0 = None, 1 = Image, 2 = Color (the default is 0)
`Browser=true or false`	When set to `true`, displays a browser, called the face browser, where the faces of all system users are displayed (the default is `false`)
`ConfigAvailable =true or false`	When set to `true`, configuration option is available from the System menu (default is `false`)
`DefaultFace=imagefile`	A file, readable by the `gdm` user, containing an image that is to be displayed if a user does not have a personal picture in the `~/gnome/photo` directory (which refers to the `gnome/photo` subdirectory of the user's home directory). The default is the `/usr/share/pixmaps/nobody.png` file.
`Exclude=usernames`	Comma-separated list of user names to be excluded from the face browser; the excluded users will still be able to log in
`GlobalFaceDir=pathname`	Directory where face files (each containing an icon showing a user's face) are located (the default is `/usr/share/faces/`)
`GraphicalTheme =themename`	Name of graphical theme to use (default is `BlueCurve`)
`GraphicalThemeDir =pathname`	Directory where graphical theme files are located (the default is `/usr/share/gdm/themes/`)
`Icon=imagefile`	A file, readable by the `gdm` user, containing the image to be displayed when the login window is in iconified state (the default is `/usr/share/pixmaps/gdm.xpm`)
`LocaleFile=localefile`	Full pathname for the file in GNU locale format, with entries for all languages supported on the system (the default is `/etc/X11/gdm/locale.alias`)
`LockPosition =true or false`	When set to `true`, the user cannot move the greeter window (the default is `true`)
`Logo=imagefile`	A file, readable by the `gdm` user, with the image to be displayed in the logo area (the default is `/usr/share/pixmaps/gnome-logo-large.png`).
`MinimalUID =number`	Users with this user ID or higher can log in (the default is 500)
`PositionX =xpos` `PositionY=ypos`	Horizontal and vertical position of greeter window
`Quiver=true or false`	When set to `true`, the gdmlogin program shakes the display (not physically, but by moving the graphics output) when a user enters an incorrect password (the default is false)
`RunBackgroundProgramAlways = true or false`	When set to `true`, runs the background program specified by `BackgroundProgram` (the default is `false`)

Configuration Option	Description
SetPosition =true or false	When set to true, the gdmlogin program shakes the display (not physically, but by moving the graphics output) when a user enters an incorrect password (the default is false)
ShowGnomeChooserSession = true or false	When set to true, shows previous GNOME sessions in the chooser (the default is false)
ShowGnomeFailsafeSession = true or false	When set to true, shows the GNOME failsafe session in the chooser (the default is false)
ShowXtermFailsafeSession = true or false	When set to true, show the failsafe session that runs an xterm window (the default is false)
SystemMenu =true or false	When set to true, show the System menu on the greeter (the default is true)
TitleBar =true or false	When set to true, show a title bar on the greeter window (the default is false)
Use24Clock =true or false	When set to true, use a 24-hour clock no matter what the locale (the default is false)
UseCirclesInEntry =true or false	When set to true, echo the typed password as circles (the default is false)
Welcome=message	The English welcome message that the gdmlogin program displays next to the logo on the login screen (the default message is Welcome to %n, where %n means the node name—the hostname without the domain)
XineramaScreen =number	The Xinerama screen where greeter is displayed (default is 0)

[chooser] section

Broadcast =true or false	When set to true, an XDMCP query is broadcast to get the names of all the hosts that accept login (the default is true)
DefaultHostImg=filename	File containing an image to be displayed for those hosts that do not have a unique icon file (the default is /usr/share/pixmaps/nohost.png)
HostImageDir=pathname	Directory (the default is /usr/share/hosts/) that contains host icon files; each filename matches the host system's fully qualified domain name (such as yourhost.yourdomain.com).
Hosts=hostnames	Comma-separated names of hosts to list
ScanTime=N	Number of seconds the chooser should wait for replies to its XDMCP broadcast query (the default is 3 seconds)

[debug] section

Enable=true or false	When set to true, gdm saves information that can help isolate any bugs in gdm (the default is false)

(continued)

Table 9-1: *(continued)*

Configuration Option	Description
[servers] section	
N=ServerName	Name of the X server to start on local display number N (if your system has a single monitor, N is 0). Default is Standard
[server-Standard] section	
command=ServerPathName	Full pathname of the Standard X server (the default is /usr/X11R6/bin/X)
flexible=true or false	When set to true, the Standard server is considered a flexible server (the default is true)
name=servername	A descriptive name of the Standard server (default is Standard server)

Secret

For the default configuration (after you install Red Hat Linux and X from the companion CD-ROMs), gdm manages the login session as follows:

1. The gdm program starts the X server and looks for a script named after the local display's name (for the first display, the filename is :0) in the /etc/X11/gdm/ Init directory. If it does not find that file, gdm executes the file named Default from that directory. The /etc/X11/gdm/Init/Default script in Red Hat Linux contains the following commands:

```
#!/bin/sh
# Xsetup for Red Hat Linux
# Copyright (c) 1999, 2000, 2001 Red Hat, Inc.

sysresources=/etc/X11/Xresources

# merge in defaults
if [ -f "$sysresources" ]; then
    xrdb -merge "$sysresources"
fi

/usr/X11R6/bin/xsetroot -solid "#5477A0"

if [ -z "$RUNNING_UNDER_GDM" ] ; then
  /sbin/pidof -s kdm &> /dev/null && [ $? -eq 0 -a -x
/usr/bin/kdmdesktop ] && /usr/bin/kdmdesktop && sleep 1s

    # Only set the background if the xsri program is installed.
    if [ -x /usr/bin/xsri -a -f /etc/X11/xsrirc ]; then
```

```
            /usr/bin/xsri --redhat-login --set
    fi
fi
```

In this case, the script sets the background to a solid color and displays the Red Hat logo. The gdm program runs this script as `root` and waits until the commands finish.

2. The gdm program runs the `/usr/bin/gdmlogin` program, which displays a dialog box that contains fields in which the user can enter a name and a password.

3. After a user enters a name and password and presses Enter, gdm verifies the password and tries to execute the startup script `/etc/X11/gdm/PreSession/DisplayName`, where `DisplayName` is `:0` for the first display. If that file is not found, gdm executes the `/etc/X11/gdm/PreSession/Default` script, if it exists.

4. The gdm program runs the session script from the `/etc/X11/gdm/Sessions` directory. The exact script that gdm runs depends on the session the user selects in the Sessions menu in the login dialog box `gdmlogin` is displayed. If the user has not explicitly selected a specific type of session (GNOME or KDE), gdm runs the `/etc/X11/gdm/Default` script, which, in turn, executes the `/etc/X11/xdm/Xsession` script. This script looks for another script file, named `.xsession`, in the user's home directory and executes that script, if it exists. Next, it looks for the `.Xclients` script file in the user's home directory and executes that file, if it exists. Otherwise, `Xsession` executes the `/etc/X11/xinit/Xclients` script. When you follow through these scripts, you find that the `Xclients` script executes the `/usr/bin/gnome-session` program if the `/etc/sysconfig/desktop` file contains the line `DESKTOP="GNOME"`. The gnome-session program then starts the GNOME session (which includes a set of applications and a window manager). Initially, gnome-session uses the session file `/usr/share/gnome/default.session` (a text file) to start the applications and the window manager. Later, the GNOME session is restored to the values saved in a file in the `~/.metacity/sessions` directory (this refers to a subdirectory in the user's home directory). The default session file runs a script named `/usr/bin/gnome-wm`, which, in turn, starts an appropriate window manager. The default window manager is `metacity`, but you can specify a different window manager by defining the `WINDOW_MANAGER` environment value to the name of a window manager you want.

5. From this point on, the user can interact with the system through the X display and through the window manager (started by the gnome-session program).

6. When the user ends the GNOME session (by selecting Log out from the Main Menu button), gdm attempts to run the script `/etc/X11/gdm/PostSession/DisplayName`, where `DisplayName` is `:0` for the first display. If that file does not exist, gdm executes the `/etc/X11/gdm/PostSession/Default` script, if it exists.

Although this brief description of gdm does not show you all the details, gdm provides a user-friendly interface for user login and for starting a GNOME session. Moreover, like many other X programs, gdm is highly configurable. For example, the names of the script files in the preceding list are the typical ones, but you can specify other names through the file named `gdm.conf`, which, by default, also resides in the `/etc/X11/gdm` directory.

Switching from GNOME to KDE

GNOME and KDE are both capable GUI environments. Red Hat Linux comes with both of these GUIs, but you get GNOME as the default GUI. However, Red Hat also includes the utility script /usr/bin/switchdesk, which enables you easily to switch from one GUI to another, and vice versa. To switch from GNOME to KDE, follow these steps:

1. From your GNOME desktop, select Main Menu⇨System Settings⇨More System Settings⇨Desktop Switching Tool, or type **switchdesk** in a terminal window. The Desktop Switcher dialog box appears.

2. In the Desktop Switcher dialog box, click the KDE radio button to select it (see Figure 9-2), then click the OK button.

Figure 9-2: Switching to KDE by Using the Desktop Switching Tool.

3. A message informs you that the desktop configuration has been changed, but you must restart X for the change to take effect. Click the OK button to dismiss the dialog box.

Although the message in Step 3 states that you must restart X, all you need to do is log out of the session and log back in. To log out, select Main Menu⇨Log Out. When you log in again, you should get the KDE GUI.

The switchdesk utility changes the GUI by creating the appropriate scripts in your home directory. It leaves the display manager unchanged. This means that you use the GNOME display manager, gdm, for login, even when you switch to the KDE GUI. After you log in, gdm executes a session script that eventually executes the .Xclients script in your home directory, if that script exists.

When you run the switchdesk utility, you execute a shell script in the /usr/bin/switchdesk file that contains the following lines:

```
#!/bin/sh
echo "Red Hat Linux `basename $0` 3.9"
echo "Copyright (C) 1999-2001 Red Hat, Inc"
echo "Redistributable under the terms of the GNU General Public License"

kicker=`/sbin/pidof "kdeinit: kicker"`
[ -z "$kicker" ] && kicker=`/sbin/pidof kicker`
[ -z "$kicker" ] && kicker=`/sbin/pidof kpanel`
[ -z "$kicker" ] && kicker=`/sbin/pidof kpanel1`
```

```
good=1

if [ "$DISPLAY" != "" -a "$1" = "" ]; then
    if [ -n "$kicker" -a -x /usr/bin/switchdesk-kde ]; then
        exec switchdesk-kde
    elif [ -x /usr/bin/switchdesk-gnome ]; then
        exec switchdesk-gnome
    elif [ -x /usr/bin/switchdesk-kde ]; then
        exec switchdesk-kde
    else
        echo "Desktop Switcher GUI unavailable."
        echo "Please install the switchdesk-kde or switchdesk-gnome packages or use"
        echo "switchdesk desktopname."
        good=0;
    fi
else
    good=0;
fi

if [ "$good" = "0" ]; then
    exec switchdesk-helper $1
fi
```

Secret

If you are using GNOME, the switchdesk script runs the switchdesk-gnome application that displays the GUI from which you change the desktop. In KDE, this script runs the switchdesk-kde GUI tool. The switchdesk-gnome GUI tool creates two scripts—.Xclients and .Xclients-default—in the home directory of the user. The .Xclients script contains the following lines:

```
#!/bin/bash

# Created by Red Hat Desktop Switcher

if [ -e "$HOME/.Xclients-$HOSTNAME$DISPLAY" ]; then
    exec $HOME/.Xclients-$HOSTNAME$DISPLAY
else
    exec $HOME/.Xclients-default
fi
```

The .Xclients-default script is simpler; it contains the following commands:

```
# Created by Red Hat Desktop Switcher
exec startkde
```

The result of these changes is that when you log in the next time, gdm executes the .Xclients script in your home directory, which, in turn, executes the startkde program (/usr/bin/startkde) to start a KDE session.

Because the switchdesk utility changes the GUI by creating the .Xclients and .Xclients-default scripts in a user's home directory, these changes only affect that particular user.

To switch from KDE to GNOME, log in as `root`, open a terminal window, and type **switchdesk** at the shell prompt, then select GNOME as the desktop. After you log out of KDE and log back in, you should get GNOME as your desktop.

Note that if you want to use GNOME for one session only (as opposed to making it your default GUI), simply click Session at the bottom of the login screen, and then select Gnome from the login window menu in the initial login screen, as shown in Figure 9-3.

Figure 9-3: Switching to GNOME for the Current Session Only.

You should get the GNOME desktop for this session. The next time you log in, the system reverts to KDE.

Learning the KDE Display Manager (kdm)

If you install only the KDE desktop or set the `DISPLAYMANAGER` variable in the `/etc/sysconfig/desktop` file to `KDE`, the kdm program starts the X server for the local display and displays the graphical login window through which you log in to the system. Figure 9-4 shows the graphical login screen that you see when you run the kdm display manager.

When kdm runs, it reads various configuration parameters from the configuration file `/usr/share/config/kdm/kdmrc`, which has a structure similar to a Windows `INI` file. For example, here is a typical `kdmrc` file:

```
# KDM configuration example.
[General]
Xservers=/usr/share/config/kdm/Xservers
PidFile=/var/run/kdm.pid

[Xdmcp]
Enable=false
Xaccess=/usr/share/config/kdm/Xaccess
Willing=/usr/share/config/kdm/Xwilling

[Shutdown]
HaltCmd=/sbin/poweroff

[X-*-Core]
# Core config for all displays
Setup=/usr/share/config/kdm/Xsetup
Startup=/usr/share/config/kdm/Xstartup
Reset=/usr/share/config/kdm/Xreset
Session=/usr/share/config/kdm/Xsession
AutoReLogin=false
```

```
AllowRootLogin=true
AllowNullPasswd=true
AllowShutdown=Root

[X-*-Greeter]
# Greeter config for all displays
SessionTypes=default,kde,failsafe,gnome
GUIStyle=Bluecurve
LogoArea=Clock
GreetFont=Sans,12,-1,5,75,0,0,0,0,0
StdFont=Sans,10,-1,5,50,0,0,0,0,0
FailFont=Sans,10,-1,5,75,0,0,0,0,0
AntiAliasing=true
ShowUsers=None
MinShowUID=500
SortUsers=true
PreselectUser=None
FocusPasswd=false
EchoMode=OneStar
[X-:*-Core]
# Core configurations for local displays
# place local display core configurations here
[X-:*-Greeter]
# Greeter configurations for local displays
# place local display greeter configurations here
```

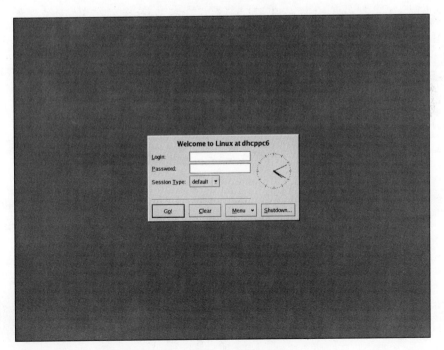

Figure 9-4: Graphical Login Screen Managed by kdm.

As you can see, the file is organized into sections, with each section identified by labels within square brackets. Each section specifies a related set of options that affects some aspect of the GUI login process.

Secret

You can configure the look and feel of the kdm greeter—the login dialog box—on each X display individually. The configuration of each display is specified by a section name that has the following format:

```
[X-host:number_class-subsection]
```

where `host` refers to the hostname of the system to which the display is attached (can be empty for a local display), `number` is the display number (0, if you have only one display), `class` is a display class (it's optional and ignored in most cases), and `subsection` identifies the element of the display manager to which the options apply. For example, if the options apply to the desktop, subsection is `Desktop`. If the options are for the greeter, the subsection is `Greeter`. You can use an asterisk (*) for any of these elements—host, number, and class—as a wildcard.

Thus, to specify the options for the greeter for all displays, place the options in a section named `[X-*-Greeter]`. To change some of these greeter options for the local displays, place the changed options in the `[X-:*-Greeter]` section. On the other hand, if you want to customize some aspect of the greeter for the first local display (which is display number 0), place those options in the section labeled `[X-:0-Greeter]`.

Table 9-2 summarizes some common `kdm` configuration options, organized by sections. I show the X display options for all displays. To customize these for a specific display, you can add a section with a name that reflects the X display to which the options apply.

Table 9-2: Common kdm Configuration Options

Configuration Option	Description
[General] section	
LockPidFile=true or false	If set to true, kdm locks the PidFile to prevent multiple instances of kdm from running simultaneously
PidFile=/var/run/kdm.pid	File where kdm should store its process ID (ID)
Xservers= /usr/share/config/ kdm/Xservers	File containing list of X servers to start (one per display)
[Xdmcp] section	
ChoiceTimeout=seconds	Number of seconds to wait for display to respond after the user has selected a host from the chooser (default is 15 seconds)
Enable=true or false	If set to true, kdm listens on port 177 and supports the X Display Manager Control Protocol (XDMCP) that enables users to log in to other hosts on the network (the default is true)
Port=177	The UDP port number where kdm listens for XDMCP requests (default is 177)

Configuration Option	Description
RemoveDomainname=true or false	If set to true, strips domain name from remote display names if it is equal to the local domain (default is true)
SourceAddress=true or false	Use the numeric IP address of the incoming connection instead of the hostname (useful on multihomed hosts, the default is false)
Willing= /usr/share/config/ kdm/Xwilling	Program to run to generate replies to XDMCP BroadcastQuery requests (the Xwilling program is a shell script that displays the number of users and current load average)

[Shutdown] section

HaltCmd=/sbin/poweroff	Full pathname of command to run to halt the system
RebootCmd=/sbin/reboot	Full pathname of command to run to reboot the system (default is /sbin/reboot)

[X-*-Core] section (core configuration for all displays)

AllowNullPasswd=true or false	If set to true, kdm allows users with empty passwords to log in (default is true)
AllowRootLogin=true or false	If set to true, kdm allows logins by root (default is true)
AllowSdForceNow=Root or All	Specifies who can abort all currently running programs when shutting down system; choices are All for anyone or Root for root user (default is All)
AllowShutdown=Root or All	Specifies who can shut down the system; possible values are All to enable anyone to shut down the system, None to prevent shutdown from the login screen, and Root to require root password for shutdown (default is All)
AutoReLogin=true or false	If set to true, kdm will automatically restart a session after the X server crashes or if it is killed by pressing Ctrl-Alt-Backspace (default is false)
DefaultSdMode=ForceNow or TryNow or Schedule	The default mode for shutdown; choices are ForceNow to shut down immediately, Schedule to shut down after the session exits, or TryNow to shutdown if no session is open and do nothing otherwise (default is Schedule)
OpenDelay=seconds	Number of seconds to wait before retrying to open the display after any error (default is 15 seconds)
OpenRepeat=seconds	How many seconds to wait before trying to open display again (default is 5 seconds)
OpenTimeout=seconds	Number of seconds to wait before timing out on the attempt to open the display (default is 120 seconds)
PingInterval=seconds	How many minutes between successive pinging of remote displays (ping checks if network connection is up and running; default interval is 5 minutes)
Reset= /usr/share/config/ kdm/Xreset	Program to run after a user session ends

(continued)

Table 9-2: *(continued)*

Configuration Option	Description
`ResetSignal=1`	The signal to send to reset the local X server (default is `1`, which stands for SIGHUP)
`Session= /usr/share/config/ kdm/Xsession`	Program that accepts the `SessionTypes` argument and starts an appropriate session
`SessSaveFile=.wmrc`	Filename (in user's home directory) where the last session type is stored (default is `.wmrc`)
`Setup= usr/share/config/ kdm/Xsetup`	Program to run before showing the greeter window
`StartAttempts=number`	The maximum number of times to try opening a display before the display is disabled (default is 4)
`StartInterval=seconds`	How many seconds to wait before resetting the `StartAttempts` counter (default is 30 seconds)
`Startup= usr/share/config/ kdm/Xstartup`	Program to run before starting a user session
`TerminateServer=true or false`	If set to true, restart the local X server instead of resetting after session ends (default is false)
`TermSignal=signum`	The signal to send to terminate the local X server (default is 15, which stands for SIGTERM)

[X-*-Greeter] section (greeter configuration for all displays)

`AntiAliasing=true or false`	If set to true, fonts shown in the greeter should be antialiased (default is `false`)
`DefaultUser=username`	User preselected for login if `PreselectUser=Default`
`EchoMode=OneStar or ThreeStar or NoEcho`	What to show as user types the password; choices are `NoEcho` to show nothing at all, `OneStar` to show a * for each letter typed, or `ThreeStars` to show *** for each letter typed (default is `OneStar`)
`FailFont= Sans,10,-1,5,75, 0,0,0,0,0`	Font used for the "Login Failed" message
`FocusPasswd=true or false`	If set to true, the password input line is automatically selected to receive the keyboard input (default is `false`)
`GreeterPosFixed=true or false`	If set to `true`, the position of the greeter window is fixed and specified by `GreeterPosX` and `GreeterPosY` (default is `false`)
`GreeterPosX=pixels`	Horizontal position, in pixels, of greeter window
`GreeterPosY=pixels`	Vertical position, in pixels, of greeter window
`GreetFont=Sans,12,-1,5,75, 0,0,0,0,0`	The font to use for the welcome text

Configuration Option	Description
GreetString= welcometext	Welcome text in greeter window (default is "Welcome to %s at %n"); use following special characters strings: %d = current display %h = hostname, possibly with domain name %n = node name, most probably the hostname without domain name %s = operating system (Linux) %r = operating system's version %m = machine (hardware) type %% = a single %
GUIStyle=Bluecurve	The look and feel of the greeter (other choices are Default, Windows, Motif, CDE, and any other styles installed on the system)
HiddenUsers=user1,user2,...	List of user names not to be listed in the greeter when ShowUsers is NotHidden
Language=en_US	Language to use in the greeter (default is en_US)
LogoArea=Clock	What to show in the area to the right of the text input line (other options are Logo to display an image specified by LogoPixmap, Clock to display an analog clock, and None to display nothing)
LogoPixmap= /usr/share/apps/kdm/pics/kdelogo.png	The image to show when LogoArea is set to Logo
MinShowUID=500	Users with UID less than the specified number are not shown
NumLock=Off	What to do with the Num Lock key during the time when the greeter is running; choices are On to turn it on, Off to turn it off, and Keep to leave it at its previous state
PreselectUser=None or Previous or Default	User name to be preselected for login; choices are Previous to preselect the previous user, Default to select user listed in DefaultUser field, or None to not preselect at all (default is None)
SelectedUsers=user1,user2,...	List of users to show when ShowUsers=Selected
SessionTypes= default,kde, failsafe,gnome	Names of session types that the user can select from the GUI login window
ShowUsers=None	Which user names, along with pictures, to show in the greeter; choices are NotHidden to show all users except those listed in HiddenUsers, Selected to show only those users listed in SelectedUsers, and None to show no users at all (default is NotHidden)
SortUsers=true or false	If set to true, sort user names alphabetically (default is true)
StdFont= Sans,10,-1,5,50, 0,0,0,0,0	Normal font used in the greeter

Using GNOME

GNOME stands for GNU Network Object Model Environment; and GNU, as you probably know, stands for GNU's Not Unix. GNOME is a GUI and a programming environment. From the user's perspective, GNOME is like the Motif-based Common Desktop Environment (CDE) or Microsoft Windows. Behind the scenes, GNOME has many features that enable programmers to write graphical applications that work together well. The next few sections provide a quick overview of GNOME, highlighting the key features of the GNOME GUI. You can explore the details on your own.

You can always find out the latest information about GNOME by visiting the GNOME home page at http://www.gnome.org.

Taking Stock of GNOME

Although what you see of GNOME is the GUI, there is much more to GNOME than the GUI. To help you appreciate it better, note the following points and key features of GNOME:

◆ GNOME is officially pronounced "guh-NOME," but many people pronounce the word as "NOME." Note that "guh-NOME" stems from "guh-NU," the way people pronounce GNU.

◆ The latest GNOME release is 2.x, also known as GNOME 2 for short.

◆ GNOME runs on several UNIX systems, including Linux, BSD (FreeBSD, NetBSD, and OpenBSD), Solaris, HP-UX, AIX, and Silicon Graphics IRIX.

◆ GNOME uses the Gimp Tool Kit (GTK+) as the graphics toolkit for all graphical applications. GTK+ relies on X for output and supports multiple programming languages, including C, C++, Perl, and others. Users can easily change the look and feel of all GTK+ applications running on a system. GTK+ is licensed under the GNU Library General Public License (LGPL). See Chapter 23 for more information about GPL and LGPL.

◆ GNOME also uses Imlib, another library that supports displaying images on an X display. Imlib supports many different image formats, including XPM and PNG (Portable Network Graphics).

◆ GNOME uses the Object Management Group's Common Object Request Broker Architecture (CORBA) Version 2.2 to enable GNOME software components to communicate with one another regardless of where the components are located or what programming language is used to implement the components.

◆ GNOME applications support drag-and-drop operations.

◆ GNOME application developers write documentation using DocBook, which is a Document Type Definition (DTD) based on Standard General Markup Language (SGML). This means that you can view the manual for a GNOME application on a Web browser, such as Mozilla.

◆ GNOME supports standard internationalization and localization methods. This means that you can easily configure a GNOME application for a new native language.

◆ GNOME uses Mesa, an implementation of OpenGL (an application programming interface—API—for 3D graphics) to support 3D graphics.

◆ GNOME uses libxml2, a free XML library that also includes libxslt, a complete implementation of the XSLT specification (for transforming XML documents to other XML documents)

Exploring GNOME

Assuming that you have enabled a graphical login screen during Red Hat Linux installation, you should get the GNOME GUI whenever you log in to your Linux system. The exact appearance of the GNOME display depends on the current session. The session is nothing more than the set of applications (including a window manager) and the state of these applications. The metacity window manager, which is the default window manager in GNOME, stores the session information in files located in the `~/.metacity/sessions` directory (this is in your home directory). The session files are text files; if you are curious, you can browse these file with the `more` command.

Initially, when you don't yet have a session file, the GNOME session comes from the `/usr/share/gnome/default.session` file. However, as soon as the session starts, the GNOME session manager (`/usr/bin/gnome-session`) saves the current session information in the `~/.metacity/sessions` directory. A typical initial GNOME desktop produced by the session description in the default session file is shown in Figure 9-5.

Figure 9-5: The Initial GNOME Desktop, with the Default Session File.

As you can see from the icons on the left side of the GNOME desktop, GNOME enables you to place folders and applications directly on the desktop. This is similar to the way in which you can place icons directly on the Microsoft Windows desktop.

---

insider insight   The default GNOME session also starts the magicdev daemon, which is designed to monitor devices, such as the floppy drive and the CD-ROM drive, and to detect events, such as the user inserting a CD-ROM into the drive. When magicdev detects a new CD-ROM, it mounts the CD-ROM and communicates with the GNOME file manager to display the contents of the CD-ROM.

When you are running a GUI, you need the window manager as part of your session. A window manager is a special X application that handles interactions for various applications that are displaying windows onscreen. You need a window manager to control the placement and size of each application's window. Without a window manager, you cannot change a window's location or alter its size.

To see why a window manager is necessary, consider the case of two X applications—A and B—that are displaying on the same screen. Neither application has any idea of the other's needs. Suppose that you run application B after A, and B takes over the entire screen (the root window) as its output window. At this point, A's window is obscured underneath B's, and you have no way to reach A's window.

A window manager enables you to switch from B to A, even when B is ill-behaved. (For example, if B's window fills the entire screen, you have no way of accessing A's window without a window manager). The window manager adds a decorative frame to the main window of each application. This frame enables you to move and resize the windows. You can click and drag a corner of the frame to shrink B's window. The window manager shows an outline of the window that changes in size as you move the mouse. This outline enables you to make the topmost window smaller to expose windows underneath it. Additionally, the window manager adds a pull-down menu that you can get by clicking the upper-left corner of the window's frame. This menu contains options that enable you to resize the window, reduce the window to an icon, and quit the application.

As in the window frames in Microsoft Windows, the right-hand corner of the title bar includes three buttons: The leftmost button reduces the window to an icon, the middle button maximizes the window to fill up the entire screen, and the rightmost button closes the window. Unlike Windows, the locations of these buttons, as well as the appearance of the entire window frame, are configurable in GNOME.

Using the GNOME Panel

A key feature of the GNOME desktop is the long bar along the bottom edge of the screen. This is known as the GNOME panel or simply the panel. The panel is a separate GNOME application. As you can see from the bottom edge of Figure 9-5, the panel provides a display area for menus and small panel applets. Each panel applet is a small program designed to work inside the panel. For example, the clock applet on the panel's far right displays the current date and time.

The GNOME panel includes several other applets:

- Launcher applets display buttons with icons of applications. Clicking a button starts (launches) that application. For example, click the earth icon to launch the Mozilla Web browser. Clicking the icon showing sheets of paper next to a pen launches OpenOffice.org Writer—a Microsoft Word-like word-processing program.

- The GNOME Pager applet provides a virtual desktop that's larger than the physical dimensions of your system's screen. The pager displays four pages in a small display area. Each page represents an area equal to the size of the X display screen. To go to a specific page, click that page in the pager window. If you want a window to always appear on each virtual screen page, simply select Put on All Workspaces from its window menu. The window then appears at the same location on each virtual screen page. The GNOME Pager applet also displays buttons for each window being displayed in the current virtual page.

◆ You can add other applets to the GNOME panel. For example, to add the GNOME weather applet, which displays the local weather, right-click on an unused area of the GNOME panel, and then select Add to Panel⇨Accessories⇨ Weather Report from the pop-up menu. In the Add to Panel pop-up menu, you will find many more categories of applets that you can try out.

The GNOME panel also displays the Main Menu button (the red hat icon) that behaves like the Windows Start menu.

Exploring the Main Menu Button

In Figure 9-5, the left-hand side of the panel includes a button with the image of a red hat. That is the Main Menu button. As with the Start button in Microsoft Windows, you can launch applications from the menu that pops up when you click the left mouse button on the foot. Typically, this menu lists items that start an application. Some of the menu items have an arrow; another pop-up menu appears when you place the mouse pointer on an item with an arrow. Figure 9-6 shows a typical view of the Main Menu on a Red Hat Linux system.

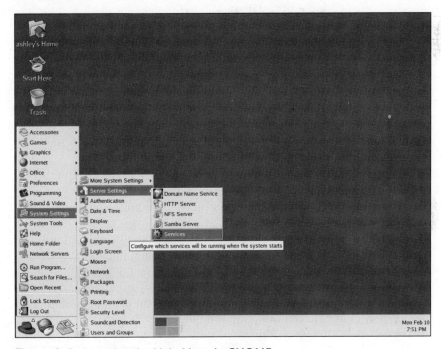

Figure 9-6: Accessing the Main Menu in GNOME.

Explore all the items in the Main menu to see all the tasks you can perform from this menu. As you can see from Figure 9-6, pausing the mouse on a menu item displays pop-up help with information about that menu item.

KDE applications can also run under GNOME. Many KDE applications are organized under Main Menu⇨Extras. Even if you use the GNOME desktop, you can always start a KDE application by selecting Main Menu⇨Extras. Thus, you are in no way limited to running only GNOME applications when you use the GNOME GUI.

Setting GNOME Preferences

You can configure certain aspects of the GNOME desktop by selecting Main Menu➪ Preferences➪Control Center. The Preferences window appears, and it displays a number of icons. Each icon is meant for customizing one aspect of the GNOME desktop. For example, the Background icon enables you to customize the desktop's background.

Using KDE

KDE stands for the K Desktop Environment. The KDE project started in October 1996, with an intention to develop a common GUI for UNIX systems that use the X Window System. The first beta version of KDE was released a year later in October 1997, and KDE Version 1.0 was released in July 1998. KDE 2.0 was released on October 23, 2000. KDE 3.0 was released on April 3, 2002, and KDE 3.1 was released on January 28, 2003. Red Hat Linux comes with KDE 3.1.

From the user's perspective, KDE provides a graphical desktop environment that includes a window manager, the Konqueror Web browser and file manager, a panel for starting applications, a help system, configuration tools, and many applications, including the KOffice office suite, image viewer, PostScript viewer, and mail and news programs.

From the developer's perspective, KDE has class libraries and object models for easy application development in C++. KDE is a large development project with many collaborators.

The following sections provide an overview of KDE, but the best way to learn about KDE is to use it for a while. Follow the instructions in the section "Switching from GNOME to KDE" to change your GUI to KDE, then use it for a while to get a feel for KDE's capabilities.

You can always find out the latest information about KDE by visiting the KDE home page at http://www.kde.org.

Taking Stock of KDE

Like GNOME, KDE is meant to be a complete desktop environment for users and a programming environment for application developers. Here are some key features of KDE:

♦ KDE runs on a number of UNIX-like systems, including Linux, FreeBSD, Solaris, HP-UX, and Silicon Graphics IRIX. KDE needs the X Window System.

♦ The latest KDE release is 3.1, also known as KDE 3.1 for short.

♦ KDE is written in C++ and uses object-oriented development.

♦ KDE uses the Qt Free Edition GUI toolkit from a Norwegian company, Trolltech AS (http://www.troll.no/). Qt is a C++ class library for building GUIs; it provides the widgets such as menus, buttons, and sliders used in KDE applications. There has been some controversy over the Qt license because its terms are not the same as the GNU General Public License. However, in September 2000, Trolltech announced that it would license Qt Free Edition, Version 2.2, under the GNU General Public License.

♦ KDE provides an application development framework built on DCOP (Desktop Communications Protocol) and KParts, a compound document model. DCOP and KParts are similar to Microsoft's DCOM (Distributed Component Object Model) and ActiveX controls.

◆ KDE includes an office application suite based on the DCOP/KParts technology. The office suite, KOffice, includes a spreadsheet (KSpread), a charting program (KChart), a FrameMaker-like word processor (KWord), a presentation application (KPresenter), and a vector drawing program (Kontour).

◆ KDE supports drag-and-drop operations.

◆ KDE supports internationalization, and most KDE applications have been translated into over 25 different languages.

Exploring KDE

Assuming that you have selected KDE as your desktop (or selected a KDE session from the Session pop-up menu), you should get the KDE desktop when you log in. Figure 9-7 shows the default KDE desktop after I log in on my Red Hat Linux system.

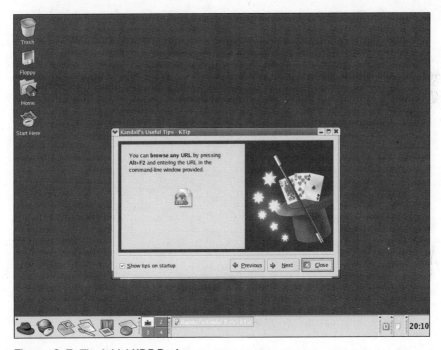

Figure 9-7: The Initial KDE Desktop.

The initial desktop looks very similar to the GNOME desktop because Red Hat has configured both desktops and menus to look similar—so as to provide a consistent look and feel no matter which desktop users select. The initial KDE session includes a window showing a helpful tip. That's the only part that makes the desktop look different from that in GNOME.

KDE is easy to use and has many similarities with the Microsoft Windows GUI. You can start applications from a menu that's similar to the Start menu in Windows. KDE also enables you to place folders and applications directly on the desktop.

As Figure 9-7 shows, KDE provides a Windows-like desktop with a panel along the bottom edge of the screen. The most important component of the panel is the red hat button on the left-hand side. That button is like the Start button in Windows. When you click the red hat button, a pop-up menu appears. From this menu, you can get to other menus by moving the mouse over items with a right-pointing arrow. For example, Figure 9-8 shows a typical menu hierarchy for changing some desktop settings.

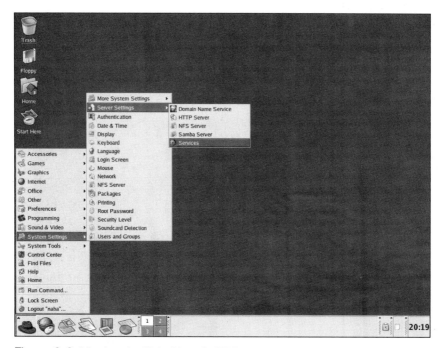

Figure 9-8: Viewing the Main Menu in KDE.

You can start applications from the main menu. That's why the KDE documentation calls this button the *Application Starter*. Just to keep everything simple, I will refer to the red hat button as Main Menu.

---

insider
insight

Red Hat has changed the Main Menu button to show a red hat icon (the Red Hat logo). In a normal KDE installation, the leftmost button is a large letter K on top of a gear. It's sometimes called the K button for short.

Next to the red hat button (Main Menu), the panel includes several other buttons. If you don't know what a button does, simply move the mouse over the button, and a small pop-up window displays a brief message about that button.

KDE supports a virtual desktop. By default, you get four virtual desktops. You can click one of the buttons on the panel (see Figure 9-8) labeled 1, 2, 3, and 4 to switch to a specific desktop. Use the desktops to organize your application windows. You needn't clutter up a single desktop with many open windows. When a desktop gets crowded, simply switch to another desktop and open the applications there.

Sometimes you want to type Linux commands at a text prompt. Select Main Menu⇨System Tools⇨Terminal and a terminal window appears. You can then type Linux commands at the shell prompt in the terminal emulation window. Chapter 7 describes the shell and some important Linux commands.

Secret

KDE includes a KDE Control Center that you can use to customize various aspects of KDE, including the desktop background, icons, and fonts. To start the KDE Control Center, select Main Menu⇨Control Center. The KDE Control Center main window has two parts. The left side of the window has a tree menu of items that you can control with this tool. The tree menu is organized into categories, such as Appearance & Themes, Internet & Network, Peripherals, Security & Privacy, and so on. Click an item to view the subcategories for that item. To change an item, go through the tree menu to locate the item, then click it. That item's configuration options then appear in a dialog box on the right side of the window. For example, Figure 9-9 shows the options for customizing the desktop background.

Figure 9-9: Customizing the Desktop Background with KDE Control Center.

You can choose the desktop whose background you want to customize, then select either a solid color background or a wallpaper (an image used as a background). After making your selections, click Apply to make the change.

To log out of KDE, select Main Menu⇨Logout, and click the Logout button on the resulting dialog box.

Summary

Newcomers and old-timers alike can benefit from a graphical point-and-click user interface. This chapter shows you how Red Hat Linux starts a graphical login screen so that you can stay in the graphical environment. This chapter also provides an overview of the GNOME and KDE graphical user interfaces and explains how to customize the appearance of X applications. The next chapter introduces you to common Linux applications.

By reading this chapter, you learn the following:

- After Linux boots, a process named init starts all the other processes. The exact set of initial processes depends on the run level, which typically is a number ranging from 0 to 6. The /etc/inittab file specifies the processes that start at each run level. The /etc/inittab file specifies that a graphical display manager starts at run level 5. In Red Hat Linux, the GNOME Display Manager (gdm) provides the graphical login prompt. The Red Hat Linux installation program can set up a graphical login for you.

- If you install KDE, you can opt to run the KDE Display Manager (KDM). To do so, add the line DISPLAYMANAGER="KDE" to the /etc/sysconfig/desktop file.

- You can configure the initial graphical login screen through configuration files for gdm and kdm. For gdm, the configuration file is /etc/X11/gdm/gdm.conf and for kdm, the file is /usr/share/config/kdm/kdmrc. This chapter explains both of these configuration files.

- GNOME and KDE are two popular GUIs for Linux. Red Hat Linux comes with both GNOME and KDE, but your system starts with GNOME as the default GUI. You can use the switchdesk utility to change your default GUI to KDE.

- Both GNOME and KDE are similar to other modern desktop environments, such as Apple Mac OS and Microsoft Windows. Therefore, you can easily learn to use GNOME and KDE. Both include control centers from which you can customize various aspects of the desktop, including the appearance.

Red Hat Linux Applications and Utilities

Chapter
10

◆ ◆

Secrets in This Chapter

◆ ◆

The Red Hat Linux distribution on this book's companion CD-ROMs includes many applications. The GNOME and KDE desktops come with a number of applications, such as calendars, calculators, CD players, and games. Red Hat Linux also comes with the GNU software packages, which include applications such as the GIMP (for working with images) and kghostview (for viewing PostScript files).

Many more Linux applications are available on the Internet or commercially from various Linux vendors. This chapter briefly describes some of the Linux applications included on the companion CD-ROMs. The chapter also introduces you to several prominent, commercially available office-productivity applications for Linux that are not included on the companion CD-ROMs.

Applications on the Companion CD-ROMs

Table 10-1 shows a selected set of Linux applications on the CD-ROMs, organized by category.

Table 10-1: Linux Applications on the CD-ROMs

Category	Applications
Editors	GNU Emacs, vim, GUI text editors, KDE Binary Editor
GUI Desktops	GNOME, KDE
Office Tools	OpenOffice.org Writer, OpenOffice.org Calc, OpenOffice.org Impress, OpenOffice.org Draw, OpenOffice.org Math, calendars, calculators, spelling checker, Dictionary
Utilities	GNU bc, gzip, Midnight Commander, patch, GnuPG (GNU Privacy Guard)
Multimedia	X Multimedia System (XMMS), CD players, gtkam, xsane
Graphics and image manipulation	The GIMP, xfig, gnuplot, ghostscript, kghostview, ImageMagick, dia, netpbm
DOS/Windows	mtools, wine
System Administration	User Manager, Printer Configuration, Network Configuration, Disk Management, Date/Time Properties, System Monitor, Gnome RPM, Nautilus, redhat-config utilities
Internet	Ximian Evolution, INN, gaim, pine, pppd, rdist, sendmail, xchat, Telnet, FTP, SSH, Mozilla, Internet Configuration Wizard, Apache Configuration, Bind Configuration, Firewall configuration
Serial communications	minicom, xminicom
Database	PostgreSQL, MySQL
Programming	Bison, flex, Gawk, GCC, GCJ, Perl, Python, RCS, CVS, Tcl/Tk, yacc
Text formatting	groff, TeX, docbook2dvi, docbook2html, docbook2man, docbook2ps, docbook2rtf, docbook2tex, docbook2texi, docbook2txt, docbook2pdf
Games	GNU Chess, chromium, Maelstrom, Mahjongg, Reversi, GNOME Mines, FreeCell, GNOME Robots, KBackgammon, AisleRiot, and many more

This list is by no means comprehensive. The Red Hat Linux distribution comes with a plethora of standard GNU utilities not shown in the list.

This chapter provides a brief summary of a smaller subset of these applications. In particular, you learn about some of the programs not covered in earlier chapters. Some applications, such as GNU Emacs and vi, are covered in detail elsewhere in the book. Also, entire categories of important applications, such as Internet applications, are covered in great detail in individual chapters within the book.

Quite a few of the listed applications are automatically installed during the Red Hat Linux installation process. Other applications have to be installed from one of the companion CD-ROMs.

You can start many of these applications from the GNOME or KDE desktop. The Main Menu button of each desktop provides a series of menus from which you can select the applications.

Editors

You can find the following text editors on the companion CD-ROMs:

- GNU Emacs, which is the one and only original Emacs
- Vim, which is a vi-like editor
- GUI text editors that are part of GNOME and KDE

As you can see, most of these editors aspire to be either GNU Emacs or vi. The look-alikes typically are smaller and have fewer features.

The GUI text editors are part of GNOME and KDE.

GNU Emacs

The companion CD-ROM includes GNU Emacs version 21.2. GNU Emacs, one of the best-known GNU products, is distributed by the Free Software Foundation. The GNU Emacs binary is /usr/bin/emacs, which works under X and provides menus for editing operations. You must have X installed to run Emacs.

cross
ref

Chapter 11 describes the features of GNU Emacs and how to use it for text-editing tasks.

Vim

Vim stands for Vi IMproved. As the name implies, Vim is an improved version of the standard UNIX text editor vi. The companion CD-ROMs include version 6.1 of Vim. In addition to the standard vi commands, Vim includes many new features, including several levels of undo, command-line history, and filename completion.

cross
ref

In Red Hat Linux, when you run the vi editor, you are running Vim. Chapter 11 shows you how to use the vi editor.

GUI Text Editors

Both of the Linux graphical desktops—GNOME and KDE—come with GUI text editors (text editors that have graphical user interfaces).

To try the GNOME text editor, gedit, select Main Menu⇨Accessories⇨Text Editor from the GNOME desktop. You can open a file by clicking the Open button on the toolbar. This brings up the Open File dialog box. You can then change directories and select the file to edit by clicking the OK button.

The gedit editor then loads the file in its window. You can open more than one file and move among them as you edit the files. Figure 10-1 shows a typical editing session with gedit.

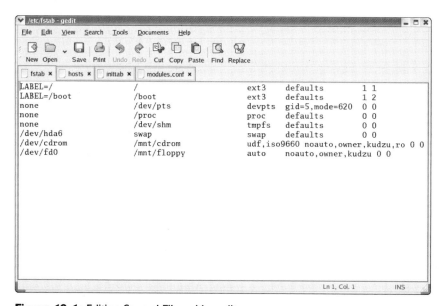

Figure 10-1: Editing Several Files with gedit.

In this case, the editor has four files open for editing: fstab, inittab, hosts, and modules.conf (all from the /etc directory). The filenames appear as tabs below the toolbar of the editor's window. You can switch among the files by clicking the tabs with the filenames.

The rest of the text-editing steps are intuitive. To enter new text, click to position the cursor and begin typing. You can select text and copy or cut it by using the buttons on the toolbar above the text-editing area. To paste the text elsewhere in the file, position the cursor, and click the Paste button.

From the KDE desktop, you can start the KDE text editor by selecting Main Menu⇨Accessories⇨Kate. To open a text file, select File⇨Open from the menu. A dialog box appears. From this dialog box, you can go to the desired directory, select the file to open, and click the OK button. The KDE text editor then opens the file and displays its contents in the window. You can then edit the file.

Office Tools

This book's companion CD-ROMs include several office tools, such as calendars, calculators, and spell checkers. The following sections describe a few of these office tools:

- ◆ **Ximian Evolution**—A personal information manager (PIM) that includes email, calendar, contact management, and an online task list
- ◆ **OpenOffice.org Writer**—A Microsoft Word-like word processor
- ◆ **OpenOffice.org Calc**—A Microsoft Excel-like spreadsheet program
- ◆ **OpenOffice.org Impress**—A Microsoft PowerPoint-like presentation program
- ◆ **KOrganizer**—KDE calendar
- ◆ **Calculators**—GNOME calculator and KDE calculator
- ◆ **Other applications**—Commercially available office applications for Linux

Managing Your Inbox with Ximian Evolution

Red Hat provides Ximian Evolution as the mail reader and organizer for appointments, contacts, and tasks. You can learn more about Evolution at Ximian's website at `http://www.ximian.com/products/evolution/`.

Select Main Menu⇨Internet⇨Email from the GNOME or KDE desktop. If this is your first time with Evolution, the Evolution Setup Assistant starts up (see Figure 10-2).

Figure 10-2: Setting Up Evolution for the First Time.

Click Next in the Welcome screen, and the Evolution Setup Assistant guides you through the following steps:

1. Enter your name and email address in the Identity screen, and click Next. For example, if your email address is `joe@someplace.com`, that's what you enter.
2. Set up the options for receiving email, and click Next. Select the type of mail download protocol—POP (Post Office Protocol) or IMAP (Internet Message Access Protocol). Then provide the name of the mail server (for example, `mail.comcast.net`). You don't have to enter the password for your email account right now; you will be prompted for a password when Evolution connects to the mail server the first time.

3. Provide further information about receiving email—how often to check for mail and whether to leave messages on the server—and then click Next. Typically, you would want to download the messages and delete them on the server; otherwise, the ISP would complain after your mail piles up.

4. Set up the options for sending email. Select the server type as SMTP (Simple Mail Transfer Protocol), then enter the name of the server such as `smtp .comcast.net`. If the server requires you to log in, click the check box that says Server requires authentication, then enter your user name (this is the user name you need to log in to your ISP's mail server). Click Next.

5. Indicate if you want this email account to be your default account. Click Next.

6. Set your time zone by clicking on a map. Click Next.

7. Click Finish to complete the Evolution setup.

Secret

After you complete the one-time setup, Evolution opens its main window, as shown in Figure 10-3.

Figure 10-3: Main Window of Ximian Evolution.

Evolution's main display area is vertically divided into two windows—a narrow Shortcuts window on the left with a number of shortcut icons and a bigger window where Evolution displays information relevant to the currently selected shortcut.

Initially, Evolution displays a summary view that shows information about your mail, appointments, and tasks, as well as other useful information such as the weather. By default, Evolution initially displays the weather for Boston, Massachusetts, USA.

Some of the information in Evolution's summary window come from Web links. For example, the list of Red Hat Errata comes from the Red Hat website.

You can click the icons on the left-hand window to switch to different views. These icons provide access to all the necessary components of a PIM—email, calendar, task list, and contacts. You will find all of these tasks intuitive to perform in Evolution.

To access your email in Evolution, click the Inbox icon. Evolution opens your Inbox. If you had turned on the feature to automatically check for mail every so often, Evolution would have already prompted you for your mail password and downloaded your mail. The email inbox looks very much like any other mail reader's inbox, such as the Outlook Express inbox.

To read a message, click on the message in the upper window of the Inbox, and the message text appears in the lower window.

To reply to the current message, click the Reply button on the toolbar. A message composition window pops up. You can write your reply and then click the Send button on the toolbar to send the reply.

To send a new email, click the New Message button on the Evolution toolbar. A new message composition window appears, and you can type your message in that window, then click Send.

To add an appointment in Evolution, click the Calendar button. Evolution then displays the calendar. You can move to the date of the appointment and double-click the time. A new window appears where you can type in the details of the appointment. When done, click the Save and Exit buttons on that window. Evolution then shows the appointment in the calendar, as shown in Figure 10-4.

insider
insight
Ximian Evolution comes with extensive online help. Select Help⇨Table of Contents from the Evolution menu and *A User's Guide to Ximian Evolution* appears in a Nautilus window.

Writing with OpenOffice.org Writer

OpenOffice.org Write is a word-processing program. It's part of an open-source office application suite, OpenOffice.org project (http://www.openoffice.org/). To start OpenOffice.org Writer, select Main Menu⇨Office⇨OpenOffice.org Writer from GNOME or KDE (you can also start OpenOffice.org Writer by clicking the panel button with icon showing papers next to a pen). OpenOffice.org Writer prompts you to register and displays a blank document in its main window. Using Writer is simple—it's similar to other word processors such as Microsoft Word. For example, you can type text into the blank document, format text, and save text when done.

You can also open documents that you have prepared with Microsoft Word on a Windows machine. Figure 10-5 shows a Microsoft Word document being opened in OpenOffice.org Writer.

Figure 10-4: Keeping Track of Appointments in Evolution's Calendar.

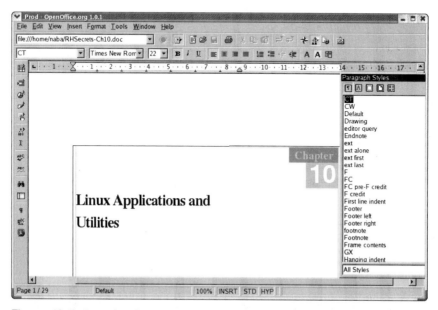

Figure 10-5: Preparing Documents in OpenOffice.org Writer.

When you save a document, by default Writer saves it in OpenOffice.org 1.0 Text Document format in a file with the .sxw extension.

insider insight

If you need to share OpenOffice.org Writer documents with Microsoft Word, save the documents in several formats including Microsoft Word 97/2000/XP, Microsoft Word 95, Microsoft Word 6.0, and Rich Text Format (.rtf). Microsoft Word can open .rtf files.

I won't explain how to use Writer because it is simple and intuitive to use. If you need it, online help is available. Select Help⇨Contents from the Writer menu. This brings up the OpenOffice.org Help window with help information on the Writer. You can then click the links to view specific help information.

Preparing Spreadsheets with OpenOffice.org Calc

Calc is the spreadsheet program in the OpenOffice.org application suite. To start Calc, select Main Menu⇨Office⇨OpenOffice.org Calc from the GNOME or KDE panel. The Calc program displays its main window, which looks similar to Windows-based spreadsheets, such as Microsoft Excel. (In fact, Calc can read and write Microsoft Excel format spreadsheet files.)

Use Calc in the same way you use Microsoft Excel. You can type entries in cells, use formulas, and format the cells (such as specifying the type of value and the number of digits after the decimal point). Figure 10-6 shows a typical spreadsheet in Calc.

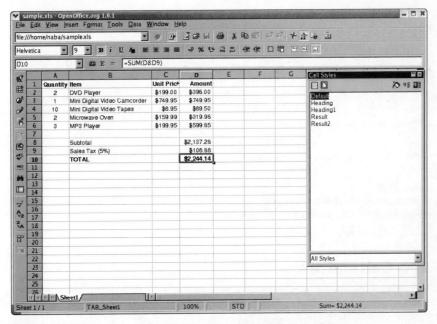

Figure 10-6: Preparing Spreadsheets Using OpenOffice.org Calc.

When preparing the spreadsheet, use formulas you normally use in Microsoft Excel. For example, use the formula SUM(D2:D6) to add up the entries from cell D2 to D6. To set cell D2 as the product of the entries A2 and C2, type **=A2*C2** in cell D2. To learn more about the functions available in OpenOffice.org Calc, select Help➪Contents from the menu. This opens the OpenOffice.org Help window, from which you can browse the functions by category and click a function to read more about it.

To save the spreadsheet, select File➪Save As. A dialog box appears, from which you can specify the file format, the directory location, and the name of the file. OpenOffice.org Calc can save the file in a number of formats, including Microsoft Excel 97/2000/XP, Microsoft Excel 95, Microsoft Excel 5.0, and text file with comma-separated values (CSV).

insider insight

If you want to exchange files with Microsoft Excel, save the spreadsheet in Microsoft Excel format (choose an appropriate version of Excel). Then you can transfer that file to a Windows system and open it in Microsoft Excel.

Presenting Information with OpenOffice.org Impress

OpenOffice.org Impress is part of the OpenOffice.org office application suite. You can prepare briefing packages (slide presentations) using Impress. It's similar to Microsoft PowerPoint. To run Impress, select Main Menu➪Office➪OpenOffice.org Impress from the GNOME or KDE desktop.

To begin working, select the type of document (paper or screen presentation) and any template you want to use. The template provides a style for the presentation package you want to prepare. You can also choose to open an existing document.

Figure 10-7 shows a typical slide presentation in Impress.

The Impress window shows the first slide. The exact appearance depends on the document type and template you select. You can begin adding text and other graphic objects such as images, text, and lines to the slide.

To insert a new slide, select Insert Slide from the floating menu. A gallery of slide layouts appears in a dialog box. Click the style of slide you want in the dialog box. You can then add text and graphics to that new slide.

To save a presentation, select File➪Save from the menu. For new documents, you have to provide a filename and select the directory in which to save the file.

insider insight

If you want to share the slides with someone who uses Microsoft PowerPoint, save the presentation in Microsoft PowerPoint 97/2000/XP format.

Using Calculators

You have a choice of the GNOME calculator or the KDE calculator. Both are scientific calculators, and you can do the typical scientific calculations such as square root and inverse, as well as trigonometric functions, such as sine, cosine, and tangent.

To run the GNOME calculator, select Main Menu➪Accessories➪Calculator in the GNOME panel. Figure 10-8 shows the GNOME calculator.

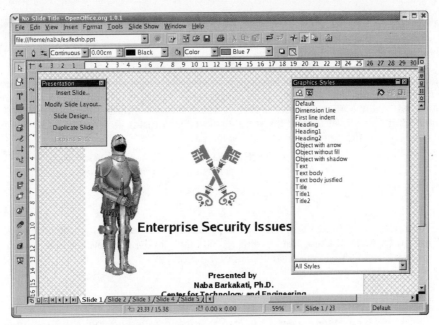

Figure 10-7: Preparing Briefing Packages in OpenOffice.org Impress.

Figure 10-8: The GNOME Calculator.

The KDE calculator has more features than the GNOME calculator. For example, it can perform calculations in hexadecimal, decimal, octal, and binary format. From the KDE desktop, you can start the KDE calculator by selecting Main Menu⇨Accessories⇨ Scientific Calculator. The KDE calculator is intuitive to use.

Commercially Available Office Applications for Linux

Because office applications are important to many businesses as well as individuals, I want to briefly mention some of the commercial office applications available for Red Hat Linux. These commercial offerings include Anyware (formerly Applixware) Office, and StarOffice. These products do cost some money, but the cost is usually less than that for Microsoft Office—the leading office application suite for Windows. (In case you don't know, Microsoft Office is a collection of several applications: Microsoft Word for word processing, Microsoft Excel for spreadsheets, Microsoft PowerPoint for presentation graphics, and Microsoft Access for databases.)

Another recent commercial product for Linux is CrossOver Office from CodeWeavers. With CrossOver Office, you can run your existing Microsoft Office applications such as Word, Excel, and PowerPoint under Linux and X Window System.

> **note**   This book's companion CD-ROMs do not include any of these commercial office applications for Red Hat Linux, but I briefly describe them in the next few sections. You can visit each vendor's website for more about the products.

Running Microsoft Office in Linux with CrossOver Office

You probably have Windows and Microsoft Office installed on your PC. When you decide to run Red Hat Linux on the PC, you can continue to run the key Microsoft Office applications from the GNOME or KDE desktop. The convenience of running Microsoft Office in Linux comes in the form of a commercial product called CrossOver Office.

Secret

CrossOver Office, from CodeWeavers, is a software package that enables you to install your Microsoft Office applications (only Office 97 or Office 2000, not Office XP) in Linux. You do not need Microsoft Windows to run the Office applications in CrossOver Office. You simply install CrossOver Office and then install Microsoft Office from the CD-ROM. After you install Microsoft Office, the Office applications will be available directly from GNOME or KDE desktop.

CrossOver Office uses Wine—an open-source implementation of the Windows Win32 and Win16 application programming interfaces (APIs) using the X Window System and designed to run in UNIX and Linux systems. Wine includes the Wine loader and WineLib. Wine loader can load and run Windows applications. WineLib is used for compiling and linking Windows applications in Linux. Wine is available free of charge from `http://www.winehq.com`.

CodeWeavers created CrossOver Office using a customized version of Wine so as to make sure that the Microsoft Office applications, especially Microsoft Word, Excel, and Powerpoint (from Office 97 or Office 2000) run properly on Wine. CodeWeavers charges a nominal amount for CrossOver Office—the list price is $54.95 for a single copy (with lower costs for multiple copies)—but all changes to Wine are returned to the Wine project. Thus, the Wine open-source project benefits from the sale of CrossOver Office.

You can learn more about CrossOver Office and purchase it at CodeWeavers website (`http://www.codeweavers.com/products/office/`).

Getting Anyware Office

Anyware Office, formerly known as Applixware Office, is another prominent office application suite for all Linux distributions, including Red Hat Linux. In April 2000, Applix, Inc., formed a separate group—VistaSource, Inc.— that focuses solely on Linux applications.

Like other office suites, Anyware Office includes Words (for word processing), Spreadsheets (for spreadsheets), and Graphics and Presents (for presentation graphics). In addition, it also has Mail (an email interface) and Data (an interactive relational database browsing tool). Anyware Office can also read and write documents in Microsoft Office and Corel WordPerfect formats, as well as in several other file formats. Although trial versions are not offered, the entire Anyware Office suite is currently priced at less than $100 in the U.S.

You can learn more about Applixware at VistaSource's website (http://www.vista source.com/products/).

Getting StarOffice

StarOffice is another commercial office applications suite; it was created by StarDivision of Hamburg, Germany, and purchased by Sun Microsystems in 1999. StarOffice is a cross-platform solution—it runs on Linux, Windows 95/98/Me/NT/2000/XP, Sun Solaris SPARC, and Sun Solaris x86. Also, StarOffice is available in several languages: English, French, German, Spanish, Italian, and Swedish.

Secret

StarOffice is a unique office productivity suite in that it combines all of its components into a common desktop from which you can open new documents, drag-and-drop documents from one application to another, and access the Internet. Here's what StarOffice 6.0 includes

- StarOffice Writer for word processing (Microsoft Word compatible)
- StarOffice Calc for spreadsheets (Microsoft Excel compatible)
- StarOffice Impress for presentations (Microsoft PowerPoint compatible)
- StarOffice Draw for vector graphics drawing
- StarOffice Base for data management

You can buy a copy of StarOffice from http://www.sun.com/staroffice/. You can also find the details of Sun's StarOffice licensing policy at the same URL.

In October 2000, Sun released the source code of StarOffice under open-source licenses. OpenOffice.org, an open-source project that Sun supports, released the OpenOffice.org 1.0 office productivity suite in May 2002. Presently, Red Hat Linux comes with OpenOffice.org 1.0.1, which has everything that StarOffice includes, except the database program. To learn more about OpenOffice.org, visit http://www.openoffice.org.

Graphics and Images

The applications in this category enable you to work with images, graphics (line drawings and shapes), and sound. Chapter 5 describes the CD players you can use to play audio CDs on your Red Hat Linux system. The following applications, summarized in this chapter, enable you to prepare, view, modify, and print graphics and images:

- **The GIMP (the GNU Image Manipulation Program)**—A program for viewing and performing image-manipulation tasks, such as photo retouching, image composition, and image creation
- **Xfig**—A drawing program capable of producing engineering drawings
- **Gnuplot**—A plotting package
- **Ghostscript**—A PostScript interpreter capable of producing output on many devices, including output in various image-file formats
- **KGhostview**—A KDE application capable of displaying PostScript and PDF files

Manipulating Images with the GIMP

The GIMP (GNU Image Manipulation Program) is an image-manipulation program written by Peter Mattis and Spencer Kimball and released under the GNU General Public License (GPL). It is installed if you select the Graphics Manipulation package when you install Red Hat Linux from this book's companion CD-ROMs. The GIMP is comparable to other image-manipulation programs, such as Adobe Photoshop and Corel Photopaint.

To try out the GIMP, select Main Menu↪Graphics↪The GIMP from the GNOME desktop or the KDE desktop. The GIMP starts and displays a window with copyright and license information. Click the Continue button to proceed with the installation. The next screen shows the directories to be created when you proceed with a personal installation of the GIMP.

GIMP installation involves creating a directory called `.gimp-1.2` in your home directory and placing a number of files in that directory. This directory essentially holds information about any changes to user preferences you might make to the GIMP. Go ahead and click the Continue button at the bottom of the window. The GIMP creates the necessary directories and copies the necessary files to those directories, then it displays an installation log.

After reading the installation log and ensuring that there are no error messages, click the Continue button. The GIMP then guides you through several screens from which you are asked to specify the values of some parameters; you can accept the defaults and click the Continue button in each screen until the installation window closes. From this time on, you won't see the installation window; you have to deal with installation only when you run the GIMP for the first time.

The GIMP then loads any plug-ins—external modules that enhance its functionality. It displays a startup window that shows a message about each plug-in as it has loaded. After finishing the startup, the GIMP displays a tip of the day in a window and a number of windows, as shown in Figure 10-9. You can browse the tips and click the Close button to close the tip window.

The initial GIMP windows include a main toolbox window titled The GIMP, a Tool Options window, a Brush Selection window, and a Layers, Channels & Paths window. Of these, the main toolbox window is the most important—in fact, you can close the other windows and work by using the menus and buttons in the toolbox.

Figure 10-9: The Initial Windows Displayed by the GIMP.

The toolbox has three menus on the menu bar: File, Xtns (extensions), and Help. The File menu has options to create a new image, open an existing image, save and print an image, mail an image, and quit the GIMP. The Xtns menu gives you access to numerous extensions to the GIMP. The exact content of the Xtns menu depends on which extensions are installed on your system. The Help menu enables you to view tips and get help on the GIMP. For example, select Help⇨Help to bring up the GIMP Help Browser with online information about the GIMP.

To open an image file in the GIMP, select File⇨Open. This brings up the Load Image dialog box from which you can select an image file. You can change directories and select the image file you want to open. GIMP can read all common image-file formats, such as GIF, JPEG, TIFF, PCX, BMP, PNG, and PostScript. After you select the file and click the OK button, the GIMP loads the image into a new window. Figure 10-10 shows a JPEG image from the file `/usr/share/wallpapers/alien-night.jpg`, which the GIMP has opened.

Figure 10-10: Opening an Image with the GIMP.

Secret

The GIMP's main toolbox also has many buttons that represent the tools you use to edit the image and apply special effects. You can get pop-up help on each tool button by placing the mouse pointer on the button. You can select a tool by clicking that tool's button, and you can apply that tool's effects on the image.

For your convenience, the GIMP displays a pop-up menu when you right-click your mouse on the image window. The pop-up menu has most of the options from the File and Xtns menus in the toolbox. You can then select specific actions from these menus.

You can do much more than just load and view images with the GIMP, but a complete discussion of all its features is beyond the scope of this book. If you want to try the other features of the GIMP, you should consult the GIMP User Manual (GUM), available online at http://manual.gimp.org/. You can also select Xtns⇨Web Browser⇨GIMP.ORG⇨Documentation to access the online documentation for the GIMP (you need an Internet connection for this to work).

Some documentation about the GIMP is installed in the /usr/share/doc directory. To go to that directory, type **cd /usr/share/doc/gimp*** (the actual directory name depends on the current version of the GIMP). The README file in that directory points you to other resources on the Web, where you can learn more about the GIMP. In particular, visit the GIMP home page at http://www.gimp.org/ to learn the latest news about the GIMP and to find links to other resources.

Drawing Figures with xfig

The xfig program is an interactive drawing program that runs under X and can generate encapsulated PostScript files suitable for inclusion in documents. To use xfig, you need to install two RPM files—first the transfig RPM and then the xfig RPM.

To install xfig, follow these steps:

1. Mount each CD-ROM and search for the `transfig` and `xfig` RPMs. Insert each CD-ROM and wait for it to be mounted (or type **mount /dev/cdrom** to mount the CD-ROM). Then, type the following commands in a terminal window and look for the files:

   ```
   cd /mnt/cdrom/RedHat/RPMS
   ls transfig*
   ls xfig*
   ```

2. After you find the files, install the transfig program with the `rpm` command as follows:

   ```
   rpm -ivh transfig*.rpm
   ```

3. Install the xfig program with the `rpm` command as follows:

   ```
   rpm -ivh xfig*.rpm
   ```

To try xfig, type **xfig &** in a terminal window. This command causes a rather large xfig window to appear. At the top edge of the window, you'll find a menu bar. To open an xfig drawing, click the File button. That action brings up a file-selection dialog box, through which you can change directories and locate `xfig` files (they usually have the `.fig` extension).

You will find a large number of `xfig` drawings, organized into subdirectories, in the `/usr/lib/X11/xfig/Libraries` directory of your Red Hat Linux system (these files are installed when you install xfig). You can open and view some of these drawing files in xfig. For example, Figure 10-11 shows the xfig window after loading the drawing file `/usr/lib/X11/xfig/Libraries/Buildings/twostory.fig`.

As is true of any other tool, learning to use all of the features of xfig takes some practice. If you are familiar with other drawing software, such as MacDraw (Macintosh) or CorelDRAW (PC), you should be able to use xfig without much trouble.

Plotting Data with Gnuplot

Gnuplot is an interactive plotting utility. You need to run Gnuplot under the X Window System because it uses an X window as the output device. Gnuplot is command-line-driven program; it prompts you and accepts your input commands. In response to those commands, Gnuplot displays various types of plots. The output appears in an X window.

Figure 10-11: A Sample Drawing That xfig Displays.

To install Gnuplot, follow these steps:

1. Mount each CD-ROM and search for the `gnuplot` RPM. Insert each CD-ROM and wait for it to be mounted (or type **mount /dev/cdrom** to mount the CD-ROM). Then, type the following commands in a terminal window and look for the file:

```
cd /mnt/cdrom/RedHat/RPMS
ls gnuplot*
```

2. After you find the file, install Gnuplot with the following `rpm` command:

```
rpm -ivh gnuplot*.rpm
```

Secret

After installing Gnuplot, run it by typing `gnuplot` & in a terminal window. Gnuplot displays an opening message and waits for further input at the prompt, as shown in Figure 10-12.

To see an immediate result, type the following Gnuplot command at the prompt:

```
plot sin(x)
```

Gnuplot opens an output window and displays a plot of the sine function, as shown in Figure 10-13.

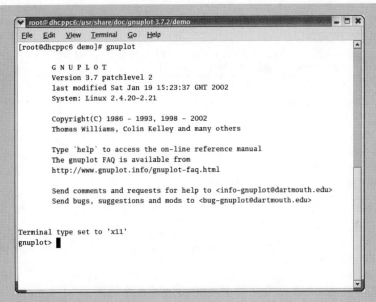

Figure 10-12: Running Gnuplot in a Terminal Window.

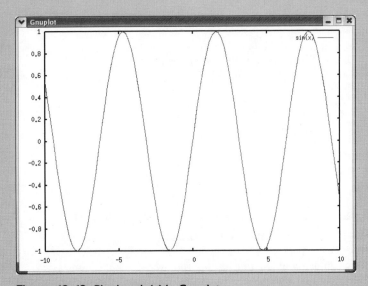

Figure 10-13: Plotting sin(x) in Gnuplot.

To quit Gnuplot, click the terminal window to make it active, then type **quit**. This example is a simple illustration of Gnuplot's capabilities.

Incidentally, although Gnuplot has "Gnu" in its name, it has nothing to do with GNU or the Free Software Foundation.

At any time in Gnuplot, you can ask for online help. The help is similar to that in the old DEC VAX/VMS system. To learn more about the `plot` command, for example, type **help plot** at the Gnuplot prompt.

Gnuplot also comes with several example files that appear in the `/usr/lib/gnuplot/demos` directory of your system. To try these demo files, type the following commands in a terminal window:

```
cd /usr/share/doc/gnuplot*
cd demo
gnuplot
```

When the Gnuplot prompt appears, load one of the demo files (the ones with the `.dem` extension) with the load command. To load the `world.dem` file, for example, type the following command at the Gnuplot prompt:

```
load "world.dem"
```

The `world.dem` Gnuplot file displays a map of the world and pauses until you press Enter. After you press Enter, Gnuplot displays the next plot, which happens to be a view of the earth in spherical coordinates, as shown in Figure 10-14.

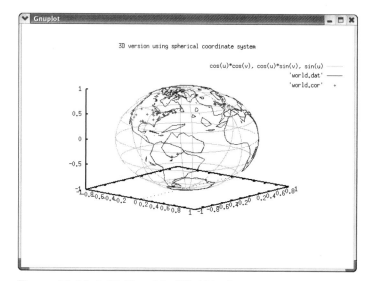

Figure 10-14: A 3D Plot of the World in Gnuplot.

If you are curious about the `world.dem` file, here's what it contains:

```
#
# $Id: world.dem.v 1.1.1.1.2.3 2001/12/04 14:12:53 lhecking Exp $
#
#
set title "Gnuplot Correspondences"
set nokey
```

```
set noborder
set noyzeroaxis
set noxtics
set noytics
#
# Plot world map and correspondent locations as a +
plot 'world.dat' with lines 3 4, 'world.cor' with points 1 2
set title ""
set key
set border
set yzeroaxis
set xtics
set ytics
pause -1 "Hit return to continue."
#
# plot a '3D version using spherical coordinate system' of the world.
set angles degrees
set title "3D version using spherical coordinate system"
set ticslevel 0
set view 70,40,0.8,1.2
set mapping spherical
set parametric
set samples 32
set isosamples 9
set urange [-90:90]
set vrange [0:360]
splot cos(u)*cos(v),cos(u)*sin(v),sin(u) with lines 5 6,\
'world.dat' with lines 3 4, 'world.cor' with points 1 2
pause -1 "Hit return to continue"

#
# Plot a '3D version using cylindrical coordinate system' of the world.
set title "3D version using cylindrical coordinate system"
set ticslevel 0.0
set view 70,40,0.8,1.2
set mapping cylindrical
set parametric
set samples 32
set isosamples 9
set urange [-180:180]
set vrange [-90:90]
splot cos(u),sin(u),v with lines 5 6,\
'world.dat' with lines 3 4, 'world.cor' with points 1 2
pause -1 "Hit return to continue."
reset
```

As the listing shows, the `world.dem` file consists of Gnuplot commands. You can learn a great deal about Gnuplot by trying each file in the Gnuplot demo directory and by studying the commands in the file.

Working with PostScript in Ghostscript

Ghostscript is a utility for previewing and printing PostScript documents. Ghostscript enables you to print PostScript documents on many non-PostScript devices.

At its heart, Ghostscript is a nearly complete implementation of the PostScript language. Ghostscript includes the interpreter that processes PostScript input and generates output on an output device. A Ghostscript device can be a printer (or display screen), as well as an image-file format, such as BMP or PCX.

Ghostscript is distributed under the GNU GPL but is copyrighted and maintained by Aladdin Enterprises. The latest version remains under Aladdin's control for one year after its release, at which point it is transferred to the Free Software Foundation and can be distributed under GPL.

Secret

To run Ghostscript, type **gs** in a terminal window. Ghostscript brings up an empty window and displays the following text in the terminal window (the version number is different if you are running a later version of Ghostscript):

```
GNU Ghostscript 7.05 (2002-04-22)
Copyright (C) 2002 artofcode LLC, Benicia, CA.  All rights reserved.
This software comes with NO WARRANTY: see the file PUBLIC for
details.
Loading NimbusRomNo9L-Regu font from
/usr/share/fonts/default/Type1/n0210031.pfb
... 2410668 1053956 1642520 347466 0 done.
Loading NimbusSanL-Regu font from
/usr/share/fonts/default/Type1/n0190031.pfb...
 2785628 1379834 1662616 358654 0 done.
Using NimbusSansL-Regu font for NimbusSanL-Regu.
GS>
```

At this point, you are interacting with the Ghostscript interpreter. Unless you know the Ghostscript language (which is like PostScript), you'll feel lost at this prompt. It's kind of like the C:> prompt under MS-DOS or the Linux shell prompt at a terminal.

If you have a PostScript file available, you can interactively load and view it in Ghostscript with a simple command. For example, try the following command:

```
GS> (/usr/share/ghostscript/7.05/examples/golfer.ps) run
>>showpage, press <return> to continue<<
```

You have typed a Ghostscript command that should cause Ghostscript to load the file /usr/share/ghostscript/7.05/examples/golfer.ps and process it. (If you are running a version of Ghostscript other than 7.05, you must change 7.05 to that version number.) The result is a picture in Ghostscript's output window. To exit Ghostscript, press Enter and type **quit**.

Fortunately, you do not have to use Ghostscript at the interpreter level (unless you know PostScript well and want to try PostScript commands interactively). Typically, you use Ghostscript to load and view a PostScript file.

Ghostscript takes several command-line arguments, including the file to be loaded. To see a list of Ghostscript options, type the `gs -h` command.

To see how Ghostscript renders a PostScript document, you can use any PostScript document you have available. You can view one of the sample PostScript files in the `/usr/share/ghostscript/7.05/examples` directory (replace 7.05 with whatever version of Ghostscript is installed on your system). Type the following command, for example, in a terminal window:

```
gs /usr/share/ghostscript/7.05/examples/golfer.ps
```

Ghostscript opens that file, processes its contents, and displays the output in another window, as shown in Figure 10-15.

Figure 10-15: Ghostscript Displaying a PostScript File.

In this case, the output happens to be a picture of a golfer. After displaying the output, Ghostscript displays the following message:

```
>>showpage, press <return> to continue<<
```

Press Enter to continue. For a multiple-page PostScript document, Ghostscript then shows the next page. After all the pages are displayed, you return to the Ghostscript prompt. Type **quit** to exit Ghostscript.

Viewing PostScript or PDF Files with KGhostview

KGhostview is a KDE application that's essentially a graphical front end to the Ghostscript interpreter. KGhostview is ideal for viewing and printing PostScript and PDF documents. For a long document, you can view and print selected pages. You can also view the document at various levels of magnification by zooming in or out.

Secret

To run KGhostview, select Main menu⇨Graphics⇨More Graphics Applications⇨PS/PDF Viewer from the GNOME or KDE desktop. This causes the KGhostview application window to appear. In addition to the menu bar and toolbar along the top edge, the main display area of the window is divided vertically into two parts.

To load and view a PostScript document in KGhostview, select File⇨Open, or click the open folder icon on the toolbar. This action causes KGhostview to display a file-selection dialog box. Use this dialog box to navigate the file system and select a PostScript file. You can select one of the PostScript files that come with Ghostscript. For example, open the file `tiger.ps` in the `/usr/share/ghostscript/7.05/examples` directory. (If your system has a version of Ghostscript later than 7.05, you have to use the new version number in place of 7.05.)

To open the selected file, click the Open File button in the file-selection dialog box. Ghostview opens the selected file, processes its contents, and displays the output in its window, as shown in Figure 10-16.

Figure 10-16: KGhostview Displaying a PostScript File.

KGhostview is useful for viewing various kinds of documentation that come in PostScript and PDF format (these files typically have the `.ps` or `.pdf` extension in their names). For example, I use Ghostview to view the documentation for the CVS program, which comes in several PostScript files you can find in the `/usr/share/doc/cvs*` directory. When viewing such documents in Ghostview, I zoom in by clicking the magnifying glass icon (with the plus sign) on the toolbar in Figure 10-16. This makes the document legible onscreen.

Summary

Red Hat Linux comes with many applications and utilities. This chapter describes some of these applications, including common office tools—spreadsheet, calendars, calculators, and email programs—as well as graphics and imaging programs, such as the GIMP and KGhostview.

By reading this chapter, you learned the following:

- ◆ The companion CD-ROMs include a variety of applications and utilities. Many of these applications are installed when you install Red Hat Linux from the companion CD-ROMs, following the steps outlined in Chapter 2. You have to install some of the applications manually from the CD-ROMs.

- ◆ Ximiam Evolution is a personal information manager that you can use to read and send email, manage your calendar, and keep track of your contact information.

- ◆ Red Hat Linux comes with the OpenOffice.org office suite—a Microsoft Office-like suite of office applications that includes among other components, the Writer word processor, Calc spreadsheet, and Impress presentation software.

- ◆ The GIMP, Ghostscript, and KGhostview are useful for working with image files of various formats. In particular, the GIMP is image-processing software with capabilities on a par with commercial packages, such as Adobe Photoshop and Corel Photopaint. KGhostview is ideal for viewing and printing PostScript and PDF documents.

- ◆ There are several commercially available office application suites for Linux — Applixware Office, and StarOffice. These commercial applications are not part of Red Hat Linux, but you can find out more about each product in case you need a Linux office suite for your home or business.

- ◆ CrossOverOffice from CodeWeavers is a unique commercial application that enables you to run Microsoft Office 97 and 2000 applications in GNOME or KDE.

Text Processing

Chapter
11

◆ ◆

Secrets in This Chapter

◆ ◆

Text processing refers to all aspects of creating, editing, and formatting textual documents. The simplest form of text processing is preparing a plaintext file, which you need to do often, because most Red Hat Linux configuration files are plaintext files. For this purpose, Red Hat Linux offers a choice of text editors, ranging from the UNIX standard, vi, to the very powerful GNU Emacs.

To prepare formatted text in Red Hat Linux, you must use a markup language such as groff or DocBook. Using a markup language, you place special formatting commands in a plaintext file, and a formatting program processes the marked-up text file to generate the formatted document for printing or viewing. You may already be familiar with a more recent markup language, HyperText Markup Language (HTML), which is as the standard document format on the World Wide Web.

insider
insight   Even if you use a Microsoft Windows- or Macintosh-based "what-you-see-is-what-you-get" application (often pronounced "whizzy-whig" for its abbreviation WYSIWYG) to prepare formatted text, you must learn the rudiments of a markup language if you want to prepare a man page—online Help text available through the man **command.**

This chapter describes the text-processing facilities in Linux. The chapter starts with the ed, vi, and GNU Emacs text editors, then it describes how to use the groff text-formatting program to prepare a man page. The chapter ends with a brief overview of the SGML- and XML-based DocBook markup language for document layout.

Text Editing with ed and vi

Text editing is an important part of all operating systems, including Linux. In Linux, you need to create and edit a variety of text files, as the following list describes:

- System configuration files, including /etc/fstab, /etc/hosts, /etc/inittab, /etc/X11/XF86Config, and many more
- User files, such as .newsrc and .bash_profile
- Mail messages and news articles
- Shell script files
- Perl, Python, and Tcl/Tk scripts
- C or C++ programs

All Unix systems, including Linux, come with the following two text editors:

- **ed**—A line-oriented text editor
- **vi**—A full-screen text editor that supports the command set of an earlier editor by the name of ex

In Red Hat Linux, another text editor, vim, emulates vi and ex, but you can invoke the editor by using the vi command.

Although ed and vi may seem more cryptic than other, more graphical text editors, you should learn the basic editing commands of these two editors, because at times, these editors may be the only ones available. If you run into a system problem and Linux refuses to boot from the hard disk, for example, you may need to boot from a floppy. In this case, you must edit system files by using the ed editor, because that editor is small enough to fit on the floppy.

As I show in the following sections, learning the basic text-editing commands of ed and vi is easy.

Using ed

The ed text editor works by using a buffer—an in-memory storage area where the actual text resides until you explicitly store the text in a file. You must use ed only if you boot a minimal version of Linux (for example, from a boot floppy), and the system doesn't support full-screen mode.

Starting ed

To start ed, use the following command syntax:

```
ed [-] [-G] [-s] [-pprompt-string] [filename]
```

The arguments in brackets are optional. The following list explains these arguments:

- ◆ `-` suppresses the printing of character counts and diagnostic messages.
- ◆ `-G` forces backward compatibility with older versions of ed.
- ◆ `-s` is the same as the single hyphen.
- ◆ `-p` prompt-string sets the text that the editor displays when waiting for a command. (The default is a null prompt string.)
- ◆ `filename` is the name of the file to be edited.

Learning ed

If you use the ed editor, you work in either command mode or text-input mode, as the following list explains:

- ◆ Command mode is what you get by default. In this mode, ed interprets anything that you type as a command. As you see in the section "Summarizing ed Commands," later in this chapter, ed uses a simple command set, wherein each command consists of a single character.
- ◆ Text-input mode enables you to enter text into the buffer. You can enter input mode by using the commands a (append), c (change), or i (insert). After entering lines of text, you can leave text-input mode by entering a period (.) on a line by itself.

The ed editor embodies the concept of the current line—the line to which ed applies the commands that you type. Each line has an address: the line number. You can apply a command to a range of lines by prefixing the command with an address range. The p command, for example, prints (displays) the current line. To see the first 10 lines, use the following command:

```
1,10p
```

In a command, the period (.) refers to the current line, and the dollar sign ($) refers to the last line in the file. Thus, the following command deletes all the lines from the current line to the last one:

```
.,$d
```

Examining a Sample Session with ed

The following example shows how to begin editing a file in ed:

```
ed -p: /etc/fstab
621
:
```

This example uses the -p option to set the prompt to the colon character (:) and opens the file /etc/fstab for editing. Turning on a prompt character is helpful, because without the prompt, determining whether ed is in input mode or command mode is difficult.

The ed editor opens the file, reports the number of characters in the file (621), displays the prompt (:), and waits for a command.

After ed opens a file for editing, the current line is the last line of the file. To see the current line number, use the .= command, as follows:

```
:.=
8
```

The output tells you that the /etc/fstab file contains eight lines. (Your system's /etc/fstab file, of course, may contain a different number of lines.) The following example shows how you can see all these lines:

```
:1,$p
LABEL=/                 /                   ext3    defaults        1 1
LABEL=/boot             /boot               ext3    defaults        1 2
none                    /dev/pts            devpts  gid=5,mode=620  0 0
none                    /proc               proc    defaults        0 0
none                    /dev/shm            tmpfs   defaults        0 0
/dev/hda6               swap                swap    defaults        0 0
/dev/cdrom              /mnt/cdrom          udf,iso9660 noauto,owner,kudzu,ro 0 0
/dev/fd0                /mnt/floppy         auto    noauto,owner,kudzu 0 0
:
```

To go to a specific line, type the line number and the editor then displays that line. Here is an example that takes you to the first line in the file:

```
:1
LABEL=/                 /                   ext3    defaults        1 1
```

Suppose that you want to delete the line that contains cdrom. To search for a string, type a slash (/) and follow it with the string that you want to locate, as follows:

```
:/cdrom
/dev/cdrom          /mnt/cdrom          udf,iso9660 noauto,owner,kudzu,ro 0 0
```

That line becomes the current line. To delete the line, use the d command, as follows:

```
:d
:
```

To replace a string with another, use the s command. To replace cdrom with the string cd, for example, use the following command:

```
:s/cdrom/cd/
:
```

To insert a line in front of the current line, use the i command, as follows:

```
:i
    (type the line you want to insert)
.   (type a single period)
:
```

You can enter as many lines as you want. After the last line, enter a period (.) on a line by itself. That period marks the end of text-input mode, and the editor switches to command mode. In this case, you can tell that ed has switched to command mode, because you see the prompt (:).

If you're happy with the changes, you can write them to the file by using the w command. If you want to save the changes and exit, type **wq** to perform both steps at the same time, as follows:

```
:wq
645
```

The ed editor saves the changes in the file, displays the number of characters that it saved, and exits.

If you want to quit the editor without saving any changes, use the Q command.

Summarizing ed Commands

The preceding sample session should give you an idea of how to use ed commands to perform the basic tasks of editing a text file. Table 11-1 lists all commonly used ed commands.

Table 11-1: Commonly Used ed Commands

Command	Meaning
!command	Execute a shell command
$	Go to the last line in the buffer
%	Apply the command that follows to all lines in the buffer (for example, %p prints all lines)
+	Go to the next line

(continued)

Table 11-1: *(continued)*

Command	Meaning
+n	Go to nth next line (n is a number)
,	Apply the command that follows to all lines in the buffer (for example, ,p prints all lines); similar to %
-	Go to the preceding line
-n	Go to nth previous line (n is a number)
.	Refer to the current line in the buffer
/regex/	Search forward for the specified regular expression (see Chapter 24 for an introduction to regular expressions)
;	Refer to a range of line (if you specify no line numbers, the editor assumes current through last line in the buffer)
=	Print the line number
?regex?	Search backward for the specified regular expression (see Chapter 24 for an introduction to regular expressions)
^	Go to the preceding line; also see the - command
^n	Go to the nth previous line (where n is a number); see also the -n command
a	Append after the current line
c	Change the specified lines
d	Delete the specified lines
e file	Edit the file
f file	Change the default filename
h	Display an explanation of the last error
H	Turn on verbose-mode error reporting
i	Insert text before the current line
j	Join contiguous lines
kx	Mark the line with letter x (later, you can refer to the line as 'x)
l	Print (display) lines
m	Move lines
n	Go to line number n
newline	Display the next line and make that line current
P	Toggle prompt mode on or off
q	Quit the editor
Q	Quit the editor without saving changes
r file	Read and insert the contents of the file after the current line
s/old/new/	Replace old string with new
Space n	A space, followed by n; nth next line (n is a number)

Command	Meaning
u	Undo the last command
W file	Append the contents of the buffer to the end of the specified file
w file	Save the buffer in the specified file (if you name no file, ed saves it in the default file—the file whose contents ed is currently editing)

You can prefix most editing commands with a line number or an address range, which you express in terms of two line numbers that you separate with a comma; the command then applies to the specified lines. To append text after the second line in the buffer, for example, use the following command:

```
2a
(Type lines of text. End with single period on a line.)
```

To print lines 3 through 15, use the following command:

```
3,15p
```

Although you may not use ed often, much of the command syntax carries over to the vi editor. As the following section on vi shows, vi accepts ed commands if it's in its command mode.

Using vi

The vi editor is a full-screen text editor that enables you to view a file several lines at a time. Most UNIX systems, including Linux, come with vi. If you learn the basic features of vi, therefore, you can edit text files on almost any UNIX system.

As does the ed editor, vi works with a buffer. As vi edits a file, it reads the file into a buffer—a block of memory—and enables you to change the text in the buffer. The vi editor also uses temporary files during editing, but it doesn't alter the original file until you save the changes by using the :w command.

Setting the Terminal Type

Before you start a full-screen text editor such as vi, you must set the TERM environment variable to the terminal type (such as vt100 or xterm). The vi editor uses the terminal type to look up the terminal's characteristics in the /etc/termcap file and then control the terminal in full-screen mode.

If you run the X Window System and a GUI, such as GNOME or KDE, you can use vi in a terminal window. The terminal window's terminal type is xterm. (To verify, type **echo $TERM** at the command prompt.) After you start the terminal window, it automatically sets the TERM environment variable to xterm. You can normally, therefore, use vi in a terminal window without explicitly setting the TERM variable.

Starting vi

If you want to consult the online manual pages for vi, type the following command:

```
man vi
```

To start the editor, use the vi name and run it with the following command syntax:

```
vi [flags] [+cmd] [filename]
```

The arguments shown in brackets are optional. The following list explains these arguments:

◆ flags are single-character flags that control the way that vi runs.

◆ +cmd causes vi to run the specified command after it starts. (You learn more about these commands in the section "Summarizing the vi Commands," later in this chapter.)

◆ filename is the name of the file to be edited.

The flags arguments can include one or more of the following:

◆ -c cmd executes the specified command before editing begins.

◆ -e starts in colon command mode (which I describe in the following section).

◆ -i starts in input mode (which I also describe in the following section).

◆ -m causes the editor to search through the file for something that looks like an error message from a compiler.

◆ -R makes the file read-only so that you can't accidentally overwrite the file. (You can also type view filename to start the editor in this mode to simply view a file.)

◆ -s runs in safe mode, which turns off many potentially harmful commands.

◆ -v starts in visual command mode (which I describe in the following section).

Most of the time, however, vi starts with a filename as the only argument, as follows:

```
vi /etc/hosts
```

Another common way to start vi is to jump to a specific line number right at startup. To begin editing at line 107 of the file /etc/X11/XF86Config, for example, use the following command:

```
vi +107 /etc/X11/XF86Config
```

This way of starting vi is useful if you edit a source file after the compiler reports an error at a specific line number.

Learning vi Concepts

If you edit a file by using vi, the editor loads the file into a buffer, displays the first few lines of the file in a full-screen window, and positions the cursor on the first line. If you type the command vi /etc/fstab in a terminal window, for example, you get a full-screen text window, as shown in Figure 11-1.

The last line shows information about the file, including the number of lines and the number of characters in the file. Later, vi uses this area as a command-entry area. It uses the rest of the lines to display the file. If the file contains fewer lines than the window, vi displays the empty lines with a tilde (~) in the first column.

The cursor marks the current line, appearing there as a small black rectangle. The cursor appears on top of a character. In Figure 11-1, the cursor is on the first character of the first line.

Figure 11-1: A File Displayed in a Full-Screen Text Window by the vi Editor.

In vi, you work in one of the following three modes:

◆ *Visual-command mode* is what you get by default. In this mode, vi interprets anything that you type as a command that applies to the line containing the cursor. The vi commands are similar to those of ed, and I list the in the section "Summarizing the vi Commands," later in this chapter.

◆ *Colon-command mode* enables you to read or write files, set vi options, and quit. All colon commands start with a colon (:). After you enter the colon, vi positions the cursor at the last line and enables you to type a command. The command takes effect after you press Enter. Notice that vi's colon-command mode relies on the ed editor. When editing a file using vi, you can press Escape at any time to enter the command mode. In fact, if you are not sure what mode vi is in, press Escape a few times to get vi into command mode.

◆ *Text-input mode* enables you to enter text into the buffer. You can enter text-input mode by using the command a (insert after cursor), A (append at end of line), or i (insert after cursor). After entering lines of text, you must press Esc to leave text-input mode and reenter visual-command mode.

One problem with all these modes is that you can't easily determine vi's current mode. Typing text, only to realize that vi isn't in text-input mode, can be frustrating. The converse situation also is common—you may end up typing text when you want to enter a command. To ensure that vi is in command mode, just press Esc a few times. (Pressing Esc more than once doesn't hurt.)

tip

To view online Help in vi, type :help while in command mode.

Examining a Sample Session with vi

To begin editing the file /etc/fstab, enter the following command (before you edit the file, please make a backup copy by typing the command cp /etc/fstab /etc/fstab-saved):

```
vi /etc/fstab
```

Figure 11-1, earlier in this chapter, shows you the resulting display, with the first few lines of the file appearing in a full-screen text window. The last line shows the file's name and statistics: the number of lines and characters.

The vi editor initially positions the cursor on the first character. One of the first things that you need to learn is how to move the cursor around. Try the following commands (each command being a single letter; just type the letter, and vi responds):

- ◆ *j* moves the cursor one line down.
- ◆ *k* moves the cursor one line up.
- ◆ *h* moves the cursor one character to the left.
- ◆ *l* moves the cursor one character to the right.

You can also move the cursor by using the arrow keys.

Instead of moving one line or one character at a time, you can move one word at a time. Try the following single-character commands for word-size cursor movement:

- ◆ *w* moves the cursor one word forward.
- ◆ *b* moves the cursor one word backward.

The last type of cursor movement affects several lines at a time. Try the following commands and see what happens:

- ◆ *Ctrl-D* scrolls down half a screen.
- ◆ *Ctrl-U* scrolls up half a screen.

The last two commands, of course, aren't necessary if the file contains only a few lines. If you're editing large files, however, the capability to move several lines at a time is handy.

You can move to a specific line number at any time by using a colon command. To go to line 1, for example, type the following and then press Enter:

```
:1
```

After you type the colon, vi displays the colon on the last line of the screen. From then on, vi uses the text that you type as a command. You must press Enter to submit the command to vi. In colon-command mode, vi accepts all the commands that the ed editor accepts— and then some.

To search for a string, first type a slash (/). The vi editor displays the slash on the last line of the screen. Type the search string, and then press Enter. The vi editor locates the string and positions the cursor at the beginning of that string. Thus, to locate the string cdrom in the file /etc/fstab, type the following:

```
/cdrom
```

To delete the line that contains the cursor, type **dd**. The vi editor deletes that line of text and makes the next line the current one.

tip	To begin entering text in front of the cursor, type i. The vi editor switches to text-input mode. Now you can enter text. After you finish entering text, press Esc to return to visual-command mode.

After you finish editing the file, you can save the changes in the file by using the :w command. If you want to save the changes and exit, you can type **:wq** to perform both steps at the same time. The vi editor saves the changes in the file and exits. You can also save the changes and exit the editor by pressing Shift-zz (press and hold the Shift key and press z twice).

To quit the editor without saving any changes, type the :q! command.

Summarizing the vi Commands

The sample editing session should give you a feel for the vi commands, especially its three modes:

- ◆ Visual-command mode (the default)
- ◆ Colon-command mode, in which you enter commands, following them with a colon (:)
- ◆ Text-input mode, which you enter by typing **a**, **A**, or **i**

In addition to the few commands that the sample session illustrates, vi accepts many other commands. Table 11-2 lists the basic vi commands, organized by task.

Table 11-2: Basic vi Commands

Command	*Meaning*
Insert Text	
a	Insert text after the cursor
A	Insert text at the end of the current line
I	Insert text at the beginning of the current line
i	Insert text before the cursor
o	Open a line below the current line
O	Open a line above the current line
Ctrl-v	Insert any special character in input mode
Delete Text	
D	Delete up to the end of the current line
dd	Delete the current line
dw	Delete from the cursor to the end of the following word
x	Delete the character on which the cursor rests

(continued)

Table 11-2: *(continued)*

Command	Meaning
Change Text	
C	Change up to the end of the current line
cc	Change the current line
cw	Change the word
J	Join the current line with the next one
rx	Replace the character under the cursor with x (x is any character)
~	Change the character under the cursor to the opposite case
Move Cursor	
$	Move to the end of the current line
;	Repeat the last f or F command
^	Move to the beginning of the current line
e	Move to the end of the current word
fx	Move the cursor to the first occurrence of character x on the current line
Fx	Move the cursor to the last occurrence of character x on the current line
H	Move the cursor to the top of the screen
h	Move one character to the left
j	Move one line down
k	Move one line up
L	Move the cursor to the end of the screen
l	Move one character to the right
M	Move the cursor to the middle of the screen
n|	Move the cursor to column *n* on current line
nG	Place cursor on line n
w	Move to the beginning of the following word
Mark a Location	
'x	Move the cursor to the beginning of the line that contains mark x
`x	Move the cursor to mark x
mx	Mark the current location with the letter x
Scroll Text	
Ctrl-b	Scroll backward by a full screen
Ctrl-d	Scroll forward by half a screen
Ctrl-f	Scroll forward by a full screen
Ctrl-u	Scroll backward by half a screen

Command	*Meaning*
Refresh Screen	
Ctrl-L	Redraw the screen
Cut and Paste Text	
"xndd	Delete n lines and move them to buffer x (x is any single lowercase character)
"Xnyy	Yank n (a number) lines and append them to buffer x
"xnyy	Yank n (a number) lines into buffer x (x is any single uppercase character)
"xp	Put the yanked lines from buffer x after the current line
P	Put the yanked line above the current line
p	Put the yanked line below the current line
yy	Yank (copy) the current line into an unnamed buffer
Colon Commands	
:!command	Execute the shell command
:e filename	Edit the file
:f	Display the filename and current line number
:N	Move to line n (n is a number)
:q	Quit the editor
:q!	Quit without saving changes
:r filename	Read the file and insert after the current line
:w filename	Write the buffer to the file
:wq	Save the changes and exit
Search Text	
/string	Search forward for string
?string	Search backward for string
n	Find the next string
View File Information	
Ctrl-g	Show the filename, size, and current line number
Miscellaneous	
u	Undo the last command
Esc	End text-input mode and enter visual-command mode
U	Undo recent changes to the current line

Working with GNU Emacs

Text editors are a matter of personal preference, and many UNIX users swear by GNU Emacs. Although it's intimidating at first, GNU Emacs is one of those software packages that grows on you; it has so many features that many users and programmers often perform all their tasks directly from within GNU Emacs.

A significant advantage of GNU Emacs is its availability on nearly every computer system imaginable, from MS-DOS PCs to any UNIX system. If a system doesn't have GNU Emacs, you can get it from any one of many sites on the Internet. For your Linux system, you get GNU Emacs on the companion CD-ROMs; you can choose to install it as you install Linux on your system. If you're just getting started with UNIX text editors, I recommend that you learn to use GNU Emacs and vi. That way, you acquire a skill that's usable on any UNIX system.

insider insight Because GNU Emacs is so versatile and powerful, describing it in detail could easily take an entire book, and quite a few books about GNU Emacs are on the market. Most notably, O'Reilly & Associates publishes a GNU Emacs book, *Learning GNU Emacs, 2nd Edition*, by Debra Cameron, Bill Rosenblatt, and Eric S. Raymond, that you may find useful.

On a text terminal, GNU Emacs runs in text-mode, full-screen display. Under X, GNU Emacs runs in a window. Either way, the basic commands remain the same. The X version also enables you to position the cursor by using the mouse.

The following sections provide a brief introduction to the text-editing features of GNU Emacs.

Starting GNU Emacs

On the Linux console, you start GNU Emacs by typing `emacs`. If you're running X, type **emacs &** in a terminal window to start GNU Emacs. This command launches GNU Emacs with its X-based interface and enables you to continue other work in the terminal window.

insider insight If you want to run Emacs in a terminal window itself—without the X-based graphical interface in a separate window—and edit a file, just type `emacs -nw` *filename*.

After it first starts, GNU Emacs displays a message in a window, as shown in Figure 11-2.

The initial GNU Emacs window also shows helpful information in the area where you normally edit the contents of a file. You can use the menus to get more Help on Emacs.

Before I tell you anything else, remember that to quit GNU Emacs, you must press C-x C-c (that's Ctrl-x, followed by Ctrl-c). As you learn in the section "Typing GNU Emacs Commands," later in this chapter, all GNU Emacs command keystrokes start with a control character or Escape (which the Emacs documentation refers to as Meta and is abbreviated as M). The left Alt key also works as the Meta key.

Figure 11-2: The Initial Window That the X Version of GNU Emacs Displays.

Learning GNU Emacs

Although I've used GNU Emacs extensively for years, I feel that I've barely scratched the surface as far as using its full capabilities. As is true of anything else, your best bet is to start with a small subset of GNU Emacs commands. Then, as you become more proficient with the software, you can gradually add to your repertoire of GNU Emacs commands and features.

GNU Emacs employs some basic concepts that, if you learn them, are helpful. Some of those concepts include the following:

- ◆ As do other text editors (vi or ed), GNU Emacs uses a buffer to maintain the text that you enter and change. You must explicitly save the buffer to update the contents of the file.

- ◆ Unlike vi and ed, GNU Emacs doesn't require you to type any special command to enter text into the buffer. By default, anything that you type goes into the buffer.

- ◆ GNU Emacs uses the concept of a cursor to indicate the current location in the file. As you type text, GNU Emacs inserts that text in front of the character on which the cursor rests.

- GNU Emacs uses long, descriptive command names that it binds to (associates with) specific key sequences—these are the key bindings for the GNU Emacs commands. C-x C-c, for example, is bound to the GNU Emacs command `save-buffers-kill-emacs`.

- All GNU Emacs key bindings start with a control character (for which you simultaneously press Ctrl and a character) or Escape.

- GNU Emacs uses several modes, each of which provides a specific type of editing environment. (In C mode, for example, GNU Emacs indents the braces that enclose blocks of C programming language statements.)

- In the GNU Emacs window, the last screen line is the minibuffer; it displays all commands and filenames that you type. The line second to the bottom is the mode line. On this line, GNU Emacs displays the name of the buffer and the current mode (the default mode being fundamental).

- You don't need to start GNU Emacs each time that you want to edit a file. Rather, you start GNU Emacs and then open one or more files for editing. You save and close files that you finish editing.

- You can use many buffers in GNU Emacs, and you can cut and paste between buffers.

Typing GNU Emacs Commands

GNU Emacs uses an extensive set of commands in which each command has a very long descriptive name, as in the following example:

```
save-buffer save-buffers-kill-emacs scroll-up previous-line
```

Most of these commands, however, are bound to somewhat cryptic keystrokes. Otherwise, you'd need to actually type these long commands and wouldn't get much editing done.

Although you can enter any of these descriptive commands in the minibuffer (at the bottom of the GNU Emacs window), the basic means of entering the commands is through special keystrokes. These keystrokes begin with one of the following characters:

- A control character that you enter by simultaneously pressing the Ctrl key and the character. GNU Emacs documentation abbreviates each control character as C-x (x is a letter). This book uses the notation Ctrl-x to denote the control character that corresponds to the letter x. The GNU Emacs online Help writes Ctrl-v as C-v.

- An Escape character. GNU Emacs abbreviates the Esc key, or the Meta key, as M. Thus you write Esc v (Escape, followed by the letter v) as M-v. Notice that, depending on the keyboard, the Meta key may also be the Alt key or some other key, such as the Windows key, on some Windows machines.

Most of the time, you enter the control commands, which require pressing the Ctrl key together with a letter. Ctrl-v or C-v, for example, causes GNU Emacs to move forward one screen.

The commands with an Esc prefix are easier to enter, because you press the keys in sequence: first the Escape key and then the letter. Esc v or M-v, for example, causes GNU Emacs to move backward one screen of text. To enter this command, press Esc first, and then press v. Although the Ctrl and Esc commands may sound complicated, you can learn a basic set very quickly.

Getting Help

The best source of information on GNU Emacs is GNU Emacs itself. For starters, GNU Emacs includes an online tutorial that teaches you its basics. To use the tutorial, type **C-h t**. GNU Emacs displays the initial screen of the tutorial in its window, as shown in Figure 11-3.

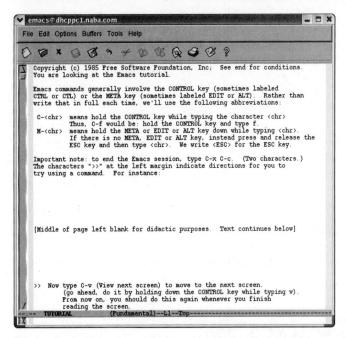

Figure 11-3: GNU Emacs Displays the Online Tutorial After You Press C-h t.

As the instructions near the bottom of Figure 11-3 show, the tutorial guides you through the steps and asks you to try GNU Emacs commands. If you're new to GNU Emacs, go through the tutorial. Because the tutorial is hands-on, it gives you a good feel for GNU Emacs.

In addition to the tutorial, you can look up the key bindings for various GNU Emacs commands. To see the key bindings, type **C-h b**. GNU Emacs splits the window and displays a list of key bindings in the bottom half, as shown in Figure 11-4.

Each line in the key binding shows the name of the key and the GNU Emacs command associated with that command. If you press the key, GNU Emacs executes the command that's bound to that key.

Figure 11-4 illustrates GNU Emacs' ability to split its window into two or more parts. After splitting, each part becomes a separate window with its own buffer.

In Figure 11-4, you can scroll the key-binding list by using the following keystrokes:

- *C-x o* switches to the other window (the bottom window, which shows the Help buffer with its key-bindings list).
- *C-v* scrolls the contents of the Help buffer.

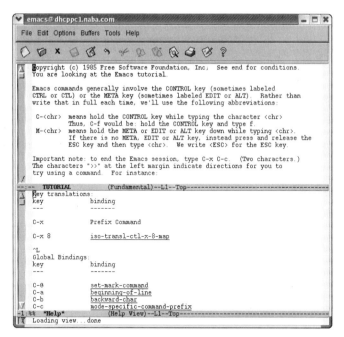

Figure 11-4: GNU Emacs Displays the Key Bindings in a Split Window After You Press C-h b.

Table 11-3 lists other GNU Emacs help commands.

Table 11-3: GNU Emacs help Commands

Command	Meaning
C-h c	Prompts you for a key sequence and briefly describes that sequence
C-h f	Prompts you for a GNU Emacs command name and describes that command
C-h k	Prompts you for a key sequence and describes what that sequence does
C-h l	Displays the last 100 characters typed
C-h m	Displays the current GNU Emacs mode
C-h s	Displays the syntax table for the current buffer
C-h v	Prompts for a variable name and describes that variable
C-h w	Prompts for a command and shows that command's key binding

Reading a File

After you start GNU Emacs, you can read in a file by typing the C-x C-f command. To open the file /usr/share/emacs/21.2/etc/COPYING, for example, follow these steps in GNU Emacs:

1. Press C-x C-f. GNU Emacs prompts you for a filename.
2. Type the filename—**/usr/share/emacs/21.2/etc/COPYING**—and press Enter. GNU Emacs reads the file into a buffer and displays that buffer in the window.

To open a file in the current directory, you don't need to type the full directory name; just type the filename. By default, GNU Emacs looks for the file in the current working directory.

---

insider insight

You don't need to type the full filename in GNU Emacs; just enter the first few characters of the filename and then press Tab. If the partial name uniquely identifies a file, GNU Emacs completes the filename for you. Thus, all you need to type is the first few characters of a filename—just enough to uniquely identify the file. You can use this shortcut feature to avoid typing long filenames.

Suppose that the current working directory contains the file Makefile, which is the only file with a name that starts with the substring Mak. To load that file in GNU Emacs, press C-x C-f, type **Mak**, and press Tab. GNU Emacs completes the filename and reads the file Makefile.

Moving around the Buffer

One of the first things that you need to do in GNU Emacs is move around the buffer. The cursor marks the current spot in the buffer; anything that you type goes into the buffer in front of the character under the cursor. Thus, to insert text into a file, you must read in the file, move the cursor to the desired spot, and type the text.

To move around the buffer, you need to move the cursor. You must use control keys to move the cursor in any direction. Following are the six basic cursor-movement commands:

- *C-b* moves the cursor backward one character.
- *C-f* moves the cursor forward one character.
- *C-n* moves the cursor to the following line (while trying to maintain the same column position as in the current line).
- *C-p* moves the cursor to the preceding line (while trying to maintain the same column position as in the current line).
- *C-a* moves the cursor to the beginning of the current line.
- *C-e* moves the cursor to the end of the current line.

If moving one character at a time is too slow, you can move one word at a time by using the following commands:

- *M-f* moves the cursor forward one word.
- *M-b* moves the cursor backward one word.

You can move in even bigger chunks through the buffer. The following two commands enable you to move one screen at a time:

- *C-v* moves forward one screen.
- *M-v* moves backward one screen.

You can use the following two other simple cursor-movement commands for really big jumps:

♦ M-< (Esc followed by the less-than key) moves the cursor to the beginning of the buffer.

♦ M-> (Esc followed by the greater-than key) moves the cursor to the end of the buffer.

A timesaving feature of GNU Emacs enables you to repeat a command a specified number of times. Suppose that you want to move 13 characters forward. You can do so by pressing C-f 13 times or by typing C-u 13 C-f. The C-u command accepts a repeat count and repeats the next command that many times. If you don't provide a count and simply type a command after C-u, GNU Emacs repeats the command four times. Thus, C-u C-f means "move forward four characters."

One exception to the behavior of the C-u command exists: If you use C-u with the M-v or C-v command, GNU Emacs doesn't repeat the screen-scrolling commands. Instead, GNU Emacs scrolls the screen up or down by the specified count. So, if you press C-u 10 C v, GNU Emacs scrolls down 10 lines (not 10 screens).

Inserting and Deleting Text

Because GNU Emacs doesn't have special command and insert modes as vi does, you just begin typing to insert text in GNU Emacs. GNU Emacs inserts the text in front of the cursor. GNU Emacs, of course, interprets control characters and Esc as the beginning of a command.

You can take advantage of the repeat-count feature to insert many copies of a character. I typically use the following line to separate sections of a C program:

```
/*-----------------------------------------------------------*/
```

I enter this line by making the following key presses:

```
/* C-u 51 - */
```

Ignore the spaces; I don't manually type them. I first type /*, then I press C-u and type 51. Finally, I press the hyphen (-), following it with the ending */.

You can delete text in GNU Emacs in the following ways:

♦ To delete the character in front of the cursor, press Del.

♦ To delete the character on which the cursor rests, press C-d.

♦ To delete the word after the cursor, press M-d.

♦ To delete the word immediately before the cursor, press M-Del.

♦ To delete from the cursor to the end of the line, press C-k. (GNU Emacs refers to this command as "kill the line.")

insider
insight Whenever you delete anything longer than one character, GNU Emacs saves it for you.
Press C-y to retrieve the saved text.

You can undo a change by typing the C-x u command. Each time that you press C-x u, GNU Emacs performs the Undo operation for a previous command. To undo the effects of the last two commands, for example, press C-x u twice.

Searching and Replacing

Every text editor offers a search-and-replace capability, and GNU Emacs is no exception. The two most common search commands are as follows:

- ♦ **C-s *string***—incrementally searches forward for string.
- ♦ **C-r *string***—incrementally searches backward for string.

If you press C-s to search forward, GNU Emacs prompts you for a search string in the minibuffer (the last line in the GNU Emacs window). As you enter the characters for the string, GNU Emacs jumps to the first occurrence of the string that you've typed so far. As soon as you finish typing the search string, GNU Emacs positions the cursor at the end of the next occurrence of the search string (providing, of course, that GNU Emacs finds the string).

To find the next occurrence of the string, press C-s again. To end the search, press Enter. You also can halt the search by using cursor-control commands, such as C-f or C-b.

Searching in the reverse direction works similarly; just press C-r instead of C-s.

GNU Emacs also enables you to replace an occurrence of one string with another. The two basic commands for replacing strings are replace-string and query-replace. The replace-string command replaces all occurrences of one string with another. The query-replace command works similarly, but GNU Emacs prompts you each time that it's about to replace a string, enabling you to decide which strings it actually replaces.

The query-replace command is bound to the M-% (Esc, followed by %) key sequence. To perform a query-replace operation, first press M-%. GNU Emacs displays the following prompt in the minibuffer:

    Query replace:

Enter the string that you want to replace—for example, 2003—and then press Enter. GNU Emacs prompts you for the replacement string, as follows:

    Query replace 2002 with:

Enter the replacement string—say, 2004—and press Enter. GNU Emacs moves the cursor to the next occurrence of the string to replace and displays the following prompt in the minibuffer:

    Query replacing 2003 with 2004: (? for help)

Type **y** or press the Spacebar to enable GNU Emacs to replace the string. Otherwise, press n or Del to stop GNU Emacs from replacing the string. In either case, GNU Emacs moves to the next occurrence of the string and repeats the prompt. If no more strings are left, GNU Emacs displays a message in the minibuffer informing you how many occurrences of the string it replaced.

Secret

No key binding exists for the `replace-string` command. You can type any GNU Emacs command, however, by following these steps:

1. Type **M-x**. GNU Emacs displays `M-x` in the minibuffer and waits for more text.
2. Type the GNU Emacs command, and press Enter. To use the `replace-string` command, for example, type **replace-string**, and then press Enter.
3. For some commands, GNU Emacs prompts you for further input; enter that input. If you use `replace-string`, for example, GNU Emacs first prompts for the string to replace and then for the replacement string.

If you type a GNU Emacs command by using M-x, you can press the Spacebar or the Tab key for command completion. To enter the `replace-string` command, for example, you may start by typing **repl** and then pressing the Spacebar. That action causes GNU Emacs to display `replace-` and then pause. Type **s** and press the spacebar again. GNU Emacs displays `replace-string`. You then can use the command by pressing Enter. Try it to see what I mean.

Copying and Moving

Another common editing function is copying blocks of text and moving that text to another location in the buffer. The first step in working with a block of text is to define the block.

GNU Emacs defines a block as the text between a mark and the current cursor position. You can think of the mark as a physical marker that GNU Emacs places in the buffer to mark a location. To set the mark, move the cursor to the beginning of the block and then press C-@ or C-Space (pressing the Ctrl key together with the Spacebar). GNU Emacs sets the mark at the current location and displays the following message in the minibuffer:

```
Mark set
```

After the mark is set, GNU Emacs treats the text between the mark and the current cursor location as a block. To copy the block, type **M-w**. That command copies the block to an internal storage area without deleting the block from the current buffer.

If you actually want to cut the block of text, type **C-w**. That command deletes the block of text from the buffer and moves it to an internal storage area.

To insert the cut (or copied) text at any location, move the cursor to the insertion point, and type **C-y**. That command causes GNU Emacs to paste the previously cut text in front of the cursor.

Secret

Between the cut and paste operations, you may switch from one buffer to another and, thereby, cut from one file and paste to another. To cut from one file and paste into another, follow these steps:

1. Open the first file by typing the `C-x C-f` command. For this exercise, assume that the first file's name is `first.txt`.
2. Open the second file by typing the `C-x C-f` command again. For this exercise, assume that the second file's name is `second.txt`.
3. Change to the first buffer by typing the `C-x b first.txt` command.
4. Move the cursor to the beginning of the text that you want to copy and press C-Space.
5. Move the cursor to the end of the block and press **C-w** to cut the text.
6. Change to the second buffer by typing `C-x b second.txt`.
7. Move the cursor to the location where you want to insert the text, and press **C-y**. GNU Emacs inserts the previously cut text from first buffer into the second one.

Saving Changes

After you edit a buffer, you must write those changes to a file to make them permanent. The GNU Emacs command for saving a buffer to its file is `C-x C-s`. This command saves the buffer to the file with the same name.

To save the buffer in another file, type the command `C-x C-w`. GNU Emacs prompts you for a filename. Type the filename, and press Enter to save the buffer in that file. Unlike many DOS or Windows word processors, GNU Emacs doesn't automatically add a file extension. You must provide the full filename.

Running a Shell in GNU Emacs

GNU Emacs is versatile enough to enable you to access anything in Linux from within a GNU Emacs session. One way to access anything in Linux is to run a shell session. You can do so by using the GNU Emacs command shell.

Secret

To see how the shell command works in GNU Emacs, type **M-x** (pressing Esc, followed by x). GNU Emacs displays `M-x` in the minibuffer and waits for further input. Type **shell**, and press Enter. GNU Emacs starts a new shell process and displays the shell prompt in the GNU Emacs window. Type any shell command that you want. The output appears in the GNU Emacs window.

You can continue to use the shell for as long as you need it. All output from the commands goes into the window where the shell prompt appears. If you no longer need the shell, type **exit**. That command terminates the shell process and returns you to GNU Emacs.

If you want to run a single shell command, use the `M-!` key binding. If you type `M-!`, GNU Emacs displays the following prompt in the minibuffer:

```
Shell command:
```

continues

> *continued*
>
> Type a shell command (such as `ls -l`), and press Enter. GNU Emacs executes that command and displays the resulting output in a separate window. To revert to a single-window display, type **C-x 1**. (That command is Ctrl-x, followed by the number 1.) The command instructs GNU Emacs to delete the other windows (excluding the one that contains the cursor).

---

insider insight

If you're in the mood for a lighthearted quote, type `M-x yow`, and Emacs displays a quote from Zippy the Pinhead in the minibuffer. Each time that you type this command, Emacs displays a different quote.

Writing Man Pages with groff

Before the days of graphical interfaces, typesetting with the computer meant preparing a text file containing embedded typesetting commands and then processing that marked-up text file with a computer program that generated commands for the output device: a printer or some other typesetter.

As you know, such markup languages still exist. A prime example is HyperText Markup Language (HTML), which you use to prepare World Wide Web pages.

In the late 1970s and early 1980s, I prepared all my correspondence and reports on a DEC VAX/VMS system, using a program named RUNOFF. That program formatted output for a line printer or a daisy-wheel printer. That VAX/VMS RUNOFF program accepted embedded commands such as the following:

```
.page size 58,80
.spacing 2
.no autojustify
```

As you may guess, the first command sets the number of lines per page and the number of characters on each line. The second command generates double-spaced output. The last command turns off justification. Essentially, I'd pepper a text file with these commands, run it through RUNOFF, and send RUNOFF's output to the line printer. The resulting output looked as good as a typewritten document, which was good enough for most work in those days.

UNIX came with a more advanced typesetting program called troff (which stands for *typesetting runoff*) that could send output to a special device called a *typesetter*. A typesetter could produce much better output than a line printer. troff enables you to choose different fonts and to print text in bold and italic.

To handle output on simpler printers, UNIX also included nroff (which stands for *non-typesetting runoff*) to process troff files and generate output, to ignore fancy output commands, and to generate output on a line printer. troff typesetting is versatile enough that many computer books were typeset by using troff.

Now that nearly every computer offers some sort of graphical interface (Microsoft Windows, Apple Macintosh, or GNOME and KDE in Linux), most word-processing programs work in WYSIWYG (what you see is what you get) mode, in which you get to work directly with the formatted document. You probably don't have any reason, therefore, to use troff for typesetting. You still use nroff for one important task, however: preparing man pages. The remainder of this chapter focuses on that aspect of using nroff.

insider insight

The groff program is the GNU version of troff and nroff. By using appropriate flags, you can use groff to typeset for several output devices, including any typewriter-like device.

Even if you don't use groff to prepare formatted documents (because using a PC-based word processor is more convenient), you may end up using groff to write the man page for any program that you write.

Man pages are the files that contain the information that users can view by typing the command `man progname`. This command shows online Help information on progname. The subject of a man page can be anything from an overview of a software package to the programming information for a specific C function. (Try typing `man fopen`, for example, on your Linux system.)

After you go through an example, you realize that writing man pages in groff is quite simple.

note

Before reading about the man page preparation process, understand that you don't really use the groff program to prepare the man page. The man page is just a text file containing embedded commands that groff recognizes. You may use groff to view a man page during preparation, but you can prepare a man page without ever running groff.

Trying an Existing man Page

Before you write a man page, look at an existing man page. A brief example is the man page for zless. Figure 11-5 shows the man page for zless in a terminal window.

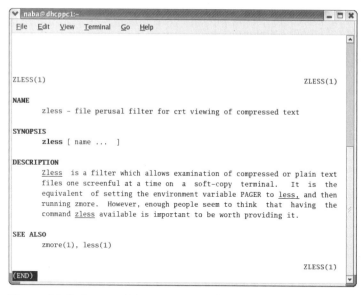

Figure 11-5: Output of the `man zless` Command in a Terminal Window.

Secret

The output of the `man zless` command may appear garbled if the `LANG` environment variable is set to use UTF-8 encoding for characters and the terminal window is unable to handle the UTF-8 encoding for characters such as the hyphen. To check the setting of `LANG`, type **locale** and look at the setting for `LANG`. For example, on my system (in the United States), the value of `LANG` is as follows:

```
LANG=en_US.UTF-8
```

In this case, the language is U.S. English with UTF-8 encoding. To fix the problem, I redefine `LANG` as plain U.S. English (represented by the code `en_US`):

```
export LANG=en_US
```

To reset `LANG` for the entire system, I edit the `/etc/sysconfig/i18n` file such that it contains the line:

```
LANG="en_US"
```

If the output of the `man` command is garbled on your system, try making similar changes to the `LANG` variable to correct the problem (the exact setting of `LANG` depends on your language—the garbling problem should disappear if you select a language name that does not end with `.UTF-8`).

Returning to the example of the man page for the `zless` command, you don't really need to pay attention to the exact content of the man page; all you care about is the layout. Take a moment to look at the layout and notice the following points:

◆ The name of the command appears at the top of the man page. The number 1 that appears in parentheses next to the command's name denotes the section of the UNIX manual where this command belongs.

- The man page contains several sections, each of which appears in boldface. The text within the section is indented.
- In this example, the sections are NAME, SYNOPSIS, DESCRIPTION, and SEE ALSO. If you try a few more man pages, you see that some man pages have many more sections. Almost all man pages, however, have these four sections.
- Some text appears in boldface.

Looking at a man Page Source

After you view a man page by using the man command, you should look at the original source file from which the man command generates the output. In your Linux system, the man page source files are in several directories. The /etc/man.config file defines these directory names.

The source file for the zless man page is /usr/share/man/man1/zless.1.gz. Look at this file to see how the man page appears in its final form, which is shown in Figure 11-5. Here is how to look at the source file for the zless man page:

```
zless /usr/share/man/man1/zless.1
.TH ZLESS 1
.SH NAME
zless \- file perusal filter for crt viewing of compressed text
.SH SYNOPSIS
.B zless
[ name ...  ]
.SH DESCRIPTION
.I  Zless
is a filter which allows examination of compressed or plain text files
one screenful at a time on a soft-copy terminal.  It is the equivalent of
setting the environment variable PAGER to
.I less,
and then running zmore.  However, enough people seem to think that having the
command
.I zless
available is important to be worth providing it.
.SH "SEE ALSO"
zmore(1), less(1)
```

One interesting feature of the marked-up text file for the man page is the haphazard manner in which lines break. The formatting program groff (the man command uses groff to process the marked-up text file) fills up the lines of text and makes everything presentable.

Most groff commands must appear on a line by themselves, and each such command starts with a period or a dot. You can, however, embed some groff font-control commands in the text; these embedded commands start with a backslash (\).

Following is a summary of the commands that you see in the zless man page source file:

- *.B* turns on boldface.
- *.I* turns on italic.
- *.SH* is the start of a new section.
- *.TH* indicates the document title.

If you use these dot commands (meaning commands that begin with a period or dot) to change the font, the man page source file tends to display many short lines, because each dot command must appear on a separate line. As the following section shows, you can use embedded font-change commands to produce a more readable source file.

Writing a Sample man Page

This section shows you how to write a man page for a sample application by the name of satview. Assume that the satview program displays a satellite image in a window. The program includes some options for specifying the map projection, the zoom level, and the name of the file that contains the satellite image data.

Use a text editor to type the man page source code shown in the following listing and save it in a file named satview.1:

```
.TH SATVIEW 1 "April 19, 2003" "Satview Version 10.1"
.SH NAME
satview \- View satellite images.
.SH SYNOPSIS
\fBsatview\fP [-p \fIprojection\fP] [-m] [-z \fIzoomlevel\fP]
\fIfilename\fP
.SH DESCRIPTION
\fBsatview\fP displays the satellite image from \fIfilename\fP.
.SS Options
.TP
\fB-p \fIprojection\fR
Set the map projection (can be \fBL\fR for Lambert Conformal or
\fBP\fR for Polar Stereographic). The default is Lambert Conformal.
.TP
\fB-m\fP
Include a map in the satellite image.
.TP
\fB-z \fIzoomlevel\fR
Set the zoom level (can be one of: 2, 4, or 8). The default
zoomlevel is 1.
.TP
\fIfilename\fR
File containing satellite data.
.SH FILES
.TP
\fC/etc/awips/satview.rc\fR
Initialization commands for \fBsatview\fR
.SH SEE ALSO
nexrad(1), contour(1)
.SH Bugs
At zoom levels greater than 2, map is not properly
aligned with image.
```

Secret

The source file of a man page contains the following significant features:

- The .TH tag indicates the man page title as well as the date and a version-number string. In the formatted man page, the version and date strings appear at the bottom of each page.
- This man page has six sections—NAME, SYNOPSIS, DESCRIPTION, FILES, SEE ALSO, and Bugs—each of which starts with the .SH tag.
- The DESCRIPTION section has an Options subsection. The .SS tag indicates the beginning of a subsection.
- In the Options subsection, each item is listed with the .TP tag.
- The \fB command changes the font to boldface.
- \fI changes the font to italic.
- \fR changes the font to Roman.
- \fP changes the font to its preceding setting.

With this information in hand, you should understand the man page source listing.

Testing and Installing the man Page

As you prepare the man page file, you want to make sure that it's formatted correctly. To view the formatted output, use the following command:

```
groff -Tascii -man satview.1 | more
```

This command runs the groff command with the ascii typesetting device (which means that it produces plain ASCII output) and with the man page macro set (that's what the -man option does).

If you find any formatting discrepancies, check the dot commands and any embedded font-change commands, and make sure that everything looks right.

After you're satisfied with the man page format, you can make the man page available to everyone by copying the file to one of the directories in which all man pages reside. Log in as root and install the man page by using the following copy command:

```
cp satview.1 /usr/share/man/man1
```

After that, try the man page by using this command:

```
man satview
```

Figure 11-6 shows the resulting output. Compare the output with the source file listing shown in the preceding section, "Writing a Sample man Page," to see the effects of the commands on the final output. The italic command generates underlined output, because the terminal window can't display an italic font.

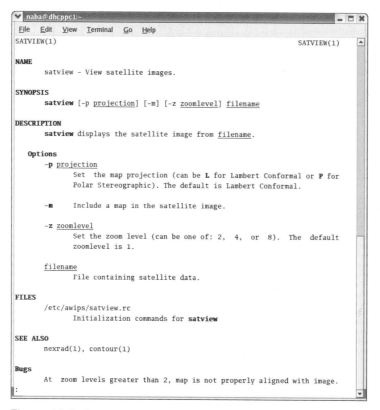

Figure 11-6: Output of the `man satview` Command in a Terminal Window.

Using the listing in this section as a guide, you can now write your own man pages.

Preparing Documentation with DocBook

The tradition of preparing formatted documentation using markup languages lives on. For example, the documentation for many open source software packages come in DocBook format. The remainder of this chapter briefly introduces you to DocBook and points you to sources where you can learn more about preparing documentation in DocBook.

Secret

DocBook is a vocubulary—a set of tags, kind of like HTML tags—for writing structured documents such as books and articles (anything that has chapters, sections, subsections, apendixes, and so forth). The DocBook vocabulary is defined in both Standard Generalized Markup Language (SGML) and the newer Extensible Markup Language (XML). Such vocabularies are formally known as Document Type Definition (DTD). Thus, DocBook is available as an SGML or XML DTD. You don't need to understand SGML or XML to use DocBook.

DocBok is gaining popularity as a markup language for documentation of open source projects such as GNOME and KDE. The publishing firm, O'Reilly & Associates, has also used DocBook to produce books. DocBook is edging out other markup languages such as Troff and LaTeX because the DocBook syntax is well-defined and easy to parse, which means that there are automated tools available to convert from DocBook format to many different types of presentation formats such as HTML for displaying on the Web browser and PostScript for printing. Another key property of DocBook is that it only lays out the structure of a document, the final formatting and presentation of the document depends on stylesheets. This enables you to generate different output formats from the same logical DocBook document.

DocBook was created in 1991 by HaL Computer Systems and O'Reilly & Associates. The DocBook DTD is now maintained by Organization for the Advancement of Structured Information Standards (OASIS). You can find more information about DocBook at http://www.oasis-open.org/committees/docbook/.

For a good book on DocBook, consult *DocBook: The Definitive Guide* by Norman Walsh and Leonard Muellner (O'Reilly & Associates).

Getting Started with DocBook

To start using DocBook, all you need are the following:

- *Text editor* to edit the DocBook file. Although automated tools can ease the burden of preparing DocBook files, you can create a DocBook using a plain text editor.
- *DocBook DTD* that defines the XML or SGML tags used to write the DocBook.
- *DocBook stylesheets*, such as the ones written in Extensible Stylesheet Language (XSL), that enable translation of DocBook from SGML or XML into other formats such as HTML, RTF, PDF, and so on.
- *Stylesheet processor* such as xsltproc that uses the stylesheets to convert the DocBook SGML or XML into other formats such as HTML.

Red Hat Linux comes with everything you need to get started with DocBook. In particular, you find both the SGML and XML DTDs for DocBook. The /usr/share/sgml/docbook directory contains the SGML and XML DTDs for different versions of DocBook as well as DocBook stylesheets.

Trying out a Sample DocBook

The best way to understand DocBook is to simply try out a sample file. You can see how the same DocBook file can be used to generate different output formats.

Use a text editor and prepare the file sample.xml with the following lines in it:

```
<?xml version="1.0"?>
<!DOCTYPE article PUBLIC "-//OASIS//DTD DocBook XML V4.2//EN"
"http://www.oasis-open.org/docbook/xml/4.2/docbookx.dtd">
<article>
  <articleinfo>
    <title>Sample DocBook</title>
  </articleinfo>
```

```
<para>This is a sample DocBook article that illustrates
      some simple DocBook XML tags.
</para>
<sect1>
  <title>Section 1</title>
  <para>Paragraph 1 of section 1</para>
  <sect2>
    <title>Section 1.1</title>
    <para>Paragraph 1 of section 1.1</para>
    <para>Paragraph 2 of section 1.1</para>
  </sect2>
  <sect2>
    <title>Section 1.2</title>
    <para>Paragraph 1 of section 1.2</para>
  </sect2>
</sect1>
<sect1>
  <title>Section 2</title>
  <para>Second high-level section in this article
  </para>
</sect1>
</article>
```

After you save the `sample.xml` file, you can use the xmllint utility to check if all the XML tags in the file are correct. Type the following command to check the syntax of the `sample.xml` file:

```
xmllint --valid --noout sample.xml
```

If everything is okay, the utility should print nothing.

Now, you can convert the `sample.xml` file into HTML and view it in a Web browser. To perform this task, type the following commands:

```
export DBS="/usr/share/sgml/docbook/xsl-stylesheets-1.58.1-1"

xsltproc -o sample.html $DBS/html/docbook.xsl sample.xml
```

The first command defines the DBS environment variable as the directory where the XSL stylesheets for DocBook are located in Red Hat Linux. The second command runs xsltproc with appropriate options to convert the `sample.xml` file into `sample.html`.

Now, you can open the `sample.html` file in Mozilla and see how the document looks. Figure 11-7 shows the `sample.html` file in Mozilla.

As Figure 11-7 shows, the DocBook is converted into a single HTML file with a table of contents at the beginning of the document. The table of contents includes links for each section and subsection.

You can also create a set of linked HTML files, one for each section. This is called chunked HTML because each section becomes a chunk. To create chunked HTML files from the `sample.xml` DocBook, type the following command (I assume that you still have the DBS environment variable defined as shown earlier in this section):

```
xsltproc $DBS/html/chunk.xsl sample.xml
```

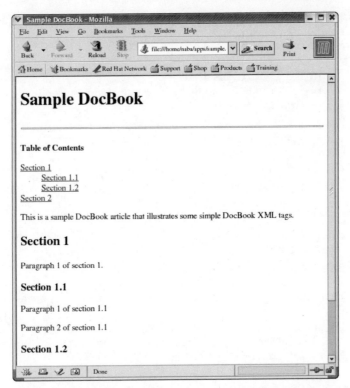

Figure 11-7: Displaying HTML Version of Sample DocBook in a Web Browser.

This generates an `index.html` file and separate HTML files for the other chunks (sections). Figure 11-8 shows the HTML chunk for section 2 of the sample DocBook.

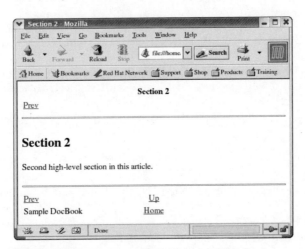

Figure 11-8: Chunked HTML Version of DocBook.

The chunked HTML output is widely used for many open source documentation, so Figure 11-8 should look familiar to you. Note that each HTML chunk contains Next, Prev, and Up links to go from section to section and go back to the first page.

Examining the Sample DocBook File

If you examine the `sample.xml` file, shown in the "Trying out a Sample DocBook" section, you should note the following points:

- All XML DocBook tags are in lowercase. Because XML is case sensitive, you must type all tags in lowercase.
- A DocBook begins with a standard header that identifies the XML version and information about the DTD. Here is a typical header:

```
<?xml version="1.0"?>
<!DOCTYPE article PUBLIC "-//OASIS//DTD DocBook XML V4.1.2//EN"
"http://www.oasis-open.org/docbook/xml/4.1.2/docbookx.dtd">
```

- Usually the entire DocBook is a `<book>` or an `<article>`. The `sample.xml` file uses a `<article>` structure.
- An `<article>` is composed of nested section elements such as `<sect1>`, `<sect2>`, and so on.
- A `<book>` is composed of multiple `<chapter>` elements, each with section elements inside.
- As with other markup languages, all indentations and white spaces are ignored, except for some elements such as `<programlisting>` and `<literallayout>` that are meant to show verbatim text.

Using Stylesheets

DocBook documents only contain the logical layout of the document. Stylesheets define how to convert a DocBook document into various formatted output. There are two sets of stylesheets:

- **XSLT**—Stands for Extensible Stylesheet Language (XSL) Transformations, which is a language used to convert XML documents into other XML documents. XSLT can convert DocBook XML into HTML, HTML Help, Java Help, XHTML, and XSL formatting objects.
- **DSSSL**—Stands for Document Style Semantics and Specification Language. The DSSSL stylesheets can convert DocBook SGML and XML into HTML, MIF, RTF, and TeX files.

Other tools can convert some of these formats such as XSL formatting objects or TeX into other formats such as PDF and PostScript.

Red Hat Linux comes with both XSL and DSSL stylesheets. These stylesheets are located in subdirectories of the `/usr/share/sgml/docbook` directory.

You can use the following stylesheet utilities to convert DocBook files into formatted output files:

- **xmllint**—Checks for correct syntax of document. Typically, you can check the correctness of an XML file with the following command:

```
xmllint --valid --noout xmlfilename
```

◆ **xsltproc**—Applies XSLT stylesheets to XML documents. A typical command-line is of the following form:

```
xsltproc stylesheetname xmlfilename
```

Thus, if you want to apply the stylesheet `mystyles.xls` to the `mydoc.xml` file, you would use the following command:

```
xsltproc mystyles.xsl sample.xml
```

Learning Some DocBook Elements

There are close to 400 DocBook elements in version 4.2. This chapter does not have enough space to cover them in detail. This section briefly touches upon some of the commonly used elements, especially those that you may want to use when writing documentation that you intend to convert to HTML.

---

insider insight

For a detailed, online reference to DocBook elements, point your Web browser to `http://www.docbook.org/tdg/en/html/ref-elements.html`.

Sections

Sections are a key organizing element in a DocBook. You can define sections either through specific numbered tags `<sect1>` through `<sect5>`, or through generic `<section>` tags nested inside one another.

When you use the specific section tags `<setc1>` through `<sect5>`, the higher numbered sections are subsections of the lower numbered ones. With these tags, a complex layout of sections would be similar to the following:

```
<sect1>
    <sect2>
        <sect3>...</sect3>
        <sect3>
            <sect4>
                <sect5>...</sect5>
                <sect5>...</sect5>
            </sect4>
            <sect4>...</sect4>
        </sect3>
    </sect2>
    <sect2>...</sect2>
</sect1>
<sect1>...</sect1>
```

On the other hand, when you use generic `<section>` tags, the layout is written in the following form:

```
<section>
    <section>
        <section> ... </section>
        <section> ... </section>
    </section>
    <section> ... </section>
</section>
```

Itemized List

Use the `<itemizedlist>` element to create a bulleted list. Such lists map to the ones created with the `<ul>` tag in HTML. Inside the list, use `<listitem>` elements to define entries in the list. Here is an example:

```
<itemizedlist mark='opencircle'>
  <listitem><para>SGML</para></listitem>
  <listitem><para>HTML B</para></listitem>
  <listitem><para>XML C</para></listitem>
</itemizedlist>
```

Use the `<itemizedlist>` element's `mark` attribute to specify the appearance of the bullets. You can also have other DocBook elements inside the `<listitem>` elements.

Ordered List

Use the `<orderedlist>` element to define a numbered list that maps to the lists displayed by the `<ol>` tag in HTML. Use the `<listitem>` element to specify each entry in the ordered list, as shown in this example:

```
<orderedlist>
  <listitem><para>Step 1</para></listitem>
  <listitem><para>Step 2</para></listitem>
  <listitem><para>Step 3</para></listitem>
</orderedlist>
```

Variable List

Use the `<variablelist>` element to create a list of terms and their definitions. The `<variablelist>` maps to a list displayed by the `<dl>` tag in HTML. Inside the variable list, the `<varlistentry>` element contains the term, identified by the `<term>` element and the definition, idenfied by a `<listitem>`. Here is an example:

```
<variablelist>
  <title>File Name Extensions</title>
  <varlistentry>
    <term>txt</term>
    <listitem><para>Text file.</para></listitem>
  </varlistentry>
  <varlistentry>
    <term>xml</term>
    <listitem><para>XML file</para></listitem>
  </varlistentry>
</variablelist>
```

Image and Multimedia Elements

You might want to insert screen shots or other images into the documentation. You can do so with the `<mediaobject>` and `<imageobject>` elements. You have to place the `<imageobject>` element inside a `<mediaobject>`. A simple example is as follows:

```
<mediaobject>
  <imageobject>
    <imagedata fileref="imagefile.jpg" format="JPG"/>
  </imageobject>
  <textobject>
```

```
    <phrase>Description of image</phrase>
  </textobject>
</mediaobject>
```

Use the `<imagedata>` element to specify the image file and format. You can associate an alternate text description of the image by adding a `<textobject>` element, as shown in this example.

Tables

Use the `<table>` element, along with `<thead>`, `<row>`, and `<entry>` elements to define tables in DocBook. The following example illustrates how all these elements fit together:

```
<table>
  <title>Sample Table</title>
  <tgroup cols="2">
    <thead>
      <row>
        <entry>Fruit</entry>
        <entry>Color</entry>
      </row>
    </thead>
    <tbody>
      <row>
        <entry>Apple</entry>
        <entry>Red</entry>
      </row>
      <row>
        <entry>Banana</entry>
        <entry>Yellow</entry>
      </row>
    </tbody>
  </tgroup>
</table>
```

As you can see, the table's content is inside a `<tgroup>` element that specifies the number of columns. Each row is defined by a `<row>` element that contains as many `<entry>` elements as there are columns.

DocBook also includes an `<informaltable>` element that defines a table without any title.

Figures

Use the `<figure>` element to add figures to documents. The figure will be numbered and have a title. You can use the `<informalfigure>` element for a figure that does not need a number and a title. Here is an example of a figure:

```
<figure>
  <title>AWIPS Software Architecture</title>
  <mediaobject>
    <imageobject>
      <imagedata fileref="awips-swarch.jpg" format="JPG"/>
    </imageobject>
  </mediaobject>
</figure>
```

Inside the `<figure>` element, you can embed the figure using a `<mediaobject>` and an `<imageobject>`, as shown in the example.

Examples

Software documentation often requires the inclusion of sample code. Use the `<example>` tag to show such samples. Such examples have a title and are numbered. Use the `<informalexample>` element for examples that do not need titles and do not have to be numbered. Here is an `<example>` element:

```
<example>
  <title>Sample Java Code</title>
  <programlisting>
    public class HelloWorld {
        public static void main(String [] args) {
            System.out.println("Hello, World!");
        }
    }
  </programlisting>
</example>
```

Enclose the program listing in a `<programlisting>` element, as shown in this example.

Notes, Tips, and Warnings

You may also want to include notes, tips, and warnings in documentation (just as this and many other books do). DocBook includes several elements for this purpose. Here are the relevant DocBook elements:

◆ **Note**—Use the `<note>` element for notes, as shown below:

```
<note><para>This is a note.</para></note>
```

◆ **Tip**—Use the `<tip>` element to add a tip in the text, like this:

```
<tip><para>This is a tip.</para></tip>
```

◆ **Warning**—Use the `<warning>` element to add a warning message, like this:

```
<warning><para>This is a warning.</para></warning>
```

◆ **Caution**—Use the `<caution>` element to add cautionary messages, like this:

```
<caution><para>This is a caution.</para></caution>
```

◆ **Important**—Use the <important> element to set aside any important message, like this:

```
<important><para>This is important.</para></important>
```

Character Formatting

Within the running text in a paragraph, you may want to emphasize some text. You can do so with the `<emphasis>` element. For example, here's how you can set apart a word in a paragraph:

```
<para>
  This is the <emphasis>most important</emphasis> part of this sentence.
</para>
```

You can use the `<filename>` element to set apart filenames that occur in the text. Here is an example:

```
<para>
The XSL stylesheets for DocBook are located in the
<filename class='directory'>
   /usr/share/sgml/docbook/xsl-stylesheets-1.58.1-1
</filename> directory.

</para>
```

Software documentation also mention commands—names of executable files—in text. To set such commands apart from the rest of the text, use the `<command>` element, as shown in the following example:

```
<para>
Type the
<command>ls -l</command> get a detailed directory listing.
</para>
```

Links

You can embed links to internal DocBook elements in a document as well as external websites and other resources. Use the <link> element to point to an internal link identified by the id attribute added to other elements. For example, suppose that you have an Introduction section, defined as follows:

```
<sect1 id="intro">
<title>Introduction</title>
<para> ... </para>
</sect1>
```

Elsewhere in the document, you can then use the `<link>` element to set up a link to this Introduction section, like this:

```
<para>See the <link linkend="intro">Introduction section</link>
for more information </para>
```

Use the `<link>` element's linkend attribute to identify the target of this link. That target should be identified by the id attribute of another element in the document.

To define an external link, use the `<ulink>` element. For example, here is how you can show a link to the DocBook home page:

```
<para>
To learn more about DocBook, visit the
<ulink url="http://www.docbook.org/">Docbook home page</ulink>
</para>
```

Use the `<ulink>` element's url attribute to specify the URL of the external link.

Summary

The configuration of many Linux features depends on settings that you store in text files. You must, therefore, know how to edit text files to set up and maintain a Linux system. Another form of text processing involves typesetting and formatting text documents. Linux includes groff for this purpose. Nowadays, you're likely to use a PC to prepare formatted documents, but you still need to prepare one kind of formatted document: the man pages that provide online help for any software that you write. Accordingly, this chapter shows you how to use several text editors. It also shows you how to prepare man pages by using groff.

By reading this chapter, you learned the following:

◆ Linux includes a variety of text editors. Learning the ed and vi editors is important, because all UNIX systems come with these editors. Although the ed editor may seem cryptic, you may need to use it to edit files if no other editor is available.

◆ The ed editor works on a text file one line at a time (which is why it's called a line editor). Each command takes the form of a range of lines, followed by a one-character command that applies to that range of lines.

◆ The vi editor is a full-screen editor that enables you to view a file several lines at a time. The vi editor has three modes: visual-command mode, colon-command mode, and text-input mode.

◆ In vi's text-input mode, you can enter text. To change to text-input mode, press i, a, or A. To return to command mode, press Esc.

◆ In vi's colon-command mode, you enter a colon (:) followed by a command that uses the same syntax as ed commands.

◆ GNU Emacs is more than just an editor—it's also an environment from which you can perform most routine tasks.

◆ As an editor, GNU Emacs doesn't have any modes; whatever you type goes into the file. Commands begin with a control character (such as Ctrl-x) or Esc.

◆ To view the online tutorial, type **C-h t** in GNU Emacs.

◆ The groff utility is useful for formatting documents. groff provides the functionality of the standard UNIX nroff and troff utilities. You must use groff to prepare man pages.

◆ The best way to learn to prepare a man page is to study an existing man page and mimic its style in your own man page. This chapter provided an example of how you can prepare a typical man page.

◆ DocBook is a markup language for structured document layout. DocBook is defined using SGML or XML document type definitions (DTDs). Red Hat Linux comes with DocBook DTDs and stylesheets. This chapter showed you how to get started with DocBook.

Basic System Administration

Chapter

12

◆ ◆

Secrets in This Chapter

◆ ◆

This chapter introduces you to some Linux system administration tasks. You learn to perform many of these system administration tasks by using graphical tools as well as commands. You can access many of these graphical utilities from the main menu as well as from the Start Here window (that opens when you double-click the Start Here icon on the desktop).

First, you will learn how to manage users and groups by using Red Hat User Manager as well as text commands. Then you will explore tasks that the Start Here window enables you to perform. This overview of Start Here should help you perform other system-administration tasks as the need arises.

Because you typically install Red Hat Linux on a PC that previously had Microsoft Windows installed on it, a common system-administration task is to access the Windows files from Linux. This chapter shows you how to mount and access DOS/Windows disks, including floppy disks. You learn about a kernel module for the NTFS file system that enables you to read from Windows XP partitions that use the NTFS file system.

You also learn about a package by the name of mtools, which enables you to access and use (copy, delete, and format) MS-DOS files (typically, on a floppy disk) in Red Hat Linux.

Revisiting Linux System Administration

Chapter 1 provides an overview of the tasks involved in Linux system administration. In this chapter, you briefly revisit the key tasks that you perform as a system administrator, learning where, in this book, you can find more information about a specific task. System administration is essentially the work required to keep your Red Hat Linux system working properly.

You can group the tasks into two broad categories: system administration and network administration. The first category refers to keeping the system itself up and running, while network administration focuses on the LAN and Internet services.

Typical system and network administration tasks include the following:

♦ **Adding and removing users**—This chapter shows you how to add or remove user accounts using Red Hat User Manager and the useradd and userdel commands.

♦ **Installing, configuring, and upgrading the operating system and various utilities**—Chapter 2 covers how to install Red Hat Linux, and Chapters 4 through 6 focus on how to configure and set up specific hardware in Red Hat Linux. Chapter 21 describes how to upgrade or reconfigure the Linux kernel.

♦ **Installing new software**—Chapter 21 shows you how to use the Red Hat Package Manager (RPM) as well as the Package Management GUI tool to install software. In that chapter, you also learn how to unpack and build software from source archives that you can download from various Internet sites.

♦ **Making backups**—Chapter 20 covers backing up and restoring files and directories by using the GNU tar utility.

♦ **Mounting and unmounting file systems**—The mount and umount commands appear in various chapters, such as Chapters 8 and 10. The current chapter shows you how to mount MS-DOS file systems. You also learn to use the mtools utilities to access Windows/DOS files. This chapter also introduces you to the User Mount Tool for mounting file systems.

- **Monitoring the system's performance**—This chapter describes a few utilities for monitoring system performance. I describe this topic further in Chapter 20.
- **Starting and shutting down the system**—Chapter 7 describes how to start and shut down your Red Hat Linux system.
- **Maintaining the network configuration files**—Chapter 6 describes various TCP/IP configuration files.
- **Setting up PPP and SLIP**—You learn about PPP and SLIP in Chapter 13.
- **Monitoring network status**—Chapter 6 presents some utility programs that you can use as network diagnostic tools.
- **Setting up host and network security**—You have to protect the system files and your network against attacks from the outside. Chapter 22 describes how to secure your system and Internet services.
- **Monitoring security**—You have to keep an eye on any intrusions, usually by checking the log files. Chapter 22 covers this topic.

note As you can see from the comments next to the items in the list of system administration tasks, I cover many of these system administration topics in other chapters of this book. For topics covered elsewhere, please turn to the referenced chapter for more information.

Becoming root

You have to be logged in as root to perform the system administration tasks. The root user is the super user and the only account with all the privileges needed to do anything in the system.

Secret The common wisdom is that you should not normally log in as root. That's because when you're root, one misstep and you could easily delete all the files—especially when typing commands. Take, for example, the command rm *.html that you may type to delete all files with the .html extension. Unfortunately, if you accidentally press the spacebar after the asterisk (*), the shell takes the command to be rm * .html and, because * matches any file name, deletes everything in the current directory. That sort of thing can happen, and the damage from any mistakes are much bigger when you are logged in as root.

You should log in as a normal user and become root when needed. Another advantage of this approach of becoming root when necessary is that there will be an entry in the /var/log/messages file every time a user becomes root (only those who know the root password can become root). Those entries in the /var/log/messages file can server as audit trail of who became super user when and did what.

Using the su - Command

If you are logged in as a normal user and need to become root, type the following command at a terminal window or console:

```
su -
```

Then enter the root password in response to the prompt. From this point on, you're root. Do whatever you have to do. To return back to your usual self, type:

```
exit
```

It's that easy to switch between being a normal user and root.

> **caution**
>
> You should always type su - to become root rather than typing su. The su - command changes the environment to root's default environment settings whereas su alone retains the current user's environment, which may contain unsafe settings for environment variables.

Becoming Root for the GUI Utilities

If you use any of Red Hat's GUI utilities to perform a system administration chore, it's even easier. Typically, the utility pops up a dialog box that prompts you for the root password (see Figure 12-1). Just type the root password and press Enter. The GUI utility should then start. If you don't want to use the utility, click Cancel.

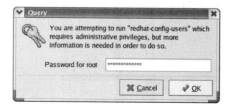

Figure 12-1: Providing the Root Password for GUI Tools That Need Root Privileges.

Recovering from a Forgotten Root Password

To perform system administration tasks, you have to know the root password. What happens if you forget the root password? There is a way to recover from a forgotten root password. Just reboot the PC and you can reset the root password. Simply follow these steps:

1. Reboot the PC (select Reboot as you log out of the GUI screen) or power up as usual. Soon, you see the graphical GRUB screen with the names of operating systems you can boot. (If you have a GRUB password, press p and enter the GRUB password now.)
2. Press a (just the letter "a"). GRUB prompts you for commands to add to its default boot command.

3. Press the spacebar, type the following word, and then press Enter:

`single`

This causes Linux to start up as usual, but run in a single-user mode that does not require you to log in. After Linux starts, you see the following command-line prompt:

`sh-2.05b#`

4. Use the `passwd` command to change the root password as follows:

`sh-2.05b# passwd`

`Changing password for user root.`
`New password:` *(type the new root password)*

Type the new root password that you want to use (it won't appear onscreen), and then press Enter. Linux asks for the password again, like this:

`Retype new password:` *(retype the new root password)*

Type the password again, and press Enter. If you enter the same password both times, the `passwd` command changes the password and displays the following message:

`passwd: all authentication tokens updated successfully`

5. Now, type **exit** or **reboot** to reboot the PC. After Linux starts, it displays the familiar login screen. Now, you should be able to log in as `root` with the new password.

caution Make sure that your Red Hat Linux PC is physically secure. As this procedure shows, anyone who can physically access your Red Hat Linux PC can simply `reboot`, set a new root password, and do whatever they want with the system. Having a password for the GRUB bootloader can provide an extra level of protection.

Managing User Accounts

Adding user accounts to the system is a key system-administration function. You get the chance to add user accounts when you boot Red Hat Linux for the first time. If you didn't add other user accounts at that time, you can do so now. You can use the Red Hat User Manager or the `useradd` command to add a new user account to your system.

insider insight A good idea is to create other user accounts besides root. Even if you're the only user of the system, logging in as a less-privileged user is good practice, because you can't damage any important system files inadvertently. If necessary, you can type the `su -` command to log in as root and perform any system-administration tasks.

Using Red Hat User Manager to Add User Accounts

You can use the Red Hat User Manager to add user accounts. To start the Red Hat User Manager, log in as root at the graphical login screen and then select Main Menu⇨ System Settings⇨Users and Groups from the GNOME or KDE Panel. If you're not logged in as `root`, the Red Hat User Manager prompts you for the root password. You can enter the password and click OK, then the Red Hat User Manager window appears.

The window shows two tabs: Users and Groups (see Figure 12-2). The Users tab displays the current list of users from the `/etc/passwd` file. The Groups tab lists the name of groups from the `/etc/group` file. Initially, the Red Hat User Manager filters out any system users and groups. However, you can turn off the filer by selecting Preferences⇨Filter system users and groups. Figure 12-2 shows the Red Hat User Manager window with a listing of all user accounts, including the system ones.

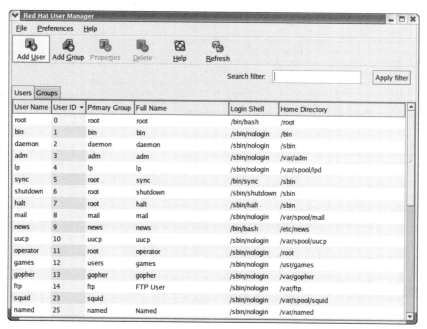

Figure 12-2: Red Hat User Manager Window.

You can add new users and groups or edit existing users and groups from the Red Hat User Manager. To edit the information for an existing user, click the user name in the list in the Users tab, and then click the Properties button on the toolbar. That user's information appears in a User Properties dialog box. You can then edit the information and click OK to make the changes.

To add a new user, click the New User button on the toolbar. This action opens the Create New User dialog box, as shown in Figure 12-3.

Figure 12-3: Entering Information for a New User.

Fill in the requested information. In particular, you must enter the user name and the password. After filling in all the fields, click the OK button. The new user should now appear in the list on the Users tab in the Red Hat User Manager window.

> **note**
>
> If you want to remove a user account, click the user name in the list on the Users tab that displays all user accounts (see Figure 12-2), then click the Delete button on the toolbar.

Secret

Notice the checkbox labeled `Create a private group for the user` in Figure 12-3. It's checked by default, and that means each new user is in a separate private user group. However, sometimes you want a user to be in a specific group so that the user can access the files owned by that group. It's easy to add a user to another group. For example, suppose that I want to add the user name `naba` to the group called `wheel`. I can do this simply by typing the following command in a terminal window:

```
usermod -G wheel naba
```

If you simply uncheck that check box labeled `Create a private group for the user` (see Figure 12-3), the new user is assigned the group named `users`. Type **more /etc/group** to see the group names and group ID.

Using Commands to Manage User Accounts

If you're working from a text console, you can create a new user account by using the `useradd` command. Follow these steps to add an account for a new user:

1. Log in as `root`. (If you're not already logged in as root, type **su -** to become root.)
2. Type the following `useradd` command with the `-c` option to create the account:

```
/usr/sbin/useradd -c "Ashley Barkakati" ashley
```

3. Set Ashley's password by using the `passwd` command, as follows:

```
passwd ashley
Changing password for user ashley
New password: (Type the password and then press Enter.)
Retype new password: (Type the password again and press Enter.)
passwd: all authentication tokens updated successfully
```

Notice that, if you type a password that someone can easily guess, the passwd program rejects it.

Secret

The `useradd` command consults the files `/etc/default/useradd` and `/etc/login.defs` to obtain default information on various parameters for the new user account. The `/etc/default/useradd` file, for example, specifies the default shell (`/bin/bash`) and default home directory location (`/home`). The `/etc/login.defs` file provides systemwide defaults for automatic group and user IDs, as well as password expiration parameters.

You can delete a user account by using the `userdel` command. Simply type **userdel username** at the command prompt to delete a user's account. To wipe out that user's home directory as well, type **userdel -r username**.

To modify any information in a user account, use the `usermod` command. For example, if I want my user name, `naba`, to have `root` as the primary group, I would type:

```
usermod -g root naba
```

To learn more about the `useradd` and `userdel` commands, type **man useradd** or **man userdel** in a terminal window.

Understanding the /etc/passwd File

The `/etc/passwd` file is a list of all user accounts. It's a text file, and any user can read it; no special privileges are needed. Each line in /etc/passwd has seven fields, separated by colons (`:`).

Here is a typical entry from the `/etc/passwd` file:

```
naba:x:500:10:Naba Barkakati:/home/naba:/bin/bash
```

Figure 12-4 uses this typical entry to explain the meaning of the seven fields.

As the example shows, the format of each line in `/etc/passwd` looks like this:

```
username:password:UID:GID:GECOS:homedir:shell
```

Table 12-1 explains the meaning of the seven fields in each /etc/passwd entry.

Figure 12-4: Meaning of Fields in a Typical /etc/passwd Entry.

Table 12-1: Meaning of the Fields in /etc/passwd File

Field	Meaning
username	An alphanumeric user name, usually eight characters long and unique (Red Hat Linux allows user names to be longer than eight characters, but some other operating systems do not)
password	When present, a 13-character encrypted password (an empty field means that no password is required to access the account, an x means the password is stored in the /etc/shadow file, which is more secure)
UID	A unique number that serves as the user identifier (root has a UID of 0 and usually the UIDs between 1 to 100 are reserved for nonhuman users, such as servers; it's best to keep the UID less that 32,767)
GID	The default group ID (GID) of the group to which the user belongs (GID 0 is for group root, other groups are defined in /etc/group and users can be and usually are in more than one group at a time)
GECOS	Optional personal information about the user (the finger command uses this field and GECOS stands for General Electric Comprehensive Operating System, a long-forgotten operating system that's immortalized by the name of this field in /etc/passwd)
homedir	The name of the user's home directory
shell	The command interpreter (shell) such as Bash (/bin/bash) that's executed when this user logs in

Managing Groups

A group is an something to which users belong. A group has a name and an identification number (GID). After a group is defined, users can belong to one or more of these groups.

You'll find all the existing groups listed in /etc/group. For example, here is the line that defines the group named wheel:

```
wheel:x:10:root,naba
```

As this example shows, each line in /etc/group has the following format with four fields separated by colons:

```
groupname:password:GID:membership
```

Table 12-2 explains the meaning of the four fields in a group definition.

Table 12-2: Meaning of Fields in /etc/group File

Field	Meaning
groupname	The name of the group (for example, wheel)
password	The group password (an x means the password is stored in the /etc/shadow file)
GID	The numerical group ID (for example, 10)
membership	A comma-separated list of user names who belong to this group (for example, root,naba)

If you want to create a new group, you can simply click the Add Group button in the Red Hat User Manager (Figure 12-2). An even quicker way is to use the groupadd command. For example, to add a new group called class with an automatically-selected group ID, just type the following command in a terminal window (you have to be logged in as root):

```
groupadd class
```

Then, you can add users to this group with the usermod command. For example, to add the users naba and ashley to the group named class, I type the following commands:

```
usermod -G class naba
usermod -G class ashley
```

That's it. Now I check /etc/group to find that it contains the following definition of class:

```
class:x:502:naba,ashley
```

If you want to remove a group, use the `groupdel` command. For example, to remove the group named `class`, type

```
groupdel class
```

Exploring the Start Here Window

Both GNOME and KDE desktops in Red Hat Linux come with a Start Here icon on the desktop that provides access to icons for performing many system- and network-administration tasks, including adding new users. This section provides an overview of some system administration tasks that you can perform through the Start Here window.

To open the Start Here window, double-click the Start Here icon on the GNOME or KDE desktop. This action opens the initial Start Here window, as shown in Figure 12-5.

Figure 12-5: The Initial Start Here Window, After You Double-Click the Start Here Icon on the Desktop.

The window shown in Figure 12-5 has three icons. Double-clicking each icon brings up further icons with which you can perform specific tasks from starting applications to configuring various aspects of your Red Hat Linux system. The three icons in Figure 12-5 serve the following purposes:

- ♦ **Applications**—Brings up icons that provide access to all the applications that are also available through the Main Menu
- ♦ **Preferences**—Displays icons through which you can configure many aspects of the desktop
- ♦ **System Settings**—Enables you to perform many system administration tasks through a number of icons

To perform system-administration tasks, double-click the System Settings icon. This action accesses a new set of icons in the System Settings window, as shown in Figure 12-6. The System Settings window is somewhat similar to the Control Panel in Microsoft Windows. You can perform various tasks by double-clicking the icons in the window.

Figure 12-6: System Settings Icons.

The System Settings icons shown in Figure 12-6 enable you to perform the following system-administration tasks through easy-to-use GUIs:

◆ **Add/Remove Applications**—Red Hat's Package Management utility through which you can install or remove package groups (I describe this utility in Chapter 21).

◆ **Authentication**—GUI utility used to configure authentication (similar to what you do during Red Hat Linux installation, described in Chapter 2).

◆ **Date & Time**—A utility that enables you to set the date and time. You can also set the time zone and enable the use of Network Time Protocol (NTP) to automatically get the date and time from an Internet time server (Red Hat provides two such time servers—clock.redhat.com and clock2.redhat.com).

◆ **Display**—The redhat-config-xfree86 GUI tool to configure the display settings (Chapter 3 describes the redhat-config-xfree86 utility).

◆ **Keyboard**—GUI tool to select the keyboard layout suitable for your language (similar to the keyboard configuration that you perform during Red Hat Linux installation, as described in Chapter 2).

◆ **Language**—Tool to select the default language out of the languages that you have installed on your system.

◆ **Login Screen**—GUI tool to configure the GNOME Display Manager (GDM). The tool enables you to set options in the /etc/X11/gdm/gdm.conf file (Chapter 9 describes the GDM configuration options).

◆ **Mouse**—Tool to select your mouse from a list of available mouse types (similar to the mouse configuration screen that you encounter when installing Red Hat Linux, as described in Chapter 2).

◆ **Network**—The Network Configuration tool for configuring, activating, and deactivating network interfaces (described in Chapter 6).

◆ **Printing**—Printer configuration tool for setting up print queues (described in Chapter 4).

◆ **Root Password**—GUI tool to set the root password, similarly to the way you set the root password during Red Hat Linux installation, as described in Chapter 2.

◆ **Security Level**—Tool to configure the security level of the firewall to one of three predefined levels—High, Medium, No Firewall (described in Chapter 22).

◆ **Server Settings**—Opens the Server Settings window with five icons for configuring the Web server, DNS, NFS, and Samba, and turning all services on or off.

◆ **Soundcard Detection**—Tool that detects the sound card and displays the information, but does not provide any way to configure the sound card (described in Chapter 5).

◆ **Users and Groups**—The Red Hat User Manager tool, which enables you to add new users and groups and edit existing user information (as I described in the section "Managing User Accounts," earlier in this chapter).

You can explore these tools by double-clicking the icons one at a time. If you're not logged in as root, each utility first prompts you for the root password and then proceeds to display the GUIs through which you can perform a specific set of tasks.

You can access some of these system administration utilities from the GNOME and KDE panels as well. The following section describes a few of these tools.

Managing the File System

The *file system* refers to the organization of files and directories. As a system administrator, you have to perform certain operations to manage the file system. For example, you have to learn how to mount—add a file system on a storage medium to the overall Red Hat Linux file system. You also need to back up important data and learn how to restore files from a backup. Other file system operations include sharing files with the Network File System (NFS) and accessing MS-DOS files. Chapter 7 introduces you to the Red Hat Linux file system, Chapter 20 describes how to back up and restore files, and Chapter 19 covers NFS. The next few sections explain how to mount file systems, and specifically, how to access DOS files in Linux.

Mounting a Device on the File System

The storage devices that you use in Red Hat Linux contain Linux file systems. Each device has its own local file system, consisting of a hierarchy of directories. Before you can access the files on a device, you have to attach the device's directory hierarchy to the tree that represents the overall Red Hat Linux file system.

Mounting is the operation that you perform to cause the file system on a physical storage device (a hard-disk partition or a CD-ROM) to appear as part of the Linux file system. Figure 12-7 illustrates the concept of mounting.

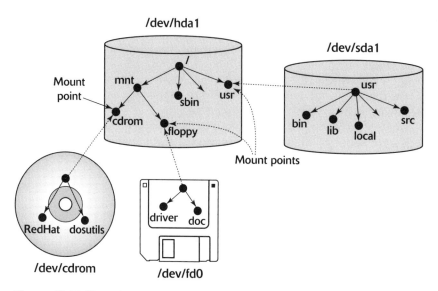

Figure 12-7: Mounting Devices on the Red Hat Linux File System.

Figure 12-7 shows each device with a name that begins with /dev. For example, /dev/cdrom is the CD-ROM drive and /dev/fd0 is the floppy drive. These physical devices are mounted at specific mount points on the Red Hat Linux file system. For example, the CD-ROM drive, /dev/cdrom, is mounted on /mnt/cdrom in the file system. After mounting the CD-ROM in this way, the RedHat directory on the CD-ROM appears as /mnt/cdrom/RedHat in the Red Hat Linux file system.

Secret

You can use the mount command to manually mount a device on the Red Hat Linux file system at a specified directory. That directory is the *mount point*. For example, to mount the CD-ROM drive at /mnt/cdrom directory, you would type the following command (after logging in as root):

```
mount /dev/cdrom /mnt/cdrom
```

The mount command reports an error if the CD-ROM device is mounted already or if no CD-ROM is in the drive. Otherwise, the mount operation succeeds, and you can access the CD-ROM's contents through the /mnt/cdrom directory.

You can use any directory as the mount point. If you mount a device on a nonempty directory, however, you cannot access the files in that directory until you unmount the device by using the umount command. You should always, therefore, use an empty directory as the mount point.

Red Hat Linux comes with the /mnt/cdrom directory for mounting CD-ROMs and /mnt/floppy for mounting floppy drives. If you have a Zip drive, the installation program detects that drive and creates a /mnt/zip directory as the mount point for the Zip drive.

To unmount a device when you no longer need it. use the umount command. For example, to unmount the CD-ROM device, type:

```
umount /dev/cdrom
```

The umount command succeeds as long as no one is using the CD-ROM. If you get an error when trying to unmount the CD-ROM, check to see if the current working directory is on the CD-ROM. If you are currently in one of the CD-ROM's directories, that also qualifies as a use of the CD-ROM.

Examining the /etc/fstab File

The mount command has the following general format:

```
mount device-name mount-point
```

However, you can mount the CD-ROM by typing one of the following commands:

```
mount /dev/cdrom
mount /mnt/cdrom
```

You can mount by specifying only the CD-ROM device name or the mount point name because of what's in a file named /etc/fstab. There is a line in the /etc/fstab file for the /mnt/cdrom mount point. That entry specifies the CD-ROM device name and the file system type. That's why you can mount the CD-ROM with a shorter mount command.

The /etc/fstab file is a configuration file—a text file containing information that the mount and umount commands use. Each line in the /etc/fstab file provides information about a device and its mount point in the Red Hat Linux file system. Essentially, the /etc/fstab file associates various mount points within the file system with specific devices, which enables the mount command to work from the command line with only the mount point or the device as argument.

Here is a /etc/fstab file from a typical Red Hat Linux system:

```
LABEL=/            /             ext3     defaults          1 1
LABEL=/boot        /boot         ext3     defaults          1 2
none               /dev/pts      devpts   gid=5,mode=620    0 0
none               /proc         proc     defaults          0 0
none               /dev/shm      tmpfs    defaults          0 0
/dev/hda6          swap          swap     defaults          0 0
/dev/cdrom         /mnt/cdrom    udf,iso9660 noauto,owner,kudzu,ro 0 0
/dev/fd0           /mnt/floppy   auto     noauto,owner,kudzu 0 0
```

The first field on each line shows a device name, such as a hard-disk partition (or it identifies a partition by a LABEL keyword). The second field is the mount point, and the third field indicates the type of file system on the device. You can ignore the last three fields for now.

This /etc/fstab file shows that the /dev/hda6 device (the second logical partition on the first IDE hard disk) functions as a swap device for virtual memory, which is why both the mount point and the file system type are set to swap.

The Linux operating system uses the contents of the /etc/fstab file to mount various file systems automatically. During Red Hat Linux startup, the init process executes a shell script that runs the mount -a command. That command reads the /etc/fstab file and mounts all listed file systems (except those with the noauto option).

The fourth field on each line of the /etc/fstab file shows a comma-separated list of options that apply to a specific device. Typically, you find the defaults option in this field. The defaults option implies—among other things—that the device mounts at boot time, that only root can mount the device, and that the device mounts for reading and writing. If the options include noauto, the device doesn't mount automatically as the system boots.

The kudzu option in the fourth field of /etc/fstab entries indicates that these lines were added to the fstab file by the kudzu hardware detection utility—kudzu runs the updfstab command to add entries in the /etc/fstab file for each removable drive that it detects. You typically find that the entries for CD-ROM (/dev/cdrom) and floppy drive (dev/fd0) have the kudzu option in the fourth field. On a PC with a IDE Zip drive, for instance, the /etc/fstab file has another entry set up by kudzu that associates the /mnt/zip mount point with the Zip drive device (/dev/hdd4), as follows:

```
/dev/hdd4   /mnt/zip   auto   noauto,owner,kudzu   0  0
```

Mounting a DOS/Windows File System

If you have Microsoft Windows 95/98/Me installed on your hard disk, you've probably already mounted the DOS partition under Red Hat Linux. If not, you can easily mount DOS partitions in Red Hat Linux. Mounting makes the DOS directory hierarchy appear as part of the Linux file system. To identify the DOS partitions easily, you may want to mount the first DOS partition as /dosc, the second one as /dosd, and so on.

To determine whether your DOS hard disk partitions are set up to mount automatically, type the following grep command to look for the string vfat in the file /etc/fstab:

```
grep vfat /etc/fstab
```

If the output shows one or more lines that contain vfat, your Red Hat Linux system mounts DOS/Windows hard-disk partitions automatically.

If the grep command doesn't show any lines that contain the string vfat in /etc/fstab, your system is not set up to mount any DOS/Windows hard-disk partitions automatically. Of course, a very good reason may be that your hard disk doesn't have any DOS partitions.

Even if you don't have any DOS partitions on your hard disk, you should learn how to access a DOS file system from Red Hat Linux because you may need to access a DOS floppy disk on your Red Hat Linux system.

To mount a DOS hard disk partition or floppy, use the mount command but include the option -t vfat to indicate the file system type as DOS. For example, if your DOS partition happens to be the first partition on your IDE drive and you want to mount it on /dosc, use the following mount command:

```
mount -t vfat /dev/hda1 /dosc
```

The `-t vfat` part of the `mount` command specifies that the device you mount—`/dev/hda1`—has an DOS/Windows file system. Figure 12-8 illustrates the effect of this `mount` command.

Figure 12-8: Mounting a DOS/Windows FAT Partition on the /dosc Directory.

Figure 12-8 shows how directories in your DOS partition map to the Linux file system. What was the `C:\DOS` directory under DOS becomes `/dosc/dos` under Red Hat Linux. Similarly, `C:\WINDOWS` now is `/dosc/windows`. You probably can see the pattern. To convert a DOS filename to Linux (when you mount the DOS partition on `/dosc`), perform the following steps:

1. Change the DOS names to lowercase.
2. Change `C:\` to `/dosc/`.
3. Change all backslashes (\) to slashes (/).

Mounting DOS Floppy Disks

Just as you mount a DOS hard disk partition on the Red Hat Linux file system, you can also mount a DOS floppy disk. You must log in as `root` to mount a floppy, but you can follow the steps shown in the latter part of this section to set up your system so that any user can mount a DOS floppy disk. You also need to know the device name for the floppy drive. By default, Linux defines the following two generic floppy device names:

♦ `/dev/fd0` is the A drive (the first floppy drive).
♦ `/dev/fd1` is the B drive (the second floppy drive, if you have one).

As for the mount point, you can use any empty directory in the file system as the mount point, but the Red Hat Linux system comes with a directory, `/mnt/floppy`, specifically mounting a floppy disk.

To mount a DOS floppy disk on the `/mnt/floppy` directory, put the floppy in the drive and type the following command:

```
mount -t vfat /dev/fd0 /mnt/floppy
```

After you mount the floppy, you can copy files to and from the floppy by using Linux's copy command (cp). To copy the file gnome1.pcx from the current directory to the floppy, type the following:

```
cp gnome1.pcx /mnt/floppy
```

Similarly, to see the contents of the floppy disk, type the following:

```
ls /mnt/floppy
```

If you want to remove the floppy disk from the drive, first unmount the floppy drive. Unmounting removes the association between the floppy disk's file system and the mount point on the Red Hat Linux file system. Use the umount command to unmount the floppy disk like this:

```
umount /dev/fd0
```

Secret

You can set up your Red Hat Linux system so that any user can mount a DOS floppy. To enable any user to mount a DOS floppy in the A drive on the /a directory, for example, perform the following steps:

1. Log in as root.
2. Create the /a directory (the mount point) by typing the following command in a terminal window:

   mkdir /a

3. Edit the /etc/fstab file in a text editor (such as vi or Emacs), insert the following line and then save the file and quit the editor:

   /dev/fd0   /a   vfat   noauto,user   0 0

   If a line already exists for /dev/fd0, simply edit that line to match what is shown previously. The first field in that line is the device name of the floppy drive (/dev/fd0), the second field is the mount directory (/a), and the third field shows the type of file system (vfat). The user option (which appears next to noauto) is what enables all users to mount DOS floppy disks.

4. Log out and log in as a normal user.
5. To confirm that you can mount a DOS floppy as a normal user and not just as root, insert a DOS floppy in the A drive and type the following command:

   mount /a

   The mount operation should succeed, and you should see a listing of the DOS floppy when you type the command ls /a.

6. To unmount the DOS floppy, type **umount /a**.

Mounting an NTFS Partition

Nowadays, many PCs come installed with Windows XP or Windows 2000. Both Windows XP and 2000, as well as Windows NT, often use the NT File System (NTFS). Linux supports read-only access to NTFS partitions, but Red Hat does not come with the kernel module needed to support NTFS.

Secret

If you have installed Red Hat Linux on a Windows XP system and want to access files on the NTFS partition, you can download a ready-to-run version of the NTFS kernel module from the Linux NTFS Project at http://linux-ntfs.sourceforge .net/info/redhat.html. Look for your version of Red Hat Linux, your kernel version (type **uname -r** to see your kernel version), and then download the RPM file for that version. The file you want has a name of the following form: kernel-ntfs-<VERSION>.i686.rpm, where <VERSION> is replaced by your kernel version number.

After downloading the file, log in as root, and type the following command to install the NTFS kernel module:

```
rpm -Uvh kernel-ntfs*.rpm
```

Load the module with the following command:

```
modprobe ntfs
```

Create a mount point for the NTFS partition. For example, you might create a mount point in the /mnt directory with the following command:

```
mkdir /mnt/windows
```

Now, you can mount the NTFS partition with the following command:

```
mount /dev/hda2 /mnt/windows -t ntfs -r -o umask=0222
```

Replace /dev/hda2 with the device name for the NTFS partition on your system. On most PCs that come with Windows XP preinstalled, the NTFS partition is the second one (/dev/hda2)—the first partition (/dev/hda1) is a hidden partition used to hold files used for Windows XP installation.

Using mtools

One way to access the MS-DOS file systems is to mount the DOS hard disk or floppy disk by using the mount command and then use regular Linux commands, such as ls and cp, to work with the mounted DOS file system. This approach of mounting a DOS file system is fine for hard disks. Linux can mount the DOS partition automatically at startup, and you can access the DOS directories on the hard disk at any time.

If you want a quick directory listing of a DOS floppy disk, however, mounting can soon become quite tedious. First, you must mount the floppy drive. Then, you must use the ls or cp command to work with the files. Finally, you must use the umount command before ejecting the floppy out of the drive.

This is where the mtools package comes to the rescue. The mtools package implements most common DOS commands; the commands use the same names as in DOS, except that you add an m prefix to each command. Thus, the command for getting a directory listing is mdir, and mcopy copies files. The best part of mtools is the fact that you don't need to mount the floppy disk to use the mtools commands.

insider
insight Because the mtools commands write to and read from the physical device (floppy disk), you must log in as root to perform these commands. If you want any user to access the mtools commands, you must alter the permission settings for the floppy drive devices. Use the following command to permit anyone to read from and write to the first floppy drive:

```
chmod o+rw /dev/fd0
```

Trying mtools

The mtools package comes with the Red Hat Linux distribution on this book's companion CD-ROMs. When you install Linux, mtools installs automatically as part of the base Linux. The mtools executable files are in the /usr/bin directory. To see whether you have mtools, type **ls /usr/bin/mdir** at the shell prompt. If the ls command shows that this file exists, mtools is available on your system.

You also can type the following rpm command to verify that mtools is on your system:

```
rpm -q mtools
mtools-3.9.8-7
```

If mtools is present, the output shows you the full name of the mtools package. The sample output shows that mtools version 3.9.8 is present on the system.

To try out mtools, follow these steps:

1. Log in as root or type **su -** and then enter the root password.
2. Place an MS-DOS floppy disk in your system's A drive.
3. Type **mdir**. You should see the directory of the floppy disk (in the standard DOS directory-listing format).

The /etc/mtools.conf File

The mtools package should work with the default setup, but if you get any errors, you should check the /etc/mtools.conf file. That file contains the definitions of the drives (such as A, B, and C) that the mtools utilities see. Following are a few lines from a typical /etc/mtools.conf file:

```
drive a: file="/dev/fd0" exclusive mformat_only
drive b: file="/dev/fd1" exclusive mformat_only

# First SCSI hard disk partition
#drive c: file="/dev/sda1"

# First IDE hard disk partition
drive c: file="/dev/hda1"

# IDE Zip drive
drive X: file="/dev/hdd4" exclusive
```

The pound sign (#) indicates the start of a comment. Each line defines a drive letter, the associated Linux device name, and some keywords that indicate how to access the device. In this example, the first two lines define drives A and B. The third noncomment line defines drive C as the first partition on the first IDE drive (/dev/hda1). If you have other DOS drives (D, for example), you can add another line that defines drive D as the appropriate disk partition.

If your system's A drive is a high-density, 3.5-inch drive, you shouldn't need to change anything in the default /etc/mtools.conf file to access the floppy drive. If you also want to access any DOS partition in the hard drive, uncomment and edit an appropriate line for the C drive.

Typically, you use the mtools utilities to access the floppy disks. Although you can define C and D drives for your DOS hard-disk partitions, you may want to access those partitions by using the Linux mount command to mount them. Because you can mount the hard-disk partitions automatically at startup, accessing them through the Linux commands is normally just as easy.

insider insight

You also can access Iomega Zip drives through mtools. Simply specify a drive letter and the appropriate device's filename. For built-in IDE (ATAPI) Zip drives, try /dev/hdd4 as the device file, and add the following line in the /etc/mtools.conf file:

```
drive e: file="/dev/hdd4"
```

After that, you should be able to use mtools commands to access the Zip drive (refer to it as the E drive). For example, to see the directory listing, place Zip disk in the Zip drive and type:

```
mdir e:
```

Learning the mtools Commands

The mtools package is a collection of utilities. So far, I have been using mdir—the mtools counterpart of the DIR command in DOS. The other mtools commands are fairly easy to use.

insider insight

If you know the MS-DOS commands, you find that using the mtools commands is very easy. Type the DOS command in lowercase letters, and remember to add m in front of each command. Because the Linux commands and filenames are case sensitive, you must use all lowercase letters as you type mtools commands.

Table 12-3 summarizes the commands available in mtools.

Table 12-3: The mtools Commands

mtools Utility	MS-DOS Command (If Any)	Action
mattrib	ATTRIB	Changes MS-DOS file-attribute flags
mbadblocks		Tests a floppy disk and marks the bad blocks in the file allocation table (FAT)
mcd	CD	Changes an MS-DOS directory

(continued)

Table 12-3: *(continued)*

mtools Utility	MS-DOS Command (If Any)	Action
mcopy	COPY	Copies files between MS-DOS and Linux
mdel	DEL or ERASE	Deletes an MS-DOS file
mdeltree	DELTREE	Recursively deletes an MS-DOS directory
mdir	DIR	Displays an MS-DOS directory listing
mdu		Lists space that a directory and its contents occupy
mformat	FORMAT	Places an MS-DOS file system on a low-level-formatted floppy disk (Use fdformat to low-level-format a floppy in Red Hat Linux)
minfo		Gets information about an MS-DOS file system
mkmanifest		Makes a list of short name equivalents
mlabel	LABEL	Initializes an MS-DOS volume label
mmd	MD or MKDIR	Creates an MS-DOS directory
mmove		Moves or renames an MS-DOS file or subdirectory
mmount		Mounts an MS-DOS disk
mpartition		Creates an MS-DOS file system as a partition
mrd	RD or RMDIR	Deletes an MS-DOS directory
mren	REN or RENAME	Renames an existing MS-DOS file
mshowfat		Shows FAT entries for an MS-DOS file
mtoolstest		Tests and displays the current mtools configuration
mtype	TYPE	Displays the contents of an MS-DOS file
mwrite	COPY	Copies a Linux file to MS-DOS
mzip		Performs certain operations on SCSI Zip disks

You can use the mtools commands just as you'd use the corresponding DOS commands. The mdir command, for example, works the same as the DIR command in DOS. The same goes for all the other mtools commands shown in Table 12-3.

Secret

You can use wildcard characters (such as *) with mtools commands, but you must remember that the Linux shell is the first program to see your command. If you don't want the shell to expand the wildcard character, use quotation marks around file-names that contain any wildcard characters. For example, to copy all *.txt files from the A drive to your current Red Hat Linux directory, use the following command:

```
mcopy "a:*.txt".
```

If you omit the quotation marks, the shell tries to expand the string a:*.txt with filenames from the current Linux directory. It also tries to copy those files (if any) from the DOS floppy disk.

On the other hand, if you want to copy files from the Linux directory to the DOS floppy disk, you do want the shell to expand any wildcard characters. To copy all *.jpg files from the current Linux directory to the DOS floppy disk, for example, use mcopy like this:

```
mcopy *.jpg a:
```

With the mtools utilities you can use the backslash character (\) as the directory separator, just as you would in DOS. However, when you type a filename that contains the backslash character, you must enclose the name in double quotation marks. For example, here's a command that copies a file from a subdirectory on the A drive to the current Linux directory:

```
mcopy "a:\test\sample.dat".
```

Formatting a DOS Floppy

Suppose that you run Red Hat Linux on your home PC and MS-DOS is no longer on your system, but you need to copy some files onto an MS-DOS floppy disk and take the disk to your office. If you already have a formatted MS-DOS floppy, you can simply mount that floppy and copy the file to the floppy by using the Linux cp command. But what if you don't have a formatted DOS floppy? The mtools package again comes to the rescue.

The mtools package provides the mformat utility, which can format a floppy disk for use in MS-DOS. Unlike the DOS format command that formats a floppy in a single step, the mformat command requires you to follow a two-step process:

1. Use the fdformat command to low-level-format a floppy disk. The fdformat command uses the floppy device name as the argument; the device name includes all the parameters necessary for formatting the floppy disk. Figure 12-9 illustrates the device-naming convention for the floppy drive device. Based on the information shown in Figure 12-9, you use the following command to format a 3.5-inch, high-density floppy disk in your system's A drive:

```
fdformat /dev/fd0H1440
```

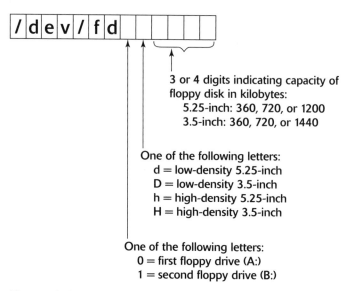

One of the following letters:
0 = first floppy drive (A:)
1 = second floppy drive (B:)

One of the following letters:
d = low-density 5.25-inch
D = low-density 3.5-inch
h = high-density 5.25-inch
H = high-density 3.5-inch

3 or 4 digits indicating capacity of
floppy disk in kilobytes:
5.25-inch: 360, 720, or 1200
3.5-inch: 360, 720, or 1440

Figure 12-9: Naming Convention for the Floppy Disk Drive in Red Hat Linux.

2. Use the `mformat` command to put an MS-DOS file system on the low-level-formatted floppy disk. If the floppy is in drive A, type the following command to create a formatted DOS floppy:

```
mformat a:
```

Summary

Even if you're the only user of your Red Hat Linux system, you must perform some system-administration tasks to keep the system up and running. Moreover, if your PC has a DOS partition in addition to the Linux partition, or if you work with DOS floppy disks, you may want to access the DOS files directly from Linux. This chapter provides an overview of Linux system-administration and network-administration tasks. It introduces Nautilus and shows you how to use the mtools utility programs to format and access a DOS floppy disk directly from Linux.

By reading this chapter, you learned the following:

◆ GNOME comes with a Start Here window that enables you to perform some common system-administration tasks.

◆ You can add new user accounts by using the Red Hat User Manager or the `useradd` command. To remove an account, you can either use Red Hat User Manager or the `userdel` command.

◆ Linux provides built-in support for the MS-DOS file system. You can use the `mount` command to access a DOS partition or a DOS floppy from Linux. After mounting a DOS file system at a directory in your Linux system, you can use Linux commands such as `ls` and `cp` to manipulate the DOS files.

♦ You can download a kernel module and load it to enable Linux to read from NTFS partitions that are used in Windows XP, 2000, and NT.

♦ As you install Linux (following the directions in Chapter 2), you also install a set of utility programs known as mtools. The mtools programs provide a convenient way to access MS-DOS files, especially floppy disks, because you can use mtools commands without first needing to mount the floppy disk. The mtools utilities include commands such as `mdir` and `mcopy` that work the same as the DOS commands `DIR` and `COPY`.

Part III

Internetworking with Red Hat Linux

Internet Connection Setup

Chapter

13

◆ ◆

Secrets in This Chapter

◆ ◆

The Internet is fast becoming a lifeline for most of us. It seems we can't get by a day without it. I know I could not write the book without it. Sometimes I wonder how we ever managed without the Internet. You'll no doubt want to connect your Red Hat Linux system (and perhaps your own LAN) to the Internet. In this chapter, I show you how to connect to the Internet in several different ways—depending on whether you have DSL, a cable modem, or a dial-up network connection.

Two of the options for connecting to the Internet—DSL and cable modem—involve connecting a special modem to an Ethernet card on your Red Hat Linux system. In these cases, you have to set up Ethernet networking on your Red Hat Linux system. This chapter shows you how to set up a DSL and a cable modem connection. I also describe dial-up networking, which involves dialing up an Internet service provider (ISP) from your Red Hat Linux system.

---

cross ref As you read this chapter, consult Chapter 6 for discussions of networking, TCP/IP, and the Internet, as well as for terms such as Request for Comments (RFC).

Deciding How to Connect to the Internet

Nowadays, you have the following popular options for connecting a small office or home office to the Internet (of course, huge corporations and governments have many other ways to connect to the Internet):

♦ **Digital subscriber line (DSL)**—Your local telephone company as well as other telecommunications companies offer DSL—a high-speed data transmission service over a regular phone line. You can use DSL to connect your Red Hat Linux system to the Internet. In this case, you must connect a special DSL modem to an Ethernet card on your Red Hat Linux system. When you use DSL, your Red Hat Linux system is always connected to the Internet. Typically, DSL offers data transfer rates of anywhere between 128 Kbps and 1.5 Mbps. You can download from the Internet at much higher rates than when you send data from your PC to the Internet (upload). One caveat with DSL is that your home must be between 12,000 and 15,000 feet from your central office (this is a phone company facility where your phone lines end up). The distance limitation varies from provider to provider. In the United States, you can check out the distance limits for many providers at www.dslreports.com/distance.

♦ **Cable modem**—If the cable television company in your area offers Internet access over cable, you can use that service to hook up your Red Hat Linux system to the Internet. As with DSL, connect a cable modem to an Ethernet card in your Red Hat Linux system. Typically, cable modems offer higher data transfer rates than DSL for the same cost. Downloading data from the Internet is much faster than sending data from your PC to the Internet. You can expect routine download speeds of 1.5 Mbps and upload speeds of around 128 Kbps, but sometimes you may even get higher speeds than these.

♦ **Dial-up networking**—This is what most of us were using to connect to the Internet before DSL and cable modems came along. In this case, your Red Hat Linux system uses the Point-to-Point Protocol (PPP) or Serial Line Internet Protocol (SLIP) over a dial-up link to connect to another system already on the

Internet. Usually, that Internet-connected system belongs to your Internet service provider (ISP). This method of connection is referred to as dial-up networking—establishing a network connection between your Red Hat Linux PC and another network (such as the Internet) through a dial-up modem. In this case, the maximum data-transfer rate is 56 Kbps. Most dial-up users connect to their ISP using PPP; SLIP is rarely used nowadays.

As far as costs go, DSL and cable modem service connect you to the Internet and also act as your ISP—they provide you with an IP address and give you email accounts. If you use a dial-up modem to connect to the Internet, you get the phone line from the phone company and then select a separate ISP who gives you a phone number that you dial and all the other necessary goodies like an IP address and email accounts.

Table 13-1 summarizes these three options for a small office or a home office connecting to the Internet. You can consult that table and select the type of connection that's available to you and that best suits your needs.

Table 13-1: Comparison of Dial-Up, DSL, and Cable

Feature	Dial-Up	DSL	Cable
Equipment	Modem	DSL modem, Ethernet card	Cable modem, Ethernet card
Also Requires	Phone service and an ISP	Phone service and within 12,000 to 15,000 feet of central office	Cable TV connection
Connection type	Dial to connect	Always on, dedicated	Always on, Shared
Typical speed	56 Kbps maximum	640 Kbps download, 128 Kbps upload (higher speeds cost more)	1.5 Mbps download, 128 Kbps upload
One-time costs (estimate)	None	Install = $100–200, Equipment = $200–300, May require activation cost	Install = $100–200, Equipment = $200–300
Typical monthly cost (2003)	Phone charges = $20/month, ISP charges = $15–$30/month	$50/month, May require monthly modem lease	$50/month, May require monthly modem lease

Note: Costs vary by region. Costs shown are typical ones for U.S. metropolitan areas.

Connecting with DSL

DSL stands for digital subscriber line. DSL uses your existing phone line to send digital data in addition to the normal analog voice signals (analog means continuously varying whereas digital data is represented by 1s and 0). The phone line goes from your home to a central office where the line connects to the phone company's network—by the way, the connection from your home to the central office is called the local loop. When you sign up for DSL service, the phone company has to hook up your phone line to some special equipment at the central office. That equipment can separate the digital data from the voice. From then on, your phone line can carry digital data that can then be directly sent to an Internet connection at the central office.

Understanding How DSL Works

A special box called a DSL modem takes care of sending digital data from your PC to the phone company's central office over your phone line. Your PC can connect to the Internet with the same phone line that you use for your normal telephone calls—you can make voice calls even as the line is being used for DSL. Figure 13-1 shows a typical DSL connection to the Internet.

Figure 13-1: Connecting to the Internet Using DSL.

Your PC talks to the DSL modem through an Ethernet connection, which means that you need an Ethernet card in your Red Hat Linux system.

Your PC sends digital data over the Ethernet connection to the DSL modem. The DSL modem sends the digital data at different frequencies than those used by the analog voice signals. The voice signals occupy a small portion of all the frequencies that the phone line can carry. DSL uses the higher frequencies to transfer digital data, so both voice and data can travel on the same phone line.

The distance between your home and the central office—the loop length—is a factor in DSL's performance. Unfortunately, the phone line can reliably carry the DSL signals only over a limited distance—typically three miles or less. This means that you can get DSL service only if your home (or office) is located within about three miles of your phone's central office. Your phone company can tell you whether your location can get DSL or not. Often they have a website where you can type in your phone number and get a response about DSL availability. For example, try www. dslavailability.com for U.S. locations.

Learning the DSL Alphabet Soup—ADSL, IDSL, SDSL

So far this chapter has used the term DSL as if there were only one kind of DSL. There are in fact three variants of DSL, each with different features, summarized as follows:

♦ **ADSL**—Asymmetric DSL, the most common form of DSL, has much higher download speeds (from Internet to your PC) than upload speeds (from your PC to the Internet). ADSL can have download speeds of up to 8 Mbps and upload speeds of up to 1 Mbps. ADSL works best when your location is within about two and a half miles (12,000 feet) of your central office. ADSL service is priced according to the download and upload speeds you want. A popular form of ADSL called G.lite is specifically designed to work on the same line that you use for voice calls. G.lite has a maximum download speed of 1.5 Mbps and maximum upload speed of 512 Kbps.

♦ **IDSL**—ISDN DSL (ISDN is an older technology called Integrated Services Digital Network) is a special type of DSL that works at distances of up to five miles between your phone and the central office. The downside is that IDSL only offers downstream and upstream speeds of up to 144 Kbps.

♦ **SDSL**—Symmetric DSL provides the equal download and upload speeds of up to 1.5 Mbps. SDSL is priced according to the speed you want, with the higher speeds costing more. The closer your location is to the phone company's central office, the faster the connection you can get.

Secret

DSL speeds are typically specified by two numbers, like this: 1,500/384. The numbers refer to data transfer speeds in kilo bits per second (Kbps, or thousand bits per second). The first number is the download speed, the second the upload. Thus, 1,500/384 means you can expect to download from the Internet at a maximum rate of 1,500 Kbps (or 1.5 Mbps) and upload to the Internet at 384 Kbps. If your phone line's condition is not perfect, you may not get these maximum rates—both ADSL and SDSL adjust the speeds to suit the line conditions.

The price of DSL service depends on which variant—ADSL, IDSL, or SDSL—you select. For most home users, the primary choice is ADSL or, more accurately, the G.lite form of ADSL with transfer speed ratings of 1,500/128.

Setting Up a DSL Connection

To get DSL for your home or business, you have to contact a DSL provider. In addition to your phone company, there are many other DSL providers. No matter who provides the DSL service, some work has to be done at your central office—the place where your phone lines connect to the rest of the phone network. The work involves connecting your phone line to equipment that can work with the DSL modem at your home or office. The central office equipment and the DSL modem at your location can then do whatever magic is needed to send and receive digital data over your phone line.

Because of the need to set up your line at the central office, it takes some time after you place an order to get your line ready for DSL.

The first step for you is to check out the DSL providers who provide service and see if you can actually get the service. Because DSL can work only over certain distances—typically less than 2.5 miles—between your location and the central office, you have to check to see if you are within that distance limit. Contact your phone company to verify this. You may be able to check this on the Web. Try typing into Google (`http://www.google.com`) the words `DSL`, `availability`, and your local phone company's name. You should get a website where you can type in your phone number and learn if DSL is available for your number.

If DSL is available, you can look for the types of service—ADSL versus SDSL—and the pricing. The price depends on the download and upload speeds you want. Sometimes phone companies offer a simple residential DSL that's basically the G.lite form of ADSL with 1,500/128 speed rating—meaning that you can download at 1,500 Kbps and upload at 128 Kbps. Of course, these are the maximums, and your mileage may vary.

After selecting the type of DSL service and provider, you can place an order and have the provider install the necessary equipment at your home or office. Figure 13-2 shows a sample connection diagram for typical residential DSL.

Figure 13-2: Typical Residential DSL Connection.

Here are some key points to note in Figure 13-2:

♦ Connect your DSL modem's data connection to the phone jack on a wall plate.

♦ Connect the DSL modem's Ethernet connection to the Ethernet card on your PC.

♦ When you connect other telephones or fax machines on the same phone line, install a microfilter between the wall plate and each of these devices.

insider
insight
Because the same phone line carries both voice signals and DSL data, you need the microfilters to protect the DSL data from possible interference. You can buy them at electronic stores or from the DSL provider.

Secret

When you connect your Red Hat Linux PC to the Internet using DSL, the connection is always on and there is more potential for outsiders to break into the PC. You should make sure that the Red Hat Linux firewall setting is set at High Security. To configure the firewall settings, select Main Menu⇨System Settings⇨Security Level from the GNOME desktop.

There is another way to protect your Red Hat Linux system from intruders and, as an added bonus, share the high-speed connection with other PCs in a local area network (LAN). To do this you need a router that can perform network address dtranslation (NAT). The NAT router translates private Internet Protocol (IP) addresses from an internal LAN into a single public IP address and makes it possible for all the internal PCs to access the Internet. If you use a NAT router, be sure to change the administrator password from the default password after you install the router.

If you also want to set up a local area network, you'd need an Ethernet hub to connect the other PCs to the network. Figure 13-3 shows a typical setup the connects a LAN to the Internet through a NAT router and a DSL modem.

Figure 13-3: Connecting a LAN to Internet through a NAT Router and DSL Modem.

Here are the points to note when setting up a connection like the one shown in Figure 13-3:

♦ You need a NAT router with two 10Base-T Ethernet ports (the 10Base-T port looks like a large phone jack, also known as RJ-45 jack). Typically one Ethernet port is labeled Internet (or External or WAN for Wide Area Network) and the other one is labeled Local or LAN (for Local Area Network).

◆ You also need an Ethernet hub. For a small home network, you can buy a 4- or 8-port Ethernet hub. Basically, you want a hub with as many ports as the number of PCs you want to connect to your LAN.

◆ Connect the Ethernet port of the DSL modem to the Internet port of the NAT router using a 10Base-T Ethernet cable (these look like phone wires with bigger RJ-45 jacks and are often labeled Category 5 or Cat 5 wire).

◆ Connect the Local Ethernet port of the NAT router to one of the ports on the Ethernet hub using a 10Base-T Ethernet cable.

◆ Now connect each of the PCs to the Ethernet hub. Of course, you must have an Ethernet card installed in each PC.

---

insider
insight

You can also buy NAT router with built-in 4- or 8-port Ethernet hub. With combined router/hub, you need only one box to set up a LAN and connect it to Internet with a DSL modem. These boxes are typically sold under the name Cable/DSL router because they work with both DSL and cable modem.

Connecting with Cable Modem

Cable TV companies also offer high-speed Internet access over the same coaxial cable that carries television signals to your home. After the cable company installs the necessary equipment at their facility to send and receive digital data over the coaxial cables, customers can sign up for cable Internet service. You can then get high-speed Internet access over the same cable that delivers cable TV signals to your home.

Understanding How a Cable Modem Works

A box called a cable modem is at the heart of Internet access over the cable TV network. The cable modem takes digital data from your PC's Ethernet card and puts in an unused block of frequency (think of it as another TV channel, but instead of pictures and sound, this channel carries digital data).

The cable modem places upstream data—data that's being sent from your PC to the Internet—in a different channel from that used for the downstream data that's coming from the Internet to your PC. By design, the speed of downstream data transfers is much higher than upstream transfers. The assumption is that people download far more stuff from the Internet than they upload. Probably true for most of us.

Secret

The coaxial cable that carries all those hundreds of cable TV channels to your home is a very capable signal carrier. In particular, the coaxial cable can carry signals covering a huge range of frequencies—hundreds of megahertz (MHz). Each TV channel requires 6 MHz, and the coaxial cable can carry hundreds of such channels. The cable modem places the upstream data in a small frequency band and expects to receive the downstream data in another frequency band.

At the other end of your cable connection to the Internet is a cable modem termination system (CMTS) that your cable company installs at their central facility. The CMTS connects the cable TV network to the Internet. It also extracts the digital upstream data sent by your cable modem (and by your neighbors as well) and sends them to the Internet. The CMTS also puts digital data into the upstream channels so that your cable modem can extract that data and provide it to your PC via the Ethernet card. Figure 13-4 illustrates how cable companies provide high-speed Internet access over their cable TV network.

Figure 13-4: High-Speed Internet Access over the Cable TV Network.

Cable modems can receive downstream data at the rate of about 30 Mbps and send data at around 3 Mbps upstream. However, all the cable modems in a neighborhood share the same downstream capacity. Each cable modem filters out—separates—the data it needs from the stream of data that the CMTS sends out.

In practice, with cable modem you can get downstream transfer rates of around 1.5 Mbps and upstream rates of 128 Kbps.

If you want to check your downstream transfer speed, go to `http://bandwidthplace` `.com/speedtest`, and click the link to start the test. For my cable modem connection, the tests reported a downstream transfer rate of about 1.4 Mbps on good days.

Setting Up a Cable Modem Connection

To set up cable modem access, your cable TV provider must offer high-speed Internet access. If the service is available, you can call to sign up. The cable companies often have promotional offers like no installation fee or a reduced rate for three months. Look for these offers. If you are lucky, they may have a promotion going on just when you want to sign up.

The installation is typically done by a technician who splits your incoming cable into two—one side goes to the TV and the other to the cable modem. The technician provides information about the cable modem to the cable company's head end for set up at their end. When all that is done, you can plug in your PC's Ethernet card to the cable modem, and you're all set to enjoy high-speed Internet access. Figure 13-5 shows a typical cable modem hookup.

Figure 13-5: Splitting the Cable TV Signal between the TV and the Cable Modem.

The cable modem connects to an Ethernet card in your PC. So you need an Ethernet card in your PC. The cable company technician often provides an Ethernet card.

Here are some key points to note about the cable modem setup in Figure 13-5:

♦ Split the incoming cable TV signal into two parts by using a 2-way splitter (the cable company technician installs this). By the way, the 2-way splitter should be rated for 1 GHz; otherwise, it may not pass through the frequencies that contain the downstream data from the Internet.

♦ Connect one of the video output from the splitter to your cable modem's F-type video connector using a coaxial cable.

♦ Connect the cable modem's 10 Base-T Ethernet connection to the Ethernet card on your PC.

♦ Connect your TV to the other video output from the 2-way splitter.

---

caution When you use cable modem to connect your Red Hat Linux PC to the Internet, the connection is always on, so there is more chance that someone may try to break into the PC. You should set the firewall setting to High Security. To configure the firewall settings, select Main Menu⇨System Settings⇨Security Level from the GNOME desktop.

Secret You may want to add a NAT (network address translation) router between your PC and the cable modem. As an added bonus, you can even share a cable modem connection with all the PCs in your own local area network (LAN) by adding an Ethernet hub. Better yet, buy a combination NAT router and hub so you can do the job with only one box. By the way, the NAT router/hubs are typically sold under the name cable/DSL router because they work with both DSL and cable modems.

The NAT router translates private Internet Protocol (IP) addresses into a public IP address. When connected through a NAT router, any PC in the internal LAN can access the Internet as if it has its own unique IP address. The end result is that a single Internet connection is shared among many PCs. This can be an ideal solution for connecting a small LAN to the Internet.

Figure 13-6 shows what a typical setup with a cable modem connection being shared by a number of PCs in a LAN.

Here are the points to note when setting up a connection like the one shown in Figure 13-6:

♦ You need a cable/DSL NAT router with two 10Base-T Ethernet ports (the 10Base-T port looks like a large phone jack—it's also known as a RJ-45 jack). Typically, one Ethernet port is labeled Internet (or External or WAN for wide area network) and the other one is labeled Local.

♦ If you plan to set up a LAN, you also need an Ethernet hub. For a small home network, you can buy a 4- or 8-port Ethernet hub. Basically, you want a hub with as many ports as the number of PCs you want to connect to your local area network.

♦ Consider buying a single box that acts as a NAT router and also a hub with a number of Ethernet ports.

◆ Connect the video cable to the video input port of the cable modem.

◆ Connect the Ethernet port of the cable modem to the Internet port of the NAT router using a 10Base-T Ethernet cable (these look like phone wires, except that the Ethernet cables have bigger RJ-45 jacks and are often labeled Category 5 or Cat 5 wire).

◆ Connect the Local Ethernet port of the NAT router to one of the ports on the Ethernet hub using a 10Base-T Ethernet cable.

◆ Now connect each of the PCs to the Ethernet hub. Of course, each PC must have an Ethernet card.

Figure 13-6: Sharing a Cable Modem Internet Connection with Several PCs in a LAN.

Setting Up IEEE 802.11b Wireless Ethernet Networks

If you have laptop computers on your LAN or if you don't want to run wires to connect a PC to the LAN, you have the option of using a wireless Ethernet network. In a typical scenario, you have a cable modem or DSL connection to the Internet, and you want to connect one or more laptops with wireless network cards to access the Internet through the cable or DSL modem. This section shows you how to set up wireless networking for connecting to an Ethernet LAN and accessing the Internet.

Understanding Wireless Ethernet Networks

There are two popular IEEE standards—802.11a and 802.11b—for wireless Ethernet networks, also commonly referred to Wi-Fi (for Wireless Fidelity) networks. These two standards were finalized in 1999, and they specify how the wireless Ethernet network works at the physical level.

Secret

The two wireless Ethernet standards have the following characteristics:

- **802.11b**—Operates in the 2.4-GHz radio band (2.4 GHz to 2.4835 GHz) in up to three nonoverlapping frequency bands or channels. Supports a maximum bit rate of 11 Mbps per channel. One of the disadvantages of 802.11b is that the 2.4-GHz frequency band is crowded—many devices such as microwave ovens, cordless phones, medical and scientific equipment, as well as Bluetooth devices, all work within the 2.4-GHz frequency band. Nevertheless, 802.11b is very popular in corporate as well as home networks.

- **802.11a**—Operates in the 5-GHz radio band (5.725 GHz to 5.850 GHz) in up to eight nonoverlapping channels. Supports a maximum bit rate of 54 Mbps per channel. The 5-GHz band is not as crowded as the 2.4-GHz band, but the 5-GHz band is not approved for use in Europe. Products conforming to 802.11a standard are now beginning to appear, and there are wireless access points that are designed to handle both 802.11a and 802.11b connections.

In both cases, the maximum data throughput that a user sees is much less because all users of that radio channel share the capacity of the channel. Also, the data transfer rate decreases as the distance between the user's PC and the wireless access point increases.

There is a third standard—802.11g—under development that would support 54-Mbps data rates in the 2.4-GHz band (the same band that 802.11b uses). 802.11g achieves the higher bit rate by using a technology called OFDM (orthogonal frequency division multiplexing), which is also used by 802.11a. 802.11g-compliant equipment is currently becoming available on the market.

insider insight

To learn more about wireless Ethernet, visit http://www.wi-fi.org/, the home page of the Wi-Fi Alliance—a nonprofit international association formed in 1999 to certify interoperability of wireless LAN products based on IEEE 802.11 standards.

Understanding Infrastructure and Ad Hoc Modes

The 802.11 standard defines two modes of operation for wireless Ethernet networks: infrastructure and ad hoc. *Ad hoc* mode is simply two or more wireless Ethernet cards communicating with each other without an access point.

Infrastructure mode refers to the approach in which all the wireless Ethernet cards communicate with each other and to the wired LAN through an access point. For the example considered in this book, your wireless Ethernet card should be set to infrastructure mode. In the configuration files, this mode is referred to as Managed mode.

Understanding Wired Equivalent Privacy (WEP)

The 802.11 standard includes the Wired Equivalent Privacy (WEP) for protecting wireless communications from eavesdropping. WEP relies on a 40-bit or 104-bit secret key that is shared between a mobile station (such as a laptop with a wireless Ethernet card) and an access point (also called a base station). The secret key is used to encrypt packets before they are transmitted and an integrity check is performed to ensure that packets are not modified in transit. The 802.11 standard does not explain how the shared key is established. In practice, most wireless LANs use a single key that is shared between all mobile stations and access points. Such an approach, however, does not scale well to an environment such as a college campus due to the fact that the keys are shared with all users. Therefore, WEP is typically not used on large wireless networks such as the ones at universities. In such wireless networks, users should other security approaches such as using SSH (Secure Shell) to log in to remote systems.

Secret

WEP uses the RC4 encryption algorithm, which is known as a stream cipher. Such a stream cipher works by taking a short secret key and generating an infinite stream of pseudorandom bits. The sending station performs an exclusive-OR operation between the pseudorandom bits and the bits representing the data packet. The receiver has a copy of the same secret key, so it generates an identical stream of pseudo-random bits. Performing an exclusive-OR between this pseudorandom stream and the received bits regenerates the original, unencrypted data packet.

Such a method of stream cipher has a few problems. If a bit is flipped (from a 0 to 1 or vice versa) in the encrypted data stream, then the corresponding is flipped in the decrypted output. Also, if an eavesdropper intercepts two encoded messages that were encoded with the same stream, then it is possible to generate the exclusive-OR of the original messages. That knowledge is enough to mount attacks that can eventually break the encryption.

To counter against these weaknesses, WEP uses some defenses:

♦ **Integrity Check (IC) Field**—To make sure that data packets are not modified in transit, WEP uses an Integrity Check field in each packet.

♦ **Initialization Vector (IV)**—To avoid encrypting two messages with the same key stream, WEP uses a 24-bit initialization vector (IV) that augments the shared secret key to produce a different RC4 key for each packet. The IV itself is also included in the packet.

Experts say that both of these defenses are poorly implemented, making WEP ineffective. The problems with IC and IV are the following:

♦ The Integrity Check field is implemented using a checksum algorithm called 32-bit cyclic redundancy code (CRC-32), and that checksum is then included as part of the data packet. Unfortunately, it is possible for an attacker to flip arbitrary bits in an encrypted message and correctly adjust the checksum so that the resulting message appears valid.

♦ The 24-bit IV is sent in the clear. This means that there are only 2^{24} possible initialization vectors, and they have to be reused after running through all of them. In other words, after sending 2^{24}, or 16,777,216 packets, the IV has to be repeated. The number might sound like a lot, but consider the case of a busy access point that sends 1,500-byte packets at a rate of 11 Mbps. Each packet has 8×1,500 = 12,000 bits. That means each second the access point sends 11,000,000/12,000 = 916 packets. At that rate, the access point sends 16,777,216 packets in 16,777,216/916 = 18,315 seconds or 5 hours. That means the IV is reused after 5 hours, and the time may be less than that because many message are smaller than 1,500 bytes. Thus, there are ample opportunities for an attacker to collect two encrypted messages that are encrypted with the same key stream and perform statistical attacks to decrypt the message.

Thus, WEP has its weaknesses, but it's better than nothing. You can use it in smaller wireless LANs where sharing the same key among all wireless stations is not an onerous task.

insider insight

There is work underway to provide better security than WEP for wireless networks. The 802.11i standard, which is under development, would use public key encryption with digital certificates and an an authentication, authorization, and accounting RADIUS (Remote Authentication Dial-In User Service) server to provide better security for wireless Ethernet networks.

While the 802.11i standard is in progress, the Wi-Fi Alliance—a multivendor consortium that supports Wi-Fi—is publishing an interim specification called *Wi-Fi Protected Access* (WPA) that's a precursor to 11i. WPA will replace the existing WEP standard and improve security by making some changes. For example, unlike WEP, which uses fixed keys, the WPA standard uses Temporal Key Integrity Protocol (TKIP), which generates new keys for every 10K of data transmitted over the network. This makes WPA more difficult to break.

Setting Up the Wireless Hardware

To set up the wireless connection, you need a wireless access point and a wireless network card in each PC. You can also set up an ad hoc wireless network among two or more PCs with wireless network cards, but that would be a wireless LAN among those PCs only. In this section, I focus on the scenario where you want to set up a wireless connection to an established LAN that has a wired Internet connection through a cable modem or DSL.

In addition to the wireless access point, you would also need a cable modem or DSL connection to the Internet, along with a NAT router/hub, as described in the previous sections. Figure 13-7 shows a typical setup for wireless Internet access through an existing cable modem or DSL connection.

As Figure 13-7 shows, the LAN has both wired and wireless PCs. In this example, a cable or DSL modem connect the LAN to the Internet through a NAT router/hub. A wireless access point is attached to one of the RJ-45 ports on the hub. Laptops with wireless network cards connect the LAN through the wireless access point. To connect desktop PCs to the wireless network, you can use a USB wireless network card—a wireless network card that connects to a USB port.

cross ref

See Appendix F for a brief discussion of PCMCIA wireless network cards supported by Red Hat Linux.

Figure 13-7: Connecting a Mixed Wired and Wireless Ethernet LAN to the Internet.

---

insider
insight

If you have not yet purchased a NAT router/hub for your cable or DSL connection, consider buying a router/hub that has a built-in wireless access point.

Configuring the Wireless Access Point

Configuring the wireless access point involves the following:

- ◆ Setting the frequency or channel on which the wireless access point communicates with the wireless network cards. Both the access point and cards must use the same channel.

- ◆ Whether encryption is to be used or not.

- ◆ If encryption is to be used, the number of bits in the encryption key and the value of the encryption key. Twenty-four bits of the encryption key are internal to the access point; you only specify the remaining bits of the encryption key. Thus, for 64-bit encryption, you have to specify a 40-bit key, which comes to 10 hexadecimal digits (a hexadecimal digit is one of 0 through 9 and the letters A through F). For a 124-bit encryption key, you specify 104 bits, or 26 hexadecimal digits.

- ◆ Setting the access method that wireless network cards would use when connecting to the access point. The choices are open access and shared key. You typically use the open access method (even when you use encryption).

- ◆ Setting the wireless access point to operate in infrastructure mode because that's the way you should connect wireless network cards to an existing Ethernet LAN.

The exact method of configuring the wireless access point depends on the make and model of the access point. The vendor provides the instructions to configure the wireless access point. You would typically work through a graphical client application to configure the wireless access point. If you enable encryption, make a note of the encryption key because you have to specify the same key for each wireless network card.

Configuring Wireless Networking

On your Red Hat Linux laptop, the PCMCIA or PC Card manager should recognize the wireless network card and load the appropriate driver for the card. The wireless network card is treated like another Ethernet device and assigned a device name such as eth0 or eth1. If you already have an Ethernet card in the laptop, that card gets the eth0 device name, and the wireless PC card is named the eth1 device.

Secret

You do have to configure certain parameters to enable the wireless network card to communicate with the wireless access point. For example, the channel selection must be the same as that used by the wireless access point, and the encryption settings must match those on the access point.

Follow these steps to configure and activate the wireless network connection on your Red Hat Linux system:

1. Log in as root and type the iwconfig command (this command is similar to ifconfig, but meant for configuring a wireless network interface). Note the Ethernet device name for the wireless interface.

2. Assuming that the wireless network device name is eth0, edit the text file /etc/sysconfig/network-scripts/ifcfg-eth0. If the wireless device name is eth1, you have to edit /etc/sysconfig/network-scripts/ifcfg-eth1. This file contains various settings for the wireless network card. Table 13-2 explains the meaning of the settings. Here is a slightly edited version of the /etc/sysconfig/network-scripts/ifcfg-eth0 file from my laptop PC:

```
USERCTL=no
PEERDNS=yes
TYPE=Wireless
DEVICE=eth0
HWADDR=00:02:2d:8c:f8:c5
BOOTPROTO=dhcp
ONBOOT=no
DHCP_HOSTNAME=
NAME=
ESSID='UNKNOWN!!'
CHANNEL=6
MODE=Managed
KEY=aecf-a00f-03
RATE=auto
```

continues

continued

3. **Edit the text file** /etc/pcmcia/network **and locate the following line:**

    `'start')`

    Right after this line, add the following lines of text:

    ```
    [ -f /etc/sysconfig/network-scripts/ifcfg-${device} ] && \
        /etc/sysconfig/network-scripts/ifup ifcfg-${device}
    ```

    Save the file and exit.

4. **Type the following command to reactivate the wireless network interface after making changes to the configuration file:**

    `service pcmcia restart`

Table 13-2: Settings in Configuration File for a Wireless Ethernet Network Interface

Parameter	*Description*
BOOTPROTO	The name of the protocol to use to get the IP address for the interface. Should be either dhcp or bootp for Ethernet interface.
CHANNEL	Channel number (between 1 and 14 in U.S. and Canada). Must be the same as that set for the wireless access point.
DEVICE	The device name for the wireless Ethernet network interface (eth0 for the first interface, eth1 for second, and so on)
ESSID	Extended Service Set (ESS) Identifier, also known as the wireless network name. It is case sensitive and must be the same as the name specified for the wireless access point. Provide the name within single quotes (for example, 'Home').
HWADDR	The hardware address (also called the MAC address) of the wireless network card (six pairs of colon-separated hexadecimal numbers; for example, 00:02:2d:8c:f9:c4)
KEY	Encryption key; 10 hexadecimal digits for 40-bit key (for example, 1fdf-3fde-fe) or 26 hexadecimal digits for 104-bit key. The keys are in fact 64-bit and 128-bit, but the encryption algorithm automatically generates 24 bits of the key, so you need to specify only the remaining bits.
MODE	The mode of operation of the wireless network card. Set to Managed for a typical network that connects through a wireless access point.
NAME	A nickname for your wireless network. If you don't specify it, the hostname is used as the nickname.
ONBOOT	Set to yes to activate the wireless interface at boot time; otherwise set to no.
PEERDNS	Set to yes to enable the interface to modify your system's /etc/resolv.conf file to use the DNS servers obtained from the DHCP server (this is the same server that provides the IP address for the interface). If you set this to no, the /etc/resolv.conf file is left unchanged.

Parameter	Description
RATE	Bit rate for the wireless connection (set to one of 1M, 2M, 5.5M, 11M, or auto). The M means Mbps or a million bits per second. Set to auto to use the maximum possible transmission rate.
TYPE	Set to Wireless for wireless network interface
USERCTL	When set to yes, a nonroot user can control the device. Set it to no so that only root can control the device.

Now, the wireless interface should be working properly. To check the interface status, type the following command:

```
iwconfig
```

Here's a typical output on my Red Hat Linux laptop:

```
lo        no wireless extensions.

eth0      IEEE 802.11-DS  ESSID:"Test-Network"  Nickname:"localhost.localdomain"
          Mode:Managed  Frequency:2.437GHz  Access Point: 00:30:AB:06:2F:4E
          Bit Rate:11Mb/s   Tx-Power=15 dBm    Sensitivity:1/3
          RTS thr:off    Fragment thr:off
          Encryption key:AABB-CCDD-EE
          Power Management:off
          Link Quality:40/92  Signal level:-57 dBm  Noise level:-97 dBm
          Rx invalid nwid:0  Rx invalid crypt:0  Rx invalid frag:0
          Tx excessive retries:0  Invalid misc:4221    Missed beacon:0
```

Here the eth0 interface refers to the wireless network card. I have edited the encryption key and some other parameters, but the sample output shows what you should see when the wireless link is working.

Learning the Basics of Dial-Up Networking

Dial-up networking refers to connecting a PC to a remote network through a dial-up modem. If you are ancient enough to remember the days of dialing up with Procomm or some serial communications software, there is a significant difference between dial-up networking and the old days of serial communication. Both approaches use a modem to dial up a remote computer and to establish a communication path, but the serial communication software makes your computer behave like a dumb terminal connected to the remote computer. The serial-communication software exclusively uses dial-up connection. You cannot run another copy of the communication software and use the same modem connection, for example.

In dial-up networking, both your PC and the remote system run a network-protocol (called TCP/IP) software. When your PC dials up and sets up a communication path, the network protocols exchange data packets over that dial-up connection. The neat part is that any number of applications can use the same dial-up connection to send and receive data packets. So your PC becomes a part of the network to which the remote computer belongs. (If the remote computer is not on a network, dial-up networking creates a network that consists of the remote computer and your PC.)

Chapter 6 describes TCP/IP protocol some more, but I have to use the term as well as a few concepts such as Internet Protocol (IP) address and Domain Name Service (DNS) when describing how to set up dial-up networking.

Here's what you have to do to set up dial-up networking in Red Hat Linux:

♦ Install an internal or external modem in your PC. If your PC did not already come with an internal modem, you can buy an external modem and connect it to the PC's serial port.

♦ Connect the modem to the phone line. Figure 13-8 illustrates how a modem enables the PC to send digital data over the analog phone lines.

Figure 13-8: Sending Digital Data over a Modem.

♦ Get an account with an ISP. Every ISP provides you a phone number to dial, a user name, and a password. Additionally, the ISP should give you the domain names of servers for email and news. Typically, your system automatically gets an IP address from the ISP's server.

♦ Test your modem and make sure it's working. You can do this testing with a serial communication package called minicom that comes with Red Hat Linux.

♦ Run the Internet Configuration Wizard or edit appropriate configuration files to set up a PPP connection.

♦ Activate the PPP connection to connect to the Internet from a GUI tool or by typing a command.

cross ref   Appendix E describes how to set up and use modems to dial out from your Red Hat Linux system. The following sections provide an overview of PPP and show how to set up and use a PPP connection.

Understanding SLIP and PPP

Like TCP/IP networking over Ethernet, TCP/IP networking over a dial-up link involves specifying the protocol—the convention—for packaging a network packet over the communication link. There are two popular protocols for TCP/IP networking over point-to-point serial communication links:

♦ **Serial Line Internet Protocol (SLIP)**—This is a simple protocol that specifies how to frame an IP packet on a serial line. RFC 1055 describes SLIP.

♦ **Point-to-Point Protocol (PPP)**—This is a more advanced protocol for establishing a TCP/IP connection over any point-to-point link, including dial-up serial links. RFC 1661 describes PPP.

I first provide an overview of SLIP and PPP; then I show you how to use PPP to set up a network connection to a remote system. SLIP is not widely used anymore, but a brief overview is useful as a context for how PPP improves upon SLIP.

Serial Line Internet Protocol (SLIP)

SLIP originated as a simple protocol for framing an IP packet—an Internet Protocol packet that consists of an IP header (which includes the source and destination IP addresses), followed by data (the data sent from source to destination). RFC 1055, "A Nonstandard for Transmission of IP Datagrams over Serial Lines: SLIP," J. L. Romkey, June 1988, describes SLIP. As the title of RFC 1055 suggests, SLIP is not an official Internet standard; it's a de facto standard.

SLIP defines two special characters for framing—marking the beginning and ending—IP packets:

- ◆ SLIP-END is octal 300 (decimal 192); it marks the end of an IP packet.
- ◆ SLIP-ESC is octal 333 (decimal 219); it "escapes" any SLIP-END or SLIP-ESC characters that are embedded in the packet (for example, to ensure that a packet does not end prematurely because the IP packet happens to include a byte with decimal 192).

The protocol involves sending out the bytes of the IP packet one by one and marking the end of the packet with a SLIP-END character. The following convention handles any SLIP-END and SLIP-ESC characters that happen to appear in the IP packet:

- ◆ Replace a SLIP-END character with SLIP-ESC, followed by octal 334 (decimal 220).
- ◆ Replace a SLIP-ESC character with SLIP-ESC, followed by octal 335 (decimal 221).

That's it! Based on the most popular implementation of SLIP from Berkeley UNIX, SLIP also uses these conventions:

- ◆ Packets start and end with the SLIP-END character to ensure that each IP packet starts anew.
- ◆ The total size of the IP packet (including the IP header and data, but without the SLIP framing characters) is 1,006 bytes.

SLIP's simplicity led to its popularity (although PPP is used more widely nowadays). SLIP has several shortcomings, however:

- ◆ Each end of the SLIP connection has to know its and the other end's IP addresses. Although some schemes permit dynamic assignment of IP addresses, the protocol does not have any provisions for address negotiation.
- ◆ Both ends of SLIP must use the same packet size because the protocol does not permit the two ends to negotiate the packet size.
- ◆ SLIP has no support for data compression. (As you learn later in this section, Compressed SLIP (CSLIP) introduces compression in SLIP.)
- ◆ There is no way to identify the packet type in SLIP. Accordingly, SLIP can carry only one protocol—the one that both ends of SLIP are hard-wired to use. A transport mechanism such as SLIP should be capable of carrying packets of any protocol type.

CSLIP addresses the lack of data compression in SLIP, as described in RFC 1144, "Compressing TCP/IP Headers for Low-Speed Serial Links," V. Jacobson, February 1990. CSLIP compresses TCP/IP header information, which tends to be repetitive in packets exchanged between the two ends of a SLIP connection. CSLIP does not compress the packet's data. CSLIP often is referred to as the Van Jacobson compression in recognition of CSLIP's author. Van Jacobson compression is also used in PPP.

Point-to-Point Protocol (PPP)

PPP fixes the shortcomings of SLIP and defines a more complex protocol. Unlike SLIP, PPP is an official Internet standard. It is documented in RFC 1661, "The Point-to-Point Protocol," W. Simpson, July 1994 (updated in RFC 2153, "PPP Vendor Extensions," W. Simpson, May 1997).

PPP includes the following main components:

◆ A packet-framing mechanism that uses a modified version of the well-known High-Level Data Link Control (HDLC) protocol

◆ A Link Control Protocol (LCP) to establish, configure, and test the data link

◆ A family of Network Control Protocols (NCP) that enables PPP to carry more than one type of network packet—such as IP, IPX, or NetBEUI (Network BIOS Extended User Interface)—over the same connection

PPP has replaced SLIP as the protocol of choice for transporting packets over point-to-point links. In addition to the ubiquitous serial link, some versions of PPP work over several other types of point-to-point links. Some of these point-to-point links include Frame Relay, SONET/SDH (Synchronous Optical Network/Synchronous Digital Hierarchy), X.25, and ISDN (Integrated Services Digital Network).

The PPP frame has a more complex structure than SLIP has. The PPP frame structure is based on ISO (International Organization for Standardization) standard 3309, "Data Communications—High-Level Data Link Control Procedures—Frame Structure," 1979. The HDLC protocol uses a special flag character to mark the beginning and the end of a frame. Figure 13-9 shows the structure of a complete PPP frame.

Figure 13-9: The Format of a PPP Frame.

As Figure 13-9 shows, the PPP frames begin and end with a flag character whose value is always 0x7E (7E in hexadecimal notation). The Address and Control fields come from HDLC; they have the fixed values of 0xFF and 0x03, respectively. The PPP data consists of a 2-byte protocol field. (Actually, this field can be only 1 byte; the Link Control Protocol negotiates the length of the protocol field.)

Within the encapsulated network packet, PPP uses 0x7D as the escape character. To send a byte that has a special meaning (such as 0x7E, which marks the beginning and end of a frame), PPP follows these steps:

- Embeds 0x7D in the data
- Places the data byte being escaped
- Toggles the sixth bit of that data byte

Thus, if the PPP data includes 0x7E, that byte is replaced by the 2-byte sequence 0x7D, followed by 0x5E. (If you toggle the sixth bit of 0x7E, or 0111 1110 in binary, you get 0x5E, or 0101 1110 in binary.)

When you use PPP to set up a link between your Red Hat Linux PC and a remote computer, your PC first sends LCP packets to set up the data link. After the physical data link is established and any optional parameters are negotiated, your PC sends NCP packets to select one or more network protocols for use over that link. Thereafter, any of those network protocols can send packets over the PPP link.

You don't need to know the complete details of PPP to use it effectively. Later in this chapter, I describe how you can use PPP to establish a TCP/IP network connection to another computer.

Connecting to a Remote Network Using PPP

To set up a PPP networking connection between two systems, you must have PPP software running at both ends. Typically, your ISP provides you with an account already set up, so that the PPP software runs automatically upon login. In that case, simply start the PPP software on your system after you log in to the remote system. In some cases, the ISP might use another authentication protocol PAP or CHAP. Those require some additional configuration on your Red Hat Linux system.

The pppd program takes care of communicating with its peer—a remote PPP server—over a dial-up line. The pppd program's name stands for Point-to-Point Protocol daemon. (In UNIX, daemon refers to a program that runs in the background and performs some useful task.) The pppd program provides an option through which you can invoke another program, such as wvdial, that actually establishes the serial communication and completes the remote login process.

You can set up and activate a PPP connection through Red Hat's graphical Internet Configuration Wizard or by editing appropriate configuration files and then running pppd from the command line. One good way to learn about pppd and wvdial is to use the Internet Configuration Wizard to set up and activate the connection and then examine the configuration files that the graphical configuration tool creates.

Gathering Information for a PPP Connection

Most ISPs provide PPP access to the Internet through one or more systems that the ISP maintains. If you sign up for such a service, the ISP should provide you the information you need to make a PPP connection to the ISP's system. Typically, this information includes the following:

- The phone number to dial to connect to the remote system
- The user name and password you must use to log in to the remote system
- The names of the ISP's mail and news servers

◆ The IP address for your side of the PPP connection. (This IP address is associated with your PC's PPP interface—the serial port.) The ISP does not provide this address if the IP address is assigned dynamically (this means the IP address may change every time your system establishes a connection).

◆ IP addresses of the ISP's Domain Name Servers (DNS). The ISP does not provide these addresses if it assigns the IP address dynamically.

Of this information, the first two items are what you need to set up a PPP connection.

Using Red Hat's Internet Configuration Wizard

Follow these steps to set up a PPP connection using Red Hat's Internet Configuration Wizard:

1. Log in as `root` and select Main Menu⇨System Tools⇨Internet Configuration Wizard from the GNOME or KDE desktop (if you are not logged in as `root`, you'll be prompted for the root password). The Select Device Type dialog box appears (see Figure 13-10). Click the Modem connection, and then click Forward.

Figure 13-10: Configuring a New Modem Connection.

2. The Select Modem dialog box shows information about your modem. Click Forward to continue.

3. The Select Provider dialog box appears. Fill in the connection information—the ISP's phone number, your login name, and password—in the text boxes. Click Forward to continue.

4. The IP Settings dialog appears. Fill in the requested IP settings. Typically, you would set it to automatically obtain IP settings from the provider. However, if you have static IP address, you can enter that information in this dialog box.

5. Click Apply to save the dial-up configuration information and close the Internet Configuration Wizard.

6. The Network Configuration dialog appears with the name of the new dial-up connection in a list (see Figure 13-11). In this case, I have configured a PPP connection with the nickname MyISP. Click the connection name and click Activate. You can verify the PPP connection by typing the /sbin/ifconfig command (and looking for the ppp0 interface in the output) or by running a Web browser such as Mozilla to access websites on the Internet.

Figure 13-11: Click Activate in the Network Configuration Dialog Box to Establish the PPP Connection.

7. When you're done, click Deactivate to turn the PPP connection off.

Understanding the PPP Configuration Files

The Internet Configuration Wizard and the Network Configuration tool save configuration information in the /etc/sysconfig/network-scripts/ifcfg-ppp0 and /etc/wvdial .conf files. In this case, I configured a PPP connection with the nickname MyISP. For the MyISP account, the contents of the /etc/sysconfig/network-scripts/ifcfg-ppp0 file contains the following:

```
USERCTL=yes
PEERDNS=yes
TYPE=Modem
DEVICE=ppp0
BOOTPROTO=dialup
ONBOOT=no
NAME=MyISP
CCP=off
PC=off
AC=off
BSDCOMP=off
VJ=off
```

```
VJCCOMP=off
LINESPEED=57600
MODEMPORT=/dev/ttyS1
DEMAND=no
PROVIDER=MyISP
DEFROUTE=yes
PERSIST=no
PAPNAME=naba
WVDIALSECT=MyISP
MODEMNAME=Modem0
```

Table 13-3 explains the meaning of these settings.

Table 13-3: Settings in Configuration File for a PPP Network Interface

Parameter	Description
AC	Set to on to enable address compression; otherwise, set to off
BOOTPROTO	The name of the protocol to use to get the IP address for the interface. Set to dialup for PPP interface.
BSDCOMP	Set to on if the BSD (Berkeley Software Distribution) UNIX compression protocol is to be used for compressing PPP encapsulated packets. Otherwise, set this to off.
CCP	Set to on to enable the Compression Control Protocol (CCP), which is responsible for configuring, enabling, and disabling data compression algorithms at both ends of the point-to-point link. Set to off if CCP is not being used.
DEFROUTE	Set to yes if you want the PPP connection to be the default route for your system (this is true if the PPP connection is how you connect to the Internet). Otherwise, set this option to no.
DEMAND	Set to yes if you want pppd to dial out on demand (whenever there is some application attempting a connection to the Internet). Otherwise, set to no.
DEVICE	The device name for the PPP interface (ppp0 for the first interface, ppp1 for second, and so on)
LINESPEED	Causes pppd to set the modem's data rate (often called the baud rate) to the specified number of bits per second. This is not the same as the data-transfer rate between the local and the remote modem; this simply sets the highest data rate for the UART. (See Appendix E for a discussion of UART.)
MODEMNAME	Identifies the section in /etc/wvdial.conf file that defines the characteristics of the modem (for example, Modem0)
MODEMPORT	The name of the device where the modem is connected (for example, /dev/ttyS0 for first serial port, /dev/ttyS1 for the second serial port, and so on)
NAME	The nickname for the interface (for example, MyISP)
ONBOOT	Set to yes to establish the PPP connection at boot time. Set to no if you want to manually activate the PPP connection when you need it.
PAPNAME	The user name to be used to log in to the remote system (this is the user name your ISP gives you)

Parameter	Description
PC	Set to on to enable protocol field compression. Otherwise, set this to off.
PEERDNS	Set to yes if you want the interface to modify your system's /etc/resolv.conf file to use the ISP's DNS servers. Set to no, if you want the /etc/resolv.conf file unchanged.
PERSIST	Set to yes if you want the PPP link to be restarted every time it goes down. Otherwise, set it to no.
PROVIDER	Name of the ISP
TYPE	Set to Modem for dial-up PPP interface
USERCTL	Set to yes if you want any user to control the PPP interface. Set it to no if you want only root to control the interface.
VJ	Set to on to enable Van Jacobson style TCP/IP header compression. Otherwise, set this to off.
VJCCOMP	Set to on to enable the connection-ID compression option in Van Jacobson style TCP/IP header compression. With this option enabled, pppd will omit the connection-ID byte from Van Jacobson compressed TCP/IP headers and ask the other end of the PPP connection to do the same. Set the option to off if you do not want to use this compression.
WVDIALSECT	The name of the section in /etc/wvdial.conf file that should be used with /usr/sbin/wvdial to dial out (for example, MyISP refers to the [Dialer MyISP] section in /etc/wvdial.conf)

Secret

When you establish a PPP connection by clicking **Activate** in the Network Configuration tool, that GUI tool uses two programs—/usr/sbin/pppd and /usr/bin/wvdial—with appropriate options to dial out and set up the PPP connection. For the connection named MyISP PPP, the Network Configuration tool starts pppd with the following command:

```
/usr/sbin/pppd -detach lock modem crtscts asyncmap 00000000
defaultroute usepeerdns user naba remotename ppp0 /dev/ttyS1 57600
ipparam ppp0 linkname ppp0 call ppp0 noauth
```

You can look up the meanings of the pppd options by reading the pppd man page with the man pppd command. A key option here is call ppp0. That options tells pppd to dial out using the command stored in the file /etc/ppp/peers/ppp0. For the MyISP connection, the /etc/ppp/peers/ppp0 contains the following line:

```
connect "/usr/bin/wvdial --remotename ppp0 --chat 'MyISP'"
```

That line instructs pppd to connect by executing the command within double quotes following the connect option. In this example, pppd runs the /usr/bin/wvdial program with the following command line:

```
/usr/bin/wvdial --remotename ppp0 --chat MyISP
```

The —chat option causes /usr/bin/wvdial to run just like the chat program, under control of pppd. Like chat, wvdial dials the modem, connects to the remote system, looks for login prompt, and sends the appropriate user name and password.

The wvdial program looks for the phone number and other details for the `MyISP` connection in the `/etc/wvdial.conf` file—in a section named `MyISP`. Here's what the `/etc/wvdial.conf` file contains:

```
[Modem0]
Modem = /dev/ttyS1
Baud = 57600
SetVolume = 0
Dial Command = ATDT
Init1 = ATZ
FlowControl = Hardware (CRTSCTS)
[Dialer MyISP]
Area Code = 301
Username = naba
Password = mypassword
Phone = 555-1212
Stupid Mode = 1
Inherits = Modem0
```

The `[Modem0]` section lists information about the modem named `Modem0`, including any modem initialization commands (`ATZ`, in this example). This modem name also appears in the `MODEMNAME` field of the PPP configuration file such as `/etc/sysconfig/network-scripts/ifcfg-ppp0`.

---

caution

> The `[Dialer MyISP]` section contains the information needed to dial and log in to the ISP. Notice that the password is stored in plaintext form in `/etc/wvdial.conf`. To protect your ISP user name and password, you should make sure that only `root` has read and write access to the `/etc/wvdial.conf` file.

Configuring CHAP and PAP Authentication

The pppd on your system has to authenticate itself to the ISP's PPP server before the PPP connection is up and running. Authentication requires proving that you have a valid account with the ISP and essentially involves providing a user name and a secret (password). PPP specifies two ways of exchanging the authentication information between the two ends of the connection:

◆ **CHAP**—Challenge Handshake Authentication Protocol (CHAP) requires the remote end to send a randomly generated challenge string along with the remote server's name. The local system looks up the secret using the server's name and sends back a response that includes its name and a value that combines the secret and the challenge by using a one-way hash function. The remote system then checks that value against its own calculation of the expected hash value. If the values match, the authentication succeeds; otherwise, the remote system terminates the connection. In this case, the name and secret are stored in the `/etc/ppp/chap-secrets` file. Note that the remote system can repeat the CHAP authentication any time while the PPP link is up.

◆ **PAP**—Password Authentication Protocol (PAP) is like the normal login process. When using PAP, the local system repeatedly sends a user name (name) and password (secret) until the remote system acknowledges the authentication or ends the connection. The name and secret are stored in the `/etc/ppp/pap-secrets` file. Note that the user name and password are sent in the clear.

Secret

The Linux pppd server supports both types of authentication. For both PAP and CHAP, the information that the pppd server needs is a name and a secret—a user-name-password pair. This authentication information is stored in the following configuration files:

- `/etc/ppp/chap-secrets` stores the information for CHAP. Here's what a typical chap-secrets file looks like:

```
# Secrets for authentication using CHAP
# client        server  secret              IP addresses
"naba"  *       "mypassword"
```

- `/etc/ppp/pap-secrets` stores the information for PAP. Here's a typical pap-secrets file:

```
# Secrets for authentication using PAP
# client        server  secret              IP addresses
"naba"  *       "mypassword"
```

As you can see, the format of entries are the same for both `chap-secrets` and `pap-secrets`. There are four fields in each line, in the following order:

1. **client**—This field contains the name to be used during authentication. This is the user name that you get from the ISP.
2. **server**—This field contains the name of the remote system to which you are authenticating the local system. If you don't know the server's name, put an asterisk to indicate any server.
3. **secret**—This field is the secret that your system's pppd has to send to the remote system to authenticate itself. This is the password you received from the ISP.
4. **IP addresses**—This optional field can contain a list of the IP addresses that the local system may use when connecting to the specified server. Typically, this field is left blank because the local system usually gets a dynamic IP address from the server and, therefore, does not know what IP address it would use.

Testing the PPP Connection

If you have PPP access to another system (such as an ISP or a system at your employer's organization), you can set up a script as described in the preceding section and enjoy the benefits of full TCP/IP network access to another system. After you run the script, and after pppd completes the initial protocol exchanges to set up the connection, you can verify that the connection is up by typing the `ifconfig` command. You should see the `ppp0` device listed in the output. The `ifconfig` output also shows the IP addresses of the local and remote ends of the PPP connection. This output confirms that the PPP device is up and running.

To verify that the routing table is set up correctly, use the `/sbin/route` command without any arguments, as follows:

```
/sbin/route
Kernel IP routing table
Destination     Gateway         Genmask         Flags Metric Ref  Use Iface
209.100.18.4    *               255.255.255.255 UH    0      0      0 ppp0
192.168.1.200   *               255.255.255.255 UH    0      0      0 eth0
192.168.1.0     *               255.255.255.0   U     0      0      0 eth0
127.0.0.0       *               255.0.0.0       U     0      0      0 lo
default         209.100.18.4    0.0.0.0         UG    0      0      0 ppp0
```

In the routing table, the first line shows a route to the remote end of the PPP connection; this one should be set to the ppp0 device. Also, the default route should be set up so that the remote end of the PPP connection serves as the gateway for your system (as the last line of the routing table shows).

After checking the interface configuration (with the ifconfig command) and the routing table (with the route command), verify that you can reach some well-known host. If your ISP gives you the IP address of a name server or a mail server, you can try to ping those addresses. Otherwise, try to ping the IP address of a system at your workplace or university.

The following example displays the results of the ping command:

```
ping 140.90.23.100
PING 140.90.23.100 (140.90.23.100): 56 data bytes
64 bytes from 140.90.23.100: icmp_seq=0 ttl=241 time=244.3 ms
64 bytes from 140.90.23.100: icmp_seq=1 ttl=241 time=200.0 ms
64 bytes from 140.90.23.100: icmp_seq=2 ttl=241 time=220.0 ms
64 bytes from 140.90.23.100: icmp_seq=3 ttl=241 time=190.0 ms

--- 140.90.23.100 ping statistics ---
4 packets transmitted, 4 packets received, 0% packet loss
round-trip min/avg/max = 190.0/213.5/244.3 ms
```

The end of each line shows the round-trip time for a packet originating at your system to reach the designated IP address (140.90.23.100, in this case) and to return to your system. For a PPP connection over dial-up lines, you can see times in hundreds of milliseconds.

Incidentally, you do not have to have an account on a system to ping its IP address. Although a system may disable the automatic response to ping messages (ping uses Internet Control Message Protocol or ICMP messages), most systems respond to ping.

Using IP Masquerading to Share an Internet Connection

Linux supports a feature called IP masquerading, which enables you to connect an Ethernet LAN with a private IP address to the Internet. This occurs through a Linux PC (with an officially assigned IP address) that has a connection to the Internet. The Linux PC may be connected to the Internet by dial-up PPP or some other high-speed connection, such as DSL or cable modem.

Secret

With IP masquerading enabled, your Red Hat Linux PC acts as a stand-in for any of the other systems on the Ethernet LAN. As with the router setup, the Red Hat Linux PC is designated as the gateway for the Ethernet LAN. However, masquerading involves more than simply forwarding IP packets back and forth between the LAN and the Internet.

When the Red Hat Linux PC masquerades as another system on the LAN, it modifies outgoing packets so that they always appear to originate from the Red Hat Linux PC. When a response to one of the outgoing packets is received, the Red Hat Linux PC performs the reverse task—it modifies the packets so that they appear to come from the Internet, directly to the system that sends the outgoing packet. The result is that each system on the Ethernet LAN appears to have full access to the Internet, even though the Ethernet LAN uses a nonunique, private IP address.

To enable and use IP masquerading, perform the following steps:

1. Make sure the Red Hat Linux PC has an Internet connection and a network connection to your LAN. Typically, the Linux PC has two network interfaces—an Ethernet card for the LAN and a dial-up PPP connection to the Internet (through an ISP).

2. Make sure that all other systems on your LAN use the Linux PC as the default gateway for TCP/IP networking. Use the same ISP-provided DNS addresses on all systems.

3. Enable IP forwarding in the kernel by typing the following command:

```
echo "1" > /proc/sys/net/ipv4/ip_forward
```

   This is necessary because IP forwarding is disabled by default. To ensure that IP forwarding is enabled when you reboot your system, place this command in the /etc/rc.d/rc.local file.

4. Run /sbin/iptables—the IP packet filter administration program—to set up the rules that enable the Linux PC to masquerade for your LAN. For example, to enable masquerading for a LAN via the Linux PC's ppp0 network interface, you can use the following command:

```
/sbin/iptables -t nat -A POSTROUTING -o ppp0 -j MASQUERADE
```

   You can also add packet filtering to ensure that no new connections can come in through the ppp0 interface. The following two commands turn on this packet filtering:

```
/sbin/iptables -A INPUT -i ppp0 -m state --state NEW,INVALID -j DROP
/sbin/iptables -A FORWARD -i ppp0 -m state --state NEW,INVALID -j DROP
```

   If you want the IP masquerading set up at system startup, you should place these commands in the /etc/rc.d/rc.local file.

You may find IP masquerading a convenient way to provide Internet access to a small LAN (for example, a LAN at home or in the office). With IP masquerading on the Linux PC, everyone in your family or small business can access the Internet from any of the other PCs on the LAN.

Setting Up a PPP Server

The preceding sections describe how your Linux PC can establish a PPP link with another system that offers PPP service. After a PPP link is set up, both ends of the PPP link behave as peers. Before a PPP link is established, you can think of the end that initiates the dial-up connection as the client because that system asks for the connection. The other end provides the PPP connection when needed, so it's the PPP server.

If you want to enable other people to connect to your Linux PC by using PPP over a dial-up modem, log in as root and perform these steps:

1. Search through the CD-ROMs to locate the mgetty RPM. Insert each CD-ROM and mount using the mount /dev/cdrom command (or, if you are running GNOME, wait for the magicdev process to mount the CD). Then type the following commands to see if the CD contains the mgetty RPM file:

```
cd /mnt/cdrom/RedHat/RPMS
ls -l mgetty*.rpm
```

2. After you find the mgetty RPM, install it with the following command:

```
rpm -ivh mgetty*.rpm
```

3. At the end of the `/etc/mgetty+sendfax/mgetty.config` file, add the following lines for the serial port connected to a modem for dial-in users (this example assumes that the modem is connected to the second serial port, COM2):

```
# For US Robotics Sportster 56K with speaker off
port ttyS1
init-chat "" ATZ OK AT&F1M0E1Q0S0=0 OK
answer-chat "" ATA CONNECT \c \r
```

The AT&F1 modem command sets hardware flow-control mode on many modems. For other modems use appropriate initializations in the init-chat line. Note that the serial port device names may change depending on your serial communications hardware (for example, multiport serial boards would have their own device names).

4. Edit the text file `/etc/mgetty+sendfax/login.config` and search for the line that starts with `/AutoPPP/`. Uncomment it by deleting the `#` character at the beginning of the line. Edit the line so that it looks like this:

```
/AutoPPP/ - a_ppp /usr/sbin/pppd file /etc/ppp/options
```

As the last part of that line shows, automatic PPP startup involves running pppd with the options listed in the file `/etc/ppp/options`.

5. Edit the file `/etc/ppp/options` and make sure that it contains the following lines:

```
asyncmap 0
auth
crtscts
-detach
lock
login
modem
ms-dns 192.168.0.1 #put the IP address of the DNS server here
proxyarp
refuse-chap
require-pap
```

Here is what these options mean:

- **asyncmap 0**—Causes pppd not to set up and use escape control sequences
- **auth**—Causes pppd to require the peer to authenticate itself
- **crtscts**—Causes pppd to use hardware flow control
- **-detach**—Causes pppd not to become a background process (which pppd will do if a serial device is specified)
- **lock**—Creates a lock file so that pppd can have exclusive access to the particular modem
- **login**—Causes pppd to use the system password file to authenticate the peer using PAP
- **ms-dns DNS_IP**—Specifies the IP address of the name server that pppd can send to the system that dials in
- **modem**—Causes pppd to use modem control lines

- **proxyarp**—Causes the other end of the PPP connection to appear as if it is on the LAN with this system
- **refuse-chap**—Causes pppd to not use CHAP for authentication
- **require-pap**—Causes pppd to use PAP for authentication

6. Open the `/etc/ppp/pap-secrets` file in a text editor and locate the following lines:

```
# Secrets for authentication using PAP
# clientserver          secret          IP addresses
Then add the following line just below these two lines:
    *           *             " "             *
```

That basically says that pppd won't use any secrets (because it uses the system password file instead).

7. To set up a specific IP address for each serial port, create a file for that serial port with the name `/etc/ppp/options.ttyXX` where `ttyXX` is the serial port device name. In that file list the local IP address and the remote end's IP address, separated by a colon. For example, if for the `ttyS1` serial port, the local IP address is 192.168.0.100, and the remote IP address is 192.168.0.200, then add the following line to the file `/etc/ppp/options.ttyS1`:

```
192.168.0.100:192.168.0.200
```

8. Open the `/etc/inittab` file in a text editor and add a line of the following form (this example assumes that the modem is on the second serial port, `ttyS1`):

```
s1:235:respawn:/sbin/mgetty -D -x 3 ttyS1
```

The `-D` option tells `mgetty` to treat the modem as a data modem, not fax. The `-x` 3 option turns on logging—the log file is `/tmp/log_mg.ttyS1` (for modem device `/dev/ttyS1`).

9. Connect the modems to the serial ports, turn them on, and then make init reload the `/etc/inittab` file (thereby running the `mgetty` command) with the following command:

```
init q
```

Now, you can test this PPP server setup by dialing in from another PC. You will need to have your Red Hat Linux system connected to a modem, that, in turn, is connected to the phone line. You should turn on the modem, then you or a friend can dial in to that modem and establish a PPP connection using the user name and password of any existing user on the Red Hat Linux system.

Summary

Most of us do not have a direct connection to the high-bandwidth backbones of the Internet. Instead, we rely on dial-up modems, cable modems, or DSL connections to Internet service providers (ISPs), which, in turn, are connected to the backbones (typically provided by large telecommunications companies such as Sprint and AT&T). You can accomplish TCP/IP networking over serial lines with SLIP and PPP. Software for both SLIP and PPP comes with Linux. This chapter explains SLIP and PPP and shows you how to configure and use DSL, cable modem, PPP over dial-up modem, and wireless Ethernet to connect a single PC or a LAN to the Internet.

In this chapter, you learned the following:

♦ DSL and cable modem provides higher speed access to the Internet than dial-up modems. You can use a network address translation (NAT) router and a hub to connect a single PC or a small LAN to the Internet through DSL or cable modem.

♦ If you have laptops with wireless Ethernet card, you can bring them onto your LAN by connecting a wireless access point to the Ethernet hub and configuring wireless networking on the laptop. This chapter shows you how to configure wireless networking in Red Hat Linux.

♦ PPP, or Point-to-Point Protocol, is a more complex protocol for packet transport over any point-to-point link. PPP can carry packets of many protocols over the same link. PPP is the preferred way to establish a dial-up TCP/IP network connection with ISPs.

♦ Setting up a PPP link involves two basic steps. First, you must use a utility program to dial the modem and make the connection with the remote modem; then you have to start the PPP software on your system. The wvdial program functions with the pppd program to perform these two steps.

♦ You can use the Red Hat Internet Configuration Wizard to set up a PPP connection over a dial-up modem and you can use the Network Configuration utility to activate the PPP connection.

♦ You can use IP masquerading to provide Internet access to a private LAN through a Linux PC that has a PPP connection to an ISP.

♦ You also can set up your Linux PC as a PPP server so that others may dial in and establish a PPP connection with your system. This chapter describes the steps for setting up a PPP server.

Web Server

Chapter

14

◆ ◆

Secrets in This Chapter

◆ ◆

hapter 13 shows you how to connect your Red Hat Linux PC to the Internet through an Internet service provider (ISP). This chapter addresses one of the reasons the Internet has become so popular in recent years: the World Wide Web (or simply the Web), which provides an easy graphical way to browse and retrieve information from the Internet.

As a host on the Internet, all your Red Hat Linux system needs is a Web browser—an application that "knows" how to download and display Web documents—so that you can enjoy the benefits of the Web. You also can make information available to other users through Web pages—the common term for Web documents.

This chapter explains what the Web is and describes the HyperText Transfer Protocol (HTTP)—the information exchange protocol that makes the Web work. Then, it provides a brief introduction to the Mozilla Web browser, which comes with Red Hat Linux on this book's companion CD-ROMs.

Next, the chapter addresses the use of the Web as a popular way to publish information on the Internet. Red Hat Linux includes the Apache HTTP server (HTTP server being the technical term for a Web server), which you can use simply by placing your HTML files in the appropriate directory. This chapter shows you where various files should go and how to configure the Apache Web server.

Discovering the World Wide Web

If you have used a network file server of any kind, you know the convenience of being able to access files that reside at a shared location. Using a word-processing application that runs on your computer, you can easily open a document that physically resides on the file server.

Now, imagine a word processor that enables you to open and view a document that resides on any computer on the Internet. You can view the document in its full glory, with formatted text and graphics. If the document makes a reference to another document (possibly one that resides on yet another computer), you can open that linked document by clicking the reference. That kind of easy access to distributed documents is essentially what the Web provides.

Of course, the documents have to be in a standard format, so that any computer (with appropriate Web software) can access and interpret them. In addition, a standard protocol is necessary for transferring Web documents from one system to another.

The standard Web document format is HyperText Markup Language (HTML), and the standard protocol for exchanging Web documents is HyperText Transfer Protocol (HTTP).

note

A *Web server* is the software that sends HTML documents (and other files as well) to any client that makes the appropriate HTTP requests. Typically, a Web browser is the client software that actually downloads an HTML document from a Web server and displays the contents graphically.

Observing Similarity to a Giant Spider Web

The World Wide Web is a combination of Web servers and HTML documents that contain a variety of information. Imagine the Web as a giant book whose pages are scattered throughout the Internet. You use a Web browser running on your computer to view the pages.

The Web pages—HTML documents—are linked by network connections that resemble a giant spider web, so you can see how the Web got its name. The "World Wide" part refers to the fact that the Web pages are linked around the world.

Learning URLs

Like the pages of real books, Web pages contain text and graphics. Unlike the pages of real books, however, Web pages can contain multimedia information such as images, video clips, digitized sound, and cross-references, called links, that can actually take the user to the page referred to.

The links in a Web page are references to other Web pages. You follow (click) the links to go from one page to another. The Web browser typically displays these links as underlined text (in a different color) or as images. Each link is like an instruction to the reader—such as "For more information, please consult Chapter 14"—that you might find in a real book. In a Web page, all you have to do is click the link, and the Web browser brings up the page referred to, even if it's on a different computer.

> **note**
>
> The term *hypertext* refers to nonlinear organization of text (as opposed to the sequential, linear arrangement of text in most books or magazines). The links in a Web page are referred to as hypertext links; by clicking a link, you can jump to a different Web page, which is an example of nonlinear organization of text.

This arrangement raises a question. In a real book, you might ask the reader to go to a specific chapter or page. How does a hypertext link indicate the location of the Web page in question? Each Web page has a special name, called a Uniform Resource Locator (URL). A URL uniquely specifies the location of a file on a computer, as shown in Figure 14-1.

Figure 14-1: A Uniform Resource Locator (URL) Is Composed of Various Parts.

As Figure 14-1 illustrates, a URL has this sequence of components:

1. **Protocol**—This is the name of the protocol the Web browser uses to access the data that reside in the file the URL specifies. In Figure 14-1, the protocol is `http://`, which means that the URL specifies the location of a Web page. Following are the common protocol types and their meanings:

   - `file://` specifies the name of a local file that is to be opened and displayed. You can use this URL to view HTML files without having to connect to the Internet. For example, `file:///usr/share/doc/HTML/index.html` opens the file `/usr/share/doc/HTML/index.html` from your Red Hat Linux system.

   - `ftp://` specifies a file that is accessible through File Transfer Protocol (FTP). For example, `ftp://ftp.purdue.edu/pub/uns/NASA/nasa.jpg` refers to the image file `nasa.jpg` from the `/pub/uns/NASA/` directory of the FTP server `ftp.purdue.edu`. (If you want to access a specific user account by FTP, use the URL of the form `ftp://username:password@ftp.somesite.com/` with the user name and password embedded in the URL.)

   - `http://` specifies a file that is accessible through the HyperText Transfer Protocol (HTTP). This is the well-known format of URLs for all websites, such as `http://www.redhat.com/` for Red Hat's home page.

   - `https://` specifies a file that is to be accessed through a Secure Sockets Layer (SSL) connection, which is a protocol designed by Netscape Communications for encrypted data transfers across the Internet. This form of URL is typically used when the Web browser sends sensitive information such as credit card number, user name, and password to a Web server. For example, a URL such as `https://some.site.com/secure/takeorder.html` might display an HTML form that requests credit card information and other personal information such as name, address, and phone number.

   - `mailto://` specifies an email address you can use to send an email message. For example, `mailto:webmaster@someplace.com` refers to the Webmaster at the host `someplace.com`.

   - `news://` specifies a newsgroup you can read by means of the Network News Transfer Protocol (NNTP). For example, `news://news.psn.net/comp.infosystems.www.authoring.html` accesses the `comp.infosystems.www.authoring.html` newsgroup at the news server `news.psn.net`. If you have a default news server configured for the Web browser, you can omit the news server's name and use the URL `news:comp.infosystems.www.authoring.html` to access the newsgroup.

   - `telnet://` specifies a user name and a system name for remote login. For example, the URL `telnet://guest:bemyguest@someplace.com/` logs in to the host `someplace.com` with the user name `guest` and password `bemyguest`.

2. **Domain name**—This contains the fully qualified domain name of the computer on which resides the file this URL specifies. You can also specify an IP address in this field (see Chapter 6 for more information on IP addresses). The domain name is not case sensitive.

3. **Port address**—This is the port address of the server that implements the protocol listed in the first part of the URL (see Chapter 6 for a discussion of port addresses). This part of the URL is optional; there are default ports for all protocols. The default port for HTTP, for example, is 80. Some sites, however, may configure the Web server to listen to a different port. In such a case, the URL must include the port address.

4. **Directory path**—This is the directory path of the file being referred to in the URL. For Web pages, this field is the directory path of the HTML file. The directory path is case sensitive.

5. **Filename**—This is the name of the file. For Web pages, the filename typically ends with .htm or .html. If you omit the filename, the Web server returns a default file (often named index.html). The filename is case sensitive.

6. **HTML anchor**—This optional part of the URL makes the Web browser jump to a specific location in the file. If this part starts with a question mark (?) instead of a hash mark (#), the browser takes the text following the question mark to be a query. The Web server returns information based on such queries.

Understanding HyperText Transfer Protocol (HTTP)

The HyperText Transfer Protocol—the protocol that underlies the Web—is called HyperText because Web pages include hypertext links. The Transfer Protocol part refers to the standard conventions for transferring a Web page across the network from one computer to another. Although you really do not have to understand HTTP to set up a Web server or use a Web browser, I think you'll find it instructive to know how the Web works.

Before I explain anything about HTTP, you should get some firsthand experience of it. On most systems, the Web server listens to port 80 and responds to any HTTP requests sent to that port. Therefore, you can use the Telnet program to connect to port 80 of a system (if it has a Web server) to try some HTTP commands.

To see an example of HTTP at work, follow these steps:

1. Make sure your Linux PC's connection to the Internet is up and running. (If you use SLIP or PPP, for example, make sure that you have established a connection.)

2. Type the following command:

   `telnet www.gao.gov 80`

3. After you see the Connected... message, type the following HTTP command:

   `GET / HTTP/1.0`

   and press Enter twice. In response to this HTTP command, the Web server returns some useful information, followed by the contents of the default HTML file (usually called `index.html`).

The following is what I get when I try the GET command on the U.S. General Accounting Office's website:

```
telnet www.gao.gov 80
Trying 161.203.16.2...
Connected to www.gao.gov.
Escape character is '^]'.
HTTP/1.1 200 OK
Date: Sat, 15 Feb 2003 21:35:20 GMT
Server: Apache/1.3.27 (Unix) PHP/4.2.3 mod_ssl/2.8.12 OpenSSL/0.9.6g
X-Powered-By: PHP/4.2.3
Connection: close
Content-Type: text/html

<!DOCTYPE HTML PUBLIC "-//W3C//DTD HTML 4.0 Transitional//EN"
"http://www.w3.org
/TR/REC-html40/loose.dtd">

<HTML>
<HEAD>
<TITLE>The United States General Accounting Office</TITLE>
... (lines deleted) ...
</HEAD>

... (lines deleted) ...

</BODY>
</html>
Connection closed by foreign host.
```

When you try this example with Telnet, you see exactly what the Web server sends back to the Web browser. The first few lines are administrative information for the browser. The server returns this information:

◆ A line that shows that the server uses HTTP protocol version 1.1 and a status code of 200 indicating success: HTTP/1.1 200 OK

◆ The current date and time. A sample date and time string looks like this:
Date: Sat, 15 Feb 2003 21:35:20 GMT

◆ The name and version of the Web-server software. For example, for a site running the Apache Web server version 1.3.27 with the PHP hypertext processor version 4.2.3, the server returns the following string:
Server: Apache/1.3.27 (Unix) PHP/4.2.3 mod_ssl/2.8.12 OpenSSL/0.9.6g

The mod_ssl phrase refers to the fact that the Apache server has loaded the mod_ssl module that supports secure data transfers through the Secure Sockets Layer (SSL) protocol.

◆ The type of document the Web server returns. For HTML documents, the content type is reported as follows:
Content-type: text/html

The document itself follows the administrative information. An HTML document has the following general layout:

```
<title>Document's title goes here</title>
<html>
<body optional attributes go here >
... The rest of the document goes here.
</body>
</html>
```

You can identify this layout by looking through the listing that shows what the Web server returns in response to the GET command. Because the example uses a Telnet command to get the document, you see the HTML content as lines of text. If you were to access the same URL (http://www.gao.gov) with a Web browser (such as Mozilla), you would see the page in its graphical form, as shown in Figure 14-2.

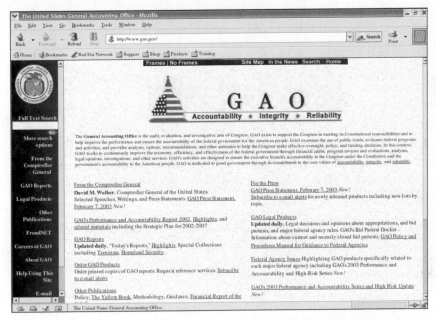

Figure 14-2: The URL www.gao.gov Viewed with the Mozilla Web Browser.

The example of HTTP commands shows the result of the GET command. GET is the most common HTTP command; it causes the server to return a specified HTML document.

The other two HTTP commands are HEAD and POST. The HEAD command is almost like GET: it causes the server to return everything in the document except the body. The POST command sends information to the server; it's up to the server to decide how to act on the information.

Surfing the Net

Like anything else, the Web is easier to understand after you have seen how it works. One of the best ways to learn about the Web is to surf it with a Web browser. Browsing Web pages is fun because the typical Web page contains both text and images. Also, browsing has an element of surprise; you can click the links and end up at unexpected Web pages. Links are the most curious aspect of the Web. You can start by looking at a page that shows today's weather; a click later, you can be reading this week's issue of *Time* magazine.

Before you can try anything, of course, you need a Web browser. (You must also have an Internet connection for your Red Hat Linux system, but I am assuming you have already taken care of that part.)

Checking out the Web Browsers in Red Hat Linux

Red Hat Linux comes with the Mozilla Web browser. Mozilla is an open-source version of Netscape Communicator, and it's replacing Netscape as the primary Web browser in Red Hat Linux.

Red Hat Linux includes several other Web browsers. I briefly mention the other browsers, but I focus on Mozilla in the rest of the discussions. Here are the major Web browsers that come with Red Hat Linux:

♦ **Mozilla**—The reincarnation of that old workhorse—Netscape Communicator—only better. It includes mail and news reader. The Web browser is called the Mozilla Navigator, or simply Navigator (just as it was in Netscape Communicator).

♦ **Galeon**—The GNOME Web browser that uses parts of the Mozilla code to draw the Web pages, but has simpler user interface than Mozilla. Galeon is not installed by default, but it should be on one of the CDs.

♦ **Konqueror**—The KDE Web browser that also doubles as a file manager and a universal viewer.

In addition to these three, many other applications are capable of downloading and displaying Web pages.

Starting Mozilla

From the GNOME or KDE desktop, you can start Mozilla in one of two ways:

- ◆ Click the Web Browser icon (the earth with a mouse) on the GNOME or KDE panel.
- ◆ Select Main Menu⇨Internet⇨Web Browser from GNOME or KDE.

If you are running Mozilla for the first time, it prompts you to select the user profile. Mozilla uses profiles to organize the bookmarks and other information for a user.

When Mozilla starts, it displays a browser window with a default home page (the main Web page on a Web server is known as the home page). You can configure Mozilla to use a different Web page as the default home page.

Learning Mozilla's User Interface

Figure 14-3 shows a Web page from the Wiley website (http://www.wiley.com), as well as the main elements of the Mozilla's browser window.

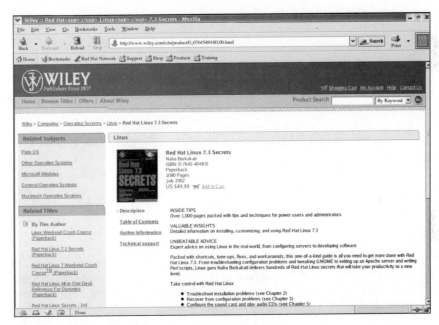

Figure 14-3: The Mozilla Web Browser in Action.

The Mozilla Web browser has lots in its user interface, but you can master it easily. You can turn off some of the items that make it look busy. You can also start with just the basics to get going with Mozilla and then gradually expand to areas that you have not yet explored.

Starting from the top of the window, you see the standard menu bar, then a Navigation toolbar, followed by thinner Personal toolbar with icons such as Home and Bookmarks. The area underneath the Personal toolbar is where the current Web page appears.

Here's what you can do with the buttons on the Navigation toolbar that appears just below the menu bar:

- **Back**—Moves to the previous Web page
- **Forward**—Moves to the page from which you may have gone backwards
- **Reload**—Reloads the current Web page
- **Stop**—Stops loading the current page
- **Location text box**—Shows the URL of the current Web page (type a URL in this box to view that Web page)
- **Search**—Searches the Netscape search site (`search.netscape.com`) with the current Web page URL as a search string
- **Print**—Prints the current Web page (you can also preview how the page would appear when printed)
- **Mozilla icon**—Takes you to the Mozilla.org website (`http://www.mozilla.org`)

Immediately below the Navigation toolbar comes the Personal toolbar with the Home and Bookmarks buttons. These two buttons serve the following purpose:

- **Home**—Takes you to the home page
- **Bookmarks**—Displays a menu from which you can bookmark the current page as well as manage your bookmarks

There are more links on the Personal toolbar. Clicking the Red Hat Network link takes you to the Red Hat Network site, where you can register to receive updates to Red Hat Linux. The rest of the links are organized into a folder. Click a folder to view the drop-down list of links, and click the link you want to visit.

You can think of the bar along the bottom edge of the Mozilla window as the status bar because the middle part of that area displays status information as Mozilla loads a Web page.

The left side of the status bar includes a number of icons. If you want a hint about what any of these icons do, simply hover the mouse cursor over the button, and Mozilla displays a small balloon help message. You can click these icons to open other Mozilla windows to perform various tasks.

Secret

In the lower-right corner of the Mozilla window is a padlock—the security padlock. Mozilla supports a secure version of the HTTP that uses Secure Sockets Layer (SSL) to transfer encrypted data. When Mozilla connects to a Web server that supports secure HTTP, the security padlock appears locked. Otherwise the security padlock is open, signifying an insecure connection. The URL for secure HTTP transfers begins with `https://` instead of the usual `http://` (note the extra s in `https`).

Mozilla displays a progress bar in the area to the left of the security key. When Mozilla is busy downloading a Web page, it displays the progress of the document it has downloaded.

Setting Up the Apache Web Server

You probably already know how it feels to use the Web, but you may not know how to set up a Web server so that you, too, can provide information to the world through Web pages. To become an information provider on the Web, you have to run a Web server on your Red Hat Linux PC on the Internet. You also have to prepare the Web pages for your website—a task that may be more demanding than the Web server setup.

Web servers provide information using HTTP. Web servers are also known as HTTP daemons (because continuously running server processes are called daemons in UNIX) or HTTPD for short. The Web server program is usually named httpd.

Among the available Web servers, the Apache Web server is the most popular. The Apache Web server started out as an improved version of the NCSA HTTPD server but soon grew into a separate development effort. Like NCSA HTTPD, the Apache server is developed and maintained by a team of collaborators. Apache is freely available over the Internet.

The following sections describe the installation and configuration of the Apache Web server.

Learning More about the Apache Web Server

The Apache Web server has too many options and configuration directives to describe in detail in this book. Whole books are devoted to configuring the Apache Web server. You should consult one of these books for more information:

- Mohammed J. Kabir, *Apache Server 2 Bible*, John Wiley & Sons, 2002.
- Mohammed J. Kabir, *Apache Server Administrator's Handbook*, Hungry Minds, Inc., 1999.
- Ken A. L. Coar, *Apache Server for Dummies*, IDG Books Worldwide, 1998.

You can also find late-breaking news and detailed information about the latest version of Apache HTTPD from Apache's website at `http://httpd.apache.org/docs-2.0/`. In particular, you can browse a complete list of Apache directives at `http://httpd.apache.org/docs-2.0/mod/directives.html`.

Installing the Apache Web Server

Installing Red Hat Linux from this book's companion CD-ROMs gives you the option to install the Apache Web server. As described in Chapter 2, simply select the Web Server package group when you are prompted for the components to install. This package group includes the Apache Web server. The Web server program is called httpd, so the Apache Web server package is called httpd.

Perform these steps to verify that the Apache Web server software is installed on your system:

1. Use the `rpm -q` command to check whether or not the Apache package is installed:

   ```
   rpm -q httpd
   httpd-2.0.40-16
   ```

   If the output shows an `httpd` package name, you have installed the Apache software.

2. Type the following command to check whether or not the httpd process is running (httpd is the name of the Apache Web server program):

```
ps ax | grep httpd
```

If the Apache Web server is running, the output should show a number of `httpd` processes. It is common to run several Web server processes—one parent and several child processes—so that several HTTP requests can be handled efficiently by assigning each request to an `httpd` process. If there is no `httpd` process, log in as `root` and start the `httpd` service with the following command:

```
service httpd start
```

3. Use the `telnet` program on your Linux system, and use the `HTTP HEAD` command to query the Web server, as follows:

```
telnet localhost 80
Trying 127.0.0.1...
Connected to localhost.
Escape character is '^]'.
HEAD / HTTP/1.0   (press Enter twice)

HTTP/1.1 403 Forbidden
Date: Sat, 15 Feb 2003 22:12:28 GMT
Server: Apache/2.0.40 (Red Hat Linux)
Accept-Ranges: bytes
Content-Length: 2898
Connection: close
Content-Type: text/html; charset=ISO-8859-1

Connection closed by foreign host.
```

If you get a response such as that in the preceding code, your system already has the Apache Web server installed and set up correctly. All you have to do is understand the configuration so that you can place the HTML documents in the proper directory.

Use a Web server to load the homepage from your system. For instance, if your system's IP address is 192.168.0.100, use the URL `http://192/168.0.100/` or try `http://localhost` and see what happens. You should see a Web page with the title "Test Page for the Apache Web Server on Red Hat Linux."

Secret

According to the information about the Apache Web server project on `http://www.apache.org/`, the Apache group was formed in March 1995 by a number of people who provided patch files that had been written to fix bugs in NCSA HTTPD 1.3. The result after applying the patches to NCSA HTTPD was what they called *a patchy* server (that's how the name Apache came about).

According to the January 2003 Netcraft Web Server Survey at `http://www.netcraft.co.uk/Survey/`, the Apache Web server is the most popular—62.23 percent of 35,424,956 sites reported using the Apache server. Microsoft Internet Information Server (IIS) is a distant second, with 27.49 percent of the sites.

Configuring the Apache Web Server

Red Hat Linux configures the Apache Web server software to use these files and directories:

- ♦ The Web server program—httpd—is installed in the /usr/sbin directory.
- ♦ The Apache Web server configuration file—httpd.conf—is located in the /etc/httpd/conf directory. The configuration file is a text file with directives that specify various aspects of the Web server (a later section describes the Apache directives).
- ♦ The Apache Web server treats files with .conf extension in the /etc/httpd/conf.d directory as configuration files for Apache modules such as mod_perl, mod_python, mod_ssl, and so on. For example, the /etc/httpd/conf.d directory contains the configuration information that SSL needs.
- ♦ The Apache Web server is set up to serve the HTML documents from the /var/www/html directory. Therefore, you should place your Web pages in this directory.
- ♦ If you have any Common Gateway Interface (CGI) programs—programs the Web server can invoke to access other files and databases—you should place these in the /var/www/cgi-bin/ directory.
- ♦ The /var/log/httpd directory is meant for Web server log files (access logs and error logs).
- ♦ The /etc/init.d/httpd script starts the httpd process as your Red Hat Linux system boots. You can type the command /etc/init.d/httpd start to run the Web server (another way is to type **service httpd start**).

---

insider insight

If you want the Apache Web server to start automatically when you boot the system, log in as root and type the following command to enable the server:

```
chkconfig --level 35 httpd on
```

To restart Apache httpd after making changes to configuration files, type:

```
service httpd restart
```

Apache Configuration Directives

The Apache httpd server's operation is controlled by the directives stored in the httpd.conf file located in the /etc/httpd/conf directory as well as separate .conf files located in the /etc/httpd/conf.d directory. The directives in these configuration files specify general attributes of the server, such as the server's name, the port number and the directory in which the server's directories are located. The configuration directives also specify information about the server resources—the documents and other information the Web server provides to users—and access control directives that control access to the entire Web server as well as to specific directories.

The next few sections show you the key information about the Apache httpd configuration directives. Typically, you do not have to change much in the configuration files to use the Apache Web server, except for setting the ServerName in the httpd.conf file. However, it is useful to know the format of the configuration files and the meaning of the various keywords used in them.

As you study the `/etc/httpd/conf/httpd.conf` file, keep these syntax rules in mind:

- The configuration file is a text file that you can edit with your favorite text editor and view with the `more` command.
- All comment lines begin with a #.
- Each line can have only one directive.
- Extra spaces and blank lines are ignored.
- All entries, except pathnames and URLs, are case insensitive.

The following sections show the Apache directives grouped into three separate categories: general HTTPD directives, resource configuration directives, and access-control directives.

General HTTPD Directives

Some interesting items from the `httpd.conf` file are

- `ServerName` specifies the host name of your website (of the form `www.your.domain`). The name should be a registered domain name other users can locate through their name servers. Here is an example:

  `ServerName www.myhost.com`

- `ServerAdmin` is the email address that the Web server provides to clients in case any errors occur. The default value for `ServerAdmin` is `root@localhost`. You should set this to a valid email address that anyone on the Internet can use to report errors your website contains.

Many more directives control the way that the Apache Web server works. The following list summarizes some of the directives you can use in the `httpd.conf` file. You can leave most of these directives in their default settings, but it's important to know about them if you are maintaining a Web server.

- **ServerType *type***—Specifies how Linux executes the HTTP server. The *type* can be `xinetd` (to run the server through the `xinetd` daemon) or `standalone` (to run the server as a standalone process). You should run the server as a standalone server for better performance. In addition, the latest Apache documentation states that the `xinetd` mode is no longer recommended and does not work properly.
- **Port *num***—Specifies that the HTTP daemon should listen to port num (a number between 0 and 65,535) for requests from clients. The default port for HTTPD is 80. You should leave the port number at its default value; clients will assume that the HTTP port is 80. If your server does not use port 80, the URL for your server must specify the port number.
- **User name [#id]**—Specifies the user name (or ID) the HTTP daemon uses when it is running in standalone mode. You can leave this directive at the default setting (apache). If you specify a user ID, use a hash (#) prefix for the numeric ID.
- **Group name [#id]**—Specifies the group name (or ID) of the HTTP daemon when the server is running in standalone mode. The default group name is `apache`.
- **ServerRoot *pathname***—Specifies the directory where the Web server is located. By default, the configuration and log files are expected to reside in subdirectories of this directory. In Red Hat Linux, `ServerRoot` is set to `/etc/httpd`.
- **ServerName www.company.com**—Sets the server's hostname to `www.company.com` instead of to its real host name. You cannot simply invent a name; the name must be a valid name from the Domain Name System (DNS) for your system.
- **StartServers *num***—Sets the number of child processes that start as soon as the Apache Web server runs. The default value is 8.

◆ **MaxSpareServers *num*—**Sets the desired maximum number of idle child-server processes (a child process is considered idle if it is not handling an HTTP request). The default value is 20.

◆ **MinSpareServers *num*—**Sets the desired minimum number of idle child server processes (a child process is considered idle if it is not handling an HTTP request). A new spare process is created every second if the number falls below this threshold. The default value is 5.

◆ **Timeout *numsec*—**Sets the number of seconds that the server waits for a client to send a query after the client establishes connection. The default Timeout is 300 seconds (five minutes).

◆ **ErrorLog *filename*—**Sets the file where httpd logs the errors it encounters. If the filename does not begin with a slash (/), the name is taken to be relative to `ServerRoot`. The default `ErrorLog` is `/var/log/httpd/error_log`. Typical error-log entries include events such as server restarts and any warning messages, such as the following:

```
[Sat Feb 15 17:12:09 2003] [notice] Apache/2.0.40 (Red Hat Linux)
configured -- resuming normal operations
[Sat Feb 15 18:38:51 2003] [error] [client 127.0.0.1] File does not
exist: /var/www/html/sample.html
```

◆ **TransferLog *filename*—**Sets the file where httpd records all client accesses (including failed accesses). The default `TransferLog` is `/var/log/httpd/access_log`. The following example shows how a typical access is recorded in the `TransferLog` file:

```
127.0.0.1 - - [15/Feb/2003:18:41:36 -0500] "GET / HTTP/1.1" 403 2898 "-
" "Mozilla/5.0 (X11; U; Linux i686; en-US; rv:1.2.1) Gecko/20030115"
127.0.0.1 - - [15/Feb/2003:18:41:36 -0500] "GET /icons/powered_by.gif
HTTP/1.1" 304 0 "http://localhost/" "Mozilla/5.0 (X11; U; Linux i686;
en-US; rv:1.2.1) Gec
ko/20030115"
```

The first entry is for the text of the file; the second entry is for embedded images.

◆ **LogFormat *formatstring formatname*—**Specifies the format of log-file entries for the `TransferLog`. This format is also used by the `CustomLog` directive to produce logs in a specific format.

◆ **CustomLog *filename formatname*—**Sets the name of the custom log file where httpd records all client accesses (including failed accesses) in a format specified by *formatname* (which you define using a `LogFormat` directive).

◆ **PidFile *filename*—**Sets the file where httpd stores its process ID. The default `PidFile` is `/var/run/httpd.pid`. You can use this information to kill or restart the HTTP daemon. The following example shows how to restart `httpd`:

```
kill -HUP `cat /var/run/httpd.pid`
```

◆ **MaxClients *num*—**Sets the limit on the number of clients that can simultaneously connect to the server. The default value is 150. The value of `MaxClients` cannot be more than 256.

◆ **LoadModule *module modules/modfile.so*—**Loads a module that was built as a Dynamic Shared Object (DSO). You have to specify the module name and the module's object file. Because the order in which modules are loaded is important, you should leave these directives as they appear in the default configuration file. Note that the `mod_ssl` module provides support for encryption using the Secure Sockets Layer (SSL) protocol.

Resource Configuration Directives

The resource configuration directives specify the location of the Web pages, as well as how to specify the data types of various files. To get started, you can leave the directives at their default settings. These are some of the resource configuration directives for the Apache Web server:

◆ **DocumentRoot *pathname***—Specifies the directory where the HTTP server finds the Web pages. In Red Hat Linux, the default DocumentRoot is /var/www/html. If you place your HTML documents in another directory, set DocumentRoot to that directory.

◆ **UserDir *dirname***—Specifies the directory below a user's home directory where the HTTP server looks for the Web pages when a user name appears in the URL (in an URL such as http://www.psn.net/~naba/, for example, which includes a user name with a tilde prefix). The default UserDir is public_html, which means that a user's Web pages are in the public_html subdirectory of that user's home directory. If you do not want to allow users to have Web pages, specify disabled as the directory name in the UserDir directive.

◆ **DirectoryIndex *filename1 filename2* ...**—Indicates the default file or files to be returned by the server when the client does not specify a document. The default DirectoryIndex is index.html. If httpd does not find this file, it returns an index (basically, a nice-looking listing of the files) of that directory.

◆ **AccessFileName *filename***—Specifies the name of the file that may appear in each directory that contains documents and that indicates who has permission to access the contents of that directory. The default AccessFileName is .htaccess. The syntax of this file is the same as that of Apache access-control directives, which the next section discusses.

◆ **AddType *type/subtype extension***—Associates a file extension with a MIME (Multipurpose Internet Mail Extensions) data type of the form type/subtype, such as text/plain or image/gif. Thus, to have the server treat files with the .lst extension as plaintext files, specify the following:

```
AddType text/plain .lst
```

The default MIME types and extensions are listed in the /etc/mime.types file.

◆ **AddEncoding *type extension***—Associates an encoding type with a file extension. To have the server mark files ending with .gz or .tgz as encoded with the x-gzip encoding method (the standard name for the GZIP encoding), specify the following:

```
AddEncoding x-gzip gz tgz
```

◆ **DefaultType *type/subtype***—Specifies the MIME type that the server should use if it cannot determine the type from the file extension. If you do not specify DefaultType, httpd assumes the MIME type to be text/html. In the default httpd.conf file that you get from the companion CD-ROMs, DefaultType is specified as text/plain.

◆ **Redirect *requested-file actual-URL***—Specifies that any requests for requested-file are to be redirected to actual URL.

- **Alias *requested-dir actual-dir*—**Specifies that the server use `actual-dir` to locate files in the `requested-dir` directory (in other words, `requested-dir` is an alias for `actual-dir`). To have requests for the `/icons` directory go to `/var/www/icons`, specify the following:

  `Alias /icons/ /var/www/icons/`

- **ScriptAlias *requested-dir actual-dir*—**Specifies the real name of the directory where scripts for the Common Gateway Interface (CGI) are located. For example, the following directive specifies the location of the `/cgi-bin/` directory:

  `ScriptAlias /cgi-bin/ /var/www/cgi-bin/`

  This directive means that when a Web browser requests a script, such as `/cgi/bin/test-cgi`, the HTTP server runs the script `/var/www/cgi-bin/test-cgi`.

- **FancyIndexing on [off]—**Enables or disables the display of fancy directory listings, with icons and file sizes.

- **DefaultIcon *iconfile*—**Specifies the location of the default icon that the server should use for files that have no icon information. By default, `DefaultIcon` is `/icons/unknown.gif`.

- **ReadmeName *filename*—**Specifies the name of a README file whose contents are added to the end of an automatically generated directory listing. The default `ReadmeName` is `README`.

- **HeaderName *filename*—**Specifies the name a header file whose contents are prepended to an automatically generated directory listing. The default `HeaderName` is `HEADER`.

- **AddDescription *"file description" filename*—**Specifies that the file description string be displayed next to the specified filename in the directory listing. You can use a wildcard, such as `*.html`, as the filename. For example, the following directive describes files ending with `.tgz` as `GZIP compressed tar archives`:

  `AddDescription "GZIP compressed tar archive" .tgz`

- **AddIcon *iconfile extension1 extension2 ...*—**Associates an icon with one or more file extensions. The following directive associates the icon file `/icons/text.gif` with the file extension `.txt`:

  `AddIcon /icons/text.gif .txt`

- **AddIconByType *iconfile MIME-types*—**Associates an icon with a group of file types specified as a wildcard form of MIME types (such as `text/*` or `image/*`). To associate an icon file of `/icons/text.gif` with all text types, specify the following:

  `AddIconByType (TXT,/icons/text.gif) text/*`

  This directive also tells the server to use `TXT` in place of the icon for clients that cannot accept images. (Browsers tell the server what types of data they can accept.)

- **AddIconByEncoding *iconfile encoding1 encoding2 ...*—**Specifies an icon to be displayed for one or more encoding types (such as `x-compress` or `x-gzip`).

♦ **IndexIgnore** *filename1 filename2 ...*—Instructs the server to ignore the specified filenames (they typically contain wildcards) when preparing a directory listing. To leave out README, HEADER, and all files with names that begin with a period (.), a trailing tilde (~), or a trailing hash mark (#), specify the following:

```
IndexIgnore .??* *~ *# HEADER* README* RCS CVS *,v *,t
```

♦ **IndexOptions** *option1 option2 ...*—Indicates the options you want in the directory listing prepared by the server. Options can include one or more of the following:

- FancyIndexing turns on the fancy directory listing that includes filenames and icons representing the files' types, sizes, and last-modified dates.
- IconHeight=N specifies that icons are N pixels tall.
- IconWidth=N specifies that icons are N pixels wide.
- NameWidth=N makes the filename column N characters wide.
- IconsAreLinks makes the icons act like links.
- ScanHTMLTitles shows a description of HTML files.
- SuppressHTMLPreamble does not add a standard HTML preamble to the header file (specified by the HeaderName directive).
- SuppressLastModified stops the displaying of the last date of modification.
- SuppressSize stops the displaying of the file size.
- SuppressDescription stops the displaying of any file description.
- SuppressColumnSorting stops the column headings from being links that enable sorting the columns.

♦ **ErrorDocument** *errortype filename*—Specifies a file the server should send when an error of a specific type occurs. You can also provide a text message for an error. Here are some examples:

```
ErrorDocument 403 "Sorry, you cannot access this directory"
ErrorDocument 404 /cgi-bin/bad_link.pl
ErrorDocument 401 /new_subscriber.html
```

If you do not have this directive, the server sends a built-in error message. The *errortype* can be one of the following HTTP/1.1 error conditions (see RFC 2616 at http://www.ietf.org/rfc/rfc2616.txt or http://www.cis.ohio-state .edu/htbin/rfc/rfc2616.html for more information):

- **400**—Bad Request
- **401**—Unauthorized
- **402**—Payment Required
- **403**—Forbidden
- **404**—Not Found
- **405**—Method Not Allowed
- **406**—Not Acceptable
- **407**—Proxy Authentication Required
- **408**—Request Timeout
- **409**—Conflict
- **410**—Gone
- **411**—Length Required
- **412**—Precondition Failed

- **413**—Request Entity Too Large
- **414**—Request-URI Too Long
- **415**—Unsupported Media Type
- **416**—Requested Range Not Satisfiable
- **417**—Expectation Failed
- **500**—Internal Server Error
- **501**—Not Implemented
- **502**—Bad Gateway
- **503**—Service Unavailable
- **504**—Gateway Timeout
- **505**—HTTP Version Not Supported

♦ **TypesConfig** *filename*—Specifies the file that contains the mapping of file extensions to MIME data types. (MIME stands for Multipurpose Internet Mail Extensions, which defines a way to package attachments in a single message file.) The server reports these MIME types to clients. If you do not specify a `TypesConfig` directive, httpd assumes that the `TypesConfig` file is `/etc/mime.types`. The following are a few selected lines from the default `/etc/mime.types` file:

```
application/msword            doc
application/pdf               pdf
application/postscript        ai eps ps
application/x-tcl             tcl
audio/mpeg                    mpga mp2 mp3
audio/x-pn-realaudio          ram rm
audio/x-wav                   wav
image/gif                     gif
image/jpeg                    jpeg jpg jpe
image/png                     png
text/html                     html htm
text/plain                    asc txt
video/mpeg                    mpeg mpg mpe
```

Each line shows the MIME type (such as `text/html`), followed by the file extensions for that type (`html` or `htm`).

Access-Control Directives

Access-control directives enable you to control who can access different directories in the system. These are the global access-configuration directives. In each directory containing documents served by the Apache Web server, you can have another access-configuration file with the name specified by the `AccessFileName` directive. (That per directory access-configuration file is named `.htaccess` by default.)

Stripped of most of the comment lines, the access-control directive has this format:

```
# First, we configure the "default" to be a
# very restrictive set of permissions.
<Directory />
Options None
AllowOverride None
</Directory>
```

```
# The following directory name should
# match DocumentRoot in httpd.conf
<Directory /var/www/html>
    Options Indexes Includes FollowSymLinks
    AllowOverride None
    order allow,deny
    allow from all
</Directory>

# The directory name should match the
# location of the cgi-bin directory
<Directory "/var/www/cgi-bin">
    AllowOverride None
    Options ExecCGI
    Order allow,deny
    Allow from all
</Directory>
```

Access-control directives use a different syntax from the other Apache directives. The syntax is like that of HTML. Various access-control directives are enclosed within pairs of tags, such as `<Directory> ... </Directory>`.

The following list describes some of the access-control directives. In particular, notice the `AuthUserFile` directive; you can have password-based access control for specific directories.

♦ **Options *opt1 opt2 ...*** —Specifies the access-control options for the directory section in which this directive appears. The options can be one or more of the following:

- `None` disables all access-control features.
- `All` turns on all features for the directory.
- `FollowSymLinks` enables the server to follow symbolic links.
- `SymLinksIfOwnerMatch` follows symbolic links, only if the same user of the directory owns the linked directory.
- `ExecCGI` enables execution of CGI scripts in the directory.
- `Includes` enables server-side include files in this directory (the term server-side include refers to directives, placed in an HTML file, that the Web server processes before returning the results to the Web browser).
- `Indexes` enables clients to request indexes (directory listings) for the directory.
- `IncludesNOEXEC` disables the `#exec` command in server-side includes.

♦ **AllowOverride *directive1 directive2 ...*** —Specifies which access-control directives can be overridden on a per directory basis. The directive list can contain one or more of the following:

- `None` stops any directive from being overridden.
- `All` enables overriding of any directive on a per directory basis.
- `Options` enables the use of the Options directive in the directory-level file.
- `FileInfo` enables the use of directives controlling document type, such as `AddType` and `AddEncoding`.
- `AuthConfig` enables the use of authorization directives, such as `AuthName`, `AuthType`, `AuthUserFile`, and `AuthGroupFile`.
- `Limit` enables the use of `Limit` directives (`allow`, `deny`, and `order`) in a directory's access-configuration file.

◆ **AuthName** *name*—Specifies the authorization name for a directory.

◆ **AuthType** *type*—Specifies the type of authorization to be used. The only supported authorization type is Basic.

◆ **AuthUserFile** *filename*—Specifies the file in which usernames and passwords are stored for authorization. For example, the following directive sets the authorization file to /etc/httpd/conf/passwd:

```
AuthUserFile /etc/httpd/conf/passwd
```

You have to create the authorization file with the /usr/sbin/htpasswd support program. To create the authorization file and add the password for a user named jdoe, specify the following:

```
/usr/bin/htpasswd -c /etc/httpd/conf/passwd jdoe
New password: (type the password)
Re-type new password: (type the same password again)
Adding password for user jdoe
```

◆ **AuthGroupFile** *filename*—Specifies the file to consult for a list of user groups for authentication.

◆ **order** *ord*—Specifies the order in which two other directives—allow and deny—are evaluated. The order is one of the following:

- deny,allow causes the Web server to evaluate the deny directive before allow.
- allow,deny causes the Web server to evaluate the allow directive before deny.
- mutual-failure enables only hosts in the allow list.

◆ **deny from** *host1 host2 ...*—Specifies the hosts denied access.

◆ **allow from** *host1 host2 ...*—Specifies the hosts allowed access. To enable all hosts in a specific domain to access the Web documents in a directory, specify the following:

```
order deny,allow
allow from .nws.noaa.gov
```

◆ **require entity** *en1 en2 ...*—This directive specifies which users can access a directory. entity is one of the following:

- user enables only a list of named users.
- group enables only a list of named groups.
- valid-user enables all users listed in the AuthUserFile access to the directory (provided that they enter the correct password).

Supporting Virtual Hosts with the Apache HTTP Server

A useful feature of the Apache HTTP server is its ability to handle virtual Web servers. This ability enables a single server to respond to many different IP addresses and to serve Web pages from different directories, depending on the IP address. That means that you can set up a single Web server to respond to both www.big.org and www.tiny.com and serve a unique home page for each hostname. A server with this capability is known as multihomed Web server, a virtual Web server, or a server with virtual host support.

As you might guess, ISPs use virtual host capability to offer virtual websites to their customers. You must meet the following requirements to support virtual hosts:

◆ The Web server must be able to respond to multiple IP addresses (each with a unique domain name) and must enable you to specify document directories, log files, and other configuration items for each IP address.

◆ The Linux system must associate multiple IP addresses with a single physical network interface. Red Hat Linux enables you to associate multiple IP addresses with a single physical interface.

◆ Each domain name associated with the IP address must be a unique registered domain name with proper DNS entries.

For the latest information on how to set up virtual hosts in an Apache HTTP server, consult the following URL:

```
http://httpd.apache.org/docs-2.0/vhosts/index.html
```

The Apache HTTP server can respond to different host names with different home pages. You have two options when supporting virtual hosts:

◆ Run multiple copies of the httpd program, one for each IP address—In this case, you create a separate copy of the `httpd.conf` configuration file for each host and use the `BindAddress` directive to make the server respond to a specific IP address.

◆ Run a single copy of the httpd program with a single `httpd.conf` file—In the configuration file, set `BindAddress` to * (so that the server responds to any IP address), and use the `VirtualHost` directive to configure the server for each virtual host.

You should run multiple HTTP daemons only if you do not expect heavy traffic on your system; the system may not able to respond well because of the overhead associated with running multiple daemons. However, you may need multiple HTTP daemons if each virtual host has a unique configuration need for the following directives:

◆ `ServerType`, which specifies whether the server runs as a standalone process or through `xinetd`.

◆ `UserId` and `GroupId`, which are the user and group ID for the `HTTP` daemon.

◆ `ServerRoot`, which is the root directory of the server.

◆ `TypesConfig`, which is the MIME type configuration file.

For a site with heavy traffic, you should configure the Web server so that a single `HTTP` daemon can serve multiple virtual hosts. Of course, this recommendation implies that there is only one configuration file. In that configuration file, use the `VirtualHost` directive to configure each virtual host.

Most ISPs use the `VirtualHost` capability of Apache HTTP server to provide virtual websites to their customers. Unless you pay for a dedicated Web host, you typically get a virtual site where you have your own domain name, but share the server and the actual host with many other customers.

The syntax of the `VirtualHost` directive is as follows:

```
<VirtualHost hostaddr>
    ... directives that apply to this host
    ...
</VirtualHost>
```

With this syntax, you use `<VirtualHost>` and `</VirtualHost>` to enclose a group of directives that will apply only to the particular virtual host identified by the `hostaddr` parameter. The `hostaddr` can be an IP address, or the fully qualified domain name of the virtual host.

You can place almost any Apache directives within the `<VirtualHost>` block. At a minimum, Webmasters include the following directives in the `<VirtualHost>` block:

- ♦ `DocumentRoot`, which specifies where this virtual host's documents reside
- ♦ `Servername`, which identifies the server to the outside world (this should be a registered domain name DNS supports)
- ♦ `ServerAdmin`, which is the email address of this virtual host's Webmaster
- ♦ `Redirect`, which specifies any URLs to be redirected to other URLs
- ♦ `ErrorLog`, which specifies the file where errors related to this virtual host are to be logged
- ♦ `CustomLog`, which specifies the file where accesses to this virtual host are logged

When the server receives a request for a document in a particular virtual host's `DocumentRoot` directory, it uses the configuration parameters within that server's `<VirtualHost>` block to handle that request.

Here is a typical example of a `<VirtualHost>` directive that sets up the virtual host `www.lnbsoft.com`:

```
<VirtualHost www.lnbsoft.com>
    DocumentRoot    /home/naba/httpd/htdocs
    ServerName   www.lnbsoft.com
    ServerAdmin   webmaster@lnbsoft.com
    ScriptAlias   /cgi-bin/   /home/naba/httpd/cgi-bin/
    ErrorLog /usr/home/naba/httpd/logs/error_log
    CustomLog   /home/naba/httpd/logs/access_log common
</VirtualHost>
```

Here, the name common in the `CustomLog` directive refers to the name of a format defined earlier in the `httpd.conf` file by the `LogFormat` directive, as follows:

```
LogFormat "%h %l %u %t \"%r\" %>s %b" common
```

This format string for the log produces lines in the log file that look like this:

```
dial236.dc.psn.net - - [29/Oct/2002:18:09:00 -0500] "GET / HTTP/1.0" 200 1243
```

The format string contains two letter tokens that start with a percent sign (%). The meaning of these tokens is shown in Table 14-1.

Table 14-1: LogFormat Tokens

Token	Meaning
%b	The number of bytes sent to the client, excluding header information
%h	The hostname of the client machine
%l	The identity of the user, if available
%r	The HTTP request from the client (for example, GET / HTTP/1.0)
%s	The server response code from the Web server
%t	The current local date and time
%u	The user name the user supplies (only when access-control rules require user name/password authentication)

Configuring Apache for Server-Side Includes (SSI)

"Server-side include" (SSI) refers to a feature of the Apache Web server whereby it can include a file or the value of an environment variable in an HTML document. The feature is like the include files in many programming languages such as C and C++. Just as a preprocessor processes the include files in a programming language, the Web browser reads the HTML file and parses the server-side includes before returning the document to the Web browser.

Server-side includes provide a convenient way to include date, file size, and any file into an HTML document. The SSI directives look like special comments in the HTML file. For example, you can show the size of a graphics file by placing the following SSI directive in the HTML file:

```
File size = <!--#fsize file="nbphoto.gif"-->
```

The Web server replaces everything to the right of the equal sign with the size of the file nbphoto.gif.

Similarly, to display today's date, you can use the following SSI directive:

```
Today is <!--#echo var="DATE_LOCAL" -->
```

To enable SSI on the Apache Web server, place the following directive in the /etc/httpd/conf/httpd.conf file:

```
Options +Includes
```

Apache directives can apply to specific directories. Therefore, it's best if you place this directive in the block of directives that apply to the directory where you want to allow SSI.

Secret

You also have to tell Apache which files to parse for SSI. The convention is to use the `.shtml` extension for SSI files. To instruct Apache about the `.shtml` files, you need the following directives in `/etc/httpd/conf/httpd.conf`:

```
AddType text/html .shtml
AddOutputFilter INCLUDES .shtml
```

The only drawback of using the `.shtml` extension for SSI files is that you need to change the file extension if you decide SSI directives to a plain HTML file. Unfortunately, changing a file's extension requires all links to that file to be updated. A way out of this quandary is to use the `XBitHack` directive. To use `XBitHack`, add the following line to the `httpd.conf` file:

```
XBitHack on
```

Then, use the `chmod` command to make those HTML files with SSI directives executable. For example, if the file welcome.html contains SSI directives, type the following command to make that file executable:

```
chmod +x welcome.html
```

When the `XBitHack` is turned on, Apache parses HTML files for SSI directives if they have the execute bit set (which is what happens when you make the file executable with the `chmod +x` command).

From the standpoint of security, one problem of server-side includes is the ability to execute a command on the server. For example, the following line of HTML includes the contents of the `/etc/passwd` file in the document returned to the browser:

```
<!--#exec cmd="/bin/cat /etc/passwd"-->
```

If you want to retain some of the benefits of server-side includes but minimize the security risks, you can turn off the `#exec` keyword with the following directive on an Options line in `httpd.conf`:

```
Options IncludesNoExec
```

Supporting CGI Programs in Apache

Sometimes an HTML document's content may not be known in advance. For example, if a website provides a search capability, the result of a search depends on which keywords the user enters in the search form. To handle these needs, the Web server relies on external programs called gateways.

A gateway program accepts the user input and responds with the requested data formatted as an HTML document. Often, the gateway program acts as a bridge between the Web server and some other repository of information such as a database.

Gateway programs have to interact with the Web server. To allow anyone to write a gateway program, the method of interaction between the Web server and the gateway program had to be specified completely. Common Gateway Interface (CGI) is the standard method used by gateway programs to exchange information with the Web server. The Apache Web server supports CGI programs.

The URL specifying a CGI program looks like any other URL, but the Apache Web server can examine the directory name and determine whether the URL is a normal document or a CGI program. Typically, a directory is set aside for CGI programs, and you specify that directory through the ScriptAlias directive in the /etc/httpd/conf/httpd.conf file. You can use multiple ScriptAlias directives to specify multiple directories for CGI programs. Here's a typical ScriptAlias directive:

```
ScriptAlias /cgi-bin/ "/var/www/cgi-bin/"
```

This tells Apache that CGI URLs use the /cgi-bin/ directory name. The ScriptAlias directive also specifies that Apache should substitute the full pathname /var/www/cgi-bin/ for /cgi-bin/.

For example, if a URL specifies http://www.someplace.com/cgi-bin/dbquery, then the Apache server at www.someplace.com recognizes this as a CGI URL and invokes the dbquery program. The ScriptAlias directive in that Web server's httpd.conf configuration file indicates which directory on the server's system contains the CGI programs. In other words for the example ScriptAlias directive, the Web server translates the CGI program name /cgi-bin/dbquery to the full pathname /var/www/cgi-bin/dbquery.

Secret

You can also permit CGI execution in specific directories by placing an explicit Options directive in that directory's configuration. For example, suppose you want to permit CGI execution in the /var/www/special directory. You could do so by adding the following block of directives to the httpd.conf file:

```
<Directory /var/www/special>
    Options +ExecCGI
... other directives for this directory...
</Directory>
```

In addition to this, you also have to indicate which files in that directory are CGI files. Suppose that the CGI files have .cgi and .pl extensions (Perl scripts are often stored in files with .pl extension and CGI programs are often written in Perl). Then, you should add the following directive to the httpd.conf file:

```
AddHandler cgi-script cgi pl
```

You also have to make sure that the CGI files are executable and have appropriate permissions.

Using Java Servlets with Apache

Servlets are Java programs that execute in a Web server in response to requests from a Web browser. Servlets are more powerful than CGI programs commonly used as gateways between Web servers and other services such as databases. One drawback of CGI programs is that the Web server has to start a new process to run a standalone CGI program whenever the server receives data from an HTML form.

Servlets provide functionality similar to that of CGI programs, but servlets avoid the overhead of new process startup. Typically, the Web server runs a Java Virtual Machine (JVM), and that JVM, in turn, loads and runs the servlets. The JVM runs a servlet in a Java thread, which is faster and requires fewer operating system resources than a new process. Additionally, the JVM can keep a servlet loaded and running so that a single instance can handle many future requests. This makes servlets more responsive than other CGI programs, especially ones written in scripting languages such as Perl. At the same time, servlets are portable to any system that supports Java, just as Perl CGI programs can run on any system with a Perl interpreter.

Many websites already use servlets extensively. While browsing the Web, you may have accessed some servlets without even realizing it. A giveaway that the Web server is using a servlet is the occurrence of /servlet/ in the URL (in the same way that /cgi-bin/ commonly appears in URLs that refer to CGI programs).

Many websites use another Java-based approach to generate dynamic content. That approach is based on what is known as JavaServer Pages (JSP) technology. A Web page based on JSP uses XML tags and Java scripts along with other HTML tags. Typically, a JSP page has the .jsp file extension, which tells the Web server that the page should be processed by a server that understands JSP.

If you want to support Java servlets and JSP on your Apache Web server, you have to download and install the following software on your Red Hat Linux system, in the order shown:

1. **Java Development Kit (JDK) release (version 1.2 or later)**—For writing Java servlets. Download the binary distribution for Linux from http://java.sun.com/j2se/downloads.html. You can download the RPM distribution, which is easy to install with the rpm command (after an additional step of unpacking). After installing JDK, set the environment variable JAVA_HOME to the pathname of the directory where you installed the JDK release.

2. **Apache Tomcat**—A server that runs servlets and can execute JSP documents. Tomcat version 5.0 implements the Servlet 2.4 and JSP 2.0 specifications from the Java Community Process (http://www.jcp.org). More information about Tomcat is available from the home page of the Apache Jakarta project at http://jakarta.apache.org/tomcat/. Download the Tomcat binary distribution from http://jakarta.apache.org/site/binindex.cgi. You should download what the Jakarta project calls Release Builds because they are considered ready to use by anyone.

3. **Jakarta-Tomcat-Connector mod_jk**—An Apache Web server module that enables the Apache Web server to communicate with Tomcat. Download the latest source files from http://jakarta.apache.org/builds/jakarta-tomcat-connectors/jk/release/. Online information about the jk connector is available at http://jakarta.apache.org/builds/jakarta-tomcat-connectors/jk/doc/.

note   You also need the Apache httpd source files before you can build the mod_jk module.

The following sections show how to install JDK, Tomcat, the Apache httpd source RPM, and build the mod_jk2 module that connects the Apache Web server to Tomcat.

Installing the Java 2 Software Development Kit

After you download and save the Linux RPM binaries for Java, you'll see a file with a name ending in `.bin`. You have to go through an extra step before you can use RPM commands to install this file.

Secret

Sun provides the RPM file wrapped in a shell script. You have to make the file executable by using the `chmod +x` command. Execute the file (by typing its name on the command line), accept the license agreement, and the script generates a RPM file that you can install.

For example, when I downloaded the Linux RPM distribution of JDK 1.4.0 binaries, the file name was `j2sdk-1_4_0_03-linux-i586-rpm.bin` (the file was about 39MB in size, so it can take you a while to download unless you have a high-speed Internet connection). I logged in as `root` and made that file executable by typing:

```
chmod +x j2sdk*.bin
```

Then, I executed the file with the following command:

```
./j2sdk*.bin
```

That displayed the license agreement, a page at a time, followed by the prompt:

```
Do you agree to the above license terms? [yes or no]
```

I typed `yes` and that started the unpacking and ended with the RPM file:

```
j2sdk-1_4_0_03-fcs-linux-i586.rpm
```

Then, I installed the JDK with the following command:

```
rpm -ivh j2sdk*.rpm
```

In this case, the JDK is installed in the directory `/usr/java/j2sdk1.4.0_03`. Therefore, I set the environment variable `JAVA_HOME` to this directory with the command `export JAVA_HOME=/usr/java/j2sdk1.4.0_03`.

insider insight

To make sure that this definition is available to everyone who use the Bash shell, create a text file named `java.sh` in `/etc/profile.d` directory and add the following lines in that file:

```
export JAVA_HOME=/usr/java/j2sdk1.4.0_03

PATH=$JAVA_HOME/bin:$PATH
```

The `/etc/profile` script will then read and execute the `java.sh` script at login and set the `JAVA_HOME` environment variable and add the JDK binaries to the `PATH`.

cross ref

To learn about Java programming on Red Hat Linux, consult Chapter 26.

Installing Apache Tomcat

Download the latest binary for the Release Build of Tomcat. If you have JDK 1.4, you should download the file with a name that ends in `-LE-jdk14`. That's the lightweight binary that does not include the XML parser—the XML parser is already included in the 1.4.x versions of Java.

To install and test the Tomcat binaries, log in as `root` and follow these steps:

1. Copy the downloaded Tomcat compressed tar archive to a suitable directory such as `/usr/local` with the following command:

```
mv tomcat-*LE-jdk*.gz /usr/local
```

2. Unpack with the `tar zxvf` command in its new location (for example, `/usr/local`) with the following commands:

```
cd /usr/local
tar zxvf tomcat-*.tar.gz
```

3. Set the `CATALINA_HOME` environment variable to the full pathname of the directory where you installed Tomcat. For example, I installed version 4.1.18 of Tomcat in the directory `/usr/local/jakarta-tomcat-4.1.18-LE-jdk14`, so I define `CATALINA_HOME` as follows:

```
export CATALINA_HOME=/usr/local/jakarta-tomcat-4.1.18-LE-jdk14
```

You need the `CATALINA_HOME` environment variable in the future. Therefore, you should create a file named `tomcat.sh` in `/etc/profile.d` directory with the following line in that file:

```
export CATALINA_HOME=/usr/local/jakarta-tomcat-4.1.18-LE-jdk14
```

Then, whenever you log in, the CATALINA_HOME environment variable would be defined.

4. Start Tomcat with the following commands

```
cd $CATALINA_HOME/bin
./startup.sh
```

5. To see if Tomcat is working, start a Web browser on your system or another system on the LAN. Point the browser to your system at port 8080 by using the following URL:

```
http://localhost:8080/examples
```

If Tomcat is up and running, you should see three directories named `images`, `jsp`, and `servlets`. Browse through the `jsp` and `servlets` directories and try out the JSP and servlet examples.

6. Shut down Tomcat with the following command:

```
cd $CATALINA_HOME/bin
./shutdown.sh
```

Now, you can proceed to install the Apache httpd source files and then go on to build the `mod_jk` connector module.

Installing the Apache httpd Source RPMs

To build `mod_jk` from source files, you also need the Apache httpd source files. You can download the source files in the form of an RPM from one of the sites listed in `http://www.redhat.com/download/mirror.html`. Click one of the Distribution links, and then click the folder for the Red Hat Linux version (for example, 8.0). You will find the source RPMs in the SRPMS folder corresponding to your language (en for English) and processor architecture (i386 for Intel). For example, for Red Hat Linux 8.0, I found the source RPM for Apache httpd 2.0.40 in the 8.0/en/os/i386/SRPMS directory of the download site.

The source RPM is about 4.5MB in size. Download it and use the following command to install on your Red Hat Linux system:

```
rpm -ivh httpd-*.rpm
```

After you install the RPM, you find a compressed tar file, as well as several other files, in the /usr/src/redhat/SOURCES directory. For example, for Apache 2.0.40, the source archive is named httpd-2.0.40.tar.gz.

Unpack the file with the following command:

```
tar zxvf httpd-2.0.40.tar.gz
```

This creates a subdirectory named httpd-2.0.40 and places the Apache httpd source files, organized into further subdirectories. Type the following commands to configure the Apache httpd directory:

```
cd httpd-2.0.40
./configure
```

That's all you have to do. To build mod_jk, all you need is the full pathname of the directory where the Apache httpd source files are located. For example, in my case, the directory name is

```
/usr/src/redhat/SOURCES/httpd-2.0.40
```

Building the mod_jk Module

You have to download and build the mod_jk module (also referred to as JK) before you can use Tomcat with the Apache httpd server. Point your Web browser to http://jakarta.apache.org/builds/jakarta-tomcat-connectors/jk/release/ and download the latest source files for JK. For example, for version 1.2.2 of JK, the source file is at http://jakarta.apache.org/builds/jakarta-tomcat-connectors/jk/release/v1.2.2/src/. From this location, I downloaded jakarta-tomcat-connectors-jk-1.2.2-src.tar.gz, which is about 559K in size.

After downloading the source archive, follow these steps to build the mod_jk.so file:

1. Log in as root and copy the file to a suitable directory. I moved it to /usr/local directory with the command:

   ```
   mv jakarta-tomcat-connectors-jk-1.2.2-src.tar.gz /usr/local
   ```

2. Unpack the file in the /usr/local directory by typing commands such as the following:

   ```
   cd /usr/local
   tar zxvf jakarta-tomcat-connectors-jk-1.2.2-src.tar.gz
   ```

   The files are now in /usr/local/jakarta-tomcat-connectors-jk-1.2.2-src directory.

3. Type the following commands:

```
cd jakarta-tomcat-connectors*
cd jk/native
./buildconf.sh
```

This will create a file called `configure` in that directory.

4. Run the `configure` file with the following command:

```
./configure --with-java-home=${JAVA_HOME} --with-
apache=/usr/src/redhat/SOURCES/httpd-2.0.40
```

5. Type the following commands to build `mod_jk.so` module:

```
make
cd apache-2.0
make mod_jk.so
```

6. Type the following command to copy the module to the location where all Apache `httpd` modules are stored:

```
cp mod_jk.so /usr/lib/httpd/modules
```

Now, all you have to do is configure Apache `httpd`, Tomcat, and `mod_jk` to complete the connection between Apache httpd and Tomcat.

Connecting Apache httpd Server to Tomcat

The first step is to configure Tomcat. Edit the `server.xml` file located in the `$CATALINA_HOME/conf` directory (you should define the `CATALINA_HOME` environment variable as the directory where Tomcat is installed). Make the following changes in `$CATALINA_HOME/conf/server.xml`:

♦ Look for a line that begins with `<Server port="8005"`. Add the following directly below that line:

```
<Listener className="org.apache.ajp.tomcat4.config.ApacheConfig"
modJk="/usr/lib/httpd/modules/mod_jk.so" />
```

Make sure that the last pathname matches the directory where you have placed the `mod_jk.so` file.

♦ Locate the line that starts with `<Host name="localhost"`. Add the following immediately after this line:

```
<Listener className="org.apache.ajp.tomcat4.config.ApacheConfig"
append="true" forwardAll="false"
modJk="/usr/lib/httpd/modules/mod_jk.so" />
```

Make sure that the last pathname matches the directory where you have placed the `mod_jk.so` file.

♦ Change the name parameter in the `<Host name="localhost"` line from localhost to whatever name you have used in the `ServerName` directive in the Apache `httpd.conf` file.

Next, edit the Apache `httpd` configuration file—/etc/httpd/conf/httpd.conf—as follows:

♦ Make sure that the name specified with the `ServerName` directive matches the name used in the `<Host name=` line in Tomcat's `server.xml` file.

◆ At the very end of the configuration file, add the following line:

```
Include /usr/local/jakarta-tomcat-4.1.18-LE-jdk14/conf/auto/mod_jk.conf
```

Make sure that the first part of the directory name—/usr/local/jakarta-tomcat-4.1.18-LE-jdk14—matches the definition of the CATALINA_HOME environment variable (the directory where you installed Tomcat).

---

insider insight Everytime Tomcat starts, it creates the mod_jk.conf file referenced in the last line in httpd.conf file. Thus, the configuration of mod_jk module is all done automatically.

The final configuration step is to create the workers.properties file in the $CATALINA_HOME/conf/jk directory (if the directory does not exist, first create it). Here's an example of that file from my installation (the comments tell you what you have to change):

```
# workers.tomcat_home should point to the location where you
# installed Tomcat. Change as necessary.
workers.tomcat_home=/usr/local/jakarta-tomcat-4.1.18-LE-jdk14

# workers.java_home should point to your Java installation. Change
# as needed.
workers.java_home=/usr/java/j2sdk1.4.0_03
ps=/
# Workers to be created
worker.list=ajp13
#
# Define a worker named ajp13 and of type ajp13.
# Note that the name and the type do not have to match.
#
worker.ajp13.port=8009
# Make sure the hostname matches what's in ServerName (httpd.conf)
# and Host name (server.xml). Change if necessary.
worker.ajp13.host=localhost
worker.ajp13.type=ajp13
```

Testing Apache httpd with Tomcat

To test whether Apache httpd is working with Tomcat, perform the following steps:

1. Log in as root and start Tomcat with the following command:
   ```
   cd $CATALINA_HOME/bin
   ./startup.sh
   ```

2. Wait 10 seconds or so for Tomcat to start up.

3. Start Apache httpd with the following command:
   ```
   service httpd start
   ```

4. Open a Web browser on the same system and point the Web browser to the URL http://localhost:8080/examples. You should see the jsp and servlets directory and be able to execute the examples. This shows that Tomcat is working correctly.

5. Now, type the following URL in the Web browser:

`http://localhost/examples`

You should again see the same directories as you did when you connected to port 8080. This shows that Apache `httpd` is correctly handing over the JSP and servlet requests to Tomcat.

Creating a Secure Server with SSL

You have no doubt noticed the URLs that begin with `https://` (instead of the usual `http://`)—those are HTTPS requests that use HTTP together with encryption performed using the SSL. HTTPS requests are commonly used to securely send sensitive information such as your date of birth or a credit card number to a website. The "s" in the protocol name https means that the Web server communicates with your Web browser using HTTP over an SSL connection.

The Apache Web server supports SSL through the `mod_ssl` module that, in turn, relies on the OpenSSL toolkit to perform the encryption function. Red Hat Linux comes with everything you need to turn Apache into a secure server. The configuration file `/etc/httpd/conf.d/ssl.conf` loads the `mod_ssl` module and configures various parameters that mod_ssl needs. You do not have to do anything to the `ssl.conf` configuration file to enable HTTPS support, but you do have to create some additional files required for encryption using SSL.

The same Apache server can handle both HTTP and HTTPS requests because these two protocols use two different ports by default. HTTP uses port 80, whereas HTTPS uses port 443.

The following sections provide an overview of how to create a secure Apache server using SSL. In addition to the simple setup I show in the following sections, there are many different ways to configure SSL. For more information on SSL configuration of Apache, consult the online documentation at `http://httpd.apache.org/docs-2.0/ssl/`.

Secret

Secure Sockets Layer (SSL) is a client/server protocol that enables the client and server to use *public key cryptography* to authenticate each other and exchange a 40-bit or 128-bit shared secret key. That secret key is then used to encrypt and decrypt data sent between the client and the server.

Public key cryptography relies on each party having a key pair—a private key and a public key—that are related in such a way that a message encrypted with one key can only be decrypted with the other. The public and private keys are usually 1,024 bits long. The public keys are available to anyone, while the private key is kept secret, known only to the owner of the key. Then anyone can send a message securely by encrypting the message with the recipient's public key because only the recipient can decrypt the message with the corresponding private key.

A digital certificate, or simply a certificate, associates information about a recipient and the corresponding public key. It's basically a well-defined format so that the public key information can be distributed easily.

continues

continued

The only catch is how do you know that a public key truly belongs to your intended recipient? That's where the certificate authority (CA) comes in. The CA is the trusted third party that verifies the identity of a certificate's owner and assures that the certificate contains the public key and identifying information of that owner.

How does the CA assure the integrity of a certificate? It does so by digitally signing the certificate. The CA creates the digital signature by first computing a message digest—a short fixed-length number from a message from arbitrary length—of the certificate and then encrypting the digest with the CA's private key. Then anyone can verify the authenticity of the certificate by decrypting the digital signature with the CA's public key and computing the message digest again and comparing with what the digest in the CA's signature.

For more information about SSL, visit Netscape's website at `http://developer` `.netscape.com/docs/manuals/security/sslin/contents.htm.`

There are two versions of SSL:

- **SSL v2.0**—This is the original version of SSL protocol, developed by Netscape Communications. This version of SSL uses only RSA keys.
- **SSL v3.0**—A version of the SSL protocol revised to prevent certain security attacks and to support non-RSA keys and certificate chains.

SSL 3.0 is the basis for the Transport Layer Security (TLS) protocol, which is currently being developed by the Internet Engineering Task Force (IETF).

Establishing an SSL session involves a handshake sequence between the client and the server, followed by encrypted data exchange using an agreed upon secret key. The overall sequence has the following key steps:

1. The client sends a client hello message to which the server must respond with a server hello message, or else a fatal error will occur and the connection will fail. The client hello and server hello establish the following attributes: SSL protocol version, a session ID, and the cipher suite—the method to exchange the key, the secret key, and the message digest algorithm to be used to create the message authentication code that ensures integrity.

2. Optionally, the server sends its certificate to the client for authentication. The server may also send a key exchange message, and it may request a certificate from the client. The details of the exchanges between the server and the client depend on the cipher suite selected and whether the client had a digital certificate or not.

3. The client sends a change cipher message and uses the secret key to send an encrypted message indicating it's done.

4. The client and server begin to exchange encrypted data using the secret key.

To support SSL, your Apache server needs a public-private key pair and a digital certificate to provide the public key to any Web browser that connects to the server with a

HTTPS request. Ideally the certificate should be signed by a well-known certificate authority so that anyone coming to your website can trust the certificate. The next section explains how to set up the keys and the certificate.

Generating Digital Certificates

To support SSL, the Apache Web server needs a public-private key pair and a digital certificate with its public key. You can perform these tasks by using the `make` command and the `Makefile` in the `/etc/httpd/conf` directory.

Secret

Before you can use the `Makefile`, you have to remove the keys and certificate that were generated during Apache installation. To remove the key and certificate, type the following commands while logged in as `root`:

```
cd /etc/httpd/conf
rm ssl.key/server.key
rm ssl.crt/server.crt
```

Next, generate the keys by typing the following command:

```
make genkey
```

You should see some output similar to the following that ends with a prompt for a pass phrase:

```
umask 77 ; \
/usr/bin/openssl genrsa -des3 1024 >
/etc/httpd/conf/ssl.key/server.key
Generating RSA private key, 1024 bit long modulus
.......................++++++
.......++++++
e is 65537 (0x10001)
Enter PEM pass phrase:
```

Type a long pass phrase—it can be a sentence with spaces and punctuations—and press Enter. You will be prompted to reenter the pass phrase. The new key is now in the `/etc/httpd/conf/ssl.key/server.key` file.

Generating a Certificate Request

The next step is to generate a certificate request that you can send to a Certificate Authority requesting a signed digital certificate. Typically, you have to pay an annual fee for the CA's services. Verisign, Entrust, Thawte are some of the well-known CAs in the United States. You can find links to other CAs at the PKI Page (`http://www.pki-page.org/`). To generate the certificate request, type:

```
cd /etc/httpd/conf
make certreq
```

You will be prompted for the pass phrase—enter the same pass phrase you typed when creating key. You will also be prompted for the following information:

- **Country name**—Enter the two-letter country code (for example, US for the United States). For the official list of two-letter country codes, consult `http://www.iso.org/iso/en/prods-services/iso3166ma/02iso-3166-code-lists/list-en1.html`.
- **State or province name**—Enter the full name (for example, Maryland).
- **Locality name**—Enter the name of your city or town (for example, North Potomac).
- **Organization name**—Enter the name of your organization.
- **Organization unit name**—Enter the name of division or section where you work (or type anything you want).
- **Common name**—Enter the server's hostname.
- **Email address**—Enter the email address of the person responsible for the server.

When you finish entering this information, the certificate request is created and saved in the file `/etc/httpd/conf/ssl.csr/server.csr`.

---

insider insight

After you create the certificate request, select a CA and visit its website for further instructions on how to send the certificate request and how to pay for the certificate.

After the CA is satisfied about your identity and receives payment for the certificate, it will send the signed certificate back to you by email. You should save the certificate in the file `/etc/httpd/conf/ssl.crt/server.crt` (overwrite the existing file).

Creating a Test Certificate

For the purposes of testing, you can create a self-signed certificate. To generate the test certificate, log in as `root`, and type the following commands:

```
cd /etc/httpd/conf
make testcert
```

You will see output similar to the following:

```
umask 77 ; \
/usr/bin/openssl req -new -key /etc/httpd/conf/ssl.key/server.key -x509 -
days 365 -out /etc/httpd/conf/ssl.crt/server.crt
Using configuration from /usr/share/ssl/openssl.cnf
Enter PEM pass phrase:
```

You have to type the same pass phrase that you used when generating the key. After you enter the pass phrase and press Enter, you have to provide the same set of information that you enter when preparing the certificate request (see the "Generating a Certificate Request" section). Provide the requested information and, at the end, a test certificate should be created and saved in the `/etc/httpd/conf/ssl.crt/server.crt` file.

Testing the Secure Server

After installing a CA-signed certificate or creating a test certificate, you can try out the secure server. Assuming that Apache is already running, log in as `root` and type the following command to restart the server:

```
service httpd restart
```

Because your server key is encrypted, you will be prompted for the pass phrase, like this:

```
Starting httpd: Apache/2.0.40 mod_ssl/2.0.40 (Pass Phrase Dialog)
Some of your private key files are encrypted for security reasons.
In order to read them you have to provide us with the pass phrases.

Server new.host.name:443 (RSA)
Enter pass phrase:
```

Type the pass phrase you used when creating the key and press Enter. The Apache server should now be up and running.

You can now try connecting to the secure server from a Web browser on another PC on the LAN. For example, if the IP address of your Red Hat Linux system (the one running the Apache secure server) is 192.168.0.8, then type the following URL:

```
https://192.168.0.8/
```

Make sure that you type **https** and not **http**. If you are using a test certificate, the browser displays a dialog box explaining that the certificate is from an unknown certificate authority. You can view the certificate and accept it. Because this is only a test, you can accept the certificate, and the Web browser should then show you the home page on your Red Hat Linux system.

Summary

The World Wide Web (WWW or the Web) has propelled the Internet into the mainstream because Web browsers make it easy for users to browse documents stored on various Internet hosts. Whether you run a small business or manage computer systems and networks for a large company, chances are good that you have to set up and maintain a Web server. Because of its built-in networking support, a Red Hat Linux PC makes an affordable Web server. This chapter describes how to configure the Apache Web server on a Red Hat Linux PC.

By reading this chapter, you learned:

♦ The Web is made possible by the standard format for documents and the standard protocol for transferring a document across the network. The document format is HyperText Markup Language, or HTML. The standard document exchange protocol is HyperText Transfer Protocol, or HTTP.

♦ The Web has a client/server architecture, with Web servers providing the HTML documents (often referred to as Web pages) to Web-browser clients.

◆ The Uniform Resource Locator (URL) syntax uniquely identifies Web pages and other network resources. A URL identifies the location of the document (machine name and directory), as well as the protocol to be used to transfer the document (such as HTTP or FTP).

◆ Among Web servers, the most popular is the Apache Web server. You can install the Apache Web server during Red Hat Linux installation. This chapter describes the Apache Web server configuration files and some of the configuration directives.

◆ The Apache Web server is also referred to as the Apache httpd server or simply httpd.

◆ The main Apache httpd configuration file is `/etc/httpd/conf/httpd.conf`. Other configuration files are located in the `/etc/httpd/conf.d` directory, and these configuration files have file names with the `.conf` extension.

◆ You can install Apache Tomcat and the `mod_jk` connector to enable the Apache httpd server to run Java servlets (small Java applications that run on the server and usually provide access to databases or perform some computations and return a HTML document with the results). This chapter showed you the steps to install and configure Apache Tomcat with Apache httpd.

◆ You can set up Apache for secure sockets layer (SSL) support by generating public-private key pair and obtaining a digital certificate signed by a certificate authority. This chapter showed you how to set up the secure server.

Mail Server

Chapter

15

♦ ♦

Secrets in This Chapter

♦ ♦

Electronic mail (email) is the mainstay of the Internet. Email enables you to exchange messages and documents with anyone on the Internet. One of the most common ways people use the Internet is to keep in touch with friends, acquaintances, loved ones, and strangers through email. You can send a message to a friend thousands of miles away and get a reply within a couple of minutes. Essentially, you can send messages anywhere in the world from an Internet host, and that message typically makes its way to its destination within minutes—something you cannot do with paper mail, which is why paper mail is also called snail mail.

Because email can be stored and forwarded, you can arrange to send and receive email without making your Linux system a full-time host on the Internet. You won't get the benefits of nearly immediate delivery of messages, however, if your system is not an Internet host.

This chapter introduces you to the sendmail mail server for transferring mail. You learn about its configuration files and how to use its features to create mailing lists.

Installing Mail Software

During Red Hat Linux installation from this book's companion CD-ROMs, you have the option to install the necessary packages for the email. As described in Chapter 2, select the Mail Server package group when you are prompted for which components to install. The mail readers such as Ximian Evolution and Mozilla Mail come as part of the Graphical Internet package group. The mail readers such as pine and fetchmail are part of the Text Internet package group.

> **cross ref**
> If you install the mail software during Red Hat Linux installation, you do not have to do much more to begin using the mail service. Otherwise, you can use the Red Hat Package Manager (RPM) to install individual packages. Chapter 21 describes how to use the **rpm** program to install new software.

To access the RPM files for mail, mount each CD-ROM with the following command:

```
mount /mnt/cdrom
```

Then, change the directory to /mnt/cdrom/RedHat/RPMS, where you will find the RPM files. Because Red Hat often moves RPMs around on the CDs, please check all the CDs to locate the RPMs. After mounting the CD-ROM at /mnt/cdrom, the RPMs are always in /mnt/cdrom/RedHat/RPMS. Some of the RPMs you may want to install are as follows (I show the RPM name; the actual filename starts with the RPM name, has a version number, and ends with a .rpm extension):

- ◆ fetchmail (a mail retrieval and forwarding utility)
- ◆ imap (an Internet Message Access Protocol server)
- ◆ mailx (a mail-user agent)
- ◆ pine (a versatile mail and news program)
- ◆ procmail (a local mail-delivery package, meant to be invoked directly by sendmail or from a .forward file to process mail automatically; for example, to delete all mail from a specific address)

+ sendmail (a complex mail-transport agent)
+ sendmail-cf (configuration files for sendmail)
+ sendmail-doc (documentation for sendmail)

You probably have already installed many of these packages. For this chapter, you should install sendmail.

---

insider insight

To determine whether **sendmail** is installed on your system, type the following command:

```
rpm -q sendmail
sendmail-8.12.7-4
```

If the output shows **sendmail**, it's installed. In the preceding example, **sendmail** version 8.12 is installed on the system.

Understanding Electronic Mail

Email is one of the most popular services on the Internet. Everyone likes the convenience of being able to communicate without having to play the game of "phone tag," in which two people leave telephone messages for each other without successfully making contact. When you send an email message, it waits in the recipient's mailbox to be read at the recipient's convenience.

Email started as a simple mechanism in which messages were copied to a user's mailbox file. That simple mechanism is still used. In Red Hat Linux, your mail messages are stored in the /var/spool/mail directory, in a text file with the same name as your user name.

Messages are addressed to a user name. That means if John Doe logs in with the user name jdoe, email to him is addressed to jdoe. The only other piece of information needed to identify the recipient uniquely is the fully qualified domain name of the recipient's system. Thus, if John Doe's system is named someplace.com, his complete email address becomes jdoe@someplace.com. Given that address, anyone on the Internet can send email to John Doe.

Red Hat Linux comes with all the software you need to set up and use email on your Linux system. The following sections guide you through various aspects of setting up and using email on your Red Hat Linux system.

Understanding Mail Software

To set up and use email on your Red Hat Linux PC, you need two types of mail software:

+ **Mail User Agent (MUA)**—This software enables you to read your mail messages, write replies, and compose new messages. Typically, the mail-user agent retrieves messages from the mail server by using the POP3 or IMAP4 protocol. POP3 is the Post Office Protocol Version 3, and IMAP4 is the Internet Message Access Protocol Version 4. Red Hat Linux comes with mail-user agents such as pine and Ximian Evolution. Mozilla also includes a mail-user agent and a news-reader, besides the Web browser.

◆ **Mail Transport Agent (MTA)**—This software actually sends and receives mail messages. The exact method used for mail transport depends on the underlying network. In TCP/IP networks, the mail-transport agent delivers mail using the Simple Mail Transfer Protocol (SMTP). Red Hat Linux includes sendmail, a powerful and popular mail-transport agent for TCP/IP networks.

Figure 15-1 shows how the MUAs and MTAs work with one another when Alice sends an email message to Bob.

Figure 15-1: Interactions between MUAs and MTAs When Sending Email.

The scenario in Figure 15-1 is typical of email exchanges. Alice and Bob both connect to the Internet through an ISP and get and send their email through their ISPs. When Alice types a message and sends it, her mail user agent (MUA) sends the message to her ISP's mail transfer agent (MTA) using the Simple Mail Transfer Protocol (SMTP). The sending MTA then sends that message to the receiving MTA—Bob's ISP's MTA—using SMTP. When Bob connects to the Internet, his MUA downloads the message from his ISP's MTA using the POP3 (or IMAP4) protocol. That's the way mail moves around the Internet—from sending MUA to sending MTA to receiving MTA to receiving MUA.

Secret

Most mail-transport agents run as daemons, background processes that run as long as your system is up. Because you or another user on the system might send mail at any time, the transport agent has to be there to deliver the mail to its destination. The mail-user agent runs only when the user starts the mail reader and wants to check mail.

Typically, a mail-transport agent is started after the system boots. The system startup files for Red Hat Linux are configured so that the sendmail mail-transport agent starts when the system is in multiuser mode. The shell script file /etc/init.d/sendmail starts sendmail.

Because the system is already set up to start sendmail at boot time, all you have to do is use an appropriate sendmail configuration file to get email going on your Red Hat Linux system.

Learning More about sendmail

This chapter shows you how to use a predefined sendmail configuration file to get email going on your system. sendmail, however, is a very complex mail system. *sendmail, 3rd Edition* by Bryan Costales with Eric Allman (O'Reilly & Associates, December 2002) will help you learn to configure sendmail.

You should also visit http://www.sendmail.org/ and http://www.sendmail.net/ for a thorough description of sendmail features and configuration examples.

cross ref
For answers to commonly asked questions about **sendmail** or to ask a question yourself, visit the newsgroup comp.mail.sendmail (see Chapter 16 for more on reading newsgroups and posting articles to them).

Using sendmail

To set up your system as a mail server, you must configure the sendmail mail-transport agent properly and start the sendmail server. If you installed sendmail, it should already be configured to run when you boot Red Hat Linux. To check if this is true, type the following command:

```
chkconfig --list sendmail
sendmail        0:off   1:off   2:on    3:on    4:on    5:on    6:off
```

The output shows whether sendmail is turned on or off for each of the run levels from 1 through 6 (consult Chapter 20 to learn more about run levels). If sendmail is configured to run automatically, you should see it set to on for at least the run levels 3 and 5. If it's off for all run levels, type the following command to turn it on:

```
chkconfig --level 35 sendmail on
```

To restart sendmail after making changes to configuration files, type the following command:

```
service sendmail restart
```

sendmail has the reputation of being a complex but complete mail-delivery system. If you take a quick look at sendmail's configuration file, `/etc/mail/sendmail.cf`, you'll immediately agree that sendmail is indeed complex. Luckily, you do not have to be an expert on the sendmail configuration file (a whole book has been written on that subject; see the "Learning More about sendmail" section). All you need is one of the predefined configuration files from this book's companion CD-ROMs.

Secret

Your system should already have a working sendmail configuration file—`/etc/mail/sendmail.cf`. The default file assumes you have an Internet connection and a name server. Provided you have an Internet connection, you should be able to send and receive email from your Red Hat Linux PC.

To ensure that mail delivery works correctly, your system's name must match the system name your ISP has assigned to you. Although you can give your system any hostname you want, other systems can successfully deliver mail to your system only if your system's name is in the ISP's name server.

Testing Mail Delivery

I have been able to send and receive email immediately after installing Red Hat Linux because sendmail is installed as part of the basic operating system package. To try out the sendmail mail-transfer agent, I have used the `mail` command to compose and send a mail message to myself at a different address, as follows:

```
mail naba@comcast.net
Subject: Testing email
This is from my Red Hat Linux system.
.
Cc: Press Ctrl+D
```

The `mail` command is a simple mail-user agent. In the preceding example, I specify the addressee—`naba@comcast.net`—in the command line. The mail program prompts me for a subject line. Following the subject, I enter my message and end it with a line that contains only a period. After I end the message, the mail-user agent passes the message to sendmail—the mail-transport agent—for delivery to the specified address. Because my system is already connected to the Internet, sendmail delivers the mail message immediately.

To verify the delivery of mail, I check my ISP mail account and I also send a short reply. (You cannot send a reply if your system does not have a hostname in the ISP's DNS database.) I can then read the reply on the Red Hat Linux PC by using the `mail` command.

Thus, the initial sendmail configuration file that comes with Red Hat Linux should be adequate for sending and receiving email, provided that your Red Hat Linux system has an Internet connection and a registered domain name.

Understanding the Mail-Delivery Mechanism

On an Internet host, the sendmail mail-transport agent delivers mail using the Simple Mail Transfer Protocol (SMTP). SMTP is documented in RFC 821, "Simple Mail Transfer Protocol," by Jonathan Postel, 1982.

SMTP-based mail-transport agents listen to the TCP port 25 and use a small set of text commands to interact with other mail-transport agents. In fact, the commands are simple enough that you can use them directly to send a mail message. The following example shows how I use SMTP commands to send a mail message to my account on the Linux PC from a Telnet session running on the same system:

```
telnet localhost 25
Trying 127.0.0.1...
Connected to localhost.
Escape character is '^]'.
220 dhcppc6.naba.com ESMTP Sendmail 8.12.7/8.12.7; Sun, 16 Feb 2003
11:44:19 -000
help
214-2.0.0 This is sendmail version 8.12.7
214-2.0.0 Topics:
214-2.0.0      HELO    EHLO    MAIL    RCPT    DATA
214-2.0.0      RSET    NOOP    QUIT    HELP    VRFY
214-2.0.0      EXPN    VERB    ETRN    DSN     AUTH
214-2.0.0      STARTTLS
214-2.0.0 For more info use "HELP <topic>".
214-2.0.0 To report bugs in the implementation send email to
214-2.0.0      sendmail-bugs@sendmail.org.
214-2.0.0 For local information send email to Postmaster at your site.
214 2.0.0 End of HELP info
HELP DATA
214-2.0.0 DATA
214-2.0.0      Following text is collected as the message.
214-2.0.0      End with a single dot.
214 2.0.0 End of HELP info
HELO localhost
250 dhcppc6.naba.com Hello localhost.localdomain [127.0.0.1], pleased to
meet you
MAIL FROM: naba
553 5.5.4 naba... Domain name required for sender address naba
MAIL FROM: naba@localhost
250 2.1.0 naba@localhost... Sender ok
RCPT TO: naba
250 2.1.5 naba... Recipient ok
DATA
354 Enter mail, end with "." on a line by itself
Testing... 1 2 3
Sending mail by telnet to port 25
.
250 2.0.0 h0BIAs8E004713 Message accepted for delivery
quit
221 2.0.0 dhcppc6.naba.com closing connection
Connection closed by foreign host.
```

The `telnet` command opens a Telnet session on port 25—the port on which sendmail expects SMTP commands. The sendmail server on the Red Hat Linux system immediately replies with an announcement.

I type **HELP** to view a list of SMTP commands. To get help on a specific command, I can type **HELP** *commandname*. The listing shows the help information sendmail prints when I type HELP DATA.

I type **HELO localhost** to initiate a session with the host. The sendmail process replies with a greeting. To send the mail message, I start with the MAIL FROM: command that specifies the sender of the message (I enter the user name on the system from which I am sending the message). sendmail requires a domain name along with the user name.

Next, I type the RCPT TO: command to specify the recipient of the message. If I want to send the message to several recipients, all I have to do is provide each recipient's address with the RCPT TO: command.

To enter the mail message, I type the DATA command. In response to the DATA command, sendmail displays an instruction that I should end the message with a period on a line by itself. I enter the message and end it with a single period on a separate line. The sendmail process displays a message indicating that the message has been accepted for delivery. Finally, I quit the sendmail session by typing the QUIT command.

Afterward, I log in to my Red Hat Linux system and check mail with the mail command. The following is what I see when I display the mail message I have sent through the sample SMTP session with sendmail:

```
mail
Mail version 8.1 6/6/93.  Type ? for help.
"/var/spool/mail/naba": 1 message 1 new
>N  1 naba@dhcppc6.naba.co  Sun Feb 16 13:14  12/454
& 1
Message 1:
From naba@dhcppc6.naba.com  Sun Feb 16 13:14:07 2003
Date: Sun Feb 16 2003 13:10:54 -0500
From: Naba Barkakati <naba@dhcppc6.naba.com>

Testing... 1 2 3
Sending mail by telnet to port 25

& q
Saved 1 message in mbox
```

As this example shows, the SMTP commands are simple enough to understand. This example should help you understand how a mail-transfer agent uses SMTP to transfer mail on the Internet. Of course, this whole process is automated by email programs and the sendmail program (through settings in the sendmail configuration file /etc/mail/sendmail.cf).

Learning the sendmail Configuration File

You don't need to understand everything in the sendmail configuration file, /etc/mail/sendmail.cf, but you should know how that file is created. That way, you can make minor changes if necessary and regenerate the /etc/mail/sendmail.cf file.

Secret

To be able to regenerate the sendmail.cf file, you have to install the `sendmail-cf` package. To check whether the sendmail-cf package is installed, type **rpm -q send-mail-cf**. If the command does not print the name of the sendmail-cf package, you have to install the package. This RPM file is in one of the CD-ROMs bundled with this book. To install that package, log in as `root` and mount the CD-ROM with the following command:

```
mount /mnt/cdrom
```

Then change to the `/mnt/cdrom/RedHat/RPMS` directory and install the package by using the following code:

```
cd /mnt/cdrom/RedHat/RPMS
rpm -ivh sendmail-cf*
```

The sendmail-cf package installs in the `/usr/share/sendmail-cf` directory all the files needed to generate a new sendmail.cf configuration file. As you learn in the next few sections, the `sendmail.cf` file is generated from a number of m4 macro files. These macro files are organized into a number of subdirectories under `/usr/share/sendmail-cf`. You can read the `README` file in `/usr/share/sendmail-cf` to learn more about the creation of sendmail configuration files.

While you're at it, you can also install the sendmail documentation from the sendmail-doc package. To install that RPM, type the following command:

```
rpm -ivh sendmail-doc*
```

The sendmail-doc package installs a number of documentation files in the `/usr/share/doc/sendmail` directory of your system. You can find a Sendmail Installation and Operation Guide in a PostScript file, `/usr/share/doc/sendmail/doc/op/op.ps`. To run kghostview, select Main Menu⇨Graphics⇨More Graphics Applications⇨ PS/PDF Viewer. Then, open the file `/usr/share/doc/sendmail/doc/op/op.ps`).

Now that you have taken care of the prerequisites, you can learn how to regenerate the `sendmail.cf` file.

Using the m4 Macro Processor

The m4 macro processor is used to generate the `sendmail.cf` configuration file, which comes with the sendmail package in Red Hat Linux. The main macro file, `sendmail.mc`, is included with the sendmail package, but that file needs other m4 macro files that are in the sendmail-cf package. To be able to process the `sendmail.mc` file, you have to install the sendmail-cf package, as explained in the previous section. This section introduces you to the m4 macro processor.

A *macro* is a symbolic name for some action or a long string of characters. A macro processor such as m4 usually reads its input file and copies it to the output, processing the macros along the way. The processing of a macro generally involves performing some action and generating some output. Because a macro generates a lot more text in the output than merely the macro's name, the processing of macros is referred to as macro expansion.

cross
ref

The m4 macro processor is the GNU implementation of the standard UNIX macro processor. Only a few simple m4 macros are described in this section, but there is much more to m4 than the simple examples shown here. It's essentially a new scripting language for generating configuration files. You can read the online manual about m4 by typing the command `info m4` at a shell prompt. Chapter 23 describes how to read online help by using `info`.

Secret

Note that m4 is stream based (like the sed editor, described in Chapter 8). That means it copies the input characters to the output, while expanding any macros. The m4 macro processor does not have any concept of lines, so it copies newline characters to the output. That's why you see the word `dnl` in most m4 macro files; `dnl` is an m4 macro that stands for *delete through newline*. The `dnl` macro deletes all characters starting at the dnl up to and including the next newline character. The newline characters in the output don't cause any harm; they merely create unnecessary blank lines. The `sendmail` macro package uses `dnl` to avoid such blank lines in the output configuration file. Because `dnl` basically means delete everything up to the end of the line, m4 macro files also use `dnl` as the prefix for comment lines.

To see a very simple use of m4, consider the following m4 macro file that defines two macros—`hello` and `bye`—and uses them in a form letter:

```
dnl #############################################
dnl #  File: ex.m4
dnl #  A simple example of m4 macros
dnl #############################################
define(`hello', `Dear Sir/Madam')dnl
define(`bye',
`Sincerely,


Customer Service')dnl
dnl Now type the letter and use the macros
hello,

This is to inform you that we received your recent inquiry.
We will respond to your question soon.

bye
```

Type this text using your favorite text editor, and save it in a file named `ex.m4`. You can name a macro file anything you like, but it is customary to use the `.m4` extension for m4 macro files.

Before you process the macro file by using m4, note the following key points the preceding example illustrates:

◆ Use the `dnl` macro to start all the comment lines (for example, the first four lines in the example).

◆ End each macro definition with the `dnl` macro. Otherwise, when m4 processes the macro file, it produces a blank line for each macro definition.

♦ Use the built-in m4 command `define` to define a new macro. The macro name and the value are both enclosed between a pair of left and right quotes (`` ` ``...'). Note that you cannot use the plain single quote to enclose the macro name and definition.

Now process the macro file `ex.m4` by using m4 as follows:

```
m4 ex.m4
Dear Sir/Madam,

This is to inform you that we received your recent inquiry.
We will respond to your question soon.

Sincerely,


Customer Service
```

As you can see, m4 prints the form letter on standard output, expanding the macros `hello` and `bye` into their defined values. If you want to save the form letter in a file called `letter`, use the shell's output redirection feature, like this:

```
m4 ex.m4 > letter
```

What if you want to use the word `hello` or `bye` in the letter without expanding them? You can do so by enclosing these macros in a pair of left- and right-quotes (`` ` ``...'). You have to do this for other predefined m4 macros, such as `define`. To use define as a plain word, not as a macro to expand, write `` `define' ``.

sendmail.mc file

The simple example in the preceding section should give you an idea of how m4 macros are defined and used to create configuration files such as the `sendmail.cf` file. Essentially, many complex macros are written and stored in files in the `/usr/share/sendmail-cf` directory. A top-level macro file, `sendmail.mc`, described later in this section, brings in these macro files with the include macro (used to copy a file into the input stream).

By defining its own set of high-level macros in files located in the `/usr/share/sendmail-cf` directory, sendmail essentially creates its own macro language. The sendmail macro files use the `.mc` extension. The primary sendmail macro file you should configure is `sendmail.mc`, located in the `/etc/mail` directory.

Unlike the `/etc/mail/sendmail.cf` file, the `/etc/mail/sendmail.mc` file is short and should be easier to work with. Here is the full listing of the `/etc/mail/sendmail.mc` file that comes with Red Hat Linux:

```
divert(-1)dnl
dnl #
dnl # This is the sendmail macro config file for m4. If you make changes to
dnl # /etc/mail/sendmail.mc, you will need to regenerate the
dnl # /etc/mail/sendmail.cf file by confirming that the sendmail-cf package is
dnl # installed and then performing a
dnl #
dnl #     make -C /etc/mail
dnl #
```

```
include(`/usr/share/sendmail-cf/m4/cf.m4')dnl
VERSIONID(`setup for Red Hat Linux')dnl
OSTYPE(`linux')dnl
dnl #
dnl # Uncomment and edit the following line if your outgoing mail needs to
dnl # be sent out through an external mail server:
dnl #
dnl define(`SMART_HOST',`smtp.your.provider')
dnl #
define(`confDEF_USER_ID',``8:12'')dnl
dnl define(`confAUTO_REBUILD')dnl
define(`confTO_CONNECT', `1m')dnl
define(`confTRY_NULL_MX_LIST',true)dnl
define(`confDONT_PROBE_INTERFACES',true)dnl
define(`PROCMAIL_MAILER_PATH',`/usr/bin/procmail')dnl
define(`ALIAS_FILE', `/etc/aliases')dnl
dnl define(`STATUS_FILE', `/etc/mail/statistics')dnl
define(`UUCP_MAILER_MAX', `2000000')dnl
define(`confUSERDB_SPEC', `/etc/mail/userdb.db')dnl
define(`confPRIVACY_FLAGS', `authwarnings,novrfy,noexpn,restrictqrun')dnl
define(`confAUTH_OPTIONS', `A')dnl
dnl #
dnl # The following allows relaying if the user authenticates, and disallows
dnl # plaintext authentication (PLAIN/LOGIN) on non-TLS links
dnl #
dnl define(`confAUTH_OPTIONS', `A p')dnl
dnl #
dnl # PLAIN is the preferred plaintext authentication method and used by
dnl # Mozilla Mail and Evolution, though Outlook Express and other MUAs do
dnl # use LOGIN. Other mechanisms should be used if the connection is not
dnl # guaranteed secure.
dnl #
dnl TRUST_AUTH_MECH(`EXTERNAL DIGEST-MD5 CRAM-MD5 LOGIN PLAIN')dnl
dnl define(`confAUTH_MECHANISMS', `EXTERNAL GSSAPI DIGEST-MD5 CRAM-MD5 LOGIN PLA
IN')dnl
dnl #
dnl # Rudimentary information on creating certificates for sendmail TLS:
dnl #     make -C /usr/share/ssl/certs usage
dnl #
dnl define(`confCACERT_PATH',`/usr/share/ssl/certs')
dnl define(`confCACERT',`/usr/share/ssl/certs/ca-bundle.crt')
dnl define(`confSERVER_CERT',`/usr/share/ssl/certs/sendmail.pem')
dnl define(`confSERVER_KEY',`/usr/share/ssl/certs/sendmail.pem')
dnl #
dnl # This allows sendmail to use a keyfile that is shared with OpenLDAP's
dnl # slapd, which requires the file to be readable by group ldap
dnl #
dnl define(`confDONT_BLAME_SENDMAIL',`groupreadablekeyfile')dnl
dnl #
dnl define(`confTO_QUEUEWARN', `4h')dnl
dnl define(`confTO_QUEUERETURN', `5d')dnl
dnl define(`confQUEUE_LA', `12')dnl
```

```
dnl define(`confREFUSE_LA', `18')dnl
define(`confTO_IDENT', `0')dnl
dnl FEATURE(delay_checks)dnl
FEATURE(`no_default_msa',`dnl')dnl
FEATURE(`smrsh',`/usr/sbin/smrsh')dnl
FEATURE(`mailertable',`hash -o /etc/mail/mailertable.db')dnl
FEATURE(`virtusertable',`hash -o /etc/mail/virtusertable.db')dnl
FEATURE(redirect)dnl
FEATURE(always_add_domain)dnl
FEATURE(use_cw_file)dnl
FEATURE(use_ct_file)dnl
dnl #
dnl # The -t option will retry delivery if e.g. the user runs over his quota.
dnl #
FEATURE(local_procmail,`',`procmail -t -Y -a $h -d $u')dnl
FEATURE(`access_db',`hash -T<TMPF> -o /etc/mail/access.db')dnl
FEATURE(`blacklist_recipients')dnl
EXPOSED_USER(`root')dnl
dnl #
dnl # The following causes sendmail to only listen on the IPv4 loopback address
dnl # 127.0.0.1 and not on any other network devices. Remove the loopback
dnl # address restriction to accept email from the internet or intranet.
dnl #
DAEMON_OPTIONS(`Port=smtp,Addr=127.0.0.1, Name=MTA')dnl
dnl #
dnl # The following causes sendmail to additionally listen to port 587 for
dnl # mail from MUAs that authenticate. Roaming users who can't reach their
dnl # preferred sendmail daemon due to port 25 being blocked or redirected find
dnl # this useful.
dnl #
dnl DAEMON_OPTIONS(`Port=submission, Name=MSA, M=Ea')dnl
dnl #
dnl # The following causes sendmail to additionally listen to port 465, but
dnl # starting immediately in TLS mode upon connecting. Port 25 or 587 followed
dnl # by STARTTLS is preferred, but roaming clients using Outlook Express can't
dnl # do STARTTLS on ports other than 25. Mozilla Mail can ONLY use STARTTLS
dnl # and doesn't support the deprecated smtps; Evolution <1.1.1 uses smtps
dnl # when SSL is enabled-- STARTTLS support is available in version 1.1.1.
dnl #
dnl # For this to work your OpenSSL certificates must be configured.
dnl #
dnl DAEMON_OPTIONS(`Port=smtps, Name=TLSMTA, M=s')dnl
dnl #
dnl # The following causes sendmail to additionally listen on the IPv6 loopback
dnl # device. Remove the loopback address restriction listen to the network.
dnl #
dnl # NOTE: binding both IPv4 and IPv6 daemon to the same port requires
dnl #       a kernel patch
dnl #
dnl DAEMON_OPTIONS(`port=smtp,Addr=::1, Name=MTA-v6, Family=inet6')dnl
dnl #
dnl # We strongly recommend not accepting unresolvable domains if you want to
```

```
dnl # protect yourself from spam. However, the laptop and users on computers
dnl # that do not have 24x7 DNS do need this.
dnl #
FEATURE(`accept_unresolvable_domains')dnl
dnl #
dnl FEATURE(`relay_based_on_MX')dnl
dnl #
dnl # Also accept email sent to "localhost.localdomain" as local email.
dnl #
LOCAL_DOMAIN(`localhost.localdomain')dnl
dnl #
dnl # The following example makes mail from this host and any additional
dnl # specified domains appear to be sent from mydomain.com
dnl #
dnl MASQUERADE_AS(`mydomain.com')dnl
dnl #
dnl # masquerade not just the headers, but the envelope as well
dnl #
dnl FEATURE(masquerade_envelope)dnl
dnl #
dnl # masquerade not just @mydomainalias.com, but @*.mydomainalias.com as well
dnl #
dnl FEATURE(masquerade_entire_domain)dnl
dnl #
dnl MASQUERADE_DOMAIN(localhost)dnl
dnl MASQUERADE_DOMAIN(localhost.localdomain)dnl
dnl MASQUERADE_DOMAIN(mydomainalias.com)dnl
dnl MASQUERADE_DOMAIN(mydomain.lan)dnl
MAILER(smtp)dnl
MAILER(procmail)dnl
```

As the comments (the lines that begin with `dnl`) in the beginning of the file explain, you can generate the `/etc/mail/sendmail.cf` file by running the `sendmail.mc` file through the m4 macro processor with the following command (you have to log in as `root`):

```
m4 /etc/mail/sendmail.mc > /etc/mail/sendmail.cf
```

The comments also tell you that you need the sendmail-cf package to process this file.

From the previous section's description of m4 macros, you can see that the `sendmail.mc` file uses define to create new macros. You can also see the liberal use of `dnl` to avoid inserting too many blank lines into the output.

The other uppercase words such as `OSTYPE`, `FEATURE`, and `MAILER` are sendmail macros. These are defined in the `.m4` files located in the subdirectories of the `/usr/share/sendmail-cf` directory and are incorporated into the `sendmail.mc` file with the following include macro:

```
include(`/usr/share/sendmail-cf/m4/cf.m4')
```

The `/usr/share/sendmail-cf/m4/cf.m4` file, in turn, includes the `cfhead.m4` file, which includes other m4 files, and so on. The net effect is that, as the m4 macro processor processes the `sendmail.mc` file, the macro processor incorporates many m4 files from various subdirectories of `/usr/share/sendmail-cf`.

Note the following key points about the `/etc/mail/sendmail.mc` file:

- The `VERSIONID(`linux setup for Red Hat Linux')` macro inserts the version information enclosed in quotes into the output.

- `OSTYPE(`linux')` specifies Linux as the operating system. You have to specify this early to ensure proper configuration. It is customary to place this macro right after the VERSIONID macro.

- `MAILER(smtp)` describes the mailer. According to the `/usr/share/sendmail-cf/README` file, MAILER, declarations should always be placed at the end of the `sendmail.mc` file, and `MAILER(`smtp')` should always precede `MAILER` `(`procmail')`. The mailer `smtp` refers to the SMTP mailer.

- `FEATURE` macros request various special features. For example, `FEATURE` `(`blacklist_recipients')` turns on the capability to block incoming mail for certain user names, hosts, or addresses. The specification for what mail to allow or refuse is placed in the access database (`/etc/mail/access.db` file). You also need the `FEATURE(`access_db')` macro to turn on the access database.

- `MASQUERADE_AS(`mydomain.com')` causes sendmail to label outgoing mail as having come from the host `mydomain.com` (replace this with your domain name). The idea is for a large organization to set up a single sendmail server that handles the mail for many subdomains and makes everything appear to come from a single domain (for example, mail from many departments in a University would appear to come from the University's main domain name).

- `MASQUERADE_DOMAIN(subdomain.mydomain.com)` instructs sendmail to send mail from an address such as `user@subdomain.mydomain.com` as having originated from the same user name at the domain specified by the MASQUERADE_AS macro.

---

insider insight

The sendmail macros such as FEATURE and MAILER are described in the `/usr/share/sendmail-cf/README` file. Consult that file to learn more about the **sendmail** macros before you make changes to the `sendmail.mc` file.

Learning the sendmail.cf File Syntax

The `sendmail.cf` file's syntax is designed to be easy to parse by the sendmail program because sendmail reads this file whenever it starts. Human readability was not a primary consideration when the file's syntax was designed. Still, with a little explanation, you can understand the meaning of the control lines in `sendmail.cf`.

Secret

Each sendmail control line begins with a single-letter operator that defines the meaning of the rest of the line. A line that begins with a space or a tab is considered a continuation of the previous line. Blank lines and lines beginning with a pound sign (#) are comments.

continues

continued

Often, there is no space between the single-letter operator and the arguments that follow the operator. This makes the lines even harder to understand. For example, `sendmail.cf` uses the concept of a class—essentially a collection of phrases. You can define a class named P and add the phrase `REDIRECT` to that class with the following control line:

```
CPREDIRECT
```

Because everything is jumbled together, it's hard to decipher. On the other hand, to define a class named `Accept` and set it to the values `OK` and `RELAY`, write the following:

```
C{Accept}OK RELAY
```

This may be slightly easier to understand because the delimiters (such as the class name, `Accept`) are enclosed in curly braces.

Other more recent control lines are even easier to understand. For example, the line

```
O HelpFile=/etc/mail/helpfile
```

defines the option `HelpFile` as the filename `/etc/mail/helpfile`. That file contains help information sendmail uses when it receives a `HELP` command.

Table 15-1 summarizes the one-letter control operators used in `sendmail.cf`. Each entry also shows an example of that operator. This table should help you understand some of the lines in `sendmail.cf`.

Table 15-1: Control Operators Used in sendmail.cf

Operator	Description
C	Defines a class; a variable (think of it as a set) that can contain several values. For example, `Cwlocalhost` adds the name `localhost` to the class w.
D	Defines a macro, a name associated with a single value. For example, `DnMAILER-DAEMON` defines the macro n as `MAILER-DAEMON`.
F	Defines a class read from a file. For example, `Fw/etc/mail/local-host-names` reads the names of hosts from the file `/etc/mail/local-host-names` and adds them to the class w.
H	Defines the format of header lines that sendmail inserts into a message. For example, `H?P?Return-Path: <$g>` defines the `Return-Path:` field of the header.
K	Defines a map (a key-value pair database). For example, `Karith arith` defines the map named `arith` as the compiled-in map of the same name.
M	Specifies a mailer. The following lines define the `procmail` mailer:`Mprocmail, P=/usr/bin/procmail,F=DFMSPhnu9,S=EnvFromSMTP/HdrFromSMTP, R=EnvToSMTP/HdrFromSMTP,T=DNS/RFC822/X-Unix, A=procmail -Y -m $h $f $u`

Operator	Description
O	Assigns a value to an option. For example, O AliasFile=/etc/aliases defines the AliasFile option to /etc/aliases, which is the name of the sendmail alias file.
P	Defines values for the precedence field. For example, Pjunk=-100 sets to -100 the precedence of messages marked with the header field Precedence: junk.
R	Defines a rule (a rule has a left-hand side and a right-hand side; if input matches the left-hand side, it's replaced with the right-hand side—this is called rewriting). For example, the rewriting rule R$* ; $1 strips trailing semicolons.
S	Labels a ruleset you can start defining with subsequent R control lines. For example, Scanonify=3 labels the next ruleset as canonify or ruleset 3.
T	Adds a user name to the trusted class (class t). For example, Troot adds root to the class of trusted users.
V	Defines the major version number of the configuration file. For example, V10/Berkeley defines the version number as 10.

Exploring Other sendmail Files

The /etc/mail directory contains other files that sendmail uses. These files are referenced in the sendmail configuration file, /etc/mail/sendmail.cf. For example, here's the result of searching for the /etc/mail string in the /etc/mail/sendmail.cf file:

```
grep "\/etc\/mail" /etc/mail/sendmail.cf
Fw/etc/mail/local-host-names
FR-o /etc/mail/relay-domains
Kmailertable hash -o /etc/mail/mailertable.db
Kvirtuser hash -o /etc/mail/virtusertable.db
Kaccess hash -T<TMPF> -o /etc/mail/access.db
#O ErrorHeader=/etc/mail/error-header
O HelpFile=/etc/mail/helpfile
O StatusFile=/etc/mail/statistics
O UserDatabaseSpec=/etc/mail/userdb.db
#O ServiceSwitchFile=/etc/mail/service.switch
#O DefaultAuthInfo=/etc/mail/default-auth-info
Ft/etc/mail/trusted-users
```

You can ignore the lines that begin with a hash mark or number sign (#) because sendmail treats those lines as comments. The other lines are sendmail control lines that refer to other files in the /etc/mail directory.

Secret

Following are brief descriptions of files in the `/etc/mail` directory that are referenced in the `sendmail` configuration file (note that not all of these files need to be present in your `/etc/mail` directory and even when present, the file may be empty):

- **/etc/mail/access**—Access list database to stop spam (unwanted mail)
- **/etc/mail/helpfile**—Help information for SMTP commands
- **/etc/mail/local-host-names**—List of alternate names for this host (the list is usually the domains for which this sendmail server accepts mail)
- **/etc/mail/mailertable**—Table that specifies routing of email for specific domains
- **/etc/mail/relay-domains**—Domains for which sendmail allows relaying (relaying refers to the process of sending mail to others by using your sendmail server as an intermediary)
- **/etc/mail/userdb.db**—User database file that specifies where a user receives incoming email
- **/etc/mail/virtusertable**—Database of incoming users

The next few sections briefly describe a few of these sendmail configuration files in the `/etc/mail` directory.

Preparing the User Database

The user database helps sendmail deliver incoming mail when there is no centralized mail server. For example, suppose mail addressed to `jdoe@someplace.net` should really be sent to `jd@home.someplace.net`. This involves identifying a user's *maildrop*—the location where a user receives mail—to sendmail. You can accomplish this task by creating the user database.

sendmail expects the user database in a binary file `/etc/mail/userdb.db` in the Berkeley database format. Follow these steps to create the binary user database file:

1. Edit the text file `/etc/mail/userdb` and add lines for each user for whom you need to identify a maildrop location. The lines look like this:

   ```
   loginname:mailname      emailname@someplace.net
   emailname:maildrop      loginname@home
   ```

2. Convert the text file `/etc/mail/userdb` into a Berkeley database file that sendmail can use by running the `makemap` with the following command:

   ```
   makemap btree /etc/mail/userdb < /etc/mail/userdb
   ```

   This creates the database file `/etc/mail/userdb.db` from the text file `/etc/mail/userdb`.

caution You must remember to run `makemap` **every time you change** `/etc/mail/userdb`, otherwise sendmail will not be using your latest user database when sending mail.

Preparing the Mailer Table

The mailer table database specifies how to route email messages destined for specific domains. You specify these mail routings in a text file `/etc/mail/mailertable`. For example, suppose all mail meant for the mydomain.net should be sent to the host mailhost.mydomain.net. You can specify this with the following entry in /etc/mail/mailertable:

```
.mydomain.net          smtp:mailhost.mydomain.net
```

The left-hand side of each line is a domain name. The right-hand side is of the form mailer:host, where mailer is a mail transfer agent and host is the hostname to be provided to that mailer.

After editing the text file /etc/mail/mailertable, you have to convert it into a binary database by running makemap with the following command:

```
makemap hash /etc/mail/mailertable < /etc/mail/mailertable
```

Preparing the Access Database

The access database causes sendmail to accept or refuse mail from specified domains and also control the behavior of sendmail in various situations. The database is a list of names (user names, hostnames, or network addresses) and codes that specify the action sendmail performs.

Secret

You can use the access database to stop spam (unsolicited email). You prepare the access database by editing the text file /etc/mail/access. Like other sendmail databases, each line in that file has two fields. On each line, the left-hand side is an email address, a domain name, or an IP address (IPv6 addresses have to be prefixed with Ipv6:). The right-hand side is typically a code that specifies what sendmail should do.

Here is an example of a /etc/mail/access file:

```
spammer@somewhere.net          DISCARD
spam.com                       REJECT
mybuddy.com                    RELAY
192.168.15                     REJECT
IPv6:2002:c0a8:02c5            REJECT
some.unresolvable.domain.net   OK
junkmail.com                   ERROR:550 "Junk mail not allowed"
```

The codes on the right-hand side tell sendmail what to do for each case. For example, all messages from spammer@somewhere.net are discarded without any error message. On the other hand, when the action is REJECT, sendmail rejects the email with a general message. You can even use the access database to accept messages even when some errors occur. In this example, the OK keyword causes sendmail to accept messages from some.unresolvable.domain.net even though DNS could not translate that domain name to an IP address.

After editing the text file /etc/mail/access, you must convert it to a binary database with the following command:

```
makemap hash /etc/mail/access < /etc/mail/access
```

Using the .forward File

Users can redirect their own mail by placing a .forward file in their home directory. The .forward file is a plaintext file with a comma-separated list of mail addresses. Any mail sent to the user is then forwarded to these addresses. If the .forward file contains a single address, all email for that user is redirected to that single email address. For example, suppose that the following .forward file is placed in the home directory of a user named emily:

```
ashley
```

All email addressed to emily is automatically sent to the user name ashley on the same system. User emily does not receive mail at all.

You can also forward to a user name on another system by listing the complete email address. For example, I have added a .forward file with the following line to send my messages (addressed to my user name, naba) to the mail address naba@comcast.net:

```
naba@comcast.net
```

Now, suppose I want to keep a copy of the message on this system, in addition to forwarding to the address naba@comcast.net. I can do so by adding the following line to the .forward file:

```
naba@comcast.net, naba\
```

I simply append my user name and end the line with a backslash. The backslash (\) at the end of the line stops sendmail from repeatedly forwarding the message (because when a copy is sent to my user name on the system, sendmail processes my .forward file again—the backslash tells sendmail not to forward the message repeatedly).

Secret

Another use of the .forward file is to run procmail to handle some mail messages automatically. For example, suppose that you want to delete any email message that comes from an address containing the string mailing_list. Here's what you do to achieve that:

1. Create a .forward file in your home directory, and place the following line in it:
   ```
   "| /usr/bin/procmail"
   ```

   This line causes sendmail to run the external program /usr/bin/procmail and to send the email messages to the input stream of that program.

2. Create a text file named .procmailrc in your home directory, and place the following lines in that file:
   ```
   # Delete mail from an address that contains mailing_list
   :0
   * ^From:.*mailing_list
   /dev/null
   ```

3. Log in as root and set up a symbolic link in /etc/smrsh to the /usr/bin/procmail program with the following command:
   ```
   ln -s /usr/bin/procmail /etc/smrsh/procmail
   ```

This step is necessary because sendmail uses the SendMail Restricted Shell—smrsh—to run external programs. Instead of running `/usr/bin/procmail`, smrsh runs `/etc/smrsh/procmail`. That's why you need the symbolic link. This is a security feature of sendmail that controls what external programs it can run.

That's it! Now if you receive any messages from an address containing `mailing_list`, the message will be deleted.

insider insight

With procmail, you can perform other chores, such as automatically storing messages in a file or forwarding messages to others. All you have to do is create an appropriate `.procmailrc` file in your home directory. To learn more about procmail, type `man procmail`; to see examples of .procmailrc, type `man procmailex`.

Understanding the sendmail Alias File

In addition to the `sendmail.cf` file, sendmail also consults an alias file named `/etc/aliases` to convert a name into an address. The location of the alias file appears in the `sendmail` configuration file.

Each alias is typically a shorter name for an email address. The system administrator uses the sendmail alias file to forward mail, to create mailing lists (a single alias that identifies several users), or to refer to a user by several different names. For example, here are some typical aliases:

```
barkakati: naba
naba: naba@lnbsoft
all: naba, leha, ivy, emily, ashley
```

The first line says that mail addressed to `barkakati` should be delivered to the user named `naba` on the local system. The second line indicates that mail for `naba` should really be sent to the user name `naba` on the `lnbsoft` system. The last line defines `all` as the alias for the five users `naba`, `leha`, `ivy`, `emily`, and `ashley`.

As the next section explains, you can set up a mailing list simply by defining an alias in the `/etc/aliases` file.

Creating a sendmail Alias Mailing List

You can implement a simple mailing list through a sendmail alias. In its simplest form, all you have to do is define an alias for the addresses in the `/etc/aliases` file. For example, suppose a large company has several websites (one in each major department), and the Webmasters decide to keep in touch through a mailing list. One of the Webmasters, Emily, volunteers to set up a mailing list for the group. To set up the mailing list, Emily (who logs in with the user name `emily`) adds the following alias to the `/etc/aliases` file:

```
webmasters: emily, webmaster@sales, webmaster@mktg,
        webmaster@appdev, ...,
        ...,
        webmaster@admin
```

In this case, the address list includes Emily and the Webmasters at all websites in the company (typically, mail to the Webmaster is addressed to the user name `webmaster`). If the list of addresses gets too long, end a line with a comma, and indent the next line with a tab character.

After defining an alias in the `/etc/aliases` **file, you must log in as** `root` **and make the new alias active by typing the following command:**

```
/usr/lib/sendmail -bi
```

You can use the absolute path name `/usr/lib/sendmail` **to run sendmail because** `/usr/lib/sendmail` **is a symbolic link to the actual sendmail program file** `/usr/sbin/sendmail`.

In addition to the `webmasters` alias, it's conventional to define two other aliases:

◆ The alias `listname-request` is where users send mail to subscribe to (or unsubscribe from) the list.
◆ The alias `owner-listname` is where errors (such as bounced messages) are sent.

In this case, because Emily sets up the Webmasters list, she might define the two aliases as follows:

```
webmasters-request: emily
owner-webmasters: emily
```

For a simple mailing list, one person is usually responsible for everything about the list.

Storing the Address List in a Separate File

Although defining an alias with all the addresses works, the drawback is that you must edit the `/etc/aliases` file whenever you want to add a new name to the list. You need to log in as `root` to edit the `/etc/aliases` file (or ask the system administrator to edit the file for you). A better solution is to store the address list in a separate file in your home directory and make sendmail read that file with the `:include:` directive in the alias definition.

For example, Emily might put the address list for the `webmasters` alias in the `/home/emily/mlist/webms` file (assuming that `/home/emily` is the login directory of user `emily`). Then the `/etc/aliases` file would reference the address list as follows:

```
webmasters: :include:/home/emily/mlist/webms
```

In the `/home/emily/mlist/webms` file, each address appears on a separate line:

```
emily (Emily B. -- list owner)
webmaster@appdev (Webmaster, Application Development Group)
webmaster@mktg (Webmaster, Marketing Department)
```

As you can see, you can put helpful comments in parentheses.

Every time sendmail sends a message to the `webmasters` alias, it reads the `/home/emily/mlist/webms` file. Thus, you can add a new user by simply editing this file.

If you use an address file, make sure that only the owner can modify it. Use the command `chmod 644 filename` to set the permission properly.

Ensuring That Replies Go to the List

When you set up a mailing list, you want any replies to go to everyone in the list so that discussions can take place among the group. However, when you use a sendmail alias to define a mailing list, the reply goes to the person who has sent the message instead of to the entire list. You can correct this problem by making the alias start a new sendmail process and by changing the sender's address through the -f option of sendmail.

Here's how you define the webmasters list by using this approach:

```
webmasters: "|/usr/lib/sendmail -fwebmasters -oi dist-webmasters"
dist-webmasters: :include:/home/emily/mlist/webms
```

This definition of webmasters runs sendmail with the -f option (this option sets the From address of the message) and sends mail to another alias, dist-webmasters, that points to the file containing the actual addresses. The -f option works only when a trusted user, such as root, sends mail.

 insider insight

When mail for the list arrives from another system, sendmail runs under a trusted user name. Therefore, the mail is sent out with webmasters as the return address. Unfortunately, when a user on the local system sends mail, the -f option does not work because sendmail runs under that user's name (and the user probably is not considered a trusted user). A solution to this problem is to set up the mailing list on a system where none of the list members have an account (this ensures that mail to the list always comes from a remote system).

Summary

The Internet has become an essential part of everyday life, as ISPs have sprung up all over the United States and in much of the world. Online services, such as AOL and Microsoft's MSN, now offer Internet mail and Web browsing, bringing even more people to the Internet. Because of its support for TCP/IP networking—the universal language of the Internet—a Linux PC is an ideal Internet host. This chapter describes the email service and shows you how to configure the sendmail server on a Red Hat Linux PC.

By reading this chapter, you learned the following:

- ♦ Email is one of the important services available on Internet hosts. This chapter describes email service available on a Red Hat Linux PC.
- ♦ Email software comes in two parts: a mail-transport agent (MTA), which physically sends and receives mail messages; and a mail-user agent (MUA), which reads messages and prepares new messages.
- ♦ The companion CD-ROMs contain several mail-transfer agents and mail-user agents. This chapter describes how to use sendmail as a mail-transport agent.
- ♦ The sendmail configuration is complex, but you can get going with the configuration file that comes with Red Hat Linux. All you may need to do is set your Red Hat Linux PC's hostname properly.
- ♦ To read email, you can use mail or Ximian Evolution. Mozilla also includes a mail reader you can use.

◆ You can automatically forward messages to another address by placing a `.forward` file in your home directory. The `.forward` file should contain a comma-separated list of email addresses.

◆ You can run the `procmail` mailer by invoking it from the `.forward` file. The typical use of procmail is to delete unwanted messages automatically and to sort messages into different files.

◆ You can set up a mailing list by using the `/etc/aliases` file, which stores aliases for sendmail.

News Server

Chapter

16

♦ ♦

Secrets in This Chapter

♦ ♦

The Internet helps you communicate in many ways. With email, you generally exchange messages with people whom you already know. Sometimes, however, you may want or need to participate in group discussions. If you are looking for help in setting up XFree86 on a system with the ATI Radeon 7000 video chipset, for example, you may want to question someone who knows something about this subject. For that sort of communication, you can post a message on the appropriate Internet newsgroup; someone is likely to give you an answer.

Internet newsgroups are like the bulletin boards or forums on other online systems, such as AOL and MSN. Essentially, newsgroups provide a bulletin-board system that spans the globe. You'll find a wide variety of newsgroups—covering subjects ranging from politics to computers. For Linux-related questions, you can read and post articles to newsgroups, such as `comp.os.linux.networking` and `comp.os.linux.setup`. You can think of an Internet newsgroup as a gathering place—a virtual meeting place where you can ask questions and discuss various issues.

Red Hat Linux comes with the software you need to read newsgroups and to set up your own system as a news server. This chapter introduces you to newsgroups and describes how to configure and run the InterNetNews (INN) server, a popular news server. You also learn how to set up local newsgroups for your corporate intranet.

Using Simple News Strategies

Although using news is reasonably simple, a news server requires some effort on your part if it is to be set up and maintained properly. Newsgroups in particular need a great deal of disk space and access to a news server that provides a news feed to your server. You need a large amount of disk space because so many newsgroups exist, and the volume of messages can be quite high. In addition, the news articles must be purged periodically; otherwise, the disk becomes filled. Even if you choose a subset of newsgroups, you may need tens of gigabytes, if not hundreds, just to keep the news items on your system. Running a news server can be one of the most demanding Internet services you provide because of the bandwidth requirements, disk space, and the in-memory indexes and caches that news servers require for fast access to news articles.

Secret

If you get your Internet access from an ISP, the ISP gives you access to a mail server and a news server. Then, you can use mail software that downloads messages from the mail server and a newsreader that reads newsgroups directly from the ISP's news server. If you are the sole user of your Red Hat Linux PC, I strongly recommend this strategy for reading news. That way, you get to read news and post articles without the headache of having to maintain a news server.

Another option is to read news at a website, such as Google's Usenet discussion forums at `http://groups.google.com/`. At that website, you can select a newsgroup to browse, and you can post replies to articles posted on various newsgroups. In this case, you don't even need access to a news server. Another similar service is offered by Mailgate (`http://www.mailgate.org`) where you can read, search, and post messages to the newsgroups using a Web browser.

All these options may not be enough if you want to set up a news server for a company intranet and manage your newsgroups. You might do this to provide a forum for employees to discuss various topics and to exchange knowledge with others. Internal newsgroups can be a good way to facilitate knowledge sharing and knowledge management within a company. Internal newsgroups can provide a virtual gathering place (or what are often called *communities of practice*) for employees to share their knowledge with others. To set up your own newsgroups, you have to set up a news server, such as innd, which uses the Network News Transfer Protocol (NNTP). You will learn about the news server later in this chapter.

The next section briefly describes the news-related software packages you can install in Red Hat Linux.

Installing News Software

During the installation of Red Hat Linux from this book's companion CD-ROMs, you have the option to install the necessary packages for news. As described in Chapter 2, select the News Server package group when you are prompted for which package groups to install.

cross ref

If you install the mail and news software during Linux installation, you do not have to do much more to begin using the mail and news services. Otherwise, you can use the Red Hat Package Manager (RPM) to install individual packages. Chapter 21 describes how to use the **rpm** program to install new software.

To access the RPM files for news, mount the appropriate CD-ROM by using the following command:

```
mount /mnt/cdrom
```

Then change the directory to /mnt/cdrom/RedHat/RPMS. You will find the RPM files in that directory. Following are some of the RPMs you may want to install (I show the RPM name; the actual filename starts with the RPM name, has a version number, and ends with an .rpm extension):

♦ cleanfeed (a spam filter for news servers)
♦ inews (an Internet news program to post news)
♦ inn (InterNetNews, a TCP/IP-based news server)
♦ slrn (a simple, NNTP-based newsreader)

You have probably already installed most of these packages. For this chapter, you need only inn and a news reader such as Mozilla (as well as any other mail or news reader you want to try).

Understanding Newsgroups

Newsgroups originated in Usenet—a store-and-forward messaging network for exchanging email and news items. Usenet works like a telegraph in that news and mail are relayed from one system to another. In Usenet, the systems are not on any network; they simply dial up and use the UNIX-to-UNIX Copy Protocol (UUCP) to transfer text messages.

Secret

Usenet is a very loosely connected collection of computers that has worked well and continues to be used because very little expense is involved in connecting to it. All you need is a modem and a site willing to store and forward your mail and news. You have to set up UUCP on your system, but you do not need a sustained network connection; just a few phone calls are all it takes to keep the email and news flowing. The downside is that you cannot use TCP/IP services, such as the Web, Telnet, or FTP.

From their Usenet origins, the newsgroups have migrated to the Internet (even though the name Usenet is still used to refer to news). Instead of UUCP, the news is transported by means of the Network News Transfer Protocol (NNTP), which is described in RFC 977, "Network News Transfer Protocol: A Proposed Standard for the Stream-Based Transmission of News," by B. Kantor and P. Lapsley, 1986.

Although the news transport protocol has changed from UUCP to NNTP (although some sites still use UUCP), the store-and-forward concept of news transfer remains. Thus, if you want to get news on your Red Hat Linux system, you have to find a news server from which your system can download news.

insider insight If you have signed up with an ISP, it should provide you with access to a news server. Such Internet news servers communicate by using NNTP. Then, you can use an NNTP-capable newsreader, such as slrn, to access the news server and read selected newsgroups. You can also read news by using the news reader that comes with Mozilla (included with Red Hat Linux). This is the easiest way to access news on your Linux Internet host.

The following discussion about reading newsgroups assumes that you have obtained access to a news server from your ISP.

Reading News from Your ISP

To read news from your ISP, you need a newsreader—a program that enables you to select a newsgroup and view the items in that newsgroup. You also need to understand the newsgroup hierarchy and naming convention, which is described in the "Understanding the Newsgroup Hierarchy" section of this chapter. First, you should try reading news from a news server.

Reading Newsgroups with Mozilla Mail

You can browse newsgroups and post articles from Mozilla Mail, one of the components of Mozilla—the Web browser that comes with Red Hat Linux on this book's companion CD-ROMs. You can start Mozilla by selecting Main Menu⇨Internet⇨Mozilla Web Browser or by clicking the earth icon on the panel. When you start to read newsgroups for the first time, follow these steps to set up the news account:

1. Select Windows⇨Mail & Newsgroups from the Mozilla menu. The Mozilla Mail and News (called Mozilla Mail, for short) window appears.
2. Select Edit⇨Mail & Newsgroups Account Settings from the Mozilla Mail menu. A dialog box appears.
3. Click Add Account. The Account Wizard appears.
4. Click the Newsgroup account radio button, and click Next.
5. Fill in your identity information—name and email address—and click Next.
6. Enter your news server name (provided by your ISP), and click Next.
7. Enter a descriptive name of the newsgroup account, and click Next.
8. Click Finish to complete the newsgroup account setup.

The new newsgroup account now appears in the list of accounts on the left-hand side of the Mozilla Mail window. Click the newsgroup's account name, and the right-hand side shows the options for the newsgroup account.

Click the Subscribe to newsgroups link. Mozilla Mail starts to download the list of newsgroups from the news server.

If your ISP's news server requires a user name and password, you are prompted for that information. After that, Mozilla Mail downloads the list of newsgroups and displays them in the Subscribe dialog box. You can enter a search string in a text box to narrow down the list. When you find the newsgroups you want, click the check box to subscribe to these newsgroups, then click OK to close the dialog box.

After you subscribe to newsgroups, those newsgroups appear under the newsgroup account name in the left-hand side of the Mozilla Mail window. You can then read a newsgroup using these steps:

1. Click a newsgroup name (for example, `comp.os.linux.announce`). This brings up a dialog box that asks you how many message headers you want to download.
2. Specify the number of headers (for example, 500) you want, and then click OK to proceed. Mozilla Mail downloads the headers from the newsgroup and displays a list in the upper-right area of the window.
3. From the list of headers, click an item to read that article.

To select other subscribed newsgroups, click on the newsgroup's name in the left-hand side of the window.

Understanding the Newsgroup Hierarchy

News items are organized in a hierarchy of newsgroups for ease of maintenance as well as ease of use. A typical newsgroup name looks like the following:

```
comp.os.linux.announce
```

This name says that `comp.os.linux.announce` is a newsgroup for announcements (`announce`) about the Linux operating system (`os.linux`) and that these subjects fall under the broad category of computers (`comp`).

As you can see, the format of a newsgroup name is a sequence of words separated by periods. These words denote the hierarchy of the newsgroup.

Secret

To understand the newsgroup hierarchy, compare the newsgroup's name with the pathname of a file (such as `/usr/lib/X11/xinit/Xclients`) in Linux. Just as a file's pathname shows the directory hierarchy of the file, the newsgroup name shows the newsgroup hierarchy. In filenames, a slash (/) separates the names of directories; in a newsgroup's name, a period (.) separates the different levels in the newsgroup hierarchy.

In a newsgroup's name, the first word represents the newsgroup category. The `comp.os.linux.announce` newsgroup, for example, is in the `comp` category, whereas `alt.books.technical` is in the `alt` category.

Table 16-1 lists some of the major newsgroup categories.

Table 16-1: Major Newsgroup Categories

Category	Subject
alt	"Alternative" newsgroups (not subject to any rules), which run the gamut from the mundane to the bizarre
bionet	Biology newsgroups
bit	Bitnet newsgroups
biz	Business newsgroups
clari	Clarinet news service (daily news)
comp	Computer hardware and software newsgroups
ieee	Newsgroups for the Institute of Electrical and Electronics Engineers
k12	Newsgroups devoted to elementary and secondary education
linux	Newsgroups about Linux (includes a `linux.redhat` hierarchy)
misc	Miscellaneous newsgroups
news	Newsgroups about Internet news administration (`news.software.nntp` newsgroup covers INN)
rec	Recreational and art newsgroups
sci	Science and engineering newsgroups
soc	Newsgroups for discussing social issues and various cultures
talk	Discussions of current issues (such as "talk radio")

This short list of categories is deceptive because it does not really tell you about the wide-ranging variety of newsgroups available in each category. Because each newsgroup category contains several levels of subcategories, the overall count of newsgroups runs into several thousands. The comp category alone has more than 500 newsgroups.

Typically, you have to narrow your choice of newsgroups according to your interests. If you are interested in Linux, for example, you can pick one or more of these newsgroups:

◆ `comp.os.linux.admin`—Information about Linux system administration

◆ `comp.os.linux.advocacy`—Discussions about promoting Linux

◆ `comp.os.linux.announce`—Important announcements about Linux. This newsgroup is moderated, which means that you must mail the article to the moderator, who then posts it to the newsgroup if the article is appropriate for the newsgroup.

◆ `comp.os.linux.answers`—Questions and answers about Linux. All the Linux HOWTOs are posted in this moderated newsgroup. (See Chapter 7 for a list of Linux HOWTOs.)

◆ `comp.os.linux.development`—Current Linux development work

◆ `comp.os.linux.development.apps`—Linux application development

◆ `comp.os.linux.development.system`—Linux operating-system development

◆ `comp.os.linux.hardware`—Discussions about Linux and various types of hardware

◆ `comp.os.linux.help`—Help with various aspects of Linux

◆ `comp.os.linux.misc`—Miscellaneous Linux-related topics

◆ `comp.os.linux.networking`—Networking under Linux

◆ `comp.os.linux.redhat`—Red Hat Linux-related topics

◆ `comp.os.linux.setup`—Linux setup and installation

◆ `comp.os.linux.x`—Discussions about setting up and running the X Window System under Linux

◆ `linux.redhat`—Discussions about Red Hat Linux

You have to be selective about what newsgroups you read because it's impossible to keep up with all the news, even in a specific area such as Linux. When you first install and set up Linux, you might read newsgroups such as `comp.os.linux.setup`, `comp.os.linux.hardware`, and `comp.os.linux.x` (especially if you are having problems with X). After you have Linux up and running, you may want to learn only about new things happening in Linux. For such information, read the `comp.os.linux.announce` newsgroup.

Subscribing to Newsgroups

Unlike magazines or newspapers, newsgroups do not require that you subscribe to them; you can read any newsgroup that is available on the news server. The news server administrator may decide to exclude certain newsgroups, however; in that case, you cannot read them.

The only thing to which you come close to "subscribing" is the `.newsrc` file in your home directory. All newsreaders consult this file to determine which newsgroups you want to read. From inside the newsreader, you can use its menus or commands to subscribe to a newsgroup. When you subscribe to the newsgroup, the newsreader simply adds the name of that newsgroup to the `.newsrc` file.

Posting to Newsgroups

You can use any newsreader to post a news item (a new item or a reply to an old posting) to one or more newsgroups. Posting a news item to a newsgroup is basically similar to sending an email message. The exact command for posting a news item depends on the newsreader. For example, in the Mozilla Mail newsreader, follow these steps to post an article:

1. Click Reply on the toolbar to post a follow-up to a news item you are reading. To post a new news article, click New Msg.

2. A window appears where you can compose the message. You should type the names of the newsgroups, just as you would type the addresses of recipients when sending email. Then enter the subject and your message. For this test posting, type a subject line with the word ignore in it, and enter misc.test as the name of the newsgroup. Otherwise, any site that receives your article replies by mail to tell you the article has reached the site; that's in keeping with the purpose of the misc.test newsgroup.

3. After you finish composing the message, click Send on the toolbar. Mozilla sends the message to the news server, which in turn sends it to other news servers.

4. To verify that the test message has reached the newsgroup, click File⇨ Subscribe; then subscribe to the misc.test newsgroup (that's where you've recently posted the new article). Look at the latest article in misc.test, which should be the article you've recently posted.

Verifying Your Newsgroup Posting

If you post an article and read the newsgroup immediately, you'll see the new article, but that does not mean the article has reached other sites on the Internet. After all, your posting shows up on your news server immediately because that's where you have posted the article. Because of the store-and-forward model of news distribution, the news article gradually propagates from your news server to others around the world.

Secret

The misc.test newsgroup provides a way to see whether or not your news posting is really getting around. If you post to that newsgroup and do not include the word "ignore" in the subject, news servers acknowledge receipt of the article by sending an email message to the address listed in the Reply-To field of the article's header.

If you have your Linux host on the Internet, try posting to the misc.test newsgroup to verify that articles are getting out. Be prepared to receive a dozen or so replies from various sites, acknowledging the arrival of your article at those sites.

Configuring and Starting the INN Server

So far, you have seen how to read news from an existing news server. Now, you can turn to the subject of setting up an INN server on your system. Much of the InterNetNews (INN) software, bundled with Red Hat Linux, is already set up for you. You need to understand the various components of INN, edit the configuration files, and start innd—the INN server. Sometimes I refer to the INN server as the *news server*.

Secret

If you want to support a selection of Internet newsgroups, you also have to arrange for a *news feed*—this is the source from which your news server gets the newsgroup articles. Typically, you can get a news feed from an ISP, for an additional monthly fee, to cover the cost of resources required to provide the feed. You need the name of the upstream server that provides the news feed, and you have to provide that server with your server's name and the newsgroups you want to receive.

Based on the newsgroups you want to receive and the number of days you want to retain articles, you have to set aside disk space for the articles. The newsgroups are stored in a directory hierarchy (based on the newsgroup names) in the /var/spool/news directory of your system. If you are setting up a news server, you may want to devote a large disk partition to the /var/spool/news directory.

In your news server's configuration files, enter the name of the server providing the news feed. At the same time, add to the configuration files the names of any down-stream news servers, if any, that receive news feeds from your server. Then, you can start the news server and wait for news to arrive. Monitor the log files to ensure that the news articles are being sorted and stored properly in the /var/spool/news directory on your system.

Once you have news up and running, you must run news maintenance and cleanup scripts. These are run using the cron jobs (see Chapter 20 for more information about cron jobs). On Red Hat Linux, a cron job is already set up to run the /usr/lib/news/bin/news.daily script to perform the news maintenance tasks.

insider insight

The following sections introduce you to INN setup, but you can learn more about INN from the Internet Software Consortium (ISC), a nonprofit corporation dedicated to developing and maintaining open source Internet software, such as BIND (an implementation of Domain Name System), DHCP (Dynamic Host Configuration Protocol), and INN. Rich Salz originally wrote INN; ISC took over the development of INN in 1996. You can learn more about INN and can access other resources at ISC's INN Web page (http://www.isc.org/products/INN/).

Taking Stock of INN Components

INN includes several programs that perform specific newsgroup-delivery and -management tasks. It also includes a number of files that control how the INN programs work. The most important INN programs are the following:

◆ **innd**—The news server. It runs as a *daemon*—a background process that keeps itself running to provide a specific service—and listens on the NNTP port (TCP port 119). The innd server accepts connections from other feed sites, as well as from local newsreader clients, but it hands off local connections to the nnrpd.

◆ **nnrpd**—A special server invoked by innd to handle requests from local newsreader clients.

◆ **expire**—Removes old articles based on the specifications in the text file /etc/news/expire.ctl.

♦ **nntpsend**—Invokes the innxmit program to send news articles to a remote site by using NNTP. The configuration file /etc/news/nntpsend.ctl controls the nntpsend program.

♦ **ctlinnd**—Enables you to control the innd server interactively. The ctlinnd program can send messages to the control channel of the innd server.

Secret

Some of the important components of INN are its control files. Most of these files are in the /etc/news directory of your Red Hat Linux system, but a few are in the /var/lib/news directory also. Between the two directories, there are over 30 INN control files. Some of the important files include the following:

- **/etc/news/inn.conf**—Specifies configuration data for the innd server. (To view online help for this file, type **man inn.conf**.)

- **/etc/news/newsfeeds**—Specifies what articles to feed downstream to other news servers. (The file is complicated, but you can get help by typing man newsfeeds.)

- **/etc/news/incoming.conf**—Lists the names and addresses of hosts that provide news feeds to this server. (To view online help for this file, type **man incoming.conf**.)

- **/etc/news/storage.conf**—Specifies the storage methods to be used when storing news articles. (To view online help for this file, type **man storage.conf**.)

- **/etc/news/expire.ctl**—Controls expiration of articles, on a per newsgroup level, if desired. (To view online help for this file, type **man expire.ctl**.)

- **/var/lib/news/active**—Lists all active newsgroups, showing the oldest and newest article number for each, and each newsgroup's posting status. (To view online help for this file, type **man active**.)

- **/var/lib/news/newsgroups**—Lists newsgroups, with a brief description of each.

- **/etc/news/readers.conf**—Specifies hosts and users are permitted to read news from this news server and post news to newsgroups. The default file allows only the localhost to read news; you have to edit it if you want to allow other hosts in your local area network to read news. (To view online help for this file, type **man readers.conf**.)

The next few sections describe how to set up some of the control files.

Understanding inn.conf

This file holds configuration data for all INN programs and, as such, is the most important file. Each line of the file has the value of a parameter in the following format:

```
parameter:     value
```

Depending on the parameter, the value is a string, a number, or true or false. As in many other configuration files, comment lines begin with a number or pound sign (#).

Most of the parameters in the default inn.conf file in the /etc/news directory should not require changes. You might want to edit one or more of the parameters shown in Table 16-2.

Table 16-2: Configuration Parameters in /etc/news/inn.conf

Parameter Name	Description
mta	Set this to the mail transfer agent that will be used by innd to transfer messages. The default is to use sendmail.
organization	Set this to the name of your organization in the way you want it to appear in the Organization: header of all news articles posted from your system. Users may override this by defining the ORGANIZATION environment variable.
ovmethod	Sets the type of overview storage method (the overview is an index of the news articles in the newsgroup). The default method is tradindexed, which is fast for reading news, but slow for storing news items.
pathhost	Set this to the name of your news server as you want it to appear in the Path header of all postings that go through your server. If pathhost is not defined, the fully qualified domain name of your system is used.
pathnews	Set this to the full pathname of the directory that contains INN binaries and libraries. In Red Hat Linux, pathnews is set to /usr/lib/news.
domain	Set this to the domain name for your server.
allownewnews	Set this to true if you want INN to support the NEWNEWS command from news readers. Because this command can drastically reduce your server's performance, INN documentation recommends that you set this to false.
storageapi	Set this to true if you want articles to be stored using the Storage Manager application programming interface (API). The default setting of false causes INN to use the traditional article storage method of storing one article per file. If you set this to true, you have to choose between the storage methods timehash and cnfs, and you have to create new spool and database files (type **man storage.conf** to read more about cnfs and timehash storage methods). For a small number of newsgroups, you can leave this option at its default value of false.
hiscachesize	Set this to the size in kilobytes that you want INN to use for caching recently used history file entries. The default setting of 0 disables history caching. Because history caching can greatly increase the number of articles your server can process per second, you may want to set a value of 256 (for 256KB).
innflags	Set this to any flags you want to pass to the INN server process when it starts up.

Understanding News Feeds

The `newsfeeds` file specifies how incoming news articles are redistributed to other servers and to INN processes. If you provide news feeds to other servers, you have to list these news feeds in this file. (You also must have an entry labeled ME, which serves a special purpose explained later in this section.)

The `newsfeeds` file contains a series of entries, one for each feed. Each feed entry has the following format:

```
site[/exclude,exclude...]\
      :pattern,pattern...[/distrib,distrib...]\
      :flag,flag...\
      :param
```

Each entry has four fields separated by colons (:). Usually, the entries span multiple lines, and a backslash (\) at the end of the line is used to continue a line to the next. Following are the four fields in each entry in the `newsfeeds` file:

1. The first field, site, is the name of the feed. Each name must be unique, and for feeds to other news servers, the name is set to the hostname of the remote server. Following the name is an optional slash and an exclude list (`/exclude,exclude...`) consisting of a list of names. If any of the names in this list appear in the Path line of an article, that article will not be forwarded to the feed. You can use an exclude list if you don't want to receive articles from a specific source.

2. The second field consists of a comma-separated list of newsgroup patterns, such as `*,@alt.binaries.warez.*,!control*,!local*`, followed by an optional distribution list. The distribution list is a list of comma-separated keywords, with each keyword specifying a specific set of sites to which the articles are distributed. The newsgroup patterns essentially define a subscription list of sites that receive this news feed. An asterisk (*) matches all newsgroups. A pattern beginning with an @ causes newsgroups matching that pattern to be dropped. A pattern that begins with an exclamation mark (!) means the matching newsgroups are not sent. By the way, the simple pattern-matching syntax used in INN configuration files is referred to as a *wildmat* pattern.

3. The third field is a comma-separated list of flags. These flags determine the feed-entry type and set certain parameters for the entry. There are numerous flags; you should type **man newsfeeds** and read the man page for more information about the flags.

4. The fourth field is for parameters whose values depend on the settings in the third field. Typically, this field contains names of files or external programs that the INN server uses. You can learn more about this field from the newsfeeds man page.

Now that you know the layout of the `/etc/news/newsfeeds` file, you can study that file as an example. The default file contains many sample feed entries, but all but the following two are commented out:

◆ ME is a special feed entry that's always required. It serves two purposes. First, the newsgroup patterns listed in this entry are preprended to all newsgroup patterns in all other entries. Second, the ME entry's distribution list determines what distributions your server accepts from remote sites.

♦ The `controlchan` feed entry is used to set up INN so that an external program is used to handle control messages (these messages are used to create new newsgroups and remove groups). For example, the following `controlchan` entry specifies the external program `/usr/bin/controlchan` to handle all control messages, except cancel messages (meant for canceling an article):

```
controlchan!\
            :!*,control,control.*,!control.cancel\
            :Tc,Wnsm:/usr/lib/news/bin/controlchan
```

In addition to these feed entries, you add entries for any actual sites to which your news server provides news feed. Such entries have the format

```
feedme.domain.com\
                  :!junk,!control/!foo\
                  :Tm:innfeed!
```

where `feedme.domain.com` is the fully qualified domain name of the site to which your system sends news articles.

Understanding incoming.conf

The `incoming.conf` file describes which hosts are allowed to connect to your host to feed articles (in versions of INN prior to 2.2.3, a file named `hosts.nntp` was used to specify remote hosts allowed to transfer articles to the local site). For a single feed, you can add an entry like

```
peer myfeed {
    hostname: myfeedsite.com
}
```

where `myfeed` is a label for the peer and `myfeedsite.com` identifies the peer—the site that feeds your site.

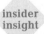

insider insight

Keep in mind that simply adding a site's name in the `incoming.conf` file does not cause that remote site to start feeding your site news—it simply enables your server to accept news articles from the remote site. At the remote site, the server must be configured to send articles to your site.

Understanding readers.conf

This file specifies the hostnames or IP addresses from which newsreader clients (such as Mozilla) can retrieve newsgroups from your server. For example, the following `readers.conf` file allows read access and post access (meaning you can submit articles) from localhost and any from host in the network 192.168.0.0:

```
auth "localhost" {
    hosts: "localhost, 127.0.0.1, stdin"
    default: "<localhost>"
}
access "localhost" {
    users: "<localhost>"
    newsgroups: "*"
```

```
    access: RPA
}
auth "localnet" {
    hosts: 192.168.0.0/24
    default: "<localnet>"
}
access "localnet" {
    users: "<localnet>"
    newsgroups: "*"
    access: RPA
}
```

Starting INN

In addition to the configuration files, you also need to initiate cron jobs that perform periodic maintenance of the news server. In Red Hat Linux, these cron jobs are already set up. Therefore, you are now ready to start the INN server—innd.

Before you start innd, you must run `makehistory` and `makedbz` to initialize and rebuild the INN history database. Type **man makehistory** and **man makedbz** to learn more about these commands. You can use the following commands to create an initial history database and associated index:

```
/usr/lib/news/bin/makehistory -b -f history -O -l 30000 -I
cd /var/lib/news
/usr/lib/news/bin/makedbz -s `wc -l < history` -f history
chown news.news *
chown news.news /var/spool/news/overview/group.index
chmod 664 /var/spool/news/overview/group.index
```

As with any other standalone servers (these are servers that do not run under `xinetd`) in Red Hat Linux, you can set up innd to start at boot time by typing the following command:

```
chkconfig --level 35 innd on
```

To start innd right now, log in as `root` and type the following command:

```
service innd start
```

If you change any configuration file (such as `inn.conf` or `newsfeeds`), restart the innd server with the following command:

```
service innd restart
```

You can type **ps ax** to see if the innd process is up and running. If all goes well, you should see two processes such as the following listed in the output of the `ps ax` command:

```
23789 ?        S        0:00 /usr/lib/news/bin/innd -p4
23794 ?        S        0:00 /usr/bin/perl /usr/lib/news/bin/controlchan
```

The /var/log/spooler **file contains all status and error messages from innd. Type the following command to see the last few messages in that file:**

```
tail /var/log/spooler
```

Setting Up Local Newsgroups

If you want to use newsgroups as a way to share information within your company, you can set up a hierarchy of local newsgroups. Then, you can use these newsgroups to create virtual communities within your company, where people with shared interests can informally discuss issues and exchange knowledge.

Defining a Newsgroup Hierarchy

The first task is to define a hierarchy of newsgroups and decide what each newsgroup will discuss. For example, if your company's name is XYZ Corporation, here's a partial hierarchy of newsgroups you might define:

- **xyz.general**—General items about XYZ Corporation
- **xyz.weekly.news**—Weekly news
- **xyz.weekly.menu**—The weekly cafeteria menu and any discussions about it
- **xyz.forsale**—A listing of items offered for sale by employees
- **xyz.jobs**—Job openings at XYZ Corporation
- **xyz.wanted**—Wanted (help, items to buy, and so on) postings by employees
- **xyz.technical.hardware**—Technical discussions about hardware
- **xyz.technical.software**—Technical discussions about software

Updating Configuration Files

Add descriptive entries for each of these newsgroups to the /var/lib/news/newsgroups file. Here are some entries from the /var/lib/news/newsgroups file:

```
control              Various control messages (no posting).
control.cancel       Cancel messages (no posting).
control.checkgroups  Hierarchy check control messages (no posting).
control.newgroup     Newsgroup creation control messages (no posting).
control.rmgroup      Newsgroup removal control messages (no posting).
junk                 Unfiled articles (no posting).
```

Add a line for each newsgroup—type its name, followed by a brief description.

Next, edit the ME entry in the /etc/news/newsfeeds file and add the phrase !xyz.* to the comma-separated list of newsgroup patterns. This ensures that your local newsgroups are not distributed outside your site.

You must also add a storage method to be used for the local newsgroups. For example, you can add the following lines in /etc/news/storage.conf to define the storage method for the new xyz hierarchy of newsgroups (change xyz to whatever you name your local newsgroups):

```
method tradspool {
```

```
    class: 1
    newsgroups: xyz.*
}
```

After making changes to configuration files, remember to restart the news server with the command:

```
service innd restart.
```

Adding the Newsgroups

The final step is to add the newsgroups. Once you have innd running, it's very easy to add a local newsgroup. Log in as `root` and use ctlinnd to perform this task. For example, here's how you add a newsgroup named `xyz.general`:

```
/usr/lib/news/bin/ctlinnd newgroup xyz.general
```

That command adds the `xyz.general` newsgroup to your site. If you use the traditional storage method, the innd server creates the directory `/var/spool/news/articles/xyz/general` and stores articles for that newsgroup in that directory.

Once you have created all the local newsgroups, users from your intranet should be able to post news articles and read articles in the local newsgroups. If they have problems accessing the newsgroups, make sure that the `/etc/news/readers.conf` file contains the IP addresses or names of the hosts that should be able to access the innd server.

Testing Your Newsgroups

For example, I have added a newsgroup named `local.news` on an INN server running on my Red Hat Linux system by using the instructions explained in the previous sections. Then, I start Mozilla Mail on another system on the LAN and edit the preferences so that the news server is set to my INN server. Next, I access the local.news newsgroup by typing `news:local.news` as the URL.

Summary

Internet newsgroups provide a convenient way to discuss various topics and to share your knowledge with others. This chapter describes newsgroups and shows you how to set up a news server on your Red Hat Linux PC.

By reading this chapter, you learned the following:

◆ Newsgroups originated in Usenet, which is a store-and-forward network. News items travel around the world from one system to another. Nowadays, news is transported over the Internet by means of the Network News Transport Protocol (NNTP).

◆ Because thousands of newsgroups exist, storing all the news articles takes a great deal of disk space. Moreover, the articles must be purged periodically; otherwise, the disk becomes filled. It's best to read news from a news server maintained by an Internet service provider (ISP).

◆ This chapter shows you how to use Mozilla to read news from a designated news server.

♦ Red Hat Linux comes with all the software and configuration files you need for the InterNetNews (INN) server. If you want to provide all Internet newsgroups, you have to find a site willing to provide you with a news feed. This chapter shows you how to set up the INN configuration files and start the innd server.

♦ You can use local newsgroups to provide discussion forums to employees in your company. Once innd is running, it's simple to add local newsgroups. This chapter shows you how to add such local newsgroups.

FTP Server

Chapter

17

♦ ♦

Secrets in This Chapter

♦ ♦

File Transfer Protocol (FTP) is a popular client/server software for transferring files from one system to another. If you have an ISP account that provides you with a home page, you've probably used FTP to upload your Web pages to the ISP's server. Using an FTP client, you log in to your ISP account and copy the files from your home system to the ISP's server.

You can also use FTP to download other files, such as open source software from Internet hosts. In this case, you don't need an account on the remote system. You simply log in using the anonymous user name and provide your email address as the password. This is called anonymous FTP. If you want to enable others to download files from your system by using FTP, you can set up anonymous FTP on your system so that users can log in with the user name "anonymous."

Red Hat Linux comes with several FTP clients and the Very Secure FTP daemon (vsftpd), written by Chris Evans. Red Hat Linux also includes a package called anonftp that sets up the files you need to support anonymous FTP. This chapter introduces you to a few FTP clients and, for the command-line FTP client, describes the commands you use to work with remote directories. It also shows you how to configure the FTP server through text configuration files and how to control access to the FTP server. Finally, this chapter describes anonymous FTP—how it's set up and how to ensure that it's secure.

Installing FTP Software

During the installation of Red Hat Linux from this book's companion CD-ROMs, you have the option to install the packages necessary for FTP. As described in Chapter 2, select the FTP Server package group when you are prompted for which packages to install.

---

cross ref

If you install the FTP Server package group during Linux installation, you do not have to do much more than start **vsftpd** to begin using FTP. Otherwise, you can use the Red Hat Package Manager (RPM) to install individual packages. Chapter 21 describes how to use the **rpm** program to install new software.

To access the RPM files for FTP, mount the appropriate CD-ROM with the following command:

```
mount /mnt/cdrom
```

Then, change the directory to /mnt/cdrom/RedHat/RPMS, where you will find the RPM files. Following are some of the RPMs you may want to install (shown is the RPM name; the actual filename starts with the RPM name, has a version number, and ends with an .rpm extension):

- ♦ vsftpd (the Very Secure FTP daemon—an FTP server)
- ♦ anonftp (anonymous FTP setup files)
- ♦ ftp (an FTP client)
- ♦ gftp (X Window System–based graphical FTP client)
- ♦ ncftp (another FTP client)

You have probably already installed all of these packages. For this chapter, you should install vsftpd, anonftp, and ftp. The gftp package should be installed when you install the GNOME package group.

Understanding FTP

As the name implies, the File Transfer Protocol (FTP) enables users to transfer files between systems on the Internet. FTP is client/server software—you can use the FTP client on a system to access files on another Internet host. The FTP server on that host acts on commands you send via the FTP client.

Secret

The FTP clients and servers exchange information by using the FTP, described in RFC 959, "File Transfer Protocol," by J. Postel and J. K. Reynolds, October 1985. FTP uses two TCP ports—data is transferred on port 20, while control information is exchanged on port 21.

With FTP, you can download files from other Internet hosts or from hosts in your local area network. Reciprocally, users on other systems also can download files from your system, typically through a feature known as anonymous FTP. You learn how to set up anonymous FTP service in the section "Setting up Secure Anonymous FTP."

Before you can try out the FTP client, log in as `root` and start the vsftpd server on your system with the following command:

```
service vsftpd start
```

In pervious versions of Red Hat Linux, the FTP server was run under xinetd. Starting in Red Hat Linux 9, the FTP server runs as a standalone server, just like Apache httpd and the innd news server. To automatically start vsftpd when you boot the Red Hat Linux system, you must turn it on with the following command:

```
chkconfig --level 35 vsftpd on
```

The next few sections introduce you to FTP for transferring files and working with remote directories. In addition to the FTP commands, you also learn about the graphical FTP clients and how to use FTP through your Web browser.

Using the Command-Line FTP Client

After you have started vsftpd, you can see how FTP works by using the command-line FTP client. You can try out the FTP commands from another system on a local area network or on your Red Hat Linux system. For example, the following sample FTP session shows how I use the command-line FTP client to log in using my user name (naba) and browse the directories on my system (my comments appear in italics):

```
ftp localhost
Connected to localhost (127.0.0.1).
220 (vsFTPd 1.1.3)
Name (localhost:naba):    (I press Enter)
331 Please specify the password.
Password:        (I type my password)
230 Login successful. Have fun.
```

```
Remote system type is UNIX.
Using binary mode to transfer files.
ftp> help
Commands may be abbreviated.  Commands are:

!               debug           mdir            sendport        site
$               dir             mget            put             size
account         disconnect      mkdir           pwd             status
append          exit            mls             quit            struct
ascii           form            mode            quote           system
bell            get             modtime         recv            sunique
binary          glob            mput            reget           tenex
bye             hash            newer           rstatus         tick
case            help            nmap            rhelp           trace
cd              idle            nlist           rename          type
cdup            image           ntrans          reset           user
chmod           lcd             open            restart         umask
close           ls              prompt          rmdir           verbose
cr              macdef          passive         runique         ?
delete          mdelete         proxy           send
ftp> cd /var/ftp (This changes directory to /var/ftp)
250 Directory successfully changed.
ftp> ls          (This command lists the contents of the directory)
227 Entering Passive Mode (127,0,0,1,121,193)
150 Here comes the directory listing.
d--x--x--x    2 0          0              4096 Jan 09 19:31 bin
d--x--x--x    2 0          0              4096 Jan 09 19:31 etc
drwxr-xr-x    2 0          0              4096 Jan 09 19:31 lib
drwxr-sr-x    2 0          50             4096 Dec 13 16:13 pub
226 Directory send OK.
ftp> bye          (This command ends the session)
221 Goodbye.
```

As the listing shows, you can start the command-line FTP client by typing the command
ftp *hostname*, where *hostname* is the name of the system you want to access. Once the
FTP client establishes a connection with the FTP server at the remote system, the FTP
server prompts you for a user name and password. After you've supplied the information,
the FTP client displays the ftp> prompt, and you can begin typing commands to perform
specific tasks. If you can't remember a specific FTP command, type **help** to view a list of
them. You can get additional help for a specific command by typing **help** *command*.

Secret

Many of the FTP commands are similar to UNIX commands for navigating the file
system. For example, cd changes directory, pwd prints the name of the current working directory, and ls lists the contents of the current directory. Two other common
commands are get and put—get downloads a file from the remote system to your
system, and put uploads (sends) a file from your system to the remote host.

You can use the mget command to download multiple files. However, you cannot
conveniently download entire directory hierarchies by using the command-line FTP
client. Graphical FTP clients are much better at downloading entire directories and
subdirectories.

Table 17-1 describes some commonly used FTP commands. Note that you do not have to type the entire FTP command. For a long command, you have to type the first characters only—enough to identify the command uniquely. For example, to delete a file, you can type **dele**, and to change the file transfer mode to binary, you can type **bin**.

Table 17-1: List of Commonly Used FTP Commands

Command	Description
!	Executes a shell command on the local system. For example, `!ls` lists the contents of the current directory on the remote system.
?	Displays list of commands (same as `help`)
append	Appends a local file to a remote file
ascii	Sets the file transfer type to ASCII (or plaintext). This is the default file transfer type.
binary	Sets the file transfer type to binary
bye	Ends the FTP session with the remote FTP server and quits the FTP client
cd	Changes directory on the remote system. For example, `cd /pub/Linux` changes the remote directory to `/pub/Linux`.
chmod	Changes the permission settings of a remote file. For example, `chmod 644 index.html` changes the permission settings of the `index.html` file on the remote system.
close	Ends the FTP session with the FTP server and returns to the FTP client's prompt
delete	Deletes a remote file. For example, `delete bigimage.jpg` deletes that file on the remote system.
dir	Lists the contents of the current directory on the remote system
disconnect	Ends the FTP session and returns to the FTP client's prompt. (This is the same as close.)
get	Downloads a remote file. For example, `get junk.tar.gz junk.tgz` downloads the file `junk.tar.gz` from the remote system and saves it as the file `junk.tgz` on the local system.
hash	Turns on or off hash mark (#) printing showing the progress of file transfer. When turned on, a hash mark is printed for every 1,024 bytes transferred from the remote system.
help	Displays a list of commands
image	Same as binary
lcd	Changes the current directory on the local system. For example, `lcd /var/ftp/pub` changes the current local directory to `/var/ftp/pub`.
ls	Lists the contents of the current remote directory
mdelete	Deletes multiple files on a remote system. For example, `mdelete *.jpg` deletes all remote files with names ending in `.jpg` in the current directory.

(continued)

Table 17-1: (continued)

Command	Description
mdir	Lists multiple remote files and saves the listing in a specified local file. For example, mdir /usr/share/doc/w* wlist saves the listing in the local file named wlist.
mget	Downloads multiple files. For example, mget *.jpg downloads all files with names ending in .jpg. If prompt is turned on, the FTP client asks for confirmation before each file is downloaded.
mkdir	Creates a directory on the remote system. mkdir images creates a directory named images in the current directory on the remote system.
mls	Same as mdir
mput	Uploads multiple files. For example, mput *.jpg sends all files with names ending in .jpg to the remote system. If prompt is turned on, the FTP client asks for confirmation before each file is sent.
open	Opens a connection to the FTP server on the specified host. For example, open ftp.netscape.com connects to the FTP server on the host ftp.netscape.com.
prompt	Turns prompt on or off. When prompt is on, the FTP client prompts you for confirmation before downloading or uploading each file during a multifile transfer.
put	Sends a file to the remote system. For example, put index.html sends the index.html file from the local system to the remote system.
pwd	Displays the full path name of the current directory on the remote system. When you log in as a user, the initial current working directory is your home directory.
quit	Same as bye
recv	Same as get
rename	Renames a file on the remote system. For example, rename old.html new.html renames the file old.html to new.html on the remote system.
rmdir	Deletes a directory on the remote system. For example, rmdir images deletes the images directory in the current directory of the remote system.
send	Same as put
size	Shows the size of a remote file. For example, size bigfile.tar.gz shows the size of that remote file.
status	Shows the current status of the FTP client
user	Sends new user information to the FTP server. For example, user naba sends the user name naba; the FTP server then prompts for the password for that user name.

Using a Graphical FTP Client

GNOME comes with gFTP, a graphical FTP client. To start gFTP, select from the GNOME desktop Main Menu➪Internet➪More Internet Applications➪gFTP. This starts the gFTP application to run and display its main window.

Secret

The gFTP window (Figure 17-1) has a menu bar with menus for performing various tasks. Just below the menu bar is a toolbar with a number of buttons and text fields. Here, you can type the name of the remote host, the user name, and the password needed to log in to the remote host. After you supply the host and user information, click the button with the icon of two computers to the left of the Host field. This causes gFTP to connect to that host and to log in with the user name and password you have provided.

Figure 17-1 shows the gFTP window after you have connected to the remote FTP site and moved around the remote directories in prepartion for downloading some files.

Figure 17-1: The gFTP Window after Connecting to a Remote FTP Server.

The middle part of the gFTP window is divided into two parts. The left side shows the contents of the current local directory; after establishing a connection, the right side shows the contents of the remote directory. Once the directories are listed, transferring files is simple. Simply select the desired files in the list, clicking the left arrow button to download or the right arrow button to upload.

The best part about using gFTP is that you can download entire directories by simply selecting the directories on the right-hand side window and clicking the left arrow.

To disconnect, click the computer button again. You can then quit the gFTP application by selecting FTP➪Quit from the menu.

Using a Web Browser as an FTP Client

Any Web browser can act as an FTP client, but they are best for anonymous FTP downloads, where the Web browser can log in using the anonymous user name and any password.

In Red Hat Linux, you can use the Mozilla Web browser as an FTP client. All you need to do is provide the URL that tells the Web browser to download a file using FTP. The syntax of the FTP URL is

```
ftp://username:password@hostname/pathname
```

The first part (`ftp://`) indicates that you want an FTP transfer. The `hostname` part should be the name of the FTP server (the name often starts with an `ftp`—for example, `ftp.beta.redhat.com`). The `pathname` is the full directory path and filename of the file you want to download. The `username:password` is the username and password required to log in to the FTP server. You can leave them out if you want to log in as anonymous user.

caution   When you provide the username and password in the URL, the password is in plaintext and can be read by anyone who looks at the URL.

If the URL has only the hostname for the FTP server, the Web browser displays the contents of the anonymous FTP directory. If you want to try this on your Red Hat Linux system, start Mozilla (click the Mozilla icon on the GNOME panel), and then type the following line in the location text box:

```
ftp://localhost
```

Then press Enter. Mozilla shows the contents of the anonymous FTP directory on your Red Hat Linux system. You can click on folders to see their contents and download any files.

When you use the `ftp://localhost` URL, you won't get a response from your system if you are not running an FTP server or if you have set up your firewall such that no FTP connections are allowed.

The same approach of accessing anonymous FTP sites would work if you were to type the hostname of some other anonymous FTP server. For example, try typing the following URL:

```
ftp://ftp.netscape.com
```

You should get the directory of the `ftp.netscape.com` server.

Configuring the FTP Server

Red Hat Linux comes with the Very Secure FTP daemon (vsftpd), written by Chris Evans. The executable file for vsftpd is /usr/sbin/vsftpd, and it uses a number of configuration files in the /etc and /etc/vsftpd directories.

In previous versions of Red Hat Linux, the vsftpd server was set up to run under xinetd—the Internet super server. This required editing a configuration file in /etc/xinetd.d directory to enable the vsftpd server. However, starting in Red Hat Linux 9, the vsftpd server is configured to run stand-alone and there is an initialization script (or *initscript*)—/etc/init.d/vsftpd—to start and stop the server. As explained earlier in this chapter, you can start the server with the command:

```
service vsftpd start
```

You can type the following command as root to turn vsftpd on so that it starts at system startup:

```
chkconfig --level 35 vsftpd on
```

After you start the vsftpd server, the default settings should be adequate to begin using the server. However, you should learn about the configuration files in case you need to customize them.

Learning the vsftpd Configuration Files

The vsftpd server consults a number of configuration files located in the /etc directory. These directories control many aspects of the FTP server such as whether it runs stand-alone, who can download files, and whether to allow anonymous FTP.

Secret

The key configuration files for vsftpd are the following:

- /etc/vsftpd/vsftpd.conf controls how the vsftpd server works (for example, should it allow anonymous logins, should it allow file uploads, should it run standalone, and so on).
- /etc/vsftpd.ftpusers lists the names of users who cannot access the FTP server.
- /etc/vsftpd.user_list lists the names of users who are denied access (not even prompted for password). However, if the userlist_deny option is set to NO in /etc/vsftpd/vsftpd.conf, then these users are allowed to access the FTP server.

You can usually leave most of these configuration files with their default settings. However, just in case you need to change something to make vsftpd suit your needs, the next few sections briefly explain the configuration files.

Understanding the /etc/vsftpd/vsftpd.conf File

To learn what you can have in the /etc/vsftpd/vsftpd.conf file and how these lines affect the vsftpd server's operation, start by looking at the /etc/vsftpd/vsftpd.conf file that's installed by default in Red Hat Linux. The comments in this file tell you what each option does.

insider insight   **By default, vsftpd allows almost nothing. Through the options in** /etc/vsftpd/ vsftpd.conf **you can loosen the restrictions so that users can use FTP. It's up to you to decide how loose the settings should be. Note that most of the options are set to** YES. **That's because most of the default settings are** NO. **To reverse the intent of an option, just comment out that option by placing a** # **at the beginning of that line.**

Here are the options you can set in /etc/vsftpd/vsftpd.conf:

- anon_mkdir_write_enable=YES enables anonymous FTP users to create new directories. This is another risky option and you may want to set this to NO, even if you allow anonymous users to upload files.

- anon_upload_enable=YES means anonymous FTP users can upload files. This option takes effect only if write_enable is already set to YES and the directory has write permissions for everyone. Remember that allowing anonymous users to write on your system can be very risky because someone could fill up the disk or use your disk for their personal storage.

- anonymous_enable=YES enables anonymous FTP (so users can log in with the user name anonymous and provide their email address as password). Comment out this line if you do not want anonymous FTP.

- ascii_download_enable=YES enables file downloads in ASCII mode. Unfortunately, a malicious remote user can issue the SIZE command with the name of a huge file and essentially cause the FTP server to waste huge amounts of resources opening that file and determining its size. This can be used by malicious users as a denial of service attack.

- ascii_upload_enable=YES enables file uploads in ASCII mode (for text files).

- async_abor_enable=YES causes vsftpd to recognize ABOR (abort) requests that arrive at any time. You may need to enable it to allow older FTP clients to work with vsftpd.

- banned_email_file=/etc/vsftpd.banned_emails specifies the file with the list of banned email addresses (used only if deny_email_enable is set to YES).

- chown_uploads=YES causes uploaded anonymous files to be owned by a different user specified by the chown_username option. Don't enable this, unless absolutely necessary and don't make the chown_username be root.

- chown_username=name specifies the user name that would own files uploaded by anonymous FTP users.

- chroot_list_enable=YES causes vsftpd to confine all users except those on a list specified by the chroot_list_file to their home directories when they log in for FTP service. This prevents these users from getting to any other files besides what's in their home directories.

- chroot_list_file=/etc/vsftpd.chroot_list is the list of users who are either confined to their home directories or not, depending on the setting of chroot_local_user.

- connect_from_port_20=YES causes vsftpd to make sure that data transfers occur through port 20 (the FTP data port).

- data_connection_timeout=120 is the time in seconds after which an inactive data connection is timed out.

◆ `deny_email_enable=YES` causes vsftpd to check a list of banned email addresses and denies access to anyone who tries to log in anonymously with a banned email address as password.

◆ `dirmessage_enable=YES` causes vsftpd to display messages when FTP users change to certain directories.

◆ `ftpd_banner=Welcome to my FTP service.` sets the banner that vsftpd displays when a user logs in. You can change the message to anything you want.

◆ `idle_session_timeout=600` is the time (in seconds) after which an idle session (refers to the situation where someone connects and does not do anything) times out and vsftpd logs the user out.

◆ `listen=YES` causes vsftpd to listen for connection requests and, consequently, run in standalone mode. Set this to `NO` if you want to run vsftpd under xinetd.

◆ `local_enable=YES` causes vsftpd to grant local users access to FTP.

◆ `local_umask=022` means whatever files FTP writes will have a permission of 644 (read access for everyone, but write access for owner only). You can set it to any file permission mask setting you want. For example, if you want no permissions anyone but the owner, change this to 077.

◆ `ls_recurse_enable=YES` enables FTP users to recursively traverse directories using the `ls -R` command.

◆ `nopriv_user=ftp` identifies a unprivileged user that the FTP server can use.

◆ `pam_service_name=vsftpd` is the name of the Pluggable Authentication Module (PAM) configuration file that is used when vsftpd needs to authenticate a user. By default the PAM configuration files are in `/etc/pam.d` directory. That means vsftpd's PAM configuration file is `/etc/pam.d/vsftpd`.

◆ `userlist_deny=YES` causes vsftpd to deny access to the users listed in the `/etc/vsftpd.user_list` file. These users are not even prompted for a password.

◆ `write_enable=YES` causes vsftpd to allow file uploads to the host.

◆ `xferlog_enable=YES` turns on the logging of file downloads and uploads (always a good idea, but takes disk space).

◆ `xferlog_file=/var/log/vsftpd.log` specifies the full pathname of the vsftpd log file. The default is `/var/log/vsftpd.log`.

◆ `xferlog_std_format=YES` causes vsftpd to generate log files in a standard format used by other FTP daemons.

Secret

Understanding the /etc/vsftpd.ftpusers File

The vsftpd server uses the Pluggable Authentication Module (PAM) to authenticate users when they try to log in (just as the normal login process uses PAM to do the job). The PAM configuration file for vsftpd is `/etc/pam.d/vsftpd`. That PAM configuration file refers to `/etc/vsftpd.ftpusers` like this:

```
auth       required      pam_listfile.so item=user sense=deny
file=/etc/vsftpd.ftpusers onerr=succeed
```

continues

continued

This basically says that anyone listed in the `/etc/vsftpd.ftpusers` should be denied login. The default `/etc/vsftpd.ftpusers` file contains the following list of users:

```
root
bin
daemon
adm
lp
sync
shutdown
halt
mail
news
uucp
operator
games
nobody
```

If you want to deny FTP access to any other user names, simply add those names to the `/etc/vsftpd.ftpusers` file.

Understanding the /etc/vsftpd.user_list File

If the `userlist_deny` option is set to `YES`, vsftpd does not allow users listed in the `/etc/vsftpd.user_list` file any access to FTP services. It does not even prompt them for a password. However, if `userlist_deny` is set to `NO`, the meaning is reversed and these users are the only ones allowed access (but the PAM configuration still denies anyone on the `/etc/vsftpd.ftpusers` list).

Setting up Secure Anonymous FTP

Anonymous FTP refers to the use of the user name anonymous, which anyone can use with FTP to transfer files from a system. Anonymous FTP is a common way to share files on the Internet.

If you have used anonymous FTP to download files from Internet sites, you already know the convenience of that service. Anonymous FTP makes information available to anyone on the Internet. If you have a new Linux application that you want to share with the world, set up anonymous FTP on your Linux PC, and place the software in an appropriate directory. After that, all you need to do is announce to the world (probably through a posting in the comp.os.linux.announce newsgroup) that you have a new program available. Now, anyone can get the software from your system at his or her convenience.

Even if you run a for-profit business, you can use anonymous FTP to support your customers. If you sell a hardware or software product, you may want to provide technical information or software "fixes" through anonymous FTP.

Unfortunately, the convenience of anonymous FTP comes at a price. If you do not configure the anonymous FTP service properly, intruders and pranksters may gain access to your system. Some intruders may simply use your system's disk as a temporary holding place for various files; others may fill your disk with junk files, effectively making your system inoperable (this sort of attack is called a denial-of-service—DoS—attack). At the other extreme, an intruder may gain user-level (or, worse, root-level) access to your system and do much more damage.

> **note**   If you have installed Red Hat Linux from this book's companion CD-ROMs, you already have anonymous FTP on your system. The default setup also employs the necessary security precautions.

Trying Anonymous FTP

To see anonymous FTP in action, try accessing your system by using an FTP client. For example, in the following sample session, I have accessed my system from another PC on the LAN (my input appears in boldface):

```
ftp localhost
Connected to localhost (127.0.0.1).
220 (vsFTPd 1.1.3)
Name (localhost:naba): anonymous
331 Please specify the password.
Password:        <-- I can type anything as password.
230 Login successful. Have fun.
Remote system type is UNIX.
Using binary mode to transfer files.
ftp> ls -l
227 Entering Passive Mode (127,0,0,1,87,69)
150 Here comes the directory listing.
d--x--x--x    2 0        0            4096 Jan 19 19:31 bin
d--x--x--x    2 0        0            4096 Jan 19 19:31 etc
drwxr-xr-x    2 0        0            4096 Jan 19 19:31 lib
drwxr-sr-x    2 0        50           4096 Dec 13 16:13 pub
226 Directory send OK.
ftp> bye
221 Goodbye.
```

When you successfully log in for anonymous FTP, you access the home directory of the user named ftp (the default directory is /var/ftp). Place the publicly accessible files— the ones you want to enable others to download from your system—in the /var/ftp/pub directory.

Learning the Key Features of Anonymous FTP

The key features of an anonymous FTP setup are as follows:

- There is a user named `ftp` whose home directory is `/var/ftp`. The user does not have a shell assigned. Here is what you get when you search for `ftp` in the `/etc/passwd` file:

```
grep ftp /etc/passwd
ftp:x:14:50:FTP User:/var/ftp:/sbin/nologin
```

  The `x` in the second field means that no one can log in with the user name `ftp`. The login shell for this account, listed in the last field as `/sbin/nologin`, also ensures that the `ftp` user cannot log in (type **man nologin** to see what the `nologin` shell does).

- Here is the full permission setting and owner information for the `/var/ftp` directory:

```
drwxr-xr-x    6 root      root          4096 Jan 18 14:31 ftp
```

  As this line shows, the `/var/ftp` directory is owned by `root`, and the permission is set to 755 (only `root` can read and write; everyone else can only read; for more information on permission settings, see the `chmod` command described in Appendix A).

- To view the contents of the `/var/ftp` directory, type the `ls -la` command. The output of this command is as follows:

```
total 24
drwxr-xr-x    6 root      root          4096 Jan 18 21:20 .
drwxr-xr-x   21 root      root          4096 Jan 18 21:33 ..
d--x--x--x    2 root      root          4096 Jan 18 21:20 bin
d--x--x--x    2 root      root          4096 Jan 18 21:20 etc
drwxr-xr-x    2 root      root          4096 Jan 18 21:20 lib
drwxr-sr-x    2 root      ftp           4096 Dec 13 11:13 pub
```

  The permission settings of the `bin` and `etc` directories are 111 (execute only). All files inside the `bin` directory are also execute-only (permission setting 111). All files in the `etc` directory are `read-only` (permission setting 444).

- The `pub` directory is where you place any files you want to enable others to download from your system through anonymous FTP.

Summary

File Transfer Protocol (FTP) is a popular Internet service for transferring files from one system to another. This chapter describes the FTP service and shows you how to configure the vsftpd server that comes with Red Hat Linux.

By reading this chapter, you learn the following:

- ♦ FTP is an important Internet service for transferring files from one system to another. FTP is documented in RFC 959.
- ♦ You must set up and run an FTP server if you want your system's users to transfer files to and from the system. Red Hat Linux comes with the Very Secure FTP daemon (`vsftpd`), a popular FTP server.

♦ The vsftpd server is set up to run standalone. You can start it with the command `service vsftpd start`. You can set the vsftpd server to start at boot time by typing the command `chkconfig —level 35 vsftpd on`.

♦ You can configure the vsftpd server by editing the files `/etc/vsftpd/vsftpd.conf`, `/etc/vsftpd.ftpusers`, and `/etc/vsftpd.user_list`.

♦ Anonymous FTP is another popular Internet service for distributing files. With anonymous FTP, anyone can use FTP with the anonymous user ID and can download files from your system. Although anonymous FTP is useful for distributing data, it poses a security risk if it is not set up properly.

♦ The default Red Hat Linux installation includes everything needed to support anonymous FTP. The default anonymous FTP setup incorporates the necessary security precautions.

DNS and NIS

Chapter

18

♦ ♦

Secrets in This Chapter

♦ ♦

Domain Name System (DNS) is an Internet service that converts a fully qualified domain name, such as www.redhat.com, into its corresponding IP address. You can think of DNS as the directory of Internet hosts—DNS is what enables you to refer to a host by its name even though TCP/IP requires IP addresses for data transfers. DNS is implemented by a hierarchy of distributed DNS servers. This chapter provides an overview of DNS and shows you how to set up a caching DNS server on your Red Hat Linux system.

Network Information System (NIS) is a client/server service designed to manage information shared among several host computers on a network. Typically, NIS is used on UNIX (and Linux) systems to maintain a common set of user accounts and other system files for a group of hosts. This, among other things, enables a user to log in on all hosts with the same user name and password. This chapter describes the NIS client and server software and shows you how to use them on a Red Hat Linux system.

Using the Domain Name System (DNS)

In TCP/IP networks, each network interface (for example, an Ethernet card on a host computer) is identified by an IP address. Because IP addresses are hard to remember, an association is made between an easy-to-remember name and the IP address—much like the association between a name and a telephone number. For example, instead of having to remember that the IP address of Red Hat's Web server is 216.148.218.195, you can simply refer to that host by its name, www.redhat.com. When you type **www.redhat.com** as the URL in a Web browser, the name www.redhat.com has to be translated into its corresponding IP address. This is where the concept of DNS comes in.

Secret

DNS is a distributed, hierarchical database that holds information about computers on the Internet. The information includes the hostname, the IP address, and mail routing information. This information resides in many DNS hosts on the Internet; that's why the DNS database is called a distributed database. The primary job of DNS is to associate hostnames to IP addresses and vice versa.

In ARPANET—the precursor to today's Internet, the association between hostnames and IP addresses was maintained in a text file named HOSTS.TXT, which was managed centrally and distributed to each host. As the number of hosts grew, it became clear that a static host table was unreasonable. DNS was proposed by Paul Mockapetris to alleviate the problems associated with using a static host table. As formally documented in RFCs 882 and 883 (November 1983), DNS introduced two key concepts:

- **Use of hierarchical domain names,** such as www.ee.umd.edu and www.redhat.com
- **Distributed responsibility** for managing the host database by using DNS servers throughout the Internet

DNS, as we know it today, is an Internet standard documented in RFCs 1034 and 1035. The standard has been updated and extended by several other RFCs—1101, 1183, 1348, 1876, 1982, 1996, 2065, 2181, 2136, 2308, 2535, 2845, 2929, 2930, 2931, 3007, 3008, 3090, 3110, and 3130. The earlier updates define data encoding, whereas later ones focus on improving DNS security. To read these and other RFCs online, visit Ohio State University's Internet RFC page at http://www.cis.ohio-state.edu/hypertext/information/rfc.html.

DNS defines the following:

- ♦ A hierarchical domain-naming system for hosts
- ♦ A distributed database that associates a name with an IP address
- ♦ Library routines that network applications can use to query the distributed DNS database (this library is called the resolver library)
- ♦ A protocol for DNS clients and servers to exchange information about names and IP addresses

Nowadays, all hosts on the Internet rely on DNS to access various Internet services on remote hosts. As you may know from personal experience, when you obtain Internet access from an Internet service provider (ISP), the ISP provides you with the IP addresses of name servers. These are the DNS servers your system accesses whenever hostnames have to be mapped to IP addresses.

If you have a small LAN, you may decide to run a DNS server on one of the hosts or to use the name servers provided by the ISP. For medium-sized networks with several subnets, you can run a DNS server on each subnet to provide efficient DNS lookups. On a large corporate network, the corporate domain (such as `microsoft.com`) is further subdivided into a hierarchy of subdomains, and several DNS servers may be used in each subdomain.

The following sections provide an overview of the hierarchical domain-naming convention, and describe BIND—the implementation of DNS used on most UNIX systems, including Red Hat Linux.

Understanding Hierarchical Domain Names

DNS uses a hierarchical tree of domains to organize the namespace—the entire set of names. Each higher-level domain has authority over its lower-level subdomains. Each domain represents a distinct block of the namespace and is managed by a single administrative authority. Figure 18-1 illustrates the hierarchical organization of the DNS namespace.

Figure 18-1: Sample Domain Names Illustrating the Hierarchical DNS Namespace.

The root of the tree is called the root domain and is represented by a single dot (.). The top-level, or root-level, domains come next. The top-level domains are further divided into second-level domains, which, in turn, can be broken into further subdomains.

Secret

The top-level domains are relatively fixed and include well-known domains such as com, net, org, edu, gov, and mil. These are the commonly used top-level domains in the United States. These top-level domains came about as the Internet became widely used in the early 1990s. More recently, however, there have been many newer top-level domains such as aero, biz, coop, info, museum, and name. To learn about these and other top-level domains, visit http://www.iana.org/gtld/gtld.htm.

There is another set of top-level domain names for the countries, called *country code domains*. These domain names use the two-letter country codes assigned by the International Organization for Standardization (abbreviated as ISO, see http://www.iso.ch/). For example, the top-level country code domain for the United States is us. In the United States, many local governments and organizations use the us domain. For example, mcps.k12.md.us is the domain name of the Montgomery County Public Schools in the state of Maryland in United States. To see a list of the top-level country code domain names, please see http://www.iana.org/cctld/cctld-whois.htm.

The fully qualified domain name (FQDN) is constructed by stringing together the sub-domain names, from lower to higher level, using dots (.) as separators. For example, REDHAT.COM is a fully qualified domain name; so is EE.UMD.EDU. Note that each of these may also refer to a specific host computer. Figure 18-2 illustrates the components of a fully qualified domain name.

ee.umd.edu

Top level domain

Second level domain

Subdomain or host name

Figure 18-2: Components of a Fully Qualified Domain Name.

Domain names are case insensitive. Therefore, as far as DNS is concerned, the domains UMD.EDU and umd.edu both represent University of Maryland's domain. The norm, however, is to type domain names in all lowercase.

Using the Berkeley Internet Domain Name (BIND) System

Most UNIX systems, including Red Hat Linux, come with the BIND system—a well-known implementation of DNS. The BIND software is installed during Red Hat Linux installation, as long as you select the DNS Name Server package group when selecting the packages for installation.

To see which version of BIND is installed on your Red Hat Linux system, type the following command:

```
rpm -q bind
bind-9.2.1-16
```

As the output shows, BIND Version 9.2.1 is installed on my system.

BIND includes three major components:

♦ The `named` daemon—the name server— that responds to queries about hostnames and IP addresses

♦ A resolver library that applications can use to resolve hostnames into IP addresses and vice versa

♦ Command-line DNS utility programs (DNS clients), such as dig (Domain Internet Groper) and host, that users can use to query DNS

The next few sections describe these components of BIND. Later sections describe how to configure the resolver and the name server.

Secret

Learning More about DNS and BIND

This chapter only briefly describes DNS and BIND, but entire books have been devoted solely to them. For example, *DNS and BIND, 4th Edition*, by Paul Albitz and Cricket Liu (O'Reilly & Associates, April 2001), can help you learn more about DNS and BIND.

BIND also comes with a lot of online documentation that's installed on your Red Hat Linux system when you install the DNS Name Server package group. To read the online documentation about BIND, change the current directory with the command `cd/usr/share/doc/bind*` (the directory name depends on which version of BIND is installed on your system), and look at the files in that directory.

The Internet Software Consortium (ISC)—a nonprofit corporation—supports BIND. Visit their website at `http://www.isc.org/` to learn more about the latest release of BIND.

To ask questions online about DNS and BIND, or to participate in related discussions, read the following newsgroups (see Chapter 16 for more information about reading newsgroups):

• comp.protocols.dns.bind—Discussions about using BIND

• comp.protocols.dns.ops—Discussions about DNS operations

• comp.protocols.dns.std—Discussions about DNS standards

Understanding named—the BIND Name Server

The `named` daemon is the name server that responds to queries about hostnames and IP addresses. Based on the configuration files and the local DNS database, named either provides answers to queries or asks other servers and caches their responses. The named server also performs a function referred to as *zone transfer*, which involves copying data among the name servers in a domain.

Secret

The `named` name server can be configured to operate in one of three modes:

• **Primary or Master**—This is the authoritative name server that keeps the master copy of the domain's data on disk. There is one primary server for each domain or subdomain.

• **Secondary or Slave**—A secondary name server copies its domain's data from the primary server using a zone transfer operation. There can be one or more secondary name servers for a domain.

continues

continued

- **Caching**—A caching name server loads the addresses of a few authoritative servers for the root domain and gets all domain data by caching responses to queries resolved by contacting other name servers. Primary and secondary servers also cache responses. The Time To Live (TTL) field associated with each resource record controls the length of time for which a record may be retained in the cache of a caching name server. As you see later in this chapter, you can easily extend a caching-only name server into a primary name server.

A name server can be authoritative or not. As the term implies, the response from an authoritative name server is supposed to be accurate. The primary and secondary name servers are authoritative for their own domains, but they are not authoritative for responses provided from cached information. Caching name servers are never authoritative because all of their responses come from cached information.

To run a name server on your Red Hat Linux system, you have to run `named` with the appropriate configuration files. Later in this chapter, you learn about the configuration files and data files that control how the name server operates.

Understanding Resolver Library

Finding an IP address for a hostname is referred to as *resolving the hostname*. Network-aware applications, such as a Web browser or an FTP client, use a resolver library to perform the conversion from the name to an IP address. Depending on the settings in the `/etc/host.conf` file, the resolver library consults the `/etc/hosts` file or makes a DNS query to resolve a hostname to its IP address. The resolver library queries the name servers listed in the `/etc/resolv.conf` file.

You do not need to learn much about the resolver library unless you are writing network-aware applications. To run Internet services properly, all you need to learn is how to configure the resolver. Subsequent sections in this chapter show you how to configure this and other aspects of DNS.

Using DNS Utility Programs

You can use the DNS utility programs—dig and host—to try out DNS from the shell prompt interactively. These utility programs are DNS clients. You can use them to query the DNS database and debug any name server you might set up on your system. By default, these programs query the name server listed in your system's `/etc/resolv.conf` file.

Using dig

You can use dig, the Domain Internet Groper program, to look up IP addresses for a domain name or vice versa. For example, to look up the IP address of `addlab.nws.noaa.gov`, type:

```
dig addlab.nws.noaa.gov
```

dig prints the results of the DNS query with a great amount of detail. Here's the output of that `dig` command on my Red Hat Linux system:

```
; <<>> DiG 9.2.1 <<>> addlab.nws.noaa.gov
;; global options:  printcmd
;; Got answer:
;; ->>HEADER<<- opcode: QUERY, status: NOERROR, id: 18561
;; flags: qr rd ra; QUERY: 1, ANSWER: 1, AUTHORITY: 6, ADDITIONAL: 6

;; QUESTION SECTION:
;addlab.nws.noaa.gov.           IN      A

;; ANSWER SECTION:
addlab.nws.noaa.gov.    86400   IN      A       140.90.141.131

;; AUTHORITY SECTION:
nws.noaa.gov.           86400   IN      NS      netinfo.hqnoc.noaa.gov.
nws.noaa.gov.           86400   IN      NS      ns3.noc.noaa.gov.
nws.noaa.gov.           86400   IN      NS      nwrns.noaa.gov.
nws.noaa.gov.           86400   IN      NS      serns.noaa.gov.
nws.noaa.gov.           86400   IN      NS      merns.noaa.gov.
nws.noaa.gov.           86400   IN      NS      mwrns.noaa.gov.

;; ADDITIONAL SECTION:
netinfo.hqnoc.noaa.gov. 86400   IN      A       140.90.148.33
ns3.noc.noaa.gov.       86400   IN      A       140.90.143.33
nwrns.noaa.gov.         67000   IN      A       161.55.32.3
serns.noaa.gov.         69806   IN      A       192.111.123.245
merns.noaa.gov.         68814   IN      A       192.94.173.133
mwrns.noaa.gov.         68801   IN      A       140.172.253.1

;; Query time: 50 msec
;; SERVER: 192.168.0.1#53(192.168.0.1)
;; WHEN: Sun Feb 16 17:59:12 2003
;; MSG SIZE  rcvd: 279
```

The answer you are looking for—the IP address of the host—is in the in the part of the output labeled ANSWER SECTION:. Here's what that section looks like for this sample query:

```
;; ANSWER SECTION:
addlab.nws.noaa.gov.    86400    IN       A       140.90.141.131
```

Thus, the IP address of addlab.nws.noaa.gov is 140.90.141.131. The other sections in dig's output shows details such as the server it queried, the authoritative name servers for the hostname it queried, the time it took to perform the query, and so on. In this example, the SERVER line near the end of dig's output shows that dig queries the name server at the IP address 192.168.0.1—that's the first name server listed in my system's /etc/resolv.conf file.

Reverse lookups (finding hostnames for IP addresses) are also easy with dig. All you have to do is use dig with the -x option. For example, to find the hostname corresponding to the IP address 140.90.141.131, type the following:

```
dig -x 140.90.141.131
```

On my system, the output from this query looks like this:

```
; <<>> DiG 9.2.1 <<>> -x 140.90.141.131
;; global options:  printcmd
;; Got answer:
;; ->>HEADER<<- opcode: QUERY, status: NOERROR, id: 22285
;; flags: qr aa rd ra; QUERY: 1, ANSWER: 1, AUTHORITY: 6, ADDITIONAL: 6

;; QUESTION SECTION:
;131.141.90.140.in-addr.arpa.   IN      PTR

;; ANSWER SECTION:
131.141.90.140.in-addr.arpa. 86400 IN   PTR     addlab.nws.noaa.gov.

;; AUTHORITY SECTION:
141.90.140.in-addr.arpa. 86400  IN      NS      merns.noaa.gov.
141.90.140.in-addr.arpa. 86400  IN      NS      mwrns.noaa.gov.
141.90.140.in-addr.arpa. 86400  IN      NS      nwrns.noaa.gov.
141.90.140.in-addr.arpa. 86400  IN      NS      serns.noaa.gov.
141.90.140.in-addr.arpa. 86400  IN      NS      netinfo.hqnoc.noaa.gov.
141.90.140.in-addr.arpa. 86400  IN      NS      ns3.noc.noaa.gov.

;; ADDITIONAL SECTION:
ns3.noc.noaa.gov.        86400   IN      A       140.90.143.33
merns.noaa.gov.          86400   IN      A       192.94.173.133
mwrns.noaa.gov.          86400   IN      A       140.172.253.1
nwrns.noaa.gov.          86400   IN      A       161.55.32.3
serns.noaa.gov.          86400   IN      A       192.111.123.245
netinfo.hqnoc.noaa.gov. 86400   IN      A       140.90.148.33

;; Query time: 56 msec
;; SERVER: 192.168.0.1#53(192.168.0.1)
;; WHEN: Sun Feb 16 18:03:06 2003
;; MSG SIZE  rcvd: 304
```

As you can see, dig prints a lot of information in addition to the result. The answer you want comes right after the label ANSWER SECTION:, which in this case shows the hostname to be addlab.nws.noaa.gov.

You can use dig to query other types of DNS records than name-to-address and address-to-name lookups. For example, DNS also contains mail exchanger (record type MX) to enable delivery of mail to a specific doman. The MX record instructs querying computers where to send messages meant for a domain. To look up an MX record for a host, simply prefix the hostname with the record type. Here is an example that queries the MX record for the domain name comcast.net:

```
dig MX comcast.net
```

Here's the resulting output on my system:

```
; <<>> DiG 9.2.1 <<>> MX comcast.net
;; global options:  printcmd
;; Got answer:
```

```
;; ->>HEADER<<- opcode: QUERY, status: NOERROR, id: 34566
;; flags: qr rd ra; QUERY: 1, ANSWER: 1, AUTHORITY: 2, ADDITIONAL: 3

;; QUESTION SECTION:
;comcast.net.                    IN      MX

;; ANSWER SECTION:
comcast.net.            229297  IN      MX      0 mx00.comcast.net.

;; AUTHORITY SECTION:
comcast.net.            12924   IN      NS      NS01.JDC01.PA.comcast.net.
comcast.net.            12924   IN      NS      NS02.JDC01.PA.comcast.net.

;; ADDITIONAL SECTION:
mx00.comcast.net.         5742  IN      A       24.153.64.1
NS01.JDC01.PA.comcast.net. 6437 IN      A       66.45.25.71
NS02.JDC01.PA.comcast.net. 2332 IN      A       66.45.25.72

;; Query time: 1459 msec
;; SERVER: 192.168.0.1#53(192.168.0.1)
;; WHEN: Sun Feb 16 18:05:21 2003
;; MSG SIZE  rcvd: 145
```

Again, the ANSWER SECTION shows the MX record, which says that mail addressed to comcast.net should be sent to mx00.comcast.net.

Using the host Command

You can also query DNS by using the host command. The host program produces output in a compact format. For example, here's a typical use of host to look up information about a host:

```
host www.gao.gov
www.gao.gov has address 161.203.16.2
```

By default, host prints the IP address and any MX record (these records list the names of mail handlers for the host).

For a reverse lookup, use the -t ptr option, along with the IP address as an argument, as follows:

```
host -t ptr 161.203.16.2
2.16.203.161.in-addr.arpa. domain name pointer www.gao.gov.
```

In this case, host prints the PTR record that shows the hostname corresponding to the specified IP address.

You can also try other types of records, such as CNAME (for canonical name), as follows:

```
host -t cname www.ee.umd.edu

www.ee.umd.edu. is an alias for www.ece.umd.edu.
```

This indicates that the canonical name for www.ee.umd.edu is www.ece.umd.edu.

Configuring DNS

You configure DNS by using a number of configuration files. The exact set of files depends on whether or not you are running a name server and, if so, the type of name server—caching or primary. Some configuration files are needed whether you run a name server or not.

Configuring the Resolver

You do not need a name server running on your system to use the DNS clients—dig and host. You can use them to query one of your domain's name servers. Typically, your ISP provides you with this information. You have to list the IP addresses of these name servers in the /etc/resolv.conf file—the resolver library reads this file to determine how to resolve hostnames. The format of this file is

```
domain your-domain.com
search your-domain.com
nameserver A.B.C.D
nameserver X.Y.Z.W
```

where A.B.C.D and X.Y.Z.W are the IP addresses (dotted-decimal IP addresses, such as 192.168.0.1) of the primary and secondary name servers your ISP provides you.

Secret

The domain line in /etc/resolv.conf lists the local domain name. The search line specifies the domains on which a hostname is searched first (usually, you put your own domain in the search line). The domain listed on the search line is appended to any hostname before the resolver library tries to resolve it. For example, if the search line contains your-domain.com, then when you look for a host named mailhost, the resolver library first tries mailhost.your-domain.com; if that fails, it tries mailhost. The search line applies to any hostname you try to access. For example, if you are trying to access www.redhat.com, the resolver first tries www.redhat.com.your-domain.com and then www.redhat.com.

Another important configuration file is /etc/host.conf—this file tells the resolver what to do when attempting to resolve a hostname. A typical /etc/host/conf file contains the following line:

```
order hosts,bind
```

This tells the resolver to consult the /etc/hosts file first and, if that fails, to query the name server listed in the /etc/resolv.conf file. As explained in Chapter 6, the /etc/hosts file associates IP addresses to hostnames. A typical line from the /etc/hosts file looks like the following:

```
127.0.0.1    lnbp200   localhost.localdomain   localhost
```

This line says that the IP address 127.0.0.1 is assigned to the hostnames lnbp200, localhost.localdomain, and localhost.

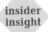

insider
insight

In the latest version of Linux, which uses GNU C Library version 2 (glibc 2) or later, the name service switch (NSS) file, /etc/nsswitch.conf, specifies how services such as the resolver library, NIS, NIS+, and local files such as /etc/hosts and /etc/shadow interact. For example, the following hosts entry in the /etc/nsswitch.conf file specifies that the resolver library should first try the /etc/hosts file, then try NIS+, and finally try DNS:

```
hosts:        files nisplus dns
```

To learn more about the /etc/nsswitch.conf file and what it does, type info libc "Name Service Switch" at the shell prompt in a terminal window.

Configuring a Caching Name Server

A simple, but useful name server is one that finds answers to hostname queries by using other name servers and then remembers the answer (by saving it in a cache) the next time you need it. This can shorten the time it takes to access hosts you have accessed recently because the answer is already in the cache.

When you install the DNS Name Server package group during Red Hat Linux installation, the configuration files for a caching name server are also installed. That means you can start running the caching name server without much work on your part. This section describes the configuration files and what you have to do to start the caching name server.

Examining the /etc/named.conf File

The first configuration file you need is /etc/named.conf. The named server reads this configuration file when it starts. You already have this file if you have installed the DNS Name Server when you installed Red Hat Linux in Chapter 2. Here's what the default /etc/named.conf file contains:

```
// generated by named-bootconf.pl

options {
        directory "/var/named";
        /*
         * If there is a firewall between you and nameservers you want
         * to talk to, you might need to uncomment the query-source
         * directive below.  Previous versions of BIND always asked
         * questions using port 53, but BIND 8.1 uses an unprivileged
         * port by default.
         */
        // query-source address * port 53;
};

//
// a caching only nameserver config
//
controls {
        inet 127.0.0.1 allow { localhost; } keys { rndckey; };
```

```
};
zone "." IN {
        type hint;
        file "named.ca";
};

zone "localhost" IN {
        type master;
        file "localhost.zone";
        allow-update { none; };
};

zone "0.0.127.in-addr.arpa" IN {
        type master;
        file "named.local";
        allow-update { none; };
};


include "/etc/rndc.key";
```

Comments are C-style (/* ... */) or C++-style (start with //). The file contains block statements enclosed in curly braces ({...}) and terminated by a semicolon (;). A block statement, in turn, contains other statements, each ending with a semicolon.

This /etc/named.conf file begins with an options block statement with a number of option statements. The directory option statement tells named where to look for all other files that appear on file lines in the configuration file. In this case, named looks for the files in the /var/named directory.

Secret

The controls statement in /etc/named.conf contains security information so that the rndc command can connect to the named service at port 953 and interact with named. In this case, the controls statement contains the following line:

```
inet 127.0.0.1 allow { localhost; } keys { rndckey; };
```

This says the rndc can connect from localhost with the key named rndc (the file /etc/rndc.key defines the key and the encryption algorithm to be used).

The rndc (remote name daemon control) utility is a successor to the older ndc (name daemon controller) utility used to control the named server by sending it messages over a special control channel, a TCP port where named listens for messages. The rndc utility uses a cryptographic key and authenticates itself to the named server by using a fast MD5 secure hash algorithm called HMAC-MD5 (see RFCs 2085 and 2104 for more information on HMAC-MD5). The named server has the same cryptographic key so that it can decode the authentication information sent by rndc.

After the options and controls statements, the /etc/named.conf file contains several zone statements, each enclosed in curly braces and terminated by a semicolon. Each zone statement defines a zone. The first zone is named "." (root zone); it's a hint zone that specifies the root name servers.

The next two `zone` statements in `/etc/named.conf` are master zones. The syntax for a master `zone` statement for an Internet class zone (indicated by the IN keyword) is as follows:

```
zone "zone-name" IN {
        type master;
        file "zone-file";
        [...other optional statements...]
};
```

The `zone-name` is the name of the zone, and `zone-file` is the zone file that contains the resource records (RR)—the database entries—for that zone.

The `/etc/named.conf` file ends with an `include` statement:

```
include "/etc/rndc.key";
```

This statement inserts the contents of the `/etc/rndc.key` file into the `/etc/named.conf` file. This enables you to place sensitive configuration data (such as encryption keys) in a separate file with appropriate permissions to prevent nonroot users from accessing it. In this case, the `/etc/rndc.key` file contains the key named `rndc`, which was referenced in the `options` statement eariler in the `/etc/named.conf` file. Here is what the key definition looks like:

```
key "rndckey" {
        algorithm        hmac-md5;
        secret "AbigLongEncryptionKey";
};
```

The `algorithm` option specifies the type of algorithm, which can be `dsa` or `hmac-md5`. The `secret` option specifies the encryption key.

---

insider insight

To generate your own HMAC-MD5 key, use the `dnssec-keygen` command with the following syntax:

```
dnssec-keygen -a hmac-md5 -b 128 -n HOST yourhost.domain.
```

You should replace `yourhost.domain` with your host's fully qualified domain name. The `dnssec-keygen` command generates two files whose names begin with K followed by the hostname. One of the files has a `.key` extension and the other .private. Use the `cat` command to look at the content of either file and copy the cryptic looking key to the secret option of the `/etc/rndc.key` file.

Understanding the Zone File Format

The zone file typically starts with a number of directives, each of which begins with a dollar sign ($) followed by a keyword. Two commonly used directives are `$TTL` and `$ORIGIN`.

For example, the line

```
$TTL    86400
```

uses the $TTL directive to set the default time to live (TTL) for subsequent records with undefined TTLs. The value is in seconds, and the valid TTLs are in the range 0 to 2147483647 seconds. In this case, the directive sets the default TTL as 86400 seconds (or one day). The time specified in the time-to-live directive indicates how long the information in that record should be considered valid.

The $ORIGIN directive sets the domain name that will be appended to any unqualified records. For example, the following $ORIGIN directive sets the domain name to localhost:

```
$ORIGIN localhost.
```

insider insight
If there is no $ORIGIN directive, the initial $ORIGIN is the same as the zone name that comes after the `zone` keyword in the `/etc/named.conf` file.

After the directives, the zone file contains one or more resource records. These records follow a specific format, which is outlined in the next section.

Understanding Resource Record (RR) Format

You have to understand the format of the resource records before you can understand and intelligently work with zone files. Each resource record has the following format (the optional fields are shown in square brackets):

```
[domain] [ttl] [class] type data [;comment]
```

Secret

In a resource record the fields are separated by tabs or spaces and may contain some special characters, such as an @ symbol for the domain and a semicolon (;) to indicate the start of a comment.

The first field, which must begin at the first character of the line, identifies the domain. You can use the @ symbol to use the current $ORIGIN for the domain name for this record. If you have multiple records for the same domain name, leave the first field blank.

The optional `ttl` field specifies the time to live—the duration for which the data can be cached and considered valid. You can specify the duration in one of the following formats:

- *N*, where *N* is a number meaning *N* seconds
- *N*W, where *N* is a number meaning *N* weeks
- *N*D, where *N* is a number meaning *N* days
- *N*H, where *N* is a number meaning *N* hours
- *N*M, where *N* is a number meaning *N* minutes
- *N*S, where *N* is a number meaning *N* seconds

The letters W, D, H, M, and S can also be in lowercase. Thus, you can write 86400 or 1D (or 1d) to indicate a duration of one day. You can also combine these to specify more precise durations, such as 5w6d16h to indicate 5 weeks, 6 days, and 16 hours.

The `class` field specifies the network type. The most commonly used value for this field is `IN` for Internet. Other values are `CH` for ChaosNet (an obsolete network used long ago by Symbolics Lisp computers), and `HS` for Hesiod (an NIS-like database service based on BIND).

Next in the resource record is the `type` field, which denotes the type of record (such as `SOA`, `NS`, `A`, or `PTR`). Table 18-1 lists many commonly used DNS resource record types. The data field comes next, and it depends on the type field.

Table 18-1: Common DNS Resource Record Types

Type	Name	Description
A	Address	Specifies the host address corresponding to a name
A	IPv6 Address	Specifies the IPv6 host address corresponding to a name
CERT	Digital Certificate	Holds a digital certificate
CNAME	Canonical Name	Defines the nickname or alias for a hostname
DNAME	Delegation Name	Replaces specified domain name with another name to be looked up
HINFO	Host Info	Identifies the hardware and operating system for a host
KEY	Public Key	Stores a public key associated with a DNS name
MX	Mail Exchanger	Identifies the host that accepts mail meant for a domain (used to route email)
NS	Name Server	Identifies authoritative name servers for a zone
PTR	Pointer	Specifies the name corresponding to an address (used for reverse mapping—converting an IP address to a hostname)
RP	Responsible Person	Provides the name of a technical contact for a domain
SIG	Signature	Contains data authenticated in the secure DNS (see RFC 2535 for details)
SOA	Start of authority	Indicates that all subsequent records are authoritative for this zone
SRV	Services	Lists well-known network services provided by the domain
TXT	Text	Used to include comments and other information in the DNS database
WKS	Well Known Services	Lists services provided by a host (this has been deprecated and is no longer used)

You should learn to read the resource records, at least the ones of type `SOA`, `NS`, `A`, `PTR`, and `MX`, which are some of the most commonly used. The next few sections briefly describe these records, illustrating each record type through an example.

SOA Record

A typical SOA record has the following format:

```
@       1D IN SOA       @ root (
                        42                      ; serial
                        3H                      ; refresh -- 3 hours
                        15M                     ; retry -- 15 minutes
                        1W                      ; expiry -- 1 week
                        1D )                    ; minimum -- 1 day
```

The first field specifies the domain as an @, which means the current domain (by default, the zone name, as shown in the /etc/named.conf file). The next field specifies a TTL of one day for this record. The class field is set to IN, which means that the record is for Internet. The type field specifies the record type as SOA. The rest of the fields constitute the data for the SOA record. The data includes the name of the primary name server (in this case, @, or the current domain), the email address of the technical contact, and five different times enclosed in parentheses.

NS Record

The NS record specifies the authoritative name servers for a zone. A typical NS record looks like the following:

```
.                       3600000   IN   NS    A.ROOT-SERVERS.NET.
```

In this case, the NS record lists the authoritative name server for the root zone (notice that the name of the first field is a single dot). The TTL field specifies the record to be valid for 1,000 hours (3600000 seconds). The class is IN, for Internet, and the record type is NS. The final field lists the name of the name server (A.ROOT-SERVERS.NET.), which ends with a dot.

A Record

An A record specifies the address corresponding to a name. For example, the following A record shows the address of A.ROOT-SERVERS.NET. as 198.41.0.4:

```
A.ROOT-SERVERS.NET.     3600000       A       198.41.0.4
```

In this case, the network class is not specified because the field is optional, and the default is IN.

PTR Record

PTR records are used for reverse mapping—converting an address to a name. Consider the following example:

```
1       IN      PTR     localhost.
```

This record comes from a file for a zone named 0.0.127.in-addr.arpa. Therefore, this record says that the name associated with the address 127.0.0.1 is localhost.

MX Record

An MX record specifies the name of a host that accepts mail on behalf of a specific domain. For example, here's a typical MX record:

```
naba    IN      MX      10      mailhub.lnbsoft.com.
```

This says that mail addressed to the hostnamed `naba` in the current domain should be sent to `mailhub.lnbsoft.com` (this host is called a *mail exchanger*). The number `10` is the preference value. For a list of multiple MX records with different preference values, the ones with lower preference values are tried first.

Now that you know a bit about resource records, you can go through the zone files for the caching name server.

Understanding the /var/named/named.ca File

Information about the root name servers is in the file `/var/named/named.ca`, as specified in the `zone` statement for the root zone in the `/etc/named.conf` file. The following listing shows the `/var/named/named.ca` file from a Red Hat Linux system:

```
;       This file holds the information on root name servers needed to
;       initialize cache of Internet domain name servers
;       (e.g. reference this file in the "cache  .  <file>"
;       configuration file of BIND domain name servers).
;
;       This file is made available by InterNIC
;       under anonymous FTP as
;           file                /domain/named.cache
;           on server           FTP.INTERNIC.NET
;
;       last update:    Nov 5, 2002
;       related version of root zone:   2002110501
;
;
; formerly NS.INTERNIC.NET
;
.                           3600000  IN  NS   A.ROOT-SERVERS.NET.
A.ROOT-SERVERS.NET.         3600000      A    198.41.0.4

; formerly NS1.ISI.EDU
;
.                           3600000      NS   B.ROOT-SERVERS.NET.
B.ROOT-SERVERS.NET.         3600000      A    128.9.0.107

; formerly C.PSI.NET
;
.                           3600000      NS   C.ROOT-SERVERS.NET.
C.ROOT-SERVERS.NET.         3600000      A    192.33.4.12
;
; formerly TERP.UMD.EDU
;
.                           3600000      NS   D.ROOT-SERVERS.NET.
D.ROOT-SERVERS.NET.         3600000      A    128.8.10.90

; formerly NS.NASA.GOV
;
.                           3600000      NS   E.ROOT-SERVERS.NET.
E.ROOT-SERVERS.NET.         3600000      A    192.203.230.10
;
```

```
; formerly NS.ISC.ORG
;
.                           3600000    NS    F.ROOT-SERVERS.NET.
F.ROOT-SERVERS.NET.         3600000    A     192.5.5.241
;
; formerly NS.NIC.DDN.MIL
;
.                           3600000    NS    G.ROOT-SERVERS.NET.
G.ROOT-SERVERS.NET.         3600000    A     192.112.36.4
;
; formerly AOS.ARL.ARMY.MIL
;
.                           3600000    NS    H.ROOT-SERVERS.NET.
H.ROOT-SERVERS.NET.         3600000    A     128.63.2.53
;
; formerly NIC.NORDU.NET
;
.                           3600000    NS    I.ROOT-SERVERS.NET.
I.ROOT-SERVERS.NET.         3600000    A     192.36.148.17
;
; operated by VeriSign, Inc.
;
.                           3600000    NS    J.ROOT-SERVERS.NET.
J.ROOT-SERVERS.NET.         3600000    A     192.58.128.30
;
; housed in LINX, operated by RIPE NCC
;
.                           3600000    NS    K.ROOT-SERVERS.NET.
K.ROOT-SERVERS.NET.         3600000    A     193.0.14.129
;
; operated by IANA
;
.                           3600000    NS    L.ROOT-SERVERS.NET.
L.ROOT-SERVERS.NET.         3600000    A     198.32.64.12
;
; housed in Japan, operated by WIDE
;
.                           3600000    NS    M.ROOT-SERVERS.NET.
M.ROOT-SERVERS.NET.         3600000    A     202.12.27.33
; End of File
```

This file contains NS and A resource records that specify the names of authoritative name servers and their addresses for the root zone (indicated by the " . " in the first field of each NS record).

The comment lines in the file begin with a semicolon. These comments give you hints about the location of the root name servers. There are 13 root name servers for the Internet, most of the root servers are located in the United States. This file is a necessity for any name server because the name server has to be able to reach at least one root name server.

Understanding the /var/named/localhost.zone File

The /etc/named.conf file includes a zone statement for the localhost zone that specifies the zone file as localhost.zone. That file is located in the /var/named directory of your Red Hat Linux system. The /var/named/localhost.zone file contains the following resource records:

```
$TTL    86400
$ORIGIN localhost.
@               1D IN SOA       @ root (
                                42                      ; serial (d. adams)
                                3H                      ; refresh
                                15M                     ; retry
                                1W                      ; expiry
                                1D )                    ; minimum


                1D IN NS        @
                1D IN A         127.0.0.1
```

This zone file starts with a $TTL directive that sets the default TTL to one day (86400 seconds) for subsequent records with undefined TTLs. Next, a $ORIGIN directive sets the domain name to localhost.

After these two directives, the /var/named/localhost.zone file contains three resource records (RRs): an SOA record, an NS record, and an A record. The SOA and the NS record specify the localhost as the primary authoritative name server for the zone. The A record specifies the address of localhost as 127.0.0.1.

Understanding the /var/named/named.local File

The third zone in the /etc/named.conf file specifies a reverse-mapping zone named 0.0.127.in-addr.arpa. For this zone, the zone file is /var/named/named.local, which contains the following:

```
$TTL    86400
@       IN      SOA     localhost. root.localhost.  (
                                        1997022700 ; Serial
                                        28800      ; Refresh
                                        14400      ; Retry
                                        3600000    ; Expire
                                        86400 )    ; Minimum
        IN      NS      localhost.

1       IN      PTR     localhost.
```

The SOA and NS records specify localhost as the primary name server.

---

insider insight

The SOA record also shows root.localhost. as the email address of the technical contact for the domain. Note that the DNS zone files use a user.host. format for the email address. When sending any email, you have to replace the first dot with an @ and remove the final dot.

Starting and Testing the Caching Name Server

Now that you have studied the configuration files for the caching name server, you can start the name server and see it in operation. To start the name server, log in as `root` and type the following command at the shell prompt:

```
service named start
```

This starts `named`—the name server daemon.

---

insider insight

To ensure that the server starts every time you reboot the system, log in as `root` and type the following command:

```
chkconfig --level 35 named on
```

The named server writes diagnostic log messages in the `/var/log/messages` file. After you start named, you can check the log messages by opening `/var/log/messages` in a text editor. Following are some typical log messages from named when started on my Red Hat Linux system:

```
Feb 14 18:02:09 localhost named[16400]: starting BIND 9.2.1 -u named
Feb 14 18:02:09 localhost named[16400]: using 1 CPU
Feb 14 18:02:10 localhost named[16400]: loading configuration from '/etc/named.conf'
Feb 14 18:02:10 localhost named: named startup succeeded
Feb 14 18:02:10 localhost named[16400]: no IPv6 interfaces found
Feb 14 18:02:10 localhost named[16400]: listening on IPv4 interface lo, 127.0.0.1#53
Feb 14 18:02:10 localhost named[16400]: listening on IPv4 interface eth1,
192.168.0.7#53
Feb 14 18:02:10 localhost named[16400]: command channel listening on 127.0.0.1#953
Feb 14 18:02:10 localhost named[16400]: zone 0.0.127.in-addr.arpa/IN: loaded serial
1997022700
Feb 14 18:02:10 localhost named[16400]: zone localhost/IN: loaded serial 42
Feb 14 18:02:10 localhost named[16400]: running
```

If there are no error messages from named, you can proceed to test the name server.

Now, you can use the `host` command to test the name server. For example, to look up the IP address of `www.gao.gov` by using the caching name server on `localhost`, type the following command:

```
host www.gao.gov localhost
Using domain server:
Name: localhost
Address: 127.0.0.1#53
Aliases:

www.gao.gov has address 161.203.16.2
```

As the output shows, the host command uses `localhost` as the DNS server and returns the IP address of `www.gao.gov`.

If you want to use the caching name server as your name server, you have to specify that name server as your primary one. To do this, make sure that the first line in the /etc/resolv.conf file is the following:

```
nameserver 127.0.0.1
```

Configuring a Primary Name Server

The best way to configure a primary name server is to start by configuring a caching name server, as explained in the previous sections. Then, add master zones for the domains for which you want this to be the primary name server. For example, suppose that I want to define a primary name server for the naba.net domain. Here are the steps I go through to configure that primary name server (after I log in as root):

1. Add the following zone statements to /etc/named.conf file:

```
zone "naba.net" IN {
    type master;
    file "naba.zone";
};
zone "0.168.192.in-addr.arpa" IN {
    type master;
    file "0.168.192.zone";
};
```

2. Create the zone file var/named/naba.zone with the following lines in it:

```
$TTL     86400
$ORIGIN naba.net.
@            1D IN SOA       @ root.naba.net (
                             100          ; serial
                             3H           ; refresh
                             15M          ; retry
                             1W           ; expiry
                             1D )         ; minimum

          1D IN NS        @
          1D IN A         192.168.0.7

wxp    IN    A    192.168.0.2
```

3. Create the zone file var/named/0.168.192.zone with the following lines in it:

```
$TTL     86400
; Remember zone name is: 0.168.192.in-addr.arpa
@       IN      SOA     naba.net. root.naba.net  (
                                 1          ; Serial
                                 28800      ; Refresh
                                 14400      ; Retry
                                 3600000    ; Expire
                                 86400 )    ; Minimum
        IN      NS      naba.net.

7       IN      PTR     naba.net.
2       IN      PTR     wxp.naba.net.
```

To test the new configuration, restart the named server with the following command:

```
service named restart
```

Now, use dig or host to query the DNS server. For example, here's how I use host to check the address of the host wxp.naba.net at the DNS server running on localhost:

```
host wxp.naba.net localhost
Using domain server:
Name: localhost
Address: 127.0.0.1#53
Aliases:

wxp.naba.net has address 192.168.0.2
```

If you want to use dig to check the DNS server, type the following command:

```
dig @localhost wxp.naba.net
```

That @localhost part specifies the DNS server that dig should contact.

Here is an example of when I try a reverse lookup with the IP address 192.168.0.2:

```
host 192.168.0.2 localhost
Using domain server:
Name: localhost
Address: 127.0.0.1#53
Aliases:

2.0.168.192.in-addr.arpa domain name pointer wxp.naba.net
```

Using Network Information Service (NIS)

Network Information Service (NIS) was developed by Sun Microsystems as a way to share information among all computers in a local area network. The types of information NIS most commonly uses include the following:

♦ User names and passwords from files such as /etc/passwd and /etc/shadow
♦ Group information from the /etc/group file

Normally, each system has its own copy of information in respective files, and any changes require updating the files on each system individually. Using NIS, you can maintain a single set of configuration files for a collection of computers in an NIS server. All other computers running NIS clients can then access the files. For example, if your user name and password are in the NIS password database, you will be able to log in on all computers on the network running NIS client programs.

Secret

NIS was originally called Sun Yellow Pages (YP), but the name Yellow Pages is a registered trademark of British Telecom in the United Kingdom, so Sun Microsystems had to change the name. However, many NIS commands, and the NIS package names, begin with the letters yp.

If you want to use NIS in a network, you must set up at least one NIS server. You can have multiple NIS servers in a network, each serving a different collection of computers. You can also have a master NIS server and one or more slave NIS servers that receive a copy of the master's database. The group of computers a master NIS server supports is called an NIS domain or YP domain.

The master NIS server runs the ypserv daemon (this is the NIS server daemon) that maintains the shared information in DBM databases. (DBM refers to Data Base Management, a library of functions that maintain key-value pairs in a database.) The NIS databases are called maps. You can create these NIS maps directly from the text configuration files—such as /etc/passwd and /etc/group—by using the /usr/lib/yp/makedbm program that comes with the NIS server software. More accurately, the ypserv daemon uses the Makefile in the /var/yp directory to create the maps for all shared configuration files.

The master NIS server provides the maps to all NIS client computers. The clients run the ypbind daemon through which various client programs access the master NIS server. In addition to a master server, one or more NIS slave servers may be set up to provide the NIS maps in case the master is unavailable or down. The NIS slave servers periodically copy the NIS maps from the master server (using the /usr/lib/yp/ypxfr command) and are able to provide these maps to clients when the master is down.

You can think of NIS as a way of distributing the same set of configuration files among all computers in an NIS domain. You get the benefits of sharing the same files (such as the same user name and password for all machines), yet you can still edit and maintain just one set of files—the files on the master NIS server.

The next few sections describe how to set up your Red Hat Linux system as an NIS client and as an NIS server.

Setting up an NIS Client

If your network uses NIS centrally to administer users and passwords, you can set up your Red Hat Linux PC as an NIS client. In fact, when you install Red Hat Linux from this book's companion CD-ROMs, you can enable NIS from the Authentication Configuration screen in the GUI installer.

cross ref

During Red Hat Linux installation (see Chapter 2 for details), the Authentication Configuration screen shows you a number of different options for authenticating users—the default being shadow passwords and the MD5 password (which are discussed in Chapter 22). One of these options is a button labeled Enable NIS. You can click this button to set up your Red Hat Linux PC as an NIS client. Of course, you should do this only if your network is set up with an NIS server.

If you do select the Enable NIS option, you have to provide the following information:

◆ Specify the NIS domain name. The domain name refers to the group of computers the NIS server serves.

◆ Specify the name of the NIS server.

◆ Indicate whether or not you want your PC to use IP broadcast to find NIS servers in the local network.

If you did not configure your system as an NIS client during Red Hat Linux installation, you can do so by performing the following tasks:

◆ Define your NIS domain name.

◆ Set up the NIS configuration file (/etc/yp.conf). In this file, you specify the master NIS and slave servers that provide NIS maps to your Red Hat Linux PC.

◆ Configure the NIS client daemon—ypbind—to start when your system boots.

The next three sections show you how to perform these tasks.

Setting the NIS Domain Name

The NIS domain name identifies the group of computers that a particular NIS server supports. You can set the NIS domain name of your system by using the domainname command. For example, to set your NIS domain name to admin, log in as root, and type the following at the shell prompt:

```
domainname admin
```

If you type **domainname** without any arguments, the command prints the current NIS domain name.

Secret

To ensure that the NIS domain name is set as soon as your system boots, the command should be run from one of the startup scripts. You can do this by adding the following line to the /etc/sysconfig/network file on your Red Hat Linux system:

```
NISDOMAIN="admin"
```

Of course, you should use the NIS domain name appropriate to your network.

The NIS domain is different from the DNS domain names discussed earlier in this chapter. It's best if you pick an NIS domain name that's not related to the DNS domain name. Doing so makes it harder for crackers to guess your NIS domain name (if they know the NIS domain name, there is a risk that they can get the NIS password database).

Preparing the /etc/yp.conf File

The ypbind daemon, described in the next section, needs information about the NIS domains and NIS servers to do its job. It finds this information in the /etc/yp.conf configuration file. The ypbind daemon reads the /etc/yp.conf file when it starts up or when it receives the SIGHUP signal (for example, when you restart ypbind with the command kill -HUP ypbind).

To specify one or more NIS servers for the local domain (which you have already set with the `domainname` command), all you need in `/etc/yp.conf` are lines such as the following:

```
ypserver nisadmin
ypserver 192.168.0.7
```

You can use a name such as `nisadmin` if that name is listed in the `/etc/hosts` file (that way, `ypbind` can resolve the name into an IP address without having to use NIS). Otherwise, you should specify the NIS server's IP address.

In `/etc/yp.conf`, you can also specify specific NIS servers for specific NIS domains, like this:

```
domain sales server nissales
domain admin server nisadmin
```

A third type of entry in the `/etc/yp.conf` file specifies that `ypbind` should use IP broadcast in the local network to find an NIS server for a specified domain. To do this, add a line such as the following to `/etc/yp.conf`:

```
domain admin broadcast
```

Configuring the ypbind Daemon

Every computer in an NIS domain, including the server, runs the `ypbind` daemon. Various NIS client applications, such as `ypwhich`, `ypcat`, and `yppoll`, need the `ypbind` daemon to obtain information from the master NIS server. More precisely, the C library contacts the `ypbind` daemon to locate the NIS server for the domain. Then the C library contacts the server directly to obtain administrative information. The client applications get the information through functions in the C library.

To interactively start `ypbind`, log in as `root` and type the following command:

```
service ypbind start
```

If you want `ypbind` to start when the system boots, log in as `root` and type the following command to turn `ypbind` on:

```
chkconfig --add ypbind
chkconfig --level 35 ypbind on
```

Setting up the NIS Server

To set up your Red Hat Linux system as an NIS server, you should first set it up as an NIS client—set the NIS domain name, configure the `/etc/yp.conf` file, and configure the `ypbind` daemon. (Note that the `ypbind` daemon won't work until you have an NIS server up and running.) After the client configuration, you can configure the NIS server. This requires that you perform the following tasks:

- ◆ Create the NIS maps using `ypinit`.
- ◆ Configure the master NIS server—`ypserv`
- ◆ Optionally, configure one or more slave NIS servers

The next two sections explain these steps.

Creating the NIS Maps

Creating NIS maps involves converting the text files, such as /etc/passwd and /etc/group into DBM files by using makedbm. The map creation is controlled by /var/yp/Makefile, a file that can be used by the make command to perform specific tasks (see Chapter 23 for more information on make and Makefile).

You can configure what you want the NIS server to share with the clients in the NIS domain. You do so by editing the Makefile in the /var/yp directory. Open /var/yp/Makefile in a text editor, and locate the line that begins with all:. Here is a typical excerpt from the Makefile showing the comments before the all: line:

```
# If you don't want some of these maps built, feel free to comment
# them out from this list.


all:  passwd group hosts rpc services netid protocols mail \
      # netgrp shadow publickey networks ethers bootparams printcap \
      # amd.home auto.master auto.home auto.local passwd.adjunct \
      # timezone locale netmasks
```

As the comment lines (the ones that begin with #) indicate, you can comment out any maps you do not want to build. In the preceding example, the maps listed in the last three lines will not be built.

Next, you should edit the /var/yp/securenets file to specify the IP addresses of client computers that can access the NIS maps. The default file has the following lines:

```
# securenets    This file defines the access rights to your NIS server
#               for NIS clients. This file contains netmask/network
#               pairs. A clients IP address needs to match with at
#               least one of those.
#
#               One can use the word "host" instead of a netmask of
#               255.255.255.255. Only IP addresses are allowed in this
#               file, not hostnames.
#
# Always allow access for localhost
255.0.0.0       127.0.0.0

# This line gives access to everybody. PLEASE ADJUST!
0.0.0.0         0.0.0.0
```

As the last comment line shows, the default configuration grants access to all IP addresses. For example, to limit access to the class C network 192.168.0.0, change the last line as follows:

```
255.255.255.0     192.168.0.0
```

This allows only those computers on the local network with IP addresses in the range 192.168.0.1 through 192.168.0.254 access to the NIS maps.

Next, you should generate the NIS map database by running the /usr/lib/yp/ypinit program with the -m option. Here is a sample session with that program:

```
/usr/lib/yp/ypinit -m
At this point, we have to construct a list of the hosts which will run NIS
servers. lnbp200 is in the list of NIS server hosts. Please continue to add
the names for the other hosts, one per line. When you are done with the
list, type a <control D>.
        next host to add: lnbp200
        next host to add: <Press Ctrl-D here>
The current list of NIS servers looks like this:

lnbp200

Is this correct?  [y/n: y]  y
We need some  minutes to build the databases...
Building /var/yp/admin/ypservers...
Running /var/yp/Makefile...
gmake[1]: Entering directory `/var/yp/admin'
Updating passwd.byname...
Updating passwd.byuid...
...lines deleted...
```

The /usr/lib/yp/ypinit program automatically selects your host as an NIS server and
prompts for the names of any other NIS servers. You can add the server names one at a
time and press Ctrl-D when you are done. Then, you have to verify that the list of NIS
servers is correct (type **y**). After that, make runs with the /var/yp/Makefile and generates the NIS maps as specified by the all: line in the Makefile. The map files are stored
in a subdirectory of /var/yp that has the same name as the NIS domain name you have
previously set for your system. For example, for the NIS domain admin, the map files are
in the /var/yp/admin directory.

Configuring the Master NIS Server

To configure the NIS server daemon, ypserv, you have to prepare the configuration file
/etc/ypserv.conf. You can learn about the syntax of this file by reading its man page,
which you can access by typing the command man ypserv.conf. Among other options,
you can use the following option to specify that DNS should not be used to look up hostnames that are not in the maps of the /etc/hosts file:

```
dns: no
```

You can also add other lines in /etc/ypserv.conf that specify access rules—which hosts
can access which maps. The format of the access rules is as follows:

```
Host : Map : Security : mangle [: field_to_mangle]
```

The field_to_mangle is optional; it indicates which field in the map file should be man-
gled (the default is the second field because the password is in the second field of most
files, such as /etc/passwd). To mangle a field is to replace it with an x if the request
comes from an unprivileged host. The rest of the fields have the following meanings:

> ♦ **Host**—IP address or a wildcard (*) indicating to whom the rule applies
>
> ♦ **Map**—Name of the map to which the rule applies (the names of the maps are the
> same as those of the map files in the /var/yp/domainname directory, where
> domainname is your NIS domain name)

♦ **Security**—One of the following: `none` (to allow access always), `port` (to access from a port less than 1024), `deny` (to deny access to the map), or `des` (to require DES authentication—this may not be supported by all C libraries)

♦ **mangle**—One of the following: `yes` (the field specified by `field_to_mangle` should be replaced by an `x` if the request is from unauthorized host) or `no` (do not mangle)

For example, the following lines in the `/etc/ypserv.conf` file restrict access to the password map to systems in the 192.168.0 network:

```
192.168.0    :    passwd.byname    : port    : yes
192.168.0    :    passwd.byuid     : port    : yes
```

If you do not specify any access rules, `ypserv` allows all computers to access all maps.

Once you have set up the `/etc/ypserv.conf` file, you can start the NIS server with the following command:

```
service ypserv start
```

insider
insight

To ensure that `ypserv` starts whenever you reboot the system, log in as `root` and type the following command to enable it:

```
chkconfig --level 35 ypserv on
```

Secret

To handle password changes from clients, you must also run the `rpc.yppasswdd` server on the master NIS server for the domain. The `rpc.yppasswdd` server enables users on client systems to type the `yppasswd` command and change their password in the NIS database. If you do not have the `rpc.yppasswdd` server running on the master NIS server, users will get the following error message when they type the `yppasswd` command:

```
yppasswd: yppasswdd not running on NIS master host
```

You can correct this problem by starting `rpc.yppasswdd`; log in as `root`, and type the command:

```
service yppasswdd start
```

To start `yppasswd` automatically at run levels 3 and 5, type:

```
chkconfig --level 35 yppasswdd on
```

Once you have the master NIS server up and running, you can test it by using various NIS client programs, such as `ypwhich`, `yppoll`, `ypcat`, and `ypmatch`.

Configuring a Slave NIS Server

To set up a system as a slave NIS server, first set it up as an NIS client and verify that the client works. In particular, type **ypwhich -m** and look for a list of NIS maps and the name of the master NIS server for each map (the next section shows how the `ypwhich -m` command works).

After you confirm that the system is configured as an NIS client, type the following command to set up the system as a slave NIS server:

```
/usr/lib/yp/ypinit -s nismaster
```

where `nismaster` is the name of the master NIS server for the domain.

Testing NIS

If you do not have a master NIS server in your network, first perform the client configurations to create one, then start the master NIS server, as explained in earlier sections. Next, start the `ypbind` daemon as follows:

```
service ypbind start
```

Now, you can try out various NIS client programs and other utilities to see if everything is working correctly.

NIS servers and clients use Remote Procedure Call (RPC) to exchange information. Network File System (NFS), described in Chapter 19, also uses RPC. RPC requires the `portmap` service, which maps RPC services to TCP and UDP ports. When a server that supports RPC starts up, it registers itself with `portmap` and lists both the services it supports and the ports it uses. Your Red Hat Linux system should already have `portmap` up and running. You can check for it with the following command:

```
ps ax | grep portmap
 371 ?         S      0:00 portmap
6755 pts/0     S      0:00 grep portmap
```

You should see a line showing the `portmap` process and its ID in the output. In this case, the `portmap` process has an ID of 371.

To see if the `ypserv` and `ypbind` processes are running on the master NIS server, use the `/usr/sbin/rpcinfo` program to check if `ypserv` and `ypbind` were able to register with the portmap service. For example, here is a sample output:

```
/usr/sbin/rpcinfo -p
   program vers proto   port
    100000    2   tcp    111  portmapper
    100000    2   udp    111  portmapper
    100021    1   udp   1024  nlockmgr
    100021    3   udp   1024  nlockmgr
    100024    1   udp   1025  status
    100024    1   tcp   1024  status
    100007    2   udp    647  ypbind
    100007    1   udp    647  ypbind
    100007    2   tcp    650  ypbind
    100007    1   tcp    650  ypbind
    100004    2   udp    894  ypserv
    100004    1   udp    894  ypserv
    100004    2   tcp    897  ypserv
    100004    1   tcp    897  ypserv
```

Each line shows the RPC program number, a version number, the protocol (TCP or UDP), the port number, and the service. As you can see, both ypbind and ypserv are registered.

To determine which NIS server your system is using, try the ypwhich command. Here is a typical example:

```
ypwhich
lnbp200
```

You can also use the ypwhich command to view the master NIS server for a specified map. If you want to see the master NIS server for the available maps, type the following command:

```
ypwhich -m
mail.aliases lnbp200
protocols.bynumber lnbp200
services.byservicename lnbp200
netid.byname lnbp200
services.byname lnbp200
rpc.bynumber lnbp200
rpc.byname lnbp200
hosts.byaddr lnbp200
hosts.byname lnbp200
group.bygid lnbp200
group.byname lnbp200
passwd.byname lnbp200
protocols.byname lnbp200
ypservers lnbp200
passwd.byuid lnbp200
```

The output shows a list of the available NIS maps and, for each map, the name of the master NIS server.

To view the name of the master NIS server and information about a specific NIS map, use the yppoll command. For example, here is the result of a yppoll query for the passwd.byname map:

```
yppoll passwd.byname
Domain admin is supported.
Map passwd.byname has order number 972760603. [Sat Oct 27 15:16:43 2001]
The master server is lnbp200
```

Use the ypcat command to print the values of the keys in an NIS map. For example, here is a ypcat query for the NIS map group.byname:

```
ypcat group.byname
ivy:!:503:
ashley:!:502:
emily:!:501:
naba:!:500:
```

You can use `ypmatch` to look at the entries in an NIS map that match a specific key. For example, here is a `ypmatch` command line that looks for entries that match the key `naba` in the `group.byname` map:

```
ypmatch naba group.byname
naba:!:500:
```

If you compare this with the output from `ypcat` showing all the groups, you see that `ypmatch` shows the line corresponding to the group name `naba`.

Summary

Domain Name System (DNS) is a key Internet service, one that enables us to use easy-to-remember names for websites and servers on the Internet, even though TCP/IP requires numeric IP addresses for data transfers. Network Information Service (NIS) is another useful service for local networks to share configuration files, such as users, groups, and passwords. Red Hat Linux comes with everything needed to run the servers and clients for DNS and NIS. This chapter describes how to use DNS and NIS in Red Hat Linux.

By reading this chapter, you learn the following:

♦ DNS is a distributed database that holds information about hostnames, IP addresses, and mail routing. Internet applications use DNS to convert hostnames, such as `www.redhat.com` into IP addresses.

♦ DNS is documented in RFCs 1034 and 1035. Many other RFCs document various updates and extensions to DNS.

♦ All hosts on the Internet use DNS. Each host needs a name server it can query to resolve hostnames into IP addresses. Typically, the ISP provides the name servers. The IP addresses of the name servers are listed in the `/etc/resolv.conf` file.

♦ Red Hat Linux comes with the Berkeley Internet Domain (BIND) system, a well-known implementation of DNS.

♦ To set up a name server, you have to prepare the `/etc/named.conf` configuration files and zone files referenced in that configuration file. The zone files are usually stored in the `/var/named` directory.

♦ Red Hat Linux comes with the configuration files for a caching name server that loads the addresses of a few authoritative servers for the root domain and gets all its data by caching responses to queries resolved by contacting other name servers. This chapter walks you through the process of setting up the caching name server and explains the configuration files the server uses.

♦ You can easily extend the caching name server to a primary name server for your domain by adding a master zone to the `/etc/named.conf` file and preparing the appropriate zone files.

♦ You can use BIND utilities such as `dig` and `host` interactively query the DNS database interactively.

♦ NIS was developed by Sun Microsystems as a way of sharing configuration files among a number of computers in a local area network. The password file and group information files are typically shared by using NIS. This enables users to log in by using the same user name and password on all computers in the local network.

◆ NIS clients have to define their NIS domain (a name for all the computers an NIS server serves); set up the NIS configuration file `/etc/yp.conf`; and run the `ypbind` daemon. All NIS client applications access the NIS server through the local `ypbind` process.

◆ To set up a master NIS server, you have to create the NIS maps—the NIS databases—by running `/usr/lib/yp/ypinit`; set up the configuration file `/etc/ypserv.conf`, and start the NIS server, `ypserv`.

◆ You can test the NIS server by running NIS client applications, such as `ypwhich`, `yppoll`, `ypcat`, and `ypmatch`.

◆ If you want users to be able to set or change NIS passwords by using the `yppasswd` command, you must also run the `rpc.yppasswdd` daemon on the master NIS server.

Samba and NFS

Chapter
19

♦ ♦

Secrets in This Chapter

♦ ♦

A low-end Pentium PC configured with Red Hat Linux (from this book's companion CD-ROMs) makes a very capable workgroup (or office) server. By workgroup, I mean a small local area network (LAN) of perhaps a dozen or so PCs. You can configure the Linux PC to be the file and print server and have the other PCs be the clients. The client PCs do not have to run Linux; they can run Windows. Linux comes with the Samba package, which provides you with everything you need to set up your Linux PC as a server in a Windows network. This chapter introduces you to Samba—a software package that makes a Linux server look like a Windows server with shared drives (Samba can act as a Windows NT Primary Domain Controller, but, as of version 2.2, it does not yet support Active Directory). Also, you learn about file sharing through Network File System (NFS), which is built into Linux.

Sharing Files with NFS

Sharing files through NFS is simple and involves two basic steps:

◆ On the Linux server, export one or more directories by listing them in the `/etc/exports` file and by running the `exportfs` command. In addition, you must run the NFS server by logging in as `root` and typing the command `service nfs start`.

◆ On each client system, use the `mount` command to mount the directories the NFS server has exported.

The only problem in using NFS is that each client system must support it. Most PCs do not come with NFS. That means you have to buy NFS software separately if you want to share files by using NFS. However, it makes sense to use NFS if all systems on your LAN run Linux (or other variants of UNIX with built-in NFS support).

caution   You should also note that NFS has security vulnerabilities. Therefore, you should not set up NFS on systems directly connected to the Internet.

The next subsections walk you through NFS setup, using an example of two Linux PCs on a LAN.

Exporting a File System with NFS

Start with the server system that exports—makes available to the client systems—the contents of a directory. On the server, you must run the NFS service and also designate one or more file systems that are to be exported—made available to the client systems.

To export a file system, you have to add an appropriate entry to the `/etc/exports` file. For example, suppose that you want to export the `/home` directory and you want to enable the host named LNBP75 to mount this file system for read and write operations. You can do this by adding the following entry to the `/etc/exports` file:

```
/home LNBP75(rw, sync)
```

If you want to give access to all hosts on a LAN such as 192.168.0.0, you could change this line to:

```
/home 192.168.0.0/24(rw,sync)
```

Secret

Each line in the `/etc/exports` file has this general format:

```
directory    host1(options)  host2(options)  ...
```

The first field is the directory being shared via NFS, followed by one or more fields that specify which hosts can mount that directory remotely and a number of options within parentheses. You can specify the hosts with names or IP addresses, including ranges of addresses.

The options within parentheses denote the kind of access each host is granted and how user and group IDs from the server are mapped to IDs the client (for example, if a file is owned by `root` on the server, what owner should that be on the client). Within the parentheses, the options are separated by commas. For example, if a host is allowed both read and write access and all IDs are to be mapped to the anonymous user (by default this is the user named `nobody`), then the options would look like this:

```
(rw,all_squash)
```

Table 19-1 shows the options you can use in the `/etc/exports` file. There are two types of options—general options and user ID mapping options.

Table 19-1: Options in /etc/exports

Option	Description
General Options	
secure	Allows connections only from ports 1024 or lower (default)
insecure	Allows connections from 1024 or higher
ro	Allows read-only access (default)
rw	Allows both read and write access
sync	Performs write operations (this means writing information to the disk) when requested (default)
async	Performs write operations when the server is ready
no_wdelay	Performs write operations immediately
wdelay	Waits a bit to see if related write requests arrive and then performs then together (default)
hide	Hides an exported directory that's a subdirectory of another exported directory (default)
no_hide	Behaves exactly the opposite of hide
subtree_check	Performs subtree checking, which involves checking parent directories of an exported subdirectory whenever a file is accessed (default)
no_subtree_check	Turns off subtree checking (opposite of `subtree_check`)
insecure_locks	Allows insecure file locking

(continued)

Table 19-1: *(continued)*

Option	Description
User ID Mapping Options	
all_squash	Maps all user IDs and group IDs to the anonymous user on the client
no_all_squash	Maps remote user and group IDs to similar IDs on the client (default)
root_squash	Maps remote root user to the anonymous user on the client (default)
no_root_squash	Maps remote root user to the local root user
anonuid=UID	Sets the user ID of anonymous user to be used for the all_squash and root_squash options
anongid=GID	Sets the group ID of anonymous user to be used for the all_squash and root_squash options

After adding the entry in the /etc/exports file, manually export the file system by typing the following command in a terminal window:

```
exportfs -a
```

This command exports all file systems defined in the /etc/exports file.

Now, you can start the NFS server processes. To do this, log in as root and type the following command in a terminal window:

```
service nfs start
```

insider insight

If you want the NFS server to start when the system boots, type the following command to turn it on:

```
chkconfig --level 35 nfs on
```

When the NFS service is up, the server side of NFS is ready. Now you can try to mount the exported file system from a client system and access the exported file system.

If you ever make any changes to the exported file systems listed in the /etc/exports file, remember to restart the NFS service. To do this, log in as root and type the following command in a terminal window:

```
service nfs restart
```

Mounting an NFS File System

To access an exported NFS file system on a client system, you have to mount that file system on a mount point. The *mount point* is nothing more than a local directory. For example, suppose that you want to access the /home directory exported from the server named LNBP200 at the local directory /mnt/lnbp200 on the client system. To do this, follow these steps:

1. Log in as `root`, and create the directory with the command

   `mkdir /mnt/lnbp200`

2. Type the following command to mount the directory from the remote system (LNBP200) on the local directory `/mnt/lnbp200`:

   `mount lnbp200:/home /mnt/lnbp200`

After these steps, you can view and access exported files from the local directory `/mnt/lnbp200`.

To confirm that the NFS file system is indeed mounted, log in as `root` on the client system and type **mount** in a terminal window. You should see a line similar to the following one about the NFS file system:

```
lnbp200:/home/public on /mnt/lnbp200 type nfs (rw,addr=192.168.1.200)
```

> **note**
>
> NFS supports two types of mount operations—hard and soft. By default a mount is hard, which means that if the NFS server does not respond, the client will keep trying to access the server indefinitely until the server responds. You can soft mount an NFS volume by adding the `-o soft` option to the `mount` command. For a soft mount, the client returns an error if the NFS server fails to respond.

Setting Up a Windows Server Using Samba

If you rely on Windows for file sharing and print sharing, you probably use Windows in your servers and clients. You can move to a Linux PC as your server without losing the Windows file and printer sharing because a Linux PC can be set up as a Windows server. When you install Red Hat Linux from this book's companion CD-ROMs, you also get a chance to install the Samba software package, which performs that setup. All you have to do is select the Windows File Server package group during installation.

> **note**
>
> After you install and configure Samba on your Linux PC, client PCs (running Windows for Workgroups or Windows 95/98/NT/2000/XP) can access disks and printers on the Linux PC by using the Server Message Block (SMB) protocol, the underlying protocol in Windows file and print sharing.

With the Samba package installed, you can make your Linux PC a Windows client, which means that the Linux PC can access disks and printers a Windows server manages.

The Samba software package has these major components:

- **/etc/samba/smb.conf**—The Samba configuration file the SMB server uses
- **/etc/samba/smbusers**—A Samba configuration file that shows the Samba user names corresponding to user names on the local Red Hat Linux PC
- **nmbd**—The NetBIOS name server, which clients use to look up servers (NetBIOS stands for Network Basic Input/Output System—an interface that applications use to communicate with network transports, such as TCP/IP)

◆ **nmblookup**—A command that returns the IP address of a Windows PC identified by its NetBIOS name

◆ **smbadduser**—A program that adds users to the SMB password file

◆ **smbcacls**—A program that manipulates Windows NT access control lists (ACLs) on shared files

◆ **smbclient**—The Windows client, which runs on Linux and allows Linux to access the files and printer on any Windows server

◆ **smbcontrol**—A program that sends messages to the smbd, nmbd, or winbindd processes

◆ **smbd**—The SMB server, which accepts connections from Windows clients and provides file and print sharing services

◆ **smbmount**—A program that mounts a Samba share directory on a Red Hat Linux PC

◆ **smbpasswd**—A program that changes the password for an SMB user

◆ **smbprint**—A script that enables printing on a printer on a SMB server

◆ **smbstatus**—A command that lists the current SMB connections for the local host

◆ **smbtar**—A program that backs up SMB shares directly to tape drives on the Red Hat Linux system

◆ **smbumount**—A program that unmounts a currently mounted Samba share directory

◆ **testparm**—A program that ensures that the Samba configuration file is correct

◆ **winbindd**—A server for resolving names from Windows NT servers

The following subsections describe how to install Samba from the companion CD-ROM and how to set up a printer on the Linux PC to print through Windows.

Checking Whether Samba Is Installed

Check whether Samba is installed, by typing the following command in a terminal window:

```
rpm -q samba
samba-2.2.7a-2
```

If the `rpm` command displays a package name that begins with `samba`, Samba is already installed on your system, and you should skip this subsection. Otherwise, follow these steps to install Samba from this book's companion CD-ROM:

1. Log in as `root`, and make sure that the appropriate companion CD-ROM is in the drive and mounted. If it is not, use the `umount /mnt/cdrom` command to dismount the current CD-ROM; replace it with the correct CD-ROM, and mount that CD-ROM with the `mount /mnt/cdrom` command.

2. Change the directory to the CD-ROM—specifically to the directory where the Red Hat Package Manager (RPM) packages are located—with the following command:

   ```
   cd /mnt/cdrom/RedHat/RPMS
   ```

3. Use the following `rpm` command to install Samba:

   ```
   rpm -ivh samba*
   ```

   If Samba is already installed, this command returns an error message. Otherwise, the `rpm` command installs Samba on your system by copying various files to their appropriate locations.

These steps complete the unpacking and installation of the Samba software. Now, all you have to do to use Samba is configure it.

insider insight

Samba comes with documentation on configuring it for SSL support. To read this documentation, change directory with the command `cd /usr/share/doc/samba*/docs/textdocs`, and type `more Samba-OpenSSL.txt` to browse through the text file on OpenSSL—a free implementation of the SSL protocol.

Configuring Samba

To set up the Windows file-sharing and print-sharing services, you have to provide a configuration file named `/etc/samba/smb.conf`. The configuration file is a text file that looks like a Microsoft Windows 3.1 INI file. You can prepare the file in any text editor on your Red Hat Linux system.

Secret

Like the old Windows `INI` files, the `/etc/samba/smb.conf` file consists of sections, with a list of parameters in each section. Each section of the `smb.conf` file begins with the name of the section in brackets. The section continues until the next section begins or until the file ends.

Each line in a section specifies the value of a parameter, using the following syntax:

```
name = value
```

As in Windows `INI` files, comment lines begin with a semicolon (;). In the `/etc/samba/smb.conf` file, comments may also begin with a hash (#).

The Samba software comes with a configuration file you can edit to get started. To prepare the configuration file, log in as `root`, and use your favorite text editor to edit the file `/etc/samba/smb.conf`. Here's a sample configuration file without any comments:

```
[global]
    netbios name = LNBP200
    workgroup = LNB SOFTWARE
    server string = LNB Software-Red Hat Linux-Samba Server
    hosts allow = 192.168.0.  127.
    guest account = naba
    log file = /var/log/samba/l%m.log

# Log files can be at most 50KB
    max log size = 50

    security = user
    smb passwd file = /etc/samba/smbpasswd

# Leave the next option as is - it's for performance
    socket options = TCP_NODELAY SO_RCVBUF=8192 SO_SNDBUF=8192

    remote browse sync = 192.168.0.255
    remote announce = 192.168.0.255/LNB SOFTWARE
```

```
        local master = yes
        os level = 33

        name resolve order = lmhosts bcast

        dns proxy = no
        unix password sync = no

[homes]
    comment = Home Directories
    browseable = no
    writable = yes

[printers]
    comment = All Printers
    path = /var/spool/samba
    browseable = no
    guest ok = no
    writable = no
    printable = yes

[tmp]
    comment = Temporary file space
    path = /tmp
    read only = no
    public = yes

[public]
    comment = Public Stuff
    path = /home/samba
    browseable = yes
    public = yes
    guest ok = yes
    writable = yes
    printable = no
    available = yes
    guest only = no
    user = naba
    only user = yes
```

Change the user name from `naba` to your user name. Also make sure that all directories mentioned in the configuration file actually exist. For example, create the `/home/samba` directory with the command `mkdir /home/samba`.

After editing the Samba configuration file, add two users to the Samba password file. First add your user name. Here's how I add myself:

```
smbadduser naba:naba
------------------------------------------------------------
ENTER password for naba
New SMB password:          (I enter the password.)
Retype new SMB password:   (I enter password again.)
Password changed for user naba.
```

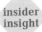

insider insight

After making the changes to the `/etc/samba/smb.conf file,` type the following command to verify that the file is okay:

```
testparm
```

If the command says that it loaded the files okay, you're all set to go.

Start the SMB services with the following command:

```
service smb start
```

To start the SMB services automatically when the system reboots, type the following command:

```
chkconfig --level 35 smb on
```

Secret

Accessing the Samba Server from Windows

You can try to access the Samba server on the Red Hat Linux system from one of the Windows systems on your LAN. Double-click the Network Neighborhood icon on the Windows 95/98/ME desktop. On Windows XP, select Start⇨My Network Places, and then click View workgroup computers. This should show all the computers on the same workgroup.

If you are accessing the Samba server from Windows 95/98/ME, you should be able to view the shared folders simply by double-clicking the icon. For the example, you should see two folders: `tmp` and `public`. You can then open these folders to explore the contents of the directories further.

Unfortunately, it's difficult to access the Samba server from Windows XP or Windows 2000. Samba emulates a Windows NT primary domain controller (PDC), and XP expects a Windows 2000 network. In a Windows XP Professional system, you can edit a key in the registry to enable the XP system to access the Samba server, but Windows XP Home Edition is simply unable to connect to the Samba server.

Accessing Windows Resources with smbclient

You can use the smbclient program to access shared directories and printers on Windows systems on the LAN and to ensure that your Linux Samba server is working. One quick way to check is to use the `smbclient -L` command to view the list of services on the Red Hat Linux Samba server itself. This is what I get when I run `smbclient` on my Linux Samba sever:

```
smbclient -L LNBP200
added interface ip=192.168.1.200 bcast=192.168.1.255 nmask=255.255.255.0
added interface ip=172.16.128.1 bcast=172.16.128.255 nmask=255.255.255.0
Got a positive name query response from 192.168.1.200 ( 192.168.1.200 )
Password: (I press Enter)
Anonymous login successful
Domain=[LNB SOFTWARE] OS=[Unix] Server=[Samba 2.2.7]
```

```
Sharename      Type      Comment
---------      ----      -------
tmp            Disk      Temporary file space
public         Disk      Public Stuff
IPC$           IPC       IPC Service (LNB Software-Red Hat Linux-Samba Server)
ADMIN$         Disk      IPC Service (LNB Software-Red Hat Linux-Samba Server)

      Server            Comment
      ---------         -------
      LNBP200           LNB Software-Red Hat Linux-Samba Server
      NABA-DELL-4400

      Workgroup         Master
      ---------         -------
      LNB SOFTWARE      NABA-DELL-4400
```

The output of smbclient shows shared resources and lists the names of the other Windows servers on the local network.

If you have other Windows servers around, you can look at their services with the smbclient program. Here is what I get when I view the shared resources on a Windows 98 PC:

```
smbclient -L LNBP933
added interface ip=192.168.0.2 bcast=192.168.0.255 nmask=255.255.255.0
Got a positive name query response from 192.168.0.3 ( 192.168.0.3 )
Password: (I press Enter)

      Sharename      Type      Comment
      ---------      ----      -------
      PRINTER$       Disk
      HP NEW         Printer   HP Photosmart on new Dell
      C              Disk      C drive on Dell (2001)
      IPC$           IPC       Remote Inter Process Communication

      Server            Comment
      ---------         -------
      LNBP200           LNB Software-Red Hat Linux-Samba Server
      LNBP400           Dell Dimension XPS-400
      LNBP933           Dell Dimension 4100 (2001)
      NABA-DELL-4400

      Workgroup         Master
      ---------         -------
      LNB SOFTWARE      NABA-DELL-4400
```

You can do much more than simply look at resources with the smbclient program: you can also use it to access a disk on a Windows server or to send a file to a Windows printer. The smbclient program is like FTP—you connect to a Windows server and use commands to get or put files and to send files to the printer.

The following example shows how I use smbclient to access a disk on my Windows XP PC and view its directory:

```
smbclient //naba-dell-4400/Share naba mypassword
added interface ip=192.168.0.2 bcast=192.168.0.255 nmask=255.255.255.0
Got a positive name query response from 192.168.0.4 ( 192.168.0.4 )
Domain=[LNB SOFTWARE] OS=[Windows 5.1] Server=[Windows 2000 LAN Manager]
smb: \> dir
  .                                  DA      0  Sun Jan 12 15:47:36 2003
  ..                                 DA      0  Sun Jan 12 15:47:36 2003
  Ashley                             DA      0  Sat Nov 23 11:32:04 2002
  bookmark.htm                       A  114785  Sun Jun 23 13:48:22 2002
  brother-mfc-10-22-02.rms           A  132633  Tue Oct 22 18:31:36 2002
... lines deleted...
  Photos                             D       0  Mon Jan  6 19:54:54 2003

        38154 blocks of size 2097152. 30719 blocks available
smb: \> quit
```

To see a list of smbclient commands, type **help** at the prompt. Table 19-2 is a brief summary of commonly used `smbclient` commands. To familiarize yourself with `smbclient`, try as many of these commands as you can.

Table 19-2: Common smbclient Commands

Command	Description
!	Executes a shell command (remember that you run `smbclient` on Linux)
? cmd	Displays a list of commands or help on a specific command
cancel id	Cancels a print job identified by its ID
cd dir	Changes the remote directory
del file	Deletes the specified file
dir file	Displays the directory listing
exit	Logs off the Windows server
get rfile lfile	Copies a remote file (`rfile`) to a local file (`lfile`)
help cmd	Provides help on a command (or displays a list of commands)
lcd newdir	Changes the local directory (on the Linux PC)
lowercase	Toggles automatic lowercase conversion of filenames when executing the get command
ls files	Lists files on the server
mask name	Applies a mask (such as `*.c`) to all file operations
md dirname	Makes a directory on the server
mget name	Gets all files with matching names (such as `*.doc`)
mkdir dirname	Makes a directory
mput name	Copies files from the Linux PC to the server

(continued)

Table 19-2: *(continued)*

Command	Description
`newer file`	Gets only the files that are newer than the specified file
`print name`	Prints the named file
`printmode mode`	Sets the print mode (the mode must be text or graphics)
`prompt`	Toggles prompt mode off (similar to the command in `ftp`)
`put lfile rfile`	Copies a local file (`lfile`) to a remote file (`rfile`)
`queue`	Displays the print queue
`quit`	Logs off the Windows server
`rd dir`	Deletes the specified directory on the server
`recurse`	Toggles directory recursion during file get and put operations
`rm name`	Deletes all files with the specified name
`rmdir name`	Deletes the specified directory
`translate`	Toggles text translation (converts a line feed to a carriage return–line-feed pair).

Summary

Red Hat Linux includes two prominent file-sharing services: NFS for sharing files with other UNIX systems (or PCs with NFS client software) and Samba for file sharing and print sharing with Windows systems. This chapter described both NFS and Samba.

By reading this chapter, you learned:

♦ Network File System (NFS) enables you to mount a file system from a remote computer on your local system. Red Hat Linux includes everything you need to set up your system as a NFS server.

♦ To export a file system, add that file system in the `/etc/exports` file, and type **/usr/sbin/exportfs -a** to export the file systems. You also have to start the NFS servers by typing the command `service nfs start`. After that, other NFS client systems on the network can mount the exported file systems by using the `mount` command.

♦ For PC networks that use Windows networking, you can configure a Red Hat Linux PC as a Windows server: all you have to do is use the Samba software package from the companion CD-ROMs. This chapter shows you how to install and use Samba.

♦ Samba configuration is somewhat complex—you configure using settings in the text file `/etc/samba/smb.conf`.

♦ You can access Windows servers and their resources from a Samba server with the `smbclient` program.

Part IV

Managing Red Hat Linux

Advanced
System
Administration

Chapter

20

♦ ♦

Secrets in This Chapter

♦ ♦

Chapter 12 introduced the basics of systems and network administration on the Red Hat Linux system. In several other chapters, you learned many other systems-administration tasks, such as configuring X, setting up printers, connecting to the Internet, and managing Internet services. This chapter introduces you to a number of other important system-administration tasks that I do not cover elsewhere in this book.

This chapter starts with a description of how Red Hat Linux boots, so you know how to start and stop services automatically at boot time. Then, you learn about automating system tasks with the `at` command or the `crontab` facility of Linux. Next, this chapter focuses on another important systems-administration task—backing up and restoring files from backup storage media. Finally, the chapter discusses monitoring system performance.

Understanding How Red Hat Linux Boots

It is important to learn the sequence in which Red Hat Linux starts processes as it boots. You can use this knowledge to start and stop services, such as the Web server and Network File System (NFS). The next few sections provide you with an overview of how Red Hat Linux boots and starts the initial set of processes. These sections also familiarize you with the shell scripts, called *initscripts*, that start various services on a Red Hat Linux system.

Understanding the init Process

When Red Hat Linux boots, it loads and runs the Linux kernel—the core operating-system program—from the hard disk. The Linux kernel is designed to run other programs. The kernel starts a process named init, which, in turn, starts the initial set of processes on your Linux system.

To see the processes currently running on the system, type the command `ps ax | more`. The first column in the output has the heading "PID"; that column shows a number for each process. PID stands for process ID (identification), which is a sequential number assigned by the Linux kernel. Right at the beginning of the list of processes, you notice a process with a process ID (PID) of 1:

```
PID TTY     STAT   TIME COMMAND
  1 ?        S     0:04 init
```

As you can see, init is the first process, and it has a PID of 1. Also, init starts all other processes in your Linux system. That's why init is referred to as the mother of all processes.

What the init process starts depends on the following:

◆ The *run level*, which designates a system configuration in which only a selected group of processes exists

◆ The contents of the `/etc/inittab` file, a text file that specifies the processes to start at different run levels

◆ A number of shell scripts (called *initscripts* and located in the `/etc/rc.d` directory and its subdirectories) that are executed at a specific run level

Secret

The current run level, together with the contents of the /etc/inittab file, controls which processes init starts. Red Hat Linux, for example, has seven run levels: 0, 1, 2, 3, 4, 5, and 6. By convention, some of these levels indicate specific processes that run at that level. Run level 1, for example, denotes a single-user, standalone system. Run level 0 means the system is halted, and run level 6 means the system is being rebooted. Run levels 2 through 5 are multiuser modes with various levels of capabilities, but run level 4 is not currently used.

init runs a specific sequence of shell scripts at each run level. Those scripts are often referred to as *initscripts* because they are run by init.

To check the current run level, type the runlevel command (type **/sbin/runlevel** if you are not logged in as root). Here is a typical output from runlevel:

```
N 5
```

The first character of the output shows the previous run level (N means there is no previous run level), and the second character shows the current level (5), indicating that the system is currently at run level 5.

The initial default run level is 3 for text-mode login screens and 5 for the graphical login screen. A line in the /etc/inittab file with the initdefault action indicates the default run level. Here is the line from /etc/inittab file that sets the default run level to 5:

```
id:5:initdefault:
```

If you change that 5 to a 3, the system would boot into a text-mode login screen.

Before you rush in and edit the /etc/inittab file, you should try out the run level by using the init command. For example, to switch to run level 3, log in as root and type the following command:

```
init 3
```

Examining the /etc/inittab File

The /etc/inittab file is the key to understanding the processes that init starts at various run levels. You can look at the contents of the file by using the more command as follows:

```
more /etc/inittab
```

To see the contents of the /etc/inittab file with the more command, you do not have to log in as root.

The following is a listing of the /etc/inittab file on my Red Hat Linux system, which is set up for a graphical login screen:

```
#
# inittab       This file describes how the INIT process should set up
#               the system in a certain run-level.
#
# Author:       Miquel van Smoorenburg, <miquels@drinkel.nl.mugnet.org>
#               Modified for RHS Linux by Marc Ewing and Donnie Barnes
#
```

```
# Default runlevel. The runlevels used by RHS are:
#   0 - halt (Do NOT set initdefault to this)
#   1 - Single user mode
#   2 - Multiuser, without NFS (The same as 3, if you do not have networking)
#   3 - Full multiuser mode
#   4 - unused
#   5 - X11
#   6 - reboot (Do NOT set initdefault to this)
#
id:5:initdefault:

# System initialization.
si::sysinit:/etc/rc.d/rc.sysinit

l0:0:wait:/etc/rc.d/rc 0
l1:1:wait:/etc/rc.d/rc 1
l2:2:wait:/etc/rc.d/rc 2
l3:3:wait:/etc/rc.d/rc 3
l4:4:wait:/etc/rc.d/rc 4
l5:5:wait:/etc/rc.d/rc 5
l6:6:wait:/etc/rc.d/rc 6

# Trap CTRL-ALT-DELETE
ca::ctrlaltdel:/sbin/shutdown -t3 -r now

# When our UPS tells us power has failed, assume we have a few minutes
# of power left.  Schedule a shutdown for 2 minutes from now.
# This does, of course, assume you have powerd installed and your
# UPS connected and working correctly.
pf::powerfail:/sbin/shutdown -f -h +2 "Power Failure; System Shutting Down"

# If power was restored before the shutdown kicked in, cancel it.
pr:12345:powerokwait:/sbin/shutdown -c "Power Restored; Shutdown Cancelled"


# Run gettys in standard runlevels
1:2345:respawn:/sbin/mingetty tty1
2:2345:respawn:/sbin/mingetty tty2
3:2345:respawn:/sbin/mingetty tty3
4:2345:respawn:/sbin/mingetty tty4
5:2345:respawn:/sbin/mingetty tty5
6:2345:respawn:/sbin/mingetty tty6

# Run xdm in runlevel 5
# xdm is now a separate service
x:5:respawn:/etc/X11/prefdm -nodaemon
```

Lines that start with a hash mark (#) are comments. The first noncomment line in the /etc/inittab file specifies the default run level as follows:

```
id:5:initdefault:
```

Even though you do not know the syntax of the /etc/inittab file (and you really do not have to learn the syntax), you probably can guess that the 5 in that line denotes the default run level for the graphical login screen. Thus, if you want your system to run at level 3 after startup (for a plaintext-mode login screen), all you have to do is change 5 to 3.

---

insider insight

Each entry in the /etc/inittab file specifies a process that init should start at one or more specified run levels. You simply concatenate all the run levels (for example, 235 for run levels 2, 3, and 5) at which the process should run. Each entry in the inittab file has four fields—separated by colons—in the following format:

```
id:runlevels:action:process
```

Type man inittab to see the detailed syntax of the entries in the inittab file.

The fields in each entry of the inittab file have the following meanings:

♦ The *id* field is a unique, 1- to 4-character identifier. The init process uses this field internally. You can employ any identifier you want, as long as you do not use the same identifier on more than one line. For example, si, x, and 1 are all valid identifiers.

♦ The *runlevels* field is a sequence of zero or more characters, each denoting a run level. The line with the identifier 1, for example, applies to run levels 1 through 5; so the *runlevels* field for this entry is 12345. This field is ignored if the *action* field is set to sysinit, boot, or bootwait.

♦ The *action* field tells the init process what to do with the entry. If this field is initdefault, for example, init interprets the *runlevels* field as the default run level. If this field is set to wait, init starts the process specified in the process field and waits until that process exits. Table 20-1 summarizes the valid action values you can use in the *action* field.

♦ The *process* field specifies the process that init has to start. Of course, some settings of the *action* field require no process field. (When *action* is set to initdefault, for example, you don't need a *process* field.)

Table 20-1: Valid Actions in /etc/inittab

Action	Description
Respawn	Restarts the process whenever it terminates
Wait	Restarts the process once at the specified run level; init waits until that process exits
Once	Executes the process once at the specified run level
Boot	Executes the process as the system boots, regardless of the run level (the *runlevels* field is ignored)
Bootwait	Executes the process as the system boots; init waits for the process to exit (the *runlevels* field is ignored)

(continued)

Table 20-1: *(continued)*

Action	Description
Off	Nothing happens for this action
Ondemand	Executes the process at the specified run level, which must be one of a, b, or c
Initdefault	Starts the system at this run level after it boots. The process field is ignored for this action.
Sysinit	Executes the process as the system boots before any entries with the boot or bootwait actions (the *runlevels* field is ignored)
Powerwait	Executes the process when init receives the SIGPWR signal, indicating that there is something wrong with the power. Then, init waits until the process exits.
Powerfail	Similar to powerwait, except that init does not wait for the process to exit
Powerfailnow	Executes the process when init receives a signal that the battery of the external uninterruptible power supply (UPS) is almost empty and the power is failing (provided that the external UPS and the monitoring process can detect this condition)
Powerokwait	Executes the process when init receives the SIGPWR signal and the /etc/powerstatus file contains the word OK (indicating that the power is back on)
Ctrlaltdel	Executes the process when init receives the SIGINT signal, which occurs when you press Ctrl-Alt-Del. Typically, the process field should specify the /sbin/shutdown command with the -r option to reboot the PC.
Kbdrequest	Executes the process when init receives a signal from the keyboard driver that a special key combination has been pressed. The key combination should be mapped to KeyboardSignal in the keymap file.

The *process* field is typically specified in terms of a shell script, which, in turn, can start several processes. The l5 entry in /etc/inittab, for example, is specified as follows:

```
l5:5:wait:/etc/rc.d/rc 5
```

This entry specifies that init should execute the file /etc/rc.d/rc with 5 as an argument. If you look at the file /etc/.rc.d/rc, you notice that it is a shell-script file. You can study this file to see how it starts various processes for run levels 1 through 5.

The last line of the /etc/inittab file starts the graphical login process with the following entry:

```
x:5:respawn:/etc/X11/prefdm -nodaemon
```

This command runs /etc/X11/prefdm, which is a shell script that starts the graphical display manager. The display manager, in turn, displays the graphical login dialog box that enables you to log into the system.

If you do not enable the graphical login screen during Red Hat installation (covered in Chapter 2), you can do so by editing the /etc/inittab file. Locate the line containing initdefault, and make sure that it reads as follows (the run level appearing between the two colons should be 5):

```
id:5:initdefault:
```

Before you edit the /etc/inittab file, you should know that any errors in this file may prevent Red Hat Linux from starting up to a point at which you can log in. If you cannot log in, you cannot use your system. You should always try out a specific run level with the init command before you actually change the default run level by editing the /etc/inittab file. In case of errors in the /etc/inittab file, you can type init 1 to enter single-user mode, and then edit the file to correct the error.

Trying out a New Run Level with the init Command

To try a new run level, you do not have to change the default run level in the /etc/inittab file. If you log in as root, you can change the run level (and, consequently, the processes that run in Red Hat Linux) with the init command, which has the following format:

```
init runlevel
```

Here, *runlevel* must be a single character denoting the run level you want. To put the system in single-user mode, for example, type the following:

```
init 1
```

Thus, if you want to try run level 5 (assuming that your system is not set up for a graphical login screen yet) without changing the /etc/inittab file, enter the following command at the shell prompt:

```
init 5
```

The system should end all current processes and enter run level 5. By default, the init command waits 20 seconds before stopping all current processes and starting the new processes for run level 5.

To switch to run level 5 immediately, type the command init -t0 5. The number after the -t option indicates the number of seconds init waits before changing the run level.

You can also use the telinit command, which is simply a symbolic link to init. If you make changes to the /etc/inittab file and want init to reload its configuration file, use the command telinit q.

Understanding the Red Hat Linux initscripts

The init process runs a number of scripts at system startup. Notice the following lines that appear near the beginning of the `/etc/inittab` file:

```
# System initialization.
si::sysinit:/etc/rc.d/rc.sysinit
```

As the comment on the first line indicates, the second line causes init to run the `/etc/rc.d/rc.sysinit` script—the first Red Hat Linux startup script that init runs.

Secret

The `rc.sysinit` script performs many initialization tasks, such as mounting the file systems, setting the clock, configuring the keyboard layout, starting the network, and loading many other driver modules. The `rc.sysinit` script performs these initialization tasks by calling many other scripts and reading configuration files located in the `/etc/sysconfig` directory.

After executing the `/etc/rc.d/rc.sysinit` script, the init process runs the `/etc/rc.d/rc` script with the run level as argument. For example, for run level 5, the following line in `/etc/inittab` specifies what init has to execute:

```
l5:5:wait:/etc/rc.d/rc 5
```

This says that init should execute the command `/etc/rc.d/rc 5` and wait until that command completes.

The `/etc/rc.d/rc` script is somewhat complicated. Here is how it works:

- It changes to the subdirectory corresponding to the run level—`rc0.d` for run level 0, `rc1.d` for run level 1, and so on. For example, for run level 5, the script changes to the `/etc/rc.d/rc5.d` directory.
- In the directory that corresponds with the run level, `/etc/rc.d/rc` looks for all files that begin with a `K` and executes each of them with the argument `stop`. This kills currently running processes. Then, it locates all files that begin with an `S` and executes each file with an argument of `start`. This starts the processes needed for the specified run level.

All the scripts in run level directories—`rc0.d`, `rc1.d`, `rc2.d`, and so on—are symbolic links to scripts located in the `/etc/rc.d/init.d` directory. These scripts are called *initscrtips* and they can start, stop, and restart services.

To see what is executed at a run level, look at the contents of that run level's subdirectory with the `ls` command. For example, to see what scripts `/etc/rc.d/rc` runs at run level 5, type the following command:

```
ls -l /etc/rc.d/rc5.d | cut -c57-
```

Here's a partial list of files shows by that command (the `cut` command extracts only 57th character onwards of each line):

```
K05innd -> ../init.d/innd
K05saslauthd -> ../init.d/saslauthd
K15httpd -> ../init.d/httpd
... Lines Deleted ...
K74ntpd -> ../init.d/ntpd
```

```
K74ypserv -> ../init.d/ypserv
K74ypxfrd -> ../init.d/ypxfrd
K95firstboot -> ../init.d/firstboot
S05kudzu -> ../init.d/kudzu
S08iptables -> ../init.d/iptables
S09isdn -> ../init.d/isdn
S10network -> ../init.d/network
... Lines Deleted ...
S90cups -> ../init.d/cups
S90xfs -> ../init.d/xfs
S95anacron -> ../init.d/anacron
S95atd -> ../init.d/atd
S97rhnsd -> ../init.d/rhnsd
S99local -> ../rc.local
```

As this listing of the `/etc/rc.d/rc5.d` directory shows, all files with names starting with `K` and `S` are symbolic links to scripts that reside in the `/etc/rc.d/init.d` directory—except for `S99local`, which is a link to `/etc/rc.d/rc.local`. The K scripts stop ("kill") servers, whereas the S scripts start servers. The `/etc/rc.d/rc` script executes these files exactly in the order that they appear in the directory listing. Thus, the prefixes `S05`, `S10`, `S90`, and so on have been selected judiciously to ensure that services start in the correct order.

insider insight Note that the S99local file is a symbolic link to the /etc/rc.d/rc.local script. This means that /etc/rc.d/rc.local is executed after all other scripts. So you can place in that script any command you want executed whenever your Red Hat Linux system boots, regardless of run level.

Manually Starting and Stopping Servers

The Red Hat Linux initscripts reside in the `/etc/rc.d/init.d` directory. You can manually invoke scripts in this directory to start, stop, or restart specific processes—usually servers. For example, to stop the Apache Web server (the program's name is httpd), type the following command:

```
/etc/rc.d/init.d/httpd stop
```

The `/etc/init.d` file is defined as a symbolic link to `/etc/rc.d/init.d`. Therefore, you can also execute the previous command as follows:

```
/etc/init.d/httpd stop
```

If httpd is already running and you want to restart it, all you have to do is change the stop to restart, like this:

```
/etc/init.d/httpd restart
```

/sbin/service **provides a more logical way to start, stop, and restart services. When you log in as root,** /sbin **is already in your** PATH **environment, so you can execute the initscripts by using the** service **command with the following syntax:**

```
service servicename action
```

where *servicename* **is the name of the service and** *action* **is one of** start, stop, **or** restart. **The** *servicename* **is the name of the initscript in** /etc/init.d **directory. Typically, the initscript name is the same as the name of the server. For example, the initscript for the Web server (httpd) is also named httpd. Thus, you restart the Web service by typing** service httpd restart.

You can enhance your systems-administration skills by familiarizing yourself with the initscripts in the /etc/init.d directory. To see its listing, type the following command:

```
ls /etc/init.d
```

Here's the output of that command on a Red Hat Linux 9 system:

```
aep1000    firstboot   isdn       network    pxe         snmpd       xfs
anacron    functions   kdcrotate  nfs        random      snmptrapd   xinetd
apmd       gpm         keytable   nfslock    rawdevices  squid       ypbind
atd        halt        killall    nscd       rhnsd       sshd        yppasswdd
autofs     httpd       kudzu      ntpd       saslauthd   syslog      ypserv
bcm5820    innd        lisa       pcmcia     sendmail    tux         ypxfrd
crond      iptables    named      portmap    single      vsftpd
cups       irda        netfs      postgresql smb         winbind
```

The script names give you some clue about which server the script can start and stop. For example, the nfs script starts and stops the processes required for NFS (Network File System) services. At your leisure, you may want to study some of these scripts to see what each one does. You don't have to understand all the shell programming; the comments should help you learn the purpose of each script.

The servers that initscripts start are often referred to as daemons. In UNIX, daemon is just a term used to describe background processes that monitor and perform many critical system functions. Typically, a daemon is started when the system boots, and daemon processes run as long as the system is up. Most daemons have the capability to restart copies of themselves to handle specific tasks. Also, although this is not a rule, most daemons have names that end with d, such as crond, syslogd, klogd, xinetd, cupsd (the printer daemon), named, and httpd. Another characteristic of daemons is that they do not require user interaction, so no terminal devices are associated with a daemon.

Configuring Servers to Start Automatically at Boot Time

Although you can start, stop, and restart servers manually by using the scripts in the `/etc/rc.d/init.d` directory, you have to set up symbolic links in the scripts for an appropriate run level. For example, to start the DNS server—named—in run level 5, you need an S script in the run level 5 directory (`/etc/rc.d/rc5.d`). Furthermore, that S script should be a symbolic link to the `/etc/rc.d/init.d/named` file. You set up such symbolic links to configure servers to start automatically at boot time. Luckily, you do not have to do this job by hand. Instead, you can use the `/sbin/chkconfig` or `/usr/sbin/ntsysv` program.

Using chkconfig

The chkconfig program is a command-line utility for querying and updating the run-level scripts in Red Hat Linux. I introduce you to the chkconfig utility next, but you can learn more about its options by reading the chkconfig man page with the `man chkconfig` command.

For example, suppose that you want to automatically start the named server at run levels 3 and 5. All you need to do is log in as `root`, and type the following command at the shell prompt:

```
chkconfig --level 35 named on
```

To see the status of the named server, type the following command:

```
chkconfig --list named
```

```
named    0:off  1:off  2:off  3:on   4:off  5:on   6:off
```

The output shows you the status of the named server at run levels 0 through 6. As you can see, named is set to run as run levels 3 and 5. If you now look at the directories `/etc/rc.d/rc3.d` and `/etc/rc.d/rc5.d`, you see two new S scripts that are symbolic links to `/etc/rc.d/init.d/named`. Both of these S scripts are symbolic links to the same script; each link looks like this:

```
lrwxrwxrwx  1 root    root    15 Jan 20 21:08 S55named -> ../init.d/named
```

If you want to turn named off, you can do so with the following command:

```
chkconfig --level 35 named off
```

You can use chkconfig to see the status of all services, including the ones started through xinetd. For example, you can view the status of all services by typing the following command:

```
chkconfig --list | more
```

The output shows the standalone services started by initscripts as well as those managed by the xinetd server:

```
snmpd           0:off   1:off   2:off   3:off   4:off   5:off   6:off
snmptrapd       0:off   1:off   2:off   3:off   4:off   5:off   6:off
iptables        0:off   1:off   2:on    3:on    4:on    5:on    6:off
gpm             0:off   1:off   2:on    3:on    4:on    5:on    6:off
kudzu           0:off   1:off   2:off   3:on    4:on    5:on    6:off
winbind         0:off   1:off   2:off   3:off   4:off   5:off   6:off
ntpd            0:off   1:off   2:off   3:off   4:off   5:off   6:off
syslog          0:off   1:off   2:on    3:on    4:on    5:on    6:off
atd             0:off   1:off   2:off   3:on    4:on    5:on    6:off
netfs           0:off   1:off   2:off   3:on    4:on    5:on    6:off
network         0:off   1:off   2:on    3:on    4:on    5:on    6:off
random          0:off   1:off   2:on    3:on    4:on    5:on    6:off
... many lines of output deleted ...
xinetd based services:
        chargen-udp:    off
        rsync:  off
        chargen:        off
        daytime-udp:    off
        daytime:        off
        echo-udp:       off
        echo:   off
        services:       off
        servers:        off
        time-udp:       off
        time:   off
        cups-lpd:       off
        sgi_fam:        on
        kotalk: off
        ktalk:  off
        imap:   off
        imaps:  off
        ipop2:  off
        ipop3:  off
        pop3s:  off
        finger: off
        ntalk:  off
        talk:   off
        telnet: on
        rexec:  off
        rlogin: off
        rsh:    off
```

The output shows the status of each service for each of the run levels from 0 through 6. For each run level, the service is either on or off. At the very end of the listing, chkconfig displays a list of the services that xinetd controls (see Chapter 6 for more information on xinetd). Each xinetd-based service is also marked on or off, depending on whether or not xinetd is configured to start the service.

Using the Red Hat Service Configuration Utility

If you don't like typing the chkconfig commands, you can use a graphical service configuration utility program to configure the services. To run the service configuration utility,
log in as root and select Main Menu⇨System Settings⇨Server Settings⇨Services from the
GNOME desktop. You can then turn services on or off from the service configuration window (see Figure 20-1).

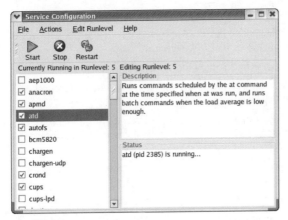

Figure 20-1: Using the Red Hat Service Configuration Utility to Select the Services You Want
to Start Automatically.

The service configuration utility shows the names of services in a scrolling list. Each line
in the list shows the name of a service with a box in front of the name. A check mark in the
box indicates that the service is already selected to start at boot time for the current run
level. When the dialog box first appears, many services are already selected.

You can scroll up and down the list and click on the box to select or deselect a service. If
you click the box, the check mark alternately turns on and off. To learn more about a service, click the service name and a brief description appears in the right-hand side of the
window. For example, Figure 20-1 shows the help text for the atd service. Additionally,
the utility also shows you whether the selected service is currently running or not.

After you select all the servers you want to start when the system boots, select File⇨
Save Changes to save the changes. Then, select File⇨Quit to exit.

caution   By default, the service configuration utility configures the selected services for the current run level. This means that if you are accessing it from the graphical desktop, the
system is in run level 5 and the services you configure are set to start at run level 5. If
you want to set up the services for a different level, select that run level from the Edit
Runlevel menu.

Table 20-2 shows a list of the services, along with a brief description of each one. The first
column shows the name of the service, which is the same as the name of the program that
has to run to provide the service. You may not see all of these services listed when you run
the service configuration utility on your system because the exact list of services depends
on what is installed on your Red Hat Linux system.

Table 20-2: Some Common Services in Red Hat Linux

Service Name	Description
aep1000	Loads and unloads the driver for the Accelerated Encryption Processing card called the AEP1000, which can do encryption fast (use this only if you have the card installed in your system)
anacron	Executes commands that are scheduled to run periodically
apmd	Monitors the Advanced Power Management (APM) BIOS and logs the status of electric power (AC or battery backup)
atd	Runs commands scheduled by the at and cron commands
autofs	Automatically mounts file systems (for example, when you insert a CD-ROM in the CD-ROM drive)
bcm5820	Loads and unloads the driver for Broadcom's BCM5820 Cryptonet SSL (Secure Sockets Layer) accelerator chip (use this service only if you have the hardware installed)
crond	Runs user-specified programs according to a periodic schedule the crontab command has set
cups	Runs the Common UNIX Printing System (CUPS) daemon (cupsd)
cups-lpd	Enables applications to use the legacy LPD (line prinetr daemon) protocol to communicate with CUPS
finger	Answers finger protocol requests (for user information, such as login name and last login time). You have to enable xinetd for this service to run.
firstboot	Runs the first time you boot Red Hat Linux and enables you to set the date and time, create user accounts, register with Red Hat Network, and install other CD-ROMs
gpm	Enables use of mouse in text-mode screens
httpd	This is the Apache Web server
imap	Allows remote IMAP (Internet Message Access Protocol) clients to download mail messages. You have to enable xinetd for this service to run.
imaps	Allows remote IMAP (Internet Message Access Protocol) clients with secure sockets layer (SSL) support to securely download mail messages. You have to enable xinetd for this service to run.
innd	This is the InterNetNews daemon—the Internet news server you can use to support local newsgroups on your system.
ipop3	Allows remote POP3 (Post Office Protocol version 3) clients to download mail messages. You have to enable xinetd for this service to run.
iptables	Automates a packet-filtering firewall with iptables
irda	Supports communications with IrDA-compliant infrared devices in Linux (IrDA is a standard for infrared wireless communication at speeds ranging from 2400 bps to 4 Mbps.)
isdn	Starts and stops ISDN (Integrated Services Digital Network) services—a digital communication service over regular phone lines (enable only if you have ISDN service)

Service Name	Description
keytable	Loads selected keyboard map as specified in the file /etc/sysconfig/ keyboard. You should leave this service running on your system.
kudzu	Probes for new hardware and configures changed hardware
lpd	Server that manages the queue of print jobs and sends the print jobs to the printer. You need this server if you want to do any printing from the Red Hat Linux system.
named	This is a server for the Domain Name System (DNS) that translates host names into IP addresses. You can run a copy on your system if you want.
netfs	Enables you to mount and unmount all network file systems (NFS, Samba, and Netware)
network	Enables you to activate or deactivate all network interfaces configured to start at system boot time
nfs	Enables sharing of file systems specified in the /etc/exports file using the Network File System (NFS) protocol
nfslock	Provides file-locking capability for file systems exported using the Network File System (NFS) protocol, so that other systems (running NFS) can share files from your system
ntalk	Provides support for chatting with users on different systems
ntpd	This is the server for Network Time Protocol version 4 (NTPv4), which is used for synchronizing clocks on computers in a network
pcmcia	Provides support for PCMCIA devices
pop3s	Allows remote POP3 (Post Office Protocol version 3) clients that support SSL to securely download mail messages. You have to enable xinetd for this service to run.
portmap	Server used by any software that relies on Remote Procedure Calls (RPC). For example, NFS requires the portmap service.
postgresql	Starts or stops the PostgreSQL server that handles database requests. (PostgreSQL is a free database that comes with Red Hat Linux.)
pxe	Server for preboot execution environment (PXE) that's used to boot other systems over the network
random	Server needed to generate high-quality random numbers on the Red Hat Linux system
rawdevices	Assigns raw devices to block devices (needed for applications such as Oracle)
rexec	Supports remote execution with authentication based on user name and password. You have to enable xinetd for this service to run.
rhnsd	Periodically connects to the Red Hat Network Services servers to check for updates and notifications
rlogin	Server that supports remote login. You have to enable xinetd for this service to run.

(continued)

Table 20-2: *(continued)*

Service Name	Description
rsh	Server that supports remote execution of commands. You have to enable xinetd for this service to run.
rsync	Server that supports remote copying of files. You have to enable xinetd for this service to run.
saslauthd	Supports authentication using the Cyrus-SASL (Simple Authentication and Security Layer) software
sendmail	Moves mail messages from one machine to another. Start this service if you want to send mail from your Red Hat Linux system. If you do not plan to use your Red Hat Linux system as a mail server, do not start the sendmail server because it can slow down the booting process and consume unnecessary resources.
sgi_fam	Implements a file alternation monitor (FAM) that can be used to get reports when files change
smb	Starts and stops the Samba smbd and nmbd services that support LAN Manager services on a Red Hat Linux system
snmpd	Simple Network Management Protocol (SNMP) service used for network management functions
squid	A caching server for Internet objects—anything that can be accessed through HTTP and FTP
sshd	Server for the OpenSSH (Secure Shell) secure remote login facility
syslog	Service used by many other programs (including other services) to log various error and status messages in a log file (usually, the /var/log/messages file). You should always run this service.
talk	Server that supports chatting with users on other systems. You have to enable xinetd for this service to run.
telnet	Server that supports telnet remote login sessions. You have to enable xinetd for this service to run.
tux	This is the kernel-based HTTP server
vsftpd	Very Secure FTP daemon for file transfers using the File Transfer Protocol (FTP)
winbind	Starts and stops the Samba winbindd server that provides a name switch capability similar to that provided by the /etc/nsswitch.conf file
xfs	Server that starts and stops the X Font Server
xinetd	This is the Internet superserver, a replacement for the older inetd. It starts other Internet services, such as Telnet and FTP, whenever they are needed.
yppasswdd	Service needed for password changes in Network Information System (NIS). You do not need to start yppasswdd unless you are using NIS.
ypserv	The server for Network Information System (NIS). You do not need to start ypserv unless you are using NIS.
ypxfrd	A server that helps ypserv. Start this service only if you are using Network Information System (NIS).

Scheduling Jobs in Red Hat Linux

As a system administrator, you may need to run some programs automatically at regular intervals or execute one or more commands at a specified time in the future. Your Linux system includes the facilities to schedule jobs to run at any future date or time you want. You can set up the system to perform a task periodically or just once. Here are some typical tasks you can perform by scheduling jobs on your Linux system:

- ◆ Back up the files in the middle of the night
- ◆ Download large files in the early morning when the system is not busy
- ◆ Send yourself messages as reminders of meetings
- ◆ Analyze the system logs periodically and look for any abnormal activities

You can perform these tasks by using the at command or the crontab facility of Red Hat Linux. The next few sections introduce these job-scheduling features of Red Hat Linux.

Scheduling One-Time Jobs

You can use the at command to schedule the execution of one or more commands at a later time. The atd daemon—a program designed to process jobs submitted using at—executes the commands at the specified time, and mails the output to you.

---

insider insight Before you try out the at command, note that the following configuration files control, which users can schedule tasks using the at command:

- ◆ /etc/at.allow contains the names of the users who may submit jobs using the at command.
- ◆ /etc/at.deny contains the names of users not allowed to submit jobs using the at command.

If these files are not present, or if there is an empty /etc/at.deny file, any user can submit jobs using the at command. The default in Red Hat Linux is an empty /etc/at.deny file, so anyone can use the at command. If you do not want some users to use at, simply list those usernames in the /etc/at.deny file.

To use at to schedule a one-time job for execution at a later time, follow these steps:

1. Run the at command with the date or time when you want your commands executed. When you press Enter, the at> prompt appears, as follows:

```
at 21:30
at>
```

This is the simplest way to indicate the time when you want to execute one or more commands—simply specify the time in a 24-hour format. In this case, you want to execute the commands at 9:30 p.m. tonight (or tomorrow, if it's already past 9:30 p.m.). You can, however, specify the execution time in many different ways (see Table 20-3 for examples).

2. At the at> prompt, type the commands you want to execute as if typing input at the shell prompt. After each command, press Enter and continue with the next command. When you are finished entering the commands you want to execute, press Ctrl-D to indicate the end. Here is an example showing a single command:

```
at> ps
at> <EOT>
job 1 at 2003-01-21 21:30
```

After you press Ctrl-D, the at command responds with a job number and the date and time when the job will execute.

Table 20-3: Specifying the Time of Execution with the at Command

Command	When the Job Is Run
at now	Immediately
at now + 15 minutes	15 minutes from the current time
at now + 4 hours	4 hours from the current time
at now + 7 days	7 days from the current time
at noon	At noontime today (or tomorrow, if already past noon)
at now next hour	Exactly 60 minutes from now
at now next day	At the same time tomorrow
at 17:00 tomorrow	At 5:00 P.M. tomorrow
at 4:45pm	At 4:45 P.M. today (or tomorrow, if already past 4:45 P.M.)
at 3:00 Aug 16, 2003	At 3:00 A.M. on August 16, 2003

After you enter one or more jobs, you can view the current list of scheduled jobs with the atq command:

```
atq
4        2003-04-19 03:00 a
5        2003-08-16 21:57 a
6        2003-10-26 16:45 a
```

The first field on each line shows the job number—the same number that the at command displays when you submit the job. The next field shows the year, month, day, and time of execution. The last field shows the jobs pending in the queue named a.

If you want to cancel a job, use the atrm command to remove that job from the queue. When removing a job with the atrm command, refer to the job by its number, as follows:

```
atrm 4
```

This deletes job 4 scheduled for 3:00 a.m. April 19, 2003.

When a job executes, the output is mailed to you. Type **mail** to read your mail and to view the output from your jobs.

Note that at is useful for scheduling jobs that need to run irregularly—for instance, if you want to clean up the /var/logs directory because the /var filesystem is over 85 percent full, you might use at to archive the old log files and then delete them to reclaim the disk space.

Scheduling Recurring Jobs

Although at is good for running commands at a specific time, it's not useful for running a program automatically at repeated intervals. You have to use crontab to schedule such recurring jobs, also called *cron jobs* because they are processed by the cron daemon (crond). You need to do this, for example, if you want to back up your files to tape at midnight every day.

Two files control who can schedule cron jobs using crontab:

♦ /etc/cron.allow contains the names of the users who may submit jobs using the crontab command.

♦ /etc/cron.deny contains the names of users not allowed to submit jobs using the crontab command.

If the /etc/cron.allow file exists, only users listed in this file can schedule cron jobs. If only the /etc/cron.deny file exists, users listed in this file cannot schedule cron jobs. Neither file exists in Red Hat Linux, so any user can submit cron jobs.

Secret

You schedule recurring jobs by placing job information in a file with a specific format and submitting this file with the crontab command. The cron daemon—crond—checks the job information every minute and executes the recurring jobs at the specified times.

Any output from the job is mailed to the user who submits the job. (In the submitted job-information file, you may specify a different recipient for the mailed output.)

To submit a cron job, perform the following steps:

1. Prepare a shell script (or an executable program in any programming language) that can perform the recurring task you want to perform. You can skip this step if you want to execute an existing program periodically.

2. Prepare a text file with information about the times when you want the shell script or program (from Step 1) to execute. Submit this file using crontab. You can submit several recurring jobs with a single file. Each line with timing information about a job has a standard format with six fields—the first five specify when the job runs, and the sixth and subsequent fields constitute the actual command that runs. For example, here is a line that executes the myjob shell script in a user's home directory at 5 minutes past midnight each day:

```
5 0 * * * $HOME/myjob
```

Table 20-4 shows the meaning of the first five fields. Note that an asterisk (*) means all possible values for that field. Also, an entry in any of the first five fields can be a single number, a comma-separated list of numbers, a pair of numbers separated by a dash (indicating a range of numbers), or an asterisk.

continues

continued

3. Suppose the text file `jobinfo` (in the current directory) contains the job information. Submit this information to crontab with the following command:

```
crontab jobinfo
```

That's it! You should be set with the cron job. From now on, the cron job should run at regular intervals (as specified in the job information file), and you should receive mail messages with the output from the job.

To verify that the job is indeed scheduled, type the following command:

```
crontab -l
```

The output of the `crontab -l` command shows the cron jobs currently installed in your name. To remove your cron jobs, type **crontab −r**.

Table 20-4: Specifying the Time of Execution in crontab Files

Field Number	Meaning of Field	Acceptable Range of Values*
1	Minute	0–59
2	Hour of the day	0–23
3	Day of the month	0–31
4	Month	1–12 (1 means January, 2 means February, and so on) or the names of months using the first letters (Jan, Feb, Mar, Apr, May, Jun, Jul, Aug, Sep, Oct, Nov, Dec)
5	Day of the week	0–6 (0 means Sunday, 1 means Monday, and so on) or the three-letter abbreviations of the week (Sun, Mon, Tue, Wed, Thu, Fri, Sat)

* An asterisk in a field means all possible values for that field. For example, if an asterisk appears in the third field, the job is executed every day.

If you log in as `root`, you can also set up, examine, and remove cron jobs for any user. To set up cron jobs for a user, use this command:

```
crontab -u username filename
```

Here, *username* is the user for whom you install the cron jobs, and *filename* is the file that contains information about the jobs.

Use the following form of `crontab` command to view the cron jobs for a user:

```
crontab -u username -l
```

Secret

Looking at the /etc/crontab File

The cron daemon (crond) also executes the cron jobs listed in the systemwide cron-job file /etc/crontab. Here's the default /etc/crontab file in Red Hat Linux (type cat **/etc/crontab** to view the file):

```
SHELL=/bin/bash
PATH=/sbin:/bin:/usr/sbin:/usr/bin
MAILTO=root
HOME=/

# run-parts
01 * * * * root run-parts /etc/cron.hourly
02 4 * * * root run-parts /etc/cron.daily
22 4 * * 0 root run-parts /etc/cron.weekly
42 4 1 * * root run-parts /etc/cron.monthly
```

The first four lines set up several environment variables for the jobs listed in this file. Note that the MAILTO environment variable specifies the user who receives the mail message with the output from the cron jobs in this file.

The line that begins with a # is a comment line. The four lines following the run-parts comment execute the run-parts shell script (located in the /usr/bin directory) at various times with the name of a specific directory as argument. Each of the arguments to run-parts—/etc/cron.hourly, /etc/cron.daily, /etc/cron.weekly, and /etc/cron.monthly—are directories. Essentially, run-parts executes all scripts located in the directory that you provide as an argument. This means that you can place scripts in these directories and get crond to execute them at the appointed time. For example, a script placed in the /etc/cron.daily gets executed at a certain time every day. Table 20-5 lists the directories and when they are executed. You have to look at the scripts in these directories to learn what gets executed at these periodic intervals.

To remove a user's cron jobs, use the following command:

```
crontab -u username -r
```

Table 20-5: Script Directories for run-parts

Directory Name	Contents
/etc/cron.hourly	Scripts executed every hour
/etc/cron.daily	Scripts executed each day at 4:02 A.M.
/etc/cron.weekly	Scripts executed weekly on Sunday at 4:22 A.M.
/etc/cron.monthly	Scripts to be executed at 4:42 A.M. on the first day of each month

Backing Up and Restoring Files

By now, you know how to perform a number of systems-administration tasks, from automatically starting servers to scheduling periodic jobs. The next few sections introduce you to another systems-administration task—backing up and restoring files. You learn about backup strategies, backup media, and how to back up and restore files by using the tape archiver (tar) program that comes with Red Hat Linux. Also, you learn how to perform incremental and automatic backups on tapes.

Selecting a Backup Strategy and Media

Your Linux system's hard disk contains everything needed to keep the system running, as well as other files, such as documents and databases you need to keep your business running. You need to back up these files so that you can recover quickly and bring the system back to normal in case the hard disk crashes. Typically, you have to follow a strict regimen of regular backups because you can never tell when the hard disk might fail or the file system might get corrupted. To implement such a regimen, you need to decide which files you want to back up, how often, and what backup storage media to use. This is what I mean by selecting a backup strategy and backup media.

Your choice of backup strategy and backup media depends on your assessment of the risk of business disruption due to hard disk failure. Depending on how you use your Linux system, a disk failure may or may not have much impact on you.

For example, if you use your Linux system as a learning tool (to learn about Linux or programming), all you may need are backup copies of some system files required to configure Linux. In this case, your backup strategy can be to save important system-configuration files on one or more floppies every time you change any system configuration.

On the other hand, if you use your Linux system as an office server that provides shared file storage for many users, the risk of business disruption due to disk failure is much higher. In this case, you have to back up all the files every week and back up any new or changed files every day. You should perform these backups in an automated manner (this is where you can use the job-scheduling features from earlier in this chapter). Also, you probably need a backup storage medium that can store large amounts (multiple gigabytes) of data on a single tape. In other words, for high-risk situations, your backup strategy is more elaborate and requires additional equipment (such as a tape drive).

Your choice of backup media depends on the amount of data you have to back up. For a small amount of data, such as system-configuration files, you can use floppy disks as the backup media. If your PC has a Zip drive, you can use Zip disks as backup media; these are good for backing up a single-user directory. To back up servers, you should use a tape drive, typically a 4-mm or 8-mm tape drive that connects to a SCSI controller. Such tape drives can store several gigabytes of data per tape, and you can use them to back up an entire file system on a single tape.

When backing up files to these backup media, you have to refer to the backup device by name. Table 20-6 lists device names for some common backup devices.

Table 20-6: Device Names for Common Backup Devices

Backup Device	Linux Device Name
Floppy disk	/dev/fd0
IDE Zip drive	/dev/hdc4 or /dev/hdd4
IDE floppy tape (Ftape) drive	/dev/qft0
SCSI Zip drive	/dev/sda (assuming it's the first SCSI drive; otherwise, the device name depends on the SCSI ID)
SCSI tape drive	/dev/st0 or /dev/nst0 (the n prefix means that the tape is not rewound after files are copied to the tape)

Taking Stock of Commercial Backup Utilities for Linux

This chapter describes how to back up and restore files using the tape archiver (tar) program that comes with Red Hat Linux. Although you can manage backups with tar, a number of commercial backup utilities come with GUIs and other features to simplify backups. Here are some well-known backup utilities for Red Hat Linux:

- **BRU**—Backup and Restore Utility from The TOLIS Group, Inc. (http://www.tolisgroup.com/)
- **LONE-TAR**—Tape-backup software package from Lone Star Software Corporation (http://www.cactus.com/)
- **Arkeia**—Backup and recovery software for heterogeneous networks from Knox Software (http://www.knox-software.com/)
- **CTAR**—Backup and recovery software for UNIX systems from UniTrends Software Corporation (http://www.unitrends.com/products.html)
- **BrightStor ARCserve Backup for Linux**—Data protection technology for Linux systems from Computer Associates (http://www3.ca.com/Solutions/Product.asp?ID=3370)

Using the Tape Archiver—tar

You can use the tar command to archive files to a device such as a floppy disk or tape. The tar program creates an archive file that can contain other directories and files and (optionally) compress the archive for efficient storage. The archive is then written to a specified device or another file. In fact, many software packages are distributed in the form of a compressed tar file.

The command syntax of the tar program is as follows:

```
tar options destination source
```

Here, *options* are usually specified by a sequence of single letters, with each letter specifying what tar should do. *destination* is the device name of the backup device. And *source* is a list of file or directory names denoting the files to back up. Optionally, you can add a hyphen prefix for the options.

Backing Up and Restoring a Single-Volume Archive

For example, suppose you want to back up the contents of the /etc/X11 directory on a floppy disk. Log in as root, place a disk in the floppy drive, and type the following command:

```
tar zcvf /dev/fd0 /etc/X11
```

The tar program displays a list of filenames as each file is copied to the compressed tar archive on the floppy disk. In this case, the options are zcvf, the destination is /dev/fd0 (the floppy disk), and the source is the /etc/X11 directory (which implies all its subdirectories and their contents). You can use a similar tar command to back up files to a tape— simply replace /dev/fd0 with the tape device—such as /dev/st0 for a SCSI tape drive.

Table 20-7 defines a few common tar options.

Table 20-7: Common tar Options

Option	Definition
c	Creates a new archive
f	Specifies the name of the archive file or device on the next field in the command line
M	Specifies a multivolume archive (the next section describes multivolume archives)
t	Lists the contents of the archive
v	Displays verbose messages
x	Extracts files from the archive
z	Compresses the tar archive using gzip

To view the contents of the tar archive you create on the floppy disk, type the following command:

```
tar ztf /dev/fd0
```

You should see a list of the filenames (each begins with /etc/X11) indicating what's in the backup. In this tar command, the t option lists the contents of the tar archive.

To learn how to extract the files from a tar backup, try the following steps while logged in as root:

1. Change the directory to /tmp by typing this command:
   ```
   cd /tmp
   ```

   This is where you extract the files from the tar backup.

2. Type the following command:
   ```
   tar zxvf /dev/fd0
   ```

   This tar command uses the x option to extract the files from the archive stored on /dev/fd0 (the floppy disk).

If you check the contents of the /tmp directory, notice that the tar command creates an etc/X11 directory tree in /tmp and restores all the files from the tar archive into that directory. The tar command strips off the leading / from the filenames in the archive and restores the files in the current directory. If you want to restore the /etc/X11 directory from the archive on the floppy, use this command:

```
tar zxvf /dev/fd0 /
```

The / at the end of the command denotes the directory where you want to restore the backup files.

As you can see, the tar command enables you to create, view, and restore an archive. You can store the archive in a file or in any device you specify with a device name.

Backing Up and Restoring a Multivolume Archive

Sometimes the capacity of a single storage medium is less than the total storage space needed to store the archive. In this case, you can use the M option for a multivolume archive—meaning the archive can span multiple tapes or floppies. Note, however, that you cannot create a compressed, multivolume archive. You have to drop the z option. To see how multivolume archives work, log in as root, place one disk in the floppy drive, and type the following tar command:

```
tar cvfM /dev/fd0 /usr/share/doc/ghostscript*
```

Note the M option in the option letters; it tells tar to create a multivolume archive. The tar command prompts you for a second floppy when the first one is filled. Take out the first floppy, and insert another floppy when you see the following prompt:

```
Prepare volume #2 for `/dev/fd0' and hit return:
```

When you press Enter, the tar program continues with the second floppy. In this example, you need only two floppies to store the archive; for larger archives, the tar program continues to prompt you for floppies if more floppies are needed.

To restore from this multivolume archive, type **cd /tmp** to change the directory to /tmp. Then type:

```
tar xvfM /dev/fd0
```

The tar program prompts you to feed the floppies as necessary.

 insider insight

Use the du -s command to determine the amount of storage you need to archive a directory. For example, here's how you can get the total size of the /etc directory in kilobytes:

```
du -s /etc
14532   /etc
```

The resulting output shows that the /etc directory requires at least 14,532K of storage space to back up. If you plan to back up on multiple high-density floppies, you need about 14,532/1,440 = 11 floppies.

Backing Up on Tapes

Although backing up on tapes is as simple as using the right device name in the `tar` command, you do need to know some nuances of the tape device to use it well. When you use `tar` to back up to the device named `/dev/st0` (the first SCSI tape drive), the tape device automatically rewinds the tape after the tar program finishes copying the archive to the tape. The `/dev/st0` device is called a rewinding tape device because it rewinds tapes by default.

Secret

If your tape can hold several gigabytes of data, you may want to write several `tar` archives—one after another—to the same tape (otherwise, much of the tape may be empty). To do this, you do not want the tape device to rewind the tape after the tar program finishes. To help you with this, there are several Linux tape devices that are nonrewinding. The nonrewinding SCSI tape device is called `/dev/nst0`. Use this device name if you want to write one archive after another on a tape.

After each archive, the nonrewinding tape device writes an end-of-file (EOF) marker to separate one archive from the next. You can use the `mt` command to control the tape—you can move from one marker to the next or rewind the tape. For example, after you finish writing several archives to a tape using the `/dev/nst0` device name, you can rewind the tape with the following command:

```
mt -f /dev/nst0 rewind
```

After rewinding the tape, you can use the following command to extract files from the first archive to the current disk directory:

```
tar xvf /dev/nst0
```

After that, you must move past the EOF marker to the next archive. To do this, use the following `mt` command:

```
mt -f /dev/nst0 fsf 1
```

This positions the tape at the beginning of the next archive. You can now use the `tar` `xvf` command again to read this archive.

note   If you save multiple archives on a tape, you have to keep track of the archives yourself.

Performing Incremental Backups

Suppose that you back up your system's hard disk on a tape by using tar. Because such a full backup can take quite some time, you do not want to repeat this task every night. (Besides, only a small number of files may have changed during the day.) You can use the `find` command to list those files that have changed in the past 24 hours:

```
find / -mtime -1 -type f -print
```

This command prints a list of files that have changed within the last day. The -mtime -1 option means that you want the files that were last modified less than one day ago. You can now combine this find command with the tar command to back up only those files that have changed within the last day:

```
tar cvf /dev/st0 `find / -mtime -1 -type f -print`
```

When you place a command between single back quotes, the shell executes that command and places the output at that point in the command line. The net result is that the tar program saves only the changed files in the archive. Thus, you get an incremental backup that includes files that have changed since the previous day.

Performing Automated Backups

Earlier in this chapter, you learn to use crontab to set up recurring jobs (called cron jobs). The Linux system performs these tasks at regular intervals. Backing up your system is a good use of the crontab facility. Suppose your backup strategy is as follows:

- Every Sunday at 1:15 A.M., your system backs up the entire disk on the tape.
- Monday through Saturday, your system performs an incremental backup at 3:10 A.M. by saving only those files that have changed during the past 24 hours.

To set up this automated backup schedule, log in as root and type the following lines in a file named backups (this example assumes that you use a SCSI tape drive):

```
15 1 * * 0 tar zcvf /dev/st0 /
10 3 * * 1-6 tar zcvf /dev/st0 `find / -mtime -1 -type f -print`
```

Next, submit this job schedule by using the following crontab command:

```
crontab backups
```

Now, you should be set for an automated backup. All you need to do is place a new tape in the tape drive everyday. You should also give each tape an appropriate label.

Managing Devices

Everything you use to work with your computer is a device. The keyboard you use to type and the mouse you click, the hard disk where you store everything, and the printer where you get your hard copies—these are all devices. You often have to load device drivers to use the device in Linux.

To manage devices, you need to understand device drivers a bit and learn to use the tools Red Hat Linux includes to help you manage devices. The next few sections provide a brief overview of device drivers and explain how to manage driver modules.

Understanding Device Drivers

The Linux kernel treats all devices as files and uses a device just as it would use a file—opens it, writes data to it, reads data from it, and closes it when done. This ability to treat every device as a file comes through the use of device drivers. A *device driver* is a special program that controls a particular type of hardware. When the kernel writes data to the device, the device driver does whatever is appropriate for that device. For example, when the kernel writes data to the floppy drive, the floppy device driver puts that data onto the physical medium of the floppy disk. On the other hand, if the kernel writes data to the parallel port device, the parallel port driver sends the data to the printer connected to the parallel port.

Thus, the device driver isolates the device-specific code from the rest of the kernel and makes a device look like a file. Any application can access a device by opening the file specific to that device. Figure 20-2 illustrates this concept of Linux device drivers.

Figure 20-2: Application Accessing Devices through Device Drivers.

Device Files

As Figure 20-2 shows, applications can access a device as if it were a file. These files are special files called device files, and they appear in the /dev directory in the Red Hat Linux file system.

If you use the ls command to look at the list of files in the /dev directory, you'll see several thousand files. This does not mean that your system has several thousand devices. The /dev directory has files for all possible types of devices—that's why the number of device files is so large.

So how does the kernel know which device driver to use when an application opens a specific device file? The answer is in two numbers called the major and minor device numbers. Each device file is mapped to a specific device driver through these numbers.

To see an example of the major and minor device numbers, type the following command in a terminal window:

```
ls -l /dev/hda
```

You should see a line of output similar to the following:

```
brw-rw----   1 root    disk     3,   0 Feb 16 14:50 /dev/hda
```

In this line, the major and minor device numbers appear just before the date. In this case, the major device number is 3 and the minor device number is 0. The kernel selects the device driver for this device file by using the major device number.

You don't really need to learn much about the device files and the device numbers, except to be aware of their existence.

Block Devices

The first letter in the listing of a device file also provides an important clue. For the /dev/hda device, the first letter is a b, which indicates that /dev/hda is a *block* device—one that can accept or provide data in chunks (typically 512 bytes or 1KB). By the way, /dev/hda refers to the first IDE hard disk on your system (the C drive in Windows). Hard drives, floppy drives, and CD-ROM drives are all examples of block devices.

Character Devices

If the first letter in the listing of a device file is a c, then the device is a character device—one that can receive and send data one character (1 byte) at a time. For example, the serial port and parallel ports are character devices. To see the listing of a character device, type the following command in a terminal window:

```
ls -l /dev/ttyS0
```

The listing of this device should be similar to the following:

```
crw-rw----    1 root       uucp       4,  64 Feb 16 14:50 /dev/ttyS0
```

Notice that the very first letter is a c because /dev/ttyS0—the first serial port—is a *character* device.

Network Devices

The network devices, such as Ethernet and dial-up point-to-point protocol (PPP) connections, are somewhat special in that they do not have a file corresponding to the device; instead the kernel uses a special name for the device. For example, the Ethernet devices are named eth0 for the first Ethernet card, eth1 for the second one, and so on. The PPP connections are named ppp0, ppp1, and so on.

Because the network devices are not mapped to device files, there are no files corresponding to these devices in the /dev directory.

Managing Loadable Driver Modules

To use any device, the Linux kernel must contain the driver. If the driver code is linked into the kernel as a monolithic program—a program that's in the form of a single large file, then adding a new driver means rebuilding the kernel with the new driver code. Rebuilding the kernel means you have to reboot the PC with the new kernel before you can use the new device driver. Luckily, the Linux kernel uses a modular design that does away with all the rebooting hassles. Linux device drivers can be created in the form of modules that the kernel can load and unload without having to restart the PC.

note

Driver modules are one type of a broader category of software modules called loadable kernel modules (LKM). Other types of kernel modules include code that can support new types of file systems, modules for network protocols, and modules that interpret different formats of executable files.

Loading and Unloading Modules

You can manage the loadable device driver modules by using a set of commands. Table 20-8 summarizes these commands. You have to log in as `root` to use some of these commands. I explain a few of the commonly used module commands.

Table 20-8: Commands to Manage Kernel Modules

Command	Description
insmod	Inserts a module into the kernel
rmmod	Removes a module from the kernel
depmod	Determines interdependencies between modules
ksyms	Displays a list of symbols along with the name of the module that defined the symbol
lsmod	Lists all currently loaded modules
modinfo	Displays information about a kernel module
modprobe	Inserts or removes a module or a set of modules intelligently. For example, if module A requires B, then modprobe will automatically load B when asked to load B.

If you need to use any of these commands, log in as `root` or type **su -** in a terminal window to become `root`.

To see what modules are currently loaded, type:

```
lsmod
```

You should see a list of modules. For example, here is a list on one of my PCs:

```
Module          Size  Used by    Not tainted
ide-cd          35772   0 (autoclean)
cdrom           33696   0 (autoclean) [ide-cd]
parport_pc      19076   1 (autoclean)
lp               8996   0 (autoclean)
parport         37056   1 (autoclean) [parport_pc lp]
autofs          13276   0 (autoclean) (unused)
ds               8680   1
yenta_socket    13440   1
pcmcia_core     57216   0 [ds yenta_socket]
3c59x           30832   1
keybdev          2976   0 (unused)
mousedev         5492   1
hid             22148   0 (unused)
input            5888   0 [keybdev mousedev hid]
usb-uhci        26444   0 (unused)
usbcore         78880   1 [hid usb-uhci]
ext3            88168   2
jbd             51828   2 [ext3]
```

As you may expect, the list of modules depends on the types of devices installed on your system.

The first column lists the names of the modules in the last-to-first order. Thus, the first module in the list is the last one to be loaded. The Size column shows the number of bytes that the module occupies in your PC's memory. The remaining columns show other information about each module such as how many applications are currently using the module and the names of the modules that require the module.

The list displayed by lsmod includes all types of Linux kernel modules, not just device drivers. For example, the last two modules—jbd and ext3—are both part of the EXT3 file system (the latest file system for Linux).

Secret

Besides lsmod, one commonly used module command is modprobe. Use modprobe whenever you need to manually load or remove one or more modules. The best thing about modprobe is that you don't need to worry if a module requires other modules to work. The modprobe command automatically loads any other modules that are needed by a module. For example, on my system I can manually load the sound driver with the command:

```
modprobe sound-slot-0
```

This command causes modprobe to load everything needed to make sound work. On one of my PCs with a OPL3SA2 sound card, the modprobe sound-slot-0 command loads soundcore, sound, ad1848, mpu401, and opl3sa2—in that order.

You can use modprobe with the -r option to remove modules. For example, to remove the sound modules, I use the following command:

```
modprobe -r sound-slot-0
```

This command gets rid of all the modules that the modprobe sound-slot-0 command has loaded.

Understanding the /etc/modules.conf File

How does the modprobe command know that it should load the opl3sa2 driver module when I use a module name sound-slot-0? The answer is in the /etc/modules.conf configuration file. That file contains a line that tells modprobe what it should load when it sees the module name sound-slot-0.

To view the contents of /etc/modules.conf, type

```
cat /etc/modules.conf
```

On my Red Hat Linux PC, the file contains the following lines:

```
alias parport_lowlevel parport_pc
alias eth0 eepro100
alias usb-controller usb-uhci
alias sound-slot-0 opl3sa2
```

Secret

The `modprobe` command consults the `/etc/modules.conf` file to convert an alias to the real name of a driver module as well as for other tasks such as obtaining parameters for driver modules. For example, you can insert lines that begin with the `options` keyword to provide values of parameters that a driver may need.

For example, to set the interrupt request (IRQ) parameter for the sound card to 5, I would add the following line to the `/etc/modules.conf` file:

```
options opl3sa2 irq=5
```

This line specifies 5 as the value of the parameter named `irq` in the `opl3sa2` module.

If you want to know the names of the parameters that a module accepts, use the `modinfo` command. For example, to view information about the `opl3sa2` driver module, I type **modinfo opl3sa2** and look in the output for lines that begin with the word `parm`, like these:

```
parm:           irq int
parm:           dma int, description "Set MSS (audio) first DMA channel
(0, 1, 3)"
```

From the resulting output I can guess that `irq` is the name of the parameter for the Interrupt Request parameter.

Unfortunately, the information shown by the `modinfo` command can be somewhat cryptic. The only saving grace is that you may not need to do much more than use a graphical utility to configure the device, and the utility will take care of adding whatever is needed to configuration files such as `/etc/modules.conf`.

Each line that begins with the keyword `alias` defines a standard name for an actual driver module. For example, the second line defines `eepro100` as the actual driver name for the alias `eth0`, which stands for the first Ethernet card. Similarly, the fourth line defines `opl3sa2` as the module to load when I use the name `sound-slot-0`.

Monitoring System Performance

A key systems-administration task is to keep track of how well your Red Hat Linux system performs. You can monitor the overall performance of your Linux system by gathering information such as:

- ◆ Central Processing Unit (CPU) usage
- ◆ Physical memory usage
- ◆ Virtual memory (swap space) usage
- ◆ Hard disk usage

Red Hat Linux comes with a number of utilities you can use to monitor one or more of these performance parameters. The following sections introduce you to a few of these utilities and show you how to understand the information they present.

Understanding Load Averages

The system performance is often expressed in terms of the *load averages*, which refers to the average number of processes ready to run in the last 1, 5, and 15 minutes. You can think of the load averages as the number of processes waiting to run.

The load averages give you an indication of how busy the system is. In addition to several system monitoring programs, you can get the load averages with the `uptime` command, as follows:

```
uptime
   2:16pm  up 31 days, 22:30,  2 users,  load average: 0.29, 0.16,
0.11
```

The `uptime` command's output shows the current time, how long the system has been up, the number of users, and, finally, the three load averages. Load averages greater than one imply that many processes are competing for the CPU time simultaneously. You can then look at the top CPU processes and try to run these processes one after another rather than all at the same time.

Using top

To view the top CPU processes—the ones that use most of the CPU time—you can employ the top program. To start this program, type **top** in a terminal window (or text console). The top program then displays a text screen listing the current processes, arranged in the order of CPU usage, along with other information, such as memory and swap-space usage. Figure 20-3 shows typical output from the top program.

```
  root@ dhcppc6:/etc/profile.d                                          _ □ ✕
File   Edit   View   Terminal   Go    Help
 12:29:22  up 48 min,  3 users,  load average: 0.00, 0.00, 0.00
65 processes: 62 sleeping, 3 running, 0 zombie, 0 stopped
CPU states:    1.6% user   0.4% system   0.0% nice   0.0% iowait   98.0% idle
Mem:    254748k av,  192848k used,   61900k free,      0k shrd,   16296k buff
                     166580k actv,    1260k in_d,   6980k in_c
Swap:  522072k av,       0k used,  522072k free                 103908k cached

  PID USER     PRI  NI  SIZE   RSS SHARE STAT %CPU %MEM   TIME CPU COMMAND
 2544 root      15   0 45340  11M  2120 R    1.3  4.7   0:06   0 X
 2653 root      15   0 13692  13M  8892 S    0.1  5.3   0:00   0 rhn-applet-gu
 2728 root      15   0   608  608   500 S    0.1  0.2   0:00   0 in.telnetd
 2889 root      20   0   908  908   768 S    0.1  0.3   0:00   0 xwd
    3 root      15   0     0    0     0 SW   0.0  0.0   0:00   0 kapmd
    4 root      34  19     0    0     0 SWN  0.0  0.0   0:00   0 ksoftirqd_CPU
    7 root      25   0     0    0     0 SW   0.0  0.0   0:00   0 bdflush
    5 root      15   0     0    0     0 SW   0.0  0.0   0:00   0 kswapd
    6 root      15   0     0    0     0 SW   0.0  0.0   0:00   0 kscand
    8 root      15   0     0    0     0 SW   0.0  0.0   0:00   0 kupdated
    9 root      25   0     0    0     0 SW   0.0  0.0   0:00   0 mdrecoveryd
   13 root      15   0     0    0     0 SW   0.0  0.0   0:00   0 kjournald
   71 root      25   0     0    0     0 SW   0.0  0.0   0:00   0 khubd
 1715 root      15   0     0    0     0 SW   0.0  0.0   0:00   0 kjournald
 2015 root      24   0  1016 1016   744 S    0.0  0.3   0:00   0 dhclient
 2058 root      15   0   748  748   648 S    0.0  0.2   0:00   0 syslogd
```

Figure 20-3: Viewing top CPU Processes.

The top utility updates the display every 5 seconds. You can keep top running in a window so that you can continually monitor the status of your Linux system. You quit top by pressing q or Ctrl-C or by closing the terminal window.

The first six lines of the output screen provide summary information about the system. Here is what these six lines show:

1. The first line shows the current time, how long the system has been up, how many users are logged in, and three load averages (the average number of processes ready to run during the last 1, 5, and 15 minutes).

2. The second line lists the total number of processes and the status of these processes.

3. The third line shows CPU usage—what percentage of CPU time user processes employ, what percentage of CPU time system (kernel) processes employ, and what percentage of time the CPU is idle.

4. The fourth and fifth lines show how the physical memory is used—the total amount, how much is used, how much is free, how much is shared, and how much is allocated to buffers (for reading from disk, for instance).

5. The sixth line shows how the virtual memory (or swap space) is used—the total amount of swap space, how much is used, how much is free, and how much is cached.

The following table the summary data lists information about the current processes arranged in decreasing order of CPU time usage. Table 20-9 summarizes the meanings of the column headings in the table that top displays.

Table 20-9: Column Headings in the Top Utility's Display Screen

Heading	Meaning
PID	The process ID of the process
USER	Username under which the process runs
PRI	Priority of the process—the value ranges from -20 (highest priority) to 19 (lowest priority); the default is 0.
NI	Nice value of the process (same as negative PRI values)
SIZE	Total size of the process in kilobytes
RSS	Total physical memory used by task (typically shown in kilobytes, but an M suffix indicates megabytes)
SHARE	Amount of shared memory the process uses
STAT	State of the process (S for sleeping, D for uninterruptible sleep, R for running, W for swapped out, Z for zombies (processes that should be dead but are still running), or T for stopped; a trailing < means the process has a negative nice value)

Heading	Meaning
%CPU	Percentage of CPU time used since last screen update
%MEM	Percentage of physical memory the process uses
TIME	Total CPU time the process has used since it started
COMMAND	Shortened form of the command that starts the process

insider insight

If the RSS field is drastically smaller than the SIZE field for a process, the process is using too little physical memory compared with what it needs. The result is a lot of swapping as the process runs. You can use the vmstat utility (which you try later in this chapter) to find out how much your system is swapping.

Secret

You should also know that you can use combinations of other Linux commands to find the processes that are consuming the most system resources. For example, to find the top five processes that are using the most resources, type the following command line:

```
ps -A -o sz.cmd | sort -bgr | head -5
```

That command line uses ps with appropriate options to display all processes and their size, sort to sort them in decreasing numerical order of size, and finally, use head to display the first five lines of output. Here is typical output from this command line on my system:

```
15000 nautilus --no-default-window --sm-client-id default3
11849 /usr/X11R6/bin/X :0 -auth /var/gdm/:0.Xauth vt7
 6098 /usr/bin/python /usr/bin/rhn-applet-gui --sm-client-id default5
 5306 gnome-panel --sm-client-id default2
 5042 gnome-terminal
```

Using the GNOME System Monitor

Like the text-mode top utility, the GNOME System Monitor tool also enables you to view the system load in terms of the number of processes currently running, their memory usage, and the free disk space on your system. To run this tool, select Main Menu⇨ System Tools⇨System Monitor. The System Monitor starts and displays its output in a window (Figure 20-4).

The output is similar to the output you see when you type **top** in a text-mode console or terminal window. In fact, the column headings in the table match what the top utility uses in its output. (See Table 20-9 for the meaning of the column headings.) As with the text-mode top utility, the display is continuously updated to reflect the current state of the system.

You can click the columns to sort the processes in different ways. You can use the drop-down list on the upper-right corner of the window to select which processes you want to see. Figure 20-4 shows a list of processes sorted in descending order of their memory usage. For each process, the GNOME System Monitor shows a number of details including the process ID (PID), the user who starts the process, and the command used to start the process.

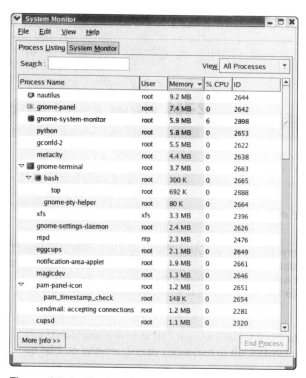

Figure 20-4: Viewing Current Processes in the System Monitor.

The GNOME System Monitor window has another tab that displays the CPU and memory usage history and the free space on the file system. To view this information, click the System Monitor tab. Figure 20-5 shows the typical graphical output in the System Monitor tab. You will find the plots easy to understand. At the bottom of the tab, you see the amount of free and used space on the file systems.

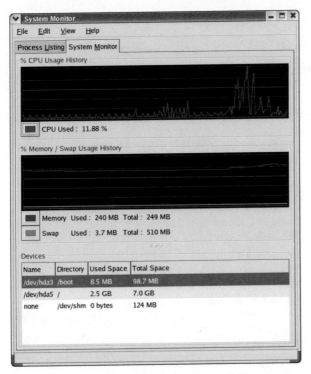

Figure 20-5: Graphical Display of CPU and Memory Usage History.

Using the vmstat Utility

You can get summary information about the overall system usage with the vmstat utility. To view system-usage information averaged over 5-second intervals, type the following command (the second argument indicates the total number of lines of output vmstat should display):

```
vmstat 5 8
      procs                   memory     swap        io    system          cpu
 r  b  w   swpd   free   buff  cache  si  so    bi   bo   in    cs  us  sy  id
 1  0  0  46100   5304   2740  12572   0   0     2    5   11     9  10   5   7
 0  0  0  46100   5304   2748  12572   0   0     0    6  104    69   3   5  92
 0  0  0  46100   5304   2756  12572   0   0     0    5  103    71   4   6  91
 1  0  0  46100   5304   2764  12572   0   0     0    3  104    62   3   6  91
 1  0  0  46100   5304   2772  12572   0   0     0    3  103    63   2   4  94
 0  0  0  46100   5304   2780  12572   0   0     0    3  104    69   2   7  91
 0  0  0  46100   5300   2788  12572   0   0     0    3  103    64   2   7  91
 1  0  0  46100   5292   2796  12572   0   0     0    6  104    66   2   3  94
```

The tabular output is grouped into six categories of information, as the fields in the first line of output indicate. The second line shows further details for each of the six major fields. You can interpret the six major fields, as well as the detailed fields in each category, using Table 20-10.

Table 20-10: vmstat Utility Output Fields

Field Name	Description
procs	Number of processes and their types: r = processes waiting to run; b = processes in uninterruptible sleep; w = processes swapped out, but ready to run
memory	Information about physical memory and swap space usage (all numbers in kilobytes): swpd = virtual memory used; free = free physical memory; buff = memory used as buffers; cache = virtual memory that's cached
swap	Amount of swapping (the numbers are in kilobytes per second): si = amount of memory swapped in from disk; so = amount of memory swapped to disk
io	Information about input and output (the numbers are in blocks per second; the block size depends on the disk device): bi = rate of blocks sent to disk; bo = rate of blocks received from disk
system	Information about the system: in = number of interrupts per second (including clock interrupts); cs = number of context switches per second—the number of times the kernel changes which process is running
cpu	Percentages of CPU time used: us = percentage of CPU time used by user processes; sy = percentage CPU time used by system processes; id = percentage of time CPU is idle

The first line of vmstat output following the two header lines shows the averages since the last reboot. After that, vmstat displays the 5-second average data seven more times over the next 35 seconds. In the vmstat utility's output, high values in the si and so fields indicate too much swapping. High numbers in the bi and bo fields indicate too much disk activity.

Checking Disk Performance and Disk Usage

Red Hat Linux comes with the /sbin/hdparm program, which you can use to control IDE or ATAPI hard disks common on most PCs. One feature of the hdparm program is that the -t option enables you to determine the rate at which data can be read from the disk into a buffer in memory. For example, here's the result of the command on my system:

```
/sbin/hdparm -t /dev/hda
```

```
/dev/hda:
 Timing buffered disk reads:  64 MB in 3.05 seconds =  21.00 MB/sec
```

As you can see, the command requires the IDE drive's device name (/dev/hda) as an argument. If you have an IDE hard disk, you can try this command to see how fast data can be read from your system's disk drive.

insider
insight
During system startup, the /etc/rc.sysinit script runs /sbin/hdparm to set the hard disk parameters based on settings in the /etc/sysconfig/harddisks file. Type man hdparm to learn more about the hard disk parameters you can set. To set a parameter at boot time, you can place an appropriate line in the /etc/sysconfig/harddisks file.

To display the space available in the currently mounted file systems, use the df command. If you want a more human-readable output from df, type the following command:

```
df -h
Filesystem          Size  Used Avail Use% Mounted on
/dev/hda5           7.1G  2.6G  4.2G  38% /
/dev/hda3            99M  8.6M   86M  10% /boot
none                125M     0  125M   0% /dev/shm
```

As this example shows, the -h option causes the df command to show the sizes in gigabytes (G) and megabytes (M).

To check the disk space a specific directory uses, employ the du command. You can specify the -h option to view the output in kilobytes (k) and megabytes (M), as shown in the following example:

```
du -h /var/log
4.0K    /var/log/vbox
20M     /var/log/cups
4.0K    /var/log/samba
4.0K    /var/log/news/OLD
8.0K    /var/log/news
12K     /var/log/httpd
4.0K    /var/log/squid
532K    /var/log/gdm
23M     /var/log
```

The du command displays the disk space each directory uses, and the last line shows the total disk space that directory uses. If you want to see only the total space a directory uses, use the -s option, like this:

```
du -sh /var
71M     /var
```

This says that the /var directory uses 71M of disk space.

Exploring the /proc File System

You can find out a great deal about your Linux system by consulting the contents of a special file system known as /proc. Knowing about the /proc file system is useful because it can help you monitor a wide variety of information about your system. In fact, you can even change kernel parameters through the /proc file system and thereby modify the system's behavior.

The /proc file system is not a real directory on the disk but a collection of data structures in memory, managed by the Linux kernel, that appears to the user as a set of directories and files. The purpose of /proc (also called the *process file system*) is to enable users to access information about the Linux kernel and the processes currently running on your system.

You can access the /proc file system just as you access any other directory, but you have to know the meaning of various files to interpret the information. Typically, you can use the cat or more command to view the contents of a file in /proc; the file's contents provide information about some aspect of the system.

As with any directory, you may want to start by looking at a detailed directory listing of /proc. To do so, type **ls -l /proc**. In the output, the first set of directories (indicated by the letter d at the beginning of the line) represents the processes currently running on your system. Each directory that corresponds to a process has the process ID (a number) as its name.

Also notice a very large file named /proc/kcore; that file represents the entire physical memory of your system. Although /proc/kcore appears in the listing as a huge file, there is no physical file occupying that much space on your hard disk. You should not try to remove this file to reclaim disk space.

Several files and directories in /proc contain interesting information about your Linux system. The /proc/cpuinfo file, for example, lists the key characteristics of your system, such as processor type and floating-point processor information. You can view the processor information by typing cat /proc/cpuinfo. For example, here is what I get when I type the command on my system:

```
cat /proc/cpuinfo
processor       : 0
vendor_id       : GenuineIntel
cpu family      : 15
model           : 2
model name      : Mobile Intel(R) Celeron(R) CPU 1.50GHz
stepping        : 7
cpu MHz         : 1495.631
cache size      : 256 KB
fdiv_bug        : no
hlt_bug         : no
f00f_bug        : no
coma_bug        : no
fpu             : yes
fpu_exception   : yes
cpuid level     : 2
wp              : yes
flags           : fpu vme de pse tsc msr pae mce cx8 sep mtrr pge mca cmov
pat pse36 clflush dts acpi mmx fxsr sse sse2 ss ht tm
bogomips        : 2981.88
```

This output is from a 1.4GHz Intel Celeron system. The listing shows many interesting characteristics of the processor. Notice the line that starts with fdiv_bug. Remember the infamous Pentium floating-point-division bug? The bug is in an instruction called fdiv (for floating-point division). Thus, the fdiv_bug line indicates whether or not this particular Pentium has the bug (fortunately, my system's processor does not).

Table 20-11 summarizes some of the files in the /proc file system from which you can get information about your Linux system. You can view some of these files on your system to see what they contain. Note that not all the files shown in Table 20-11 are present on your system—the contents of the /proc file system depend on the kernel configuration and the driver modules loaded (which, in turn, depend on your PC's hardware configuration).

You can navigate the /proc file system just as you work with any other directories and files in Linux. Use the more or cat command to view the contents of a file.

Table 20-11: Typical Files and Directories in /proc

File Name	Content
/proc/apm	Information about Advanced Power Management (APM)
/proc/bus	Directory with bus-specific information for each bus type, such as PCI
/proc/cmdline	The command line used to start the Linux kernel (for example, `auto BOOT_IMAGE=linux ro root=303`)
/proc/cpuinfo	Information about the CPU (the microprocessor)
/proc/devices	Available block and character devices in your system
/proc/dma	Information about DMA (direct memory access) channels that are used
/proc/driver	Directory with information about various drivers (for example, you will find information about the `rtc` driver for PC's real-time clock in this directory)
/proc/fb	Information about any frame buffer devices
/proc/filesystems	List of supported file systems
/proc/fs	Directory with file-system parameters
/proc/ide	Directory containing information about IDE devices
/proc/interrupts	Information about interrupt request (IRQ) numbers, how they are used, and how many interrupts were generated for each IRQ
/proc/iomem	Memory map showing how various ranges of physical memory addresses are being used
/proc/ioports	Information about input/output (I/O) port addresses and how they are used
/proc/irq	Directory that contains subdirectories for each interrupt request (IRQ) number, with the `smp_affinity` file that indicates which of several CPUs should handle that interrupt (applies only to systems with multiple CPUs)
/proc/kcore	Image of the physical memory
/proc/kmsg	Kernel messages
/proc/ksyms	Kernel symbol table
/proc/loadavg	Load average (average number of processes waiting to run in the last 1, 5, and 15 minutes)
/proc/locks	Current kernel locks (used to ensure that multiple processes do not write to a file at the same time)
/proc/meminfo	Information about physical memory and swap-space usage
/proc/misc	Miscellaneous information
/proc/modules	List of loaded driver modules
/proc/mounts	List of mounted file systems
/proc/net	Directory with many subdirectories that contain information about networking
/proc/partitions	List of partitions known to the Linux kernel

(continued)

Table 20-11: *(continued)*

File Name	Content
/proc/pci	Information about PCI devices found on the system
/proc/scsi	Directory with information about SCSI devices, if any, found on the system
/proc/sound	Information about the sound driver module, if any
/proc/stat	Overall statistics about the system
/proc/swaps	Information about the swap space and how much is used
/proc/sys	Directory with information about the system (You can change kernel parameters by writing to files in this directory. This is one way to tune the system's performance, but it requires expertise to do it properly.)
/proc/sysvipc	Information about System V interprocess communication (IPC) resources such as shared memory
/proc/tty	Information about tty drivers
/proc/uptime	Information about how long the system has been up
/proc/version	Kernel version number

Using sysctl to View and Set Kernel Parameters

As the entry for /proc/sys in Table 20-11 explains, you can change kernel parameters by writing to files in the /proc/sys directory. This is one way to tune the system's performance. Red Hat Linux also comes with the /sbin/sysctl program that enables you to read and write kernel parameters without having to overwrite files manually in the /proc/sys directory.

In Chapter 13, you encounter an instruction that asks you to log in as root and enable IP forwarding in the kernel by typing the following command:

```
echo "1" > /proc/sys/net/ipv4/ip_forward
```

This is the manual way to set the value of a parameter—using the echo command to copy the value into a file in the /proc/sys directory.

You can perform this same step by running sysctl as follows:

```
/sbin/sysctl -w net.ipv4.ip_forward=1
net.ipv4.ip_forward = 1
```

This sysctl command sets the value of the parameter and echoes the new value for your information. As you can see, you refer to the parameter by using the last part of the pathname excluding /proc/sys, but you use periods (.) instead of slashes (/) as separators. Note that, if you prefer, you can continue to use slashes as separators and can refer to this variable as net/ipv4/ip_forward.

You can use sysctl to both query and set the value of a parameter. To see the value of a parameter, use the parameter's name as an argument like this:

```
/sbin/sysctl dev.cdrom.info
```

The command `/sbin/sysctl dev.cdrom.info` displays the contents of that parameter. In this case, `dev.cdrom.info` is a structure that contains many different fields; `sysctl` shows these fields as separate lines in the output.

For a simple parameter, such as `fs.file-max`, `sysctl` displays the single value as shown in the following example:

```
/sbin/sysctl fs.file-max
fs.file-max = 26163
```

The `fs.file-max` variable denotes the maximum number of file handles the Linux kernel can allocate. If you get error messages about running out of file handles, you may want to increase this value with a command, such as `/sbin/sysctl -w fs.file-max=65535`.

Secret

To use `sysctl` to modify kernel variables and tune the kernel's performance, you need to know what each parameter means. You can find some documentation on these parameters in the `/usr/src/linux*/Documentation/sysctl` directory of your system (provided you install the `kernel-source` RPM). In particular, look at the `/usr/src/linux*/Documentation/sysctl/kernel.txt` file for information on the kernel parameters.

You can see the values of all parameters in the `/proc/sys` directory by typing the `/sbin/sysctl -a` command. It's instructive to look through the names of the parameters and their values. You should try the `/sbin/sysctl -a` command on your system. Table 20-12 lists some of these parameters.

Before you use `sysctl` to change any of the parameters listed in Table 20-12, you should know that changing some kernel parameters can adversely affect your system's performance and even cause the system to hang. You should play with these parameters only if you know what you are doing. In particular, never play around with kernel parameters on a production system.

If you have a number of parameters to alter using `sysctl`, you can place the parameters and their values in a file and use the command `/sbin/sysctl -p filename` to load the settings from that file. For example, when Red Hat Linux boots, a startup script sets some parameters with the following command:

```
/sbin/sysctl -p /etc/sysctl.conf
```

On my Red Hat Linux system, the `/etc/sysctl.conf` file contains the following lines:

```
# Disables packet forwarding
net.ipv4.ip_forward = 0
# Enables source route verification
net.ipv4.conf.all.rp_filter = 1
# Disables automatic defragmentation (needed for masquerading)
net.ipv4.ip_always_defrag = 0
# Disables the magic-sysrq key
kernel.sysrq = 0
# Appends the PID to the core filename during core dumps
kernel.core_uses_pid = 1
```

Table 20-12 describes some of the interesting kernel parameters from the `/proc/sys` directory, as well as the meaning of these parameters.

Table 20-12: Some Kernel Parameters in the /proc/sys Directory

Parameter Name	Meaning
fs.file-max	Maximum number of file handles the Linux kernel can allocate
fs.file-nr	Three values representing the number of allocated file handles, the number of used file handles, and the maximum number of file handles
fs.super-max	Maximum number of superblocks, and thus the maximum number of mounted file systems the kernel can support (default value is 256)
kernel.acct	Three values specifying high, low, and frequency that control the logging of process accounting information—when free space on file system goes below the low (percent), accounting is suspended; it resumes when free space goes above high (percent), and frequency specifies how many seconds the free space information is valid (default values are 4% for high, 2% for low, and 30 seconds for frequency)
kernel.ctrl-alt-del	When set to 0, a Ctrl-Alt-Del keypress is handled by using the init program to restart the system; when set to 1, Ctrl-Alt-Del performs an immediate reboot without even saving any dirty buffers to the disk
kernel.domainname	The NIS domain name of the system
kernel.hostname	The hostname of the system
kernel.modprobe	Name of the program that the kernel uses to load one or more modules (for example, /sbin/modprobe)
kernel.osrelease	The version number of the operating system (for example, 2.4.20-2.48)
kernel.ostype	Name of operating system (for example, Linux for all Linux systems)
kernel.panic	Number of seconds the kernel waits before rebooting in case of a panic (default is 0)
kernel.printk	Values that affect the printing or logging of error messages by the kernel
kernel.rtsig-max	Maximum number of POSIX real-time signals that can be outstanding in the system (default is 1024)
kernel.rtsig-nr	Number of real-time signals currently queued

Parameter Name	Meaning
`kernel.shmall`	Total amount, in bytes, of shared memory segments that can be created (default is `33554432 bytes`)
`kernel.shmmax`	Maximum size, in bytes, of shared memory segments that can be created (default is `33554432 bytes`; kernel supports shared memory segments up to 1GB)
`kernel.sysrq`	When set to 0, the SysRq key is disabled; when set to 1, user can perform specific tasks by pressing Alt-SysRq and a command key (see the file `/usr/src/linux*/Documentation/sysrq.txt` for more information)
`kernel.version`	The build number and the date the kernel was built (for example, `#1 Thu Feb 13 11:52:55 EST 2003`)
`net.core.netdev_max_backlog`	Maximum number of packets that can be queued on input when a network interface receives packets faster than the kernel can process them (default is `300`)
`net.core.optmem_max`	Maximum size of ancillary buffer allowed per socket (default is `10240 bytes`, or 10K)
`net.core.rmem_default`	Default size of socket receive buffer in bytes (default is `65535 bytes`, or 64K)
`net.core.rmem_max`	Maximum size of socket receive buffer in bytes (default is `65535 bytes`, or 64K)
`net.core.wmem_default`	Default size of socket send buffer in bytes (default is `65535 bytes`, or 64K)
`net.core.wmem_max`	Maximum size of socket send buffer in bytes (default is `65535 bytes`, or 64K)
`net.ipv4.conf.all.accept_redirects`	When set to 1, the kernel accepts ICMP redirect messages (should be set to 0 for a system configured as a router)
`net.ipv4.conf.all.accept_source_route`	When set to 1, accepts source routed packets (should be set to 1 for a system configured as a router)
`net.ipv4.conf.all.forwarding`	When set to 1, enables IP forwarding for all interfaces
`net.ipv4.conf.all.hidden`	When set to 1, hides network addresses from other systems
`net.ipv4.conf.all.log_martians`	When set to 1, logs all packets with source addresses with no known route

(continued)

Table 20-12: (continued)

Parameter Name	Meaning
`net.ipv4.conf.all.rp_filter`	When set to 0, turns off source validation; when set to 1, performs source validation using reverse path (as specified in RFC 1812)
`net.ipv4.conf.all.secure_redirects`	When set to 1, accepts ICMP redirect messages only for gateways listed in default gateway list
`net.ipv4.conf.all.send_redirects`	When set to 1, sends ICMP redirect messages to other hosts
`net.ipv4.conf.all.shared_media`	When set to 1, assumes that different subnets share the media and can communicate directly
`net.ipv4.conf.eth0.accept_redirects`	When set to 1, accepts ICMP redirect messages (must be 0 for a system used as a router)
`net.ipv4.conf.eth0.forwarding`	When set to 1, turns on IP forwarding for the `eth0` network interface
`net.ipv4.conf.eth0.hidden`	When set to 1, keeps the address hidden from other devices
`net.ipv4.conf.eth0.log_martians`	When set to 1, logs packets with impossible addresses in the log file
`net.ipv4.conf.eth0.rp_filter`	When set to 0, turns off source validation; when set to 1, performs source validation using reverse path (as specified in RFC 1812)
`net.ipv4.icmp_echo_ignore_all`	When set to 1, kernel ignores all ICMP ECHO requests sent to it
`net.ipv4.icmp_echo_ignore_broadcasts`	When set to 1, kernel ignores all ICMP ECHO requests sent to broadcast or multicast addresses
`net.ipv4.ip_always_defrag`	When set to 1, automatically reassembles all fragmented packets (this is enabled when masquerading is enabled)
`net.ipv4.ip_autoconfig`	Contains 1 if the host receives its IP address by using a mechanism such as RARP, BOOTP, or DHCP; otherwise, it is 0
`net.ipv4.ip_default_ttl`	Time-to-live (TTL) for IP packets (default value is 64; this is the maximum number of routers through which the packet can travel)
`net.ipv4.ip_forward`	When set to 1, packets are forwarded among interfaces

Parameter Name	Meaning
net.ipv4.ip_local_port_range	Two numbers denoting the range of port numbers used by TCP and UDP for the local port (default range 1024-4999; you can change this to 32768-61000 if you need more ports)
net.ipv4.ip_masq_debug	When set to 1, enables debugging of IP masquerading
net.ipv4.ipfrag_high_thresh	Maximum memory for use in reassembling IP fragments (default is 262144 bytes)
net.ipv4.ipfrag_low_thresh	When maximum amount of memory (net.ipv4.ipfrag_high_thresh) is already being used to reassemble fragmented IP packets, further packets are discarded until the memory usage comes down to this value (default is 196608 bytes)
net.ipv4.ipfrag_time	Time in seconds to keep an IP fragment in memory (default is 30 seconds)
net.ipv4.tcp_fin_timeout	Number of seconds to wait for a final FIN before the socket is closed—this occurs to prevent denial-of-service attacks (default is 180 seconds)
net.ipv4.tcp_keepalive_probes	Number of keepalive probes TCP sends out before it decides that the connection is broken (default value is 9)
net.ipv4.tcp_keepalive_time	Time in seconds between keepalive messages (default is 7200 seconds, or two hours)
net.ipv4.tcp_max_ka_probes	Maximum number of keepalive probes to send in one interval of the slow timer (default is 5)
net.ipv4.tcp_max_syn_backlog	Length of the backlog queue for each socket (default is 128)
net.ipv4.tcp_retries1	Number of times an answer to a TCP connection request is retransmitted before giving up (default is 7)
net.ipv4.tcp_retries2	Number of times a TCP packet is retransmitted before giving up (default is 15)
net.ipv4.tcp_sack	When set to 1, enables select acknowledgments as specified in RFC 2018
net.ipv4.tcp_syn_retries	Number of times initial SYNs for a TCP connection attempt are retransmitted (default value is 10)

(continued)

Table 20-12: *(continued)*

Parameter Name	Meaning
net.ipv4.tcp_syncookies	When set to 1, sends out SYN cookies when the SYN backlog queue of a socket overflows (this prevents the common SYN flood attack)
net.ipv4.tcp_timestamps	When set to 1, enables timestamps as defined in RFC 1323
net.ipv4.tcp_window_scaling	When set to 1, enables window scaling as defined in RFC 1323
vm.bdflush	Settings that control the operation of the bdflush daemon that handles flushing of dirty buffers; dirty indicates that a buffer's contents have changed and still remain to be written to the disk (see the file /usr/src/linux*/Documentation/ sysctl/vm.txt for more details)
vm.buffermem	The first value denotes the minimum percentage of memory that should be used for the buffers (default is 2%)
vm.freepages	Three values provide minimum, low, and high threshold values for the number of free pages that control swapping—when the number of free pages reaches the minimum, only the kernel can allocate more memory; if the number of free pages drops below the low threshold, kernel starts swapping aggressively; the high threshold is the number of pages the kernel tries to keep available (the default values are 128 for minimum, 256 for low, and 384 for high threshold)
vm.kswapd	The three values specify base, minimum, and cluster values that control the operation of kswapd, the kernel swap out daemon that frees memory when needed—the base value computes how many pages kswapd tries to free in one round; the minimum value is the minimum number of times kswapd tries to free a page; and the cluster value is the number of pages kswapd writes to the disk in one turn (the default values are 512 for base, 32 for minimum tries, and 32 for the cluster)
vm.overcommit_memory	If this value is set to 1, the system pretends that there is always enough memory; when it's 0, the kernel checks before each memory allocation request to determine if enough memory remains

Parameter Name	Meaning
vm.pagecache	Similar to vm.buffermem, but this one controls the amount of memory used for page cache
vm.page-cluster	If this value is n, the Linux virtual memory subsystem reads 2n pages at once (default is 4, which means the VM subsystem reads 16 pages at a time)
vm.pagetable_cache	The range of values that specify the size of the cache for page tables—primarily used for multiprocessor systems (default is between 25 and 50)

Summary

If you use your Red Hat Linux system for production work (to run an Internet server or an office server, for example), you have to perform some advanced systems-administration tasks. This chapter introduces you to some systems-administration tasks I do not cover elsewhere in the book.

By reading this chapter, you learned the following:

♦ After Linux boots, a process named init starts all other processes. The exact set of initial processes depends on the run level, which typically is a number ranging from 0 to 6. The /etc/inittab file specifies the processes that start in each run level.

♦ The /etc/inittab file specifies that a graphical display manager starts at run level 5. In Red Hat Linux, the display manager provides the graphical login prompt.

♦ The init process executes Red Hat Linux startup scripts in the /etc/rc.d directory and its subdirectories.

♦ You can use the /sbin/chkconfig program to set up servers to start automatically at various run levels.

♦ You can use the at command to execute one or more commands at a future time and have the output mailed to you.

♦ You can use the crontab facility to set up periodic jobs (called *cron jobs*) that are executed at recurring intervals. Then, you can have the output mailed to you.

♦ If you use your Red Hat Linux system for anything important, you have to back up your files. You should select a backup strategy and backup media based on your needs and your level of tolerance for the risk of business interruption from a hard disk failure.

♦ You can use the tape archiver program—tar—to back up and restore files. This chapter shows you how to set up cron jobs for automated full and incremental backups.

♦ Red Hat Linux comes with utilities and commands you can use to keep an eye on your system's performance. You learn to use and interpret the displays produced by top, the GNOME System Monitor, and vmstat. Also, you learn some commands to check available disk space and your hard disk's performance.

♦ The /proc file system contains extensive information about the system. The /proc file system is not a disk-based file system; it is a collection of data structures in memory, managed by the Linux kernel, that appears to the user as a set of directories and files.

♦ In the /proc/sys directory are a number of files whose values you can set to modify the kernel's behavior at run time. You can either directly write to these files or use the /sbin/sysctl program to view or set the parameters. If you know what you are doing, you can tune the performance of your system by modifying the parameters in the /proc/sys directory.

Software Installation and Update

Chapter 21

♦ ♦

Secrets in This Chapter

♦ ♦

Y ou should know how to install or remove software packages distributed in the form of Red Hat Package Manager (RPM) files because most Red Hat Linux software comes in RPM files. This chapter shows you how to work with RPM files.

Many open-source software packages come in source-code form, usually in compressed archives. You have to build and install the software to use it. This chapter describes the steps you ordinarily follow when downloading, building, and installing source-based software packages.

Next, I briefly describe the Red Hat Network and how, after registering with it, you can use Red Hat's Update agent to update specific Red Hat Linux packages.

Finally, this chapter turns to the subject of configuring and rebuilding the kernel. The last part of this chapter explains how to apply a kernel patch and how to rebuild the Linux kernel.

Working with the Red Hat Package Manager

A significant innovation from the people at Red Hat is the Red Hat Package Manager (RPM)—a system for packaging all the necessary files for a software product in a single file (referred to as an RPM file or simply an RPM). Red Hat Linux is distributed in the form of a lot of RPMs. In the following sections, you will learn to install, remove, and query RPMs by using Red Hat's Package Management graphical tool and the rpm commands.

insider
insight
The rpm commands are a must when you have to work from a text-mode command line. The graphical package management utility, however, is better than using rpm commands when it comes to installing or uninstalling entire package groups (a package group is a collection of related RPMs).

Using the Package Management Utility

Red Hat's Package Management utility is a graphical tool for installing and uninstalling RPMs. With this utility you can check what's installed on your system and also add or remove packages—as a group or individually.

To start the Package Management utility, choose Main Menu⇨System Settings⇨Add Remove Applications. If you are not logged in as root, a dialog box prompts you for the root password. Enter that password, and press Enter. The Package Management utility starts and gathers information about the status of packages installed on your system. After it sorts through the information about all the installed packages, the Package Management utility displays a list of all the packages (see Figure 21-1).

The Package Management window displays information about the packages organized into package groups such as Desktops and Applications. Each package group has a graphical icon, a label such as X Window System or GNOME Desktop Environment, and a brief description as well. A check box precedes each package group's name. If the package is already installed, a check mark appears in the check box. For example, in Figure 21-1, the X Window System and GNOME Desktop Environment package groups are installed, but the KDE Desktop Environment is not yet installed.

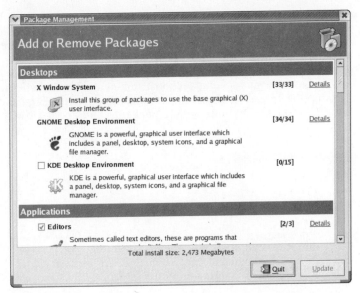

Figure 21-1: The Main Window of the Package Management Utility.

For the installed package groups (the ones with check marks), notice the hypertext link labeled Details on the right side of the package's name and description. If you click on Details, the Package Management utility brings up a new window in which it displays further details about the contents of that package group. For example, Figure 21-2 displays the detailed contents of the GNOME Desktop Environment package group. Click Close after you finish examining the details of a package group.

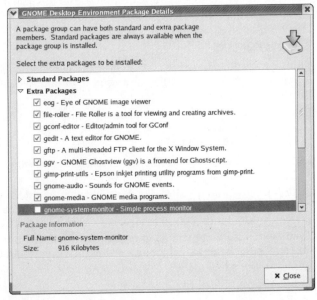

Figure 21-2: Viewing a Package Group's Detailed Contents.

To install an uninstalled package group, simply click the check box so that a check mark appears there. Then, click the Update button to proceed with the installation. The Package Management utility figures out what specific files have to be installed for that package group. (Because of interdependencies among package groups, installing one package group may require installing quite a few other package groups.) After it finishes gathering information, a dialog box informs you what will be installed and how much disk space will be needed For example, Figure 21-3 shows the information about package and space requirements for the KDE Desktop Environment (12 packages and about 161MB of disk space).

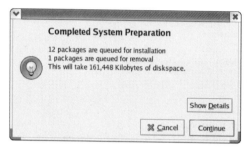

Figure 21-3: Information about Disk Space Required to Install a Package Group.

Click Continue to proceed. The Package Management utility then updates the system and displays the progress as it installs files. If a new CD-ROM is needed, the Package Management utility prompts you for the next CD-ROM. Insert the requested CD-ROM, and click OK.

To remove one or more package groups, uncheck the check marks for those package groups in the Package Management window, and then click the Update button. A dialog box shows you the details of what will be removed. Click Continue, and the packages will be removed.

Using the RPM Commands

When you install Red Hat Linux from the companion CD-ROMs, the installation program uses the `rpm` command to unpack the packages (RPM files) and to copy the contents to appropriate locations on the disk.

Although you do not need to understand the internal structure of an RPM file, you should know how to use the `rpm` command to work with RPM files. Specifically, you may want to perform one or more of the following tasks with RPMs:

- ◆ Find out the version numbers and other information about RPMs installed on your system
- ◆ Install a new software package from an RPM. For example, you might install a package you have skipped during the initial installation. In particular, you have to install the source files for the Linux kernel before you can rebuild the kernel.
- ◆ Remove (uninstall) unneeded software you have previously installed from an RPM. You might uninstall a package to reclaim the disk space, if you find that you rarely (or never) use the package.

♦ Upgrade an older version of an RPM with a new one. You might upgrade after you download a new version of a package from Red Hat's FTP server. Often, you must upgrade an RPM to benefit from the fixes in the new version.

♦ Verify that an RPM is in working order. You can verify a package to ensure that all necessary files are in the correct locations.

You can perform all of these tasks with the rpm command—it's just a matter of using different options. The next few subsections briefly introduce you to the rpm command.

---

insider insight

If you ever forget the rpm options, type the following command to see a list:

```
rpm --help | more
```

The number of options rpm has will amaze you!

Understanding RPM Filenames

An RPM contains a number of files, but it appears as a single file on your Red Hat Linux system. By convention, the RPM filenames have a specific structure. To see the names of RPM files available on the companion CD-ROMs, use the following steps:

1. Place the first CD-ROM in the CD-ROM drive. If you are using GNOME or KDE graphical desktops, the CD should be mounted automatically. Otherwise, mount it by typing the following command in a terminal window:

```
mount /mnt/cdrom
```

2. Go to the directory in which the RPMs are located, and view the listing using the ls command. For example to see RPMs with names that start with cups, type:

```
cd /mnt/cdrom/RedHat/RPMS
ls cups*.rpm | more
```

Here is a typical output from my system:

```
cups-1.1.17-13.i386.rpm
cups-libs-1.1.17-13.i386.rpm
```

As you might guess from the listing, all RPM files end with an .rpm extension. To understand the various parts of the filename, consider the following RPM:

```
cups-1.1.17-13.i386.rpm
```

This filename has the following parts, separated by dashes (-):

♦ **Package name**—cups
♦ **Version number**—1.1.17
♦ **Release number**—13 (this is a Red Hat–assigned release number)
♦ **Architecture**—i386 (this package is for Intel 80386–compatible processors)

Usually, the package name is descriptive enough for you to guess what the RPM might contain. The version number is the same as that of the software package's current version number (even when it is distributed in some other form, such as a tar file). Red Hat assigns the release number to keep track of changes. The architecture should be i386 or noarch for the RPMs you want to install on a PC with an Intel x86–compatible processor.

Finding Information about RPMs

As it installs packages, the `rpm` command builds a database of installed RPMs. You can use the `rpm -q` command to query this database to find out information about packages installed on your system.

For example, to find out the version number of the Linux kernel installed on your system, type the following `rpm -q` command:

```
rpm -q kernel
kernel-2.4.20-6
```

The response is the name of the RPM for the kernel (this is the executable version of the kernel, not the source files). The name is the same as the RPM filename, except that the last part—`.i386.rpm`—is not shown. In this case, the version part of the RPM tells you that the kernel is `2.4.20`.

You can see a list of all installed RPMs by using the following command:

```
rpm -qa
```

You will see a long list of RPMs scroll by your screen. To view the list one screen at a time, type:

```
rpm -qa | more
```

If you want to search for a specific package, feed the output of `rpm -qa` to the `grep` command. For example, to see all packages with `kernel` in their names, type:

```
rpm -qa | grep kernel
kernel-pcmcia-cs-3.1.31-13
kernel-source-2.4.20-6
kernel-2.4.20-6
kernel-utils-2.4-8.29
```

You can query much more than a package's version number with the `rpm -q` command. By adding single-letter options, you can find out other useful information. For example, try the following command to see the files in the kernel package:

```
rpm -ql kernel | more
/boot/System.map-2.4.20-6
/boot/config-2.4.20-6
/boot/module-info-2.4.20-6
/boot/vmlinux-2.4.20-6
/boot/vmlinuz-2.4.20-6
/dev/shm
/lib/modules
/lib/modules/2.4.20-6
/lib/modules/2.4.20-6/build
/lib/modules/2.4.20-6/kernel
/lib/modules/2.4.20-6/kernel/arch
/lib/modules/2.4.20-6/kernel/arch/i386
/lib/modules/2.4.20-6/kernel/arch/i386/kernel
/lib/modules/2.4.20-6/kernel/arch/i386/kernel/cpuid.o
/lib/modules/2.4.20-6/kernel/arch/i386/kernel/edd.o
/lib/modules/2.4.20-6/kernel/arch/i386/kernel/microcode.o
/lib/modules/2.4.20-6/kernel/arch/i386/kernel/msr.o
(rest of the listing deleted)
```

Following are several useful forms of `rpm -q` commands to query information about a package (to use any of these `rpm -q` commands, type the command, followed by the package name):

- `rpm -qc`—Lists all configuration files in a package
- `rpm -qd`—Lists all documentation files in a package. These are usually the online manual pages (also known as man pages).
- `rpm -qf`—Lists the package that owns a specified file. This is a good way to find out which package installed a specific file.
- `rpm -qi`—Displays detailed information about a package, including version number, size, installation date, and a brief description
- `rpm -ql`—Lists all the files in a package. For some packages, this can be a very long list.
- `rpm -qs`—Lists the state of all files in a package

Secret

These `rpm -q` commands provide information about installed packages only. If you want to find information about an uninstalled RPM file, add the letter p to the command-ine option of each command. For example, to view the list of files in the RPM file named `cups-1.1.17-13.i386.rpm`, use the following command:

```
rpm -qpl cups-*.rpm
```

Of course, this works only if the current directory contains that RPM file.

If you are curious which package installed a specific file, use the `rpm -qf` command. For example, if you notice the file `/etc/foomatic` and wonder which package installed it, you can type **rpm -qf /etc/foomatic**. The resulting display is not much of a surprise:

```
foomatic-2.0.2-15
```

Installing an RPM

To install an RPM, use the `rpm -i` command. You have to provide the name of the RPM file as the argument. A typical example is installing an RPM from this book's companion CD-ROMs containing the Red Hat Linux RPMs. As usual, you have to mount the CD-ROM and change to the directory in which the RPMs are located. Then use the `rpm -i` command to install the RPM. If you want to view the progress of the RPM installation, use `rpm -ivh`. A series of hash marks (#) are displayed as the package is unpacked.

For example, to install the kernel-source RPM (which contains the source files for the Linux operating system) from the first companion CD-ROM, I type the following commands:

```
mount /mnt/cdrom
cd /mnt/cdrom/RedHat/RPMS
rpm -ivh kernel-source*
```

insider
insight

You do not have to type the full RPM filename—you can use a few characters from the beginning of the name followed by an asterisk (*). Make sure you type enough of the name to identify the RPM file uniquely.

If you try to install an RPM already installed, the `rpm` command displays an error message. For example, here is what happens when I try to install the man package on my system:

```
rpm -i man-*
package man-1.5k-6 is already installed
```

To force the `rpm` command to install a package even if errors are present, just add `−force` to the `rpm -i` command, as follows:

```
rpm -i --force man-*
```

Removing an RPM

You might want to remove—uninstall—a package if you realize you don't really need the software. For example, if you have installed the X Window System development package but discover you are not interested in writing X applications, you can easily remove the package by using the `rpm -e` command.

You need to know the name of the package before you can remove it. One good way to find the name is to use `rpm -qa` in conjunction with `grep` to search for the appropriate RPM file. For example, to locate the X Window System development RPM, you might try the following command:

```
rpm -qa | grep XFree86
XFree86-truetype-fonts-4.3.0-2
XFree86-devel-4.3.0-2
XFree86-ISO8859-14-75dpi-fonts-4.3.0-2
XFree86-xfs-4.3.0-2
XFree86-base-fonts-4.3.0-2
XFree86-4.3.0-2
XFree86-xdm-4.3.0-2
XFree86-ISO8859-2-100dpi-fonts-4.3.0-2
XFree86-libs-data-4.3.0-2
XFree86-Mesa-libGLU-4.3.0-2
XFree86-cyrillic-fonts-4.3.0-2
XFree86-ISO8859-15-75dpi-fonts-4.3.0-2
XFree86-ISO8859-9-75dpi-fonts-4.3.0-2
XFree86-Mesa-libGL-4.3.0-2
XFree86-100dpi-fonts-4.3.0-2
XFree86-xauth-4.3.0-2
XFree86-tools-4.3.0-2
XFree86-ISO8859-15-100dpi-fonts-4.3.0-2
XFree86-ISO8859-9-100dpi-fonts-4.3.0-2
XFree86-font-utils-4.3.0-2
XFree86-75dpi-fonts-4.3.0-2
XFree86-twm-4.3.0-2
```

In this case, XFree86-devel happens to be the name of the package you need. To remove the package, type:

```
rpm -e XFree86-devel
```

Note that you do not need the full RPM filename; all you need is the package name—the first part of the filename up to the dash (-) before the version number.

The rpm -e command does not remove a package other packages need. For example, when I try to remove the vim-common package, I get the following error messages:

```
rpm -e vim-common
error: Failed dependencies:
        vim-common is needed by (installed) vim-minimal-6.1-29
        vim-common is needed by (installed) vim-enhanced-6.1-29
```

Upgrading an RPM

Use the rpm -U command to upgrade an RPM. You must provide the name of the RPM file that contains the new software. For example, if I have version 2.0.36 of Apache httpd (Web server) installed on my system but I want to upgrade to version 2.0.40, I download the RPM file httpd-2.0.40-20.i386.rpm from one of Red Hat update sites listed at http://www.redhat.com/download/mirror.html and use the following command:

```
rpm -U httpd-2.0.40-20.i386.rpm
```

The rpm -U command performs the upgrade by removing the old version of the netscape-communicator package and installing the new RPM.

insider insight You should upgrade, whenever possible, rather than remove the old package; then you should install the new version. Upgrading automatically saves the old configuration files, which saves you the hassle of configuring the software after a fresh installation.

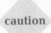

caution When you are upgrading the kernel and the kernel module packages that contain a ready-to-run Linux kernel, you should install it by using the rpm -i command (instead of the rpm -U command). That way you won't overwrite the current kernel.

Verifying an RPM

You may not do this often, but if you suspect that a software package is not properly installed, use the rpm -V command to verify it. For example, to verify the kernel package, type the following:

```
rpm -V kernel
```

Secret

The `rpm -V` causes `rpm` to compare the size and other attributes of each file in the package against those of the original files. If everything verifies correctly, the `rpm -V` command does not print anything. If there are any discrepancies, you will see a report of them. For example, I have modified the configuration files for the Apache httpd (Web) server. Here is what I see when I verify the httpd package:

```
rpm -V httpd
S.5....T c /etc/httpd/conf/httpd.conf
```

In this case, the output from `rpm -V` shows that a configuration file has changed. Each line of this command's output consists of three parts:

- The line starts with eight characters: each character indicates the type of discrepancy found. For example, S means the size is different, and T means the time of last modification is different. Table 21-1 shows each character and its meaning. A period (.) means that that specific attribute matches the original.

- For configuration files, a c appears next; otherwise, this field is blank. That's how you can tell whether or not a file is a configuration file. Typically, you shouldn't worry if a configuration file has changed; you have probably made the changes yourself.

- The last part of the line is the full pathname of the file. From this part, you can tell exactly where the file is located.

Table 21-1: Characters Used in RPM Verification Reports

Character	Meaning
S	Size has changed
M	Permissions and file type are different
5	Checksum computed with the MD5 algorithm is different
D	Device type is different
L	Symbolic link is different
U	File's user is different
G	File's group is different
T	File's modification time is different

Building Software Packages from Source Files

In the previous sections, you have seen how to install software packages distributed in the RPM format. RPM files bundle everything—all the executable binary files and configuration files—needed to install a software package. Many open-source software packages, however, are distributed in source-code form, without executable binaries. Before you can use such software, you have to build the executable binary files by compiling them, and you have to follow some instructions to install the package. This section shows you how to build software packages from source files.

Downloading and Unpacking the Software

Open-source software source files are typically distributed in compressed `tar` archives. These archives are created by the tar program and compressed with the gzip program. The distribution is in the form of a single large file with the `.tar.gz` or `.tar.Z` extension—often referred to as a *compressed tarball*. If you want the software, you have to download the compressed tarball and unpack it.

Download the compressed `tar` file by using anonymous FTP or through your Web browser. Typically, this involves no effort on your part beyond clicking a link and saving the file in an appropriate directory on your system.

To try your hand at downloading and building a software package, practice on the X Multimedia System (XMMS)—a graphical X application for playing MP3 and other multimedia files. XMMS is bundled with Red Hat Linux and should already be installed on your system if you have selected the Multimedia Support package group during Red Hat Linux installation. However, there is no harm in downloading and rebuilding the XMMS package again.

The source files for XMMS are available from `http://www.xmms.org/download.html` in the form of a compressed `tar` archive. In addition, you can also download the files from the `xmms/1.2.x` directory of the anonymous FTP server `ftp.xmms.org`.

Click the `ftp` link for the `.tar.gz` format on the `http://www.xmms.org/download.html` page and save the compressed source tarball in the `/usr/local/src` directory in your Red Hat Linux system (be sure to log in as `root`, otherwise you cannot save in the `/usr/local/src` directory).

After downloading the compressed `tar` file, examine the contents with the following `tar` command:

```
tar ztf xmms*.gz | more
```

You should see a listing similar to the following:

```
xmms-1.2.7/
xmms-1.2.7/Makefile.in
xmms-1.2.7/README
xmms-1.2.7/stamp-h1.in
xmms-1.2.7/ABOUT-NLS
xmms-1.2.7/AUTHORS
xmms-1.2.7/COPYING
xmms-1.2.7/ChangeLog
xmms-1.2.7/INSTALL
xmms-1.2.7/Makefile.am
xmms-1.2.7/NEWS
xmms-1.2.7/TODO
xmms-1.2.7/acconfig.h
xmms-1.2.7/acinclude.m4
xmms-1.2.7/aclocal.m4
xmms-1.2.7/config.guess
xmms-1.2.7/config.h.in
xmms-1.2.7/config.sub
xmms-1.2.7/configure
... rest of the output not shown ...
```

The output of this `tar` command shows you what's in the archive and gives you an idea of the directories that will be created after you unpack the archive. In this case, a directory named `xmms-1.2.7` will be created in the current directory, which, in my case, is `/usr/local/src`. From the listing, you'll also learn the programming language used to write the package. If you see `.c` and `.h` files, which means that the source files are in the C programming language, which is used to write many open-source software packages.

To extract the contents of the compressed `tar` archive, type the following `tar` command:

```
tar zxvf xmms*.gz
```

You'll again see the long list of files as they are extracted from the archive and copied to the appropriate directories on your hard disk.

Now, you are ready to build the software.

Building the Software from Source Files

After you unpack the compressed `tar` archive, all source files will be in a directory whose name is usually that of the software package with a version-number suffix. For example, the XMMS version 1.2.7 source files are extracted to the `xmms-1.2.7` directory. To start building the software, change directories with the following command:

```
cd xmms*
```

You don't have to type the entire name—the shell can expand the directory name and change to the `xmms-1.2.7` directory.

Secret

Nearly all software packages come with some sort of `README` or `INSTALL` file—a text file that tells you how to build and install the package. XMMS is no exception; it comes with a `README` file you can peruse by typing more `README`. There is also an `INSTALL` file, which contains instructions for building and installing XMMS.

Most open-source software packages, including XMMS, also come with a file named `COPYING`. This file contains the full text of the GNU General Public License (GPL), which spells out the conditions under which you can use and redistribute the software. If you are not familiar with the GNU GPL, read this file and show the license to your legal counsel for a full interpretation and an assessment of applicability to your business.

To build the software package, follow the instructions in the `README` or `INSTALL` file. For the XMMS package, the `README` file lists some of the prerequisites (such as libraries) and tells you what commands to type to build and install the package. In the case of XMMS, the instructions tell you to use the following steps:

1. Type **./configure** to run a shell script that checks your system configuration and creates a file named `Makefile`—a file the `make` command uses to build and install the package. (You can type **./configure —help** to see a list of options that `configure` accepts.)

2. Type **make** to build the software. This step compiles the source files in all the sub-directories (compiling source code converts each source file into an object file—a file containing binary instructions that your PC's processor can understand).

3. Type **make install** to install the software. This step copies libraries and executable binary files to appropriate directories on your system.

Although these steps are specific to XMMS, most other packages follow these steps—configure, make, and install. The `configure` shell script guesses system-dependent variables and creates a `Makefile` with commands needed to build and install the software.

---

note

Usually, you do not have to do anything but type the commands to build the software, but you must install the software-development tools on your system. This means that you must install the Software Development package when you install Red Hat Linux. To build and run XMMS, you must also install the X Software Development package because it's an X application.

Building and Testing XMMS

To begin building XMMS, type the following command to run the configure script (you must be in the `xmms-1.2.7` directory when you type this command):

```
./configure
```

The configure script starts running and prints lots of messages as it checks various features of your system—from the existence of the C compiler to various libraries needed to build XMMS. Finally, the configure script creates a `Makefile` you can use to build the software.

---

insider insight

If the `configure` script displays error messages and fails, review the `INSTALL` and `README` files to find any clues to solving the problem. You may be able to circumvent it by providing some information to the `configure` script through command-line arguments.

After the configure script finishes, build the software by typing make. This command runs the GNU make utility, which reads the `Makefile` and starts compiling the source files according to information specified in the `Makefile`. The `make` command goes through all the source directories, compiles the source files, and creates the executable files and libraries needed to run XMMS. You'll see a lot of messages scroll by as each file is compiled. These messages show the commands used to compile and link the files.

The `make` command can take 3 to 10 minutes to complete, depending on how fast your PC is. After `make` is done, you can install the XMMS software with the following command:

```
make install
```

This command also runs GNU `make`, but the `install` argument instructs GNU `make` to perform a specific set of commands from the `Makefile`. These instructions essentially go through all the subdirectories and copy various files to their final locations. For example, the binary executable files `xmms`, `wmxmms`, and `xmms-config` are copied to the `/usr/bin` directory.

Secret

XMMS already comes with Red Hat Linux and you can run it by selecting Main Menu⇨Sound & Video⇨Audio Player. However, after you build and install XMMS again, you should get the new version of XMMS.

Try running XMMS from the GNOME or KDE desktop by selecting Main Menu⇨Sound & Video⇨Audio Player or by typing xmms in a terminal window. From the XMMS window, press L to get the Load File dialog and select an MP3 file to play. Your PC must have a sound card, and that the sound card must be configured correctly for XMMS to work.

Figure 21-4 shows a typical view of XMMS playing an MP3 music clip.

Figure 21-4: Playing MP3 Music with XMMS.

If you get an error message saying that the MPEG support has been removed, select Window menu⇨Options⇨Preferences and in the dialog box that appears select MPEG Layer 1/2/3 Placeholder Plugin. Then click off the Enable Plugin check box to disable that plug-in. The XMMS source that downloaded builds a working MP3 plug-in.

Summarizing the Steps in Building Software from Source Code

Now, that you have tried the entire process of downloading and building a software package, here's an overview of the steps you follow to download, unpack, build, and install a typical software package:

1. Use a Web browser to download the source code, usually in the form of a .tar.gz file, from the anonymous FTP site or website.

2. Unpack the file with a tar zxvf filename command.

3. Change the directory to the new subdirectory where the software is unpacked, with a command such as cd software_dir.

4. Read any README or INSTALL files to learn any specific instructions you must follow to build and install the software.

5. The details of building the software may differ slightly from one software package to another, but typically you type the following commands to build and install the software:

```
./configure
make
make install
```

6. Read any other documentation that comes with the software to learn how to use the software and whether you must configure the software further before using it.

Installing SRPMS

If you have the source CDs for Red Hat Linux (you can download the source CD images from one of the sites listed on `http://www.redhat.com/download/mirror.html`), you can install the source files and build various applications directly from the source files. Red Hat provides the sources files in RPMs and these RPMs are generally known as SRPMS (for source RPMs).

To install a specific source RPM and build the application, follow these steps:

1. Mount the CD-ROM by typing mount `/mnt/cdrom` or waiting for GNOME desktop to mount the CD.

2. Typically source RPMs would be in the SRPMS directory. Change to that directory by typing the following command:

   `cd /mnt/cdrom/SRPMS`

3. Install the source RPM file by using the `rpm -i` command. For example, to install the Web server (`httpd`) source, type

   `rpm -ivh httpd*.src.rpm`

   The files would be installed in the `/usr/src/redhat/SOURCES` directory. A spec file with a `.spec` extension would be placed in the `/usr/src/redhat/SPECS` directory. The *spec file* describes the software and also contains information that is used to build and install the software.

4. Use the `rpmbuild` command with the spec file to build the software. You perform different tasks from unpacking the source files to building and installing the binaries by using different options with `rpmbuild` command. For example, to execute the instructions in the `%prep` section of the spec file, type:

   `rpmbuild -bp packagename.spec`

   where *packagename* is the name of the RPM. The `%prep` section should typically unpack the source files. The unpacked source files appear in a subdirectory in the `/usr/src/redhat/BUILD` directory. The subdirectory usually has the name of the software package, including a version number.

   If you want to run the whole spec file, type:

   `rpmbuild -ba packagename.spec`

   This command should typically build the software and install the binary files,

A number of single-letter options that go with `-b` are very useful. Here is a summary of these `rpmbuild -b` options:

- `rpmbuild -bp` means just run the `%prep` section of the specfile.
- `rpmbuild -bl` performs a list check that expands the `%files` section of a spec file and checks to see if all files exist.
- `rpmbuild -bc` executes the `%build` section after the `%prep`. This is equivalent to a `make` command that compiles the source code.
- `rpmbuild -bi` performs the `%prep`, `%build`, and then `%install`. This is equivalent to the `make install` command.
- `rpmbuild -bb` builds a binary package after completing the `%prep`, `%build`, and `%install` sections of the spec file.
- `rpmbuild -ba` builds both binary and source packages after completing the `%prep`, `%build`, and `%install` sections of the spec file.

Upgrading Red Hat Linux with the Update Agent

Red Hat Linux comes with a service called Red Hat Network. The idea behind Red Hat Network is to enable registered users to keep their Red Hat Linux system and applications current. The idea is that you register with the Red Hat Network and provide information about your system's hardware and the RPMs currently installed on your system. After you've done this, an Update Agent can download any new RPM files your system requires and install those files for you.

I briefly provide an overview of how to update your system by using the Update Agent and the Red Hat Network.

Registering with Red Hat Network

To take full advantage of the Red Hat Network's facilities, you must register with the Red Hat Network and provide information about your Red Hat Linux system. To register, follow these steps:

1. Make sure that your Internet connection is up; then select Main Menu⇨System Tools⇨Red Hat Network. If this is the first time, a configuration dialog appears from which you can configure some options such as what to do with downloaded packages, what packages to skip, and whether to verify authenticity of packages. You can typically click OK to proceed. You also get a prompt that asks you if you want to install Red Hat's GPG key (used to verify that packages are securely signed by Red Hat). You should click Yes to install the key.

2. The Red Hat Update Agent runs and displays a message explaining the purpose of the program. Click Forward to continue.

3. When you run the Red Hat Update Agent for the first time, it registers you with the Red Hat Network. It starts by displaying a privacy statement explaining the information to be collected and sent to Red Hat's server during registration. The information includes an inventory of RPM files on your system and an inventory of your system hardware. Read the privacy policy; if you want to continue, click the Forward button.

4. You are prompted for a user name and password to establish a new user account with Red Hat, as shown in Figure 21-5. Fill in the requested information, and click Forward to continue.

5. The next screen asks you to enter more information about yourself, including your name, address, and phone number. Fill in the information, and click the Forward button.

6. The Red Hat Update Agent shows some information about your system and asks you to provide a name for the system profile (the collection of information about your system). Enter a descriptive name, and then click Forward.

7. The Red Hat Update Agent displays a list of RPMs (names of software packages) to be included in the profile information. When the Update Agent checks for updated software, it uses this list. If you don't care about updating some of the packages, uncheck these names, then click Forward.

8. The Red Hat Update Agent informs you that it's about to send your system information to the Red Hat Network. Click Forward to continue.

Figure 21-5: Creating a New Account with the Red Hat Network.

9. The Red Hat Update Agent sends your information (the information mentioned in the privacy statement) to the Red Hat Network. If all goes well, the upload begins and a progress bar shows the percentage sent so far. Otherwise, you may get a message from the server that due to high load access to the Red Hat Network is limited to subscription customers only. If this happens, you have to try to register after waiting for some time.

10. After the Red Hat Update Agent successfully uploads your system profile to the Red Hat Network, the final window displays a message telling you to visit `http://rhn.redhat.com`, to log in, and to access Red Hat Network. That website is where you can buy subscriptions to the Red Hat Network also. Click the Finish button to complete the registration process.

Updating Red Hat Linux Packages

After you're registered with Red Hat Network, you can use the Red Hat Update Agent to update Red Hat Linux. Red Hat gives you a free subscription to Red Hat Network for one PC, but you have to pay for anything beyond that. If you want to buy a subscription, visit `rhn.redhat.com`, log in, and follow the directions.

To update software packages, follow these steps:

1. Log in as `root`, and select Main Menu⇨System Tools⇨Red Hat Network. The Red Hat Update Agent starts, and a dialog box that prompts you to install Red Hat's public key in your GPG key ring. (GPG refers to GNU Privacy Guard or GnuPG, a program for encrypting, decrypting, and signing email and other data using the OpenPGP Internet standard.) Red Hat's public GPG key is used to verify that Red Hat has securely signed the packages the Update Agent has downloaded.

2. Click the Yes button to install Red Hat's key.

3. The Red Hat Update Agent displays a window with a welcome message. Click the Forward button to proceed. The Update Agent retrieves a list of all available packages from the Red Hat Network. (This may take a few minutes.) Then, the Update Agent downloads the headers for all available packages. For each download, a progress bar shows the percentage of data downloaded so far. The header download takes quite a bit of time over a slow connection to the Internet.

4. After the Red Hat Update Agent downloads the headers, it displays a list of packages to be skipped. You can accept the list and click the Forward button to continue.

5. The Update Agent displays a list of all the packages available for updating from Red Hat Network. Scroll through the list and pick the package updates you want to download. Click the box to the left of a package's name to select it. As you select packages, the Update Agent displays the total size of the packages you have selected so far.

6. After selecting the packages, click the Forward button to proceed with the download.

7. The Update Agent then checks for any package dependencies and begins downloading the packages. Progress bars show the status of the download. After the download is finished, click the Forward button to proceed with the installation.

8. The Update Agent displays progress bars as it installs each package update. Click the Forward button when the installation is complete.

9. The Update Agent displays a message about the package or packages it has installed successfully. Click the Finish button to exit the Red Hat Update Agent.

After you have registered with the Red Hat Network, you can use the Red Hat Update Agent to keep Red Hat Linux up to date.

Upgrading and Customizing the Linux Kernel

One reason that Linux is so exciting is that many programmers are constantly improving it. Some programmers, for example, write drivers that add support for new hardware, such as a new sound card or a new networking card. All these innovations come to you in the form of new versions of the Linux kernel.

Although you do not have to upgrade or modify the Linux operating system—the kernel—every time a new version is available, sometimes you need to upgrade simply because the new version corrects some problems or supports your hardware better. On the other hand, if an earlier kernel version has everything you need, there is no need to rush out and upgrade.

Sometimes you may want to rebuild the kernel even when there are no fixes or enhancements. The Linux kernel on the companion CD-ROM is generic and uses modules to support all types of hardware. You may want to build a new kernel that links in the drivers for only the devices installed on your system. In particular, if you have a SCSI hard disk, you may want to create a kernel that supports your SCSI adapter. Depending on your needs, you may also want to change some of the kernel-configuration options, such as creating a kernel that's specific for your Pentium processor (instead of a generic Intel 386 processor).

The rest of this chapter explains how to upgrade a kernel using a kernel RPM provided by Red Hat as well as how to rebuild and install a new Linux kernel.

Secret

In the past it was possible to apply kernel patches—alterations to the kernel source code—and rebuild the kernel. You would typically download the Linux kernel patches (as well as the latest versions of the kernel sources) from the website `http://www.kernel.org`, decompress the files, and apply the patches by using the `patch` command. Unfortunately, these steps do not usually work with Red Hat Linux because Red Hat has modified some of the kernel files. In Red Hat Linux, you can still upgrade the kernel to newer versions—you just have to get the newer kernels from Red Hat's FTP server. If a Red Hat RPM for a newer kernel is not available yet, you can download the entire new kernel source from `http://www.kernel.org` and build the kernel by following the directions in the next section.

Upgrading with a Red Hat Kernel RPM

Red Hat distributes all software updates, including new versions of kernels, in the form of RPM files. To download and install the kernel RPMs, follow these steps:

1. Use a Web server to download the kernel RPM files from Red Hat's FTP server (the next section explains the details). If you want to rebuild the kernel, you have to download the `kernel-source` RPM corresponding to the new version of the kernel.
2. Install the RPMs by using the `rpm -i` command.
3. Create a new, initial RAM disk by running the `/sbin/mkinitrd` command.
4. Reconfigure GRUB to boot the new kernel.
5. Try out the new kernel by rebooting the system.

The next few sections further describe these steps.

Downloading New Kernel RPMs

Red Hat makes software updates available in the form of RPMs—packages—at its FTP server or one of the mirror sites listed at `http://www.redhat.com/download/mirror.html`. The updates are organized in directories according to Red Hat Linux version numbers. For example, any updates for Red Hat Linux 9 for Intel x86 systems reside in the `9/en/os/i386` directory. Use a Web browser (for example, Mozilla) to visit the FTP site and download any kernel RPMs available at that site.

Installing the Kernel RPMs

To install the kernel and the modules, follow these steps:

1. Log in as `root`.
2. Use the `cd` command to change directory to where the RPM files (the ones you have downloaded from Red Hat's FTP server) are located.
3. Type the following command to install the kernel RPM:

```
rpm -ivh kernel*.rpm
```

You need to install the `kernel-source` RPM only if you want to build a new kernel.

Making a New, Initial RAM Disk

Next, you have to make a new, initial RAM disk image—a file that the kernel can copy into a block of memory and use as a memory-resident disk.

Usually, the initial RAM disk image is stored in a file whose name begins with initrd. initrd is shorthand for initial RAM disk; the mkinitrd command is so named because it makes an initrd file.

Log in as root and type a command-line of the following form to create the initrd file:

```
mkinitrd /boot/initrd-filename.img  module-dir-name
```

The initrd file has to be in the /boot directory where the kernel is located. You can use any filename for initrd-filename. The module-dir-name is the name of the directory in /lib/modules where the module files are located. By convention, the module directory name is the same as the kernel version number. For example, if your kernel version (type the uname -r command to see the version number) is 2.4.20-2.48, the module directory name is 2.4.20-2.48. Another common practice is to use an initrd filename created by appending the version number to the initrd- prefix. Thus, for kernel version 2.4.20-2.48, the initrd file is initrd-2.4.20-2.48.img.

To create the initial RAM disk image for kernel version 2.4.20-2.48, type the following command:

```
/sbin/mkinitrd /boot/initrd-2.4.20-2.48.img 2.4.20-2.48
```

This creates the file initrd-2.4.20-2.48.img in the /boot directory. You refer to this initrd file in the GRUB configuration file (/etc/grub.conf).

Reconfiguring GRUB

After you install the kernel RPMs and create the initial RAM disk image, you have to reconfigure GRUB so that it can boot the new kernel.

Use a text editor such as vi or Emacs to edit the /etc/grub.conf file. Add the following lines near the beginning of that file right after the splashimage line:

```
title Red Hat Linux (NEW)
        root (hd0,0)
        kernel /vmlinuz-2.4.20-2.48 ro root=/dev/hda2

        initrd /initrd-2.4.20-2.48.img
```

In the kernel line where it says root=/dev/hda2, change /dev/hda2 to the correct device name for the disk partition where your Linux system's root file system (/) is located. Also, make sure that the correct names are used for the kernel and initrd filenames—these names depend on the version number of the kernel you have downloaded.

After editing and saving the /etc/grub.conf file, you can reboot the system and try out the new version of kernel.

Trying out the New Kernel

After installing the new kernel RPM, creating the initial RAM disk file, and reconfiguring GRUB, it's time to try the new kernel. To restart the system, log in as `root` and type the following command from the Linux prompt:

```
reboot
```

You may also reboot the system as you log out of the GNOME or KDE desktop. Select Restart the computer from the dialog box, and click OK.

When the system reboots and you see the GRUB screen, press the arrow key to select the new kernel's name. If you have added the new kernel description before all other operating systems in the GRUB configuration file, that kernel should boot even if you don't do anything at the boot screen.

After Red Hat Linux starts, you should see the usual graphical login screen. Log in as a user, open a terminal window, and type the `uname -sr` command to see the version number. The response should show that your system is running the new version of the kernel.

Rebuilding the Kernel

Rebuilding the kernel refers to creating a new binary file for the core Linux operating system. This binary file is the one that runs when Linux boots. You may have to rebuild the kernel for various reasons:

♦ After you initially install Linux, you may want to create a new kernel that includes support for only the hardware installed on your system. In particular, if you have a SCSI adapter, you may want to create a kernel that links in the SCSI driver. The kernel in the companion CD-ROM includes the SCSI driver as an external module you load at start up.

♦ If you have a system with hardware for which only experimental support is available, you have to rebuild the kernel to include that support into the operating system.

♦ You may want to recompile the kernel and generate code that works well on your specific Pentium processor (instead of the generic 386 processor code that comes in the standard Red Hat Linux distribution).

Secret

Before you rebuild the kernel, make sure you have the emergency boot floppy (covered in Chapter 2) you have prepared when installing Red Hat Linux. If the system does not boot after you rebuild the kernel, you can use the emergency boot floppy to start the system and repeat the kernel build process.

Never rebuild and install a new kernel without first making sure you have an emergency boot floppy. If you have not createed the boot floppy during Red Hat Linux installation, use the `/sbin/mkbootdisk` command to create the boot floppy. Type **man mkbootdisk** to learn the syntax of that command. The exact command line to build the emergency boot floppy depends on the kernel version number. For example, to create a boot floppy for version **2.4.20-2.48**, log in as `root`, and type the following command at the shell prompt (you have to insert a blank floppy disk when prompted):

```
mkbootdisk -device /dev/fd0 2.4.20-2.48
```

Replace `2.4.20-2.48` with the version number of your Linux kernel, as displayed by the `uname -r` command.

To rebuild the Linux kernel, you need the kernel source files. The kernel source files are not normally installed. Use the following steps to install the kernel source files on your system:

1. Log in as `root` and insert the second Red Hat Linux CD-ROM into the CD-ROM drive.

2. If the CD-ROM drive does not mount automatically, type the following command to mount the CD-ROM drive:

   ```
   mount /mnt/cdrom
   ```

   If you are using GNOME or KDE, the CD-ROM is automatically mounted, and you should not have to perform this step manually.

3. Change the directory to the `RedHat/RPMS` directory on the CD-ROM, and use the `rpm` command to install the kernel source files. Type the following commands:

   ```
   cd /mnt/cdrom/RedHat/RPMS
   rpm -ivh kernel-source*
   ```

   After the `rpm` command finishes installing the kernel source package, the source files appear in the `/usr/src/linux-2.4` directory.

---

note

If you cannot find the kernel-source RPM on this book's CD-ROMs, you have to download that file from one of the mirror sites listed at `www.redhat.com/download/mirror.html`. Click on the Distribution link next to one of the listed FTP sites and then look in the directory corresponding to the Red Hat Linux version number. For example, the RPM files for Red Hat Linux 9 should be in the `9/en/os/i386/RedHat/RPMS` directory. Use a Web browser to download the kernel-source RPM file and install it by following the steps outlined above.

Building the kernel involves the following key phases:

◆ Configuring the kernel
◆ Building the kernel
◆ Building and installing the modules (if any)
◆ Installing the kernel and setting up GRUB

The next section describes the use of modules versus linking hardware support directly into the kernel. Subsequent sections describe the phases of kernel building.

---

insider insight

When you create a custom kernel for your hardware configuration, you may want to link all required device drivers into the kernel. In this case, you can keep the size of such a monolithic kernel under control because you link in device drivers only for the hardware installed on your system.

Secret

Creating a Monolithic versus a Modular Kernel

Before you start configuring the kernel, understand that you have two options for the device drivers needed to support various hardware devices in Linux:

- **Link in support**—You can link the drivers for all hardware on your system into the kernel. As you might imagine, the size of the kernel grows as device-driver code is incorporated into the kernel. A kernel that links in all necessary support code is called a *monolithic kernel*.

- **Use modules**—You can create the necessary device drivers in the form of modules. A module is a block of code the kernel can load after it starts running. A typical use of modules is to add support for a device without having to rebuild the kernel for each new device. Modules do not have to be device drivers; they can also serve to add new functionality to the kernel. A kernel that uses modules is called a *modular kernel*.

You do not have to create a fully monolithic or fully modular kernel. In fact, it is common practice to link some support directly into the kernel. Conversely, you can build infrequently used device drivers in the form of modules. For a company such as Red Hat, it makes sense to distribute a modular kernel. Red Hat provides a generic kernel, along with a large number of modules, to support many different types of hardware. Then, the Red Hat installation program configures the system to load only modules needed to support the hardware installed in a user's system.

Configuring the Kernel

The first phase in rebuilding a kernel is configuring it. To configure the kernel, log in as root. Then change the kernel source directory by using the cd command as follows:

```
cd /usr/src/linux*
```

To configure the kernel, you have to indicate which features and device drivers you want to include in your Linux system. In essence, you build a copy of Linux with the mix-and-match features you want.

Linux provides several ways for you to configure the kernel:

- Type **make menuconfig** to enter the kernel-configuration parameters through a text-based interface similar to the one the Red Hat installation program uses.

- Type **make xconfig** to use an X Window System-based configuration program to configure the kernel. You have to run X to use this configuration program with a graphical interface.

- Type **make config** to use a shell script that prompts you for each configuration option one by one. You can use this configuration program from the Linux command prompt. When you use this option, you undergo a long question-and-answer process to specify the configuration parameters.

- Type **make oldconfig** to use a shell script to reconfigure the kernel after upgrading the sources. This configuration script keeps the existing options and prompts you only for new or changed options.

Secret

The `make menuconfig,` `make xconfig,` `make config,` **and** `make oldconfig` commands achieve the same end result—each stores your choices in a text file named `.config` located in the `/usr/src/linux-2.4` directory. Because the filename starts with a period, you don't see it when you use the `ls` command alone to list the directory. Instead, type **ls -a** to see the `.config` file in the directory listing.

The kernel-configuration step merely captures your choices in the `.config` file. (In fact, the `.config` file does not exist until you configure the kernel once.) The kernel file does not change until you compile the kernel with the `make` command. That means you can go through the kernel-configuration option as many times as you want. If you want to start over with default settings, type the following command before you start configuring the kernel:

```
make mrproper
```

Here are some lines from the `.config` file on my system (after I configure the kernel):

```
more .config
#
# Automatically generated make config: don't edit
#

#
# Code maturity level options
#
CONFIG_EXPERIMENTAL=y

#
# Loadable module support
#
CONFIG_MODULES=y
CONFIG_MODVERSIONS=y
CONFIG_KMOD=y

#
# Processor type and features
#
# CONFIG_M386 is not set
# CONFIG_M486 is not set
# CONFIG_M586 is not set
# CONFIG_M586TSC is not set
# CONFIG_M586MMX is not set
# CONFIG_M686 is not set
# CONFIG_MPENTIUMIII is not set
CONFIG_MPENTIUM4=y
(rest of the file not shown)
```

Essentially, each configuration option has a name, and each one is assigned a value. The name begins with CONFIG_ followed by a word that identifies the option. Each selected option has a value of y (to link in support for that feature) or m (to use a module for that feature). Lines beginning with # are comments. Comment lines list features not selected.

> **note**
>
> I describe the configuration process through the make config command. Although this approach is somewhat tedious because it walks you through each option one by one, it is ideal as a learning tool. As you step through the groups of configuration options, I provide notes explaining what most of the options mean. You can then use any configuration tool (make xconfig, make menuconfig, make config, or make oldconfig) to configure the kernel.

As you configure the kernel with the make config command, you have to select how to include support for specific devices. Typically, for each configuration option, you have to respond with one of the following choices:

- ◆ **y** to link support into the kernel
- ◆ **m** to use a module
- ◆ **n** to skip the support for that specific device
- ◆ **?** to get help on that kernel-configuration option

If a device does not have a modular device driver, you won't see the m option. For some configuration options, you may have to type a specific answer. For example, when responding to the processor type, type **Pentium-4** to indicate that you have a Pentium 4 PC.

Starting the Kernel Configuration

To start configuring the kernel, type:

```
rm -f include/asm
( cd include ; ln -sf asm-i386 asm)
/bin/sh scripts/Configure arch/i386/config.in
#
# Using defaults found in configs/kernel-2.4.20-i686.config
#
*
* Code maturity level options
*
Prompt for development and/or incomplete code/drivers (CONFIG_EXPERIMENTAL) [Y/n/?]
```

Press Enter to accept the default Yes answer. This causes the configuration process to show all experimental device drivers.

> **insider insight**
>
> The possible answers to each prompt appear in square brackets with the default answer in uppercase. Thus, [Y/n/?] means the default answer is Yes, and two other possible answers are n and ?. To accept the default, press Enter. For help on this option, press ?. If you have questions about any option, press ? and carefully read the help text before you decide what to do.

Enabling Support for Loadable Modules

The next group of options asks you about support for loadable modules. A loadable module is a block of code that the Linux kernel can load and execute as if it were a part of the operating system.

```
*
* Loadable module support
*
Enable loadable module support (CONFIG_MODULES) [Y/n/?]
  Set version information on all module symbols (CONFIG_MODVERSIONS) [Y/n/?]
  Kernel module loader (CONFIG_KMOD) [Y/n/?]
```

You want to include support for modules, so answer Yes to the first question. The next question asks you about including version information in each module. If modules have version information, the module is checked for compatibility with the current kernel version. Because it is easy to unload a module that does not work, I tend to answer No to this option. However, you may safely accept the default and press Enter. The third question asks whether or not you want the kernel to be capable of loading required modules. You should answer Yes to this option.

Configuring Processor-Related Features

The next set of questions involves the processor type and support for specific processor-related features. The first question of this set queries you about a new configuration parameter—CONFIG_LOLAT—when this parameter is set to y, the kernel uses code that tries to lower the latency (the time elapsed between an interrupt and starting the interrupt handler). You can press Enter to accept the default Yes answer.

The next question asks about your system's processor family. If you answer 386, the compiled kernel can run on any other processor (such as a 486 or any type of Pentium). However, if you are creating a kernel specifically for your system, enter your processor type from the choices shown in parentheses. If you have an older 386 or 486SX PC that does not have a math coprocessor, you should answer Yes to the math-emulation question and have the kernel perform floating-point arithmetic in software. You can also enable symmetric multiprocessing (SMP) support, but you should do so only if your system's motherboard has two or more processors.

There are a host of other processor-specific options in this section. You can read the help for each option and select the ones that apply to your system.

Configuring General Options

Next, comes a set of general options that deal with networking, PCI bus, MCA bus, PCM-CIA, parallel port, and advanced power management (APM) BIOS support.

You can simply press Enter to accept the default answers for these options. If you don't understand what an option means, press **?** to get help on that option.

---

cross ref One of the general options is CONFIG_SYSCTL. By answering Yes to this option, you enable the necessary support in the kernel so you can use the /sbin/sysctl program to view or set kernel parameters. Chapter 20 shows you how to use the sysctl program.

Enabling Plug and Play Support

The next two questions ask if you want to enable Plug and Play (PnP) support in the kernel. If you enable PnP support, the kernel automatically configures PnP devices (just as Windows does). You should press Enter to accept the default choices for these two questions.

```
*
* Plug and Play configuration
*
Plug and Play support (CONFIG_PNP) [Y/m/n/?]
   ISA Plug and Play support (CONFIG_ISAPNP) [Y/m/n/?]
```

Configuring Floppy and Parallel Port IDE Devices

The next set of questions involves the floppy and IDE (Integrated Drive Electronics) devices connected to the PC's parallel port.

```
*
* Block devices
*
Normal floppy disk support (CONFIG_BLK_DEV_FD) [Y/m/n/?]
XT hard disk support (CONFIG_BLK_DEV_XD) [M/n/y/?]
Parallel port IDE device support (CONFIG_PARIDE) [M/n/?]
```

The first question asks if you want floppy-drive support. Because most PCs do have a floppy drive, your answer generally is Yes. You should press Enter to accept the default for the third question if you have external CD-ROM or disk devices that connect through your PC's parallel port. Some IDE devices use a parallel port IDE adapter—that's what the PARIDE in the CONFIG_PARIDE option refers to.

The next set of options is for various parallel IDE drivers. You may want to build in support for parallel port IDE devices through loadable modules. That way, the modules are there if you need them, but the kernel doesn't become bloated with extra code.

Configuring Additional Block Devices

Next comes another set of options for block devices, which refers to devices that transfer data in chunks (as opposed to a keyboard that transfers data one character at a time). The CONFIG_BLK_DEV_LOOP option is for loopback device. Enabling the loopback device lets Linux manipulate an entire file system inside a single large file. The multiple devices driver (CONFIG_BLK_DEV_MD option) allows Linux to combine several hard-disk partitions into a single logical device. This option supports RAID (Redundant Array of Independent Disks) devices. The RAM disk support allows the kernel to use a portion of your system's memory as a disk capable of storing a file system. Typically, a RAM disk functions only during system startup when the hard disk may not yet be available. The RAM disk is essential if you are booting a SCSI disk and you haven't compiled the SCSI drivers into the kernel.

Enabling Cryptography Support

Next comes a set of options for enabling cryptography support in the kernel. You can build them as modules, as the default selections of the following options show:

```
*
* Cryptography support (CryptoAPI)
*
CryptoAPI support (CONFIG_CRYPTO) [M/n/y/?]
Cipher Algorithms (CONFIG_CIPHERS) [M/n/?]
*
```

```
* 128 bit blocksize
*
 AES (aka Rijndael) cipher (CONFIG_CIPHER_AES) [M/n/?]
 Identity Function cipher (CONFIG_CIPHER_IDENTITY) [M/n/?]
Crypto Devices (CONFIG_CRYPTODEV) [M/n/?]
 Loop Crypto support (CONFIG_CRYPTOLOOP) [M/n/?]
```

Configuring the Network

The next set of options deals with networking. How you answer depends on how you want to use your Linux system in a network. Here are some guidelines:

♦ Answer Yes to enable CONFIG_NETFILTER if you want to use your Linux system as a firewall—an intermediary system that controls information flowing between a local area network (LAN) and the Internet. When you enable CONFIG_NETFILTER, you can use the Linux PC as a packet-filtering firewall. (See Chapter 22 for more information on packet filters.) You should also turn on this option if you want to use IP masquerading, which allows many systems on a private LAN to access the Internet through a Linux system with a single public IP address. Also, you have to turn on CONFIG_IP_NF_CONNTRACK, CONFIG_IP_NF_IPTABLES, and CONFIG_IP_NF_NAT. Chapter 13 explains IP masquerading.

♦ If you answer Yes to CONFIG_IP_ALIAS, you can assign multiple IP addresses to a single network interface card.

♦ You should always enable CONFIG_INET for TCP/IP networking.

♦ Answer Yes to CONFIG_IP_ADVANCED_ROUTER if you want to use your Linux system as a router—a gateway between two LANs.

♦ You should turn on CONFIG_IP_MULTICAST if you employ the Linux system to address several networked computers at once using IP multicasting.

♦ You can enable CONFIG_SYN_COOKIES if you want Linux to resist a type of attack known as SYN flooding, which can overwhelm the network connection.

♦ You can safely answer No to the IP tunneling (CONFIG_NET_IPIP) option. You need to address this option only in certain situations, such as moving a laptop from one network to another, without changing its IP address.

Note that the Linux kernel now supports the next version of the Internet Protocol: IP version 6 (IPv6, also called IPng or IP next generation).

Configuring Telephony Support

Next come two options for telephony support in Linux. With the right hardware and software, telephony support enables you to use the Linux system for making phone calls over the Internet (also known as voice over IP or VoIP).

```
*
* Network testing
*
Packet Generator (USE WITH CAUTION) (CONFIG_NET_PKTGEN) [N/y/m/?]
*
* Telephony Support
*
Linux telephony support (CONFIG_PHONE) [M/n/y/?]
QuickNet Internet LineJack/PhoneJack support (CONFIG_PHONE_IXJ) [M/n/?]
QuickNet Internet LineJack/PhoneJack PCMCIA support (CONFIG_PHONE_IXJ_PCMCIA) [M/n/?]
```

You can accept the default choices to build driver modules for telephony support if you have a telephony card, such as the Internet PhoneJACK or Internet LineJACK manufactured by Quicknet Technologies, Inc. If you do not have any Quicknet telephony cards, you can safely ignore this option.

Configuring IDE Devices

The next set of questions involves IDE devices, such as hard disks and ATAPI CD-ROM drives.

```
*
* ATA/IDE/MFM/RLL support
*
ATA/IDE/MFM/RLL support (CONFIG_IDE) [Y/m/n/?]
*
* IDE, ATA and ATAPI Block devices
*
Enhanced IDE/MFM/RLL disk/cdrom/tape/floppy support (CONFIG_BLK_DEV_IDE) [Y/m/n/?]
```

This set of questions has four acronyms: ATA, IDE, MFM, and RLL. All of these relate to hard disks or interface of disk drives to the PC. Here's what they mean:

- ♦ **ATA** stands for *Advanced Technology Attachment* and refers to the PC-AT style interface used to connect hard disks and CD-ROM drives to the PC's motherboard.
- ♦ **IDE** stands for *Integrated Drive Electronics* and refers to the original PC hard disks that integrated the disk controller onto the hard disk itself. The IDE interface is more accurately described as AT Attachment Packet Interface, or ATAPI. You typically see the terms IDE, ATA, and ATAPI used interchangeably.
- ♦ **MFM** stands for *modified frequency modulation* and refers to the way data was encoded on older hard drives. These hard drives can work over an IDE interface.
- ♦ **RLL** stands for *run length limited* and is also a technique for storing data on hard disk. RLL disks can work over an IDE interface.

The first question asks if you want the kernel to support IDE devices. The second question asks if you want to use the full-featured IDE device that can control up to 10 IDE interfaces. Because each IDE interface can have a master and a slave device, this enables Linux to access a total of up to 20 IDE devices, such as disks or CD-ROM drives. You can press Enter to accept the default choices of Yes for both of these options.

---

insider insight The next set of options concerns various IDE drivers. The initial comment starts with a note that refers to the file `/usr/src/linux-2.4/Documentation/ide.txt`. **You can find many useful help files (these are all text files) in the** `/usr/src/linux-2.4/Documentation` **directory.**

You can accept the default answers for these options. Note that `IDE/ATAPI FLOPPY` refers to IDE floppy drives, such as Iomega Zip drive or Imation Superdisk LS-120 drive. The questions about CMD640 and RZ1000 bug fixes refer to some known problems with specific chipsets used in IDE interfaces.

Configuring SCSI Devices

Next follows an entire set of options that has to do with SCSI devices. SCSI stands for *Small Computer Systems Interface* and refers to a type of interface through which you can connect multiple devices such as hard disks and scanners to the PC. If your system has a SCSI adapter, you should start by answering Yes to the CONFIG_SCSI option. After that, you have to answer questions about the types of devices (disk, tape, CD-ROM) connected to the SCSI adapter. Finally, you must enable support for the specific SCSI adapter model on your system.

---

insider insight

If your system has a SCSI adapter, always press y in response to all the needed SCSI options. Do not press m to create SCSI modules. You have to go through several extra steps to install a kernel that has to load modular SCSI device drivers. The easiest approach is to simply link in the SCSI support by answering y to options such as CONFIG_SCSI, CONFIG_BLK_DEV_SD and the configuration option corresponding to your SCSI adapter.

Configuring IEEE 1394 Support

The next set of options is for enabling IEEE 1394 support, either as a module or linked into the kernel. IEEE 1394 is a high-speed serial bus for connecting peripherals to PCs. Apple calls this bus FireWire; Sony calls it i.Link. IEEE 1394 is similar to USB, but it can transfer data at rates up to 400 Mbps, which is more than 30 times the data rate of the older USB version 1.1 (note that USB 2.0 is much faster; it can transfer data at rates of up to 480 Mbps). Because of its high data-transfer rates, IEEE 1394 is ideal for connecting high-speed peripherals such as digital audio and video devices and external hard drives to the PC.

The Linux kernel includes experimental support for the IEEE 1394 bus. Currently, Linux supports IEEE 1394 chipsets that are compatible with Texas Instruments PCILynx/ PCILynx2 and OHCI chipsets. If your PC has an IEEE 1394 adapter, you can build the necessary drivers through the following options:

```
*
* IEEE 1394 (FireWire) support (EXPERIMENTAL)
*
IEEE 1394 (FireWire) support (EXPERIMENTAL) (CONFIG_IEEE1394) [M/n/y/?]
*
* Device Drivers
*
  Texas Instruments PCILynx support (CONFIG_IEEE1394_PCILYNX) [N/m/?]
  OHCI-1394 support (CONFIG_IEEE1394_OHCI1394) [M/n/?]
*
* Protocol Drivers
*
  OHCI-1394 Video support (CONFIG_IEEE1394_VIDEO1394) [M/n/?]
  SBP-2 support (Harddisks etc.) (CONFIG_IEEE1394_SBP2) [M/n/?]
    Enable Phys DMA support for SBP2 (Debug) (CONFIG_IEEE1394_SBP2_PHYS_DMA) [Y/n/?]
  Ethernet over 1394 (CONFIG_IEEE1394_ETH1394) [M/n/?]
  OHCI-DV I/O support (CONFIG_IEEE1394_DV1394) [M/n/?]
  Raw IEEE1394 I/O support (CONFIG_IEEE1394_RAWIO) [M/n/?]
  IEC61883-1 Plug support (CONFIG_IEEE1394_CMP) [M/n/?]
    IEC61883-6 (Audio transmission) support (CONFIG_IEEE1394_AMDTP) [M/n/?]
Excessive debugging output (CONFIG_IEEE1394_VERBOSEDEBUG) [N/y/?]
```

To learn more about using IEEE 1394 peripherals in Linux, visit the website of the IEEE 1394 for Linux project at `http://www.linux1394.org/`.

Configuring I2O drivers

Pronounced *eye-two-oh*, I2O refers to Intelligent Input/Output—a new device driver architecture independent of the operating system and the controlled device. I2O functions by logically separating the part responsible for managing the device from the part that contains operating system-specific details (it's called the I2O Split Driver model). The two parts of an I2O driver are the OS Services Module (OSM), which works with the operating system, and the Hardware Device Module (HDM) that interfaces with the particular device the driver manages. The OSM and HDM communicate by passing messages to each other. To learn more about I2O, visit the Intelligent-IO.com website at `http://www.intelligent-io.com/`.

Linux comes with some I2O drivers for SCSI and PCI devices. You can build the I2O drivers through the following configuration options:

```
*
* I2O device support
*
I2O support (CONFIG_I2O) [M/n/y/?]
  I2O PCI support (CONFIG_I2O_PCI) [M/n/?]
  I2O Block OSM (CONFIG_I2O_BLOCK) [M/n/?]
  I2O LAN OSM (CONFIG_I2O_LAN) [M/n/?]
  I2O SCSI OSM (CONFIG_I2O_SCSI) [M/n/?]
  I2O /proc support (CONFIG_I2O_PROC) [M/n/?]
```

Configuring Network Adapters

The next group of options involves networking. It includes the configuration of LAN adapters such as Ethernet (10/100 Mpbs as well as Gigabit Ethernet), ATM (Asynchronous Transfer Mode), Token ring, ARCnet, and AppleTalk network adapters. You can also enable dial-up and wide area network (WAN) support by using SLIP and PPP through options in this category.

For Ethernet, you can build support for the Ethernet card installed on your system. This category also includes support for wireless networking and drivers for wireless Ethernet cards.

Network adapters also includes support for modems built into sound cards.

Enabling Support for Infrared Devices

The Linux kernel now supports IrDA-compliant infrared (IR) devices. This set of options allows you to enable support for IrDA devices. If your PC has any IrDA interfaces, you can build the modules needed to support such devices.

Many IR interfaces are in the form of dongles—small adapters that typically attach to the serial port of the PC. You can use the options in this section to enable support for several common types of dongles.

Enabling Support for ISDN

The next set of options enables you to include support for ISDN (Integrated Services Digital Network)—a digital telephone line you can use to connect the Linux system to the Internet. These ISDN-related options include the configuration of specific ISDN adapters.

You should build the ISDN driver only if your PC has an ISDN card. If you anticipate adding an ISDN card and purchase ISDN service from the phone company, you can build the driver as a module. Read the file `/usr/src/linux-2.4/Documentation/isdn/README` for more information on how to set up and use the ISDN driver in Linux.

Configuring CD-ROM Drives with Proprietary Interfaces

If you have a CD-ROM drive with a proprietary interface—not a SCSI or IDE (ATAPI) CD-ROM drive—you should select your CD-ROM interface from the following set of options:

```
   *
 * Old CD-ROM drivers (not SCSI, not IDE)
   *
 Support non-SCSI/IDE/ATAPI CDROM drives (CONFIG_CD_NO_IDESCSI) [Y/n/?]
```

If you enter y for that option, you can select the specific model of proprietary CD-ROM drive that your system has.

Typically, you can ignore the CD-ROM options, unless you have an old non-IDE and non-SCSI CD-ROM drives.

Configuring Character Devices

The next few options deal with configuring character devices, which include devices connected to the serial and parallel ports. These options also include configuration of multiport serial interface cards that enable you to connect multiple terminals or other devices to your Linux system. Answer No if you do not have any such devices on your system. Near the end of the list, you see a question about parallel-printer support (CONFIG_PRINTER). If you plan to connect a printer to the parallel port, answer Yes to this option.

Configuring I2C Protocol

I2C—pronounced *eye-squared-see*—is a protocol Philips has developed for communication over a pair of wires at rates between 10 and 100 kHz. System Management Bus (SMBus) is a subset of the I2C protocol. Many modern motherboards have an SMBus meant for connecting devices such as EEPROM (electrically erasable programmable read-only memory) and chips for hardware monitoring. Linux supports the I2C and SMBus protocols. You need this support for Video for Linux. If you have any hardware sensors or video equipment that needs I2C support, answer m to the CONFIG_I2C option, and answer m to the specific driver for your hardware. For example, if you want to use a BT848 frame-grabber board (to capture video), you should answer m to the CONFIG_I2C_ALGOBIT option.

To learn more about the I2C, read the documentation in the /usr/src/linux-2.4/ Documentation/i2c directory. In particular, the summary file briefly describes the I2C and SMBus protocols.

Specifying the Type of Mouse

From the next set of options, specify the type of mouse on your PC:

```
   *
 * Mice
   *
 Bus Mouse Support (CONFIG_BUSMOUSE) [M/n/y/?]
   ATIXL busmouse support (CONFIG_ATIXL_BUSMOUSE) [M/n/?]
   Logitech busmouse support (CONFIG_LOGIBUSMOUSE) [M/n/?]
   Microsoft busmouse support (CONFIG_MS_BUSMOUSE) [M/n/?]
 Mouse Support (not serial and bus mice) (CONFIG_MOUSE) [Y/m/n/?]
   PS/2 mouse (aka "auxiliary device") support (CONFIG_PSMOUSE) [Y/n/?]
   C&T 82C710 mouse port support (as on TI Travelmate) (CONFIG_82C710_MOUSE) [M/n/y/?]
   PC110 digitizer pad support (CONFIG_PC110_PAD) [M/n/y/?]
   MK712 touch screen support (CONFIG_MK712_MOUSE) [M/n/y/?]
```

Enabling Support for Joysticks

If you have a joystick or a special game controller (steering wheel, game pad, six-degrees-of-freedom controller), you can build the driver modules for your game controller from the options in this section.

Enabling Support for a Non-SCSI Tape Drive

If you have a non-SCSI tape drive that uses the QIC-02 format, you should answer Yes to the next question; otherwise, answer No:

```
QIC-02 tape support (CONFIG_QICO2_TAPE) [N/y/m/?]
```

Configuring the Watchdog Timer

Configuration options in the next set enable you to turn on support for the watchdog timer. Essentially, this causes the kernel to create a special file; failure to open the file and write to it every minute causes the system to reboot. Some watchdog boards can monitor the PC's status (including the temperature). You can also enable support for specific watchdog cards from this set of options.

If you want access to the PC's nonvolatile (battery-backed) memory—NVRAM—in the real-time clock, answer Yes to the CONFIG_NVRAM option. You can get access to the real-time clock by enabling the CONFIG_RTC configuration option.

Configuring Floppy Tape Drive

If you have a tape drive connected to your floppy controller, answer y or m to the next option, and select the other parameters appropriately (or accept the default choices):

```
*
* Ftape, the floppy tape device driver
*
Ftape (QIC-80/Travan) support (CONFIG_FTAPE) [M/n/y/?]
  Zftape, the VFS interface (CONFIG_ZFTAPE) [M/n/?]
  Default block size (CONFIG_ZFT_DFLT_BLK_SZ) [10240]
```

You can also enable several parameters related to floppy tape drives.

Configuring Graphics Support

The next set of options configures support for advanced video cards that can perform hardware-accelerated, 3D graphics. You can enable the first option to build the AGP (Accelerated Graphics Port) driver and can answer Yes to the option for your specific chipset.

```
/dev/agpgart (AGP Support) (CONFIG_AGP) [M/n/y/?]
  Intel 440LX/BX/GX and I815/I820/I830M/I830MP/I840/I845/I850/I860 support (CONF
IG_AGP_INTEL) [Y/n/?]
  Intel I810/I815/I830M (on-board) support (CONFIG_AGP_I810) [Y/n/?]
  VIA chipset support (CONFIG_AGP_VIA) [Y/n/?]
  AMD Irongate, 761, and 762 support (CONFIG_AGP_AMD) [Y/n/?]
  AMD 8151 support (CONFIG_AGP_AMD_8151) [Y/n/?]
  Generic SiS support (CONFIG_AGP_SIS) [Y/n/?]
  ALI chipset support (CONFIG_AGP_ALI) [Y/n/?]
  Serverworks LE/HE support (CONFIG_AGP_SWORKS) [Y/n/?]
```

Next, you have to configure a set of options for the *Direct Rendering Manager* (DRM)—a device-independent driver that supports the XFree86 *Direct Rendering Infrastructure* (DRI). DRI is meant for direct access to 3D graphics hardware in advanced graphics cards, such as 3Dfx Banshee and Voodoo3. To learn more about DRI, use your Web browser to visit the URL http://dri.sourceforge.net/.

If you have a 3D graphics card, you can answer Yes to CONFIG_DRM and build the module for the graphics card in your system. If you do not have one of the listed graphics cards, you should answer No to these options.

Configuring Audio and Video Devices

The next set of options involves audio and video devices, including FM radio cards. For more information on these devices, consult the documentation in the /usr/src/linux-2.4/Documentation/video4linux directory.

Enabling Support for Specific File Systems

The next set of options enables you to turn on support for specific types of file systems. You can make your choices based on the guidelines shown in Table 21-2.

Table 21-2: Common File System Configuration Options

Option	Description
CONFIG_ADFS_FS	Enables Linux to read from the ADFS—the Acorn Disc Filing System—the standard file system of the RiscOS operating system that runs on Acorn's ARM-based Risc PC systems and the Acorn Archimedes systems. Answer y if you want Linux to read from ADFS partitions on hard drives and from ADFS floppy disks.
CONFIG_AFFS_FS	Enables support for the Fast File System (FFS)—the file system used by Amiga systems since AmigaOS version 1.3 (34.20). Answer y if you need to read from and write to an Amiga FFS partition on your hard drive. Note that this support does not enable Linux to read from Amiga floppy disks because of an incompatibility of the floppy controller used in an Amiga and the standard floppy controller in PCs.
CONFIG_CODA_FS	Enables support for Coda, an advanced network file system that is similar to NFS but that better supports disconnected operation (for example, laptops) and is a better security model. Answer y only if you need your Linux system to act as a Coda client. Consult the file /usr/src/linux-2.4/Documentation/filesystems/coda.txt for more information.
CONFIG_EXT2_FS	Enables support for the second extended file system. You should definitely answer y to turn on this option.
CONFIG_EXT3_FS	Enables support for the journaling version of the second extended file system—the current standard file system for Linux. You should definitely answer y to turn on this option. The use of journaling means that you do not have to check the file system after a crash—the journal keeps track of all changes and can keep the file system consistent even if there is a crash.
CONFIG_FAT_FS	Turns on support for any File Allocation Table (FAT)-based file system (including MS-DOS and Windows 95 VFAT file systems). Answer y if you want to access MS-DOS or VFAT files.

Option	Description
CONFIG_HFS_FS	Enables Linux to mount Macintosh-formatted floppy disks and hard drive partitions with full read/write access. Answer y if you want to access Macintosh file systems.
CONFIG_HPFS_FS	Enables your Linux system to access and read an OS/2 HPFS file system (you can only read HPFS files). Answer y if you have an OS/2 partition on your hard disk.
CONFIG_ISO9660_FS	Turns on support for the standard ISO 9660 file system used on CD-ROMs (this is also known as the High Sierra File System and is referred to as hsfs on some UNIX workstations). If you have a CD-ROM drive, answer y here.
CONFIG_JOLIET	Enables support for Microsoft's Joliet extension for the ISO 9660 CD-ROM file system, which allows for long filenames in Unicode format (Unicode is the new 16-bit character code that can encode the characters of almost all languages of the world.) Answer y if you want to be able to read Joliet CD-ROMs under Linux.
CONFIG_MINIX_FS	Supports the Minix file system—the original file system of Linux. This simple file system still functions on floppy disks, so you should answer m to include support in the form of a module.
CONFIG_MSDOS_FS	Supports MS-DOS file systems. Press y if you want to read an MS-DOS partition on the hard disk or an MS-DOS floppy.
CONFIG_NFS_FS	Enables you to mount Network File System (NFS) directories from other systems on a network. Answer y if you want to access NFS directories.
CONFIG_NTFS_FS	Enables Linux to read from the NT file system (NTFS)—the file system used by Microsoft Windows NT. Answer y here for read-only access to an NTFS partition on the hard disk.
CONFIG_PROC_FS	Turns on support for the /proc virtual file system through which you can get information about the kernel. (For example, type the cat /proc/interrupts command to list the IRQs used by the system.) The /proc file system does not exist on the disk; files are created when you access them. You should answer y to enable this option because it is useful and several Linux system utilities rely on the /proc file system.
CONFIG_QNX4FS_FS	Supports the file system used by the QNX 4 operating system—a popular real-time operating system (http://www.qnx.com/). Answer y if you intend to mount QNX hard disks or floppies for read-only access.
CONFIG_QUOTA	Turns on disk quota so you can limit each user's disk space. Answer y only if your system has many users and you want to implement disk quota for the ext2 file system.
CONFIG_ROMFS_FS	Turns on support for a very small, read-only, memory-resident file system used in the initial RAM disk (initrd) during Red Hat Linux installation. Answer y to include support for this file system. Consult the file /usr/src/linux-2.4/ Documentation/filesystems/romfs.txt for more information.

(continued)

Table 21-2: *(continued)*

Option	Description
CONFIG_SMB_FS	Enables your Linux system to access shared directories from networked PCs running Windows 95/98/NT/2000 or Windows for Workgroups. Answer y if you want to access shared directories on Windows systems.
CONFIG_SYSV_FS	Turns on support for the System V file system used by SCO, Xenix, and Coherent variants of UNIX for Intel PCs. If you need to access a System V file system, answer y here.
CONFIG_UFS_FS	Allows your Linux system to read to (but not write to) the UFS file system used by the BSD (Berkeley Software Distribution) variants of UNIX (such as SunOS, FreeBSD, NetBSD, and NeXTstep). Answer y if you need to access any UFS file system. If you also want to write to UFS file systems, answer y to the experimental CONFIG_UFS_FS_WRITE option.
CONFIG_UMSDOS_FS	Supports the UMSDOS file system, which stores a Linux file system in a FAT or VFAT partition. You have to also include support for FAT or VFAT file system to support the UMSDOS file system.
CONFIG_VFAT_FS	Supports Windows 95/98/NT/2000 VFAT file systems with long filenames. Answer y if your system has partitions with VFAT file systems, or you expect to read floppy disks with Windows files.

Linux can read and manipulate disk partitions created by many different systems. The next option enables you to include support for specific partition types:

```
*
* Partition Types
*
Advanced partition selection (CONFIG_PARTITION_ADVANCED) [Y/n/?]
  Acorn partition support (CONFIG_ACORN_PARTITION) [N/y/?]
  Alpha OSF partition support (CONFIG_OSF_PARTITION) [Y/n/?]
  Amiga partition table support (CONFIG_AMIGA_PARTITION) [N/y/?]
  Atari partition table support (CONFIG_ATARI_PARTITION) [N/y/?]
  Macintosh partition map support (CONFIG_MAC_PARTITION) [Y/n/?]
  PC BIOS (MSDOS partition tables) support (CONFIG_MSDOS_PARTITION) [Y/n/?]
    BSD disklabel (FreeBSD partition tables) support (CONFIG_BSD_DISKLABEL) [Y/n/?]
    Minix subpartition support (CONFIG_MINIX_SUBPARTITION) [Y/n/?]
    Solaris (x86) partition table support (CONFIG_SOLARIS_X86_PARTITION) [Y/n/?]

    Unixware slices support (CONFIG_UNIXWARE_DISKLABEL) [Y/n/?]
  Windows Logical Disk Manager (Dynamic Disk) support (EXPERIMENTAL)
(CONFIG_LDM_PARTITION) [N/y/?]
  SGI partition support (CONFIG_SGI_PARTITION) [Y/n/?]
  Ultrix partition table support (CONFIG_ULTRIX_PARTITION) [N/y/?]
  Sun partition tables support (CONFIG_SUN_PARTITION) [Y/n/?]
  EFI GUID Partition support (CONFIG_EFI_PARTITION) [N/y/?]
```

Selecting a Native Language Character Set

Next comes a set of configuration options that requires you to select a native language character set. The Microsoft FAT file systems use these character sets to store and display filenames in one of several languages. The character sets are stored in files called DOS codepages. You have to include the appropriate codepages so that the Linux kernel can read and write filenames correctly in any DOS partitions in the hard disk. Note that the codepages apply only to filenames; they have nothing to do with the actual contents of files.

You can include support for as many codepages as you want. Simply answer Yes to the codepages for your selection of languages.

Configuring the Console Drivers

After selecting the natural language support for DOS file systems, you have to configure the console drivers that the kernel can use to display text output without the X Window System. You definitely want to answer Yes to the CONFIG_VGA_CONSOLE option, which allows the kernel to display output in text mode using generic VGA mode (supported by nearly all video cards). Most of the other console drivers are experimental. A new feature is the CONFIG_FB option, which can enable support for frame-buffer devices. A frame buffer is an abstraction for the graphics hardware so that the kernel and other software can produce graphical output without having to rely on low-level details (such as hardware registers) of a video card. Frame buffer support is available for a few specific video cards.

Configuring the Sound Card

The next set of options involves sound-card support. If you have a sound card installed, start by answering y or m to the CONFIG_SOUND option. After that, you have to answer a number of questions about various sound cards. You can always answer m to build the sound support in the form of modules you can load when needed.

Enabling USB Support

The next set of options enables support for the Universal Serial Bus (USB)—a serial bus that comes built into most new PCs. USB version 1.1 supports data-transfer rates as high as 12 Mbps—12 million bits per second or 1.5 megabytes per second—compared with 115 Kbps or the 0.115 Mbps transfer rate of a standard serial port (such as COM1). You can daisy-chain up to 127 devices on a USB bus. The bus also provides power to the devices, and you can attach or remove devices while the PC is running—a capability commonly referred to as hot swapping. USB version 2.0 (or USB 2.0 or USB2, for short) ups the ante by raising the data transfer rates to a whopping 480 Mbps, slightly faster than the competing IEEE 1394 (FireWire) bus.

USB can replace the functionality of the PC's serial and parallel ports, as well as the keyboard and mouse ports. Nowadays, many PC peripherals—such as mouse, keyboard, printer, scanner, modem, digital camera, memory card, and so on—are designed to connect to the PC through a USB port.

If your PC has a USB port, you should answer y or m to the CONFIG_USB option. Then, you have to answer m to the CONFIG_USB_UHCI or CONFIG_USB_OHCI option, depending on the type of USB interface—UHCI (Intel) or OHCI (Compaq and others) —your PC has. To determine the type of USB interface, type the /sbin/lspci command, and look for the USB controller's make and model in the output. For example, here's the output from /sbin/lspci for a PC with a USB port:

```
/sbin/lspci
00:00.0 Host bridge: Intel Corp. 82845 845 (Brookdale) Chipset Host Bridge (rev
05)
```

```
00:01.0 PCI bridge: Intel Corp. 82845 845 (Brookdale) Chipset AGP Bridge (rev 05)
00:1d.0 USB Controller: Intel Corp. 82801CA/CAM USB (Hub #1) (rev 02)
00:1d.1 USB Controller: Intel Corp. 82801CA/CAM USB (Hub #2) (rev 02)
00:1e.0 PCI bridge: Intel Corp. 82801BAM/CAM PCI Bridge (rev 42)
00:1f.0 ISA bridge: Intel Corp. 82801CAM ISA Bridge (LPC) (rev 02)
00:1f.1 IDE interface: Intel Corp. 82801CAM IDE U100 (rev 02)
00:1f.3 SMBus: Intel Corp. 82801CA/CAM SMBus (rev 02)
00:1f.5 Multimedia audio controller: Intel Corp. 82801CA/CAM AC'97 Audio (rev 02)
00:1f.6 Modem: Intel Corp. 82801CA/CAM AC'97 Modem (rev 02)
01:00.0 VGA compatible controller: nVidia Corporation NV11 [GeForce2 Go] (rev b2)
02:01.0 Ethernet controller: 3Com Corporation 3c905C-TX/TX-M [Tornado] (rev 78)
02:04.0 CardBus bridge: O2 Micro, Inc. OZ6912 Cardbus Controller
```

As the output shows, this PC has an Intel USB controller. Therefore, I need the driver module for the Intel UHCI support (CONFIG_USB_UHCI option).

After you select the UHCI or OHCI interface support, you have to build the driver modules for specific USB devices on your system. Linux supports a huge number of USB devices. For more information on USB devices, consult the documentation in the `/usr/src/linux-2.4/Documentation/usb` directory—especially the links in the `usb-help.txt` file.

Enabling Bluetooth Support

The next few options are for enabling support for Bluetooth—a low-power, short-range wireless technology for connecting devices on the 2.4 GHz frequency band. Devices that use Bluetooth can usually connect when they are within 10 meters of one another. To learn more about Bluetooth, visit `http://www.bluetooth.com/`.

Linux supports Bluetooth through a core driver and several other modules. You can answer y to the `CONFIG_BLUEZ` option to enable Bluetooth support and then select other options specific to your Bluetooth devices.

Enabling Support for Kernel Debugging

The next and final set of options enables you to use the SysRq key (equivalent to pressing Alt-PrintScreen) to get important status information right after a system crash. This information is useful if you are a Linux developer who expects to debug the kernel. Most users answer No (because most users run a stable version of the kernel and do not expect to fix kernel errors) to disable these options.

The kernel configuration session ends with the following message, which tells you to type the command `make dep` before building the kernel.

```
*** End of Linux kernel configuration.
*** Check the top-level Makefile for additional configuration.
*** Next, you must run 'make dep'.
```

Building the Kernel

You should initiate the next three tasks by using a single command line (Linux enables you to enter multiple semicolon-separated commands on the same line) so that you can type the line, then press Enter, and take a break. This part takes a while.

Depending on your system, making a new kernel can take anywhere from a few minutes to over an hour. Type the following on a single line to initiate the process:

```
make dep; make clean; make zImage
```

The `make dep` command determines which files have changed and what needs to be compiled again. The `make clean` command deletes old, unneeded files (such as old copies of the kernel). Finally, `make zImage` creates the new kernel in a compressed file and places it in a certain directory.

Secret

If you link too many features into the kernel (by answering Yes to configuration options), the kernel file size may be too big to fit in the 640K of memory a PC can use as it boots up. This 640K limit exists because Intel x86 processors start in real mode and can only access 1MB of memory, of which 640K is available for programs. This limit is a leftover from the old MS-DOS days, and it applies only as the Linux kernel is initially loaded as the PC starts. In this case, the `make` command displays an error message such as the following:

```
System is too big. Try using bzImage or modules.
```

If you get a "System too big" error, type **make bzImage** to use a different type of compressed kernel that may fit within the memory limits. Otherwise, go through the `make config` step again, and eliminate unnecessary features by answering No to those configuration questions. For other features you really need or may want to try out, type **m** to create modules. Although the kernel size is limited at startup, the kernel can load as many modules as it needs once the boot process is complete.

As the kernel is built, you see a lot of messages on the screen. When it's all over, there is a new kernel in the form of a compressed file named `zImage` in the `/usr/src/linux-2.4/arch/i386/boot` directory.

To use the new kernel, you have to copy the kernel to the `/boot` directory under a specific name and edit the `/etc/grub.conf` file to set up GRUB—the new boot loader. You learn these steps in the section, "Installing the New Kernel and Setting up GRUB" later in this chapter. Before you proceed with the kernel installation, however, you have to build and install the modules.

Building and Installing the Modules

If you select any modules during the kernel configuration, you have to build the modules and install them. Perform these tasks with the following steps:

1. Type the following commands to build the modules:
   ```
   cd /usr/src/linux
   make modules
   ```

2. The current set of modules in a directory is named after the version of Linux kernel your system is running. For example, if your system runs kernel version 2.4.20-2.48, the modules are in the following directory:
   ```
   /lib/modules/2.4.20-2.48
   ```
   Move the module directory to a new location as follows:
   ```
   mv /lib/modules/2.4.20-2.48 /lib/modules/2.4.20-2.48-old
   ```

3. Install the new modules with the following command:
   ```
   make modules_install
   ```

Now you can install the kernel and make it available for GRUB to boot.

Installing the New Kernel and Setting up GRUB

Red Hat Linux uses GRUB to load the Linux kernel from the disk. The configuration file /etc/grub.conf lists the kernel binary that GRUB runs. You can examine the contents of the GRUB configuration file by typing the following command:

```
cat /etc/grub.conf
```

Here is what I see when I try this command on one of my systems with a SCSI adapter:

```
# grub.conf generated by anaconda
#
# Note that you do not have to rerun grub after making changes to this file
# NOTICE:  You have a /boot partition.  This means that
#          all kernel and initrd paths are relative to /boot/, eg.
#          root (hd0,2)
#          kernel /vmlinuz-version ro root=/dev/hda5
#          initrd /initrd-version.img
#boot=/dev/hda
default=0
timeout=10
splashimage=(hd0,2)/grub/splash.xpm.gz
title Red Hat Linux (2.4.20-2.48)
        root (hd0,2)
        kernel /vmlinuz-2.4.20-2.48 ro root=LABEL=/
        initrd /initrd-2.4.20-2.48.img
title Windows XP
        rootnoverify (hd0,1)
        chainloader +1
```

You learn more about GRUB and its configuration file (/etc/grub.conf) by typing info grub in a terminal window. For this discussion, you should note the following:

♦ The default=0 line specifies the first boot entry as the default one that GRUB should boot.

♦ The timeout=10 command causes GRUB to boot the default entry automatically after waiting for 10 seconds. If other boot entries are in the file, the user may select another one from a boot menu GRUB displays.

♦ The four lines starting with title Red Hat Linux (2.4.20-2.48) define a specific kernel file GRUB can boot. You can make GRUB boot another kernel by adding a similar section to the configuration file.

♦ The root (hd0,2) line sets the root device to the third partition of the first hard disk.

♦ The kernel /vmlinuz-2.4.20-2.48 ro root=LABEL=/ line identifies the kernel GRUB loads. In this case, the kernel file is vmlinuz-2.4.20-2.48, which is located in the root device—the third partition on the first hard disk. In my system, that partition is mounted on the /boot directory. In other words, GRUB loads the kernel file /boot/vmlinuz-2.4.20-2.48. The root=LABEL=/ part of the line specifies that the Linux root file system is on the device whose label is /. This location may differ on your system.

- The `initrd /initrd-2.4.20-2.48.img` line specifies a file that contains an initial RAM disk (`initrd` stands for initial RAM disk) image that serves as a file system before the disks are available. The Linux kernel uses the RAM disk—a block of memory used as a disk—to get started, then it loads other driver modules and begins using the hard disk.

On systems that have a Windows partition, the GRUB configuration file typically includes another section with details for the operating system (perhaps Windows 98, Windows 2000, or Windows XP) on that partition.

To configure GRUB to boot yet another kernel (the one you just built), you need to follow these steps:

1. Copy the new kernel binary to the `/boot` directory. The new, compressed kernel file is in the `/usr/src/linux-2.4/arch/i386/boot` directory. If you have typed the command `make zImage`, the kernel filename is `zImage`; if you have built the kernel with the `make bzImage` command, the filename is `bzImage`. I simply copy that file to the `/boot` directory with the same name:

   ```
   cp /usr/src/linux-2.4/arch/i386/boot/zImage /boot
   ```

   If the kernel filename is `bzImage`, make sure you use `bzImage` instead of `zImage`. You can use any other filename you want, as long as you use the same filename when referring to the kernel in the `/etc/grub.conf` file in Step 3.

2. Save the old `System.map` file in the `/boot` directory, and copy the new map file. (I assume you have rebuilt kernel version 2.4.20-2.48 after changing some configuration options):

   ```
   mv /boot/System.map-2.4.20-2.48 /boot/System.map-2.4.20-2.48-old
   cp /usr/src/linux*/System.map /boot/System.map-2.4.20-2.48
   cd /boot
   ln -s System.map-2.4.20-2.48 System.map
   ```

3. Use your favorite text editor to edit the `/etc/grub.conf` file to add the following lines just after the `splashimage` line in the file. (If you need help with a text editor, consult Chapter 14 to learn about vi and Emacs—two popular text editors for Linux):

   ```
   title Red Hat Linux (2.4.20-2.48 NEW)
           root (hd0,2)
           kernel /zImage ro root=LABEL=/
   ```

   Note that I do not show the `initrd` line anymore because I assume you are no longer using a modular SCSI driver even if your system has a SCSI adapter.

4. Save the `grub.conf` file, and exit the editor.

---

caution

On your system, you should make sure the `root (hd0,2)` line is correct—instead of `(hd0,2)`, you should list the correct disk partition where the Linux `/boot` file system is located. Also, make sure that you use the correct filename for the kernel image file (for example, `/boot/bzImage` if the kernel file is so named).

After preparing the `/etc/grub.conf` file, you are ready to reboot the system and try out the new kernel.

Rebooting the System to Test the New Kernel

While you are still logged in as root, type the following command to reboot the system:

```
reboot
```

When you see the GRUB screen, select the name you have assigned to the new kernel in the /etc/grub.conf file.

Secret

After the system reboots with the new kernel, you should see the familiar graphical login screen. To see proof that you are indeed running the new kernel, log in as a user, open a terminal window, and type **uname -srv**. This command shows you the kernel version, as well as the date and time when this kernel was built. If you have upgraded the kernel source, you should see the version number for the new kernel. If you have simply rebuilt the kernel for the same old kernel version, the date and time should match the time when you rebuilt the kernel. That's your proof that the system is running the new kernel.

If the system hangs (nothing seems to happen—there is no output on the screen and no disk activity), you may have skipped a step during the kernel rebuild. You can power the PC off and on to reboot. This time, select the name of the old working kernel at the GRUB screen.

If you cannot boot the older version of Red Hat Linux either, use the emergency boot disk (containing an earlier, but working, version of Linux) to start the system. Then, you can repeat the kernel rebuild and installation process, making sure you follow all the steps correctly.

Summary

Most Red Hat Linux software comes in Red Hat Package Manager (RPM) files, and many open-source software packages are provided in source-code form (usually in compressed archives). Therefore, you need to know how to work with RPM files and how to build software from source code. In addition, from time to time, you may have to get some updates or bug fixes and rebuild the Linux kernel. This chapter showed you how to install RPM files, download source code and build programs, and use the Red Hat Update Agent to update Red Hat Linux packages. Also, you learned how to build and install a new kernel. Moreover, this chapter showed you how to download and install new updates from Red Hat in the form of Red Hat Package Manager (RPM) files.

By reading this chapter, you learned the following:

♦ Red Hat Package Manager (RPM) is a system for packaging all the necessary files for a software product in a single file. The file is referred to as an RPM file, a package, or simply an RPM. Red Hat Linux is distributed in the form of a lot of RPMs.

♦ You can use the rpm commands or the Red Hat Package Management graphical tool to work with RPM files. You learn to use the Package Management graphical utility with which you can install and uninstall entire package groups—collections of many related RPM files. In addition, you learn the syntax of a number of RPM commands used to query, install, upgrade, remove, and verify RPMs.

◆ To download and install open-source software distributed in source-code form, use FTP to download and tar to unpack; then read the README file for installation instructions. Typically, you have to run a configure script to create a Makefile and to run the make command to build the software. Using the X Multimedia System (XMMS) package as an example, this chapter shows you how to build the software and install it.

◆ You can register with the Red Hat Network and use the Red Hat Update Agent to download and install any updates to various packages that make up Red Hat Linux. This chapter shows you how to register and use the Red Hat Update Agent.

◆ The term kernel refers to the core Linux operating system—the program that makes your PC a Linux PC.

◆ You can upgrade to a new version of the Linux kernel for Red Hat Linux from one of the mirror sites listed at http://www.redhat.com/download/mirror. html. The updates are organized in directories according to Red Hat Linux version numbers. For example, any updates for Red Hat Linux 9 for Intel x86 systems appear in the 9/en/os/i386 directory.

◆ You can rebuild the Linux kernel to add support for experimental devices or build a kernel customized to include support for only devices that your PC has.

◆ Before rebuilding the kernel, you should prepare an emergency boot disk so that you can restart the system if something goes wrong with the kernel rebuild process.

◆ To rebuild the kernel, change the directory to /usr/src/linux-2.4 and use the make command. You have to follow the sequence make config; make dep; make clean; make zImage (in that order). If you get a "System too big" error, you should try the make bzImage command. You have also to use the commands make modules and make modules_install.

◆ To make a new kernel available for booting, you have to copy the new kernel file to the /boot directory and edit the GRUB configuration file /etc/grub.conf so that it includes information about the new kernel file.

System and Network Security

◆ ◆

Secrets in This Chapter

◆ ◆

As a systems administrator, you have to worry about your Red Hat Linux system's security. For a standalone system, or a system used in an isolated local area network (LAN), you have to focus on protecting the system from the users and the users from one another. In other words, you do not want a user to modify or delete system files, whether intentionally or unintentionally. Also, you do not want a user destroying another user's files.

If your Linux system is connected to the Internet, you must worry about securing the system from unwanted access by outsiders over the Internet. These intruders, also known as *crackers*, typically impersonate a user, steal or destroy information, and even deny you access to your own system (this is known as a denial-of-service attack).

By its very nature, an Internet connection makes your system accessible to any other system on the Internet. After all, the Internet connects many networks across the globe. In fact, the client/server architecture of Internet information services, such as HTTP (Web) and FTP, rely on the wide-open network access the Internet provides. Unfortunately, the easy accessibility to Internet services running on your system also means anyone on the Net can easily access your system.

If you operate an Internet host that provides information to others, you certainly want everyone to access your system's Internet services, such as FTP and Web servers. However, these servers often have vulnerabilities that crackers can exploit in order to cause harm to your system. You need to know about the potential security risks of Internet services and the precautions you can take to minimize the risk of someone exploiting the weaknesses of your FTP or Web server.

You may also want to protect your company's internal network from outsiders, even though your goal is to provide information to the outside world through a Web server. You can protect your internal network by setting up an Internet firewall—a controlled access point to the internal network—and placing the Web and FTP servers on a host outside the firewall.

This chapter takes you through the basic steps you should follow in securing your Red Hat Linux system. You also learn about setting up an Internet firewall and running Web and FTP servers outside the firewall, where users cannot break through and access your company's internal network. As you'll see, Red Hat Linux already includes many of the tools you need to maintain system security. You can even set up a packet-filtering firewall by using the iptables software that comes with Red Hat Linux.

insider insight

To learn more about Linux security, consult the Linux Security HOWTO at `http://www.ibiblio.org/pub/Linux/docs/HOWTO/Security-HOWTO`. **Another good resource is the Linux Administrator's Security Guide, which you can read online at** `http://www.seifried.org/lasg/`.

Establishing a Security Framework

The first step in securing your Linux system is to set up a security policy. The security policy is your guide to what you enable users (as well as visitors over the Internet) to do on the Linux system. The level of security you establish depends on how you use the Linux system and how much is at risk if someone gains unauthorized access to your system.

If you are a system administrator for Linux systems at an organization, you probably want to involve the management, as well as the users, in setting up the security policy. Obviously, you cannot create an imposing policy that prevents everyone from working on the system. On the other hand, if the users are creating or using data valuable to the organization, you have to set up a policy that protects the data from disclosure to outsiders. In other words, the security policy should strike a balance between the users' needs and the need to protect the system.

For a standalone Linux system or a home system you occasionally connect to the Internet, the security policy can be just a listing of the Internet services you want to run on the system and the user accounts you plan to set up on the system.

Secret

For a larger organization that has one or more Linux systems on a LAN connected to the Internet—preferably through a firewall (a device that controls the flow of Internet Protocol (IP) packets between the LAN and the Internet)—it is best to think of computer security across the entire organization systematically. Figure 22-1 shows the key elements of an organization-wide framework to computer security (some call this the *security architecture*).

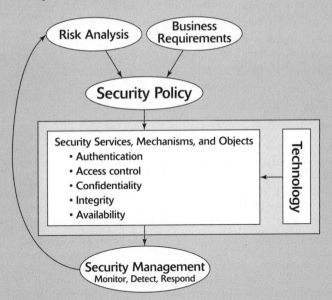

Figure 22-1: An Organization-wide Framework for Computer Security.

Such an organization-wide computer security framework includes the following key elements:

- Determining business requirements for security
- Performing risk analysis
- Establishing a security policy
- Implementing security solutions to mitigate identified security risks
- Managing security continuously

The next few sections explain these elements of the security framework.

Determining Business Requirements for Security

The security framework outlined in Figure 22-1 starts with the development of a security policy based on business requirements and risk analysis. The business requirements identify the security needs of the business—the computer resources and information you have to protect (including any requirements imposed by applicable laws, such as the requirement to protect the privacy of some types of data). Typical security requirements might include items such as the following:

◆ Enable access to information by authorized users.

◆ Implement business rules that specify who has access to what information.

◆ Employ a strong user-authentication system.

◆ Deny malicious or destructive actions on data.

◆ Protect data from end to end as it moves across networks.

◆ Implement all security and privacy requirements that applicable laws impose.

Performing Risk Analysis

Risk analysis involves determining the following and performing some analysis to establish the priority of handling the risks:

◆ **Threats**—What you are protecting against

◆ **Vulnerabilities**—The weaknesses that might be exploited (these are the risks)

◆ **Probability**—The likelihood that a vulnerability will be exploited

◆ **Impact**—The effect of exploiting a specific vulnerability

◆ **Mitigation**—What to do to reduce the vulnerabilities

Before I describe risk analysis, here are some typical threats to computer security:

◆ **Denial of service**—The computer and network are tied up so that legitimate users cannot make use of the systems. For businesses, denial of service can mean loss of revenue.

◆ **Unauthorized access**—Use of the computer and network by someone who is not an authorized user. The unauthorized user can steal information or maliciously corrupt or destroy data. Some businesses may be hurt by the negative publicity from the mere act of an unauthorized user gaining access to the system, even if there is no explicit damage to any data.

◆ **Disclosure of information to the public**—The unauthorized release of information to the public. For example, the disclosure of a password file enables potential attackers to figure out user name and password combinations for accessing a system. Exposure of other sensitive information, such as financial and medical data, might be a potential liability for a business.

These threats come from exploitation of vulnerabilities in your organization's computer and human resources. Some common vulnerabilities are the following:

◆ People (divulging passwords, losing security cards, and so on)

◆ Internal network connections (routers, switches)

◆ Interconnection points (gateways—routers and firewalls—between the Internet and the internal network)

◆ Third-party network providers (ISPs, long-distance carriers)

- Operating-system security holes (potential holes in Internet servers, such as sendmail, named, bind, and so on)
- Application security holes (known security holes in specific applications)

Secret

To perform risk analysis, assign a numeric value to the probability and impact of each potential vulnerability. A workable risk analysis approach is to do the following for each vulnerability or risk:

1. Assign subjective ratings of Low, Medium, and High for the probability of a risk. As the ratings suggest, Low means a lesser chance that the vulnerability will be exploited; High means there is a greater chance.

2. Assign similar ratings to the impact of a risk. What you consider impact is up to you. Businesses often assess the impact by estimating the monetary damages resulting from a risk event. If the exploitation of a vulnerability will affect your business greatly, assign it a High impact.

3. Assign a numeric value to the three levels—Low = 1, Medium = 2, and High = 3—for both probability and impact.

4. Compute a numerical risk level by multiplying the numerical values of probability and impact. Then, make a decision to develop and implement protections for vulnerabilities that exceed a specific threshold for the risk level—the product of probability and impact. For example, you may choose to handle all vulnerabilities with a probability times impact—risk level—greater than 6.

If you want to characterize the probability and impact with a finer level of granularity, pick a scale of 1 through 5, for example, and follow the same steps as before.

Establishing a Security Policy

Based on the risk analysis and any business requirements you may need to address regardless of risk level, you can craft a security policy for the organization. The security policy typically addresses the following areas:

- **Authentication**—What method will be used to ensure that a user is the real user? Who gets access to the system? What is the minimum length and complexity of passwords? How often do users change passwords? How long can a user be idle before that user is logged out automatically?

- **Authorization**—What can different classes of users do on the system? Who can have the root password?

- **Data protection**—What data must be protected? Who has access to the data? Is encryption necessary for some data?

- **Internet access**—What are the restrictions on users (from the LAN) accessing the Internet? What Internet services (such as Web, Internet Relay Chat, and so on) can users access? Are incoming emails and attachments scanned for viruses? Is there a network firewall? Are virtual private networks (VPNs) used to connect private networks across the Internet?

- **Internet services**—What Internet services are allowed on each Linux system? Are there any file servers? Mail servers? Web servers? What services run on each type of server? What services, if any, run on Linux systems used as desktop workstations?

⬩ **Security audits**—Who tests whether the security is adequate? How often is the security tested? How are problems found during security testing handled?

⬩ **Incident handling**—What are the procedures for handling any computer security incidents? Who must be informed? What information must be gathered to help with the investigation of incidents?

⬩ **Responsibilities**—Who is responsible for maintaining security? Who applies patches and upgrades system software to fix security holes? Who monitors log files and audit trails for signs of unauthorized access? Who maintains the database of security policy?

Implementing Security Solutions

After you analyze the risks—vulnerabilities—and develop a security policy, you have to select the mitigation approach: how to protect against specific vulnerabilities. This is where you develop an overall security solution based on security policy, business requirements, and available technology—a solution that consists of the following:

⬩ Services (authentication, access control, encryption)

⬩ Mechanisms (user name/password, firewalls)

⬩ Objects (hardware, software)

Managing Security Continuously

In addition to implementing security solutions, you have to set up security management that continually monitors, detects, and responds to any security incidents.

The combination of the risk analysis, security policy, security solutions, and security management provides the overall security framework. Such a framework helps establish a common level of understanding of security and a common basis for the design and implementation of security solutions.

The remainder of this chapter shows you some of the ways in which you can enhance and maintain the security of your Red Hat Linux system and any network.

Securing Red Hat Linux

After you have defined a security policy, you can proceed to secure the system according to the policy. The exact steps depend on what you want to do with the system—whether it is a server or a workstation and how many users must access the system.

To secure the Red Hat Linux system, you have to handle two broad categories of security issues:

⬩ *Host security* issues that relate to securing the operating system and the files and directories on the system.

⬩ *Network security* issues that refer to the threat of attacks over the network connection.

Understanding the Host Security Issues

Here are some high-level guidelines to address host security (The "Securing the Host" section covers some of these topics in detail):

♦ When installing Red Hat Linux, select only those package groups you need for your system. Do not install unnecessary software. For example, if your system is used as a workstation, you do not need to install most of the servers (Web server, news server, and so on).

♦ Create initial user accounts and make sure all passwords are strong ones that password-cracking programs can't "guess." Red Hat Linux includes tools to enforce strong passwords.

♦ Set file ownerships and permissions to protect important files and directories. In particular, understand which programs are set-UID and set-GID and remove such permissions from files where they are not needed. Use the new access control lists (ACLs) to manage who gets to use which files and directories.

♦ Use the GNU Privacy Guard (GnuPG) to encrypt or decrypt files with sensitive information and to authenticate files that you download from Red Hat. GnuPG comes with Red Hat Linux, and you can use the gpg command to perform the tasks such as encrypting or decrypting a file and digitally sign a file.

♦ Regularly apply patches and upgrades that correct known security problems. When downloading and installing upgrades, check the MD5 checksums and digital signatures to ensure the integrity of the downloaded files.

♦ Use file-integrity checking tools, such as Tripwire, to monitor any changes to crucial system files and directories.

♦ Periodically check various log files for signs of any break-ins or attempted break-ins. These log files are in the /var/log directory of your system.

♦ Install security updates from Red Hat, as soon as they become available. These security updates fix known vulnerabilities in Red Hat Linux.

Understanding Network Security Issues

The issue of security comes up as soon as you connect your organization's internal network to the Internet. This is true even if you connect a single computer to the Internet, but security concerns are more pressing when an entire internal network is opened to the world.

If you are an experienced system administrator, you already know that it's not the cost of managing an Internet presence that worries corporate management; their main concern is security. To get your management's backing for the website, you need to lay out a plan to keep the corporate network secure from intruders.

You may think that you can avoid jeopardizing the internal network by connecting only the external servers, such as Web and FTP servers, to the Internet. However, this simplistic approach is not wise. It is like deciding not to drive because you may have an accident. Not having a network connection between your Web server and your internal network also has the following drawbacks:

♦ You cannot use network file transfers, such as FTP, to copy documents and data from your internal network to the Web server.

♦ Users on the internal network cannot access the corporate Web server.

♦ Users on the internal network do not have access to Web servers on the Internet. Such a restriction makes a valuable resource—the Web—inaccessible to the users in your organization.

A practical solution to this problem is to set up an Internet firewall and to put the Web server on a highly secured host outside the firewall.

In addition to using a firewall, here are some of the other steps you should take to address network security (the "Securing the Network" section explain these further):

- Enable only those Internet services you need on a system. In particular, do not enable services that are not properly configured.
- Use secure shell (ssh) for remote logins. Do not use the "r" commands, such as rlogin and rsh.
- Secure any Internet services such as FTP or Telnet that you want to run on your system. You can use the TCP wrapper access control files—/etc/hosts.allow and /etc/hosts.deny—to secure some of these services.
- Promptly fix any known vulnerabilities of Internet services that you choose to run. Typically, you'd do this by downloading and installing the latest server RPM file from Red Hat.

Learning Computer Security Terminology

Computer books, magazine articles, and experts on computer security use a number of terms with unique meanings. You need to know these terms to understand discussions about computer security (and to communicate effectively with security vendors). Table 22-1 describes some of the commonly used computer security terms.

Table 22-1: Commonly Used Computer Security Terminology

Term	Description
Application gateway	A proxy service that acts as a gateway for application-level protocols, such as FTP, Telnet, and HTTP
Authentication	The process of confirming that a user is indeed who he or she claims to be. The typical authentication method is a challenge-response method, wherein the user enters a user name and secret password to confirm his or her identity.
Backdoor	A security weakness a cracker places on a host in order to bypass security features
Bastion host	A highly secured computer that serves as an organization's main point of presence on the Internet. A bastion host typically resides on the perimeter network, but a dual-homed host (with one network interface connected to the Internet and the other to the internal network) is also a bastion host.
Buffer overflow	A security flaw in a program that enables a cracker to send an excessive amount of data to that program and to overwrite parts of the running program with code in the data being sent. The result is that the cracker can execute arbitrary code on the system and possibly gain access to the system as a privileged user.
Certificate	An electronic document that identifies an entity (such as an individual, an organization, or a computer) and associates a public key with that identity. A certificate contains the certificate holder's name, a serial number, expiration dates, a copy of the certificate holder's public key, and the digital signature of the Certificate Authority so that a recipient can verify that the certificate is real.

Term	Description
Certificate Authority (CA)	An organization that validates identities and issues certificates
Cracker	A person who breaks into (or attempts to break into) a host, often with malicious intent
Confidentiality	Of data, a state of being accessible by no one but you (usually achieved by encryption)
Decryption	The process of transforming encrypted information into its original, intelligible form
Denial of service (DoS)	An attack that uses so many of the resources on your computer and network that legitimate users cannot access and use the system
Digital signature	A one-way MD5 or SHA-1 hash of a message encrypted with the private key of the message originator, used to verify the integrity of a message and ensure nonrepudiation
DMZ	Another name for the perimeter network. (DMZ stands for demilitarized zone, the buffer zone separating North and South Korea.)
Dual-homed host	A computer with two network interfaces (think of each network as a home)
Encryption	The process of transforming information so that it is unintelligible to anyone but the intended recipient. The transformation is accomplished by a mathematical operation between a key and the information.
Firewall	A controlled-access gateway between an organization's internal network and the Internet. A dual-homed host can be configured as a firewall.
Hash	A mathematical function converts a message into a fixed-size numeric value known as a message digest or hash. The MD5 algorithm produces a 128-bit message digest, whereas the Secure Hash Algorithm-1 (SHA-1) generates a 160-bit message digest. The hash of a message is encrypted with the private key of the sender to produce the digital signature.
Host	A computer on any network (so called because it offers many services)
Integrity	Of received data, a state of being the same data that were sent (unaltered in transit)
IPSec (IP Security Protocol)	A security protocol for the network layer that is designed to provide cryptographic security services for IP packets. IPSec provides encryption-based authentication, integrity, access control, and confidentiality (visit `www.ietf.org/html.charters/ipsec-charter.html` for the list of RFCs related to IPSec).
IP spoofing	An attack in which a cracker figures out the IP address of a trusted host and then sends packets that appear to come from the trusted host. The attacker can only send packets, but cannot see any responses. However, the attacker can predict the sequence of packets and essentially send commands that will set up a back door for future break-ins.

(continued)

Table 22-1: (continued)

Term	Description
Nonrepudiation	A security feature that prevents the sender of data from being able to deny ever having sent the data
Packet	A collection of bytes that serve as the basic unit of communication on a network. On TCP/IP networks, the packet may be referred to as an IP packet or a TCP/IP packet.
Packet filtering	Selective blocking of packets based on the type of packet (as specified by the source and destination IP address or port)
Perimeter network	A network between the Internet and the protected internal network. The bastion host resides on the perimeter network (also known as the DMZ).
Port scanning	A method for discovering which ports are open (in other words, which Internet services are enabled) on a system. Performed by sending connection requests to the ports one by one. This is usually a precursor to further attacks.
Proxy server	A server on the bastion host that enables internal clients to access external servers (and enables external clients to access servers inside the protected network). There are proxy servers for various Internet services, such as FTP and HTTP.
Public-key cryptography	An encryption method that uses a pair of keys, a private key and a public key, to encrypt and decrypt the information. Anything encrypted with the public key can be decrypted with the corresponding private key, and vice versa.
Public Key Infrastructure (PKI)	A set of standards and services that enables the use of public-key cryptography and certificates in a networked environment. PKI facilitates tasks, such as issuing, renewing, and revoking certificates, and generating and distributing public-private key pairs.
Screening router	An Internet router that filters packets
Setuid program	A program that runs with the permissions of the owner regardless of who runs the program. For example, if a setuid program is owned by root, that program has root privileges regardless of who has started the program. Crackers often exploit vulnerabilities in setuid programs to gain privileged access to a system.
Symmetric-key encryption	An encryption method wherein the same key is used to encrypt and decrypt the information
Threat	An event or activity, deliberate or unintentional, with the potential for causing harm to a system or network
Trojan horse	A program that masquerades as a benign program, but, in fact is a back door used for attacking a system. Attackers often install a collection of Trojan horse programs that enable the attacker to freely access the system with root privileges, yet hide that fact from the system administrator. Such collections of Trojan horse programs are called rootkits.

Term	Description
Virus	A self-replicating program that spreads from one computer to another by attaching itself to other programs
Vulnerability	A flaw or weakness that may cause harm to a system or network
Worm	A self-replicating program that copies itself from one computer to another over a network

Securing the Host

A key aspect of computer security is to secure the host—your Red Hat Linux system. The next few sections describe a few key steps you should follow in securing your Red Hat Linux host. These steps include

- ♦ Installing operating system updates
- ♦ Protecting passwords
- ♦ Protecting the files and directories
- ♦ Using encryption if necessary
- ♦ Monitoring the security of the system

You can monitor host security by examining log files for any suspicious activities and by using the Tripwire tool to see if anyone has messed with important files on your system.

Installing Operating System Updates

Red Hat Linux and related application updates come in RPM files. To manually download and install the updates, follow these steps:

1. Log in as `root` and create a directory for the updates:
   ```
   mkdir /usr/local/updates
   cd /usr/local/updates
   ```

2. Use the `wget` command to download the updates from Red Hat's FTP site. For example, to download the updates for the i386 version of Red Hat Linux version 8.0, type
   ```
   wget ftp://updates.redhat.com/8.0/en/os/i386/\*.rpm
   wget ftp://updates.redhat.com/8.0/en/os/noarch/\*.rpm
   ```

3. Install all updates with the following command:
   ```
   rpm -F *
   ```

4. Delete the update files with the command:
   ```
   rm -fr /usr/local/updates
   ```

Securing Passwords

Historically, UNIX passwords are stored in the /etc/passwd file, which any user can read. For example, a typical old-style /etc/passwd file entry for the root user looks like this:

```
root:t6Z7NWDK1K8sU:0:0:root:/root:/bin/bash
```

The fields are separated by colons (:), and the second field contains the password in encrypted form. To check if a password is valid, the login program encrypts the plaintext password the user enters and compares the password with the contents of the /etc/passwd file. If there is a match, the user is allowed to log in.

Password-cracking programs work just like the login program, except that these programs pick one word at a time from a dictionary, encrypt the word, and compare the encrypted word with the encrypted passwords in the /etc/passwd file for a match. Crackers often use multiple password-cracking programs, and some of these programs also try various manipulations of the words in the dictionary. For example, password-cracking programs try obvious manipulations of words such as:

◆ A word with a single punctuation character at the end
◆ A word with punctuation character at the beginning
◆ A word with letters in a mix of uppercase and lowercase
◆ A word written backwards
◆ Two words with a number in between

To crack the passwords, the intruder needs the /etc/passwd file. Often, crackers use weaknesses of various Internet servers (such as mail and FTP) to get a copy of the /etc/passwd file.

Recently, several improvements have made passwords more secure in Red Hat Linux. These include shadow passwords and pluggable authentication modules, and you can install these easily as you install Red Hat Linux. During Red Hat Linux installation, one step involves making selections in an Authentication Configuration screen. If you accept the default selections—Enable MD5 passwords and Enable shadow passwords—you automatically enable more-secure passwords in Red Hat Linux.

Learning the Role of Shadow Passwords

Instead of storing them in the /etc/passwd file, which any user can read, passwords are now stored in a shadow password file. On Red Hat Linux, the shadow passwords are in /etc/shadow file. Only the super user (root) can read this file, which makes it harder for crackers to get their hands on the encrypted passwords. For example, here is the entry for root in the new-style /etc/passwd file:

```
root:x:0:0:root:/root:/bin/bash
```

In this case, the second field contains an x, instead of an encrypted password.

Secret

When you use shadow passwords, the encrypted passwords are stored in the /etc/shadow file where the entry for root is like this:

```
root:$1$AAAni/yN$uESHbzUpy9Cgfoo1BfOtSO:11077:0:99999:7:-1:-
1:134540356
```

The format of the /etc/shadow entries with colon-separated fields resembles the entries in the /etc/passwd file, but the meanings of most fields differ. The first field, however, is still the user name, and the second one is the encrypted password.

In addition to improving the password file's security by storing it in the /etc/shadow file that only root can read, Red Hat Linux also improves the actual encryption of the passwords stored in the /etc/shadow file. Password encryption is now done using the MD5 message-digest algorithm that converts a plaintext password into a 128-bit fingerprint or digest. The MD5 algorithm, described in RFC 1321 (http://www .faqs.org/rfcs/rfc1321.html or http://www.cis.ohio-state.edu/cgi-bin/rfc/rfc1321.html), reduces a message of any length to a 128-bit message digest. MD5 is used to create message digests for documents so that you can digitally sign them through encryption with your private key. MD5 works quite well for password encryption, too.

Another advantage of MD5 over the older-style password encryption is that the older passwords were limited to a maximum of eight characters; new passwords (encrypted with MD5) can be much longer. Longer passwords are harder to guess, even if the /etc/shadow file falls into the wrong hands.

A clue to the use of MD5 encryption in the /etc/shadow file is the increased length of the encrypted password and the 1 prefix, as in the second field of each entry.

The remaining fields in each /etc/shadow entry control when the password expires. You do not need to interpret or change these entries in the /etc/shadow file. Instead, use the chage command to change the password-expiration information. For starters, you can check a user's password-expiration information by using the chage command with the -l option, as follows (in this case, you have to be logged in as root):

```
chage -l root
```

This command displays various expiration information, including how long the password lasts and how often you can change the password.

If you want to ensure that the user is forced to change password every 90 days, you can use the -M option to set the maximum number of days the password stays valid. For example, to make sure that user naba is prompted to change the password in 90 days, I log in as root and type the following command:

```
chage -M 90 naba
```

You can do this for each user account to ensure that all passwords expire when appropriate and that all users must pick new passwords.

Another password integrity check is to run the `pwck` command. The `pwck` command checks the entries in the `/etc/passwd` and `/etc/shadow` files for proper format and valid data in each field. To run `pwck`, type `pwck`. and follow any suggestions that the command makes.

Understanding Pluggable Authentication Modules (PAMs)

A Pluggable Authentication Module (PAM) performs the actual MD5 encryption, described in the "Learning the Role of Shadow Passwords" section. PAM provides a flexible method for authenticating users on Red Hat Linux systems. Through settings in configuration files, you can change the authentication method on the fly, without having to actually modify programs, such as `login` and `passwd`, which verify a user's identity.

Red Hat Linux uses PAM extensively, and the configuration files are in the `/etc/pam.d` directory of your system. Check out the contents of this directory on your system by typing the following command:

```
ls /etc/pam.d
```

Each configuration file in this directory specifies how users are authenticated for a specific utility. For example, there is a file for each of `login`, `passwd`, `su`, and a whole host of the GUI redhat-config utlities. Here's what I see when I type **cat /etc/pam.d/passwd file** on my system:

```
#%PAM-1.0
auth        required      pam_stack.so service=system-auth
account     required      pam_stack.so service=system-auth
password    required      pam_stack.so service=system-auth
```

These lines indicate that authentication, account management, and password checking should all be done by using the pam_stack module (`/lib/security/pam_stack.so`) with the argument `service=system-auth`. Essentially, the pam_stack module refers to another configuration file in the `/etc/pam.d` directory. In this case, the configuration file is `/etc/pam.d/system-auth`. Here's the content of the `/etc/pam.d/system-auth` file on my Red Hat Linux PC:

```
#%PAM-1.0
# This file is auto-generated.
# User changes will be destroyed the next time authconfig is run.
auth        required      /lib/security/$ISA/pam_env.so
auth        sufficient    /lib/security/$ISA/pam_unix.so likeauth nullok
auth        required      /lib/security/$ISA/pam_deny.so
account     required      /lib/security/$ISA/pam_unix.so
password    required      /lib/security/$ISA/pam_cracklib.so retry=3 type=
password    sufficient    /lib/security/$ISA/pam_unix.so nullok use_authtok md5 shadow
password    required      /lib/security/$ISA/pam_deny.so
session     required      /lib/security/$ISA/pam_limits.so
session     required      /lib/security/$ISA/pam_unix.so
```

Although I won't go over all the details, here's a brief explanation of PAM configuration files.

Secret

Each line in a PAM configuration file specifies the rules to be used for a specific type of authentication service. The general syntax of each line in a PAM configuration file is the following:

```
module-type control module-path module-arguments
```

The meaning of these four fields are as follows:

- module-type denotes the type of service being controlled by this line. The acceptable module types are: account for verifying the account (for example, whether the user's password has expired or whether a user is permitted access to the requested service); auth for authenticating a user's claimed identity, typically by using some challenge-response method where the user is asked for a password; password for updating passwords; and session for performing tasks before he user is given access to a service and after the user is done with the service.

- control determines the behavior of a PAM in case the module does not succeed in the authentication task. Typically, the control field is set to required or sufficient. If the control field is set to required, the module must be successful for the authentication to continue. If the control field is set to sufficient and the module is successful, no other checks are needed and the authentication is considered complete.

- module-path specifies the pathname of a PAM module—a shared library object—that implements the service. In the pathname /lib/security/$ISA/, ISA refers to an environment variable that you can set to a subdirectory where you decide to organize the PAM modules for your system. Typically, ISA is not defined and the PAM modules are located in the /lib/security directory.

- module-arguments lists any module-specific options that are then passed to the module. It is up to the module to parse and interpret these options. Everything after the first three fields is interpreted as module arguments.

In the /etc/pam.d/system-auth file, the first three lines are for auth service:

```
auth        required    /lib/security/$ISA/pam_env.so
auth        sufficient  /lib/security/$ISA/pam_unix.so likeauth nullok
auth        required    /lib/security/$ISA/pam_deny.so
```

Here the first auth line loads the PAM module pam_env.so that can set or unset environment variables. The second auth line specifies an authentication module that checks the user's identity by using the PAM module pam_unix.so with the arguments likeauth nullok. The options in the argument string have the following meanings:

♦ likeauth—Returns same value whether the module is used to set new credentials or authenticate an existing user name

♦ nullok—Allows blank password

The third auth line in the /etc/pam.d/system-auth file uses the pam_deny.so module to deny access to the requested service if the pam_unix.so module's authentication is unsuccessful.

Following the `auth` lines in the `/etc/pam.d/system-auth` file comes an `account` line:

```
account     required     /lib/security/$ISA/pam_unix.so
```

The `account` service uses pam_unix.so module to make sure that the user account has not expired, that the user is allowed to log in at a given time of day, and so on.

The next two `password` lines in the `/etc/pam.d/system-auth` file specify how passwords are set:

```
password    required     /lib/security/$ISA/pam_cracklib.so retry=3 type=
password    sufficient   /lib/security/$ISA/pam_unix.so nullok use_authtok md5 shadow
```

The first `password` line uses the pam_cracklib.so module to try to crack the new password (that's what the `cracklib` in the module's name indicates). The `retry=3` argument indicates that the user can try to enter a new password three times at most. The second password line indicates that the MD5 encryption is used to store the password in the `/etc/shadow` file.

The `/etc/pam.d/passwd` configuration file applies when you use the `passwd` command to change passwords. Here's an example where I am trying to change my password (the text in italic is my comment):

```
passwd
Changing password for naba
(current) UNIX password:  I type my current password
New UNIX password: I type "xyzz"
BAD PASSWORD: it is too short
New UNIX password:  I type "transport" as password
BAD PASSWORD: it is based on a dictionary word
New UNIX password:  I type "naba12" as the new password
BAD PASSWORD: it is based on your username
passwd: Authentication token manipulation error
```

In this case, the passwd program is using the PAM module to check my identity (when I first type my current password) and making sure that each of the new passwords I try are strong. Finally, the PAM modules abort the passwd program after I fail to select a good password in three tries.

Protecting Files and Directories

One important aspect of securing the host is to protect important system files and the directories that contain these files. You can protect the files through the file ownership and through the permission settings that control who can read, write, or execute (in case of executable programs) the file.

Setting File Ownership and Permissions

The default Red Hat Linux file security is controlled through the following settings for each file or directory:

- ♦ User ownership
- ♦ Group ownership
- ♦ Read, write, execute permissions for owner
- ♦ Read, write, execute permissions for group
- ♦ Read, write, execute permissions for others (everyone else)

Viewing Ownerships and Permissions

You can see these settings for a file when you look at the detailed listing with the `ls -l` command. For example, type the following command to see the detailed listing of the `/etc/inittab` file:

```
ls -l /etc/inittab
```

The resulting listing should look something like this:

```
-rw-r--r--    1 root     root         1698 Aug 16 17:00 /etc/inittab
```

The first set of characters describe the file permissions for user, group, and others. The third and fourth fields show the user and group that own this file. In this case, both user and group names are the same: `root`.

Changing File Ownerships

You can set the user and group ownerships with the `chown` command. For example if the file `/dev/hda` should be owned by the user root and the group disk, then you would type the following command as root to set up this ownership:

```
chown root.disk /dev/hda
```

To change the group ownership alone, use the `chgrp` command. For example, here's how you can change the group ownership of a file to the group named accounting:

```
chgrp accounting ledger.xls
```

Changing File Permissions

Use the `chmod` command to set the file permissions. To use `chmod` effectively, you have to learn how to specify the permission settings. One way is to concatenate one or more letters from each of the following tables in the order shown (Who/Action/Permission), as shown in Table 22-2:

Table 22-2: File Permission Codes

Who	Action	Permission
u user	+ add	r read
g group	- remove	w write
o others	= assign	x execute
a all	s set user ID	

To give everyone read and write access to all files in a directory, type **chmod a+rw ***. On the other hand, to permit everyone to execute a specific file, type **chmod a+x filename**.

Secret

Another way to specify a permission setting is to use a three-digit sequence of numbers. In a detailed listing, the read, write, and execute permission settings for the user, group, and others appear as the sequence

`rwxrwxrwx`

with hyphens (-) in place of letters for disallowed operations. Think of `rwxrwxrwx` as three occurrences of the string `rwx`. Now, assign the values `r=4`, `w=2`, and `x=1`. Assign zero to a hyphen. To get the value of the sequence `rwx`, simply add the values of r, w, and x. Thus, `rwx` = 7, `rw-`=6, and `r--`=4. Using this formula, you can assign a three-digit value to any permission setting. For example, if the user can read and write the file but everyone else can only read the file, the permission setting is `rw-r--r--` (that's how it appears in the listing), and the value is 644. Thus, if you want all files in a directory to be readable by everyone but writeable by only the user, use the command:

`chmod 644 *`

Setting Default File Permissions

What permission setting does a file get when you (or a program) create a new file? The answer is in what is known as the user file-creation mask that you can see and set using the `umask` command.

Type **umask**, and it prints out a number showing the current file-creation mask. The default setting is different for the `root` user and other normal users. For the `root` user the mask is set to 022 whereas the mask for normal users is 002. To see the effect of this file-creation mask and to interpret the meaning of the mask, follow these steps:

1. Log in as `root` and type the following command:

`touch junkfile`

This creates a file named `junkfile` with nothing in it.

2. Type **ls -l junkfile** to that file's permissions. You should see a line similar to the following:

`-rw-r--r--     1 root      root             0 Apr 19 10:56 junkfile`

Interpret the numerical value of the permission setting by converting each three-letter permissions in the first field (excluding the very first letter) into a number between 0 and 7. For each letter that's present, the first letter gets a value of 4, second letter is 2, and the third is 1. For example, `rw-` translates to 4+2+0 (because the third letter is missing) or 6. Similarly, `r--` is 4+0+0 = 4. Thus the permission string `-rw-r--r--` becomes 644.

3. Subtract the numerical permission setting from 666 and what you get is the `umask` setting. In this case, 666 - 644 gives us a `umask` of 022.

So, a `umask` of 022 results in a default permission setting of 666 − 022 = 644. When you rewrite 644 in terms of a permission string, it becomes `rw-r--r--`.

Secret

To set a new umask, **type umask** followed by the numerical value of the mask. Here is how you can select a umask and set it:

1. Figure out what permission settings you want for new files. For example, if you want new files that can be read and written by the owner only and nothing else, then the permission setting would look like

   rw-------

2. Convert the permissions into a numerical value by using the conversion method that takes the permission setting in groups of three characters each and then assigns 4 to the first field, 2 to the second, and 1 to the third. Thus, for files that are readable and writable by owner only, the permission setting is 600.

3. Subtract the desired permission setting from 666 to get the value of the mask. For a permission setting of 600, the mask then becomes 666 − 600 = 066.

4. Use the umask command to set the file-creation mask, like this:

   umask 066

A default umask of 022 is good for system security because it translates to files that have read and write permission for the owner and read permissions for everyone else. The bottom line is that you don't want a default umask that results in files that are writable by the whole wide world.

Checking for the Set User ID Permission

There is another permission setting that can be a security hazard. This permission setting, called the set user ID (or *setuid* for short), applies to executable files. When the setuid permission is enabled, the file is executed under the user ID of the file's owner. In other words, if an executable program is owned by root and the setuid permission is set, then no matter who executes that program, it runs as if being executed by root. This means that that program can do a lot more (for example, read all files, create new files, and delete files) than what a normal user program could do. Another risk is that if a setuid program file has some security hole, crackers can do a lot more damage through such programs than through other vulnerabilities.

You can find all setuid programs with a simple find command:

```
find / -type f -perm +4000 -print
```

You should see a list of files such as the following:

```
/usr/X11R6/bin/XFree86
/usr/bin/chage
/usr/bin/gpasswd
/usr/bin/at
/usr/bin/passwd
/usr/bin/chfn
/usr/bin/chsh
/usr/bin/newgrp
/usr/bin/crontab
/usr/bin/lppasswd
... lines deleted ...
```

Many of the programs have the setuid permission because they need it, but check the complete list and make sure that there are no strange setuid programs (for example, setuid programs in a user's home directory).

If you want to see how these permissions are listed by the `ls` command, type **ls -l /usr/bin/passwd**, and you should see the permission settings:

```
-r-s--x--x   1 root     root        15104 Aug 16 20:44 /usr/bin/passwd
```

The s in the owner's permission setting (r-s) tells you that the setuid permission is set.

To remove the setuid bit from a program's permission, type

```
chmod ug-s progname
```

Encrypting and Signing Files with GnuPG

Red Hat Linux comes with the GNU Privacy Guard (GnuPG, or simply GPG) encryption and authentication utility. With GPG, you can create your public and private key pair, encrypt files using your key, and also digitally sign a message to authenticate that it's really from you. If you send a digitally signed message to someone who has your public key, the recipient can verify that it was you who signed the message.

Understanding Public-Key Encryption

The basic idea behind public-key encryption is to use a pair of keys—one private and the other public—that are related, but one cannot be guessed from the other. Anything encrypted with the private key can be decrypted with the corresponding public key, and vice versa. The public key is for distribution to other people, while you keep the private key in a safe place.

Secret

You can use public-key encryption for securely communicating with others. Figure 22-2 illustrates the basic idea. Suppose that Alice wants to send secure messages to Bob. Each of them generate public-private key pairs and exchange their public keys. When Alice wants to send a message to Bob, she simply encrypts the message using Bob's public key and sends the encrypted message to him. Now, the message is secure from any eavesdropping because only Bob's private key can decrypt the message, and only Bob has that key. When Bob receives the message, he uses his private key to decrypt the message and read it.

If you think about it, you'd realize a fundamental problem in using public key encryption. In the scenario of Figure 22-2, how does Bob know the message really came from Alice? What if someone else uses Bob's public key and sends a message as if it came from Alice? Also, how does Alice assure herself that she is indeed using Bob's public key and not some impostor's key. This is where digital signature, certificates, and certificate authority come in.

The following section describes digital signatures and then goes on to explain how to use gpg to digitally sign a message. I don't describe certificates, but a *certificate* is an electronic file that associates a public key with the identity of that public key's owner, which can be an individual, an organization, a computer, or an application running on a computer. The certificate is issued and digitally signed by a *certificate authority* (CA)—an organization whose public key we apparently trust. The whole purpose of a

CA-issued certificate is to assure someone like Alice that before she encrypts a message for Bob's eyes only by using Bob's public key she (or a program that she uses) can verify the authenticity of Bob's public key.

Figure 22-2: Bob and Alice Can Communicate Securely with Public-Key Encryption.

Understanding Digital Signatures

The purpose of digital or electronic signatures is the same as pen-and-ink signatures, but how you sign digitally is completely different. Unlike pen-and-ink signatures, your digital signature depends on the message you are signing. The first step is to apply a mathematical function on the message and reduce it to a fixed-size message digest (also called hash). No matter how big your message is, the message digest is always around 128 or 160 bits, depending on the hashing function.

The next step is to apply public key encryption. Simply encrypt the message digest with your private key, and you get the digital signature for the message. Typically, the digital signature is appended to the end of the message and you've got an electronically signed message.

Secret

What good does the digital signature do? Well, anyone who wants to verify that the message is indeed signed by you takes your public key and decrypts the digital signature. What they get is the message digest of the message. Then, they apply the same hash function to the message and compare the computes hash with the decrypted the value. If the two match, no one has tampered with the message. Because your public key was used to verify the signature, the message must have been signed with the private key known only to you. So the message must be from you!

In the theoretical scenario of Alice sending private messages to Bob, Alice can digitally sign her message to make sure that Bob can tell that the message is really from her. Figure 22-3 illustrates the use of digital signature along with normal public-key encryption.

continues

continued

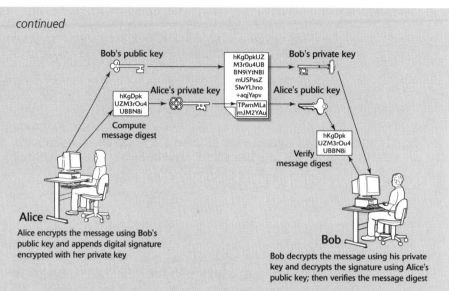

Figure 22-3: Alice Can Digitally Sign Her Message So That Bob Can Tell It's Really from Her.

Here's how Alice sends her private message to Bob with the assurance that Bob can really tell it's from her:

1. Alice uses some software to computer the message digest of the message and then encrypts the digest using her private key. This is her digital signature for the message.

2. Alice encrypts (again, using some convenient software) the message using Bob's public key.

3. She sends both the encrypted message and the digital signature to Bob.

4. Bob decrypts the messages using his private key.

5. Bob decrypts the digital signature using Alice's public key. This gives him the message digest.

6. Bob computes the message digest of the message and compares with what he got by decrypting the digital signature.

7. If the two message digests match, Bob can be sure that the message really came from Alice.

Using GPG

GPG includes the tools you need to use public-key encryption and digital signatures. What you'd use is the gpg command. You can learn to use GPG gradually as you begin using encryption. I show you some of the typical tasks you may perform with GPG.

Generating the Key Pair

The first thing you have to do is generate your own private-public key pair. Type the following command in a terminal window to generate the key pairs:

```
gpg --gen-key
```

If this is your first time with `gpg`, it creates a `.gnupg` directory in your home directory. The steps for generating the key pairs go like this:

1. Type the `gpg —gen-key` command again. You should see a message similar to the following:

   ```
   Please select what kind of key you want:
      (1) DSA and ElGamal (default)
      (2) DSA (sign only)
      (5) RSA (sign only)
   Your selection?
   ```

2. Press Enter for the default choice because it's good enough.

3. GPG then prompts you for the key size (the number of bits). Again, press Enter to accept the default value of 1,024 bits.

4. GPG asks you when the keys should expire. The default is to never expire. If that's what you want (and why not?), press Enter.

5. GPG asks if you really want the keys to never expire. Press y to confirm.

6. GPG prompts you for your name, then your email address, and finally a comment so that the key pair can be associated with your name. Type the requested information and press Enter.

7. GPG gives you a chance to change the information or confirm it as is. To confirm it, type **o** and then press Enter.

8. GPG prompts you for a passphrase that will be used to protect your private key. Type a long phrase that includes lowercase and uppercase letters, numbers, and punctuation marks—the longer the better. Careful though, pick a passphrase that you can easily remember as well. Type the passphrase, and press Enter.

9. GPG generates the keys. It may ask you to perform some work on the PC so that the random number generator can generate enough random numbers for the key-generation process.

Exchanging Keys

To communicate with others, you have to give them your public key. You also have to get public keys from those who may send you a message (or to verify the signature of someone who might sign a file). GPG keeps the public keys in your key ring. To list the keys in your key ring, type

```
gpg --list-keys
```

To send your public key to someone or place it on a website, you have to export the key to a file. The best way is to put the key in what GPG documentation calls a ASCII-armored format with a command like this:

```
gpg --armor --export naba@comcast.net > nabakey.asc
```

This command saves my public key in an ASCII-armored format (it basically looks like garbled text) in the file named nabakey.asc. Of course, you should replace the email address with your email address (the one you used when you created the keys) and the output filename to something different.

After you export the public key to a file, you can mail that file to others or place it on a website for use by others.

When you import a key from someone else, you typically get it in an ASCII-armored format as well. For example, if I have Red Hat's GPG public key in a file named redhatkey.asc, I would import it into my key ring with the following command:

```
gpg --import redhatkey.asc
```

Use the gpg —list-keys command to verify that the key is in your key ring.

The next step is to check the fingerprint of the new key. For example, to get the fingerprint of the Red Hat key, type the following command:

```
gpg --fingerprint security@redhat.com
```

This causes GPG to print the fingerprint:

```
pub  1024D/DB42A60E 1999-09-23 Red Hat, Inc <security@redhat.com>
     Key fingerprint = CA20 8686 2BD6 9DFC 65F6  ECC4 2191 80CD DB42 A60E
sub  2048g/961630A2 1999-09-23
```

At this point, you should verify the key fingerprint with someone at Red Hat. For a company like Red Hat, you can verify the fingerprint from a Web page (http://www.redhat.com/solutions/security/news/publickey.html). If you think the key fingerprint is good, you can sign the key and validate it. Here's the command you use to sign the key:

```
gpg --sign-key security@redhat.com
```

GPG displays a message and prompts you on the level of key verification you have performed:

```
gpg: Warning: using insecure memory!
gpg: please see http://www.gnupg.org/faq.html for more information

gpg: checking the trustdb
gpg: checking at depth 0 signed=0 ot(-/q/n/m/f/u)=0/0/0/0/0/1
pub  1024D/DB42A60E  created: 1999-09-23 expires: never     trust: -/-
sub  2048g/961630A2  created: 1999-09-23 expires: never
(1). Red Hat, Inc <security@redhat.com>


pub  1024D/DB42A60E  created: 1999-09-23 expires: never     trust: -/-
             Fingerprint: CA20 8686 2BD6 9DFC 65F6  ECC4 2191 80CD DB42 A60E

     Red Hat, Inc <security@redhat.com>

How carefully have you verified the key you are about to sign actually belongs
to the person named above?  If you don't know what to answer, enter "0".
```

```
(0) I will not answer. (default)
(1) I have not checked at all.
(2) I have done casual checking.
(3) I have done very careful checking.

Your selection?
```

After you answer and press Enter, GPG asks for confirmation and then prompts you for your passphrase. After that GPG signs the key.

> **caution** Because the key verification and signing is a potential weak link in GPG, be careful about what keys you sign. By signing a key, you basically say that you trust the key to be from that person or organization.

Signing a File

You'd find it useful to sign files if you send out a file to someone and want to assure the recipient that no one has tampered with the file and that it was you who sent the file. GPG makes it very easy to sign a file. You can compress and sign a file named `message` with the following command:

```
gpg -o message.sig -s message
```

To verify the signature, type

```
gpg --verify message.sig
```

To get back the original document, simply type

```
gpg -o message --decrypt message.sig
```

Sometimes you don't care about keeping a message secret, but simply want to sign it to indicate that the message is from you. In this case, you can generate and append a clear text signature with the following command:

```
gpg -o message.asc --clearsign message
```

This command basically appends a clear text signature to the text message. Here's a typical clear-text signature block:

```
-----BEGIN PGP SIGNATURE-----
Version: GnuPG v1.0.7 (GNU/Linux)

iD8DBQE9ZYUtjre6e89JIhURAmUzAKDAK8tdQMRrA2qSpaG8rKpYO5dZuACeI9kT
26EaLE5s/zHDiapiW+geXdo=
=U26+
-----END PGP SIGNATURE-----
```

When a message has a clear-text signature appended, you can use GPG to verify the signature with the command like this:

```
gpg --verify message.asc
```

The last line of the output should say that it's a good signature.

Encrypting and Decrypting Documents

To encrypt a message meant for a recipient, you can use the −encrypt (or -e) GPG command. Here's how you might encrypt a message for me if you had my public GPG key:

```
gpg -o message.gpg -e -r naba@comcast.net message
```

The message would be encrypted using my public key (without any signature, but you can add the signature with an -s command).

When I receive the message.gpg file, I have to decrypt it using my private key. Here's the command I would use:

```
gpg -o message --decrypt message.gpg
```

GPG then prompts me for the passphrase to unlock my private key and then decrypts the message and saves the output in the file named message.

If you simply want to encrypt a file and no one else has to decrypt the file, you can use GPG to perform what is called symmetric encryption. In this case, you provide a passphrase to encrypt the file with the following GPG command:

```
gpg -o secret.gpg -c somefile
```

GPG prompts you for the passphrase and asks you to repeat the passphrase (to make sure that you didn't mistype anything). Then, GPG encrypts the file using a key generated from the passphrase.

To decrypt a file encrypted with a symmetric key, type

```
gpg -o myfile --decrypt secret.gpg
```

GPG prompts you for the passphrase. If you enter the correct passphrase, GPG decrypts the file and saves the output (in this example) in the file named myfile.

Monitoring System Security

Even if you have secured your system, you have to monitor the log files periodically for signs of intrusion. You should also install the Tripwire software to monitor the integrity of critical system files and directories.

I will briefly describe how to use Tripwire and what log files to check periodically.

Using Tripwire to Monitor the Integrity of System Files

The worst security breaches are the ones that go undetected. A savvy cracker may manage to get access to a system, replace critical system programs with Trojan horses, and hide his or her tracks by modifying the log files (the Trojan horse programs are often called *root kits* because they allow the cracker to get root access to your system). Later on, the cracker may use the Trojan horse programs to access the system at will. The problem is that the system administrator may never even suspect that anything is out of the ordinary. Using software such as Tripwire to monitor file integrity can help avoid this type of problem.

Red Hat Linux comes with the Tripwire package. It is not installed by default, but you can easily install it and configure it to monitor any changes to specified system files and directories.

Installing Tripwire

To install the Tripwire package, place each CD-ROM in the CD-ROM drive and mount it with the `mount /mnt/cdrom` command (or, if you are running the GNOME desktop, wait until the `magicdev` device automatically mounts the CD-ROM). Then, look for the Tripwire package with the following commands:

```
cd /mnt/cdrom/RedHat/RPMS
ls tripwire*
```

> **note** This book comes with the Publisher's Edition version of Red Hat Linux that was provided by Red Hat. Unfortunately, these CD-ROMs do not include all the software that comes with the full Red Hat Linux distribution. If you cannot find the `tripwire` RPM file in this book's CD-ROMs, you have to download that file from one of the mirror sites listed at `http://www.redhat.com/download/mirror.html`. Click on the Distribution link next to one of the listed FTP sites and then look in the directory corresponding to the Red Hat Linux version number. For example, the RPM files for Red Hat Linux 9 should be in the `9/en/os/i386/RedHat/RPMS` directory. Use a Web browser to download the `tripwire` RPM file and install it by following the steps outlined next.

If the file exists, then type the following command to install the Tripwire package:

```
rpm -ivh tripwire*
```

The Tripwire installation does the following:

- ◆ Installs the programs siggen, tripwire, twadmin, and twprint in the `/usr/sbin` directory
- ◆ Creates the `/etc/tripwire` directory and places some files in it, including the shell script `/etc/tripwire/twinstall.sh`, which you have to run after installing the package
- ◆ Installs the `tripwire-check` script in the `/etc/cron.daily` directory. This causes the `tripwire-check` script to be executed daily.
- ◆ Installs the man pages for `twconfig`, `twpolicy`, `twfiles`, `siggen`, `tripwire`, `twadmin`, `twintro`, and `twprint`. You can read these man pages with commands, such as `man tripwire`.
- ◆ Installs some Tripwire documentation in the `/usr/share/doc` directory. To change to the Tripwire documentation directory, type **cd /usr/share/doc/ tripwire***.
- ◆ Creates the `/var/lib/tripwire/report` directory in which to store Tripwire reports.

After installing the Tripwire package, you have to run the `/etc/tripwire/twinstall.sh` script to generate cryptographic keys. Type the following command:

```
/etc/tripwire/twinstall.sh
```

You have to enter a site passphrase and a local passphrase. The necessary keys are then generated, the policy file is signed, and the Tripwire installation ends with the following message:

```
A clear-text version of the Tripwire policy file
/etc/tripwire/twpol.txt
has been preserved for your inspection.  This implements
a minimal policy, intended only to test essential
Tripwire functionality.  You should edit the policy file
to describe your system, and then use twadmin to generate
a new signed copy of the Tripwire policy.
```

You can examine the /etc/tripwire/twpol.txt file to see how Tripwire policy is specified. The policy file identifies the program and configuration files that are critical to system security. Tripwire then periodically checks the integrity of these files.

Initializing the Tripwire Database

After installing Tripwire, you have to initialize the Tripwire database with the following command:

```
/usr/sbin/tripwire --init
```

Tripwire prompts you for the local passphrase and then works for a while as it creates a database file. This can take a while to complete.

You may get a few error messages for files that are not in your system but are referred to in the Tripwire policy file /etc/tripwire/twpol.txt. At the end of all the processing, Tripwire writes a database file named after your system's hostname and saves that file in the /var/lib/tripwire directory. The database file is digitally signed with the key generated during the step when you ran the /etc/tripwire/twinstall.sh script (remember that a digital signature is a hash of a file's contents, encrypted with the local private key—the hash is a fixed-length binary number computed with a mathematical function such as the MD5 or SHA-1).

Checking File Integrity

After the Tripwire database is initialized, you should periodically run Tripwire in integrity-checking mode with the command /usr/sbin/tripwire —check. In this mode, Tripwire uses the policy file, /etc/tripwire/tw.pol, and compares the state of the current files against what's stored in the initial database. Tripwire prints a report on the standard output and saves the report in the /var/lib/tripwire/report directory.

For example, when I log in as root and type the following command:

```
/usr/sbin/tripwire --check
```

Tripwire displays some error messages about missing files (the same ones I get when I initialize the Tripwire database with the /usr/sbin/tripwire —init command). After that, Tripwire prints the report to the standard output and writes it to a file.

The name of the Tripwire report file depends on your system's hostname and the date and time when you run the /usr/sbin/tripwire —check command. You can see the report files in the /var/lib/tripwire/report directory.

Each report file's name is created by appending the date and time to the hostname, with dashes as separators, and then appending a `.twr` as file extension. The report is in binary format. To print the report, follow these steps:

1. Change directory to the Tripwire report directory by typing

   `cd /var/lib/tripwire/report`

2. Use the `ls` command to look at the list of report files in that directory.

3. Print the report using the `/usr/sbin/twprint` command with the following syntax:

   `/usr/sbin/twprint --print-report -r reportfilename.twr`

   Replace `reportfilename.twr` with the report that you want to view. If it's scrolling by too fast, simply pipe the output through the `more` command (append `|` `more` to the command).

The Tripwire report file lists any violations of the Tripwire policy—basically any files that have changed since the last time the Tripwire database was generated. You should always verify that the changes are expected and not suspicious.

---

insider insight When you install Tripwire, your system is already set up to run the `/etc/cron.daily/` `tripwire-check` script every day. The `/etc/cron.daily/tripwire-check` script executes the `/usr/sbin/tripwire —check` command to generate a report. All you need to do is log in as `root` and use the `/usr/sbin/twprint` command to review the latest report each day.

Examining Log Files

Many Red Hat Linux applications, including some servers, write log information using the logging capabilities of syslogd. On Red Hat Linux systems, the log files written by syslogd reside in the `/var/log` directory. Make sure that only the `root` user can read and write these files.

---

insider insight The syslogd configuration file is `/etc/syslog.conf`. The default configuration of syslogd should generate the necessary log files; however, if you want to examine and understand the configuration file, type `man syslog.conf` for more information.

You should routinely monitor the following log files:

- `/var/log/messages` contains a wide variety of logging messages, from user logins to messages from services started by the TCP wrapper.
- `/var/log/secure` contains reports from services such as in.telnetd that xinetd starts through the TCP wrapper.
- `/var/log/maillog` contains reports from sendmail.
- `/var/log/xferlog` contains a log of all FTP file transfers.

Red Hat Linux comes with a graphical log file viewer utility. To use this tool, select Main Menu⇨System Tools⇨System Logs from the GNOME panel. The System Logs utility is simple to use. Click the log filename in the left window and view the contents in the scrolling text window to the right.

Because many potential intruders use port-scanning tools in an attempt to establish TCP/IP connections to well-known ports on your system, you should look for messages that indicate attempted connections from unknown hosts (indicated by names or IP addresses). To do this, click Security Log on the left window and then browse the log messages that appears in the right window. You'll see lines such as the following:

```
Feb  7 20:46:04 dhcppc6 xinetd[2240]: START: telnet pid=2870 from=192.168.0.4
```

These lines show you the type of connection such as `telnet` and the IP addresses from where the connections originated. If you want to browse through these messages using a text editor, they are in the `/var/log/secure` file.

Securing the Network

To secure your Red Hat Linux system, you have to pay attention to both host security and network security. The distinction between the two types of security is somewhat arbitrary because securing the network involves fixing up things on the host that relate to what Internet services your system offers. The next few sections explain how you can secure the Internet services (mostly by not running unnecessary services), how you can use firewall to stop unwanted network packets from reaching your network, and how to use secure shell for secure remote logins.

Securing Internet Services

For an Internet-connected Red Hat Linux system (or even one on a TCP/IP LAN that's not connected to the Internet), a significant threat is the possibility that someone will use one of many Internet services to gain access to your system. Each service—such as mail, Web, or FTP—requires running a server program that responds to client requests arriving over the TCP/IP network. Some of these server programs have weaknesses that can allow an outsider to log in to your system—maybe with root privileges. Luckily, Red Hat Linux comes with some facilities that you can use to make the Internet services more secure.

---

caution   Potential intruders can employ a port-scanning tool—a program that attempts to establish a TCP/IP connection at a port and to look for a response—to check which Internet servers are running on your system. Then, to gain access to your system, the intruder can potentially exploit any known weaknesses of one or more services

---

Using the chkconfig Command to Disable Services

To provide Internet services such as Web, mail, and FTP, your Red Hat Linux system has to run server programs that listen to incoming TCP/IP network requests. Some of these servers are started when your system boots, and they run all the time. We call such servers standalone servers. The Web server and mail server are examples of standalone servers. The other servers are started on demand by another server called xinetd.

You can turn both standalone servers and the ones started by xinetd on or off using the `chkconfig` command. Here's how you should use `chkconfig` to stop unneeded services:

- Log in as `root` and type **chkconfig —list** to view all the services set to start automatically at the run levels 0 through 6. At the end of the list you see the services started by xinetd. Note that the xinetd-controlled services do not depend on the run level; they run at those run levels when xinetd itself is turned on.

- The services that are turned on for run levels 3 and 5 matter most because your Red Hat Linux system is usually at run level 3 (text mode) or 5 (graphical login). Type **runlevel** to see the current run level.

- Decide which services you don't need. What you need or don't need depends on how you use your Red Hat Linux system. For example, if it's just a personal workstation, you don't need to run most services.

- To stop a service, use the following form of the `chkconfig` command:

  ```
  chkconfig --level 345 service_name off
  ```

  where `service_name`, is the name of the service you want to turn off. For example to prevent the `vsftpd` service (this is the FTP service) from automatically starting at run levels 3, 4, and 5, type the following command:

  ```
  chkconfig --level 345 vsftpd off
  ```

  You can also use `chkconfig` to turn on or off xinetd-controlled services. For example, to turn the Telnet service on, type:

  ```
  chkconfig telnet on
  ```

You use `chkconfig` to stop services from starting at boot time, but if you want to immediately stop a service that's currently running, use the `service` command like this:

```
service service_name stop
```

where `service_name` is the name of the service to stop. For example, if the mail server (`sendmail`) is already running, you can stop it with the command:

```
service sendmail stop
```

Configuring the xinetd Server to Disable Services

In addition to the stand-alone servers such as Web server (`httpd`), mail (`sendmail`), and domain name server (`named`), you have to configure another server separately. That other server, `xinetd` (the Internet super server), starts a host of other Internet services, such as TELNET, POP3, and so on whenever a client makes a request over the network. The `xinetd` server includes some security features that you can use to disable the services that it can start on demand.

The `xinetd` server reads a configuration file named `/etc/xinetd.conf` at startup. This file, in turn, incorporates all the configuration files stored in the `/etc/xinetd.d` directory. The configuration files in `/etc/xinetd.d` tell `xinetd` which ports to listen to and which server to start for each port. Type **ls /etc/xinetd.d** to see a list of the files in `/etc/xinetd.d` directory on your system. On my system, here's what the `ls /etc/xinetd.d` command lists:

```
chargen       daytime-udp  imap   kotalk  rexec   servers    telnet
chargen-udp   echo         imaps  ktalk   rlogin  services   time
cups-lpd      echo-udp     ipop2  ntalk   rsh     sgi_fam    time-udp
daytime       finger       ipop3  pop3s   rsync   talk
```

This list shows all the services `xinetd` can start. However, the configuration file for a service can also turn off a service simple by having a `disable = yes` line in the file. For example, here's the `telnet` file's content:

```
# default: on
# description: The telnet server serves telnet sessions:
#       it uses unencrypted username/password pairs for
#       authentication.
service telnet
{
        flags            = REUSE
        socket_type      = stream
        wait             = no
        user             = root
        server           = /usr/sbin/in.telnetd
        log_on_failure  += USERID
        disable          = yes
}
```

Notice the last line in the configuration file—that line disables the Telnet service.

I won't explain the format of the `xinetd` configuration files here (Chapter 6 covers `xinetd` configuration files), except to reiterate that you can turn off a service simply by adding the following line in the configuration file somewhere between the two curly braces { . . . }:

```
        disable          = yes
```

Conversely, to turn a service on, change that line to `disable = no` or comment is out by placing a number sign (#) at the beginning of the line.

---

caution   After you make any changes to any `xinetd` configuration file, you must restart the xinetd server; otherwise the changes won't take effect. To restart the xinetd server, type the following command:

```
service xinetd restart
```

This stops the xinetd server and then starts it again. When it restarts, it'll read the configuration files, and the changes will take effect.

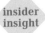

If you don't feel like editing the configuration file for a service in /etc/xinetd.d directory, you can use the chkconfig command to turn these services on or off. To turn one of these services off, type chkconfig servicename off. There is no need to specify any run levels because these services are activated by xinetd and can run only when xinetd is running.

Depending on how you use your system, you may be able to disable many of the services. If you do not want anyone to log in remotely or download files from your system, simply disable the Telnet and FTP services. Note that to disable FTP, you have to type **chkconfig —level 35 vsftpd off** because FTP service is now a standalone service and the name of the server is vsftpd.

Another security feature of xinetd is its use of TCP wrapper library to start various services. The TCP wrapper provides an access-control facility for Internet services. The TCP wrapper can start other services, such as FTP and Telnet, but before starting a service, it consults the /etc/hosts.allow file to see if the host requesting service is allowed that service. If nothing appears in /etc/hosts.allow about that host, TCP wrapper checks the /etc/hosts.deny file to see if it should deny the service. If both files are empty, TCP wrapper provides access to the requested service.

Follow these steps to tighten access to the services that xinetd is configured to start:

1. Use a text editor to edit the /etc/hosts.deny file, adding the following line into that file:

   ALL:ALL

   This denies all hosts access to any Internet services on your system.

2. Edit the /etc/hosts.allow file and add to it the names of hosts that can access services on your system. For example, to enable only hosts from the 192.168.1.0 network and the localhost (IP address 127.0.0.1) access the services on your system, place the following line in the /etc/hosts.allow file:

   ALL: 192.168.1.0/255.255.255.0 127.0.0.1

3. If you want to permit access to a specific Internet service to a specific remote host, you can do so using the following syntax for a line in /etc/hosts.allow:

   server_program_name: hosts

   Here, server_program_name is the name of the server program (for example, in.telnetd for Telnet), and hosts is a comma-separated list of hosts that can access the service. You may also write hosts as a network address or an entire domain name, such as .mycompany.com. For example, here's how you can give Telnet access to all systems in the mycompany.com domain:

   in.telnetd: .mycompany.com

You should edit configuration files in /etc/xinetd.d directory to turn off unneeded services and use the /etc/hosts.deny and /etc/hosts.allow files to control access to the services that are allowed to run on your system. After you edit the files in the /etc/xinetd.d directory, remember to type **service xinetd restart** to restart the xinetd server.

Using Secure Shell (SSH) for Remote Logins

Red Hat Linux comes with the Open Secure Shell (OpenSSH) software, a suite of programs that provide a secure replacement for the Berkeley r commands: rlogin (remote login), rsh (remote shell), and rcp (remote copy). OpenSSH uses public-key cryptography to authenticate users and to encrypt the communication between two hosts, so users can securely log in from remote systems and copy files securely.

In this section, I briefly describe how to use the OpenSSH software in Red Hat Linux. To learn more about OpenSSH and read the latest news about it, visit www.openssh.com or www.openssh.org.

The OpenSSH software is installed during Red Hat Linux installation. Table 22-3 lists the main components of the OpenSSH software.

Table 22-3: Components of the OpenSSH Software

Component	Description
/usr/sbin/sshd	The secure shell daemon that must run on a host if you want users on remote systems to use the ssh client to log in securely. When a connection from an ssh client arrives, sshd performs authentication using public-key cryptography and establishes an encrypted communication link with the ssh client.
/usr/bin/ssh	The secure shell client that users can run to log in to a host that is running sshd. Users can also use ssh to execute a command on another host.
/usr/bin/slogin	A symbolic link to /usr/bin/ssh
/usr/bin/scp	The secure copy program that works like rcp, but securely. The scp program uses ssh for data transfer and provides the same authentication and security as ssh.
/usr/bin/ssh-keygen	The program you use to generate the public and private key pairs you need for the public-key cryptography used in OpenSSH. The ssh-keygen program can generate key pairs for both RSA and DSA (Digital Signature Algorithm) authentication.
/etc/ssh/sshd_config	The configuration file for the sshd server. This file specifies many parameters for sshd, including the port to listen to, the protocol to use (there are two versions of SSH protocols, SSH1 and SSH2, both supported by OpenSSH), and the location of other files.
/etc/ssh/ssh_config	The configuration file for the ssh client. Each user can also have a ssh configuration file named config in the .ssh subdirectory of the user's home directory.

OpenSSH uses public-key encryption where the sender and receiver both have a pair of keys—a public key and a private key. The public keys are freely distributed, and each party knows the other's public key. The sender encrypts data by using the recipient's public key. Only the recipient's private key can then decrypt that data.

To use OpenSSH, do the following:

◆ If you want to support SSH-based remote logins on a host, start the sshd server on your system. Type **ps ax | grep sshd** to see if the server is already running. If not, log in as `root`, and type the following command at the shell prompt to immediately start the sshd server:

```
service sshd start
```

Then type the following command to ensure that the sshd server starts when the system reboots:

```
chkconfig --level 35 sshd on
```

◆ Generate the host keys with the following command:

```
ssh-keygen -d -f /etc/ssh/ssh_host_key -N ''
```

The `-d` flag causes the ssh-keygen program to generate DSA keys, which the SSH2 protocol uses. If you see a message saying that the file `/etc/ssh/ssh_host_key` already exists, that means that the key pairs were generated during Red Hat Linux installation. You can then use the existing file without having to regenerate the keys.

A user who wants to log in using `ssh` also has to generate the public-private key pair. For example, here is what I do so that I can log in from another system on my Red Hat Linux system using SSH:

1. I type the following command to generate the DSA keys for use with SSH2:

```
ssh-keygen -d
```

I am prompted for a passphrase and the last message informs me that my public key is saved in `/home/naba/.ssh/id_dsa.pub`.

2. I copy my public key—the `/home/naba/.ssh/id_dsa.pub` file—to the remote system and save it as the `~/.ssh/authorized_keys2` file (this refers to the `authorized_keys2` file in the `.ssh` subdirectory of my home directory on the other system, assuming that the remote system is also another Red Hat Linux system). Note that the 2 in the name of the `authorized_keys2` file refers to the SSH2 protocol.

3. To log in to my account on my Red Hat Linux system (with hostname `lnbp200`), I type the following command on the remote system:

```
ssh lnbp200 -l naba
naba@lnbp200's password: (I type my password and press Enter.)
```

I am prompted for my password on `lnbp200`. After I enter my password, I have a secure login session with that system. I can also log in to this account with the following equivalent command:

```
ssh naba@lnbp200
```

If I simply want to copy a file securely from the `lnbp200` system, I can use `scp` like this:

```
scp lnbp200:/etc/ssh/ssh_config .

naba@lnbp200's password: (I type my password.)
ssh_config          100% |*****************************|  1167       00:00
```

This command securely copies the `/etc/ssh/ssh_config` file from the `lnbp200` host to the system from which I type the `scp` command.

Setting up Simple Firewalls

An Internet firewall is an intermediary between your internal network and the Internet. The firewall controls access to and from the protected internal network.

If you connect an internal network directly to the Internet, you have to make sure that every system on the internal network is properly secured—which can be nearly impossible, because it takes only one careless user to render the entire internal network vulnerable. A firewall is a single point of connection to the Internet: you can direct all of your efforts toward making that firewall system a daunting barrier to unauthorized external users.

To be useful, a firewall should have the following general characteristics:

♦ It must control the flow of packets between the Internet and the internal network.

♦ It must not provide dynamic routing, because dynamic routing tables are subject to route spoofing—use of fake routes by intruders. Instead, the firewall should use static routing tables (which you can set up with the route or ip command on Red Hat Linux systems).

♦ It must not allow any external user to log in as root. That way, even if the firewall system is compromised, the intruder will not be able to become root from a remote login.

♦ It must be kept in a physically secure location.

♦ It must distinguish between packets that come from the Internet and packets that come from the internal protected network. This feature allows the firewall to reject packets that come from the Internet, but have the IP address of a trusted system on the internal network (an attack wherein packets use fake IP addresses is known as IP spoofing).

♦ It should act as the SMTP mail gateway for the internal network. The sendmail software should be set up so that all outgoing mail appears to come from the firewall system.

♦ It should not have any user accounts. However, the firewall system may need to have a few user accounts for those internal users who need access to external systems. External users who need access to the internal network should use SSH for remote login (see discussion of SSH earlier in this chapter).

♦ It should keep a log of all system activities, such as successful and unsuccessful login attempts.

♦ It should provide DNS name lookup service to the outside world to resolve any host names that should be known to the outside world.

♦ It should provide good performance so that it does not hinder the internal users' access to specific Internet services (such as HTTP and FTP).

A firewall can take many different forms. Here are three common forms of a firewall:

♦ **Screening router with packet filtering**—This simple firewall uses a router capable of filtering (blocking) packets based on IP addresses.

♦ **Dual-homed host with proxy services**—In this case, a host with two network interfaces—one on the Internet and the other on the internal network—runs proxy services that act as a gateway for services, such as FTP and HTTP.

♦ **Perimeter network with bastion host**—This firewall configuration includes a perimeter network between the Internet and the protected internal network. A secure bastion host resides on the perimeter network and provides various services.

In a large organization, you may also need to isolate smaller internal networks from the corporate network. You can set up such internal firewalls the same way you set up Internet firewalls.

In the next few sections, I describe the common forms of firewall: a screening router with packet filtering, a dual-homed host, a perimeter network with bastion host, and an application gateway.

Screening Router with Packet Filtering

If you were to directly connect your organization's internal network to the Internet, you would have to use a router to ensure proper exchange of packets between the internal network and the Internet. Most routers can block a packet based on its source or its destination IP address (as well as its port number). The router's packet-filtering capability can serve as a simple firewall. Figure 22-4 illustrates the basic concept of packet filtering.

Figure 22-4: Packet Filtering with a Screening Router Provides a Simple Firewall.

Many router vendors, such as Cisco and 3Com, offer routers that can be programmed to perform packet filtering. The exact details of filtering depend on the router vendor, but all routers operate according to rules that refer to the basic attributes of an Internet packet:

- Source IP address
- Destination IP address
- Protocol (TCP, UDP, or ICMP)
- Source port number (if protocol is TCP or UDP)
- Destination port number (if protocol is TCP or UDP)
- ICMP message type

In addition, the router knows the physical interface on which the packet arrived and the interface on which the packet will go out (if it is not blocked by the filtering rules).

Most packet filters operate in the following sequence:

1. You define the rules for allowing or blocking specific types of packets based on IP addresses and port numbers. These packet-filtering rules are stored in the router.
2. The screening router examines the header of each packet that arrives for the information (such as IP addresses and port numbers) to which your rules apply.

3. The screening router applies the rules in the order in which they are stored.

4. If a rule allows the packet to be forwarded, the router sends the packet to its destination.

5. If a rule blocks the packet, the router drops the packet (stops processing it).

6. If none of the rules applies, the packet is blocked. This rule epitomizes the security philosophy that one should "deny unless expressly permitted."

Although packet filtering with a screening router is better than no security, packet filtering suffers from the following drawbacks:

♦ It is easy for the network administrator to introduce errors inadvertently into the filtering rules.

♦ Packets are filtered on the basis of IP addresses, which represent specific hosts. Essentially, packet filtering either blocks or routes all packets from a specific host. That means that anyone who breaks into a trusted host can immediately gain access to your protected network.

♦ Because it is based on IP addresses, packet filtering can be defeated by a technique known as IP spoofing, whereby a cracker sends packets with the IP address of a trusted host (by appropriating the IP address of a trusted host and setting up an appropriate route).

♦ Packet filtering is susceptible to routing-attack programs that can create a bogus route that allows an intruder to receive all packets meant for the protected internal network.

♦ Screening routers that implement packet filtering do not keep logs of activities. That makes it hard for you to determine if anyone is attempting to break into the protected network. As you see in the next section, a dual-homed host can provide logging.

♦ A screening router does not hide the hostnames and IP addresses of the internal network. Outsiders can access and use this information to mount attacks against the protected network.

A more sophisticated approach is to use an application gateway that controls network traffic, based on specific applications instead of on a per packet basis. You can implement an application gateway with a dual-homed host known also as a bastion host.

Dual-Homed Host

A dual-homed host is a system with two network interfaces—one connected to the Internet and the other on an internal network that needs protection. The term dual-homed refers to the fact that the host "lives" in two networks.

In fact, if your operating system supports IP routing—the ability to forward network packets from one interface to another—the dual-homed host can serve as a router. However, you must turn off the IP forwarding feature to use the dual-homed host as a firewall system.

The Linux kernel supports the IP forwarding feature. If you plan to use a dual-homed host as a firewall, you have to use the sysctl command (or write directly to a file in the /proc file system) to disable IP forwarding.

With IP forwarding turned off, systems on both networks—the internal network as well as the Internet—can reach the dual-homed host, but no one from the Internet can access the internal network (nor can anyone from the internal network access the Internet). In this configuration, the dual-homed host completely isolates the two networks. Figure 22-5 shows the basic architecture of a dual-homed host.

Figure 22-5: A Dual-Homed Host Can Act as an Internet Firewall.

The dual-homed host is turned into a firewall by running application gateways—proxy services—on the dual-homed host. These proxy services allow specific applications, such as FTP and HTTP, to work across the dual-homed host. That means that you can configure the firewall so that internal clients (on the internal network) are able to access Web and FTP servers on the Internet.

Your public website can also run on the dual-homed host and be accessible to everyone on the Internet.

caution | Don't allow user logins on the dual-homed host. Anyone logged in to the host can have access to both the internal network, as well as the Internet. Because the dual-homed host is your only barrier between the Internet and the internal network, it's best not to increase the chances of a break-in by allowing users to log in to the firewall system. By having user accounts, you increase the chances of an intruder gaining access to the firewall by cracking a user's password.

Perimeter Network with a Bastion Host

An Internet firewall is often more complicated than a single dual-homed host that connects to both the Internet and the protected internal network. In particular, if you provide a number of Internet services, you may need more than one system to host them. Imagine that you have two systems: one to run the Web and FTP servers and the other to provide mail (SMTP) and domain name system (DNS) lookups. In this case, you place these two systems on a network that sits between the Internet and the internal network. Figure 22-6 illustrates this concept of an Internet firewall.

In this case, the firewall includes a perimeter network that connects to the Internet through an exterior router. The perimeter network, in turn, connects to the internal network through an interior router. The perimeter network has one or more hosts that run Internet services, including proxy services that allow internal hosts to access Web servers on the Internet.

insider insight | The term *bastion host* refers to any system on the perimeter network, because such a system is on the Internet and has to be well fortified. The dual-homed host is also a bastion host because the dual-homed host is also accessible from the Internet and has to be protected.

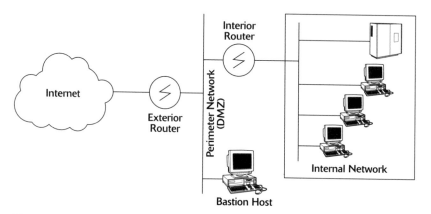

Figure 22-6: A More Complete Internet Firewall Includes a Perimeter Network and Bastion Hosts.

In the firewall configuration shown in Figure 22-6, the perimeter network is known as a DMZ (demilitarized zone) network because that network acts as a buffer between the Internet and the internal network (just as the real-life DMZ is a buffer between North and South Korea).

Usually, you would combine a packet-filtering router with a bastion host. Your Internet service provider typically provides the external router, which means that you do not have much control over that router's configuration. But you provide the internal router, which means you can choose a screening router and employ some packet-filtering rules. For example, you might employ the following packet-filtering rules:

♦ From the internal network, allow only packets addressed to the bastion host.

♦ From the DMZ, allow only packets originating from the bastion host.

♦ Block all other packets.

This ensures that the internal network communicates only with the bastion host (or hosts).

Like the dual-homed host, the bastion host also runs an application gateway that provides proxy services for various Internet services, such as Telnet, FTP, SMTP, and HTTP.

Application Gateway

The bastion host or the dual-homed host is the system that acts as the intermediary between the Internet and the protected internal network. As such, that system serves as the internal network's gateway to the Internet. Toward this end, the system runs software to forward and filter TCP/IP packets for various services, such as Telnet, FTP, and HTTP. The software for forwarding and filtering TCP/IP packets for specific applications are known as proxy services. Figure 22-7 illustrates a proxy server's role in a firewall.

A proxy server accepts a connection for a specific protocol, such as FTP, and forwards the request to another server. In other words, the proxy server acts as a proxy for an actual server. Because it acts as a gateway for a specific application (such as HTTP or FTP), a proxy server is also known as an application gateway.

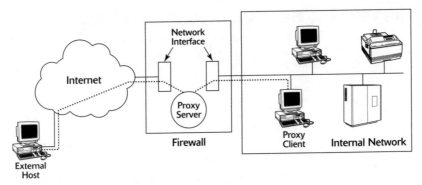

Figure 22-7: A Proxy Server Lets Internal Hosts Access Internet Servers.

Unlike a screening router, which blocks packets only on the basis of information in the packet header (such as source and destination IP addresses), a proxy server uses the packet's data to decide what to do. For example, a proxy server does not blindly forward packets to an Internet service. The proxy server can enforce a site's security policy and disallow certain operations, depending on the specific application. For example, an FTP proxy server may prevent users from internal networks from using the FTP put command to send files to the Internet.

Accessing an Internet service through a proxy server can be a bit more involved than accessing that service directly. For example, a user on the internal network establishes a Telnet session with an Internet host with the following steps:

1. The user establishes a Telnet session with the firewall host—the system that runs the Telnet proxy. To do this, the user has to enter a user name and password so that the firewall host can verify that the user has permission to connect to the Internet.

2. The user enters a command (which the Telnet proxy accepts) to connect to the Internet host. The Telnet proxy, in turn, establishes a Telnet connection between itself and the Internet host.

3. The Telnet proxy on the firewall begins passing packets back and forth between the Internet host and the user's system (until the user ends the Telnet session with the Internet host).

Besides acting as a gateway, the Telnet proxy also logs the user's session with the Internet host. The logging is part of an application gateway's security feature because the log file keeps track of all firewall accesses (as well as attempted accesses that may fail because of a wrong user name or password).

Although the Telnet session involves two steps—first Telnet to the firewall host and then connect to the Internet host—the process of accessing services through a proxy need not be too cumbersome. The exact steps you take to access services through a firewall depend on the proxy software and the client program you use to access a service. With the right client program, proxies can be transparent to the user. For example, many Web browsers make it easy to access a website through an HTTP proxy. All you need to do is indicate through a menu choice the HTTP proxy you want to use.

Enabling Packet Filtering in Red Hat Linux

Red Hat Linux comes with built-in packet filtering software in the form of something called *netfilter* that's in the Linux kernel. All you have to do is use the `iptables` command to set up the rules for what happens to the packets based on the IP addresses in their header and the network connection type.

The built-in packet-filtering capability is handy when you do not have a dedicated firewall between your Red Hat Linux system and the Internet. This is the case, for example, when you connect your Red Hat system to the Internet through a DSL or cable modem. You can essentially have a packet-filtering firewall inside your Red Hat Linux system, sitting between the kernel and the applications.

Setting the Security Level with a GUI Tool

You can turn on different levels of packet filtering through the a graphical Security Level Configuration tool. To run the tool, log in as `root` and select Main menu⇨System Settings⇨Security Level. The Security Level Configuration window appears (see Figure 22-8).

Figure 22-8: Setting the Security Level with a GUI Tool.

You can select three predefined levels of simple firewalling (more precisely, packet filtering) with the Security Level Configuration tool:

♦ **High**—Rejects all connection requests except DNS (for querying IP addresses corresponding to names) and DHCP (for obtaining an IP address for a network interface).

♦ **Medium**—Rejects connection requests to ports lower than 1023 (these are the standard reserved ports used by Internet services such as FTP, SSH, Telnet, and HTTP). Some other ports used by NFS, the X Window System, and the X Font Server are also blocked.

♦ **No firewall**—Does not perform any filtering, and all connections are allowed (you can still turn off Internet services by not running the servers or disabling them in the `xinetd` configuration files). This security level is fine if your Red Hat Linux system is inside a protected local area network.

With High and Medium settings, you can also click the Customize radio button and then select one or more trusted devices (network interfaces) or allow incoming packets meant for specific Internet services such as SSH, Telnet, and FTP. If you select a network interface such as `eth0` (the first Ethernet card) as trusted, then all network traffic over that interface will be allowed without any filtering.

Behind the scenes, the GUI security level tool uses `iptables` rules to implement the packet filerting implied by the selections you make.

Filtering IP Packets with iptables

You can set up packet filtering manually using the `iptables` command. The `iptables` command works with the netfilter software, built into the Linux kernel, to intercept network packets and apply filtering rules to the packets. With the `iptables` command, you can set up, view, and manage tables of rules for filtering IP packets.

Packet filtering with `iptables` relies on the concept of a chain—a sequence of rules—to filter packets. Each rule says what to do with a packet if the header contains certain information (such as the source or destination IP address). If a rule does not apply, `iptables` consults the next rule in the chain. By default, there are three chains:

- **INPUT chain**—The first set of rules against which packets are tested. The packets continue to the next chain only if the input chain does not specify `DROP` or `REJECT`.
- **FORWARD chain**—Contains the rules that apply to packets attempting to pass through this system to another system (for example, when you use the Red Hat Linux system as a router between your LAN and the Internet).
- **OUTPUT chain**—Includes the rules applied to packets before they are sent out (either to another network or to an application)

Figure 22-9 shows a high-level depiction of how IP packets are processed by `iptables` through these three chains.

Figure 22-9: Simplified View of the `iptables` Processing Chains.

continues

continued

When an incoming packet arrives, the kernel uses `iptables` to make a routing decision based on the destination IP address of the packet. If the packet is for this server, the kernel passes the packet to the `INPUT` chain. If the packet satisfies all the rules in the `INPUT` chain, then the packet is processed by local processes such as an Internet server that is listening for packets of this type.

If the kernel had IP forwarding enabled and the packet has a destination IP address of a different network, the kernel passes the packet to the `FORWARD` chain. If the packet satisfies the rules in the `FORWARD` chain, it's sent out to the other network. If the kernel does not have IP forwarding enabled and the packet's destination address is not for this server, then the packet is dropped.

If the local processing progams that received the input packets want to send network packets out, then those packets pass through the `OUTPUT` chain. If those packets are accepted by the `OUTPUT` chain, they are sent out to the specified destination network.

You can view the current chains, add rules to the existing chains, or create new chains of rules by using the `iptables` command. When you view the current chains, you can also save them to a file. For example, if you have done nothing else and your system has no firewall configured, typing the `iptables -L` command should show the following:

```
Chain INPUT (policy ACCEPT)
target      prot opt source                  destination

Chain FORWARD (policy ACCEPT)
target      prot opt source                  destination

Chain OUTPUT (policy ACCEPT)
target      prot opt source                  destination
```

In this case, all three chains—INPUT, FORWARD, and OUTPUT—show the same ACCEPT policy, which means that everything is wide open.

If you are setting up a packet filter, the first thing you do is specify the packets that you want to accept. For example, to accept packets only from the 192.168.0.0 network, add the following rule to the INPUT chain:

```
iptables -A INPUT -s 192.168.0.0/24 -j ACCEPT
```

Now, add rules to drop everything except local loopback (the `lo` network interface) traffic and stop all forwarding with the following commands:

```
iptables -A INPUT -i ! lo -j REJECT
iptables -A FORWARD -j REJECT
```

The first `iptables` command, for example, appends to the INPUT chain (`-A INPUT`) the rule that if the packet does not come from the `lo` interface (`-i ! lo`), iptables should reject the packet (`-j REJECT`).

Before rejecting all other packets, you should also add more rules to each of the INPUT chains to allow specific packets in. Otherwise, you cannot effectively use the Internet. For example, packets coming from Internet servers such as name servers and Web servers will not be accepted by your system. You can further configure the firewall by adding rules to accept or reject packets based on many different parameters such as source and destination IP addresses, protocol types (TCP, UDP), network interface, and port numbers.

You can do all sorts of specialized packet filtering with iptables. For example, suppose that you are setting up a Web server and you want to accept packets meant for only HTTP (port 80) and secure shell (SSH) services. The secure shell service (port 22) is for you to securely log in and adminsiter the server. Suppose that the server's IP address is 192.168.0.10. Here is how you might set up the rules for this server:

```
iptables -P INPUT DROP
iptables -A INPUT -s 0/0 -d 192.168.0.10 -p tcp --dport 80 -j ACCEPT
iptables -A INPUT -s 0/0 -d 192.168.0.10 -p tcp --dport 22 -j ACCEPT
```

In this case, the first rule sets up the default policy of the INPUT chain to DROP, which means that if none of the specific rules match, the packet will be dropped. The next two rules say that packets addressed to 192.168.0.10 and meant for ports 80 and 22 are accepted.

caution

Don't type iptables commands from a remote login session. A rule that begins denying packets from all addresses can also stop what you type from reaching the system; once that happens, you may have no way of accessing the system over the network. To avoid unpleasant surprises, always type iptables rules at the console—the keyboard and monitor that are connected directly to your Red Hat Linux PC that is running the packet filter. If you want to delete all filtering rules in a hurry, flush all the rules by typing the following command:

```
iptables -F
```

I won't provide all the details of the iptables commands in this section. Type **man iptables** to read a summary of the commands. You can also read about netfilter and iptables at http://www.iptables.org.

After you define the rules by using the iptables command, they are in the memory and will be gone when you reboot the system. To save them, use the iptables-save command to store the rules in a file. For example, you can save the rules in a file named iptables .rules by using the following commands:

```
iptables-save > iptables.rules
```

Here's a listing of the iptables.rules file, generated on a Red Hat Linux system:

```
# Generated by iptables-save v1.2.7a on Fri Feb  7 20:47:16 2003
*filter
:INPUT ACCEPT [480:30210]
:FORWARD ACCEPT [0:0]
:OUTPUT ACCEPT [3266:217223]
-A INPUT -s 192.168.0.0/255.255.255.0 -j ACCEPT
-A INPUT -i ! lo -j REJECT --reject-with icmp-port-unreachable
-A FORWARD -j REJECT --reject-with icmp-port-unreachable
COMMIT
# Completed on Fri Feb  7 20:47:16 2003
```

In case you are curious, these rules correspond to the following `iptables` commands I used to configure the filter:

```
iptables -A INPUT -s 192.168.0.0/24 -j ACCEPT
iptables -A INPUT -i ! lo -j REJECT
iptables -A FORWARD -j REJECT
```

If you want to load these saved rules into `iptables`, use the following command:

```
iptables-restore < iptables.rules
```

---

insider insight

On a Red Hat Linux system, the process of saving and restoring firewall rules is automated by saving the `iptables` rules in the file `/etc/sysconfig/iptables` and by enabling `iptables` with the following command:

```
chkconfig iptables on
```

That should ensure that the `/etc/init.d/iptables start` command is executed at system startup. The `/etc/init.d/iptables` script then runs the `/sbin/iptables-restore` command to restore the `iptables` rules from the `/etc/sysconfig/iptables` file.

Performing Security Audits

The purpose of a computer security audit is to basically test your system and network security. For larger organizations, the security audit may be done by an independent auditor (much like the auditing of financial statements). If you have only a few Red Hat Linux systems or a small network, you can do the security audit as a self-assessment, just to figure out if you are doing everything okay or not.

The following sections explain how to perform computer security audits and show you a number of free tools and resources to help you test your system's security.

Understanding Computer Security Audits

An audit is simply an independent assessment of whatever it is you are auditing. So a computer security audit is an independent assessment of computer security.

Secret

A typical computer security audit of your organization would focus on two areas:

- Independent verification of whether your organization is complying with its existing policies and procedures for computer security. This is the *nontechnical* part of the security audit.

- Independent testing of the effectiveness of your security controls, which refer to any hardware and software security mechanisms you use to secure the system. This is the *technical* part of the security audit.

You might wonder why you need security audits. You need them for the same reason an organization needs financial audits—mainly to verify that everything is being done the way it is supposed to be done. For public as well as private organizations, management may want independent security audits to assure themselves that their security is adequate. Regardless of your organization's size, you can always perform security audits on your own, either to prepare for independent security audits or simply to verify that you're doing everything right.

No matter whether you have independent security audits or a self-assessment, here are some of the benefits you get from security audits:

♦ Periodic risk assessments that consider internal and external threats to systems and data

♦ Periodic testing of the effectiveness of security policies, security controls, and techniques

♦ Identification of any significant deficiencies in your system's security (so you know what to fix)

♦ In case of self-assessments, preparation for any annual independent security testing that your organization might have to face

The nontechnical side of computer security audits focuses on your organization-wide security framework. The audit examines how well the organization has set up and implemented the policies, plans, and procedures for computer security. Some of the items to be verified include

♦ Risks are periodically assessed.

♦ There is an entity-wide security program plan.

♦ A security program management structure is put in place.

♦ Computer security responsibilities are clearly assigned.

♦ Effective security-related personnel policies are in place.

♦ The security program's effectiveness is monitored and changes are made when needed.

As you may expect, the nontechnical aspects of the security audit involves reviewing documents and interviewing appropriate individuals to learn how the organization manages computer security. Of course, for a small organization or a home PC, it's ridiculous to expect plans and procedures to be captured in documents. In those cases, all you need to do is make sure is that you have some technical controls in place to secure your system and your network connection.

The technical side of computer security audits focus on testing the technical controls that secure your hosts and network. The testing involves determining:

♦ **How well the host is secured.** Are all operating system patches applied? Are the file permissions set correctly? Are user accounts protected? Are file changes monitored? Are log files monitored? And so on.

♦ **How well the network is secured.** Are unnecessary Internet services turned off? Is a firewall installed? Are remote logins secured with tools such as SSH? Are TCP wrapper access controls used? And so on.

Typically security experts use automated tools to perform these two security reviews—host and network.

Learning a Security Test Methodology

A key element of computer security audit is the security test that checks the technical mechanisms used to secure a host and the network. The security test methodology follows these high-level steps:

1. Take stock of the organization's networks, hosts, network devices (routers, switches, firewalls, and so on), and how the network is connected to the Internet.
2. If there are many hosts and network connections, determine what are the important hosts and network devices that should be tested. The importance of a host depends on the kind of applications it runs.
3. Test the hosts individually. Typically, this involves logging in as a system administrator and then performing checking various aspects of host security from passwords to system log files.
4. Test the network. This is usually done by attempting to break through the network defenses from another system on the Internet. If there is a firewall, the testing checks that the firewall is indeed configured correctly.
5. Analyze the test results of both host and network tests to determine the vulnerabilities and risks.

Each of the two types of testing—host and network—focuses on three areas that comprise overall computer security:

♦ **Prevention**—This includes the mechanisms (nontechnical and technical) that help prevent attacks on the system and the network

♦ **Detection**—This refers to techniques such as monitoring log files, checking file integrity, and using intrusion detection systems that can detect when someone is about to break into, or has already broken into, your system

♦ **Response**—This includes the steps, such as reporting an incident to authorities and restoring important files from backup, that you perform when a computer security incident has occurred.

These host and network security areas have some overlaps. For example, prevention mechanisms for host security, such as good passwords or file permissions, can also provide network security. Nevertheless, it helps to think in terms of the three areas—prevention, detection, and response.

Before you can think of prevention, however, you need to know the types of problems that you are trying to prevent. In other words, what are the common security vulnerabilities? The prevention and detection steps typically depend on what these vulnerabilities are.

Understanding Common Computer Vulnerabilities

The specific tests of the host and network security depend on the common vulnerabilities. Basically, the idea is to check if a host or a network has the vulnerabilities that crackers are most likely to exploit.

Online Resources on Computer Vulnerabilities

There are several online resources that identify and categorize computer security vulnerabilities:

♦ *SANS Institute* publishes a list of Top 20 most critical Internet security vulnerabilities at `http://www.sans.org/top20/`.

♦ *CVE* (Common Vulnerabilities and Exposures) is a list of standardized names of vulnerabilities. For more information on CVE, see `http://cve.mitre.org` (the list has over 2,200 names of vulnerabilities). It's common practice to use the CVE name to describe vulnerabilities.

♦ The *ICAT Metabase* is a searchable index of information on computer vulnerabilities, published by National Institute of Standards and Technology (NIST), a United States government agency. The ICAT vulnerability index is online at `http://icat.nist.gov`. ICAT has nearly 5,400 vulnerabilities and it provides links to vulnerability advisory and patch information for each vulnerability. ICAT also a Top Ten List that lists the vulnerabilities that were most queried during the past year.

Typical Top 20 Computer Vulnerabilities

The SANS Top 20 vulnerabilities list includes three types of vulnerabilities—general ones that affect all systems, Windows vulnerabilities, and UNIX vulnerabilities. Of these, the general and UNIX vulnerabilities are relevant to Red Hat Linux. Table 22-4 summarizes the general and UNIX vulnerabilities that apply to Red Hat Linux. The information in the table is based on past SANS Top 20 lists. You can read the complete details about these vulnerabilities at `http://www.sans.org/top20`.

Table 22-4: Some Common Computer Vulnerability Types

Vulnerability Type	Description
General Vulnerabilities	
Default install options	These are the vulnerabilities introduced by the default installation options that often install unneeded software or configure software with insufficient security
Weak or no password	Many user accounts have weak passwords that can be easily cracked by password-cracking programs. Also, some software packages may add user accounts with no password or a standard password that everyone knows.
Incomplete or no backups	If a security incident occurs, the files may have to be restored from backups. However, it's a common mistake to either not do backups regularly or not test the backups for completeness.
Large number of open ports	The open ports refer to Internet services that are enabled on a system. Sometimes there are many unnecessary Internet services running on a system.
Incorrect or no filtering of packets	An IP address-based packet filter can cut back on attacks, but many systems do not have any packet filtering enabled. With iptables, it's easy to turn on packet filtering in Red Hat Linux.
Incomplete or no logging	The system logs are the only way to figure out the sequence of events that led to someone breaking into your system. Unfortunately, sometimes the logging is not set up correctly.
Vulnerable CGI programs	This vulnerability refers to the common gateway interface (CGI) that's used on Web servers to process interactive Web pages (for example, forms that request input from users). A CGI program with vulnerability (such as buffer flow) can provide attackers a way to do bad things to your system.

(continued)

Table 22-4: *(continued)*

Vulnerability Type	Description
UNIX Vulnerabilities	
RPC buffer overflows (NFS, NIS)	Services such as Network File System (NFS) and Network Information System (NIS) use remote procedure calls (RPC), and there are some known vulnerabilities in RPC.
Sendmail vulnerabilities	Sendmail is a complex program used to transport mail messages from one system to another, and some versions of Sendmail have vulnerabilities.
BIND (DNS) weaknesses	Berkeley Internet Name Domain (BIND) is a package that implements Domain Name System (DNS), the Internet's name service that translates a name to an IP address. Some versions of BIND have vulnerabilities.
r command (rlogin, rsh, rcp) vulnerabilities	The so-called r commands allow an attacker to easily access any system that has an implicit trust relationship with others (the r commands assume a trust relationship).
LPD (remote printing) vulnerabilities	LPD is the print server process and it listens on port 515 for remote printing requests. Unfortunately, the remote printing capability has a buffer overflow vulnerability.
Default SNMP strings	Simple Network Management Protocol (SNMP) is used to remotely monitor and administer various network-connected systems ranging from routers to computers. SNMP lacks good access control, so, if SNMP is running on your system, an attacker may be able to reconfigure or shut down your system.

Reviewing Host Security

When reviewing host security, focus on assessing the security mechanisms in each of the following areas:

- ◆ **Prevention.** Install operating system updates, secure passwords, improve file permissions, set up password for boot loader, and use encryption.
- ◆ **Detection.** Capture log messages and check file integrity with Tripwire.
- ◆ **Response.** Make routine backups and develop incident response procedures.

I describe how to review a few of these host security mechanisms.

Operating System Updates

Red Hat issues Red Hat Linux updates as soon they learn of any security vulnerabilities, but it's up to you or a system administrator to download and install the updates. One way to keep up with the Red Hat Linux security patches is to sign up for the Red Hat Network service (it's free for a single machine, but costs for a subscription for other machines).

You can install them using the rpm command. If you place all current updates in a single directory, you can use the following command to install them:

```
rpm -F *.rpm
```

On larger organizations, an authorized system administrator should install the operating system updates.

To assess whether the operating system updates are current, an auditor gets a current list of updates for key Red Hat Linux components and then uses the `rpm` command to check if they are installed. For example, if a list shows that `glibc` version 2.2.5 is what the system should have, the auditor types the following `rpm` command to view the current `glibc` version number:

```
rpm -q glibc
```

If the version number is less than 2.2.5, the conclusion is that operating system updates are not being installed.

File Permissions

Key system files should be protected with appropriate file ownerships and file permissions. The key steps in assigning file system ownerships and permissions are to:

- ♦ Figure out which files contain sensitive information and why. Some files may contain sensitive data related to your work or business, whereas many other files are sensitive because they control the Red Hat Linux system configuration.
- ♦ Maintain a current list of authorized users and what they are authorized to do on the system.
- ♦ Set up passwords, groups, file ownerships, and file permissions to allow only authorized users access the files.

Table 22-5 lists some of the important system files in Red Hat Linux. The table also shows the numeric permission setting for each file.

Table 22-5: Important System Files and Their Permissions

File Pathname	Permission	Description
`/boot/grub/grub.conf`	600	GRUB bootloader configuration file
`/etc/cron.allow`	400	List of users permitted to use cron to submit periodic jobs
`/etc/cron.deny`	400	List of users who cannot use cron to submit periodic jobs
`/etc/crontab`	644	System-wide periodic jobs
`/etc/hosts.allow`	644	List of hosts allowed to use Internet services that are started using TCP wrappers
`/etc/hosts.deny`	644	List of hosts denied access to Internet services that are started using TCP wrappers
`/etc/logrotate.conf`	644	File that controls how log files are rotated
`/etc/pam.d`	755	Directory with configuration files for pluggable authentication modules (PAM)

(continued)

Table 22-5: *(continued)*

File Pathname	Permission	Description
/etc/passwd	644	Old-style password file with user account information but not the passwords
/etc/rc.d	755	Directory with system startup scripts
/etc/securetty	600	TTY interfaces (terminals) from which root can login
/etc/security	755	Policy files that control system access
/etc/shadow	400	File with encrypted passwords and password expiry information
/etc/shutdown.allow	400	Users who can shutdown or reboot by pressing Ctrl-Alt-Delete
/etc/ssh	755	Directory with configuration files for the Secure Shell (SSH)
/etc/sysconfig	755	System configuration files
/etc/sysctl.conf	644	Kernel configuration parameters
/etc/syslog.conf	644	Configuration file for syslogd server that logs messages
/etc/vsftpd	600	Configuration file for the very secure FTP server
/etc/vsftpd.ftpusers	600	List of users who cannot use FTP to transfer files
/etc/xinetd.conf	644	Configuration file for the xinetd server
/etc/xinetd.d	755	Directory containing configuration files for specific services that the xinetd server can start
/var/log	755	Directory with all log files
/var/log/lastlog	644	Information about all previous logins
/var/log/messages	644	Main system message log file
/var/log/secure	400	Security related log file
/var/log/wtmp	664	Information about current logins

Another important check is to look for executable program files that have the setuid permission. If a program has setuid permission and it's owned by `root`, then the program runs with `root` privileges, no matter who runs the program. You can find all setuid programs with the following `find` command:

```
find / -perm +4000 -print
```

You may want to save the output in a file (just append > filename to the command) and then examine the file for any unusual setuid programs. For example, a setuid program in a user's home directory would be unusual.

Password Security

Verify that the password, group, and shadow password files are protected. In particular, the shadow password file should be write-protected and readable only by root. The file-names and their recommended permissions are shown in Table 22-6.

Table 22-6: Ownership and Permission of Password Files

File Pathname	Ownership	Permission
/etc/group	root.root	644
/etc/passwd	root.root	644
/etc/shadow	root.root	400

Incident Response

Incident response is the answer to the question of what to do if something does happen. In other words, if someone has broken into your system, what you need to do.

Your response to an incident depends on how you use your system and how important it is to you or your business. For a comprehensive incident response, here are some key points to remember:

- Figure out how critical and important your computer and network are and iden-tify who or what resources can help you protect your system.
- Take steps to prevent and minimize potential damage and interruption.
- Develop and document a comprehensive contingency plan.
- Periodically test the contingency plan and revise the procedures as appropriate.

Reviewing Network Security

Network security review focuses on assessing the security mechanisms in each of the fol-lowing areas:

- **Prevention.** Set up firewall, enable packet filtering, disable unnecessary xinetd services, turn off unneeded Internet services, use TCP wrappers access control, and use SSH for secure remote logins.
- **Detection.** Use network intrusion detection and capture system logs.
- **Response.** Develop incident response procedures.

I briefly describe some key steps in assessing the network security.

Services Started by xinetd

Many Internet services such as Telnet and POP3 are started by the xinetd server. The decision to turn on some of these services depends on factors such as how the system is connected to the Internet and how the system is being used. You can usually turn off most xinetd services.

Check which xinetd services are turned on by using one of the following ways:

♦ Check the configuration files in the /etc/xinetd.d directory for all the services that xinetd can start. If a service is turned off, the configuration file has a line like this:

```
disable = yes
```

Remember that the disable = yes line doesn't count if it's commented out by placing a # at the beginning of the line.

♦ Type the following command:

```
chkconfig --list | more
```

In the output, look for the lines that follow:

```
xinetd based services:
```

These lines list all the services that xinetd can start and whether they are on or off. For example, here are a few lines showing status of xinetd services on a system:

```
chargen-udp:    off
rsync:  off
chargen:        off
daytime-udp:    off
daytime:        off
echo-udp:       off
echo:   off
services:       off
servers:        off
time-udp:       off
time:   off
cups-lpd:       off
sgi_fam:        on
kotalk: off
ktalk:  off
imap:   off
imaps:  off
ipop2:  off
ipop3:  off
... lines deleted ...
```

In this case, the sgi_fam (a server that reports changes to any file) service is on, but everything else is off.

Also check the following files for any access controls used with the xinetd services:

♦ /etc/hosts.allow lists hosts allowed to access specific services.
♦ /etc/hosts.deny lists hosts that should be denied access to services.

Standalone Services

Many services such as the httpd (Web server) and sendmail (mail server) start automatically at boot time, assuming that they are configured to start that way. You can use the chkconfig command to check which standalone servers are set to start at various run levels. Typically, your Red Hat Linux system starts up at run level 3 (for text login) or 5 (for graphical login). Therefore, what matters is the setting for the servers in levels 3 and 5. To view the list of servers, type the following command:

```
chkconfig --list | more
```

Here's a partial listing of what you might see:

```
snmpd           0:off   1:off   2:off   3:off   4:off   5:off   6:off
snmptrapd       0:off   1:off   2:off   3:off   4:off   5:off   6:off
iptables        0:off   1:off   2:on    3:on    4:on    5:on    6:off
gpm             0:off   1:off   2:on    3:on    4:on    5:on    6:off
kudzu           0:off   1:off   2:off   3:on    4:on    5:on    6:off
winbind         0:off   1:off   2:off   3:off   4:off   5:off   6:off
ntpd            0:off   1:off   2:off   3:off   4:off   5:off   6:off
syslog          0:off   1:off   2:on    3:on    4:on    5:on    6:off
atd             0:off   1:off   2:off   3:on    4:on    5:on    6:off
netfs           0:off   1:off   2:off   3:on    4:on    5:on    6:off
network         0:off   1:off   2:on    3:on    4:on    5:on    6:off
random          0:off   1:off   2:on    3:on    4:on    5:on    6:off
rawdevices      0:off   1:off   2:off   3:on    4:on    5:on    6:off
saslauthd       0:off   1:off   2:off   3:off   4:off   5:off   6:off
xinetd          0:off   1:off   2:off   3:on    4:on    5:on    6:off
...lines deleted...
```

The first column shows the names of the servers. Look at the column of entries that begin with 3: and the ones that begin with 5:. These are the ones that show the status of the server for run levels 3 and 5. The ones that appear as on are automatically started when your Red Hat Linux system starts.

If you are doing a self-assessment of your network security and you find that some servers should not be running, you can turn them off for run levels 3 and 5 with the chkconfig command like this:

```
chkconfig --level 35 servicename off
```

Replace servicename with the name of the service you want to turn off.

If you are auditing network security, make a note of all the servers that are turned on and then try to determine if they should really be on, based on what you know about the system. The decision to turn on services depends on how a system is used (as a Web server or a desktop system) and how it is connected to the Internet (through a firewall or directly).

Penetration Testing

A penetration test is the best way to tell what services are really running on a Red Hat Linux system. Penetration testing involves trying to get access to your system from an attacker's perspective. Typically, you perform this test from a system on the Internet and try to see if you can break in or, at a minimum, get access to services running on your Red Hat Linux system.

Secret

One aspect of penetration testing is to see what ports are open on your Red Hat Linux system. The port number is simply a number that identifies specific TCP/IP network connections to the system. The attempt to connect to a port succeeds only if a server is running on that port (or put another way, if a server is "listening on that port"). A port is considered to be open if a server responds when a connection request for that port arrives.

The first step in penetration testing is to perform a port scan. The term port scan is used to describe the automated process of trying to connect to each port number and see if a valid response comes back. There are many automated tools available to perform port scanning—Red Hat Linux comes with a popular port scanning tool called `nmap` (I describe it later in this chapter).

After performing a port scan, you know the potential vulnerabilities that could be exploited. Not all servers have security problems, but many servers have well-known vulnerabilities, and an open port provides a cracker a way to attack your system through one of the servers. In fact, you can use automated tools called vulnerability scanners to identify vulnerabilities that exist in your system. (I describe some vulnerability scanners next.) Whether your Red Hat Linux system is connected to the Internet directly (through DSL or cable modem) or through a firewall, use the port scanning and vulnerability scanning tools to figure out if you have any holes in your defenses. Better you than them!

Exploring Security-Testing Tools

There are many automated tools available to perform security testing. Some tools are meant for finding the open ports on every system in a range of IP addresses. Others are meant to find the vulnerabilities associated with the open ports. Yet other tools can capture (or sniff) and help you analyze them so you can glean useful information about what's going on in your network.

You can browse a list of top 50 security tools (based on informal poll of nmap users) at `http://www.insecure.org/tools.html`. Table 22-7 lists a number of tools by category. I describe a few of the freely available vulnerability scanners in the next few sections.

Table 22-7: Some Popular Computer Security Tools

Type	Names of Tools
Port scanners	nmap, Strobe
Vulnerability scanners	Nessus Security Scanner, SAINT, SARA, Whisker (CGI scanner), ISS Internet Scanner, CyberCop Scanner, Vetescan, Retina Network Security Scanner
Network utilities	Netcat, hping2, Firewalk, Cheops, ntop, ping
Host security tools	Tripwire, lsof
Packet sniffers	tcpdump, Ethereal, dsniff, sniffit
Intrusion detection system (IDS)	Snort, Abacus portsentry, scanlogd, NFR, LIDS
Password checking tools	John the Ripper, LC4
Log analysis and monitoring tools	logcolorise, tcpdstats, nlog, logcheck, Swatch

nmap

nmap (short for Network Mapper) is a port scanning tool. It can rapidly scan large networks and determine what hosts are available on the network, what services they are offering, what operating system (and the operating system version) they are running, what type of packet filters or firewalls are in use, and dozens of other characteristics. Red Hat Linux comes with nmap. You can read more about nmap at www.insecure.org/nmap.

If you want to try out nmap to scan your local area network, just type a command similar to the following (replace the IP address range with addresses appropriate for your network):

```
nmap -O -sS 192.168.0.2-10
```

Here's part of a typical output listing from that nmap command:

```
Starting nmap V. 3.00 ( www.insecure.org/nmap/ )
Interesting ports on dhcppc1 (192.168.0.2):
(The 1595 ports scanned but not shown below are in state: closed)
Port        State        Service
21/tcp      open         ftp
22/tcp      open         ssh
23/tcp      open         telnet
111/tcp     open         sunrpc
1024/tcp    open         kdm
6000/tcp    open         X11
Remote operating system guess: Linux Kernel 2.4.0 - 2.5.20
Uptime 3.322 days (since Tue Feb  4 14:07:38 2003)

Interesting ports on dhcppc2 (192.168.0.3):
(The 1600 ports scanned but not shown below are in state: closed)
Port        State        Service
139/tcp     open         netbios-ssn
Remote OS guesses: Turtle Beach AudioTron Firmware 3.0, Windows NT4 or 95/98/98SE
... lines deleted ...
```

As you can see, nmap displays the names of the open ports and hazards a guess at the operating system name and version number.

Nessus

The Nessus Security Scanner is a modular security auditing tool that uses plugins written in Nessus scripting language to test for a wide variety of network vulnerabilities. Nessus uses a client-server software architecture with a server called nessusd and a client called nessus.

insider insight   Before you try to install Nessus, you must install the sharutils RPM. That package includes the uudecode utility that the Nessaus installation script needs. For some reason, the sharutils package is no longer installed with any of the standard package groups.

To install sharutils, follow these steps:

1. Mount the companion CDs one by one and locate the package whose name starts with `sharutils`. You can try the following sequence commands after mounting the CD on `/mnt/cdrom`:

   ```
   cd /mnt/cdrom/RedHat/RPMS
   ls sharutils*
   ```

2. After you find the sharutils package, install it with the following command:

   ```
   rpm -ivh sharutils*.rpm
   ```

To download and install Nessus, follow these steps:

1. Read the instructions on `http://www.nessus.org/posix.html`. Then scroll down on that page, click a link to an appropriate FTP site, and download the files `nessus-installer.sh` and `MD5`.

2. Type the following command to install Nessus (you must have the development tools, including the GIMP Toolkit, installed):

   ```
   sh nessus-installer.sh
   ```

   This should extract the Nessus files and build all the executables and libraries. I have had some compilation errors sometimes, but I hope the steps complete without any problems when you try it.

After the installation is complete, here are the steps to use Nessus:

1. Log in as `root` and type the following command to create the Nessus SSL certificate used for secure communication between the Nessus client and the Nessus server:

   ```
   nessus-mkcert
   ```

2. Provide the requested information to complete the certificate generation process.

3. Create a `nessusd` account with the following command:

   ```
   nessus-adduser
   ```

4. When prompted, enter your user name, password, and any rules (press Ctrl-D if you don't know what rules to enter).

5. If you want to, you can configure `nessusd` by editing the configuration file `/usr/local/etc/nessus/nessusd.conf`. If you want to try out Nessus, you can proceed with the default configuration file.

6. Start the Nessus server with this command:

   ```
   nessusd -D
   ```

7. Run the Nessus client by typing the following command in a terminal window:

   ```
   nessus
   ```

   The Nessus Setup window appears.

8. Type a nessusd user name and password, and then click Log In. Nessus displays the certificate used to establish the secure connection and asks if you accept it. Click Yes. After the client connects to the server, the Log in button changes to Log out, and a Connected label appears at its left.

9. Click the Target selection tab. Enter a range of IP addresses to scan all hosts in a network. For example, to scan the first eight hosts in a private network 192.168.0.0, I enter the address as:

   `192.168.0.0/29`

10. Click Start the Scan. Nessus starts scanning the IP addresses and checks for many different vulnerabilities. Progress bars show the status of the scan.

After Nessus completes the vulnerability scan of the hosts, it displays the result in a nice combination of graphical and text formats. The report is interactive—you can click on a host address to view the report on that host, and you can drill down on a specific vulnerability (including the CVE number that identifies the vulnerability).

SAINT

Security Administrator's Integrated Network Tool (SAINT) scans hosts for a variety of security vulnerabilities. For the vulnerabilities it finds, SAINT shows the Common Vulnerabilities and Exposures (CVE) identifier. Older versions of SAINT are free, but the latest version is available to only those who purchase SAINTWriter or SAINTexpress.

You can download a crippled (limited to scanning two hosts only) 15-day trial version of SAINT from `http://www.saintcorporation.com/products/download.html` and see what it can do. You can decide whether to buy the full version or not.

I won't describe the steps for downloading and installing the trial version. You will find the instructions on the page from which you download the free trial version of SAINT.

SARA

Security Auditor's Research Assistant (SARA) is a vulnerability-scanning tool based on SAINT. SARA scans for known vulnerabilities, including those in the CVE list and the SANS Top 20 List (`http://www.sans.org/top20.htm`).

To try out SARA, download the latest version of SARA from `http://www-arc.com/sara/downloads/`. After downloading the compressed `tar` file, build and install the software using these steps:

1. Unpack tar file with the command:

   `tar zxvf sara*`

2. To configure SARA, type the following commands:

   ```
   cd sara*
   ./configure
   ```

3. To build the software, type:

   `make`

After SARA is built, run it with the following command:

`./sara`

SARA starts a Web browser and displays its user interface in the Web browser. You can perform various tasks by clicking the links along the left-hand side of the Web browser. For example, to perform a vulnerability scan, click the Target Selection link. SARA brings up a form where you can provide information about hosts and networks to scan. You can also specify the scanning level—anywhere from light to extreme.

After filling in the information, click the Start the Scan button at the bottom of the form. SARA starts to perform the vulnerability scan. During the scan, SARA displays a data collection page that indicates progress of the scan.

After the scan is complete, you can proceed to data analysis and view the vulnerability information.

Keeping up with Security News and Updates

To keep up with the latest security alerts, you may want to visit one or more of the following sites on a daily basis:

 * CERT Coordination Center at http://www.cert.org
 * Computer Incident Advisory Capability (CIAC) at http://www.ciac.org/ciac/
 * National Infrastructure Protection Center at http://www.nipc.gov/

If you have access to Internet newsgroups, you can periodically browse the following:

 * **comp.security.announce**—A moderated newsgroup that includes announcements from CERT about security.
 * **comp.security.unix**—A newsgroup that includes discussions of UNIX security issues, including items related to Red Hat Linux

If you prefer to receive regular security updates through email, you can also sign up for, or subscribe to, various mailing lists:

 * **redhat-watch-list**—Follow the directions in www.redhat.com/mailing-lists/ to subscribe to this mailing list.
 * **linux-security**—Follow the directions in www.redhat.com/mailing-lists/ to subscribe to this mailing list.
 * **FOCUS-LINUX**—Fill out the form in http://online.securityfocus.com/cgi-bin/sfonline/subscribe.pl to subscribe to this mailing list focused on Linux security issues.
 * **Cert Advisory mailing list**—Follow the directions in http://www.cert.org/contact_cert/certmaillist.html to subscribe to this mailing list.

Finally, you should check Red Hat's website at www.redhat.com/apps/support/errata/index.html for updates that may fix any known security problems with Red Hat Linux.

Summary

As the system administrator, your primary concern is the security of your Red Hat Linux system and the local network. You may also have to worry about securing it from unwanted access from the Internet. This chapter introduces you to the subjects of system and network security and shows you how to use some of the security features of Red Hat Linux.

By reading this chapter, you learn the following:

♦ It is helpful to think of an organization-wide security framework. In such a framework, you first establish a security policy based on business requirements and risk analysis. Then, you develop an overall security solution based on security policy, business requirements, and available technology. Finally, you put in place the management practices to continually monitor, detect, and respond to any security problems.

♦ Risk analysis means identifying threats and vulnerabilities. Then, you can assess the probability and impact of each vulnerability and decide to mitigate those vulnerabilities that are most likely to be exploited and whose exploitation will cause the most harm.

♦ To secure the Red Hat Linux system, you have to secure the passwords and the network services, such as FTP, NFS, and HTTP. You can use the chkconfig command to disable unnecessary services. For services started by xinetd you can also edit the configuration files in /etc/xinetd.d directory to turn services off or on.

♦ Use secure shell (SSH) for secure remote logins. This chapter shows you how to use SSH.

♦ For a system connected to the Internet (including a local network), you can meet network security needs by setting up a firewall between the internal network and the Internet. Any publicly accessible servers, such as Web and FTP servers, should be placed outside the firewall in a perimeter network or the demilitarized zone (DMZ).

♦ There are many kinds of firewalls—packet filters, dual-homed hosts, and application gateways (or proxy servers). This chapter provides an overview of firewalls. You can implement a packet-filtering firewall by using the iptables software that comes with Red Hat Linux.

♦ You can monitor the integrity of system files and directories by installing and setting up the Tripwire software that comes on the companion CD-ROMs.

♦ You should periodically review the log files in the /var/log directory of your Red Hat Linux system for any signs of intrusion attempts.

♦ You should also perform a periodic security audit of your system and network. You can use some automated tools such as nmap and Nessus to test your network security.

♦ The chapter provides some online resources from which you can learn more about securing your Red Hat Linux system. You can use these online resources to keep up with late-breaking security news.

Part V

Programming Red Hat Linux

Software
Development
in Linux

Chapter
23

◆ ◆

Secrets in This Chapter

◆ ◆

Many Linux users happen to be software developers. If you want to develop software as a hobby or want to add features to Linux, you'll find that Linux includes everything you need to create UNIX and X applications. You can use the GNU C and C++ compilers to write conventional programs (that you compile and link into an executable). As an alternative, you can use the Tcl/Tk scripting language to write interpreted graphical applications.

This chapter discusses software development on a Linux PC. The focus is not on any specific programming language. Instead, this chapter describes how to use various software-development tools, such as compilers, makefiles, and version-control systems.

The chapter also describes the implications of Free Software Foundation's GNU Public License on any plans you might have to develop Linux software. You need to know this because you usually use GNU tools and GNU libraries to develop software in Linux.

Also, I discuss dynamic linking and the Executable and Linking Format (ELF), which makes dynamic linking easier. These topics are of interest to Linux programmers because dynamic linking reduces the size of executables and may enable programmers to distribute software in binary form, even if software uses the GNU libraries.

Software Development Tools in Linux

As expected, as a UNIX look-alike, Linux includes these traditional UNIX software-development tools:

- ✦ A text editor, such as `vi` or `emacs`, for editing the source code (described in Chapter 11)
- ✦ A C compiler for compiling and linking programs written in C—the programming language of choice for writing UNIX applications (although nowadays, many programmers are turning to C++). Linux includes the GNU C and C++ compilers. Originally, the GNU C Compiler was known as GCC. The acronym GCC now stands for GNU Compiler Collection (see description in `http://gcc .gnu.org/`).
- ✦ The GNU make utility for automating the software build process—the process of combining object modules into an executable or a library
- ✦ A debugger for debugging programs. Linux includes the GNU debugger `gdb`.
- ✦ A version-control system to keep track of various revisions of a source file. Linux comes with RCS (Revision Control System) and CVS (Concurrent Versions System). Nowadays, most open-source projects use CVS as the version-control system.

These tools are installed automatically if you select the *Development Tools* package group when you install Red Hat Linux from this book's companion CD-ROMs, following the steps outlined in Chapter 2. The next few sections briefly describe how to use these tools to write applications for Linux.

Using info for Help on GNU Tools

You may have noticed that most of the Linux software-development tools are from the Free Software Foundation's GNU project. The online documentation for all these tools comes as `info` files. The `info` program is GNU's hypertext help system.

To see info in action, type **info** at the shell prompt, or type **Esc-x** followed by **info** in GNU Emacs. Typically, I access info from GNU Emacs; doing so enables me to use online help while editing a program. However, you can always type **info** in a separate terminal window. Figure 23-1 shows the terminal window after I type **info** at the shell prompt.

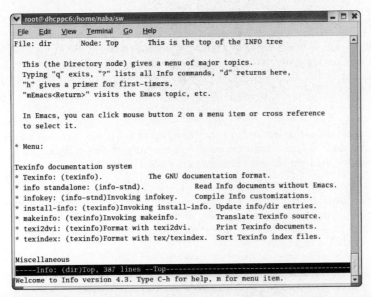

Figure 23-1: The Terminal Window after Typing info at the Shell Prompt.

In info, the online help text is organized in nodes; each node represents information on a specific topic. The first line shows the header for that node.

Figure 23-1 shows the initial info screen, with a directory of topics. This directory is an info file: /usr/share/info/dir, a text file that contains embedded special characters. The following are a few lines from the /usr/share/info/dir file that correspond to the screen shown in Figure 23-1:

```
$Id: dir.v 1.2 1996/09/24 18:43:01 karl Exp $
This is the file .../info/dir, which contains the topmost node of the
Info hierarchy.  The first time you invoke Info you start off
looking at that node, which is (dir)Top.
^_  (This is the Ctrl+_ character)
File: dir       Node: Top       This is the top of the INFO tree

  This (the Directory node) gives a menu of major topics.
  Typing "q" exits, "?" lists all Info commands, "d" returns here,
  "h" gives a primer for first-timers,
  "mEmacs<Return>" visits the Emacs topic, etc.

  In Emacs, you can click mouse button 2 on a menu item or cross reference
  to select it.

* Menu:
```

```
Texinfo documentation system
* Standalone info program: (info-stnd).    Standalone Info-reading program.
* Texinfo: (texinfo).            The GNU documentation format.
* install-info: (texinfo)Invoking install-info. Update info/dir entries.
* makeinfo: (texinfo)makeinfo Preferred.       Translate Texinfo source.
(...Lines deleted...)
```

A comparison of this listing with the screen shown in Figure 23-1 shows that info displays only the lines that follow the Ctrl+_ character. In your system, the /usr/share/info directory contains this info file, as well as others, with the text for each topic. Usually, these info files are stored in compressed format. You really don't have to know these details to use the info files.

---

insider insight You have to use several single-letter commands to navigate info files. The best way to learn the commands is to type h from the initial info directory, shown in Figure 23-1. Type d after reading the help screens to return to the initial directory of topics.

From the directory screen of Figure 23-1, type **m**, followed by the name of a menu item (shown with an asterisk prefix). For example, to view the online help for GCC, type **m**; then type **gcc**, and press Enter. The info system, in turn, displays the top-level menu of items for GCC, as shown in Figure 23-2.

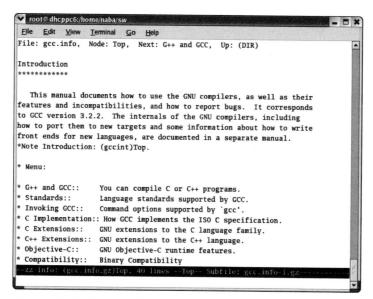

Figure 23-2: The Info Window, Showing the Top-Level Help on GCC.

You can explore further by typing **m**, followed by one of the menu items shown in Figure 23-2.

While you're at it, you may want to type **m**, then **copy**; then press Enter in the screen shown in Figure 23-2. That action displays the GNU General Public License (GPL), shown in Figure 23-3.

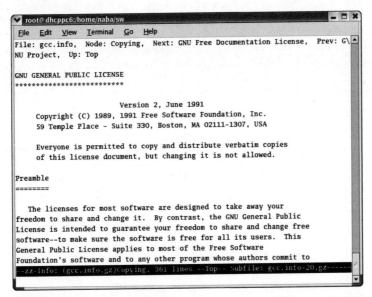

Figure 23-3: The Info Window, Showing the First Page of the GNU General Public License (GPL).

GPL covers Linux and the gcc compiler. GPL requires distribution of the source code (that's why all Linux distributions come with source code). In the "Implications of GNU Licenses" section, you learn that you can still use GNU tools to develop commercial applications and to distribute applications in binary form (without source code), as long as they link with selected GNU libraries only.

At any time in `info`, you can type **d** to return to the `info` topic directory shown in Figure 23-1. From that screen, you can view help on other GNU tools, such as make and the GNU debugger.

To quit info, type **q**. If you access `info` from the Emacs editor, press Ctrl+X, followed by Ctrl+C, to quit the Emacs editor.

Running the GNU C and C++ Compilers

The most important software-development tool in Linux is GCC, which is the GNU C and C++ compiler. In fact, GCC can compile three languages: C, C++, and Objective-C (a language that adds object-oriented extensions to C). You use the same `gcc` command to compile and link both C and C++ source files. The GCC compiler supports ANSI standard C, making it easy to port any ANSI C program to Linux. In addition, if you've ever used a C compiler on other UNIX systems, you are right at home with GCC.

Running GCC

Use the gcc command to run GCC. By default, when you use the gcc command on a source file, GCC preprocesses, compiles, and links the executable. However, you can use GCC options to stop this process at an intermediate stage. For example, you might invoke gcc by using the -c option to compile a source file and to generate an object file, but not to perform the link step.

Using GCC to compile and link a few C source files is very simple. Suppose you want to compile and link a simple program made up of two source files. The following listing shows the file area.c (the main program that computes the area of a circle whose radius is specified through the command line):

```
#include <stdio.h>
#include <stdlib.h>

/* Function prototype */
double area_of_circle(double r);

int main(int argc, char **argv)
{
  if(argc < 2)
  {
    printf("Usage: %s radius\n", argv[0]);
    exit(1);
  }
  else
  {
    double radius = atof(argv[1]);
    double area = area_of_circle(radius);
    printf("Area of circle with radius %f = %f\n",
        radius, area);
  }
  return 0;
}
```

The following listing shows the file circle.c, which provides a function that computes the area of a circle.

```
#include <math.h>

#define SQUARE(x) ((x)*(x))

double area_of_circle(double r)
{
  return 4.0 * M_PI * SQUARE(r);
}
```

For such a simple program, of course, I can place everything in a single file, but this contrived example lets me show you how to handle multiple files.

To compile these two programs and to create an executable file named area, you might use this command:

```
gcc -o area area.c circle.c
```

This invocation of GCC uses the -o option to specify the name of the executable file. (If you do not specify the name of an output file, GCC creates a file named a.out.)

If there are too many source files to compile and link, compile the files individually, and generate object files (that have the .o extension). That way, when you change a source file, you need to compile only that file and to link all the object files. The following example shows how to separate the compile and link steps for the example program:

```
gcc -c area.c
gcc -c circle.c
gcc -o area area.o circle.o
```

The first two invocations of gcc with the -c option compile the source files. The third invocation links the object files into an executable named area.

In case you are curious, here's how you run the sample program (to compute the area of a circle with a radius of 1):

```
./area 1
Area of circle with radius 1.000000 = 12.566371
```

insider insight

Incidentally, you have to add the ./ prefix to the program's name (area) only if the current directory is not in the PATH environment variable. There is no harm in adding the prefix, even if your PATH contains the current directory.

Compiling C++ programs

GNU CC is a combined C and C++ compiler, so the gcc command also can compile C++ source files. GCC uses the file extension to determine whether a file is C or C++. C files have a lowercase .c extension, whereas C++ files end with .C or .cpp.

Although the gcc command can compile a C++ file, that command does not automatically link with various class libraries that C++ programs typically require. That's why it's easier to compile and link a C++ program by using the g++ command, which invokes gcc with appropriate options.

Suppose you want to compile the following simple C++ program stored in a file named hello.C (it's customary to use an uppercase C extension for C++ source files):

```
#include <iostream>

int main()
{
  using namespace std;
  cout << "Hello from Red Hat Linux!" << endl;
}
```

To compile and link this program into an executable program named hello, use this command:

```
g++ -o hello hello.C
```

This command creates the hello executable, which you can run as follows:

```
./hello
Hello from Red Hat Linux!
```

As you see in the following section, a host of GCC options controls various aspects of compiling C++ programs.

Exploring GCC Options

Following is the basic syntax of the gcc command:

```
gcc options filenames
```

Each option starts with a hyphen (-) and usually has a long name, such as -funsigned-char or -finline-functions. Many commonly used options are short, however, such as -c, to compile only, and -g, to generate debugging information, (needed to debug the program by using the GNU debugger).

You can view a summary of all GCC options by using info. Type **info** at the shell prompt, and press m, followed by gcc. Then follow the menu items: Invoking GCC⇨Option Summary. Usually, you do not have to specify GCC options explicitly; the default settings are fine for most applications. Table 23-1 lists some of the GCC options you might use.

Table 23-1: Commonly Used GCC Options

Option	Meaning
-ansi	Support ANSI standard C syntax only. (This option disables some GNU C-specific features, such as the asm and typeof keywords.)
-c	Compile and generate object file only
-DMACRO	Define the macro with the string "1" as its value
-DMACRO=DEFN	Define the macro as *DEFN* where *DEFN* is some text
-E	Run only the C preprocessor
-fallow-single-precision	Perform all math operations in single precision
-fpack-struct	Pack all structure members without any padding
-fpcc-struct-return	Return all struct and union values in memory, rather than in registers. (Returning values this way is less efficient, but is compatible with other compilers.)
-fPIC	Generate position-independent code (PIC) suitable for use in a shared library
-freg-struct-return	When possible, return struct and union values in registers
-g	Generate debugging information. (The GNU debugger can use this information.)
-IDIRECTORY	Search the specified directory for files you include by using the #include preprocessor directive
-LDIRECTORY	Search the specified directory for libraries
-lLIBRARY	Search the specified library when linking
-mcpu=cputype	Optimize code for a specific processor (*cputype* can take many different values—some common ones are i386, i486, i586, i686, pentium2, pentium3, and pentium4).

Option	Meaning
-o FILE	Generate the specified output file (used to designate the name of an executable file)
-O0	Do not optimize
-O or -O1	Optimize the generated code
-O2	Optimize even more
-O3	Perform optimizations beyond those done for -O2
-pedantic	Generate errors if any non-ANSI standard extensions are used
-pg	Add extra code to the program so that, when run, it generates information the gprof program can use to display timing details for various parts of the program
-shared	Generate a shared object file (typically used to create a shared library)
-UMACRO	Undefine the specified macro (MACRO)
-v	Display the version number of GCC
-w	Don't generate any warning messages
-Wl,OPTION	Pass the OPTION string (containing multiple comma-separated options) to the linker. To create a shared library named libXXX.so.1, for example, use the following flag: -Wl,-soname,libXXX.so.1

Using the GNU make Utility

When an application is made up of more than a few source files, compiling and linking the files by manually typing the gcc command is inconvenient. Also, you do not want to compile every file whenever you change something in a single source file. The GNU make utility is helpful in this situation because make can compile only those files that really must be compiled.

The make utility works by reading and interpreting a *makefile*: a text file you have to prepare according to a specified syntax. The makefile describes which files constitute a program and explains how to compile and link the files to build the program. Whenever you change one or more files, make determines which files should be recompiled and issues the appropriate commands for compiling those files and rebuilding the program.

The make utility is, in fact, specified in Section 6.2 of the POSIX.2 standard (IEEE Standard 1003.2-1992) for shells and tools. GNU make conforms to the POSIX.2 standard.

Learning makefile Names

By default, GNU make looks for a makefile that has one of the following names, in the order shown:

- ◆ GNUmakefile
- ◆ makefile
- ◆ Makefile

In UNIX systems, using Makefile as the name of the makefile is customary because it appears near the beginning of directory listings where the uppercase names appear before the lowercase names.

When you download software from the Internet, you usually find a Makefile, together with the source files. To build the software, you have only to type **make** at the shell prompt; make takes care of all the steps necessary to build the software.

If your makefile does not have a standard name, such as Makefile, you have to use the -f option to specify the makefile's name. If your makefile is called webprog.mak, for example, you have to run make using the following command line:

```
make -f webprog.mak
```

GNU make also accepts several other command-line options, which are summarized in the "How to Run make" section of this chapter.

Understanding the makefile

For a program that consists of several source and header files, the makefile specifies the following:

- The items make will create—usually the object files and the executable. The term target is used for an item to be created.
- The files or other actions required to create the target.
- Which commands should be executed to create each target.

Suppose you have a C++ source file named form.C that contains the following preprocessor directive:

```
#include "form.h"  // Include header file
```

The object file form.o clearly depends on the source file form.C and the header file form.h. In addition to these dependencies, you must specify how make should convert the form.C file to the object file form.o. Suppose you want make to run g++ (because the source file is in C++) with these options:

- -c (compile only)
- -g (generate debugging information)
- -O2 (optimize some)

In the makefile, you can express this with the following rule:

```
# This a comment in the makefile
# The following lines indicate how form.o depends
# form.C and form.h and how to create form.o.

form.o: form.C form.h
        g++ -c -g -O2 form.C
```

In this example, the first noncomment line shows form.o as the target and form.C and form.h as the dependent files.

insider insight

The line following the dependency indicates how to build the target from its dependents. This line must start with a Tab; otherwise `make` will not work.

Secret

The benefit of using `make` is that it prevents unnecessary compilations. After all, you can invoke g++ (or gcc) in a shell script to compile and link all the files that make up your application, but the shell script compiles everything, even if the compilations are unnecessary. GNU `make`, on the other hand, builds a target, only if one or more of its dependents have changed since the last time the target was built. `make` verifies this change by examining the time of the last modification of the target and the dependents.

`make` treats the target as the name of a goal to be achieved; the target does not have to be a file. You can have a rule such as this:

```
clean:
        rm -f *.o
```

This rule specifies an abstract target named clean that does not depend on anything. This dependency statement says that to make clean, GNU make should invoke the command `rm -f *.o`, which deletes all files that have the .o extension (these are the object files). Thus, the net effect of creating the target named clean is to delete the object files.

Using Variables (or Macros)

In addition to the basic service of building targets from dependents, GNU `make` includes many nice features that make it easy for you to express the dependencies and rules for building a target from its dependents. If you need to compile a large number of C++ files by using GCC with the same options, for example, typing the options for each file is tedious. You can avoid this task by defining a variable or macro in `make` as follows:

```
# Define macros for name of compiler
CXX= g++

# Define a macro for the GCC flags
CXXFLAGS= -O2 -g -mcpu=i686

# A rule for building an object file
form.o: form.C form.h
        $(CXX) -c $(CXXFLAGS) form.C
```

In this example, `CXX` and `CXXFLAGS` are `make` variables. GNU `make` prefers to call them variables, but most UNIX `make` utilities call them macros.

To use a variable anywhere in the makefile, start with a dollar sign ($) followed by the variable within parentheses. GNU `make` replaces all occurrences of a variable with its definition; thus, it replaces all occurrences of $(CXXFLAGS) with the string `-O2 -g -mcpu=i686`.

GNU `make` has several predefined variables that have special meanings. Table 23-2 lists these variables. In addition to the variables listed in Table 23-2, GNU `make` considers all environment variables predefined.

Table 23-2: Some Predefined Variables in GNU make

Variable	Meaning
$%	Member name for targets that are archives. If the target is libDisp.a(image.o), for example, $% is image.o, and $@ is libDisp.a.
$*	Name of the target file without the extension
$+	Names of all dependent files with duplicate dependencies, listed in their order of occurrence
$<	The name of the first dependent file
$?	Names of all dependent files (with spaces between the names) that are newer than the target
$@	Complete name of the target
$^	Names of all dependent files, with spaces between the names. Duplicates are removed from the dependent filenames.
AR	Name of the archive-maintaining program (Default value: ar)
ARFLAGS	Flags for the archive-maintaining program (Default value: rv)
AS	Name of the assembler program that converts the assembly language to object code (Default value: as)
ASFLAGS	Flags for the assembler
CC	Name of the C compiler. (Default value: cc)
CFLAGS	Flags to be passed to the C compiler
CO	Name of the program that extracts a file from RCS (Default value: co)
COFLAGS	Flags for the RCS co program
CPP	Name of the C preprocessor (Default value: $(CC) -E)
CPPFLAGS	Flags for the C preprocessor.
CXX	Name of the C++ compiler (Default value: g++)
CXXFLAGS	Flags to be passed to the C++ compiler
FC	Name of the FORTRAN compiler (Default value: f77)
FFLAGS	Flags for the FORTRAN compiler
GET	Name of the program to extract a file from SCCS (Default value: get)
GFLAGS	Flags for the SCCS get program
LDFLAGS	Flags for the compiler when it is supposed to invoke the linker ld
LEX	Name of the program to convert Lex grammar to C program (Default value: lex)
LFLAGS	Flags for Lex
MAKEINFO	Name of the program that converts Texinfo source files to info files (Default value: makeinfo)
RM	Name of the command to delete a file (Default value: rm -f)

Variable	Meaning
TEX	Name of the program to generate TeX DVI files from TeX source files (Default value: tex)
TEXI2DVI	Name of the program to generate TeX DVI files from the Texinfo source (Default value: texi2dvi)
YACC	Name of the program to convert YACC grammars to C programs (Default value: yacc -r)
YFLAGS	Flags for yacc

Taking Stock of Implicit Rules

GNU make also includes built-in, or implicit, rules that define how to create specific types of targets from various dependencies. An example of an implicit rule is the command that make should execute to generate an object file from a C source file.

GNU make supports two types of implicit rules:

♦ **Suffix rules** —Suffix rules define implicit rules for make. A suffix rule defines how to convert a file that has one extension to a file that has another extension. Each suffix rule is defined with the target showing a pair of suffixes (file extensions). The suffix rule for converting a .c (C source) file to a .o (object) file, for example, might be written as follows:

```
.c.o:
$(CC) $(CFLAGS) $(CPPFLAGS) -c -o $@ $<
```

This rule uses the predefined variables CC, CFLAGS and CPPFLAGS. For filenames, the rule uses the variables $@ (the complete name of the target) and $< (the name of the first dependent file).

♦ **Pattern rules**—These rules are more versatile because you can specify more complex dependency rules by using pattern rules. A pattern rule looks just like a regular rule, except that a single percent sign (%) appears in the target's name. The dependencies also use % to indicate how the dependency names relate to the target's name. The following pattern rule specifies how to convert any file X.c to a file X.o:

```
%.o: %.c
$(CC) $(CFLAGS) $(CPPFLAGS) -c -o $@ $<
```

GNU make has a large set of implicit rules, defined as both suffix and pattern rules. To see a list of all known variables and rules, run make by using the following command:

```
make -p -f/dev/null
```

The output includes the names of variables, as well as implicit rules.

Writing a Sample makefile

You can write a makefile easily if you use GNU make's predefined variables and its built-in rules. Consider, for example, a makefile that creates the executable xdraw from three C source files (xdraw.c, xviewobj.c, and shapes.c) and two header files (xdraw.h and shapes.h). Assume that each source file includes one of the header files. Given these facts, here is what a sample makefile might look like:

```
####################################################
# Sample makefile
# Comments start with '#'
#
####################################################

# Use standard variables to define compile and link flags

CFLAGS= -g -O2
# Define the target "all"
all: xdraw

OBJS=xdraw.o xviewobj.o shapes.o

xdraw: $(OBJS)

# Object files
xdraw.o: Makefile xdraw.c xdraw.h

xviewobj.o: Makefile xviewobj.c xdraw.h

shapes.o: Makefile shapes.c shapes.h
```

This makefile relies on GNU make's implicit rules. The conversion of .c files to .o files uses the built-in rule. Defining the variable CFLAGS passes the flags to the C compiler.

Secret

The target named all is defined as the first target in a makefile for a reason—if you run GNU make without specifying any targets in the command line (see the make syntax described in the following section), it builds the first target it finds in the makefile. By defining the first target all as xdraw, you can ensure that make builds this executable file, even if you do not explicitly specify it as a target. UNIX programmers traditionally use all as the name of the first target, but the target's name is immaterial; what matters is that it is the first target in the makefile.

If you have a directory that contains the appropriate source files and header files, you can try the makefile. Here's what happens when I try the sample makefile:

```
make
cc -g -O2   -c xdraw.c -o xdraw.o
cc -g -O2   -c xviewobj.c -o xviewobj.o
cc -g -O2   -c shapes.c -o shapes.o
cc  xdraw.o xviewobj.o shapes.o  -o xdraw
```

As the output of make shows, make uses the cc command (which happens to be a symbolic link to GCC in your Red Hat Linux system) with appropriate options to compile the source files and, finally, to link the objects to create the xdraw executable.

Running make

Typically, you run `make` with a single command in the command line; that is, you run make by typing `make`. When run this way, GNU make looks for a file named `GNUmakefile`, `makefile`, or `Makefile`—in that order. If `make` finds one of these makefiles, it builds the first target specified in that makefile. However, if `make` does not find an appropriate makefile, it displays the following error message and exits:

```
make: *** No targets.  Stop.
```

If your makefile happens to have a different name from the default names, you have to use the `-f` option to specify the makefile. The syntax of this `make` option is the following:

```
make -f filename
```

where `filename` is the name of the makefile.

Even when you have a makefile with a default name such as Makefile, you may want to build a specific target out of several targets defined in the makefile. In that case, you have to run make by using this syntax:

```
make target
```

If the makefile contains the target named `clean`, you can build that target with this command:

```
make clean
```

Another special syntax overrides the value of a `make` variable. For example, GNU make uses the `CFLAGS` variable to hold the flags used when compiling C files. You can override the value of this variable when you invoke `make`. Here is an example of how you can define `CFLAGS` to be the option `-g -O2`:

```
make CFLAGS="-g -O2"
```

In addition to these options, GNU make accepts several other command-line options. Table 23-3 lists the GNU `make` options.

Table 23-3: Options for GNU make

Option	Meaning
-b	Ignore but accept for compatibility with other versions of `make`
-C *DIR*	Change to the specified directory before reading the makefile
-d	Print debugging information
-e	Allow environment variables to override definitions of similarly named variables in the makefile
-f *FILE*	Read *FILE* as the makefile
-h	Display the list of `make` options
-i	Ignore all errors in commands executed when building a target

(continued)

Table 23-3: *(continued)*

Option	Meaning
-I DIR	Search specified directory for included makefiles (the capability to include a file in a makefile is unique to GNU make)
-j NUM	Specify the number of commands that make can run simultaneously
-k	Continue to build unrelated targets, even if an error occurs when building one of the targets
-l LOAD	Don't start a new job if load average is at least LOAD (a floating-point number)
-m	Ignore but accept for compatibility with other versions of make
-n	Print the commands to be executed, but do not execute them
-o FILE	Do not rebuild the file named FILE, even if it is older than its dependents
-p	Display the make database of variables and implicit rules
-q	Do not run anything, but return zero if all targets are up to date; return 1 if anything needs updating and 2 if an error occurs
-r	Get rid of all built-in rules
-R	Get rid of all built-in variables and rules
-s	Work silently (without displaying the commands as they are executed)
-t	Change the timestamp of the files
-v	Display the version number of make and a copyright notice
-w	Display the name of the working directory before and after processing the makefile
-W FILE	Assume that the specified file has been modified (used with -n to see what happens if you modify that file)

The GNU Debugger

Although make automates the process of building a program, that task is the least of your worries when a program does not work correctly or when a program suddenly quits with an error message. You need a debugger to find the cause of program errors. This book's companion CD-ROMs include gdb—the versatile GNU debugger with a command-line interface.

Like any debugger, gdb lets you perform typical debugging tasks, such as the following:

- ◆ Set the breakpoint so that program execution stops at a specified line.
- ◆ Watch the values of variables in the program.
- ◆ Step through the program one line at a time.
- ◆ Change variables in an attempt to fix errors.

The gdb debugger can debug C and C++ programs.

Preparing a Program for Debugging

If you want to debug a program by using gdb, you have to ensure that the compiler generates and places debugging information in the executable. The debugging information contains the names of variables in your program and the mapping of addresses in the executable file to lines of code in the source file. gdb needs this information to perform its functions, such as stopping after executing a specified line of source code.

---

insider insight

To ensure that the executable is properly prepared for debugging, use the -g **option with GCC. You can do this by defining the variable CFLAGS in the makefile as:**

```
CFLAGS= -g
```

Running gdb

The most common way to debug a program is to run gdb by using the following command:

```
gdb progname
```

progname is the name of the program's executable file. After it runs, gdb displays the following message and prompts you for a command:

```
GNU gdb Red Hat Linux (5.3post-0.20021129.7rh)
Copyright 2002 Free Software Foundation, Inc.
GDB is free software, covered by the GNU General Public License, and you are
welcome to change it and/or distribute copies of it under certain conditions.
Type "show copying" to see the conditions.
There is absolutely no warranty for GDB.  Type "show warranty" for details.
This GDB was configured as "i386-redhat-linux-gnu".
(gdb) help
List of classes of commands:

aliases -- Aliases of other commands
breakpoints -- Making program stop at certain points
data -- Examining data
files -- Specifying and examining files
internals -- Maintenance commands
obscure -- Obscure features
running -- Running the program
stack -- Examining the stack
status -- Status inquiries
support -- Support facilities
tracepoints -- Tracing of program execution without stopping the program
user-defined -- User-defined commands

Type "help" followed by a class name for a list of commands in that class.
Type "help" followed by command name for full documentation.
Command name abbreviations are allowed if unambiguous.
(gdb) q
```

When you type **help**, gdb displays the classes of gdb commands. You can get further help on a specific class of commands or a specific command by following the instructions. To see the list of commands you use to run the program you are debugging, type **help running** at the gdb prompt.

To quit gdb, type **q**, and press Enter.

gdb has a large number of commands, but you need only a few to find the cause of an error quickly. Table 23-4 lists the commonly used gdb commands.

Table 23-4: Commonly Used gdb Commands

Command	Description
break *NUM*	Set a breakpoint at the specified line number (the debugger stops at breakpoints)
bt	Display a trace of all stack frames. (This command shows you the sequence of function calls so far.)
clear *FILENAME:NUM*	Delete the breakpoint at a specific line in a source file. For example, clear xdraw.c:8 clears the breakpoint at line 8 of file xdraw.c.
Continue	Continue running the program being debugged. (Use this command after the program has stopped due to a signal or breakpoint.)
display *EXPR*	Display value of expression (consisting of variables defined in the program) each time the program stops
file *FILE*	Load specified executable file for debugging
help *NAME*	Display help on the command named *NAME*
info break	Display a list of current breakpoints, including information on how many times each breakpoint has been reached
info files	Display detailed information about the file being debugged
info func	Display all function names
info local	Display information about local variables of current function
info prog	Display the execution status of the program being debugged
info var	Display all global and static variable names
Kill	End the program you are debugging
List	List a section of the source code
Make	Run the make utility to rebuild the executable without leaving gdb
Next	Advance one line of source code in the current function without stepping into other functions
print *EXPR*	Show the value of the expression *EXPR*
Quit	Quit gdb
Run	Start running the currently loaded executable
set variable *VAR=VALUE*	Set the value of the variable *VAR* to *VALUE*
shell *CMD*	Execute a Linux command *CMD*, without leaving gdb

Command	Description
Step	Advance one line in the current function, stepping into other functions, if any
watch *VAR*	Show the value of the variable named *VAR* whenever the value changes
Where	Display the call sequence. Use this command to locate where your program died.
x/F *ADDR*	Examine the contents of the memory location at address *ADDR* in the format specified by the letter F, which can be o (octal); x (hex); d (decimal); u (unsigned decimal); t (binary); f (float); a (address); i (instruction); c (char); or s (string). You can append a letter indicating the size of data type to the format letter. Size letters are b (byte); h (halfword, 2 bytes), w (word, 4 bytes); and g (giant, 8 bytes). Typically, *ADDR* is the name of a variable or pointer.

Finding Bugs by Using gdb

To understand how you can find bugs by using gdb, you need to see an example. The procedure is easiest to show with a simple example, so I start with a rather contrived program that contains a typical bug.

This is the contrived program, which I store in the file dbgtst.c:

```c
#include <stdio.h>

static char buf[256];
void read_input(char *s);

int main(void)
{
    char *input = NULL; /* Just a pointer, no storage for string */

    read_input(input);

/* Process command. */
    printf("You typed: %s\n", input);

/* ... */
    return 0;
}

void read_input(char *s)
{
    printf("Command: ");
    gets(s);
}
```

This program's main function calls the read_input function to get a line of input from the user. The read_input function expects a character array in which it returns what the user types. In this example, however, main calls read_input with an uninitialized pointer—that's the bug in this simple program.

Build the program by using gcc with the -g option:

```
gcc -g -o dbgtst dbgtst.c
```

Ignore the warning message about the gets() function being dangerous; we are trying to use the shortcoming of the gets() function to show how gdb can be used to track down errors.

To see the problem with this program, run it:

```
./dbgtst
Command: test
Segmentation fault
```

The program dies after displaying the Segmentation fault message. For this small program, you can find the cause by examining the source code. In a real-world application, however, you may not immediately know what causes the error. That's when you use gdb to find the cause of the problem.

To use gdb to locate a bug, follow these steps:

1. Load the program under gdb. To load a program named dbgtst in gdb, type the following:

   ```
   gdb dbgtst
   ```

2. At the (gdb) prompt, type **run**. When the program prompts for input, type some input text. The program should fail as it has previously. Here's what happens with the dbgtst program:

   ```
   (gdb) run
   Starting program: /home/naba/apps/dbgtst
   Command: test

   Program received signal SIGSEGV, Segmentation fault.
   0x420632cc in gets () from /lib/tls/libc.so.6
   (gdb)
   ```

3. Type the where command to determine where the program died. For the dbgtst program, this command yields this output:

   ```
   (gdb) where
   #0  0x420632cc in gets () from /lib/tls/libc.so.6
   #1  0x080483bc in read_input (s=0x0) at dbgtst.c:22
   #2  0x0804837e in main () at dbgtst.c:10
   #3  0x420154a0 in __libc_start_main () from /lib/tls/libc.so.6
   (gdb)
   ```

   The output shows the sequence of function calls. Function call #0—the most recent one—is to a C library function, gets. The gets call originates in the read_input function, which in turn is called from the main function.

4. Type the list command with the name of a file and line number to inspect the lines of suspect source code. In dbgtst, you might start with line 22 of dbgtst.c file, as follows:

   ```
   (gdb) list dbgtst.c:22
   17          }
   18
   19          void read_input(char *s)
   ```

```
20      {
21        printf("Command: ");
22        gets(s);
23      }
24
(gdb)
```

After looking at this listing, if you have some experience writing C programs, you should be able to tell that the problem might be the way read_input is called. Then you list the lines around line 10 in dbgtst.c (where the read_input call originates):

```
(gdb) list dbgtst.c:10
5
6       int main(void)
7       {
8         char *input = NULL; /* Just a pointer, no storage for string */
9
10        read_input(input);
11
12      /* Process command. */
13        printf("You typed: %s\n", input);
14
(gdb)
```

At this point, you should be able to narrow the problem to the variable named input. That variable should be an array, not a NULL pointer.

Fixing Bugs in gdb

Sometimes you can try a bug fix directly in gdb. For the example program in the preceding section, you can try this fix immediately after the program dies after displaying an error message. Because the example is contrived, I have an extra buffer named buf defined in the dbgtst program, as follows:

```
static char buf[256];
```

I can fix the problem of the uninitialized pointer by setting the variable input to buf. The following session with gdb corrects the problem of the uninitialized pointer (this example picks up immediately after the program has run and died, due to the segmentation fault):

```
(gdb) file dbgtst
A program is being debugged already.  Kill it? (y or n) y

Load new symbol table from "dbgtst"? (y or n) y
Reading symbols from dbgtst...
done.
(gdb) list
1       #include <stdio.h>
2
3       static char buf[256];
4       void read_input(char *s);
```

```
5
6        int main(void)
7        {
8            char *input = NULL; /* Just a pointer, no storage for string
*/
9
10           read_input(input);
(gdb) break 9
Breakpoint 1 at 0x8048373: file dbgtst.c, line 9.
(gdb) run
Starting program: /home/naba/apps/dbgtst

Breakpoint 1, main () at dbgtst.c:10
10           read_input(input);
(gdb) set var input=buf
(gdb) cont
Continuing.
Command: test
You typed: test

Program exited normally.
(gdb) q
```

As the previous listing shows, if I stop the program just before read_input is called and set the variable named input to buf (which is a valid array of characters), the rest of the program runs fine.

After trying in gdb a fix that works, you can make the necessary changes to the source files and can make the fix permanent.

Implications of GNU Licenses

You have to pay a price for the bounty of Linux—to protect its developers and users, Linux is distributed under the GNU GPL (General Public License), which stipulates the distribution of the source code.

This does not mean, however, that you cannot write commercial software for Linux that you want to distribute (either for free or for a price) in binary form only. You can follow all the rules and still sell your Linux applications in binary form.

When writing applications for Linux, be aware of two licenses:

◆ The GNU General Public License (GPL), which governs many Linux programs, including the Linux kernel and GCC.
◆ The GNU Library General Public License (LGPL), which covers many Linux libraries.

caution   The following sections provide an overview of these licenses and some suggestions on how to meet their requirements. Because I am not a lawyer, however, you should not take anything in this book as legal advice. The full text for these licenses is in text files on your Red Hat Linux system; show these licenses to your legal counsel for a full interpretation and an assessment of applicability to your business.

Understanding the GNU General Public License

The text of the GPL is in a file named COPYING in various directories in your Red Hat Linux system. For example, type **cd /usr/share/doc/gdb***, and type **more COPYING** to read the GPL.

The GPL has nothing to do with whether you charge for the software or distribute it for free; its thrust is to keep the software free for all users. GPL does this by requiring that the software is distributed in source-code form and by stipulating that any user can copy and distribute the software in source-code form to anyone else. In addition, everyone is reminded that the software comes with absolutely no warranty.

The software that GPL covers is not in the public domain; such software is always copyrighted, and the GPL spells out the restrictions on the software's copying and distribution. From a user's point of view, of course, GPL's restrictions are not really restrictions; they are benefits because the user is guaranteed access to the source code.

caution   If your application uses parts of any software the GPL covers, your application is considered a derived work; because the GPL covers it, you must distribute the source code to your application.

Secret

Although the GPL covers the Linux kernel, the GPL does not cover your applications that use the kernel services through system calls. Those applications are considered normal use of the kernel.

If you plan to distribute your application in binary form (as most commercial software is distributed), you must make sure your application does not use any parts of any software the GPL covers. Your application may end up using parts of other software when it calls functions in a library. Most libraries, however, are covered by a different GNU license, which is described in the following section.

You have to watch out for only a few library and utility programs the GPL covers. The GNU dbm (gdbm) database library is one of the prominent libraries GPL covers. The GNU bison parser-generator tool is another utility the GPL covers. If you allow bison to generate code, the GPL covers that code.

Other alternatives for the GNU dbm and GNU bison are not covered by GPL. For a database library, you can use the Berkeley database library db in place of gdbm. For a parser-generator, you might use yacc instead of bison.

Understanding the GNU Library General Public License

The text of the GNU LGPL is in a file named COPYING.LIB. If you have the kernel source installed, a copy of COPYING.LIB file is in one of the source directories. To locate a copy of the COPYING.LIB file, use this find command:

```
find /usr/share/doc -name "COPYING*" -print
```

This command lists all occurrences of COPYING and COPYING.LIB in your system. The COPYING file contains the GPL, whereas COPYING.LIB has the LGPL.

Secret

The LGPL is intended to allow use of libraries in your applications, even if you do not distribute source code for your application. The LGPL stipulates, however, that users must have access to the source code of the library you use and that users can make use of modified versions of those libraries.

The LGPL covers most Linux libraries, including the C library (`libc.a`). Thus, when you build your application on Linux by using the GCC compiler, your application links with code from one or more libraries the LGPL covers. If you want to distribute your application in binary form only, you need to pay attention to LGPL.

One way to meet the intent of the LGPL is to provide the object code for your application and a makefile that relinks your object files with any updated Linux libraries the LGPL covers.

A better way to satisfy the LGPL is to use dynamic linking, in which your application and the library are separate entities, even though your application calls functions in the library when it runs. With dynamic linking, users immediately get the benefit of any updates to the libraries without ever having to relink the application.

Version Control

When you write applications with a few files, it is simple enough to prepare a makefile to automate the software-build process and to avoid worrying about keeping track of changes. Typically, for small projects, you might keep track of changes through comments at the beginning of a file.

This approach works well for a small project, but for larger software projects, you should use some tools that help manage different versions of your applications. In fact, you can benefit from version-control tools even if you are the sole author of a small application. Eventually, you may have trouble remembering what changes you have made. Software version control can help you track these changes.

The Linux software distribution comes with RCS and CVS. Both of these products are collections of tools that help you control software revisions.

The next few sections provide an overview of RCS through some simple examples. A later section briefly discusses CVS and lists some other sources of information about CVS.

Controlling Source Files Using RCS

Source control refers to saving a version of the source code so you can recover a specific version or revision of a file whenever you need it. Essentially, when you modify a source file, the sequence goes something like this:

1. When you have an initial version of the source file, you archive it—place it under source control.
2. When you want to make changes in the file, you first get a copy of the current revision. (When you get it this way, the tools should ensure that no one else can modify that revision.)
3. You make the changes in the source file, test the code, and store the modified file as a new revision.
4. The next time you want to make changes in the file, you start with the latest revision of the file.

RCS provides the tools that enable you to archive file revisions and update them in a controlled manner. Table 23-5 lists the tools.

Table 23-5: RCS Tools

Tool	Purpose
ci	Creates a new revision of a file, or adds a working file to an RCS file (co stands for check in)
co	Gets a working version of a file for reading. (co -l provides a working file and locks the original so you can modify the working file.) co stands for check out.
ident	Searches for identifiers in a file
merge	Incorporates changes from two files into a third file
rcsdiff	Compares a working file with its RCS file
rcsmerge	Merges different revisions of a file
rlog	Views the history of changes in a file

Suppose you have just finished developing the initial working version of an application and want to use RCS to manage the revisions from now on. The following sections outline the steps to follow to use RCS for your development effort.

Creating Initial RCS Files

The first step in managing source-file revisions by using RCS is to enable RCS to archive the current revision of your files. Follow these steps to put the source file under the control of RCS:

1. In the directory where you keep your application's source files, create a subdirectory named RCS by typing mkdir RCS. If the RCS subdirectory exists, RCS archives file revisions in this directory.

2. In each file you plan to place under revision control, add a comment by adding the following RCS identification keyword:

   Id

   In a C source file, for example, add the following:

   ```
   /*
    * $Id$
    */
   ```

   In a makefile, on the other hand, use the following:

   ```
   # $Id$
   ```

   Later, RCS expands these identifier keywords to include information about the file revision and date.

3. Check in each file with RCS; use the ci command, and provide a brief description of each file as prompted by ci. Following is how you might check in Makefile:

   ```
   ci Makefile
   RCS/Makefile,v  <--  Makefile
   enter description, terminated with single '.' or end of file:
   ```

```
NOTE: This is NOT the log message!
>> Makefile for sample programs.
>> .
initial revision: 1.1
done
```

When a file is checked in, the `ci` command creates a corresponding RCS file in the RCS subdirectory. The RCS file's name is the same as the original file, except a `.v` is appended to the name. Thus, the RCS file for `Makefile` is `Makefile.v`. Also, `ci` deletes the original source file after it creates the RCS file. To use or edit the file again, you have to extract it by using the `co` command.

After you follow these steps, all your files are safely stored in RCS files in the RCS sub-directory.

Using the Archived Files

Now suppose you want to edit one of the files (for example, to add a new feature) and rebuild the application. For starters, you need all the source files and the makefile for the compile and link step.

You should extract all these files by using the `co` command for read-only access (except for the file you want to change). Using the `co` command is straightforward. To get a working copy of `Makefile` for read-only use, for example, use the following command:

```
co Makefile
RCS/Makefile.v --> Makefile
revision 1.1
done
```

By default, this command looks for an RCS file named `RCS/Makefile.v` and creates a read-only working copy of it named `Makefile`.

A copy of `Makefile` is in the directory. Examine that copy of `Makefile` to see what happens to the Id keyword that you add as a comment. Here's what my example Makefile shows:

```
# $Id: Makefile.v 1.1 2003/02/08 03:06:56 naba Exp $
```

As this example shows, RCS expands each identifier keyword into a string with information. The exact information depends on the identifier.

If you want to modify a file, you have to check it out by using the `-l` option. If you want to check out a copy of the file `xmutil.c` for editing, use this command:

```
co -l xmutil.c
RCS/xmutil.c,v --> xmutil.c
revision 1.1 (locked)
done
```

Compare this output with that from the previous example of `co`; the current output confirms that the RCS file is locked. No one else can modify the archived file until you check in the copy you have checked out for editing.

When you check out a file and put a lock on it, no one else can check out the same file for editing. However, anyone can get a copy of the file for read-only use.

After you make changes in a file, you can check it in again by using the ci command, just as you do when you create the RCS file.

Using RCS Identification Keywords

You can use RCS identification keywords—each of which is a string delimited by dollar signs ($...$)—to record information in source files. RCS expands the Id keyword, for example, into summary information about the file, including the filename, revision number, date, and author. All you have to do is put the keyword in the file; RCS takes care of expanding that keyword into the appropriate information. Table 23-6 lists the identification keywords RCS supports.

Table 23-6: Identification Keywords RCS Supports

Keyword	Purpose
$Author$	Login ID of the user who checked in the revision
$Date$	Date and time when the revision was checked in
$Header$	Expands to summary information, including full path name of the RCS file, revision number, date, author, and the state of file revision
Id	Same as $Header$, except the RCS filename does not have a directory prefix
$Locker$	Login ID of the user who locked the file (empty if the file is not currently locked)
Log	Expands to a log of changes made in the file
$RCSfile$	Name of the RCS file without the directory names
$Revision$	Revision number of the RCS file
$Source$	Expands to the full path name of the RCS file
$State$	Indicates the state of the file revision (whether it is locked or not)

insider insight

At minimum, you may want to use the Id keyword in your files to include summary information about the latest revision.

RCS expands the identifier keywords anywhere in a file. Thus, you might mark an object file (and the executable that uses that object file) by placing the identifier keyword in a string variable. A common practice is to define a string named rcsid as follows:

```
static const char rcsid[] = "$Id";
```

Defining the rcsid string causes the object and executable file to contain a string such as the following:

```
$Id: xmutil.c,v 1.1 2003/02/08 03:09:56 naba Exp naba $
```

Viewing the Changes Made So Far

Most of the time, the `ci` and `co` commands are used to maintain file revisions with RCS. RCS, however, includes several other tools for managing various aspects of version control, such as comparing two revisions, viewing the history of changes, and examining identifiers in files.

If you have checked out a file for modification, you might want to know what changes you have made thus far. You can use the `rcsdiff` program to see a list of changes. If you've been editing a file named `xmutil.c`, for example, you can compare the working file against its RCS file, by using this command:

```
rcsdiff xmutil.c
```

The `rcsdiff` program runs the UNIX `diff` utility to find the differences between the working file and the RCS file.

If necessary, you can even find the differences between two specific revisions of a file by using a command such as the following:

```
rcsdiff -r1.1 -r1.2 xmutil.c
```

This command lists the differences between revision 1.1 and 1.2 of the file `xmutil.c`.

Discarding Changes Made So Far

Sometimes after making changes in a file, you realize the changes are either wrong or unnecessary. In such a case, you want to discard the changes you have made so far.

To discard changes, all you have to do is unlock the RCS file and delete the working copy of the file. To unlock an RCS file, use the `rcs` command with the `-u` (unlock) option. The following command discards the current changes in the file named `xmutil.c`:

```
rcs -u xmutil.c
```

Another, more convenient, way to discard changes is to overwrite the current working file with a copy of the former RCS file. To do this, use the `co` command with `-u` and `-f` flags:

```
co -f -u xmutil.c
```

The `-u` option unlocks the checked-out revision, and `-f` forces co to overwrite the working file with the former revision of that file.

Viewing the Change Log

As you make changes in a file and keep checking in revisions, RCS maintains a log of changes. You can view this log by using the `rlog` command. The following example shows how to view the log of changes for the file `xmutil.c`:

```
rlog xmutil.c

RCS file: RCS/xmutil.c,v
Working file: xmutil.c
head: 1.2
branch:
locks: strict
```

```
access list:
symbolic names:
keyword substitution: kv
total revisions: 2;      selected revisions: 2
description:
Motif utilities
----------------------------
revision 1.2
date: 2003/02/08 01:16:47;  author: naba;  state: Exp;  lines: +10 -6
Added new header file
----------------------------
revision 1.1
date: 2002/10/26 01:10:27;  author: naba;  state: Exp;
Initial revision
===========================================================================
```

The first part of the `rlog` output displays some summary information about the RCS file. The lines following the `description:` line show the description I enter when I create the RCS file. Following this description is an entry for each revision, with the most recent revision appearing first. Each revision's entry shows the date, the author, and a brief description the author has entered.

Examining Identifier Keywords

If any identifier keywords are embedded in a file, you can view them by using the `ident` command. If `Makefile` contains the `$Id$` keyword, you can examine the keyword by using this command:

```
ident Makefile
Makefile:
        $Id: Makefile,v 1.1 2003/02/08 01:06:26 naba Exp $
```

If you define a string variable with a keyword that eventually gets embedded in a binary file (an object file or an executable file), `ident` displays those identifiers as well. You can try `ident` in any binary file to see whether it contains any embedded keywords. This is what I find when I try ident on the file `/usr/bin/ident` (the executable program for the `ident` command itself):

```
ident /usr/bin/ident
/usr/bin/ident:
        $Id: rcsbase.h,v 5.20 1995/06/16 06:19:24 eggert Exp $
        $Id: ident.c,v 5.9 1995/06/16 06:19:24 eggert Exp $
        $Id: rcsmap.c,v 5.3 1995/06/16 06:19:24 eggert Exp $
```

From this output, you can tell the exact versions of source files that are used to build this version of the `ident` program.

Performing Concurrent Version Control with CVS

CVS is another source-control tool designed to keep track of changes made by a group of developers working on the same set of files. CVS keeps track of collections of files in a shared directory. An entire collection of files is given a module name; a developer can check out an entire collection of files by using the module name.

CVS uses RCS to save the version-control information in RCS files stored in a directory hierarchy called the repository, which is separate from the developer's working directory. Unlike RCS, CVS does not lock the files when they are checked out. In fact, CVS enables multiple developers to check out an entire collection of files. When developers commit the files back to the repository, CVS tries to merge the changes various developers have made. If CVS cannot successfully merge the changes, the developers are notified, and they have to resolve any conflicting changes manually.

To use an existing CVS repository, first set the CVSROOT environment variable to that repository. The repository can even be on a different system. For example, to work on GNOME as a developer, set CVSROOT as follows:

```
export CVSROOT=':pserver:anonymous@anoncvs.gnome.org:/cvs/gnome'
```

You also must log in to the CVS server by using this command:

```
cvs login
Logging in to :pserver:anonymous@anoncvs.gnome.org:2401/cvs/gnome
CVS password:  (There is no password, simply press Enter)
```

You will be back at the shell prompt, but you are now logged in and can use the cvs command to access this CVS repository. Use the cvs checkout command to extract the packages you need from the repository. When extracting files from a remote CVS server, you can specify a compression level with -z option (the recommended level is -z3). Thus, you might use the following command to get the gnome-xml package from the GNOME CVS repository:

```
cvs -z3 checkout gnome-xml
```

You see a whole lot of message as the copy of CVS on your system downloads from the repository the latest version of each file in the gnome-xml module, creates a directory named gnome-xml in the current directory, and places the files in that directory. You can simply type **cd gnome-xml** to change the directory and to begin working on these files.

If you have checked out a module to a working directory, you can use the cvs update command to bring your copy current. The cvs update command essentially merges the changes in the repository with whatever changes you may have made in the working directory. If conflicting changes exist, you have to resolve the problem manually.

After you work on these files, you can use the cvs commit command to incorporate your changes to the files in the repository. You can either commit specific files or commit the entire module.

When you no longer want your working copy of a module, use the cvs release command to indicate that you no longer need the module. To remove the files, use the cvs release -d command; the -d flag means you want to delete the files.

When you are done working with a CVS repository, type **cvs logout** to log out of that repository.

That, in short, is how CVS works. To learn more about CVS, consult these resources:

- Type **info cvs** to browse help information on CVS.
- Type **cd /usr/share/doc/cvs*** to change to the CVS documentation directory. In that directory is a file named FAQ (Frequently Asked Questions) and several PostScript files about CVS. The FAQ file may be a bit out of date, but you can still use it as a source of information about CVS.

◆ Visit one of these websites to read the latest online information about CVS:

- `http://www.cvshome.org/`
- `http://www.gnu.org/software/cvs/`
- `http://www.gnu.org/manual/cvs/index.html`

Linux Programming Topics

Developing software under Linux is quite similar to developing software under any UNIX system. Most C and UNIX programming issues are generic and apply to all UNIX systems. There are, however, a few topics you want to know about if you are developing software for Linux.

This section covers the most significant topic: the Executable and Linking Format (ELF) binary in Linux. The other topic—the use of dynamic linking in applications—is related to ELF. Also, I describe how you can exploit dynamic linking and how you can create a dynamically linked library in Linux.

Understanding the Executable and Linking Format

If you have programmed in UNIX, you probably know that when you compile and link a program, the default executable file is named `a.out`. What you may not have realized is that a file format is associated with the `a.out` file. The operating system has to know this file format so it can load and run an executable. In the early days, Linux used the `a.out` format for its binaries.

Although the `a.out` format has served its purpose adequately, it has two shortcomings:

◆ Shared libraries are difficult to create.

◆ Dynamically loading a shared library is cumbersome.

Using shared libraries is desirable because a shared library enables many executable programs to share the same block of code. Also, the dynamic loading of modules is becoming increasingly popular because it enables an application to load blocks of code only when needed, thus reducing the memory requirement of the application.

Secret

The UNIX System Laboratories (USL) had developed the Executable and Linking Format or ELF, a new binary format, for use in System V Release 4 (SVR4). The ELF format is much more flexible than the `a.out` format. In particular, ELF has these advantages over the old `a.out` format in Linux:

- Shared libraries for the ELF format are simpler to create. You compile all source files with the `gcc -fPIC -c` command and link them by using a command such as the following, which creates the library `libXXX.so.1.0`:

  `gcc -shared -Wl,-soname,libXXX.so.1 -o libXXX.so.1.0 *.o`

- Dynamic loading (wherein a program loads code modules at runtime) is simpler. With dynamic loading, you can design an application to be extensible so that users can add new code in the form of shared libraries.

continues

continued

Because of ELF's increased flexibility, Linux developers (in particular, the GCC developers) decided to move to ELF as the standard binary-format Linux. By default, the new GCC compilers—gcc version 2.7 and later—generate ELF binaries.

Note that GCC continues to use a.out as the default name of the executable file (used only if you do not specify an output filename by using the -o option). Although the executable may be named a.out, the binary format is ELF, not the old a.out format.

If you want to check the binary format of an executable file, use the file command. The following example shows how to check the file type of /bin/ls (the executable file for the ls command):

```
file /bin/ls
/bin/ls: ELF 32-bit LSB executable, Intel 80386, version 1 (SYSV), for GNU/Linux
  2.2.5, dynamically linked (uses shared libs), stripped
```

On the other hand, the file command reports the following for an older a.out format executable (the default name of executable files is still a.out, but the format is ELF):

```
file a.out
a.out: Linux/i386 demand-paged executable (QMAGIC)
```

Using Shared Libraries in Linux Applications

Most Linux programs use shared libraries. At minimum, most C programs use the C shared library libc.so.X, wherein X is a version number. When a program uses one or more shared libraries, you need the program's executable file, as well as all the shared libraries, to run the program. In other words, your program won't run if all shared libraries are not available on a system.

If you sell an application, you need to make sure all necessary shared libraries are distributed with your software.

Examining Shared Libraries that a Program Uses

Use the ldd utility to determine which shared libraries an executable program needs. The following is what ldd reports for a typical C program that uses the ELF binary format:

```
ldd a.out
    libc.so.6 => /lib/tls/libc.so.6 (0x42000000)
    /lib/ld-linux.so.2 => /lib/ld-linux.so.2 (0x40000000)
```

For a more complex program, such as gimp (ELF version), ldd shows more shared libraries:

```
ldd /usr/bin/gimp
    libgtk-1.2.so.0 => /usr/lib/libgtk-1.2.so.0 (0x40029000)
    libgdk-1.2.so.0 => /usr/lib/libgdk-1.2.so.0 (0x40171000)
    libgmodule-1.2.so.0 => /usr/lib/libgmodule-1.2.so.0 (0x401a9000)
    libglib-1.2.so.0 => /usr/lib/libglib-1.2.so.0 (0x401ac000)
    libdl.so.2 => /lib/libdl.so.2 (0x401d1000)
    libXi.so.6 => /usr/X11R6/lib/libXi.so.6 (0x401d4000)
    libXext.so.6 => /usr/X11R6/lib/libXext.so.6 (0x401dd000)
```

```
libX11.so.6 => /usr/X11R6/lib/libX11.so.6 (0x401eb000)
libm.so.6 => /lib/tls/libm.so.6 (0x402ca000)
libc.so.6 => /lib/tls/libc.so.6 (0x42000000)
/lib/ld-linux.so.2 => /lib/ld-linux.so.2 (0x40000000)
```

In this case, the program uses several shared libraries, including the X11 library (libX11.so.6), the GIMP toolkit (libgtk-1.2.so.0), the General Drawing Kit (GDK) library (libgdk-1.2.so.0), the Math library (libm.so.6), and the C library (libc.so.6).

Thus, almost any Linux application requires shared libraries to run. In addition, the shared libraries must have the same binary format an application uses.

Creating a Shared Library

With ELF, creating a shared library for your own application is simple enough. Suppose you want to implement an object in the form of a shared library. A set of functions in the shared library represents the object's interfaces. To use the object, load its shared library, and invoke its interface functions (you learn how to do this in the following section).

Here is the C source code for this simple object, implemented as a shared library (you might also call it a dynamically linked library)—save this in a file named dynobj.c:

```c
/*-----------------------------------------------------------*/
/* File: dynobj.c
 *
 * Demonstrate use of dynamic linking.
 * Pretend this is an object that can be created by calling
 * init and destroyed by calling destroy.
 */
#include <stdio.h>
#include <stdlib.h>
#include <string.h>

/* Data structure for this object */
typedef struct OBJDATA
{
  char *name;
  int version;
} OBJDATA;

/*-----------------------------------------------------------*/
/* i n i t
 *
 * Initialize object (allocate storage).
 *
 */
void* init(char *name)
{
  OBJDATA *data = (OBJDATA*)calloc(1, sizeof(OBJDATA));
  if(name)
    data->name = malloc(strlen(name)+1);
  strcpy(data->name, name);

  printf("Created: %s\n", name);
```

```
  return data;
}
/*----------------------------------------------------------*/
/* s h o w
 *
 * Show the object.
 *
 */
void show(void *data)
{
  OBJDATA *d = (OBJDATA*)data;
  printf("show: %s\n", d->name);
}
/*----------------------------------------------------------*/
/* d e s t r o y
 *
 * Destroy the object (free all storage).
 *
 */
void destroy(void *data)
{
  OBJDATA *d = (OBJDATA*)data;
  if(d)
  {
    if(d->name)
    {
      printf("Destroying: %s\n", d->name);
      free(d->name);
    }
    free(d);
  }
}
```

The object offers three interface functions:

- ◆ init to allocate any necessary storage and initialize the object
- ◆ show to display the object (here, it simply prints a message)
- ◆ destroy to free any storage

To build the shared library named libdobj.so, follow these steps:

1. Compile all source files with the -fPIC flag. In this case, compile the dynobj.c file by using this command:

```
gcc -fPIC -c dynobj.c
```

2. Link the objects into a shared library with the -shared flag, and provide appropriate flags for the linker. To create the shared library named libdobj.so.1, use the following:

```
gcc -shared -Wl,-soname,libdobj.so.1 -o libdobj.so.1.0 dynobj.o
```

3. Set up a sequence of symbolic links so that programs that use the shared library can refer to it with a standard name. For the sample library, the standard name is libdobj.so, and the symbolic links are set up by using these commands:

```
ln -sf libdobj.so.1.0 libdobj.so.1
ln -sf libdobj.so.1 libdobj.so
```

4. When you test the shared library, define and export the LD_LIBRARY_PATH environment variable by using the following command:

```
export LD_LIBRARY_PATH=`pwd`:$LD_LIBRARY_PATH
```

After you test the shared library and are satisfied that the library works, copy it to a standard location, such as /usr/local/lib, and run the ldconfig utility to update the link between libdobj.so.1 and libdobj.so.1.0. These are the commands you use to install your shared library for everyone's use (you have to be root to perform these steps):

```
cp libdobj.so.1.0 /usr/local/lib
/sbin/ldconfig
cd /usr/local/lib
ln -s libdobj.so.1 libdobj.so
```

Dynamically Loading a Shared Library

ELF makes it simple to load a shared library in your program and to use the functions within the shared library. The header file <dlfcn.h> declares the functions for loading and using a shared library. Four functions are declared in the file dlfcn.h for dynamic loading:

♦ void *dlopen(const char *filename, int flag);—loads the shared library specified by filename and returns a handle for the library. The flag can be RTD_LAZY (resolve undefined symbols as the library's code is executed); or RTD_NOW (resolve all undefined symbols before dlopen returns and fail if all symbols are not defined). If dlopen fails, it returns NULL.

♦ const char *dlerror (void);—if dlopen fails, call dlerror to get a string that contains a description of the error.

♦ void *dlsym (void *handle, char *symbol);—returns the address of the specified symbol (function name) from the shared library identified by the handle (that was returned by dlopen).

♦ int dlclose (void *handle);—unloads the shared library if no one else is using it.

Here is the dlfcn.h file with the appropriate function declarations:

```
/*-------------------------------------------------------*/
/* File: dlfcn.h
 *
 * Header file with function prototypes.
 */
void *dlopen(const char *filename, int flag);
const char *dlerror (void);
void *dlsym (void *handle, char *symbol);
int dlclose (void *handle);
```

When you use any of these functions, include the header file <dlfcn.h> with this pre-processor directive:

```
#include <dlfcn.h>
```

The following is a simple test program—dltest.c—that shows how to load and use the object defined in the shared library libdobj.so, which you create in the preceding section:

```
/*------------------------------------------------------------*/
/* File: dltest.c
 *
 * Test dynamic linking.
 *
 */
#include <dlfcn.h>   /* For the dynamic loading functions */
#include <stdio.h>

int main(void)
{
    void *dlobj;
    void * (*init_call)(char *name);
    void (*show_call)(void *data);
    void (*destroy_call)(void *data);

/* Open the shared library and set up the function pointers */
    if(dlobj = dlopen("libdobj.so.1",RTLD_LAZY))
    {
        void *data;

        init_call=dlsym(dlobj,"init");
        show_call=dlsym(dlobj,"show");
        destroy_call=dlsym(dlobj,"destroy");

/* Call the object interfaces */
        data = (*init_call)("Test Object");
        (*show_call)(data);
        (*destroy_call)(data);
    }
    return 0;
}
```

The program is straightforward: it loads the shared library, gets the pointers to the functions in the library, and calls the functions through the pointers.

You can compile and link this program in the usual way, but you must link with the -ldl option so you can use the functions declared in <dlfcn.h>. Here is how you build the program dltest:

```
gcc -o dltest dltest.c -ldl
```

To see the program in action, run dltest:

```
./dltest
Created: Test Object
show: Test Object
Destroying: Test Object
```

Although this demonstration is not exciting, you now have a sample program that uses a shared library.

To see the benefit of using a shared library, return to the preceding section, and make some changes in the shared library (print some other message in a function, for example). Rebuild the shared library alone. Then run `dltest` again. The resulting printout should show the effect of the changes you make in the shared library, which means you can update the shared library independently of the application. You should also note that a change in a shared library can affect many applications installed on your system. Therefore, you should be careful when making changes to any shared library.

Summary

Your Red Hat Linux system comes loaded with all the tools you need to develop software. In particular, it has all the GNU software-development tools, such as GCC, the GNU debugger, GNU make, and the RCS version-control utility. This chapter describes these software-development tools and shows you how to use them.

By reading this chapter, you learn that:

♦ The GNU tools compose the software-development environment on your Linux® PC. These tools include GNU Emacs for text editing; GCC for compiling C and C++ programs; GNU make for automating software builds; the GNU debugger for debugging; and the RCS for version control.

♦ A utility named `info` provides online help information on the GNU tools. You can run info alone in a terminal window or under GNU Emacs by using the Ctrl+h i command.

♦ GCC is the GNU C and C++ compiler. You can use the `gcc` command to compile and link C programs. Use `g++` to compile and link C++ programs.

♦ GCC has a plethora of options, but you need to use only a few. Some of the common options are `-c` (for compiling only) and `-o` (for specifying the name of the output executable file).

♦ The GNU make utility enables you to automate the build process. You specify the modules that compose an executable, as well as any dependencies; make takes care of compiling only files that need recompilation. The input file for make is known as a *makefile* and is commonly named `Makefile`.

♦ The GNU debugger enables you to locate errors in your programs. Use the `gdb` command to run the debugger. You have to compile the program by using GCC's `-g` option to generate debugging information the GNU debugger can use.

♦ When you use GNU tools to develop software (as you do in Linux), you should be aware of the GNU licenses: the GNU General Public License (GPL) and the GNU Library General Public License (LGPL). The LGPL covers GNU libraries. If you distribute your software in binary form, you should use dynamic linking to comply with the terms of the LGPL. You should not take anything in this book as legal advice, of course; always consult your own legal counsel for a definitive answer.

♦ Version control is an important aspect of software development. In Linux, you get the RCS (Revision Control System) to manage revisions of source files.

♦ Concurrent Versions System (CVS) is a versatile RCS-based, version-control system that manages multiple directories of files. CVS enables multiple developers to work simultaneously on the same set of files. Open-source projects, such as GNOME, use CVS to enable many developers to work on various parts of the project.

♦ Shared libraries are commonly used in Linux applications to reduce the memory requirements of executables. Applications are dynamically linked with a shared library at runtime, and many applications can share a single library.

♦ The Linux development community has adopted the Executable and Linking Format (ELF) for binaries. ELF makes dynamic linking simpler to program. This chapter shows an example of how to use dynamic linking in your own applications.

Shell and Perl Scripting

Chapter 24

he fundamental philosophy of UNIX, which Linux continues to follow, is to give the user many small and specialized commands, along with the plumbing necessary to connect these commands. By plumbing, I mean the way in which one command's output functions as a second command's input. Bash, the default shell in Linux, provides this plumbing in the form of I/O redirection and pipes. Bash also includes features such as the `if` statement, which runs commands only when a specific condition is true, and the `for` statement, which repeats commands a specified number of times. You can use these features of Bash when writing interpreted programs called shell scripts.

This chapter shows you how to write simple shell scripts: a collection of shell commands stored in a file. Shell scripts are used to automate various tasks. For example, when your Red Hat Linux boots, many shell scripts stored in various subdirectories in the `/etc` directory (for example, `/etc/init.d`) perform many initialization tasks.

When it comes to writing scripts, the Perl language is also popular among UNIX system administrators. Because you probably are the system administrator of your Linux system, this chapter also introduces you to Perl scripting.

---

cross
ref

Chapter 25 covers Tcl/Tk, another popular scripting language you can use to build applications with a graphical interface.

Looking at Some Shell Scripts

If you are not a programmer, you may feel apprehensive about programming. But shell scripting (or programming) can be as simple as storing a few commands in a file. In fact, you can have a useful shell program that has a single command.

While writing this book, for example, I have captured screens from the X Window System and have used the screen shots in figures. I have used the X screen-capture program, xwd, to store the screen images in the X Window Dump (XWD) format. The book's production team, however, wanted the screen shots in TIFF format. Therefore, I used the Portable Bitmap (PBM) toolkit to convert the XWD images to TIFF format. To convert each file, I run two programs and delete a temporary file, by using the following commands:

```
xwdtopnm < file.xwd > file.pnm
pnmtotiff < file.pnm > file.tif
rm file.pnm
```

These commands assume that the `xwdtopnm` and `pnmtotiff` programs are in the `/usr/bin` directory—one of the directories listed in the PATH environment variable. By the way, `xwdtopnm` and `pnmtotiff` are two programs in the PBM toolkit.

After converting a few XWD files to TIFF format, I get tired of typing the same sequence of commands for each file, so I prepare a file named `totif` and saved the following lines in it:

```
#!/bin/sh
xwdtopnm < $1.xwd > $1.pnm
pnmtotiff < $1.pnm > $1.tif
rm $1.pnm
```

Then, I make the file executable by using this command:

```
chmod +x totif
```

The chmod command enables you to change the permission settings of a file. One of those settings determines whether the file is executable or not. The +x option means that you want to mark the file as executable. You need to do this because Bash runs only executable files. (See the chmod command reference in Appendix A for more information on permission settings for files.)

Finally, I convert the file figure1.xwd to figure1.tif by using the following command:

```
./totif figure1
```

The ./ prefix indicates that the totif file is in the current directory—you don't need the ./ prefix if the PATH environment variable includes the current directory. The totif file is called a *shell script* or *shell program*. When you run this shell program with the command totif figure1, the shell substitutes figure1 for each occurrence of $1.

That, in a nutshell, is why you might create shell programs—to have your Linux shell perform repetitive chores.

Here is another interesting example of a shell program. Suppose that you occasionally have to use MS-DOS text files on your Linux system. Although you might expect to use a text file on any system without any problems, there is one catch: DOS uses a carriage return followed by a line feed to mark the end of each line, whereas Linux (and other UNIX systems) use only a line feed. As a result, if you use the vi editor with the -b option to open a DOS text file (for example, type **vi -b filename** to open the file), you see ^M at the end of each line. That ^M stands for Ctrl-M, which is the carriage-return character.

On your Linux system, you can easily rid the DOS text file of the extra carriage returns by using the tr command with the -d option. Essentially, to convert the DOS text file filename.dos to a Linux text file named filename.linux, type the following:

```
tr -d '\015' < filename.dos > filename.linux
```

In this command, '\015' denotes the ASCII code for the carriage-return character in octal notation. In this command, the < symbol is used to read from a file and > is used to save output to a file.

> **insider insight**
> You can use the tr command to translate or delete characters from the input. When you use tr with the -d option, it deletes all occurrences of a specific character from the input data. Following the -d option, you must specify the character to be deleted. Like many UNIX utilities, tr reads the standard input and writes its output to standard output. As the sample command shows, you must employ input and output redirection to use tr to delete all occurrences of a character in a file and save the output in another file.

If you don't want to remember all this information every time you convert a DOS file to UNIX, store the following in a file named dos2unix:

```
tr -d '\015' < $1 > $2
```

Then, make the file executable by using this command:

```
chmod +x dos2unix
```

That's it! Now you have a shell program named `dos2unix` that converts a DOS text file to a UNIX text file. If you have the MS-DOS partition mounted as `/dosc`, you can try the `dos2unix` shell program with the following command:

```
dos2unix /dosc/autoexec.bat aexec.bat
```

The preceding command creates a file named `aexec.bat` in the current directory. If you open this file with the `vi -b aexec.bat` command, you should not see any `^M` characters at the ends of lines.

---

insider insight

If you are familiar with MS-DOS, you may notice that shell scripts closely resemble MS-DOS batch files, except for some syntax differences. Shell scripts, however, are much more powerful.

Secret

Shell scripts are popular among system administrators. If you are a system administrator, you can build a collection of custom shell scripts that help you automate tasks you perform often. If a disk seems to be getting full, for example, you may want to find all files that exceed some size (say, 10MB) and that have not been accessed in the past 30 days. In addition, you may want to send an email message to all users who have large files, requesting that they archive and clean up those files. You can perform all these tasks with a shell script. You might start with the following `find` command to identify large files:

```
find / -type f -atime +30 -size +10000k -exec ls -l {} \; >
/tmp/largefiles
```

This command creates a file named `/tmp/largefiles`, which contains detailed information about the old files taking up too much space. After you get a list of the files, you can use a few other Linux commands—such as `sort`, `cut`, and `sed`—to prepare and send mail messages to users who have large files that they should clean up. Instead of typing all these commands manually, place them in a file, and create a shell script. That, in a nutshell, is the essence of shell scripts—to gather shell commands in a file so that you can easily perform or even automate repetitive systems-administration tasks.

Learning the Basics of Shell Scripting in Bash

Now that you have seen examples of simple shell scripts, the next few sections provide an overview of Bash programming.

Secret

As you try out simple shell programs, don't name your sample programs test. Linux includes an important program named test (/usr/bin/test). This program tests for various conditions in shell scripts, such as whether or not a file exists and whether or not a file is readable. If you create a sample program named test, some scripts may end up calling your program instead of calling the system's test program.

Writing a Simple Shell Script

Earlier in this chapter, you learn how to place frequently used commands in a file and use the chmod command to make the file executable. Voila—you have a shell script. Just as most Linux commands accept command-line options, a Bash script accepts command-line options. Inside the script, you can refer to the options as $1, $2, and so on. The special name $0 refers to the name of the script itself.

Consider the following Bash script:

```
#!/bin/sh
echo "This script's name is: $0."
echo Argument 1: $1
echo Argument 2: $2
```

The first line causes Linux to run the /bin/sh program, which subsequently processes the rest of the lines in the script. The name /bin/sh traditionally refers to the Bourne shell—the first UNIX shell. In Linux, /bin/sh is a symbolic link to /bin/bash, which is the executable program for Bash. Therefore, in Linux, Bash runs Bourne shell scripts (Bash happens to be compatible with the Bourne shell).

If you save this simple script in a file named simple, and you make that file executable with the command chmod +x simple, you can run the script as follows:

```
./simple
This script's name is: ./simple
Argument 1:
Argument 2:
```

The script file's name appears relative to the current directory, which is represented by a period. Because you have run the script without arguments, the script does not display any arguments.

Now, try running the script with a few arguments, as follows:

```
./simple "This is one argument." second-argument third
This script's name is: ./simple
Argument 1: This is one argument

Argument 2: second-argument
```

As this example shows, the shell treats the entire string within double quotation marks as a single argument. Otherwise, the shell uses spaces as separators between arguments on the command line.

Note that this sample script ignores the third argument because the script is designed to print only the first two arguments. The script ignores all arguments after the first two.

Getting an Overview of Bash Programming

Like any programming language, Bash includes the following features:

◆ Variables that store values, including special built-in variables for accessing command-line arguments passed to a shell script and other special values

◆ The capability to evaluate expressions

◆ Control structures that enable you to loop over several shell commands or to execute some commands conditionally

◆ The capability to define functions that can be called in many places within a script. Bash also includes many built-in commands that you can use in any script.

The next few sections illustrate some of Bash's programming features through simple examples. Because you are already running Bash, you can try the examples by typing them at the shell prompt in a terminal window.

Understanding Bash Variables

You define variables in Bash just as you define environment variables. Thus, you might define a variable as follows:

```
count=12  # note no embedded spaces allowed
```

To use a variable's value, prefix the variable's name with a dollar sign ($). $PATH, for example, is the value of the variable PATH (yes, the famous PATH environment variable that contains the list of directories to search for any commands the user types). To display the value of the variable count, use the following command:

```
echo $count
```

Bash has some special variables for accessing command-line arguments. In a shell script, $0 refers to the name of the shell script. The variables $1, $2, and so on refer to the command-line arguments. The variable $* stores all the command-line arguments as a single variable, and $? contains the exit status of the last command the shell executes.

In addition, you can prompt the user for input and use the read command to read the input into a variable. Following is an example:

```
echo -n "Enter value: "
read value
echo "You entered: $value."
```

insider insight   The `-n` option prevents the echo command from automatically adding a new line at the end of the string that it displays.

Writing Shell Functions

You can group a number of shell commands into a function and assign it a name. Later, you can execute that group of commands by using the single name assigned to the function. Here is a simple script that illustrates the syntax of shell functions:

```
#!/bin/sh

hello() {
        echo -n "Hello, "
        echo $1 $2
}

hello Jane Doe
```

When you run this script, it displays the following output:

```
Hello, Jane Doe
```

This script defines a shell function named `hello`. The function expects two arguments; in the body of the function, these arguments are referenced by $1 and $2. The function definition begins with `hello()`—the name of the function, followed by parentheses. The body of the function is enclosed in curly braces—`{...}`. In this case, the body uses the echo built-in command (see Table 24-1 for a list of built-in commands).

Using Bash Control Structures

In Bash scripts, the control structures—such as `if`, `case`, `for`, and `while`—depend on the exit status of a command to decide what to do next. When any command executes, it returns an exit status: a numeric value that indicates whether or not the command has succeeded. By convention, an exit status of zero means the command has succeeded. (Yes, you read it right: zero indicates success.) A nonzero exit status indicates that something has gone wrong with the command.

As an example of using control structures, consider the following script, which makes a backup copy of a file before opening it with the vi text editor:

```
#!/bin/sh
if cp "$1" "#$1"
then
    vi "$1"
else
    echo "Failed to create backup copy"
fi
```

This script illustrates the syntax of the `if-then-else` structure and shows how the exit status of the `cp` command is used by the if structure to determine the next action. If `cp` returns zero, the script invokes vi to edit the file; otherwise, the script displays a message and exits. By the way, the script names the backup file whose name is the same as that of the original, except for a number sign (#) added at the beginning of the filename.

---

insider insight Don't forget the final `fi` that terminates the `if` structure. Forgetting `fi` is a common source of errors in Bash scripts.

Bash includes the `test` command to enable you to evaluate any expression and to use the expression's value as the exit status of the command. Suppose that you want a script that enables you to edit a file only if it exists. Using `test`, you might write such a script as follows:

```
#!/bin/sh
if test -f "$1"
then
    vi "$1"
else
    echo "No such file"
fi
```

Secret

A shorter form of the `test` command omits `test` and places the `test` command's options in square brackets ([. . .]). Using this notation, you can write the script that enables you to edit only existing files, as follows:

```
#!/bin/sh
if [ -f "$1" ]
then
    vi "$1"
else
    echo "No such file"
fi
```

The left square bracket ([) is in fact a symbolic link to `/usr/bin/test`. You can confirm this fact by typing `ls -l /usr/bin/[`.

Another common control structure is the for loop. The following script adds the numbers 1 through 10:

```
#!/bin/sh
sum=0
for i in 1 2 3 4 5 6 7 8 9 10
do
    sum=`expr $sum + $i`
done
echo "Sum = $sum"
```

This example also illustrates the use of the `expr` command to evaluate an expression.

The `case` statement is used to execute a group of commands based on the value of a variable. For example, consider the following script:

```
#!/bin/sh
echo -n "What should I do -- (Y)es/(N)o/(C)ontinue? [Y] "
read answer
case $answer in
  y|Y|"")
    echo "YES"
  ;;
```

```
     c|C)
        echo "CONTINUE"
     ;;
     n|N)
        echo "NO"
     ;;
     *)
        echo "UNKNOWN"
     ;;
 esac
```

Save this in a file named `confirm`, and type **chmod +x confirm** to make it executable. Then, try it out like this:

```
./confirm
What should I do -- (Y)es/(N)o/(C)ontinue? [Y] c
CONTINUE
```

The script displays a prompt and reads the input you type. Your input is stored in a variable named answer. Then the `case` statement executes a block of code based on the value of the answer variable. For example, when I type **c**, the following block of commands is executed:

```
     c|C)
        echo "CONTINUE"
     ;;
```

The `echo` command causes the script to display `CONTINUE`.

From this example, you can see that the general syntax of the `case` command is as follows:

```
case $variable in
    value1 | value2)
    command1
    command2
    ...other commands...
    ;;

    value3)
    command3
    command4
    ...other commands...
    ;;
 esac
```

Essentially, the `case` command begins with the word `case` and ends with `esac`. Separate blocks of code are enclosed between the values of the variable, followed by a right parenthesis and terminated by a pair of semicolons (`;;`).

---

insider insight   **Don't forget the final** `esac` **that terminates the** `case` **structure. Forgetting** `esac` **is a common source of errors in Bash scripts.**

Taking Stock of Built-in Commands In Bash

Bash has more than 50 built-in commands, including common commands such as cd and pwd, as well as many others that are used infrequently. You can use these built-in commands in any Bash script or at the shell prompt. Appendix A describes many of the built-in commands that you use typically at the shell prompt.

Although this chapter does not have enough space to cover all built-in Bash commands, Table 24-1 describes most of these commands and their arguments. After looking through this information, type **help *cmd*** (where *cmd* is a command's name) to read more about a specific built-in command. For example, to learn more about the built-in command test, type the following:

```
help test | more
test: test [expr]
        Exits with a status of 0 (trueness) or 1 (falseness) depending on
        the evaluation of EXPR.  Expressions may be unary or binary.  Unary
        expressions are often used to examine the status of a file.  There
        are string operators as well, and numeric comparison operators.

        File operators:

            -b FILE       True if file is block special.
            -c FILE       True if file is character special.
            -d FILE       True if file is a directory.
            -e FILE       True if file exists.
            -f FILE       True if file exists and is a regular file.
            -g FILE       True if file is set-group-id.
            -h FILE       True if file is a symbolic link.
            -L FILE       True if file is a symbolic link.
            -k FILE       True if file has its `sticky' bit set.
            -p FILE       True if file is a named pipe.
            -r FILE       True if file is readable by you.
            -s FILE       True if file exists and is not empty.
            -S FILE       True if file is a socket.
            -t FD         True if FD is opened on a terminal.
            -u FILE       True if the file is set-user-id.
            -w FILE       True if the file is writable by you.
            -x FILE       True if the file is executable by you.
            -O FILE       True if the file is effectively owned by you.
(... Lines deleted ...)
```

Where necessary, the online help from the help command includes a considerable amount of detail.

Note that some external programs may have the same name as Bash built-in commands. If you want to run any such external program, you have to specify explicitly the full pathname of that program. Otherwise, Bash executes the built-in command of the same name.

Table 24-1: Summary of Built-in Commands in Bash Shell

Function	Description
. *filename* [*arguments*]	Reads and executes commands from the specified file using the optional arguments (same as source)
: [*arguments*]	Expands the arguments but does not process them
[*expr*]	Evaluates the expression *expr* and returns zero status if *expr* is true
alias [*name*[=*value*] ...]	Defines an alias or lists all aliases if no arguments provided
bg [*job*]	Puts the specified job in the background. If no job is specified, it puts the currently executing command in the background.
bind [-m *keymap*] [-lvd] [-q *name*]	Binds a key sequence to a macro
break [n]	Exits from a for, while, or until loop. If n is specified, the *n*th enclosing loop is exited.
builtin *builtin_command* [*arguments*]	Executes a shell built-in command
cd [*dir*]	Changes the current directory to *dir* or to user's home directory if no arguments provided
command [-pVv] *cmd* [*arg* ...]	Runs the command *cmd* with the specified arguments (ignoring any shell function named *cmd*)
continue [n]	Starts the next iteration of the for, while, or until loop. If n is specified, the next iteration of the *n*th enclosing loop is started.
declare [-frxi] [*name*[=*value*]]	Declares a variable with the specified *name* and, optionally, assigns it a value
dirs [-l] [+/-n]	Displays the list of currently remembered directories
echo [-neE] [*arg* ...]	Displays the arguments on standard output
enable [-n] [-all] [*name* ...]	Enables or disables the specified built-in commands
eval [*arg* ...]	Concatenates the arguments and executes them as a command
exec [*command* [*arguments*]]	Replaces the current instance of the shell with a new process that runs the specified command
exit [n]	Exits the shell with the status code n
export [-nf] [*name*[=*word*]] ...	Defines a specified environment variable and exports it to future processes
fc -s [*pat=rep*] [*cmd*]	Reexecutes the command after replacing the pattern pat with rep
fg [*jobspec*]	Puts the specified job in the foreground. If no job is specified, it puts the most recent job in the foreground.

(continued)

Table 24-1: *(continued)*

Function	Description
getopts optstring name [args]	Gets optional parameters (called in shell scripts to extract arguments from the command line)
hash [-r] [name]	Remembers the full pathname of a specified command
help [*cmd* ...]	Displays help information for specified built-in commands
history [n]	Displays past commands or past n commands, if you specify a number n
jobs [-lnp] [*jobspec* ...]	Lists currently active jobs
kill [-s *sigspec* | -*sigspec*] [*pid* | *jobspec*] ...	Sends a specified signal to one or more processes
let *arg* [*arg* ...]	Evaluates each argument and returns 1 if the last *arg* is 0
local [*name*[=*value*] ...]	Creates a local variable with the specified *name* and *value* (used in shell functions)
logout	Exits a login shell
popd [+/-n]	Removes entries from the directory stack
pushd [*dir*]	Adds a specified directory to the top of the directory stack
pwd	Prints the full pathname of the current working directory
read [-r] [*name* ...]	Reads a line from standard input and parses it
readonly [-f] [*name* ...]	Marks the specified variables as read-only, so that the variables cannot be changed later
return [n]	Exits the shell function with the return value n
set [—abefhkmnptuvxldCHP] [-o option] [arg ...]	Sets various flags
shift [n]	Makes the n+1 argument $1, the n+2 argument $2, and so on
source filename [arguments]	Reads and executes commands from a file
suspend [-f]	Stops execution until a SIGCONT signal is received
test *expr*	Evaluates the expression *expr* and returns zero if *expr* is true
times	Prints the accumulated user and system times for processes run from the shell
trap [-l] [*cmd*] [*sigspec*]	Executes *cmd* when the signal *sigspec* is received
type [-all] [-type | -path] name [name ...]	Indicates how the shell interprets each name
ulimit [-SHacdfmstpnuv [limit]]	Controls resources available to the shell
umask [-S] [*mode*]	Sets the file creation mask—the default permission for files

Function	Description
`unalias [-a] [name ...]`	Undefines a specified alias
`unset [-fv] [name ...]`	Removes the definition of specified variables
`wait [n]`	Waits for a specified process to terminate

Perl as a Scripting Language

Perl stands for Practical Extraction Report Language. Larry Wall created Perl to extract information from text files and to use that information to prepare reports. Programs written in Perl, the language, are interpreted and executed by perl, the program. This book's companion CD-ROMs include Perl, and you can install it at the same time as you install Red Hat Linux (simply select the *Development Tools* package group).

Perl is available on a wide variety of computer systems because, like Linux, Perl can be distributed freely. In addition, Perl is popular as a scripting language among many users and system administrators, which is why I introduce Perl and describe its strengths. In Chapter 25, you learn about another scripting language (Tcl/Tk) that provides the capability to create GUIs for the scripts.

Secret

The term *script* is simply a synonym for program. Unlike programs written in languages such as C and C++, you do not have to compile Perl programs; the perl program simply interprets and executes the Perl programs. The term script often is used for such interpreted programs written in a shell's programming language or in Perl. (Strictly speaking, perl does not interpret a Perl program; it converts the Perl program to an intermediate form before executing the program.)

If you are familiar with shell programming or the C programming language, you can pick up Perl quickly. If you have never programmed, becoming proficient in Perl may take a while. I encourage you to start with a small subset of Perl's features and to ignore anything you do not understand. Then, slowly add Perl features to your repertoire.

Determining Whether You Have Perl

Before you proceed with the Perl tutorial, check whether you have Perl installed on your system. Type the following command:

```
which perl
```

The `which` command tells you whether it finds a specified program in the directories listed in the `PATH` environment variable. If perl is installed, you should see the following output:

```
/usr/bin/perl
```

If the `which` command complains that no such program exists in the current `PATH`, this does not necessarily mean you do not have perl installed; it may mean that you do not have the `/usr/bin` directory in `PATH`. Ensure that `/usr/bin` is in `PATH`; either type **echo $PATH** or look at the message displayed by the `which` command (that message includes the directories in `PATH`). If `/usr/bin` is not in `PATH`, use the following command to redefine `PATH`:

```
export PATH=$PATH:/usr/bin
```

Now, try the `which perl` command again. If you still get an error, you may not have installed Perl. You can install Perl from the companion CD-ROMs by performing the following steps:

1. Log in as `root`.

2. Mount each CD and look for the `perl` RPM package. Mount the CD with the `mount /dev/cdrom` command or wait until GNOME's `magicdev` device mounts the CD. Then search for the `perl` RPM with the following commands:
   ```
   cd /mnt/cdrom/RedHat/RPMS
   ls perl*.rpm
   ```

3. After you find the `perl` RPM file, type the following `rpm` (Red Hat Package Manager) command to install Perl:
   ```
   rpm -ivh perl*
   ```

After you have `perl` installed on your system, type the following command to see its version number:

```
perl -v
```

Following is typical output from that command:

```
This is perl, v5.8.0 built for i386-linux-thread-multi
(with 1 registered patch, see perl -V for more detail)

Copyright 1987-2002, Larry Wall

Perl may be copied only under the terms of either the Artistic License or the
GNU General Public License, which may be found in the Perl 5 source kit.

Complete documentation for Perl, including FAQ lists, should be found on
this system using `man perl' or `perldoc perl'. If you have access to the
Internet, point your browser at http://www.perl.com/, the Perl Home Page.
```

This output tells you that you have Perl Version 5.8, patch Level 0, and that Larry Wall, the originator of Perl, holds the copyright. Perl is distributed freely under the GNU General Public License, however.

You can get the latest version of Perl by pointing your World Wide Web browser to the Comprehensive Perl Archive Network (CPAN). The following address connects you to the CPAN site nearest to you:

```
http://www.perl.com/CPAN/
```

Writing Your First Perl Script

Perl has many features of C, and, as you may know, most books on C start with an example program that displays Hello, World! on your terminal. Because Perl is an interpreted language, you can accomplish this task directly from the command line. If you enter:

```
perl -e 'print "Hello, World!\n";'
```

the system responds

```
Hello, World!
```

This command uses the -e option of the perl program to pass the Perl program as a command-line argument to the Perl interpreter. In this case, the following line constitutes the Perl program:

```
print "Hello, World!\n";
```

To convert this line to a script, simply place the line in a file, and start the file with a directive to run the perl program (as you do in shell scripts, when you place a line such as #!/bin/sh to run the Bourne shell to process the script).

To try a Perl script, follow these steps:

1. Use a text editor, such as vi or emacs, to save the following lines in the file named hello:

```
#!/usr/bin/perl
# This is a comment.
print "Hello, World!\n";
```

2. Make the hello file executable by using the following command:

```
chmod +x hello
```

3. Run the Perl script by typing the following at the shell prompt:

```
./hello
Hello, World!
```

That's it! You have written and tried your first Perl script.

Secret

The first line of a Perl script starts with #!, followed by the full pathname of the perl program. If the first line of a script starts with #!, the shell simply strips off the #!, appends the script file's name to the end, and runs the script. Thus, if the script file is named hello and the first line is #!/usr/bin/perl, the shell executes the following command:

```
/usr/bin/perl hello
```

You can also add other perl options on the first line of the Perl script. For example, the -w option causes the Perl interpreter to print warning messages about any bad constructs in the Perl script. It's a good idea to include the -w option on the line that invokes the Perl interpreter. Thus, you should use the following line as the first line of your Perl scripts:

```
#!/usr/bin/perl -w
```

Learning More about Perl

I devote a few sections of this chapter to giving you an overview of Perl and to showing a few simple examples. However, this discussion does not do justice to Perl. If you want to use Perl as a tool, consult one of the following books:

◆ Larry Wall, Tom Christiansen, and Jon Orwant, *Programming Perl, 3rd Edition* (O'Reilly & Associates, 2000)

◆ Randal L. Schwartz and Tom Phoenix, *Learning Perl, 3rd Edition* (O'Reilly & Associates, 2001)

◆ Paul E. Hoffman, *Perl For Dummies* (John Wiley & Sons, 2000)

Programming Perl, 3rd Edition, is the authoritative guide to Perl (although it may not be the best resource for learning Perl). The book by Randal Schwartz focuses more on teaching Perl programming. Paul Hoffman's book is a good introduction for nonprogrammers wanting to learn Perl.

Getting an Overview of Perl

Most programming languages, including Perl, have some common features:

◆ **Variables** to store different types of data. You can think of each variable as a placeholder for data—kind of like a mailbox, with a name and room to store data. The content of the variable is its value.

◆ **Expressions** that combine variables by using operators. One expression might add several variables; another might extract a part of a string.

◆ **Statements** that perform some action, such as assigning a value to a variable or printing a string.

◆ **Flow-control statements** that enable statements to be executed in various orders, depending on the value of some expression. Typically, flow-control statements include for, do-while, while, and if-then-else statements.

◆ **Functions** (also called *subroutines* or *routines*) that enable you to group several statements and give them a name. This feature enables you to execute the same set of statements by invoking the function that represents those statements. Typically, a programming language provides some predefined functions.

◆ **Packages and modules** that enable you to organize a set of related Perl subroutines that are designed to be reusable. (Modules were introduced in Perl 5).

The next few sections provide an overview of these major features of Perl and illustrate the features through simple examples.

Learning Basic Perl Syntax

Perl is free-form, like C; no constraints exist on the exact placement of any keyword. Often, Perl programs are stored in files with names that end in .pl, but there is no restriction on the filenames you use.

As in C, each Perl statement ends with a semicolon (;). A number sign or hash mark (#) marks the start of a comment; the perl program disregards the rest of the line beginning with the number sign.

Groups of Perl statements are enclosed in braces ({ . . . }). This feature also is similar in C.

Using Variables in Perl

You don't have to declare Perl variables before using them, as you do in C. You can recognize a variable in a Perl script easily, because each variable name begins with a special character: an at symbol (@), a dollar sign ($), or a percent sign (%). These special characters denote the variable's type.

Secret

The three variable types in Perl are as follows:

- *Scalar* variables represent the basic data types: integer, floating-point number, and string. A dollar sign ($) precedes a scalar variable. Following are some examples:
  ```
  $maxlines = 256;
  $title = "Red Hat Linux Professional Secrets";
  ```
- *Array* variables are collections of scalar variables. An array variable has an at symbol (@) as a prefix. Thus, the following are arrays:
  ```
  @pages = (62, 26, 22, 24);
  @commands = ("start", "stop", "draw", "exit");
  ```
- *Associative arrays* are collections of *key-value* pairs, in which each *key* is a string and the *value* is any scalar variable. A percent-sign (%) prefix indicates an associative array. You can use associative arrays to associate a name with a value. You might store the amount of disk space each user occupies in an associative array, such as the following:
  ```
  %disk_usage = ("root", 147178, "naba", 28547, "emily", 55);
  ```

Because each variable type has a special character prefix, you can use the same name for different variable types. Thus, %disk_usage, @disk_usage, and $disk_usage can appear within the same Perl program.

Using Scalars

A scalar variable can store a single value, such as a number, or a text string. Scalar variables are the basic data type in Perl. Each scalar's name begins with a dollar sign ($). Typically, you start using a scalar with an assignment statement that initializes it. You even can use a variable without initializing it; the default value for numbers is zero, and the default value of a string is an empty string. If you want to see whether a scalar is defined, use the defined function as follows:

```
print "Name undefined!\n" if !(defined $name);
```

The expression (defined $name) is 1 if $name is defined. You can "undefine" a variable by using the undef function. You can undefine $name, for example, as follows:

```
undef $name;
```

Variables are evaluated according to context. Following is a script that initializes and prints a few variables:

```
#!/usr/bin/perl
$title = "Red Hat Linux Professional Secrets";
$count1 = 650;
$count2 = 425;

$total = $count1 + $count2;

print "Title: $title -- $total pages\n";
```

When you run the preceding Perl program, it produces the following output:

```
Title: Red Hat Linux Professional Secrets -- 1075 pages
```

As the Perl statements show, when the two numeric variables are added, their numeric values are used; but when the `$total` variable is printed, its string representation is displayed.

Another interesting aspect of Perl is that it evaluates all variables in a string within double quotation marks (`"..."`). However, if you write a string inside single quotation marks (`'...'`), Perl leaves that string untouched. If you write

```
print 'Title: $title -- $total pages\n';
```

with single quotes instead of double quotes, Perl displays

```
Title: $title -- $total pages\n
```

and does not generate a new line.

<table>
<tr><td>insider insight</td><td>A useful Perl variable is <code>$_</code> (the dollar sign followed by the underscore character). This special variable is known as the default argument. The Perl interpreter determines the value of <code>$_</code> depending on the context. When the Perl interpreter reads input from the standard input, <code>$_</code> holds the current input line; when the interpreter is searching for a specific pattern of text, <code>$_</code> holds the default search pattern.</td></tr>
</table>

Using Arrays

An array is a collection of scalars. The array name begins with an at symbol (@). As in C, array subscripts start at zero. You can access the elements of an array with an index. Perl allocates space for arrays dynamically.

Consider the following simple script:

```
#!/usr/bin/perl
@commands = ("start", "stop", "draw" , "exit");

$numcmd = @commands;
print "There are $numcmd commands.\n";
print "The first command is: $commands[0]\n";
```

When you run the script, it produces the following output:

```
There are 4 commands.
The first command is: start
```

Secret

Equating a scalar to an array sets the scalar to the number of elements in the array. The first element of an array is referenced by changing the @ sign to $ and then appending the index 0 in square brackets. Thus, the first element of the @commands array is referenced as $commands[0] because the index starts at zero. Thus, the fourth element in the @commands array is $commands[3].

Two special scalars are related to an array. The $[variable is the current base index (the starting index), which is zero by default. The scalar $#arrayname (in which arrayname is the name of an array variable) has the last array index as the value. Thus, for the @commands array that has three elements, $#commands is 3.

You can print an entire array with a simple print statement like this:

```
print "@commands\n";
```

When Perl executes this statement for the @commands array used in this section's examples, it displays the following output:

```
start stop draw exit
```

Using Associative Arrays

Associative array variables, which are declared with a percent sign (%) prefix, are unique features of Perl. Using associative arrays, you can index an array with a string, such as a name. A good example of an associative array is the %ENV array, which Perl automatically defines for you. In Perl, %ENV is the array of environment variables you can access by using the environment-variable name as an index. The following Perl statement prints the current PATH environment variable:

```
print "PATH = $ENV{PATH}\n";
```

When Perl executes this statement, it prints the current setting of PATH. In contrast to indexing regular arrays, you have to use braces to index an associative array.

Perl has many built-in functions—such as delete, each, keys, and values—that enable you to access and manipulate associative arrays.

Listing the Predefined Variables in Perl

Perl has several predefined variables that contain useful information you may need in a Perl script. Following are a few important predefined variables:

♦ @ARGV is an array of strings that contains the command-line options to the script. The first option is $ARGV[0], the second one is $ARGV[1], and so on.

♦ %ENV is an associative array that contains the environment variables. You can access this array by using the environment-variable name as a key. Thus, $ENV{HOME} is the home directory, and $ENV{PATH} is the current search path that the shell uses to locate commands.

- $_ is the default argument for many functions. If you see a Perl function used without any argument, the function probably is expecting its argument in the $_ variable.
- @_ is the list of arguments passed to a subroutine.
- $0 is the name of the file containing the Perl program.
- $^V is the version number of Perl you are using (for example, if you use Perl Version 5.8.0, $^V will be v5.8.0).
- $< is the user ID (an identifying number) of the user running the script. This is useful on UNIX and Linux, where each user has an ID.
- $$ is the script's process ID.
- $? is the status the last system call has returned.

Using Operators and Expressions

Operators are used to combine and compare Perl variables. Typical mathematical operators are addition (+), subtraction (-), multiplication (*), and division (/). Perl and C provide nearly the same set of operators. When you use operators to combine variables, you end up with expressions. Each expression has a value.

Following are some typical Perl expressions:

```
error < 0
$count == 10
$count + $i
$users[$i]
```

These expressions are examples of the comparison operator (the first two lines), the arithmetic operator, and the array-index operator.

Secret

In Perl, don't use the == operator to determine whether two strings match; the == operator works only with numbers. To test the equality of strings, Perl includes the FORTRAN-style eq operator. Use eq to see whether two strings are identical, as follows:

```
if ($input eq "stop") { exit; }
```

Other FORTRAN-style, string-comparison operators include ne (inequality), lt (less than), gt (greater than), le (less than or equal), and ge (greater than or equal). Also, you can use the cmp operator to compare two strings. The return value is -1, 0, or 1, depending on whether the first string is less than, equal to, or greater than the second string.

Perl also provides another unique operators. C lacks an exponentiation operator, which FORTRAN includes; Perl uses ** as the exponentiation operator. Thus, you can enter the following:

```
$x = 2;
$y = 3;
$z = $x**$y;   # z should be 8 (2 raised to the power 3)
$y **= 2;      # y is now 9 (3 raised to the power 2)
```

You can initialize an array to null by using ( )—the null-list operator—as follows:

```
@commands = ();
```

The dot operator (.) enables you to concatenate two strings, as follows:

```
$part1 = "Hello, ";
$part2 = "World!";
$message = $part1.$part2;  # Now $message = "Hello, World!"
```

The repetition operator, denoted by x=, is curious but useful. You can use the x= operator to repeat a string a specified number of times. Suppose that you want to initialize a string to 65 asterisks (*). The following example shows how you can initialize the string with the x= operator:

```
$marker = "*";
$marker x= 65;  # Now $marker is a string of 65 asterisks.
```

Another powerful operator in Perl is range, which is represented by two periods (..). You can initialize an array easily by using the range operator. Following are some examples:

```
@numerals = (0..9); # @numerals = 0, 1, 2, 3, 4, 5, 6, 7, 8, 9
@alphabet = ('A'..'Z'); # @alphabet = capital letters A through Z
```

Learning Regular Expressions

If you have used Linux (or any variant of UNIX) for a while, you probably know about the grep command, which enables you to search files for a pattern of strings. Following is a typical use of grep to locate all files that have any occurrences of the string blaster or Blaster—on any line of all files with names that end in .c:

```
cd /usr/src/linux*/drivers/cdrom
grep "[bB]laster"  *.c
```

The preceding commands produce the following output on my system:

```
sbpcd.c: *          Works with SoundBlaster compatible cards and with "no-sound"
sbpcd.c:          0x230, 1, /* Soundblaster Pro and 16 (default) */
sbpcd.c:          0x250, 1, /* OmniCD default, Soundblaster Pro and 16 */
sbpcd.c:          0x270, 1, /* Soundblaster 16 */
sbpcd.c:          0x290, 1, /* Soundblaster 16 */
sbpcd.c:static const char *str_sb_l = "soundblaster";
sbpcd.c:static const char *str_sb = "SoundBlaster";
sbpcd.c: *              sbpcd=0x230,SoundBlaster
sbpcd.c:          msg(DBG_INF,"   LILO boot: ... sbpcd=0x230,SoundBlaster\n");
sjcd.c: * the SoundBlaster/Panasonic style CDROM interface. But today, the
```

As you can see, grep has found all occurrences of blaster and Blaster in the files with names ending in .c.

The grep command's "[bB]laster" argument is known as a *regular expression*, a pattern that matches a set of strings. You construct a regular expression with a small set of operators and rules that resemble the ones for writing arithmetic expressions. A list of characters inside brackets ([...]), for example, matches any single character in the list. Thus, the regular expression "[bB]laster" is a set of two strings, as follows:

```
blaster    Blaster
```

Secret

Perl supports regular expressions, just as the `grep` command does. Many other UNIX programs, such as the vi editor and sed (the stream editor), also support regular expressions. The purpose of a regular expression is to search for a pattern of strings in a file. That's why editors support regular expressions.

Perl enables you to construct complex regular expressions. The rules, however, are fairly simple. Essentially, the regular expression is a sequence of characters in which some characters have special meaning. Table 24-2 describes the basic rules for interpreting the characters.

If you want to match one of the characters $, |, *, ^, [,], \, and /, you have to place a backslash before them. Thus, you type these characters as \$, \|, *, \^, \[, \], \\, and \/. Regular expressions often look confusing because of the preponderance of strange character sequences and the generous sprinkling of backslashes. As with anything else, however, you can start slowly and use only a few of the features in the beginning.

Table 24-2: Rules for Interpreting Regular Expression Characters

Expression	Meaning
.	Matches any single character except a newline
x*	Matches zero or more occurrences of the character x
x+	Matches one or more occurrences of the character x
x?	Matches zero or one occurrence of the character x
[...]	Matches any of the characters inside the brackets
x{n}	Matches exactly n occurrences of the character x
x{n,}	Matches n or more occurrences of the character x
x{,m}	Matches zero or, at most, m occurrences of the character x
x{n,m}	Matches at least n occurrences, but no more than m occurrences of the character x
$	Matches the end of a line
\0	Matches a null character
\b	Matches a backspace
\B	Matches any character not at the beginning or end of a word
\b	Matches the beginning or end of a word—when not inside brackets
\cX	Matches Ctrl-X (where X is any alphabetic character)
\d	Matches a single digit
\D	Matches a nondigit character
\f	Matches a form feed
\n	Matches a newline (line-feed) character
\ooo	Matches the octal value specified by the digits ooo (where each o is a digit between 0 and 7)

Expression	Meaning
\r	Matches a carriage return
\S	Matches a non-white-space character
\s	Matches a white-space character (space, tab, or newline)
\t	Matches a tab
\W	Matches a nonalphanumeric character
\w	Matches an alphanumeric character
\x*hh*	Matches the hexadecimal value specified by the digits *hh* (where each *h* is a digit between 0 and f)
^	Matches the beginning of a line

So far, this section has summarized the syntax of regular expressions. But, you have not seen how to use regular expressions in Perl. Typically, you place a regular expression within a pair of slashes and use the match (=~)or not-match (!~) operators to test a string. You can write a Perl script that performs the same search as the one done with grep earlier in this section. The following steps help you complete this exercise:

1. Use a text editor to type and save the following script in a file named lookup:

```
#!/usr/bin/perl

while (<STDIN>)
{
    if ( $_ =~ /[bB]laster/ ) { print $_; }
}
```

2. Make the lookup file executable by using the following command:

```
chmod +x lookup
```

3. Try the script by using the following command:

```
cat /usr/src/linux*/drivers/cdrom/sbpcd.c | ./lookup
```

My system responds with this:

```
 *      Works with SoundBlaster compatible cards and with "no-sound"
        0x230, 1, /* Soundblaster Pro and 16 (default) */
        0x250, 1, /* OmniCD default, Soundblaster Pro and 16 */
        0x270, 1, /* Soundblaster 16 */
        0x290, 1, /* Soundblaster 16 */
static const char *str_sb_l = "soundblaster";
static const char *str_sb = "SoundBlaster";
 *              sbpcd=0x230,SoundBlaster
            msg(DBG_INF,"   LILO boot: ...
sbpcd=0x230,SoundBlaster\n");
 *      Works with SoundBlaster compatible cards and with "no-sound"
        0x230, 1, /* Soundblaster Pro and 16 (default) */
        0x250, 1, /* OmniCD default, Soundblaster Pro and 16 */
        0x270, 1, /* Soundblaster 16 */
        0x290, 1, /* Soundblaster 16 */
```

```
static const char *str_sb_l = "soundblaster";
static const char *str_sb = "SoundBlaster";
*               sbpcd=0x230,SoundBlaster
            msg(DBG_INF,"   LILO boot: ...
sbpcd=0x230,SoundBlaster\n");
```

The `cat` command feeds the contents of a specific file (which, as you know from the `grep` example, contains some lines with the regular expression) to the lookup script. The script simply applies Perl's regular expression-match operator (=~) and prints any matching line.

The $_ variable in the script needs some explanation. The `<STDIN>` expression gets a line from the standard input and, by default, stores that line in the $_ variable. Inside the `while` loop, the regular expression is matched against the $_ string. The following single Perl statement completes the lookup script's work:

```
if ( $_ =~ /[bB]laster/ ) { print $_; }
```

This example illustrates how you might use a regular expression to search for occurrences of strings in a file.

After you use regular expressions for a while, you can better appreciate their power. The trick is to find the regular expression that performs the task you want. Following is a search that looks for all lines that begin with exactly seven spaces and end with a right parenthesis:

```
while (<STDIN>)
{
    if ( $_ =~ /\)\n/ && $_ =~ /^ {7}\S/ )  { print $_; }
}
```

Using Flow-Control Statements

So far, you have seen Perl statements intended to execute in a serial fashion, one after another. Perl also includes statements that enable you to control the flow of execution of the statements. You already have seen the `if` statement and a `while` loop. Perl includes a complete set of flow-control statements just like those in C, but with a few extra features.

In Perl, all conditional statements take the following form:

```
conditional-statement
{ Perl code to execute if conditional is true }
```

Notice that you must enclose within braces ({...}) the code that follows the conditional statement. The conditional statement checks the value of an expression to determine whether to execute the code within the braces. In Perl, as in C, any nonzero value is considered true, whereas a zero value is false.

The following sections briefly describe the syntax of the major conditional statements in Perl.

Using if and unless Statements

The Perl `if` statement resembles the C `if` statement. For example, an `if` statement might check a count to see whether the count exceeds a threshold, as follows:

```
if ( $count > 25 ) { print "Too many errors!\n"; }
```

You can add an else clause to the `if` statement, as follows:

```
if ($user eq "root")
{
    print "Starting simulation...\n";
}
else
{
    print "Sorry $user, you must be \"root\" to run this program.\n.";
    exit:
}
```

If you know C, you can see that Perl's syntax looks quite a bit like that in C. Conditionals with the `if` statement can have zero or more elsif clauses to account for more alternatives, such as the following:

```
print "Enter version number:"; # prompt user for version number
$os_version = <STDIN>;          # read from standard input
chop $os_version; # get rid of the newline at the end of the line
# Check version number
if ($os_version >= 10 ) { print "No upgrade necessary\n";}
elsif ($os_version >= 6 && $os_version < 9)
                                    { print "Standard upgrade\n";}
elsif ($os_version > 3 && $os_version < 6) { print "Reinstall\n";}
else { print "Sorry, cannot upgrade\n";}
```

Secret

The `unless` **statement is unique to Perl. This statement has the same form as** `if`, **including the use of** `elsif` **and** `else` **clauses. The difference is that** `unless` **executes its statement block only if the condition is false. You can, for example, use the following:**

```
unless ($user eq "root")
{
    print "You must be \"root\" to run this program.\n";
    exit;
}
```

In this case, unless the string user is `"root"`**, the script exits.**

Using the while Statement

Use Perl's `while` statement for looping—the repetition of some processing until a condition becomes false. To read a line at a time from standard input and to process that line, you might use the following:

```
while ($in = <STDIN>)
{
# Code to process the line
    print $in:
}
```

Secret

If you read from the standard input without any argument, Perl assigns the current line of standard input to the `$_` variable. Thus, you can write the while loop to read lines from the standard input, as follows:

```
while (<STDIN>)
{
# Code to process the line
    print $_;
}
```

Perl's `while` statements are more versatile than those of C because you can use almost anything as the condition to be tested. If you use an array as the condition, for example, the while loop executes until the array has no elements left, as in the following example:

```
# Assume @arglist has the current set of command arguments
while (@arglist)
{
    $arg = shift @arglist;  # this extracts one argument
# Code to process the current argument
    print $arg;
}
```

The `shift` function removes the first element of an array and returns that element.

You can skip to the end of a loop with the `next` keyword; the `last` keyword exits the loop. The following `while` loop adds the numbers from 1 to 10, skipping 5:

```
while (1)
{
    $i++;
    if($i == 5) { next;}  # Jump to the next iteration if $i is 5
    if($i > 10) { last;}  # When $i exceeds 10, end the loop
    $sum += $i;           # Add the numbers
}
# At this point $sum should be 50.
```

Using for and foreach Statements

Perl and C's `for` statements have similar syntax. Use the `for` statement to execute a state-ment any number of times, based on the value of an expression. The syntax of the `for` statement is as follows:

```
for (expr_1; expr_2; expr_3) { statement block }
```

`expr_1` is evaluated one time, at the beginning of the loop; the statement block is exe-cuted until expression `expr_2` evaluates to zero. The third expression, `expr_3`, is evalu-ated after each execution of the statement block. You can omit any of the expressions, but you must include the semicolons. In addition, the braces around the statement block are required. Following is an example that uses a for loop to add the numbers from 1 to 10:

```
for($i=0, $sum=0; $i <= 10; $sum += $i, $i++) {}
```

In this example, the actual work of adding the numbers is done in the third expression, and the statement the for loop controls is an empty block (( )).

Secret

The `foreach` statement is most appropriate for processing arrays. Following is the syntax of the `foreach` statement:

```
foreach Variable (Array) { statement block }
```

The `foreach` statement assigns to `Variable` an element from the `Array` and executes the statement block. The `foreach` statement repeats this procedure until no array elements remain. The following `foreach` statement adds the numbers from 1 to 10:

```
foreach $i (1..10) { $sum += $i;}
```

Notice that I declare the array with the range operator (..). You also can use a list of comma-separated items as the array.

If you omit the `Variable` in a `foreach` statement, Perl implicitly uses the `$_` variable to hold the current array element. Thus, you can use the following:

```
foreach (1..10) { $sum += $_;}
```

Using the goto Statement

The `goto` statement transfers control to a statement label. Following is an example that prompts the user for a value and repeats the request, if the value is not acceptable:

```
ReEnter:
print "Enter offset: ";
$offset = <STDIN>;
chop $offset;
unless ($offset > 0 && $offset < 512)
{
    print "Bad offset: $offset\n";
    goto ReEnter;
}
```

Accessing Linux Commands

You can execute any Linux command from Perl in several ways:

- Call the `system` function with a string that contains the Linux command you want to execute.
- Enclose a Linux command within backquotes (`` `command` ``), which also are known as grave accents. You can run a Linux command this way and capture its output.
- Call the `fork` function to copy the current script and process new commands in the child process. (If a process starts another process, the new one is known as a child process.)
- Call the `exec` function to overlay the current script with a new script or Linux command.
- Use `fork` and `exec` to provide shell-like behavior. (Monitor user input, and process each user-entered command through a child process.) This section presents a simple example of how to accomplish this task.

The simplest way to execute a Linux command in your script is to use the `system` function with the command in a string. After the system function returns, the exit code from the command is in the `$?` variable. You can easily write a simple Perl script that reads a string from the standard input and processes that string with the `system` function. Follow these steps:

1. Use a text editor to enter and save the following script in a file named `rcmd.pl`:

```perl
#!/usr/bin/perl
# Read user input and process command

$prompt = "Command (\"exit\" to quit): ";
print $prompt;

while (<STDIN>)
{
    chop;
    if ($_ eq "exit") { exit 0;}

# Execute command by calling system
    system $_;
    unless ($? == 0) {print "Error executing: $_\n";}
    print $prompt;
}
```

2. Make the `rcmd.pl` file executable by using the following command:

```
chmod +x rcmd.pl
```

3. Run the script by typing `./rcmd.pl` at the shell prompt in a terminal window. The following listing shows some sample output from the rcmd.pl script (the output depends on what commands you enter):

```
Command ("exit" to quit): ps
  PID TTY          TIME CMD
  767 pts/0    00:00:00 bash
  940 pts/0    00:00:00 rcmd.pl
  945 pts/0    00:00:00 ps
Command ("exit" to quit): exit
```

Also, you can run Linux commands by using `fork` and `exec` in your Perl script. Following is an example script—psh.pl—that uses `fork` and `exec` to execute commands the user enters:

```perl
#!/usr/bin/perl

# This is a simple script that uses "fork" and "exec" to
# run a command entered by the user

$prompt = "Command (\"exit\" to quit): ";
print $prompt;

while (<STDIN>)
{
    chop;    # remove trailing newline
    if($_ eq "exit") { exit 0;}
```

```
    $status = fork;
    if($status)
    {
# In parent... wait for child process to finish...
        wait;
        print $prompt;
        next;
    }
    else
    {
        exec $_;
    }
}
```

The following example shows how the psh.pl script executes the ps command (remember to type **chmod +x psh.pl** before typing **./psh.pl**):

```
Command ("exit" to quit): ps
  PID TTY          TIME CMD
  767 pts/0     00:00:00 bash
  949 pts/0     00:00:00 psh.pl
  950 pts/0     00:00:00 ps
Command ("exit" to quit): exit
```

Linux shells, such as Bash, use the fork and exec combination to run commands.

Working with Files

You may have noticed the <STDIN> expression in various examples in this chapter. That's Perl's way of reading from a file. In Perl, a file handle, also known as an identifier, identifies a file. Usually, file handles are in uppercase characters. STDIN is a predefined file handle that denotes the standard input—by default, the keyboard. STDOUT and STDERR are the other two predefined file handles. STDOUT is used for printing to the terminal, and STDERR is used for printing error messages.

To read from a file, write the file handle inside angle brackets (<>). Thus, <STDIN> reads a line from the standard input.

You can open other files by using the open function. The following example shows you how to open the /etc/passwd file for reading and how to display the lines in that file:

```
open (PWDFILE, "/etc/passwd");   # PWDFILE is the file handle
while (<PWDFILE>) { print $_;}   # By default, input line is in $_
close PWDFILE;                   # Close the file
```

By default, the open function opens a file for reading. You can add special characters at the beginning of the filename to indicate other types of access. A > prefix opens the file for writing, whereas a >> prefix opens a file for appending. Following is a short script that reads the /etc/passwd file and creates a new file, named output, with a list of all users who lack shells (the password entries for these users have : at the end of each line):

```
#!/usr/bin/perl
# Read /etc/passwd and create list of users without any shell

open (PWDFILE, "/etc/passwd");
open (RESULT, ">output");                    # open file for writing
```

```
while (<PWDFILE>)
{
    if ($_ =~ /:\n/) {print RESULT $_;}
}

close PWDFILE;
close RESULT;
```

After you execute this script, you should find a file named `output` in the current directory. Following is what the `output` file contains when I run this script on a Red Hat Linux system:

```
news:x:9:13:news:/etc/news:
```

Secret

One interesting filename prefix is the pipe character—the vertical bar (|). If you call `open` with a filename that begins with |, the rest of the filename is treated as a command. The Perl interpreter executes the command, and you can use `print` calls to send input to this command. The following Perl script sends a mail message to a list of users:

```
#!/usr/bin/perl
# Send mail to a list of users.

foreach ("root", "naba")
{
    open (MAILPIPE, "| mail -s
Greetings $_");
    print MAILPIPE "Remember to
send in your weekly report
today!\n";
    close MAILPIPE;
}
```

If a filename ends with a pipe character (|), that filename is executed as a command; you can read that command's output with the angle brackets (⟨...⟩) as shown in the following example:

```
open (PSPIPE, "ps ax |");
while (<PSPIPE>)
{
# Process the output of the ps command here.
# This example simply echoes each line.
    print $_;
}
```

Writing Perl Subroutines

Although Perl includes a large assortment of built-in functions, you can add your own code modules in the form of subroutines. In fact, the Perl distribution comes with a large set of subroutines. Following is a simple script that illustrates the syntax of subroutines in Perl:

```perl
#!/usr/bin/perl
sub hello
{
# Make local copies of the arguments from the @_ array.
    local ($first,$last) = @_;

    print "Hello, $first $last\n";
}

$a = Jane;
$b = Doe;

&hello($a, $b);      # Call the subroutine.
```

When you run the preceding script, it displays the following output:

```
Hello, Jane Doe
```

Secret

Note the following points about subroutines:

- The subroutine receives its arguments in the array @_ (the at symbol, followed by an underscore character).
- Variables used in subroutines are global by default. Use the local function to create a local set of variables.
- Call a subroutine by placing an ampersand (&) before its name. Thus, subroutine hello is called by typing &hello.

If you want, you can put a subroutine in its own file. The hello subroutine, for example, can reside in a file named hello.pl. When you place a subroutine in a file, remember to add a return value at the end of the file—just type **1**; at the end to return 1. Thus, the hello.pl file appears as follows:

```perl
sub hello
{
# Make local copies of the arguments from the @_ array.
    local ($first,$last) = @_;

    print "Hello, $first $last\n";
}
1;      # return value
```

continues

continued

Then, you can write a script that uses the hello subroutine, as follows:

```
#!/usr/bin/perl
require 'hello.pl';    # Include the file with the subroutine.
$a = Jane;
$b = Doe;
&hello($a, $b);       # Call the subroutine.
```

This script uses the `require` function to include the `hello.pl` file that contains the definition of the `hello` subroutine.

Taking Stock of the Built-in Functions in Perl

Perl has nearly 200 built-in functions (also referred to as Perl functions), including functions that resemble the ones in the C Run-Time Library, as well as functions that access the operating system. You really need to go through the list of functions to appreciate the breadth of capabilities available in Perl. Table 24-3 briefly describes each of the Perl functions.

insider insight

This chapter does not have enough space to cover these functions, but you can learn about the Perl functions by pointing your World Wide Web browser to the following address:

```
http://www.perl.com/CPAN//doc/manual/html/pod/perlfunc.html
```

This address connects you to the Comprehensive Perl Archive Network (CPAN)—actually, it connects to the CPAN site nearest to you—so you can download the page with an overview of the Perl built-in functions. Click a function's name to view more detailed information about that function.

Table 24-3: A Quick Reference Guide to Perl Functions

Function Call	Description
abs(VALUE)	Returns the absolute value of the argument
accept(NEWSOCKET, GENERICSOCKET)	Waits for a connection on a socket
alarm(SECONDS)	Sends an alarm signal after a specified number of seconds
atan2(Y,X)	Returns the arctangent of Y/X
bind(SOCKET,NAME)	Associates a name to an already opened socket
binmode(FILEHANDLE)	Arranges for a file to be treated as binary
bless(REF,PACKAGE)	Makes a referenced item an object in a package
caller(EXPR)	Returns information about current subroutine calls

Function Call	Description
chdir(EXPR)	Changes the directory to the directory specified by EXPR
chmod(LIST)	Changes the permissions of a list of files
chomp(VARIABLE)	Removes trailing characters that match the current value of the special variable $/
chop(VARIABLE)	Chops off the last character (useful for removing the trailing newline character in a string)
chown(LIST)	Changes the owner of a list of files
chr(NUMBER)	Returns the character whose ASCII code is NUMBER
chroot(FILENAME)	Changes the root directory to the specified FILENAME
close(FILEHANDLE)	Closes the specified file
closedir(DIRHANDLE)	Closes the directory that had been opened by opendir
connect(SOCKET,NAME)	Initiates a connection to another system using a socket
cos(EXPR)	Returns the cosine of the angle EXPR (radians)
crypt(PLAINTEXT, SALT)	Encrypts a string
dbmclose(ASSOC_ARRAY)	Disassociates an associative array from a DBM file. (DBM, or data base manager, is a library of routines that manages DBM files—data files that contain key/data pairs.)
dbmopen(ASSOC, DBNAME, MODE)	Associates an associative array with a DBM file
defined(EXPR)	Returns true if EXPR is defined
delete $ASSOC{KEY}	Deletes a value from an associative array
die(LIST)	Prints LIST to standard error and exits the Perl program
do SUBROUTINE (LIST)	Calls a subroutine
dump(LABEL)	Causes a core dump
each(ASSOC_ARRAY)	Returns next key-value pair of an associative array
endgrent	Closes the /etc/group file in UNIX
endhostent	Closes the /etc/hosts file in UNIX
endnetent	Closes the /etc/networks file in UNIX
endprotoent	Closes the /etc/protocols file in UNIX
endpwent	Closes the /etc/passwd file in UNIX
endservent	Closes the /etc/services file in UNIX
eof(FILEHANDLE)	Returns true if end of file is reached
eval(EXPR)	Executes the EXPR as if it were a Perl program
exec(LIST)	Terminates the current Perl program by running another program (specified by LIST) in its place
exists($ASSOC($KEY))	Returns true if the specified key exists in the associative array

(continued)

Table 24-3: *(continued)*

Function Call	Description
exit(EXPR)	Exits the Perl program and returns EXPR
exp(EXPR)	Returns *e* raised to the power EXPR
fcntl(FILEHANDLE, FUNCTION, SCALAR)	Performs various control operations on a file
fileno(FILEHANDLE)	Returns the file descriptor for a file handle
flock(FILEHANDLE, OPERATION)	Locks a file so other processes cannot change the file (useful when multiple processes need to access a single file)
fork	Creates a child process and returns the child process ID
format NAME = picture line value list	Defines an output format to be used by the write function
formline(PICTURE, LIST)	Formats a list of values according to the contents of PICTURE
getc(FILEHANDLE)	Reads the next character from the file
getgrent	Returns group information from /etc/group
getgrgid(GID)	Looks up a group file entry by group number
getgrnam(NAME)	Looks up a group file entry by group name
gethostbyaddr(ADDR, ADDRTYPE)	Translates a network address to a name
gethostbyname(NAME)	Translates a network hostname to corresponding addresses
gethostent	Gets entries from the /etc/hosts file on UNIX
getlogin	Returns current login information in UNIX
getnetbyaddr(ADDR, ADDRTYPE)	Translates a network address to its corresponding network name
getnetbyname(NAME)	Translates a network name to its corresponding network address
getnetent	Gets entries from the /etc/networks file (or equivalent on non-UNIX systems)
getpeername(SOCKET)	Returns the socket address of the other end of a socket connection
getpgrp(PID)	Returns the current process group for the specified process ID
getppid	Returns the process ID of the parent process
getpriority(WHICH, WHO)	Returns the current priority of a process
getprotobyname(NAME)	Translates a protocol name into a number
getprotobynumber(NUMBER)	Translates a protocol number into a name
getprotoent	Gets networking protocol information from the /etc/networks file in UNIX

Function Call	Description
getpwent	Gets entry from the password file (/etc/passwd in UNIX)
getpwnam(NAME)	Translates a user name into the corresponding entry in the password file
getpwuid(UID)	Translates a numeric user ID into the corresponding entry in the password file
getservbyname(NAME, PROTO)	Translates a service (port) name into the corresponding port number
getservbyport(PORT, PROTO)	Translates the service (port) number into a name
getservent	Gets entries from the /etc/services file in UNIX
getsockname(SOCKET)	Returns the address of this end of a socket connection
getsockopt(SOCKET, LEVEL, OPTNAME)	Returns the requested socket options
glob(EXPR)	Returns filenames corresponding to a wildcard expression
gmtime(EXPR)	Converts binary time into a nine-element list corresponding to Greenwich Mean Time (GMT)
goto(LABEL)	Jumps to the statement identified by the LABEL
grep(EXPR, LIST)	Searches LIST for occurrences of the expression
hex(EXPR)	Returns the decimal value corresponding to hexadecimal EXPR
index(STR, SUBSTR, POSITION)	Returns the position of the first occurrence of a string (the search begins at the character location specified by POSITION)
int(EXPR)	Returns the integer portion of EXPR
ioctl(FILEHANDLE, FUNCTION, SCALAR)	Controls various aspects of FILEHANDLE
join(EXPR, LIST)	Returns a single string by joining list elements
keys(ASSOC_ARRAY)	Returns an array of keys for an associative array
kill(LIST)	Sends a signal to a list of processes
last(LABEL)	Exits the loop identified by LABEL
lc(EXPR)	Returns the lowercase version of EXPR
lcfirst(EXPR)	Returns EXPR, after changing the first character to lowercase
length(EXPR)	Returns length in number of characters
link(OLDFILE, NEWFILE)	Creates NEWFILE as a link to OLDFILE
listen(SOCKET, QUEUESIZE)	Waits for incoming connections on a socket
local(LIST)	Makes a list of variables local to a subroutine
localtime(EXPR)	Converts binary time into a nine-element list corresponding to local time

(continued)

Table 24-3: *(continued)*

Function Call	Description
lock SHAREDVAR	Locks a shared variable
log(EXPR)	Returns the logarithm (to base *e*) of EXPR
lstat(FILEHANDLE)	Returns file statistics for a file (if the file refers to a symbolic link, returns information about the symbolic link)
m/PATTERN/gimosx	Performs pattern matching
map(EXPR, LIST)	Evaluates the expression EXPR for each item of LIST
mkdir(FILENAME, MODE)	Creates the directory specified by FILENAME
msgctl(ID, CMD, ARG)	Performs message control operations on message queues
msgget(KEY, FLAGS)	Gets a message queue identifier corresponding to KEY
msgrcv(ID, VAR, SIZE, TYPE, FLAGS)	Receives a message from the message queue identifier ID
msgsnd(ID, MSG, FLAGS)	Sends a message-to-message queue identifier ID
my(EXPR)	Declares one or more private variables that exist in a subroutine or a block enclosed in curly braces ({...})
next(LABEL)	Starts the next iteration of the loop identified by LABEL
no(Module LIST)	Stops using a Perl module
oct(EXPR)	Returns the decimal equivalent of an octal number in EXPR
open(FILEHANDLE, EXPR)	Opens a file whose name is in EXPR, and associates that file with FILEHANDLE
opendir(DIRHANDLE, EXPR)	Opens a directory whose name is in EXPR, and associates that directory with DIRHANDLE
ord(EXPR)	Returns the numeric ASCII code of the first character in EXPR
our EXPR	Declares the listed variables in EXPR as valid global variables within the enclosing block (similar to my, but does not create any local variables)
pack(TEMPLATE, LIST)	Takes a list of values and returns a string containing a packed binary structure (TEMPLATE specifies the packing)
package PACKAGENAME	Declares current file to be part of the specified package
pipe(READHANDLE, WRITEHANDLE)	Opens a pipe for reading and writing
pop(ARRAY)	Removes and returns the last element of an array
pos(SCALAR)	Returns the position where the last pattern match occurred (applies when a global search is performed with /PATTERN/g)
print(FILEHANDLE LIST)	Prints a list of items to a file identified by FILEHANDLE
printf(FILEHANDLE LIST)	Prints formatted output to a file

Function Call	Description
`prototype FUNCTION`	Returns the prototype of a function as a string (the *prototype* shows the declaration of the function, including its arguments)
`push(ARRAY, LIST)`	Appends values in LIST to the end of ARRAY
`q/STRING/`	Quotes a STRING, without replacing variable names with values (similar to a single quoted string)
`qq/STRING/`	Quotes a STRING, but replaces variable names with values (similar to a double-quoted string)
`quotemeta(EXPR)`	Returns the value of EXPR, after adding a backslash prefix for all characters that take on special meaning in regular expressions
`qw/STRING/`	Quotes a word list (similar to parentheses used in patterns)
`qx/STRING/`	Quotes a command (similar to backquotes)
`rand(EXPR)`	Returns a random value between 0 and EXPR
`read(FILEHANDLE, SCALAR, LENGTH)`	Reads a specified number of bytes from the file
`readdir(DIRHANDLE)`	Reads directory entries from a directory handle
`readlink(EXPR)`	Returns the filename pointed to by a symbolic link
`readpipe(EXPR)`	Returns the output after executing EXPR as a system command
`recv(SOCKET, SCALAR, LEN, FLAGS)`	Receives a message from a socket
`redo(LABEL)`	Restarts the loop identified by LABEL
`ref(EXPR)`	Returns true if EXPR is a reference (a reference points to an object)
`rename(OLDNAME, NEWNAME)`	Changes the name of a file from OLDNAME to NEWNAME
`require(FNAME)`	Includes the file specified by FNAME, and executes the Perl code in that file
`reset(EXPR)`	Clears global variables
`return(LIST)`	Returns from subroutine with the specified values
`reverse(LIST)`	Reverses the order of elements in LIST
`rewinddir(DIRHANDLE)`	Sets the current position to the beginning of the directory identified by DIRHANDLE
`rindex(STR, SUBSTR)`	Returns the last position of a substring in a string
`rindex(STR, SUBSTR, POSITION)`	Returns the position of the last occurrence of a substring in a string
`rmdir(FILENAME)`	Deletes the directory specified by FILENAME

(continued)

Table 24-3: *(continued)*

Function Call	Description
s/PATTERN/REPLACEMENT/ egimosx	Replaces PATTERN (a regular expression) with REPLACEMENT
scalar(EXPR)	Evaluates the expression EXPR in a scalar context
seek(FILEHANDLE, POSITION, WHENCE)	Moves to a new location in a file
seekdir(DIRHANDLE, POS)	Moves to a new position in a directory
select(FILEHANDLE)	Returns the currently selected file handle, and sets FILEHANDLE as the default file handle for output
select(RBITS, WBITS, EBITS, TIMEOUT)	Checks if one or more files are ready for input or output
semctl(ID, SEMNUM, CMD, ARG)	Controls the semaphores used for interprocess communication
semget(KEY, NSEMS, FLAGS)	Returns the semaphore ID corresponding to a key
semop(KEY, OPSTRING)	Performs a semaphore operation (semaphores are used for interprocess communications in UNIX System V)
send(SOCKET, MSG, FLAGS, TO)	Sends a message to a socket
setgrent	Sets group information in /etc/group
sethostent(STAYOPEN)	Opens the host database (the /etc/hosts file in UNIX)
setnetent(STAYOPEN)	Opens the network database (the /etc/networks file in UNIX)
setpgrp(PID,PGRP)	Sets the current process group of a process
setpriority(WHICH, WHO, PRIORITY)	Sets the priority for a process
setprotoent(STAYOPEN)	Opens the protocol database (the /etc/protocols file in UNIX)
setpwent	Opens the /etc/passwd file in UNIX
setservent(STAYOPEN)	Opens the /etc/services file in UNIX
setsockopt(SOCKET, LEVEL, OPTNAME, OPTVAL)	Sets the specified socket options
shift(ARRAY)	Removes the first value of the array and returns it
shmctl(ID, CMD, ARG)	Controls shared memory settings, such as permission
shmget(KEY, SIZE, FLAGS)	Allocates a shared memory segment
shmread(ID, VAR, POS, SIZE)	Reads from the shared memory segment identified by ID
shmwrite(ID, STRING, POS, SIZE)	Writes to the shared memory segment identified by ID
shutdown(SOCKET, HOW)	Shuts down a socket connection

Function Call	Description
sin(EXPR)	Returns the sine of the angle specified by EXPR (in radians)
sleep(EXPR)	Sleeps for EXPR seconds
socket(SOCKET, DOMAIN, TYPE, PROTOCOL)	Opens a socket for a specified type and attaches it to the file handle SOCKET
socketpair(SOCKET1, SOCKET2, DOMAIN, TYPE, PROTOCOL)	Creates an unnamed pair of sockets
sort(LIST)	Sorts a list and returns the sorted list in an array
splice(ARRAY, OFFSET, LENGTH, LIST)	Replaces some ARRAY elements with LIST
split(/PATTERN/, EXPR, LIMIT)	Splits EXPR into an array of strings
sprintf(FORMAT, LIST)	Returns a string containing formatted output consisting of LIST elements formatted according to the FORMAT string
sqrt(EXPR)	Returns the square root of EXPR
srand(EXPR)	Sets the seed for random number generation
stat(FILEHANDLE)	Returns a 13-element list with statistics for a file
study(STRING)	Examines STRING in anticipation of doing many pattern matches on the string
substr(EXPR, OFFSET, LEN)	Returns a substring from the string EXPR
symlink(OLDFILE, NEWFILE)	Creates NEWFILE as a symbolic link to OLDFILE
syscall(LIST)	Calls the system function specified in the first element of LIST (and passes to that call the remaining list elements as arguments)
sysopen(FILEHANDLE, FILENAME, MODE, PERMS)	Opens a file named FILENAME and associates it with FILEHANDLE
sysread(FILEHANDLE, SCALAR, LENGTH, OFFSET)	Reads a specified number of bytes from a file
sysseek(FILEHANDLE, POSITION, WHENCE)	Sets FILEHANDLE's position to the specified POSITION in bytes (WHENCE refers to the reference point for setting the position and it can be one of SEEK_SET, SEEK_CUR, and SEEK_END)
system(LIST)	Executes the shell commands in LIST
syswrite(FILEHANDLE, SCALAR, LENGTH, OFFSET)	Writes a specified number of bytes to a file
tell(FILEHANDLE)	Returns the current file position in bytes from the beginning of a file
telldir(DIRHANDLE)	Returns the current position where the readdir function can read from a directory handle

(continued)

Table 24-3: *(continued)*

Function Call	Description
`tie(VARIABLE, PACKAGENAME, LIST)`	Associates a variable to a package that implements the variable
`time`	Returns the number of seconds since 00:00:00 GMT 1/1/1970
`times`	Returns time in seconds for this process
`tr/SEARCHLIST/ REPLACE_LIST/cds`	Translates a search list into a replacement list
`truncate(FILEHANDLE, LENGTH)`	Truncates the file FILEHANDLE to a specified LENGTH
`uc(EXPR)`	Returns the uppercase version of EXPR
`ucfirst(EXPR)`	Returns EXPR after changing the first character to uppercase
`umask(EXPR)`	Sets the permission mask to be used when creating a file (this specifies what operations are not allowed on the file)
`undef(EXPR)`	Undefines EXPR
`unlink(LIST)`	Deletes a list of files
`unpack(TEMPLATE, EXPR)`	Unpacks a string into an array and returns the array
`unshift(ARRAY, LIST)`	Prepends LIST to the beginning of ARRAY
`untie(VARIABLE)`	Breaks the binding between a variable and a package
`use(MODULE)`	Starts using a Perl module
`utime(LIST)`	Changes the access and modification time of a list of files
`values(ASSOC_ARRAY)`	Returns an array containing all values from an associative array
`vec(EXPR, OFFSET, BITS)`	Treats the string EXPR as a vector of integers, and returns a specified element of the vector
`wait`	Waits for a child process to terminate
`waitpid(PID, FLAGS)`	Waits for a specific child process (identified by PID) to terminate
`wantarray`	Returns if the current subroutine has been called in an array context
`warn(LIST)`	Produces a warning message (specified by LIST) on the standard error
`write(FILEHANDLE)`	Writes a formatted record to a file
`y/SEARCHLIST/ REPLACE_LIST/cds`	Translates a search list into a replacement list

Understanding Perl Packages and Modules

A Perl package is a way to group together data and subroutines. Essentially, it's a way to use variable and subroutine names without conflicting with any names used in other parts of a program. The concept of a package existed in Perl 4.

A Perl package provides a way to control the *namespace*—a term that refers to the collection of variable and subroutine names. Although you may not be aware of this, when you write a Perl program, it automatically belongs to a package named main. Besides main, there are other Perl packages in the Perl library (these packages are in the /usr/lib/perl5 directory of your Red Hat Linux system, under a subdirectory whose name is the same as the Perl version you are running), and you can define your own package, as well.

Perl modules, as you'll learn soon, are packages that follow specific guidelines.

You can think of a Perl package as a convenient way to organize a set of related Perl subroutines. Another benefit is that variable and subroutine names defined in a package do not conflict with names used elsewhere in the program. Thus, a variable named $count in one package remains unique to that package and does not conflict with a $count used elsewhere in a Perl program.

A Perl package is in a single file. The package statement is used at the beginning of the file to declare the file as a package and to give the package a name. For example, the file ctime.pl defines a number of subroutines and variables in a package named ctime. The ctime.pl file has the following package statement in various places:

```
package ctime;
```

The effect of this package declaration is that all subsequent variable names and subroutine names are considered to be in the ctime package. You can put such a package statement at the beginning of the file that implements the package.

What if you are implementing a package and you need to refer to a subroutine or variable in another package? As you might guess, all you need to do is specify both the package name and the variable (or subroutine) name. Perl 5 provides the following syntax for referring to a variable in another package:

```
$Package::Variable
```

Here Package is the name of the package, and Variable is the name of the variable in that package. If you omit the package name, Perl assumes you are referring to a variable in the main package. Note that C++ happens to use a similar syntax when referring to variables in another C++ class (a class is basically a collection of data and functions—a template for an object).

To use a package in your program, you can simply call the require function with the package filename as an argument. For instance, there is a package named ctime defined in the file ctime.pl. That package includes the ctime subroutine that converts a binary time into a string. The following simple program uses the ctime package from the ctime.pl file:

```
#!/usr/bin/perl -w

# Use the ctime package defined in ctime.pl file.
require 'ctime.pl';

# Call the ctime subroutine.
$time = ctime(time());

# Print the time string.
print $time;
```

As you can see, this program uses the require function to bring the ctime.pl file into the program. When you run this program, it should print the current date and time formatted, as shown in the sample output:

```
Sun Feb  9 18:25:46 2003
```

Perl 5 takes the concept of a package one step further and introduces the module, a package that follows certain guidelines and is designed to be reusable. Each module is a package that is defined in a file with the same name as the package but with a .pm extension. Each Perl object is implemented as a module. For example, the Shell object is implemented as the Shell module, stored in the file named Shell.pm.

Perl 5 comes with a large number of modules. You'll find these modules in the /usr/lib/perl5 directory under a subdirectory corresponding to your Perl version. For Perl Version 5.8.0, the Perl modules are in the /usr/lib/perl5/5.8.0 directory (the last part of the pathname is the Perl version number). Look for files with names that end in .pm (for Perl module).

Using a Perl Module

You can call the require function, or the use function, to include a Perl module in your program. For example, a Perl module named Cwd (defined, as expected, in the Cwd.pm file) provides a getcwd subroutine that returns the current directory. You can call the require function to include the Cwd module and call getcwd as follows:

```
require Cwd;  # You do not need the full filename.
$curdir = Cwd::getcwd();
print "Current directory = $curdir\n";
```

The first line brings the Cwd.pm file into this program—you do not have to specify the full filename; the require function automatically appends .pm to the module's name to figure out which file to include. The second line shows how you call a subroutine from the Cwd module. When you use require to include a module, you must invoke each subroutine with the Module::subroutine format.

If you were to rewrite this example program with the use function in place of require, it would take the following form:

```
use Cwd;
$curdir = getcwd(); # no need for Cwd:: prefix
print "Current directory = $curdir\n";
```

The most significant difference is that you no longer need to qualify a subroutine name with the module name prefix (such as Cwd::).

You can call either `require` or `use` to include a module in your program. You need to understand the following nuances when you use these functions:

- When you include a module by calling `require`, the module is included only when the `require` function is invoked as the program runs. You must use the `Module::subroutine` syntax to invoke any subroutines from a module you include with the `require` function.
- When you include a module by calling `use`, the module is included in the program as soon as the use statement is processed. Thus, you can invoke subroutines and variables from the module as if they were part of your program. You do not need to qualify subroutine and variable names with a `Module::` prefix.

You may want to stick to the `use Module;` syntax to include modules in your program, because this lets you use a simpler syntax when you call subroutines from the module.

Using Perl Objects

An *object* is a data structure that includes both the data and the functions that operate on that data. Each object is an instance of a class that defines the object's type. For example, a rectangle class may have the four corners of the rectangle as data, and functions such as one that computes the rectangle's area and another that draws the rectangle. Then, each rectangle object can be an instance of the rectangle class, with different coordinates for the four corners. In this sense, an object is an instance of a class.

The functions (or subroutines) that implement the operations on an object's data are known as *methods*. That's terminology borrowed from Smalltalk, one of the earliest object-oriented programming languages.

Classes also suggest the notion of inheritance. You can define a new class of objects by extending the data or methods (or both) of an existing class. A common use of inheritance is to express the *is a* relationship among various classes of objects. Consider, for example, the geometric shapes. Because a circle *is a* shape and a rectangle *is a* shape, you can say that the circle and rectangle classes inherit from the shape class. In this case, the shape class is called a parent class or base class.

The basic idea behind *object-oriented programming* is that you can package the data and the associated methods (subroutines) of an object as a black box. Programmers access the object only through advertised methods, without having to know the inner workings of the methods. Typically, a programmer can create an object, invoke its methods to get or set attributes (that's another name for the object's data), and destroy the object. This section shows you how to use objects in Perl 5. With this knowledge in hand, you'll be able to exploit objects as building blocks for your Perl programs.

Perl 5 implements objects by using modules, which package data and subroutines in a file. Perl 5 presents the following simple model of objects:

- An object is denoted by a reference (objects are implemented as references to a hash).
- A class is a Perl module that provides the methods to work with the object.
- A method is a Perl subroutine that expects the object reference as the first argument.

continues

continued

Object implementers have to follow certain rules and provide certain methods in a module that represents a class. However, you really don't need to know much about an object's implementation to use it in your Perl program. All you need to know are the steps you have to follow when you use an object.

Creating and Using Perl Objects

A useful Perl object is `Shell` object, which is implemented by the Perl module `Shell.pm`. That module comes with the Perl distribution and is in the `/usr/lib/perl5/5.8.0` directory (for Perl Version 5.8.0).

As the name implies, the `Shell` object is meant for running shell commands from within Perl scripts. You can create a `Shell` object and have it execute commands.

To use the `Shell` object, follow these general steps:

1. Place the following line to include the CGI module in your program:

```
use Shell;
```

You must include this line before you create a `Shell` object.

2. To create a Shell object, use the following syntax:

```
my $sh = Shell->new;
```

where `$sh` is the reference to the `Shell` object.

3. Run Linux commands by using the `Shell` object and capture any outputs by saving to an appropriate variable. For example, to save the directory listing of the `/usr/lib/perl5/5.8.0` directory in an array named `@modules`, write the following:

```
@modules = $sh->ls("/usr/lib/perl5/5.8.0/*.pm");
```

Then you can work with this array of Perl module file names (that's what `*.pm` files are) any way you want. For example, to simply go through the array and print each string out, use the following while loop:

```
while(@modules)
{
  $mod = shift @modules;
  print $mod;
}
```

How do you know which methods of an object to call and in what order to call them? You have to read the object's documentation before you can use the object. The method names and the sequences of method invocation depend on what the object does.

Using the English Module

Perl includes several special variables with strange names, such as `$_` for the default argument and `$!` for error messages corresponding to the last error. When you read a program, it can be difficult to guess what a special variable means. The result is that you may end up avoiding a special variable that could be useful in your program.

As a helpful gesture, Perl 5 provides the English module (`English.pm`), which enables you to use understandable names for various special variables in Perl. To use the English module, include the following line in your Perl program:

```
use English;
```

After that, you can refer to `$_` as `$ARG` and `$!` as `$ERRNO` (these "English" names can still be a bit cryptic, but they're definitely better than the punctuation marks).

The following program uses the `English` module and prints a few interesting variables:

```perl
#!/usr/bin/perl -w
# File: english.pl

use English;
if($PERL_VERSION ge v5.8.0)
{
    print "Perl version 5.8.0 or later\n";
}
else
{
    print "Perl version prior to 5.8.0\n";
}
print "Perl executable = $EXECUTABLE_NAME\n";
print "Script name = $PROGRAM_NAME\n";
```

When I run this script, the output appears as follows:

```
Perl version 5.8.0 or later
Perl executable = /usr/bin/perl
Script name = ./english.pl
```

The `English` module is handy because it lets you write Perl scripts in which you can refer to special variables by meaningful names. To learn more about the Perl special variables and their English names, type **man perlvar** at the shell prompt.

Summary

Scripts or interpreted programs are often used to automate various tasks in Linux. This chapter focused on writing scripts in Bash—the Bourne Again shell—as well as in the scripting language Perl.

By reading this chapter, you learned the following:

♦ A shell script is nothing more than a sequence of Linux commands in a file. Typically, you have to place a special line at the beginning of the script file and make it executable. Then you can run the script by typing its name at the shell prompt.

♦ When your Red Hat Linux system boots, shell scripts stored in various subdirectories in the `/etc` directory (for example, `/etc/init.d`) perform many initialization tasks.

◆ There are many built-in shell commands you can use in shell scripts. You already know some of the built-in commands, such as `cd` and `pwd`, but this chapter describes many more built-in shell commands.

◆ Perl is a popular scripting language that appears on this book's companion CD-ROMs. You can use Perl to write powerful scripts on your Red Hat Linux system.

◆ Perl contains features comparable to those of other programming languages, such as C. A powerful feature of Perl is its capability to use regular expressions and to search files for occurrences of a search pattern.

◆ Perl 5, the latest version of Perl (and the one that comes with Red Hat Linux), includes a number of helpful features. A key feature is the Perl module, a package of subroutines that follows certain guidelines. Modules make it possible to implement objects in Perl.

◆ You can download the latest version of Perl (as well as Perl documentation) from the Comprehensive Perl Archive Network (CPAN) at `http://www.perl.com/CPAN/`.

Tcl/Tk Scripting

Chapter

25

◆ ◆

Secrets in This Chapter

◆ ◆

I f you are already a C and X Window system programmer, you will be surprised by the ease with which you can create graphical applications with *Tcl (Tool Command Language)* and its associated X toolkit, *Tk*—collectively referred to as Tcl/Tk (pronounced "tickle/tee kay"). Tcl is a scripting language like Perl. The biggest strength of Tcl is its X toolkit, Tk, which enables you to develop scripts with GUIs.

When I started using Tcl/Tk, I was pleasantly surprised by how few lines of Tcl/Tk it takes to create a functioning graphical interface. To a newcomer, a Tcl/Tk script still looks rather complicated, but if you have used C-based toolkits, such as Xt and Motif, to write programs, you can appreciate the high-level abstractions of Tk. Creating a user-interface component such as a button is much simpler in Tk than in Motif. In Tk, you still have to tend to many details, such as how to lay out the components of the user interface, but you can see results faster than you can with a C program that calls the Motif library.

insider insight

If you have never programmed, don't avoid this chapter out of fear. The examples in this chapter teach you the basics of Tcl and Tk. You are bound to become a believer in Tcl/Tk after you see how quickly you can use Tcl/Tk's interpreter to create applications with graphical interfaces.

Introducing Tcl

The creator of Tcl, John Ousterhout, intended it to be a simple, embeddable scripting language whose interpreter could be linked with any C program, so that the C program could use Tcl scripts. The term *embeddable* refers to this property of Tcl—the capability of any C program to use the Tcl interpreter and run Tcl scripts.

John Ousterhout created Tcl and Tk when he was at the University of California at Berkeley. Tcl first appeared in 1989; Tk followed in 1991. Tcl/Tk are freely available for unrestricted use, including commercial use. At the time of this writing, the current Tcl version is 8.3; Tk is also 8.3. Red Hat Linux comes with Tcl/Tk.

The following sections provide an overview of Tcl, its syntax, and some of its important commands. Because Tcl underlies the Tk toolkit, you should become familiar with Tcl before jumping into Tk, although Tk undoubtedly is more fun because you can use it to create graphical interfaces.

Writing Your First Tcl Script

In Chapter 24, you learned how to write shell scripts and Perl scripts. You write Tcl scripts the same way. Unlike Perl, Tcl includes a shell—an interactive interpreter of Tcl commands. The Tcl shell program's name is tclsh; it should be in the /usr/bin directory.

When you log in, the PATH environment variable should include the /usr/bin directory. Thus, you can start the Tcl shell by typing tclsh at a text console or in a terminal window in GNOME or KDE. A percent sign (%) appears on the next line; this is the Tcl shell program's prompt. To see which version of Tcl you have, type **info tclversion** at the Tcl shell prompt. The Tcl shell program responds by printing the version of Tcl. Here is an example of how you interact with the Tcl shell:

```
tclsh
% info tclversion
8.3
%
```

Now you can interactively try the following Tcl program, which prints `Hello, World!` on the standard output (the display screen or the terminal window):

```
% puts "Hello, World!"
Hello, World!
% exit
```

Type **exit** to quit the Tcl shell.

> **note** Note that I don't show the shell prompt in previous chapters, but I show the Tcl prompt (%) in many of this chapter's code listings. That's because the Tcl prompt looks different from the Bash prompt, which should tell you that you aren't working in Bash.

The Tcl shell immediately processes the Tcl command you enter and displays the results, then it prompts you for the next input. At this point, you can type **exit** to quit the Tcl shell (`tclsh`).

To prepare and run a Tcl script, follow these steps:

1. Use a text editor to enter and save the following lines in a file named `hellotcl` (this file will be the Tcl script):

   ```
   #!/usr/bin/tclsh
   # A simple Tcl script
   puts "Hello, World!"
   ```

2. Type the following command at the shell prompt to make the `hellotcl` file executable (that's what the +x in the `chmod` command means):

   ```
   chmod +x hellotcl
   ```

3. To run the `hellotcl` script, type the following at the shell prompt:

   ```
   ./hellotcl
   Hello, World!
   ```

Use these basic steps to create and run any Tcl script. You still have to learn the nuances of Tcl syntax, of course—as well as many rules. This section gets you started with an overview of Tcl.

Getting More Information on Tcl/Tk

This chapter provides an overview of Tcl and Tk, highlights many key points, and shows simple examples. However, there isn't enough room in this chapter to list all the information you need to fully exploit the power of Tcl and Tk. Because of Tcl/Tk's popularity, you can find quite a few resources about it, ranging from books to Internet sites. Following is a short list of Tcl/Tk resources:

- **Books** —Two prominent books on Tcl/Tk are available. The first book is *Tcl and the Tk Toolkit* (Addison Wesley 1994) by John K. Ousterhout, the originator of Tcl and Tk. John's book provides a broad overview of Tcl and Tk, including an explanation of the way that Tcl command strings are parsed. The other book is *Practical Programming in Tcl and Tk, Third Edition* (Prentice Hall 2000) by Brent B. Welch. This book provides more Tcl and Tk examples.

- **Internet resources**—Several FTP and websites contain the latest Tcl/Tk distributions and information about Tcl/Tk development. Following are the URLs for a few key sites:

  - `ftp://ftp.scriptics.com/pub/tcl/`—(Tcl/Tk master distribution site)
  - `http://www.scriptics.com/`—(Tcl developer site)
  - `http://www.neosoft.com/tcl/`—(Tcl/Tk contributed sources archive)

Getting an Overview of Tcl

True to its name (Tool Command Language), Tcl consists of a set of commands you can combine according to a set of rules. To write Tcl scripts, you have to understand two broad subjects:

- **Tcl syntax**—Tcl syntax is the set of rules the Tcl command interpreter follows when it interprets a command string (a line that contains a command and its arguments).

- **Tcl commands**—Although the syntax is the same for all commands, each Tcl command is meant to perform a specific task. To exploit Tcl fully, you have to know what commands are available and what each command does. The Tcl command set can be extended by applications. In fact, Tk itself is an extension of Tcl; Tk adds commands that manipulate components of GUIs.

Start by learning the Tcl syntax, a handful of rules that determine the way each Tcl command is parsed. Because Tcl has many commands, learning all of them can take a while. Even after you become proficient in the Tcl syntax and a small set of commands, you may need to keep a reference manual nearby so that you can check the exact format of the arguments that each command requires.

Tcl commands include the following basic programming facilities that you expect from any programming language:

- *Variables*, which store data. Each variable has a name and a value. Tcl also allows you to define arrays of variables.

- *Expressions*, which combine values of variables with operators. An expression might add two variables, for example. Tcl uses the `expr` command to evaluate expressions.

- *Control-flow commands*, which enable commands to be executed in various orders, depending on the value of some expression. Tcl provides commands such as `for`, `foreach`, `break`, `continue`, `if`, `while`, and `return` to implement flow control in Tcl scripts.

- *Procedures*, which enable you to group several commands and give them a name. Procedures also accept arguments. Tcl provides the `proc` command to enable you to define procedures. You can use a procedure to execute the same set of commands (usually with different arguments) by invoking the procedure that represents those commands.

The next few sections provide an overview of the Tcl syntax and the core Tcl commands.

Learning the Basic Tcl Syntax

To understand the basic Tcl syntax, you have to know a bit about how the Tcl interpreter processes each command string. The steps are as follows:

1. The Tcl interpreter parses (breaks down) the command string into words—the constituent parts, including variables and operators.

2. The Tcl interpreter applies rules to substitute the values of variables and replace certain commands with their results.

3. The Tcl interpreter executes the commands, taking the first word as the command name and calling a command procedure to execute the command. The command procedure receives the rest of the words as strings.

When writing Tcl command strings, you have to use *white space* (a space or a tab) to separate a command's name from its arguments. A newline or a semicolon (;) marks the end of a command string. You can put two commands on the same line if you insert a semicolon after the first command. Thus, you can use the following:

```
% puts Hello, ; puts World!
Hello,
World!
```

The resulting output appears on separate lines because the puts command adds a newline by default.

Use a backslash (\ ) at the end of a line to continue that command string on the next line (this is a standard convention in UNIX). Thus, you can write a command string to print Hello, World! as follows:

```
puts "Hello, \
World!"
```

Substitutions

The Tcl interpreter replaces certain parts of the command string with an equivalent value. If you precede a variable's name with a dollar sign ($), for example, the interpreter replaces that word with the variable's value. As you learn in the "Variables" section, you can define a variable in a Tcl script by using the set command, as follows:

```
set count 100
```

This command defines a variable named count with the value 100. Suppose that you type the following:

```
puts $count
```

The interpreter first replaces $count with its value, 100. Thus, that command string becomes:

```
puts 100
```

When the interpreter executes the puts command, it prints 100. This is an example of *variable substitution*.

In all, the Tcl interpreter supports three kinds of substitutions:

◆ **Variable substitution**—As the preceding example shows, if the Tcl interpreter finds a dollar sign ($), it replaces the dollar sign as well as the following variable name with that variable's value.

◆ **Backslash substitution**—You can embed special characters, such as the newline and tab, in a word by using backslash substitution. Type a backslash, followed by one or more characters; the interpreter replaces that sequence with a non-printable character. These sequences are patterned after ANSI Standard C's escape sequences. Table 25-1, which follows this list, summarizes the backslash sequences that the Tcl interpreter understands.

◆ **Command substitution**—This type of substitution refers to the mechanism that enables you to specify that a command be evaluated and replaced by its result before the interpreter processes the command string. The command `string length "Hello, World!"`, for example, returns 13, the length of the string. To set a variable named `len` to the length of this string, type the following:

```
set len [string length "Hello, World!"]
```

The interpreter processes the command inside the square brackets and replaces that part of the command string with the value of the command. Thus, this command becomes

```
set len 13
```

and the `set` command sets the `len` variable to 13.

Table 25-1: Backslash Sequences and Their Meanings in Tcl

Sequence	Replacement Character *
\a	Bell character (0x7)
\b	Backspace (0x8)
\f	Form feed (0xc)
\n	Newline (0xa)
\r	Carriage return (0xd)
\t	Horizontal tab (0x9)
\v	Vertical tab (0xb)
\<newline>	Replace the newline and white space on the next line with a single space
\\	Interpret as a single backslash (\)
\"	Interpret as double quotation marks (")
\ooo	Use the value specified by the octal digits ooo (up to three)
\xhh	Use the value specified by the hexadecimal digits hh (up to two)

* Hexadecimal values are shown in parentheses (for example, 0xd means hexadecimal d)

Comments

A pound sign (#) marks the start of a comment; the Tcl interpreter disregards the rest of the line, beginning with the pound sign. Tcl does, however, have a peculiar requirement for comments: you cannot start a comment within a command. The command string must end before you start a comment.

To understand this problem, try the following Tcl command at the `tclsh` prompt:

```
% puts "Hello, World!" # This is a comment
wrong # args: should be "puts ?-nonewline? ?channelId? string"
%
```

Essentially, the `puts` command processes the remainder of the line and complains about the number of arguments. The solution is to put a semicolon just before the pound sign (#), as follows:

```
% puts "Hello, World!" ;# This is a comment
Hello, World!
```

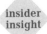

> **insider insight**
>
> If you put comments at the end of a Tcl command, remember to precede the pound sign (#) with a semicolon (;). The semicolon terminates the preceding command and enables you to start a comment.

Braces and Double Quotation Marks

You can use braces ({...}) and double quotation marks ("...") to group several words. Use double quotes to pass arguments that contain an embedded space or a semicolon, which otherwise ends the command. The quotes are not part of the group of words; they simply serve to mark the beginning and end of a group of words. Following are some examples of using double quotes to group words:

```
% puts "Hello, World!"
Hello, World!
% puts "Enter 1; otherwise file won't be saved!"
Enter 1; otherwise file won't be saved!
```

When you group words with double quotes, all types of substitutions still take place, as the following example illustrates:

```
% puts "There are [string length hello] characters in 'hello'"
There are 5 characters in 'hello'
```

The Tcl interpreter replaces everything inside the brackets with the result of the `string length hello` command, whose return value is the number of characters in `hello` (5). In the expression `[string length hello]`, you can replace the string `hello` with any variable to determine the length of that variable's value.

Also, you can use braces to group words. The Tcl interpreter does not perform any substitutions when you group words with braces (if you enclose words in double quotes, the interpreter does perform a substitution). Consider the preceding example with braces instead of double quotes:

```
% puts {There are [string length hello] characters in 'hello'}
There are [string length hello] characters in 'hello'
```

As the result shows, the Tcl interpreter simply passes everything, unchanged, as a single argument.

insider insight   Use braces as a grouping mechanism when you have to pass expressions to control commands, such as while loops, for loops, or procedures.

Understanding Tcl Variables

Everything is a string in Tcl. Variable names, as well as values, are stored as strings. To define a variable, use the built-in Tcl command set. The following commands, for example, define the variable book as "Red Hat Linux Professional Secrets"; the variable year as 2003; and the variable price as $49.99:

```
set book "Red Hat Linux Professional Secrets"
set year 2003
set price \$49.99
```

To refer to the value of a variable, add a dollar sign ($) prefix to the variable's name. Therefore, to print the variable book, use the following format:

```
% puts $book
Red Hat Linux Professional Secrets
```

If you use set with a single argument, set returns the value of that argument. Thus, set book is equivalent to $book, as the following example shows:

```
% puts [set book]
Red Hat Linux Professional Secrets
```

Writing Expressions

You can write expressions by combining variables with mathematical operators, such as + (add), - (subtract), * (multiply), and / (divide). Here are some examples of expressions:

```
set count 1
$count+1
$count + 5 - 2
2 + 3.5
```

You can use numbers, as well as variable names, in expressions. Use white space to enhance readability. Use parentheses to specify how you want an expression to be evaluated.

In addition to the basic mathematical operators, Tcl includes several built-in mathematical functions, such as sin, cos, tan, log, and sqrt. Call these functions just as you do in C, with arguments in parentheses, as follows:

```
set angle 1.5
2*sin($angle)
```

In addition, you can use Boolean operators, such as ! (not), && (and), and || (or). Comparison operators—such as < (less than), > (greater than), <= (less than or equal to), == (equal to), and != (not equal to)—also are available. Expressions that use Boolean or comparison operators evaluate to 1 if true and 0 if false. You can write expressions, such as the following:

```
count == 10
angle < 3.1415
```

Expressions are not commands by themselves. You can use expressions as arguments only for commands that accept expressions as arguments. The if and while commands, for example, expect expressions as arguments.

Tcl also provides the expr command to evaluate an expression. The following example shows how you might evaluate an expression in a Tcl command:

```
% set angle 1.5
1.5
% puts "Result = [expr 2*sin($angle)]"
Result = 1.99498997321
```

Although Tcl stores everything as a string, you have to use numbers where numbers are expected. If book is defined as "Red Hat Linux Professional Secrets", for example, you cannot write an expression $book+1, because it does not make sense.

Using Control-Flow Commands in Tcl

Tcl's control-flow commands enable you to specify the order in which the Tcl interpreter executes commands. You can use the if command to test the value of an expression; and if the value is true (nonzero), you can make the interpreter execute a set of commands. Tcl includes control-flow commands similar to those in C, such as if, for, while, and switch. This section provides an overview of the control-flow commands.

Secret

A Tcl control-flow command typically has a *command block* (a group of commands) that the control-flow command executes after evaluating an expression. To avoid substitutions (such as replacing variables with their values), you must enclose the entire command block in braces. The following if-else control-flow commands illustrate the style of braces that works properly:

```
if { expression } {
# Commands to execute when expression is true
  command_1
  command_2
} else {
# Commands to execute when expression is false
# ...
}
```

You should follow this style of braces religiously in Tcl scripts. In particular, remember to include a space between the control-flow command (such as if) and the left brace ({) that follows the command.

Using the if Command

In its simplest form, Tcl's if command evaluates an expression and executes a set of commands if that expression is nonzero (true). You might compare the value of a variable with a threshold as follows:

```
if { $errorCount > 25 } {
    puts "Too many errors!"
}
```

You can add an `else` clause to process commands if the expression evaluates to zero (false). Following is an example:

```
if { $user == "root" } {
    puts "Starting system setup ..."
} else {
    puts "Sorry, you must be \"root\" to run this program!"
}
```

Tcl's `if` command can be followed by zero or more `elseif` commands if you need to perform more complicated tests, such as the following:

```
puts -nonewline "Enter version number: "   ;# Prompt user
set version [gets stdin]                    ;# Read version number

if { $version >= 10 } {
    puts "No upgrade necessary"
} elseif { $version >= 6 && $version < 9} {
    puts "Standard upgrade"
} elseif { $version >= 3 && $version < 6} {
    puts "Reinstall"
} else {
    puts "Sorry, cannot upgrade"
}
```

Using the while Command

The `while` command executes a block of commands until an expression becomes false. The following `while` loop keeps reading lines from the standard input until the user presses Ctrl+D:

```
while { [gets stdin line]  != -1 } {
    puts $line
# Do whatever you need to do with $line.
}
```

Although this `while` command looks simple, you should realize that it has two arguments inside two sets of braces. The first argument is the expression; the second argument contains the Tcl commands to be executed if the expression is true. You must always use braces to enclose both of these arguments. The braces prevent the Tcl interpreter from evaluating the contents; the `while` command is the one that processes what's inside the braces.

If you use a variable to keep count inside a while loop, you can use the `incr` command to increment that variable. You can skip to the end of a loop by using the `continue` command; the `break` command exits the loop. The following Tcl script uses a while loop to add all the numbers from 1 to 10, except 5:

```
#!/usr/bin/tclsh

set i 0
set sum 0

while { 1 } {
    incr i                              ;# Increment i
```

```
        if {$i == 5} { continue }   ;# Skip if i is 5
        if {$i > 10} {break }       ;# End loop if i exceeds 10
        set sum [expr $sum+$i]      ;# Otherwise, add i to sum
    }
    puts "Sum = $sum";
```

When you run this script, it should display the following result:

```
Sum = 50
```

Using the for Command

Tcl's for command takes four arguments, which you should type in the following manner:

```
for {expr1} { expr2} { expr3} {
    commands
}
```

The for command evaluates expr1 once at the beginning of the loop and executes the commands inside the final pair of braces, until the expression expr2 evaluates to zero. The for command evaluates the third expression—expr3—after each execution of the commands. You can omit any of the expressions, but you must use all the braces. The following example uses a for loop to add the numbers from 1 to 10:

```
#!/usr/bin/tclsh
for {set i 0; set sum 0} {$i <= 10} {set sum [expr $sum+$i]; incr i} {
}
puts "Sum = $sum";
```

When you run this script, it displays the following result:

```
Sum = 55
```

Using the foreach Command

You have not seen a command like foreach in C, but foreach is handy when you want to perform some action for each value in a list of variables. You can add a set of numbers with the foreach command as follows:

```
set sum 0
foreach i { 1 2 3 4 5 6 7 8 9 10} {
    set sum [expr $sum+$i]
}
puts "Sum = $sum"
```

When you run this script, this one also prints Sum = 55 because the script is adding the numbers 1 through 10.

If you have a list in a variable, you can use that variable's value in place of the list shown within the first pair of braces. Following is a foreach loop that echoes the strings in a list:

```
set users "root naba"
foreach user $users {
    puts "$user"
}
```

Using the switch Command

Tcl's switch command is different from C's switch statement. Instead of evaluating a mathematical expression, Tcl's switch command compares a string with a set of patterns and executes a set of commands, depending on which pattern matches. Often, the pattern is expressed in terms of a regular expression.

cross ref   See Chapter 24 for an introduction to regular expressions.

The following script illustrates the syntax and a typical use of the switch command:

```
#!/usr/bin/tclsh
# This script reads commands from the user and processes
# the commands using a switch statement.

set prompt "Enter command (\"quit\" to exit): "

puts -nonewline "$prompt"; flush stdout

while { [gets stdin cmd]  != -1 } {
    switch -exact -- $cmd {
        quit    { puts "Bye!"; exit}
        start   { puts "Started"}
        stop    { puts "Stopped"}
        draw    { puts "Draw.."}
        default { puts "Unknown command: $cmd" }
    }
# Prompt user again
    puts -nonewline $prompt; flush stdout
}
```

Following is a sample session with this script (user input is in boldface):

```
Enter command ("quit" to exit): help
Unknown command: help
Enter command ("quit" to exit): start
Started
Enter command ("quit" to exit): stop
Stopped
Enter command ("quit" to exit): quit
Bye!
```

As this example shows, the switch statement enables you to compare a string with a set of other strings and to activate a set of commands, depending on which pattern matches. In this example, the string is $cmd (which is initialized by reading the user's input with a gets command), and the patterns are literal strings: quit, start, stop, and draw.

Secret

When you want the `switch` statement to compare a string with a set of other strings and look for an exact match, use the `-exact` flag on the first line of the `switch` command, as follows:

```
switch -exact -- $cmd {
    ...
}
```

The two hyphens (–) immediately after the `-exact` flag mark the end of the flags. When you use the `switch` command, you should always use the double hyphens at the end of the flag to prevent the test string (in this example, the test string is `$cmd`) from matching a flag inadvertently.

You can use the `switch` command with the `-regexp` flag to compare a string with a regular expression, as in the following example:

```
# Assume that $cmd is the string to be matched.

switch -regexp -- $cmd {
    ^q.*    { puts "Bye!"; exit}
    ^x.*  { puts "Something x..."}
    ^y.*  { puts "Something y..."}
    ^z.*  { puts "Something z..."}
    default { puts "Unknown command: $cmd" }
}
```

In this example, each regular expression has a similar form. The pattern `^z.*` means any string that starts with a single `z`, followed by any number of other characters.

Writing Tcl Procedures

You can use the `proc` command to add your own commands. Such commands are called *procedures*; the Tcl interpreter treats them just as though they were built-in Tcl commands. The following example shows how easy it is to write a procedure in Tcl:

```
#!/usr/bin/tclsh

proc total items {
    set sum 0
    foreach i $items {
        set sum [expr $sum+$i]
    }
    return $sum
}

set counts "5 4 3 5"
puts "Total = [total $counts]"
```

When you run the preceding script, it prints the following:

```
Total = 17
```

In this example, the procedure's name is total, and it takes a list of numbers as the argument. The procedure receives the arguments in the variable named items. The body of the procedure extracts each item and returns a sum of the items. Thus, to add numbers from 1 to 10, you have to call the total procedure as follows:

```
set sum1_10 [total {1 2 3 4 5 6 7 8 9 10}]
```

Secret

In a Tcl procedure, the argument name args has special significance; if you use args as the argument name, you can pass a variable number of arguments to the procedure. For example, write the total procedure with the argument name as args, as follows:

```
proc total args {
    set sum 0
    foreach i $args {
        set sum [expr $sum+$i]
    }
    return $sum
}
```

Now, you can call total in the following manner:

```
set sum1_10 [total 1 2 3 4 5 6 7 8 9 10]   ;# Variable arguments
```

This should set sum1_10 to the sum of the numbers from 1 through 10.

If you want to access a global variable (a variable defined outside a procedure) in the Tcl procedure, you have to use the global command inside the procedure. The global command makes a global variable visible within the scope of a procedure. If a variable named theCanvas holds the current drawing area in a Tk (Tcl's X toolkit) program, a procedure that uses theCanvas must include the following command:

```
global theCanvas
```

Taking Stock of Built-in Tcl Commands

You have seen many Tcl commands in the preceding examples. Knowing the types of commands that are available in Tcl helps you decide which commands are most appropriate for the task at hand. Although this chapter does not have enough room to cover all Tcl commands, Table 25-2 summarizes Tcl's built-in commands.

insider insight   To get online help about any Tcl command listed in Table 25-2, type man n, followed by the command name. To get online help about Tcl's file command, for example, type man n file.

Table 25-2: Built-in Tcl Commands

Command	Action
append	Appends an argument to a variable's value
array	Performs various operations on an array variable
break	Exits a loop command (such as while and for)
catch	Executes a script and traps errors to prevent errors from reaching the Tcl interpreter
cd	Changes the current working directory
close	Closes an open file
concat	Joins two or more lists in a single list
continue	Immediately begins the next iteration of a for or while loop
eof	Checks to see whether end-of-file is reached in an open file
error	Generates an error
eval	Concatenates lists (as concat does), and then evaluates the resulting list as a Tcl script
exec	Starts one or more processes that execute the command's arguments
exit	Terminates the Tcl script
expr	Evaluates an expression
file	Checks filenames and attributes
flush	Flushes buffered output to a file
for	Implements a for loop
foreach	Performs a specified action for each element in a list
format	Formats output and stores it in a string (as the sprintf function in C does)
gets	Reads a line from a file
glob	Returns the names of files that match a pattern (such as *.tcl)
global	Accesses global variables
history	Provides access to the *history list* (the list of past Tcl commands)
if	Tests an expression and executes commands if the expression is true (nonzero)
incr	Increments the value of a variable
info	Returns internal information about the Tcl interpreter
join	Creates a string, by joining all items in a list
lappend	Appends elements to a list
lindex	Returns an element from a list at a specified index. (Index 0 refers to the first element.)

(continued)

Table 25-2: *(continued)*

Command	Action
linsert	Inserts elements into a list before a specified index
list	Creates a list composed of the specified arguments
llength	Returns the number of elements in a list
lrange	Returns a specified range of adjacent elements from a list
lreplace	Replaces elements in a list with new elements
lsearch	Searches a list for a particular element
lsort	Sorts a list in a specified order
open	Opens a file and returns a file identifier
pid	Returns the process identifier (ID)
proc	Defines a Tcl procedure
puts	Sends characters to a file
pwd	Returns the current working directory
read	Reads a specified number of bytes from a file. (You can read the entire file in a single read.)
regexp	Matches a regular expression with a string
regsub	Substitutes one regular expression pattern for another
rename	Renames or deletes a command
return	Returns a value from a Tcl procedure
scan	Parses a string, using format specifiers patterned after C's sscanf function
seek	Changes the *access position* (where the next input or output operation occurs) in an open file
set	Sets a variable's value or returns its current value
source	Reads a file and processes it as a Tcl script
split	Breaks a string into a Tcl list
string	Performs various operations on strings
switch	Processes one of several blocks of commands, depending on which pattern matches a specified string
tell	Returns the current access position for an open file
time	Returns the total time needed to execute a script
trace	Executes a specified set of Tcl commands whenever a variable is accessed
unknown	Handles any unknown command. (The Tcl interpreter calls this command whenever it encounters any unknown command.)
unset	Removes the definition of one or more variables
uplevel	Executes a script in a different context

Command	Action
upvar	References a variable outside a procedure. (This is used to implement the pass-by-reference style of procedure call, in which changing a procedure argument changes the original copy of the argument.)
while	Implements a while loop that executes a set of Tcl commands repeatedly, as long as an expression evaluates to a nonzero value (true)

Manipulating Strings in Tcl

If you browse through the Tcl commands listed in Table 25-2, you find quite a few—such as append, join, split, string, regexp, and regsub—that operate on strings. This section summarizes a few string-manipulation commands.

Secret

When you set a variable to a string, the Tcl interpreter considers that string to be a single entity, even if that string contains embedded spaces or special characters. Sometimes you need to access the string as a list of items. The split command is a handy way to separate a string into its components. The lines in the /etc/passwd file, for example, look like the following:

```
root:x:0:0:root:/root:/bin/bash
```

The line is composed of fields separated by colons (:). Suppose that you want to extract the first field from each line (because that field contains the login name). You can read the file one line at a time, split each line into a list, and extract the first element (the item at index 0) of each list. Following is a Tcl script that does this:

```
#!/usr/bin/tclsh

set fid [open "/etc/passwd" r]     ;# Open file for read-only access

while { [gets $fid line] != -1 } {
    set fields [split $line ":"]   ;# Split the string into a list
# Just print out the first field
    puts [lindex $fields 0]        ;# Extract item at a index 0
}
```

When you run this script, it prints all the login names from your system's /etc/passwd file.

The join command is the opposite of split; you can use it to create a single string from the items in a list. Suppose that you have a list of six items, defined as follows:

```
set x {1 2 3 4 5 6}
```

When you join the elements, you can select what character you want to use between fields. To join the elements without anything in between them, use the following format:

```
set y [join $x ""]
```

Now the y string is "123456".

The string command is a group of commands for working with strings; the first argument of string specifies the operation to be performed. The string compare command, for example, compares two strings, returning zero when the two strings are identical. A return value of -1 indicates that the first string argument is lexicographically less than the second one, which means it appears before the second one in a dictionary. Similarly, a 1 return value indicates that the first string is lexicographically greater than the second one. Thus, you might use string compare in an if command as follows:

```
if { [string compare $command "quit"] == 0} {
    puts "Exiting..."
    exit 0
}
```

Table 25-3 lists the operations you can perform with Tcl's string command.

Table 25-3: Operations You Can Perform with String in Tcl

String Command	Description
string compare *string1* *string2*	Returns -1, 0, or 1 after comparing strings
string first *string1* *string2*	Returns the index of the first occurrence of *string1* in *string2*
string index *string* *charIndex*	Returns the character at index *charIndex*
string last *string1* *string2*	Returns the index of the last occurrence of *string1* in *string2*
string length *string*	Returns the length of the *string*
string match *pattern* *string*	Returns 1 if the *pattern* matches the *string*, and 0 if it does not
string range *string* *first* *last*	Returns a range of characters from *string*
string tolower *string*	Returns the *string* in lowercase characters
string toupper *string*	Returns the *string* in uppercase characters
string trim *string* *chars*	Returns the *string* after trimming the leading or trailing characters
string trimleft *string* *chars*	Returns the *string* after trimming the leading characters
string trimright *string* *chars*	Returns the *string* after trimming the trailing characters

Using Arrays

In Tcl, an *array* is a variable with a string index. An array contains elements; the string index of each element is called the element name. In other words, you can access an element of an array by using its name. Internally, Tcl implements arrays with an efficient data structure known as a *hash table*, which enables the Tcl interpreter to look up any array element in a relatively constant period of time.

Declare an array variable by using the `set` command. The following example shows how you might define the `disk_usage` array that holds the amount of disk space a system's users consume:

```
set disk_usage(root)        147178
set disk_usage(naba)        28574
set disk_usage(emily)       73
set disk_usage(ivy)         61
set disk_usage(ashley)      34
```

After you define the array, you can access its individual elements by element name, as in the following example:

```
set user "naba"
puts "Disk space used by $user = $disk_usage($user)K"
```

Accessing Environment Variables in Tcl

Tcl provides the environment variables in a predefined global array named `env`, with the environment-variable names used as element names. In other words, you can look up the value of an environment variable by using the variable name as an index. The following command prints the current `PATH`:

```
puts "$env(PATH)"
```

Secret

You can manipulate the environment variable array, `env`, just as you do any other variables. You can add a new directory to `PATH`, for example, as follows:

```
set env(PATH) "$env(PATH):/usr/sbin"
```

Any changes to the environment variable do not affect the parent process (for example, the shell from which you start the Tcl script). Any new processes the script creates by means of the `exec` command, however, inherit the altered environment variable.

Performing File Operations in Tcl

Most of the examples presented so far in this chapter use Tcl's `puts` command to display output. By default, `puts` writes to the standard output, the terminal window or text console, when you use X. You can write to a file, however, by providing a file identifier as the first argument of `puts`. To get a file identifier, you first have to open the file by using Tcl's `open` command. The following example shows how you open a file, write a line of text to the file, and close the file (in this example `fid` is a variable that stores the file identifier):

```
set fid [open "testfile" w]  ;# Open "testfile" for writing
puts $fid "Testing 1..2..3"  ;# Write to this file
close $fid                   ;# Close the file
```

When you use `puts` to display a string on the standard output, you do not have to provide a file-identifier argument. In addition, `puts` automatically appends a newline character to the end of the string. If you do not want the newline, use `puts` with the `-nonewline` argument, as follows:

```
puts -nonewline "Command> "  ;# This is good for command prompts.
flush stdout ;# Make sure output appears right away
```

You have seen the use of the `gets` command to read a line of input from the standard input. The following invocation of `gets`, for example, reads a line from the standard input (the command returns when you press Enter):

```
set line [gets stdin]  ;# Read a line from standard input.
```

The keyword `stdin` is a predefined file identifier that represents the standard input, which by default is your keyboard. Other predefined file IDs are `stdout`, for the standard output; and `stderr`, for the standard error-reporting device. By default, both `stdout` and `stderr` are connected to the display screen.

Following is a different way to call `gets` and read a line of input into a variable named `line`:

```
gets stdin line  ;# Read a line of input into the line variable
```

To read from another file, you should open the file for reading and then use `gets` with that file's ID. To read all lines from `/etc/passwd` and display them on the standard output, for example, use the following:

```
set fpass [open "/etc/passwd" r]    ;# Open /etc/passwd.
while { [gets $fpass line] != -1} {  ;# Read the lines one by one
    puts $line                      ;# and print each line.
}
```

The `gets` command is good for reading text files because it works one line at a time; in fact, it looks for the newline character as a marker that indicates the end of a line of text. If you want to read binary data, such as an image file, use the `read` command instead. To read and process a file in 2,048-byte chunks, you might use read in the following manner:

```
# Assume fid is the file ID of an open file.
while { ![eof $fid]} {             ;# Until end-of-file is reached
    set buffer [read $fid 2048] ;# read 2048 bytes into buffer
# process the data in buffer      ;# and process the buffer.
}
```

The second argument of the `read` command is the maximum number of bytes to be read. If you omit this argument, the `read` command reads the entire file. You can use this feature to process entire text files. After reading the contents of the file, use the `split` command to separate the input data into lines of text. Following is an example:

```
set fid [open "/etc/passwd" r]  ;# Open file for reading
set buffer [read $fid 100000]   ;# Read entire file into buffer
split $buffer "\n"              ;# Split buffer into lines
foreach line $buffer {
    puts $line                 ;# Process each line.
}
```

Secret

If you want to process several files (such as all files whose names end with .tcl), use the glob command to expand a filename, such as *.tcl, into a list. Then, you can use the open command to open and process each file in the following manner:

```
foreach filename [glob *.tcl] { ;# Create list of filenames
    puts -nonewline $filename   ;# Print the filename.
    set file [open $filename r] ;# Open that file.
    gets $file line             ;# Read the first line
    puts $line                  ;# and print it (for testing).
# process rest of the file as necessary
    close $file                 ;# Remember to close the file.
}
```

This is a good example of how to use the glob command in a script.

Executing Linux Commands in Tcl

Instead of duplicating the large number of Linux commands, Tcl simply provides the mechanism to run any Linux command. If you know Linux commands, you can use them directly in Tcl scripts.

Use the exec command to execute a Linux command in a Tcl script. In the command's simplest form, you provide the Linux command as an argument of exec. To show the current directory listing, for example, type the following:

```
exec ls
```

The output appears on the standard output (the monitor), just as it does when you enter the ls command at the shell prompt.

When you run Linux commands from the shell, you can redirect the input and output by using special characters, such as < (redirect input), > (redirect output), and | (pipe). These options are available in Tcl as well; the exec command accepts a complete command line, including any input or output redirections. Thus, you can send the directory listing to a file named dirlist as follows:

```
exec ls > dirlist
```

Secret

Tcl's `exec` command does not expand wildcard characters (such as an asterisk or a question mark) in filenames passed to a Linux command. If you use wildcards in filenames, you have to perform an additional step: You must process the filename specification through the `glob` command to expand it properly before providing the command to `exec`. In addition, you must pass the entire `exec` command to `eval` as an argument. To see a list of all files with names that end in `.tcl`, for example, you have to use the `exec` command with `glob` and feed the entire command to `eval` as follows:

```
eval exec ls [glob *.tcl]    ;# this is equivalent to "ls *.tcl"
```

Introducing Tk

Tk (pronounced *tee-kay*) is an extension of Tcl. Tk provides an X Window system–based toolkit you can use in Tcl scripts to build GUIs. As you might expect, Tk provides a set of Tcl commands beyond the core built-in set. You can use these Tk commands to create windows, menus, buttons, and other user-interface components and to provide a GUI for your Tcl scripts.

Secret

Tk uses the X Window system for its graphic components, known as widgets. A widget represents a user-interface component, such as a button, scroll bar, menu, list, or even an entire text window. Tk widgets provide a Motif-like, three-dimensional appearance.

If you are familiar with the Motif widgets, you may know that Motif relies on Xt Intrinsics—an X toolkit used to build widgets. Unlike Motif, the Tk toolkit is not based on any other toolkit; it uses only Xlib, which is the C-language library for the X Window system. The upshot is that you need only the freely available X Window system to use Tk.

As with anything new, you can best learn Tk through examples, which the following sections provide.

Saying "Hello, World!" in Tk

Tk is a major-enough extension to Tcl to warrant its own shell, called `wish` (the *windowing shell*). The `wish` shell interprets all built-in Tcl commands, as well as the Tk commands. You must start X before you can run `wish`; after all, `wish` enables you to use X to create graphical interfaces.

The wish program should be in the `/usr/bin` directory, which should be in your PATH environment variable by default. To start `wish`, all you have to do is type the following at the shell prompt in a terminal window:

```
wish
%
```

The wish program displays its prompt (the percent sign) and a small window, as shown in the upper-right corner of Figure 25-1.

Figure 25-1: The Result of Running wish from a Terminal Window.

Therefore, wish provides an interactive prompt from which you can enter Tk commands to create a graphical interface. As wish interprets the commands, it displays the resulting graphical interface in the window.

To see how this interactive creation of graphical interface works, try the following commands at the wish prompt):

```
% label .msg -text "Hello, World!"
.msg
% button .bye -text "Bye" -command { exit }
.bye
% pack .msg .bye
%
```

Figure 25-2 shows the result of these commands; wish displays a Hello, World! label with a Bye button below it.

Notice that the label and the button do not appear until you enter the pack command. In addition, the wish window shrinks to a size just large enough to hold the label and the button.

Click the Bye button; the wish program exits. This is because the -command { exit } argument of the button command associates the Tcl command exit with a click of the Bye button.

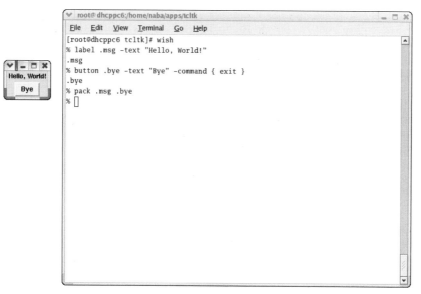

Figure 25-2: Interactively Creating a Label and a Button in wish.

To create a Tk program or script that displays the Hello, World! label and the Bye button, all you have to do is place the Tk commands in a file and add a special line at the beginning to ensure that the wish shell processes the file. To do so, follow these steps:

1. Use a text editor to enter and save the following lines in a file named hellotk:

```
#!/usr/bin/wish
# A simple Tk script
label .msg -text "Hello, World!"
button .bye -text "Bye" -command { exit }
pack .msg .bye
```

2. Type the following command at the shell prompt to make the hellotk file executable (that's what the +x in the chmod command means):

```
chmod +x hellotk
```

3. To run the hellotk script, type the following at the shell prompt in a terminal window:

```
./hellotk
```

Figure 25-3 shows the window with a Hello, World! label and the Bye button that should appear when you run the hellotk script. Click the Bye button to close the window and end the script.

Figure 25-3: The Result of Running the hellotk Script.

As this example shows, the basic steps for writing a Tk script are the same as those for creating and running any Tcl script. The only difference is that the Tk commands generate graphical output.

Learning Tk Widget Basics

Now that you have been exposed to Tcl, you can begin writing Tk scripts. What you need to know are the Tk commands used to create and configure widgets.

Secret

The term *widget* has the same meaning in Tk as it does in an X toolkit, such as Motif—a widget is a user interface component, such as a push button, list box, or dialog box.

As the examples in the preceding section show, you use the `label` command to create a label and the `button` command to create a button widget. This is a general guideline for working with all Tk widgets—the command for creating a widget is the same as the widget's name. Table 25-4 lists the names of Tk's widgets, which are also the widget-creation commands.

Table 25-4: Tk Commands for Creating Widgets

Command	Action
button	Creates a button widget
canvas	Creates a canvas widget on which you can display text, bitmaps, lines, boxes, polygons, and other widgets
checkbutton	Creates a toggle button and associates it with a Tcl variable
entry	Creates a one-line text-entry widget
frame	Creates a frame widget that is capable of holding other widgets
label	Creates a read-only, one-line label widget
listbox	Creates a list-box widget that is capable of scrolling lines of text
menu	Creates a menu
menubutton	Creates a menu-button widget that pops up an associated menu when clicked
message	Creates a read-only, multiple-line message widget
radiobutton	Creates a radio-button widget that is linked to a Tcl variable
scale	Creates a scale widget that can adjust the value of a variable
scrollbar	Creates a scroll bar widget that you can link to another widget
text	Creates a text widget where the user can enter and edit text
toplevel	Creates a top-level widget (a widget whose window is a child of the X Window system's root window)

As you create a widget, you can specify many of its characteristics as arguments of the command. You can, for example, create a blue button with a red label (test) and display the button by using the following commands:

```
button .b -text test -fg red -bg blue
pack .b
```

The pack command does not create a widget; rather, it positions a widget in relation to others. Table 25-5 lists all the widget-manipulation commands.

insider insight To look up online help about any Tk command listed in Tables 25-4 and 25-5, type man n, followed by the command name. To get online help about the bind command, for example, type man n bind.

Table 25-5: Tk Commands for Manipulating Widgets

Command	Action
after	Executes a command after a specified amount of time elapses
bind	Associates a Tcl command with an X event, so that the Tcl command is automatically invoked whenever the X event occurs
destroy	Destroys one or more widgets
focus	Directs keyboard events to a particular window (gives that window the input focus)
grab	Confines pointer and keyboard events to a specified widget and its children
lower	Lowers a window in the stacking order. (The stacking order refers to the order in which various windows overlap one another on the display screen.)
option	Provides access to the X resource database
pack	Automatically positions widgets in a frame, based on specified constraints
place	Allows manual positioning of a widget relative to another widget
raise	Raises a window's position in the stacking order
selection	Manipulates the X PRIMARY selection (the standard name of a selection in X)
send	Sends a Tcl command to a different Tk application (used for interprocess communications)
tk	Provides information about the internal state of the Tk interpreter
tkerror	Handles any error that occurs in Tk applications (the interpreter calls this command when errors occur in Tk applications)
tkwait	Waits for an event, such as the destruction of a window, or a change in the value of a variable
update	Processes all pending events and updates the display
winfo	Returns information about a widget
wm	Provides access to the window manager. (You can send commands to the window manager, requesting a size for your top-level window, for example.)

Defining Widget Hierarchies in Tk

From the example that creates a label and a button, you may have guessed that the argument that follows the widget-creation command is the widget's name. If you are wondering why all the names start with a period, which is required at the beginning of a widget's name, it is because widgets are organized in a hierarchy.

Suppose that you have a main window that contains a menu bar, a text area, and a scroll bar. The menu bar has two buttons, labeled File and Help. Figure 25-4 shows this widget hierarchy as it appears onscreen; it also shows how the widget names relate to this hierarchy.

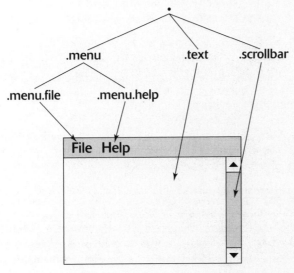

Figure 25-4: Relationship between Widget Names and the Widget Hierarchy.

Secret

The root of the widget hierarchy is the main window of the application; a single period (dot) is used to denote the main window. This main window is a child of the root window of the X display. Each child of the main window has a name that begins with a dot. Thus, .menu is a child of the main window.

The names of other widgets depend on their positions in the hierarchy. The buttons in the menu bar have names—.menu.file and .menu.help—that indicate that they are child widgets of the .menu widget. As you create widgets, you specify the name of each widget, in turn defining the widget hierarchy.

If you think about it, you can see that the widget-naming scheme is similar to the pathname of a file in Linux. The period (.) in a widget's name is analogous to the slash (/) in a file's pathname. In fact, the Tk documentation and online manual pages use the term *Tk pathname* to indicate the widget hierarchy.

All widget names must start with a lowercase letter or a number. The name cannot include a period, because the period indicates the widget's location in the hierarchy. Names that start with an uppercase letter denote a class used in specifying resources; the meaning of the term resources is the same as in X.

Configuring Widgets

Tk treats each widget name as a command name. You can perform operations on a specific widget by using that widget's name, followed by arguments that make sense for that widget. If you have a button named .b, for example, use the following command to set that button's background to blue:

```
.b config -fg blue
```

You can change the button's label to Goodbye! by using the following command:

```
.b config -text Goodbye!
```

The arguments -fg blue and -text Goodbye! specify the attributes of a widget. Each attribute name begins with a hyphen (-), as in -text. The next argument is that attribute's value.

Displaying Widgets

Tk does not display a widget, until you use a command to position the widget in the main window. To display the widgets, you have to use a geometry manager—a Tk procedure that arranges one or more child widgets in a parent widget.

Secret

Tk provides two geometry-management commands for organizing and displaying widgets:

- The place command enables you to position a widget at a fixed location in the window of a designated master widget (which does not necessarily have to be a parent widget). The master widget is used as a reference—other widgets are positioned relative to the master widget. Also, you can specify relative positions, such as a horizontal position half the width of the master widget.
- The pack command arranges child widgets around the edges of the master window. You can specify the side of the parent on which the child widget is placed, as well as any extra space you want to use around the child. As the name suggests, the pack command packs widgets together as tightly as possible.

Although the pack and place commands take many different options, their basic use is straightforward. I suggest you start wish, create a few widgets, and try the place and pack commands to see their effects. After that, you can consult the online manual for the exact options whenever you need them. Type **man n pack** for the pack command's online help; for help on the place command, type **man n place**.

insider insight
The pack and place commands have a form—pack forget and place forget — that you can use to hide a widget. If you want to hide a button named .btn1, for example, use the command pack forget .btn1. To make the button reappear, use the pack .btn1 command again.

Using the pack Command

The pack command is the most commonly used geometry-management command in Tk. As some of the simple examples in this chapter show, to make a button named .btn1 appear, use pack as follows:

```
pack .btn1
```

You can specify several widget names on the same pack command line. To display the buttons .btn1, .btn2, and .btn3, arranged in a vertical line in that order, use the following:

```
pack .btn1 .btn2 .btn3
```

On a menu bar, for instance, this type of pack command makes the most efficient use of the available space.

Table 25-6 summarizes the pack command's syntax. As Table 25-6 shows, you can use the pack command to position widgets and get information about the widget hierarchy.

Table 25-6: Different Forms of the pack Command

Command	Description
pack *widgetNames options*	Packs the listed widgets according to the specified *options* (same as pack configure). Table 25-7 shows the list of available options.
pack configure *widgetNames options*	Packs the listed widgets according to the specified options
pack forget *widgetNames*	Hides (unpacks) the specified widgets
pack info *widget*	Returns the packing configuration (a list of options and values) of the specified *widget*
pack propagate *widget boolean*	If *boolean* is 1, this enables geometry propagation for the specified widget; otherwise, this command disables propagation. (When geometry propagation is enabled, the size of a widget's window is determined by the sizes of the widgets contained in that window.)
pack slaves *widget*	Returns the list of widgets managed by a specified widget

If you want a more complicated layout of widgets, you have to use the packing options shown in Table 25-7.

Table 25-7: Options for Packing Widgets

Option	Description
-after *widgetName*	Places the widget that is being packed after the widget specified by *widgetName*
-anchor *anchorPos*	Determines where the managed widget is placed. (This applies only when the containing widget is larger than the managed widget.) The *anchorPos* value can be center, e, n, ne, nw, s, se, sw, or w; the default is center.
-before *widgetName*	Places the widget that is being packed before the widget specified by *widgetName*
-expand *boolean*	If *boolean* is 1, the contained widget expands to use any space left over in the containing widget
-fill *style*	Indicates how to expand the containing widget, if it becomes bigger than what the widgets contained in it require. The *style* value can be both, none, x, or y.
-in *widgetName*	Indicates the widget in which the widgets specified in the pack command line are placed. If you do not use this option, widgets are packed in their parent widget (.f.b is packed in .f).
-ipadx *amount*	Specifies extra horizontal space inside the widget being packed (in addition to the space that it already needs). The *amount* value is a number, in screen units.
-ipady *amount*	Specifies extra vertical space inside the widget being packed (in addition to the space it already needs). The *amount* value is a number, in screen units.
-padx amount	Specifies extra horizontal space outside the border of the widget that is being packed. The *amount* value is a number, in screen units.
-pady *amount*	Specifies extra vertical space outside the border of the widget being packed. The *amount* value is a number, in screen units.
-side *sideName*	Packs against the specified side. The *sideName* value is bottom, left, right, or top; the default is top.

insider insight

If you are wondering how to remember all these options, my advice is that you not remember them. Usually, you can get by with just a few of these options, and you will begin to remember them after a while. To become familiar with what each option does, start wish, create a few widgets, and try packing them with different options. From then on, whenever you need the exact syntax of an option, consult the online manual by typing man n pack or simply man pack.

Using the place Command

The place command is a simpler way to specify the placement of widgets as compared to the pack command, but you have to position all the windows yourself. It is simpler than pack because the place command gives you direct control of the widget positions. On the other hand, direct control of widget placement is fine for a few windows, but it can get tedious in a hurry when you have many widgets in a user interface.

Using place, you can position a widget at a specific location. For example, to place .btn1 at the coordinate (100, 50) in its parent widget, use the following command:

```
place .btn1 -x 100 -y 50
```

A good use of place is to center a widget within its parent widget. For this purpose, use the -relx and -rely options of place. If .f is a frame widget (a widget that contains other widgets), you can display it at the center of the parent window by using the following commands:

```
frame .f
button .f.b1 -text Configure
button .f.b2 -text Quit
pack .f.b1 .f.b2 -side left
place .f -relx 0.5 -rely 0.5 -anchor center
```

As the code fragment shows, the buttons inside the frame are packed with the pack command. Only the frame, .f, is positioned with the place command. The -relx and -rely options enable you to specify the relative positions in terms of a fraction of the containing widget's size. A zero value for -relx means the left edge; 1 is the right edge; and 0.5 means the middle.

Like pack, the place command has several forms, listed in Table 25-8.

Table 25-8: Forms of the place Command

Command	Description
place *widgetNames options*	Positions the listed widgets according to the specified *options* (same as place configure). Table 25-9 shows the list of available options.
place configure *widgetNames options*	Positions the listed widgets according to the specified options
place forget *widgetNames*	Stops managing the specified widgets and unmaps (hides) them
place info *widget*	Returns the list of options and their values for the specified widget
place slaves *widget*	Returns the list of widgets managed by the specified widget

In addition, place takes several options, summarized in Table 25-9. Use these options with the plain place command or the place configure command.

Table 25-9: Options for Placing Widgets

Option	Description
-anchor *anchorPos*	Specifies which point of the managed widget is placed in the specified position in the managing window. The *anchorPos* value can be center, e, n, ne, nw, s, se, sw, or w; the default is nw (upper-left corner).
-bordermode *bmode*	Indicates how the managing widget's borders are used when the managed widgets are positioned. The bordermode value must be ignore, inside, or outside.
-height *size*	Specifies the height of the managed widget
-in *widgetName*	Indicates the widget relative to which the positions of the widgets specified in the place command line are specified. If you do not use this option, widgets are placed relative to their parent widgets (.f.b is positioned relative to .f).
-relheight *fraction*	Specifies the height of the managed widget as a fraction of the managing widget. The fraction is a floating-point value.
-relwidth *fraction*	Specifies the width of the managed widget as a fraction of the managing widget. The fraction is a floating-point value.
-relx *fraction*	Specifies the horizontal position of the managed widget as a fraction of the managing widget's width. The *fraction* is a floating-point value; 0.0 means the left edge, and 1.0 means the right edge.
-rely *fraction*	Specifies the vertical position of the managed widget as a fraction of the managing widget's height. The *fraction* is a floating-point value; 0.0 means the top edge, and 1.0 means the bottom edge.
-x *coord*	Specifies the horizontal position of the managed widget's anchor point in the managing widget. The *coord* value is specified in screen coordinates.
-y *coord*	Specifies the vertical position of the managed widget's anchor point in the managing widget. The *coord* value is specified in screen coordinates.
-width *size*	Specifies the width of the managed widget

Binding Actions to Events

When you write a program that has a graphical user interface, various program actions are initiated by events, such as the user clicking a button in the user interface. In a Tk script, you indicate what the program does by associating actions with events. In this case, an action is simply a Tcl script that performs some task. In the case of a Quit button, for example, a logical action is the Tcl command exit, which ends the Tk script.

For buttons, a click of the button is a simple way to form this association. Use the command option of the button command to specify a Tcl command to be executed when the user clicks the button. The exit command is associated with the Quit button as follows:

```
button .b -text Quit -command { exit }
```

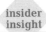

The curly braces are not necessary when you have only one Tcl command, but you must enclose multiple commands inside braces.

The `bind` command is the most common way to associate an action with an event. Following is the general syntax of the `bind` command:

```
bind widgetName <eventSpecification> TclCommand
```

The `widgetName` argument is usually the pathname of a widget, although you can bind an event to a class of widgets, such as all buttons. Typically, you have to consult online help to specify eventSpecification. (In this section, I show you an example and explain event specifications.) The last argument—`TclCommand`—refers to the Tcl commands you want to execute when the specified event occurs. These Tcl commands can be any Tcl script, ranging from a simple `puts` command to a complete Tcl script stored in a separate file.

To see a more detailed example of how to bind an action to an event, consider this scenario. You may have noticed that many Microsoft Windows applications, as well as GNOME and KDE applications, sport a toolbar—essentially, a collection of buttons, each of which is meant to perform a specific task. Typically, each button bears an icon that indicates its purpose. To help users learn the meaning of a button quickly, many Windows applications have a feature called *tool help*. If you place the mouse pointer on a button, a small window pops up, displaying a short help message that tells you what the button does.

You can use Tk to implement a similar tool-help feature. Follow these steps:

1. Create the button.
2. Prepare the help message as a label (preferably with a bright background, such as yellow).
3. When the mouse pointer enters a button, an Enter event occurs. Bind the Enter event to a command that makes the help label visible. Use the `place` command to position the label relative to the button, so that the tool help label always appears near the associated button. The following example shows how `bind` is used to associate the `place` command (shown within braces) with the Enter event:

```
bind .f.q <Enter> { place .bh -in .f.q -relx 0.5 -rely 1.0 }
```

4. When the mouse pointer leaves the button, a Leave event occurs. Bind the Leave event to the `place forget` command to hide the help message, as follows:

```
bind .f.q <Leave> { place forget .bh }
```

The following sample toolhelp script demonstrates how to implement tool help in Tk:

```
#!/usr/bin/wish -f
# Demonstrates a "tool help" window that appears when you
# place the mouse pointer inside the Quit button.

wm geometry . 180x60

frame .f
button .f.b -text File
```

```
label .bh -text "Quit program"
.bh config -bg yellow
button .f.q -text Quit -command { exit }

bind .f.q <Enter> { place .bh -in .f.q -relx 0.5 -rely 1.0 }
bind .f.q <Leave> { place forget .bh }


pack .f.b .f.q -side left
pack .f -fill x
```

Make the toolhelp script file executable by using the `chmod +x toolhelp` command. Then run that script by typing `./toolhelp` at the shell prompt in a terminal window. Figure 25-5 shows the window that results after you place the mouse pointer on the Quit button.

Figure 25-5: A Tk Script That Demonstrates How to Implement toolhelp Messages.

When you use `bind` to associate a Tcl script with an event, you need to know how to specify the event. Most are either keyboard events or mouse events. A smaller number of events are related to the state of a widget's window. `<Map>` and `<Unmap>` events, for example, occur when a widget is managed or unmanaged (when you use pack forget or place forget).

Understanding Keyboard Events

There are two keyboard events:

- ◆ `<KeyPress>` occurs when you press a key.
- ◆ `<KeyRelease>` occurs when you release a key.

You can specify a keyboard event for a specific key by appending that key's *keysym* (which is the X Window system's standard name for a key) to the string `KeyPress-` and enclosing everything in angle brackets. The event associated with pressing the q key, for example, is specified by `<Keypress-q>`. Tk provides a shorter format for keyboard events. You can simply place the keysym inside angle brackets, as follows:

```
<q>
```

For most key presses, the event specification is straightforward. If you want to exit when the user presses Ctrl-C inside a widget named `.text`, use the `bind` command as follows:

```
bind .text <Control-c> exit
```

Table 25-10 shows some other commonly used keysyms.

Table 25-10: Some Commonly Used Keysyms

Keysym	Name of Key
BackSpace	Backspace
comma	Comma
Down	Down arrow
dollar	Dollar sign ($)
Escape	Escape
exclam	Exclamation mark
Left	Left arrow
numbersign	Number sign (#)
period	Period
Return	Enter
Right	Right arrow
Tab	Tab
Up	Up arrow

Secret

Inside the Tcl commands that are bound to a key event, use the %A keyword to refer to the printable character the user presses. For any nonprintable character, %A is replaced by {} (a pair of empty braces). The %W keyword is replaced by the name of the widget that receives the keypress. Thus, you can use the following code to insert text into a text widget named .text1:

```
# Assume .text1 is a text widget
bind .text1 <KeyPress> {
    if { "%A" != "{}"} { %W insert insert %A}
}
```

Remember that a widget's name itself is a command and that the command's argument depends on the type of widget. For a text widget, the command %W insert insert %A, as shown in the example, inserts the character into the text widget.

Understanding Mouse Events

Use <ButtonPress> and <ButtonRelease> to denote mouse-button click and release events, respectively. You have to append the button number to make the event specific. Thus, clicking the left mouse button (which is button 1 in X terminology) is denoted by <ButtonPress-1>. A shorthand notation for button presses is to omit Press; thus, you can write <Button-1> to denote the event generated by clicking the left mouse button.

Secret

In the Tcl commands that are bound to a mouse event, the keywords %x and %y denote the x and y coordinates of the mouse pointer (relative to the widget's window) at the time of the mouse event. Thus, you can track the position of mouse clicks on a widget .text1 as follows:

```
bind .text1 <Button-1> { puts "Click at (%x, %y) on widget: %W"}
```

Other mouse events include the Enter and Leave events, which occur when you move the mouse pointer into or out of a widget, respectively. These two events are denoted by <Enter> and <Leave>. The toolhelp example shown in "Binding Actions to Events," earlier in this chapter, illustrates a way to use the <Enter> and <Leave> events.

Another event related to the mouse pointer is <Motion>, which occurs when you move the mouse pointer within a widget.

Understanding Window Events

In addition to keyboard and mouse events, X includes many events that occur when a window is manipulated. The X server generates <Map> and <Unmap> events, for example, when a widget is displayed or hidden (by the pack or place command).

A <Configure> event occurs when the user resizes a window. Thus, you can bind a <Configure> event to a redisplay procedure that redraws the contents of a widget based on the new size.

A <Destroy> event occurs when a window is about to be destroyed. Bind a procedure to the <Destroy> event, and intercept requests to delete a window.

Summary

The combination of Tool Command Language (Tcl) and its X Window system–based graphical toolkit, Tk, is ideal for quickly developing applications with a graphical interface. This chapter introduces Tcl/Tk through simple examples.

By reading this chapter, you learned the following:

♦ Tcl is an interpreted language with a set of commands you can combine, according to a set of rules. Tcl comes with the Red Hat Linux distribution on the companion CD-ROMs.

♦ You can learn the Tcl syntax and develop Tcl scripts interactively by running the Tcl command interpreter, tclsh, and entering Tcl commands at the tclsh prompt.

♦ Tcl includes built-in commands for most routine tasks, such as reading and writing files, manipulating strings, and running any Linux command. Also, Tcl includes control-flow commands—such as if, for, and while—that enable you to control the sequence of commands the interpreter processes. Finally, you can use Tcl's proc command to write new Tcl commands that use combinations of existing commands.

◆ Tk, the Tcl toolkit, is an extension of Tcl that uses the X Window system to enable you to build graphical user interfaces. Tk provides the three-dimensional appearance of Motif, but Tk does not require the Motif toolkit or any other X toolkit. Tk is built on Xlib, which is the C-language Application Programming Interface (API) for X.

◆ Tk includes commands for creating many common widgets (user-interface elements), such as buttons, labels, list boxes, and scrollbars. A widget-naming convention specifies the widget hierarchy (the organization of the widgets).

◆ To make the graphical interface active, you have to use the `bind` command to associate Tcl commands with specific keyboard events and mouse events.

◆ You can interactively experiment with and create Tk programs by running `wish`, the windowing shell that can interpret all Tcl and Tk commands.

Java Programming

Chapter

26

♦ ♦

Secrets in This Chapter

♦ ♦

J ava is an object-oriented programming language that began life as a language for embedded systems—small computers that control electronic devices. Java became popular as way of embedding small application progams called *applets* into the HTML code of Web pages. When the browser downloads a Web page with an applet, the browser also downloads the applet and executes that application program. To be more precise, these Java applets are transmitted as sequences of bytes that can be executed by a Java Virtual Machine (JVM) embedded in a Web browser. Thus, a Java program can be executed anywhere a JVM and the Java libraries are available.

Java's use has extended beyond applets to general-purpose applications that do not have to run inside a Web browser. Many organizations now use Java for developing mission-critical applications, including three-tiered Web applications that provide access to the corporate databases that often reside on older mainframe systems. These three-tiered Web applications use Java *servlets*—Java code that runs on the Web server and provides access to corporate databases through Java Database Connectivity (JDBC) application programming interface (API).

This chapter provides you an overview of the Java language and shows you a few simple examples. As you might guess, a single chapter cannot do justice to Java; all this chapter can do is get you started with Java. With that goal in mind, this chapter focuses immediately on the tools you need to create Java applications and shows you several small examples to illustrate specific Java programming techniques.

Getting Ready for Java Programming

Like any programming language, the best way to learn Java is to begin writing some programs. Of course, you need an overview of the language as well, but if you already know C++ and understand the basics of object-oriented programming, you can quickly become proficient in Java.

This section gets you started with the hands-on aspects of Java programming by briefly describing GCJ—the GNU Java compiler that comes with Red Hat Linux. Then, it describes how to download and install the Java Development Kit (JDK).

Using GCJ

Red Hat Linux comes with GCJ—the GNU Compiler for the Java Programming Language. GCJ should be installed if you selected the *Development Tools* package during Red Hat Linux installation.

You can use the GCJ to compile and run simple Java programs. For example, to build a simple Java program that prints `Hello, World!`, follow these steps from a text console or a terminal window (I explain Java programming further in the latter part of this chapter):

1. Use a text editor such as vi or Emacs to create a file named `HelloWorld.java` and add the following lines to that file:

```
public class HelloWorld {
    public static void main(String [] args) {
        System.out.println("Hello, World!");
    }
}
```

2. Compile and create an executable program named HelloWorld by running gcj (that's the name of the GNU Java compiler's executable) with the following command line:

```
gcj --main=HelloWorld -o HelloWorld HelloWorld.java
```

3. Run the program with the following command:

```
./HelloWorld
```

The program should display the following line of output:

```
Hello, World!
```

You can compile more complex Java programs using GCJ, but you run into a roadblock because GCJ does not yet include all the Java libraries.

insider insight Although Java code can theoretically run wherever a JVM is available, all but the simplest Java applications also require one or more of the Java libraries that may not necessarily be available in a JVM. The Java libraries provide the application programming interfaces (APIs) that Java programs use to perform tasks such as displaying graphical output or exchanging data over the network. To run typical Java programs, at minimum you need the libraries that come with Sun's Java 2 Standard Edition (J2SE). This means that you need the JVM and the JJ2SE libraries to develop Java applications. You can download the latest J2SE by following the links at Sun's Java home page (http://java.sun.com/).

Downloading and Installing Java 2 SDK

To develop Java applications, you need the Java 2 Software Development Kit. You can download the latest version of this kit by following the links at the following website:

```
http://java.sun.com/j2se/downloads.html
```

Secret Sun has two Java development products—Java 2 Standard Edition (J2SE) and Java 2 Enterprise Edition (J2EE). The J2SE Software Development Kit (SDK)—also known as Java 2 SDK—includes the Java compiler, APIs, and other tools you need to develop Java applications and applets.

J2EE is meant for developing Java applications that run on Web servers. Such server-side applications include *servlets*—Java applications that run under the control of a Web server and perform computations or provide access to databases. J2EE includes the servlet APIs as well the APIs needed to support Web services and application servers. *Web services* refer to software systems with public interfaces defined in the Extensible Markup Language (XML). Other applications can discover information about a Web service by using well-defined protocols and then make use of whatever services the Web service provides. *Application servers* refer to the tools and utilities that can be used on a Web server to run Java servlets, maintain session and state information, access databases, perform database transactions, process new content such as XML, and generate dynamic HTML documents. J2EE relies on J2SE.

continues

continued

You should download the J2SE SDK because it has all the tools you need to develop Java applications. If you also plan to develop servlets and other server-side Java applications, you need the J2EE as well.

At its J2SE download website (http://java.sun.com/j2se/downloads.html), Sun Microsystems provides the J2SE SDK for the following systems:

- Linux (32-bit Intel processors)
- Linux (64-bit Itanium processors)
- Microsoft Windows 95/98/Me/200/NT/XP
- Sun Solaris SPARC—both 32 bit and 64 bit
- Sun Solaris x86
- 64-bit Windows for Itanium

For Red Hat Linux, you should download the 32-bit Linux version of the J2SE SDK.

To download and install J2SE SDK for Linux, follow these steps from your Red Hat Linux system:

1. Make sure that your system is connected to the Internet. Start the Web browser and point the Web browser to the following URL:

```
http://java.sun.com/j2se/downloads.html
```

Click the link for the latest version of J2SE SDK.

2. Select the SDK download link for the item labeled "Linux RPM in self-extracting file." Read the license agreement and, if you agree, click Accept.

3. Click the link for the J2SE SDK file, and save it a convenient directory on your Red Hat Linux system (for example, /usr/local). The SDK is typically close to 40 MB in size, so the download can take a while if you have a slow dial-up Internet connection. After the download is completed, you end up with a file whose name ends in .rpm.bin. This file is a shell script that you must execute to extract the RPM file for J2SE SDK.

4. From a terminal window, change directory to where you saved the J2SE SDK file and type the following command to make that file executable:

```
chmod +x j2sdk*.bin
```

5. Execute the file by typing the following command:

```
./j2sdk*.bin
```

This displays the license agreement a page at a time. After reading each page, press Enter to move forward. After the last page, you see the following prompt:

```
Do you agree to the above license terms? [yes or no]
```

6. Type **yes**, and press Enter. This starts the unpacking and ends with an RPM file.

7. Install the RPM file with the following command:

```
rpm -ivh j2sdk*.rpm
```

This command installs the Java 2 SDK in the /usr/java directory under a subdirectory whose name depends on the version you are installing. For example, when I installed J2SE SDK version 1.4.1, everything is installed in the following directory:

```
/usr/java/j2sdk1.4.1_01
```

Set the PATH environment variable to include the directory where the Java 2 SDK binaries are located. For example, if you install the Java 2 SDK in the /usr/java/j2sdk1.4.1_01 directory, add the following lines at the end of the /etc/profile file:

```
PATH=$PATH:/usr/java/j2sdk1.4.1_01/bin
```

Taking Stock of the Java 2 SDK

The Java 2 SDK comes with a number of files organized into several directories. The top-level directory contains the files and subdirectories shown in Table 26-1.

Table 26-1: Java 2 SDK Content Summary

Name	Description
LICENSE	The license agreement under which Sun Microsystems is providing you the Java 2 SDK. You should read this file before using the Java 2 SDK.
COPYRIGHT	The copyright information for this release of the Java 2 SDK
README	Information about the Java 2 SDK contents
README.html	HTML version of README file with links to Sun's websites
src.zip	JDK source code in a ZIP archive. You don't need the source files to write Java applets or applications.
bin	Directory containing the executable programs. You should add the full pathname of this directory to your PATH environment variable.
demo	Directory with many sample Java programs with source code
include	Directory with the header files for the Java 2 SDK source (you don't need these to write Java programs)
lib	Directory with Java class libraries
man	Directory with man pages for Java 2 SDK tools such as the javac compiler and java—the Java interpreter

The tools you'll use most are in the bin subdirectory. Here are some of the tools that you'll use when creating Java applications:

- **appletviewer**—Java applet viewer program to load and run Java applets that are designed to be embedded in an HTML document (you can also load applets in a Java-capable browser by embedding the applet in an HTML document using the `<applet>` tag).

- **java**—Java interpreter that runs standalone Java programs specified by a class name (it expects to find the class in a file with same name as the class, but with a `.class` extension). Standalone Java applications are Java classes with a `main` method (in Java, functions are called *methods*).

- **javac**—Java compiler that converts Java source code into "byte code" (that's the instruction set of the Java Virtual Machine). The compiler takes source code in a `.java` file and generates compiled code in a `.class` file.

- **jdb**—Java debugger with a command syntax like that of the Linux gdb debuggers.

- **javadoc**—Java API documentation generator that extracts documentation from source files with special comments that begin with `/**` and ends with a `*/`.

- **javah**—Java C file generator that generates C `.h` and `.c` files for a Java class. Such C files are needed to implement the native methods that make the APIs work on a particular operating system.

- **javap**—Java class file disassembler that takes a class name and prints a human-readable description of the class.

Of these programs, the three that you'll use most are the following:

- You'll use `javac` a lot because that's the Java compiler program. The `javac` program converts a Java source file (you'll see some examples in the next section) into a binary file that contains Java byte code—the instruction set of the Java Virtual Machine.

- If you write a standalone Java application—one that can run without being embedded in a Web browser, you'll use the Java interpreter program, java, to run the application.

- If you write Java applets—miniapplications that run inside a Web browser, you'll use the appletviewer program to test the applets. Of course, you can also test applets using a Java-capable Web browser such as Mozilla (after you install the Java plug-in).

Writing Your First Java Program

In the grand old tradition of C programming books, I'll begin by showing you how to display "`Hello, World!`" from a Java program. However, before I proceed, I should point out the difference between three types of Java programs:

- **Standalone Java application**—This is a Java program that can be executed by a Java interpreter. A Java standalone application is just like the standalone C or C++ programs that you might know. The application has a main method and the java interpreter can run the application. General-purpose Java applications take the form of standalone applications.

- **Java applet**—This is a Java class that can be loaded and executed by the appletviewer program or by a Java-capable Web browser. You have to first embed the applet inside an HTML document using the `<applet>` tag and then load that HTML document to activate the applet. As a Webmaster, you'll mostly write Java applets.

♦ **Java servlet**—This is a Java class loaded and executed by a Web server (or a server that helps the Web server such as the Apache Tomcat server). To develop servlets, you need the Java 2 Enterprise Edition.

Whether you write a standalone application or an applet or a servlet, the basic steps are similar except for the last step when you execute the program. You use the java interpreter to run standalone programs and appletviewer to test applets. For servlets, you simply place them in a specific directory and insert HTML code to refer to the servlets. These development steps are as follows:

1. Use a text editor to create the Java source file. A Java application is a class (a type of object—collection of data and methods). The source file's name must be the class name with a .java extension.

2. Process the source file with javac (the Java compiler) to generate the class file with a .class extension.

3. If it's a standalone application, run the class with the java interpreter with the following command:

```
java classname
```

4. If the program is an applet, create an HTML document and embed the applet using the <applet> tag (see "The <applet> Tag" section for the syntax). Then, load that HTML document using appletviewer or a Java-capable Web browser. When the browser loads the HTML document, it also activates all embedded Java applets.

Writing a Standalone "Hello, World!" Program

The classic C-style "Hello, World!" application is easy to write in Java. That's because many of Java's syntactical details are similar to that of C and C++. The following code implements a simple "Hello, World!" program in Java (you have seen this in an earlier section, but it's so short that I'll just show you again):

```
public class HelloWorld
{
    public static void main(String[] args)
    {
        System.out.println("Hello, World!");
    }
}
```

Even this simple Java program illustrates some key features of Java:

♦ Every Java program is a public class definition.

♦ A standalone application contains a main method that must be declared public static void. The interpreter starts execution at the main method.

Save this program in a file named HelloWorld.java. Then, compile it with the following command:

```
javac HelloWorld.java
```

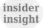

If you get an error saying "command not found," then you need to add the Java 2 SDK binary directory to the `PATH` environment variable. If you installed the Java2 SDK in the `/usr/java/j2sdk1.4.1_01`, then type the following command to add the binary directory to `PATH`:

```
PATH=$PATH:/usr/java/j2sdk1.4.1_01/bin
```

The `javac` compiler creates a class file named `HelloWorld.class`. To run the application, use the Java interpreter and specify the class name as a parameter, like this:

```
java HelloWorld
```

The program prints the following output:

```
Hello, World!
```

Writing a Simple Java Applet

The other model of a Java program is the applet that runs inside the `appletviewer` program or a Java-capable Web browser. Specifically, a Java applet is a class in the Java Abstract Windowing Toolkit (AWT). In an applet, you do not have to provide a `main` method. Instead, you provide a `paint` method where you place code to draw in an area of a window. You can use the applet model to implement GUIs and other graphical programs.

For a "`Hello, World!`" applet, I'll do the following:

- ◆ Instead of displaying the message in a default font, pick a specific font to display the message.
- ◆ Use the information about the font sizes to center the message within the area where the applet is required to display its output.
- ◆ Draw the text in red instead of the default black color.

Listing 26-1 shows the Java code that implements the "`Hello, World!`" applet.

Listing 26-1: The HelloWorld Java Applet

```
//------------------------------------------------------------
// File: HelloWorld.java
//
// Displays "Hello, World!" in Helvetica font and in red color.
//------------------------------------------------------------

import java.applet.*;
import java.awt.*;

//------------------------------------------------------------
// H e l l o W o r l d
//
// Applet class to display "Hello, World!"

public class HelloWorld extends java.applet.Applet
```

```
{
    String hellomsg = "Hello, World!";

//----------------------------------------------------------------
// p a i n t
//
// Method that paints the output

    public void paint(java.awt.Graphics gc)
    {
// Draw a rectangle around the applet's bounding box
// so we can see the box.
        gc.drawRect(0, 0, getSize().width-1,
                          getSize().height-1);

// Create the font to be used for the message.
        Font helv = new Font("Helvetica", Font.BOLD, 24);

// Select the font into the Graphics object.
        gc.setFont(helv);

// Get the font metrics (details of the font size).
        FontMetrics fm = gc.getFontMetrics();
        int mwidth = fm.stringWidth(hellomsg);
        int ascent = fm.getAscent();
        int descent = fm.getDescent();

// Compute starting (x.y) position to center string
// The size() method returns size of the applet's
// bounding box.
        int xstart = getSize().width/2 - mwidth/2;
        int ystart = getSize().height/2 + ascent/2 - descent/2;

// Set the color to red.
        gc.setColor(Color.red);

// Now draw the string.
        gc.drawString(hellomsg, xstart, ystart);
    }
}
```

By browsing through this code, you can learn a lot about how to display graphics output in Java. Here are the key points to note:

◆ The `import` statement lists external classes that this program uses. The name that follows the import statement can be the name of a class or can be a name with a wildcard (*), which tells the Java compiler to import all the classes in a package. This example uses the `Applet` class as well as a number of graphics classes that are in the `java.awt` package.

◆ The `HelloWorld` applet is defined as an extension of the `Applet` class. That's what the statement `public class HelloWorld extends java.applet.Applet` means.

◆ An applet's `paint` method contains the code that draws the output. The `paint` method receives a `Graphics` object as argument. You have to call methods of the `Graphics` object to display output.

◆ The `getSize` method returns the size of the applet's drawing area.

◆ To use a font, you have to first create a `Font` object and then call the `setFont` method of the `Graphics` object.

◆ To draw text in a specific color, invoke the `setColor` method of the `Graphics` object with an appropriate `Color` object as argument.

◆ If you know C++, you'll notice that Java's method invocation is similar to the way you call the member function of a C++ object. Indeed, there are many similarities between C++ and Java.

Save the listing in a file named `HelloWorld.java`. Then, compile it with the command:

```
javac HelloWorld.java
```

This step creates the applet class file: `HelloWorld.class`. To test the applet, you have to create an HTML document and embed the applet in that document, as shown in the following example:

```
<html>
<head>
<title>Hello, World! from Java</title>
</head>

<body>

<h3>"Hello, World!" from Java</h3>

A Java applet is given an area where it displays
its output. In this example, the applet draws a
border around its assigned area and then displays
the "Hello, World!" message centered in that box.
<br>

<applet code=HelloWorld width=200 height=60>
If you see this message, then you do not have a
Java-capable browser.
</applet>

Here is the applet!
</body>
</html>
```

As this HTML source shows, you have to use the `<applet>` tag to insert an applet in an HTML document. In the "Using the <applet> Tag" section, you'll learn the detailed syntax of the `<applet>` tag.

You can use two tools to test the applet. The first one is `appletviewer`, which comes with JDK. To view the `HelloWorld` applet, you have to run the `appletviewer` program and provide the name of the HTML document that includes the applet. Suppose that the

HTML document is in the file named `hello.html`. Then, you'd run `appletviewer` with the following command:

```
appletviewer hello.html
```

Figure 26-1 shows how the `appletviewer` displays the applet.

Figure 26-1: Running the "Hello, World!" Java Applet in `appletviewer`.

Notice that `appletviewer` displays only the applet; the rest of the text in the HTML document is ignored. However, the appearance is quite different in a Java-capable Web browser.

To view the applet in a Web browser, start the Mozilla Web browser and select File⇨ Open File from the menus. From the Open File dialog, go to the directory where you have the `hello.html` file and the `HelloWorld.class` file (for the applet). Then, select the `hello.html` file, and click Open. Mozilla then renders the HTML document containing the `HelloWorld` applet.

Unlike the `appletviewer`, Mozilla should display the entire HTML document and the Java applet appears embedded in the document just like an image. The applet draws inside the rectangle assigned to it through the width and height attributes of the `<applet>` tag.

Secret

If Mozilla fails to display the applet when you load an HTML document with an embedded applet, the most likely cause is that you have not yet installed Sun's Java plug-in for Netscape (Mozilla was derived from Netscape). The Java plug-in comes with the Java 2 SDK that you have already downloaded. To install the plug-in, you have to copy a file from the Java 2 SDK directory to the Mozilla plug-in directory. Here are the commands I type (after logging in as `root`) to install the Java plug-in file for J2EE version 1.4.1:

```
cd /usr/java/j2sdk1.4.1_01/jre/plugin/i386/ns610

cp libjavaplugin_oji.so /usr/lib/mozilla-1.2.1/plugins
```

To check that the plug-ins are loaded, start Mozilla and select Help⇨About Plug-ins from the menus. Mozilla then displays information about the installed plug-ins in its window. In particular, you should see a plug-in that can handle the MIME data type `application/x-java-vm` because that's the data type for a Java applet.

For the latest information about the Java plug-in, point your Mozilla browser to `http://java.sun.com/products/plugin/`.

Learning Java

Now that you have seen some examples of Java programming, this section provides an overview of Java. Previous examples show that Java can be used to create both stand-alone applications and applets that can be embedded in an HTML document. As you learn the features of Java, you'll notice that Java has everything you need from a general-purpose programming language. Although Java has been associated mostly with the creation of applets to be embedded in Web pages, many people have come to realize that Java is also ideal for developing general-purpose applications. Nowadays, Java is also extensively used for server-side programs such as Java servlets that work with Web servers.

One of the reasons for Java's popularity is the portability of Java code. The compiled Java code runs on any system for which a Java interpreter and the Java libraries are available. It's not trivial to build the Java libraries, but once the Java interpreter and libraries are available on an operating system, you can run most Java applications unchanged on that system.

Objects in Java

Java is an object-oriented language. So much so that Java does not allow any standalone procedures at all; all data and procedures must be inside an object. In fact, the entire Java application is an object as well.

The basic concepts of object-based programming are the same as those of other object-oriented programming languages such as Smalltalk or C++. There are three underlying concepts:

◆ Data abstraction
◆ Inheritance
◆ Polymorphism

Data Abstraction

To understand data abstraction, consider the file input/output (I/O) routines in the C run-time library. These routines allow you to view the file as a stream of bytes and allow you to perform various operations on this stream by calling the file I/O routines. For example, you can call `fopen` to open a file, `fclose` to close it, `fgetc` to read a character from it, and `fputc` to write a character to it. This abstract model of a file is implemented by defining a data type named `FILE` to hold all relevant information about a file. The C constructs `struct` and `typedef` are used to define `FILE`. You can think of this definition of `FILE`, together with the functions that operate on it, as a new data type just like C's `int` or `char`.

To use the `FILE` data type in C, you do not have to know the data structure that defines it. In fact, the underlying data structure of `FILE` can vary from one system to another. Yet, the C file I/O routines work in the same manner on all systems. This is possible because you never access the members of the `FILE` data structure directly. Instead you rely on functions and macros that essentially hide the inner details of `FILE`. This is known as *data hiding*.

Data abstraction is the process of defining a data type, often called an abstract data type (ADT), together with the principle of data hiding. The definition of an ADT involves specifying the internal representation of the ADT's data as well as the functions to be used by others to manipulate the ADT. Data hiding is used to ensure that the the internal structure of the ADT can be altered without any fear of breaking the programs that call the functions that are provided for operations on that ADT. Thus, C's FILE data type is an example of an ADT (see Figure 26-2).

Figure 26-2: C's FILE Type as an Example of Abstract Data Type (ADT).

In object-oriented languages, you create an object from an ADT. Essentially, an ADT is a collection of variables together with the procedures necessary to operate on those variables. The variables represent the information contained in the object while the procedures define the operations that can be performed on that object. You can think of the ADT as a template from which specific instances of objects can be created as needed. The term *class* is often used for this template, consequently class is synonymous with an ADT. In fact, Java provides the class keyword precisely for the purpose of defining an ADT—the template from which objects are created. The ADT is a template for objects in the sense that creating an object involves setting aside a block of memory for the variables of that object.

In Java, the procedures that operate on an object are known as *methods*. This term comes from the object-oriented language Smalltalk. The methods define the behavior of an object. Another common term of object-oriented programming also originated in Smalltalk—the idea of sending messages to an object causing it to perform an operation by invoking one of the methods. In Java, you do this is by calling the appropriate method of the object.

In Java, you use the class keyword to define the blueprint of an object. That means a class defines the data and methods that constitute a type of object. Then, you can create instances of the object by using the new keyword. For example, you might create an instance of a Circle class as follows:

```
Circle c1 = new Circle(100.0, 60.0, 50.0);
```

This example invokes the Circle class constructor that accepts three floating-point numbers as argument (presumably, the coordinates of the center and the radius of the circle). You'll see a complete example of classes in the "Geometric Shapes in Java" section, later in this chapter.

Inheritance

Data abstraction does not cover an important characteristic of objects. Real-world objects do not exist in isolation. Each object is related to one or more other objects. In fact, you can often describe a new kind of object by pointing out how the new object's characteristics and behavior differ from those of a class of objects that already exists. This is what you do when you describe an object with a sentence such as: B is just like A, except that B has ... and B does ... . Here you are defining objects of type B in terms of those of type A.

This notion of defining a new object in terms of an old one is an integral part of object-oriented programming. The term *inheritance* is used for this concept because you can think of one class of objects as inheriting the data and behavior from another class. Inheritance imposes a hierarchical relationship among classes where a child class inherits from its parent. In Java terminology, the parent class is known as the *superclass*; the child is the *subclass*. In a Java program, you use the extends keyword to indicate that one class is a subclass of another.

insider insight

Unlike C++, Java does not support multiple inheritance (multiple inheritance allows a class to inherit from multiple superclasses). Java allows a class to have only one superclass. In Java, all classes inherit from a single root class named Object. (The Smalltalk programming language also provides a class hierarchy of this type). Here the term root class refers to a class that does not have any superclass.

Polymorphism

In a literal sense, polymorphism means the quality of having more than one form. In the context of object-oriented programming, *polymorphism* refers to the fact that a single operation can have different behavior in different objects. In other words, different objects react differently to the same message. For example, consider the operation of addition. For two numbers, addition should generate the sum. In a programming language that supports object-oriented programming, you should be able to express the operation of addition by an operator, say, +. When this is possible, you can use the expression x+y to denote the sum of x and y, for many different types of x and y: integers, floating-point numbers, and, even strings (for strings the + operation means the concatenation of two strings).

Similarly, suppose a number of geometrical shapes all support a method, draw. Each object reacts to this method by displaying its shape on a display screen. Obviously, the actual mechanism for displaying the object differs from one shape to another, but all shapes perform this task in response to the same method.

Polymorphism helps by allowing you to simplify the syntax of performing the same operation on a collection of objects. For example, by exploiting polymorphism, you can compute the area of each geometrical shape in an array of shapes with a simple loop like this:

```
// Assume "shapes" is an array of shapes (rectangles, circles,
// etc.) and "computeArea" is a function that computes the
// area of a shape.

for(int i=0; i < shapes.length; i++)
{
```

```
    double area = shapes[i].computeArea();
    System.out.println("Area = "+area);
}
```

This is possible because regardless of the exact geometrical shape, each object supports the computeArea method and computes the area in a way appropriate for that shape.

Geometric Shapes in Java: An Example

For a concrete illustration of object-oriented programming in Java, consider the following example. Suppose that you want to write a computer program that handles geometric shapes such as rectangles and circles. The program should be able to draw any shape and compute its area.

Shape Class

The first step in implementing the geometric shapes in Java is to define the classes. I'll start with an abstract class that simply defines the behavior of the shape classes by defining the common methods. The following listing shows the abstract Shape class, which you should save in the Shape.java file:

```
//------------------------------------------------------------
// File: Shape.java
//
// Abstract class for Shape objects

abstract public class Shape
{
    abstract public void draw();
    abstract public double computeArea();
}
```

As this listing shows, you use the abstract keyword to indicate that a class cannot be instantiated because it does not implement all the methods.

---

caution If you know C++, you'll notice some superficial similarities between C++ and Java class definitions. Note, however, that the similarities are really superficial. As an experienced C++ programmer, I would say that you'll be better off if you approach Java as a brand-new object-oriented language rather than as a mutation of C++. You can still use your knowledge of C syntax, but when it comes to the object-oriented features of Java, you should not try to extrapolate from your knowledge of C++.

Circle Class

After you define the abstract Shape class, you can create concrete versions of Shape classes such as a Circle and Rectangle. Here is a simple implementation of the Circle class that you should save in a file named Circle.java:

```
//------------------------------------------------------------
// File: Circle.java
//
// Circle class
```

```
public class Circle extends Shape
{
    double x, y;
    double radius;

    public Circle(double x, double y, double r)
    {
        this.x = x;
        this.y = y;
        this.radius = r;
    }

    public double computeArea()
    {
        return Math.PI * radius * radius;
    }

    public void draw()
    {
        System.out.println("Circle of radius "+radius+
                            " at ("+x+", "+y+")");
    }
}
```

As this definition of the `Circle` class shows, this shape class implements the `computeArea` and `draw` methods that were declared as abstract in the `Shape` class. The `Circle` class also defines three `double` variables—x, y, and `radius`—that denote the coordinates of the center and the radius of the circle. Such variables are referred to as *instance variables* of the class.

The `extends` keyword in the `Circle` class definition indicates that `Circle` is a subclass of the `Shape` class. The `public` qualifier specifies that the `Circle` class is accessible from other packages (in Java, a *package* is a collection of classes).

Rectangle Class

Following the pattern of the `Circle` class, I defined the `Rectangle` class as shown in the following listing:

```
//---------------------------------------------------------------
// File: Rectangle.java
//
// Rectangle class

public class Rectangle extends Shape
{
    double x1, y1;
    double x2, y2;

    public Rectangle(double x1, double y1,
                     double x2, double y2)
    {
        this.x1 = x1;
        this.y1 = y1;
```

```
        this.x2 = x2;
        this.y2 = y2;
    }

    public double computeArea()
    {
        return Math.abs((x1-x2)*(y1-y2));
    }

    public void draw()
    {
        System.out.println("Rectangle with corners "+
                           "("+x1+", "+y1+") and "+
                           "("+x2+", "+y2+")");
    }
}
```

Just as the `Circle` class is saved in the `Circle.java` file, the `Rectangle` class should be saved in the `Rectangle.java` file—at least that's how Sun's Java 2 SDK expects the class definitions.

insider insight

The `computeArea` method of the `Rectangle` class calls the `Math.abs` method to get the absolute value of an argument. Although this looks like the invocation of an object's method, there is no object named `Math`; instead `Math` is the name of a class. The `abs` method is a static method in the `Math` class. You can invoke a static method without having to create an instance of the class.

MakeShape Class—The Test Program

Now that I have defined the `Circle` and `Rectangle` classes, it's time to test them with a simple program. In Java, the program itself must be another class, and for a standalone Java program, the class must include a `public static void` method called `main` (this is akin to the main function in a C program).

The following listing shows the `MakeShape` class (in a file named `MakeShape.java`) that includes a `main` method to test the geometric shapes:

```
//-------------------------------------------------------------
// File: MakeShape.java
//
// Java application to try out various shapes

public class MakeShape
{
    public static void main(String args[])
    {
        Shape shapes[] = new Shape[2];

        shapes[0] = new Circle(100.0, 100.0, 50.0);
        shapes[1] = new Rectangle(80., 40., 120., 60.);
```

```
        System.out.println("\n"+shapes.length+" shapes\n");

        for(int i=0; i < shapes.length; i++)
        {
            double area = shapes[i].computeArea();
            System.out.println("Shape #"+i);
            shapes[i].draw();
            System.out.println("Area = "+area);
            System.out.println("-----------");
        }
    }
}
```

The main method creates an array of Shape objects and initializes the array with different shapes. Then, the computeArea and draw methods of each shape are invoked.

---

insider insight   You use the new keyword to create instances of objects in Java. There is no correspon-ding delete or free keyword to get rid of objects when you no longer need them. Instead, Java supports a technique called *garbage collection* to automatically destroy objects that are no longer needed (Java keeps track of all references to an object and removes the object when there are no more references to it). That means you never have to worry about freeing memory in Java. Because memory management is a source of many errors in C and C++ programs, Java's support for garbage collection helps eliminate a major source of potential errors in your applications.

In this example, the MakeShape class is the Java application. To compile the program, type the following command:

```
javac MakeShape.java
```

This step takes care of compiling the MakeShape.java file and all the related classes (the Shape.java, Circle.java, and Rectangle.java files). In other words, the Java compiler (javac) acts a bit like the make utility in UNIX—javac determines the dependencies among classes and compiles all necessary classes.

To run the MakeShape program, use the Java interpreter, as follows:

```
java MakeShape
```

The following listing shows the result of running the MakeShape program in a terminal window in Red Hat Linux:

```
2 shapes

Shape #0
Circle of radius 50.0 at (100.0, 100.0)
Area = 7853.981633974483
-----------
Shape #1
Rectangle with corners (80.0, 40.0) and (120.0, 60.0)
Area = 800.0
-----------
```

Java Program Structure

A Java program consists of one or more classes. For standalone applications, you must have a class with a `public void static main` method. Applets require only a subclass of the `Applet` class.

The Java 2 SDK expects the source files to have the same name as the class, but with a `.java` extension (thus, a class named `Circle` is defined in the file `Circle.java`). However, other Java development environments may have a different convention for naming files.

Within each source file, the parts of the program are laid out in the following manner:

1. The file starts with some comments that describe the purpose of the class and provide other pertinent information such as the name of author and revision dates. Java supports both C and C++-style comments. As in ANSI C, comments may start with a `/*` and end after a `*/` pair. Or, you may simply begin a line of comment with a pair of slashes (`//`). A special type of comment, known as *doc comment*, begins with a `/**` and ends with `*/`. The doc comments can be extracted by the `javadoc` utility program to create online documentation for classes.

2. One or more `import` statements that allow you to use abbreviated class names. For example, if you use the `java.applet.Applet` class, you can refer to that class by the short name `Applet` provided you include the following `import` statement in the source file:

   ```
   import java.applet.*;
   ```

   Note that the `import` statement does not really bring in any extra code into a class; it's simply a way to save typing so you can refer to a class by a shorter name (for example, `Applet` instead of `java.applet.Applet`).

3. The class definition that includes instance variables and methods. All variables and methods must be inside the class definition.

Primitive Data Types in Java

Java supports the standard C data types of `char`, `short`, `int`, `long`, `float`, and `double`. Additionally, Java introduces the byte and boolean types. Unlike C, however, Java also specifies the exact size of all primitive data types (in C, the size of the `int` type varies from one system to another). Table 26-2 summarizes Java's primitive types.

Table 26-2: Java's Primitive Data Types

Type	Description
boolean	A 1-bit value that contains `true` or `false`. A `boolean` value is not an integer.
byte	An 8-bit signed integer with values between −128 and 127
char	A 16-bit unsigned integer value representing a Unicode character (Unicode is a character encoding system designed to support storage and processing of written texts of many diverse languages). You can initialize a `char` variable with the notation `\uxxxx`, where *xxxx* is a sequence of hexadecimal digits (for example, `char c = \u00ff;`).

(continued)

Table 26-2: *(continued)*

Type	Description
double	A 64-bit, double-precision floating-point value in the IEEE 754 format (a standard format that expresses a floating-point number in binary format)
float	A 32-bit, single-precision floating-point value in IEEE 754 format
int	A 32-bit signed integer with values between −2,147,483,648 and 2,147,483,647.
long	A 64-bit signed integer with values between −9,223,372,036,854,775,808 and 9,223,372,036,854,775,807.
short	A 16-bit signed integer with values between −32,768 and 32,767.

Although most of the primitive types should be familiar to C programmers, the following C-style usage are not allowed in Java:

◆ There is no `unsigned` keyword in Java; all integer values are signed.

◆ You cannot write `short int` or `long int` (these combinations are often used in C programs).

Nonprimitive Data Types in Java

The nonprimitive data types in Java are objects and arrays. All nonprimitive types are handled by reference—that means when you pass a nonprimitive type to a method, the address of the object is passed to the method. The primitive types, however, are passed by value—that means a copy of the data is passed to the method.

Secret

Unlike C, Java does not have any pointer type. So, you cannot work with addresses of variables with the &, *, and -> operators. By eliminating pointers, Java gets rid of a common source of bugs and also prevents programmers from performing tricks with pointers that bypass Java's security mechanisms.

Instead of pointers, you have to work with references to objects (a *reference* is the address of an object). You need to understand the following implications of the fact that you have to handle objects through references:

● When you assign one object to another, Java does not actually copy the value of the object. All that happens is that you end up with two references to the same object. Consider the following example:

```
Circle c1 = new Circle(0., 0., 20.);
Circle c2 = new Circle(100.0, 60.0, 20.0);
c1 = c2; // c1 now refers to the same Circle as does c2.
```

Here, both c1 and c2 end up referring to the same `Circle` object. The `Circle` object that c1 originally referred to is lost after you assign c2 to c1. (The Java garbage collector automatically reclaims the memory allocated to the lost object.)

● To actually copy an object's value into another, you have to call the `clone` method of the object (this assumes that the object supports the `clone` method). Here is an example:

```
Vector x = new Vector();
Vector y = x.clone();  // Vector y is a copy of Vector x.
```
- **When you use the == operator, you check whether two variables refer to the same object. In other words, the == operator checks whether two objects are identical. To check if two separate objects contain the same value, you must use a special method for that object type. For example, many Java classes provide an** equals **method to check for equality of object values.**

String Type

Java includes a built-in String type, and the compiler treats a String almost like a primitive type. Java's String class is a part of the java.lang package, which the Java compiler uses by default.

The Java compiler automatically converts text within double quotes ("...") into a String. Also, the + operator concatenates String objects. For example, you can write code such as the following:

```
String welcome = "Welcome to " + "Java.";
int numchars = welcome.length();
System.out.println("There are "+numchars+
                   " characters in: "+welcome);
```

When executed, this code prints the following:

```
There are 16 characters in: Welcome to Java.
```

The String class supports a number of other methods that provide the functionality of the C's string manipulation functions (that are defined in the C header file <string.h>). Java includes two related classes for handling text strings:

- ♦ String to hold a string of characters that cannot be individually manipulated (in other words, you cannot insert or replace characters in the string).
- ♦ StringBuffer to represent a string of characters that may be manipulated as necessary. You can append, insert, and replace characters in a StringBuffer object.

Table 26-3 summarizes the methods of the String class.

Table 26-3: Methods of the String Class

Method	Description
char charAt(int index);	Returns character at a specified index
int compareTo(String s);	Compares this String with another String s
String concat(String s);	Concatenates this String with another String
String copyValueOf (char[] ca);	Returns a String equivalent to the specified array of characters. This is a static method of the String class.

(continued)

Table 26-3: *(continued)*

Method	Description
`boolean endsWith (String suffix);`	Returns `true` if `String` ends with suffix
`boolean equals(String s);`	Returns `true` if this `String` matches another `String` s (case-sensitive comparison)
`boolean equalsIgnoreCase (String s);`	Returns `true` if this `String` matches another `String` s regardless of case (case-insensitive comparison)
`byte[] getBytes();`	Copies characters from a `String` into a new `byte` array (uses the default character-encoding of the system)
`byte[] getBytes(String encodingName);`	Copies characters from a `String` into a new `byte` array according to the character encoding specified by a name such as US-ASCII, ISO-8859-1, UTF-8, UTF-16, and so on
`void getChars(int srcBegin, int srcEnd, char[] dest, int destBegin);`	Copies characters from a `String` into a `char` array
`int hashcode();`	Returns hash code for the `String`
`int indexOf(int c);`	Returns index of first occurrence of a character
`int indexOf(String s);`	Returns index of first occurrence of `String` s in the current `String`
`String intern();`	Returns a unique instance of `String` from a global shared pool of `String` objects
`int lastIndexOf(int c);`	Returns index of the last occurrence of a character
`int lastIndexOf(String s);`	Returns index of last occurrence of `String` s in the current `String`
`int length();`	Returns the length of the `String` (the number of characters in the `string`)
`boolean regionMatches (int offset, String s, int soffset, int length);`	Returns true if a region of the `String` matches the specified region of another `String` s
`String replace(char old, char new);`	Replaces all occurrences of old character with new
`boolean startsWith (String prefix);`	Returns true if `String` starts with specified prefix
`String substring(int begin, int end);`	Returns a substring of this `String`
`char[] toCharArray();`	Returns a character array from the `String`
`String toLowerCase();`	Converts `String` to lowercase
`String toString();`	Returns another `String` with the same contents
`String toUpperCase();`	Converts `String` to uppercase

Method	Description
`String trim();`	Removes any leading and trailing white space from `String`
`String valueOf(type obj);`	Returns the `String` representation of an object's value (type may be any object of primitive type such as `boolean`, `char`, `int`, `long`, `float`, and `double`). This is a static method of the `String` class.

insider insight

The `String` class is defined with a `final` keyword. That means you cannot subclass `String`. The Java compiler can optimize a final class so that the class can be used as efficiently as possible. To declare a class as `final`, use the following syntax:

```
public final class ClassName extends SuperClassName

{

// Body of class

}
```

Arrays in Java

An *array* is an ordered collection of one or more elements. Java supports arrays of all primitive as well as nonprimitive data types. As in C, you can declare an array variable by appending square brackets to the variable name, as follows:

```
byte buffer[] = new byte[256]; // Create an array for 256 byte variables.

Shape shapes[] = new Shape[10];  // Create an array to hold 10 Shape objects.
```

Secret

In Java creating an array for a specific type of object does not actually create the objects that are stored in the array. All that Java creates is an array capable of holding references to objects of a specified type. All array elements are initialized with the value `null` (which is a Java keyword that means a variable that does not refer to any object). You must individually create the objects that you want to store in the array.

Here is how you might create and initialize an array of `String` objects:

```
String language[] = new String[4];
language[0] = "C";
language[1] = "C++";
language[2] = "Java";
// language[3] == null (the default value)
```

As this example illustrates, you access array elements the same way you use arrays in C—by putting an integer-values expression within square brackets after the array's name. The array indexes start at 0.

continues

continued

You can always get the length of an array—the number of elements the array can hold—by accessing the length instance variable of the array. Here is an example:

```
String names[] = new String[5];
int len = names.length; // len = 5
```

Exception-Handling in Java

Exceptions refer to unusual conditions in a program. They can be outright errors that cause the program to fail or conditions that can lead to errors. Typically, you can always detect when certain types of errors are about to occur. For instance, when indexing an array with the [] operator, you could detect if the index is beyond the range of valid values. Although you could check for such an error, it's tedious to check for errors whenever you index into an array. Java's exception-handling mechanism allows you to place the exception-handling code in one place and avoid having to check for errors all over your program.

Secret

Java's exception-handling mechanism is similar to that in C++. The basic features are as follows:

- When a block of code generates an error, it uses the throw keyword to throw an exception. When an exception is thrown, the Java interpreter stops executing that block of code and transfers control to a block that is designated as the handler for that exception (there are many types of exceptions).

- Enclose inside a try block any code that may throw an exception.

- Immediately following the try block, place one or more catch blocks that handle specific exceptions thrown by the code inside the try block.

- Inside a finally block place any code that should be executed to clean up before exiting the try block (regardless of whether there is an exception or not). In the finally block, you may include code to close files and network connections before the program exits.

The following code fragment illustrates the syntax of try, catch, and finally blocks in Java:

```
try
{
    // Code that may generate exceptions of type AnException and
    // AnotherException
}
catch(AnException e1)
{
    // Handle exception of type AnException
}
catch(AnotherException e2)
{
```

```
    // Handle exception of type AnotherException
}
finally
{
    // This block of code is always executed after exiting the try block
    // regardless of how the try block exits.
}
```

Interfaces

Java does not support multiple inheritance, so each class can have only one superclass. However, sometimes you may want to inherit other types of behavior. For example, you may want to support a specific set of methods in a class (this is akin to saying that your class can do x, y, and z). Java provides the interface keyword that allows a class to implement a specific set of capabilities.

An interface looks like an abstract class declaration. For example, the run method is used by the Thread class (see the "Threads" section) to start a thread of execution in a Java program. The Runnable interface specifies this capability through the following interface declaration:

```
public interface Runnable
{
    public abstract void run();
}
```

If you implement all the methods of an interface, you can declare this fact by using the implements keyword in the class definition. For example, if a class defines the run method (which constitutes the Runnable interface), the class definition specifies this fact as follows:

```
import java.applet.*;
public class MyApplet extends Applet implements Runnable
{
// Must include the run() method
    public void run()
    {
// This can be the body of a thread.
    }

// Other methods of the class
// ...
}
```

Threads in Java

Java includes built-in support for threads. A *thread* refers to a single flow of control—a single sequence of Java byte codes being executed by the Java Virtual Machine. Just as an operating system can execute multiple processes (by allocating short intervals of processor time to each process in turn), the Java Virtual Machine can execute multiple threads within a single application. You can think of threads as "multitasking within a single process."

Secret

Threads can be very useful because you can turn individual threads loose on different sets of tasks. For example, one thread might monitor all user inputs to an applet, while another thread periodically updates the display. The problem with threads is that they all share the same set of variables within the program. That means, each thread must be careful when accessing and updating any variable. As a thread changes parts of an object, it may lose its time slice and another may become active and use the partially updated object. Java includes the `synchronized` keyword that allows you to mark objects and methods that should not be accessed simultaneously by multiple threads. For example, you'd write the following code to ensure that a thread acquires a lock on `myObject` before executing the statements within the curly braces (`{...}`):

```
synchronized(myObject)
{
// Some task that needs to be synchronized among threads
// ...
}
```

Using Threads in an Applet

The best way to understand threads is to go through a simple example. The following listing shows the `DigitalClock` applet that uses a thread to display the current date and time:

```
//------------------------------------------------------------
// File: DigitalClock.java
//
// Displays a digital clock using a thread.

import java.util.*;
import java.awt.*;
import java.applet.*;

public class DigitalClock extends Applet implements Runnable
{
    private volatile Thread clockThread;
    int interval = 1000;

// The run method is required by the Runnable interface.
    public void run()
    {
        Thread curThread = Thread.currentThread();
        while(curThread == clockThread)
        {
            try
            {
                curThread.sleep(interval);
            }
            catch(InterruptedException e) {}
```

```
// Repaint the clock.
        repaint();
    }
}

    public void start()
    {
// Create and start the clock thread.
        clockThread = new Thread(this);
        clockThread.start();
    }

    public void stop()
    {
// Get rid of the clock thread.
        clockThread = null;
    }

// The paint method displays the date and time.
    public void paint(Graphics gc)
    {
        Font helv = new Font("Helvetica", Font.ITALIC, 16);
        gc.setFont(helv);
        gc.drawString(new Date().toString(), 4, 20);
    }
}
```

Save this listing in the `DigitalClock.java` file and compile the applet with the following command:

```
javac DigitalClock.java
```

Next, create an HTML document, `DigitalClock.html`, and embed the applet as follows:

```
<html>
<body>

<applet width=200 height=24 code=DigitalClock>
A Java clock applet.
</applet>

</body>

</html>
```

Now, type the following command to run the applet using the `appletviewer`:

```
appletviewer DigitalClock.html
```

Figure 26-3 shows the resulting appletviewer window with the output from the Clock applet.

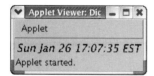

Figure 26-3: Running the Clock Applet in the `appletviewer`.

As the applet runs, it should update the clock display every second.

Understanding Thread Usage in an Applet

After you have seen the `DigitalClock` applet in action, you should go through its listing to see how a thread works. When going through the `DigitalClock` applet's code, you should note the following:

- To create a thread, you need an instance of a class that implements the `Runnable` interface. Typically, you would implement the `Runnable` interface in your applet by providing a `run` method. Then, you can create the `Thread` object by calling its constructor as follows:

  ```
  myThread = Thread(this);
  ```

- The Java Virtual Machine (JVM) calls the `start` method of the applet when the applet should run and the JVM calls the `stop` method when the applet should stop running. Thus, the applet's `start` method is a good place to create the `Thread` object.

- After you create the `Thread` object, you must call that `Thread` object's `start` method (note that this is different from the `start` method of the applet) to start running the thread.

- When started, the `Thread` executes the body of the `run` method. Thus, the `run` method should include code to perform whatever task you want the thread to perform.

- When you want to stop the thread, set the Thread's reference to null, as follows:

  ```
  myThread = null;
  ```

  The Java garbage collection mechanism would clean up the `Thread` at an appropriate time.

Writing GUI Applications in Java

You can also write standalone GUI applications in Java. Unlike applets, you do not need a Web browser to run standalone applications. Also, these applications are not burdened by the strict security restrictions that are imposed on applets. Like other applications on your system, these Java applications can perform all operations. For example, standalone Java applications can read and write files and establish a TCP/IP connection with any Internet host.

Java GUI applications use the Swing GUI components that are part of Java 2 SDK. The applet example shown in the "Writing a Simple Java Applet" section uses GUI components from the older Abstract Windowing Toolkit (AWT). The AWT includes a limited selection of components that may have been adequate for applets, but standalone GUI applications require many more user interface components, such as menu bars and tables, that the older AWT lacks. Swing extends AWT by adding an extensive collection of GUI components that are on a par with other popular windowing systems. Additionally, the Swing architecture supports what is known as *pluggable look-and-feel* that allows users to change the appearance of the user interface without having to restart the application.

---

insider insight   You will see the word `plaf` in the package name of Swing classes. That word is an acronym for "pluggable look-and-feel."

The next few sections briefly introduce the Swing GUI components, including a description of the modified Model-View-Controller (MVC) architecture of the Swing classes. Then a sample GUI application illustrates how to use many Swing GUI components. The sample GUI application shown is designed to run either as an applet or a standalone application.

An Overview of Swing

To understand the Swing class library, you need to know a bit about how Java's GUI classes came about. Java 1.0 came with the Abstract Windowing Toolkit, or AWT for short. AWT is a set of classes that allows you to build GUIs for applets and applications. AWT classes include the basic components such as buttons, labels, checkboxes, frames, text-input areas, scrollbars, and panels. AWT also provides graphics classes to handle drawing and image rendering.

Each of the GUI components in AWT has two parts: a Java class representing the component and a peer object that renders the component using the capabilities of the native windowing system on which the Java Virtual Machine is running. For example, in Microsoft Windows, AWT's Button component is drawn using a button from a Microsoft Windows library. This means that the button should look the same as other buttons in Microsoft Windows. On the other hand, the Button on a Macintosh will look like other buttons in the Macintosh user interface. The AWT components are known as heavyweight components because each component has a platform-specific implementation that is directly supported by a user interface component of the underlying windowing system. Typically, each component is rendered in a window from the windowing system.

The Swing components are a high-level collection of GUI components, implemented entirely in Java. (Swing was the name of the project that developed these components.) Swing renders components such as buttons and labels in a container such as a frame or a dialog box. The container is a heavyweight component that does rely on the underlying windowing system, but the components themselves do not make use of any user interface components from the underlying windowing system. The container provides the drawing area where various Swing components render themselves. Swing components are called lightweight because they do not have any representation in the underlying windowing system. For example, on a Microsoft Windows system, a Swing button does not use a Windows button. Instead, the button is drawn using graphics primitives such as lines and rectangles. This means that a Swing component should look the same on any system. In fact, as you will see later in this section, Swing allows you to change the look and feel of the user interface (UI) on the fly.

The following sections summarize the Swing classes, describe the modified Model-View-Controller architecture used in Swing and provide some Swing programming tips.

Java Foundation Classes (JFC) and Swing

Java Foundation Classes (JFC) is a collection of classes that provide everything you need to develop GUI applications. Swing happens to be a part of JFC, and JFC itself is incorporated into Java 2.

Secret

JFC includes the following major components:

- Swing GUI components are lightweight GUI components for Java applications and applets. For the latest information on Swing classes and some programming tips, see *The Swing Connection*, an online newsletter at http://java.sun .com/products/jfc/tsc/. Swing does not replace AWT. Rather, Swing extends AWT by adding more class libraries that support all aspects of GUI programming.

- Accessibility APIs allow developers to create GUI applications that can support people with disabilities such as limited sight or the inability to operate a mouse. For more information on the accessibility features, visit Sun's website at http:// java.sun.com/products/jfc/jaccess-1.2/doc/ and browse the online accessibility documentation.

- Java 2D API is a set of classes for two-dimensional (2D) graphics and imaging. In particular, Java 2D API provides more control over the image rendering process. For more information on Java 2D API, visit the Java 2D API home page at http://java.sun.com/products/java-media/2D/. If you have JDK 1.2 installed, you can see what Java2D offers by running the Java2Demo program, which should be in the demo\jfc\Java2D subdirectory of the location where you installed JDK 1.2. (Use the command java Java2Demo to start the demo program.)

- Drag and drop refers to the ability to cut and paste text and images between Java applications (as well as other applications running on your system). You can download the latest Drag and Drop specification from http://java.sun.com/ beans/glasgow/#draganddrop. In Java 2, the java.awt.dnd package includes the interfaces and classes for supporting drag-and-drop operations.

Swing happens to be the largest part of JFC. Originally, Swing was released as a separate class library that could be used with Java 1.1 class libraries. However, when Java 2 was officially released in December 1998, the Swing classes were included in it. The Swing classes are in various packages with names that begin with javax.swing.

JFC is essentially layered on the AWT, which, in turn, relies on the native windowing system (such as Microsoft Windows or Motif) to render the user interface on the display. Figure 26-4 illustrates the layered model of JFC. As the figure shows, the Swing components rely on parts of the AWT but not all of it. AWT components use the native windowing system to display output and receive user input from the mouse and keyboard. AWT components such as buttons, labels, panels, and frames are still available for use. The Accessibility APIs are closely tied to Swing components, but the Java2D API and Drag and Drop also rely on the native windowing system. Finally, Java GUI applications rely on the Swing components and they can also use the AWT components, if necessary.

Figure 26-4: The Layered Model of Java Foundation Classes (JFC).

Swing Classes

Because this book focuses on explaining Java programming through sample programs, you may not encounter all of the Swing classes here. Only the most commonly used Swing components show up in the various examples. However, it's useful to know the names of the various components, so you know what's available in Swing. Accordingly, Table 26-4 summarizes the Swing classes.

Table 26-4: Summary of Some Swing Component Classes

Class	Description
JApplet	Implements a Java applet capable of using Swing components. Any applet that uses Swing classes must be a subclass of JApplet.
JButton	Displays a button with some text and, optionally, an icon
JCheckBox	Displays a check box
JCheckBoxMenuItem	Displays a menu item that can be selected or deselected
JColorChooser	Displays a complex dialog box from which the user can select a color
JComboBox	Displays a combo box that includes a text field and a button to view a drop-down list of items
JComponent	Represents the superclass of most Swing classes
JDesktopPane	Implements a DesktopManager object that can be plugged into a JInternalFrame object
JDialog	Provides a container in which Swing components can be laid out to create custom dialog boxes

(continued)

Table 26-4: *(continued)*

Class	Description
JEditorPane	Provides a text component to edit various types of content such as plaintext, HTML, and Rich Text Format (RTF)
JFileChooser	Displays a complex dialog box in which the user can browse through folders and select a file
JFormattedTextField	Provides a single-line text entry and editing area, with the ability to format arbitrary values (extends JTextField)
JFrame	Provides a container in which other Swing components can be laid out. Most standalone GUI applications use a JFrame as the top-level container for laying out other Swing components.
JInternalFrame	Implements a lightweight frame object that can be placed inside a JDesktopPane object
JLabel	Displays a label showing text or an image or both
JLayeredPane	Allows the display of multiple layered panes in a frame so that components can be overlaid
JList	Displays a list of objects (text or icons) from which the user can select one or more items
JMenu	Implements a drop-down menu that can be attached to a menu bar (the menu can show text or images or both)
JMenuBar	Implements a menu bar
JMenuItem	Implements a menu item that appears in a JMenu
JOptionPane	Displays a dialog box that prompts the user for input and then provides that input to the program
JPanel	Provides a lightweight container for arranging other components such as JButton, JLabel, and JComboBox
JPasswordField	Displays a text field in which the user can type a password (the characters typed by the user are not displayed)
JPopupMenu	Implements a pop-up menu
JProgressBar	Displays a progress bar that can be used to indicate the progress of an operation
JRadioButton	Implements a radio button that can display text or an image or both
JRadioButton MenuItem	Implements a menu item that is part of a group of menu items, only one of which can be selected at any time
JRootPane	Creates an object with a glass pane, a layered pane, an optional menu bar, and a content pane
JScrollBar	Displays a scroll bar
JScrollPane	Implements a scrolled pane that can scroll objects placed inside the pane

Class	Description
JSeparator	Implements a separator that can be placed in a JMenu to separate one group of menu items from another
JSlider	Displays a slider bar from which the user can select a value
JSpinner	Displays a single line input field with a pair of tiny arrow buttons that enable the user to step through a sequence of values and select one (functionality is similar to that of JComboBox, but without a drop-down list)
JSplitPane	Implements a pane that can be split horizontally or vertically
JTabbedPane	Implements tabbed pane components that allow the user to view different pages by clicking on tabs (much like the tabs on file folders)
JTable	Implements a table that can display tabular data (ideal for displaying the results of database searches)
JTableHeader	Implements the column header part of a JTable (shares the same TableColumnModel with the JTable)
JTextArea	Implements a multiline text area that can be used to display read-only or editable text
JTextField	Provides a single-line text entry and editing area
JTextPane	Provides a text component that can be marked up with attributes that are represented graphically
JToggleButton	Implements a button that can display text or an image and that can be in one of two states (on or off)
JToolBar	Implements a toolbar that can either be attached to a frame or stand alone
JToolTip	Displays a short help message (attached to a component to provide help when the user moves the mouse onto that component)
JTree	Displays a set of hierarchical data in the form of a tree (similar to the directory structure in Windows Explorer)
JViewport	Displays a clipped view of a component (used by JScrollPane)
JWindow	Implements a container that can be displayed anywhere on the user's desktop (JWindow) does not have the title bar and window-management buttons associated with a JFrame)

The Model-View-Controller (MVC) Architecture and Swing

Swing components use a modified form of the Model-View-Controller (MVC) architecture. The classic MVC architecture of Smalltalk-80 breaks an application up into three separate layers:

◆ **Model**—This is the application layer that implements the application's functionality. All application-specific code is in this layer.

◆ **View**—This is the presentation layer that implements whatever is needed to present information from the application layer to the user. In a GUI, the view provides the windows.

◆ **Controller**—This is the virtual terminal layer that handles the user's interactions with the application. This is a graphics library that presents a device-independent interface to the presentation layer.

Figure 26-5 illustrates this classic MVC architecture of Smalltalk-80.

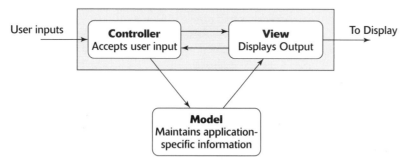

Figure 26-5: The Model-View-Controller (MVC) Architecture of Smalltalk-80.

Smalltalk's MVC architecture does an excellent job of separating the responsibilities of the objects in the system. The application-specific details are insulated from the user interface. Also, the user interface itself is broken down into two parts, with the presentation handled by the view and the user interaction (mouse and keyboard input) handled by the controller.

Each Smalltalk-80 application consists of a model and an associated view-controller pair. Figure 26-5 shows the usual interactions in Smalltalk-80's MVC architecture. The controller accepts the user's inputs and invokes the appropriate methods from the model to perform the task requested by the user. When the work is done, the method in the model sends messages to the view and controller. The view updates the display in response to this message, accessing the model for further information, if necessary. Thus, the model has a view and a controller, but it never directly accesses either of them. The view and controller, on the other hand, access the model's functions and data when necessary. The shaded box enclosing the view and controller in Figure 26-5 is meant to emphasize that in actual implementations, the view and controller are tightly coupled and typically treated as a single view-controller pair.

Swing uses a modified form of Smalltalk's MVC model. Each Swing component collapses the view and controller into a single user interface (UI) object, but retains the model as a separate entity. The model maintains state information such as the maximum, minimum, and current values of a scrollbar. The UI object handles the view and controller responsibilities by rendering the component and processing user input in the form of mouse and keyboard events. Additionally, Swing introduces a UI manager that handles the look-and-feel characteristics of each component. Figure 26-6 depicts the Model-UI object-UI manager architecture of Swing components.

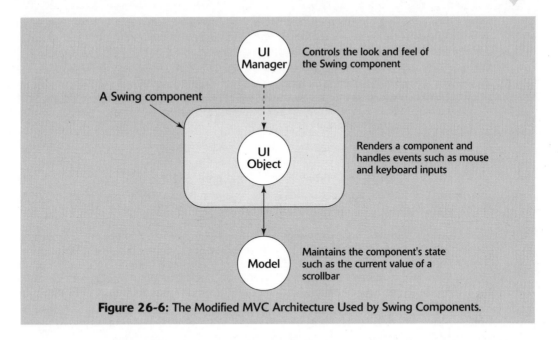

Figure 26-6: The Modified MVC Architecture Used by Swing Components.

The UI manager controls the look-and-feel capabilities of a Swing component by communicating with the component's UI object, as shown in Figure 26-6.

If you think about look and feel, *look* refers to how the component appears on the display, and *feel* refers to how the component reacts to user inputs. In other words, look and feel are the responsibilities of the view and controller components of the MVC architecture. In each Swing component, the UI object handles the look and feel of the component. Because the class representing the component delegates the look-and-feel responsibilities to the UI object, that object is also referred to as the UI delegate.

You should remember that all Swing components use a separate model. Many simple components provide a default model that maintains the information you provide when you create the Swing component. For more complex Swing components, such as JTable, you have to provide a model that represents the tabular data and implements the interface expected by JTable.

Swing Programming Tips

When you use AWT components to create a user interface, you place AWT components such as buttons, labels, and checkboxes inside various AWT containers such as frames and panels. Typically, you end up with a hierarchical containment structure, grouping several components in a panel and then placing several panels inside another panel. You do not have to worry much about how the components paint themselves, because the AWT components are heavyweight components that rely on the underlying windowing system for rendering themselves.

The situation changes when you create a user interface with the lightweight Swing components. Swing components rely on Java code (as opposed to the underlying windowing system) to support the windowing features such as showing, hiding, moving, and resizing the components. The upshot is that you have to follow certain rules when constructing user interfaces with Swing components, and you have to follow a few key rules to ensure that the user interface is painted properly.

The first rule is to avoid mixing heavyweight and lightweight components when they may overlap. In other words, do not place an AWT component inside a Swing component and vice versa. When these two types of components overlap, they are not painted correctly. (If you must use both AWT and Swing components, the article at http://java.sun.com/ products/jfc/tsc/articles/mixing/index.html explains the rules for doing so.)

To use Swing components properly, you must start with one of the container classes in Swing. The most commonly used container classes are

- ◆ JApplet for any applet that uses Swing components
- ◆ JFrame for GUI applications that use Swing components
- ◆ JDialog for dialog boxes that contain Swing components

These Swing containers use an appropriate heavyweight AWT component to create the display area where the lightweight Swing components can be arranged. Each of these containers has a content pane in which the rest of the components are placed. You must add other Swing components to the content pane. Call the getContentPane() method of the Swing container to get the content pane and then add the components to that pane. For example, here is how you would create a JFrame and add a JDesktopPane to that frame:

```
JFrame frame = new JFrame("Main Application Frame");
JDesktopPane jdp = new JDesktopPane();
frame.getContentPane().add(jdp);
```

To add lightweight components to other lightweight components, such as JPanel, you simply need to call the add() method of the JPanel object.

Whenever you want to redraw any Swing component, call that component's repaint() method. As with AWT components, do not call paint() directly. For example, here's how the repaint() method of a JButton is called in a mouse listener to repaint the button as the user presses and releases the button:

```
MouseListener l = new MouseAdapter()
{
    public void mousePressed(MouseEvent ev)
    {
        JButton b = (JButton)ev.getSource();
        b.setSelected(true);
        b.repaint();
    }
    public void mouseReleased(MouseEvent ev)
    {
        JButton b = (JButton)ev.getSource();
        b.setSelected(false);
        b.repaint();
    }
};
```

When you define any class as a subclass of the Swing container classes (JApplet, JFrame, or JDialog) and override the paint() method, you must insert a call to super.paint(), as shown in the following example:

```
public class MyApplet extends JApplet
{
    public void paint(Graphics g)
    {
        // Paint my applet's contents first. Then make sure
        // lightweight Swing components are painted.
            super.paint(g);
    }
}
```

If you do not call super.paint(),the lightweight Swing components inside the container won't show up. This is a common problem with beginners to Swing programming.

Additionally, each Swing component breaks down the paint() processing into three distinct parts by calling three methods in the following sequence:

1. paintComponent() to draw this component
2. paintBorder() to draw this component's border
3. paintChildren() to draw this component's children

When you define any class as a subclass of a lightweight Swing component such as JPanel , you should override the paintComponent() method to perform any additional painting you want done. You should first call super.paintComponent() to properly draw the component, as shown in the following example:

```
public class MyPanel extends JPanel
{
    protected void paintComponent(Graphics g)
    {
        // First call the superclass' paintComponent() to
        // ensure correct painting of the component
        super.paintComponent(g);
        // Now paint anything MyPanel needs ...
    }
}
```

Because Swing components draw themselves in a pane—a drawing area—provided by a container, Swing uses double buffering to avoid flickering when components are drawn. This means that the user interface is drawn in an off-screen buffer and then the off-screen image is copied to the screen. The doubleBuffered property of the JComponent class controls whether double buffering is enabled. By default, the doubleBuffered property is set to true. Although you can change this property by calling the setDoubleBuffered() method, you should leave double buffering enabled for all Swing components.

Displaying a Calendar Using Swing

This section presents ViewCal, a GUI application that displays a calendar for any selected month of a year. You can run ViewCal in two ways—as an applet inside an HTML document or as a standalone application by typing a command from a terminal window. By studying this application, you will learn how to use a number of different Swing components. You will also learn how to convert an applet to an application by providing a static main() method that creates the frame necessary to display the calendar.

Listing 26-2 shows the ViewCal.java file that implements the ViewCal application. I describe the code in the section that follows the listing.

Listing 26-2: A GUI Application to Display the Calendar for Any Month

```java
//-------------------------------------------------------------
// ViewCal.java
//
// A calendar applet that you can run as a standalone
// application. Uses a GUI built with the Swing classes in
// Java 2. Shows how you can convert an applet into a
// standalone GUI application.
//-------------------------------------------------------------
import java.applet.*;
import java.awt.*;
import java.util.*;
import java.awt.event.*;
import javax.swing.*;
/** ViewCal is an applet that includes a main() method so it
 *  can run as a standalone application. Use the command
 *  "java ViewCal" to run the application. Note that ViewCal
 *  is a subclass of JApplet because it uses Swing components.
 */
public class ViewCal extends JApplet implements ActionListener,
                                                 ItemListener
{
    private JComboBox    monthChoice;
    private JTextField   year;
    private JButton      previousButton;
    private JButton      nextButton;
    private int          currentMonth;
    private int          currentYear;
    private String       currentDayString;
    private String       currentDateString;
    private Font helvB16 =
               new Font("Helvetica", Font.BOLD, 16);
    private String days[] = {"SUN", "MON", "TUE", "WED", "THU",
                             "FRI", "SAT"};
    private String months[] = {"January", "February", "March",
                    "April", "May", "June", "July",
                    "August", "September", "October",
                    "November", "December"};
    private int daysInMonth[] = {31, 28, 31, 30, 31, 30, 31, 31,
                                 30, 31, 30, 31};
    private JButton[][] monthButtons = new JButton[6][7];
    private JButton highlightedBtn = null;
    private JLabel[] dayLabels = new JLabel[7];
```

```
/** Initializes the calendar's user interface */
public void init()
{
    Calendar today = new GregorianCalendar();
    currentMonth = today.get(Calendar.MONTH);
    currentYear = today.get(Calendar.YEAR);
    currentDayString = ""+today.get(Calendar.DAY_OF_MONTH);
    // In JApplet everything is inside a ContentPane
    Container cp = this.getContentPane();
    cp.setLayout(new BorderLayout());

    JPanel pTop = new JPanel();
    pTop.setLayout(new GridLayout(1, 4));
    previousButton = new JButton("<-Prev");
    previousButton.addActionListener(this);
    previousButton.setToolTipText("Previous month");
    pTop.add(previousButton);
    monthChoice = new JComboBox();
    for(int i = 0; i < months.length; i++)
        monthChoice.addItem(months[i]);
    monthChoice.setSelectedIndex(currentMonth);
    monthChoice.setMaximumRowCount(6);
    monthChoice.addItemListener(this);
    pTop.add(monthChoice);
    year = new JTextField("" + currentYear, 4);
    year.setFont(helvB16);
    year.setBackground(Color.lightGray);
    year.setHorizontalAlignment(JTextField.CENTER);
    year.addActionListener(this);
    year.setToolTipText("Enter number, then press <Enter>.");
    pTop.add(year);
    nextButton = new JButton("Next->");
    nextButton.addActionListener(this);
    nextButton.setToolTipText("Next month");
    pTop.add(nextButton);
    cp.add("North", pTop);

    JPanel pButtons = new JPanel();
    pButtons.setLayout(new GridLayout(7,7));
    for(int i=0; i < days.length; i++)
    {
        dayLabels[i] = new JLabel(days[i], JLabel.CENTER);
        pButtons.add(dayLabels[i]);
    }
    for(int i=0; i < 6; i++)
        for(int j=0; j < 7; j++)
        {
            monthButtons[i][j] = new JButton("");
            monthButtons[i][j].setBackground(Color.lightGray);
            monthButtons[i][j].addActionListener(this);
```

(continued)

Listing 26-2: *(continued)*

```
                pButtons.add(monthButtons[i][j]);
            }
    cp.add("Center", pButtons);
    validate();
    repaint();
}
/** Returns true if the year is a leap year */
public boolean isLeapYear(int year)
{
    if((year % 400) == 0) return(true);
    if((year > 1582) && ((year % 100) == 0)) return(false);
    if((year % 4) == 0) return(true);
    return(false);
}
/** Displays the calendar for a specific month of a year */
public void displayMonth(int month, int year)
{
    int day = 1; // first of the month
    //  Compute firstWeekday =>  0=Sun, 1=Mon, 2=Tue, ...
    Calendar cal = new GregorianCalendar(year, month, 1);
    int firstWeekday = cal.get(Calendar.DAY_OF_WEEK)-1;

    // Now draw the dates on the buttons in the calendar
    int maxDate = daysInMonth[month];
    if(month == 1 && isLeapYear(year)) maxDate += 1;
    int dateNow = 1;
    if(highlightedBtn != null)
        highlightedBtn.setBackground(Color.lightGray);
    String ds;
    for(int i=0; i < 6; i++)
    {
        for(int j=0; j < 7; j++)
        {
            if(dateNow == 1 && j < firstWeekday)
                monthButtons[i][j].setText("");
            else if(dateNow > maxDate)
                monthButtons[i][j].setText("");
            else
            {
                ds = ""+dateNow;
                monthButtons[i][j].setText(ds);
                if(ds.equals(currentDayString))
                {
                    monthButtons[i][j].setBackground(
                                        Color.gray);
                    highlightedBtn = monthButtons[i][j];
                }
                dateNow++;
```

```
            }
          }
        }
    }
/** Processes the year entered by the user */
public int processYear(String yearString)
{
    if((yearString.length() == 4))
    {
        try
        {
            int year = Integer.parseInt(yearString);
            return year;
        }
        catch(NumberFormatException e)
        {
            return currentYear;
        }
    }
    return -1;
}
/** Calls displayMonth() to display the calendar */
public void paint(Graphics g)
{
    g.setColor(Color.black);
    Dimension d = getSize();
    g.drawRect(0, 0, d.width-1,d.height-1);
    displayMonth(currentMonth, currentYear);
    super.paint(g);    // Important step for Swing components
}
/** Handles mouse clicks in the buttons and drop-down menus*/
public void actionPerformed(ActionEvent ev)
{
    if(ev.getSource().equals(previousButton))
    {
        if((currentYear > 1) || (currentMonth > 0))
        {
            currentMonth--;
            if(currentMonth < 0)
            {
                currentMonth = 11;
                currentYear--;
            }
            monthChoice.setSelectedIndex(currentMonth);
            year.setText(""+currentYear);
            currentDayString = "1";
            repaint();
        }
    }
    else if(ev.getSource() == nextButton)
```

(continued)

Listing 26-2: *(continued)*

```
{
    if((currentYear < 9999) || (currentMonth < 11))
    {
        currentMonth++;
        if(currentMonth > 11)
        {
            currentMonth = 0;
            currentYear++;
        }
        monthChoice.setSelectedIndex(currentMonth);
        year.setText(""+currentYear);
        currentDayString = "1";
        repaint();
    }
}
else if(ev.getSource() == year)
{
// Called when user presses Enter in text field
    int y = processYear(year.getText());
    if((y > 0) && (y != currentYear))
    {
        currentYear = y;
        currentDayString = "1";
        repaint();
    }
}
else
{   // Check for click on a day of the month
    String ds;
    for(int i=0; i < 6; i++)
    {
        for(int j=0; j < 7; j++)
        {
            if(ev.getSource() == monthButtons[i][j])
            {
                ds = ev.getActionCommand();
                if(!ds.equals(""))
                {
                    highlightedBtn.
                        setBackground(Color.lightGray);
                    highlightedBtn = monthButtons[i][j];
                    monthButtons[i][j].setBackground(
                                        Color.gray);
                    currentDayString = ds;
                }
            }
        }
    }
```

```
                }
            }
        }
        /** Handles selections from the month list */
        public void itemStateChanged(ItemEvent ev)
        {
            if(ev.getSource() == monthChoice)
            {
                int m = monthChoice.getSelectedIndex();
                year.setText(""+currentYear);
                if(m != currentMonth)
                {
                    currentMonth = monthChoice.getSelectedIndex();
                    currentDayString = "1";
                    repaint();
                }
            }
        }
        /** Makes room for a 1-pixel border */
        public Insets getInsets()
        {
            return new Insets(1,1,1,1); // 1-pixel border
        }
        /** Provides a frame so ViewCal can run standalone */
        public static void main(String s[])
        {
            WindowListener l = new WindowAdapter()
            {
                public void windowClosing(WindowEvent e)
                {System.exit(0);}
            };

            JFrame frame = new JFrame("Calendar");
            frame.addWindowListener(l);
            ViewCal c = new ViewCal();
            c.init();
            frame.getContentPane().add("Center", c);
            frame.pack();
            frame.setVisible(true);
        }
}
```

To compile and run ViewCal, type the following commands (I assume that you have the Java 2 SDK binary directory in the PATH environment variable):

```
javac ViewCal.java
java ViewCal
```

You should see the ViewCal application's window, as shown in Figure 26-7.

Figure 26-7: The ViewCal Application Displaying a Monthly Calendar.

Here is how you can interact with the ViewCal application's user interface:

♦ Clicking on the drop-down menu (implemented using a Choice component) displays a list of months from which you can select a specific month. That month's calendar is then displayed.

♦ You can type in a year (such as 2003) in the text field next to the drop-down menu for selecting a month. After you press Enter, ViewCal updates the monthly calendar to reflect the change in year.

♦ Clicking the Prev and Next buttons change the calendar to the previous or next month.

The ViewCal application's user interface is organized using Panel objects, where each panel holds other components such as Label, Choice, and Button objects. Typically, each panel uses a GridLayout layout manager to arrange its components into rows and columns. The Panel objects, in turn, are placed in the applet using a BorderLayout layout manager.

To display the calendar, the application needs the day of the week for the first day of any month. The ViewCal application uses the GregorianCalendar class to create a Gregorian calendar. Then it calls the get(Calendar.DAY_OF_WEEK) method of the GregorianCalendar object to get the day of the week for a specific date.

Recall that ViewCal is designeds to be an applet as well as a standalone GUI application. Essentially, ViewCal is an applet first. That's why Listing 26-2 shows the ViewCal class as a subclass of JApplet (any applet that uses Swing components must be defined as a subclass of JApplet):

```
public class ViewCal extends JApplet implements ActionListener,
                                                 ItemListener
```

ViewCal also implements the ActionListener and ItemListener interfaces to handle mouse clicks on various GUI components. The ViewCal class implements these interfaces by providing the required actionPerformed() and itemStateChanged() methods.

As is typical in an applet, the init() method in Listing 26-2 lays out the user interface. Because ViewCal is a subclass of JApplet, you must add all GUI components to its content pane. The following lines of code from Listing 26-2 show how to get the content pane (which is a Container object) and set the layout manager for the content pane:

```
Container cp = this.getContentPane();
cp.setLayout(new BorderLayout());
```

Later on, other high-level containers are added to the content pane named cp. For example, here is a line that adds a JPanel named pTop to the north position of the content pane (in the BorderLayout manager, the north position is the top edge of the container):

```
cp.add("North", pTop);
```

To enable `ViewCal` to run as a standalone application, you need a `static main()` method that prepares a frame and provides the context where the applet can run. The following lines show the `main()` method:

```
public static void main(String s[])
{
    WindowListener l = new WindowAdapter()
    {
        public void windowClosing(WindowEvent e)
        {System.exit(0);}
    };

    JFrame frame = new JFrame("Calendar");
    frame.addWindowListener(l);
    ViewCal c = new ViewCal();
    c.init();
    frame.getContentPane().add("Center", c);
    frame.pack();
    frame.setVisible(true);
}
```

As these lines of code show, the `main()` method accepts an array of `String` objects as argument—these are the arguments that the user might have specified on the command line. For example, if the user were to start the application with a command such as `java ViewCal arg1 arg2`, the `String` array would contain `arg1` and `arg2`. (Although `ViewCal` does not make any use of command-line arguments, the `main()` method must be declared with a `String` array for the arguments.)

The `main()` method defines a `WindowListener` of type `WindowAdapter` and provides the `windowClosing()` method, which handles a window closing event by exiting the application. The rest of `main()` creates a `JFrame` object that provides the window where `ViewCal`'s user interface is displayed. The `WindowListener` object is associated with the `JFrame` so that the application exits when the user closes the `JFrame`.

Then `main()` creates an instance of `ViewCal` and initializes it by calling the `init()` method. It then adds the applet to the center of the `JFrame` (notice that you have to add the applet to the `JFrame`'s content pane). Finally, the `main()` method makes the `JFrame` visible (this causes the `ViewCal` user interface to appear on the display screen).

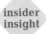

insider insight   You can use the technique of providing a `main()` method to convert any applet to a standalone application. In the `main()` method, create a frame. Then, create an instance of the applet and call its `init()` method. Add that instance to the frame. You should also provide a `WindowListener` that handles the window closing event that occurs when the user closes the frame.

Writing Java Servlets

In concept, servlets are analogous to applets. Both applets and servlets reside on a server, but an applet runs in a Java-capable Web browser after the browser downloads the applet from the Web server. Because the Web browser is a client to the Web server, applets are referred to as client-side applications. A servlet, on the other hand, runs in a Java Virtual Machine (JVM) on the Web server. Thus, servlets are server-side applications.

Another difference between applets and servlets is that an applet typically produces some visible output, whereas servlets do not display anything. Instead, servlets perform specific tasks for the Web server. They are commonly used at websites to support interactive and dynamic Web pages, which are then displayed by the Web browser that downloads the pages.

A Web search engine such as Google (http://www.google.com/) is a good example of an interactive Web page; the user enters one or more keywords, and the Google search engine returns an HTML document containing links to other Web pages that contain the search words. The HTML document returned by the search engine is dynamic because the contents of that page depend on what search words the user types; it's not a prede-fined, static document.

To create an interactive Web page, you have to use certain HTML codes (to display the form that solicits user input) and implement special computer programs on the Web server. These programs process the user input (sent by the Web browser) and return requested information to the user, usually in the form of a dynamic Web page—a page that is constructed on the fly by a computer program. Such programs are known as gate-ways because they typically act as a conduit between the Web server and an external source of information such as a database (even if the database is simply a collection of files).

Traditionally, websites have used gateway programs that are started by the Web server and that exchange information with the Web server using a standard protocol known as Common Gateway Interface (CGI). These standalone CGI programs can be written in any language (C, C++, Perl, Tcl/Tk, and even Java). One drawback of CGI programs is that the Web server has to start a new process to run a standalone CGI program whenever the server receives data from an HTML form.

Servlets provide functionality similar to that of CGI programs, but servlets avoid the over-head of new process startup. Typically, the Web server runs a JVM, and that JVM, in turn, loads and runs the servlets. The JVM runs a servlet in a Java thread, which is faster and requires fewer operating system resources than a new process. Additionally, the JVM can keep a servlet loaded and running so that a single instance can handle many future requests. This makes servlets more responsive than other CGI programs, especially ones written in scripting languages such as Perl. At the same time, servlets are portable to any system that supports Java, just as Perl CGI programs can run on any system with a Perl interpreter.

Many websites already use servlets extensively. While browsing the Web, you may have accessed some servlets without even realizing it. Typically, a giveaway that the Web server is using a servlet is the occurrence of /servlet/ in the URL (in the same way that /cgi-bin/ commonly appears in URLs that refer to CGI programs). The next few sections explain how Java servlets work and what you need to develop servlets.

The Role of Java Servlets

A servlet performs specific tasks for a Web server and typically returns the results format-ted as an HTML document (if necessary, servlets can also return images and other multi-media content). Often, the servlet program acts as a bridge between the Web server and some other repository of information such as a database. Typically, you use a servlet engine such as Apache Tomcat in conjuction with a Web server such as Apache httpd to set up a Java capable Web server. Figure 26-8 highlights the interrelationships among the Web browser, Web server, servlets, database, and HTML documents, using the Apache httpd and Apache Tomcat as examples. Web servers also serve images and other multimedia content, but the figure does not show these.

Figure 26-8: The Interrelationships among the Web Browser, Web Server, and Servlets.

As Figure 26-8 shows, the Web browser running on the user's system uses the HyperText Transfer Protocol (HTTP) to exchange information with the Web server. The Web server (also called the HTTP deamon or `httpd`) has access to the HTML documents and other content. Depending on the type of request from the browser, the Web server either serves an HTML document or passes the request to run a servlet thread to its Java servlet engine. The servlets run in the servlet engine and results are communicated to the Web server. If necessary, the servlets may access other system resources such as disk files or databases. Typically, a servlet generates a dynamic HTML document that the Web server sends back to the Web browser.

Secret

In a typical scenario, the user interacts with an HTML form that, in turn, contains a reference to a servlet that processes whatever the user enters into the form. Here is the basic sequence of events:

1. The user clicks on some link on a Web page, and that causes the Web browser to request an HTML document that contains a form.

2. The Web server sends the HTML document with the form, which the browser displays.

3. The user fills in the fields of the form and clicks the Submit button. The browser, in turn, sends the form's data using the GET or POST method (as specified by the `<form>` tag in the HTML form). In either method, the browser sends to the Web server the URL specified in the `<form>` tag's action attribute. That URL refers to the servlet that should process the form's data.

4. From the URL the Web server determines that it should pass along the form's data and the URL for the servlet to the Java servlet engine.

continues

continued

5. The servlet engine runs the servlet listed in the URL and sends the form's data to that servlet.

6. The servlet processes the form's data and returns a new MIME document to the Web browser through the servlet engine. (MIME refers to Multipurpose Internet Mail Extension, an Internet standard described in RFC 1521 for attaching any type of data to a mail message. It is also used by Web servers when sending documents back to the Web browser.)

7. The Web browser displays the document received from the Web server. The information contained in that document depends on what the user entered in the HTML form. (Often the information may be nothing more than a confirmation from the server that the user's input has been received.)

To understand how servlets process data from an HTML form, you need to know how a Web browser sends form data to the Web server. The Web browser uses the `method` attribute of the `<form>` tag to determine how to send the form's data to the Web server. There are two submission methods:

◆ In the `GET` method, the Web browser submits the form's data as part of the URL.

◆ In the `POST` method, the Web browser sends the form's data separately from the URL.

The `GET` and `POST` methods are so called because the browser uses the HTTP `GET` and `POST` command to submit the data. The `GET` command sends a URL to the Web server. This means that to send a form's contents to the server using the `GET` method, the browser must include all data in the URL. Because there is typically an upper limit on the length of a URL, the `GET` method cannot be used to transfer large amounts of form data from the browser to the server. The `POST` command, on the other hand, sends the form's data in a separate stream. Therefore, the `POST` method can send much larger amounts of data to the server.

Regardless of which method—GET or POST—is specified in the HTML form, a servlet can get the form's data by overriding specific methods in the `HttpServlet` class and calling other servlet API methods to retrieve specific parameters from the HTML form.

Because you, as the developer, design the form as well as the servlet that will process the form's data, you can select the method that best suits your needs. The basic guidelines for choosing a data submission method are as follows:

◆ Use `GET` to transfer a small amount of data, and use `POST` to send potentially large amounts of data. For example, `GET` is appropriate for a search form that solicits a few keywords from the user. On the other hand, you'd want to use `POST` for a feedback form with a free-form text-entry area because the user might enter considerable amounts of text.

◆ Use the `GET` method if you want to access the servlet without using a form. For example, if you want to access a servlet at the URL `http://www.someplace.com/servlet/dbquery` with a parameter named `keyword` as input, you could invoke the servlet with a URL such as `http://www.someplace.com/servlet/dbquery?keyword=Linux`. In this case, `Linux` is the value of the `keyword` parameter. If a servlet is designed to receive data with the `POST` method only, you cannot activate that servlet with a URL alone.

What You Need to Develop Servlets

To try out Java servlets and learn how to write a servlet, you need the following:

- ◆ Java 2 Enterprise Edition (J2EE) SDK
- ◆ A Web server that supports Java servlets or a Java servlet engine that works with a Web server

The J2EE SDK provides the APIs for writing servlets. In particular, J2EE SDK includes the servlet classes in the javax.servlet and javax.servlet.http packages. You also need the Java 2 Standard Edition (J2SE) SDK, which you already installed earlier in this chapter.

cross
ref

As for a Web server that can run Java servlets, your best bet is to use Apache Tomcat along with the Apache httpd server. Chapter 14 shows you how to download, install, and configure Apache Tomcat to work with the Apache httpd server. If you plan to try out some servlets, please set up Apache Tomcat by following the instructions in Chapter 14.

Downloading and Installing J2EE SDK

You can download the latest version of J2EE SDK from:

`http://java.sun.com/products/servlet/download.html`

The file that you eventually download is a shell script that you have to execute on your system. For example, here are the steps I followed to download and install J2EE SDK 1.4 (beta version):

1. On the Web page `http://java.sun.com/products/servlet/download.html`, I click on the link for J2EE SDK 1.4. This brings up a new Web page where I can register and set up a user ID and password.
2. I register and then enter my new user ID and password. The J2EE SDK download page appears.
3. I select "Linux Install" from the drop-down list near the end of the page and then click Download. The license agreement appears.
4. I click Accept to accept the license agreement. A new page appears with the link to the file to be downloaded.
5. I click the link labeled "Download j2sdkee-1_4-beta-linux.sh." It's a file close to 32 MB in size. The file starts to download and I save it in the `/usr/local` directory.

6. After downloading is complete, I make the file executable with the following command:

   ```
   chmod +x j2sdkee*.sh
   ```

7. I execute the shell script with the following command:

   ```
   ./j2sdkee*.sh
   ```

   A GUI installer screen appears informing me that Java 2 SDK Enterprise Edition will be installed on my system.

8. I click Next. The installer displays the license agreement again. I click the Approve radio button and then click Next. The installer shows the name of the directory where the current Java 2 SDK Standard Edition runtime environment is installed.

9. I make sure that the J2SE SDK directory is correct and then click Next. The installer asks for the name of the directory where to install J2EE and shows a suggested directory (/usr/local/j2sdkee1.4).

10. I accept the suggested directory and click Next. The installer installs the J2EE files. When done, I click Finish to exit the installer.

---

insider insight

After installing J2EE SDK, I had to copy the `j2ee.jar` file from the lib subdirectory of the J2EE installation to the `jre/lib/etc` subdirectory of the Java 2 SDK install directory. For example, on my system the `JAVA_HOME` environment variable is set to the directory where the Java 2 SDK is installed. So I type the following commands to copy the `j2ee.jar` file to the appropriate location:

```
cd /usr/local/j2sdkee1.4/lib

cp j2ee.jar $JAVA_HOME/jre/lib/ext
```

After completing these steps, I am able to write and compile servlets on my Red Hat Linux system.

Linking HTML Forms to Servlets

Before you jump into servlet programming, you need to understand how to associate servlets to an HTML form. A key relationship between servlets and HTML forms is that the servlet processes the data that users enter on the form. One of the attributes of the form specifies the name of the servlet that receives the input from the form. Additionally, each element of the form has an identifying name that helps the servlet isolate the user's input for that element. This section highlights the aspects of an HTML form that are important when you are writing a servlet to handle the form's data.

Consider a typical book order form that lets the user sign in using an ID and password, select one or more books, select the payment option, fill out the credit card information, and submit the order. Figure 26-9 shows a simple book order form.

Figure 26-9: A Book Order Form in HTML.

Listing 26-3 shows the HTML text used to display the book order form. You should save this HTML text in a file named `OrderBooks.html`.

Listing 26-3: The OrderBooks.html File, Which Displays the Book Order Form

```
<html>
<head>
<title>Book Order Form</title>
</head>
<body>
<form action="../servlet/OrderBooks/" method=post>
<h3> Book Order Form</h3>
<hr>
<b>Please sign in and order</b>
<pre>
Your ID: <input type=text size=10 name=id>
Password:<input type=password size=10 name=passwd>
```

(continued)

Listing 26-3: *(continued)*

```
Select books to purchase:
        <select name=books size=4 multiple>
          <option>Red Hat Linux Professional Secrets
          <option>Discover Perl 5
          <option>UNIX Webmaster Bible
          <option>Success with Windows 95
          <option>X Window System Programming
          <option>Object-oriented programming in C++
          <option>Visual C++ Developer's Guide
          <option>Borland C++ Developer's Guide
          <option>Turbo C++ Bible
          <option>Microsoft Macro Assembler Bible
        </select>

Special Instructions:
        <textarea name=instructions rows=2 cols=35></textarea>

Charge:  <input type=radio checked name=card value="Visa">Visa
         <input type=radio name=card value="MC">MasterCard
         <input type=radio name=card value="Amex">American Express

Acct No: <input type=text name=acct size=16>
Exp Date:<input type=text name=expire size=5>
<hr>
        <input type=submit value="Order">  <input type=reset>
</pre>
</form>
</body>
</html>
```

This is a good example of the typical HTML elements that you can use in interactive forms. You can also see how the `<form>` element associates a servlet URL with a form. Here are the key points to note in this HTML sample:

- The entire form is enclosed within `<form>` and `</form>` tags. The `action` attribute of the `<form>` tag specifies the URL of the servlet that processes this form's data. The `method` attribute specifies how the Web browser sends the form's data to the Web server.
- The `<input>` tag defines a number of common form elements, such as single-line text fields, password fields, radio buttons, and submit buttons.
- The `<select>` element defines menus. An `<option>` tag defines each menu item.
- The `<textarea>` element allows the user to enter multiple lines of text.
- Most importantly, each of the tags—`<input>`, `<select>`, and `<textarea>`—has a `name` attribute that identifies that input parameter. In the servlet that handles this form's data, you have to use the value of the `name` attribute to indicate which input parameter's value you want to retrieve.

Secret

At the heart of the HTML form is the ⟨form⟩ tag whose attributes specify the servlet that processes this form's input and how the Web browser sends the user's input to the Web server. A typical ⟨form⟩ element definition has the following structure:

```
<form method="post" action="../servlet/servletName">
...(other form elements appear here)

</form>
```

The ⟨form⟩ tag's action attribute specifies a URL for the servlet that you have designed to handle the form's input. You can use an absolute URL that specifies the full server name as well as the path name for the servlet. Often, however, you'd use a relative URL that identifies the directory on your Web server where the servlets reside.

The exact directory where you must place the Java servlets depends on the Web server. In Apache Tomcat, you typically place the servlets in the WEB-INF/classes subdirectory of the server's root directory. The exact location of servlet classes depends on the package name of the class and how Apache Tomcat is configured.

The method attribute indicates how the Web browser sends form input back to the server. You can specify one of the following submission methods:

- POST causes the browser to send the data in a two-step process. First the browser contacts the server specified in the action attribute. Then, after a successful connection is established, the browser sends the form's data to the server, which in turn provides the data to the servlet.

- GET causes the browser to append the form's data to the URL specified in the action attribute and send everything to the Web server in a single step. A question mark (?) separates the data from the URL.

If you don't specify a method, the browser uses the GET method by default.

A Servlet That Reads an HTML Form

The previous sections explain how servlets work, what you need to use and develop servlets, and how HTML forms are linked to servlets. This section shows you a simple Java servlet that retrieves the parameters that the user enters in the book order form shown in the section "Linking HTML Forms to Servlets" (see Figure 26-9).

The book order form uses a ⟨form⟩ tag that begins with the following:

```
<form action="../servlet/OrderBooks/" method=post>
```

This tells you that you need a servlet named OrderBooks to process the data sent by this form. Listing 26-4 of the OrderBooks.java file that implements the servlet:

Listing 26-4: The OrderBooks Servlet, Which Processes a Book Order Form

```
//-------------------------------------------------------------
// File: OrderBooks.java
// A servlet that demonstrates how to process data from
// a form.
```

(continued)

Listing 26-4: *(continued)*

```
//-------------------------------------------------------------
import java.util.*;
import java.io.*;
import javax.servlet.*;
import javax.servlet.http.*;
public class OrderBooks extends HttpServlet
{
    public void doPost(HttpServletRequest  request,
                       HttpServletResponse response)
                              throws ServletException, IOException
    {
        StringBuffer buffer = new StringBuffer();
        String title = "Received book order";
        // Set content type to HTML
        response.setContentType("text/html");
        // Write the response using HTML tags.
        PrintWriter out = response.getWriter();
        buffer.append("<html><head><title>");
        buffer.append(title);
        buffer.append("</title></head><body bgcolor=\"#ffffff\">");
        buffer.append("<h2>" + title + "</h2>");
        buffer.append("Customer ID: ");
        buffer.append(request.getParameter("id"));
        buffer.append("<br>");
        buffer.append("Password: ");
        buffer.append(request.getParameter("passwd"));
        buffer.append("<br>");
        buffer.append("Books Ordered: ");
        String books[] = request.getParameterValues("books");
        if(books == null)
            buffer.append("NONE<br>");
        else
        {
            buffer.append("<ul>");
            for(int i = 0; i < books.length; i++)
            {
                buffer.append("<li>");
                buffer.append(books[i]);
            }
            buffer.append("</ul>");
        }
        buffer.append("Charge to: ");
        buffer.append(request.getParameter("card"));
        buffer.append("<br>");
        buffer.append("Account Number: ");
        buffer.append(request.getParameter("acct"));
        buffer.append("<br>");
        buffer.append("<br>");
```

```
        buffer.append("Expiration Date: ");
        buffer.append(request.getParameter("expire"));
        buffer.append("<br>");
        buffer.append("Special Instructions = ");
        buffer.append(request.getParameter("instructions"));
        buffer.append("<hr>");
        buffer.append("<em>Order received at: ");
        buffer.append(new Date().toString());
        buffer.append("</em>");
        buffer.append("</body></html>");
        out.println(buffer.toString());
        out.close();
    }
}
```

A real-life `OrderBooks` servlet would use the customer's ID and password to authenticate the customer and retrieve the customer record from a database. Then, the servlet should probably display all of the information that will be used to process the order and allow the customer to confirm that information. Only then should the servlet actually record the order in the database. In this case, the `OrderBooks` servlet simply sends back the parameters received from the order form in another HTML document.

As Listing 26-4 illustrates, to use the servlet classes, you need to include the following `import` statements in a servlet:

```
import javax.servlet.*;
import javax.servlet.http.*;
```

Like everything else in Java, a servlet is also a class. Listing 26-4 defines `OrderBooks` as a subclass of the `HttpServlet` class (from the javax.servlet.http package):

```
public class OrderBooks extends HttpServlet
```

This is how you declare a servlet that is designed to work with the HTTP protocol (which is how the Web server communicates with the Web browser).

You implement the servlet by overriding the appropriate methods of the `HttpServlet` class. If you are designing the servlet to handle HTML form data, the method of form data submission—GET or POST—determines the method you have to override. If the form's data is submitted using the `GET` method, you should override the `doGet()` method. On the other hand, if the `method` attribute of the `<form>` tag is `POST`, you should override the `doPost()` method.

The `OrderBooks` servlet expects the form data to be sent by the `POST` method, so it overrides the `doPost()` method of the `HttpServlet` class. The `doPost()` declaration is as follows:

```
public void doPost(HttpServletRequest  request,
                   HttpServletResponse response)
                        throws ServletException, IOException
```

As this declaration shows, the `doPost()` method receives two arguments: an `HttpServletRequest` and an `HttpServletResponse`. The `doPost()` method throws two exceptions: `ServletException` and `IOException`. Apart from declaring the function like this, there is no need to handle any exceptions in the method.

In the body of the doPost() method, you use the HttpServletRequest interface to access HTTP-protocol-specified header information and any parameters sent by the Web browser. In particular, you would call this interface's getParameter() method to obtain the value of a parameter whose name matches the name assigned with the name attribute in the HTML tag. Recall from the discussion in the section "Linking HTML Forms to Servlets" that the name attribute of the <input>, <select>, and <textarea> HTML tags identifies the input parameter. You have to use the name of each as an argument when retrieving the parameter value with the getParameter() method. For example, to get the value that the user had entered for the HTML form element <input type=text size=10 name=id>, you would call request.getParameter("id").

The HttpServletResponse interface is used to send data back to the Web browser. You would set the MIME type of the servlet response by calling a method of this interface. For example, the following line of code sets the response type to text/html (this means that the servlet sends back a text file with HTML tags):

```
response.setContentType("text/html");
```

To actually send the response to the Web browser, you would get an output stream by calling a method of the HttpServletResponse interface, and then you would write the servlet's response to that output stream. For example, the OrderBooks servlet calls the getWriter() method of the HttpServletResponse interface named response to get a PrintWriter stream for formatted text output:

```
PrintWriter out = response.getWriter();
```

You can send HTML text to the Web browser client by calling the println() or print() method of this PrintWriter class. However, instead of writing text a line at a time, it's better to accumulate the text in a StringBuffer and then send the accumulated text with a single call to the println() method. The OrderBooks servlet illustrates this approach. For example, here is a line that initializes a StringBuffer named buffer:

```
StringBuffer buffer = new StringBuffer();
```

The servlet's response is then accumulated in this buffer through calls to the append() method of StringBuffer. For example, the following lines of code append the HTML <head> and <body> tags to the buffer:

```
buffer.append("<html><head><title>");
buffer.append(title);
buffer.append("</title></head><body
            bgcolor=\"#ffffff\">");
```

If a parameter can have multiple values, you have to call the getParameterValues() method. In the book order form, the customer may select multiple books from the selection menu (in the HTML form that menu is assigned the name books). For example, the following code shows how to get the values of the books parameter and format them in an unnumbered list enclosed in the HTML tags <ul> and </ul>:

```
String books[] = request.getParameterValues("books");
if(books == null)
    buffer.append("NONE<br>");
else
{
```

```
        buffer.append("<ul>");
        for(int i = 0; i < books.length; i++)
        {
            buffer.append("<li>");
            buffer.append(books[i]);
        }
        buffer.append("</ul>");
    }
```

The first line calls `getParameterValues()` to get the values in a `String` array named `books[]`. If the return value is `null`, the string `NONE` is appended to the buffer. Otherwise, the for each returned value is appended to the buffer as an entry in an unnumbered list.

After everything has been appended to the `StringBuffer`, the `println()` method of the `PrintWriter` class is used to send the response to the client:

```
    out.println(buffer.toString());
```

After the response has been written to the `PrintWriter`, you should close the stream like this:

```
    out.close();
```

Testing Java Servlet with Apache httpd and Tomcat

To test the `OrderBooks` servlet, you need a Web server capable of running Java servlets. I tested the servlet by using a Apache `httpd` server that used the Apache Tomcat server to support servlets.

---

cross ref Consult Chapter 14 for detailed instructions on how to download and configure Apache Tomcat to work with Apache `httpd` server. You need to complete that step before you can try out the servlet.

I log in as `root` and follow these steps to compile and test the `OrderBooks` servlet shown in Listing 26-4:

1. Check that the `CATALINA_HOME` environment variable is set to the directory where Apache Tomcat is installed (as explained in Chapter 14). On my system, `CATALINA_HOME` is set as follows:
   ```
   export CATALINA_HOME=/usr/local/jakarta-tomcat-4.1.18-LE-jdk14
   ```

2. Copy the `OrderBooks.java` file to the location where the classes for the servlet examples should be located. In my case, I type the following command:
   ```
   cp OrderBooks.java $CATALINA_HOME/webapps/examples/WEB-INF/classes
   ```

3. Change directory to where the `OrderBooks.java` file is saved and then compile the file. Here are the commands I type:
   ```
   cd $CATALINA_HOME/webapps/examples/WEB-INF/classes
   javac OrderBooks.java
   ```

4. Copy the HTML file shown in Listing 26-3—`OrderBooks.html`—to the directory where the Apache Tomcat servlet examples are located. In my case, I type the following command to copy the HTML file to the correct location:

```
cp OrderBooks.html $CATALINA_HOME/webapps/examples/servlets
```

5. Start Apache Tomcat with the following command:

```
$CATALINA_HOME/bin/startup.sh
```

6. Wait ten seconds or so and then start Apache `httpd` server with the following command:

```
service httpd start
```

7. Start the Mozilla Web browser and point the Web browser to the following URL:

```
http://localhost/examples/servlets/OrderBooks.html
```

This causes the HTML form that was shown in Figure 26-9 to appear.

8. I fill in some information the information in the form and click Order. Mozilla displays some dialog boxes about sending unencrypted information. I click OK, and Mozilla displays the HTML document returned by the `OrderBooks` servlet. Figure 26-10 shows the servlet's response to what I entered on the book order form.

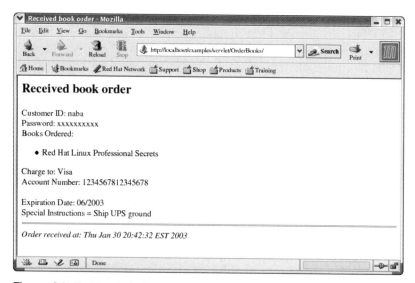

Figure 26-10: The OrderBooks Servlet Displays What the User Entered in the Book Order Form.

Becoming Proficient in Java

To become a proficient Java programmer, you have to become familiar with the Java language as well as the classes and methods available in various Java APIs. The best way to do so is to begin using some of these classes in your Java programs—whether you are writing applets, servlets, or standalone programs. Unfortunately, this chapter simply does not have enough room to cover all of the Java APIs in detail. It really takes an entire book (maybe more) to cover Java programming in detail. Because Java is very popular, there is no shortage of reference material on Java. In fact, the problem is in deciding which one of the many Java books best suits your needs. Here are a few suggestions for reference books on Java programming:

♦ Ken Arnold, James Gosling, and David Holmes, *The Java Programming Language*, 3rd Edition (Addison-Wesley, 2000). You may want a copy of this book for the very reason that C++ programmers may want a copy of *The C++ Programming Language* by Bjarne Stroustrup (Addison-Wesley, 1997)—James Gosling is the originator of Java. This book provides a concise and precise presentation of how Java works and why. It's not a tutorial guide, but professional Java developers will find this book worthwhile.

♦ Barry Burd, *Java 2 For Dummies* (John Wiley & Sons, 2001). This is a good introduction to Java 2 in the popular and well-known Dummies style.

For Java APIs, look for API documentations, tutorials, and code samples at Sun's Java website at the following URL:

```
http://developer.java.sun.com/developer/infodocs/
```

Summary

Java is an object-oriented programming language that you can use to develop applets, servlets, and standalone applications. This chapter provides you an overview of Java and gets you started with a few simple programming examples.

By reading this chapter, you learned the following:

♦ To write Java programs, you need a Java development environment. One freely available Java environment is the Java 2 Standard Edition Software Developers Kit (Java 2 SDK or J2SE SDK) from Sun Microsystems. You can download the Java 2 SDK from `http://java.sun.com/j2se/downloads.html`.

♦ If you want to develop servlets, you also need the Java 2 Enterprise Edition (J2EE) SDK. You can download the J2EE SDK by following the links from `http://java.sun.com/products/servlet/download.html`.

♦ The compiled Java code is known as Java byte code.

♦ There are several types of Java programs—standalone Java applications, applets, and servlets. Standalone applications can be executed using the Java interpreter that comes with the Java 2 SDK. Java applets must be embedded in an HTML document and run under the `appletviewer` (a program that comes with the Java 2 SDK) or a Java-capable Web browser. Java servlets run on the Web server and typically perform tasks such as process HTML forms, access a database, and prepare dynamic HTML documents.

♦ To embed a Java applet in an HTML document, you use the `<applet>` tag.

♦ Java has a syntax that's similar to that of C and C++. Like C++, Java is an object-oriented programming language. Everything in Java must be an object. Unlike C and C++, Java does not allow any standalone functions.

◆ Java supports both C-style comments (enclosed within /*...*/) and C++-style comments (comment begins with //). Additionally, Java also supports a third-style comment that begins with /** and ends with */ (this style of comment is called a doc comment).

◆ A Java class defines an object type. The class is the template from which an object can be created (or instantiated). The class includes data and procedures that operate on the data. These procedures are referred to as methods.

◆ A class can inherit from another class thereby establishing a parent-child relationship. The parent class is referred to as the superclass, and the child class is called the subclass. Unlike C++, Java supports single inheritance only—that means a subclass can inherit from at most one superclass.

◆ Java supports the primitive C data types (such as int, char, float, double) as well as the basic programming C constructs (such as for, while, if...else). Java introduces two new primitive types: boolean and byte.

◆ Java does not include any pointers. Unlike C and C++, you cannot manipulate pointers to access blocks of memory.

◆ Java introduces the interface keyword, which is a set of methods that any class may implement. The interface defines a set of capabilities.

◆ Java supports multiple threads, where each thread is an independent sequence of execution. That means a single application or applet may have multiple independent threads of execution—it's multitasking at the individual process level. You can have a thread download data from the server while another thread updates the applet's display.

◆ Like the run-time library in C, Java comes with a number of class packages— these are the foundation classes on which you build a Java application. For example, Java applets are subclassed from the Applet class in the java.applet package. Applets display user interfaces (such as buttons and menus) and generate graphics output by using classes from the java.awt package.

◆ Java Foundation Classes (JFC), included in the Java 2 SDK, includes the Swing classes that enable you to create more complex GUIs in Java.

Part VI

Appendixes

Linux Commands

A

♦ ♦

This appendix presents alphabetically arranged reference entries for the most important Linux commands. The goal here is to provide you with an overview of all commands needed to manage files and directories, start and stop processes, find files, work with text files, and access online help.

If you are looking for a command for a specific task, but don't know which command to use, you may find it helpful to browse through the commands by category. Table A-1 shows the Linux commands organized by categories.

Table A-1: Linux Commands

Command Name	Action
Getting Online Help	
apropos	Finds man pages for a specified keyword
info	Displays online help information about a specified command
man	Displays online help information
whatis	Similar to apropos, but searches for complete words only
Making Commands Easier	
alias	Defines an abbreviation for a long command
type	Shows the type and location of a command
unalias	Deletes an abbreviation defined using alias

(continued)

Table A-1: *(continued)*

Command Name	Action
Managing Files and Directories	
cd	Changes the current directory
chattr	Changes file attributes in Linux ext2 and ext3 file systems
chgrp	Changes group ownership of file
chmod	Changes file permissions
chown	Changes file owner and group
cp	Copies files
ln	Creates symbolic links to files and directories
ls	Displays the contents of a directory
mkdir	Creates a directory
mv	Renames a file as well as moves a file from one directory to another
rm	Deletes files
rmdir	Deletes directories
pwd	Displays the current directory
touch	Updates a file's time stamp
Finding Files	
find	Finds files based on specified criteria such as name, size, and so on
lsof	List open files
locate	Finds files using a periodically updated database
whereis	Finds files based in the typical directories where executable (also known as binary) files are located
which	Finds files in the directories listed in the PATH environment variable
Processing Files	
cat	Displays a file on standard output (can be used to concatenate several files into one big file)
cut	Extracts specified sections from each line of text in a file
dd	Copies blocks of data from one file to another (used to copy data from devices)
diff	Compares two text files and finds any differences
expand	Converts all tabs into spaces
file	Displays the type of data in a file
fold	Wraps each line of text to fit a specified width
grep	Searches for regular expressions within a text file
less	Displays a text file, one page at a time (can go backwards also)

Command Name	Action
lpr	Prints files
more	Displays a text file, one page at a time (goes forward only)
nl	Numbers all nonblank lines in a text file and prints the lines to standard output
paste	Concatenates corresponding lines from several files
patch	Updates a text file using the differences between the original and revised copy of the file
sed	Copies a file to standard output while applying specified editing commands
sort	Sorts lines in a text file
split	Breaks up a file into several smaller files with specified size
tac	Reverses a file (last line first and so on)
tail	Displays the last few lines of a file
tr	Substitutes one group of characters for another throughout a file
uniq	Eliminates duplicate lines from a text file
wc	Counts the number of lines, words, and characters in a text file
zcat	Displays a compressed file (after decompressing)
zless	Displays a compressed file one page at a time (can go backwards also)
zmore	Displays a compressed file one page at a time

Archiving and Compressing Files

compress	Compresses files
cpio	Copies files to and from an archive
gunzip	Decompresses files compressed with GNU ZIP (gzip) or compress
gzip	Compresses files (more powerful than compress)
tar	Creates an archive of files in one or more directories (originally meant for archiving on tape)
uncompress	Decompresses files compressed with compress

Managing Processes

bg	Runs an interrupted process in the background
fg	Runs a process in the foreground
free	Displays the amount of free and used memory in the system
halt	Shuts down Linux and halts the computer
kill	Sends a signal to a process (usually used to terminate a process)
ldd	Displays the shared libraries needed to run a program
nice	Runs a process with lower priority (referred to as *nice mode*)

(continued)

Table A-1: *(continued)*

Command Name	Action
ps	Displays a list of currently running processes
printenv	Displays the current environment variables
pstree	Similar to ps, but shows parent-child relationships clearly
reboot	Stops Linux and then restarts the computer
shutdown	Shuts down Linux
top	Displays a list of most processor- and memory-intensive processes
uname	Displays information about the system and the Linux kernel

Managing Users

chsh	Changes the shell (command interpreter)
groups	Prints the list of groups that includes a specified user
id	Displays the user and group ID for a specified user name
passwd	Changes the password
su	Starts a new shell as another user or root (when invoked without any argument)

Managing the File System

df	Summarizes free and available space in all mounted storage devices
du	Displays disk usage information
fdformat	Formats a diskette
fdisk	Partitions a hard disk
fsck	Checks and repairs a file system
mkfs	Creates a new file system
mknod	Creates a device file
mkswap	Creates a swap space for Linux in a file or a disk partition
mount	Mounts a device (for example, the CD-ROM) on a directory in the file system
swapoff	Deactivates a swap space
swapon	Activates a swap space
sync	Writes buffered data to files
tty	Displays the device name for the current terminal
umount	Unmounts a device from the file system

Working with Date and Time

cal	Displays a calendar for a specified month or year
date	Shows the current date and time or sets a new date and time

The rest of this appendix covers individual reference entries for each command shown in Table A-1. Each reference entry is organized as follows:

◆ *Purpose* tells you when to use the command.

◆ *Syntax* shows the syntax of the command with a few common options. Also, typical option values are shown. All optional items are shown in square brackets.

◆ *Options* lists most options, along with a brief description of each option. For many commands, you will find all options listed in this section. However, some commands have too many options to cover here. For those commands, I describe the most commonly used options.

◆ *Description* describes the command and provides more details about how to use it.

alias

Purpose Define an abbreviation for a long command or view the current list of abbreviations.

Syntax `alias [abbrev=command]`

Options None

Description If you type **alias** alone, you get a listing of all currently defined abbreviations. Typically, you use `alias` to define easy-to-remember abbreviations for longer commands. For example, if you type **ls -l** often, you might add a line with `alias ll='ls -l'` in the .bashrc file in your home directory. Then, you can type **ll** instead of **ls -l** to see a detailed listing of a directory. `alias` is a built-in command of the bash shell and is described in Chapter 7.

apropos

Purpose View a list of all man pages that contain a specific keyword.

Syntax `apropos keyword`

Options None

Description The `apropos` command looks up the keyword in a database (known as the `whatis` database) the `/usr/sbin/makewhatis` program creates. The `whatis` database is an index of keywords contained in all of the man pages in the system. Unfortunately, when you try `apropos` with a simple keyword such as find, you may end up with a long listing of man pages because the word find appears in many man pages.

bg

Purpose Run an interrupted process in the background.

Syntax `bg`

Options None

Description After you type a command that takes a long time to finish, you can press Ctrl-Z to interrupt the process. Then, you can type **bg** to continue that command in the background while you type other commands at the shell prompt. `bg` is a built-in command of the Bash shell.

cal

Purpose View the calendar of any month in any year.

Syntax `cal`
`cal [-jy] [[month_number] year]]`

Options `-j` displays Julian dates (days numbered between 1 and 366).

`-y` displays the calendar for all months of the current year.

Description	If you type **cal** without any options, it prints a calendar for the current month. If you type **cal** followed by a number, `cal` treats the number as the year and prints the calendar for that year. To view the calendar for a specific month in a specific year, provide the month number (1 = January, 2 = February, and so on) followed by the year. Thus, to view the calendar for April 2003, type the following:

```
cal 4 2003
      April 2003
Su Mo Tu We Th Fr Sa
       1  2  3  4  5
 6  7  8  9 10 11 12
13 14 15 16 17 18 19
20 21 22 23 24 25 26
27 28 29 30
```

cat

Purpose	Copy contents of a file to standard output (the screen).
Syntax	`cat [-benstvA]` *files*
Options	`-b` numbers nonblank lines.
	`-e` shows each end-of-line (as $) and all nonprinting characters.
	`-n` numbers all output lines starting with number 1.
	`-s` replaces multiple blank lines with a single blank line.
	`-t` shows tabs as ^I .
	`-v` shows nonprinting characters.
	`-A` shows all characters (including nonprinting ones).
Description	Typically, `cat` is used to display the contents of a file or to concatenate several files into a single file. For example, `cat file1 file2 file3 > all` combines three files into a single file named `all`.

cd

Purpose	Change the current directory.
Syntax	`cd [`*directory*`]`
Options	None
Description	Typing `cd` without a directory name changes the current directory to your home directory. Otherwise, `cd` changes to the specified directory. `cd` is a built-in command of the Bash shell.

chattr

Purpose	Change file attributes in Linux ext2 and ext3 file systems.
Syntax	`chattr [ -RV ] [ -v `*version*` ] [ `*mode*` ] `*files*`...`
Options	`-V` verbosely displays permission changes.
	`-v` *version* sets the version number of the file to *version*.
Description	The attribute is defined by the *mode* argument and mode is of the form +-=[ASacdisu], where the + causes the specified attributes to be added to the existing attributes of the files, - causes them to be removed from the existing attributes, and = causes the file attributes to be set to only the specified attributes. The letters ASacdisu specify the attributes for the files: A means do not update `atime` (`atime` is the time when file was accessed), S means synchronous updates, a means append only, c means compressed, i means immutable (file cannot be changed), d means no dump, s means secure deletion (file contents are completely wiped out when it is deleted), and u means undeletable (file cannot be removed).

chgrp

Purpose	Change the group ownership of one or more files.
Syntax	chmod [-cfvR] *group files*
Options	-c lists only files whose permissions have changed.
	-f stops any error message displays.
	-v verbosely displays permission changes.
	-R recursively changes permissions of files in all subdirectories.
Description	To change the group ownership of one or more files, invoke chgrp with the group name followed by the filenames (you can also change the group ownership by using the chown command).

chmod

Purpose	Change the permission settings of one or more files.
Syntax	chmod [-cfvR] *permission files*
Options	-c lists only files whose permissions have changed.
	-f stops any error message displays.
	-v verbosely displays permission changes.
	-R recursively changes permissions of files in all subdirectories.
Description	To use chmod effectively, you have to learn how to specify the permission settings. One way is to concatenate one letter from each of the following tables in the order shown (*Who/Action/Permission*):

Who	Action	Permission
u user	+ add	r read
g group	- remove	w write
o others	= assign	x execute
a all	s set user ID	

To give everyone read access to all files in a directory, type **chmod a+r ***. On the other hand, to permit everyone to execute a specific file, type **chmod +x filename**.

Another way to specify a permission setting is to use a three-digit sequence of octal numbers. In a detailed listing, the read, write, and execute permission settings for the user, group, and others appear as the sequence rwxrwxrwx (with dashes in place of letters for disallowed operations). Think of rwxrwxrwx as three occurrences of the string rwx. Now, assign the values r=4, w=2, and x=1. To get the value of the sequence rwx, simply add the values of r, w, and x. Thus, rwx = 7. Using this formula, you can assign a three-digit value to any permission setting. For example, if the user can read and write the file but everyone else can only read the file, the permission setting is rw-r—r— (that's how it appears in the listing), and the value is 644. Thus, if you want all files in a directory to be readable by everyone but writable by only the user, use the command chmod 644 *.

chown

Purpose	Change the user and group ownership of a file.
Syntax	chown [cvfR] *username.groupname files*
Options	-c lists only files whose ownership have changed.
	-f stops any error message displays.
	-v verbosely displays ownership changes.
	-R recursively changes the ownership of files in all subdirectories.

Description To make a user the owner of one or more files, invoke chown with the user name followed by the filenames. To change the group ownership as well, append the new group name to the user name with a period as separator. For example, to make user naba the owner of all files in a directory, type **chown naba ***. To change both the owner and group to naba, type **chown naba.naba ***. Note that you have to be logged in as root to change the ownership of files.

chsh

Purpose Change the default shell started at login.

Syntax chsh [-s *shell*] [*username*]

Options -s shell specifies the name of the shell executable to use (shell can be any program listed in the /etc/shells file, such as /bin/bash and /bin/csh).

Description A user's default shell is stored in the /etc/passwd file. The chsh command lets you change the default shell to any of the shells listed in the /etc/shells file. If you type **chsh** without any arguments, chsh prompts you for the name of a shell.

compress

Purpose Compress one or more files by using Lempel-Ziv compression.

Syntax compress [-cdrvV] *files*

Options -c writes the compressed file to the standard output and retains the original file.

-d decompresses the file.

-r recursively compresses files in all subdirectories.

-v displays a message as each file is compressed.

-V prints the version number and exits.

Description The compress command compresses each specified file and replaces the original with the compressed version (with a .Z suffix appended to the name). You can decompress the file with the compress -d command or the uncompress command.

cp

Purpose Copy files and directories.

Syntax cp [*options*] *source_files destination_directory*
cp [*options*] *source_file destination_file*

Options -a preserves all file attributes.

-b makes a backup copy before copying.

-d copies a link but not the file pointed to by the link.

-i asks for confirmation before overwriting files.

-l creates hard links instead of copying files.

-p preserves ownership, permissions, and the file time stamp.

-R recursively copies files in all subdirectories.

-s creates soft links instead of copying files.

-u copies a file only when the file being copied is newer than the destination.

-v displays verbose messages as copying progresses.

-help displays a Help message about cp.

Description The cp command copies one file to another. You can also copy several files from one directory to another.

cpio

Purpose Copy files in from, or out to, an archive that can be on a storage medium such as tape or a file on the disk.

Syntax	`cpio [-icdv] pattern`
	`cpio [-ocBv] pattern`
	`cpio [-padm] pattern`

Options	`-i` extracts files whose names match the *pattern*.

`-o` copies files to archive files whose names are provided on standard input.

`-p` copies files to another directory on the same system.

`-a` resets access times of input files.

`-B` copies files using 5,120 bytes per record (the default is 512 bytes per record).

`-c` reads or writes header information as ASCII characters.

`-d` creates directories as needed.

`-m` retains the previous file-modification time.

`-v` prints a list of filenames.

Description The `cpio` command copies files in from, and out to, archives. There are three distinct variants of the `cpio` command: `cpio -o` creates an archive, `cpio -i` extracts from an archive, and `cpio -p` copies from one directory to another. `cpio` is not that popular among Linux users; `tar` is much more commonly used. However, some installation programs use `cpio` during the installation process.

cut

Purpose	Copy selected parts of each line of text from a file to standard output.
Syntax	`cut [options] file`
Options	`-b list` extracts the characters at positions specified in the *list*.

`-f list` extracts the fields (assumed to be Tab-separated) specified in *list*.

`-d char` specifies the character that delimits the fields (the default is Tab).

`-s` skips lines that do not contain delimited fields (see the `-f` option).

Description The `cut` command extracts specified parts from each line of text in a file and writes those lines out to standard output. You can extract either a range of characters (specified by their positions) from each line or specific fields, where the fields are separated by a special character such as the Tab. For example, to extract characters 1 through 11 and the 56th character onward from a detailed directory listing, use the following command:

```
ls -l | cut -b 1-11,56- | more
total 2056
-rw-r—r—  a2ps.cfg
-rw-r—r—  a2ps-site.cfg
-rw-r—r—  adjtime
drwxr-xr-x  aep
-rw-r—r—  aep.conf
-rw-r—r—  aeplog.conf
drwxr-xr-x  alchemist
-rw-r—r—  aliases
-rw-r—-  aliases.db
(... lines deleted)
```

date

Purpose	Display the current date and time or set a new date and time.
Syntax	`date [options] [+format]` `date [-su] [MMDDHHMM[[CC]YY][.SS]]`
Options	`-u` displays or sets the time using Greenwich Mean Time (GMT).

Description The `date` command alone displays the current date and time. Using the `+format` argument, you can specify a display format for the date and time. For a complete listing of the format specification, type **man date**.

To set the date, use `date` followed by the date and time in the MMDDHHMM format, where each character is a digit (MM is the month, DD is the day, HH the hour, and MM the minutes). You can optionally specify the year (YY) and century (CC) as well.

dd

Purpose Copy blocks of data from standard input to standard output (and optionally convert the data from one format to another).

Syntax `dd option1=value1 option2=value2 option3=value3 ...`

Options `if=file` reads from the specified file instead of standard input.

`of=file` writes to the specified file instead of standard output.

`ibs=nbytes` reads blocks of `nbytes` bytes at a time.

`ibs=nbytes` writes blocks of `nbytes` at a time.

`bs=nbytes` reads and writes blocks of `nbyte` bytes at a time.

`cbs=nbytes` converts `nbytes` bytes at a time.

`skip=nblocks` skips `nblocks` input blocks from the beginning of the input file.

`seek=nblocks` skips `nblocks` output blocks in the output file.

`count=nblocks` copies `nblocks` blocks from input to output.

`conv=code` performs conversion; `code` can be one of following:

  `ascii` converts EBCDIC to ASCII.

  `ebcdic` converts ASCII to EBCDIC.

  `lcase` converts to lowercase.

  `ucase` converts to uppercase.

  `swab` swaps every pair of input bytes.

  `noerror` continues after read errors.

  (Note: EBCDIC is a character-encoding format used in IBM mainframes.)

Description The `dd` command copies blocks of data from standard input to standard output, optionally converting the data as the copying proceeds. Typically, `dd` is used to copy data directly from one device to another. For example, you can copy the Linux kernel (`/boot/vmlinuz`) to a diskette with the following command: `dd if=/boot/vmlinuz of=/dev/fd0`

df

Purpose Display the amount of free and used storage space on all mounted file systems.

Syntax `df [options] [filesystem]`

Options `-a` displays information for all file systems.

`-i` displays inode information (the disk is organized into inodes).

`-T` prints the type of file system.

`-t type` displays information about specified types of file systems only.

`-x type` excludes specified types of file systems from the output.

`—help` displays a Help message.

Description The `df` command shows the amount of free and used space on a specified file system. If you want to know how filled up all of your disks are, use the `df` command without any arguments. The `df` command then displays information about used and available storage space on all currently mounted file systems.

diff

Purpose   Show the difference between two text files (or all files with the same names in two directories).

Syntax   `diff [options]` *from_file* *to_file*

Options   `-a` treats all files as text even if they aren't text files.

`-b` ignores blank lines and repeated blanks.

`-c` produces output in a different format.

`-d` tries to find a smaller set of changes (this makes `diff` slower).

`-e` produces a script for the `ed` editor to convert `from_file` to `to_file`.

`-f` produces output similar to that of `-e`, but in reverse order.

`-i` ignores case.

`-l` passes the output to the `pr` command to paginate it.

`-n` works like `-f`, but counts the number of changed lines.

`-r` recursively compares files with the same name in all subdirectories.

`-s` reports when two files are the same.

`-t` expands tabs to spaces in the output.

`-u` uses the unified output format.

`-v` displays the version of `diff`.

`-w` ignores spaces and tabs when comparing lines.

Description   The `diff` command compares *from_file* with *to_file* and displays the lines that differ. The output is in a format the patch command can use to convert *from_file* to *to_file*.

du

Purpose   Display summary information about disk usage (in kilobytes).

Syntax   `du [options] [`*directories_or_files*`]`

Options   `-a` displays usage information for all files (not just directories).

`-b` displays usage in bytes (instead of kilobytes).

`-c` displays a grand total of all usage information.

`-k` displays usage information in kilobytes (default).

`-s` displays total disk usage without per directory details.

Description   The `du` command displays the disk space (in kilobytes) the specified files or directories use. By default, `du` displays the disk space that each directory and subdirectory uses. A common use of `du` is to view the total space the current directory uses. For example, here is how you might check the details of disk space the `/var/log` directory uses:

```
du /var/log
4       /var/log/vbox
4       /var/log/httpd
4       /var/log/squid
4       /var/log/samba
3312    /var/log/cups
8       /var/log/gdm
4       /var/log/news/OLD
8       /var/log/news
3696    /var/log
```

expand

Purpose   Write files to standard output after expanding each tab into an appropriate number of spaces.

Syntax   `expand [options] [files]`

Options   `-n` (where *n* is a number) sets the tabs *n* spaces apart.

                 `-n1 [n2, ...]` (where *n1*, *n2*,... are numbers) specifies the tab stops.

                 `-i` converts only the initial tab into spaces.

Description   The `expand` command reads from the specified files (or standard input, if no files are specified) and writes them to standard output, with each tab character expanded to an appropriate number of spaces. By default, `expand` assumes that the tab positions are eight spaces apart (equivalent to the `-8` option).

fdformat

Purpose   Format a diskette specified by device name (such as `/dev/fd0H1440` for a 3.5-inch, high-density diskette in drive A).

Syntax   `fdformat [-n] device_name`

Options   `-n` disables the verification performed after formatting.

Description   The `fdformat` command formats a diskette. Use an appropriate device name to identify the diskette drive (see Chapter 12 for naming conventions for diskette drives). After formatting a diskette with `fdformat`, you can use `mkfs` to install a Linux file system or `tar` to store an archive.

fdisk

Purpose   Partition a disk or display information about existing partitions.

Syntax   `fdisk [options] [device_name]`

Options   `-l` displays partition tables and exits.

                 `-s device` displays the size of the specified partition.

                 `-v` displays the version number of the `fdisk` program.

Description   The `fdisk` command partitions a specified hard disk (see Appendix B for disk-drive naming conventions). You can also use `fdisk` to display information about existing partitions. You should never run `fdisk` and alter the partitions of a hard disk while one or more of its partitions are mounted on the Linux file system. Instead, you should boot from an installation diskette (or a boot diskette) and perform the partitioning. Remember that partitioning typically destroys all existing data on a hard disk.

fg

Purpose   Continue an interrupted process in the foreground.

Syntax   `fg`

Options   None

Description   After you interrupt a process by pressing Ctrl-Z, you can continue that process in the foreground by typing the `fg` command. Note that `fg` is a built-in command of the Bash shell.

file

Purpose   Display the type of data in a file based on rules defined in the `/usr/lib/magic` file (this is known as the *magic file*).

Syntax   `file [options] files`

Options   `-c` displays a parsed form of a magic file (or the default one) and exits.

                 `-m file1[:file2 : . . .]` specifies other magic files.

-v displays the version number and exits.

-z looks inside compressed files.

Description   The file command uses rules specified in the /usr/lib/magic file to determine the type of data in the specified files. For example, you can use the file command to check the type of each file in the /usr/lib directory, as shown here:

```
file * | more
alchemist:                          directory
ao:                                 directory
appletproxy.la:                     ASCII English text, with
                                    very long lines
appletproxy.so:                     ELF 32-bit LSB shared
                                    object, Intel 80386,
                                    version 1 (SYSV),
                                    stripped
aspell:                             directory
autofs:                             directory
bash:                               directory
bcc:                                directory
bonobo:                             directory
bonobo-2.0:                         directory
bonobo_confConf.sh:                 ASCII English text, with
                                    very long lines
bonoboConf.sh:                      ASCII English text, with
                                    very long lines
bonoboxConf.sh:                     ASCII English text, with
                                    very long lines
bonobox_printConf.sh:               ASCII English text, with
                                    very long lines
cracklib_dict.hwm:                  data
cracklib_dict.pwd:                  data
cracklib_dict.pwi:                  data
(. . . lines deleted)
```

find

Purpose   Display a list of files that match a specified set of criteria.

Syntax   find [*path*] [options]

Options   -depth processes the current directory first, then subdirectories.

-maxdepth *n* restricts searches to *n* levels of directories.

-follow processes directories included through symbolic links.

-name *pattern* finds files whose names match the *pattern*.

-ctime *n* matches files modified exactly *n* days ago.

-user *uname* finds files the specified user owns.

-group *gname* finds files the specified group owns.

-path *pattern* finds files whose pathname matches the *pattern*.

-perm *mode* finds files with the specified permission setting.

-size +*n*K finds files bigger than *n* kilobytes.

-type *x* finds files of a specified type, where *x* is one of the following:

    f matches files.

    d matches directories.

    l matches symbolic links.

-print displays the names of the files found.

-exec *command* [*options*] {} \; executes the specified command by passing it the name of the file that was found.

Description The find command is useful for finding all files that match a specified set of criteria. If you type **find** without any arguments, the output is a listing of every file in all sub-directories of the current directory. To view all files whose names end with .gz, type **find . -name "*.gz"**.

fold

Purpose Wrap lines of text to a specified width (the default is 80 characters).

Syntax fold [options] [*files*]

Options -b counts bytes instead of columns, so backspaces and tabs are counted.

-s breaks lines at word boundaries.

-w *N* (where *N* is a number) sets line width to *N* characters.

Description The fold command wraps each input line to a specified number of characters and displays the results on the screen (standard output). If you do not specify any file-name, fold reads lines from the standard input.

free

Purpose Display the amount of free and used memory in the system.

Syntax free [options]

Options -b displays memory in number of bytes.

-k displays memory in kilobytes (default).

-m displays memory in megabytes.

-s *n* repeats the command every *n* seconds.

-t displays a line containing a summary of the total amounts.

Description The free command displays information about the physical memory (RAM) and the swap area (on the disk). The output shows the total amount of memory, as well as the amount used and the amount free.

fsck

Purpose Check and repair a Linux file system.

Syntax fsck [options] *device_name*

Options -A checks all file systems listed in the /etc/fstab file.

-R skips the root file system (when checking all file systems).

-T does not show the title on startup.

-N shows what might be done but does not actually do anything.

-V produces verbose output.

-t *fstype* specifies the file-system type (such as ext2).

-n answers all confirmation requests with no (only for the ext2 file system).

-p carries out all repairs without asking for confirmation (for ext2).

-y answers all confirmation requests with yes (only for the ext2 file system).

Description The fsck command checks the integrity of a file system and carries out any necessary repairs. Depending on the type of file system, fsck runs an appropriate command to check and repair the file system. For example, to check an ext2 file system, fsck runs the e2fsck program. You have to run fsck when you power down your system without running the shutdown command. Typically, fsck is automatically run during system startup.

grep

Purpose Search one or more files for lines that match a regular expression (a search pattern).

Syntax `grep [options]` *pattern files*

Options `-N` (where *N* is a number) displays *N* lines around the line containing *pattern*.

`-c` shows the number of lines that contain the search pattern.

`-f` *file* reads options from a specified file.

`-i` ignores case.

`-l` displays the filenames that contain *pattern*.

`-n` displays a line number next to lines that contain *pattern*.

`-q` returns a status code but does not display any output.

`-v` displays the lines that do not contain *pattern*.

`-w` matches only whole words.

Description The `grep` command searches the specified files for a pattern. The pattern is a regular expression that has its own rules. Typically, you use `grep` to search for a specific sequence of characters in one or more text files.

groups

Purpose Show the groups to which a user belongs.

Syntax `groups [`*username*`]`

Options None

Description The `groups` command displays the names of groups to which a user belongs. If you do not specify a user name, the command displays your groups.

gunzip

Purpose Decompresses files the `gzip` or the `compress` command compresses.

Syntax `gunzip [options]` *files*

Options See the options for `gzip`.

Description The `gunzip` command decompresses compressed files (these files have the `.gz` or `.Z` extension). After decompressing, `gunzip` replaces the compressed files with their decompressed versions and removes the `.gz` or `.Z` extension in the filenames. The `gunzip` command is the same as `gzip` with the `-d` option.

gzip

Purpose Compress one or more files.

Syntax `gzip [options]` *files*

Options `-c` writes output to standard output and retains the original file.

`-d` decompresses the file (same as `gunzip`).

`-h` displays a Help message.

`-l` lists the contents of a compressed file.

`-n` does not save the original name and time stamp.

`-r` recursively compresses files in all subdirectories.

`-v` displays verbose output.

`-V` displays the version number.

Description The `gzip` command compresses files using Lempel-Ziv (LZ77) coding, which produces better compression than the algorithm the `compress` command uses. After compressing a file, `gzip` replaces the original file with the compressed version and appends a `.gz` to the filename.

halt

Purpose Terminate all processes and halt the system (you must log in as `root`).

Syntax `halt [options]`

Options `-n` does not flush out in-memory buffers to disk before halting the system.

`-f` forces a halt without calling the `/sbin/shutdown` command.

`-i` shuts down all network interfaces before halting the system.

Description The `halt` command lets the super user (root) terminate all processes and halt the system. The `halt` command invokes `/sbin/shutdown` with the `-h` option.

id

Purpose List the user ID, group ID, and groups for a user.

Syntax `id [options] [username]`

Options `-g` displays group ID only.

`-n` displays group name instead of ID.

`-u` displays user ID only.

Description The `id` command displays the user ID, the group ID, and the groups for a specified user. If you do not provide a user name, `id` displays information about the current user.

info

Purpose View online help information about any Linux command.

Syntax `info [options] command`

Options `-d dirname` adds a directory to a list of directories to be searched for files.

`-f infofile` specifies the file to be used by `info`.

`-h` displays usage information about info.

Description The `info` command displays online help information about a specified command in a full-screen text window. You can use Emacs commands to navigate the text displayed by `info`. To learn more about `info`, type **info** without any arguments.

kill

Purpose Send a signal to a process.

Syntax `kill [options] process_id`

Options `-signum` (where `signum` is a number or name) sends the specified signal.

`-l` lists the signal names and numbers.

Description The `kill` command sends a signal to a process. Typically, the signal is meant to terminate the process. For example, `kill -9 123` terminates the process with ID 123. To see process IDs, use the `ps` command. To see a list of signal names and numbers, type **kill -l** (that's a lowercase "L").

ldd

Purpose Display the names of shared libraries required to run a program.

Syntax `ldd [options] programs`

Options `-v` prints the version number of `ldd`.

`-V` prints the version number of the dynamic linker (`ld.so`).

`-d` relocates functions and reports missing functions.

`-r` relocates both data and functions and reports missing objects.

Description   The ldd command lets you determine which shared libraries are needed to run the specified programs. For example, to determine what you need to run the Bash shell (/bin/bash), type the following:

```
ldd /bin/bash
        libtermcap.so.2 => /lib/libtermcap.so.2 (0x40029000)
        libdl.so.2 => /lib/libdl.so.2 (0x4002d000)
        libc.so.6 => /lib/tls/libc.so.6 (0x42000000)
        /lib/ld-linux.so.2 => /lib/ld-linux.so.2 (0x40000000)
```

less

Purpose   View text files one screen at a time (and scroll backwards if necessary).

Syntax   less [options] *filenames*

Options   -? displays a list of commands you can use in less.

-p *text* displays the first line where *text* is found.

-s reduces multiple blank lines to a single blank line.

Description   The less command displays the specified files one screen at a time. Unlike when you use more, you can press b, Ctrl-B, or Esc-V to scroll backwards. To view the commands you can use to interact with less, press h while you are viewing a file in less.

ln

Purpose   Set up a hard or symbolic link (pseudonyms) to files and directories.

Syntax   ln [options] *existing_file new_name*

Options   -b makes backup copy of files about to be removed.

-d creates a hard link to a directory (only root can do this).

-f removes the existing file with *new_name*.

—help displays a Help message.

-s creates a symbolic link.

-v displays verbose output.

Description   The ln command assigns a new name to an existing file. With the -s option, you can create symbolic links that can exist across file systems. Also, with symbolic links, you can see the link information with the ls -l command. Otherwise, ls -l shows two distinct files for a file and its hard link.

locate

Purpose   From a periodically updated database, list all files that match a specified pattern.

Syntax   locate *pattern*

Options   None

Description   The locate command searches a database of files for any name that matches a specified pattern. Your Linux system is set up to update the file database periodically. If you are not sure about the location of a file, just type **locate** followed by a part of the filename. For example, here's how you can search for the XF86Config file:

```
locate XF86Config
/etc/X11/XF86Config
/usr/X11R6/lib/X11/XF86Config
/usr/X11R6/man/man5/XF86Config.5x.gz
```

lpr

Purpose	Print one or more files.
Syntax	lpr [options] [*files*]
Options	-P*printer* prints to the specified printer (the name appears in /etc/printcap).
	-#*N* (where *N* is a number) prints that many copies of each file.
	-h suppresses the burst page (the first page, with user information).
	-m sends mail upon completion of a print job.
	-r removes the file after printing.
	-J *jobname* prints this job name on the burst page.
	-U *username* prints this user name on the burst page.
Description	The lpr command prints the specified files by using your system's print-spooling system. If no filenames are specified, lpr reads input from the standard input. You can print to a specific printer with the -P option.

ls

Purpose	List the contents of a directory.
Syntax	ls [options] [*directory_name*]
Options	-a displays all files, including those that start with a period (.).
	-b displays unprintable characters in filenames with octal code.
	-c sorts according to file creation time.
	-d lists directories like any other file (rather than listing their contents).
	-f lists directory contents without sorting (exactly as they are in the disk).
	-i shows the inode information.
	-l shows the file listing in the long format, with detailed information.
	-p appends a character to a filename to indicate its type.
	-r sorts the listing in reverse alphabetical order.
	-s shows the size (in kilobytes) of each file next to the filename.
	-t sorts the listing according to the file's time stamp.
	-1 displays a one-column listing of filenames.
	-R recursively lists the files in all subdirectories.
Description	The ls command displays the listing of a specified directory. If you omit the directory name, ls displays the contents of the current directory. By default, ls does not list files whose names begin with a period (.); to see all files, type **ls -a**. You can see full details of files (including size, user and group ownership, and read-write-execute permissions) with the ls -l command.

lsof

Purpose	List open files and network connections.
Syntax	lsof [options] [*names*]
Options	-h displays a Help message.
	-c *X* displays files for commands that begin with letter *X*.
	-i *IP* shows network connections whose IP address matches *IP*.
	-s shows the file size (when available).
	-t displays terse output.
	-u *names* lists the open files for the specified users.
	-R lists the parent process ID.

Description	The lsof command displays a list of all the open files for a user. An open file may be a regular file, a directory, a device file, a library, or a network file (Internet socket, NFS file, or UNIX domain socket). You can use this command to see who is using a specific file. You can also use lsof as an intrusion detection tool to browse the current Internet connections and see if there are any unexpected connections.

man

Purpose	View online manual pages (also called *man pages*).
Syntax	man [options] [*section*] *command*
Options	-C *cfile* specifies the man configuration file (the default is /etc/man.config).
	-P *pager* specifies the program to use to display one page at a time (for example, less).
	-a displays all man pages matching a specific *command*.
	-h displays a Help message and exits.
	-w shows the location of the man pages to be displayed.
Description	The man command displays the man pages for the specified command. If you know the section for a man page, you can provide the section as well. For example, all Tcl/Tk man pages are in section n. Thus, you can view the man page for the Tcl/Tk command pack with the command man n pack.

mkdir

Purpose	Create a directory.
Syntax	mkdir [options] *directory_name*
Options	-m *mode* assigns the specified permission setting to the new directory.
	-p creates the parent directories if they do not already exist.
Description	The mkdir command creates the specified directory.

mkfs

Purpose	Create a Linux file system on a hard-disk partition or a diskette.
Syntax	mkfs [-V] [-t] [options] *device_name* [*blocks*]
Options	-V produces verbose output needed for testing.
	-t *fstype* specifies the file system type (such as ext2).
	-c checks the device for bad blocks before creating the file system.
	-l *filename* reads the bad-block list from specified file.
Description	The mkfs command creates a Linux file system on a specified device. The device is typically a hard-disk partition or a diskette (that has been formatted with fdformat).

mknod

Purpose	Create a device file with specified major and minor numbers.
Syntax	mknod *device_file* {b|c} *major minor*
Options	None
Description	The mknod command creates a device file (such as the ones in the /dev directory) through which the operating system accesses physical devices, such as hard disk, serial port, keyboard, and mouse. To create a device file, you have to log in as root, and you have to know the major and minor numbers of the device for which you are creating the device file. In addition, you must specify either b or c to indicate whether the device is block oriented or character oriented. Typically, you perform this step following specific instructions in a HOWTO document.

mkswap

Purpose	Create a swap space for Linux.
Syntax	mkswap [options] *device_or_file numblocks*
Options	-c checks the device for bad blocks before creating the swap space.
	-f forces creation of swap space even if there are errors, such as the requested size being greater than space available on the device.
	-P *NNN* uses *NNN* as the page size for the swap space.
	-v*N* (where *N* is 0 or 1) creates an old-style swap space if *N* is 0; if *N* is 1, creates a new-style swap space.
Description	The mkswap command creates a swap space for use by the Linux kernel. If you are creating swap space in a disk partition, specify the partition's device name (such as /dev/hda2) as the second argument to mkswap. If you want to use a file as swap space, create the file with a command such as dd if=/dev/zero of=swapfile bs=1024 count=16384. Then, type **mkswap swapfile 16384** to create the swap space. You have to use the swapon command to activate a swap space.

more

Purpose	View text files one screen at a time.
Syntax	more [options] *filenames*
Options	+*N* (where *N* is a number) displays the file starting at the specified line number
	+/*pattern* begins displaying two lines before the *pattern*.
	-s reduces multiple blank lines to a single blank line.
Description	The more command displays the specified files one screen at a time. To view the commands you can use in more, press h while you are viewing a file using more. For more advanced file viewing, use the less command.

mount

Purpose	Associate a physical device to a specific directory in the Linux file system.
Syntax	mount [options] *device directory*
Options	-a mounts all devices listed in the /etc/fstab file.
	-h displays a Help message and exits.
	-r mounts the device for read-only (no writing allowed).
	-t *fstype* specifies the file system type on the device.
	-v displays verbose messages.
	-V displays the version number and exits.
Description	The mount command attaches the contents of a physical device to a specific directory on the Linux file system. For example, you may mount a CD-ROM at the /mnt/cdrom directory. Then, you can access the contents of the CD-ROM at the /mnt/cdrom directory (in other words, the root directory of the CD-ROM appears as /mnt/cdrom after the mount operation). To see the listing of the RedHat directory on the CD-ROM, type **ls /mnt/cdrom/RedHat**.

mv

Purpose	Rename files and directories or move them from one directory to another.
Syntax	mv [options] *source destination*
Options	-b makes backup copies of files being moved or renamed.
	-f removes existing files without prompting.

-i prompts before overwriting any existing files.

-v displays the name of the file before moving it.

Description   The mv command either renames a file or moves it to another directory. The command works on either plain files or directories. Thus, you can rename the file sample to sample.old with the command mv sample sample.old. On the other hand, you can move the file /tmp/sample to /usr/local/sample with the command mv /tmp/sample /usr/local/sample.

nice

Purpose   Run a program at a lower or higher priority level.

Syntax   nice [options] *program*

Options   +*n* (*n* = number) adds *n* to the nice value (positive values are lower priority).

-*n* (*n* = number) subtracts *n* from the nice value (negative nice value indicates a higher priority).

Description   The nice command enables you to run a program at lower or higher priority. By default, programs run at the nice value of zero. Adding to the nice value decreases the priority, whereas subtracting from the nice value increases the program's priority. Only root can decrease the nice value.

nl

Purpose   Add line numbers to nonblank lines of text in a file and write to standard output.

Syntax   nl [options] [*file*]

Options   -ba numbers all lines.

-bt numbers text lines only (the default).

-s*c* separates text from line numbers with the character *c* (the default is tab).

-w*n* uses *n* columns to show the line numbers.

Description   The nl command adds a line number to each nonblank line of text from a file and writes the lines to standard output. Suppose the file sample.txt has the following lines:

A line followed by a blank line and

then another non-blank line.

The nl command applied to this file produces the following result:

nl sample.txt

    1 A line followed by a blank line and

    2 then another non-blank line.

passwd

Purpose   Change password.

Syntax   passwd [*username*]

Options   None

Description   The passwd command changes your password. It prompts for the old password, followed by the new password. If you log in as root, you can change another user's password by specifying the user name as an argument to the passwd command.

paste

Purpose   Write to standard output corresponding lines of each file, separated by a tab.

Syntax   paste *file1 file2* [. . .]

Options	`-s` pastes the lines from one file at a time, instead of one line from each file.
	`-d` *delim* uses delimiters from the list of characters, instead of a tab.
	`-` causes paste to use standard input as a file.
Description	The `paste` command takes one line from each of the listed files and writes them out to standard output, separated by a tab. With the `-s` option, the `paste` command can also concatenate all lines from one file into a single gigantic line.

patch

Purpose	Apply the output of the `diff` command to an original file.
Syntax	`patch [options] < patch_file`
Options	`-c` causes the patch file to be interpreted as a context `diff`.
	`-e` forces `patch` to interpret the patch file as an `ed` script.
	`-f` forces patch to be applied regardless of any inconsistencies.
	`-n` causes the patch file to be interpreted as a normal `diff`.
	`-p`*n* strips everything up to *n* slashes in the pathname.
	`-R` indicates that patch file has been created with new and old files swapped.
	`-u` causes the patch file to be interpreted as a unified `diff`.
	`-v` displays the version number.
Description	The `patch` command is used to update an original file by applying all the differences between the original and a revised version. The differences are in the form of an output from the `diff` command, stored in the *patch_file*. Changes to Linux kernel source code are distributed in the form of a patch file. Chapter 21 discusses how to apply patches to the kernel source.

printenv

Purpose	View a list of environment variables.
Syntax	`printenv`
Options	None
Description	The `printenv` command displays a list of all current environment variables.

ps

Purpose	Display status of processes (programs) running in the system.
Syntax	`ps [options]`
Options	Note that unlike other commands, `ps` options do not have a `-` prefix.
	`a` displays processes of other users.
	`f` displays a family tree of processes.
	`j` displays output using jobs format.
	`l` displays in long format, with many details for each process.
	`m` displays memory usage information for each process.
	`u` displays the user name and start time.
	`x` displays processes that are not associated with any terminal.
Description	The `ps` command displays the status of processes running in the system. Typing `ps` alone produces a list of processes you are running. To see a list of all processes in the system, type **ps ax** (or **ps aux**, if you want more details about each process).

pstree

Purpose	Display all running processes in the form of a tree.
Syntax	`pstree [options] [pid]`
Options	`-a` shows command-line arguments.
	`-c` does not compact subtrees.
	`-l` displays long lines.
	`-n` sorts processes by process ID (instead of by name).
	`-p` shows process IDs.
Description	The `pstree` command shows all of the processes in the form of a tree, which makes it easy to understand the parent-child relationships among the processes.

pwd

Purpose	Display the current working directory.
Syntax	`pwd`
Options	None
Description	The `pwd` command prints the current working directory. `pwd` is a built-in command of the Bash shell.

reboot

Purpose	Terminate all processes and reboot the system (you must log in as `root`).
Syntax	`reboot [options]`
Options	`-n` reboots the system without flushing out in-memory buffers to disk.
	`-f` forces a halt without calling the `/sbin/shutdown` command.
	`-i` shuts down all network interfaces before rebooting the system.
Description	The `reboot` command lets the super user (`root`) terminate all processes and reboot the system. The `reboot` command invokes `/sbin/shutdown` with the `-r` option.

rm

Purpose	Delete one or more files.
Syntax	`rm [options] files`
Options	`-f` removes files without prompting.
	`-i` prompts before removing a file.
	`-r` recursively removes files in all subdirectories, including the directories.
	`-v` displays the name of each file before removing it.
Description	The `rm` command deletes the specified files. To remove a file, you must have write permission to the directory that contains the file.

rmdir

Purpose	Delete a specified directory (provided that the directory is empty).
Syntax	`rmdir [options] directory`
Options	`-p` removes any parent directories that become empty.
Description	The `rmdir` command deletes empty directories. If a directory is not empty, you should use the `rm -r` command to delete the files, as well as the directory.

sed

Purpose	Copy a file to standard output after editing according to a set of commands.
Syntax	`sed [options] [editing_commands] [file]`

Options	`-e'instructions'` applies the editing instructions to the file.
	`-f scriptfile` applies editing commands from `scriptfile`.
	`-n` suppresses default output.
Description	The `sed` command is known as the stream editor—it copies a file to standard output while applying specified editing commands. If you do not specify a file, it reads from the standard input. To use the stream editor, you have to learn its editing commands, which are very similar to the ones the `ed` editor uses (described in Chapter 11).

shutdown

Purpose	Terminate all processes and shut down (or reboot) the system.
Syntax	`shutdown [options] time [messages]`
Options	`-t seconds` specifies the time between the message and the kill signal.
	`-h` halts the system after terminating all the processes.
	`-r` reboots the system after terminating all the processes.
	`-f` performs a fast reboot.
	`-k` sends warning messages but does not shut down the system.
	`-c` cancels a shutdown that's in progress.
Description	The `shutdown` command (the full pathname is `/sbin/shutdown`) brings down the Linux system in an orderly way. You must specify a time when shutdown begins; use the keyword `now` to shutdown immediately. You must be logged in as `root` to run the `shutdown` command.

sort

Purpose	Sort or merge lines from a file, and write to standard output.
Syntax	`sort [options] [files]`
Options	`-c` checks if files are already sorted and prints error message if not.
	`-m` merges files by sorting them as a group.
	`-b` ignores leading blanks.
	`-d` sorts in phone directory order (using only letters, digits, and blanks).
	`-f` treats lowercase letters as equivalent to uppercase letters.
	`-k pos1[,pos2]` specifies the sort field as characters between the two positions `pos1` and `pos2`.
	`-o file` writes output to the specified file instead of standard output.
	`-r` sorts in reverse order.
	`-g` sorts numerically after converting the prefix of each line into a floating-point number.
	`-i` ignores unprintable characters.
	`-n` sorts numerically (used when a number begins each line).
	`-tc` specifies the separator character.
	`+n` only considers characters from position n onwards (0 = first position).
Description	The `sort` command sorts the lines in one or more files and writes them out to the standard output. The same command can also merge several files (when used with the `-m` option) and can produce an appropriately sorted and merged output.

split

Purpose	Split a file into several smaller files.
Syntax	`split [options] file [prefix]`

Options   -l *n* (where *n* is a number) puts *n* lines in each file.

-*n* (where *n* is a number) puts *n* lines in each file.

-b *n*k (where *n* is a number) splits the file every *n* kilobytes.

-c *n*k (where *n* is a number) puts as many lines as possible in a split file without exceeding *n* kilobytes per file.

Description   The split command breaks up a large file into smaller files. By default, split puts 1,000 lines into each file. The files are named by groups of letters such as aa, ab, ac, and so on. You can specify a prefix for the filenames. For example, to split a large archive into smaller files that fit into several high-density, 3.5-inch diskettes, use split as follows:

split -C 1440k bigfile.tar disk.

This creates files named disk.aa, disk.ab, and so on.

su

Purpose   Become another user.

Syntax   su [options] [*username*]

Options   -c *command* passes the *command* to the shell.

-f prevents reading the startup file (.cshrc) when the shell is csh or tcsh.

-l makes the new shell a login shell by reading the user's startup file.

-p preserves the environment variables HOME, USER, LOGNAME, and SHELL.

-s *shell* runs the specified *shell* instead of the user's default shell.

Description   The su command lets you assume the identity of another user. You have to provide the password of that user before you can continue. If you do not provide a user name, su assumes you want to change to the root user.

swapoff

Purpose   Deactivate the specified swap device or file.

Syntax   swapoff *device*

Options   None

Description   The swapoff command stops Linux from using the specified device or file as a swap space.

swapon

Purpose   Activate the specified swap device or file.

Syntax   swapon [-a] *device*

Options   -a enables all swap devices listed in the /etc/fstab file.

Description   The swapon command activates the specified device or file as a swap space. During system startup, all swap spaces are activated by the swapon -a command, which is invoked by the script file /etc/rc.d/rc.sysinit.

sync

Purpose   Write buffers to disk.

Syntax   sync

Options   None

Description   When you cannot shut down your Linux system in an orderly manner (for example, when you cannot execute shutdown, halt, or reboot commands), you should type **sync** before switching off the computer.

tac

Purpose Copy a file, line by line, to the standard output in reverse order (last line first).

Syntax tac *file*

Options -b places the separator at the beginning of each line.

-r treats the separator string specified by -s as a regular expression.

-s *sep* specifies a separator (instead of the default newline character).

Description The tac command displays the specified text file in reverse order, copying the lines to standard output in reverse order. By default, tac treats each line as a record and uses the newline character as the record separator. However, you can specify a different separator character, in which case tac copies those records to standard output in reverse order.

tail

Purpose View the last few lines of a file.

Syntax tail [options] *file*

Options -*N* (where *N* is a number) displays last *N* lines.

-n *N* (where *N* is a number) displays last *N* lines.

-f reads the file at regular intervals and displays all new lines.

Description The tail command displays lines from the end of the specified file. By default, tail displays the last 10 lines from the file. To view the last 24 lines from a file named /var/log/messages, type **tail -24 /var/log/messages**.

tar

Purpose Create an archive of files or extract files from an archive.

Syntax tar [options] *files_or_directories*

Options -c creates a new archive.

-d compares files in an archive with files in the current directory.

-r extends the archive with more files.

-t lists the contents of an archive.

-x extracts from the archive.

-C *directory* extracts files into the specified directory.

-f *file* uses the specified file as the archive, instead of a tape.

-L *n* specifies the capacity of the tape as *n* kilobytes.

-N *date* only archives files newer than the specified date.

-T *file* archives or extracts the filenames specified in *file*.

-v displays verbose messages.

-z compresses or decompresses the archive with gzip.

Description The tar command creates an archive of files, or extracts files from an existing archive. By default, tar assumes the archive to be on a tape. However, you can use the -f option to specify a file as the archive.

top

Purpose List currently running processes, arranged in order by their share of CPU time.

Syntax top [q] [d *delay*]

Options q causes top to run with the highest possible priority (you have to be root).

d *delay* specifies the delay between updates, in seconds.

Description   The `top` command produces a full-text screen with the processes arranged according to their share of the CPU time. By default, `top` updates the display every five seconds. Press q or Ctrl-C to quit `top`.

touch

Purpose   Change a file's time stamp.

Syntax   `touch [options] `*`files`*

Options   `-c` stops `touch` from creating a file that does not exist.

`-d `*`time`* uses the specified time.

`-r `*`file`* uses the time stamp from the specified file.

`-t `*`MMDDhhmm[[CC]YY][.ss]`* uses the specified date and time.

Description   The `touch` command lets you change the date and time of the last modification of a file (this information is stored with the file). If you use `touch` without any options, the current date and time are used as the time stamp for the file. If the specified file does not exist, `touch` creates a new file of size 0 bytes.

tr

Purpose   Copies from standard input to standard output, while substituting one set of characters with another.

Syntax   `tr [options] `*`string1`*` [`*`string2`*`]`

Options   `-c` complements characters in *`string1`* with ASCII codes 001–377.

`-d` deletes from the input all characters specified in *`string1`*.

`-s` replaces repeated sequences of any character in *`string1`* with a single character.

Description   The `tr` command substitutes all characters in *`string1`* in the input with the corresponding characters in *`string2`*. For example, to convert the file `sample.lc` to all uppercase and store in `sample.uc`, type the following:

`tr [a-z] [A-Z] < sample.lc > sample.uc`

To replace repeated occurrences of newlines in a file with a single newline character, type the following:

`tr -s '\n' < infile > outfile`

tty

Purpose   Display the device name of the terminal.

Syntax   `tty`

Options   None

Description   The `tty` command displays the name of the terminal connected to the standard input. This is useful in shell scripts that may need the terminal name.

type

Purpose   Display the type of a command (whether it is a built-in shell command or a separate executable program).

Syntax   `type `*`command`*

Options   None

Description   The `type` command tells you the type of a command—whether it is a built-in shell command, an alias, or an executable program. For example, I use `alias ll='ls -l'` to define the alias `ll`. Here is what I get when I check the type of the command `ll`:

`type ll`
`ll is aliased to `ls -l``

umount

Purpose Disassociate a device from the Linux file system.

Syntax `umount device`

Options None

Description The `umount` command removes the association between a device and a directory in the Linux file system. Only the root can execute the `umount` command.

unalias

Purpose Delete an abbreviation defined earlier with `alias`.

Syntax `unalias abbreviation`

Options None

Description The `unalias` command removes an abbreviation defined earlier with the `alias` command. `unalias` is a built-in command of the Bash shell.

uname

Purpose Display system information, such as type of machine and operating system.

Syntax `uname [options]`

Options `-a` displays all information.

`-m` displays the hardware type (for example, `i586`).

`-n` displays the machine's hostname.

`-p` displays the processor type (this appears as `unknown`).

`-r` displays the operating system release (for example, 2.4.0-0.43.12).

`-s` displays the operating system name.

`-v` displays the operating system version (shown as date of compilation).

Description The `uname` command displays a variety of information about your machine and the operating system (Linux).

uncompress

Purpose Decompress one or more files that have been compressed using the `compress` command.

Syntax `uncompress [-cdrvV] files`

Options `-c` writes the result to the standard output and retains the original.

`-r` recursively decompresses files in all subdirectories.

`-v` displays a message as each file is decompressed.

`-V` prints the version number and exits.

Description The `uncompress` command decompresses each specified file and replaces the compressed version with the original (also removes the `.Z` suffix appended to the name of the compressed file). Using the `uncompress` command yields the same result as running `compress` with the `-d` option.

uniq

Purpose Write all unique lines from an input file to standard output.

Syntax `uniq [options] file`

Options `-n` (where *n* is a number) ignores the first *n* fields on each line.

`+n` (where *n* is a number) ignores the first *n* characters on each line.

-c writes the number of times each line occurred in file.

-d writes only duplicate lines.

-u writes only unique lines (the default).

Description   The uniq command removes duplicate lines from an input file and copies the unique lines to the standard output. If you do not specify an input file, uniq reads from standard input.

wc

Purpose   Display the byte, word, and line count of a file.

Syntax   wc [options] [*files*]

Options   -c displays only the byte count.

-w displays only the word count.

-l displays only the line count.

Description   The wc command displays the byte, word, and line count of a file. If you do not specify an input file, wc reads from standard input.

whatis

Purpose   Search whatis database (see apropos) for complete words.

Syntax   whatis *keyword*

Options   None

Description   The whatis command searches the whatis database (see the entry for apropos) for the specified keyword and displays the result. Only complete word matches are displayed.

whereis

Purpose   Find the source, binary, and man page for a command.

Syntax   whereis [options] *command*

Options   -b searches only for binaries.

-m searches only for man pages.

-s searches only for sources.

Description   The whereis command searches the usual directories (where binaries, man pages, and source files are located) for binaries, man pages, and source files for a command. For example, here is the result of searching for the files for the rpm command:

whereis rpm

rpm: /bin/rpm /usr/lib/rpm /usr/include/rpm
/usr/man/man8/rpm.8

which

Purpose   Search the directories in the PATH environment variable for a command.

Syntax   which *command*

Options   None

Description   The which command searches the directories in the PATH environment variable for the file that will be executed when you type the command. This is a good way to check what will be executed when you type a specific command.

zcat, zless, zmore

Purpose   View the contents of a compressed text file without having to first decompress the file.

Syntax   `zcat` *filename*
            `zless` *filename*
            `zmore` *filename*

Options   None

Description   The `zcat`, `zless`, and `zmore` commands work the same way as `cat`, `less`, and `more`. The only difference is that the z-commands can directly read files compressed with `gzip` or `compress` (without having to first decompress the files with `gunzip`). These commands are particularly useful for reading compressed text files, such as the ones in `/usr/info` directory.

Disk Drives

◆ ◆

When it comes to disk drives and Linux, what matters is whether or not Linux supports the disk controller: the card that connects the disk drive to your PC's motherboard. Linux supports most common disk controllers. This appendix gives you information about various disk controllers and some operations you can perform on disks.

Disk Controller Types

The disk controller is the adapter card that acts as an intermediary between your PC's motherboard and one or more hard disk drives. Typically, you can connect up to two hard drives and two floppy drives to a single disk controller. The Small Computer System Interface (SCSI) controller is an exception to this norm; you can connect as many as seven or 15 SCSI devices (anything that has a SCSI interface, such as a disk drive, CD-ROM drive, tape drive, or scanner) in a series.

Over the years, several types of hard disk controllers have appeared for the PC. Following are some of the disk controllers you may find in a PC:

- ◆ *ST-506* disk controllers, which originally appeared in IBM XT and AT computers, became the common disk controller of the PC industry in its early years (remember that the IBM PC-AT came out in 1984). Many PCs have disk controllers that are compatible with the ST-506. Seagate's ST-506 was the original hard drive for PCs; Western Digital's WD1003 was the controller card. Thus, these controllers are often referred to as WD1003-compatible controllers. The original ST-506 drives used a recording method known as modified frequency modulation (MFM). Many ST-506 disk controllers also support drives that use another type of data-recording technique known as run length limited (RLL). This technology is outdated and not used in new PCs anymore.

◆ The *Integrated Drive Electronics (IDE)* or *AT Attachment Packet Interface (ATAPI)* emulates the ST-506 interface. IDE drives, however, have the necessary controller circuitry built into them. The motherboard typically contains an IDE interface for connecting the drive to the motherboard. For many years now, IDE drives have been the most widespread in PCs. Nowadays, the term AT attachment (ATA) is used to refer to IDE. The original IDE interface could support only two drives, and it limited the maximum disk size to approximately 500MB. You needed third-party drivers to use disks larger than 500MB. Today's PCs with large disk drives use the Enhanced IDE interface (described next). You can learn more about ATA standards at http://www.t13.org/.

◆ The *Enhanced IDE (EIDE)* interface supports up to four internal IDE devices (which include hard drives as well as CD-ROM drives), higher-capacity drives, and higher speeds of data transfer. Typical EIDE interfaces consist of two IDE interfaces: primary and secondary, each of which is capable of supporting up to two drives. EIDE interfaces are popular because of their low cost. Many PCs use the EIDE interface to connect both the hard disk and the CD-ROM drive to the PC's motherboard.

◆ The *Ultra ATA* or *Ultra DMA (UDMA)* interface is a newer version of the IDE interface that utilizes bus direct memory access (DMA) techniques to provide much faster data transfer rates, as much as 33 or 66MB per second, depending on the mode operation. These data transfer rates are twice to four times that of EIDE. Many new PCs come with Ultra ATA interfaces.

◆ The *Enhanced Small Device Interface (ESDI)* controllers emulate the ST-506 interface but provide higher data-transfer rates. This technology is outdated and not used in new PCs anymore.

◆ *Small Computer System Interface (SCSI)* controllers provide a separate bus onto which you can connect up to seven SCSI devices. You can find hard drives, CD-ROM drives, tape drives, and scanners that support SCSI. You can connect multiple SCSI devices to the computer by daisy-chaining (connecting first to second, second to third, and so on) the devices with a SCSI cable. All UNIX workstations (such as the ones from Hewlett-Packard, IBM, and Sun Microsystems) use SCSI. Lately, SCSI is becoming popular on PCs as well. The only drawback is that SCSI controllers are relatively expensive compared with EIDE controllers. There are many variants of the SCSI bus, as summarized in the following list:

   • **SCSI 1**—The original SCSI standard (ANSI specification X3.131-1986) specifies an 8-bit parallel bus that can transfer data asynchronously at 1.5MB/sec and synchronously at 5MB/sec.

   • **Fast SCSI**—The SCSI 2 standard (ANSI specification X3.131-1994) increased the maximum synchronous data transfer rate to 10MB/sec and defined a differential bus that enables cable lengths to increase to 25 meters.

   • **Wide SCSI**—SCSI 2 standard increased the width of the bus allowing 16-bit and 32-bit parallel data transfers. Typical wide SCSI buses use 16-bit data transfers. Wide SCSI buses enable up to 16 SCSI devices to be connected to the bus (at least one of these device is the host adapter, so you can attach only 15 more devices to the controller). The letter W in SCSI controller names reflects the use of wide bus.

   • **Ultra SCSI**—Uses a technique to double the maximum data transfer rate from 10MB/sec to 20MB/sec. SCSI controllers that support ultra SCSI often have the letter U as a qualifier in their name.

- **Ultra Wide SCSI**—Combines the ultra technique to 16-bit wide SCSI bus, resulting in a maximum data transfer rate of 40MB/sec. This bus is abbreviated as UW in many SCSI controller names.
- **Ultra 2 Wide SCSI**—Uses a technology called "low voltage differential (LVD) signaling" that further doubles the data transfer rate of Ultra Wide SCSI to support rates of 80MB/sec when using a 16-bit wide bus. In this case, the maximum SCSI bus length is 12 meters. Ultra 2 Wide SCSI controllers often have the U2W designation in their names.
- **Ultra 160 SCSI**—Doubles the data transfer rate, raising it to 160MB/sec. Uses cyclic redundancy check (CRC) to improve data integrity and adjusts transfer rates if the error rate is too high.
- **Ultra 320 SCSI**—Further doubles the data transfer rate to 320MB/sec. You can find more information about Ultra 320 SCSI at the SCSI Trade Association website (`http://www.scsita.org`). That website mentions Ultra 640 SCSI, capable of 640MB/sec data transfer rates, which should be appearing on the market soon.

> **note** Linux supports all these common disk controllers. Even though several disk controllers appear in the preceding list, there are essentially two types: IDE or ATA (where IDE refers to all ST-506-compatible interfaces) and SCSI.

Most Pentium systems use a motherboard that supports the Peripheral Component Interconnect (PCI) bus. Both IDE and SCSI controllers can connect to the PCI bus. Linux supports the PCI bus. The PCI bus is now dominant in the PC marketplace, replacing the outdated ISA bus.

Disk Drive Concepts

When you read about disk drives, you run into some terms and concepts unique to the world of hard disks. The following sections explain some of these concepts.

Cylinders, Heads, and Sectors

The physical organization of the disk is expressed in terms of cylinders, heads, and sectors. A hard disk consists of several platters of magnetic material. In physical terms, you can think of cylinder, head, and sector as follows:

- A *cylinder* is a set of matching tracks on both sides of all the platters in the disk drive, where each track is one of a series of concentric rings on one side of a disk platter.
- The total number of *heads* is the number of sides of all the magnetic platters.
- A *sector* is a pie-shaped wedge on the platter. Each cylinder is divided into sectors.

Any location on the disk can be expressed in terms of the cylinder, the head, and the sector. Identifying a disk location in terms of cylinder (C), head (H), and sector (S) is known as CHS addressing.

The physical geometry of a hard disk usually is expressed in terms of cylinders, heads, and sectors (CHS). A disk may have a geometry of CHS = 8,894/15/63, which means that the disk has 8,894 cylinders, 15 heads, and 63 sectors. Usually, each sector can store 512 bytes (or half a kilobyte) of data. Thus, the capacity of this disk is (8,894×15×63)÷2 kilobytes, or 4,202,415 kilobytes (about 4,103MB).

> **note**
>
> PC hard disk controllers include a read-only memory (ROM) basic input/output system (BIOS) on the controller. By convention (and for compatibility with the original IBM PC architecture), the BIOS uses CHS addressing to access the hard disk. The disk BIOS, however, uses a 10-bit value as the cylinder address. Because 10 bits can hold numbers between 0 and 1,023, the BIOS can address, at most, 1,024 cylinders. Nowadays, the BIOS supports what are called Int 13h (that's interrupt number 13 in hexadecimal) extensions that use logical block address to get around the 1,024 cylinder limitation.

Logical Block Address (LBA)

Many large disks have more than 1,024 cylinders. To accommodate the 1,024-cylinder limit, the disk controllers as well as newer BIOS use what is known as logical block address (LBA) to handle disks with more than 1,024 cylinders.

Instead of thinking of in terms of cylinder, head, and sector—CHS addresses—for each block, the idea behind LBA is to address each 512-byte block sequentially and not think of any artificial limit on the number of cylinders. In fact, with LBA, you do not have to think of a physical cylinder, head, sector model for the hard disk; a disk can simply be some storage medium organized into same-size blocks and the blocks are numbered sequentially.

Master Boot Record (MBR)

The first sector of the hard disk (cylinder 0, head 0, sector 1) is called the master boot record (MBR). This 512-byte storage area contains important information about the disk, such as the partition table, and a small amount of code that the PC's BIOS loads and runs when you boot the PC.

The small program in the MBR reads the partition table; determines which partition is active (that's just an attribute of a partition), reads the active partition's first sector, or boot sector, and runs whatever program resides in that boot sector. The program in a partition's boot sector usually loads whatever operating system is installed on that partition.

When you install a boot loader such as GRUB on the hard disk, the GRUB program resides on the hard disk's MBR or the boot sector of the partition on which the Linux root directory (/) is located.

Partitions

Partitions are a way of dividing up a hard disk and treating each part separately. By dividing your PC's hard disk into partitions, you can install different operating systems in different partitions. Even if you use the entire disk for Linux, you need, at minimum, a partition Linux can use as swap space—an extension of memory, so that you can have more virtual memory than the physical memory on your system. The Red Hat Linux installer creates three partitions: a swap partition, a small (100MB) partition for /boot file system that holds the Linux kernel files, and the remaining disk space is assigned to a large partition that holds the main Linux file system (/).

Although you can set up a Linux system with a swap parital and a single large partition for the entire Linux file system, there are circumstances in which you may want to place specific parts of the file system in their own partitions to limit their growth or for performance reasons. When you place a file system such as /var in a partition by itself, that file system cannot grow beyond the physical size of the partition and fill up the entire file system.

In practice, most production Linux installations use quite a few partitions. Here's a typical example of the file systems that could be placed in their own disk partitions:

- ◆ **swap**—Used as virtual memory (typically twice the amount of physical memory or at least 64MB)
- ◆ **/**—Is the root file system and provides the mount points for all other file systems. When there are no other partitions, the root partition also holds the entire Linux file system.
- ◆ **/boot**—A primary partition to hold the Linux kernel files (typically around 100MB). In cases where the BIOS can only access the first 1,024 cylinders, you can place this small /boot partition within the first 1,024 cylinders (this constraint does not affect new PCs that access disks using logical block address).
- ◆ **/var**—Contains the spool directories for mail and print scheduler as well as error logs. The Web server and anonymous FTP directories are also in /var. You could place this in its own partition to ensure that the entire file system does not get filled up by too many error messages (in case something goes wrong).
- ◆ **/usr**—Contains most executable files (binaries)
- ◆ **/tmp**—Holds temporary files for many programs. Any process and any user can write to this directory, so it is wise to keep /tmp in a different partition than /.
- ◆ **/home**—Contains the home directories of the users. Placing /home in a separate partition ensures that users do not inadvertently fill up the whole file system and bring the system down.

insider insight

The master boot record contains the partition table, starting at byte number 446 (or 0x1be, which means 1be in hexadecimal). The partition table can have up to four 16-byte entries at bytes 446, 462, 478, 494, respectively, followed by a signature in the two bytes with offset 510 and 511. The signature has the hexadecimal value 0x55 in byte 510 and 0xaa in byte 511.

Each 16-byte value in the partition table defines a partition. Each partition is specified by a starting and ending cylinder number. The partition entry also includes a type that identifies the operating system that creates the partition. The concept of partitions is a convention that all PC-based operating systems, ranging from MS-DOS to Linux, follow.

In MS-DOS, you use the FDISK program to manipulate the partitions. In Windows XP/2000, use the DISKPART program (located in the \WINDOWS\SYSTEM32 directory) to work with disk partitions. Linux includes a program with the same name—fdisk (lowercase)—to alter the disk partitions. In addition to fdisk, Linux includes another disk-partitioning program called sfdisk.

The partitions described in the partition table in the MBR are the primary partitions. Because there is room for only four entries, there can be at most four primary partitions on a hard disk. However, a primary partition can be marked as an extended partition and then the first sector of that extended partition will contain another partition table that subdivides the extended partition. The partitions in the extended primary partition are called *logical* partitions.

Linux Device Names for Disks

In Linux, each device is represented by a device file in the /dev directory. The device name for the hard disk depends on the type of disk controller. For IDE and EIDE drives, the device name is /dev/hda for the first disk, /dev/hdb for the second disk, and so on.

On an EIDE interface, if you have a hard disk on the primary interface and a CD-ROM drive as the first device on the secondary interface, the device names are /dev/hda for the hard disk drive and /dev/hdc for the CD-ROM drive.

The Linux disk drivers treat each disk partition as a separate device. The first primary partition in the first IDE disk is /dev/hda1, the second partition is /dev/hda2, the third one is /dev/hda3, and so on. The first logical partition is /dev/hda5, the second one /dev/hda6, and so on. Similarly, the device names for the partitions on the second IDE drive are /dev/hdb1, /dev/hdb2, and so on.

The SCSI disk devices are named /dev/sda, /dev/sdb, and so on. If a SCSI device is a hard disk, its partitions are named by appending the partition number to the device name. Thus, the partitions of the first SCSI hard disk are named /dev/sda1, /dev/sda2, /dev/sda3, and so on.

Floppy Disks in Linux

Chapter 12 describes several ways to access MS-DOS floppy disks under Linux; you can mount the floppy and use Linux commands, or use the mtools utility programs to read from or write to the floppy. You also can create a Linux file system on a floppy disk. In fact, you'll find Linux file systems on the boot and root floppies that you use to install Linux.

Formatting and creating a Linux file system on a floppy is a straightforward process. To format a 3.5-inch high-density floppy in the A drive, for example, use the following command (for more on floppy drive naming conventions, see the "How to Format a DOS Floppy" section in Chapter 12):

```
fdformat /dev/fd0H1440
```

If you have an old PC with a 5.25-inch high-density floppy as the A drive, you can access that floppy with the device name /dev/fd0h1200. On the B drive, change the first 0 in the device name to 1.

---

insider insight

After you format the floppy, use the following command to create a Linux file system on the floppy:

```
mke2fs -m 0 /dev/fd0H1440 1440
```

The -m option is used to specify what percentage of blocks should be reserved for the use of super user (root). By specifying the -m 0 option, you ensure that mke2fs does not reserve space on the floppy disk for the super user. If you do not explicitly specify the -m option, mke2fs reserves five percent of the disk space for the super user.

After you create the file system on the floppy drive, you can mount the floppy at a mount point (an empty directory) in the Linux file system. The following example shows how you mount the floppy drive at the `/mnt/floppy` directory:

```
mount /dev/fd0H1440 /mnt/floppy
```

Now you can use Linux commands, such as `cp` and `mv`, to copy or move files to the floppy disk. Before you eject the floppy disk from the drive, use the following command to dismount the floppy:

```
umount /dev/fd0H1440
```

Hard Disk Operations in Linux

You must perform some disk operations to install and use Linux on your system. Chapter 2 explains some of the disk operations you perform when you set up Linux. The next few sections provide some additional information about these disk operations.

When you first get a PC, the hard disk usually is set up as one huge partition, and DOS and Windows are already installed on it. (If you have bought your PC recently, it probably comes with Windows 2000 or Windows XP preinstalled.) To install Red Hat Linux, you have to start by creating at least three partitions for Linux: one for the swap space, a `/boot` partition for the Linux kernel files, and a / partition for the Linux file system.

If you want to retain the existing Windows operating system, you have to resize the Windows partition and create disk space for Red Hat Linux. When you install Red Hat Linux, you can use the unused disk space for all the Linux partitions.

Resizing Partitions

If you do not want to go through the trouble of reinstalling Windows, you have to alter the existing partition somehow. FIPS, which can split an existing FAT or FAT32 partition into two separate partitions, enables you to perform this task. By the way, FAT and FAT32 partitions were used in MD-DOS and Windows 95/98/Me. Windows NT, 2000, and XP also support FAT and FAT32, but they typically use the NT file system (NTFS). Chapter 2 describes how to use FIPS. You can also use one of the following utilities to repartition your hard disk:

- ◆ **PowerQuest's PartitionMagic**—This commercial utility enables you to resize, split, merge, delete, undelete, and convert partitions without destroying existing data. PartitionMagic works on Windows XP and can resize partitions containing FAT, FAT32, NTFS, and Linux ext2 file systems. For more information, visit `http://www.powerquest.com`.
- ◆ **Acronis PartitionExpert**—This commercial utility enables you to resize, copy, and move partitions without losing data. It can resize partitions containing FAT, FAT32, and NTFS, and Linux ext2 file systems, among others. For more information, visit `http://www.acronis.com`.
- ◆ **GNU parted**—Red Hat Linux includes the GNU parted utility that can manipulate FAT, FAT32, and Linux ext2 partitions. Using parted, you can resize partitions from within Linux. For more information, visit `http://www.gnu.org/software/parted/`.

Partitioning Using fdisk

Partitioning the disk involves creating several smaller logical devices within a single hard disk. In Linux, you can use the partitioning program fdisk to view and alter a disk's partition table.

Even if you have already partitioned your hard disk, you can always run fdisk just to see the current partition table of a hard disk. If you have an IDE disk drive with the device name /dev/hda, for example, you can look at its partition table with fdisk as follows:

```
/sbin/fdisk /dev/hda
Command (m for help): m
Command action
   a   toggle a bootable flag
   b   edit bsd disklabel
   c   toggle the dos compatibility flag
   d   delete a partition
   l   list known partition types
   m   print this menu
   n   add a new partition
   o   create a new empty DOS partition table
   p   print the partition table
   q   quit without saving changes
   s   create a new empty Sun disklabel
   t   change a partition's system id
   u   change display/entry units
   v   verify the partition table
   w   write table to disk and exit
   x   extra functionality (experts only)

Command (m for help): p

Disk /dev/hda: 4320 MB, 4320862208 bytes
255 heads, 63 sectors/track, 525 cylinders
Units = cylinders of 16065 * 512 = 8225280 bytes

   Device Boot    Start      End    Blocks   Id  System
/dev/hda1   *         1       13    104391   83  Linux
/dev/hda2            14      501   3919860   83  Linux
/dev/hda3           502      525    192780   82  Linux swap

Command (m for help): q
```

The m command shows you a list of the single-letter commands that fdisk accepts. You can see the current partition table with a p command. This example's IDE disk has three partitions, all for Linux.

The Id field in the table of partitions the fdisk program prints (when you type **p** at the fdisk prompt) is a number that denotes a partition type. That partition ID is a hexadecimal number. If you want to see a list of all known partition IDs, type **l** (a lowercase L) at the fdisk prompt, as follows:

```
Command (m for help): l
  0  Empty            1c  Hidden Win95 FA 70  DiskSecure Mult bb  Boot Wizard hid
  1  FAT12            1e  Hidden Win95 FA 75  PC/IX           be  Solaris boot
  2  XENIX root       24  NEC DOS         80  Old Minix       c1  DRDOS/sec (FAT-
  3  XENIX usr        39  Plan 9          81  Minix / old Lin c4  DRDOS/sec (FAT-
  4  FAT16 <32M       3c  PartitionMagic  82  Linux swap      c6  DRDOS/sec (FAT-
  5  Extended         40  Venix 80286     83  Linux           c7  Syrinx
  6  FAT16            41  PPC PReP Boot    84  OS/2 hidden C:  da  Non-FS data
  7  HPFS/NTFS        42  SFS             85  Linux extended  db  CP/M / CTOS / .
  8  AIX              4d  QNX4.x          86  NTFS volume set de  Dell Utility
  9  AIX bootable     4e  QNX4.x 2nd part 87  NTFS volume set df  BootIt
  a  OS/2 Boot Manag  4f  QNX4.x 3rd part 8e  Linux LVM       e1  DOS access
  b  Win95 FAT32      50  OnTrack DM      93  Amoeba          e3  DOS R/O
  c  Win95 FAT32 (LB  51  OnTrack DM6 Aux 94  Amoeba BBT      e4  SpeedStor
  e  Win95 FAT16 (LB  52  CP/M            9f  BSD/OS          eb  BeOS fs
  f  Win95 Ext'd (LB  53  OnTrack DM6 Aux a0  IBM Thinkpad hi ee  EFI GPT
 10  OPUS             54  OnTrackDM6      a5  FreeBSD         ef  EFI (FAT-12/16/
 11  Hidden FAT12     55  EZ-Drive        a6  OpenBSD         f0  Linux/PA-RISC b
 12  Compaq diagnost  56  Golden Bow      a7  NeXTSTEP        f1  SpeedStor
 14  Hidden FAT16 <3  5c  Priam Edisk     a8  Darwin UFS      f4  SpeedStor
 16  Hidden FAT16     61  SpeedStor       a9  NetBSD          f2  DOS secondary
 17  Hidden HPFS/NTF  63  GNU HURD or Sys ab  Darwin boot     fd  Linux raid auto
 18  AST SmartSleep   64  Novell Netware  b7  BSDI fs         fe  LANstep
 1b  Hidden Win95 FA  65  Novell Netware  b8  BSDI swap       ff  BBT
```

Booting from the Hard Disk

To automatically boot Linux from a hard disk, you need a boot loader. Red Hat Linux comes with two boot loaders—the Linux Loader (LILO) and the GNU Grand Unified Bootloader (GRUB).

The boot loader programs usually reside in the master boot record of a disk and are the first to be loaded. The boot loader program, in turn, prompts you for the operating system to start (which typically means a disk partition from which to boot). Starting an operating system basically involves loading that operating system's main program into memory and running it. For Linux, this step involves loading the Linux kernel into memory and giving control to the kernel.

> **note** GRUB is the default boot loader for Red Hat Linux, but you can opt to install LILO instead of GRUB. You get the option to select the boot loader as you install Red Hat Linux following the steps outlined in Chapter 2.

If you decide to install LILO, you'll find the LILO documentation in the /usr/share/doc directory on your system. Type **cd /usr/share/doc/lilo*** to change to the LILO documentation directory (the exact name depends on the current version of LILO). You should consult the README file in that directory for the latest word on installing and configuring LILO.

To configure LILO to boot an operating system, you have to perform two steps:

1. Prepare the LILO configuration file, which contains information that is necessary for installing LILO. The default LILO configuration file is /etc/lilo.conf.
2. Run the /sbin/lilo program (referred to as the map installer in LILO's README file) to update the boot sector and create the /boot/map file, which contains information that LILO uses during the boot process.

---

cross ref   Chapter 21 describes how to configure GRUB to install a new kernel. You can consult that chapter to learn more about GRUB.

If, during installation, you forget to assign a label to the Windows XP partition in the Boot Loader Installation screen, GRUB will not show the Windows XP partition as an option when it starts. That leaves with you with the problem that you cannot boot Windows XP anymore, even though the XP partition is intact. To recover from this problem, you have to edit the GRUB configuration file, /etc/grub.conf.

---

insider insight   Assuming that the XP partition is /dev/hda2, here's what you add to the end of the /etc/grub.conf: to enable GRUB to boot the Windows XP partition:

```
title Windows XP
        root (hd0,1)
        makeactive
        chainloader +1
```

For most PCs that come with Windows XP preinstalled, the second disk partition (/dev/hda2) is the one with the Windows XP file system; the first disk partition is a hidden one used to store files needed to install Windows XP. You do not have to restart GRUB or do anything special for these changes to take effect. Simply save the /etc/grub.conf file and reboot. This time GRUB should display a menu that includes Windows XP as an option. To boot Windows XP, all you have to do is select that option.

Creating Swap Space

Swap space is a disk partition Linux uses as an extension of its memory. When some memory-resident data is not needed immediately, Linux stores that data in the swap space. To create the swap space, you have to create a disk partition using fdisk. Make sure that you set the type of that disk partition to Linux swap (partition ID 82 in hexadecimal). Typically, you set up the swap partition and turn on swapping as you install Red Hat Linux from this book's CD-ROMs.

If you have to set up the swap space outside the installation program, you have to use the mkswap command to initialize the swap partition. You need the size of the swap partition (in number of blocks) before you use the mkswap command. Use the Linux fdisk program, and type the p command at the fdisk prompt to find the size of the swap partition.

For example, to initialize /dev/hda4 as a swap partition, type the following command:

```
/sbin/mkswap -c /dev/hda4 192772
```

In this case, 192772 is the block size of the swap partition. You can skip the size parameter because the mkswap command can determine the size from the partition table.

The size of the swap partition depends on the amount of virtual memory you need. To Linux, the total amount of memory in your PC is the combined total of the swap partition's size and the amount of physical RAM. Although there is no formula to tell you how much virtual memory you need, the conventional wisdom is that you should have at least as much swap space as physical memory.

You can have a swap partition as large as 2GB, and you can have up to eight swap partitions. All you have to do is run the mkswap command for each swap partition you create.

After mkswap finishes, use the /sbin/swapon command to turn on swapping. Linux then begins to use the swap space.

The /proc/swaps file contains information about the swap spaces your Linux system is using. For example, here's what I get when I check /proc/swaps on my system:

```
cat /proc/swaps
Filename                    Type        Size    Used    Priority
/dev/hda3                   partition   192772  59528   -1
```

The output shows the current swap spaces. Although it is customary to use a disk partition as the swap space, you can also use a file as swap space. The first column in the list of swap spaces is labeled Filename because the swap space can be a file. If you want to use a file as swap space, create the file with a command, such as the following:

```
dd if=/dev/zero of=swapfile bs=1024 count=131072
```

This creates a file named swapfile of size 131,072. Type **/sbin/mkswap -c swapfile** to initialize that file, then type **/sbin/swapon swapfile** to use the file for swapping.

---

insider insight

To ensure that Linux uses the swap space every time it boots, you need a line in the /etc/fstab file that indicates the swap partition's name. If the swap partition is /dev/hda3, for example, add the following line to /etc/fstab:

```
/dev/hda3        swap        swap      defaults      0 0
```

If you create a swap space when you install Linux, the installation program adds the appropriate line in the /etc/fstab file. You may need to add such a line if you create additional swap spaces later.

If you put a partition's name in /etc/fstab but forget to run mkswap on that partition, Linux displays the following error message:

```
Unable to find swap-space signature
```

The fix is to run mkswap to initialize the swap partition.

Creating File Systems

To use a disk partition in Linux, you have to create a file system on that partition. You can think of this procedure as formatting the partition for Linux. When you install Linux by following the steps described in Chapter 2, one of the steps creates the file system; the setup program asks you whether or not you want to format a partition. For a Linux partition, the setup program uses the mke2fs command to create a Linux file system.

Linux supports several types of file systems, including the following:

♦ **MS-DOS file system**—This DOS file system is based on the file allocation table (FAT). This file system type is designated by the keyword msdos.

♦ **Microsoft Windows file system with support for long filenames**—This is a DOS-compatible FAT file system with support for long filenames. This file type is identified by the keyword vfat. You should use this file system to access all DOS/Windows disks from Linux.

♦ **Minix file system**—Minix is the original UNIX clone that inspired the creation of Linux. Linux started by using the Minix file system, which limits filenames to 14 or 30 characters. The minix keyword identifies this file-system type.

♦ **Extended file system**—This old Linux file system goes by the keyword ext. You should not use this file system anymore.

♦ **Second extended file system**—This is the latest and greatest Linux file system. The keyword ext2 refers to this file-system type. You can use longer filenames in this file system.

♦ **Third extended file system**—This is an enhancement of the ext2 file system with journaling to enable rapid recovery in case of any errors. The keyword ext3 refers to this file-system type.

The Red Hat Linux installation program automatically creates an ext3 file system on the Linux partition. To create an ext3 file system manually, you have to use the mke2fs command as follows:

```
/sbin/mke2fs -c -j /dev/hda3
```

This command creates an ext3 file system on the /dev/hda3 partition. The mke2fs command automatically figures out the size of the partition and uses it to size the file system. The -c option forces mke2fs to check for bad blocks (using a fast read-only test) before creating the file system. The -j option causes mke2fs to create the file system with an ext3 journal.

insider insight

When you install Linux on a hard disk that uses standard IDE, MFM, or RLL controllers, always install the ext3 file system and use the bad-block-checking options when you create the file system.

SCSI Disk Controllers and Linux

SCSI (pronounced "scuzzy") is an increasingly popular interface for connecting up to seven different devices on the SCSI bus. Each device, and the SCSI controller, has a unique SCSI identifier (ID) in the range 0 through 7. The controller usually is set to SCSI

ID 7; the other devices use numbers between 0 and 6 (that means you can connect up to seven devices to a SCSI controller). Typically, a SCSI hard disk is set to SCSI ID 0.

Table B-1 lists the SCSI controllers that the version of Linux kernel on the companion CD-ROMs supports. The table also shows the name of the driver module that supports each specific set of controllers. If necessary, you can manually load the driver for your SCSI controller with the command /sbin/modprobe *modname*, where *modname* refers to the name of the driver module.

Table B-1: Supported SCSI Controllers

SCSI Controller	Linux Driver Module
3ware Storage Controller	3w-xxx
ACARD ATP870U	atp870u
Adaptec AHA-1460 (AHA152X-compatible) PCMCIA SCSI card	aha152x_cs
Adaptec AHA-1510/152x (ISA)	aha152x
Adaptec AHA-154x (ISA) (all models)	aha1542
Adaptec AHA-174x (EISA) (in enhanced mode)	aha1740
Adaptec AHA-274x/274xT (EISA), AHA-284x (VLB), AHA-2910B (PCI), AHA-2920C (PCI), AHA-2930/U/U2/CU, AHA-2940/U/W/AU/UW/U2W (PCI), AHA-294160M, AHA-2944D/WD/UD/UWD (PCI), AHA-2950U2/U2W/U2B, AHA-39160M, AHA-3940/U/W/UW (PCI), AHA-3950U2D, AHA-3960D, AHA-398x/U/W/UW (PCI)	aic7xxx
Adaptec AHA-2920A (PCI) with Future Domain chipset	fdomain
Adaptec AVA-1502E (ISA/VLB), AVA-1505/1515 (ISA), AVA-282x—all are Adaptec AHA-152x compatible	aha152x
Adaptec I2O RAID	dpt_i2o
AdvanSys ABP510/5150 Bus-Master ISA, ABP5140 Bus-Master ISA PnP (Plug and Play), ABP5142 Bus-Master ISA PnP with floppy, ABP542 Bus-Master ISA with floppy (single channel), ABP742 Bus-Master EISA (single channel), ABP752 Dual Channel Bus-Master EISA (dual channel), ABP842 Bus-Master VL (single channel), ABP852 Dual Channel Bus-Master VL (dual channel), ABP920 Bus-Master PCI, ABP930/U Bus-Master PCI/Ultra, ABP940/U Bus-Master PCI/Ultra (single channel), ABP950 Dual Channel Bus-Master PCI (dual channel), ABP960/U Bus-Master PCI/ULTRA MAC/PC, ABP970/U Bus-Master PCI/Ultra MAC/PC (single channel)	advansys
AIC-777x, AIC-785x, AIC-786x, AIC-787x, AIC-788x, AIC-789x, and AIC-3860 chipsets	aic7xxx
Always IN2000 (ISA)	in2000
AMD AM53/79C974	AM53C974
AMI Fast Disk VLB/EISA (BusLogic-compatible), BusLogic FlashPoint LT/DL/LW/DW PCI	BusLogic

(continued)

Table B-1: *(continued)*

SCSI Controller	Linux Driver Module
Compaq 64-bit/66Mhz PCI Fibre Channel HBA	cpqfc
Domex DMX3191D	dmx3191d
DPT SmartRAID V I2O	dpt_i2o
DPT PM2001, PM2012A (EATA-PIO)	eata_pio
DPT EATA-DMA controllers such as Smartcache/ SmartRAID Plus, III,IV families (ISA/EISA/PCI)	eata_dma
Data Technology Corp DTC 3180/3280	dtc
DTC 329x (EISA) (Adaptec 154x-compatible)	aha1542
Future Domain TMC-1800, TMC-18C50, TMC-18C30, TMC-36C70, TMC-16x0, TMC-3260 (PCI)	fdomain
Future Domain TMC-8xx, TMC-950	seagate
Future Domain-compatible PCMCIA SCSI card	fdomain_cs
IBM ServeRAID controller	ips
ICP-Vortex GDT ISA and EISA SCSI Controllers, GDT PCI SCSI Disk array Controllers (many RAID levels supported)	gdth
IDE/ATAPI adapters (SCSI emulation for IDE devices, so SCSI driver can be used to access IDE devices such as CD-ROM drives)	ide-scsi
Initio INI-9X00U/UW SCSI host adapters	initio
Initio INI-A100U2W SCSI host adapters	a100u2w
Intraserver ITI-6200U2 Dual Channel Ultra2 SCSI Host Adapter (uses the NCR53C896 chipset)	ncr53c8xx
Iomega Match Maker parallel-port SCSI Host Bus Adapter embedded in ZIP Plus drive	imm
Iomega PPA3 parallel-port SCSI Host Bus Adapter embedded in ZIP drive	ppa
LSI Logic MegaRAID 418, 428, 438, 466, 762, 467, 471, 490, and 493	megaraid
Mylex (formerly BusLogic) A Series (ISA/EISA), C Series (ISA/EISA/VLB/PCI), S Series (ISA/EISA/VLB), W Series (PCI)	BusLogic
NCR 5380 and 53C400 generic cards	sim710
NCR 53C406a (Acculogic ISApport / Media Vision Premium 3D SCSI)	NCR53c406a
NCR53c710 (simple driver)	g_NCR5380
NCR 53c810, 53c810A, 53c815, 53c825, 53c825A, 53c860, 53c875, 53c876 53c895 53c400, NCR5380, 53c810, 53c810A, 53c815, 53c820, 53c825, 53c810, 53c820, 53c720, 53c700, 53c710 (PCI), 53c700-66	53c7,8xx
NCR 53C875 and 53C876 chipsets	ncr53c8xx
NinjaSCSI-32Bi CardBus, NinjaSCSI-32UDE PCI/CardBus SCSI controllers	nsp32

SCSI Controller	Linux Driver Module
OnStream SCSI Tape	osst
Perceptive Solutions PCI-2000 IntelliCache	pci2220i
Perceptive Solutions PCI-2220I EIDE RAID	pci2000
Perceptive Solutions PSI-240I EIDE	psi240i
Pro Audio Spectrum/Studio 16 (ISA)	pas16
QLogic ISP1x80/1x160	qla1280
Qlogic / Control Concepts ISP2100 SCSI-FCP	qlogicfc
Qlogic Fast SCSI FASXXX family of chips (ISA/VLB/PCMCIA)	qlogicfas
QLogic ISP1020 Intelligent SCSI cards IQ-PCI, IQ-PCI-10, IQ-PCI-D (PCI)	qlogicisp
QLogic PCMCIA SCSI card	qlogic_cs
Quantum ISA-200S, ISA-250MG	fdomain
Seagate ST-01/ST-02 (ISA)	seagate
SoundBlaster 16 SCSI-2 (Adaptec 152x–compatible) (ISA)	aha152x
Symbios Logic SYM53C416 Chip	sym53c416
Symbios Logic SYM53C896 (also supports the 538XX controller family, except 53C815 and versions lower than 16 of the 53C810 and 53C825 controllers)	sym53c8xx
Tekram DC-390, DC-390W/U/F (AMD53C974 chipset)	tmscsim
Trantor T128/T128F/T228 (ISA)	t128
Trantor T130B (NCR 53C400 chipset)	g_NCR5380
UltraStor 14F (ISA), 24F (EISA), 34F (VLB)	u14-34f
Western Digital WD7000-FAST, WD7000-FASST2, WD7000-ASC, WD7000-AX/MX/EX	wd7000

Cable and Termination Problems

The SCSI bus needs terminators at both ends to work reliably. A terminator is a set of resistors that indicate the end of the SCSI bus. One end is the controller card itself, which typically has the terminator on it. Often, a SCSI device has two SCSI connectors, so that you can daisy-chain several external SCSI devices. You are supposed to place a terminator on the last connector on the chain.

insider insight

Some SCSI controllers—such as Adaptec AHA 154xC, 154xCF, and 274x (x is any digit)—are sensitive to the type of cable and terminator you use. If the cables are not perfect or the terminator is not used properly, these SCSI cards may fail intermittently or may not work at all.

To avoid problems with overly sensitive SCSI cards, use cables that come from a reputable vendor, and use cables from the same vendor to connect all SCSI devices. The cables should be SCSI 2–compliant and should have an impedance of 132 ohms (a characteristic of the cable; all you have to do is make sure the specified value is 132 ohms).

Most SCSI problems are due to bad cables or improper termination. You should check the cables and the terminator before trying anything else.

SCSI Device at All SCSI IDs

If a SCSI device shows up at all possible SCSI IDs, you must have configured that device with the same SCSI ID as the SCSI controller (usually, 7). Change the ID of that device to another value. (Many devices have a simple switch for setting the SCSI ID; on others, you have to change a jumper.)

SCSI Device at All LUNs

If a SCSI device shows up at all possible SCSI logical unit numbers (LUNs), the device probably has errors in the firmware—the built-in code in the device's SCSI interface. To verify these errors, use the following command line during boot:

```
max_scsi_luns=1
```

If the device works with this option, you can add it to the list of blacklisted SCSI devices in the array of structures named `device_list` in the file `/usr/src/linux-2.4/drivers/scsi/scsi_scan.c`. The definition of that structure and some parts of the array are as follows:

```
struct dev_info{
    const char * vendor;
    const char * model;
    const char * revision; /* Latest revision known to be bad. Not used yet */
    unsigned flags;
};
/*
 * This is what was previously known as the blacklist.  The concept
 * has been expanded so that we can specify other types of things we
 * need to be aware of.
 */
static struct dev_info device_list[] =
{
/* The following devices are known not to tolerate a lun != 0 scan for
 * one reason or another.  Some will respond to all luns, others will
 * lock up.
 */
{"Aashima","IMAGERY 2400SP","1.03",BLIST_NOLUN},/* Locks up if polled for lun !=  0 */
{"CHINON","CD-ROM CDS-431","H42", BLIST_NOLUN}, /* Locks up if polled for lun !=
  0 */
{"CHINON","CD-ROM CDS-535","Q14", BLIST_NOLUN}, /* Locks up if polled for lun !=
  0 */
{"DENON","DRD-25X","V", BLIST_NOLUN},      /* Locks up if probed for lun != 0 */
{"HITACHI","DK312C","CM81", BLIST_NOLUN},  /* Responds to all lun - dtg */
{"HITACHI","DK314C","CR21" , BLIST_NOLUN}, /* responds to all lun */
{"IMS", "CDD521/10","2.06", BLIST_NOLUN},  /* Locks-up when LUN>0 polled. */
```

```
{"MAXTOR","XT-3280","PR02", BLIST_NOLUN},  /* Locks-up when LUN>0 polled. */
... lines deleted ...
        {"HITACHI", "DF600", "*", BLIST_SPARSELUN},
        {"IBM", "ProFibre 4000R", "*", BLIST_SPARSELUN | BLIST_LARGELUN},
/*
 * Must be at end of list...
 */
{NULL, NULL, NULL}
};
```

From this list, you can get an idea of the types of SCSI devices that have the problem of showing up at all LUNs. If you have the same problem with a SCSI device, you can add that device's name to this list before the last line before rebuilding the kernel. You may not want to do this, however, if you are not familiar with the C programming language.

Sense Errors on an Error-Free SCSI Device

The cause of this problem usually is bad cables or improper termination. Check all cables, and make sure the SCSI bus is terminated at both ends.

Networking Kernel Problems with a SCSI Device

If a Linux kernel with networking support does not work with SCSI devices, the problem may be the autoprobe function of the networking drivers. The autoprobe capability is meant to detect the type of networking hardware automatically; the network drivers read from and write to specific I/O addresses during autoprobing. If an I/O address happens to be the same as that a SCSI device uses, the system may have a problem. In this case, you have to check the I/O address, IRQ, and DMA values of the network cards and of the SCSI controller and make sure no conflicts exist. Most SCSI controllers (and even network adapters) allow you to configure these parameters (I/O address, IRQ, and DMA) through setup software that comes with the adapter.

Device Is Detected but Not Accessible

If the kernel detects a SCSI device (as reported in the boot messages, which you can see by typing the command dmesg | more) but you cannot access the device, the device file may be missing from the /dev directory.

---

insider insight

To add the device file, log in as root, change the directory to /dev, and use the MAKEDEV script to create the device file. To add a device for a SCSI tape drive, for example, use the following command:

```
cd /dev

./MAKEDEV st0
```

When you log in as root, the current directory is typically not in the PATH environment variable. That's why you need to add the ./ prefix when executing the MAKEDEV script. You can find more information about the MAKEDEV script with the following command:

```
man MAKEDEV
```

SCSI Lockup

If the SCSI system locks up, check the SCSI controller card, using any diagnostic software that came with the card (usually, the diagnostic software runs under DOS). Look for conflicts in I/O address, IRQ, or DMA with other cards. Some sound cards, for example, use a 16-bit DMA channel in addition to an 8-bit DMA; make sure you have not inadvertently used the same 16-bit DMA for the SCSI card.

The Linux SCSI driver for some SCSI cards supports only one outstanding SCSI command at a time. With such a SCSI card, if a device such as a tape drive is busy rewinding, the system may not be able to access other SCSI devices (such as a hard disk or a CD-ROM drive) that are daisy-chained with that tape drive. A solution to this problem is to add a second SCSI controller to take care of the tape drives.

SCSI Devices Not Found

If the Linux kernel does not detect your SCSI devices at startup, you get the following message when Linux boots:

```
scsi : 0 hosts
scsi : detected total
```

If you see this message, but you know that the SCSI devices are there (and that they work under DOS), the problem may be the lack of a BIOS on the SCSI controller; the autoprobe routines that detect SCSI devices rely on the BIOS.

This problem occurs for the following SCSI cards:

- ◆ Adaptec 152x, 151x, AIC-6260, and AIC-6360
- ◆ Future Domain 1680, TMC-950, and TMC-8xx
- ◆ Trantor T128, T128F, and T228F
- ◆ Seagate ST01 and ST02
- ◆ Western Digital 7000

---

insider insight Even if a SCSI controller has a BIOS, jumpers often are available for disabling the BIOS. If you have disabled the BIOS for some reason, you may want to reenable it (read the documentation of your SCSI controller for directions) so that Linux can detect the SCSI devices automatically.

For a SCSI card, such as the Adaptec 151x, that does not have any BIOS, use the following command line during boot to force detection of the card:

```
aha152x=0x340,11,7,1
```

CD-ROM Drives

◆ ◆

If you have installed or are planning to install Red Hat Linux from this book's companion CD-ROMs, chances are good that your system already has a CD-ROM drive. You are probably reading this appendix because you have questions about using your CD-ROM drive to install Linux. In this appendix, you can find answers to some common questions about CD-ROM drives. In particular, this appendix describes specific types of Linux-supported CD-ROM drives, categorized by interface type.

CD-ROM as a Storage Media

Typically each CD-ROM can hold up to 650MB of data (the equivalent of over 450 high-density 3.5-inch floppy disks) and does not cost much to produce. The physical medium of the CD-ROM is the same as that used for audio compact discs (CDs): a polycarbonate disc with an aluminized layer. A laser reads the data, which is encoded in microscopic pits on the aluminized layer. CD-ROM media are more robust and reliable than other magnetic media, such as floppy disks. All these factors make CD-ROM an attractive medium for distributing data and programs. In fact, most Linux books (including this one) bundle CD-ROMs with a complete Linux distribution that includes the operating system and lots of popular software. In this case, the CD-ROMs contain Red Hat Linux—a popular Linux distribution.

In that list of good properties of a CD-ROM—high capacity, low cost, and reliability—you don't see any mention of speed; the data-transfer rates of CD-ROM drives are not as fast as those of hard disk drives. When CD-ROM drives first appeared, they could transfer data at rates of approximately 150KB per second. These drives were known as single-speed (also referred to as 1X) CD-ROM drives. Double-speed (or 2X) CD-ROM drives, which provide data-transfer rates of 300KB per second, were soon widely available. Currently, most systems come with 24X, 32X, or even 40X CD-ROM drives, which can sustain data-transfer rates of up to 3,600KB per second and average access times of 95 milliseconds (compare this with hard-drive access times of around 10 milliseconds).

> **note** Most CD-ROMs contain information in an ISO-9660 file system (formerly known as High Sierra). This file system supports only the MS-DOS-style 8.3 filenames, such as README.TXT, which have names up to eight characters and optional three-character filename extensions, such as .DOC or .TXT. An extension to the ISO-9660 file system, called the Rock Ridge Extensions, uses unused fields to support longer filenames and additional UNIX-style file attributes, such as ownership and symbolic links.

Most CD-ROM drives enable you to play audio CDs via an external headphone jack. Also, you will find an output line you can connect to the sound card so that you can play an audio CD on the speakers attached to the sound card.

Supported CD-ROM Drives

As with hard disks, Linux's support for a CD-ROM drive depends on the interface through which that CD-ROM drive connects to the PC's motherboard. CD-ROM drives come with three types of interfaces:

- ♦ **IDE or AT Attachment Packet Interface (ATAPI)**—ATAPI is a recent specification for accessing and controlling a CD-ROM drive connected to the PC through the AT Attachment (ATA). ATAPI is gaining popularity because it is built on the cheaper IDE interface. (ATA is the new name for IDE.)
- ♦ **Small Computer System Interface (SCSI)**—SCSI is popular because of its relatively high data rates and because it can support multiple devices. The only drawback is that you need a relatively expensive SCSI controller card for the PC.
- ♦ **Universal Serial Bus (USB)**—USB is a popular interface for attaching various devices from printers to scanners to PCs. There are CD-ROM drives as well as CD-R (recordable CD) and CD-RW (rewritable CD) drives that attach to USB ports. USB CD-R and CD-RW drives are popular because they can be quickly and easily moved between systems. To support USB CD drives, all you need is to enable USB mass storage support in the kernel. This causes the USB CD drives to appear as SCSI drives, but with different device names.
- ♦ **Proprietary interfaces**—Many CD-ROM vendors provide their own proprietary interfaces between the CD-ROM drive and the PC's motherboard. Many sound cards include a built-in CD-ROM-drive interface, which is typically proprietary. The problem with proprietary interfaces is that someone has to develop a Linux driver specifically for each interface, whereas with a SCSI interface you can use a SCSI driver to access any SCSI device.

ATAPI CD-ROM Drives

ATA (AT Attachment) is the official ANSI (American National Standards Institute) standard name for the commonplace IDE interface, which is commonly used to connect hard-disk drives to the PC. ATAPI (ATA Packet Interface) is a protocol (similar to SCSI) for controlling storage devices, such as CD-ROM drives and tape drives. Although ATAPI is relatively new, it is rapidly becoming the most popular type of interface for CD-ROM drives, because ATAPI is based on the ATA (or IDE) interface and does not need any expensive controller card or cable. Also, an ATAPI CD-ROM can simply be connected as the second drive on the same interface on which the PC's hard drive is connected. That means that the ATAPI CD-ROM drive does not require a separate interface card.

The Linux kernel includes an ATAPI driver that should work with any ATAPI CD-ROM drive. ATAPI CD-ROM drives are available from many vendors, such as Aztech, Mitsumi, NEC, Philips, Sony, and Toshiba. Most new PCs (such as those from Gateway and Dell) come configured with ATAPI CD-ROM drives.

insider insight

Linux also comes with the `ide-scsi` driver that emulates a SCSI interface for IDE devices. In Linux IDE CD-R (CD-recordable) or CD-RW (CD-rewritable) drives work through the SCSI emulation driver (`ide-scsi`). If you have an IDE CD-R or CD-RW drive, add the following line to the `/etc/modules.conf` file:

```
alias scsi_hostadapter ide-scsi
```

SCSI CD-ROM Drives

Linux supports a SCSI CD-ROM drive connected to one of the supported SCSI controller cards (see Appendix B for more information). The only restriction is that the block size (for data transfers) of the SCSI CD-ROM drive should be 512 or 2,048 bytes, which covers all CD-ROM drives on the market.

Some CD-ROM drives include a controller with a modified interface that's not fully SCSI-compatible. These interfaces are essentially proprietary, and you cannot use such CD-ROM drives with the SCSI driver.

SCSI CD-ROM drives are available from many vendors, such as Plextor, Sanyo, and Toshiba.

Proprietary CD-ROM Drives

Although the ATAPI and SCSI CD-ROM drives fall into neat categories and work well in Linux, the situation is much more confusing when it comes to CD-ROM drives with a proprietary interface. Following are two of the biggest sources of confusion:

♦ Some vendors, such as Creative Labs (of SoundBlaster fame), have sold CD-ROM drives with all types of interfaces: ATAPI, SCSI, and proprietary interfaces on a sound card. Thus, the vendor's name alone does not mean anything; you have to know what type of interface the CD-ROM drive uses.

♦ PC vendors sometimes categorize the CD-ROM-drive interface as IDE, even though the interface is really proprietary. Like the IDE (or ATAPI) interface, the proprietary CD-ROM-drive interface is cheap and popular.

As you may have guessed, proprietary CD-ROM-drive interfaces are popular because they tend to be much simpler than SCSI interfaces, which were the primary alternative to proprietary interfaces before ATAPI came along. Because of the popularity of the relatively inexpensive ATAPI, most new PCs do not use proprietary interfaces for CD-ROM drives. Because a proprietary CD-ROM interface can be built into a sound card at little cost, however, some Linux users may have PCs with proprietary CD-ROM drives.

If you have a choice, avoid proprietary CD-ROM-drive interfaces. They're more trouble than they're worth. Of course, if you have an older PC with a proprietary CD-ROM interface, you may be stuck with it.

Table C-1 lists CD-ROM drives with proprietary interfaces and the drivers you need to support those drives.

Table C-1: CD-ROM Drives with Proprietary Interfaces

Driver	CD-ROM Drive
aztcd	Aztech CDA268-01A (other models are ATAPI drives), Orchid CDS-3110, Okano/Wearnes CDD-110, Conrad TXC, CyCDROM CR520ie/CR940ie
cdu31a	Sony CDU31A/CDU33A
cm206cd	Philips/LMS CM 206
gscd	GoldStar R420 (may be sold as part of the Reveal Multimedia kit)
isp16	CD-ROM drives attached to the interface on an ISP16, MAD16, or Mozart sound card
mcd	Mitsumi CRMC LU005S, FX001
mcdx	Mitsumi CRMC LU005S, FX001 (new driver)
optcd	Optics Storage Dolphin 8000AT, Lasermate CR328A
sbpcd	Matsushita/Panasonic (Panasonic CR-521, CR-522, CR-523, CR-562, and CR-563), Kotobuki, Creative Labs (CD-200), Longshine LCS-7260, Teac CD-55A
sjcd	Sanyo H94A
sonycd535	Sony CDU-535/CDU-531

Linux uses a unique device name for each type of proprietary CD-ROM interface. The CD-ROM devices are block devices like the disk devices, such as /dev/hda and /dev/sda. Table C-2 lists the CD-ROM device names for the proprietary CD-ROM interfaces.

Table C-2: CD-ROM Device Names for Proprietary Interfaces

Device Name	CD-ROM Type
/dev/aztcd	Aztech CD-ROM drive interface
/dev/cdu31a	Sony CDU31A/CDU33A CD-ROM drive interface
/dev/cm206cd	Philips/LMS CD-ROM drive interface
/dev/gscd	GoldStar CD-ROM interface
/dev/hdc	ATAPI CD-ROM drive on the secondary IDE interface on an EIDE controller

Device Name	CD-ROM Type
/dev/mcd	Mitsumi CD-ROM drive interface
/dev/optcd	Optics Storage CD-ROM drive interface
/dev/sbpcd	Sound Blaster Pro CD-ROM drive interface
/dev/sjcd	Sanyo CD-ROM drive interface
/dev/sonycd535	Sony CDU-535/CDU-531 CD-ROM drive interface

CD-ROM Troubleshooting

You need a CD-ROM drive that works under Linux to install Red Hat Linux from this book's companion CD-ROM. The initial Linux kernel comes with CD-ROM driver modules for all supported CD-ROM drives; therefore, you should not have any problem as long as Linux supports your CD-ROM. Remember that the CD-ROM drive's interface is what counts, not the brand name. For example, any CD-ROM drive with the IDE interface works under Linux, because Linux supports the IDE interface.

If Linux does not seem to recognize the CD-ROM drive after you reboot the system, try the following steps to fix the problem:

1. If Linux has not loaded the CD-ROM driver module, you can manually load the driver by logging in as root and typing the command modprobe cdrom. Then check if the CD-ROM drive works by typing eject /dev/cdrom—the CD-ROM drive door should open if it's working. You can then try to mount a CD-ROM.

2. If you have rebuilt the kernel with support for your CD-ROM drive, verify that you are indeed running the new kernel. To see the version number, type the uname -srv (or uname -a) command. This output from the uname command shows the kernel's version number, as well as the date on which the kernel was built. If that date does not match the date on which you rebuilt the kernel, you may not be running the new kernel. Go through the steps outlined in Chapter 21, and make sure you have really installed the new kernel. One common problem is forgetting to reboot, so try that as well.

3. Look at the contents of the /proc/devices file to verify that the CD-ROM device is present. Use the following procedure to view the contents of a /proc/devices file:

```
cat /proc/devices | more
Character devices:
  1 mem
  2 pty
  3 ttyp
  4 ttyS
  5 cua
  6 lp
  7 vcs
 10 misc
 13 input
```

```
 29 fb
 36 netlink
... lines deleted ...
Block devices:
  1 ramdisk
  2 fd
  3 ide0
  9 md
 12 unnamed
 14 unnamed
 22 ide1
 38 unnamed
 39 unnamed
```

This listing corresponds to the devices on one of my Red Hat Linux PCs. It shows two lists of devices—*character devices*, such as serial ports that transfer data one or more characters at a time, and *block devices*, such as hard disks that transfer data in fixed-size blocks. You should look for the CD-ROM device in the list of block devices. I know my CD-ROM drive is connected to the secondary IDE interface. The two IDE interfaces correspond to the devices ide0 and ide1 in /proc/devices. Because ide1 appears in the listing, I know that the CD-ROM driver is in the kernel.

If you have a CD-ROM connected to a Sound Blaster Pro or compatible interface, look for a device number of 25 and the device name sbpcd.

If you don't see a device that corresponds to your CD-ROM drive, you have not configured the kernel properly to include the CD-ROM driver. Reconfigure and rebuild the kernel, making sure that you include support for your CD-ROM drive.

For some SCSI CD-ROM drives, you have to specify the SCSI adapter as a boot option before the Linux kernel can access the CD-ROM drive.

4. Verify that the CD-ROM driver detected the CD-ROM drive when the system started. Type the dmesg | more command to look at the boot messages and to see whether a line reports that the CD-ROM drive has been found. On my system, which has an ATAPI CD-ROM drive, the message looks like this:

```
hdc: SAMSUNG CD-ROM SN-124, ATAPI CD/DVD-ROM drive
```

If you find no boot message about the CD-ROM drive, make sure that the CD-ROM is physically installed. For an external CD-ROM drive, make sure that the drive is powered on and the cables are connected. Check any drive ID or jumpers, and make sure that they are set correctly. You may want to first make sure that the CD-ROM drive works under DOS; if you see the CD-ROM work under DOS, you can be sure that the drive is physically sound. Next, verify that you have rebuilt the kernel with support for the correct CD-ROM-drive interface.

5. Verify that you can read from the CD-ROM drive. Try the following command, and see whether the drive's activity light comes on (it should) and whether any error messages are present (they shouldn't be):

```
dd bs=1024 count=5000 < /dev/cdrom > /dev/null
5000+0 records in
5000+0 records out
```

The /dev/null device is what you might call the bit bucket. Output directed to /dev/null simply vanishes.

If the dd command does not work, the device file for the CD-ROM device may not be set properly. Type the ls -l /dev/cdrom command to view detailed information about your CD-ROM device. The Red Hat Linux installation program sets up /dev/cdrom as a symbolic link to the actual CD-ROM device. For an ATAPI CD-ROM drive on the secondary IDE interface, for example, I look at the /dev/cdrom symbolic link to make sure that it points to the real CD-ROM device (/dev/hdc in this case), as follows:

```
ls -l /dev/cdrom
lrwxrwxrwx   1 root    root     3 Feb 17 13:49 /dev/cdrom -> hdc
```

6. Verify that you can mount the CD-ROM. Place a good CD-ROM (such as the CD-ROM from this book) in the CD-ROM drive, and try to mount it by using the following command:

```
mount -t iso9660 -r /dev/cdrom /mnt/cdrom
```

The -t iso9660 option specifies that the CD-ROM has an ISO-9660 file system, and the -r option says you want to mount the file system as read-only.

If you can read from the CD-ROM drive with the dd command but cannot mount the CD-ROM, you may have configured the kernel without support for the ISO-9660 file system. To verify the currently supported file systems, use the following command:

```
cat /proc/filesystems
```

If you do not see iso9660 listed in the output, you have to rebuild the kernel and add support for the ISO-9660 file system.

7. If nothing works, you may want to read the latest CDROM-HOWTO document. To read the HOWTO documents, point your Web browser to http://www.ibiblio.org/pub/Linux/docs/HOWTO/CDROM-HOWTO (your Red Hat Linux system must be connected to the Internet for this to work).

cross ref

If you still cannot get the CD-ROM drive to work under Linux, you may want to post a news item to one of the comp.os.linux newsgroups. Chapter 16 describes how to post to newsgroups.

The following sections suggest solutions for a few more common problems.

Kernel Configuration for Specific CD-ROM Drives

If you are rebuilding the kernel and you have an ATAPI CD-ROM drive, you should answer yes to the following questions as you configure the kernel (see Chapter 21 for more on configuring the kernel):

```
Enhanced IDE/MFM/RLL disk/cdrom/tape/floppy support (CONFIG_BLK_DEV_IDE) [Y/m/n/?] y
    Include IDE/ATAPI CDROM support (CONFIG_BLK_DEV_IDECD) [Y/m/n/?] y
```

The possible responses are shown in brackets: y means yes (that means include support in the kernel); m means use a driver module, and n means no.

For SCSI CD-ROM drives, answer yes to the following questions:

```
*
* SCSI support
*
SCSI support (CONFIG_SCSI) [Y/m/n/?] y
*
* SCSI support type (disk, tape, CD-ROM)
*
SCSI CD-ROM support (CONFIG_BLK_DEV_SR) [Y/m/n/?] y
```

Of course, you must specify your SCSI controller type; otherwise, the SCSI CD-ROM won't work. If you have an Adaptec AHA1542 SCSI controller, for example, answer yes to the following question:

```
Adaptec AHA1542 support (CONFIG_SCSI_AHA1542) [M/n/y/?] y
```

If your CD-ROM drive has a proprietary interface, you must enable support for that specific CD-ROM drive interface. Start by answering yes to the following question during kernel configuration:

```
*
* Old CD-ROM drivers (not SCSI, not IDE)
*
Support non-SCSI/IDE/ATAPI CDROM drives (CONFIG_CD_NO_IDESCSI) [Y/n/?] y
```

After that, answer yes to the question about the specific CD-ROM drive in your PC. If you have a Mitsumi CD-ROM drive (with a proprietary interface, not ATAPI), for example, answer yes to the line that starts with Mitsumi (standard).

Newer versions of the Linux kernel may support other types of proprietary CD-ROM-drive interfaces. Check the prompts carefully before answering the questions the kernel-configuration program has posted.

Because most CD-ROMs use the ISO-9660 file system, you must enable support for this file system in the kernel. To do this, answer yes to the following question during kernel configuration:

```
ISO 9660 CDROM filesystem support (CONFIG_ISO9660_FS) [Y/m/n/?] y
```

IDE (ATAPI) CD-ROM Troubles

When a PC has an ATAPI CD-ROM drive, its ATA (IDE) adapter has two interfaces, primary and secondary, each of which is capable of supporting two drives. In Linux, the two primary devices are /dev/hda and /dev/hdb, typically used for hard-disk drives. The secondary IDE devices are /dev/hdc and /dev/hdd. Thus, if you have an IDE hard drive connected to the primary interface and an IDE CD-ROM drive connected to the secondary interface, the hard drive will be /dev/hda and the CD-ROM drive will be /dev/hdc.

---

insider insight   Often, of the two devices on an IDE interface, one is designated the master and the other the slave. When only one IDE device is attached to an interface, it must be designated the master (or single). Typically, the IDE device has a jumper (a connector that connects a pair of pins) to indicate whether the device is a master or a slave.

If Linux refuses to recognize your IDE CD-ROM drive, however, you should check the CD-ROM drive's parameters, making sure the drive uses the secondary IDE interface (IRQ 15 and I/O address 170H) and is set to be the master.

Some interface cards support more than two IDE interfaces. In such a case, you should know that the Linux IDE CD-ROM driver might not recognize anything but the primary and secondary IDE interfaces. The Creative Labs Sound Blaster 16 CD-ROM interface is, by default, set to be the fourth IDE interface. If you are connecting a CD-ROM drive to a Sound Blaster 16 for use in Linux, you have to set the jumpers on the Sound Blaster 16 so that the IDE interface is the secondary interface instead of the fourth interface.

Boot-Time Parameters for CD-ROM Drives

Usually, Linux drivers find CD-ROM drives (and other peripherals) by probing—reading from and writing to various I/O addresses. Linux drivers also use any available information from the PC's CMOS memory. CMOS stands for complementary metal-oxide semiconductor—a type of semiconductor. Each PC has a small amount of battery-backed, nonvolatile CMOS storage, where vital pieces of information about the PC, such as the number of types of disk drives, are stored. The real-time clock is also stored in the CMOS.

One problem with probing is that it involves reading from or writing to specific I/O addresses. Depending on what device uses that I/O address, probing can cause the system to hang (become unresponsive). When the Sound Blaster Pro CD driver, sbpcd, probes for a CD-ROM drive, it may access an I/O address used in an NE2000 Ethernet card; if this happens, the system hangs.

To avoid probing at boot time, you can pass specific device parameters for the device corresponding to your CD-ROM drive.

If you have a CD-ROM drive with the Sound Blaster Pro CD interface, the device name is sbpcd, and you can provide settings at boot loader's prompt as follows:

```
sbpcd=0x230,SoundBlaster
```

This command tells the sbpcd driver that the I/O address of the CD-ROM drive is 230H. The exact boot-time parameters for a device depend on that device driver.

If you use LILO, you can put the boot-time parameters in the /etc/lilo.conf file with the following command:

```
append = "sbpcd=0x230,SoundBlaster"
```

If you use GRUB, you can add options such as sbpcd=0x230,SoundBlaster to the kernel line in the /etc/grub.conf file.

Ethernet Cards

Appendix
D

◆ ◆

Ethernet is a good choice for the physical data-transport mechanism in local area networks (LANs) for the following reasons:

♦ Ethernet is proven technology (it has been in use since the early 1980s).

♦ Ethernet provides good data-transfer rates: typically 10 million bits per second (10 Mbps), although there is now 100-Mbps Ethernet and Gigabit Ethernet (1,000 Mbps).

♦ Ethernet runs on many different media from copper to fiber to wireless media.

♦ Ethernet hardware is relatively low-cost (PC Ethernet cards cost about $20).

Typically, Linux effectively supports affordable hardware, and Ethernet is no exception. This appendix describes the physical setup of an Ethernet LAN and summarizes the Ethernet cards Linux supports.

Ethernet Basics

Ethernet is a standard way to move packets of data between two or more computers connected to a single cable. (Larger networks are constructed by connecting multiple Ethernet segments with gateways.) Because a single wire is used, a protocol has to be used for sending and receiving data, because only one data packet can exist on the cable at any time. An Ethernet LAN uses a data-transmission protocol known as Carrier Sense Multiple Access/Collision Detection (CSMA/CD) to ensure that multiple computers can share the single transmission cable. Ethernet controllers embedded in the computers follow the CSMA/CD protocol to transmit and receive Ethernet packets.

The idea behind the CSMA/CD protocol is similar to the way in which you have a conversation at a party. You listen for a pause (carrier sense) and talk when no one else is speaking. If you and another person begin talking at the same time, both of you realize the problem (collision detection) and pause for a moment, then one of you starts speaking again. As you know from experience, everything works out.

In an Ethernet LAN, each Ethernet controller checks the cable for signals—that's the carrier-sense part. If the signal level is low, a controller sends its packets on the cable; the packet contains information about the sender and the intended recipient. All Ethernet controllers on the LAN listen to the signal, and the recipient receives the packet. If two controllers send out a packet simultaneously, the signal level in the cable rises above a threshold, and the controllers know a collision has occurred (two packets have been sent out at the same time). Both controllers wait for a random amount of time before sending their packets again.

Ethernet was invented in the early 1970s at the Xerox Palo Alto Research Center (PARC) by Robert M. Metcalfe. In the 1980s, Ethernet was standardized by the cooperative effort of three companies: Digital Equipment Corporation (DEC), Intel, and Xerox. Using the first initials of the company names, that Ethernet standard became known as the DIX standard. Later, the DIX standard was included in the 802-series standards developed by the Institute of Electrical and Electronics Engineers (IEEE). The final Ethernet specification is formally known as IEEE 802.3 CSMA/CD, but people continue to call it Ethernet.

Ethernet sends data in packets (also known as *frames*) with a standard format that consists of the following sequence of components:

- ◆ 8-byte preamble
- ◆ 6-byte destination address
- ◆ 6-byte source address
- ◆ 2-byte length of the data field
- ◆ 46- to 1,500-byte data field
- ◆ 4-byte frame-check sequence (used for error checking)

You don't need to know much about the innards of Ethernet packets except to note the 6-byte source and destination addresses. Each Ethernet controller has a unique 6-byte (48-bit) address. At the physical level, packets must be addressed with these 6-byte addresses.

Address Resolution Protocol

In an Ethernet LAN, two Ethernet controllers can communicate only if they know each other's 6-byte physical Ethernet address. You may wonder how IP addresses are mapped to physical addresses. This problem is solved by the Address Resolution Protocol (ARP), which specifies how to obtain the physical address that corresponds to an IP address. Essentially, when a packet has to be sent to an IP address, the TCP/IP protocol uses ARP to find the physical address of the destination.

When the packet is meant for an IP address outside your network, that packet is sent to the gateway that has a physical presence on your network. Therefore, that gateway can respond to an ARP request for a physical address.

Ethernet Cables

The original Ethernet standard used a thick coaxial cable, nearly half an inch in diameter. That wiring is called thickwire or thick Ethernet, although the IEEE 802.3 standard calls it 10Base5. That designation means several things: The data-transmission rate is 10 megabits per second (10 Mbps); the transmission is baseband (which simply means that the cable's signal-carrying capacity is devoted to transmitting Ethernet packets only); and the total length of the cable can be no more than 500 meters. Thickwire was expensive, and the cable was rather unwieldy.

Nowadays, two other forms of Ethernet cabling are more popular. The first alternative to thick Ethernet cable is *thinwire*, or 10Base2, which uses a thin, flexible coaxial cable. A thinwire Ethernet segment can be, at most, 185 meters long. The other, more recent, alternative is Ethernet over unshielded twisted-pair cable (UTP), known as 10BaseT.

To set up a 10BaseT Ethernet, you need an Ethernet *hub*—a hardware box with RJ-45 jacks. You build the network by running twisted-pair wires (usually, Category 5, or Cat5, cables) from each PC's Ethernet card to this hub. You can get a 4-port 10BaseT hub for about $50 U.S. Figure D-1 shows a typical small 10BaseT Ethernet LAN that you might set up at a small office or your home.

Figure D-1: A 10BaseT Ethernet LAN Using a Hub.

Supported Ethernet Cards

To set up an Ethernet LAN, you need an Ethernet card for each PC. Linux supports a wide variety of Ethernet cards for the PC. Table D-1 lists the supported Ethernet cards and their Linux drivers. The table includes wireless Ethernet cards as well as PCMCIA Ethernet cards. The driver name is useful when you load the Ethernet driver module (log in as root and type **modprobe *drivername*** to load a driver module).

Table D-1: Ethernet Cards and Their Linux Drivers

Ethernet Card	Driver Name
3Com 3C501* (obsolete and very slow)	3c501
3Com EtherLink II, 3C503, 3C503 (16-bit)	3c503 **and** 8390

(continued)

Table D-1: *(continued)*

Ethernet Card	Driver Name
3Com Etherlink Plus 3C505*	3c505
3Com Etherlink-16 3C507*	3c507
3Com Etherlink III, 3C509 / 3C509B (ISA)	3c509
3Com 3C515 Fast EtherLink Ethercard (ISA)	3c515
3Com 3C529 9MCA bus equivalent of 3C509)	3c509
3Com 3C579 (EISA version of 3C509)	3c509
3Com 3C574TX, 3CCFE574BT, 3CXFE574BT, 3CCSH572BT, 3CXSH572BT PCMCIA Card	3c574_cs
3Com 3C562 B/C/D, 3C563 B/C/D, 3C589 B/C/D, Megahertz 3CXE589 D/EC, 3CCE589EC/ET PCMCIA Card	3c589_cs
3Com Etherlink III Vortex (3C590, 3C592, 3C595, 3C597) (PCI)	3c59x
3Com 3C689 TokenLink III (PCMCIA) token ring card	ibmtr_cs
3Com Etherlink XL Boomerang Ethercards (3C900, 3C905), 3C905B Cyclone, 3C905C Tornado (PCI)	3c59x
3Com 3C985	acenic
Accton MPX	ne and 8390
Accton EN1203, EN1207, EtherDuo-PCI	de4x5, tulip
Adaptec DuraLAN (also known as Starfire) ANA-6915, 62022, and 62044	starfire
Aironet 4500 PCI-ISA-i365	aironet4500_card
Aironet 4500 PCMCIA	aironet4500_cs
Aironet 4500 and 4800 series wireless Ethernet PCI	airo
Aironet 4500 and 4800 series wireless Ethernet PCMCIA	airo_cs
Aironet Arlan 655	arlan
Allied Telesis AT1500	lance
Allied Telesis AT1700	at1700
Allied Telesis AT2450	pcnet32
Allied Telesis AT2540FX*	eepro100
Alteon AceNIC Gigabit Ethernet card and other Tigon based cards	acenic
AMD LANCE (7990, 79C960/961/961A, PCnet-ISA)	lance
AMD 79C965 (PCnet-32) and 79C970/970A (PCnet-PCI)	pcnet32
AMD 79C971 (PCnet-FAST), 79C972 (PCnet-FAST+)	pcnet32
AMD 79C974 (PCnet-SCSI)	pcnet32
AMD 8111E	amd8111e
Ansel Communications AC3200* (EISA)	ac3200

Ethernet Card	Driver Name
Apricot 82596 bus-master Ethernet	lp486e
Asix AX88190-based PCMCIA Ethernet	axnet_cs
Boca BEN (ISA, VLB, PCI)	lance, pcnet32
Broadcom BCM570x (Tigon3) Gigabit Ethernet controller	tg3
Cabletron E21xx*	ne and 8390
Cabletron E2100*	e2100 and 8390
Cabletron E22xx*	lance
Cirrus Logic (previously Crystal Semiconductor) CS89x0	cs89x0
Cogent EM100* ISA/EISA	smc9194
Cogent eMASTER+, EM100-PCI, EM400, EM960, EM964	de4x5, tulip
Compaq Deskpro / Compaq XL (Embedded AMD Chip)	pcnet32
Compaq Fast Ethernet Server Adapter	e100
Compaq Nettelligent/NetFlex (Embedded TI ThunderLAN Chip)	tlan
Compex RL100-ATX	winbond-840
Danpex EN9400	de4x5, tulip
D-Link DE-100, DE-200, DE-220-T, DE-250	ne and 8390
D-Link DE-520	pcnet32
D-Link DE-528	ne, ne2k-pci, and 8390
D-Link DE-530	de4x5, tulip
D-Link DE-600	de600
D-Link DE-620	de620
D-Link DFE-550 and DFE-580 with Sundance ST201 Alta and Kendin KS8723	sundance
D-Link DL2000-based Gigabit Ethernet Adapter	dl2k
Davicom DM9102, DM9102A, DM9102A and DM9801, DM9102A and DM9802 Fast Ethernet	dfme
DEC DEPCA, DE100/1, DE200/1/2, DE210, DE422	depca
DEC EtherWorks 3 (DE203, DE204, DE205)	ewrk3
DEC FDDIcontroller (EISA and PCI)	defxx
DEC DE425 EISA, DE434, DE435, DE500	de4x5, tulip
DEC 21040, 21041, 2114x, Tulip	de4x5, tulip
DFINET-300 and DFINET-400	ne and 8390
Digi RightSwitch SE-X	dgrs
Farallon Etherwave	3c509
Fujitsu FMV-181/182/183/184	fmv18x

(continued)

Table D-1: *(continued)*

Ethernet Card	Driver Name
Fujitsu FMV-J18x series PCMCIA Ethernet	`fmvj18x_cs`
HP 27245A	`hp` and 8390
HP EtherTwist, PC LAN+ (27247, 27252A)	`hp-plus` and 8390
HP-J2405A	`lance`
HP-Vectra On Board Ethernet	`lance`
HP 10/100 VG Any LAN (27248B, J2573, J2577, J2585, J970, J973)	`hp100`
HP NetServer 10/100TX PCI (D5013A)	`eepro100`
IBM Thinkpad 300 built-in adapter	`znet`
IBM Token Ring PCMCIA	`ibmtr_cs`
ICL EtherTeam 16i/32 (EISA)	`eth16i`
Intel EtherExpress	`eexpress`
Intel EtherExpress PRO/10	`eepro`
Intel EtherExpress PRO 100	`eepro100`
Intel PRO/100, 8255x-based Ethernet Adapter, 82559 Fast Ethernet LAN on Motherboard, 82562 based Fast Ethernet Connection	`e100`
Kingston - KNE100TX (Fast EtherRx PCI)	`de4x5` or `tulip`
LinkSys Etherfast 10/100 cards	`tulip`
LinkSys Pocket Ethernet Adapter Plus	`de620`
LinkSys WMP11 (Prism II) PCI wireless Ethernet	`orinoco_pci`
Mylex LNE390A, LNE390B	`lne390` and 8390
Mylex LNP101, LNP104*	`de4x5` or `tulip`
Myson MTD-8xx 100/10Mbps PCI	`fealnx`
Novell Eagle NE1000, NE2000	`ne` and 8390
National Semiconductor 83820 chip (10/100/1000 Mbps 64-bit PCI Ethernet)	`ns83820`
National Semiconductor NS8390-based PCMCIA Ethernet	`pcnet_cs`
National Semiconductor DP8381x series	`natsemi`
NE2000-PCI (RealTek/Winbond/Compex)	`ne`, `ne2k-pci` and 8390
NE1500, NE2100	`lance`
NE/2* (MCA bus)	`ne2`
NE3210	`ne3210` and 8390
NE5500	`pcnet32`
Orinoco wireless Ethernet cards (based on Hermes chipset)	`orinoco_cs`
Packet Engines Yellowfin G-NIC Gigabit Ethernet	`yellowfin`

Ethernet Card	Driver Name
Packet Engines GNIC-II PCI Gigabit Ethernet	`hamachi`
Proteon P1370-EA	`ne` and 8390
Proteon P1670-EA	`de4x5`, `tulip`
Pure Data PDUC8028, PDI8023	`wd` and 8390
Racal-Interlan ES3210*	`es3210`
Racal-Interlan NI5010*	`ni5010`
Racal-Interlan NI5210	`ni52`
Racal-Interlan NI6510* (not EB)	`ni65`
Racal-Interlan EtherBlaster (also known as NI6510EB)	`lance`
Raytheon Raylink Wireless LAN card	`ray_cs`
RealTek RTL8002/8012 (AT-Lan-Tec) Pocket adaptor	`atp`
RealTek 8009, 8019	`ne` and 8390
RealTek 8029	`ne`, `ne2k-pci` and 8390
RealTek RTL-8139C+ series 10/100 PCI Ethernet	`8139cp` and 8139too
RealTek RTL-8169 Gigabit Ethernet	`r8169`
RedCreek Communications PCI	`rcpci`
Sager NP943*	`3c501`
Schneider & Koch SK G16	`sk_g16`
SEEQ 8005	`seeq8005`
SMC SMC91c92-based PCMCIA Ethernet cards (Megahertz, Motorola, Ositech, and Psion Dacom)	`smc91c92_cs`
SMC Elite Ultra/EtherEZ (ISA)	`smc-ultra` and 8390
SMC Elite Ultra32 EISA	`smc-ultra32` and 8390
SMC PCI EtherPower 10/100	`de4x5`, `tulip`
SMC EtherPower II* PCI	`epic100`
SMC-9000 / SMC 91c92/4, 91c100	`smc9194`
Sparc HME/BigMac 10/100BaseT (also known as Happy Meal Ethernet)	`sunhme`
Sun GEM Gigabit Ethernet	`sungem`
Texas Instruments ThunderLAN	`tlan`
Toshiba TC35815CF PCI 10/100Mbps Ethernet	`tc35815`
VIA 86C926 Amazon	`ne`, `ne2k-pci` and 8390
VIA 86C100A Rhine I, 6102 Rhine II, and 6105/6105M Rhine III	`via-rhine`
WaveLAN 2.4GHz Wireless Ethernet PCMCIA card (version 2.0)	`wavelan_cs`
WaveLAN/IEEE 802.11 Wireless Ethernet PCMCIA card	`wvlan_cs`

(continued)

Table D-1: *(continued)*

Ethernet Card	Driver Name
Western Digital WD8003 (SMC Elite) and WD8013 (SMC Elite Plus)	wd and 8390
Winbond W89c840 PCI Ethernet chip	winbond-840
Xircom Cardbus Ethernet card	xircom_cb
Xircom Cardbus Ethernet CBE-100	xircom_tulip_cb
Xircom CreditCard Ethernet Adapter (CE2, CE IIps, RE-10, CEM28, CEM33, CE33, CEM56, CE3-100, CE3B, RE-100, REM10BT, and REM56G-100)	xirc2ps_cs
Zenith Z-Note built-in adapter	znet
Znyx ZX342 (DEC 21040 based)	de4x5, tulip

*Cards marked with an asterisk have either buggy drivers or drivers that have not been fully tested.

If you have upgraded the Linux kernel, the new kernel may support even more cards than the ones shown in this list.

If you have not bought an Ethernet card yet, you want to buy a 16-bit card, not an 8-bit card. A 16-bit card transfers data faster and has a larger onboard buffer. The cards come with different types of connectors, as follows:

♦ A DB-15 connector for thick Ethernet. (You need an additional transceiver to connect thickwire to other types of Ethernet, such as thinwire or 10BaseT.)

♦ A thinwire BNC connector

♦ An RJ-45 connector for 10BaseT. (The RJ-45 connector looks like a common RJ-11 phone jack, but the RJ-45 version has eight positions instead of six.)

Nowadays, most Ethernet cards come with a 10BaseT connector. If you have more than one PC with 10BaseT Ethernet cards, you can easily set up a small LAN—all you need is a 10BaseT Ethernet hub. A wire goes from each PC's Ethernet card to the hub, and the hub sets up the proper connections for Ethernet.

You can use Ethernet cards with a DB-15 thick Ethernet connector in a thinwire or 10BaseT network. All you need is a transceiver that attaches to the DB-15 port and provides the right type of connector (BNC for thinwire, and RJ-45 for 10BaseT).

Ethernet Driver Modules

Red Hat Linux ships with very few drivers built into the kernel. Instead, most drivers, including Ethernet drivers, are provided in the form of dynamically loadable modules. When you set up networking during Red Hat Linux installation, the installation program adds appropriate entries to the text file /etc/modules.conf. These entries tell the modprobe command what modules to load. For Ethernet drivers, the important entries are lines that define the driver aliases eth0, eth1, and so on. If you have only one Ethernet card, the alias eth0 should be set to the name of the driver for your Ethernet card (refer to Table D-1 for a list of cards and their corresponding drivers).

For example, my PC has a 3Com 3C905C PCI Ethernet card. For this card, the installation program adds the following alias entry in the /etc/modules.conf file:

```
alias eth0 3c59x
```

For some older Ethernet cards, you may need another entry in the /etc/modules.conf file to specify various options, such as I/O port address and interrupt number (IRQ) for your Ethernet card. For example, the following line in /etc/modules.conf specifies an IRQ of 5 and an I/O port address of 0x300 (hexadecimal 300) for the 3Com 3C503 card:

```
options 3c503 irq=5 io=0x300
```

insider insight For PCI and EISA Ethernet cards, it is safe to let the driver probe for various parameters of the card. Consult the files in /usr/src/linux-2.4/Documentation/networking for the options various Ethernet driver modules accept.

Ethernet Autoprobing

At boot time, a kernel with Ethernet support or an Ethernet driver module (being loaded by modprobe) attempts to probe and detect the Ethernet card. The probing involves reading from and writing to specific I/O port addresses.

Although you specify a single I/O port address for a device, most devices use a block of I/O addresses for their operation. The I/O address you specify is the base address; the rest of the I/O addresses are consecutive I/O ports, starting at the base address.

note Depending on the number of I/O addresses a device uses, two devices may end up with overlaps in the range of I/O addresses they use. The NE2000 card, for example, uses 32 I/O ports (that's 0x20 in hexadecimal notation). If you select 0x360 as the base I/O address for a NE2000 card, the card uses the ports from 0x360 to 0x37F. Unfortunately, the PC's parallel port (LPT1) uses the base I/O address of 0x378, and the secondary IDE controller uses the addresses 0x376–0x376. Thus, the NE2000 configured at 0x360 now has an overlap with the I/O addresses the first parallel port and the secondary IDE controller use. In this case, you can prevent any problems by configuring the NE2000 card at a different I/O address, such as 0x280.

Overlapping I/O port addresses cause problems; during autoprobing, the kernel may perform operations that might be harmless for some devices, but that may cause another device to lock up the system. Typically, however, if your Ethernet card and other devices are working under DOS or Windows, you should have no problem with them under Linux (assuming, of course, that your Ethernet card is supported under Linux).

If your system hangs during autoprobing, you can exclude a specific range of I/O addresses from being probed. To exclude a range of addresses during autoprobing, use the reserve command during the boot loader boot prompt. The reserve command has the following syntax:

```
reserve=BASE-IO-PORT1,NUMPORTS1[,BASE-IO-PORT2,NUMPORTS2,...]
```

Here, BASE-IO-PORT1 is an I/O port address in hexadecimal notation (for example, 0x300), and NUMPORTS1 is the number of ports (for example, 32) to be excluded when autoprobing. The arguments in brackets are optional; they are used to specify additional exclusion regions.

If you prevent a range of I/O addresses from being autoprobed, a device that may be at that address may not be detected. Thus, you must specify that device's parameters explicitly on the boot command line.

For Linux kernels with Ethernet support linked into the kernel, the boot command for specifying device parameters is ether, which takes the following format:

```
ether=IRQ,BASE-IO-PORT,PARAM-1,PARAM-2,NAME
```

Table D-2 explains the meanings of the arguments. All arguments are optional. The Ethernet driver takes the first nonnumeric argument as NAME.

Table D-2: Arguments for ether

Argument	Meaning
IRQ	The IRQ of the Ethernet card. Specify a zero IRQ to make the driver autodetect the IRQ.
BASE-IO-PORT	The base I/O port address of the Ethernet card. Specify a zero BASE-IO-PORT to make the driver autodetect the base I/O port address.
PARAM-1	The meaning depends on the Ethernet driver. Some drivers use the least significant 4 bits of this value as the debug message level. The default is 0; set this argument to a value of 1 to 7 to indicate how verbose the debug messages should be (7 means most verbose). A value of 8 stops debug messages. The AMD LANCE driver uses the low-order 4 bits as the DMA channel.
PARAM-2	The meaning depends on the Ethernet driver. The 3Com 3c503 drivers use this value to select between an internal and external transceiver—0 means the internal transceiver, and 1 means that the card uses an external transceiver connected to the DB-15 thick Ethernet port.
NAME	The name of the Ethernet driver (eth0, eth1, and so on). By default, the kernel uses eth0 as the name of the first Ethernet card it autoprobes. The kernel does not probe for more than one Ethernet card; that would increase any chance of conflicts with other devices during autoprobing.

If you have an Ethernet card at the I/O address 0x300 and do not want this card to be autoprobed, use a command line such as the following at the boot prompt:

```
reserve=0x300,32 ether=0,0x300,eth0
```

The reserve command prevents 32 I/O ports starting at 0x300 from being autoprobed, whereas the ether command specifies the base I/O port address for the Ethernet card. The exact I/O addresses depend on your Ethernet card and the range of addresses for which an overlap with some other device exists. Most of the time, you should not have to use these commands.

note

The I/O addresses and IRQs of PCI cards are assigned by the PCI BIOS when the system powers up. Thus, you cannot set the I/O address or IRQ of any PCI card through the boot commands. Even if you specify these parameters through boot commands, they are ignored for a PCI device.

Multiple Ethernet Cards

You might use a Linux PC as a gateway between two Ethernet networks. In that case, you might have two Ethernet cards in the PC. The Linux kernel can support more than one Ethernet card; however, it does not detect multiple cards automatically. The kernel looks for only the first Ethernet card. If you happen to have two Ethernet cards, you should specify the parameters of the cards on the boot command line. (The two cards must have different IRQs and I/O addresses, of course.) Following is a typical boot command line for two Ethernet cards:

```
ether=10,0x220,eth0 ether=5,0x300,eth1
```

If you happen to have two Ethernet cards and you use LILO as your boot loader, you can place the necessary LILO boot parameters in the /etc/lilo.conf file so that you don't have to enter the arguments every time you boot Linux. For the preceding example, the line in /etc/lilo.conf looks like the following:

```
append="ether=10,0x220,eth0 ether=5,0x300,eth1"
```

If you use GRUB as the boot loader, you can add the option on the kernel line in /etc/grub.conf.

If you plan to use a Linux PC with two network interfaces as a TCP/IP gateway, you have to recompile the kernel with IP forwarding enabled. Chapter 21 explains how to rebuild the kernel. During the rebuilding process, when you use the make config command, you should enable CONFIG_NETFILTER, CONFIG_IP_ADVANCED_ROUTER, CONFIG_IP_MULTIPLE_TABLES, CONFIG_IP_ROUTE_NAT, and CONFIG_IP_ROUTE_FWMARK.

Modems and Terminals

◆ ◆

If you have installed Red Hat Linux on your home PC, you may want to use a modem to dial out to your Internet service provider (ISP) and connect to the Internet. To use a modem, you have to learn how Linux works with the PC's serial ports—the ports through which the modem communicates with the PC. You need also to get cables to connect the modem to the PC, to select the proper serial device to use in Linux, and to set up configuration files that control the communication parameters for the serial port.

Terminals—devices that have a display screen and a keyboard—also connect to the PC through serial ports. In that sense, terminals are similar to modems. Terminals are ideal for simple data-entry tasks and are often used in point-of-sale systems. Linux also supports multiport serial boards that enable you to connect many terminals or modems to your PC running Linux.

This appendix explains how to connect, set up, and use modems and terminals. Much of the information applies to any device connected to the serial port, but some information is specific to modems. This appendix focuses primarily on modems because modems are more popular than dumb terminals connected to a Linux system.

Serial Ports

If you have used communications software, such as Procomm or Crosstalk, under MS-DOS or Windows, you have used your PC's modem and serial port. These communications programs transfer bytes of data from the PC to the modem over the serial port. The serial port is so named because each byte of data is sent serially—one bit at a time. Serial data communication comes with its own set of terminology. To understand how to set up the serial port, you need to understand the terminology.

UART

A chip named the universal asynchronous receiver/transmitter (UART), which is at the heart of all serial communication hardware, takes care of converting each byte to a stream of ones and zeros. That stream of ones and zeros is then sent over the communications medium (for example, the telephone line). At the receiving end, another UART reconstitutes bytes of data from the stream of ones and zeros.

The original IBM PC's motherboard did not include serial communication capabilities. Instead, the serial communication function was provided through a separate serial adapter card (or *serial board*) called the IBM Asynchronous Communications Adapter. This serial board used National Semiconductor's INS8250 UART chip.

Later, PCs began including the serial communication hardware on the motherboard, but the same 8250 or compatible UART was used for a long time. Still later, an improved version of the 8250—the 16450—was introduced, but the improvements were in the chip's fabrication details, not in its basic capability.

A problem with the 8250 and 16450 UARTs is that they do not have any way to buffer received characters. If the PC cannot keep up with the character stream, some characters may be lost. At high data-transfer rates (more than 9,600 bits per second), the PC may have trouble keeping up with the arrival of characters, especially with operating systems that keep the PC busy (such as Microsoft Windows).

The solution was to add a first in, first out (FIFO) buffer on the UART, enabling the PC to fall behind occasionally, without losing any incoming characters. The newer 16550A UARTs have send and receive buffers, each of which is capable of storing up to 16 characters. The 16550A UART is compatible with the old 8250 and 16450, but it can support higher data-transfer rates because the built-in buffers can store incoming and outgoing characters directly on the UART.

On a historical note, National Semiconductor's original 16550 UART had the FIFO buffers, but the FIFO circuits had some bugs. The 16550A (and later versions of that UART) fixed the problems of the original 16550. By now, however, the 16550 name is often used to refer to any UART with an onboard receive and transmit buffer. You don't have to worry about the distinctions between the 16550 and 16550A, except in the case of the original 16550 UARTs from National Semiconductor; those chips are marked NS16550 (without an A).

note

Linux supports PC serial ports and serial I/O boards that use a 8250, 16450, 16550, 16550A, or compatible UART. However, you really need a 16550A or better UART to keep up with today's high-speed modems, which can transfer data at rates of up to 56,000 bits per second. Most new Pentium PCs should already have 16550A UARTs. If you are buying a new PC to run Linux, you should check with the vendor and make sure that the serial interface uses 16550A UARTs. Newer UARTs, such as the 16654 and 16750, come with a 64-byte buffer. These UARTs should also work with Linux.

Communications Parameters

In serial communications, the transmission medium (such as the telephone line) is kept at a logical 1 when it is idle (1 is represented by the presence of a signal on the line). In this case, the line is said to be marking. On the other hand, when the line is at a logical 0, it is said to be spacing. Thus, logical 1 and 0 are also referred to as *mark* and *space*, respectively.

A sequence of ones and zeros makes up a single 8-bit character. A change in the condition of the line from mark to space indicates the start of a character. That change in line condition is referred to as the *Start* bit. Following the Start bit is a pattern of bits that represents the character and then a bit known as the *Parity* bit. Finally, the line reverts to its idling mark condition, which represents the *Stop* bit and indicates the end of the current character. The number of bits used to represent the character is known as the word length and is usually either seven or eight.

The Parity bit is used to perform rudimentary error detection. When even parity is selected, for example, the Parity bit is set so that the total number of ones in the current word is even (the logic is similar for odd parity). At the receiving end, the parity is recalculated and compared with the received parity bit. If the two disagree, the receiver declares a parity error. One problem of error detection with the parity check is that it can detect only errors that affect a single bit. The bit pattern 0100 0001 0 (the ASCII code for the letter A), for example, transmitted with an 8-bit word length and even parity, may change (due to noise in the telephone line) to 0100 0111 0 (ASCII G); the receiver, however, does not see the error, because the parity is still even. Thus, parity error detection is rarely used nowadays.

In serial communications, the transmitter and the receiver both must have some knowledge of how long each bit lasts; otherwise, they cannot detect the bits correctly. The duration of each bit is determined by data clocks at the receiver and the transmitter. Notice, however, that although the clocks at the receiver and the transmitter must have the same frequency, they do not have to be synchronized. The Start bit signals the receiver that a new character follows; the receiver then begins detecting the bits until it sees the Stop bit.

A particular condition of the line is sometimes used to gain the attention of the receiver. The normal state of the line is mark (1), and the beginning of a character is indicated by a space (0). If the line stays in the space condition for a period of time longer than it would have taken to receive all the bits of a character, a *break* is assumed to have occurred. When the receiver sees the break condition, it can get ready to receive characters again.

The selection of the clock frequency depends on the *baud rate* (or simply baud), which refers to the number of times that the line changes state every second. Typically, the serial I/O hardware uses a clock rate of 16 times the baud rate so that the line is sampled often enough to detect reliably.

Baud versus BPS

The data-transfer rate is expressed in terms of bits per second, or bps. In the early days of modems, the data-transfer rate was the same as the baud rate—the rate of change of the line's state—because each line state carried a single bit of information. Nowadays, modems use different technology that can send several bits of information each time the line state changes. In other words, you can get a high bps with a relatively low baud rate. The fastest modems today use a baud rate of 2,400, even though the bits per second can be as high as 56,000.

Thus, baud and bits per second are not the same. Most of us, however, ignore the exact definition of baud rate and simply use baud to mean bits per second. Even though I'll stick to bps when I speak of data-transfer rates, you'll run across Linux settings that use baud rate to mean bps.

Serial-Port IRQs and I/O Addresses

The PC typically has two serial ports, called COM1 and COM2 in MS-DOS parlance. The PC can also support two more serial ports: COM3 and COM4. Because of these port names, the serial ports are often referred to as COM ports.

Like other devices, the serial ports need interrupt request (IRQ) numbers and I/O port addresses. Two IRQs—3 and 4—are shared among the four COM ports. Table E-1 lists the IRQs and I/O port addresses assigned to the four serial ports.

Table E-1: IRQ and I/O Port Addresses Assigned to Serial Ports

Port	IRQ	I/O Address
COM1	4	0x3f8
COM2	3	0x2f8
COM3	4	0x3e8
COM4	3	0x2e8

Serial-Device Names in Linux

Like other devices in Linux, the serial-port devices are represented by device files in the /dev directory. Each serial port has two names: one for incoming connections and one for outgoing connections. Table E-2 lists the device names for incoming and outgoing serial ports, including the major and minor device numbers.

Table E-2: Device Names for Incoming and Outgoing Serial Ports

COM Port	Device Name*	Major Device Number	Minor Device Number
Incoming COM1	/dev/ttyS0	4	64
Incoming COM2	/dev/ttyS1	4	65
Incoming COM3	/dev/ttyS2	4	66
Incoming COM4	/dev/ttyS3	4	67
Outgoing COM1	/dev/cua0	5	64
Outgoing COM2	/dev/cua1	5	65
Outgoing COM3	/dev/cua2	5	66
Outgoing COM4	/dev/cua3	5	67
USB serial port #1	/dev/usb/ttyUSB0	188	0
USB serial port #2	/dev/usb/ttyUSB1	188	1

COM Port	Device Name*	Major Device Number	Minor Device Number
... 16 serial ports ...	...	188	...
USB serial port #16	/dev/usb/ttyUSB15	188	15

* You should now use the /dev/ttySx devices for both incoming and outgoing serial communications. The /dev/cuax devices only exist to provide backwards compatibility with older programs. The plan is to abolish the /dev/cuax devices in the future.

If you have installed Red Hat Linux from this book's companion CD-ROM, all these devices should already be in your system. If you check the /dev directory, you'll find the /dev/ttyS* and /dev/cua* devices, where * is 0, 1, 2, 3, and so on.

> **note** Historically, Linux used the /dev/ttyS* devices for dialing in and the /dev/cua* devices for dialing out. However, the current version of the Linux kernel does not distinguish between /dev/ttyS* and /dev/cua* devices. My recommendation is to use the /dev/ttyS* device names wherever you need to refer to serial devices.

Modems

Modem is a contraction of modulator/demodulator—and is a device that converts digital signals (string of 1s and 0s) into continuously varying analog signals that can be transmitted over telephone lines and radio waves. Thus, the modem is the intermediary between the digital world of the PC and the analog world of telephones. Figure E-1 illustrates the concept of a modem.

01001011

Modem

Figure E-1: A Modem Bridges the Digital World of PCs and the Analog World of Telephones.

Inside the PC, 1s and 0s are represented with voltage levels, but signals carried over telephone lines are usually tones of different frequencies. The modem sits between the PC and the telephone line and makes data communication possible over the phone lines. The modem converts information back and forth between the voltage/no voltage representation of digital circuits and different frequency tones that are appropriate for transmission over phone lines.

caution   A quick word of caution about Winmodems that come with many new PCs and laptops. These are largely software-based internal modems and totally different from the
traditional hardware modems. Winmodems work only with special software, so they are
often called software modems. See the "Winmodems and Linux" section for more on
Linux support for Winmodems.

The communication between the PC and the modem follows the RS-232C standard (often
stated as RS-232, without the C). The communications protocol established between two
modems also follows one of several international modem standards. The next few sections
briefly describe these standards.

RS-232C Standard

The RS-232C standard, set forth by the Electronic Industries Association (EIA), specifies a
prescribed method of information interchange between the modem and the PC's serial-
communication hardware.

note   In EIA terminology, the modem is data communications equipment (DCE), and the PC
is data terminal equipment (DTE). You'll see references to DCE and DTE in discussions
of the RS-232C standard.

A modem can communicate in one of two modes:

♦ **Half-duplex mode**—Data transmission can occur in only one direction at a time
♦ **Full-duplex mode**—Enables independent two-way communications

Most modems communicate in full-duplex mode.

RS-232C Cables

The RS-232C standard also provides control signals, such as Request to Send (RTS) and
Clear to Send (CTS), that can be used to coordinate the transmission and reception of data
between the PC and the modem. Handshaking refers to the coordination of the data
exchange.

Handshaking signals, as well as data transmission and reception, occur through wires in
the cable that connects the PC to the modem. The RS-232C specifies a 25-pin connector,
with a specific function assigned to each pin.

A typical modem has a female 25-pin, D-shell connector (called the DB-25 connector),
whereas the PC's serial port provides a male nine-pin, D-shell (DB-9) connector. Thus, to
connect a PC's serial port to a modem, you need a cable with a female DB-9 connector at
one end and a male DB-25 connector at the other end. The typical PC-to-modem cable is
often sold in computer stores as an *AT Modem Cable*.

Some PCs have a DB-25 connector for the serial port. For these machines, you need a
cable that has DB-25 connectors on both ends.

Of the 25 pins available in a DB-25 connector, only nine are used in the PC's serial port. In
the Serial/Parallel Adapter card for the PC-AT, IBM decided to save space by introducing
a DB-9 connector.

Using Modem Cables (DTE to DCE)

When you connect a PC (DTE) to a modem (DCE), the cable should connect the like signals at both ends. A cable that has such connections is often called a straight-through cable, as it connects like signals to each other.

Using Null Modem Cables (DTE to DTE)

If you want to connect two PCs through the serial port, you cannot use a straight-through cable like the one that connects the PC to a modem. The reason is that each PC expects to send data on the TD line and receive data on the RD line. If both PCs send data on the same line, neither PC can hear the other. A solution is to create a cable that connects one PC's output (TD) to the other one's input (RD), and vice versa. Such a cable is known as a null modem cable.

Choosing Serial Cables

When you connect two devices that support RS-232C serial communications, the choice of cable depends on the type of each device: DTE or DCE. As I mention previously, the PC is a DTE, and a modem is a DCE. Many printers and terminals are DTEs.

Use a straight-through modem cable to connect a DTE to a DCE. To connect a DTE to a DTE, you need a null modem cable. Many computer stores sell null modem adapters. You can connect two DTE devices by using a modem cable with a null modem adapter.

> **insider insight**
>
> Notice that the serial interface on the Hewlett-Packard LaserJet family of printers is configured as a DTE. Thus, you need a null modem–style cable to connect a PC's serial port to a LaserJet printer. Unfortunately, serial printer cables (for connecting a printer to the serial port) introduce a further complication. Printer manufacturers interpret some of the RS-232C signals in a printer-specific way. Thus, you may have to connect various signals in a specific way to use a printer with a serial interface.

Flow Control

The RS-232C standard includes the RTS/CTS signals for hardware handshaking between the communicating devices (such as the PC and the modem). In addition to this hardware flow control, special ASCII control characters (Ctrl-Q/Ctrl-S, or XON/XOFF) are typically used to implement flow control in software. Flow control is necessary because sometimes the receiver may not be able to keep up with the rate of data arrival and should be able to inform the sender to stop data transmission while it catches up.

Suppose that a receiver has a buffer to store incoming characters. As the buffer gets full, the receiver can send the XOFF character (Ctrl-S) to the transmitter, indicating that transmission should stop. If the transmitter understands the meaning of the XOFF character, it can stop sending data.

Then, when the receiver empties the buffer, it can send an XON character (Ctrl-Q) to indicate that transmission can resume. This scheme of flow control is used in many communications programs because it is simple. This is unfortunate; when the XON/XOFF protocol is used, the XON and XOFF characters cannot be part of the data because of their special meaning.

<table>
<tr><td>note</td><td>The software-based XON/XOFF flow control is not used with modem speeds faster than 9,600 bps because it slows down data transfers. Most high-speed modem connections use hardware flow control only.</td></tr>
</table>

Modem Standards

As the Internet and online services have grown in popularity, the demand for modems that offer high data-transfer rates has grown accordingly. Early modems transferred data at the rate of 300 bits per second (bps), whereas the latest modems can transfer at rates of up to 56,000 bps—which represents an increase of more than a hundredfold in modem performance. To achieve these high data-transfer rates, modems use many tricks, including compressing the data before sending it. As you might expect, two modems can communicate successfully only if both modems understand how to interpret the signal being exchanged between the two. This is where the standard modem protocols come into play.

<table>
<tr><td>note</td><td>The International Telecommunications Union (ITU) has ratified several modem standards in use today. These standards have names that start with V. The latest standard is V.90, which supports data-transfer rates of 56,000 bps (more precisely, 56,000 bps downstream and up to 33,600 bps upstream). The V.90 standard is also called V.PCM because it uses a technique known as pulse code modulation (PCM). Table E-3 lists some of the common modem standards used today.

If you need the exact text of the ITU Series V recommendations, as these data communication standards are called, you can purchase copies from ITU's website at http://www.itu.ch/itudoc/itu-t/rec/v/. The site offers the files in English, French, and Spanish, and in a number of file formats, including Microsoft Word for Windows, Adobe's Portable Document Format (PDF), and PostScript.</td></tr>
</table>

Table E-3: Modem Standards

Standard Name	Maximum Data-Transfer Rate (bps)
Bell 103	300
Bell 212A	1,200
V.17 (Group III Fax)	14,400
V.21	300
V.22	1,200
V.22bis	2,400
V.23	1,200
V.27ter (Group III Fax)	4,800
V.29 (Group III Fax)	9,600
V.32	9,600

Standard Name	Maximum Data-Transfer Rate (bps)
V.32bis	14,400
V.34	28,800
V.90	56,000 downstream and up to 33,600 bps upstream
V.91	Up to 64,000 bps for use on a 4-wire circuit-switched connection and on leased point-to-point 4-wire digital circuits

When you buy a modem, make sure that it conforms to these international standards. Currently, the ITU V.90–compliant 56K modems are the norm.

Modem Commands (AT Commands)

The now-famous AT command set first appeared in the 300-baud Hayes Smartmodem, a name coined and trademarked by Hayes Microcomputer Products, Inc. The Smartmodem worked in two distinct modes:

- ◆ **Command mode**—Characters sent from the PC (DTE) are interpreted as commands for the modem.
- ◆ **Online mode**—After receiving a dial command and establishing a connection, the modem sends all received data out on the phone lines.

The Hayes Smartmodem commands start with the characters AT (for attention). The initial command set included those to dial a number, turn the modem's speaker on or off, and set the modem to answer an incoming call.

Modern manufacturers have widely copied the AT command system, making it a de facto standard. Although virtually all modems use a core command set, each modem manufacturer has its own proprietary commands that control some of the exotic and advanced features of the modem.

The AT Command Line

I have found it very helpful to know at least a few of the AT commands for controlling a modem. Although many communications programs hide the details of the AT commands, you can end up in a situation in which the communications software is primitive—all the software does is send the other modem whatever you type. In such situations, you can enter AT commands to set up the modem, dial out, and establish a connection. The following sections briefly cover the AT command set.

As the name implies, each command in the AT command set starts with the letters AT. Following these letters, you can enter one or more valid commands and end the command line with a carriage return (press Enter on the PC's keyboard). Thus, the command line has the following format:

```
AT[command1][command2]...<CR>
```

[command1] and [command2] denote optional commands, each of which has appropriate arguments. The ending <CR> is a required carriage return (the Enter key).

Suppose that you want to use the following commands:

- ◆ The E command with an argument of 1 to force the modem to echo the commands
- ◆ The V command with 1 as the argument to make the modem provide verbose result codes (instead of numeric codes)

You can send these commands to the modem with the following AT command line:

```
ATE1V1
```

As with any AT command line, of course, you have to end this command by pressing Enter. If you enter this command through a communications software package, you see that the modem replies with the string OK.

> **note**
>
> All modems accept at least 40 characters per command line, in which the character count includes the AT and the final carriage return. Many modems, however, can accept up to 255 characters on an AT command line.

If an internal modem stops responding to the AT commands, you may have to shut down the system and power it off to reset the modem.

The A/ Command

The A/ command is an exception to the AT command syntax. If you enter A/ as the only command on a line by itself (no need to press Enter), the modem immediately repeats the last command line it has received.

Configuration Commands

These commands specify how the modem should operate and how it responds to commands. Following are some useful configuration commands:

- ◆ **Echo commands**—ATE1 causes the modem to display a command as you type it; ATE0 disables the display of the command.
- ◆ **Speaker volume**—The ATLn (n being a number between 0 and 3) command sets the volume of the modem's built-in speaker. ATL0 and ATL1 set the volume to low, ATL2 sets it to medium, and ATL3 sets it to high.
- ◆ **Speaker control**—ATMn (n being a number between 0 and 2) controls whether and when the modem's speaker is turned on. ATM0 turns the speaker off, ATM1 turns it on until a call is established, and ATM2 turns it on always.
- ◆ **Quiet mode**—When quiet mode is enabled, the modem does not acknowledge commands or report call status. ATQ0 disables quiet mode and causes the modem to respond to commands and show call status. ATQ1 enables quiet mode.
- ◆ **Verbose mode**—When verbose mode is enabled, the modem acknowledges commands and reports call status with words. Otherwise, it responds with numeric codes (which may be more suitable for communications software than for humans). The ATV1 command turns on verbose mode; ATV0 turns it off. A typical modem generates the nine responses listed in Table E-4.

Table E-4: Responses* from a Typical Modem

Numeric Response	Word Response
0	OK
1	CONNECT
2	RING
3	NO CARRIER
4	ERROR
5	CONNECT 1200
6	NO DIALTONE
7	BUSY
8	NO ANSWER

* Most modems include several other responses for reporting successful connections at higher data rates.

♦ **Result code selection**—The ATXn command selects the type of reports the modem should send back. The argument n can be one of the following:

```
0   CONNECT
1   CONNECT bits-per-sec
2   CONNECT bits-per-sec, NO DIALTONE
3   CONNECT bits-per-sec, BUSY
4   CONNECT bits-per-sec, NO DIALTONE, BUSY
```

♦ **View stored profiles**—The AT&V command causes the modem to display the current values of a selected set of configuration parameters and the values of internal registers. Some modems have nonvolatile memory to store groups of settings, known as profiles. On such modems, AT&V displays the stored profiles.

Action Commands

Each action command causes the modem to perform some action immediately. The most important action command is the dial command: ATDTnumber. Two other useful action commands are ATZn and AT&Fn, which reset the modem's configuration. Following are some of the important action commands:

♦ **Pulse dial**—The ATDPnumber command causes the modem to use the pulse-dialing system to dial a specified phone number. The pulse-dialing system was used by rotary telephones. Nowadays, you typically use the ATDT command to dial a number by using the tone-dialing system.

♦ **Tone dial**—Use the ATDTnumber command to dial a specified phone number by using the tone-dialing system. To dial the number 555-1234, for example, use the command ATDT555-1234. You should enter whatever other digits you may need to dial the number you want to reach. If you need to dial 9 for an outside line, simply use ATDT9,555-1234. The comma introduces a slight pause (typically, two seconds), which may be necessary to get an outside line.

◆ **Dial last number**—The ATDL command causes the modem to execute the last dial command.

◆ **Hook control**—The ATH command simulates lifting or putting down the handset of a regular telephone. ATH0 hangs up the phone; ATH1 makes the modem go online (as though you have picked up the handset).

◆ **Answer call**—Use the ATA command to make the modem answer the phone. You can put the modem in answer mode (by setting register S0—a storage area in the modem—to a nonzero value), so that it answers the phone when someone calls. With the ATA command, you can force the modem to answer the phone even if register S0 is set to 0 (which means the modem won't answer the phone).

◆ **Return to online**—The ATO command returns the modem to online mode. Use this command after you press **+++** (rapidly enter three plus signs in sequence with some pause before and after the sequence) to take the modem offline.

◆ **Software reset**—If the modem stores configuration profiles in nonvolatile memory, you can recall one of the configuration profiles with the ATZn command (n being the number of the configuration profile). If you enter ATZ without any argument, the modem is reset. The ATZ command terminates any existing connection.

◆ **Factory-default setting**—The AT&F command causes the modem to restore the factory-default settings. Some modems take a numeric argument with AT&F; consult your modem's documentation for more information on the meaning of the numeric arguments.

The ATSr=n Commands

In addition to the AT command set, Hayes Smartmodem pioneered the use of internal modem registers to configure the modem. All current modems have registers, called the S registers, that control many aspects of the modem (including features that may be unique to a specific brand of modem).

> **note** A typical modem has anywhere from 30 to 60 S registers, denoted by S0, S1, S2, and so on. The ATSr=n command sets the S register numbered r to the value n. To view the current contents of the S register numbered r, use the ATSr? command.

Register S0, for example, contains the number of rings after which the modem answers the phone. When S0 is 0, the modem does not answer the phone at all. The following listing shows how you might query and set the S0 register with the ATS command:

```
ATS0?
000
OK
ATS0=1
OK
ATS0?
001
```

The exact set of S registers varies from one brand of modem to another, but most modems seem to provide and interpret the following 13 S registers consistently, as follows:

- **S0, ring to answer on**—The number of rings after which the modem answers the phone. When S0 is 0, the modem does not answer the phone.

- **S1, counts number of rings**—The count of incoming rings. When S1 equals S0, the modem answers the phone (assuming that S0 is nonzero). The modem resets S1 to 0 a few seconds after the last ring.

- **S2, escape code character**—The character used as the escape sequence to switch the modem from online mode to command mode. The default value is 43, which is the ASCII code for the plus (+) character. To go from online mode to command mode, enter this escape character three times in rapid succession.

- **S3, carriage-return character**—The ASCII code of the character used as the carriage return (this character terminates the AT command lines). The default value is 13.

- **S4, line-feed character**—The ASCII code of the character used as the line-feed character when the modem generates word responses to commands. The default value is 10.

- **S5, backspace character**—The ASCII code of the character used as the backspace. The modem echoes this character to implement the "erase preceding character" function. The default value is 8.

- **S6, wait time for dial tone (seconds)**—The number of seconds to wait before dialing the first digit in a dial command. The default value is 2.

- **S7, wait time for carrier (seconds)**—The number of seconds the modem waits for a carrier. If the modem does not detect a carrier after waiting for this many seconds, it displays the NO CARRIER message. The default value depends on the modem. Typically it will be anywhere from 30 to 60.

- **S8, comma time (seconds)**—The number of seconds to pause when the modem finds a comma in the phone number to dial. The default value is 2.

- **S9, carrier detect time (tenths of a second)**—The amount of time, in tenths of a second, that the carrier must be present before the modem declares that a carrier has been detected. The default value is 6, which means the carrier must be present for 0.6 seconds before the modem detects it.

- **S10, carrier loss time (tenths of a second)**—The amount of time, in tenths of a second, that the carrier must be lost before the modem disconnects. The default value is anywhere from 7 to 15, which means the carrier must be lost for 0.7 to 1.5 seconds before the modem disconnects.

- **S11, dial-tone spacing (milliseconds)**—The duration of each dial tone and the spacing between adjacent tones. The default value is typically somewhere between 50 and 100 milliseconds (50 is considered the minimum necessary for dial tones to be recognized by the phone system).

- **S12, escape sequence guard time (fiftieths of a second)**—The amount of guard time, in fiftieths of a second, that must occur before and after the escape-code sequence (the default sequence is +++) that switches the modem from online mode to command mode. The default value is 50, which means the guard time is one second.

Online Help

In response to the AT$ command, U.S. Robotics modems display online help information on the basic modem command sets. You'll find the help information instructive because it shows you the breadth of commands that a typical modem accepts. You can enter the command in a serial communication program such as Minicom, which I describe briefly later in the "Dialing out with a Communication Program" section of this chapter.

Linux and Modems

If you're using Linux at home or in a small office, you probably want to use the modem for one or more of the following reasons:

- ◆ To dial out to another computer, an online service (such as America Online), or another UNIX system, perhaps at your university or company.
- ◆ To enable other people to dial in and use your Linux system. If your home PC runs Linux and you have a modem set up, you might even dial in to your home system from work.
- ◆ To use dial-up networking with Serial Line Internet Protocol (SLIP) or Point-to-Point Protocol (PPP) to connect to the Internet (typically through an Internet service provider).

cross ref
The following sections describe how to use a modem to dial out from your Linux PC. Dial-up networking with SLIP or PPP is an important topic in itself: Chapter 13 covers that subject in detail.

Winmodems and Linux

Many PCs and laptops come with Winmodems that turn over much of the modem's signal-processing functions to the main CPU. These modems work only with special software that performs the necessary parts of the modem's functions. For this reason, they are often called software modems. Initially, such software modems came with special driver software for Microsoft Windows only; hence the name Winmodem (for Windows modem). Lately, Linux software necessary to operate these modems has become available. If your system has a Winmodem, you should visit the Linux Winmodem Support homepage at http://www.linmodems.org/ to learn more about Linux support for various models of Winmodems. For a list of Linux-compatible Winmodems—or Linmodems, as they are often called—visit the Web page at http://www.idir.net/~gromitkc/winmodem.html.

USB Modem Support in Linux

You should be able to use USB modems in Linux provided that you load the acm module that supports the Abstract Control Model (ACM) of the USB Communication Device Class (CDC) specification. The USB modem must also comply with the CDC specification; otherwise, it will not work with the acm driver module.

You also must set up the device node entries for the modems. You can use up to 32 modems with the acm driver. For example, the following commands set up the first four modem devices:

```
mknod /dev/usb/ttyACM0 c 166 0
mknod /dev/usb/ttyACM1 c 166 1
mknod /dev/usb/ttyACM2 c 166 2
mknod /dev/usb/ttyACM3 c 166 3
```

After you set up the devices and load the `acm` driver (type the command `modprobe acm` while logged in as `root`), you should be able to use a serial communication program such as minicom to dial out of a USB modem by specifying `/dev/usb/ttyACM0` as the device name for the modem.

Dialing out with a Modem

When you install Red Hat Linux from this book's companion CD-ROMs, you automatically install some tools you can use to dial out from your Linux system with a modem. Before you can dial out, however, you have to make sure you have a modem properly connected to one of the serial ports of your PC and that the Linux devices for the serial ports are set up correctly.

Examining a Modem's Hardware Setup

Make sure that your modem is properly connected to the power supply and the telephone line.

Buy the right type of cable to connect the modem to the PC. As explained in earlier sections of this chapter, you need a straight-through serial cable to connect the modem to the PC. The types of connectors at the ends of the cable depend on the type of serial connector on your PC. The modem end of the cable needs a male DB-25 connector. The PC end of the cable often is a female DB-9 connector, but, in addition, some PCs need a female DB-25 connector at the PC end of the cable.

You can buy modem cables at most computer stores. In particular, the DB-9 to DB-25 modem cables are often sold as AT modem cables.

> **note**
>
> If your PC's serial port is a DB-25, the connector at the back of the PC (not the one on the cable) is a male DB-25 connector. Don't confuse this connector with the parallel port's DB-25 connector, which is female. If you use the wrong connector, no damage should occur, but serial communication won't work.

If your PC has an internal modem, all you have to do is make sure the IRQ and I/O addresses are set properly (assuming that the modem card has jumpers for setting these values). For COM1, set the IRQ to 4 and the I/O address to 0x3f8; for COM2, set the IRQ to 3 and the I/O address to 0x2f8. You also have to connect the phone line to the phone jack at the back of the modem card.

Checking Linux's Serial Devices

When you install Red Hat Linux from this book's CD-ROMs, following the directions in Chapter 2, the necessary Linux serial devices are automatically created for you. You should have the `/dev/ttyS*` devices for dialing in and out through the modem.

The installation process creates the /dev/ttyS* files with a permission setting that does not enable everyone to read the device. If you want any user to be able to dial out with the modem, type the following command while you are logged in as root:

```
chmod o+rw /dev/ttyS*
```

This command gives all users access to the dial-out devices.

Another approach is to create a group named ppp and to make it the owner of the /dev/ttyS* files. Then, you can add to the ppp group those users you trust to use the dial-out capability.

To verify that the Linux kernel has detected the serial port correctly, check the boot messages by typing dmesg | grep ttyS in a terminal window. If you see a message about the serial driver being loaded, the next few lines should show information about one or more serial ports on your system. On one of my PCs, for example, I get the following message for the first serial port (COM1):

```
ttyS0 at 0x03f8 (irq = 4) is a 16550A
```

You can also check for the serial ports with the setserial command. Type **setserial -g /dev/ttyS?** to see detailed information about the serial ports. A telltale sign of a problem is a message from setserial of the form:

```
/dev/ttyS0, UART: unknown, Port: 0x03f8, IRQ: 4
```

---

insider insight

If the UART is shown as unknown, this means the serial port was not detected. This usually occurs because your PC's BIOS is set up to expect a Plug and Play (PnP) operating system. You should reboot your PC and, as it powers up, press a key (typically you have to press a function key such as F2, but the exact key depends on your PC's BIOS) to enter BIOS setup. In the setup screen, locate the option for PnP operating system (often labeled "Plug & Play O/S") and turn that option off. Then, save the BIOS settings and exit. This causes the PC to reboot. This time, when Linux boots again, the kernel should be able to detect the PC's serial port correctly.

Dialing out with a Communication Program

After you complete the physical installation of the modem and verify that the necessary Linux device files exist, you can try to dial out through the modem. The best approach is to use the Minicom serial communications program included in the Linux distribution on this book's CD-ROM and installed in the /usr/bin directory. The Minicom program is a serial communication program with a text-based interface that emulates a VT102 terminal. Minicom is similar to other communication software, such as Procomm or Crosstalk, which you may have used under MS-DOS or Windows.

To run Minicom, type **minicom** at the shell prompt in a terminal window or in a virtual console. If you run Minicom as a normal user (not root), Minicom may display the following error message and exit:

```
minicom
minicom: there is no global configuration file /etc/minirc.dfl
Ask your sysadm to create one (with minicom -s).
```

Log in as `root`, and type:

```
minicom -s
```

Minicom starts and displays a dialog box that lets you configure various aspects of Minicom, including serial-port commands and the modem-dialing commands. Make any changes you want, and then use the up and down arrow keys to highlight the item labeled `Save as dfl` (meaning save as default); then, press Enter. Minicom saves the settings in the `/etc/minirc.dfl` file—the default configuration file for Minicom. After that, you can exit Minicom by selecting Exit from Minicom and pressing Enter.

You also need to do the following before any user can run Minicom:

♦ Make sure that the text file `/etc/minicom.users` has a line containing the word `ALL`. (This enables all users to access Minicom's default configuration file.)

♦ Assuming that you want all users to be able to dial out using the modem, enable any user to read from and write to the serial port where the modem is connected. For example, if the modem is on COM1 (`/dev/ttyS0`), type **chmod o+rw /dev/ttyS0** to give everyone write permission for that device.

♦ Establish a link between the `/dev/modem` and the serial port device where the modem is connected. If the modem is on COM1 (`/dev/ttyS0`), you should type the following command:
```
ln -s /dev/ttyS0 /dev/modem
```

After that, you can run Minicom as an ordinary user. When Minicom first runs, it resets the modem.

The Minicom program is similar to an older shareware communication program named Telix. As in that program, you can press Ctrl-A to get the attention of the Minicom program. After you press Ctrl-A, if you press Z, a help screen appears in the form of a text window.

In the help screen, you can get information about other Minicom commands. From the help screen, press Enter to return to online mode. In online mode, you can use the modem's AT commands to dial out. In particular, you can use the `ATDT` command to dial the phone number of another modem (for example, your Internet service provider's computer or a system at work). Once you get the login prompt, you can log in as usual and use the remote system.

When you log out of the other system and want to exit Minicom, press Ctrl-A, then type **X** to exit the program. Press Enter again in response to the Minicom prompt.

Setting up Linux for Dial-In

You can set up the same modem for dial-in use as well as dial-out use (only one operation is allowed at any one time, of course). Setting up a modem for dial-in use involves setting up a program that monitors the serial port for any incoming calls; this program provides the login prompt. You can use the `mgetty` program for this purpose.

Chapter 13 describes how to set up Red Hat Linux as a dial-in PPP server. That description also tells you how to set up the `mgetty` program for dial-in. You can learn more about setting up dial-in modems by reading the latest Modem-HOWTO at the URL `http://www.ibiblio.org/pub/Linux/docs/HOWTO/Modem-HOWTO`. You should also read the `mgetty` manual—just type **kghostview /usr/share/doc/mgetty*/mgetty.ps** in a terminal window from the GUI screen to read the PostScript manual that comes with the `mgetty` software distribution. If mgetty is not installed on your system, you'll find the `mgetty` RPM on one of the CD-ROMs (see Chapter 21 for information on how to install RPMs).

Terminals and Multiport Serial Boards

The previous sections show you how to set up and use a modem in Linux for dialing out. The rest of this appendix briefly describes the steps involved in setting up terminals connected to the PC's serial port. You'll also find a list of multiport serial boards Linux supports.

You can learn more about connecting terminals to Linux systems by reading the Text-Terminal-HOWTO, available online at `http://www.ibiblio.org/pub/Linux/docs/HOWTO/Text-Terminal-HOWTO`.

> **note**
>
> Note that you might want to use other x86 PCs (especially older 486 and Pentium PCs) as terminals connected to your Linux system. To convert a PC to a terminal, all you need on the PC is a serial-communications package, such as Procomm Plus or Telix.

Setting up a Terminal on a Serial Port

To set up a terminal on a serial port, you have to set up a getty process, just as you do when you set up a dial-in modem. Follow these steps:

1. Make sure that you use the correct serial cable to connect the terminal to the serial port. Most terminals need a null modem cable in which the TD (transmit data) and RD (receive data) signal lines are reversed in going from one end of the cable to the other. (See earlier sections of this chapter for further discussions of serial cables.)

2. Set up the terminal's communication parameters. The exact steps depend on the terminal type.

3. Log in as `root` and edit the `/etc/inittab` file, and add a line to start the `agetty` process on the line connected to the terminal. If you have a VT102-compatible terminal on the line `ttyS1` (COM2), you might add the following line to your system's `/etc/inittab`:

   `S1:23:respawn:/sbin/getty -L 9600 ttyS1 vt102`

   This assumes that the terminal operates at a baud rate of 9,600. If the terminal is set to some other rate, change 9600 to that number.

4. Force the init process to reexamine the `/etc/inittab` file, as follows:

   `init q`

5. A login prompt should appear on the terminal's screen, and you should be able to log in using an existing user name.

Setting up Multiport Serial Boards in Linux

If you plan to support a small business with a Linux PC and dumb terminals (terminals are cheaper than complete PCs, although you can also use old PCs as terminals), you want more than two serial ports. With another serial board, the PC can support four serial ports. If you want more than four serial ports, you have to buy special serial I/O boards known as multiport serial boards. These boards typically support anywhere from 4 to 32 serial ports. The serial ports share one IRQ, but each port has a unique I/O address.

To add support for a specific multiport serial board, you have to add appropriate commands in the /etc/rc.serial file. That file is automatically executed by the /etc/rc .sysinit script as your Red Hat Linux system boots. For specific information on what to place in the /etc/rc.serial file, consult the multiport serial board's documentation or contact the vendor. The Linux kernel's serial port driver supports the following 16450 or 16550A UART–based multiport serial boards:

- AST FourPort and clones (4 ports)
- Accent Async-4 (4 ports)
- Arnet Multiport-8 (8 ports)
- Bell Technologies HUB6 (6 ports)
- Boca BB-1004 (4 ports), BB-1008 (8 ports), BB-2016 (16 ports)
- Boca IOAT66 (6 ports)
- Boca 2by4 (four serial and two parallel ports)
- Byte Runner
- Computone ValuePort V4-ISA (AST FourPort-compatible)
- Digi PC/8 (eight ports)
- Dolphin
- Globetek
- GTEK BBS-550 (eight ports)
- Hayes ESP
- Longshine LCS-8880, Longshine LCS-8880+ (AST FourPort-compatible)
- Moxa C104, Moxa C104+ (AST FourPort-compatible)
- National Instruments NI-SERIAL
- PC-COMM (four ports)
- Sealevel Systems COMM-2 (two ports), COMM-4 (four ports), and COMM-8 (eight ports)
- SIIG I/O Expander 2S IO1812 (four ports)
- STB-4COM (four ports)
- Twincom ACI/550
- Usenet Serial Board II (four ports)
- VScom (same driver as Byte Runner)

The Boca BB-1004 and BB-1008 boards do not support the Carrier Detect (CD) and Ring Indicator (RI) signals necessary to make dial-in modems work. Thus, you cannot use the BB-1004 and BB-1008 boards with dial-in modems.

Some multiport serial boards use special processors instead of the 16450 or 16550A UART. Table E-5 lists some intelligent multiport serial boards Red Hat Linux supports. It also shows the name of the driver module you must load to add support for a specific type of multiport serial board. These driver modules are located in the `/lib/modules/VERSION/kernel/drivers/char` directory of your Red Hat Linux system, *VERSION* being the Linux kernel version. Thus, for kernel version 2.4.20-2.48, these driver modules are in the `/lib/modules/2.4.20-2.48/kernel/drivers/char` directory.

Table E-5: Linux Drivers for Intelligent Multiport Serial Boards

Multiport Serial Board	Linux Driver Module
Computone IntelliPort II	ip2main
Comtrol RocketPort	rocket
COSA or SRP synchronous serial card	cosa
Cyclades Cyclom-Y and Cyclades-Z series multiport serial boards	cyclades
Digi International PC/Xe, PC/Xi, PC/Xr, and PC/Xem	epca
Hayes ESP serial card	esp
ISI series of cards by MultiTech	isicom
Microgate SyncLink ISA and PCI high-speed multiprotocol serial adapters	synclink
MOXA Intellio family of multiport serial cards	moxa
MOXA Smartio family of multiport serial cards	mxser
SDL RISCom/8	riscom8
Specialix IO8+	specialix
Stallion Intelligent Multiport Serial Boards	istallion
Stallion Multiport Serial Driver	stallion
Winbond W83977AF Super I/O chip multiport boards	w83977af_ir

note To learn more about setting up a multiport serial board, you may want to read the latest Serial-HOWTO document. To read the Serial-HOWTO document, use your Web browser to go to `http://www.ibiblio.org/pub/Linux/docs/HOWTO/Serial-HOWTO`.

PC Cards

◆ ◆

Laptop computers typically include PCMCIA slots for attaching peripherals. PCMCIA stands for Personal Computer Memory Card International Association, a nonprofit organization that has standardized the interface for adding memory cards to laptop computers. Although originally conceived for memory cards, PCMCIA devices became popular for a wide variety of add-ons for laptops. Today, laptop computers use many PCMCIA devices, such as modems, network cards, SCSI controllers, and sound cards. Using Linux on a laptop means having to use the PCMCIA devices, or *PC Cards*, as the popular press calls them nowadays. Thanks to the efforts of David Hinds, you can now use PCMCIA devices under Linux with his PCMCIA Card Services for Linux. This appendix briefly describes PC Cards that use the PCMCIA interface and the PCMCIA support package for Linux.

> **note** I refer to the actual cards as PC Cards because that's the proper name for the devices. PCMCIA refers to the industry organization that specifies the standard for PC Cards. However, I use the term PCMCIA Card in one context—when referring to PCMCIA Card Services for Linux (or Card Services, for short), the software that supports PC Cards under Linux.

PC Card Basics

PC Cards originated as static random access memory (SRAM) and flash RAM cards used to store data on small laptop computers. The credit-card-sized cards fit into a slot on the side of the laptop. The flash memory cards used electrically erasable programmable read-only memory (EEPROM) to provide laptop storage capability that might have been too small for other conventional storage media.

Vendors soon realized the convenience of the memory-card slot as a general-purpose expansion slot for laptop computers. The Personal Computer Memory Card International Association (PCMCIA) standardized various aspects of PC Cards, including the electrical interface, card dimensions, and card-slot sizes. This standardization has contributed to the proliferation of PC Cards in the laptop market.

By now, PCMCIA slots are a feature of almost all laptops, and the memory card is a small part of the overall PC Card market. Most laptops provide PCMCIA slots so that users can add hardware, such as fax/modems, sound cards, network cards, SCSI cards, and even hard disks.

---

insider insight To learn more about PCMCIA (the association) and PC Card specifications, point your favorite Web browser to `http://www.pc-card.com/`. **For information about PCM-CIA support in Linux, visit the Linux PCMCIA Information page at** `http://pcmcia-cs.sourceforge.net/`.

PC Card Physical Specifications

PC Cards are divided into three different classifications, according to the thickness of the card. Following are the standard physical dimensions for each type of PC Card, in terms of width by length by thickness:

- **Type I PC Card**—54 mm by 85.6 mm by 3.3 mm
- **Type II PC Card**—54 mm by 85.6 mm by 5 mm
- **Type III PC Card**—54 mm by 85.6 mm by 10.5 mm

All three types of PC Cards have the same length and width—the size of a standard credit card, except that credit card corners are rounded. The cards, however, are thicker than credit cards, and the card types are differentiated by thickness.

The term *form factor* is often used to refer to the dimensions of PC Cards.

All PC Cards use the same 68-pin connector. Because of this connector, a thinner card (Type I, for example) can be used in a thicker slot (Type II, for example). As you might guess, a thicker card cannot be used in a thinner slot, because you cannot physically insert a thick card into a thin slot.

Typical PC Card Applications

Each type of PC Card is used for a specific type of application. Following are the typical applications of PC Cards, by card type:

- **Type I PC Card**—These thin cards are used for memory devices, such as static RAM (SRAM) and flash RAM.
- **Type II PC Card**—These cards are used for input and output (I/O) devices, such as fax/modems, network adapters, and sound cards.
- **Type III PC Card**—These cards are used for devices that need the added thickness, such as hard disks with rotating components (hard to believe, isn't it?).

A PC Card can have a maximum length of 135.6 mm (slightly longer than 5.25 inches), meaning the card can extend outside the host. Such extended cards are used for devices such as removable media, transceivers, and antennas.

PCMCIA Standards

All these specifications are described in the PCMCIA Standard, of which there have been three major releases:

♦ **PCMCIA Standard Release 1.0 (June 1990)**—The initial standard defined the 68-pin connector and Type I and Type II PC Cards. This standard also defined the Card Information Structure (CIS) that has been the basis for interoperability of PC Cards. The first release of the PCMCIA Standard did not account for any I/O cards; only memory cards were considered.

♦ **PCMCIA Standard Release 2.0, 2.01, 2.1 (1991–94)**—The second release of the standard defined an I/O interface for the 68-pin connector. Release 2.01 added the PC Card AT Attachment (ATA) specification and provided an initial version of the Card and Socket Services (CSS) Specification. Release 2.1 further enhanced the CSS Specification.

♦ **PC Card Standard (February 1995)**—The current release of the standard has a new name: it is called the *PC Card Standard*, instead of the PCMCIA Standard. This release of the standard adds information to improve compatibility among different types of PC Cards and includes support for features such as 3.3-volt operation, DMA support, and 32-bit CardBus bus mastering.

PC Card Terminology

As all laptop vendors have adopted PC Card slots, the PC Card market has experienced explosive growth. Thanks to the PCMCIA Standards, the PC Card devices can be used in any PC Card slot. As you use PC Cards, you'll run into some special terms, including the following:

♦ **Card information structure (CIS)**—This describes the characteristics and capabilities of a PC Card, so that the operating system or driver software can configure the card.

♦ **CardBus**—This is an electrical specification that describes the use of 32-bit bus mastering technology and enables PC Cards to operate at up to 33 MHz.

♦ **Direct Memory Access (DMA)**—This has the same meaning as in other peripherals; now PC Cards can use DMA technology.

♦ **Execute in Place (XIP)**—This refers to the feature that enables operating-system and application software to run directly from the PC Card without having to be loaded into the system's RAM, which eliminates the need for too much system RAM.

♦ **Low-voltage operation**—This refers to the ability of PC Cards to operate at 3.3 volts (as well as at 5 volts). The connector has a physical key to ensure that you do not inadvertently insert a 3.3-volt card into a 5-volt slot.

♦ **Multifunction capability**—This enables a PC Card to support several functions. 3Com's 3C562, for example, is a 10Base-T Ethernet card and a 28,800-bps modem in a Type II form-factor PC Card.

♦ **Plug and Play**—This enables you to insert or remove a PC Card while the system is turned on (this is known as *hot-swapping*). You can hot-swap PC Cards by making the power-connection pins the longest, so that the data lines disconnect before the power.

♦ **Power management**—This refers to the capability of PC Cards to interface with the Advanced Power Management (APM) capabilities of laptops through the Card Services Specification.

♦ **Zoomed video (ZV)**—This refers to a connection between a PC Card and the system's video controller that enables the card to write video data directly to the video controller.

PCMCIA Card Services for Linux

The standardization of PC Cards means Linux developers can get their hands on the programming information they need to write device drivers for PC Cards. In particular, the Card Services Specification provides an application programming interface (API) that's independent of the hardware that controls the PC Card sockets—the receptacles or slots for PC Cards.

The Socket Services Specification, a related specification, also provides an API that enables software applications to access the hardware that controls the sockets for PC Cards.

You do not have to learn about the PC Card and Socket Services APIs. David Hinds has already done the work in his PCMCIA Card Services for Linux, a software package that you can use to access PC Card devices under Linux. All you need to do is turn on the PCMCIA support when you need it.

Activating Card Services

PCMCIA Card Services software will be installed on your system if you select the Laptop Support package group when you install Red Hat Linux following the steps outlined in Chapter 2. If you have not installed the Laptop Support package group, you can install the PCMCIA software by installing the `kernel-pcmcia-cs` RPM from the first CD-ROM (see Chapter 21 for information on how to install RPMs).

Assuming that PCMCIA support is installed, the following files control the activation of the Card Services:

♦ `/etc/init.d/pcmcia` is the shell script that starts the PCMCIA Card Services. Essentially, the command `/etc/init.d/pcmcia start (or service pcmcia start)` activates the Card Services when you boot the system. The script loads the appropriate PCMCIA driver modules by using the `modprobe` command. Then the script runs the `/sbin/cardmgr` program, which handles all card-insertion and card-removal events. Running the `cardmgr` program enables you to hot-swap PC Cards so that you can insert or eject a card at any time. To stop Card Services, type **/etc/init.d/pcmcia stop or service pcmcia stop**.

♦ `/etc/sysconfig/pcmcia` contains a number of variables the `/etc/init.d/pcmcia` script uses. In particular, the Card Services are not activated unless the line `PCMCIA=yes` appears in the `/etc/sysconfig/pcmcia` file. Lines such as the following specifies the name of the PC Card Interface Controller (PCIC) as well as any options that the PCIC may need:

```
PCIC=yenta_socket
PCIC_OPTS=
```

If your system does not have any PCMCIA interface, you will find the line `PCMCIA=no` in the `/etc/sysconfig/pcmcia` file.

You can activate the Card Services at system startup by ensuring that the line PCMCIA=yes appears in the /etc/sysconfig/pcmcia file. Of course, you want to do this only if your PC has a PCMCIA slot (most laptop PCs do).

Using the cardctl Program

If you have PCMCIA Card Services running, you can use the /sbin/cardctl program to monitor and control a PCMCIA socket. To view the status of a PCMCIA slot, type:

```
/sbin/cardctl status
```

The output should show the current socket-status flags.

The cardctl program takes many more arguments. With different arguments, you can suspend a card, resume it, or view the configuration parameters, such as interrupts and configuration registers. To learn more about cardctl from the online manual, type **man cardctl** to view the manual page.

Using Supported PC Cards

In the PCMCIA Card Services documentation directory, you'll find a file named SUPPORTED .CARDS. (You can change to that directory by typing cd /usr/share/doc/kernel-pcmcia*.) That file lists some of the PCMCIA Cards that are known to work with at least one system. Unfortunately, that list is somewhat dated by now. To search for specific types of PC Card, visit the PC Card Resource Directory at http://www.pc-card.com/.

The list of supported cards has become too numerous to include here. The categories of cards supported by the Card Services are as follows:

- ◆ **Ethernet cards**—Close to a hundred different models of Ethernet cards are supported, including popular models such as 3Com 3c589, 3c589B, 3c589C, and 3c589D; Megahertz XJ10BT, and CC10BT; and Xircom CreditCard CE2.
- ◆ **Fast Ethernet (10/100BASET) cards**—Over 20 cards are supported, including 3Com 3c574TX, 3c575TX, 3CCFE575B, and 3CXFE575B; Linksys EtherFast 10/100; NetGear FA410TXC and FA411; and Xircom CreditCard CE3-100, CE3B, RE-100, R2E-100BTX, and XE2000.
- ◆ **Token Ring cards**—IBM Token Ring Adapter and 3Com 3c689 TokenLink III cards are supported.
- ◆ **Wireless network cards**—Lucent Orinoco WaveLAN/IEEE 802.11b, Dell TrueMobile 1150 Series, Linksys WPC11, and Xircom CreditCard Netwave are supported.
- ◆ **Modem and serial cards**—All modem and serial-port cards should work. The only exceptions are modems such as Compaq 192, New Media WinSurfer, Megahertz XJ/CC2560, 3Com 3CXM356/3CCM356 and 3CXM656/3CCM656, and other WinModems that require special Windows drivers. The Trimble Mobile GPS card is supported through the serial/modem driver.
- ◆ **Memory cards**—All static RAM (SRAM) memory cards should work.
- ◆ **SCSI adapter cards**—Over 30 different models of SCSI cards are supported, including models such as Adaptec APA-1460, APA-1460A, APA-1450A, and APA-1460B SlimSCSI; IBM SCSI; Iomega Zip and Jaz Cards; NEC PC-9801N-J03R; and Toshiba NWB0107ABK and SCSC200B.
- ◆ **ATA/IDE disk drive cards**—All ATA/IDE disk-drive PC Cards are supported.

- **ATA/IDE CD-ROM adapter cards**—Many ATA/IDE CD-ROM adapters are supported, including Argosy EIDE CD-ROM, Caravelle CD-36N, Creative Technology CD-ROM, IBM Max 20X CD-ROM, Sony PCGA-CD5 CD-ROM, Digital Mobile Media CD-ROM, some EXP models, and several IO-DATA models.

- **Multifunction cards**—Several multifunction Ethernet/Modem cards are supported, including 3Com 3c562, 3c562B/C/D, and 3c563B/C/D; IBM Home and Away Card; Linksys LANmodem 28.8, 33.6; Megahertz EM1144, EM3288, and EM3336; Motorola Mariner and Marquis; Ositech Jack of Diamonds; and Xircom CreditCard CEM28, CEM33, CEM56 models.

Further Reading

To learn more about the PCMCIA Card Services software, consult the PCMCIA-HOWTO. To read this HOWTO document, type **cd /usr/share/doc/kernel-pcmcia*** to change to the directory where that HOWTO file is located (if you cannot find the file, type **locate PCMCIA-HOWTO** to find the file). Then, type **more PCMCIA-HOWTO** to view the PCMCIA-HOWTO file. This file contains the latest information about the Card Services software, including common problems and suggested fixes.

In particular, you should look through the PCMCIA-HOWTO file for any information that applies to your specific PC Card.

Linux Resources

◆ ◆

This appendix lists some resources where you can get more information about specific topics. Most of the resources are on the Internet because that's where you can get the latest information on Linux. Often, you'll be able to download the files necessary for a specific task.

Some Internet resources appear in the standard Uniform Resource Locator (URL) syntax— Chapter 14 explains URLs. If you have used a Web browser such as Mozilla or Microsoft Internet Explorer, you are probably already familiar with URLs.

Instead of providing a long listing of URLs, this appendix describes a few key websites you can use as a starting point for your search.

Web Pages

If you browse the Internet, you may notice that there are quite a few Web pages with Linux-related information. A good starting point for locating information about Linux is the Linux Online page at:

```
http://www.linux.org/
```

You can click the buttons to access more information about the topic that button's label identifies. At this page, you also find an organized collection of links to Linux-related websites.

To browse recent news about Linux, visit the Linux Resources page at:

```
http://www.linuxresources.com/
```

Specialized Systems Consultants (SSC), Inc., the publisher of the *Linux Journal*, maintains this page. You can scan the articles in the latest issue of *Linux Journal* and find out other information, such as the latest version of the kernel and links to other Linux resources.

Another popular and definitive source of Linux information is the home page of The Linux Documentation Project (LDP) at the following URL:

```
http://www.tldp.org/
```

On this website, you can find many more pointers to other Linux resources on the Internet. In particular, you can browse and download the latest HOWTO documents from `http://www.ibiblio.org/pub/Linux/docs/HOWTO/`.

For Red Hat Linux–specific questions, you can visit Red Hat's Support website at:

```
http://www.redhat.com/apps/support/
```

This website provides links such as Product Updates and Errata, Hardware Compatibility List, and Installation Guides and Manuals. In particular, you can find the manuals and FAQs (frequently asked questions) at `http://www.redhat.com/apps/support/resources/`.

---

insider insight   If you are interested in open source development, including Linux, a good resource is the SourceFirge.net website at `http://sourceforge.net/`.

Newsgroups

To keep up with Linux developments, you need access to the Internet, especially to the newsgroups. You can find discussions on specific Linux-related topics in the newsgroups listed in Table G-1.

Table G-1: Linux Newsgroups on the Internet

Newsgroup	Provides the Following
comp.os.linux.admin	Information about Linux system administration
comp.os.linux.advocacy	Discussions about promoting Linux
comp.os.linux.announce	Important announcements about Linux. (This is a moderated newsgroup, which means you must mail an article to the moderator, who then posts it to the newsgroup.)
comp.os.linux.answers	Questions and answers about Linux. (All the Linux HOWTOs are posted in this moderated newsgroup.)
comp.os.linux.development	Current Linux development work
comp.os.linux.development.apps	Linux application development
comp.os.linux.development.system	Linux operating system development
comp.os.linux.hardware	Discussions about Linux and various hardware
comp.os.linux.help	Help with various aspects of Linux
comp.os.linux.misc	Miscellaneous topics about Linux

Newsgroup	Provides the Following
comp.os.linux.networking	Networking under Linux
comp.os.linux.setup	Linux setup and installation
comp.os.linux.x	Discussions about setting up and running the X Window System under Linux
linux.redhat	Discussions about Red Hat Linux

You can use Mozilla to read the newsgroups. For a newsgroup, use a URL of the form news://my.newsserver.com/newsgroup, in which my.newsserver.com is the fully qualified domain name of your news server (your Internet service provider should give you this name), and newsgroup is the name of the newsgroup you want to read. For example, assuming that your news server is news.myisp.net, you can browse the comp.os.linux.setup newsgroup by typing the following URL in the Location field of the Netscape Web browser:

```
news://news.myisp.net/comp.os.linux.setup
```

> **note**
>
> You can also use the Google Groups page at http://groups.google.com/ to search for specific items in the comp.os.linux newsgroups or browse that newsgroup.

FTP Archive Sites

You can download Red Hat Linux and other Linux distributions from one of several FTP sites around the world. In addition to the Linux distribution itself, these sites also contain many other software packages that run under Linux.

For the latest list of Red Hat Linux FTP sites worldwide, visit the following Web page that Red Hat maintains:

```
http://www.redhat.com/download/mirror.html
```

This page displays a table of URLs of sites that maintain the Red Hat distribution for downloading. In that table, the Updates column lists the URLs for downloading specific Red Hat Package Manager (RPM) files for the latest Red Hat Linux version (for Intel-based PCs).

> **note**
>
> Red Hat provides many of the fixes and improvements—these updates are in the form of Red Hat packages distributed from Red Hat's FTP server. (Try ftp://ftp.redhat.com/pub/redhat/linux/updates/; if it's busy, consult http://www.redhat.com/download/mirror.html for a mirror site near you.) To install these packages, you have to use the Red Hat Package Manager (RPM).

Magazines

Linux Journal is a monthly magazine devoted entirely to Linux. On the Web, the magazine's home page can be found at `http://www.linuxjournal.com/`. There, you can find information about how to subscribe to this magazine.

Linux Magazine is another monthly magazine that covers everything about Linux. Visit its home page at `http://www.linux-mag.com/` to learn more about the magazine and to subscribe.

About the CD-ROMs

◆ ◆

The companion CD-ROMs contain Red Hat Linux 9 with the Linux 2.4.20 kernel, which is the latest version of Linux available as of this writing (Spring 2003). Linux is a complete UNIX-like operating system for your PC. The Red Hat Linux distribution includes over 2GB of files. The companion CDs, which accompany this book, contain the Red Hat Linux software. The last page of the book contains a source-code coupon that you can use to obtain the sorce code. By installing Linux on a PC, you can turn that PC into a full-fledged UNIX workstation.

> **note** Please note that the software contained in these CD-ROMs is distributed under a variety of license agreements. Some of the software (such as the Linux kernel) is distributed in full source and binary format under the GNU General Public License. In all cases, the software is copyrighted by the respective authors. After installing Red Hat Linux, you should consult the README.* files (or files with names such as COPYING and COPYRIGHT) in various subdirectories of the /usr/share/doc directory for information on the licensing terms for each software package.

This appendix provides you with information on the contents of the CD-ROMs that accompany this book. (For late-breaking information, please see the ReadMe file located at the root of the CD-ROMs.) Here is what you'll find in this appendix:

- ◆ System requirements
- ◆ CD-ROM installation instructions
- ◆ What's on the CD-ROMs
- ◆ Troubleshooting

System Requirements

Make sure that your computer meets the minimum system requirements listed in this section. If your computer doesn't match up to most of these requirements, you may have a problem using the contents of the CD-ROMs.

- PC with a Pentium processor running at 200MHz or faster
- At least 64MB of total RAM installed on your computer; for best performance, we recommend at least 128MB
- At least 4GB of free space on your hard disk
- Ethernet network interface card (NIC) or a modem with a speed of at least 56 Kbps
- A CD-ROM drive

CD-ROM Installation Instructions

Installation can be a tricky step in Linux. You need some specific information about hardware, such as the disk controller, video card, and CD-ROM drive. Linux controls the hardware through drivers, so you need to make sure that the current release of Linux includes drivers for your hardware. Because Linux is free, you cannot really demand—or expect—support for some specific hardware. Linux is, however, continually improving through collaboration among programmers throughout the world. If your hardware is popular enough, there's a good chance that someone has developed a driver for it. In any case, the Red Hat Linux on the companion CD-ROMs already supports such a wide variety of hardware that all your PC's peripherals probably are supported.

The following steps describe the general procedure for installing and configuring Linux and the X Windows System.

1. Gather information about your PC's hardware, such as the graphics card, network card, and SCSI card before you install Linux.

2. Create space for Linux by reducing the size of the existing Windows partition. For Windows 95/98/Me use the nondestructive repartitioning program, FIPS, to repartition your hard disk without destroying the existing contents. For Windows NT/2000/XP systems that use an NTFS partition, use a commercial disk-partitioning program, such as PowerQuest's PartitionMagic (http://www.powerquest.com/partitionmagic/), to shrink the NTFS partition and create room for Linux. Skip this step if you plan to use Linux as the sole operating system or if you plan to install Red Hat Linux on a DOS/Windows partition or on an empty second hard disk.

3. If your PC cannot boot directly from the CD-ROM, create a Linux installer boot disk under DOS or Windows.

4. Boot your PC from the first CD-ROM or boot with the Linux installer boot disk (in either case, make sure that the first CD-ROM is in the CD-ROM drive). This procedure automatically runs the Red Hat Linux installer. From this point on, you must respond to a number of dialog boxes as the Red Hat installer takes you through the steps. Here are some of the key installation steps:
    - Identify any SCSI adapters installed on your PC.
    - Let the installer automatically create partitions for Red Hat Linux by using the free space you had created by shrinking the existing Windows partition.

- Configure the Ethernet network, if any. You may have to specify parameters, such as the IP address and hostname for your Red Hat Linux system.
- Specify the local time zone and set the root password.
- Install the GRUB boot loader program on your hard disk's master boot record (MBR) so that you can boot Linux when you power up your PC after shutting it down.
- Select the specific software package groups that you want to install, such as the X Window System and the GNOME Desktop Environment.
- Configure the X Window System and enable the graphical login screen so that when you boot your Linux system, it displays a login dialog box and goes directly into the GNOME or KDE graphical desktop after successful login.

To install specific items from the CD-ROM to your hard drive, follow these steps:

1. Log in as `root`.
2. Insert the CD-ROM into your computer's CD-ROM drive.
3. If you are using GNOME or KDE GUI, wait for the CD to mount. Otherwise, open a terminal window and at the command prompt type:

   `mount /dev/cdrom /mnt/cdrom`

4. Browse the CD-ROM and follow the instructions in Chapter 21 to install individual software packages.
5. To remove the CD-ROM from your CD-ROM drive, at the command prompt type:

   `umount /mnt/cdrom`

   You can also right-click on the CD-ROM icon on the desktop and choose Eject from the selections. This will unmount your CD-ROM and eject it.

What's on the CD-ROMs

You can find the following software on the Red Hat Linux 9 CD-ROMs:

- Linux kernel 2.4.20 with driver modules for all major PC hardware configurations, including IDE/ATA and SCSI drives, PCMCIA devices, and CD-ROMs
- A complete set of installation and configuration tools for setting up devices (such as the keyboard and mouse) and services
- A graphical user interface based on the XFree86 4.3.0 package, with GNOME and KDE desktops
- Full TCP/IP networking for Internet, LANs, and intranets
- Tools for connecting your PC to your Internet service provider (ISP) using PPP, SLIP, or dial-up serial communications programs
- A complete suite of Internet applications, including electronic mail (sendmail and mail), news (inn), Telnet, FTP, DNS, and NFS
- Apache httpd (Web) server 2.0.40, to turn your PC into a Web server; and Mozilla 1.2.1, to surf the Net
- Ximian Evolution 1.2.2 email and calendar application
- OpenOffice.org 1.0.2 office suite with word processor, spreadsheet, presentation software, and more

- Samba 2.2.7a LAN Manager software for Microsoft Windows connectivity and incorporate Linux systems into a Windows network
- Several text editors (for example, GNU Emacs 21.2; vim)
- Graphics and image manipulation software, such as The GIMP, XPaint, Xfig, Gnuplot, Ghostscript, Ghostview, and ImageMagick
- Programming languages (GNU C and C++ 3.2.2, Perl 5.8.0, Tcl/Tk 8.3.5, Python 2.2.2, GNU AWK 3.1.1) and software development tools (GNU Debugger 5.3, CVS 1.11.2, RCS 5.7, GNU Bison 1.35, flex 2.5.4a, TIFF, and JPEG libraries)
- Support for industry standard Executable and Linking Format (ELF) and Intel Binary Compatibility Specification (iBCS)
- A complete suite of standard UNIX utilities from the GNU project
- Tools to access and use DOS files and applications (mtools 3.9.8)
- Text-formatting and typesetting software (DocBook, groff, TeX, and LaTeX)

Source Code Coupon

To provide you with CD-ROMss that are packed with more software, we're offering the source code (which usually comes packaged with the Linux operating system) via mail. This offer is valid for a period of one year from the date of purchase. Mail in the coupon located on the companion CD-ROM with a dated cash register receipt and a money order for $9.95 for orders within the U.S. or $13.95 for orders outside the United States (U.S. funds only). Please make sure that you list the ISBN 4133-1 on your check or money order so that we can ensure that you receive the CD-ROM that corresponds to your book. Please allow 4 to 6 weeks for delivery.

Troubleshooting

If you have difficulty installing or using any of the materials on the companion CD-ROMs, consult the detailed installation and troubleshooting instructions in Chapter 2.

If you still have trouble with the CD-ROMs, please call the Customer Care phone number: (800) 762-2974. Outside the United States, call 1 (317) 572-3994. You can also contact Customer Service by email at techsupdum@wiley.com. Wiley Publishing Inc. will provide technical support only for installation and other general quality control items; for technical support on the applications themselves, consult the program's vendor or author.

Index

continued

continued

continued

Wiley Publishing, Inc.
End-User License Agreement

READ THIS. You should carefully read these terms and conditions before opening the software packet(s) included with this book "Book". This is a license agreement "Agreement" between you and Wiley Publishing, Inc."WPI". By opening the accompanying software packet(s), you acknowledge that you have read and accept the following terms and conditions. If you do not agree and do not want to be bound by such terms and conditions, promptly return the Book and the unopened software packet(s) to the place you obtained them for a full refund.

1. **License Grant.** WPI grants to you (either an individual or entity) a nonexclusive license to use one copy of the enclosed software program(s) (collectively, the "Software" solely for your own personal or business purposes on a single computer (whether a standard computer or a workstation component of a multi-user network). The Software is in use on a computer when it is loaded into temporary memory (RAM) or installed into permanent memory (hard disk, CD-ROM, or other storage device). WPI reserves all rights not expressly granted herein.

2. **Ownership.** WPI is the owner of all right, title, and interest, including copyright, in and to the compilation of the Software recorded on the disk(s) or CD-ROM "Software Media". Copyright to the individual programs recorded on the Software Media is owned by the author or other authorized copyright owner of each program. Ownership of the Software and all proprietary rights relating thereto remain with WPI and its licensers.

3. **Restrictions On Use and Transfer.**

   (a) You may only (i) make one copy of the Software for backup or archival purposes, or (ii) transfer the Software to a single hard disk, provided that you keep the original for backup or archival purposes. You may not (i) rent or lease the Software, (ii) copy or reproduce the Software through a LAN or other network system or through any computer subscriber system or bulletin-board system, or (iii) modify, adapt, or create derivative works based on the Software.

   (b) You may not reverse engineer, decompile, or disassemble the Software. You may transfer the Software and user documentation on a permanent basis, provided that the transferee agrees to accept the terms and conditions of this Agreement and you retain no copies. If the Software is an update or has been updated, any transfer must include the most recent update and all prior versions.

4. **Restrictions on Use of Individual Programs.** You must follow the individual requirements and restrictions detailed for each individual program in the About the CD-ROM appendix of this Book. These limitations are also contained in the individual license agreements recorded on the Software Media. These limitations may include a requirement that after using the program for a specified period of time, the user must pay a registration fee or discontinue use. By opening the Software packet(s), you will be agreeing to abide by the licenses and restrictions for these individual programs that are detailed in the About the CD-ROM appendix and on the Software Media. None of the material on this Software Media or listed in this Book may ever be redistributed, in original or modified form, for commercial purposes.

GNU General Public License

Version 2, June 1991

Preamble

The licenses for most software are designed to take away your freedom to share and change it. By contrast, the GNU General Public License is intended to guarantee your freedom to share and change free software—to make sure the software is free for all its users. This General Public License applies to most of the Free Software Foundation's software and to any other program whose authors commit to using it. (Some other Free Software Foundation software is covered by the GNU Library General Public License instead.) You can apply it to your programs, too.

When we speak of free software, we are referring to freedom, not price. Our General Public Licenses are designed to make sure that you have the freedom to distribute copies of free software (and charge for this service if you wish), that you receive source code or can get it if you want it, that you can change the software or use pieces of it in new free programs; and that you know you can do these things.

To protect your rights, we need to make restrictions that forbid anyone to deny you these rights or to ask you to surrender the rights. These restrictions translate to certain responsibilities for you if you distribute copies of the software, or if you modify it.

For example, if you distribute copies of such a program, whether gratis or for a fee, you must give the recipients all the rights that you have. You must make sure that they, too, receive or can get the source code. And you must show them these terms so they know their rights.

We protect your rights with two steps: (1) copyright the software, and (2) offer you this license which gives you legal permission to copy, distribute and/or modify the software.

Also, for each author's protection and ours, we want to make certain that everyone understands that there is no warranty for this free software. If the software is modified by someone else and passed on, we want its recipients to know that what they have is not the original, so that any problems introduced by others will not reflect on the original authors' reputations.

Finally, any free program is threatened constantly by software patents. We wish to avoid the danger that redistributors of a free program will individually obtain patent licenses, in effect making the program proprietary. To prevent this, we have made it clear that any patent must be licensed for everyone's free use or not licensed at all.

The precise terms and conditions for copying, distribution and modification follow.

Terms and Conditions for Copying, Distribution, and Modification

0. This License applies to any program or other work which contains a notice placed by the copyright holder saying it may be distributed under the terms of this General Public License. The "Program", below, refers to any such program or work, and a "work based on the Program" means either the Program or any derivative work under copyright law: that is to say, a work containing the Program or a portion of it, either verbatim or with modifications and/or translated into another language. (Hereinafter, translation is included without limitation in the term "modification".) Each licensee is addressed as "you".

Activities other than copying, distribution and modification are not covered by this License; they are outside its scope. The act of running the Program is not restricted, and the output from the Program is covered only if its contents constitute a work based on the Program (independent of having been made by running the Program). Whether that is true depends on what the Program does.

1. You may copy and distribute verbatim copies of the Program's source code as you receive it, in any medium, provided that you conspicuously and appropriately publish on each copy an appropriate copyright notice and disclaimer of warranty; keep intact all the notices that refer to this License and to the absence of any warranty; and give any other recipients of the Program a copy of this License along with the Program.

You may charge a fee for the physical act of transferring a copy, and you may at your option offer warranty protection in exchange for a fee.

2. You may modify your copy or copies of the Program or any portion of it, thus forming a work based on the Program, and copy and distribute such modifications or work under the terms of Section 1 above, provided that you also meet all of these conditions:

(a) You must cause the modified files to carry prominent notices stating that you changed the files and the date of any change.

(b) You must cause any work that you distribute or publish, that in whole or in part contains or is derived from the Program or any part thereof, to be licensed as a whole at no charge to all third parties under the terms of this License.

(c) If the modified program normally reads commands interactively when run, you must cause it, when started running for such interactive use in the most ordinary way, to print or display an announcement including an appropriate copyright notice and a notice that there is no warranty (or else, saying that you provide a warranty) and that users may redistribute the program under these conditions, and telling the user how to view a copy of this License. (Exception: if the Program itself is interactive but does not normally print such an announcement, your work based on the Program is not required to print an announcement.)

These requirements apply to the modified work as a whole. If identifiable sections of that work are not derived from the Program, and can be reasonably considered independent and separate works in themselves, then this License, and its terms, do not apply to those sections when you distribute them as separate works. But when you distribute the same sections as part of a whole which is a

10. If you wish to incorporate parts of the Program into other free programs whose distribution conditions are different, write to the author to ask for permission. For software which is copyrighted by the Free Software Foundation, write to the Free Software Foundation; we sometimes make exceptions for this. Our decision will be guided by the two goals of preserving the free status of all derivatives of our free software and of promoting the sharing and reuse of software generally.

NO WARRANTY

11. BECAUSE THE PROGRAM IS LICENSED FREE OF CHARGE, THERE IS NO WARRANTY FOR THE PROGRAM, TO THE EXTENT PERMITTED BY APPLIC-ABLE LAW. EXCEPT WHEN OTHERWISE STATED IN WRITING THE COPY-RIGHT HOLDERS AND/OR OTHER PARTIES PROVIDE THE PROGRAM "AS IS" WITHOUT WARRANTY OF ANY KIND, EITHER EXPRESSED OR IMPLIED, INCLUDING, BUT NOT LIMITED TO, THE IMPLIED WARRANTIES OF MER-CHANTABILITY AND FITNESS FOR A PARTICULAR PURPOSE. THE ENTIRE RISK AS TO THE QUALITY AND PERFORMANCE OF THE PROGRAM IS WITH YOU. SHOULD THE PROGRAM PROVE DEFECTIVE, YOU ASSUME THE COST OF ALL NECESSARY SERVICING, REPAIR OR CORRECTION.

12. IN NO EVENT UNLESS REQUIRED BY APPLICABLE LAW OR AGREED TO IN WRITING WILL ANY COPYRIGHT HOLDER, OR ANY OTHER PARTY WHO MAY MODIFY AND/OR REDISTRIBUTE THE PROGRAM AS PERMITTED ABOVE, BE LIABLE TO YOU FOR DAMAGES, INCLUDING ANY GENERAL, SPECIAL, INCIDENTAL OR CONSEQUENTIAL DAMAGES ARISING OUT OF THE USE OR INABILITY TO USE THE PROGRAM (INCLUDING BUT NOT LIMITED TO LOSS OF DATA OR DATA BEING RENDERED INACCURATE OR LOSSES SUSTAINED BY YOU OR THIRD PARTIES OR A FAILURE OF THE PROGRAM TO OPERATE WITH ANY OTHER PROGRAMS), EVEN IF SUCH HOLDER OR OTHER PARTY HAS BEEN ADVISED OF THE POSSIBILITY OF SUCH DAMAGES.

CD-ROM Installation Instructions

Insert the CD-ROMs into your CD-ROM drive. The setup program on the CD-ROMs should start automatically, displaying a dialog with the options that you can install. Select the options that you want to install and the drive and subdirectory into which you want to install the software.

For more information about installing the CD-ROMs, please refer to Appendix H.